BUSINESS
STATISTICS
A FIRST COURSE

Canadian Edition

Norean R. Sharpe
Georgetown University

Richard D. De Veaux
Williams College

Paul F. Velleman
Cornell University

Jonathan Berkowitz
Sauder School of Business
University of British Columbia

PEARSON

Toronto

Managing Editor, Business Publishing: Claudine O'Donnell
Acquisition Editor: Megan Farrell
Marketing Manager: Michelle Bish
Supervising Developmental Editor: Suzanne Schaan
Developmental Editors: Darryl Kamo and Lori McLellan
Project Manager: Sarah Gallagher
Production Editor: Vastavikta Sharma, Cenveo® Publisher Services
Copy Editor: Cat Haggert
Proofreader: Susan Adlam
Full Service Vendor: Cenveo Publisher Services
Permissions Project Manager: Joanne Tang
Photo Researcher: Aptara
Permissions Researcher: Aptara
Cover Designer: Anthony Leung
Interior Designer: Anthony Leung
Cover Image: serp77/Veer

For permission to use copyrighted material, grateful acknowledgment has been made to the copyright holders within each page.

Many of the designations used by manufacturers and sellers to distinguish their products are claimed as trademarks. Where those designations appear in this book, and Pearson Education was aware of a trademark claim, the designations have been printed in initial caps or all caps.

10 9 8 7 6 5 4 3 2 1 [WC]

Library and Archives Canada Cataloguing in Publication

Sharpe, Norean Radke, author
      Business statistics : a first course / Norean Sharpe, Richard
De Veaux, Paul Velleman, Jonathan Berkowitz. — Canadian edition.
Includes bibliographical references and index.
ISBN 978-0-321-82483-7 (pbk.)

      1. Commercial statistics—Textbooks. I. Berkowitz, Jonathan,
1956-, author II. Velleman, Paul F., 1949-, author III. De Veaux, Richard
D., author IV. Title.
HF1017.S467 2015   519.5   C2014-904870-X

ISBN 978-0-321-82483-7

To my parents, who taught me the importance of education
—Norean

To my parents
—Dick

To my father, who taught me about ethical business practice by
his constant example as a small businessman and parent
—Paul

To my wife, Heather, who provides the quality in my quantitative life;
and to my sons, Matthew and Joshua, two outliers
in the best sense of the word
—Jonathan

MEET THE AUTHORS

As a researcher of statistical problems in business and a professor of Statistics at a business school, **Norean Radke Sharpe** (Ph.D. University of Virginia) understands the challenges and specific needs of the business student. She is currently teaching at the McDonough School of Business at Georgetown University, where she is also Associate Dean and Director of Undergraduate Programs. Prior to joining Georgetown, she taught business statistics and operations research courses to both undergraduate and MBA students for fourteen years at Babson College. Before moving into business education, she taught mathematics for several years at Bowdoin College and conducted research at Yale University. Norean is coauthor of the recent text, *A Casebook for Business Statistics: Laboratories for Decision Making*, and she has authored more than 30 articles—primarily in the areas of statistics education and women in science. Norean currently serves as Associate Editor for the journal *Cases in Business, Industry, and Government Statistics*. Her research focuses on business forecasting and statistics education. She is also co-founder of DOME Foundation, Inc., a nonprofit foundation that works to increase diversity and outreach in mathematics and engineering for the greater Boston area. She has been active in increasing the participation of women and underrepresented students in science and mathematics for several years and has two children of her own.

Richard D. De Veaux (Ph.D. Stanford University) is an internationally known educator, consultant, and lecturer. Dick has taught statistics at a business school (Wharton), an engineering school (Princeton), and

a liberal arts college (Williams). While at Princeton, he won a Lifetime Award for Dedication and Excellence in Teaching. Since 1994, he has been a professor of statistics at Williams College, although he returned to Princeton for the academic year 2006–2007 as the William R. Kenan Jr. Visiting Professor of Distinguished Teaching. Dick holds degrees from Princeton University in Civil Engineering and Mathematics and from Stanford University in Dance Education and Statistics, where he studied with Persi Diaconis. His research focuses on the analysis of large data sets and data mining in science and industry. Dick has won both the Wilcoxon and Shewell awards from the American Society for Quality and is a Fellow of the American Statistical Association. Dick is well known in industry, having consulted for such *Fortune* 500 companies as American Express, Hewlett-Packard, Alcoa, DuPont, Pillsbury, General Electric, and Chemical Bank. He was named the "Statistician of the Year" for 2008 by the Boston Chapter of the American Statistical Association for his contributions to teaching, research, and consulting. In his spare time he is an avid cyclist and swimmer. He also is the founder and bass for the doo-wop group, Diminished Faculty, and is a frequent soloist with various local choirs and orchestras. Dick is the father of four children.

Paul F. Velleman (Ph.D. Princeton University) has an international reputation for innovative statistics education. He designed the Data Desk® software package and is also the author and designer of the award-winning ActivStats® multimedia software, for which he received the EDUCOM Medal for innovative uses of computers in teaching statistics and the

ICTCM Award for Innovation in Using Technology in College Mathematics. He is the founder and CEO of Data Description, Inc. (www.datadesk.com), which supports both of these programs. He also developed the Internet site, *Data and Story Library* (DASL; www.dasl.datadesk.com), which provides data sets for teaching Statistics. Paul coauthored (with David Hoaglin) the book *ABCs of Exploratory Data Analysis*. Paul has taught Statistics at Cornell University on the faculty of the School of Industrial and Labor Relations since 1975. His research often focuses on statistical graphics and data analysis methods. Paul is a Fellow of the American Statistical Association and of the American Association for the Advancement of Science. He is also baritone of the barbershop quartet Alchemy. Paul's experience as a professor, entrepreneur, and business leader brings a unique perspective to the book.

Richard De Veaux and Paul Velleman have authored successful books in the introductory college and AP High School market with David Bock, including *Intro Stats,* Third Edition (Pearson, 2009), *Stats: Modeling the World*, Third Edition (Pearson, 2010), and *Stats: Data and Models*, Second Edition (Pearson, 2008).

For the past 25 years **Jonathan Berkowitz** (Ph.D. University of Toronto) has had a full-time practice as a consulting statistician as president of the aptly named Berkowitz & Associates Consulting Inc. But Jonathan leads a double life, because he is also a full-time instructor with the Sauder School of Business and an Associate Member of the Department of Family Practice (Faculty of Medicine), both at the University of British Columbia.

Jonathan is recognized as an outstanding teacher, having won the Killam Teaching Prize for undergraduate teaching and CGA Graduate Master Teacher Award for MBA teaching, both at the Sauder School, as well as many awards and commendations from students. In addition he teaches short courses and workshops for a number of public and private sector groups. His passion for teaching also extends to younger audiences, regularly performing shows on math magic, word games, and puzzles in school classrooms.

In his consulting life, Jonathan has been involved in a wide range of collaborative and interdisciplinary research in health care and medical research, social science, engineering, biotechnology, transportation, law, management consulting, market research, and accounting. His clients enthusiastically describe him as a "user-friendly" statistician! He has contributed to numerous successful research grant applications, and has co-written many peer-reviewed journal articles and other publications. He has also helped more than 100 graduate students complete their degrees.

While numbers are his vocation, words are his avocation. A passion for puzzles, word games, and puns infiltrates all aspects of his life, including the classroom. He is an active member of the National Puzzlers' League, and for six years was the puzzle composer and editor for the American Statistical Association's *CHANCE* magazine.

Jonathan and his wife have two children, both of whom graduated from Canadian business schools and have careers in quantitative fields, a classic illustration of the power of both nature and nurture.

CONTENTS

Part II   Understanding Data and Distributions   177

Appendixes

From the Classroom...

Providing Real Business Context

Chapter Openers

Each chapter opens with an interesting business example. The stories of companies such as Mountain Equipment Co-op, Canada Goose, and Rogers Communication enhance and illustrate the message of each chapter, showing students how and why statistical thinking is vital to modern business decision-making. We analyze data from these examples throughout the chapter.

Random Variables and Probability Models

CHAPTER 8

CONNECTIONS: CHAPTER

With the ideas of probability we discussed in Chapter 7 we now have the tools to create specific models that describe where the data came from. In this chapter we will learn about two types of models—discrete and continuous—that correspond to the two types of data we have worked with—categorical and quantitative. The models will be used all the way through the rest of the text; they are the key to understanding and interpreting data. This is also where the famous bell-shaped curve will be introduced.

LEARNING OBJECTIVES

1. Find the expected value and standard deviation of a random variable or combination of random variables.
2. Use the Binomial and Geometric models to find probabilities.
3. Use the 68–95–99.7 Rule to find probabilities or cutoff values.
4. Use the Normal model to find probabilities, cutoff values, and the mean and standard deviation.
5. Compute and use z-scores for comparisons.
6. Use the Normal model to approximate the Binomial and compute probabilities.

Manulife Financial

What company could be more Canadian than one whose first president was the first Prime Minister of Canada, Sir John A. Macdonald? The Manufacturers Life Insurance Company was founded in 1887, and a mere ten years later expanded its operations into China and Hong Kong. Manulife now operates in 21 countries, most notably in the United States, through its subsidiary, John Hancock Insurance.

Manulife Financial is the largest insurance company in Canada, the second largest in the North Americ... known because of their use of Snoopy... strip "Peanuts"), and the world's fifth lar... capitalization. At the end of 2011, its to... $450 billion and total employees surpa... a financial services provider and holds N... a wholly-owned subsidiary.

Manulife changed from a joint stock... company, privately owned by its policyh... demutualized in 1999 and shares of the... Financial Corporation began trading on... Exchange (TSX), New York Stock Excha...

In 2002, China gave approval to Ma... Insurance Co. Ltd. to open a branch off...

In-Text Examples

Real business examples motivate the discussions, often returning to the chapter-opening company.

99.9%?
If you are careful to add the percentages in Table 4.2, you will notice the total is 99.99%. Of course the real total has to be 100.00%. The discrepancy is due to individual percentages being rounded. You'll often see this in tables of percents, sometimes with explanatory footnotes.

It is often also very useful to rearrange the order of the categories, and the bars, so that they go from highest to lowest (or lowest to highest). This version is referred to as a Pareto chart, but it is just a variation of the bar chart we have discussed. Here is another look at Figure 4.3, with reordered, and horizontal, bars.

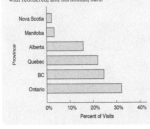

4.3 Charts

The Area Principle

Now that we have a frequency table, we're ready to follow the three rules of data analysis and make a picture of the data. But we can't just make any picture; a bad picture can distort our understanding rather than help it. For example, here's a graph of the frequencies of Table 4.1. What impression do you get of the relative frequencies of visits from each province?

The figure does not accurately represent the information in the table. What's gone wrong? The height of the images in the figure do match the percentages in the table. But our eyes tend to be more impressed by the *area* (or perhaps even the *volume*) than by other aspects of each image, and it's that aspect of the image that we notice.

Since there were nearly three times as many visits from Ontario and BC as from Quebec, the images depicting the number from Ontario and from BC is almost three times higher than the image for Quebec, but it occupies almost nine times the area, since both the height and the width were increased three-fold to keep the image looking proportional. As you can see from the frequency table, that isn't a correct impression.

The best data displays observe a fundamental principle of graphing data called the **area principle**, which says that the area occupied by a part of the graph should correspond to the magnitude of the value it represents.

Applying the Concepts

The Sharpe Edge: PLAN, DO, REPORT

There are three simple steps to doing Statistics right: *Plan, Do,* and *Report.*

We lead students through the process of making business decisions with data. The first step is planning how to tackle a problem, the second is doing the calculations, and the third is reporting the results and conclusions. In each chapter, we apply the new concepts learned in *Guided Example*. Examples are structured to the way statisticians approach and solve problems. These step-by-step examples show students how to produce the kind of solutions and reports that clients expect to see.

PLAN first. Know where you're headed and why. Clearly defining and understanding your objective will save you a lot of work. What do you know? What do you hope to learn? Are the assumptions and conditions satisfied?

DO is the mechanics of calculating statistics. This is what most people think Statistics is about. But the computations don't tell the whole story.

REPORT what you've learned. Until you've explained your results in the context of the business question in your Plan, the job isn't done. We present the report step as a memo to emphasize the decision aspect of each example.

GUIDED EXAMPLE	New York Stock Exchange Trading Volume

Are some months on the NYSE busier than others? Boxplots of the number of shares traded by month are a good way to see such patterns. We're interested not only in the centres, but also in the spreads. Are volumes equally variable from month to month, or are they more spread out in some months?

PLAN	**Setup** Identify the variables, report the time frame of the data, and state the objective.	We want to compare the daily volume of shares traded from month to month on the NYSE during 2006. The daily volume is quantitative and measured in number of shares. We can partition the values by month and use side-by-side boxplots to compare the volume across months.
DO	**Mechanics** Plot the side-by-side boxplots of the data.	
REPORT	**Conclusion** Report what you've learned about the data and any recommended action or analysis.	MEMO: **Re: Research on trading volume of the NYSE** We have examined the daily sales volume on the NYSE (number of shares traded) for each month of 2006. As the attached display shows, sales volume follows a seasonal pattern with lower volume in March and August. The highest median trading activity is found in November. The variability of trading volume also shows a pattern. June and December have higher variability than the rest, and March has noticeably less variability. There were several unusually high-volume days that bear investigation and one extremely low-volume day in November.

Promoting Understanding

What Can Go Wrong?

The most common mistakes for those new to statistical analysis usually involve misusing a method, not miscalculating a statistic. We acknowledge these mistakes with *What Can Go Wrong?*, found at the end of each chapter. Our goal is to arm students with the tools to detect statistical errors and offer practice in debunking misuses of statistics.

Math Box

The mathematical underpinnings of statistical methods and concepts are set apart to avoid interrupting the explanation of the topic at hand. We use these derivations to increase students' understanding of the underlying mathematics, but they can be skipped by less mathematically inclined students.

By Hand

Although we encourage using technology to perform statistical calculations, we recognize the benefits of knowing how to compute by hand. *By Hand* boxes explain formulas and help students through the calculation of a worked example.

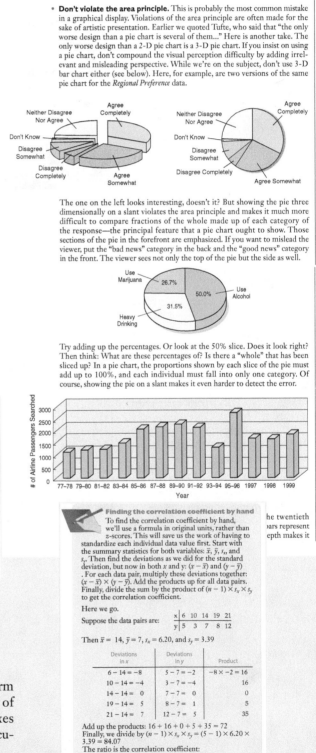

WHAT CAN GO WRONG?

- **Don't violate the area principle.** This is probably the most common mistake in a graphical display. Violations of the area principle are often made for the sake of artistic presentation. Earlier we quoted Tufte, who said that "the only worse design than a pie chart is several of them..." Here is another take. The only worse design than a 2-D pie chart is a 3-D pie chart. If you insist on using a pie chart, don't compound the visual perception difficulty by adding irrelevant and misleading perspective. While we're on the subject, don't use 3-D bar chart either (see below). Here, for example, are two versions of the same pie chart for the *Regional Preference* data.

The one on the left looks interesting, doesn't it? But showing the pie three dimensionally on a slant violates the area principle and makes it much more difficult to compare fractions of the whole made up of each category of the response—the principal feature that a pie chart ought to show. Those sections of the pie in the forefront are emphasized. If you want to mislead the viewer, put the "bad news" category in the back and the "good news" category in the front. The viewer sees not only the top of the pie but the side as well.

Try adding up the percentages. Or look at the 50% slice. Does it look right? Then think: What are these percentages of? Is there a "whole" that has been sliced up? In a pie chart, the proportions shown by each slice of the pie must add up to 100%, and each individual must fall into only one category. Of course, showing the pie on a slant makes it even harder to detect the error.

MATH BOX

We want to find the mean (expected value) of random variable X, using a geometric method with probability of success p.

First write the probabilities:

x	1	2	3	4	...
$P(X = x)$	p	qp	$q^2 p$	$q^3 p$	...

The expected value is: $E(X) = 1p + 2qp + 3q^2 p + 4q^3 p + \cdots$

Let $p = 1 - q$: $\qquad = (1-q) + 2q(1-q) + 3q^2(1-q) + 4q^3(1-q) + \cdots$

Simplify: $\qquad = 1 - q + 2q - 2q^2 + 3q^2 - 3q^3 + 4q^3 - 4q^4 + \cdots$

That's an infinite geometric series, with first term 1 and common ratio q:

$\qquad = 1 + q + q^2 + q^3 + \cdots$

$\qquad = \dfrac{1}{1-q}$

So, finally $\qquad E(X) = \dfrac{1}{p}$.

Finding the correlation coefficient by hand

To find the correlation coefficient by hand, we'll use a formula in original units, rather than z-scores. This will save us the work of having to standardize each individual data value first. Start with the summary statistics for both variables: $\bar{x}$, $\bar{y}$, s_x, and s_y. Then find the deviations as we did for the standard deviation, but now in both x and y: $(x - \bar{x})$ and $(y - \bar{y})$. For each data pair, multiply these deviations together: $(x - \bar{x}) \times (y - \bar{y})$. Add the products up for all data pairs. Finally, divide the sum by the product of $(n-1) \times s_x \times s_y$ to get the correlation coefficient.

Here we go.

Suppose the data pairs are:

x	6	10	14	19	21
y	5	3	7	8	12

Then $\bar{x} = 14$, $\bar{y} = 7$, $s_x = 6.20$, and $s_y = 3.39$

Deviations in x	Deviations in y	Product
$6 - 14 = -8$	$5 - 7 = -2$	$-8 \times -2 = 16$
$10 - 14 = -4$	$3 - 7 = -4$	16
$14 - 14 = 0$	$7 - 7 = 0$	0
$19 - 14 = 5$	$8 - 7 = 1$	5
$21 - 14 = 7$	$12 - 7 = 5$	35

Add up the products: $16 + 16 + 0 + 5 + 35 = 72$
Finally, we divide by $(n-1) \times s_x \times s_y = (5-1) \times 6.20 \times 3.39 = 84.07$
The ratio is the correlation coefficient:

$$r = 72/84.07 = 0.856$$

Integrating Technology

Technology Help

In business, Statistics is practised with computers. We offer specific guidance for Excel®, often with an annotated example to help students get started with the technology of their choice.

TECHNOLOGY HELP: Displaying and Summarizing Quantitative Variables

Almost any program that displays data can make a histogram, but some will do a better job of determining where the bars should start and how they should partition the span of the data (see the art on the next page).

Many statistics packages offer a prepackaged collection of summary measures. The result might look like this:

```
Variable: Weight
N = 234
Mean = 143.3      Median = 139
St. Dev = 11.1    IQR = 14
```

Alternatively, a package might make a table for several variables and summary measures:

Variable	N	mean	median	stdev	IQR
Weight	234	143.3	139	11.1	14
Height	234	68.3	68.1	4.3	5
Score	234	86	88	9	5

It is usually easy to read the results and identify each computed summary. You should be able to read the summary statistics produced by any computer package.

Packages often provide many more summary statistics than you need. Of course, some of these may not be appropriate when the data are skewed or have outliers. It is your responsibility to check a histogram or stem-and-leaf display and decide which summary statistics to use.

It is common for packages to report summary statistics to many decimal places of "accuracy." Of course, it is rare to find data that have such accuracy in the original measurements. The ability to calculate to six or seven digits beyond the decimal point doesn't mean that those digits have any meaning. Generally, it's a good idea to round these values, allowing perhaps one more digit of precision than was given in the original data.

Displays and summaries of quantitative variables are among the simplest things you can do in most statistics packages.

The vertical scale may be counts or proportions. Sometimes it isn't clear which. But the shape of the histogram is the same either way.

Most packages choose the number of bars for you automatically. Often you can adjust that choice.

The axis should be clearly labelled so you can tell what "pile" each bar represents. You should be able to tell the lower and upper bounds of each bar.

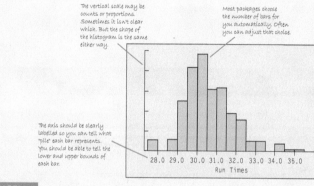

EXCEL

To calculate summaries, Click on an empty cell. Type an equals sign and choose " **Average**" from the popup list of functions that appears to the left of the text editing box. Enter the data range in the box that says " **Number 1**." Click the **OK** button. To compute the standard deviation of a column of data directly, use the **STDEV** from the popup list of functions in the same way.

Comments

Excel's Data Analysis add-in does offer something called a histogram, but it isn't a statistically appropriate histogram. Excel cannot make histograms, boxplots, or dotplots without a third-party add in. Excel's STDEV function should not be used for data values larger in magnitude than 100 000 or for lists of more than a few thousand values. It is fine for smaller data sets.

MINI CASE STUDY PROJECT

Eddie's Hang-Up Display

Chances are very high that when you walk into a retail store you notice the merchandise. But do you notice the store fixtures: hangers and size dividers, clothing racks, display cases, signs, tagging and price labels, mannequins, and the myriad of supplies that retailers need to run a business? Eddie's Hang-Up Display Ltd. (www.eddies.com) is one of Canada's leading importers and distributors of store fixtures and retail supplies. They have suppliers in Taiwan, China, Korea, Thailand, Italy, Turkey, France, and the United States. Eddie's has stores in Vancouver and Edmonton and offers over 3000 different display and supply items in addition to custom manufacturing.

Like MEC in the chapter's opening illustration, Eddie's relies on Google Analytics to analyze web traffic and a variety of other data. The Excel spreadsheet **ch04_MCPS_Eddies** has data on *Visits*, *Pages*, and *New Visits* for each of ten regions for March and October 2012. These are two peak months in their business as retailers prepare for spring and Christmas sales periods. The spreadsheet also has 2012 monthly data on these variables for British Columbia and Alberta, where Eddie's has retail stores.

Using Excel or your statistics package, create frequency tables and bar charts of the three variables by region, for each of the two months separately. Next, create a bar chart that compares the two months on the same graph. Then create frequency tables and bar charts to compare data from British Columbia and Alberta across the year. Write a case report summarizing your analysis and results.

Mini Case Study Projects

Each chapter includes one or more *Mini Case Study Projects* that use real data and ask students to investigate a question or make a decision. Students define the objective, plan the process, complete the analysis, and report their conclusion. Data for the *Mini Case Study Projects* are available on MyStatLab, formatted for various technologies. Solutions for the *Mini Case Study Projects* are found in the Instructor's Solutions Manual.

Checking Understanding

Just Checking

Once or twice per chapter, *Just Checking* asks students to stop and think about what they've read. These questions are designed to check student understanding and involve little calculation. Answers are provided at the end of the chapter so students can easily check their work.

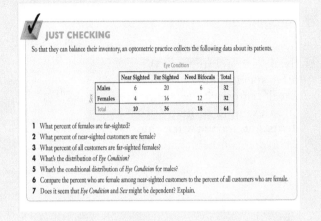

So that they can balance their inventory, an optometric practice collects the following data about its patients.

		Eye Condition			
		Near Sighted	Far Sighted	Need Bifocals	Total
Sex	Males	6	20	6	32
	Females	4	16	12	32
	Total	10	36	18	64

1 What percent of females are far-sighted?
2 What percent of near-sighted customers are female?
3 What percent of all customers are far-sighted females?
4 What's the distribution of *Eye Condition*?
5 What's the conditional distribution of *Eye Condition* for males?
6 Compare the percent who are female among near-sighted customers to the percent of all customers who are female.
7 Does it seem that *Eye Condition* and *Sex* might be dependent? Explain.

What Have We Learned?

These chapter-ending summaries highlight the concepts introduced in the chapter, define new terms, and list the skills presented in the chapter. If students understand all these parts, they're probably ready for the exam.

WHAT HAVE WE LEARNED?

We've learned that data are information in a context.

• The W's help nail down the context: *Who, What, Why, Where, When*.
• We must know at least the *Who, What,* and *Why* to be able to say anything useful based on the data. The *Who* are the *cases*. The *What* are the *variables*. A variable gives information about each of the cases. The *Why* helps us decide which way to treat the variables.

We treat variables in two basic ways, as *categorical* or *quantitative*.

• Categorical variables identify a category for each case. Usually we think about the counts of cases that fall in each category. (An exception is an identifier variable that just names each case.)
• Quantitative variables record measurements or amounts of something.
• Sometimes we treat a variable as categorical or quantitative depending on what we want to learn from it, which means some variables can't be pigeonholed as one type or the other. That's an early hint that in Statistics we can't always pin things down precisely.

Terms

Case	A case is an individual about whom or whic
Categorical variable	A variable that names categories (whether v categorical.
Context	The context ideally tells *Who* was measured were collected, *Where* the data were collect performed.
Cross-sectional data	Data taken from situations that vary over ti instant are said to be a cross-section of the
Data	Systematically recorded information, wheth context.
Data table	An arrangement of data in which each row represents a variable.
Experiment	A study in which the researcher *manipulates* factor on the response.
Experimental unit	An individual in a study for which or for wh experimental units are usually called subject
Identifier variable	A categorical variable that records a unique value for each case, used to name or identify it.
Nominal variable	The term "nominal" can be applied to data whose values are used only to name categories.

Skills

PLAN
• Recognize when a variable is categorical and choose an appropriate display for it.
• Understand how to examine the association between categorical variables by comparing conditional and marginal percentages.

DO
• Summarize the distribution of a categorical variable with a frequency table.
• Display the distribution of a categorical variable with a bar chart.
• Construct and examine a contingency table.
• Construct and examine displays of the conditional distributions of one variable for two or more groups.

REPORT
• Describe the distribution of a categorical variable in terms of its possible values and relative frequencies.
• Describe any anomalies or extraordinary features revealed by the display of a variable.
• Describe and discuss patterns found in a contingency table and associated displays of conditional distributions.

Tackling Problems

Exercises

We have worked hard to ensure that the exercises contain relevant and modern questions with real data. The exercises generally start with a straightforward application of the ideas, then tackle larger problems. Many break a problem into several parts to help guide the student through the logic of a complete analysis. Finally, there are exercises that ask students to synthesize and incorporate their ideas with less guidance. Data sets for exercises marked with **T** can be found on MyStatLab.

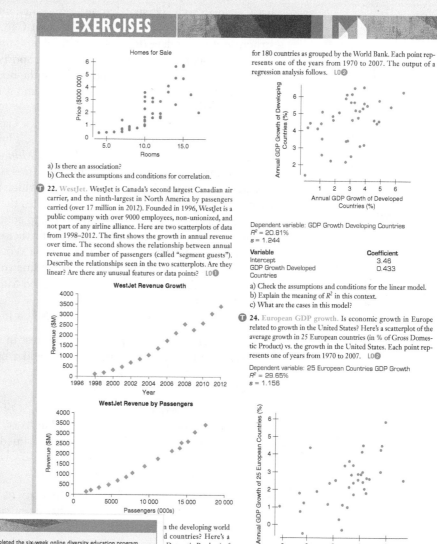

EXERCISES

a) Is there an association?
b) Check the assumptions and conditions for correlation.

T 22. WestJet. WestJet is Canada's second largest Canadian air carrier, and the ninth-largest in North America by passengers carried (over 17 million in 2012). Founded in 1996, WestJet is a public company with over 9000 employees, non-unionized, and not part of any airline alliance. Here are two scatterplots of data from 1998–2012. The first shows the growth in annual revenue over time. The second shows the relationship between annual revenue and number of passengers (called "segment guests"). Describe the relationships seen in the two scatterplots. Are they linear? Are there any unusual features or data points? **LO❶**

for 180 countries as grouped by the World Bank. Each point represents one of the years from 1970 to 2007. The output of a regression analysis follows. **LO❷**

Dependent variable: GDP Growth Developing Countries
$R^2 = 20.81\%$
$s = 1.244$

Variable	Coefficient
Intercept	3.46
GDP Growth Developed Countries	0.433

a) Check the assumptions and conditions for the linear model.
b) Explain the meaning of R^2 in this context.
c) What are the cases in this model?

T 24. European GDP growth. Is economic growth in Europe related to growth in the United States? Here's a scatterplot of the average growth in 25 European countries (in % of Gross Domestic Product) vs. the growth in the United States. Each point represents one of years from 1970 to 2007. **LO❷**

Dependent variable: 25 European Countries GDP Growth
$R^2 = 29.65\%$
$s = 1.156$

Ethics in Action

Our ethics vignettes in each chapter illustrate some of the judgments needed in statistical analysis, identify possible errors, link the issues to the ASA's Ethical Guidelines, and then propose ethically and statistically sound alternatives.

This book recognizes both the changing curriculum and the changing pedagogy for teaching introductory Statistics. It focuses on application, streamlines and reorganizes topics, sheds unneeded theoretical details, and recognizes learning styles of the current generation of students, making it an attractive choice for single-term courses at Canadian business schools.

The Canadian edition uses illustrative case studies and chapter exercises that focus on business and management of Canadian companies, large and small. The writing has Canadian style, perspective, and sensibility, not just changes to spelling and metric measurements. The book recognizes that Canada has public policy, governmental structure and mandate (federal, provincial, and municipal), economic systems (banking and finance), social services, health care, sports, and entertainment that are different from those of the United States. While the book is indeed Canadian, it also shows how Statistics has no geographical borders and is a vital part of building and enhancing the global community.

Most chapter-opening examples reflect a Canadian situation that is then used within the chapter to illustrate new concepts. Throughout the chapters, exercises use Canadian sources and examples, as do most *Mini Case Study Projects*.

The Canadian edition has two new features on the chapter opener, to help map the chapter content: Learning Objectives, which are then tied to the end-of-chapter exercises, and a Connections box that situates the content within the text as a whole. New and expanded topics, new sidebars, and added warnings in *What Can Go Wrong* features throughout the chapters provide further clarity and context for students.

Chapter 16, Statistical Modelling and the World of Business Statistics, is a brand-new capstone chapter. It provides both a framework for the inference methods developed in Chapters 9 through 15 and a method for choosing an appropriate procedure for a given data analysis situation.

Here are some highlights of what else is new in the Canadian edition:

- **Chapter 1** encourages students' interest in and understanding of the discipline through the revised chapter opener and a brand-new Section 1.1, The Role of Statistics in the World. This chapter also includes new material to explain and expand on the concept of variation.

- **Chapter 2** expands Section 2.2, Types of Variables (and Types of Data), to include topics such as "imaginary" units or underlying measurement scale, the creation of quantitative variables as summed ordinal scales, and string variables. The new Section 2.3, Data Quality, categorizes data as "good" versus "bad" and explores various aspects of data quality.

- **Chapter 3** provides additional explanations of *population, parameter, sample, statistic,* and *sampling frame* and sidebar discussions that help contextualize the concept of polls and surveys.

- **Chapter 4** introduces alternatives and variations on bar charts—dot plot, Pareto chart—and segmented bar charts as an alternative to pie charts.

- **Chapter 5** has new historical notes on the term *histogram*, the origins of stem-and-leaf displays, and the use of x-bar notation; an added explanation of harmonic and geometric means, with illustrative examples; and the probability explanation of the $n-1$ denominator of sample standard deviation.

- **Chapter 6** has a new discussion on regression to the mean, with graphical illustration.

- **Chapter 7** features expanded commentary about and illustrations of Bayes' Rule. The new Section 7.10, Fun with Probability!, describes three famous probability puzzles.

- **Chapter 8** has a new subsection on dependent random variables, in light of their importance in finance and portfolio diversification.

- **Chapter 9** includes stronger ties to material in previous and later chapters, to help students draw on what they have already learned.

- **Chapter 10** has a full illustration of the correspondence between the logic of hypothesis testing and proof by contradiction, as well as new explanations of concepts such as statistical versus practical significance and how the two error-type probabilities are inversely related.

- **Chapter 11** includes feature boxes that connect statistics to students' everyday life, including a *Just Checking* feature on the Canadian census administered by Statistics Canada and an *Ethics in Action* box that addresses wait times for elective medical treatment in Canada.

- **Chapter 12** has a new subsection about how the paired *t*-test works, as well as a new Section 12.9, Comparing Two Proportions, with an illustrative example on Facebook usage by teenagers.

- **Chapter 13** combines the two sections on the chi-square test of homogeneity and the chi-square test of independence into a single section, Chi-Square Tests of Two-Way Tables, showing how the two-proportion *z*-test can be recast as a two-way table and then extended to more rows and more columns.

- **Chapter 14** has two new sections: Section 14.10, A Hypothesis Test for Correlation, and Section 14.11, ANOVA and the *F*-statistic.

- **Chapter 15** has two new sections: Section 15.6, Building, Comparing, and Using Models, and Section 15.7, Extending Multiple Regression.

- **Chapter 16,** the new capstone chapter, synthesizes key material from earlier chapters. It also provides a brief description of several business statistics methods beyond the scope of this text and concludes with comments on the future of business statistics and big data.

We set out to write a book for business students that answers the simple question: "How can I make better decisions?" As entrepreneurs and consultants, we know that statistics are essential to survive and thrive in today's competitive environment. As educators, we've seen a disconnect between the way Statistics is taught to business students and the way it is used in making business decisions. In *Business Statistics: A First Course*, we try to close the gap between theory and practice by presenting statistical methods so they are both relevant and interesting to students.

The data that inform a business decision have a story to tell, and the role of statistics is to help us hear that story clearly. Like other textbooks, *Business Statistics: A First Course* teaches how to select and perform inferential tests and highlights definitions and formulas. But, unlike other textbooks, *Business Statistics: A First Course* also teaches the "why" and insists that results be reported in the context of business decisions. Students will come away knowing how to use statistics to make better business decisions and how to effectively communicate both their analysis and recommendations.

Business Statistics: A First Course is written with the understanding that today Statistics is practised with technology. This insight informs everything from our choice of forms for equations to our extensive use of real data. But more important, understanding the value of technology allows us to focus on teaching statistical thinking rather than calculation. The questions that motivate each of our hundreds of examples are not "how do you find the answer?" but "how do you think about the answer, and how does it help you make a better decision?"

Our focus on statistical thinking ties the chapters of the book together. An introductory business statistics course covers an overwhelming number of new terms, concepts, and methods. But they have a central core: how we can understand more about the world and make better decisions by understanding what the data tell us. From this perspective, students can see that the many ways to draw inferences from data are several applications of the same core concepts.

Our Goal: Read This Book!

The best textbook in the world is of little value if students don't read it. Here are some of the ways we made *Business Statistics: A First Course* more approachable:

- *Readability.* You'll see immediately that this book doesn't read like other Statistics texts. We strive for a conversational, approachable style, and we introduce anecdotes to maintain interest. In class tests, instructors report their amazement that students are voluntarily reading ahead of their assignments. Students write to tell us (to their amazement) that they actually enjoyed the book.

- *Focus on assumptions and conditions.* More than any other textbook, *Business Statistics: A First Course* emphasizes the need to verify assumptions to use statistical procedures. We reiterate this focus throughout the examples and exercises. We make every effort to provide students with templates that reinforce the practice of checking these assumptions and conditions, rather than rushing through the computations of a real-life problem.

- *Emphasis on graphing and exploring data.* Our consistent emphasis on the importance of displaying data is evident through all chapters. Examples always include data displays and often illustrate the value of examining data visually, and the exercises reinforce this. When we graph data, we are able to see structures, or patterns, that we can't see otherwise. These patterns often raise new questions and guide our statistical analysis and case analysis process. Emphasizing graphics throughout the book helps students see that the structures we look for in graphs help illuminate sophisticated concepts.

- *Consistency.* We work hard to avoid the "do as we say, not as we do" trap. Having taught the importance of plotting data and checking assumptions and conditions, we are careful to model that behaviour throughout the book. (Check the exercises in the chapter on multiple regression and you'll find us still requiring and demonstrating the plots and checks that were introduced in the early chapters.) This consistency helps reinforce these fundamental principles.

- *The need to read.* Students who plan just to skim the book may find that important concepts, definitions, and sample solutions are not always set aside in boxes. This book needs to be read, so we've tried to make the reading experience enjoyable.

Coverage

The topics covered in a Business Statistics course are generally consistent and mandated by our students' needs in their studies and in their future professions. But the *order* of these topics and the relative emphasis given to each is not well established. In *Business Statistics: A First Course*, you may encounter some topics sooner or later than you expected. Although we have written many chapters specifically so they can be taught in a different order, we urge you to consider the order we have chosen.

We've been guided in the order of topics by the fundamental principle that this should be a coherent course in which concepts and methods fit together to give students a new understanding of how reasoning with data can uncover new and important truths. We have tried to ensure that each new topic fits into the growing structure of understanding that we hope students will build. For example, we teach inference concepts with proportions first and then with means. Students have a wider experience with proportions, seeing them in polls and advertising. And by starting with proportions, we can teach inference with the Normal model and then introduce inference for means with the Student's *t*-distribution.

We introduce the concepts of association, correlation, and regression early in *Business Statistics: A First Course*. Our experience in the classroom shows that introducing students to these fundamental ideas early motivates them at the beginning of the course. Later in the semester, when we discuss inference, students recall what they have learned and find it natural and relatively easy to build on the fundamental concepts they experienced by exploring data with these methods. In an introductory course, the relative emphasis placed on topics requires planning by the instructor. Introductory Business Statistics courses often have limited time, so it can be hard to get to the important topics of multiple regression and model building with enough time to treat them thoroughly. We've been guided in our choice of what to emphasize by the GAISE (Guidelines for Assessment and Instruction in Statistics Education) Report,[1] which resulted from extensive experience in how students best learn statistics. Those recommendations, which received wide support and adoption across North America (Statistical Society of Canada and American Statistical Association), urge (among other detailed suggestions) that Statistics education should:

1. Emphasize statistical literacy and develop statistical thinking;
2. Use real data;
3. Stress conceptual understanding rather than mere knowledge of procedures;

[1] www.amstat.org/education/gaise

4. Foster active learning;
5. Use technology for developing conceptual understanding and analyzing data; and
6. Make assessment a part of the learning process.

In this sense, this book is thoroughly modern. But to be effective, a course must fit comfortably with the instructor's preferences. There are several equally effective pathways through this material depending on the emphasis a particular instructor wants to make. We describe some alternative orders that also work comfortably with these materials.

Flexible Syllabus. *Business Statistics: A First Course* follows the GAISE Guidelines. The committee that developed these guidelines was made up of innovative educators in Statistics education, including one of the authors of this textbook (Velleman). Those guidelines call for presenting students with real data early and throughout the course and emphasizing real-world decisions and understanding as the final step of any statistical analysis. Following that advice, we have placed an introductory (exploratory, non-inference) section on regression early in the text (Chapter 6).

However, we are acutely aware of the challenge that Statistics instructors face in covering essential material in a limited period of time. For that reason we offer suggested modifications that may better fit your teaching style and requirements:

- Chapter 3 (Surveys and Sampling) can be taught just before Chapter 7 (Randomness and Probability), where it would provide motivation for randomness.

- Chapter 6 (Correlation and Linear Regression [without inference]) can be taught just before Chapter 14 (Inference for Regression), where it would form a larger lesson on regression analysis through inference and can be followed immediately by Chapter 15's discussion of multiple regression.

- Chapter 7 (Randomness and Probability) can be excluded if probability is taught in a separate course (e.g. quantitative decision-making), or for a more data-focused course.

- We introduce inference with proportions. We find this works better for students (who know about polls and margins of error in that context), and makes the presentation simpler. If you prefer to introduce inference with means, you can teach Chapter 11 (Confidence Intervals and Hypothesis Tests for Means) before Chapter 10 (Testing Hypotheses about Proportions). Note, however, that we teach inference for means without the assumption that the population standard deviation is known, and thus emphasize Student's t. That reflects the almost universal practice in real business analyses and in all statistics software. It also frees students of any concern about how big a sample should be before "switching" from t to Normal—with modern technology, there is no need to switch. And no statistics package or regression analysis does switch.

- Chapters 12 (Comparing Two Groups) and 13 (Inference for Counts: Chi-Square Tests) are omitted by some instructors.

- Chapter 15 introduces multiple regression, which can also be omitted.

- Chapter 16 is designed to be a capstone chapter, by summarizing inference in the framework of statistical modelling. For courses that do not cover regression models, this chapter is optional.

Features

A textbook isn't just words on a page: it is many features that come together to form a big picture. The features in *Business Statistics: A First Course* provide a real-world context for concepts, help students apply these concepts, promote problem-solving, and integrate technology—all of which help students understand and see the big picture of Business Statistics.

Motivating Examples. Each chapter opens with a motivating example, often taken from the authors' consulting experiences. These companies—such as Angus Reid, Mountain Equipment Co-op, Manulife Financial, and Canada Goose—enhance and illustrate the story of each chapter and show students how and why statistical thinking is so vital to modern business decision-making. We analyze the data from those companies throughout the chapter.

LEARNING OBJECTIVES

Learning Objectives. Each chapter begins with a list of learning objectives. These are brief but clear statements about what students are expected to know and be able to demonstrate by the end of chapter (or the end of the course). These will also help instructors with course planning and classroom delivery. Each end-of-chapter exercise references one or more learning objectives to guide students' assessment of their progress with the material.

CONNECTIONS

Connections. Although the authors (and, we hope, the instructors) know how the chapters of a textbook are related to each other and understand the logic behind the sequencing, it may not be clear to students until they reach the end of the book. The Connections boxes explain how the current chapter is related to the previous chapter(s), and why its position in the sequence is appropriate.

Step-by-Step Guided Examples. The ability to clearly communicate statistical results is crucial to helping Statistics contribute to business decision-making. To that end, some examples in each chapter are presented as *Guided Examples*. A good solution is modelled in the right column while commentary appears in the left column. The overall analysis follows our innovative **Plan, Do, Report** template. That template begins each analysis with a clear question about a decision and ends with a report that answers that question. To emphasize the decision aspect of each example, we present the **Report** step as a business memo that summarizes the results in the context of the example and states a recommendation if the data are able to support one. In addition, whenever possible we include limitations of the analysis or models in the concluding memo.

MINI CASE STUDY PROJECTS

Mini Case Study Projects. Each chapter includes one or two *Mini Case Study Projects* that use real data and ask students to investigate a question or make a decision. Students define the objective, plan the process, complete the analysis, and report a conclusion. Data for the *Mini Case Study Projects* are available on MyStatLab.

What Can Go Wrong? Each chapter contains an innovative section called *What Can Go Wrong?* that highlights the most common statistical errors and the misconceptions people have about Statistics. The most common mistakes for the new user of statistical methods involve misusing a method, not miscalculating a statistic. Most of the mistakes we discuss have been experienced by the authors in a business context rather than a classroom situation. One of our goals is to arm students with the tools to detect statistical errors and to offer practice in recognizing when Statistics is misused, whether intentional or not. In this spirit, some of our exercises probe the understanding of such errors.

By Hand. Even though we encourage the use of technology to calculate statistical quantities, we realize the pedagogical benefits of doing a calculation by hand. The *By Hand* boxes break apart the calculation of some of the simpler formulas and help the student through the calculation of a worked example.

REALITY CHECK

Reality Check. We regularly remind students that Statistics is about understanding the world and making decisions with data. Results that make no sense are probably wrong, no matter how carefully we think we did the calculations. Mistakes are often easy to spot with a little thought, so we ask students to stop for a reality check before interpreting results.

Notation Alert. Throughout this book, we emphasize the importance of clear communication. Proper notation is part of the vocabulary of Statistics, but it can be daunting. Students who know that in Algebra n can stand for any variable may be surprised to learn that in Statistics n is always the sample size. Statisticians dedicate many letters and symbols for specific meanings (b, e, n, p, q, r, s, t, and z, along with many Greek letters all carry special connotations). Students learn more effectively when they are clear about the letters and symbols statisticians use.

Just Checking. To help students check their understanding of material they've just read, we ask questions at points throughout the chapter. These questions are a quick check and most involve little calculation. The answers are at the end of the exercise sets in each chapter so students can easily check themselves to be sure they understand the key ideas. The questions can also be used to motivate class discussion.

MATH BOX

Math Boxes. In many chapters, we present the mathematical underpinnings of the statistical methods and concepts. Different students learn in different ways, and even the same student can understand the material by more than one path. By setting these proofs, derivations, and justifications apart from the narrative, we allow the student to continue to follow the logical development of the topic at hand, yet also make available the underlying mathematics for greater depth.

WHAT HAVE WE LEARNED?

What Have We Learned? These chapter-ending summaries highlight new concepts, define new terms introduced in the chapter, and list the skills that the student should have acquired. Students can think of these as study guides. If they understand the concepts in the summary, know the terms, and have the skills, they're probably ready for the exam.

ETHICS IN ACTION

Ethics in Action. Students are often surprised to learn that Statistics is not just plugging numbers into formulas. Most statistical analyses require a fair amount of judgment. The best guidance for these judgments is that we make an honest and ethical attempt to learn the truth. Anything less than that can lead to poor and even dangerous decisions. The *Ethics in Action* vignettes in each chapter illustrate some of the judgments needed in statistical analyses, identify possible errors, link the issues to widely accepted ethical guidelines in Statistics, and then propose ethically and statistically sound alternative approaches.

Exercises. We've worked hard to ensure that exercises contain relevant, modern, and real-world questions. Many come from news stories; some come from recent research articles. Whenever possible, the data are on MyStatLab (always in a variety of formats) so students can explore them further. Sometimes, because of the size of the data set, the data are only available electronically. Throughout the book, we pair the exercises so that each odd-numbered exercise (with answer in the back of the book) is followed by an even-numbered exercise on the same Statistics topic. Exercises are roughly ordered within each chapter by both topic and by level of difficulty.

Data Sources. Most of the data used in examples and exercises are from real-world sources, and we list many sources in this edition. Whenever we can, we include references to the internet data sources used, often in the form of URLs. As internet users (and thus, our students) know well, URLs can "break" as websites evolve. To minimize the impact of such changes, we point as high in the address tree as is practical. Moreover, the data themselves often change as more recent values become available. The data we use are usually on MyStatLab. If you seek the data—or an updated version of the data—on the internet, we try to direct you to a good starting point.

TECHNOLOGY HELP

Technology Help. In business, Statistics is practised with computers, but not with a single software platform. Instead of emphasizing a particular statistics program, at the end of each chapter, we summarize what students can find in the most common packages, often with annotated output. We then offer specific guidance for one of the most common packages, Excel®, to help students get started with the software of their choice.

Supplements

Technology Resources

MyStatLab™ Online Course (access code required). MyStatLab is a course management system that delivers **proven results** in helping individual students succeed.

- MyStatLab can be successfully implemented in any environment—lab-based, hybrid, fully online, traditional—and demonstrates the quantifiable difference that integrated usage has on student retention, subsequent success, and overall achievement.

- MyStatLab's comprehensive online gradebook automatically tracks students' results on tests, quizzes, and homework, and in the study plan. Instructors can use the gradebook to provide positive feedback or intervene if students have trouble. Gradebook data can be easily exported to a variety of spreadsheet programs, such as Microsoft Excel. You can determine which points of data you want to export, and then analyze the results to determine success.

MyStatLab provides **engaging experiences** that personalize, stimulate, and measure learning for each student. In addition to the following resources, each course includes a full interactive online version of the accompanying textbook.

- **Data Sets:** Data sets are available on MyStatLab and are formatted for use with Excel® and other statistics software.

- **Tutorial Exercises with Multimedia Learning Aids:** The homework and practice exercises in MyStatLab align with the exercises in the textbook, and they regenerate algorithmically to give students unlimited opportunity for practice and mastery. Exercises offer immediate helpful feedback, guided solutions, sample problems, animations, videos, and eText clips for extra help at point-of-use.

- **StatTalk Videos:** *24 Conceptual Videos to Help You Actually Understand Statistics.* Fun-loving statistician Andrew Vickers takes to the streets of Brooklyn, New York, to demonstrate important statistical concepts through interesting stories and real-life events. These fun and engaging videos will help students actually understand statistical concepts. Available with an instructor's user guide and assessment questions.

- **Business Insight Videos:** Concept videos feature Deckers, Southwest Airlines, Starwood, and other companies and focus on statistical concepts as they pertain to the real world.

- **Getting Ready for Statistics:** A library of questions now appears within each MyStatLab course to offer the developmental math topics students need for the course. These can be assigned as a prerequisite to other assignments, if desired.

- **Conceptual Question Library:** In addition to algorithmically regenerated questions that are aligned with the textbook, there is a library of 1000 Conceptual Questions available in the assessment manager that requires students to apply their statistical understanding.

- **StatCrunch™:** MyStatLab integrates the web-based statistical software StatCrunch within the online assessment platform so that students can easily analyze data sets from exercises and the text. In addition, MyStatLab includes access to **www.StatCrunch.com**, a website where users can access more than 15 000 shared data sets, conduct online surveys, perform complex analyses using the powerful statistical software, and generate compelling reports.

- **Statistical Software Support:** Knowing that students often use external statistical software, we make it easy to copy our data sets into software such as StatCrunch, Minitab, Excel, and more. Students have access to a variety of support tools—Technology Tutorial Videos, Technology Study Cards, and Technology Manuals for select titles—to learn how to effectively use statistical software.

- **Pearson eText:** Pearson eText gives students access to the text whenever and wherever they have access to the Internet. eText pages look exactly like the printed text, offering powerful new functionality for students and instructors. Users can create notes, highlight text in different colours, create bookmarks, zoom, click hyperlinked words and phrases to view definitions, and view in single-page or two-page view. Pearson eText allows for quick navigation to key parts of the eText using a table of contents and provides full-text search. The eText may also offer links to associated media files, enabling users to access videos, animations, or other activities as they read the text.

MathXL® for Statistics Online Course (access code required). MathXL® is the homework and assessment engine that runs MyStatLab. (MyStatLab is MathXL plus a learning management system.) With MathXL for Statistics, instructors can

- Create, edit, and assign online homework and tests using algorithmically generated exercises correlated at the objective level to the textbook.

- Create and assign their own online exercises and import TestGen tests for added flexibility.

- Maintain records of all student work, tracked in MathXL's online gradebook.

With MathXL for Statistics, students can

- Take chapter tests in MathXL and receive personalized study plans and/or personalized homework assignments based on their test results.

- Use the study plan and/or the homework to link directly to tutorial exercises for the objectives they need to study.

- Access supplemental animations and video clips directly from selected exercises.

Knowing that students often use external statistical software, we make it easy to copy our data sets, both from the eText and the MyStatLab questions, into software like StatCrunch™, Minitab®, Excel®, and more.

MathXL for Statistics is available to qualified adopters. For more information, visit our website at **www.mathxl.com**, or contact your Pearson representative.

StatCrunch. StatCrunch is powerful web-based statistical software that allows users to perform complex analyses, share data sets, and generate compelling reports of their data. The vibrant online community offers more than 15 000 data sets for students to analyze.

- **Collect.** Users can upload their own data to StatCrunch or search a large library of publicly shared data sets, spanning almost any topic of interest. Also, an online survey tool allows users to quickly collect data via web-based surveys.

- **Crunch.** A full range of numerical and graphical methods allow users to analyze and gain insights from any data set. Interactive graphics help users understand statistical concepts, and are available for export to enrich reports with visual representations of data.

- **Communicate.** Reporting options help users create a wide variety of visually appealing representations of their data.

Full access to StatCrunch is available with a MyStatLab kit, and StatCrunch is available by itself to qualified adopters. StatCrunch Mobile is now available to access from your mobile device. For more information, visit our website at **www.Stat-Crunch.com**, or contact your Pearson representative.

Additional Student Supplement

CourseSmart for Students. CourseSmart goes beyond traditional expectations—providing instant, online access to the textbooks and course materials you need at significant savings over the price of a printed text. With instant access from any computer and the ability to search your text, you'll find the content you need quickly, no matter where you are. And with online tools like highlighting and note-taking, you can save time and study efficiently. See all the benefits at www.coursesmart.com/students.

Instructor Supplements

Instructor's Solutions Manual. This manual contains solutions for all end-of-chapter exercises as well as the Mini Case Study Projects. Available within MyStatLab or at http://www.pearsoncanada.ca/highered.

Instructor's Resource Guide. This guide contains chapter-by-chapter comments on the major concepts, tips on presenting topics (and what to avoid), teaching examples, suggested assignments, basic exercises, and web links and lists of other resources. Available within MyStatLab or at http://www.pearsoncanada.ca/highered.

Business Insight Video Guide to accompany *Statistics*. Written to accompany the Business Insight Videos, this guide includes a summary of the video, video-specific questions and answers that can be used for assessment or classroom discussion, a correlation to relevant chapters in *Statistics*, concept-centred teaching points, and useful web links. The Video Guide is available for download from MyStatLab or at http://www.pearsoncanada.ca/highered.

PowerPoint® Lecture Slides. The PowerPoint® package provides an outline to use in a lecture setting, presenting definitions, key concepts, and figures from the text. These slides are available within MyStatLab or at http://www.pearsoncanada.ca/highered.

TestGen® (www.pearsoned.com/testgen). TestGen software enables instructors to build, edit, print, and administer tests using a computerized bank of questions developed to cover all the objectives of the text. TestGen is algorithmically based, allowing instructors to create multiple but equivalent versions of the same question or test with the click of a button. Instructors can also modify test bank questions or add new questions. The software and testbank are available for download from Pearson Canada's online catalogue.

Test Item File. All the test questions from the TestGen testbank are also available in Microsoft Word format, available within MyStatLab or at www.pearsoncanada.ca/highered.

Image Library. An image library with electronic copies of key figures and tables from the text is available within MyStatLab or at www.pearsoncanada.ca/highered.

CourseSmart for Instructors. CourseSmart goes beyond traditional expectations—providing instant, online access to the textbooks and course materials you need at a lower cost for students. And even as students save money, you can save time and hassle with a digital eTextbook that allows you to search for the most relevant content at the very moment you need it.

Whether it's evaluating textbooks or creating lecture notes to help students with difficult concepts, CourseSmart can make life a little easier. See how when you visit www.coursesmart.com/instructors.

Pearson Custom Library. For enrollments of at least 25 students, you can create your own textbook by choosing the chapters that best suit your own course needs. To begin building your custom text, visit www.pearsoncustomlibrary.com. You may also work with a dedicated Pearson Custom editor to create your ideal text—publishing your own original content or mixing and matching Pearson content. Contact your local Pearson sales representative to get started.

Learning Solutions Managers. Pearson's Learning Solutions Managers work with faculty and campus course designers to ensure that Pearson technology products, assessment tools, and online course materials are tailored to meet your specific needs. This highly qualified team is dedicated to helping schools take full advantage of a wide range of educational resources, by assisting in the integration of a variety of instructional materials and media formats. Your local Pearson sales representative can provide you with more details on this service program.

Acknowledgments

Many people have contributed to this book from the first day of its conception to its publication. This book would not have been possible without the many contributions of David Bock, our co-author on several of our other textbooks. Many of the explanations and exercises in this book benefit from Dave's pedagogical flair and expertise. We are honoured to have him as a colleague and friend.

Business Statistics: A First Course would have never seen the light of day without the assistance of the incredible team at Pearson. We'd also like to thank our accuracy checkers whose monumental task was to make sure we said what we thought we were saying; the individuals who joined us for a weekend to discuss business statistics education, emerging trends, technology, and business ethics; and those who provided feedback through focus groups, class tests, and reviews.

Finally, we want to thank our families. This has been a long project, and it has required many nights and weekends. Our families have sacrificed so that we could write the book we envisioned.

Norean Sharpe
Richard De Veaux
Paul Velleman

My sincere thanks to Mark Wexler for his guidance and suggestions on how to successfully undertake a textbook writing project, and to Sam Shamash for his list of suggested suitable companies to profile.

Special thanks to Stephen Gaerber, Neil Cumming, Rob Philipp, and Kit Chansavang for providing interesting and illuminating data sets for chapter openers or exercises.

Thanks to Jan Wallace and Alex Micu for their early assistance and helping me get my first chapter written.

And most importantly, from a very proud father, thanks to Joshua Berkowitz and Matthew Berkowitz, who enthusiastically undertook internet research to suggest appropriate case studies and exercises, and to find relevant data sets.

Thanks to the amazing team at Pearson, in particular, Megan Farrell, Acquisitions Editor; Darryl Kamo and Lori McLellan, Developmental Editors; and Cat Haggert, Copy Editor.

The following reviewers (plus other who choose to remain anonymous) provided feedback on either the U.S. edition or the manuscript for the Canadian edition:

Peter Au, George Brown College
Charles A. Backman, Grande Prairie Regional College
Fouzia Baki, McMaster University
Walid Belassi, Athabasca University
Clare Chua, Ryerson University
Laurel A. Donaldson, Douglas College
Torben Drewes, Trent University
Bruno Fullone, George Brown College
Scott Hadley, Sheridan Institute of Technology and Advanced Learning
Darryl Hammond, Red River College of Applied Arts, Science and Technology
Ali R. Hassanlou, Kwantlen Polytechnic University
Dave Kennedy, Lethbridge College
Dennis Kira, Concordia University
Linda Lakats, York University
Lisa MacKay, SAIT Polytechnic
Colin F. Mang, Nipissing University
John Mayer, SAIT Polytechnic
Ron McCarron, Cape Breton University
Hassan Qudrat-Ullah, York University
Gerhard Trippen, University of Toronto Mississauga
Thomas Varghese, Northern Alberta Institute of Technology

Their comments helped to shape this edition of the book.

Jonathan Berkowitz

Why Statistics Is Important ... to YOU

CONNECTIONS: CHAPTER

A connection is a linkage. It comes from the Latin *com-* (with) + *nectere* (to bind). Boxes like this at the beginning of each chapter will bind the textbook together. They will tell you how the chapter you are about to start is related to the previous chapter(s) and why it fits logically into the sequence of chapters. Since this is Chapter 1, we don't have anything to connect it to, yet!

Just look at a page from the *Financial Times* website, like the one shown here. It's full of "statistics." Obviously, the writers of the *Financial Times* think all this information is important, but is this what Statistics is all about? Well, yes and no. This page may contain a lot of facts, but as we'll see, the subject is much more interesting and powerful than just spreadsheets and tables.

"Why should I learn Statistics?" you might ask. "After all, I don't plan to do this kind of work. In fact, I'm going to hire people to do this stuff." That's fine. But the decisions you make based on data are too important to delegate. You'll want to be able to interpret the data that surround you and to come to your own conclusions. And you'll want to understand how to gather the right kind and sufficient amount of data to answer questions that are important to you.

There are two parties involved in statistical decision-making: those who present the analysis and those who receive it. No matter which side you are on, you need to know about statistics.

You will find that studying Statistics is much more important and enjoyable than you thought. We hope that our book succeeds in removing the "r" from "Intro Stats" and turns you into someone who is really "into stats"!

LEARNING OBJECTIVES

❶ Recognize that knowledge of statistics is vital for the twenty-first century

❷ Think about the role of variation and uncertainty in your life

❸ Commit to READING THIS BOOK

1.1 The Role of Statistics in the World

There are lots of jokes about statistics and statisticians, and most of them are not entirely flattering. Here's one: Statisticians are like accountants, but without the sense of humour. Here's another: How many statisticians does it take to change a light bulb? Answer: What would you like the answer to be?

The first joke is totally wrong. Statisticians are fun-loving, jovial people with keen senses of humour (well, most of us). But the second joke has a strong element of truth in it. It underscores that most people are uneasy about the subject, that they don't think they'll ever understand the answer a statistician gives, and that the answers seem to change with the wind.

We live in a data-centric world. In business, organizational functions such as finance, marketing, and operations all make extensive use of data collection and statistical analysis techniques. But statistics is not just a vital part of business. Every aspect of our lives is bombarded with, and determined by, data and statistics. Statisticians have a favourite line from the fictional detective Sherlock Holmes: "Data, data, data!" he cried impatiently. "I cannot make bricks without clay." How do you make the bricks? With Statistics, the set of techniques for collecting, organizing, summarizing, analyzing, and interpreting the data.

Every section of a daily newspaper is governed by statistical thinking. The front section reports government policies that have been developed, in part, with opinion polling. The business section reports economic indicators, stock market behaviour, company earnings, real estate prices, and so on. The sports section is almost completely statistical: measurements of athletic performance, all-time records, current standings, salaries, and contracts. The entertainment section has news about films, music, television, and radio; decisions about which shows or albums are made are based on statistical ratings and box-office revenues. The lifestyle section reports on the latest news in the world of medicine and health care, diet and exercise, fashion, and consumer products. The central part of these activities involves clinical trials of medical treatments, product design and market research, or customer surveys. The classified ads have statistics, such as the price listed for an item for sale. Even the comics have statistics; many Dilbert cartoons address statistical concepts!

Florence Nightingale (1820–1910) was a British social reformer, nurse, and part-time statistician. Her knowledge of mathematics and statistics saved the lives of many in the British army during the Crimean war and provided data that led to widespread hospital reforms. She wrote, "Statistics...[is] the most important science in the whole world; for upon it depends the practical application of every other science and of every art; the one science essential to all political and social administration, all education, all organization based on experience, for it only gives results of our experience." What she said so eloquently can be restated more simply: Until you've tested an idea on a group and found out what happens in the aggregate, you can't apply it to the individual. In other words, you can't accurately predict what one person might do but you can accurately predict what a group of people might do. This is sometimes referred to as "the wisdom of crowds."

It is not an overstatement to say that virtually every area of life or field of inquiry uses statistics. Most decision-making is now quantitative. We hope this convinces you not to ask, as some high school students do about Algebra, "Why do we need to learn Statistics?" We think you need it to live as a productive member of society.

Speaking of society, societies worldwide agree that illiteracy is a fundamental barrier to development on the national and the personal level, and should be eradicated. We need to achieve the same understanding of the problems caused by innumeracy or quantitative illiteracy. The famed cognitive scientist, Douglas Hofstadter, wrote, "Our society would be unimaginably different if the average person truly understood basic mathematical concepts." A key part of numeracy (the counterpart to literacy) is statistical literacy, the ability to handle fundamental ideas of numbers and chance.

The size of numbers is crucial. The worlds of business, finance, and economics need to understand just how large a million, or a billion, or a trillion really is. The U.S. financial bailout in 2008 was close to one trillion dollars. Did the politicians and decision-makers really understand how big that was? To put it in perspective, let's change from units of money to units of time. A million seconds is 11.5 days, a billion seconds is 32 years, while a trillion seconds is 32 000 years!

The worlds of risk management, insurance, engineering, health, medicine, and law need to understand how small a one in a million or one in a billion chance is. When is a risk small enough not to worry about? The chance of winning the biggest prize in Lotto 6/49 is about one in 14 million. To put that in perspective, it is equivalent to guessing correctly which exact second I am thinking of, between now and nearly six months from now.

Basic statistical literacy includes other key concepts, such as:

◆ *Estimation – How long would it take to move a mountain if you wanted to develop the land into a shopping mall? How many circus clowns can you fit in a sports car?*

◆ *Percentages and averages – If your stock portfolio drops by 50% but rebounds by 60%, what is the combined effect on the portfolio's worth? If you have one foot in the oven and one in the freezer are you at room temperature on average?*

◆ *Randomness – When is a cluster of events simply due to chance and when is it symptomatic of some real effect?*

◆ *Uncertainty – If the meteorologist predicts a 60% chance of rain today, should the road paving crew cancel the day's paving work?*

There's much more to statistical literacy, but you'll have to read the book and take the course to discover it.

1.2 So, What Is Statistics?

It seems every time we turn around, someone is collecting data on us, from every purchase we make in the grocery store to every click of our mouse as we surf the Web. We produce data in every aspect of our lives and contribute to incredibly large data sets collected by Google, Facebook, Twitter, and credit card companies, to name just a few data collectors. United Parcel Service (UPS) tracks every package it ships from one place to another around the world and stores these records in a giant database. You can access part of it if you send or receive a UPS package. The database is about 17 terabytes—about the same size as a database that contained every book in the United States Library of Congress (the largest library in the world) would be. (But, we suspect, not quite as interesting.) What can anyone hope to do with all these data?

As we said earlier, Statistics plays a role in making sense of our complex world. Statisticians assess the risk of genetically engineered foods or of a new drug being considered by Health Canada. Statisticians predict the number of new cases of a disease by regions of the country or the number of customers likely to respond to a sale at the supermarket. And statisticians help scientists, social scientists, and business leaders understand how unemployment is related to environmental controls, whether enriched early education affects the later performance of school children, and whether vitamin C really prevents illness. Whenever you have data and a need to understand the world, you need Statistics.

Netflix uses data to determine that, if you liked a particular movie, you might also like other movies they recommend. How do they know that? They use the ratings you provide from movies you viewed and liked in the past, along with ratings from many other customers. At its core, the algorithm is based on the statistical concept of correlation. Netflix ran a contest, open to all, to design an improved system of making Netflix recommendations, with the winner to get $1 000 000 if

"It is the mark of a truly intelligent person to be moved by statistics."

—George Bernard Shaw

Q: What is Statistics?

A: Statistics is a way of reasoning, along with a collection of tools and methods, designed to help us understand the world.

Q: What are statistics?

A: Statistics (plural) are quantities calculated from data.

Q: So what is data?

A: You mean, "what *are* data?" Data is the plural form. The singular is datum.

Q: So, what are data?

A: Data are values along with their context.

they licensed the algorithm to Netflix and explained how it worked. The winning team (made up of statisticians and computer scientists from the United States, Austria, Canada, and Israel) was announced in 2009. You can read the paper that explains the new system at: www.netflixprize.com.

Credit card companies examine data on spending habits to find which customers are good credit risks, but just barely good. A customer who carries a large balance at a high interest rate generates the greatest profit, as long as they don't default on payment. J.P. Martin was a Canadian Tire executive who discovered, through his analysis of all Canadian Tire credit card transactions, that what people purchased was a good predictor of what their payment behaviour would be. His findings were written about in a *New York Times Magazine* article entitled "What Does Your Credit Card Company Know About You? People who bought cheap, generic automotive oil (not expensive, name-brand oil) were at greater risk of missing a credit card payment. People who bought carbon-monoxide monitors or felt protector pads for furniture legs rarely missed payments. Other studies showed that customers who buy premium birdseed are better credit risks than those who buy chrome skull car hood ornaments. Canadian Tire's competitor, Walmart, (where Martin now works) is credited with noticing that hurricane warnings led to a dramatic increase in sales of Pop-Tarts, which were then moved to the front of stores during hurricane season.

If we want to analyze student perceptions of business ethics, should we administer a survey to every single university student in Canada—or, for that matter, in the world? Well, that wouldn't be very practical or cost effective. What should we do instead? Give up and abandon the survey? Maybe we should try to obtain survey responses from a smaller, representative group of students. Statistics can help us make the leap from the data we have at hand to an understanding of the world at large. We talk about the specifics of sampling in Chapter 3, and the theme of generalizing from the specific to the general is one that we revisit throughout this book. We hope this text will empower *you* to draw conclusions from data and make valid business decisions in response to such questions as:

◆ *Do university students from different parts of the world perceive business ethics differently?*

◆ *What is the effect of advertising on sales?*

◆ *Do aggressive, "high-growth" mutual funds really have higher returns than more conservative funds?*

◆ *Is there a seasonal cycle in your firm's revenues and profits?*

◆ *What is the relationship between shelf location and cereal sales?*

◆ *How reliable are the quarterly forecasts for your firm?*

◆ *Are there common characteristics about your customers and why they choose your products?—and, more important, are those characteristics the same among those who aren't your customers?*

Our ability to answer questions such as these and draw conclusions from data depends largely on our ability to understand *variation*. That may not be the term you expected to find at the end of that sentence, but it is the essence of Statistics. The key to learning from data is understanding the variation that is all around us.

Data vary. People are different. So are economic conditions from month to month. We can't see everything, let alone measure it all. And even what we do measure, we measure imperfectly. So the data we wind up looking at and basing our decisions on provide, at best, an imperfect picture of the world. Variation lies at the heart of what Statistics is all about. How to make sense of it is the central challenge of Statistics.

In fact, variation is what distinguishes Statistics from other subjects in the wide area of quantitative analysis.

People have an intuitive understanding of some kinds of variation. When you weigh yourself on a bathroom scale you are quite likely to repeat it at least two more times, because you know (or hope) that the result will differ in successive weighings. Whether you take the average, the middle value, or the minimum depends on what kind of "statistician" you are.

Variation means that we can never repeat things exactly. Everything varies, but we are not sure how things vary. Is the second measurement likely to be lower or higher than the first, and by how much? This aspect of variation is called uncertainty, the lack of knowledge about an outcome or result. We are uncertain about what will happen when we roll the dice. This troubled Einstein, who wrote, "God does not play dice with the universe." Stephen Hawking contradicted Einstein when he commented that not only does God play dice with the universe, he throws them where they cannot be seen.

Statistics provides us with tools to help make decisions in the face of uncertainty. There is an expression well known to statisticians, "A person with one watch knows what time it is, a person with two watches is never sure." In his book *Picturing the Uncertain World*, Howard Wainer explains, "The correct interpretation [of this expression] is that the road to advancing knowledge runs through the recognition and measurement of uncertainty rather than through simply ignoring it." In other words, know what it is that you don't know! Understanding uncertainty is crucial in business decision-making.

We live in a world of uncertainty and variation. The French have an expression for it, too, "*Vive la différence.*" Life is in variation and there's variation in life.

1.3 How Will This Book Help?

A fair question. Most likely, this book will not turn out to be what you expect. It emphasizes graphics and understanding rather than computation and formulas. Instead of learning how to plug numbers in formulas, you'll learn the process of model development and come to understand the limitations both of the data you analyze and the methods you use. Every chapter uses real data and real business scenarios so you can see how to use data to make decisions.

Canada is the second largest country on the planet by land area. And Canada is different from the United States! "Peace, order, and good government" (Canadian Constitution Act, 1867) is not "Life, liberty and the pursuit of happiness" (U.S. Declaration of Independence, 1776). Canada has different public policy, governmental structure, and jurisdiction (federal, provincial, and municipal), economic systems (banking and finance), social services, health care, sports, and entertainment. And Canada is a "metric" country, so many of our measurement scales are different.

There is nothing inherently American or Canadian about the theory or mathematical development of statistics. However, we hope you will find the business applications more relevant and interesting by our use of illustrative examples and exercises based on Canadian companies and Canadian data.

However, Canada is a global player and Canadian businesses cross geographical borders, so our book includes business situations and data from the United States and abroad. Since the United States is our major trading partner, what happens there affects us here. As the saying goes, "When the U.S. catches cold, Canada sneezes." Statistics, too, has no geographical borders, and is a vital part of building and enhancing the global community. This text teaches how Statistics is an integral part of building the future Canadian economy. The scenarios and techniques described in this text are just like those you will encounter whether you find work with a large multinational corporation, a mid-size company, or a small business, whether it operates for profit or not for profit, or whether it is in the public or private sphere.

Learning Objectives

At the beginning of each chapter you'll see a list of skills and knowledge that represent what we hope you will acquire through that chapter. And each of the end-of-chapter exercises has one (and occasionally more) learning objective associated with it. As you begin a chapter the learning objectives will give you an idea of what to expect. When you finish a chapter, look back at the learning objectives to see how far you got. And then test yourself with the exercises (see below).

Graphs

Close your eyes and open the book at random. Is there a graph or table on the page? Do it again, say, 10 times. You probably saw data displayed in many ways, even near the back of the book and in the exercises. Graphs and tables help you understand what the data are saying. So, each story and data set and every new statistical technique will come with graphics to help you understand both the methods and the data.

Process

To help you use Statistics to make business decisions, we'll lead you through the entire process of thinking about a problem, finding and showing results, and telling others what you have discovered. The three simple steps to doing Statistics for business right are: **Plan**, **Do**, and **Report**.

Plan first. Know where you're headed and why. Clearly defining and understanding your objective will save you a lot of work.

Do is what most students think Statistics is about. The mechanics of calculating statistics and making graphical displays are important, but the computations are usually the least important part of the process. In fact, we usually turn the computations over to technology and get on with understanding what the results tell us.

Report what you've learned. Until you've explained your results in a context that someone else can understand, the job is not done.

"Get your facts first, and then you can distort them as much as you please. (Facts are stubborn, but statistics are more pliable.)"
—Mark Twain

Guided Example

Each chapter applies the new concepts taught in worked examples called **Guided Examples**. These examples model how you should approach and solve problems using the Plan, Do, Report framework. They illustrate how to plan an analysis, the appropriate techniques to use, and how to report what it all means. These step-by-step examples show you how to produce the kind of solutions and case study reports that instructors and managers or, better yet, clients expect to see. You will find a model solution in the right-hand column and background notes and discussion in the left-hand column.

Just Checking

Sometimes, in the middle of the chapter, you'll find sections called **Just Checking**, which pose a few short questions you can answer without much calculation. Use them to check that you've understood the basic ideas in the chapter. You'll find the answers at the end of the chapter exercises.

Ethics in Action

Statistics often requires judgment, and the decisions based on statistical analyses may influence people's health and even their lives. Decisions in government can affect policy decisions about how people are treated. In science and industry, interpretations of data can influence consumer safety and the environment. And in business, misunderstanding what the data say can lead to disastrous decisions. The central guiding principle of statistical judgment is the ethical search for a true understanding of the real world. In all spheres of society it is vitally important that a statistical analysis of data be done in an ethical and unbiased way. Allowing pre-conceived notions, unfair data gathering, or deliberate slanting to affect statistical conclusions is harmful to business and to society.

At various points throughout the book, you will encounter a scenario under the title **Ethics in Action** in which you'll read about an ethical issue. Think about the issue and how you might deal with it. Then read the summary of the issue and a proposed solution to the problem, which follow the scenario. We've related the ethical issues to guidelines that the American Statistical Association has developed.[1] These scenarios can be good topics for discussion. We've presented one solution, but we invite you to think of others.

What Can Go Wrong?

One of the interesting challenges of Statistics is that, unlike some math and science courses, there can be more than one right answer. This is why two statisticians can testify honestly on opposite sides of a court case. And it's why some people think that you can prove anything with statistics. But that's not true. People make mistakes using statistics, and sometimes people misuse statistics to mislead others. Most of the mistakes are avoidable. We're not talking about arithmetic. Mistakes usually involve using a method in the wrong situation or misinterpreting results. So each chapter has a section called **What Can Go Wrong?** to help you avoid some of the most common mistakes that we've seen in our years of consulting and teaching experience.

Mini Case Study Projects

At the end of each chapter you'll find an extended problem or two that use real data and ask you to investigate a question or make a decision. These mini case studies are a good way to test your ability to attack an open-ended (and thus more realistic) problem. You'll be asked to define the objective, plan your process, complete the analysis, and report your conclusion. These are good opportunities to apply the template provided by the **Guided Examples**. And they provide an opportunity to practise reporting your conclusions in written form to refine your communication skills where statistical results are involved. Data sets for these case studies can be found on MyStatLab.

Technology Help: Using the Computer

Although we show you all the formulas you need to understand the calculations, you will most often use a calculator or computer to perform the mechanics of a

---

[1] www.amstat.org/committees/ethics/index.cfm

You'll find all sorts of stuff in margin notes, such as stories and quotations. For example:

"Computers are useless. They can only give you answers."
—Pablo Picasso

While Picasso underestimated the value of good statistics software, he did know that creating a solution requires more than just *Doing*—it means you have to *Plan* and *Report*, too!

statistics problem. And the easiest way to calculate statistics with a computer is with a statistics package. Several different statistics packages are used widely. Although they differ in the details of how to use them, they all work from the same basic information and find the same results. Rather than adopt one package for this book, we present generic output and point out common features that you should look for. We also give some instructions to get you started using Excel.

> From time to time we'll take time out to discuss an interesting or important side issue. We indicate these by setting them apart like this.[2]

What have we learned?

At the end of each chapter, you'll see a brief summary of the important concepts in a section called **What have we learned?** That section includes a list of the **Terms** and a summary of the important **Skills** you've acquired in the chapter. You won't be able to learn the material from these summaries, but you can use them to check your knowledge of the important ideas in the chapter. If you have the skills, know the terms, and understand the concepts, you should be well prepared—and ready to use Statistics!

Exercises

Beware: No one can learn Statistics just by reading or listening. The only way to learn it is to do it. So, at the end of each chapter (except this one) you'll find **Exercises** designed to help you learn to use the Statistics you've just read about. As we mentioned earlier, each exercise has a learning objective (and occasionally, more than one), so even before you read the question, you'll know the purpose and aim of the question. And it will help you select questions in areas or concepts you'd like more practice on. Some exercises are marked with a red **T**. You'll find the data for these exercises on MyStatLab and download the data set to work that particular exercise.

We've paired up and grouped the exercises, so if you're having trouble doing an exercise, you'll find a similar exercise either just before or just after it. You'll find answers to the odd-numbered exercises at the back of the book. But these are only "answers" and not complete solutions. What's the difference? The answers are sketches of the complete solutions. For most problems, your solution should follow the model of the **Guided Examples**. If your calculations match the numerical parts of the answer and your argument contains the elements shown in the answer, you're on the right track. Your complete solution should explain the context, show your reasoning and calculations, and state your conclusions. Don't worry too much if your numbers don't match the printed answers to every decimal place. In fact, different technology often provides slightly different results. Because Statistics is more than computation—it's about getting the reasoning correct—pay more attention to how you interpret a result than to what the digit in the third decimal place is.

*Optional Sections and Chapters

Some sections and chapters of this book are marked with an asterisk (*). These are optional in the sense that subsequent material does not depend on them directly.

---

[2] Or in a footnote.

It doesn't mean they aren't important or potentially very useful to you. We hope you'll read them anyway, as you did this section.

Getting Started

It's only fair to warn you: You can't get there by just picking out the highlighted sentences and the summaries. This book is different. It's not about memorizing definitions and learning equations. It's deeper than that. And much more interesting. But . . .

> ***You have to read the book!***

Look what happens when you rearrange the letters of INTRO STATS. It spells STARTS INTO... That's what happens when you turn the page!

> ***So...turn the page and get started!***

Data

Indigo Books & Music Inc.

LEARNING OBJECTIVES

1. Identify cases, different types of data, and any measurement units

2. Organize a spreadsheet as a data table

3. Distinguish between time series data and cross-sectional data

4. Assess the quality of a data source

CONNECTIONS: CHAPTER

In Chapter 1 we explained that the essence of Statistics is variation. What varies? Data. So that's where we will begin. In this chapter we discuss the types, quality, and sources of data, the building blocks of Statistics.

Indigo (chapters.indigo.ca)

In 1940, a single bookstore in Toronto, Ontario, called Coles Books, opened for business. Over the years the business expanded and finally became Indigo in 1996. Through nationwide expansion and multiple mergers, **Indigo** became Canada's largest bookstore, operating in all 10 provinces, with both online and retail stores. On the website of the parent company, Indigo Books & Music, they describe themselves as "Canada's purveyor of ideas and inspiration" and "the largest book, gift, and specialty toy retailer in Canada." Its selection of merchandise also increased, expanding beyond just books, with the launch of Kobo ebooks in 2009 and IndigoKids in 2010. This led to record revenues of over $1 billion in 2010.[1]

In April 2011, Indigo launched its free Plum Rewards program. The program collects data from customers, such as contact information and purchase history, and gives customers exclusive discounts on merchandise. According to the company's Annual Information Form, the data collected serves to "expand on the Company's existing marketing and service strategies to better know and thereby better serve customers."[2] In other words, **Indigo** uses these data to match its offerings to what interests customers.

---

[1] Indigo Annual Report 2011.
[2] Indigo Information Form 2011.

This is one example of how companies collect and use data to drive their business strategies. Other Canadian retailers such as Safeway, Save-On-Foods, and HBC (Hudson's Bay Company) also collect and use sales data to align their business strategies with their customers' shopping habits. Clearly, many businesses across Canada rely on data both to operate in the short run and make strategic decisions in the long run

Based on information from www.chaptersindigo.ca

"Data! Data! Data! I cannot make bricks without clay."
—Sherlock Holmes, in *The Adventure of the Copper Beeches*, by Sir Arthur Conan Doyle

"Data is a precious thing and will last longer than the systems themselves."
— Tim Berners-Lee, inventor of the World Wide Web

"The organization of the future is held together by information— working in such an organization will require literacy to obtain the necessary internal and external information to do our jobs."
—Peter Drucker, renowned visionary economist

The word *data* is plural; the singular is *datum*, which is a Latin word meaning "thing given"; so, **data** are the "things given" for us to turn into information. To be grammatically correct, you should say the "data are" not the "data is."

Many years ago, stores in small towns knew their customers personally. If you walked into the hobby shop, the owner might tell you about a new bridge that had come in for your Lionel train set. The tailor knew your dad's size, and the hairdresser knew how your mom liked her hair. There are still some stores like that around today, but you're increasingly likely to shop at large stores, by phone, or on the internet. Even so, when you phone an 800 number to buy new running shoes, customer service representatives may call you by your first name or ask about the socks you bought six weeks ago. Or the company may send an email in October offering new head warmers for winter running. This company has millions of customers, and you called without identifying yourself. How did the sales rep know who you are, where you live, and what you had bought?

The answer to all these questions is data. Collecting data on their customers, transactions, and sales lets companies track inventory and know what their customers prefer. These data can help them predict what their customers may buy in the future so they know how much of each item to stock. The store can use the data and what they learn from the data to improve customer service, mimicking the kind of personal attention a shopper had 50 years ago.

2.1 What *Are* Data?

We bet you thought you knew this instinctively. Think about it for a minute. What exactly *do* we mean by "data"? Do data even have to be numbers? The amounts of your most recent purchases in dollars are numerical data, but some data record names or other labels. The names in the Indigo database are data, but are not numerical.

Sometimes, data can have values that look like numerical values but are just numerals serving as labels. This can be confusing. For example, the ISBN (International Standard Book Number) of a book may have a numerical value, such as 978-0321426581, but it's really just another *name* for the book *Business Statistics: A First Course.*

Data values, no matter what kind, are useless without their context. Newspaper journalists know that the lead paragraph of a good story should establish the "Five W's": Who, What, When, Where, and (if possible) Why. Often, we add How to the list as well. Answering these questions can provide a **context** for data values. The answers to the first two questions are essential. If you can't answer *Who* and *What*, you don't have data, and you don't have any useful information.

Here's an example of some of the data Indigo might collect:

1004567	Samuel L.	978-0-588-43775-9	1012345	978-0-588-75332-9	Print
19.95	Print	15.45	555	Digital	1004568
978-1-564-83423-3	Monica D.	978-1-923-34522-8	901	1005675	1004567
Rob D.	1052345	Digital	Digital	978-1-984-12955-3	Digital
1052345	Steve C.	5.45	501	Chris F.	Print

Table 2.1 An example of data with no context. It's impossible to say anything about what these values might mean without knowing their context.

Try to guess what they represent. Why is that hard? Because these data have no *context*. We can make the meaning clear if we add the context of *Who* and *What* and organize the values into a **data table** such as Table 2.2 below.

Purchase Order Number	Name	Price	Area Code	ISBN-13	Book Type
1004567	Samuel L.	19.95	604	978-0-588-75332-9	Print
1004568	Chris F.	15.45	555	978-1-343-77888-0	Digital
1005675	Monica D.	12.89	901	978-1-923-34522-8	Digital
1012345	Rob D.	9.99	876	978-1-984-12955-3	Digital
1052345	Steve C.	5.45	501	978-1-564-83423-3	Print

Table 2.2 Example of a data table. The variable names are in the top row. Typically, the Who of the table are found in the leftmost column.

Now we can see that these are five purchase records, relating to book orders from Indigo. The column titles tell *What* has been recorded. The rows tell us *Who*. But, be careful. Look at all the variables to see *Who* the variables are about. Even if people are involved, they may not be the *Who* of the data. For example, the *Who* here are the purchase orders (not the people who made the purchases) because each row refers to a different purchase order, not necessarily a different *person*. A common place to find the *Who* of the table is the leftmost column. The other W's might have to come from the company's database administrator.[3]

In general, the rows of a data table correspond to individual **cases** about *Who*m (or about which—if they're not people) we record some characteristics. These cases go by different names, depending on the situation. Individuals who answer a survey are referred to as **respondents**. People on whom we experiment are **subjects** or (in an attempt to acknowledge the importance of their role in the experiment) **participants**, but animals, plants, websites, and other inanimate subjects are often called **experimental units**. In a database, rows are called **records**—in this example, purchase records. Perhaps the most generic term is **cases**. In the table, the cases are the individual book purchase orders.

Sometimes people refer to data values as **observations**, without being clear about the *Who*. Be sure you know the *Who* of the data, or you may not know what the data say. The *characteristics* recorded about each individual or case are called **variables**. These are usually shown as the columns of a data table, and they should have a name that identifies *What* has been measured.

It is important to distinguish between values and variables. Data represent the specific **values** of variables. For example: the height of students in a university class is a variable. Once you measure each student and obtain actual values of height for each student you have data.

---

[3] In database management, this kind of information is called "metadata" or data about data.

A common term for a data table like this is a **spreadsheet**, a name that comes from bookkeeping ledgers of financial information. The data were typically spread across facing pages of a bound ledger, the book used by an accountant for keeping records of expenditures and sources of income. For the accountant, the columns were the types of expenses and income, and the cases were transactions, typically invoices or receipts. Since the advent of computers, use of spreadsheet programs has become a common skill, and the programs have become some of the most successful applications in the computer industry. It is usually easy to move a data table from a spreadsheet program to a program designed for statistical graphics and analysis, either directly or by copying the data table and pasting it into the statistics program.

Although data tables and spreadsheets are great for relatively small data sets, they are cumbersome for the complex data sets that companies must maintain on a day-to-day basis. Various other database architectures are used to store data. The most common is a relational database. In a **relational database**, two or more separate data tables are linked together so that information can be merged across them. Each data table is a *relation* because it is about a specific set of cases with information about each of these cases for all (or at least most) of the variables ("fields" in database terminology). For example, a table of customers, along with demographic information on each, is such a relation. A data table with information about a different collection of cases is a different relation. For example, a data table of all the items sold by the company, including information on price, inventory, and past history, is a relation as well (for example, as in Table 2.3). Finally, the day-to-day transactions may be held in a third database where each purchase of an item by a customer is listed as a case. In a relational database, these three relations can be linked together. For example, you can look up a customer to see what he or she purchased or look up an item to see which customers purchased it.

Customers

Customer Number	Name	City	Province	Postal Code	Plum Member
473859	Samuel L.	Victoria	BC	V1M 2R5	Yes
127389	Chris F.	Laval	QC	C4R 3D3	No
335682	Monica D.	Regina	SK	G5T 3C9	Yes

Items

ISBN	Name	Price	Genre	Stock
0-588-75332-9	Journey Home	19.89	Adventure	165
1-984-12955-3	Journey Home – eBook	12.89	Adventure	–
1-564-83423-3	Stock Market Analysis	34.98	Non-Fiction	87

Transactions

Transaction Number	Date	Customer Number	ISBN	Quantity	Shipping	Shipping Cost
T234564	9/15/11	473859	0-588-75332-9	2	UPS Overnight	12.56
T124321	9/15/12	127389	1-984-12955-3	1	Digital	–
T321312	9/20/12	335682	1-564-83423-3	1	Digital	–

Table 2.3 A relational database shows all the relevant information for three separate relations linked together by customer and product numbers.

Indigo's parent company used to maintain several systems for managing retail, online sales, and their customer loyalty program. Individual clients were tracked through multiple retail and online records. Infusion, a global software engineering firm, was hired to centralize the data systems into a single consolidated customer database, thereby making sales and customer data readily available for analysis. Sumit Oberai, VP Customer Solutions, stated "We've stopped talking about online customers and retail store customers and loyalty customers and just talk about customers."[4]

In statistics, all analyses are performed on a single data table. But often the data must be retrieved from a relational database. Retrieving data from these databases often requires specific expertise with that software. In the rest of the book, we'll assume that all data have been downloaded to a data table or spreadsheet with variables listed as columns and cases as the rows.

If you are ever presented with a spreadsheet data table having reversed orientation, where variables are row and cases are columns, you can use standard spreadsheet functions to "transpose" the rows and columns back to the usual orientation.

2.2 Types of Variables (and Types of Data)

This is the most important chapter in the book! We know what you're thinking. We are only in Chapter 2, so how can it be the most important chapter? To be specific, Section 2.2 is the most important section in the whole book. Why? Just as a physician cannot make a diagnosis or prescribe an appropriate course of treatment without knowing symptoms, statistical analysis cannot be done without knowing the type of variables or type of data to be analyzed.

Variables play different roles, and knowing the variable's *type* is crucial to knowing what to do with it and what it can tell us. The simplest and most important way to classify variables (and data) is either as *categorical* or *quantitative*.

When a variable names categories (or distinct "bins") and answers questions about how cases fall into those categories, we call it a **categorical variable**.[5] When a variable has measured numerical values and the variable tells us about the quantity of what is measured, we call it a **quantitative variable**.[6]

Generally, a quantitative variable has *units*, and involves some kind of measurement process. It is also possible and sensible to carry out arithmetic operations such as adding values or computing averages. For example, it makes sense to compute the average grade in a class, but does not make sense to compute the average ethnicity. Another way to distinguish between the two types of variables is that categorical variables take only a small number of possible values, with lots of repetition of each value, while quantitative variables take on a large number of possible values, with little repetition of each value.

Canadian postal addresses use postal codes that are six-character strings that alternate between letters and digits. Introduced in the early 1970s, they replaced numerical postal zones that began as single digits, and then grew to three digits. Postal codes contain a great deal of information. The first three characters, called a *forward sortation area* (FSA), identify a geographical region. The first letter is a postal district, which is usually a province or territory except in the two largest provinces of Quebec (which has three districts) and Ontario (which has five districts). Montreal/Laval and Toronto are so populous that each has a dedicated postal district ("H" for Montreal/Laval; and "M" for Toronto). Nunavut and Northwest Territories share a postal district. The digit indicates whether the FSA is rural (a zero) or urban (all other digits). The third character, a letter, represents a specific rural region, entire medium-sized city, or section of a major metropolitan area. The last three characters, called a *local delivery unit* (LDU), denote a specific address or range of addresses.

So, by examining the FSA component of postal codes, it is possible to determine geographical region and urban/rural status, and in this way postal codes can be considered a source of categorical variables. Of course, this would require breaking down postal codes into their component parts, not just treating them as six-character strings.

---

[4] http://www.internetretailer.com/2008/08/28/a-single-view?p=2

[5] You may also see them called *qualitative* variables, and sometimes *discrete* variables.

[6] You may also see them called *measurement* variables, and sometimes *continuous* variables.

Sometimes, the same variable may be viewed as categorical or quantitative depending on the situation. It's more a decision about what we hope to learn from a variable than a quality of the variable itself. It's the questions we ask of a variable (the *Why* of our analysis) that influence how we think about it and how we treat it. For example, *Age*, in years, is a quantitative variable, but in market segmentation studies it is usually turned into a categorical variable (e.g., Under 18, 18 to 34, 35 to 54, 55 and over). Household income is also a quantitative variable (measured in dollars, or thousands of dollars), but on surveys is only asked about as a categorical variable.

In general, there is more information in a quantitative variable than in a categorical variable. For example, a categorical letter grade in a course (A, B, C, D, F) is less informative than a quantitative percentage grade.

Descriptive responses to questions are often categories. For example, the responses to the questions "What type of mutual fund do you invest in?" or "What kind of advertising does your firm use?" yield categorical values. An important special case of categorical variables is one that has only two possible responses (usually "yes" or "no"), which arise naturally from questions like "Do you invest in the stock market?" or "Do you make online purchases from this website?" A categorical variable with only two categories is known as a *binary* variable.

Many quantitative variables do have units, which tell how each value has been measured. Even more important, units such as yen, cubits, carats, angstroms, nanoseconds, kilometres per hour, or degrees Celsius tell us the scale of measurement. The units tell us how much of something we have or how far apart two values are. Without units, the values have no meaning. It does little good to be promised a raise of 5000 a year if you don't know whether it will be paid in euros, dollars, yen, or Estonian krooni.

While it is easy to spot quantitative variables that have units, such as age in years, height in centimetres, salary in dollars, or percentage return on investments, it is not as clear for phenomena with "imaginary" units. For example, ratings of customer satisfaction or quality of work life, on 0 to 10 scales require imagining "satisfaction units" or "quality of work life units." Many tools in human resources, such as measurements of employee morale or job satisfaction, are treated as quantitative because there is an underlying scale of measurement, even though the units are imaginary.

Still other quantitative variables that are counts of things may appear to be numbers without units. For example, the number of visits to a website yesterday might be 1234. The number of shares of Toronto-Dominion Bank traded on the Toronto Stock Exchange in one day might be 1 855 528. These are numbers of website visits or shares traded, but do not have units such as centimetres or dollars. Instead their units are the "number of" or "counts" for short.

Be careful. If you treat a variable as quantitative, especially if there are no units or if there are imaginary units, make sure the values measure a quantity of something. For example, area codes are numbers, but do we use them that way? Is 403 plus 416 equal to 819? Of course, but that is irrelevant when we are speaking of area codes. We don't care that Southern Alberta (area code 403) plus Metro Toronto (area code 416) equals Northern Quebec (area code 819). The numbers assigned to the area codes are codes that *categorize* the phone

One tradition that hangs on in some quarters is to name variables with cryptic abbreviations written in uppercase letters. This can be traced back to the 1960s, when the very first statistics computer programs were controlled with instructions punched on cards. The earliest punch card equipment used only uppercase letters, and the earliest statistics programs limited variable names to six or eight characters, so variables were called things like PRSRF3. Most modern programs do not have such restrictive limits, so there is no reason for variable names that you wouldn't use in an ordinary sentence.

Addison-Wesley/Pearson Education

number into a geographical area. So we treat area code as a categorical variable. Even though Canadian postal codes have digits in them, we don't ever try to treat them as quantitative since we can't add the letters in postal codes. However, without knowing how the postal codes are assigned it is not so clear how they can be treated as categorical variables—see sidebar.

Sometimes the type of the variable is clear. Some variables can answer questions *only* about categories. If the values of a variable are words rather than numbers, it's a good bet that it is categorical. But some variables can answer both kinds of questions. For example, Indigo could ask for a customer's *Age* in years. That seems quantitative, and would be if they want to know the average age of those customers who visit their site after 3 a.m. But suppose they want to decide which book to offer a customer in a special deal and need to be sure they have adequate supplies on hand to meet the demand. Thus, thinking of a customer's age in terms of the categories child, teen, adult, or senior might be more useful. If it isn't clear whether to treat a variable as categorical or quantitative, think about *Why* you are looking at it and what you want it to tell you.

Four-point or five-point scales are very widely used for ratings of many different phenomena. For example, a typical course evaluation survey asks:

"How valuable do you think this course will be to you?"

1 = Not valuable; 2 = Slightly valuable;

3 = Moderately valuable; 4 = Extremely valuable

Is this variable categorical or quantitative? Once again we'll look to the *Why*. Teachers might simply count the number of students who gave each response for a course, treating *Educational Value* as a categorical variable. However, when they want to see whether the course is improving, they might treat the responses as the *amount* of perceived value, in effect, treating the variable as quantitative. Once again, this requires imagining that there are "educational value units." A further difficulty arises because the numbers 1, 2, 3, and 4 were essentially an arbitrary assignment. We could have chosen the numbers 1, 2, 5, and 10. Be very cautious about treating scales like this as quantitative variables.

Such scales are also used to create quantitative variables. For example, a retail clothing store might carry out a customer satisfaction survey by asking customers to rate a number of different aspects of their most recent shopping experience (e.g., price, merchandise selection, size availability, fitting room facilities, sales representative knowledge, sales representative courtesy, efficiency of checkout process, etc.). If each aspect is rated on a five-point scale 1 = Very dissatisfied; 2 = Somewhat dissatisfied; 3 = Neither dissatisfied nor satisfied; 4 = Somewhat satisfied; and 5 = Very satisfied, a quantitative variable can be created by adding up the responses to the individual items. If there are 10 items, the overall score would range from 10 to 50. There still are no natural units, but it is easier and safer to imagine "satisfaction units."

We cannot overemphasize the importance of the distinction between categorical and quantitative variables. If you do not know what type of variables you have you cannot choose appropriate analysis!

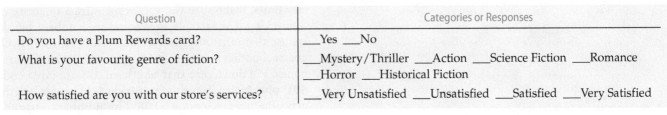

Question	Categories or Responses
Do you have a Plum Rewards card?	___Yes ___No
What is your favourite genre of fiction?	___Mystery/Thriller ___Action ___Science Fiction ___Romance ___Horror ___Historical Fiction
How satisfied are you with our store's services?	___Very Unsatisfied ___Unsatisfied ___Satisfied ___Very Satisfied

Table 2.4 Some examples of categorical variables

Counts

Earlier we discussed some quantitative variables that are counts of things. Let's have another look at the role of counting in Statistics. Counting is a natural way to summarize a categorical variable. For example, when Indigo considers a special offer of free shipping to customers, they might first analyze how purchases have been shipped in the recent past. They would use counts of each category to understand how they distribute their packages, as in Table 2.5.

Delivery Method	Number of Purchases
Ground	20 567
Second-Day	12 432
Overnight	3456
Digital	21 543

Table 2.5 A summary of the categorical variable Delivery Method that shows the counts, or number of cases for each category.

Categorical variables don't have units, only categories. We *count* the cases in each category to summarize what the variable tells us. The categories are the data values, but counts are used to summarize the distribution of the variable.

But counts *can* be data values themselves. How many songs are on your digital music player? How many classes are you taking this semester? Both of these variables (*Songs* and *Classes*) are quantitative, since they measure a quantity of usage.

So we use counts in two different ways. They can be a *summary* of the frequency of cases in a category or they can be the values of a variable whose units are "number of something."

The distinction can be subtle. Indigo might keep track of a customer's *Age*—a categorical variable one of whose categories is *Teen*. When they want to know how many of their customers are *Teens*, they summarize the variable by counting. But if they measure the number of teenagers who buy books, the new variable *Teenage Customers* is a quantitative variable whose amount is measured by counting, as shown in Table 2.6.

Month	Teenage Customers
January	20 447
February	11 988
March	23 610
April	33 343
May	...
...	...

Table 2.6 A summary of the quantitative variable Teenage Customers that shows the counts, or how many teenage customers made purchases, for each month of the year.

Identifiers, Strings, and Dates

What's your student ID number? It may be numerical, but is it a quantitative variable? No, it doesn't have units. Is it categorical? Yes, but a special kind. Look at how many categories there are and at how many individuals there are in each category. There are exactly as many categories as individuals and only one individual in each category. While it's easy to count the totals for each category, it's not very interesting. This is an **identifier variable**. Indigo wants to know who you are when you sign in again and doesn't want to confuse you with some other customer. So they assign you a unique identifier.

Identifier variables themselves don't tell us anything useful about the categories because we know there is exactly one individual in each. However, they are crucial in this era of large data sets because by uniquely identifying the cases, they make it possible to combine data from different sources, protect confidentiality, and provide unique labels. Most company databases are, in fact, relational databases. The identifier is crucial to linking one data table to another in a relational database. The identifiers in Table 2.3 are the *Customer Number*, *ISBN*, and *Transaction Number*. Variables like *UPS Tracking Number*, *Social Insurance Number*, provincial health care number, and vehicle identification number are other examples of identifiers.

You'll want to recognize when a variable is playing the role of an identifier so you won't be tempted to analyze it. Knowing that Indigo's average customer number increased 10% from one year to the next doesn't really tell you anything—any more than analyzing any categorical variable as if it were quantitative would.

A spreadsheet of grades in a university course will typically include a Student Number, which is often an eight-digit number. While a computation of the average grade is useful, computing the average ID number (even though software can do it because they are only digits) would be nonsensical.

Identifier variables are a specific type of "string" variable. Sometimes variables are just strings of letters, digits, words, or any combination and, while they do not identify individual respondents, they do contain information about the respondent. Canadian postal codes are actually string variables; they identify a postal destination but do not uniquely identify an individual. Stock-keeping units (SKUs) and abbreviations for TSX-listed companies are string variables.

A common subset of string variables are dates and times. They are not categorical or quantitative or identifier variables. But they can be transformed into quantitative variables. For example, the interval between a birth date and the current date will give current age. The interval between time stamps recorded upon entering and then exiting a secure website will give the amount of time spent at the website.

Be careful not to be inflexible in your typing of variables. Variables can play different roles, depending on the question we ask of them, and classifying variables rigidly into types can be misleading. For example, in their annual reports, Indigo refers to its database and looks at the variables *Sales* and *Year*. When analysts ask how many books Indigo sold in 2011, what role does *Year* play? There's only one row for 2011, and *Year* identifies it, so it plays the role of an identifier variable. In its role as an identifier, you might match other data from Indigo, or the economy in general, for the same year. But analysts also track sales growth over time. In this role, *Year* measures time. Now it's being treated as a quantitative variable with units of years. The difference lies in the consideration of the *Why* of our question.

Above all, you should base your decision on "meaningfulness"; in what way(s) is it useful and meaningful to treat the variables and the data they contain.

Variable Subtypes

We have focused on the critical importance of the major classification into categorical and quantitative variables. You should also know about minor sub-classifications within each of these two types.

Categorical variables have two subtypes. Categorical variables used only to name categories are sometimes called **nominal variables**. (The word "nominal" comes from the Latin "*nomen*" meaning "name.") Examples include marital status, ethnicity, and industry sector. If the categories have a natural ordering, we call them

ordinal variables. Sometimes all we want to know about a variable is the order of its values. For example, we may want to pick out the first, the last, or the middle value. Values can be individually ordered (e.g., the ranks of employees based on the number of days they've worked for the company) or ordered in classes (e.g., short, tall, grande, venti). But the ordering always depends on our purpose. Are the categories Infant, Youth, Teen, Adult, and Senior ordinal? Well, if we are ordering on age, they surely are. But if we are ordering (as Indigo might) on purchase volume, it is likely that either Teen or Adult will be the top group. Other examples include the colour of Olympic medal (gold, silver, bronze), and highest level of education.

Some people differentiate quantitative variables according to whether their measured values have a defined value for zero. This is a technical distinction and usually not one we'll need to make. (For example, it isn't correct to say that a temperature of 80°F is twice as hot as 40°F because 0 is an arbitrary value. On the Celsius scale, those temperatures are 26.6°C and 4.44°C, which is a ratio of 6:1). The term *interval scale* is sometimes applied to data such as these, and the term *ratio scale* is applied to measurements for which such ratios are appropriate. For example, the Kelvin temperature scale is a ratio scale because it has a non-arbitrary value for zero, called absolute zero. But the zero point on the Celsius scale is 273.15 K, so Celsius is not a ratio scale.

Cross-Sectional and Time Series Variables and Data

The quantitative variable *Teenage Customers* in Table 2.6 is an example of a **time series** because we have the same variable measured at regular intervals over time. So is the share price of the Royal Bank of Canada at the end of each day for the past year. Both give longitudinal data. Time series are common in business. Typical measuring points are months, quarters, or years, but virtually any consistently-spaced time interval is possible. Variables collected over time hold special challenges for statistical analysis and require special methods. Most of the methods in this book are better suited for **cross-sectional data**, where several variables are measured at the same time point. Surveys are a common method of collecting cross-sectional data.

For example, if we collect data on sales revenue, number of customers, and expenses for last month at each Tim Hortons (more than 3000 locations in Canada and 4000 worldwide as of 2011), these would be cross-sectional data. If we expanded our data collection process to include sales revenue and expenses each day over a time span of several months, we would now have a time series for sales and expenses. Because different methods are used to analyze these different types of data, it is important to be able to identify both time series and cross-sectional data sets.

2.3 Data Quality

In the previous section we classified variables into two main types: categorical and quantitative. But an equally important classification of the data values of variables is good data versus bad data! This aspect of data is called data quality.

J.M. Juran, one of the giants in the field of quality control, explained that data are of high quality "if they are fit for their intended uses in operations, decision-making and planning." Data quality refers to the accuracy, completeness, appropriateness, and overall trustworthiness of the data. Bad data lead to bad results. Bad data teach us nothing.

One of the five *W*s of data is *Where*, as in, where did the data come from? Sir Josiah Charles Stamp (1880–1941) was a British civil servant, industrialist, economist, statistician, and banker. He was the first director of the Bank of England, chairman of the London Midland and Scottish Railway, and reputedly the second richest man in England at his peak. He wrote:

> *The government [is] extremely fond of amassing great quantities of statistics. These are raised to the nth power, the cube roots are extracted, and the results are arranged into elaborate and impressive displays. What must be kept ever in mind, however, is that in every case, the figures are first put down by a village watchman, and he puts down anything he damn well pleases.*[7]

His message is that data collection is often done by the lowest person on the organizational chart (and probably the most poorly paid). Are the data accurately assessed and accurately recorded? **Always examine the data source.**

Another *W* is *What*, as in, what do the data represent? An internet search may find the exact combination of keywords you entered but the article may turn out to be unrelated to your question. The words are the same, but the meanings are different. Variables are limited by the clarity of the operational definitions used to describe them. For example, if an investigator were interested in the proportion of people in an audience wearing blue shirts, he/she would need to begin by defining the terms "blue" and "shirt". What is a shirt? How blue is blue? How much of the shirt needs to be blue? And so on. **Be careful of incompletely or poorly defined variables.**

Another journalistic word is *How*, as in, how were the data collected? Data collected by an observer can be very different from data that are self-reported. All sorts of biases can arise from self-report data. These are known by various terms: non-response bias, recall bias, social desirability bias, lack of understanding of terminology, and "rose-coloured glasses" bias. For example, self-report of height, weight, age, and income generally puts respondents in a different light than reality would indicate!

Data that are captured electronically and automatically transferred to a database (e.g., using bar codes), are likely to be higher quality than data recorded in hand-written form and subsequently manually keyed into a database. But technological glitches could make the electronic data of lower quality! Data that are recorded over time may be affected by changes in methods of measurement and categorization, as definitions, procedures, and equipment are clarified, streamlined, and enhanced.

Another aspect of data quality is the level of accuracy of measurement and reporting. For example, age is a time variable and time is measured on a continuum. If you are asked your age, you are likely to respond using "years," and it probably wouldn't even occur to you to say how many days old you are, even though that level of measurement is possible. Even more extreme would be to report how many seconds you have been alive! This leads us to the idea of "insignificant" digits and rounding, and the closely related idea of spurious accuracy.

If exam scores are reported as whole numbers, how many decimal places, if any, should be reported in the class average? Decimal places give the illusion of accuracy. For instance, if you hear that one-half of all new Canadian businesses fail within three years, that seems imprecise. But is it really more informative to report 50.4% or 50.3756%?

On the Fahrenheit scale, normal human body temperature is 98.6°F; on the Celsius scale it is 37°C. But body temperature changes during the day, so what is normal? If you had a temperature of 98.8°F, would that indicate a fever?

Suppose a guide at a museum of natural history tells you that a dinosaur skeleton is 90 million and 5 years old. When you question him about how he could be so

What is the height of Mt. Everest? In 1856, Everest's height was announced as 29 002 ft (8840 m). An Indian survey in 1955, confirmed by a Chinese measurement in 1975, pegged it as 29 029 ft (8848 m). This is the height officially recognized by Nepal and China, although Nepal is planning a new survey. For many years, encyclopedias and almanacs rounded down to 29 028 ft. But this measured the snow cap, not the rock head; a rock head elevation of 29 035 ft (8850 m) was obtained in 1999. In 2005, the Chinese Academy of Sciences announced the height of Everest as 29 017.16 ft (8844.43 m) with accuracy of 0.69 ft (0.21 m), at the actual highest point of rock, not the snow and ice covering it. The snow/ice depth was 11 ft (3.5 m); the total agrees with the next elevation of 29 029 ft (8848 m). Since the snow and ice thickness varies over time, a definitive height of the snow cap is impossible to determine. What we can safely say is that Everest is about 29 000 ft high, and not less!

---

[7] Excerpt by Sir Josiah Charles Stamp.

precise he tells you that when he started working at the museum five years ago, he was told that the skeleton was 90 million years old. That's spurious accuracy!

But data quality is not just about the data that are present. An equally important factor concerns what is missing. It is not just the obvious problem resulting from large quantities of missing data, but also the nature of *what* is missing. If data are missing in some systematic way, that is, in a way related to variables of interest, a number of biases can arise.

In practice there is no such thing as a perfectly correct and complete database. Many factors can affect data quality and hence the results of data analysis. Let's end this section with the words of Charles Babbage, the "father of the computer," who wrote, "Errors using inadequate data are much less than those using no data at all."

2.4 Data Sources—Where, How, and When

We must know *Who, What,* and *Why* to analyze data. Without knowing these three, we don't have enough to start. Of course, we'd always like to know more. The more we know, the more we'll understand. If possible, we'd like to know the *When* and *Where* of data as well. Values recorded in 1803 may mean something different than similar values recorded last year. Values measured in Tanzania may differ in meaning from similar measurements made in Mexico.

How the data are collected can make the difference between insight and nonsense. As we'll see later, data that come from a voluntary survey on the internet are almost always worthless. In an internet poll during the subprime mortgage crisis, 84% of respondents said "no" to the question of whether subprime borrowers should be bailed out. Although it may be true that 84% of those 23 418 respondents did say that, it's dangerous to assume that that group is representative of any larger group. Chapter 3 discusses sound methods for collecting data from **surveys** and polls so that you can make inferences from the data you have at hand to the world at large.

You may also collect data by performing an **experiment** in which you actively manipulate variables (called factors) to see what happens. Most of the "junk mail" credit card offers that you receive are actually experiments done by marketing groups in those companies. With the advent of the internet, researchers can assess the effects of different product offers quickly and easily by directing randomly chosen individuals to different sites and then measuring the differences between the customers' responses. Because the researcher manipulates the levels of the factors instead of simply relying on data that are available, experiments make it possible to assess the effects of the factors. For this reason, experiments are the "gold standard" for data gathering.

Sometimes, the answer to the question you have may be found in data that someone, or, more typically, some organization has already collected. Such **observational studies** may work with data that were collected for other purposes (for example, transactional data about customers), data made available by government agencies (for example, economic indicators), and data collected without the careful design of a survey. The analysis of large transactional data sets for purposes other than those for which the data were originally collected is often referred to as **data mining**. Companies, nonprofit organizations, and government agencies collect a vast amount of data that are becoming increasingly easy to access via the internet, although some organizations may charge a fee for accessing or downloading their data. Statistics Canada collects information on nearly every aspect of life in Canada, both social and economic (see www.statcan.gc.ca), as the European Union does for Europe (see ec.europa.eu/eurostat). International organizations such as the World Health Organization (www.who.org) and polling agencies such as Gallup (www.gallup.com) offer information on a variety of topics as well.

Before you begin to gather data, ask the following questions. What data are needed? Who collects them? Are they published, and, if so, by whom? Are they

> *"[Data are] the next frontier for innovation. . . .Analyzing large data sets—so-called big data— will become a key basis of competition, underpinning new waves of productivity growth, innovation, and consumer surplus."*
>
> Excerpt by James Manyika from Big data: The Next Frontier for Innovation, Competition, and Productivity. Published by McKinsey & Company,© 2011.

freely available, or contained in a commercial fee-based system? How can they be accessed? Is there a statistical interface for downloading the data? During data-gathering, remember to evaluate data quality. Is the information-provider authoritative? How current is the information? What sources were used to compile the information? Does the publication present a balanced and unbiased viewpoint?

One important source of help is research librarians and subject specialists who know where and how to retrieve information. Many academic libraries and some public libraries provide access to online databases. Here are a few statistical databases in use at many universities:

Bloomberg

Bloomberg financial service provides quotes and analysis of securities, company and industry financial data, market news, stock exchange data, and economic data. It is accessible on dedicated terminals in selected libraries.

CANSIM

CANSIM is a comprehensive database of socioeconomic data from Statistics Canada, containing more than 42 million numeric time series. Much of CANSIM's data are accessible for free at http://www5.statcan.gc.ca/cansim/home-accueil?lang=eng

Print Measurement Bureau

Survey information on Canadians' use of over 3500 products and services, including demographics, attitudes, media consumption, retail outlets, frequency of use, and the brands used (where available). It is accessible at selected libraries.

World Bank Data

The World Bank has collected statistical data for over 550 development indicators, and time series data from 1960–present for over 200 countries and 18 country groups. Data include social, economic, financial, natural resource, and environmental indicators. Freely accessible.

> Statistics Canada is undoubtedly the largest and best source of data in the country. Its mission is, "Serving Canada with high-quality statistical information that matters." Best known for the national Census, done every five years, StatCan (its well-known nickname) maintains about 350 active surveys on nearly all aspects of Canadian life: our population, resources, economy, society, and culture. It is a good starting point for virtually any research question about Canada.

One more aspect of data sources is worth noting, namely whether the source is primary or secondary. Primary data are data we collect ourselves, with a particular purpose in mind, by observation, interview, survey, or experiment. Secondary data are data collected by someone else, such as Statistics Canada, and made available for others. StatCan doesn't know what users might do with the data, but they still collect them on our behalf. When a data source is secondary it is very important to read the details about the data collection to understand fully what the data mean.

> **There's a world of data on the internet**
>
> These days, one of the richest sources of data is the internet. With a bit of practice, you can learn to find data on almost any subject. Many of the data sets we use in this book were found in this way. The internet has both advantages and disadvantages as a source of data. Among the advantages are the fact that often you'll be able to find even more current data than we present. The disadvantage is that references to internet addresses can "break" as sites evolve, move, and die.

Our solution to these challenges is to offer the best advice we can to help you search for the data, wherever they may be residing. We usually point you to a website. We'll sometimes suggest search terms and offer other guidance.

Some words of caution, though: Data found on internet sites may not be formatted in the best way for use in statistics software. Although you may see a data table in standard form, an attempt to copy the data may leave you with a single column of values. You may have to work in your favourite statistics or spreadsheet program to reformat the data into variables. You will also probably want to remove commas from large numbers and such extra symbols as money indicators ($, ¥, £, €); few statistics packages can handle these.

> **THE W'S:**
>
> **WHO**
>
> **WHAT**
>
> **WHEN**
>
> **WHERE**
>
> **WHY**

Throughout this book, whenever we introduce data, we will provide a margin note listing the W's of the data. It's a habit we recommend. The first step of any data analysis is to know why you are examining the data (what you want to know), to whom each row of your data table refers, and what the variables (the columns of the table) record. These are the *Why*, the *Who*, and the *What*. Identifying them is a key part of the *Plan* step of any analysis. Make sure you know all three before you spend time analyzing the data.

✓ JUST CHECKING

An insurance company that specializes in commercial property insurance has a separate database for their policies that involve churches and schools. Here is a small portion of that database.

Policy Number	Years Claim Free	Net Property Premium ($)	Net Liability Premium ($)	Total Property Value ($1000)	Median Age in Postal Code	School?	Territory	Coverage
4000174699	1	3107	503	1036	40	FALSE	QC580	BLANKET
8000571997	2	1036	261	748	42	FALSE	NS192	SPECIFIC
8000623296	1	438	353	344	30	FALSE	YT60	BLANKET
3000495296	1	582	339	270	35	TRUE	NS340	BLANKET
5000291199	4	993	357	218	43	FALSE	ON590	BLANKET
8000470297	2	433	622	108	31	FALSE	NB140	BLANKET
1000042399	4	2461	1016	1544	41	TRUE	NU20	BLANKET
4000554596	0	7340	1782	5121	44	FALSE	MB530	BLANKET
3000260397	0	1458	261	1037	42	FALSE	AL560	BLANKET
8000333297	2	392	351	177	40	FALSE	NL190	BLANKET
4000174699	1	3107	503	1036	40	FALSE	BC580	BLANKET

1 List as many of the W's as you can for this data set.

2 Classify each variable as to whether you think it should be treated as categorical or quantitative (or both); if quantitative, identify the units.

Harald Høiland Tjøstheim/Shutterstock

WHAT CAN GO WRONG?

- **Don't label a variable as categorical or quantitative without thinking about the data and what they represent.** The same variable can sometimes take on different roles.

- **Don't assume that a variable is quantitative just because its values are numbers.** Categories are often given numerical labels. Don't let that fool you into thinking they have quantitative meaning. Look at the context.

- **Always be skeptical.** One reason to analyze data is to discover the truth. Even when you are told a context for the data, it may turn out that the truth is a bit (or even a lot) different. The context colours our interpretation of the data, so those who want to influence what you think may slant the context. A survey that seems to be about all students may in fact report just the opinions of those who visited a fan website. The question that respondents answered may be posed in a way that influences responses.

ETHICS IN ACTION

Sarah Potterman, a doctoral student in educational psychology, is researching the effectiveness of various interventions recommended to help children with learning disabilities improve their reading skills. Among the approaches examined is an interactive software system that uses analogy-based phonics. Sarah contacted the company that developed this software, RSPT Inc., in order to obtain the system free of charge for use in her research. RSPT Inc. expressed interest in having her compare their product with other intervention strategies and was quite confident that their approach would be the most effective. Not only did the company provide Sarah with free software, but RSPT Inc. also generously offered to fund her research with a grant to cover her data collection and analysis costs.

ETHICAL ISSUE *Both the researcher and company should be careful about the funding source having a vested interest in the research result (related to Item H, ASA Ethical Guidelines).*

ETHICAL SOLUTION *RSPT Inc. should not pressure Sarah Potterman to obtain a particular result. Both parties should agree on paper before the research is begun that the research results can be published even if they show that RSPT's interactive software system is not the most effective.*

Jim Hopler is operations manager for a local office of a top-ranked full service brokerage firm. With increasing competition from both discount and online brokers, Jim's firm has redirected attention to attaining exceptional customer service through its client-facing staff, namely brokers. In particular, they wish to emphasize the excellent advisory services provided by their brokers. Results from surveying clients about the advice received from brokers at the local office revealed that 20% rated it *poor*, 5% rated it *below average*, 15% rated it *average*, 10% rated it *above average*, and 50% rated it *outstanding*. With

corporate approval, Jim and his management team instituted several changes in an effort to provide the best possible advisory services at the local office. Their goal was to increase the percentage of clients who viewed their advisory services as *outstanding*. Surveys conducted after the changes were implemented showed the following results: 5% *poor*, 5% *below average*, 20% *average*, 40% *above average*, and 30% *outstanding*. In discussing these results, the management team expressed concern that the percentage of clients who considered their advisory services *outstanding* fell from 50% to 30%. One member of the team suggested an alternative way of summarizing the data. By coding the categories on a scale from 1 = poor to 5 = outstanding and computing the average, they found that the average rating increased from 3.65 to 3.85 as a result of the changes implemented. Jim was delighted to see that their changes were successful in improving the level of advisory services offered at the local office. In his report to corporate, he only included average ratings for the client surveys.

ETHICAL ISSUE *By changing the categorical variable to a quantitative one, Jim is able to show improved customer satisfaction. However, their goal was to increase the percentage of outstanding ratings. Jim redefined his study after the fact to support a position (related to ASA Ethical Guidelines, Item C, which can be found at http://www.amstat.org/about/ethicalguidelines.cfm).*

ETHICAL SOLUTION *Jim should report the percentages for each rating category. He can also report the average. He may wish to include in his report a discussion of what those different ways of looking at the data say and why they appear to differ. He may also want to explore with the survey participants the perceived differences between "above average" and "outstanding."*

WHAT HAVE WE LEARNED?

We've learned that data are information in a context.

- The W's help nail down the context: *Who, What, Why, Where, When.*
- We must know at least the *Who, What,* and *Why* to be able to say anything useful based on the data. The *Who* are the *cases.* The *What* are the *variables.* A variable gives information about each of the cases. The *Why* helps us decide which way to treat the variables.

We treat variables in two basic ways, as *categorical* or *quantitative.*

- Categorical variables identify a category for each case. Usually we think about the counts of cases that fall in each category. (An exception is an identifier variable that just names each case.)
- Quantitative variables record measurements or amounts of something.
- Sometimes we treat a variable as categorical or quantitative depending on what we want to learn from it, which means some variables can't be pigeonholed as one type or the other. That's an early hint that in Statistics we can't always pin things down precisely.

Terms

Case	A case is an individual about whom or which we have data.
Categorical variable	A variable that names categories (whether with words or numerals) is called categorical.
Context	The context ideally tells *Who* was measured, *What* was measured, *How* the data were collected, *Where* the data were collected, and *When* and *Why* the study was performed.
Cross-sectional data	Data taken from situations that vary over time but measured at a single time instant are said to be a cross-section of the time series.
Data	Systematically recorded information, whether numbers or labels, together with its context.
Data table	An arrangement of data in which each row represents a case and each column represents a variable.
Experiment	A study in which the researcher *manipulates* factor levels to assess the effect of the factor on the response.
Experimental unit	An individual in a study for which or for whom data values are recorded. Human experimental units are usually called subjects or participants.
Identifier variable	A categorical variable that records a unique value for each case, used to name or identify it.
Nominal variable	The term "nominal" can be applied to data whose values are used only to name categories.

Observational study	A study based on data in which no manipulation of factors has been employed.
Observations	Another word for data.
Ordinal variable	The term "ordinal" can be applied to data for which some kind of order is available but for which measured values are not available.
Participant	A human experimental unit. Also called a subject.
Quantitative variable	A variable in which the numbers are values of measured quantities, usually with units.
Record	Information about an individual in a database.
Relational database	A relational database stores and retrieves information. Within the database, information is kept in data tables that can be "related" to each other.
Respondent	Someone who answers, or responds to, a survey.
Spreadsheet	A spreadsheet is a layout designed for accounting that is often used to store and manage data tables. Excel is a common example of a spreadsheet program.
Subject	A human experimental unit. Also called a participant.
Survey	A study that asks questions of a sample drawn from some population in the hope of learning something about the entire population.
Time series	Data measured over time. Usually the time intervals are equally-spaced (e.g., every week, every quarter, or every year).
Units	A quantity or amount adopted as a standard of measurement, such as dollars, hours, or grams.
Value	A piece of information on a variable, for a single case. Data are the values of variables.
Variable	A variable holds information about the same characteristic for many cases.

Skills

PLAN

- Be able to identify the *Who, What, When, Where, Why,* and *How* of data, or recognize when some of this information has not been provided.
- Be able to identify the cases and variables in any data set.
- Know how to treat a variable as categorical or quantitative depending on its use.
- For any quantitative variable, be able to identify the units, real or imaginary, in which the variable has been measured (or note that they have not been provided).

REPORT

- Be sure to describe a variable in terms of its *Who, What, When, Where, Why,* and *How* (and be prepared to remark when that information is not provided).

TECHNOLOGY HELP: Statistics Packages

Most often we find statistics on a computer using a program, or *package*, designed for that purpose. There are many different statistics packages, but they all do essentially the same things. If you understand what the computer needs to know to do what you want and what it needs to show you in return, you can figure out the specific details of most packages pretty easily.

For example, to get your data into a computer statistics package, you need to tell the computer:

- Where to find the data. This usually means directing the computer to a file stored on your computer or to data on a database. Or it might just mean that you have copied the data from

a spreadsheet program or internet site and it is currently on your computer's clipboard. Usually, the data should be in the form of a data table. Most computer statistics packages prefer the *delimiter* that marks the division between elements of a data table to be a *tab* character and the delimiter that marks the end of a case to be a *return* character.

- Where to put the data. (Usually this is handled automatically.)

- What to call the variables. Some data tables have variable names as the first row of the data, and often statistics packages can take the variable names from the first row automatically.

MINI CASE STUDY PROJECTS

Credit Card Company

Like all credit and charge card companies, this company makes money on each of its cardholders' transactions. Thus, its profitability is directly linked to card usage. To increase customer spending on its cards, the company sends many different offers to its cardholders, and market researchers analyze the results to see which offers yield the largest increases in the average amount charged.

On MyStatLab (in the file **ch02_MCSP_Credit_Card_Bank.xls**) is a small part of a database like the one used by the researchers. For each customer, it contains several variables in a spreadsheet.

Examine the data in the data file. List as many of the W's as you can for these data and classify each variable as categorical or quantitative. If quantitative, identify the units.

Left, Gregory Bajor/iStockphoto; right, Konstantin Inozemtsev/ iStockphoto

Edmonton Oilers

Sports analytics began in baseball, and was made famous in the book and movie *Moneyball*. Moneypuck is the new term being used for data analytic methods applied to hockey. The Edmonton Oilers were the first National Hockey League team to embrace it; they set up an analytics advisory group comprising university professors, business analytics experts, and hockey pundits. The benefits remain to be seen.

The file **ch02_MCSP_Oilers.xlsx** on MyStatLab has data on all Edmonton Oilers players from the 2010–2011 NHL season. A glossary of terms is also included. What types of data are contained in the file? Classify the variables according to whether they are categorical, quantitative, identifier, string, or date, and explain your choice of classification.

Student Survey

To demonstrate real-world data collection and analysis, a large undergraduate business statistics course administers an anonymous survey of its students, using an online survey tool. Participation is strictly voluntary and is not linked to grades! The survey questions can be found in the document: **ch02_MCSP_Student_Survey.docx**.

Responses to each question will give one or more variables. List the questions/variables that are categorical; then list the questions/variables that are quantitative, and identify the units where possible. If a variable could be either, choose the more likely one. Be careful with the first variable!

MyStatLab **Students! Save time, improve your grades with MyStatLab.**
The Exercises marked in red can be found on MyStatLab. You can practice them as often as you want, and most feature step-by-step guided solutions to help you find the right answer. You'll find a personalized Study Plan available to you too! Data Sets for exercises marked **T** are also available on MyStatLab for formatted technologies.

EXERCISES

For each description of data in Exercises 1 to 26, identify the W's, name the variables, specify for each variable whether its use indicates it should be treated as categorical or quantitative, and for any quantitative variable identify the units in which it was measured (or note that they were not provided or that the variable does not have units).

1. The news. Find a newspaper or magazine article in which some data are reported (e.g., see *The National Post, Financial Times, Business Week, The Economist,* or *Fortune*). For the data discussed in the article, answer the questions above. Include a copy of the article with your report. **LO❶**

2. TFSA. The Tax-Free Savings Account (TFSA) was introduced in 2009 as an investment option for Canadian residents wanting to save for the future. While there is no tax deduction for contributions, withdrawals are tax-free. Unused space until the annual cap can be carried forward. The Canadian government wants to know how many Canadians have opened these accounts and the amounts of money that have been contributed, in each year since its inception. **LO❶**

3. Oil spills. After several major ocean oil spills, oil tankers were redesigned to have thicker hulls. Further improvements in the structural design have decreased the likelihood of an oil spill and the amount of outflow in the event of a hull puncture. Infoplease (www.infoplease.com) reports the date, the spillage amount, and cause of puncture for recent major oil spills from tankers and carriers. **LO❶**

4. Sales. A major Canadian company is interested in seeing how various promotional activities are related to domestic sales. Analysts decide to measure the money spent on different forms of advertising ($ thousand) and sales ($ million) on a monthly basis for the past three years. **LO❶**

5. Food store. A food retailer that specializes in selling organic food has decided to open a new store. To help determine the best location for the new store, researchers decide to examine data from existing stores, including weekly sales ($), town population (thousands), median age of town, median income of town ($), and whether or not the store sells wine and beer. **LO❶**

6. Sales, part 2. The company in Exercise 4 is also interested in the impact of national indicators on their sales. It decides to obtain measurements for unemployment rate (%) and inflation rate (%) on a quarterly basis to compare to their quarterly sales ($ million) over the same time period. **LO❶**

7. Subway menu. A listing posted by the Subway restaurant chain gives, for each of the sandwiches it sells, the type of meat in the sandwich, number of calories, and serving size in grams. The data might be used to assess the nutritional value of the different sandwiches. **LO❶**

8. MBA admissions. A Canadian business school is concerned with the recent drop in female students in its MBA program. It decides to collect data from the admissions office on each applicant, including: sex of each applicant, age of each applicant, whether or not they were accepted, whether or not they attended, and the reason for not attending (if they did not attend). The school hopes to find commonalities among the female accepted students who have decided not to attend the business program. **LO❶**

9. Climate. In a study appearing in the journal *Science*, a research team reports that plants in southern England are flowering earlier in the spring. Records of the first flowering dates for 385 species over a period of 47 years indicate that flowering has advanced an average of 15 days per decade, an indication of climate warming according to the authors. **LO❶**

10. MBA admissions, part 2. An internationally recognized MBA program in London intends to track the GPA of the MBA students and compares MBA performance to standardized test scores over the past five years. **LO❶**

11. Schools. A provincial ministry of education requires local school districts to keep records on all students, recording: age, days absent, current grade level, standardized test scores in reading and mathematics, and any disabilities or special educational needs the student may have. **LO❶**

12. Pharmaceutical firm. Scientists at a major pharmaceutical firm conducted an experiment to study the effectiveness of an herbal compound to treat the common cold. They exposed volunteers to a cold virus, then gave them either the herbal compound or a sugar solution known to have no effect on colds. Several days later they assessed each patient's condition using a cold severity scale ranging from 0–5. They found no evidence of the benefits of the compound. **LO❶**

13. Start-up company. A Canadian start-up company is building a database of customers and sales information. For each customer, it records name, ID number, region of the country (1=West, 2=Prairies, 3=Ontario, 4=Quebec, 5=Atlantic, 6=North), date of last purchase, amount of purchase, and item purchased. LO❶

14. Cars. A survey of autos parked in executive and staff lots at a large company recorded the make, country of origin, type of vehicle (car, van, SUV, etc.), and age. LO❶

15. Vineyards. Business analysts hoping to provide information helpful to grape growers compiled these data about vineyards: size (hectares), number of years in existence, province, varieties of grapes grown, average case price, gross sales, and percent profit. LO❶

16. Environment. As research for an ecology class, each year students at a college in British Columbia collect data on streams to study the impact of the environment. They record a number of biological, chemical, and physical variables, including the stream name, the substrate of the stream (limestone, shale, or mixed), the acidity of the water (pH), the temperature (°C), and the BCI (a numerical measure of biological diversity). LO❶

17. Environics Poll. Environics Research Group conducted a representative telephone survey of 1180 Canadian voters. Among the reported results were the voter's region (West, Prairies, etc.), age, political party affiliation, whether the respondent owned any shares of stock, and their attitude (on a scale of 1 to 5) toward unions. LO❶

18. TSB. The Transportation Safety Board of Canada (TSB) monitors airlines for safety and customer service. For each flight the carrier must report the type of aircraft, number of passengers, whether or not the flights departed and arrived on schedule, and any mechanical problems. LO❶

19. Cellphones. The Print Measurement Bureau (PMB) database (see Section 2.4) was used to study cellphone use in Canada. Data are collected about the brand of cellphone (i.e., major manufacturer) and user demographics for each province. LO❶

20. Consumer Reports. The Consumer Reports website provides ratings of a wide range of consumer products. A recent rating of digital cameras examined 234 models; it provided the brand, cost, pixel count (megapixels), zoom (magnification number, e.g., 30×), weight (grams), and overall rating (excellent, very good, etc.). LO❶

21. Gasoline prices. Using Statistics Canada's CANSIM website (see Section 2.4), prices for regular unleaded gasoline at self service filling stations at major Canadian cities were recorded monthly over a one-year period. LO❶

22. Lands' End. Lands' End is a large North American retailer that depends heavily on its catalogue sales. It collects data internally and tracks the number of catalogues mailed out, the number of square inches in each catalogue, and the sales ($ thousands) in the four weeks following each mailing. The company is interested in learning more about the relationship (if any) among the timing and space of their catalogues and their sales. LO❶

23. Stock market. An online survey of students in a large MBA Statistics class at a business school in Ontario asked them to report their total personal investment in the stock market ($), total number of different shares currently held, total invested in mutual funds ($), and the name of each mutual fund in which they have invested. The data were used in the aggregate for classroom illustrations. LO❶

24. Theme park sites. A study on the potential for developing theme parks in various locations throughout Europe in 2008 collects the following information: the country where the proposed site is located, estimated cost to acquire site (in euros), size of population within a one hour drive of the site, size of the site (in hectares), mass transportation within five minutes of the site. The data will be used to present to prospective developers. LO❶

25. Indy. The 2.5-mile (4-km) Indianapolis Motor Speedway has been the home to a race on Memorial Day in the United States nearly every year since 1911. Even during the first race there were controversies. Ralph Mulford was given the checkered flag first but took three extra laps just to make sure he'd completed 500 miles. When he finished, another driver, Ray Harroun, was being presented with the winner's trophy, and Mulford's protests were ignored. Harroun averaged 74.6 mph for the 500 miles. Here are the data for the first few and three recent Indianapolis 500 races. LO❶

Year	Winner	Car	Time (hrs)	Speed (mph)	Car #
1911	Ray Harroun	Marmon Model 32	6.7022	74.602	32
1912	Joe Dawson	National	6.3517	78.719	8
1913	Jules Goux	Peugeot	6.5848	75.933	16
...					
...					
2009	Helio Castroneves	Dallara/Honda	3.3263	150.318	3
2010	Dario Franchitti	Dallara/Honda	3.0936	161.623	10
2011	Dan Wheldon	Dallara/Honda	2.9366	170.265	98

26. Kentucky Derby. The Kentucky Derby is a horse race that has been run every year since 1875 at Churchill Downs, Louisville, Kentucky. The race started as a 1.5-mile race, but in 1896 it was shortened to 1.25 miles because experts felt that 3-year-old horses shouldn't run such a long race that early in the season. (It has been run in May every year but one—1901—when it took place on April 29.) The table at the bottom of the page shows the data for the first few and a few recent races. LO**①**

Date	Winner	Margin (lengths)	Jockey	Winner's Payoff ($)	Duration (min:sec)	Track Condition
May 17, 1875	Aristides	2	O. Lewis	2850	2:37.75	Fast
May 15, 1876	Vagrant	2	B. Swim	2950	2:38.25	Fast
May 22, 1877	Baden-Baden	2	W. Walker	3300	2:38.00	Fast
May 21, 1878	Day Star	1	J. Carter	4050	2:37.25	Dusty
May 20, 1879	Lord Murphy	1	C. Shauer	3550	2:37.00	Fast
...						
May 3, 2008	Big Brown	4 3/4	K. Desormeaux	1 442 200	2:01.82	Fast
May 2, 2009	Mine That Bird	6 3/4	C. Borel	1 417 000	2:02.66	Fast
May 1, 2010	Super Saver	2 3/4	C. Borel	1 425 200	2:04.45	Fast
May 7, 2011	Animal Kingdom	2 1/2	J. Velazquez	1 411 800	2:02.04	Fast

When you organize data in a spreadsheet, it is important to lay it out as a data table. For each of these examples in Exercises 27 to 30, show how you would lay out these data. Indicate the headings of columns and what would be found in each row.

27. Mortgages. For a study of mortgage loan performance: amount of the loan, the name of the borrower. LO**②**

28. Employee performance. Data collected to determine performance-based bonuses: employee ID, average contract closed (in $), supervisor's rating (1–10), years with the company. LO**②**

29. Company performance. Data collected for financial planning: weekly sales, week (week number of the year), sales predicted by last year's plan, difference between predicted sales and realized sales. LO**②**

30. Command performance. Data collected on investments in Broadway shows: number of investors, total invested, name of the show, profit/loss after one year. LO**②**

For the following examples in Exercises 31 to 36, indicate whether the data are a time series or a cross-section.

31. Car sales. Number of cars sold by each salesperson in a dealership in September. LO**③**

32. Motorcycle sales. Number of motorcycles sold by a dealership in each month last year. LO**③**

33. Cross-sections. Average diameter of trees brought to a sawmill in each week of a year. LO**③**

34. Grey Cup. Attendance at a Grey Cup game recording the age of each fan. LO**③**

35. Bullying: You read the following statement in a newspaper article, "According to recent research, 39.57% of teens are bullied." How would you critique this statement? LO**④**

36. University grades. According to an online survey of students in a business statistics class, the average grade in the prerequisite course was 73.78%. However, the professor in the prerequisite course reported an average of 69%. How could you explain the discrepancy? LO**④**

JUST CHECKING ANSWERS

1 Who—policies on churches and schools What—policy number, years claim free, net property premium ($), net liability premium ($), total property value ($000), median age in postal code, school?, territory, coverage

How—company records

When—not given

2 Policy number: identifier (categorical)

Years claim free: quantitative

Net property premium: quantitative ($)

Net liability premium: quantitative ($)

Total property value: quantitative ($)

School?: categorical (true/false)

Territory: categorical

Coverage: categorical

Surveys and Sampling

Edhar/Shutterstock

CONNECTIONS: CHAPTER

Where do data we discussed in Chapter 2 come from? In this chapter we discuss how surveys and opinion polls are used to get data, and how to ensure we get good data. We also deal with the reality that we can never (well, almost never) have ALL possible data—that's sampling.

Angus Reid

Angus Reid is a sociologist, researcher, entrepreneur, and above all, a pollster. In 1979 he founded a market research and public opinion research company which went on to become part of Ipsos Reid, the Canadian arm of a global company. Ipsos Reid employs more than 600 people, has the largest network of call centres in Canada, and offers the largest household and online panels.

He currently runs Angus Reid Public Opinion, part of Vision Critical, a leader in using the internet to carry out public opinion polling, the process of asking questions to find out what people think, how they feel, and who they will vote for. It is a "family business," with his son Andrew as founder and co-CEO of Vision Critical. Another arm of his enterprises is the Angus Reid Forum, which recruits panel participants to ensure representation across all segments of a given population. His company provides daily summaries of polling results from around the world and helps identify the trends that influence society.

One important product of his company is an online polling program for electoral forecasting in North America. They have accurately predicted the outcome of eight Canadian provincial elections from 2006–2012, and have provided the most accurate predictions of the 2008 and 2012 Canadian federal elections.[1]

Reid has always been at the forefront of opinion research, from the early days when polling was done with face-to-face interviews,

LEARNING OBJECTIVES

1. Identify population, population parameter, sampling frame, sample, and sample statistic

2. Recognize different methods (random and non-random) of selecting a representative sample

3. Understand how to avoid bias in sampling and recognize problems in generalizing to the population

---

[1] www.angusreidforum.com

to the switch to telephone surveys in the 1970s, to his current work with online surveys and panels. With the internet, results are now available within hours, instead of the weeks it used to take with old methodologies. Reid says, "It's all about applying the traditional science of survey research and marketing research to the new world." One advantage of online research is that traditional telephone-surveying is now suffering from high refusal rates and changes in telephone technology from land-line to cellular. Telephone surveying is fast becoming "phone spam." Online research also allows richer environments for measuring public opinion, such as surveys that incorporate audio, visual, and interactive components.

The key to good survey research remains what it always has been, the use of representative samples. Angus Reid and all other successful polling companies use samples that are representative of all regions of Canada and both official languages. One remarkable fact about survey research is the surprisingly small size of samples that are used, and yet that are still representative. National surveys of 1000 to 1500 respondents are the norm.

Based on information from www.angusreidforum.com

How do the researchers at Angus Reid, or indeed any of the Canadian polling companies, know that the responses they get reflect the real attitudes of consumers? After all, they don't ask everyone, but they don't want to limit their conclusions to just the people they surveyed. Generalizing from the data at hand to the world at large is something that market researchers, investors, and pollsters do every day. To do it wisely, they need three fundamental ideas.

3.1 Three Ideas of Sampling

Idea 1: Examine a Part of the Whole

The first idea is to draw a sample. We'd like to know about an entire population of individuals, but examining all of them is usually impractical, if not impossible. So we settle for examining a smaller group of individuals—a sample—selected from the population. All of Canada is the population the Angus Reid researchers are interested in, but it's not practical, cost-effective, or feasible to survey the entire population. So they examine a sample selected from the **population**.

You take samples of a larger population every day. For example, if you want to know how the vegetable soup you're cooking for dinner tonight is going to taste, you try a spoonful. You certainly don't consume the whole pot. You trust that the taste will *represent* the flavor of the entire pot. The idea of tasting is that a small sample, if selected properly, can represent the entire population.

The Angus Reid Daily Omnibus is an example of a **sample survey**, designed to ask questions of a small group of people in the hope of learning something about

For many people, sampling is what they do at a Costco store on a weekend noon hour. One can have an entire meal just from the samples that are provided. And this type of sampling is not so unlike what we are discussing here. Consider a new brand of frozen pizza. At Costco a sample is a small taste of an entire product. The taste should be like the rest of the pizza, with some of the topping and sauce, not just a piece of the crust. And no matter how big the pizza is, the size of piece you are offered, which is what your purchasing decision will be based on, will be the same.

The W's and Sampling

The population we are interested in is usually determined by the *Why* of our study. The participants or cases in the sample we draw will be the *Who*. *When* and *How* we draw the sample may depend on what is practical.

"Poll" and "survey" both refer to data collection about a sample drawn from a larger population. The word "poll" comes from the Greek word for "citizen" and has the same root (*politikos*) as the word "politics." In the twentieth century it referred to voting and taxation and then to public opinion surveys. In contrast, the word "survey" comes from the Latin words *sur*, from *super* meaning "over," and *vey*, from *videre* meaning "to see." To survey means to oversee something; the word's meaning spread to a general or comprehensive view of anything. Survey is a somewhat broader term than poll, but now the words are intermixed.

The first political "straw poll" (i.e., unofficial poll) was probably done in 1824 by the *Harrisburg Pennsylvanian* newspaper. Using straw polls to predict U.S. presidential elections continued to 1935, when the famous names of Gallup, Roper, and Crossley changed the methods of polling to what we are familiar with today.

Social surveys can be found in the Old Testament, as when Moses carried out a census of the Israelites after the Exodus (Exodus 30:12). The first national census in Canada took place in 1871, although a census of New France was done as early as 1666 (it found 3215 inhabitants—the country is about 10 000 times as big now!).

the entire population. Most likely, you've never been selected to be part of a national opinion poll. That's true of most people. So how can the pollsters claim that a sample is representative of the entire population? Professional researchers like those who run the Angus Reid surveys work hard to ensure that the "taste"—the sample that they take—represents the population fairly. If they are not careful, the sample can produce misleading information about the population.

Selecting a sample to represent the population fairly may sound easy, but it is more difficult than it sounds. Polls or surveys most often fail because the sample fails to represent part of the population. The way the sample is drawn may overlook subgroups that are hard to find. For example, a telephone survey may get no responses from people with caller ID and may favour other groups, such as the retired or the homebound, who would be more likely to be near their phones when the interviewer calls. Samples that over- or underemphasize some characteristics of the population are said to be biased. When a sample is **biased**, the summary characteristics of a sample differ from the corresponding characteristics of the population it is trying to represent. Conclusions based on biased samples are inherently flawed. There is usually no way to fix bias after the sample is drawn and no way to salvage useful information from it.

What are the basic techniques for making sure that a sample is representative? To make the sample as representative as possible, you might be tempted to handpick the individuals included in the sample. But the best strategy is to do something quite different: We should select individuals for the sample *at random*. We will discuss the concepts of *random* and *randomness* in detail in Chapter 7.

Idea 2: Randomize

Think back to our example of sampling soup. Suppose you add some salt to the pot. If you sample it from the top before stirring, you'll get the misleading idea that the whole pot is salty. If you sample from the bottom, you'll get the equally misleading idea that the whole pot is bland. But by stirring the soup, you *randomize* the amount of salt throughout the pot, making each taste more typical of the saltiness of the whole pot. Deliberate randomization is one of the great tools of Statistics.

Randomization can protect against factors that you aren't aware of, as well as those you know are in the data. Suppose, while you aren't looking, a friend adds a handful of peas to the soup. The peas sink to the bottom of the pot, mixing with the other vegetables. If you don't randomize the soup by stirring, your test spoonful from the top won't have any peas. By stirring in the salt, you *also* randomize the peas throughout the pot, making your sample taste more typical of the overall pot *even though you didn't know the peas were there*. So randomizing protects us by giving us a representative sample even for effects we were unaware of.

How do we "stir" people in our survey? We select them at random. Randomizing protects us from the influences of *all* the features of our population by making sure that *on average* the sample looks like the rest of the population.

Michael Lamotte/Getty Images

We all think we know what it means for something to be random. Rolling dice, spinning spinners, and shuffling cards all produce random outcomes. What's the most important aspect of the randomness in these games? Randomness makes them fair.

Two things make **randomization** seem fair. First, nobody can guess the outcome before it happens. Second, when we want things to be fair, usually some underlying set of outcomes will be equally likely (although in many games, some combinations of outcomes are more likely than others). We'll soon see how to use randomness to ensure that the sample we draw is representative of the population we want to study.

Truly random values are surprisingly hard to get. Computers are a popular way to generate random numbers. Even though they often do much better than humans, computers can't generate truly random numbers either. Computers follow programs. Start a computer from the same place, and, all things being equal, it will follow the same path every time. So numbers generated by a computer program are not truly random. Technically, "random" numbers generated by computer are *pseudorandom*. Fortunately, pseudorandom values are good enough for most purposes because they are virtually indistinguishable from truly random numbers.

There *are* ways to generate random numbers that are both equally likely and truly random. If you want to select subjects for a survey at random from a list of potential respondents, you can get as many random numbers as you need online, from a source such as www.random.org, match them up with your list, sort the numbers while carrying along the respondent IDs, and start from the top of the sorted list, selecting as many respondents as you need, now at random.

◆ **Why not match the sample to the population?** Rather than randomizing, we could try to design our sample to include every possible, relevant characteristic: income level, age, political affiliation, marital status, number of children, place of residence, etc. Clearly we can't possibly think of all the things that might be important. Even if we could, we wouldn't be able to match our sample to the population for all these characteristics.

How well does a sample represent the population from which it was selected? Here's an example using the database of a philanthropic organization with a donor list of about 3.5 million people. We've taken two samples, each of 8000 individuals at random from the population. Table 3.1 shows how the means and proportions match up on seven variables.

Notice that the two samples match closely in every category. This shows how well randomizing has stirred the population. We didn't preselect the samples for these variables, but randomizing has matched the results closely. We can reasonably assume that since the two samples don't differ too much from each other, they don't differ much from the rest of the population either.

Even if a survey is given to multiple random samples, the samples will differ from each other and so, therefore, will the responses. This variability from sample-to-sample is often referred to as sampling variability or **sampling error** even though no error has occurred. In statistical terminology, the word "error" means

	Age (yr)	White (%)	Female (%)	# of Children	Income Bracket (1–7)	Wealth Bracket (1–9)	Homeowner? (% Yes)
Sample 1	61.4	85.12	56.2	1.54	3.91	5.29	71.36
Sample 2	61.2	84.44	56.4	1.51	3.88	5.33	72.30

Table 3.1 Means and proportions for seven variables from two samples of size 8000 from the organization's data. The fact that the summaries of the variables from these two samples are so similar gives us confidence that either one would be representative of the entire population.

Canadian Sources of Public Opinion Polls

The Canadian Opinion Research Archive (CORA) (est. 1992) is based at Queen's University; CORA's website provides access to information about hundreds of surveys. In addition, here is a list of major Canadian sources of public opinion polls. Many of them were established in the 1980s, only a few years before the internet made information available online.

- Angus Reid Strategies (est. 2006)
- Compas Inc. (est. 1987)
- EKOS Research Associates (est. 1980)
- Environics Research Group (est. 1970)
- Gallup Canada polls (est. 1935)
- Harris/Decima Research Inc. (est. 1979)
- Ipsos-Reid Corporation (est. 1979)
- Leger Marketing (est. 1986)
- Nanos Research (est. 1987)
- Pollara (est. 1985)

the difference or deviation between an observed value and a true value. It does not mean "mistake." The term will arise many more times.

Idea 3: The Sample Size Is What Matters

You probably weren't surprised by the idea that a sample can represent the whole. And the idea of sampling randomly makes sense when you stop to think about it, too. But the third important idea of sampling often surprises people. The third idea is that the **size of the sample** determines what we can conclude from the data *regardless of the size of the population*. Many people think that we need a large percentage, or *fraction*, of the population, but in fact all that matters is the size of the sample. The size of the *population* doesn't matter at all.[2] A random sample of 100 students in a university represents the student body just about as well as a random sample of 100 voters represents the entire electorate of Canada. This is perhaps the most surprising idea in designing surveys.

To understand how this works, let's return one last time to your pot of soup. If you're cooking for a banquet rather than just for a few people, your pot will be bigger, but you don't need a bigger spoon to decide how the soup tastes. As long as the pot is properly mixed, the same size spoonful is probably enough to make a decision about the entire pot, no matter how large the pot. What *fraction* of the population you sample doesn't matter. It's the **sample size** itself that's important. This idea is of key importance to the design of any sample survey, because it determines the balance between how well the survey can measure the population and how much the survey costs.

How big a sample do you need? That depends on how much your population varies. If you're tasting a plain broth, any spoonful will be like another. But if you're tasting a soup with chunks of vegetables, small tastes can be quite different from one another. To get a *representative* sample, you'll need a larger taste. For a survey that tries to answer questions about a population made up of several categories of respondents, you'll usually need at least several hundred respondents to be sure you see enough in each category.[3]

◆ **What do the professionals do?** How do professional polling and market research companies do their work? The most common polling method today is still to contact respondents by telephone, even though online research is growing rapidly. Computers generate random telephone numbers for telephone exchanges known to include residential customers; so pollsters can contact people with unlisted phone numbers. The person who answers the phone will be invited to respond to the survey—if that person qualifies. (For example, only adults are usually surveyed, and the respondent usually must live at the residence phoned.) If the person answering doesn't qualify, the caller will ask for an appropriate alternative. When they conduct the interview, the pollsters often list possible responses (such as product names) in randomized orders to avoid biases that might favour the first name on the list.

---

[2] Well, that's not exactly true. If sample is more than 10% of the whole population, it *can* matter. It doesn't matter whenever, as usual, our sample is a very small fraction of the population.

[3] Chapter 9 gives the details behind this statement and shows how to decide on a sample size for a survey.

Do these methods work? The Pew Research Center for the People and the Press, reporting on one survey, says that

> *Across five days of interviewing, surveys today are able to make some kind of contact with the vast majority of households (76%), and there is no decline in this contact rate over the past seven years. But because of busy schedules, skepticism and outright refusals, interviews were completed in just 38% of households that were reached using standard polling procedures.*[4]

Nevertheless, studies indicate that those actually sampled can give a good snapshot of larger populations from which the surveyed households were drawn. But it is for reasons such as this that telephone surveying is being replaced in some situations by online methods, just as the pollster Angus Reid foresaw.

3.2 A Census—Does It Make Sense?

Why bother determining the right sample size? If you plan to open a store in a new community, why draw a sample of residents to understand their interests and needs? Wouldn't it be better to just include everyone and make the "sample" be the entire population? Such a special sample is called a **census**. Although a census would appear to provide the best possible information about the population, there are a number of reasons why it might not.

First, it can be difficult to complete a census. There always seem to be some individuals who are hard to locate or hard to measure. Do you really need to contact the folks away on vacation when you collect your data? How about those with no telephone or mailing address? The cost of locating the last few cases may far exceed the budget. It can also be just plain impractical to take a census. The quality control manager for Molson Canadian beer doesn't want to census *all* the beer bottles on the production line to determine their quality. Aside from the fact that nobody could drink that much beer (although I'm sure there would be volunteers to try), it would defeat their purpose: there would be nothing left to sell. In fact, a census is impractical for every kind of destructive testing, such as the strength of steel girders, crash-testing of automobiles, leak-proof nature of condoms, etc. That is, anything of the type, "if you use it, you lose it."

Second, the population we're studying may change. For example, in any human population, babies are born, people travel, and folks die during the time it takes to complete the census. News events and advertising campaigns can cause sudden shifts in opinions and preferences. A sample, surveyed in a shorter time frame, may actually generate more accurate information.

Finally, taking a census can be cumbersome. A census usually requires a team of pollsters and/or the cooperation of the population. Some people may have multiple addresses (e.g., "snowbirds" who summer in Canada but winter in Florida or Arizona). Students often have one address while attending university and another over the summer when they live with their parents. It takes great effort to identify which is the "primary" residence so as to avoid double-counting.

The sheer size of a population also makes taking a census a daunting task. For the 2010 national census of China, more than six million census-takers were needed, a number that exceeds the population of some countries.

3.3 Populations and Parameters

A Harris Decima survey in 2012 reported that 31% of Canadian workers expressed dissatisfaction with their career progression. And 70% who did not receive a promotion were not told the reasons for the decision. What do these claims mean? We can be sure the researchers didn't take a census. They can't possibly know exactly

---

[4] Excerpt from Polls Face Growing Resistance, But Still Representative. Published by Pew Research Center for the People & the Press, © 2004.

what percentage of all Canadian workers are dissatisfied with their career progression. So what does the "31%" mean?

To generalize from a sample to the world at large, we need a model of reality. The model doesn't need to be complete or perfect. Just as a model of an airplane in a wind tunnel can tell engineers what they need to know about aerodynamics even though it doesn't include every rivet of the actual plane, models of data can give us summaries that we can learn from and use even though they don't fit each data value exactly. It's important to remember that they're only models of reality and not reality itself. But without models, what we can learn about the world at large is limited to only what we can say about the data we have at hand. Models use mathematics to represent reality. We call the key numbers in those models **parameters**. All kinds of models have parameters, so sometimes a parameter used in a model for a population is called (redundantly) a **population parameter**.

But let's not forget about the data. We use the data to try to estimate values for the population parameters. Any summary found from the data is a **statistic**. Those statistics that estimate population parameters are particularly interesting. Sometimes—and especially when we match statistics with the parameters they estimate—we use the term **sample statistic**. Since a sample statistic is used to estimate a parameter we often call the sample statistic an **estimate**.

We draw samples because we can't work with the entire population. We hope that the statistics we compute from the sample will estimate the corresponding parameters accurately, at least on average. A sample that does this is said to be **representative**. Another way to think about a representative sample is that it has similar characteristics or make-up as the population. That is, the sample is a miniature version of the population.

There is a clever mnemonic device to help remember the relationships among the four terms. Parameter goes with population—both start with "P"; statistic goes with sample—both start with "S". And here's the brilliant part—even the first syllable of estimate is pronounced "S"!

>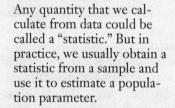
> Any quantity that we calculate from data could be called a "statistic." But in practice, we usually obtain a statistic from a sample and use it to estimate a population parameter.

> Population model parameters are not just unknown—usually they are *unknowable*. We have to settle for sample statistics.

Population	←→	Parameter
(e.g., all Canadian households)		(e.g., mean household income of population)
Sample	←→	Statistic/Estimate
(e.g., 1000 households contacted by researchers)		(e.g., mean household income of the 1000 households)

JUST CHECKING

1 Various claims are often made for surveys. Why is each of the following claims not correct?

  a) It is always better to take a census than to draw a sample.

  b) Stopping customers as they are leaving a restaurant is a good way to sample opinions about the quality of the food.

  c) We drew a sample of 100 from the 3000 students in a school. To get the same level of precision for a town of 30 000 residents, we'll need a sample of 1000.

  d) A poll taken at a popular website garnered 12 357 responses. The majority of respondents said they enjoy doing Statistics. With a sample size that large, we can be sure that most people feel this way.

  e) The true percentage of all people who enjoy doing Statistics is called a "population statistic."

3.4 Simple Random Sample (SRS)

How would you select a representative sample? It seems fair to say that every individual in the population should have an equal chance to be selected. We need that, but we also need something more. There are many ways to give everyone an equal chance that still wouldn't give a representative sample. Consider, for example, a café where half the customers pay cash and half use a credit card. The owner wants to draw a sample of customers to survey them about her new idea for offering a cash discount. She could flip a coin. If it lands heads, she'll select 100 credit-card customers; if it lands tails, she'll select 100 cash customers. Each customer has an equal chance of being selected, but the sample she draws won't be representative.

We need to do better. Suppose we insist that every possible *sample* of the size we plan to draw has an equal chance of being selected. This ensures that situations like the all cash or all credit samples are not likely to occur and still guarantees that each person has an equal chance of being selected. With this method each *combination* of individuals has an equal chance of being selected as well. A sample drawn in this way is called a **simple random sample**, usually abbreviated **SRS**. An SRS is the standard against which we measure other sampling methods, and the sampling method on which the theory of working with sampled data is based.

To select a sample at random, we first need to define a **sampling frame**, a list of individuals from which the sample will be drawn. For example, to draw a random sample of regular customers, a store might sample from its list of all "frequent buyers." In defining the sampling frame, we must deal with the details of defining the population. Are former frequent buyers who have moved away included? How about those who still live in the area but haven't shopped at our store in over a year? The answers to these questions may depend on the purpose of the survey.

Once we have a sampling frame, the easiest way to choose an SRS is with random numbers. We can assign a sequential number to each individual in the sampling frame. We then draw random numbers to identify those to be sampled. Let's look at an example.

> We want to select 5 students from the 80 enrolled in a Business Statistics class. We start by numbering the students from 00 to 79. Now we get a sequence of random digits from a table (such as the table in the back of this book), technology (most statistics packages and spreadsheets can generate random numbers), or the internet (e.g., a site like www.random.org). For example, we might get 051662930577482. Taking those random numbers two digits at a time gives us 05, 16, 62, 93, 05, 77, and 48. We ignore 93 because no one had a number that high. And to avoid picking the same person twice, we also skip the repeated number 05. Our simple random sample consists of students with the numbers 05, 16, 62, 77, and 48.

Often the sampling frame is so large that it would be awkward to search through the list to locate each randomly selected individual. An alternative method is to generate random numbers of several digits in length, assigning one to each member of the sampling frame. Then *sort* the random numbers, *carrying along* the identities of the individuals in the sampling frame. (Spreadsheets and statistics programs typically can do this kind of sort.) Now you can pick a random sample of any size you like off the top of the sorted list.

Samples drawn at random generally differ one from another. Each draw of random numbers selects *different* people for our sample. As we've seen, the different people give rise to different summary statistics for each sample, a phenomenon known as **sampling variability** or sampling error. Surprisingly, sampling variability isn't a problem; it's an opportunity. If different samples from a population vary little

---

A "cosmic" poetic way to think about the sampling frame:

Since the population is the "universe" of interest, and the universe is infinite, it means that the population might also be infinite (e.g., all components already made and those to be made in the future). Put a "frame" around the part of the population that you have access to (e.g., all components made so far), and therefore have the possibility of being in the sample. That is the sampling frame.

Sampling Errors vs. Bias

We referred to sample-to-sample variability earlier in this chapter as *sampling error*, making it sound like it's some kind of mistake. It's not. We understand that samples will vary, so "sampling errors" are to be expected. It's *bias* we must strive to avoid. Bias means our sampling method distorts our view of the population. Of course, bias leads to mistakes. Even more insidious, bias introduces errors that we cannot correct with subsequent analysis.

from each other, then most likely the underlying population harbors little variation. If the samples show much sampling variability, the underlying population probably varies a lot. In the coming chapters, we'll spend much time and attention working with sampling variability to better understand what we are trying to measure.

3.5 Other Sample Designs

Simple random sampling is not the only fair way to sample. More complicated designs may save time or money or avert sampling problems. All statistical sampling designs have in common the idea that chance, rather than human choice, is used to select the sample.

Stratified Sampling

Strata or Clusters?

We create strata by dividing the population into groups of similar individuals so that each stratum is different from the others. (For example, we often stratify by age, race, or sex.) By contrast, we create clusters that all look pretty much alike, each representing the wide variety of individuals seen in the population.

Digital Vision/Getty Images

Designs that are used to sample from large populations—especially populations residing across large areas—are often more complicated than simple random samples. Sometimes we slice the population into homogeneous groups, called **strata**, and then use simple random sampling within each stratum, combining the results at the end. This is called **stratified random sampling**.

Why would we want to stratify? Suppose we want to survey how shoppers feel about a potential new anchor store at a large suburban mall. The shopper population is 60% women and 40% men, and we suspect that men and women have different views on their choice of anchor stores. If we use simple random sampling to select 100 people for the survey, we could end up with 70 men and 30 women or 35 men and 65 women. There is even a slim chance that we might get 100 women and 0 men! Our resulting estimates of the attractiveness of a new anchor store could vary widely. To help reduce this sampling variability, we can force a representative balance, selecting 40 men at random and 60 women at random. This is no longer a simple random sample, but it does guarantee that the proportions of men and women within our sample match the proportions in the population, and that should make such samples more accurate in representing population opinion.

You can imagine that stratifying by race, income, age, and other characteristics can be helpful, depending on the purpose of the survey. When we use a sampling method that restricts by strata, additional samples are more like one another, so statistics calculated for the sampled values will vary less from one sample to another. This reduced sampling variability is the most important benefit of stratifying.

Understanding Cluster Sampling:

The M&Ms website used to publish information about the proportions of each colour in each of their products. For example, milk chocolate M&Ms were 24% blue, 14% brown, 16% green, 20% orange, 13% red, and 14% yellow. How could you investigate the proportions yourself?

If you open the spigot on a large bulk dispenser of a well-mixed collection of M&Ms and take the first kilogram's worth that come out, that would be an SRS. If you take a random sample of 50 packages of M&Ms (each is 47.9 grams), that would be cluster sampling. Each package is a cluster, since each package is similar to each other package. Stratified sampling is not possible or relevant here because you don't know the proportions of each colour. That is the point of the investigation.

Cluster and Multistage Sampling

Sometimes dividing the sample into homogeneous strata isn't practical, and even simple random sampling may be difficult. For example, suppose we wanted to assess the reading level of a product instruction manual based on the length of the sentences. Simple random sampling could be awkward; we'd have to number each sentence and then find, for example, the 576th sentence or the 2482nd sentence, and so on. Doesn't sound like much fun, does it?

We could make our task much easier by picking a few *pages* at random and then counting the lengths of the sentences on those pages. That's easier than picking individual sentences and works if we believe that the pages are all reasonably similar to one another in terms of reading level. Splitting the population in this way into parts or **clusters** that each represent the population can make sampling more practical. We select one or a few clusters at random and perform a census within each of them. This sampling design is called **cluster sampling**. If each cluster fairly represents the population, cluster sampling will generate an unbiased sample.

What's the difference between cluster sampling and stratified sampling? We stratify to ensure that our sample represents different groups in the population, and sample randomly within each stratum. This reduces the sample-to-sample variability. Strata are homogeneous, but differ from one another. By contrast, clusters are more or less alike, each heterogeneous and resembling the overall population. We cluster to save money or even to make the study practical.

Sometimes we use a variety of sampling methods together. In trying to assess the reading level of our instruction manual, we might worry that the "quick start" instructions are easy to read, but the "troubleshooting" chapter is more difficult. If so, we'd want to avoid samples that selected heavily from any one chapter. To guarantee a fair mix of sections, we could randomly choose one section from each chapter of the manual. Then we would randomly select a few pages from each of those sections. If altogether that made too many sentences, we might select a few sentences at random from each of the chosen pages. So, what is our sampling strategy? First we stratify by the chapter of the manual and randomly choose a section to represent each stratum. Within each selected section, we choose pages as clusters. Finally, we consider an SRS of sentences within each cluster. Sampling schemes that combine several methods are called **multistage samples**. Most surveys conducted by professional polling organizations and market research firms use some combination of stratified and cluster sampling as well as simple random samples.

Systematic Samples

Sometimes we draw a sample by selecting individuals systematically. For example, a **systematic sample** might select every tenth person on an alphabetical list of employees. To make sure our sample is random, we still must start the systematic selection with a randomly selected individual—not necessarily the first person on the list. When there is no reason to believe that the order of the list could be associated in any way with the responses measured, systematic sampling can give a representative sample. Systematic sampling can be much less expensive than true random sampling. When you use a systematic sample, you should justify the assumption that the systematic method is not associated with any of the measured variables.

✓ JUST CHECKING

2 We need to survey a random sample of the 300 passengers on a flight from Vancouver to Tokyo. Name each sampling method described below.

   a) Pick every tenth passenger as people board the plane.

   b) From the boarding list, randomly choose 5 people flying first class and 25 of the other passengers.

   c) Randomly generate 30 seat numbers and survey the passengers who sit there.

   d) Randomly select a seat position (right window, right centre, right aisle, etc.) and survey all the passengers sitting in those seats.

The Canadian population is very diverse with respect to geography, language, and culture. In order to ensure adequate representation, stratified sampling is widely used. For example, an SRS is likely to yield too few Prince Edward Islanders to give reliable estimates since the population of PEI is less than one percent of the Canadian population. And for surveys that require in-person data collection, cluster sampling is used to reduce travel times.

Think about the reading level sampling example again. Suppose we have chosen a section of the manual at random, then three pages at random from that section, and now we want to select a sample of 10 sentences from the 73 sentences found on those pages. Instead of numbering each sentence so we can pick a simple random sample, it would be easier to sample systematically. A quick calculation shows 73/10 = 7.3, so we can get our sample by picking every seventh sentence on the page. But where should you start? At random, of course. We've accounted for 10 × 7 = 70 of the sentences, so we'll throw the extra three into the starting group and choose a sentence at random from the first 10. Then we pick every seventh sentence after that and record its length.

Guided Example   Market Demand Survey

Tatiana Popova/ Shutterstock

In a course at a business school, the students form business teams, propose a new product, and use seed money to launch a business to sell the product on campus.

Before committing funds for the business, each team must complete the following assignment: "Conduct a survey to determine the potential market demand on campus for the product you are proposing to sell." Suppose your team's product is a 500-piece jigsaw puzzle of the map of your university campus. Design a marketing survey and discuss the important issues to consider.

PLAN

Setup State the goals and objectives of the survey (the *Why*).

Population and Parameters Identify the population to be studied and the associated sampling frame. The *What* identifies the parameters of interest and the variables measured. The *Who* is the sample of people we draw.

Sampling Plan Specify the sampling method and the sample size, *n*. Specify how the sample was actually drawn. What is the sampling frame?

The description should, if possible, be complete enough to allow someone to replicate the procedure, drawing another sample from the same population in the same manner. A good description of the procedure is essential, even if it could never practically be repeated. The question you ask is important, so state the wording of the question clearly. Be sure that the question is useful in helping you with the overall goal of the survey.

Our team designed a study to find out how likely students at our school are to buy our proposed product—a 500-piece jigsaw puzzle of the map of our university campus.

The population studied will be students at our school. We have obtained a list of all students currently enrolled to use as the sampling frame. The parameter of interest is the proportion of students likely to buy this product. We'll also collect some demographic information about the respondents.

We will select a simple random sample of students. We decided against stratifying by sex or class because we thought that students were all more or less alike in their likely interest in our product.

We will ask the students we contact:

Do you solve jigsaw puzzles for fun?

Then we will show them a prototype puzzle and ask:

If this puzzle sold for $10, would you purchase one?

We will also record the respondent's sex and class.

Sampling Practice Specify *When*, *Where*, and *How* the sampling will be performed. Specify any other details of your survey, such as how respondents were contacted, any incentives that were offered to encourage them to respond, how nonrespondents were treated, and so on.

The survey will be administered in the middle of the fall semester during October. We have a master list of registered students, which we will randomize by matching it with random numbers from www.random.org and sorting on the random numbers, carrying the names. We will contact selected students by phone or email and arrange to meet with them. If a student is unwilling to participate, the next name from the randomized list will be substituted until a sample of 200 participants is found.

We will meet with students in an office set aside for this purpose so that each will see the puzzle under similar conditions.

Summary and Conclusion This report should include a discussion of all the elements needed to design the study. It's good practice to discuss any special circumstances or other issues that may need attention.

MEMO:

Re: Survey Plans

Our team's plans for the puzzle market survey call for a simple random sample of students. Because subjects need to be shown the prototype puzzle, we must arrange to meet with selected participants. We have arranged an office for that purpose.

We will also collect demographic information so we can determine whether there is in fact a difference in interest level among classes or between men and women.

3.6 Defining the Population

The *Who* of a survey can refer to different groups, and the resulting ambiguity can tell you a lot about the success of a study. To start, you should think about the population of interest. Often, this is not a well-defined group. For example, who, exactly, is a mall "shopper": only the hurrying couples already carrying a purchase, or should we include people eating at the food court? How about teenagers outside the mall's video store, who may be carrying purchases or just hanging out, or both? Even when the population is clear, it may not be a practical group to study. For example, election polls want to sample from all those who will vote in the next election—a population that is particularly tricky to identify before election day.

Second, you must specify the sampling frame. Usually, the sampling frame is not the group you *really* want to know about, and sometimes it's actually much smaller. The sampling frame limits what your survey can find out.

Then there's your target sample. These are the individuals for whom you *intend* to measure responses. You're not likely to get responses from all of them. ("I know it's dinner time, but I'm sure you wouldn't mind answering a few questions. It'll only take 20 minutes or so. Oh, you're busy?") Nonresponse is a problem in many surveys.

> The population is determined by the *Why* of the study. Unfortunately, the sample is just those we can reach to obtain responses— the *Who* of the study. This difference could undermine even a well-designed study.

Finally, there is your sample—the actual respondents. These are the individuals about whom you *do* get data and can draw conclusions. Unfortunately, they might not be representative of either the sampling frame or the population.

At each step, the group we can study may be constrained further. The *Who* keeps changing, and each constraint can introduce biases. A careful study should address the question of how well each group matches the population of interest. One of the main benefits of simple random sampling is that it never loses its sense of who's *Who*. The *Who* in an SRS is the population of interest from which we've drawn a representative sample. That's not always true for other kinds of samples.

When people (or committees!) decide on a survey, they often fail to think through the important questions about who are the *Who* of the study and whether they are the individuals about whom the answers would be interesting or have meaningful business consequences. This is a key step in performing a survey and should not be overlooked.

Universal Uclick

3.7 The Valid Survey

It isn't sufficient to draw a sample and start asking questions. You want to feel confident your survey can yield the information you need about the population you are interested in. We want a *valid survey*.

To help ensure a valid survey, you need to ask four questions:

◆ *What do I want to know?*

◆ *Who are the right respondents?*

◆ *What are the right questions?*

◆ *What will be done with the results?*

These questions may seem obvious, but there are a number of specific pitfalls to avoid:

Know what you want to know.   Far too often, decisionmakers decide to perform a survey without any clear idea of what they hope to learn. Before considering a survey, you must be clear about what you hope to learn and about whom you hope to learn it. If you don't know that, you can't even judge whether you have a valid survey. The survey *instrument*—the questionnaire itself—can be a source of errors. Perhaps the most common error is to ask unnecessary questions. The longer the survey, the fewer people will complete it, leading to greater nonresponse bias. For each question on your survey, you should ask yourself whether you really want to know this and what you would do with the responses if you had them. If you don't have a good use for the answer to a question, don't ask it.

Use the right sampling frame. A valid survey obtains responses from appropriate respondents. Be sure you have a suitable sampling frame. Have you identified the population of interest and sampled from it appropriately? A company looking to expand its base might survey customers who returned warrantee registration cards—after all, that's a readily available sampling frame—but if the company wants to know how to make its product more attractive, it needs to survey customers who rejected its product in favour of a competitor's product. This is the population that can tell the company what about its product needs to change to capture a larger market share.

It is equally important to be sure that your respondents actually know the information you hope to discover. Your customers may not know much about the competing products, so asking them to compare your product with others may not yield useful information.

Ask specific rather than general questions. It is better to be specific. "Do you usually recall TV commercials?" won't be as useful as "How many TV commercials can you recall from last night?" or better, yet, "Please describe for me all the TV commercials you can recall from your viewing last night."

Watch for biases. Even with the right sampling frame, you must beware of bias in your sample. If customers who purchase more expensive items are less likely to respond to your survey, this can lead to **nonresponse bias**. Although you can't expect all mailed surveys to be returned, if those individuals who don't respond have common characteristics, your sample will no longer represent the population you hope to learn about. Surveys in which respondents volunteer to participate, such as online surveys, suffer from **voluntary response bias**. Individuals with the strongest feelings on either side of an issue are more likely to respond; those who don't care may not bother.

Be careful with question phrasing. Questions must be carefully worded. A respondent may not understand the question—or may not understand the question the way the researcher intended it. For example, "Does anyone in your family own a Ford truck?" leaves the term "family" unclear. Does it include only spouses and children or parents and siblings, or do in-laws and second cousins count too? A question like "Were your Timbits fresh?" might be interpreted quite differently by different people.

Be careful with answer phrasing. Respondents and survey-takers may also provide inaccurate responses, especially when questions are politically or sociologically sensitive. This also applies when the question does not take into account all possible answers, such as a true-false or multiple-choice question to which there may be other answers. Or the respondent may not know the correct answer to the question on the survey. We refer to inaccurate responses (intentional or unintentional) as **measurement errors**. One way to cut down on measurement errors is to provide a range of possible responses. But be sure to phrase them in neutral terms.

The best way to protect a survey from measurement errors is to perform a pilot test. In a **pilot test**, a small sample is drawn from the sampling frame, and a draft form of the survey instrument is administered. A pilot test can point out flaws in the instrument. For example, during a staff cutback at one of our schools, a researcher surveyed faculty members to ask how they felt about the reduction in staff support. The scale ran from "It's a good idea" to "I'm very unhappy." Fortunately, a pilot study showed that everyone was very unhappy or worse. The scale was re-tuned to run from "unhappy" to "ready to quit."

WHAT CAN GO WRONG?—OR, HOW TO SAMPLE BADLY

Bad sample designs yield worthless data. Many of the most convenient forms of sampling can be seriously biased. And there is no way to correct for the bias from a bad sample. So it's wise to pay attention to sample design—and to beware of reports based on poor samples.

Voluntary Response Sample

One of the most common dangerous sampling methods is the voluntary response sample. In a **voluntary response sample**, a large group of individuals is invited to respond, and all who do respond are counted. This method is used by call-in shows, 900 numbers, internet polls, and letters written to Members of Parliament. Voluntary response samples are almost always biased, so conclusions drawn from them are almost always wrong.

It's often hard to define the sampling frame of a voluntary response study. Practically, the frames are groups such as internet users who frequent a particular website or viewers of a particular TV show. But those sampling frames don't correspond to the population you are likely to be interested in.

Even if the sampling frame is of interest, voluntary response samples are often biased toward those with strong opinions or those who are strongly motivated—and especially from those with strong negative opinions. A request that travellers who have used the local airport visit a survey site to report on their experiences is much more likely to hear from those who had long waits, cancelled flights, and lost luggage than from those whose flights were on time and carefree. The resulting voluntary response bias invalidates the survey.

Convenience Sampling

Another sampling method that doesn't work is convenience sampling. As the name suggests, in **convenience sampling** we simply include the individuals who are convenient. Unfortunately, this group may not be representative of the population. A survey of 437 potential home buyers in Orange County, California, found, among other things, that

> all but 2 percent of the buyers have at least one computer at home, and 62 percent have two or more. Of those with a computer, 99 percent are connected to the Internet (Jennifer Hieger, "Portrait of Homebuyer Household: 2 Kids and a PC," Orange County Register, July 27, 2001).

Later in the article, we learn that the survey was conducted via the internet. That was a convenient way to collect data and surely easier than drawing a simple random sample, but perhaps home builders shouldn't conclude from this study that *every* family has a computer and an internet connection.

Many surveys conducted at shopping malls suffer from the same problem. People in shopping malls are not necessarily representative of the population of interest. Mall shoppers tend to be more affluent and include a larger percentage of teenagers and retirees than the population at large. To make matters worse, survey interviewers tend to select individuals who look "safe," or easy to interview.

Convenience sampling is not just a problem for beginners. In fact, convenience sampling is a widespread problem in the business world. When a company wants to find out what people think about its products or services, it may turn to the easiest people to sample: its own customers. But the company will never learn how those who *don't* buy its product feel about it.

Do you use the Internet?
Click here ○ for yes
Click here ○ for no

Internet convenience surveys are often worthless. As voluntary response surveys, they have no well-defined sampling frame (all those who use the internet and visit their site?) and thus report no useful information. Do not use them.

(continued)

Bad Sampling Frame?

An SRS from an incomplete sampling frame introduces bias because the individuals included may differ from the ones not in the frame. It may be easier to sample workers from a single site, but if a company has many sites and they differ in worker satisfaction, training, or job descriptions, the resulting sample can be biased. There is serious concern among professional pollsters that the increasing numbers of people who can be reached only by cell phone may bias telephone-based market research and polling.

Undercoverage

Many survey designs suffer from **undercoverage**, in which some portion of the population is not sampled at all or has a smaller representation in the sample than it has in the population. Undercoverage can arise for a number of reasons, but it's always a potential source of bias. Are people who use answering machines to screen callers (and are thus less available to blind calls from market researchers) different from other customers in their purchasing preferences? In a census, undercoverage means missing those members of the population who are homeless.

WHAT ELSE CAN GO WRONG?

- **Nonresponse bias.** No survey succeeds in getting responses from everyone. The problem is that those who don't respond may differ from those who do. And if they differ on just the variables we care about, the lack of response will bias the results. Rather than sending out a large number of surveys for which the response rate will be low, it is often better to design a smaller, randomized survey for which you have the resources to ensure a high response rate.

- **Long, dull surveys.** Surveys that are too long are more likely to be refused, reducing the response rate and biasing all the results. Keep it short.

- **Response bias.** Response bias includes the tendency of respondents to tailor their responses to please the interviewer and the consequences of slanted question wording.

THE WIZARD OF ID   parker and hart

John L. Hart/Creators Syndicate, Inc.

Push polls, which masquerade as surveys, present one side of an issue before asking a question. For example, a question like

> Would the fact that the new store that just opened by the mall sells mostly goods made overseas by workers in sweatshop conditions influence your decision to shop there rather than in the downtown store that features products made in Canada?

is designed not to gather information, but to spread ill-will toward the new store.

How to Think about Biases

- **Look for biases in any survey.** If you design a survey of your own, ask someone else to help look for biases that may not be obvious to you. Do this *before* you collect your data. There's no way to recover from a biased sample or a survey that asks biased questions.

  A bigger sample size for a biased study just gives you a bigger useless study. A really big sample gives you a really big useless study.

- **Spend your time and resources reducing biases.** No other use of resources is as worthwhile as reducing the biases.

- **If you possibly can, pretest or pilot your survey.** Administer the survey in the exact form that you intend to use it to a small sample drawn from the population you intend to sample. Look for misunderstandings, misinterpretation, confusion, or other possible biases. Then redesign your survey instrument.

- **Always report your sampling methods in detail.** Others may be able to detect biases where you did not expect to find them.

ETHICS IN ACTION

The Okanagan River Restoration Initiative is interested in applying for government agency funds to continue their restoration and conservation of the Okanagan River. While they have managed to gain significant support for their cause through education and community involvement, the executive committee is now interested in presenting more compelling evidence to the province. They decided to survey local residents regarding their attitudes toward the proposed expansion of the river restoration and conservation project. With limited time and money (the deadline for the grant application was fast approaching), the executive committee was delighted that one of its members, Harry Greentree, volunteered to undertake the project. Harry owned a local organic food store and agreed to have a sample of his shoppers interviewed during the next one-week period. The only concern that the committee had was that the shoppers be selected in a systematic fashion, for instance, by interviewing every fifth person who entered the store. Harry had no problem with this request and was eager to help the Okanagan River Restoration Initiative.

ETHICAL ISSUE *Introducing bias into the results (even if not intentional). One might expect consumers of organic food to be more concerned about the environment than the general population (related to ASA Ethical Guidelines, Item C, which can be found at http://www.amstat.org/about/ethicalguidelines.cfm).*

ETHICAL SOLUTION *Harry is using a convenience sample from which results cannot be generalized. If the Okanagan River Restoration Initiative cannot improve their sampling scheme and survey design (for example, for lack of expertise or time), they should openly discuss the weaknesses of their sampling method when they disclose details of their study. When reporting the results, they should note that their findings are from a convenience sample and include an appropriate disclaimer.*

WHAT HAVE WE LEARNED?

We've learned that a representative sample can offer important insights about populations. It's the size of the sample—and not its fraction of the larger population—that determines the precision of the statistics it yields.

We've learned several ways to draw samples, all based on the power of randomness to make them representative of the population of interest:

- A simple random sample (SRS) is our standard. Every possible group of *n* individuals has an equal chance of being our sample. That's what makes it *simple*.

- Stratified samples can reduce sampling variability by identifying homogeneous subgroups and then randomly sampling within each.
- Cluster samples randomly select among heterogeneous subgroups that each resemble the population at large, making our sampling tasks more manageable.
- Systematic samples can work in some situations and are often the least expensive method of sampling. But we still want to start them randomly.
- Multistage samples combine several random sampling methods.

We've learned that bias can destroy our ability to gain insights from our sample:

- Nonresponse bias can arise when sampled individuals will not or cannot respond.
- Response bias arises when respondents' answers might be affected by external influences, such as question wording or interviewer behaviour.

We've learned that bias can also arise from poor sampling methods:

- Voluntary response samples are almost always biased and should be avoided and distrusted.
- Convenience samples are likely to be flawed for similar reasons.
- Even with a reasonable design, sampling frames may not be representative. Undercoverage occurs when individuals from a subgroup of the population are selected less often than they should be.

Finally, we've learned to look for biases in any survey we find and to be sure to report our methods whenever we perform a survey so that others can evaluate the fairness and accuracy of our results.

Terms

Bias	Any systematic failure of a sampling method to represent its population.
Census	An attempt to collect data on the entire population of interest.
Cluster	A representative subset of a population chosen for reasons of convenience, cost, or practicality.
Cluster sampling	A sampling design in which groups, or clusters, representative of the population are chosen at random and a census is then taken of each.
Convenience sampling	A sample that consists of individuals who are conveniently available.
Measurement error	An intentional or unintentional inaccurate response.
Multistage sampling	Sampling schemes that combine several sampling methods.
Nonresponse bias	Bias introduced to a sample when a large fraction of those sampled fails to respond.
Parameter	A numerically valued attribute of a model for a population. We rarely expect to know the value of a parameter, but we do hope to estimate it from sampled data.
Pilot test	A small trial run of a study to check that the methods of the study are sound.
Population	The entire group of individuals or instances about whom we hope to learn.

Population parameter	A numerically valued attribute of a model for a population.
Randomization	A defense against bias in the sample selection process, in which each individual is given a fair, random chance of selection.
Representative sample	A sample from which the statistics computed accurately reflect the corresponding population parameters.
Response bias	Anything in a survey design that influences responses.
Sample	A subset of a population, examined in hope of learning about the population.
Sample size	The number of individuals in a sample.
Sample survey	A study that asks questions of a sample drawn from some population in the hope of learning something about the entire population.
Sampling error (or sampling variability)	The natural tendency of randomly drawn samples to differ, one from another. Sometimes called *sampling variability*.
Sampling frame	A list of individuals from which the sample is drawn. Individuals in the population of interest but who are not in the sampling frame cannot be included in any sample.
Simple random sample (SRS)	A sample in which each set of n elements in the population has an equal chance of selection.
Statistic, sample statistic, estimate	A value calculated for sampled data, particularly one that corresponds to, and thus estimates, a population parameter. The term "sample statistic" is sometimes used, usually to parallel the corresponding term "population parameter." The term "estimate" is also used since the statistic "estimates" the parameter.
Strata	Subsets of a population that are internally homogeneous but may differ one from another.
Stratified random sampling	A sampling design in which the population is divided into several homogeneous subpopulations, or strata, and random samples are then drawn from each stratum.
Systematic sampling	A sample drawn by selecting individuals systematically from a sampling frame.
Undercoverage	A sampling scheme that biases the sample in a way that gives a part of the population less representation than it has in the population.
Voluntary response bias	Bias introduced to a sample when individuals can choose on their own whether to participate in the sample.
Voluntary response sample	A sample in which a large group of individuals are invited to respond and decide individually whether or not to participate. Voluntary response samples are generally worthless.

Skills

PLAN
- Know the basic concepts and terminology of sampling.
- Be able to recognize population parameters in descriptions of populations and samples.

- Understand the value of randomization as a defence against bias.
- Understand the value of sampling to estimate population parameters from statistics calculated on representative samples drawn from the population.
- Understand that the size of the sample (not the fraction of the population) determines the precision of estimates.

- Know how to draw a simple random sample from a master list of a population, using a computer or a table of random numbers.

REPORT

- Know what to report about a sample as part of your account of a statistical analysis.
- Be sure to report possible sources of bias in sampling methods. Recognize voluntary response and nonresponse as sources of bias in a sample survey.

TECHNOLOGY HELP: Random Sampling

Computer-generated pseudorandom numbers are usually good enough for drawing random samples. But there is little reason not to use the truly random values available on the internet. Here's a convenient way to draw an SRS of a specified size using a computer-based sampling frame. The sampling frame can be a list of names or of identification numbers arrayed, for example, as a column in a spreadsheet, statistics program, or database:

1. Generate random numbers of enough digits so that each exceeds the size of the sampling frame list by several digits. This makes duplication unlikely.

2. Assign the random numbers arbitrarily to individuals in the sampling frame list. For example, put them in an adjacent column.

3. Sort the list of random numbers, *carrying* along the sampling frame list.

4. Now the first *n* values in the sorted sampling frame column are an SRS of *n* values from the entire sampling frame.

MINI CASE STUDY PROJECTS

Market Survey Research

You are part of a marketing team that needs to research the potential of a new product. Your team decides to e mail an interactive survey to a random sample of consumers. Write a short questionnaire that will generate the information you need about the new product. Select a sample of 200 using an SRS from your sampling frame. Discuss how you will collect the data and how the responses will help your market research.

Canadian Labour Force Survey

Employment and unemployment rates are among the most important measures of how the Canadian economy is performing. They are also the most timely, with results being released only 13 days after data collection is completed. The survey is carried out during the third week of the month and uses a sample size of about 54 000 households, which gives labour market information for about 100 000 individuals. In addition to employment and unemployment rates, the survey

Left, Istockphoto; right, Photodisc/Getty Images

covers hours of work and work arrangements, industry, occupation, unionization, wages and salaries, as well as demographic information about employees such as age, sex, marital status, education level, and province or territory of residence.

As the leading and public sector survey organization in the country, Statistics Canada (Statcan) provides detailed information on all its survey activities. To answer the following questions, consult the online information. You can go to www.statcan.gc.ca and search for Labour Force Survey (LFS); or you can try the following link: http://www.statcan.gc.ca/pub/71-544-x/71-544-x2012001-eng.htm

- What is the target population? Is any group of Canadians excluded?
- What sampling design is used? What challenges might be posed by using simple random sampling instead of the actual design?
- What method is used to collect the data?
- How does Statcan ensure that they get a representative sample of people from each province and territory, and from each of the demographic groups described above?
- What does Statcan say about data accuracy and possible bias from non-sampling errors?

MyStatLab **Students! Save time, improve your grades with MyStatLab.**
The Exercises marked in red can be found on MyStatLab. You can practice them as often as you want, and most feature step-by-step guided solutions to help you find the right answer. You'll find a personalized Study Plan available to you too! Data Sets for exercises marked **T** are also available on MyStatLab for formatted technologies.

EXERCISES

1. Roper. GfK Roper Consulting (www.gfkamerica.com) conducts a global consumer survey to help multinational companies understand different consumer attitudes throughout the world. In India, the researchers interviewed 1000 people aged 13–65. Their sample is designed so that they get 500 males and 500 females. **LO❷**

a. Are they using a simple random sample? How do you know?
b. What kind of design do you think they are using?

2. Coffee shop survey. For their class project, a group of Business students decide to survey the student body to assess opinions about a proposed new student coffee shop to judge how successful it might be. Their sample of 200 contained 50 students from each of the four years of their undergraduate program. **LO❷**

a) Do you think the group was using an SRS? Why?
b) What kind of sampling design do you think they used?

3. Software licences. The website www.gamefaqs.com asked, as their question of the day to which visitors to the site were invited to respond, *"Do you ever read the end-user licence agreements when installing software or games?"* Of the 98 574 respondents, 63.47% said they never read those agreements—a fact that software manufacturers might find important. **LO❷**

a) What kind of sample was this?

b) How much confidence would you place in using 63.47% as an estimate of the fraction of people who don't read software licences?

4. Drugs in baseball. Major League Baseball, responding to concerns about their "brand," tests players to see whether they are using performance-enhancing drugs. Officials select a team at random, and a drug-testing crew shows up unannounced to test all 40 players on the team. Each testing day can be considered a study of drug use in Major League Baseball. **LO❷**

a) What kind of sample is this?
b) Is that choice appropriate?

5. Environics. Environics Research Group carries out public opinion and market research studies in business, public policy, communications, and so on. An example of their work is a 2011 study that examines the Canadian public's level of concern about environmental issues (www.environics.ca/reference-library/?news_id=109). The final paragraph of the press release includes the following statement about the methodology. **LO❶**

These results are based on a syndicated Environics survey with a representative sample of 2000 Canadians (aged 18 and over) conducted by telephone in English and French from November 15 to 27, 2011.[5]

a) For this survey, identify the population of interest.
b) Telephone surveys are usually done by phoning numbers generated at random by a computer program. What is the sampling frame?
c) What problems, if any, would you be concerned about in matching sampling frame with the population?

6. Defining the survey. At its website (www.gallupworldpoll.com) the Gallup World Poll reports results of surveys conducted

---

[5] Excerpt from a Study on Environmental Issues. Published by Environics Research Group, © 2011.

in various places around the world. At the end of one of these reports, they describe their methods, including explanations such as the following: **LO❷**

Results are based on face-to-face interviews with randomly selected national samples of approximately 1000 adults, aged 15 and older, who live permanently in each of the 21 sub-Saharan African nations surveyed. Those countries include Angola (areas where land mines might be expected were excluded), Benin, Botswana, Burkina Faso, Cameroon, Ethiopia, Ghana, Kenya, Madagascar (areas where interviewers had to walk more than 20 kilometers from a road were excluded), Mali, Mozambique, Niger, Nigeria, Senegal, Sierra Leone, South Africa, Tanzania, Togo, Uganda (the area of activity of the Lord's Resistance Army was excluded from the survey), Zambia, and Zimbabwe. . . . In all countries except Angola, Madagascar, and Uganda, the sample is representative of the entire population.

a) Gallup is interested in sub-Saharan Africa. What kind of survey design are they using?
b) Some of the countries surveyed have large populations. (Nigeria is estimated to have about 130 million people.) Some are quite small. (Togo's population is estimated at 5.4 million.) Nonetheless, Gallup sampled 1000 adults in each country. How does this affect the precision of its estimates for these countries?

7–16. Survey details. For the following reports about statistical studies, identify the following items (if possible). If you can't tell, then say so—this often happens when we read about a survey. **LO❶, LO❷, LO❸**

a) The population
b) The population parameter of interest
c) The sampling frame
d) The sample
e) The sampling method, including whether or not randomization was employed
f) Any potential sources of bias you can detect and any problems you see in generalizing to the population of interest

7. HR directors. A business magazine mailed a questionnaire to the human resources directors of all Fortune 500 companies, and received responses from 23% of them. Those responding reported that they did not find that such surveys intruded significantly on their workday.

8. Senate reform. A Canadian Press-Harris/Decima survey asked Canadians whether they want to see the Senate reformed or abolished. Just over 1000 Canadians were interviewed using the company's national telephone omnibus survey.

9. Alternative medicine. Consumers Union asked all subscribers whether they had used alternative medical treatments and, if so, whether they had benefited from them. For almost all of the treatments, approximately 20% of those responding reported cures or substantial improvement in their condition.

10. Global warming. The Gallup Poll interviewed 1007 randomly selected U.S. adults aged 18 and older, March 23–25, 2007. Gallup reports that when asked when (if ever) the effects of global warming will begin to happen, 60% of respondents

said the effects had already begun. Only 11% thought that they would never happen.

11. At the bar. Researchers waited outside a bar they had randomly selected from a list of such establishments. They stopped every 10th person who came out of the bar and asked whether he or she thought drinking and driving was a serious problem.

12. Election poll. Hoping to learn what issues may resonate with voters in the coming election, the campaign director for a mayoral candidate selects one block from each of the city's election districts. Staff members go there and interview all the residents they can find.

13. Toxic waste. Environment Canada took soil samples at 16 locations near a former industrial waste dump and checked each for evidence of toxic chemicals. They found no elevated levels of any harmful substances.

14. Housing discrimination. Inspectors send trained "renters" of various races and ethnic backgrounds, and of both sexes to inquire about renting randomly assigned advertised apartments. They look for evidence that landlords deny access illegally based on race, sex, or ethnic background.

15. Quality control. A company packaging snack foods maintains quality control by randomly selecting 10 cases from each day's production and weighing the bags. Then they open one bag from each case and inspect the contents.

16. Contaminated milk. Dairy inspectors visit farms unannounced and take samples of the milk to test for contamination. If the milk is found to contain dirt, antibiotics, or other foreign matter, the milk is destroyed and the farm is considered to be contaminated pending further testing.

17. Pulse poll. A local TV station conducted a "PulsePoll" to predict the winner in the upcoming mayoral election. Evening news viewers were invited to phone in their votes, with the results to be announced on the late-night news. Based on the phone calls, the station predicted that Amabo would win the election with 52% of the vote. They were wrong: Amabo lost, getting only 46% of the vote. Do you think the station's faulty prediction is more likely to be a result of bias or sampling error? Explain. **LO❷**

18. Paper poll. Prior to the mayoral election discussed in Exercise 17, the newspaper also conducted a poll. The paper surveyed a random sample of registered voters stratified by political party, age, sex, and area of residence. This poll predicted that Amabo would win the election with 52% of the vote. The newspaper was wrong: Amabo lost, getting only 46% of the vote. Do you think the newspaper's faulty prediction is more likely to be a result of bias or sampling error? Explain. **LO❷**

19. Cable company market research. A local cable TV company with customers in 15 towns is considering offering high-speed internet service on its cable lines. Before launching the new service they want to find out whether customers would pay the $50 per month that they plan to charge. An intern has prepared several alternative plans for assessing customer demand. For each, indicate what kind of sampling strategy is involved and what (if any) biases might result. **LO❷, LO❸**

a) Put a big ad in the newspaper asking people to log their opinions on the company's website.

b) Randomly select one of the towns and contact every cable subscriber by phone.

c) Send a survey to each customer and ask them to fill it out and return it.

d) Randomly select 20 customers from each town. Send them a survey, and follow up with a phone call if they do not return the survey within a week.

20. Cable company market research, part 2. Four new sampling strategies have been proposed to help a cable TV company determine whether enough cable subscribers are likely to purchase high-speed internet service. For each, indicate what kind of sampling strategy is involved and what (if any) biases might result. **LO❷, LO❸**

a) Run a poll on the local TV news, asking people to dial one of two phone numbers to indicate whether they would be interested.

b) Hold a meeting in each of the 15 towns, and tally the opinions expressed by those who attend the meetings.

c) Randomly select one street in each town and contact each of the households on that street.

d) Go through the company's customer records, selecting every 40th subscriber. Send employees to those homes to interview the people chosen.

21. Churches. For your marketing class, you'd like to take a survey from a sample of all the Catholic Church members in your city to assess the market for a DVD about Pope Benedict, the first pope to resign in 600 years. A list of churches shows 17 Catholic churches within the city limits. Rather than try to obtain a list of all members of all these churches, you decide to pick 3 churches at random. For those churches, you'll ask to get a list of all current members and contact 100 members at random. **LO❷**

a) What kind of design have you used?

b) What could go wrong with the design that you have proposed?

22. Great Lakes aquatic invaders. According to the Ontario Ministry of Natural Resources, as of 2009, 186 non-native species, such as the sea lamprey and the zebra mussel, were present in the Great Lakes Basin. These aquatic invaders enter Ontario in many different ways, through canals, bait buckets, boats, and ballast water. In order to estimate how many of each species are present, take a sample every third day at dawn during June and July, from each of the Great Lakes. **LO❷**

a) What kind of design is this?

b) What could go wrong with this design?

23. Amusement park riders. An amusement park has opened a new roller coaster. It is so popular that people are waiting for up to three hours for a two-minute ride. Concerned about how

patrons (who paid a large amount to enter the park and ride on the rides) feel about this, they survey every 10th person on the line for the roller coaster, starting from a randomly selected individual. **LO❶**

a) What kind of sample is this?

b) Is it likely to be representative?

c) What is the sampling frame?

24. Playground. Some people have been complaining that the children's playground at a municipal park is too small and is in need of repair. Managers of the park decide to survey city residents to see if they believe the playground should be rebuilt. They hand out questionnaires to parents who bring children to the park. Describe possible biases in this sample. **LO❸**

25. Survey wording. The intern designing the study of high speed internet service for Exercises 19 and 20 has proposed some questions that might be used in the surveys. **LO❸**

Question 1: If our company offered state-of-the-art high-speed internet service for $50 per month, would you subscribe to that service?

Question 2: Would you find $50 per month—less than the cost of a daily cappuccino—an appropriate price for high-speed internet service?
a) Do you think these are appropriately worded questions? Why or why not?

b) Which one has more neutral wording? Explain.

26. More words. Here are more proposed survey questions. **LO❸**

Question 3: Do you find that the slow speed of dial-up internet access reduces your enjoyment of web services?

Question 4: Given the growing importance of high-speed internet access for your children's education, would you subscribe to such a service if it were offered?
a) Do you think these are appropriately worded questions? Why or why not?

b) Propose a question with more neutral wording.

27. Another ride. The survey of patrons waiting in line for the roller coaster in Exercise 23 asks whether they think it is worthwhile to wait a long time for the ride and whether they'd like the amusement park to install still more roller coasters. What biases might cause a problem for this survey? **LO❸**

28. Playground bias. The survey described in Exercise 24 asked,

Many people believe this playground is too small and in need of repair. Do you think the playground should be repaired and expanded even if that means raising the entrance fee to the park?

Describe two ways this question may lead to response bias. **LO❸**

29. (Possibly) Biased questions. Examine each of the following questions for possible bias. If you think the question is biased, indicate how and propose a better question. **LO❸**

a) *Should companies that pollute the environment be compelled to pay the costs of cleanup?*

b) *Should a company enforce a strict dress code?*

30. More possibly biased questions. Examine each of the following questions for possible bias. If you think the question is biased, indicate how and propose a better question. **LO❸**

a) *Do you think that price or quality is more important in selecting an MP3 player?*

b) *Given humanity's great tradition of exploration, do you favour continued funding for space exploration?*

31. Phone surveys. Any time we conduct a survey, we must take care to avoid undercoverage. Suppose we plan to select 500 names from the city phone book, call their homes between noon and 4 p.m., and interview whoever answers, anticipating contacts with at least 200 people. **LO❷**

a) Why is it difficult to use a simple random sample here?

b) Describe a more convenient, but still random, sampling strategy.

c) What kinds of households are likely to be included in the eventual sample of opinion? Who will be excluded?

d) Suppose, instead, that we continue calling each number, perhaps in the morning or evening, until an adult is contacted and interviewed. How does this improve the sampling design?

e) Random-digit dialing machines can generate the phone calls for us. How would this improve our design? Is anyone still excluded?

32. Cell phone survey. What about drawing a random sample only from cell phone exchanges? Discuss the advantages and disadvantages of such a sampling method compared with surveying randomly generated telephone numbers from non–cell phone exchanges. Do you think these advantages and disadvantages have changed over time? How do you expect they'll change in the future? **LO❷**

33. Change. How much change do you have on you right now? Go ahead, count it. **LO❶**

a) How much change do you have?

b) Suppose you check on your change every day for a week as you head for lunch and average the results. What parameter would this average estimate?

c) Suppose you ask 10 friends to average *their* change every day for a week, and you average those 10 measurements. What is the population now? What parameter would this average estimate?

d) Do you think these 10 average change amounts are likely to be representative of the population of change amounts in your class? In your university? In the country? Why or why not?

34. Fuel economy. Occasionally, when I fill my car with gas, I figure out how many litres it used to travel 100 kilometres. I wrote down those results after six fill-ups in the past few months. Overall, it appears my car uses 8.2 litres per 100 kilometres. **LO❶**

a) What statistic have I calculated?

b) What is the parameter I'm trying to estimate?

c) How might my results be biased?

d) When *Consumer Reports* checks a car like mine to predict its fuel economy, what parameter is it trying to estimate?

35. Accounting. Between quarterly audits, a company likes to check on its accounting procedures to address any problems before they become serious. The accounting staff processes payments on about 120 orders each day. The next day, the supervisor rechecks 10 of the transactions to be sure they were processed properly. **LO❷**

a) Propose a sampling strategy for the supervisor.

b) How would you modify that strategy if the company makes both wholesale and retail sales, requiring different bookkeeping procedures?

36. Happy workers? A manufacturing company employs 14 project managers, 48 foremen, and 377 labourers. In an effort to keep informed about any possible sources of employee discontent, management wants to conduct job satisfaction interviews with a simple random sample of employees every month. **LO❷, LO❸**

a) Do you see any danger of bias in the company's plan? Explain.

b) How might you select a simple random sample?

c) Why do you think a simple random sample might not provide the representative opinion the company seeks?

d) Propose a better sampling strategy.

e) Listed below are the last names of the project managers. Use random numbers to select two people to be interviewed. Be sure to explain your method carefully.

Ali	Bowman	Chen
DeLara	DeRoos	Grigorov
Gill	Mulvaney	Pagliarulo
Rosica	Smithson	Tadros
Williams	Yamamoto	

37. Quality control. Sammy's Salsa, a small local company, produces 20 cases of salsa a day. Each case contains 12 jars and is imprinted with a code indicating the date and batch number. To help maintain consistency, at the end of each day, Sammy selects three bottles of salsa, weighs the contents, and tastes the product. Help Sammy select the sample jars. Today's cases are coded 07N61 through 07N80. **LO❷**

a) Carefully explain your sampling strategy.

b) Show how to use random numbers to pick the three jars for testing.

c) Did you use a simple random sample? Explain.

38. Fish quality. Concerned about reports of discoloured scales on fish caught downstream from a newly sited chemical plant, scientists set up a field station in a shoreline public park. For one week they asked fishermen there to bring any fish they caught to the field station for a brief inspection. At the end of the week, the scientists said that 18% of the 234 fish that were submitted for inspection displayed the discolouration. From this information, can the researchers estimate what proportion of fish in the river have discoloured scales? Explain. **LO❷**

39. Sampling methods. Consider each of these situations. Do you think the proposed sampling method is appropriate? Explain. LO❷

a.) We want to know what percentage of local family doctors accept new patients. We call the offices of 50 family doctors randomly selected from local Yellow Page listings.

b.) We want to know what percentage of local businesses anticipate hiring additional employees in the upcoming month. We randomly select a page in the Yellow Pages and call every business listed there.

40. More sampling methods. Consider each of these situations. Do you think the proposed sampling method is appropriate? Explain. LO❷

a) We want to know if business leaders in the community support the development of an "incubator" site at a vacant lot on the edge of town. We spend a day phoning local businesses in the phone book to ask whether they'd sign a petition.

b) We want to know if travellers at the local airport are satisfied with the food available there. We go to the airport on a busy day and interview every 10th person in line in the food court.

JUST CHECKING ANSWERS

1 a) It can be hard to reach all members of a population, and it can take so long that circumstances change, affecting the responses. A well-designed sample is often a better choice.

   b) This sample is probably biased—people who didn't like the food at the restaurant might not choose to eat there.

   c) No, only the sample size matters, not the fraction of the overall population.

   d) Students who frequent this website might be more enthusiastic about Statistics than the overall population of Statistics students. A large sample cannot compensate for bias.

   e) It's the population "parameter." "Statistics" describe samples.

2 a) systematic
   b) stratified
   c) simple
   d) cluster

Displaying and Describing Categorical Data

CONNECTIONS: CHAPTER

In Chapter 2 we learned that data can be categorical or quantitative. In this chapter we concentrate on categorical data. We learn how to display them with graphs and describe them with numerical summaries, first examining one variable at a time. Then we learn how to display and assess the relationship between two categorical variables.

MEC Blog

LEARNING OBJECTIVES

1. Choose an appropriate display of categorical data and determine its effectiveness

2. Analyze a contingency table of counts or percentages

3. Create and analyze relative frequency distributions from tabulated data

4. Compute and interpret marginal and conditional distributions from contingency tables

5. Identify misleading results that are due to data aggregation (Simpson's paradox)

MEC: Mountain Equipment Co-op

Mountain Equipment Co-op, or MEC, is a leader in active outdoor lifestyle equipment: gear, clothing, and services. A Canadian success story founded over 40 years ago by a group of climbers at the University of British Columbia, it has grown to more than $250 million in annual sales with 3.5 million members, while retaining its co-operative member-owned structure.

It has 16 retail locations across Canada, with a global supply chain hub in Surrey, British Columbia. MEC has embraced internet sales and marketing. In 2001 the MEC website became transactional so that members could buy clothing and gear online. It is now also bilingual English/ French. In MEC's words, their aim is to provide quality gear and excellent value, and to minimize environmental impact by building products that last.

MEC is a leader in ethical sourcing, sustainability initiatives, and charitable contributions to the environmental sector. The Community Contributions page on their website details an extensive program of grants and product donations, national and regional partnerships, and outreach and advocacy programs. It is a member of 1% For the Planet, investing one percent of annual revenue to environmental causes.

MEC is a fast-growing company. Approximately 10% of adult Canadians are MEC members, and the number increased by an average of over 10 000 new members every month, as at the end of 2013. MEC employs about 1500 people and was recognized as one of Canada's Top 100 Employers in 2011.

Based on information from www.mec.ca

WHO	Visits to the MEC.ca website
WHAT	Originating province of search on MEC's website
WHEN	Jan. 1 – Dec. 31, 2012
WHERE	Canada-wide
HOW	Data compiled via Google Analytics from MEC website
WHY	To understand regional differences in where customers come from

There is a well-known saying that the three most important principles of real estate are: location, location, location. And in French cooking, the three most important principles are: use butter, use butter, use butter. A simple three-fold rule also applies to data analysis.

MEC, like most companies, collects data on visits to its website. Actual data are proprietary, and companies either need to invest in their own resources to handle the large data files, or rely on third party resources such as Google Analytics to summarize the data. Without formal access to a company's data, a researcher can turn to online resources such as Google Trends (www.google.com/trends) to analyze search volume for "Mountain Equipment Co-op," which is a useful proxy for total traffic. As well, Google AdWords (https://adwords.google.com) gives actual measures of the number of times a particular item was searched for, or can identify the most common keywords that brought a visitor to the site. In this illustration we have actual data courtesy of MEC.

Raw data are rarely informative. And rarely can we see what is going on, but seeing is exactly what we want to do. We need ways to show the data so that we can see patterns, relationships, trends, and exceptions.

4.1 The Three Rules of Data Analysis

There are three things you should always do with data:

1. **Make a picture.** A display of your data (as in Figure 4.1) will reveal things you are not likely to see in a table of numbers and will help you to *plan* your approach to

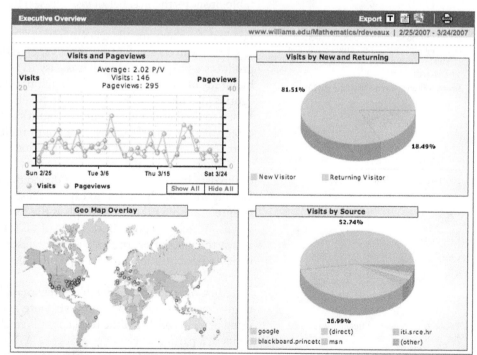

visualization.geblogs.com/visualization/kitchen

Figure 4.1 Part of the output from Google Analytics (www.google.com) for the period Feb. 25 to March 24, 2007 displaying website traffic.

the analysis and think clearly about the patterns and relationships that may be hiding in your data.

2. **Make a picture.** A well-designed display will *do* much of the work of analyzing your data. It can show the important features and patterns. A picture will also reveal things you did not expect to see: extraordinary (possibly wrong) data values or unexpected patterns.

3. **Make a picture.** The best way to *report* to others what you find in your data is with a well-chosen picture.

These are the three rules of data analysis. These days, technology makes drawing pictures of data easy, so there is no reason not to follow the three rules. Figure 4.1 has some displays showing various aspects of traffic on one of the authors' websites.

Some displays communicate information better than others. We'll discuss some general principles for displaying information honestly and effectively in this chapter.

4.2 Frequency Tables

To make an informed business decision, it is often important to know how a variable distributes it values. For example, as part of planning new retail locations and spending advertising dollars, MEC managers might want to know how much activity their website attracts from different provinces in the country. Since *Province* is a categorical variable, the possible values of the variables are just the categories, namely the provinces, and we can start by counting the number of cases in each category.

Table 4.1 has a summary of information of the originating province of search traffic to MEC.ca, created using Google Analytics. Only provinces that have bricks-and-mortar MEC retail stores are included.

Organizing the counts in this way (i.e., as in Table 4.1) is called a **frequency table**; it shows the number of visits (cases) for each category and records totals and category names. The names of the categories label each row in the frequency table. For *Province* these are "British Columbia," "Alberta," and so on.

Even with thousands of cases, a variable that doesn't have too many categories produces a frequency table that is easy to read. A frequency table with dozens or hundreds of categories would be much harder to read. When the number of categories gets too large, we often lump together values of the variable into "Other." When to do that is a judgment call, but it's a good idea to have fewer than a dozen categories. In the MEC case, we could include another category that includes searches originating in all the other provinces.

Counts are useful, but sometimes we want to know the fraction or proportion of the data in each category, so we divide the counts by the total number of cases. Usually we multiply by 100 to express these proportions as percentages. A **relative frequency table** (Table 4.2) displays the *percentages*, rather than the counts, of the values in each category. Both types of tables show how the cases are distributed across the categories. In this way, they describe the **distribution** of a categorical variable because they name the possible categories and tell how frequently each occurs.

Most often a frequency table will contain both the counts and the percentages, to give views of the data in both absolute and relative ways. But be careful about using percentages when the total count is small. Suppose you read that 67% of students in a particular class got grades of A. You would be very impressed (and surprised) if it happened in a large class of 100 students. But if the class had only three students, 67% would just mean that two of three students got an A. You wouldn't be so impressed.

Province	Organic Search Visits
British Columbia	1609 160
Alberta	1031 830
Manitoba	208 185
Ontario	2108 643
Quebec	1441 269
Nova Scotia	138 393
Total	**6537 470**

Table 4.1 Frequency table of organic search traffic to MEC.ca, Jan. 1 – Dec. 31, 2012, by province. An organic search visit originates from a search engine, not from an advertisement.
Source: MEC and Google Analytics, Feb. 2013

Province	Organic Search Visits (%)
British Columbia	24.61%
Alberta	15.78%
Manitoba	3.18%
Ontario	32.25%
Quebec	22.05%
Nova Scotia	2.12%
Total	**100.00%**

Table 4.2 A relative frequency table for the same data.

4.3 Charts

The Area Principle

Now that we have a frequency table, we're ready to follow the three rules of data analysis and make a picture of the data. But we can't make just any picture; a bad picture can distort our understanding rather than help it. For example, Figure 4.2 is a graph of the frequencies of Table 4.1. What impression do you get of the relative frequencies of visits from each province?

The figure does not accurately represent the information in the table. What's gone wrong? The height of the images in the figure do match the percentages in the table. But our eyes tend to be more impressed by the *area* (or perhaps even the *volume*) than by other aspects of each image, and it's that aspect of the image that we notice.

Since there were nearly three times as many visits from Ontario and BC as from Quebec, the images depicting the number from Ontario and from BC is almost three times higher than the image for Quebec, but it occupies almost nine times the area, since both the height and the width were increased threefold to keep the image looking proportional. As you can see from the frequency table, that isn't a correct impression.

The best data displays observe a fundamental principle of graphing data called the **area principle**, which says that the area occupied by a part of the graph should correspond to the magnitude of the value it represents.

Bar Charts

Figure 4.3 gives us a chart that obeys the area principle. It's not as visually entertaining as the shoes, but it does give a more *accurate* visual impression of the distribution. The height of each bar shows the count for its category. The bars are the same width, so their heights determine their areas, and the areas are proportional to the counts in each class. Now it's easy to see that about three times as many visits came from BC and Ontario as from Quebec—not the impression that the images in Figure 4.2 conveyed. We can also see that Manitoba and Nova

Liveshot/Shutterstock

Figure 4.2 Although the length of each shoe corresponds to the correct number, the impression we get is all wrong because we perceive the entire area of the shoe. In fact, only a little more than 50% of all website visits originated in BC or Ontario.

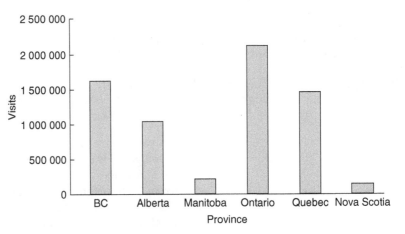

Figure 4.3 Visits to MEC website by *Province*. With the area principle satisfied, the true distribution is clear.

Scotia had about half as many as Quebec. Bar charts make these kinds of comparisons easy and natural.

A **bar chart** displays the distribution of a categorical variable, showing the counts for each category next to each other for easy comparison. Bar charts should have small spaces between the bars to indicate that these are freestanding bars that could be rearranged into any order. The bars are lined up along a common base.

Bar charts are usually drawn vertically in columns, but sometimes they are drawn with horizontal bars, like this.[1]

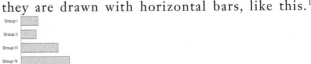

Horizontal bars are very useful when the category labels are quite long, as they are in Figure 4.3. If the spaces between bars in Figure 4.3 were reduced, the labels would either be in much smaller print or printed on an angle, making them harder to read.

It is often also very useful to rearrange the order of the categories, and the bars, so that they go from highest to lowest (or lowest to highest). This version is referred to as a Pareto chart, but it is just a variation of the bar chart we have discussed. Here is another look at Figure 4.3, with reordered, and horizontal, bars.

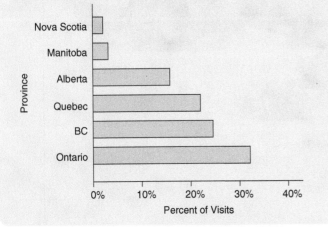

If we want to draw attention to the relative *proportion* of visits from each *Province*, we could replace the counts with percentages and use a **relative frequency bar chart**, like the one shown in Figure 4.4.

Pie Charts

Unfortunately, another display of categorical data is still in wide use. **Pie charts** were designed to show how a whole group breaks into several categories. The whole group of cases is represented as a circle, and the circle in

[1]Excel refers to this display as a bar graph.

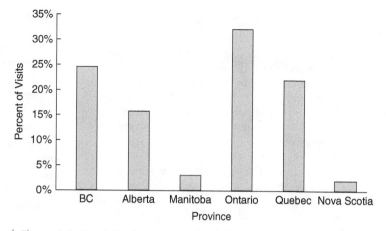

Figure 4.4 The relative frequency bar chart looks the same as the bar chart (Figure 4.3) but shows the proportion of visits in each category rather than the counts.

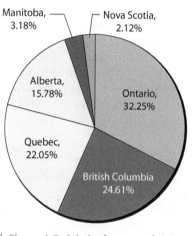

Figure 4.5 Relative frequency of visits by *Province*.

sliced into pieces whose size is proportional to the fraction of the whole in each category.

Becker and Cleveland (1996) wrote, "Pie charts have severe perceptual problems." Tufte (1983) prefers using a frequency table to a "...dumb pie chart; the only worse design than a pie chart is several of them, for then the viewer is asked to compare quantities located in spatial disarray both within and between pies....Given their low data-density and failure to order numbers along a visual dimension, pie charts should never be used." That's a very strong indictment of pie charts.

Pie charts may give a quick impression of how a whole group is partitioned into smaller groups, but mostly for seeing relative frequencies near 1/2, 1/4, or 1/8. That's because we're used to cutting up pies into 2, 4, or 8 pieces. However, in Figure 4.5 it is very difficult to compare Alberta to Ontario or British Columbia, or Quebec to Manitoba or Nova Scotia. What's worse is that since the areas are hard to interpret, the relative frequencies are included. And if you have the relative frequencies, why is the pie needed? Compare the pie chart to the bar chart in Figure 4.4 and to the dot plot to the left.

The worst examples of pie charts occur when the variable is binary so that the pie has only two pieces. For example, a pie chart of the male/female split in a population is a graph that displays one piece of information, namely the percentage of males. You might think there are two pieces, but if you know the percentage of males, you also know the percentage of females. They have to sum to 100%! And when multiple two-slice pies are shown, for example, to show the male/female split across a number of countries, it is clear that the graphic designer did not think about communicating information clearly.

Tufte makes the challenge that it is *always* possible to find a better way to display data than by pie charts. We challenge you to take up his challenge!

There are a number of alternatives to bar charts. A simple and effective one is a dot plot, where dots replace the bars. After all, it is only the height (or length) of the bars that matters, not the bars themselves. Here are the data in Table 4.2 displayed as a *dot plot*. Note that the dots should not be joined up with line segments since the data are categorical.

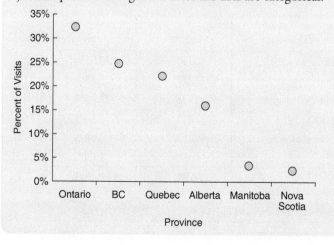

Statisticians and psychologists have studied our ability to decode quantitative information. We are best at finding positions on a common scale (e.g., dot plot or bar chart). Next best are our abilities if the scales are identical but not aligned (e.g., comparing two side-by-side but separate dot plots or bar charts). We perceive length more accurately than angles or area, which is why pie charts are hard to interpret. We are worst at perceiving volume and colour. So three-dimensional charts of single-variable data should never be used.

Beware of chartjunk, the term coined by Tufte to describe decorations in graphics that generate a lot of ink but do not tell the viewer anything new. It is possible to be both artistically interesting and accurate in communicating information, but it takes work.

For additional advice on good and bad graphs, see What Can Go Wrong near the end of this chapter.

◆ **Think before you draw.** Our first rule of data analysis is *Make a picture*. But what kind of picture? We don't have a lot of options—yet. There's more to Statistics than pie charts and bar charts, and knowing when to use every type of display we'll discuss is a critical first step in data analysis. That decision depends in part on what type of data you have and on what you hope to communicate.

We always have to check that the data are appropriate for whatever method of analysis we choose. Before you make a bar chart, always check the **Categorical Data Condition:** that the data are counts or percentages of individuals in categories.

If you want to make a relative frequency bar chart or insist on making a pie chart, you'll need to also make sure that the categories don't overlap, so that no individual is counted in two categories. If the categories do overlap, it's misleading to make a one of these charts, since the percentages won't add up to 100%. For the MEC search data, either kind of display is appropriate because the categories don't overlap—each visit comes from a unique source.

Throughout this course, you'll see that doing Statistics right means selecting the proper methods. That means you have to think about the situation at hand. An important first step is to check that the type of analysis you plan is appropriate. Our Categorical Data Condition is just the first of many such checks.

4.4 Contingency Tables

GfK Roper Consulting gathers information on consumers, attitudes about health, food, and health care products. In order to effectively market food products across different cultures, it's essential to know how people in different countries differ in their attitudes toward the food they eat. One question in the Roper survey asked respondents how they felt about the following statement: "I have a strong preference for regional or traditional products and dishes from where I come from." Here is a frequency table (Table 4.3) of the responses.

The pie chart (Figure 4.6) shows clearly that more than half of all the respondents agreed (either somewhat or completely) with the statement.

But if we want to target our marketing differently in different countries, wouldn't it be more interesting to know how opinions vary from country to country?

WHO	Respondents in the GfK Roper Reports Worldwide Survey
WHAT	Responses to questions relating to perceptions of food and health
WHEN	Fall 2005; published in 2006
WHERE	Worldwide
HOW	Data collected by GfK Roper Consulting using a multistage design
WHY	To understand cultural differences in the perception of the food and beauty products we buy and how they affect our health

Response to *Regional Food Preference* Question	Counts	Relative Frequency
Agree Completely	2346	30.51%
Agree Somewhat	2217	28.83%
Neither Disagree Nor Agree	1738	22.60%
Disagree Somewhat	811	10.55%
Disagree Completely	498	6.48%
Don't Know	80	1.04%
Total	**7690**	**100.00%**

Table 4.3   A combined frequency and relative frequency table for the responses (from all five countries represented: China, France, India, the United Kingdom, and the United States) to the statement "I have a strong preference for regional or traditional products and dishes from where I come from."

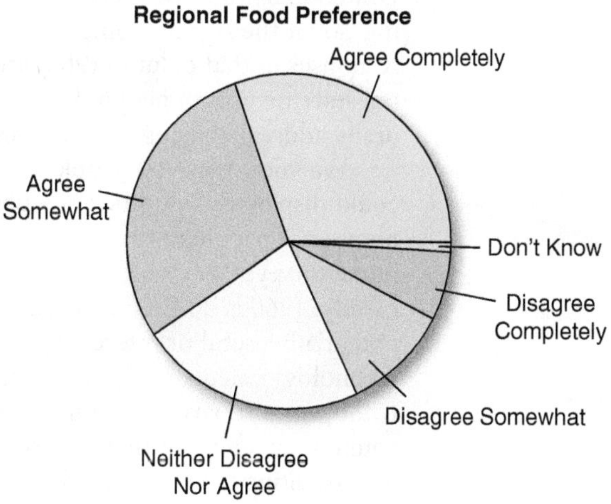

Figure 4.6 It's clear from the pie chart that the majority of respondents identify with their local foods.

A segmented or stacked 100% bar chart is another alternative to a pie chart. Instead of displaying each bar separately, the bars are "stacked" into one bar representing the 100% total. In other words, a 100% circle has become a 100% rectangle. It is even clearer from this chart that the majority of respondents identify with their local foods. In fact, this chart shows that almost 60% agree; that figure is much harder to ascertain from the pie chart.

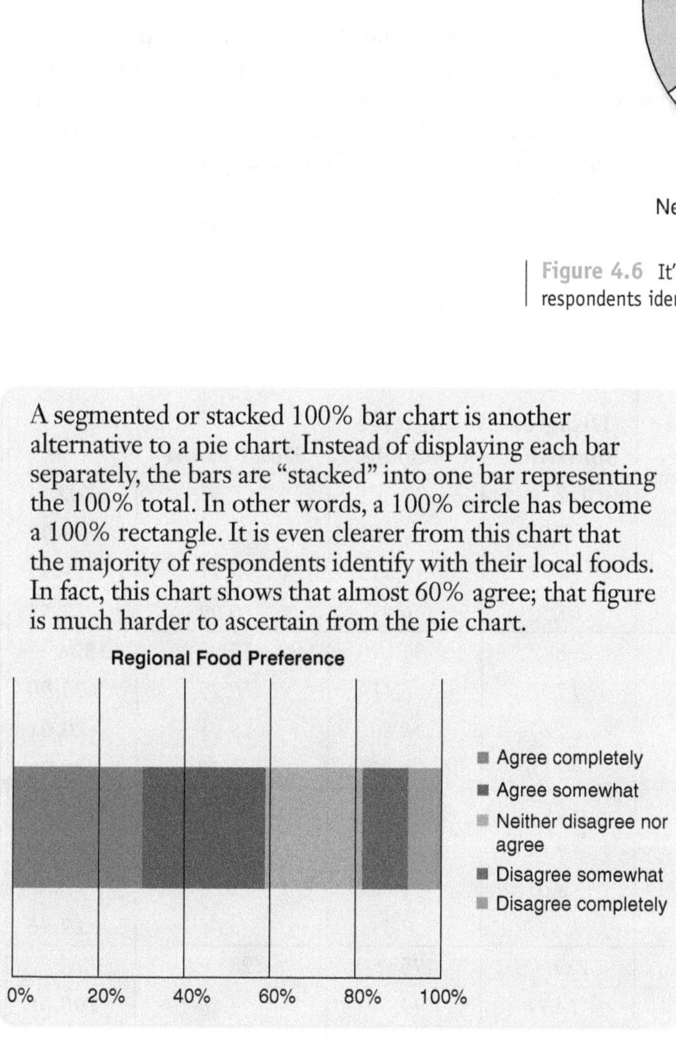

To find out, we need to look at the two categorical variables *Regional Preference* and *Country* together, which we do by arranging the data in a two-way table. Table 4.4 is a two-way table of *Regional Preference* by *Country*. Because the table shows how the individuals are distributed along each variable, depending on, or *contingent on*, the value of the other variable, such a table is called a **contingency table.**

The margins of a contingency table give totals. In the case of Table 4.4, these are shown in both the right-hand column (in bold) and the bottom row (also in bold). The totals in the bottom row of the table show the frequency distribution of the variable *Regional Preference*. The totals in the right-hand column of the table show the frequency distribution of the variable *Country*. When presented like this, at the margins of a contingency table, the frequency distribution of either one of the variables is called its **marginal distribution.**

Each cell of a contingency table (any intersection of a row and column of the table) gives the count for a combination of values of the two variables. If you look across the row in Table 4.4 for the

Country	Regional Preference: Agree Completely	Agree Somewhat	Neither Disagree Nor Agree	Disagree Somewhat	Disagree Completely	Don't Know	Total
China	518	576	251	117	33	7	**1502**
France	347	475	400	208	94	15	**1539**
India	960	282	129	65	95	4	**1535**
U.K.	214	407	504	229	175	28	**1557**
U.S.	307	477	454	192	101	26	**1557**
Total	**2346**	**2217**	**1738**	**811**	**498**	**80**	**7690**

Table 4.4 Contingency table of Regional Preference and Country. The bottom line "Totals" are the values that were in Table 4.3.

United Kingdom, you can see that 504 people neither agreed nor disagreed. Looking down the Agree Completely column, you can see that the largest number of responses in that column (960) are from India. Are Britons less likely to agree with the statement than people from India or China? Questions like this are more naturally addressed using percentages.

We know that 960 people from India agreed completely with the statement. We could display this number as a percentage, but as a percentage of what? The total number of people in the survey? (960 is 12.5% of the total.) The number of Indians in the survey? (960 is 62.5% of the row total.) The number of people who agree completely? (960 is 40.9% of the column total.) All of these are possibilities, and all are potentially useful or interesting. You'll probably wind up calculating (or letting your technology calculate) lots of percentages. Most statistics programs offer a choice of **total percent, row percent,** or **column percent** for contingency tables. Unfortunately, they often put them all together with several numbers in each cell of the table. The resulting table (Table 4.5) holds lots of information but is hard to understand.

Country	Regional Preference						
	Agree Completely	**Agree Somewhat**	**Neither Disagree Nor Agree**	**Disagree Somewhat**	**Disagree Completely**	**Don't Know**	Total
China	518	576	251	117	33	7	**1502**
% of Row	*34.49*	*38.35*	*16.71*	*7.79*	*2.20*	*0.47*	***100.00***
% of Column	*22.08*	*25.98*	*14.44*	*14.43*	*6.63*	*8.75*	***19.53***
% of Table	*6.74*	*7.49*	*3.26*	*1.52*	*0.43*	*0.09*	***19.53***
France	347	475	400	208	94	15	**1539**
% of Row	*22.55*	*30.86*	*25.99*	*13.52*	*6.11*	*0.97*	***100.00***
% of Column	*14.79*	*21.43*	*23.01*	*25.65*	*18.88*	*18.75*	***20.01***
% of Table	*4.51*	*6.18*	*5.20*	*2.70*	*1.22*	*0.20*	***20.01***
India	960	282	129	65	95	4	**1535**
% of Row	*62.54*	*18.37*	*8.40*	*4.23*	*6.19*	*0.26*	***100.00***
% of Column	*40.92*	*12.72*	*7.42*	*8.01*	*19.08*	*5.00*	***19.96***
% of Table	*12.48*	*3.67*	*1.68*	*0.845*	*1.24*	*0.05*	***19.96***
U.K.	214	407	504	229	175	28	**1557**
% of Row	*13.74*	*26.14*	*32.37*	*14.71*	*11.24*	*1.80*	***100.00***
% of Column	*9.12*	*18.36*	*29.00*	*28.24*	*35.14*	*35.00*	***20.24***
% of Table	*2.78*	*5.29*	*6.55*	*2.98*	*2.28*	*0.36*	***20.24***
U.S.	307	477	454	192	101	26	**1557**
% of Row	*19.72*	*30.64*	*29.16*	*12.33*	*6.49*	*1.67*	***100.00***
% of Column	*13.09*	*21.52*	*26.12*	*23.67*	*20.28*	*32.50*	***20.24***
% of Table	*3.99*	*6.20*	*5.90*	*2.50*	*1.31*	*0.34*	***20.24***
Total	**2346**	**2217**	**1738**	**811**	**498**	**80**	**7690**
% of Row	***30.51***	***28.83***	***22.60***	***10.55***	***6.48***	***1.04***	***100.00***
% of Column	***100.00***	***100.00***	***100.00***	***100.00***	***100.00***	***100.00***	***100.00***
% of Table	***30.51***	***28.83***	***22.60***	***10.55***	***6.48***	***1.04***	***100.00***

Table 4.5 Another contingency table of Regional Preference and Country. This time we see not only the counts for each combination of the two variables, but also the percentages these counts represent. For each count, there are three choices for the percentage: by row, by column, and by table total. There's probably too much information here for this table to be useful.

To simplify the table, let's first pull out the values corresponding to the percentages of the total.

Regional Preference—Percentage of Total

		Agree Completely	Agree Somewhat	Neither Disagree Nor Agree	Disagree Somewhat	Disagree Completely	Don't Know	Total
Country	China	6.74	7.49	3.26	1.52	0.43	0.09	19.53
	France	4.51	6.18	5.20	2.70	1.22	0.20	20.01
	India	12.48	3.67	1.68	0.85	1.24	0.05	19.96
	U.K.	2.78	5.29	6.55	2.98	2.28	0.36	20.25
	U.S.	3.99	6.20	5.90	2.50	1.31	0.34	20.25
	Total	**30.51**	**28.83**	**22.60**	**10.55**	**6.48**	**1.04**	**100.00**

Table 4.6 A contingency table of Regional Preference and Country showing only the total percentages.

These percentages tell us what percent of *all* respondents belong to each combination of column and row category. For example, we see that 3.99% of the respondents were Americans who agreed completely with the question, which is slightly more than the percentage of Indians who agreed somewhat. Is this fact useful? Is that really what we want to know?

Percent of what? The English language can be tricky when we talk about percentages. If asked, "What percent of those answering 'I Don't Know' were from India?" it's pretty clear that you should focus only on the *Don't Know* column. The question itself seems to restrict the *Who* in the question to that column, so you should look at the number of those in each country among the 80 people who replied "I don't know." You'd find that in the column percentages, and the answer would be 4 out of 80 or 5.00%.

But if you're asked, "What percent were Indians who replied 'I don't know?'" you'd have a different question. Be careful. The question really means "what percent of the entire sample were both from India and replied 'I don't know'?" So the *Who* is all respondents. The denominator should be 7690, and the answer is the table percent 4/7690 = 0.05%.

Finally, if you're asked, "What percent of the Indians replied 'I don't know'?" you'd have a third question. Now the *Who* is Indians. So the denominator is the 1535 Indians, and the answer is the row percent, 4/1535 = 0.26%.

> Always be sure to ask "percent of what." That will help define the *Who* and will help you decide whether you want *row*, *column*, or *table* percentages.

Conditional Distributions

The more interesting questions are contingent on something. We'd like to know, for example, what percentage *of Indians* agreed completely with the statement and how that compares to the percentage *of Britons* who also agreed. Equivalently, we might ask whether the chance of agreeing with the statement depended on the *Country* of the respondent. We can look at this question in two ways. First, we could ask how the distribution of *Regional Preference* changes across *Country*. To do that we look at the *row percentages*.

By focusing on each row separately, we see the distribution of *Regional Preference* under the condition of being in the selected *Country*. The sum of the percentages in each row is 100%, and we divide that up by the responses to the question.

		Regional Preference					
		Agree Completely	Agree Somewhat	Neither Disagree Nor Agree	Disagree Somewhat	Disagree Completely	Don't Know	Total
India Row percentage	960 62.54	282 18.37	129 8.40	65 4.23	95 6.19	4 0.26	**1535** **100%**
U.K. Row percentage	214 13.74	407 26.14	504 32.37	229 14.71	175 11.24	28 1.80	**1557** **100%**

Table 4.7 The conditional distribution of Regional Preference conditioned on two values of Country: India and the United Kingdom. This table shows the row percentages.

In effect, we can temporarily restrict the *Who* first to Indians and look at how their response are distributed. A distribution like this is called a **conditional distribution** because it shows the distribution of one variable for just those cases that satisfy a condition on another. Looking at how the percentages change across each row, it sure looks like the distribution of responses to the question is different in each *Country*. To make the differences more vivid, we could also display the conditional distributions. Figure 4.7 shows an example of a side-by-side bar chart, displaying the responses to the questions for India and the United Kingdom. Figure 4.8 shows the same comparison of India and the United Kingdom, but this time using pie charts. We'll leave it to you decide which graphical comparison is easier to interpret.

Of course, we could also turn the question around. We could look at the distribution of *Country* for each category of *Regional Preference*. To do this, we would look at the column percentages.

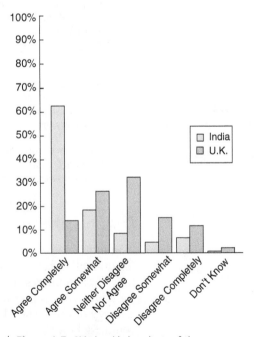

Figure 4.7 Side-by-side bar charts of the conditional distributions of *Regional Food Preference* importance for India and the United Kingdom. The percentage of people who agree is much higher in India than in the United Kingdom.

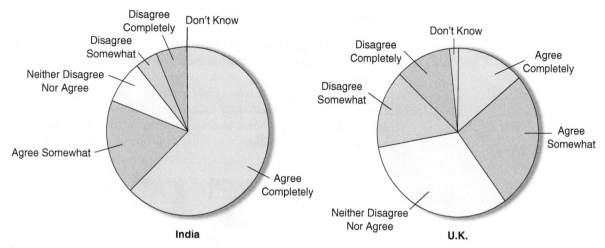

Figure 4.8 Pie charts of the conditional distributions of Regional Food Preference importance for India and the United Kingdom. It's much harder to compare percentages within each country using pie charts than with side-by-side bar charts.

From Figure 4.7, it is clear that Indians have a stronger preference for their own cuisine than Britons have for theirs. For food companies, including GfK Roper's clients, that means Indians are less likely to accept a food product they perceive as foreign, and people in Great Britain are more accepting of "foreign" foods. This could be invaluable information for marketing products.

Variables can be associated in many ways and to different degrees. The best way to tell whether two variables are associated is to ask whether they are *not*.[2] In a contingency table, when the distribution of one variable is the same for all categories of another, we say that the variables are **independent**. That tells us there's no association between these variables. We'll see a way to check for independence formally later in the book. For now, we'll just compare the distributions.

✔ **JUST CHECKING**

So that they can balance their inventory, an optometric practice collects the following data about its patients.

		Eye Condition			
		Near Sighted	**Far Sighted**	**Need Bifocals**	**Total**
Sex	**Males**	6	20	6	**32**
	Females	4	16	12	**32**
	Total	**10**	**36**	**18**	**64**

1 What percent of females are far-sighted?

2 What percent of near-sighted customers are female?

3 What percent of all customers are far-sighted females?

4 What's the distribution of *Eye Condition?*

5 What's the conditional distribution of *Eye Condition* for males?

6 Compare the percent who are female among near-sighted customers to the percent of all customers who are female.

7 Does it seem that *Eye Condition* and *Sex* might be dependent? Explain.

---

[2] This kind of "backwards" reasoning shows up surprisingly often in science—and in Statistics.

Segmented Bar Charts

We could display the Roper survey information on India and the United Kingdom comparatively, with two segmented bar charts. Instead of dividing up circles as we did when making pie charts, we divide up bars. The resulting **segmented bar chart** (Figure 4.9) treats each bar as the "whole" and divides it proportionally into segments corresponding to the percentage in each group. We can see that the distributions of responses to the question are very different in the two countries, indicating again that *Regional Preference* is not independent of *Country*.

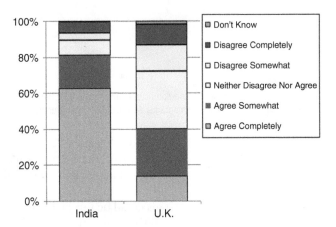

Figure 4.9 Although the totals for India and the United Kingdom are different, the bars are the same height because we have converted the numbers to percentages. Compare this display with the side-by-side bar charts in Figure 4.7 and the side-by-side pie charts of the same data in Figure 4.8.

GUIDED EXAMPLE | Food Safety

Food storage and food safety are major issues for multinational food companies. A client wants to know if people of all age groups have the same degree of concern so GfK Roper Consulting asked 1500 people in five countries how they felt about the following statement: "I worry about how safe the food I buy is." We might want to report to a client who was interested in how concerns about food safety were related to age.

PLAN

Setup

- State the objectives and goals of the study.
- Identify and define the variables.
- Provide the time frame of the data collection process.

Determine the appropriate analysis for data type.

The client wants to examine the distribution of responses to the food safety question and see whether they are related to the age of the respondent. GfK Roper Consulting collected data on this question in the fall of 2005 for their 2006 Worldwide report. We will use the data from that study.

The variable is Food Safety. The responses are in nonoverlapping categories of agreement, from Agree Completely to Disagree Completely (and Don't Know). There were originally 12 Age groups, which we can combine into five:

Teen	13–19
Young Adult	20–29
Adult	30–39
Middle Aged	40–49
Mature	50 and older

Both variables, *Food Safety* and *Age*, are ordered categorical variables. To examine any differences in responses across age groups, it is appropriate to create a contingency table and a side-by-side bar chart. Here is a contingency table of "Food Safety" by "Age."

Mechanics For a large data set like this, we rely on technology to make table and displays. Because we want to compare the response distribution by age, we will examine the row percentages for each age group.

Food Safety

Age	Agree Completely	Agree Somewhat	Neither Disagree Nor Agree	Disagree Somewhat	Disagree Completely	Don't Know	Total
Teen	16.19	27.50	24.32	19.30	10.58	2.12	**100%**
Young Adult	20.55	32.68	23.81	14.94	6.98	1.04	**100%**
Adult	22.23	34.89	23.28	12.26	6.75	0.59	**100%**
Middle Aged	24.79	35.31	22.02	12.43	5.06	0.39	**100%**
Mature	26.60	33.85	21.21	11.89	5.82	0.63	**100%**

A side-by-side bar chart is particularly helpful when comparing multiple groups.

A side-by-side bar chart shows the percent of each response to the question by *Age* group.

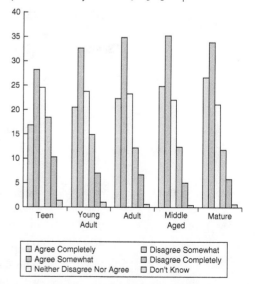

<table>
<tr><td>

REPORT

</td><td>

Summary and Conclusions Summarize the charts and analysis in context. Make recommendations if possible and discuss further analysis that is needed.

</td><td>

MEMO:

RE: FOOD SAFETY CONCERNS BY AGE

Our analysis of the GfK Roper Reports™ Worldwide survey data for 2006 shows a pattern of concern about food safety that generally increases from youngest to oldest.

Our analysis thus far has not considered whether this trend is consistent across countries. If it were of interest to your group, we could perform a similar analysis for each of the countries.

The enclosed tables and plots provide support for these conclusions.

</td></tr>
</table>

WHAT CAN GO WRONG?

- **Don't violate the area principle.** This is probably the most common mistake in a graphical display. Violations of the area principle are often made for the sake of artistic presentation. Earlier we quoted Tufte, who said that "the only worse design than a pie chart is several of them..." Here is another take. The only worse design than a 2-D pie chart is a 3-D pie chart. If you insist on using a pie chart, don't compound the visual perception difficulty by adding irrelevant and misleading perspective. While we're on the subject, don't use 3-D bar charts either (see the following page). Here, for example, are two versions of the same pie chart for the *Regional Preference* data.

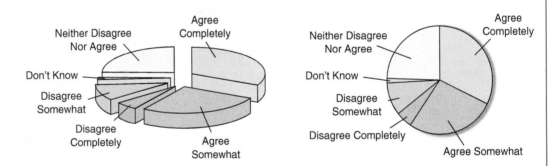

  The one on the left looks interesting, doesn't it? But showing the pie three dimensionally on a slant violates the area principle and makes it much more difficult to compare fractions of the whole made up of each category of the response—the principal feature that a pie chart ought to show. Those sections of the pie in the forefront are emphasized. If you want to mislead the viewer, put the "bad news" category in the back and the "good news" category in the front. The viewer sees not only the top of the pie but the side as well.

- **Keep it honest.** Here's a pie chart that displays data on the percentage of high school students who engage in specified dangerous behaviours. What's wrong with this plot?

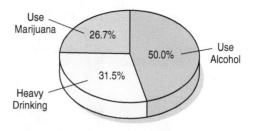

Try adding up the percentages. Or look at the 50% slice. Does it look right? Then think: What are these percentages of? Is there a "whole" that has been sliced up? In a pie chart, the proportions shown by each slice of the pie must add up to 100%, and each individual must fall into only one category. Of course, showing the pie on a slant makes it even harder to detect the error.

Here's another example. This bar chart shows the number of airline passengers searched by security screening.

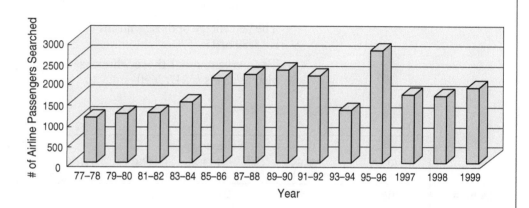

Looks like things didn't change much in the final years of the twentieth century—until you read the bar labels and see that the last three bars represent single years, while all the others are for *pairs* of years. The false depth makes it even harder to see the problem.

Here's yet another example. If the vertical axis is truncated, a slight change across bars can become a pronounced one. The following two bar charts show the change in single occupancy vehicle (SOV) trips at the University of British Columbia over the years. The first chart shows a modest decline, the second shows a strong decline, and it makes 2005 look like the Year of the Carpool!

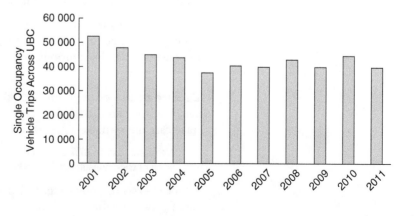

(*continued*)

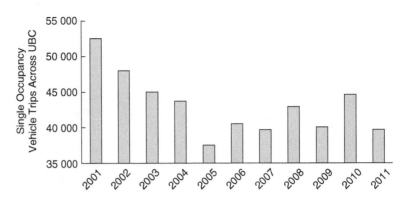

- **Don't confuse percentages.** Many percentages based on a conditional and joint distributions sound similar, but are different:

  - The percentage of French who answered "Agree Completely": This is 347/1539 or 22.5%.

  - The percentage of those who answered "Don't Know" who are French: This is 15/80 or 18.75%.

  - The percentage of those who were French *and* answered "Agree Completely": This is 347/7690 or 4.5%.

		Regional Preference					
	Agree Completely	**Agree Somewhat**	**Neither Disagree Nor Agree**	**Disagree Somewhat**	**Disagree Completely**	**Don't Know**	Total
China	518	576	251	117	33	7	**1502**
France	347	475	400	208	94	15	**1539**
India	960	282	129	65	95	4	**1535**
UK	214	407	504	229	175	28	**1557**
USA	307	477	454	192	101	26	**1557**
Total	**2346**	**2217**	**1738**	**811**	**498**	**80**	**7690**

(Country)

In each instance, pay attention to the wording that makes a restriction to a smaller group (those who are French, those who answered "Don't Know," and all respondents, respectively) before a percentage is found. This restricts the *Who* of the problem and the associated denominator for the percentage. Your discussion of results must make these differences clear.

- **Don't forget to look at the variables separately, too.** When you make a contingency table or display a conditional distribution, be sure to also examine the marginal distributions. It's important to know how many cases are in each category.

- **Be sure to use enough individuals.** When you consider percentages, take care that they are based on a large enough number of individuals (or cases). Take care not to make a report such as this one:

  We found that 66.67% of the companies surveyed improved their performance by hiring outside consultants. The other company went bankrupt.

- **Don't overstate your case.** Independence is an important concept, but it is rare for two variables to be *entirely* independent. We can't conclude that one variable has no effect whatsoever on another. Usually, all we know is that

One famous example of Simpson's Paradox arose during an investigation of admission rates for men and women at the University of California at Berkeley's graduate schools. As reported in an article in *Science*, about 45% of male applicants were admitted, but only about 30% of female applicants got in. It looked like a clear case of discrimination. However, when the data were broken down by school (Engineering, Law, Medicine, etc.), it turned out that within each school, the women were admitted at nearly the same or, in some cases, much *higher* rates than the men. How could this be? Women applied in large numbers to schools with very low admission rates. (Law and Medicine, for example, admitted fewer than 10%.) Men tended to apply to Engineering and the sciences. Those schools have admission rates above 50%. When the total applicant pool was combined and the percentages were computed, the women had a much lower *overall* rate, but the combined percentage didn't really make sense.

little effect was observed in our study. Other studies of other groups under other circumstances could find different results.

- **Don't use unfair or inappropriate percentages.** Sometimes percentages can be misleading. Sometimes they don't make sense at all. Be careful when finding percentages across different categories not to combine percentages inappropriately. The next section gives an example.

Simpson's Paradox

Here's an example showing that combining percentages across very different values or groups can give absurd results. Suppose there are two sales representatives, Peter and Katrina. Peter argues that he's the better salesperson, since he managed to close 83% of his last 120 prospects compared with Katrina's 78%. But let's look at the data a little more closely. Here (Table 4.8) are the results for each of their last 120 sales calls, broken down by the product they were selling.

| | Product | | |
Sales Rep	**Printer Paper**	**USB Flash Drive**	**Overall**
Peter	90 out of 100	10 out of 20	100 out of 120
	90%	50%	83%
Katrina	19 out of 20	75 out of 100	94 out of 120
	95%	75%	78%

Table 4.8 Look at the percentages within each Product category. Who has a better success rate closing sales of paper? Who has the better success rate closing sales of flash drives? Who has the better performance overall?

Look at the sales of the two products separately. For printer paper sales, Katrina had a 95% success rate, and Peter only had a 90% rate. When selling flash drives, Katrina closed her sales 75% of the time, but Peter only 50%. So Peter has better "overall" performance, but Katrina is better selling each product. How can this be?

This problem is known as **Simpson's Paradox**, named for the statistician who described it in the 1960s. Although it is rare, there have been a few

(continued)

Simpson's Paradox shows the perils of aggregation, which can happen in many different contexts. A political party could win a majority of seats, but lose the popular vote if in the ridings it wins, it wins by a small number of votes, and in the ridings it loses, it loses by a lot. In the 1960 World Series, the New York Yankees lost to the Pittsburgh Pirates even though the Yankees outscored the Pirates 55 to 27 in the seven-game series. New York's victories were by scores of: 16–3, 10–0, and 12–0, while Pittsburgh's victories were by scores of: 6–4, 3–2, 5–2, and 10–9. Best in the aggregate didn't mean best in wins and losses.

well-publicized cases of it. As we can see from the example, the problem results from inappropriately combining percentages of different groups. Katrina concentrates on selling flash drives, which is more difficult, so her *overall* percentage is heavily influenced by her flash drive average. Peter sells more printer paper, which appears to be easier to sell. With their different patterns of selling, taking an overall percentage is misleading. Their manager should be careful not to conclude rashly that Peter is the better salesperson.

The lesson of Simpson's Paradox is to be sure to combine comparable measurements for comparable individuals. Be especially careful when combining across different levels of a second variable. It's usually better to compare percentages *within* each level, rather than across levels.

ETHICS IN ACTION

Lyle Erhart has been working in sales for a leading vendor of Customer Relationship Management (CRM) software for the past three years. He was recently made aware of a published research study that examined factors related to the successful implementation of CRM projects among firms in the financial services industry. Lyle read the research report with interest and was excited to see that his company's CRM software product was included. Among the results were tables reporting the number of projects that were successful based on type of CRM implementation (Operational versus Analytical) for each of the top leading CRM products of 2006. Lyle quickly found the results for his company's product and their major competitor. He summarized the results into one table as follows:

	His Company	**Major Competitor**
Operational	16 successes out of 20	68 successes out of 80
Analytical	90 successes out of 100	19 successes out of 20

At first he was a bit disappointed, especially since most of their potential clients were interested in Operational CRM. He had hoped to be able to disseminate the findings of this report among the sales force so they could refer to it when visiting potential clients. After some thought, he realized that he could combine the results. His company's overall success rate was 106 out of 120 (over 88%) and was higher than that of its major competitor. Lyle was now happy that he found and read the report.

ETHICAL ISSUE *Lyle, intentionally or not, has benefited from Simpson's Paradox. By combining percentages, he can present the findings in a manner favourable to his company (related to ASA Ethical Guidelines, Item A, which can be found at http://www.amstat.org/about/ethicalguidelines.cfm).*

ETHICAL SOLUTION *Lyle should not combine the percentages as the results are misleading. If he decides to disseminate the information to his sales force, he must do so without combining.*

WHAT HAVE WE LEARNED?

We've learned that we can summarize categorical data by counting the number of cases in each category, sometimes expressing the resulting distribution as percents. We can display the distribution in a bar chart or, if you insist, a pie chart. When we want to see how two categorical variables are related, we put the counts (and/or percentages) in a two-way table called a contingency table.

- We look at the marginal distribution of each variable (found in the margins of the table).
- We also look at the conditional distribution of a variable within each category of the other variable.

- We can display these conditional and marginal distributions using bar charts or related graphs.
- If the conditional distributions of one variable are (roughly) the same for every category of the other, the variables are independent.

Terms

Area principle	A principle that helps to interpret statistical information without distortion by insisting that in a statistical display, each data value be represented by the same amount of area.
Bar chart (relative frequency bar chart)	A chart that represents the count (or percentage) of each category in a categorical variable as a bar, allowing easy visual comparisons across categories.
Categorical data condition	Data are counts or percentages of individuals in categories.
Column percent	The proportion of each column contained in the cell of a contingency table.
Conditional distribution	The distribution of a variable restricting the *Who* to consider only a smaller group of individuals.
Contingency table	A contingency table displays counts and, sometimes, percentages of individuals falling into named categories on two or more variables. The table categorizes the individuals on all variables at once, to reveal possible patterns in one variable that may be contingent on the category of the other.
Distribution	The distribution of a variable is a list of: - all the possible values of the variable - the relative frequency of each value
Frequency table	A table that lists the categories in a categorical variable and gives the number (i.e., count) of observations for each category.
Independent variables	Variables for which the conditional distribution of one variable is the same for each category of the other.
Marginal distribution	In a contingency table, the distribution of either variable alone. The counts or percentages are the totals found in the margins (usually the right-most column or bottom row) of the table.
Pie chart	Pie charts show how a "whole" divides into categories by showing a wedge of a circle whose area corresponds to the proportion in each category. We recommend not using them. Use other alternatives wherever possible.
Relative frequency table	A frequency table showing proportions (i.e., relative frequencies) or percentages instead of numbers or counts. But be careful when using percentages. Always consider the size of the base; that is, the denominator being used to compute the percentages.
Row percent	The proportion of each row contained in the cell of a contingency table.
Segmented bar chart	A bar representing the "whole" divided proportionally into segments corresponding to the percentage in each group.

Simpson's paradox	A phenomenon that arises when averages, or percentages, are taken across different groups, and these group averages appear to contradict the overall averages.
Total percent	The proportion of the total contained in the cell of a contingency table.

Skills

PLAN

- Recognize when a variable is categorical and choose an appropriate display for it.
- Understand how to examine the association between categorical variables by comparing conditional and marginal percentages.

DO

- Summarize the distribution of a categorical variable with a frequency table.
- Display the distribution of a categorical variable with a bar chart.
- Construct and examine a contingency table.
- Construct and examine displays of the conditional distributions of one variable for two or more groups.

REPORT

- Describe the distribution of a categorical variable in terms of its possible values and relative frequencies.
- Describe any anomalies or extraordinary features revealed by the display of a variable.
- Describe and discuss patterns found in a contingency table and associated displays of conditional distributions.

TECHNOLOGY HELP: Displaying Categorical Data on the Computer

Although every package makes a slightly different bar chart, they all have similar features:

Sometimes the count or a percentage is printed above or on top of each bar to give some additional information. You may find that your statistics package sorts category names in annoying orders by default. For example, many packages sort categories alphabetically or by the order the categories are seen in the data set. Often, neither of these is the best choice.

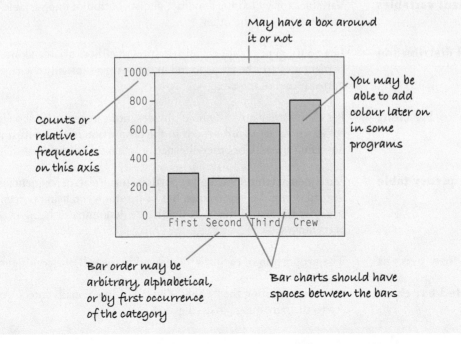

EXCEL

First make a pivot table (Excel's name for a frequency table). From the **Data** menu, choose **Pivot Table** and **Pivot Chart Report.**

When you reach the Layout window, drag your variable to the row area and drag your variable again to the data area. This tells Excel to count the occurrences of each category.

Once you have an Excel pivot table, you can construct bar charts and pie charts.

Click inside the Pivot Table.

Click the Pivot Table Chart Wizard button. Excel creates a bar chart.

A longer path leads to a pie chart; see your Excel documentation.

Comments

Excel uses the pivot table to specify the category names and find counts within each category. If you already have that information, you can proceed directly to the Chart Wizard.

EXCEL 2007

To make a bar chart:

- Select the variable in Excel you want to work with.
- Choose the **Column** command from the Insert tab in the Ribbon.
- Select the appropriate chart from the drop-down dialog.

To change the bar chart into a pie chart:

- Right-click the chart and select **Change Chart Type...** from the menu. The Chart type dialog opens.
- Select a pie chart type.
- Click the **OK** button. Excel changes your bar chart into a pie chart.

MINI CASE STUDY PROJECT

Eddie's Hang-Up Display

Eddie's Hang-Up

Chances are very high that when you walk into a retail store you notice the merchandise. But do you notice the store fixtures: hangers and size dividers, clothing racks, display cases, signs, tagging and price labels, mannequins, and the myriad of supplies that retailers need to run a business? Eddie's Hang-Up Display Ltd. (www.eddies.com) is one of Canada's leading importers and distributors of store fixtures and retail supplies. They have suppliers in Taiwan, China, Korea, Thailand, Italy, Turkey, France, and the United States. Eddie's has stores in Vancouver and Edmonton and offers over 3000 different display and supply items in addition to custom manufacturing.

Like MEC in the chapter's opening illustration, Eddie's relies on Google Analytics to analyze web traffic and a variety of other data. The Excel spreadsheet **ch04_MCSP_Eddies.xlsx** has data on *Visits, Pages,* and *New Visits* for each of ten regions for March and October 2012. These are two peak months in their business as retailers prepare for spring and Christmas periods. The spreadsheet also has 2012 monthly data on these variables for British Columbia and Alberta, where Eddie's has retail stores.

Using Excel or your statistics package, create frequency tables and bar charts of the three variables by region, for each of the two months separately. Next, create a bar chart that compares the two months on the same graph. Then create frequency tables and bar charts to compare data from British Columbia and Alberta across the year. Write a case report summarizing your analysis and results.

EXERCISES

1. Graphs in the news. Find a bar graph of categorical data from a business publication (e.g., *Financial Post, The Economist, The Wall Street Journal*, etc.). **LO❶**

a) Is the graph clearly labelled?
b) Does it violate the area principle?
c) Does the accompanying article tell the W's of the variable?
d) Do you think the article correctly interprets the data? Explain.

2. Graphs in the news, part 2. Find a pie chart of categorical data from a business publication (e.g., *Financial Post, The Economist, The Wall Street Journal*, etc.). **LO❶**

a) Is the graph clearly labelled?
b) Does it violate the area principle?
c) Does the accompanying article tell the W's of the variable?
d) Do you think the article correctly interprets the data? Explain.

3. Tables in the news. Find a frequency table of categorical data from a business publication (e.g., *Financial Post, The Economist, The Wall Street Journal*, etc.). **LO❶**

a) Is it clearly labelled?
b) Does it display percentages or counts?
c) Does the accompanying article tell the W's of the variable?
d) Do you think the article correctly interprets the data? Explain.

4. Tables in the news, part 2. Find a contingency table of categorical data from a business publication (e.g., *Financial Post, The Economist, The Wall Street Journal*, etc.). **LO❶**

a) Is it clearly labelled?
b) Does it display percentages or counts?
c) Does the accompanying article tell the W's of the variable?
d) Do you think the article correctly interprets the data? Explain.

5. Canadian market share. A report on the Canadian Soft Drink Industry, prepared by Agriculture and Agri-Food Canada (AAFC), summarized Canada's non-alcoholic beverage market in 2009. Here is a pie chart with the results. **LO❶**

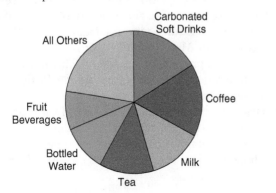

a) Is this an appropriate display for these data? Explain.
b) Compare the relative market share of carbonated soft drinks with that of coffee, tea, milk, and bottled water.
c) Approximately what percentage is in the "All Others" category?

6. World market share. An article that appeared in 2005 *The Wall Street Journal* indicated the world market share for leading distributors of total confectionery products. The following bar chart displays the values: **LO❶**

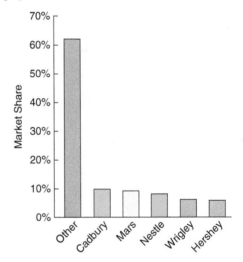

a) Is this an appropriate display for these data? Explain.
b) Which company had the largest share of the candy market?

7. Canadian market share again. Here's a bar chart of the data in Exercise 5. **LO❶**

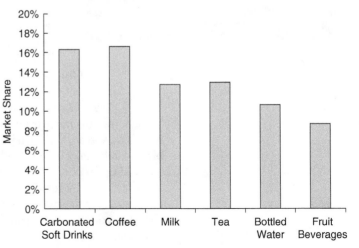

a) Compared to the pie chart in Exercise 5, which is better for displaying the relative portions of market share? Explain.

b) What is missing from this display that might make it misleading?

8. World market share again. Here's a pie chart of the data in Exercise 6. LO❶

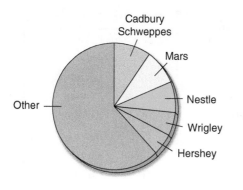

a) Which display of these data is best for comparing the market shares of these companies? Explain.

b) Does Cadbury Schweppes or Mars have a bigger market share?

9. Insurance company. An insurance company is updating its payouts and cost structure for their insurance policies. Of particular interest to them is the risk analysis for customers currently on heart or blood pressure medication. Statistics Canada reported the leading causes of death in Canada in 2009 as follows. LO❶

Cause of Death	Percent
Cancer	29.8
Heart disease	20.7
Circulatory diseases and stroke	5.9
Respiratory diseases	4.6
Accidents	4.3

a) Is it reasonable to conclude that heart or respiratory diseases were the cause of approximately 25% of Canadian deaths in 2009?

b) What percent of deaths were from causes not listed here?

c) Create an appropriate display for these data.

10. Revenue growth. A 2005 study by Babson College and The Commonwealth Institute surveyed the top women-led businesses in the state of Massachusetts in 2003 and 2004. The study reported the following results for continuing participants with a 9% response rate. (Does not add up to 100% due to rounding.) LO❶

2003–2004 Revenue Growth	
Decline	7%
Modest Decline	9%
Steady State	10%
Modest Growth	18%
Growth	54%

a) Describe the distribution of companies with respect to revenue growth.

b) Is it reasonable to conclude that 72% of all women-led businesses in the U.S. reported some level of revenue growth? Explain.

11. Web conferencing. Cisco Systems Inc. announced plans in March 2007 to buy WebEx Communications, Inc. for $3.2 billion, demonstrating their faith in the future of Web conferencing. The leaders in market share for the venders in the area of Web conferencing in 2006 were as follows: WebEx 58.4% and Microsoft 26.3%. Create an appropriate graphical display of this information and write a sentence or two that might appear in a newspaper article about the market share. LO❶

12. Mattel. In their 2011 annual report, Mattel Inc. reported that their worldwide market gross sales were broken down as follows: 60.7% Mattel Girls and Boys brand, 31.6% Fisher-Price brand and the rest of the over $6.8 billion revenues were due to their American Girl brand. Create an appropriate graphical display of this information and write a sentence or two that might appear in a newspaper article about their revenue breakdown. LO❶

13. Small business productivity. The Wells Fargo/Gallup Small Business Index asked 592 small business owners in March 2004 what steps they had taken in the past year to increase productivity. They found that 60% of small business owners had updated their computers, 52% had made other (non-computer) capital investments, 37% hired part-time instead of full-time workers, 24% had not replaced workers who left voluntarily, 15% had laid off workers, and 10% had lowered employee salaries. LO❶

a) What do you notice about the percentages listed? How could this be?

b) Make a bar chart to display the results and label it clearly.

c) Would a pie chart be an effective way of communicating this information? Why or why not?

d) Write a couple of sentences on the steps taken by small businesses to increase productivity.

14. Small business hiring. In 2004, the Wells Fargo/Gallup Small Business Index found that 86% of the 592 small business owners they surveyed said their productivity for the previous year had stayed the same or increased and most had substituted productivity gains for labour. (See Exercise 13.) As a follow-up question, the survey gave them a list of possible economic outcomes and asked if that would make them hire more employees. Here are the percentages of owners saying that they would "definitely or probably hire more employees" for each scenario: a substantial increase in sales—79%, a major backlog of sales orders—71%, a general improvement in the economy—57%, a gain in productivity—50%, a reduction in overhead costs—43%, and more qualified employees available—39%. **LO❶**

a) What do you notice about the percentages listed?
b) Make a bar chart to display the results and label it clearly.
c) Would a pie chart be an effective way of communicating this information? Why or why not?
d) Write a couple of sentences on the responses to small business owners about hiring given the scenarios listed.

15. Environmental hazard. Data from the International Tanker Owners Pollution Federation Limited (www.itopf.com) give the cause of spillage for 455 large (>700 tonnes) oil tanker accidents from 1970–2012. Here are the displays. Write a brief report interpreting what the displays show. Is a pie chart an appropriate display for these data? Why or why not? **LO❶**

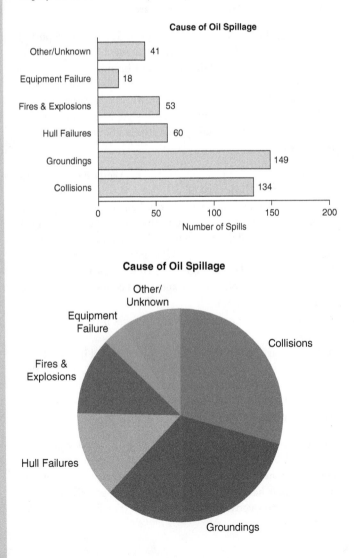

16. Winter Olympics 2010. Twenty-six countries won medals in the 2010 Winter Olympics in Vancouver-Whistler. The following table lists them, along with the total number of medals each won. Note that by virtue of winning more gold medals than any other country (including men's and women's hockey—hurray!), the Olympic Committee officially ranks Canada number one. **LO❶**

Country	Medals	Country	Medals
United States	37	Poland	6
Germany	30	Italy	5
Canada	26	Japan	5
Norway	23	Finland	5
Austria	16	Australia	3
Russia	15	Belarus	3
South Korea	14	Slovakia	3
China	11	Croatia	3
Sweden	11	Slovenia	3
France	11	Latvia	2
Switzerland	9	Great Britain	1
Netherlands	8	Estonia	1
Czech Republic	6	Kazakhstan	1

a) Try to make a display of these data. What problems do you encounter?
b) Can you find a way to organize the data so that the graph is more successful?

17. Importance of wealth. GfK Roper Reports Worldwide surveyed people in 2004, asking them "How important is acquiring wealth to you?" The percent who responded that it was of more than average importance were: 71.9% China, 59.6% France, 76.1% India, 45.5% UK, and 45.3% USA. There were about 1500 respondents per country. A report showed the following bar chart of these percentages. **LO❶**

a) How much larger is the proportion of those who said acquiring wealth was important in India than in the United States?

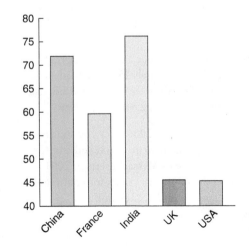

b) Is that the impression given by the display? Explain.

c) How would you improve this display?

d) Make an appropriate display for the percentages.

e) Write a few sentences describing what you have learned about attitudes toward acquiring wealth.

18. Importance of power. In the same survey as that discussed in Exercise 17, GfK Roper Consulting also asked "How important is having control over people and resources to you?" The percent who responded that it was of more than average importance are given in the following table: **LO❶**

China	49.1%
France	44.1%
India	74.2%
UK	27.8%
USA	36.0%

Here's a pie chart of the data:

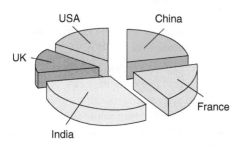

a) List the errors you see in this display.

b) Make an appropriate display for the percentages.

c) Write a few sentences describing what you have learned about attitudes toward acquiring power.

19. Google financials. Google Inc. derives revenue from three major sources: advertising revenue from their websites, advertising revenue from the thousands of third-party websites that comprise the Google Network, and licensing and miscellaneous revenue. The following table shows the percentage of all revenue derived from these sources for the period 2005 to 2012. **LO❶**

a) Are these row or column percentages?

b) Make an appropriate display of these data.

c) Write a brief summary of this information.

20. Real estate pricing. A study of a sample of 1057 houses reports the following percentages of houses falling into different *Price* and *Size* categories. **LO❸**

		Price			
		Low	**Med Low**	**Med High**	**High**
	Small	61.5%	35.2%	5.2%	2.4%
Size	**Med Small**	30.4%	45.3%	26.4%	4.7%
	Med Large	5.4%	17.6%	47.6%	21.7%
	Large	2.7%	1.9%	20.8%	71.2%

a) Are these column, row, or total percentages? How do you know?

b) What percent of the highest priced houses were small?

c) From this table, can you determine what percent of all houses were in the low price category?

d) Among the lowest prices houses, what percent were small or medium small?

e) Write a few sentences describing the association between *Price* and *Size*.

21. Stock performance. The following table displays information for 40 widely held stocks that are popular among Canadian investors, on how their one-day change on March 15, 2007, compared with their previous 52-week change. **LO❸**

		Over prior 52 weeks	
		Positive Change	**Negative Change**
March 15, 2007	**Positive Change**	14	9
	Negative Change	11	6

a) What percent of the companies reported a positive change in their share price over the prior 52 weeks?

b) What percent of the companies reported a positive change in their share price over both time periods?

c) What percent of the companies reported a negative change in their share price over both time periods?

d) What percent of the companies reported a positive change in their share price over one period and then a negative change in the other period?

e) Among those companies reporting a positive change in their share price over the prior day what percentage also reported a positive change over the prior year?

		Year							
		2005	**2006**	**2007**	**2008**	**2009**	**2010**	**2011**	**2012**
Revenue Source	**Google websites**	55%	60%	64%	66%	67%	66%	69%	68%
	Google network websites	44%	39%	35%	31%	30%	30%	27%	27%
	Licensing & other revenue	1%	1%	1%	3%	3%	4%	4%	5%

f) Among those companies reporting a negative change in their share price over the prior day what percentage also reported a positive change over the prior year?

g) What relationship, if any, do you see between the performance of a stock on a single day and its 52-week performance?

22. New product. A company started and managed by business students is selling campus calendars. The students have conducted a market survey with the various campus constituents to determine sales potential and identify which market segments should be targeted. (Should they advertise in the alumni magazine and/or the local newspaper?) The following table shows the results of the market survey. LO❹

	Buying Likelihood			
Campus Group	**Unlikely**	**Moderately Likely**	**Very Likely**	Total
Students	197	388	320	**905**
Faculty/Staff	103	137	98	**338**
Alumni	20	18	18	**56**
Town Residents	13	58	45	**116**
Total	**333**	**601**	**481**	**1415**

a) What percent of all these respondents are alumni?

b) What percent of these respondents are very likely to buy the calendar?

c) What percent of the respondents who are very likely to buy the calendar are alumni?

d) Of the alumni, what percent are very likely to buy the calendar?

e) What is the marginal distribution of the campus constituents?

f) What is the conditional distribution of the campus constituents among those very likely to buy the calendar?

g) Does this study present any evidence that this company should focus on selling to certain campus constituents?

23. Real estate. The Edmonton Real Estate Board (Realtors Association of Edmonton) website (www.ereb.com) provides data on sales activity in the Edmonton CMA (Census Metropolitan Area). The following table compares the number of sales in the January 2012 to those in January in 2013, the year over year change. LO❸

	Type of Sale				
Year	**Single Family**	**Condos**	**Multi-family**	**Rural**	Total
2012	543	219	51	52	**865**
2013	496	265	59	57	**877**
Total	**1039**	**484**	**110**	**109**	**1742**

a) What percent of all sales in January 2012 were condominiums (condos)? In January 2013?

b) What percent of all sales in January 2012 were multi-family? In January 2013?

c) Overall, what was the percentage change in January real estate sales in Edmonton from 2012 to 2013?

24. Google financials, part 2. Google Inc. divides their total costs and expenses into five categories: cost of revenues, research and development, sales and marketing, general administrative, and miscellaneous. See the table below.

a) What percent of all costs and expenses were cost of revenues in 2011? In 2012? LO❸

b) What percent of all costs and expenses were due to research and development in 2011? In 2012?

c) Have general administrative costs grown as a percentage of all costs and expenses over this time period?

Cost & Expenses (millions of $)	2007	2008	2009	2010	2011	2012
Cost of revenues	$6649	$8622	$8844	$10 417	$13 188	$20 634
Research and development	$2120	$2793	$2843	$3762	$5162	$6793
Sales and marketing	$1461	$1946	$1984	$2799	$4589	$6143
General administrative	$1279	$1803	$1668	$1962	$2724	$3845
Miscellaneous	$0	$0	$0	$0	$500	$0
Total Costs and Expenses	**$11 510**	**$15 164**	**$15 339**	**$18 940**	**$26 163**	**$37 415**

Note: 2012 cost of revenues includes Motorola Mobile.

25. Movie ratings. The movie ratings system is a voluntary system operated jointly by the Motion Picture Association of America (MPAA) and the National Association of Theatre Owners (NATO). The ratings themselves are given by a board of parents who are members of the Classification and Ratings Administration (CARA). The board was created in response to outcries from parents in the 1960s for some kind of regulation of film content, and the first ratings were introduced in 1968. Here is information on the ratings of a random sample of 120 movies that were released last year, also classified by their genre. LO❹

	Rating				
Genre	**G**	**PG**	**PG-13**	**R**	Total
Action/Adventure	4	5	17	9	**35**
Comedy	2	12	20	4	**38**
Drama	0	3	8	17	**28**
Thriller/Horror	0	0	11	8	**19**
Total	**6**	**20**	**56**	**38**	**120**

a) Find the conditional distribution (in percentages) of movie ratings for action/adventure films.

b) Find the conditional distribution (in percentages) of movie ratings for thriller/horror films.

c) Create a graph comparing the ratings for the four genres.

d) Are *Genre* and *Rating* independent? Write a brief summary of what these data show about movie ratings and the relationship to the genre of the film.

26. Smartphone use. A 2012 survey by Angus Reid/Vision Critical for Rogers asked smartphone users a variety of questions about their attitudes and behaviours with the device. The following table, adapted from the report, is a breakdown by age group of the question, "How close do you keep your cellphone/smartphone to you when you sleep at night?" LO④

	Age		
Phone location at night	18–34	35–54	55+
In the bed with me	24	11	4
Nightstand beside bed	162	138	92
In the same room	35	46	33
In the next room	22	74	129
Downstairs/on another floor	22	64	129
Other	5	21	29

a) Complete the table by calculating the marginal distributions for the rows and columns.

b) Find the conditional distribution (in percentages) for each age group.

c) Create a graph that compares location by age group (in percentages).

d) Write a brief summary of what these data show about "phone location at night" and its relationship to age.

27. MBAs. Records of entering MBA students at the University of British Columbia from 2011 to 2013 include country of birth of the students. The following table compares the full-time program (FT) and part-time program (PT) by region of birth. LO④

	Type		
Region of Birth	Full-time MBA	Part-time MBA	Total
North America	154	81	235
Asia/Pacific Rim	139	42	181
Europe	27	16	43
Middle East	6	13	19
Other	13	3	16
Total	339	155	494

a) What percent of all MBA students were from North America?

b) What percent of the full-time MBAs were from North America?

c) What percent of the part-time MBAs were from North America?

d) What is the marginal distribution of region of birth?

e) Obtain the column percentages and show the conditional distributions of region of birth by MBA program.

f) Do you think that region of birth of the MBA student is independent of the MBA program? Explain.

28. MBAs, part 2. The same university as in Exercise 27 reported the following data on the gender of their students in their two MBA programs. LO④

	Full-time MBA	Part-time MBA	Total
Men	230	106	336
Women	109	49	158
Total	339	155	494

a) What percent of all MBA students are women?

b) What percent of full-time MBAs are women?

c) What percent of part-time MBAs are women?

d) Do you see evidence of an association between the *Type* of MBA program and the percentage of women students? If so, why do you believe this might be true?

29. Top producing movies. The following table shows the Motion Picture Association of America (MPAA) (www.mpaa.org) ratings for the top 20 grossing films in the United States for each of the 10 years from 2003 to 2012. (Data are number of films.) LO④

	Rating				
Year	**G**	**PG**	**PG-13**	**R**	Total
2012	0	6	12	2	20
2011	3	3	12	2	20
2010	1	9	8	2	20
2009	0	7	12	1	20
2008	2	4	10	4	20
2007	1	5	11	3	20
2006	1	4	13	2	20
2005	1	4	13	2	20
2004	1	6	10	3	20
2003	1	3	11	5	20
Total	11	51	112	26	200

a) What percent of all these top 20 films are G rated?

b) What percent of all top 20 films in 2005 were G rated?

c) What percent of all top 20 films were PG-13 and came out in 2006?

d) What percent of all top 20 films produced in 2007 or later were PG-13?

e) What percent of all top 20 films produced from 2003 to 2006 were PG-13?

f) Compare the conditional distributions of the ratings for films produced in 2007 or later to those produced in 2003 to 2006. Write a couple of sentences summarizing what you see.

30. Movie admissions. The following table shows attendance data collected by the Motion Picture Association of America during the period 2002 to 2006. Figures are in millions of movie admissions. LO④

	Patron Age						
	12 to 24	25 to 29	30 to 39	40 to 49	50 to 59	60 and Over	Total
2006	485	136	246	219	124	124	**1334**
2005	489	135	194	216	125	122	**1281**
2004	567	132	265	236	145	132	**1477**
2003	567	124	269	193	152	118	**1423**
2002	551	158	237	211	119	130	**1406**
Total	**2659**	**685**	**1211**	**1075**	**665**	**626**	**6921**

Year (row label at left)

a) What percent of all admissions during this period were bought by people between the ages of 12 and 24?

b) What percent of admissions in 2003 were bought by people between the ages of 12 and 24?

c) What percent of the admission were bought by people between the ages of 12 and 24 in 2006?

d) What percent of admissions in 2006 were bought by people over 60 years old?

e) What percent of the admissions bought by people 60 and over were in 2002?

f) Compare the conditional distributions of the age groups across years. Write a couple of sentences summarizing what you see.

31. Tattoos. A study by a medical centre examined 626 people to see if there was an increased risk of contracting hepatitis C associated with having a tattoo. If the subject had a tattoo, researchers asked whether it had been done in a commercial tattoo parlor or elsewhere. Write a brief description of the association between tattooing and hepatitis C, including an appropriate graphical display. LO②

	Tattoo done in commercial parlor	Tattoo done elsewhere	No tattoo
Has hepatitis C	17	8	18
No hepatitis C	35	53	495

32. Working parents. In July 1991 and again in April 2001, the Gallup Poll asked random samples of 1015 adults about their opinions on working parents. The following table summarizes responses to this question: "*Considering the needs of both parents and children, which of the following do you see as the ideal family in today's society?*" Based upon these results, do you think there was a change in people's attitudes during the 10 years between these polls? Explain. LO②

	Year	
	1991	**2001**
Both work full-time	142	131
One works full-time, other part-time	274	244
One works, other works at home	152	173
One works, other stays home for kids	396	416
No opinion	51	51

Response (row label at left)

33. Revenue growth, last one. The study completed in 2005 and described in Exercise 10 also reported on education levels of the women chief executives. The column percentages for CEO education for each level of revenue are summarized in the following table. (Revenue is in $ million.) LO②

	Graduate Education and Firm Revenue Size		
	< $10 M revenue	$10–$49.999 M revenue	≥ $50 M revenue
% with High School Education only	8%	4%	8%
% with College Education, but no Graduate Education	48%	42%	33%
% with Graduate Education	44%	54%	59%
Total	**100%**	**100%**	**100%**

a) What percent of these CEOs in the highest revenue category had only a high school education?

b) From this table, can you determine what percent of all these CEOs had graduate education? Explain.

c) Among the CEOs in the lowest revenue category, what percent had more than a high school education?

d) Write a few sentences describing the association between *Revenue* and *Education*.

34. Low wage workers. Statistics Canada's Labour Force Survey 2004 data were analyzed to examine the incidence of low pay wages (defined as the percentage of employees earning less than $10.00 per hour). From the analysis, here is a table that presents the percentages, split by age and sex (www.rhdcc-hrsdc.gc.ca/eng/labour/employment_standards/fls/research/research02/page05.shtml) LO②

Age	Male	Female
17–24	60.2%	69.2%
25–34	14.5%	22.8%
35–44	8.8%	19.6%
45–54	7.1%	19.4%
55–64	12.1%	24.9%

a) Is this a contingency table? Why or why not? Are segmented bar charts appropriate here?
b) Prepare a graphical display to compare the incidence of low pay for men to the incidence for women. Write a couple of sentences summarizing what you see.

35. Moviegoers and ethnicity. The Motion Picture Association of America studies the ethnicity of moviegoers to understand changes in the demographics of moviegoers over time. Here are the numbers of moviegoers (in millions) classified as to whether they were Hispanic, African-American, or Caucasian for the years 2002 to 2006. **LO❹**

	Year					
	2002	**2003**	**2004**	**2005**	**2006**	Total
Hispanic	21	23	25	25	26	**120**
African-American	21	20	22	21	20	**104**
Caucasian	118	127	127	113	120	**605**
Total	**160**	**170**	**174**	**159**	**166**	**829**

(Ethnicity on left axis)

a) Find the marginal distribution *Ethnicity* of moviegoers.
b) Find the conditional distribution of *Ethnicity* for the year 2006.
c) Compare the conditional distribution of *Ethnicity* for all five years with a segmented bar graph.
d) Write a brief description of the association between *Year* and *Ethnicity* among these respondents.

36. Department store. A department store is planning its next advertising campaign. Because different publications are read by different market segments, they would like to know if they should be targeting specific age segments. The results of a marketing survey are summarized in the following table by *Age* and *Shopping Frequency* at their store. **LO❹**

	Age			
Shopping	**Under 30**	**30–49**	**50 and Over**	Total
Low	27	37	31	**95**
Moderate	48	91	93	**232**
High	23	51	73	**147**
Total	**98**	**179**	**197**	**474**

(Frequency on left axis)

a) Find the marginal distribution of *Shopping Frequency.*
b) Find the conditional distribution of *Shopping Frequency* within each age group.
c) Compare these distributions with a segmented bar graph.
d) Write a brief description of the association between *Age* and *Shopping Frequency* among these respondents.
e) Does this prove that customers ages 50 and over are more likely to shop at this department store? Explain.

37. Women's business centres. A study conducted in 2002 by Babson College and the Association of Women's Centers surveyed women's business centres in the United States. The data showing the location of established centres (at least five years old) and less established centres are summarized in the following table. **LO❷**

	Location	
	Urban	**Nonurban**
Less Established	74%	26%
Established	80%	20%

a) Are these percentages column percentages, row percentages, or table percentages?
b) Use graphical displays to compare these percentages of women's business centres by location.

38. Advertising. A company that distributes a variety of pet foods is planning their next advertising campaign. Because different publications are read by different market segments, they would like to know how pet ownership is distributed across different income segments. The U.S. Census Bureau reports the number of households owning various types of pets. Specifically, they keep track of dogs, cats, birds, and horses. **LO❷**

Income Distribution of Households Owning Pets (Percent)

	Pet			
	Dog	**Cat**	**Bird**	**Horse**
Under $12,500	14	15	16	9
$12,500 to $24,999	20	20	21	21
$25,000 to $39,999	24	23	24	25
$40,000 to $59,999	22	22	21	22
$60,000 and over	20	20	18	23
Total	**100**	**100**	**100**	**100**

(Income on left axis)

a) Do you think the income distributions of the households who own these different animals would be roughly the same? Why or why not?
b) The table shows the percentages of income levels for each type of animal owned. Are these row percentages, column percentages, or table percentages?
c) Do the data support that the pet food company should not target specific market segments based on household income? Explain.

39. Worldwide toy sales. Around the world, toys are sold through different channels. For example, in some parts of the world toys are sold primarily through large toy store chains, while in other countries department stores sell more toys. The following table shows the percentages by region of the distribution of toys sold through various channels in Europe and North America in 2003, accumulated by the International Council of Toy Industries (www.toy-icti.org). **LO❷**

a) Are these row percentages, column percentages, or table percentages?
b) Can you tell what percent of toys sold by mail order in both Europe and North America are sold in Europe? Why or why not?
c) Use a graphical display to compare the distribution of channels between Europe and North America.
d) Summarize the distribution of toy sales by channel in a few sentences. What are the biggest differences between these two continents?

				Channel		
	General Merchandise	**Toy Specialists**	**Department Stores**	**Mass Merchant Discounters & Food Hypermarkets**	**Mail Order**	**Other**
North America	9%	25%	3%	51%	4%	8%
Europe	13%	36%	7%	24%	5%	15%

(Location)

40. Internet users. Internet World Stats tracks internet usage and population for over 233 individual countries and world regions. The website (www.internetworldstats.com) reports that, as of June 30, 2012, there were 2.4 billion internet users worldwide. The site also reports users by World Region, as follows: **LO❸**

	Population (millions)	Internet Users (millions)
Africa	1073	167
Asia	3922	1077
Europe	821	519
Middle East	224	90
North America	348	274
Latin America/Caribbean	594	255
Oceania/Australia	36	24
World Total	7018	2406

a) What percent of North Americans use the internet?
b) What percent of internet users are from North America?
c) Draw a graph to compare the percentage of the population who are internet users across regions.

41. Health care. A provincial ministry of health is concerned that patients who undergo surgery at large hospitals have their discharges delayed for various reasons—which results in increased medical costs. The recent data for area hospitals and two types of surgery (major and minor) are shown in the following table. **LO❸, LO❺**

	Discharge Delayed	
	Large Hospital	**Small Hospital**
Major surgery	120 of 800	10 of 50
Minor surgery	10 of 200	20 of 250

(Procedure)

a) Overall, for what percent of patients was discharge delayed?
b) Were the percentages different for major and minor surgery?
c) Overall, what were the discharge delay rates at each size of hospital?
d) What were the delay rates at each size of hospital for each kind of surgery?
e) The ministry of health is considering advising patients use large hospitals for surgery to avoid postsurgical complications. Do you think they should do this?
f) Explain, in your own words, why this confusion occurs.

42. Delivery service. A company must decide which of two delivery services they will contract with. During a recent trial period, they shipped numerous packages with each service and have kept track of how often deliveries did not arrive on time. Here are the data. **LO❸, LO❺**

Delivery Service	Type of Service	Number of Deliveries	Number of Late Packages
Pack Rats	Regular	400	12
	Overnight	100	16
Boxes R Us	Regular	100	2
	Overnight	400	28

a) Compare the two services' overall percentage of late deliveries.
b) Based on the results in part a, the company has decided to hire Pack Rats. Do you agree they deliver on time more often? Why or why not? Be specific.
c) The results here are an instance of what phenomenon?

43. Graduate admissions. This case is old but it's a "classic". A 1975 article in the magazine *Science* examined the graduate admissions process at Berkeley for evidence of gender bias. The following table shows the number of applicants accepted to each of four graduate programs. LO❸, LO❺

Program	Males Accepted (of Applicants)	Females Accepted (of Applicants)
1	511 of 825	89 of 108
2	352 of 560	17 of 25
3	137 of 407	132 of 375
4	22 of 373	24 of 341
Total	**1022 of 2165**	**262 of 849**

a) What percent of total applicants were admitted?
b) Overall, were a higher percentage of males or females admitted?
c) Compare the percentage of males and females admitted in each program.
d) Which of the comparisons you made do you consider to be the most valid? Why?

44. Simpson's Paradox. Develop your own table of data that is a business example of Simpson's Paradox. Explain the conflict between the conclusions made from the conditional and marginal distributions. LO❸, LO❺

✓ **JUST CHECKING ANSWERS**

1 50.0%
2 40.0%
3 25.0%
4 15.6% Near-sighted, 56.3% Far-sighted, 28.1% Need Bifocals
5 18.8% Near-sighted, 62.5% Far-sighted, 18.8% Need Bifocals
6 40% of the near-sighted patients are female, while 50% of patients are female.
7 Since near-sighted patients appear less likely to be female, it seems that they may not be independent. (But the numbers are small.)

Displaying and Describing Quantitative Data

In Chapter 4 we dealt with categorical data. Now it is quantitative data's turn, but it will take us two chapters to explore the subject. In this chapter we learn how to display quantitative data with graphs and describe them with numerical summaries. Since there are many more numerical summaries for quantitative data than for categorical data it will take the whole chapter.

Jandke/Caro/Alamy

LEARNING OBJECTIVES

1. Identify the features that describe a data distribution
2. Find a five-number summary
3. Create and interpret a boxplot
4. Compute and interpret summary statistics of the centre and spread of a distribution
5. Create a stem-and-leaf display
6. Create and interpret a histogram
7. Evaluate appropriateness of graphical displays
8. Create and interpret a time series plot
9. Compute and interpret z-scores

Nortel Networks

Until the dot-com crash of 2000, Nortel Networks, a multinational telecommunications and data networking equipment manufacturer, was one of Canada's most valuable companies, with over 90 000 employees worldwide (more than 25 000 in Canada) and worth almost $300 billion. Its origins dated back to the late 1800s when its predecessor, Bell Telephone, began making telephone equipment. Incorporated in 1895 as Northern Electric, the name changed to Nortel Networks in 1998. In July 2000, its share price reached a high of $124.50. At the time of bankruptcy filing in January 2009, shares were worth just 39 cents, having lost more than 99% of their value.

At its peak, Nortel accounted for more than a third of the total valuation of all companies listed on the Toronto Stock Exchange (TSX). Nortel was delisted by the TSX in June 2009. The crash of Nortel stock had huge implications on Canadian investors and on pension funds, and left 60 000 Nortel employees unemployed. Were there warning signs in the data?

Based on information from www.nortel-canada.com and www.cbc.ca/news/business/nortel-failed-amid-culture-of-arrogance-1.2582136

o learn more about the behaviour and volatility of Nortel's shares, let's start by looking at Table 5.1, which gives the monthly changes in share price (in dollars) for the five years from January 2003 to December 2007.

	Jan.	Feb.	Mar.	Apr.	May	Jun.	Jul.	Aug.	Sep.	Oct.	Nov.	Dec.
2003	7.60	−2.20	−0.70	5.00	5.60	−4.40	2.50	3.00	8.50	3.50	0.60	−2.80
2004	36.30	1.10	−20.30	−22.00	0.90	11.60	−13.30	1.00	−3.60	−0.10	0.80	0.00
2005	−2.20	−5.70	0.50	−2.40	1.00	0.20	0.20	4.10	2.20	−0.10	−3.50	1.60
2006	−0.60	−1.40	1.90	−3.90	−2.80	−1.40	−2.80	1.30	2.10	−0.70	−0.80	5.23
2007	0.04	3.21	−5.93	−1.17	3.20	−2.03	−2.41	−4.17	−0.21	−1.13	0.71	−1.75

| **Table 5.1**   Monthly price change in dollars of Nortel shares for the period January 2003 to December 2007.

It's hard to tell very much from tables of values like this. You might get a rough idea of how much the share price changed from month to month—usually less than $10 in either direction—but that's about it.

<table>
<tr><td>**WHO**</td><td>Months</td></tr>
<tr><td>**WHAT**</td><td>Monthly changes in Nortel's share price in dollars</td></tr>
<tr><td>**WHEN**</td><td>2003 to 2007</td></tr>
<tr><td>**WHERE**</td><td>Toronto Stock Exchange</td></tr>
<tr><td>**WHY**</td><td>To examine Nortel share price volatility</td></tr>
</table>

5.1 Displaying Distributions

Instead, let's follow the first rule of data analysis and make a picture. What kind of picture should we make? It can't be a bar chart or a pie chart. Those are only for categorical variables, and Nortel's share price change is a *quantitative* variable, whose units are dollars. Remember that a **distribution** gives the possible values of a variable and the frequency or relative frequency of each value.

Histograms

The origin of the word *histogram* is not certain; however, it is certainly derived by combining two Greek words, "*histos*" and "*gramma*." *Gramma* means drawing or writing, as in "graph." *Histos* means "mast" or "upright beam," which suggests the columns in the graph. *Histos* also means "web" or "layers" and is the root of the medical/biological word *histology*, which is the study of tissues. So, for us, the best way to think of the word histogram is as "a picture of layers" of the distribution.

Here are the monthly price changes of Nortel shares displayed in a histogram.

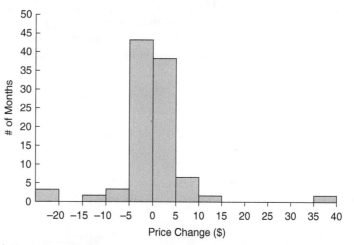

Figure 5.1 Monthly price changes of Nortel shares. The histogram displays the distribution of price changes by showing for each "bin" of price changes, the number of months having price changes in that bin.

Like a bar chart, a **histogram** plots the bin counts as the heights of bars. It counts the number of cases that fall into each bin, and displays that count as the height of the corresponding bar. In this way it displays the distribution at a glance.

In this histogram of monthly price changes, each bin has a width of $5, so, for example, the height of the second tallest bar says that there were about 20 to 25 monthly price changes with values between $0 and $5. In this way, the histogram displays the entire distribution of price changes. Unlike a bar chart, which puts gaps between bars to separate the categories, there are no gaps between the bars of a histogram *unless* there are actual gaps in the data. Gaps indicate a region where there are no values, such as the gap between $15 and $35 in Figure 5.1. Gaps can be important features of the distribution so watch out for them and point them out.

For categorical variables, each category got its own bar. The only choice was whether to combine categories for ease of display. For quantitative variables, we have to choose the width of the bins. We usually leave that choice to technology when we can.

◆ **How do histograms work?** If you were to make a histogram by hand or in Excel, you'd need to decide how wide to make the bins. Bin choice is important because some features of the distribution may appear more obvious at different bin width choices. With many statistics packages, you can easily vary the bin width interactively so you can make sure that a feature you think you see isn't just a consequence of a certain bin width choice.

You'd also need to decide where to place the endpoints of the bins. (Statistics packages and graphing calculators make these choices for you automatically.) Bins are always equal in width and are typically multiples of five or ten. But what do you do with a value of $5 if one bin spans from $0 to $5 and the next bin spans from $5 to $10? The standard rule for a value that falls exactly on a bin boundary is to put it into the next higher bin, so you'd put a month with a change of $5 into the $5 to $10 bin instead of into the $0 to $5 bin. In other words, the $0 to $5 bin is really the $0 to $4.99 bin.

From the histogram, we can see that these months typically have changes near $0. We can see that although they vary, most of the monthly price changes are less than $5 in either direction. Only in a very few months were the changes larger than $10 in either direction. There appear to be about as many positive as negative price changes—indicating that the share price went up as often as it went down.

Does the distribution look as you expected? It's often a good idea to imagine what the distribution might look like before making the display. That way you're less likely to be fooled by errors either in your display or in the data themselves.

If our focus is on the overall pattern of how the values are distributed rather than on the counts themselves, it can be useful to make a relative frequency histogram (Figure 5.2), replacing the counts on the vertical axis with the percentage of the total number of cases falling in each bin. The shape of the histogram is exactly the same;

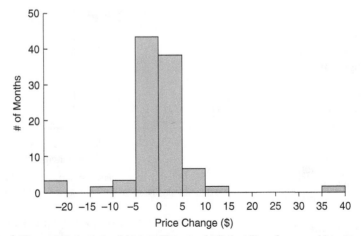

Figure 5.2 A relative frequency histogram looks just like a frequency histogram except that the *y*-axis now shows the percentage of months in each bin.

only the labels are different. A **relative frequency histogram** is faithful to the area principle by displaying the *percentage* of cases in each bin instead of the count.

Stem-and-Leaf Displays

The stem-and-leaf display may seem like an antiquated idea in the age of modern computer graphics, but it is really not an old idea. Although the underlying concept dates back to the early 1900s, the development of the stem-and-leaf display as a useful tool in exploratory data analysis is due to the great statistician John Tukey, who included them in a landmark book in 1977.

Histograms provide an easy-to-understand summary of the distribution of a quantitative variable, but they don't show the data values themselves. **Stem-and-leaf displays** are like histograms, but they also give the individual values. They are easy to make by hand for data sets that aren't too large, so they're a great way to look at a small batch of values quickly.[1] Here's a stem-and-leaf display for just the last three years of the Nortel price change data, excluding the large negative values and large positive values, alongside a histogram of the same data.

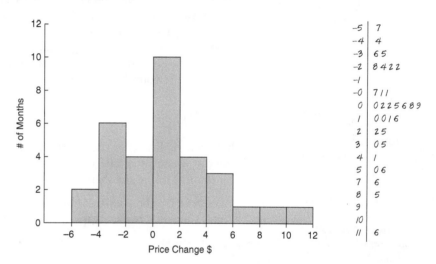

Figure 5.3 The last 36 months of Nortel monthly share price changes displayed both by a histogram (left) and stem-and-leaf display (right). Stem-and-leaf displays are typically made by hand, so we are most likely to use them for small data sets. For much larger data sets, we use a histogram.

◆ **How do stem-and-leaf displays work?** Stem-and-leaf displays use part of each number (called the stem) to name the bins. To make the "bars," they use the next digit of the number. For example, if we had a monthly price change of $2.13, we could write 2 | 1, where 2 serves as the stem and 1 as the leaf (rounding $2.13 to $2.1). To display the changes 2.1, 2.2, 2.4, 3.3, and 3.3 together, we would write

$$2|124$$

$$3|33$$

Often we put the higher numbers on top, but either way is common. Higher numbers on top is often natural, but putting the higher numbers on the bottom keeps the direction of the histogram the same when you tilt your head to look at it—otherwise the histogram appears reversed.

When you make a stem-and-leaf display by hand, make sure you give each digit about the same width, in order to satisfy the area principle. (That can lead to some fat 1s and thin 8s—but it keeps the display honest.) If you use the computer to typeset the display (e.g., with Microsoft Word), use a non-proportional font such as Courier.

---

[1] The authors like to make stem-and-leaf displays whenever data are presented (without a suitable display) at committee meetings or working groups. The insights from just that quick look at the distribution are often quite valuable.

Visually, the main difference between a bar chart and a histogram is that there are no gaps between bars in a histogram. Excel's default display has gaps; to create a proper histogram in Excel you need to close up the gaps. The other difference is that the bars in a bar chart can be displayed in any order, since the categories are not quantitative. You certainly can't rearrange the order of the bars in a histogram.

The **mode** is typically defined as the single value that appears most often. That definition is fine for categorical variables because we need only to count the number of cases for each category. For quantitative variables, the meaning of *mode* is more ambiguous. For example, what's the mode of the Nortel data? No price change occurred more than twice, but two months had drops of $2.20, two of $0.20 and two of $1.00. Should any of those be the mode? Probably not. For quantitative data, it makes more sense to use the word *mode* in the more general sense of "peak in a histogram," rather than as a single summary value.

You've heard of pie à la mode. Is there a connection between pie and the mode of a distribution? Actually, there is! The mode of a distribution is a *popular* value near which a lot of the data values gather. And à la mode means "in style"—*not* "with ice cream." That just happened to be a *popular* way to have pie in Paris around 1900.

There are both positive and negative values in the price changes. Values of $0.3 and $0.5 are displayed as leaves of "3" and "5" on the "0" stem. But values of −$0.3 and −$0.5 must be plotted below zero. So the stem-and-leaf display has a "−0" stem to hold them—again with leaves of "3" and "5." It may seem a little strange to see two zero stems, one labelled "−0." But, if you think about it, you'll see that it's a sensible way to deal with negative values.

Unlike most other displays discussed in this book, stem-and-leaf displays are great pencil-and-paper constructions. They are well-suited to moderate amounts of data—say, between 10 and a few hundred values. For larger data sets, histograms do a better job.

In Chapter 4 you learned to check the Categorical Data Condition before making a pie chart or a bar chart. Now, by contrast, before making a stem-and-leaf display, or a histogram, you need to check the **Quantitative Data Condition**: The data are values of a quantitative variable whose units are known.

Although a bar chart and a histogram may look similar, they're not the same display. You can't display categorical data in a histogram or quantitative data in a bar chart. Always check the condition that confirms what type of data you have before making your display.

5.2 Shape

Once you've displayed the distribution in a histogram or stem-and-leaf display, what can you say about it? When you describe a distribution, you should pay attention to three things: its shape, its centre, and its spread.

> We describe the **shape** of a distribution in terms of its modes, its symmetry, and whether it has any gaps or outlying values.

Mode

Does the histogram have a single, central hump (or peak) or several, separated humps? These humps are called **modes**.[2] Formally, the mode is the single, most frequent value, but we rarely use the term that way. Sometimes we talk about the mode as being the value of the variable at the centre of this hump. The Nortel share price changes have a single mode at just below $0 (Figure 5.1). We often use modes to describe the shape of the distribution. A distribution whose histogram has one main hump, such as the one for the Nortel price changes, is called **unimodal**; distributions whose histograms have two humps are **bimodal**, and those with three or more are called **multimodal**. For example, here's a bimodal distribution.

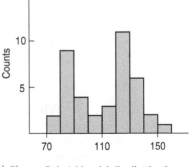

Figure 5.4 A bimodal distribution has two apparent modes.

---

[2] Technically, the mode is the value on the *x*-axis of the histogram below the highest peak, but informally we often refer to the peak or hump itself as a mode.

A bimodal histogram is often an indication that there are two groups in the data. It's a good idea to investigate when you see bimodality.

A distribution whose histogram doesn't appear to have any mode and in which all the bars are approximately the same height is called **uniform**.

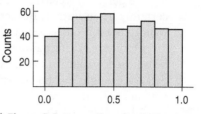

Figure 5.5 In a uniform distribution, bars are all about the same height. The histogram doesn't appear to have a mode.

Symmetry

Could you fold the histogram along a vertical line through the middle and have the edges match pretty closely, as in Figure 5.6, or are more of the values on one side, as in the histograms in Figure 5.7? A distribution is **symmetric** if the halves on either side of the centre look, at least approximately, like mirror images.

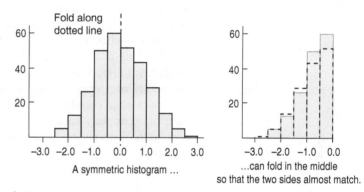

Figure 5.6 A symmetric histogram can fold in the middle so that the two sides almost match.

> Amounts of things (dollars, employees, waiting times) can't be negative and have no natural upper limit. So, they often have right skewed distributions.

The (usually) thinner ends of a distribution are called the **tails**. If one tail stretches out farther than the other, the distribution is said to be **skewed** to the side of the longer tail.

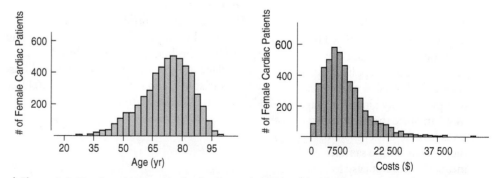

Figure 5.7 Two skewed histograms showing the age (on left) and hospital costs (on right) for all female heart attack patients in a province in one year. The histogram of Age (in blue) is skewed to the left, while the histogram of Costs (in purple) is skewed to the right.

Here is a literal "rule of thumb." Cover up one or two data points with your thumb. If your impression of the distribution changes markedly, those data points are outliers, not skewness. Outliers and skewness are two different characteristics. Outliers are unusual individual data points. Skewness is a feature of the distribution that wouldn't disappear even if you removed the outliers.

Outliers

Do any features appear to stick out? Often such features tell us something interesting or exciting about the data. You should always point out any stragglers or **outliers** that stand off away from the body of the distribution. For example, if you're studying the personal wealth of Americans and Bill Gates is in your sample, he would certainly be an outlier. Because his wealth would be so obviously atypical, you'd want to point it out as a special feature.

Outliers can affect almost every method we discuss in this book, so we'll always be on the lookout for them. An outlier can be the most informative part of your data, or it might just be an error. Either way, you shouldn't throw it away without comment. Treat it specially and discuss it when you report your conclusions about your data. (Or find the error and fix it if you can.) In the section about boxplots we'll learn a rule of thumb for how we can decide if and when a value might be considered to be an outlier and some advice for what to do when you encounter them.

◆ **Using Your Judgment.** How you characterize a distribution is often a judgment call. Does the gap you see in the histogram really reveal that you have two subgroups, or will it go away if you change the bin width slightly? Are those observations at the high end of the histogram truly unusual, or are they just the largest ones at the end of a long tail? These are matters of judgment on which different people can legitimately disagree. There's no automatic calculation or rule of thumb that can make the decision for you. Understanding your data and how they arose can help. What should guide your decisions is an honest desire to understand what is happening in the data.

Looking at a histogram at several different bin widths can help to see how persistent some of the features are. Some technologies offer ways to change the bin width interactively to get multiple views of the histogram. If the number of observations in each bin is small enough so that moving a couple of values to the next bin changes your assessment of how many modes there are, be careful. Be sure to think about the data, where they came from, and what kinds of questions you hope to answer from them.

Statistics Joke: She told me she wouldn't go out with me because I was only average. I told her she was just being mean.

5.3 Centre

Look again at the Nortel price changes in Figure 5.1. If you had to pick one number to describe a *typical* price change, what would you pick? When a histogram is unimodal and symmetric, most people would point to the centre of the distribution, where the histogram peaks. The typical price change is around $0. So **centre** means the middle of a distribution. However, there is more than one way to define "middle."

If we want to be more precise and *calculate* a number, we can *average* the data. In the Nortel example, the average price change is −$0.02, about what we might expect from the histogram. You already know how to average values, but this is a good place to introduce notation that we'll use throughout the book. We'll call a generic variable *y*, and use the Greek capital letter sigma, Σ, to mean "sum" (sigma is "S" in Greek), and write[3]:

$$\bar{y} = \frac{Total}{n} = \frac{\Sigma y}{n}$$

! **NOTATION ALERT:**
A bar over any symbol indicates the mean of that quantity. The notation $\bar{y}$ is a remnant of an old convention in applied mathematics and physics, which was to represent any kind of average by a bar. Since the early statisticians had these backgrounds they used it for the sample mean. But it is not easy to represent in modern word processing!

_____

[3] You may also see the variable called *x* and the equation written $\bar{x} = \frac{Total}{n} = \frac{\Sigma x}{n}$.

According to this formula, we add up all the values of the variable, y, and divide that sum (*Total*, or $\Sigma\, y$) by the number of data values, n. We call the resulting value the **mean** of y.[4]

Although the mean is a natural summary for unimodal, symmetric distributions, it can be misleading for skewed data or for distributions with gaps or outliers. For example, Figure 5.7 showed a histogram of the total costs for hospital stays of female heart attack patients in one year in a province. The mean value is $10 260.70. Locate that value on the histogram. Does it seem a little high as a summary of a typical cost? In fact, about two thirds of the costs are lower than that value. It might be better to use the **median**—the value that splits the histogram into two *equal* areas. We find the median by counting in from the ends of the data until we reach the middle value. So the median is resistant; it isn't affected by unusual observations or by the shape of the distribution. Because of its resistance to these effects, the median is commonly used for variables such as cost or income, which are likely to be skewed. For the female heart attack patient costs, the median cost is $8619, which seems like a more appropriate summary.

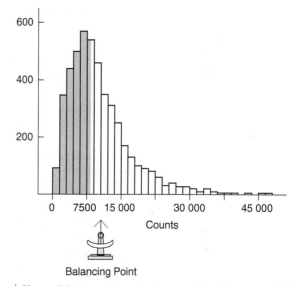

Finding the median by hand

Finding the median of a batch of n numbers is easy as long as you remember to order the values first. If n is odd, the median is the middle value. Counting in from the ends, we find this value in the $\dfrac{n+1}{2}$ position.

When n is even, there are two middle values. So, in this case, the median is the average of the two values in positions $\dfrac{n}{2}$ and $\dfrac{n}{2}+1$.

Here are two examples:

Suppose the batch has the values 14.1, 3.2, 25.3, 2.8, −17.5, 13.9, and 45.8. First we order the values: −17.5, 2.8, 3.2, 13.9, 14.1, 25.3, and 45.8. There are 7 values, so the median is the $(7+1)/2 = 4$th value counting from the top or bottom: 13.9.

Suppose we had the same batch with another value at 35.7. Then the ordered values are −17.5, 2.8, 3.2, 13.9, 14.1, 25.3, 35.7, and 45.8. The median is the average of the 8/2, or 4th, and the $(8/2) + 1$, or 5th, values. So the median is $(13.9 + 14.1)/2 = 14.0$.

Figure 5.8 The median splits the area of the histogram in half at $8619. Because the distribution is skewed to the right, the mean $10 260 is higher than the median. The points at the right have pulled the mean toward them, away from the median.

Does it really make a difference whether we choose a mean or a median? The mean price change for the Nortel shares is −$0.02. Because the distribution of the price changes is roughly symmetric, we'd expect the mean and median to be close. In fact, we compute the median to be −$0.05. But for variables with skewed distributions, the story is quite different. For a right skewed distribution like the hospital costs in Figure 5.8, the mean is larger than the median: $10 260 compared to $8619. The difference is due to the overall shape of the distribution.

---

[4] Once you've averaged the data, you might logically expect the result to be called the *average*. But average is used too colloquially as in the "average" home buyer, where we don't sum up anything. Even though average *is* sometimes used in the way we intend, as in the Dow Jones Industrial Average (which is actually a weighted average) or a batting average, we'll often use the term *mean* throughout the book.

The mean is the point at which the histogram would balance. Just like a child who moves away from the centre of a see-saw, a bar of the histogram far from the centre has more leverage, pulling the mean in its direction. It's hard to argue that a summary that's been pulled aside by only a few outlying values or by a long tail is what we mean by the centre of the distribution. That's why the median is usually a better choice for skewed data.

However, when the distribution is unimodal and symmetric, the mean offers better opportunities to calculate useful quantities and draw more interesting conclusions. It will be the summary value we work with much more throughout the rest of the book.

In fact, there are three types of means: arithmetic, geometric, and harmonic.

The arithmetic mean (call it AM), which we have computed here, is of course the familiar one, and is used for non-related values. Note that "arithmetic" is pronounced with the emphasis on the third syllable because it is an adjective here—arith-MET-ic.

The harmonic mean (call it HM) is used for rates that are *not* dependent on each other. The formula looks more complicated: $\text{HM} = \dfrac{n}{\frac{1}{y_1} + \frac{1}{y_2} + \cdots + \frac{1}{y_n}}$. For example, suppose you drive from point A to point B at 40 kph and from point B to point A at 60 kph. What is your average speed for the round trip? The AM is $\dfrac{40 + 60}{2}$ = 50, but that's not the appropriate average. The HM is $\dfrac{2}{\frac{1}{40} + \frac{1}{60}}$ = 48. If you're still dubious, assume the distance is 120 km. It will take you 3 hours to go 120 km at 40 kph and 2 hours at 60 kph. That's a total of 240 km in 5 hours, which is 48 kph!

The geometric mean (call it GM) is used for rates where each measurement depends on the previous one. If the rates are $R_1, R_2, \ldots R_n$, then the geometric mean is $\text{GM} = \sqrt{(1 + R_1) \times (1 + R_2) \times \ldots \times (1 + R_n)} - 1$. For example, suppose an investment experiences 100% growth in the first year and then a 50% loss in the second year. What is the average increase? The AM mean would be $[100\% + (-50\%)]/2 = 25\%$, but that's nonsense since you would actually be right back where you started from! However, the GM is $\sqrt{(1 + 1.0)(1 + (-0.5))} - 1 = 0$.

The harmonic and geometric means are not used very often in data analysis, but it is worthwhile knowing about them for a full understanding of the word "average."

5.4 Spread of the Distribution

We know that the typical price change of the Nortel shares is around $0, but knowing the mean or median alone doesn't tell us about the entire distribution. A share whose price change doesn't move away from $0 isn't very interesting. The more the data vary, the less a measure of centre can tell us. We need to know how spread out the data are as well. **Spread** refers to how tightly clustered the data are around the centre of the distribution.

One simple measure of spread is the **range**, defined as the difference between the extremes:

$$\text{Range} = max - min.$$

For the Nortel data, the range is $36.30 − (−$22.00) = $58.30. Notice that the range is *a single number* that describes the spread of the data, not an interval of values—as you might think from its use in common speech. If there are any unusual observations in the data, the range is not resistant and will be influenced by them. Concentrating on the middle of the data avoids this problem. The **quartiles** are the values that frame the middle 50% of the data. One quarter of the data lies below the lower quartile, Q1, and one quarter of the data lies above the upper quartile,

An easy way to find the quartiles is to first split the sorted data at the median. (If *n* is odd, include the median with each half.) Then find the median of each of these halves and use them as the quartiles. Even though quartiles are easy to find, there are at least six rules for finding them. The rules all give pretty much the same values when we have a lot of data. But when *n* is small, they can differ. If your calculator, statistics package, or friend in a different class gets a slightly different value, don't worry about it. Usually the exact value isn't important.

Why do banks favour a single line that feeds several teller windows rather than separate lines for each teller? It does make the average waiting time slightly shorter, but that improvement is very small. The real difference people notice is that the time you can expect to wait is less variable when there is a single line, and people prefer consistency.

Q3. The **interquartile range (IQR)** summarizes the spread by focusing on the middle half of the data. It's defined as the difference between the two quartiles:

$$IQR = Q3 - Q1.$$

For the Nortel data, there are 30 values on either side of the median. After ordering the data, we average the 15th and 16th values to find Q1 = −$2.30. We average the 45th and 46th values to find Q3 = $2.00. So the IQR = Q3 − Q1 = $2.00 − (−$2.30) = $4.30.

The IQR is usually a reasonable summary of spread, but because it uses only the two quartiles of the data, it ignores much of the information about how individual values vary.

A more powerful measure of spread—and the one we'll use most often—is the standard deviation, which, as we'll see, takes into account how far each value is from the mean. Like the mean, the standard deviation is appropriate only for symmetric data and can be influenced by outlying observations.

As the name implies, the standard deviation uses the *deviations* of each data value from the mean. If we tried to average these deviations, the positive and negative differences would cancel each other out, giving an average deviation of 0—not very useful. Instead, we square each deviation. The average[5] of the *squared* deviations is called the **variance** and is denoted by s^2:

$$s^2 = \frac{\sum (y - \bar{y})^2}{n - 1}.$$

![checkmark icon] **JUST CHECKING**

Thinking About Variation

1 Statistics Canada reports the median family income in its summary of census data. Why do you suppose they use the median instead of the mean? What might be the disadvantages of reporting the mean?

2 You've just bought a new car that claims to get a highway fuel efficiency of 9 litres per 100 kilometres. Of course, your fuel efficiency will "vary." If you had to guess, would you expect the IQR of fuel efficiency attained by all cars like yours to be 9, 2, or 0.1 litres per 100 kilometres? Why?

3 A company selling a new MP3 player advertises that the player has a mean lifetime of five years. If you were in charge of quality control at the factory, would you prefer that the standard deviation of lifespans of the players you produce be two years or two months? Why?

Absolute values give us another way to handle the cancelling effect of the positive and negative differences. We could compute the average absolute deviation of all the data values from the mean and call it the Mean Absolute Deviation (MAD). It seems like a natural way to measure the spread, but the MAD has a weakness. While the mean is a unique value that minimizes the standard deviation, there is no unique value that minimizes the MAD, so it doesn't help us locate the mean. For example, the four numbers –6, –4, 4, and 6 have a mean of 0. The MAD from 0 is 5. But the MAD from 1 is also 5; in fact, the MAD from any number between –4 and 4 is 5. The lack of specific minimizing value can drive one mad! Maybe that's where the name came from.

The variance plays an important role in statistics, but as a measure of spread, it has a problem. Whatever the units of the original data, the variance is in *squared* units. We want measures of spread to have the same units as the data, so we usually take the square root of the variance. That gives the **standard deviation**.

$$s = \sqrt{\frac{\sum (y - \bar{y})^2}{n - 1}}.$$

For the Nortel stock price changes, $s = \$7.17$.

---

[5] For technical reasons, we divide by $n - 1$ instead of n to take this average. Here's a non-technical explanation for the denominator of n − 1. To find the distance from each data value to the mean, you first need to use the data to compute the mean. That's like saying, "pick any five numbers you want, as long as the average is a pre-specified value." The first four numbers can be anything, but the fifth is predetermined. That is, the fifth choice must be that number that ensures that the average equals the pre-specified value.

Finding the standard deviation by hand

To find the standard deviation, start with the mean, $\bar{y}$. Then find the *deviations* by taking $\bar{y}$ from each value: $(y - \bar{y})$. Square each deviation: $(y - \bar{y})^2$.

Now you're nearly home. Just add these up and divide by $n - 1$. That gives you the variance, s^2. To find the standard deviation, s, take the square root.

Suppose the batch of values is 4, 3, 10, 12, 8, 9, and 3. The mean is $\bar{y} = 7$. So find the deviations by subtracting 7 from each value:

Original Values	Deviations	Squared Deviations
4	$4 - 7 = -3$	$(-3)^2 = 9$
3	$3 - 7 = -4$	$(-4)^2 = 16$
10	$10 - 7 = 3$	9
12	$12 - 7 = 5$	25
8	$8 - 7 = 1$	1
9	$9 - 7 = 2$	4
3	$3 - 7 = -4$	16

Add up the squared deviations:
$9 + 16 + 9 + 25 + 1 + 4 + 16 = 80$
Now, divide by $n - 1$: $80/6 = 13.33$
Finally, take the square root: $s = \sqrt{13.33} = 3.65$

How to Build a Boxplot

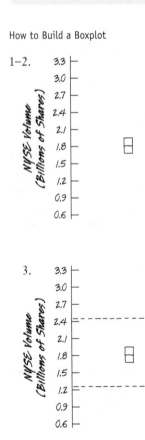

5.5 Shape, Centre, and Spread—A Summary

What should you report about a quantitative variable? Report the shape of its distribution, and include a centre and a spread. But which measure of centre and which measure of spread? The guidelines are pretty easy.

♦ If the shape is skewed, point that out and report the median and IQR. You may want to include the mean and standard deviation as well, explaining why the mean and median differ. The fact that the mean and median do not agree is a sign that the distribution may be skewed. A histogram will help you make the point.

♦ If the shape is unimodal and symmetric, report the mean and standard deviation and possibly the median and IQR as well. For unimodal symmetric data, the IQR is usually a bit larger than the standard deviation. If that's not true for your data set, look again to make sure the distribution isn't skewed or mutimodal and that there are no outliers.

♦ If there are multiple modes, try to understand why. If you can identify a reason for separate modes, it may be a good idea to split the data into separate groups.

♦ If there are any clearly unusual observations, point them out. If you are reporting the mean and standard deviation, report them computed with and without the unusual observations. The differences may be revealing.

♦ Always pair the median with the IQR and the mean with the standard deviation. It's not useful to report one without the other. Reporting a centre without a spread can lead you to think you know more about the distribution than you do. Reporting only the spread omits important information.

5.6 Five-Number Summary and Boxplots

The volume of shares traded on the New York Stock Exchange (NYSE) is important to investors, research analysts, and policymakers. It can predict market volatility, and has been used in models for predicting price fluctuations. How many shares are typically traded in a day on the NYSE? One good way to summarize a distribution with just a few values is with a five-number summary. The **five-number summary** of a distribution reports its median, quartiles, and extremes (maximum and minimum). For example, the five-number summary of NYSE volume during the entire year 2006 looks like this (in billions of shares).

Max	3.287
Q3	1.972
Median	1.824
Q1	1.675
Min	0.616

Table 5.2 The five-number summary of a NYSE daily volume (in billions of shares) for the year 2006.

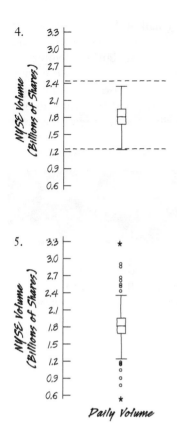

4.

5.

The five-number summary provides a good overall look at the distribution. For example, because the quartiles frame the middle half of the data, we can see that on half of the days the volume was between 1.675 and 1.972 billion shares. We can also see the extremes of over 3 billion shares on the high end and just over half a billion shares on the low end. Were those days extraordinary for some reason or just the busiest and quietest days? To answer that, we'll need to work with the summaries a bit more.

Once we have a five-number summary of a (quantitative) variable, we can display that information in a **boxplot**. To make a boxplot of the daily volumes, follow these steps:

1. Draw a single vertical axis spanning the extent of the data.

2. Draw short horizontal lines at the lower and upper quartiles and at the median. Then connect them with vertical lines to form a box. The width isn't important unless you plan to show more than one group.

3. Now erect (but don't show in the final plot) "fences" around the main part of the data, placing the upper fence 1.5 IQRs above the upper quartile and the lower fence 1.5 IQRs below the lower quartile. For the NYSE share volume data, compute:

Upper fence $= Q3 + 1.5\ IQR = 1.97 + 1.5 \times 0.29 = 2.405$ billion shares

and

Lower fence $= Q1 - 1.5\ IQR = 1.68 - 1.5 \times 0.29 = 1.245$ billion shares

4. Grow "whiskers." Draw lines from each end of the box up and down to *the most extreme data values found within the fences.* If a data value falls outside one of the fences, do *not* connect it with a whisker.

5. Finally, add any outliers by displaying data values that lie beyond the fences with special symbols. Here there are about 15 such values. (We often use one symbol for outliers that lie less than 3 IQRs from the quartiles and a different symbol for "far outliers"—data values more than 3 IQRs from the quartiles.)

Now that you've drawn the boxplot, let's summarize what it shows. The centre of a boxplot is (remarkably enough) a box that shows the middle half of the data, between the quartiles. The height of the box is equal to the IQR. If the median is roughly centred between the quartiles, then the middle half of the data is roughly symmetric. If it is not centred, the distribution is skewed. The whiskers show skewness as well if they are not roughly the same length. Any outliers are displayed individually, both to keep them out of the way for judging skewness and to encourage you to give them special attention. They may be mistakes, or they may be the most interesting cases in your data.

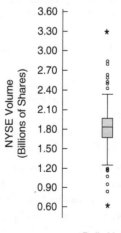

Figure 5.9 Boxplot of daily volume of shares traded on NYSE in 2006 (in billions of shares).

The boxplot for NYSE volume shows the middle half of the days—those with average volume between 1.676 and 1.970 billion shares—as the central box. From the shape of the box, it looks like the central part of the distribution of volume is roughly symmetric, and the similar length of the two whiskers shows the outer parts of the distribution to be roughly symmetric as well. We also see several high-volume and low-volume days. Boxplots are particularly good at exhibiting outliers. We also see two extreme outliers, one on each side. These extreme days may deserve more attention. (When and why did they occur?)

GUIDED EXAMPLE | Credit Card Bank Customers

Keet/Fotolia

In order to focus on the needs of particular customers, companies often segment their customers into groups with similar needs or spending patterns. A major credit card bank wanted to see how much a particular group of cardholders charged per month on their cards in order to understand the potential growth in their card use. The data for each customer was the amount he or she spent using the card during a three-month period last year. Boxplots are especially useful for one variable when combined with a histogram and numerical summaries. Let's summarize the spending of this segment.

PLAN

Setup Identify the *variable*, the time frame of the data, and the objective of the analysis.

We want to summarize the average monthly charges (in dollars) made by 500 cardholders from a market segment of interest during a three-month period last year. The data are quantitative, so we'll use histograms and boxplots, as well as numerical summaries.

DO

REALITY CHECK

Mechanics Select an appropriate display based on the nature of the data and what you want to know about it.

It is always a good idea to think about what you expected to see and to check whether the histogram is close to what you expected. Are the data about what you might expect for customers to charge on their cards in a month? A typical value is a few hundred dollars. That seems like the right ballpark.

Note that outliers are often easier to see with boxplots than with histograms, but the histogram provides more details about the shape of the distribution. This computer program "jitters" the outliers in the boxplot so they don't lie on top of each other, making them easier to see.

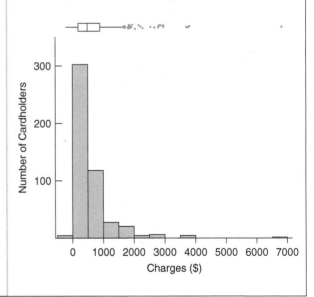

Both graphs show a distribution that is highly skewed to the right with several outliers and an extreme outlier near $7000.

Summary of Monthly Charges	
Count	500
Mean	544.749
Median	370.65
StdDev	661.244
IQR	624.125
Q1	114.54
Q3	738.665

The mean is much larger than the median. The data do not have a symmetric distribution.

REPORT

Interpretation Describe the shape, centre, and spread of the distribution. Be sure to report on the symmetry, number of modes, and any gaps or outliers.

Recommendation State a conclusion and any recommended actions or analysis.

MEMO:

Re: Report on segment spending.

The distribution of charges for this segment during this time period is unimodal and skewed to the right. For that reason, we have summarized the data with the median and interquartile range (IQR).

The median amount charged was $370.65. Half of the cardholders charged between $114.54 and $738.67.

In addition, there are several high outliers, with one extreme value at $6745.

There are also a few negative values. We suspect that these are people who returned more than they charged in a month, but because the values might be data errors, we suggest that they be checked.

Future analyses should look at whether charges during these three months were similar to charges in the rest of the year. We would also like to investigate if there is a seasonal pattern and, if so, whether it can be explained by our advertising campaigns or by other factors.

5.7 Comparing Groups

As we saw earlier, the volume on the NYSE can vary greatly from day to day, but if we step back a bit, we may be able to find patterns that can help us understand, model, and predict it. We might be interested not only in individual daily values, but also in looking for patterns in the volume when we group the days into time periods such as weeks, months, or seasons. Such comparisons of distributions can reveal patterns, differences, and trends.

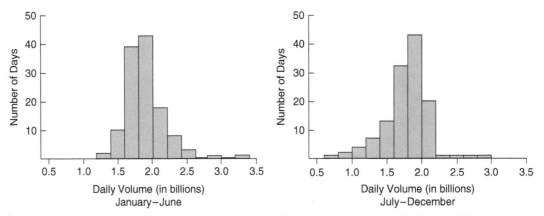

| Figure 5.10 Daily volume on the NYSE split into two halves of the year. How do the two distributions differ?

Let's start with the "big picture." We'll split the year into halves: January through June and July through December. Here are histograms of the NYSE volume for 2006.

The centres and spreads are not too different, but the shape appears to be slightly right skewed in the first half, while the second half of the year appears to be left skewed with more days on the lower end. There are several noticeable outlying values on the high side in both graphs. Notice that we have displayed the two histograms on the same scale. Histograms with very different centres and spreads may appear similar unless you do that.

Histograms work well for comparing two groups, but what if we want to compare the volume across four quarters? Or 12 months? Histograms are best at displaying one or two distributions. When we compare several groups, boxplots usually do a better job. Boxplots offer an ideal balance of information and simplicity, hiding the details while displaying the overall summary information. And we can plot them side by side, making it easy to compare multiple groups or categories.

When we place boxplots side by side, we can easily see which group has the higher median, which has the greater IQR, where the central 50% of the data is located, and which has the greater overall range. We can also get a general idea of symmetry from whether the medians are centred within their boxes and whether the whiskers extend roughly the same distance on either side of the boxes. Equally important, we can see past any outliers in making these comparisons because they've been displayed separately. We can also begin to look for trends in the medians and in the IQRs.

GUIDED EXAMPLE | New York Stock Exchange Trading Volume

Are some months on the NYSE busier than others? Boxplots of the number of shares traded by month are a good way to see such patterns. We're interested not only in the centres, but also in the spreads. Are volumes equally variable from month to month, or are they more spread out in some months?

PLAN

Setup Identify the variables, report the time frame of the data, and state the objective.

We want to compare the daily volume of shares traded from month to month on the NYSE during 2006.

The daily volume is quantitative and measured in number of shares. We can partition the values by month and use side-by-side boxplots to compare the volume across months.

	Mechanics Plot the side-by-side boxplots of the data.	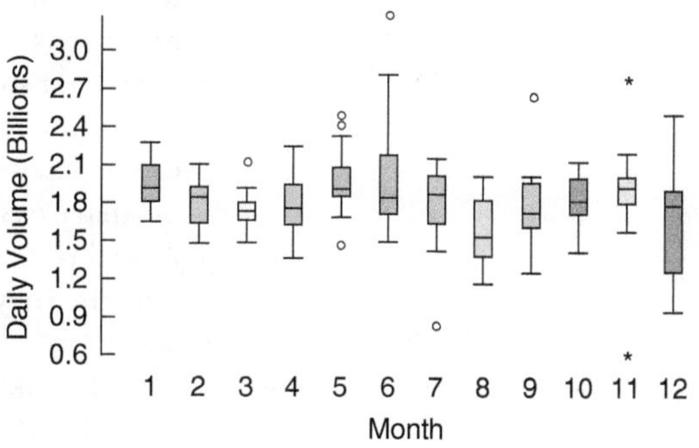

DO

	Conclusion Report what you've learned about the data and any recommended action or analysis.	MEMO: **Re: Research on trading volume of the NYSE** We have examined the daily sales volume on the NYSE (number of shares traded) for each month of 2006. As the attached display shows, sales volume follows a seasonal pattern with lower volume in March and August. The highest median trading activity is found in November. The variability of trading volume also shows a pattern. June and December have higher variability than the rest, and March has noticeably less variability. There were several unusually high-volume days that bear investigation and one extremely low-volume day in November.

REPORT

5.8 Identifying Outliers

When we looked at a boxplot for volumes of the entire year, there were 15 outliers. Now, when we group the days by *Month*, the boxplots display fewer days as outliers, and identify different days as the extraordinary ones. This change occurs because our outlier nomination rule for boxplots depends on the quartiles of the data being displayed. Days that may have seemed ordinary when placed against the entire year's data can look like outliers for the month they're in and *vice versa*. That high-volume day in March certainly wouldn't stand out in May or June, but for March it was remarkable, and that very low-volume day in November really stands out now. What should we do with such outliers?

Cases that stand out from the rest of the data deserve our attention. Boxplots have a rule for nominating extreme cases to display as outliers, but that's just a rule of thumb—not a definition. The rule doesn't tell you what to do with them.

So, what *should* we do with outliers? The first thing to do is to try to understand them in the context of the data. Look back at the boxplot in the Guided Example. The boxplot for November (month 11) shows a fairly symmetric body of data with one low-volume and one high-volume day set clearly apart from the other days. Such a large gap suggests that the volume really is quite different.

Once you've identified likely outliers, you should always investigate them. Some outliers are unbelievable and may simply be errors. A decimal point may have been misplaced, digits transposed, or digits repeated or omitted. Or, the units may be wrong. If you saw the number of shares traded on the NYSE listed as two shares for a particular day, you'd know something was wrong. It could be that it was meant as two billion shares, but you'd have to check to be sure. Sometimes a number is transcribed incorrectly, perhaps copying an adjacent value on the original data sheet. If you can identify the error, then you should certainly correct it.

Many outliers are not wrong; they're just different. These are the cases that often repay your efforts to understand them. You may learn more from the extraordinary cases than from summaries of the overall data set. There is a saying that Nobel prizes come, not from identifying unusual observations, but from figuring out why they happened.

What about that low November day? It was November 24, 2006, the Friday after Thanksgiving, a day when most likely, traders would have rather stayed home.

The high-volume day, September 15, was a "triple witching day," a day when during the final trading hour, options and futures contracts expire. Such days often experience large trading volume and price fluctuations.

14-year-old widowers?

Careful attention to outliers can often reveal problems in data collection and management. Two researchers, Ansley Coale and Fred Stephan, looking at data from the 1950 census noticed that the number of widowed 14-year-old boys had increased from 85 in 1940 to a whopping 1600 in 1950. The number of divorced 14-year-old boys had increased, too, from 85 to 1240. Oddly, the number of teenaged widowers and divorcees *decreased* for every age group after 14, from 15 to 19. When Coale and Stephan also noticed a large increase in the number of young Native Americans in the Northeast United States, they began to look for data problems. Data in the 1950 census were recorded on computer cards. (For a picture of a computer card, see p. 15.) Cards are hard to read and mistakes are easy to make. It turned out that data punches had been shifted to the right by one column on hundreds of cards. Because each card column meant something different, the shift turned 43-year-old widowed males into 14-year-olds, 42-year-old divorcees into 14-year-olds, and children of white parents into Native Americans. Not all outliers have such a colourful (or famous) story, but it is always worthwhile to investigate them. And, as in this case, the explanation is often surprising. (A. Coale and F. Stephan, "The case of the Indians and the teen-age widows." *J. Am. Stat. Assoc.* 57 [Jun 1962]: 338–347.)

5.9 Standardizing

The data we compared by groups in previous sections were all the same variable. It was easy to compare volume on the NYSE in July to volume on the NYSE in December because the data had the same units. Sometimes, however, we want to compare very different variables—apples to oranges, so to speak. For example, the Great Place to Work Institute measures more than 50 aspects of companies and publishes through *Fortune Magazine* a ranking of the top places to work. In 2007, the top honour was captured by Google.

Courtesy Google Inc.

What was the key to Google's winning? Was it the free food offered to all employees? Maybe the on-site day care? How about the salaries—do they compare favourably with other companies? Were they better on all 50 variables? Probably not, but it isn't obvious how to combine and balance all these different aspects to come up with a single number. The variables don't even have the same units; for example, average salary is in dollars, perceptions are often measured on a seven-point scale, and diversity measures are in percentages.

The trick to comparing very different-looking values is to standardize the values. Rather than working with the original values, we ask "how far is this value from the mean?" Then—and this is the key—we measure that distance with the standard deviation. The result is the standardized value that records how many standard deviations each value is above or below the overall mean. The standard deviation provides a ruler, based on the underlying variability of all the values, against which we can compare values that otherwise have little in common.

It turns out that statisticians do this all the time. Over and over during this course (and in any additional Statistics courses you may take), questions such as "How far is this value from the mean?" or "How different are these two values?" will be answered by measuring the distance or difference in standard deviations.

In order to see how standardizing works, we'll focus on just two of the 50 variables that the Great Places to Work Institute reports: the number of *New Jobs* created during the year and the reported *Average Pay* for salaried employees for two companies. We'll choose two companies that were farther down the list to show how standardization works: Starbucks and the Wrigley Company (the company that makes Wrigley's chewing gum among other things).[6]

When we compare two variables, it's always a good idea to start with a picture. Here we'll use stem-and-leaf displays (Figure 5.11), so we can see the individual distances, highlighting Starbucks in red and Wrigley in blue. The mean number of new jobs created for all the companies was 305.8. Starbucks with over 2000 jobs is well above average, as we can see from the stem-and-leaf display. Wrigley, with only 16 jobs (rounded to 0 in the stem-and-leaf), is closer to the centre. On the other hand, Wrigley's average salary was $56 350 (rounded to 6), compared with Starbuck's $44 790 (represented as 4), so even though both are below average, Wrigley is closer to the centre (see margin).

Variable	Mean (all companies)	SD (all companies)
New Jobs	305.8	1508.0
Avg Pay	$73 229.42	$34 055.24

```
                New Jobs

 4 |                                                          Average Pay
 3 | 67
 2 | 25                                                   2 | 5
 1 | 01234567                                             2 |
 0 | 11111111222222233333334445555666667778888            2 |
-0 | 65444332110000                                       1 |
-1 | 1                                                    1 |
-2 |                                                      1 | 45
-3 | 3                                                    1 | 222
-4 |                                                      1 | 000001
-5 |                                                      0 | 88889999999999
-6 |                                                      0 | 66666666666777777777
-7 |                                                      0 | 44444444455555555555
-8 |                                                      0 | 3
-9 | 1                                                    0 | 1

 3|6 represents 3600                         2|5 represents 250 000
```

Figure 5.11 Stem-and-leaf displays for both the number of new jobs created and the average pay of salaried employees at the top 100 companies to work for in 2005 from *Fortune* Magazine. Starbucks (in red) had more jobs created, but Wrigley (in blue) did better in average pay. Which company did better for both variables combined?

When we compare scores from different variables, our eye naturally looks at how far from the centre of each distribution the value lies. We adjust naturally for the fact that these variables have very different scales. Starbucks did better on *New Jobs*, and Wrigley did better on *Average Pay*. To quantify *how much* better each one did and to combine the two scores, we'll ask how many standard deviations they each are from the variable means.

---

[6] The data we analyze here are actually from 2005, the last year for which we have data and the year Wegman's Supermarkets was the number one company to work for.

To find how many standard deviations a value is from the mean we find:

$$z = \frac{y - \bar{y}}{s}.$$

We call the resulting value a **standardized value** and denote it with the letter z. Usually, we just call it a **z-score**.

A z-score of 2.0 indicates that a data value is two standard deviations above the mean. Data values below the mean have negative z-scores, so a z-score of -0.84 means that the data value is 0.84 standard deviations *below* the mean.

	New Jobs	Average Pay
Mean (All companies)	305.9	$73 299.42
SD	1507.97	$34 055.25
Starbucks	2193	$44 790
z-score	**1.25** = (2193 − 305.9)/1507.97	**−0.84** = (44 790 − 73 299.42)/34 055.25
Wrigley	16	$56 351
z-score	**−0.19** = (16 − 305.9)/1507.97	**−0.50** = (56 351 − 73 299.42)/34 055.25
Total z-score		
Starbucks	**1.25 − 0.84 = 0.41**	
Wrigley	**−0.19 − 0.50 = −0.69**	

Table 5.3   For each variable, the z-score for each observation is found by subtracting the mean from the value and then dividing that difference by the standard deviation. By adding the two z-scores, we see that even though Starbucks has a lower average salary than Wrigley, it is compensated for by the number of new jobs they offered.

Starbucks offered more new jobs than Wrigley, but Wrigley had a higher average salary. The z-score for Starbucks' *New Jobs* $(2193 - 305.9)/1507.97 = 1.25$ is 1.44 higher than Wrigley's -0.19 (see Table 5.3 for details). By comparison, Wrigley's *Average Pay* z-score of -0.50 is only 0.34 better than Starbucks' -0.84. So in terms of standardized scores, Starbucks' *New Jobs* performance dominates Wrigley's *Average Pay*.

Is this the result we wanted? Perhaps not. Adding z-scores together doesn't always make sense, or give the answer we want. Maybe we should put more weight on salary than on number of new jobs created. Our combined z-score added the two variables equally, but we could weight the variables differently. Even though the Great Places to Work Institute may not have added the z-scores together, they still had to combine scores from 50 different variables into one ranking, a task best accomplished by working with standardized scores. By using the standard deviation as a ruler to measure statistical distance from the mean, we compare values that are measured on different variables, with different scales, with different units, or for different populations.

Standardizing into z-scores:

- Shifts the mean to 0.
- Changes the standard deviation to 1.
- Does not change the shape.
- Removes the units.

*5.10 Time Series Plots

The volume on the NYSE is reported daily. Earlier, we grouped the days into months and half years, but we could simply look at the volume day by day. Whenever we have time series data, it is a good idea to look for patterns by plotting the data in time order. Figure 5.12 shows the *daily volumes* plotted over time for 2006.

A display of values against time is sometimes called a **time series plot**. This plot reflects the pattern that we saw when we plotted the daily volume by month, but without the arbitrary divisions between months we can see periods of relative calm contrasted with periods of greater activity. We can also see that the volume both became more variable and increased during certain parts of the year.

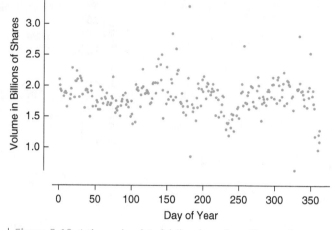

Figure 5.12 A time series plot of daily volume shows the overall pattern and changes in variation.

Time series plots often show a great deal of point-to-point variation, as Figure 5.12 does, and you'll often see time series plots drawn with all the points connected, especially in financial publications.

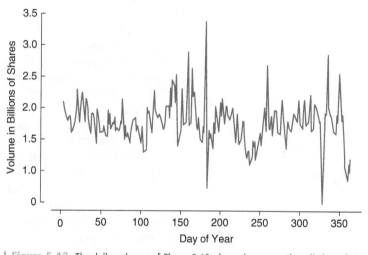

Figure 5.13 The daily volumes of Figure 5.12, drawn by connecting all the points. Sometimes this can help us see the underlying pattern.

Often it is better to try to smooth out the local point-to-point variability. After all, we usually want to see past this variation to understand any underlying trend and think about how the values vary around that trend—the time series version of centre and spread. There are many ways for computers to run a smooth trace through a time series plot. Some follow local bumps, others emphasize long-term trends. Some provide an equation that gives a typical value for any given time point, others just offer a smooth trace.

A smooth trace can highlight long-term patterns and help us see them through the more local variation. In Figure 5.14 we see the daily volumes of Figures 5.12 and 5.13 with a typical smoothing function, available in many statistics programs. With the smooth trace, it's a bit easier to see a pattern. The trace helps our eye follow the main trend and alerts us to points that don't fit the overall pattern.

It is always tempting to try to extend what we see in a timeplot into the future. Sometimes that makes sense. Most likely, the NYSE volume follows some regular patterns throughout the year. It's probably safe to predict more volume

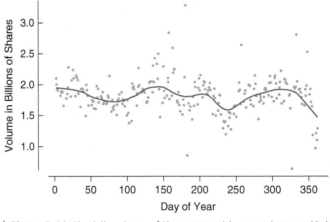

Figure 5.14 The daily volumes of Figure 5.12, with a smooth trace added to help your eye see the long-term pattern.

on triple witching days (when contracts expire) and less activity in the week between Christmas and New Year's Day. But we certainly wouldn't predict a record every June 30.

Other patterns are riskier to extend into the future. If a stock's price has been rising, how long will it continue to go up? No stock has ever increased in value indefinitely, and no stock analyst has consistently been able to forecast when a stock's value will turn around. Stock prices, unemployment rates, and other economic, social, or psychological measures are much harder to predict than physical quantities. The path a ball will follow when thrown from a certain height at a given speed and direction is well understood. The path interest rates will take is much less clear.

Unless we have strong (nonstatistical) reasons for doing otherwise, we should resist the temptation to think that any trend we see will continue indefinitely. Statistical models often tempt those who use them to think beyond the data. We'll pay close attention later in this book to understanding when, how, and how much we can justify doing that.

Let's return to the Nortel data we saw at the beginning of the chapter. The share price changes are a time series from January 2003 to December 2007 with frequency one month. The histogram (Figure 5.1) showed a symmetric, possibly unimodal distribution for the most part concentrated between −$5 and +$5 with a few outliers. The time series plot (Figure 5.15) shows a different story.

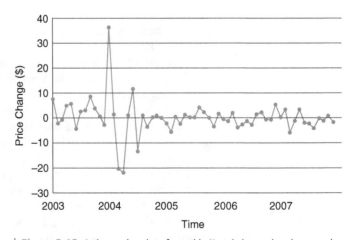

Figure 5.15 A time series plot of monthly Nortel share price changes, shows the increased volatility in 2004, and the decreased volatility in later years.

The time series plot shows stable price changes in 2003, great volatility in 2004, and a return to small and stable changes from 2005 onwards.

The histogram fails to summarize this distribution well because of the change in the behaviour of the series over time. When a time series is **stationary**[7] (without a strong trend or change in variability), then a histogram can provide a useful summary, especially in conjunction with a time series plot. However, when the time series is not stationary, a histogram is unlikely to capture much of interest. Then, a time series plot is the best graphical display to use in describing the behaviour of the data.

Sometimes a time series plot can tell an entire story. Following the 2010 Winter Olympics gold medal hockey game, the Edmonton water and power utility, EPCOR, published an incredible graph of water consumption (Figure 5.16). Nearly 80% of Canadians watched at least part of the game; the effect on toilet flushing was inevitable. The graph shows with remarkable clarity the degree to which water consumption matches the key breaks in the hockey game. For comparison, water consumption for the same period the day before is also displayed on the graph.

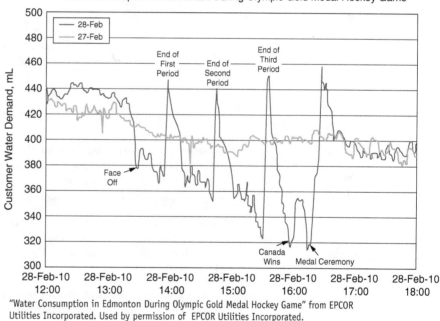

"Water Consumption in Edmonton During Olympic Gold Medal Hockey Game" from EPCOR Utilities Incorporated. Used by permission of EPCOR Utilities Incorporated.

Figure 5.16 Water usage in Edmonton during the 2010 gold medal hockey game.

While the game was played water use dropped, but then it rose during intermissions and after the medal ceremony. When Sidney Crosby scored the "golden goal" that won the gold medal for Canada, water demand had dipped to a low of 320 mL per customer, compared to about 400 mL per customer the day before. After the medal ceremony, water use spiked to 460 mL per customer. As Sarah Boesveld wrote in *The Globe and Mail*, "A nation that plays together, flushes together too." Incidentally, similar utility surges were seen across the country.

---

[7] Sometimes we separate out the properties and say the series is stationary with respect to the mean (if there is no trend) or stationary with respect to the variance (if the spread doesn't change), but unless otherwise noted, we'll assume that *all the statistical properties* of a stationary series are constant over time.

WHAT CAN GO WRONG?

A data display should tell a story about the data. To do that it must speak in a clear language, making plain what variable is displayed, what any axis shows, and what the values of the data are. And it must be consistent in those decisions.

The task of summarizing a quantitative variable requires that we follow a set of rules. We need to watch out for certain features of the data that make summarizing them with a number dangerous. Here's some advice:

- **Don't make a histogram of a categorical variable.** Just because the variable contains numbers doesn't mean it's quantitative. Here's a histogram of the insurance policy numbers of some workers. It's not very informative because the policy numbers are categorical. A histogram or stem-and-leaf display of a categorical variable makes no sense. A bar chart may do better.

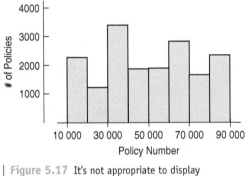

Figure 5.17 It's not appropriate to display categorical data like policy numbers with a histogram.

- **Choose a scale appropriate to the data.** Computer programs usually do a pretty good job of choosing histogram bin widths. Often, there's an easy way to adjust the width, sometimes interactively. Figure 5.18 shows the Nortel price change histogram with two other choices for the bin size.

- **Avoid inconsistent scales.** Parts of displays should be mutually consistent—no fair changing scales in the middle or plotting two variables on different scales but on the same display. When comparing two groups, be sure to draw them on the same scale.

- **Label clearly.** Variables should be identified clearly and axes labelled so a reader knows what the plot displays.

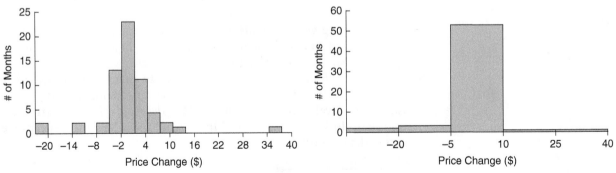

Figure 5.18 Changing the bin width changes how the histogram looks. The Nortel share price changes look very different with these two choices.

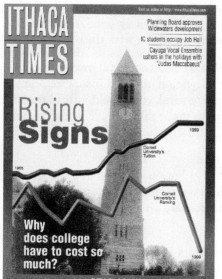

Ithaca Times

Here's a remarkable example of a plot gone wrong. It illustrated a news story about rising college costs. It uses time series plots, but it gives a misleading impression. First, think about the story you're being told by this display. Then try to figure out what has gone wrong. What's wrong? Just about everything.

- The horizontal scales are inconsistent. Both lines show trends over time, but for what years? The tuition sequence starts in 1965, but rankings are graphed from 1989. Plotting them on the same (invisible) scale makes it seem that they're for the same years.

- The vertical axis isn't labelled. That hides the fact that it's using two different scales. Does it graph dollars (of tuition) or ranking (of Cornell University)?

This display violates three of the rules. And it's even worse than that. It violates a rule that we didn't even bother to mention. The two inconsistent scales for the vertical axis don't point in the same direction! The line for Cornell's rank shows that it has "plummeted" from 15th place to 6th place in academic rank. Most of us think that's an *improvement*, but that's not the message of this graph.

- **Beware of unintended optical illusions in graphs.** Here is an example of multiple line plots or time series plots. It appears that *Profit* (*Sales* minus *Costs*) is decreasing since the lines appear to be converging, but it is an optical illusion. The vertical distance between the two lines at any point is a constant. The lines don't converge any more than two railroad tracks do!

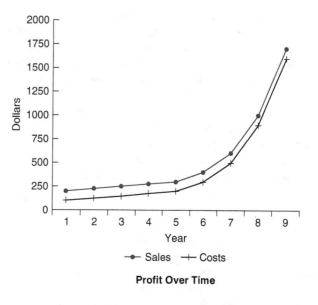

Profit Over Time

- **Do a reality check.** Don't let the computer (or calculator) do your thinking for you. Make sure the calculated summaries make sense. For example, does the mean look like it is in the centre of the histogram? Think about the spread. An IQR of 20 litres per 100 kilometres would clearly be wrong for a family car. And no measure of spread can be negative. The standard

(continued)

deviation can take the value 0, but only in the very unusual case that all the data values equal the same number. If you see the IQR or standard deviation equal to 0, it's probably a sign that something's wrong with the data.

- **Don't compute numerical summaries of a categorical variable.** The mean student ID number or the standard deviation of Social Insurance Numbers is not meaningful. If the variable is categorical, you should instead report summaries such as percentages. It is easy to make this mistake when you let technology do the summaries for you. After all, the computer doesn't care what the numbers mean.

- **Watch out for multiple modes.** If the distribution—as seen in a histogram, for example—has multiple modes, consider separating the data into groups. If you cannot separate the data in a meaningful way, you should not summarize the centre and spread of the variable.

- **Beware of outliers.** If the data have outliers but are otherwise unimodal, consider holding the outliers out of the further calculations and reporting them individually. If you can find a simple reason for the outlier (for instance, a data transcription error), you should remove or correct it. If you cannot do either of these, then choose the median and IQR to summarize the centre and spread.

ETHICS IN ACTION

Beth Tully owns Zenna's Café, an independent coffee shop located in a small city in British Columbia. Since opening Zenna's in 2002, she has been steadily growing her business and now distributes her custom coffee blends to a number of regional restaurants and markets. She operates a microroaster that offers specialty grade Arabica coffees recognized as some as the best in the area. In addition to providing the highest quality coffees, Beth also wants her business to be socially responsible. Toward that end, she pays fair prices to coffee farmers and donates funds to help charitable causes in Panama, Costa Rica, and Guatemala. In addition, she encourages her employees to get involved in the local community. Recently, one of the well-known multinational coffeehouse chains announced plans to locate shops in her area. This chain is one of the few to offer Certified Free Trade coffee products and work toward social justice in the global community. Consequently, Beth thought it might be a good idea for her to begin communicating Zenna's socially responsible efforts to the public, but with an emphasis on their commitment to the local community. Three months ago she began collecting data on the number of volunteer hours donated by her employees per week. She has a total of 12 employees, of whom 10 are full time. Most employees volunteered less than 2 hours per week, but Beth noticed that one part-time employee volunteered more than 20 hours per week. She discovered that her employees collectively volunteered an average of 15 hours per month (with a median of 8 hours). She planned to report the average number and believed most people would be impressed with Zenna's level of commitment to the local community.

ETHICAL ISSUE *The outlier in the data affects the average in a direction that benefits Beth Tully and Zenna's Café (related to ASA Ethical Guidelines, Item C, which can be found at http://www.amstat.org/about/ethicalguidelines.cfm).*

ETHICAL SOLUTION *Beth's data are highly skewed. There is an outlier value (for a part-time employee) that pulls the average number of volunteer hours up. Reporting the average is misleading. In addition, there may be justification to eliminate the value since it belongs to a part-time employee (10 of the 12 employees are full time). It would be more ethical for Beth to: (1) report the average but discuss the outlier value; (2) report the average for only full-time employees, or (3) report the median instead of the average.*

WHAT HAVE WE LEARNED?

We've learned how to display and summarize quantitative data to help us see the story the data have to tell.

- We can display the distribution of quantitative data with a histogram or a stem-and-leaf display.
- We report what we see about the distribution by talking about shape, centre, spread, outliers, and any unusual features.

We've learned how to summarize distributions of quantitative variables numerically.

- Measures of centre for a distribution include the median and the mean.
- Measures of spread include the range, IQR, and standard deviation.
- We'll report the median and IQR when the distribution is skewed. If it's symmetric, we'll summarize the distribution with the mean and standard deviation (and possibly the median and IQR as well). Always pair the median with the IQR and the mean with the standard deviation.

We've learned to think about the type of variable we're summarizing.

- All the methods in this chapter assume that the data are quantitative.
- The Quantitative Data Condition serves as a check that the data are, in fact, quantitative. One good way to be sure is to know the measurement units.

We've learned the value of comparing groups and looking for patterns among groups and over time.

- We've seen that boxplots are very effective for comparing groups graphically.
- When we compare groups, we discuss their shapes, centres, spreads, and any unusual features.

We've experienced the value of identifying and investigating outliers, and we've seen that when we group data in different ways, it can allow different cases to emerge as possible outliers.

- We've graphed data that have been measured over time against a time axis and looked for trends both by eye and with a data smoother.

We've learned the power of standardizing data.

- Standardizing uses the standard deviation as a ruler to measure distance from the mean, creating z-scores.
- Using these z-scores, we can compare apples and oranges—values from different distributions or values based on different units.
- A z-score can identify unusual or surprising values among data.

Terms

Bimodal Distributions with two modes.

Boxplot A boxplot displays the five-number summary as a central box with whiskers that extend to the non-outlying values. Boxplots are particularly effective for comparing groups.

Centre	The middle of the distribution, usually summarized numerically by the mean or the median.
Distribution	The distribution of a variable gives: • possible values of the variable • frequency or relative frequency of each value
Five-number summary	A five-number summary for a variable consists of: • The minimum and maximum • The quartiles Q1 and Q3 • The median
Histogram (relative frequency histogram)	A histogram uses adjacent bars to show the distribution of values in a quantitative variable. Each bar represents the frequency (relative frequency) of values falling in an interval of values.
Interquartile range (IQR)	The difference between the first and third quartiles. IQR = Q3 − Q1.
Mean	A measure of centre found as $\bar{y} = \Sigma y / n$.
Median	The middle value with half of the data above it and half below it.
Mode	A peak or local high point in the shape of the distribution of a variable. The apparent location of modes can change as the scale of a histogram is changed.
Multimodal	Distributions with more than two modes.
Outliers	Extreme values that don't appear to belong with the rest of the data. They may be unusual values that deserve further investigation or just mistakes; there's no obvious way to tell.
Quartile	The lower quartile (Q1) is the value with a quarter of the data below it. The upper quartile (Q3) has a quarter of the data above it. The median and quartiles divide the data into four equal parts.
Range	The difference between the lowest and highest values in a data set: Range = *max − min*.
Shape	The visual appearance of the distribution. To describe the shape, look for: • single vs. multiple modes • symmetry vs. skewness
Skewed	A distribution is skewed if one tail stretches out farther than the other.
Spread	The description of how tightly clustered the distribution is around its centre. Measures of spread include the IQR and the standard deviation.
Standard deviation	A measure of spread found as $s = \sqrt{\dfrac{\Sigma(y - \bar{y})^2}{n - 1}}$.
Standardized value	We standardize a value by subtracting the mean and dividing by the standard deviation for the variable. These values, called z-scores, have no units.

Stationary	A time series is said to be stationary if its statistical properties don't change over time.
Stem-and-leaf display	A stem-and-leaf display shows quantitative data values in a way that sketches the distribution of the data. It's best described in detail by example.
Symmetric	A distribution is symmetric if the two halves on either side of the centre look approximately like mirror images of each other.
Tail	The tails of a distribution are the parts that typically trail off on either side.
Time series plot	Displays data that change over time. Often, successive values are connected with lines to show trends more clearly.
Uniform	A distribution that's roughly flat is said to be uniform.
Unimodal	Having one mode. This is a useful term for describing the shape of a histogram when it's generally mound-shaped.
Variance	The standard deviation squared.
***z*-score**	A standardized value that tells how many standard deviations a value is from the mean; z-scores have a mean of 0 and a standard deviation of 1.

Skills

- Be able to identify an appropriate display for any quantitative variable.
- Be able to select a suitable measure of centre and a suitable measure of spread for a variable based on information about its distribution.
- Know the basic properties of the median: The median divides the data into the half of the data values that are below the median and the half that are above the median.
- Know the basic properties of the mean: The mean is the point at which the histogram balances.
- Know that the standard deviation summarizes how spread out all the data are around the mean.
- Know that standardizing uses the standard deviation as a ruler.

- Know how to display the distribution of a quantitative variable with a stem-and-leaf display or a histogram.
- Know how to make a time series plot of data that are collected at regular time intervals.
- Know how to compute the mean and median of a set of data and know when each is appropriate.
- Know how to compute the standard deviation and IQR of a set of data and know when each is appropriate.
- Know how to compute a five-number summary of a variable.
- Know how to construct a boxplot by hand from a five-number summary.
- Know how to calculate the z-score of an observation.

- Be able to describe and compare the distributions of quantitative variables in terms of their shape, centre, and spread.

- Be able to discuss any outliers in the data, noting how they deviate from the overall pattern of the data.

- Be able to describe summary measures in a sentence. In particular, know that the common measures of centre and spread have the same units as the variable that they summarize and that they should be described in those units.

- Be able to compare two or more groups by comparing their boxplots.

- Be able to discuss patterns in a time series plot, both in terms of the general trend and any changes in the spread of the distribution over time.

TECHNOLOGY HELP: Displaying and Summarizing Quantitative Variables

Almost any program that displays data can make a histogram, but some will do a better job of determining where the bars should start and how they should partition the span of the data (see the art below).

Many statistics packages offer a prepackaged collection of summary measures. The result might look like this:

```
Variable: Weight
N = 234
Mean = 143.3      Median = 139
St. Dev = 11.1    IQR = 14
```

Alternatively, a package might make a table for several variables and summary measures:

Variable	N	mean	median	stdev	IQR
Weight	234	143.3	139	11.1	14
Height	234	68.3	68.1	4.3	5
Score	234	86	88	9	5

It is usually easy to read the results and identify each computed summary. You should be able to read the summary statistics produced by any computer package.

Packages often provide many more summary statistics than you need. Of course, some of these may not be appropriate when the data are skewed or have outliers. It is your responsibility to check a histogram or stem-and-leaf display and decide which summary statistics to use.

It is common for packages to report summary statistics to many decimal places of "accuracy." Of course, it is rare to find data that have such accuracy in the original measurements. The ability to calculate to six or seven digits beyond the decimal point doesn't mean that those digits have any meaning. Generally, it's a good idea to round these values, allowing perhaps one more digit of precision than was given in the original data.

Displays and summaries of quantitative variables are among the simplest things you can do in most statistics packages.

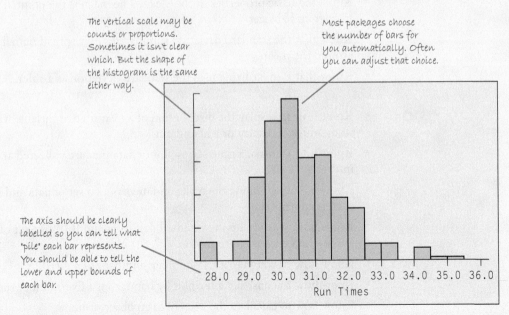

EXCEL

To calculate summaries, click on an empty cell. Type an equals sign and choose **Average** from the popup list of functions that appears to the left of the text editing box. Enter the data range in the box that says **Number 1**. Click the **OK** button. To compute the standard deviation of a column of data directly, use the **STDEV** from the popup list of functions in the same way.

Comments

Excel's Data Analysis add-in does offer something called a histogram, but it isn't a statistically appropriate histogram. Excel cannot make histograms, boxplots, or dotplots without a third-party add in. Excel's STDEV function should not be used for data values larger in magnitude than 100 000 or for lists of more than a few thousand values. It is fine for smaller data sets.

MINI CASE STUDY PROJECTS

Canada's CEO Top 100

Bloomberg/Getty Images

We have long been fascinated by wealth, and a wealth of data is available about CEO compensation in Canada and the United States. Boards of directors now pay much more attention to how much corporate executives are paid, partly in reaction to scandals at Nortel and Enron, and partly in response to the financial professionals on Wall Street, whose perception was that executive compensation was wildly out of control. The Excel spreadsheet **ch05_MCSP_CanadianCEO.xlsx** lists the total compensation package paid to the top 100 Canadian CEOs in 2010. The average is a staggering $8.4 million. By comparison, in 2010, Canadians working full-time earned an average yearly wage of about $44 000.

a. Prepare a histogram of the full set of 100 compensations. Compute summary statistics (including the five-number summary) and identify any outliers.

b. Remove the largest outlier and prepare another histogram and set of summary statistics. Comment on the shape of the distribution and how the summary statistics have changed.

c. Remove the next three largest values and prepare another histogram. Has the shape of the distribution changed?

d. For comparison (and curiosity), the pay for the top 500 US CEOs (as compiled by *Forbes* magazine) is presented in the second worksheet in the spreadsheet. Prepare a histogram and compute summary statistics for this set of 500 data values. Do the results look similar to those for Canadian CEOs?

e. One way to make a skewed distribution more symmetric is to re-express or transform the data by applying a simple function to all the data values. For distributions that are "right-skewed" (i.e., that have a long right-hand tail), taking the logarithm (base 10 or natural) or the square root is of benefit. Find the natural logarithm of the 500 US CEO salaries and prepare a histogram of the transformed data values. Comment on the shape of the transformed distribution.

Hotel Occupancy Rates

Many properties in the hospitality industry experience strong seasonal fluctuations in demand. To be successful in this industry it is important to anticipate such fluctuations and to understand demand patterns. The file **ch05_MCSP_Occupancy_Rates.xls** contains data on monthly *Hotel Occupancy Rates* (in % capacity) for Honolulu, Hawaii, from January 2000 to December 2004.

Examine the data and prepare a report for the manager of a hotel chain in Honolulu on patterns in *Hotel Occupancy* during this period. Include both numerical summaries and graphical displays and summarize the patterns that you see. Discuss any unusual features of the data and explain them if you can, including a discussion of whether the manager should take these features into account for future planning.

Value and Growth Stock Returns

Investors in the stock market have choices of how aggressive they would like to be with their investments. To help investors, stocks are classified as "growth" or "value" stocks. Growth stocks are generally shares in high quality companies that have demonstrated consistent performance and are expected to continue to do well. Value stocks on the other hand are stocks whose prices seem low compared to their inherent worth (as measured by the book to price ratio). Managers invest in these hoping that their low price is simply an overreaction to recent negative events.[8]

In the data set **ch05_MCSP_Returns.xls**[9] are the monthly returns of 2500 stocks classified as Growth and Value for the time period January 1975 to June 1997. Examine the distributions of the two types of stocks and discuss the advantages and disadvantages of each. Is it clear which type of stock offers the best investment? Discuss briefly.

---

[8] The cynical statistician might say that the manager who invests in growth funds puts his faith in extrapolation, while the value manager is putting his faith in the Law of Averages.

[9] Source: Independence International Associates, Inc. maintains a family of international style indexes covering 22 equity markets. The highest book-to-price stocks are selected one by one from the top of the list. The top half of these stocks become the constituents of the "value index," and the remaining stocks become the "growth index."

MyStatLab **Students! Save time, improve your grades with MyStatLab.**
The Exercises marked in red can be found on MyStatLab. You can practice them as often as you want, and most feature step-by-step guided solutions to help you find the right answer. You'll find a personalized Study Plan available to you too! Data Sets for exercises marked **T** are also available on MyStatLab for formatted technologies.

EXERCISES

1. Statistics in business. Find a histogram that shows the distribution of a variable in a business publication (e.g., *Financial Post, The Economist, The Wall Street Journal*, etc.). **LO❶**

a) Does the article identify the W's?
b) Discuss whether the display is appropriate for the data.
c) Discuss what the display reveals about the variable and its distribution.
d) Does the article accurately describe and interpret the data? Explain.

2. Statistics in business, part 2. Find a graph other than a histogram that shows the distribution of a quantitative variable in a business publication (e.g., *Financial Post, The Economist, The Wall Street Journal*, etc.). **LO❶**

a) Does the article identify the W's?
b) Discuss whether the display is appropriate for the data.
c) Discuss what the display reveals about the variable and its distribution.
d) Does the article accurately describe and interpret the data? Explain.

T 3. University tuition. The histogram shows the distribution of yearly tuitions in 2012–2013 for undergraduate programs in arts and humanities at 66 universities and colleges that are

members of the AUCC (Association of Universities and Colleges of Canada). Write a short description of this distribution (shape, centre, spread, unusual features). **LO❶**

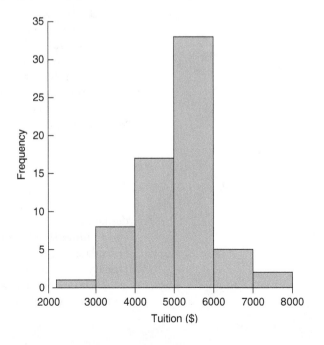

T **4.** Gas prices. Data on the average monthly retail prices for gasoline and fuel oil are available from Statistics Canada's CANSIM database (www5.statcan.gc.ca; cansim). This histogram shows the average monthly retail price of regular unleaded gasoline at self-service filling stations in Vancouver, for a three-year period from Jan. 2010 to Dec. 2012. Describe the shape, centre, spread, and unusual features of this distribution. **LO❶**

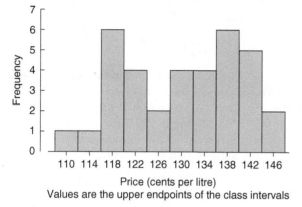

Price (cents per litre)
Values are the upper endpoints of the class intervals

5. Credit card charges. The histogram shows the December charges (in $) for 5000 customers from one marketing segment from a credit card company. (Negative values indicate customers who received more credits than charges during the month.) **LO❶**

a) Write a short description of this distribution (shape, centre, spread, unusual features).

b) Would you expect the mean or the median to be larger? Explain.

c) Which would be a more appropriate summary of the centre, the mean or the median? Explain.

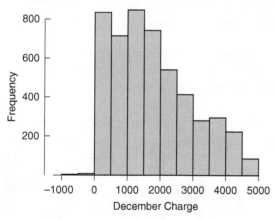

December Charge

T **6.** Vineyards. Adair Vineyard is a 10-acre vineyard in New Paltz, New York. The winery itself is housed in a 200-year-old historic Dutch barn, with the wine cellar on the first floor and the tasting room and gift shop on the second. Since they are relatively small and considering an expansion, they are curious about how their size compares to that of other vineyards. The histogram shows the sizes (in acres) of 36 wineries in upstate New York. **LO❶**

a) Write a short description of this distribution (shape, centre, spread, unusual features).

b) Would you expect the mean or the median to be larger? Explain.

c) Which would be a more appropriate summary of the centre, the mean or the median? Explain.

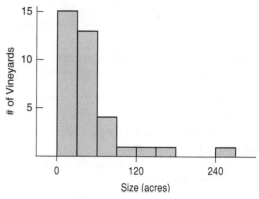

Size (acres)

T **7.** Mutual funds. The histogram displays the 12-month returns (in percent) for a collection of mutual funds in 2007. Give a short summary of this distribution (shape, centre, spread, unusual features). **LO❶**

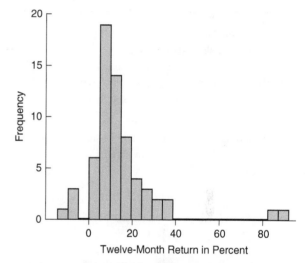

Twelve-Month Return in Percent

T **8.** Car discounts. A researcher, interested in studying gender differences in negotiations, collects data on the prices that men and women pay for new cars. Here is a histogram of the discounts (the amount in $ below the list price) that men and women received at one car dealership for the last 100 transactions (54 men and 46 women). Give a short summary of this distribution (shape, centre, spread, unusual features). What do you think might account for this particular shape? **LO❶**

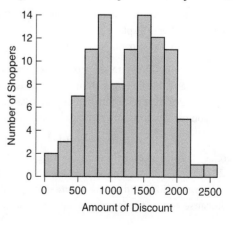

Amount of Discount

9. Mutual funds, part 2. Use the data set of Exercise 7 to answer the following questions. **LO②, LO③**

a) Find the five-number summary for these data.
b) Find appropriate measures of centre and spread for these data.
c) Create a boxplot for these data.
d) What can you see, if anything, in the histogram that isn't clear in the boxplot?

10. Car discounts, part 2. Use the data set of Exercise 8 to answer the following questions. **LO②, LO③**

a) Find the five-number summary for these data.
b) Create a boxplot for these data.
c) What can you see, if anything, in the histogram of Exercise 8 that isn't clear in the boxplot?

11. Vineyards, part 2. Here are summary statistics for the sizes (in acres) of upstate New York vineyards from Exercise 6. **LO③, LO④**

Variable	N	Mean	StDev	Minimum	Q1	Median	Q3	Maximum
Acres	36	46.50	47.76	6	18.50	33.50	55	250

a) From the summary statistics, would you describe this distribution as symmetric or skewed? Explain.
b) From the summary statistics, are there any outliers? Explain.
c) Using these summary statistics, sketch a boxplot. What additional information would you need to complete the boxplot?

12. Graduation. A survey of major universities asked what percentage of incoming first-year students usually graduate "on time" in four years. Use the summary statistics given to answer these questions. **LO③, LO④**

	% on time
Count	48
Mean	68.35
Median	69.90
StdDev	10.20
Min	43.20
Max	87.40
Range	44.20
25th %tile	59.15
75th %tile	74.75

a) Would you describe this distribution as symmetric or skewed?
b) Are there any outliers? Explain.
c) Create a boxplot of these data.

13. Vineyards, again. The data set provided contains the data from Exercises 6 and 11. Create a stem-and-leaf display of the sizes of the vineyards in acres. Point out any unusual features of the data that you can see from the stem-and-leaf. **LO⑤**

14. Gas prices again. The data set provided contains the data from Exercise 4 on the average retail price of gas in Vancouver from Jan. 2010 to Dec. 2012. Round the data to the nearest cent (e.g., 134.7 becomes 135) and create a stem-and-leaf display of the data. Because of the nature of the data, use the following

stems: 11−, 11+, 12−, 12+, 13−, 13+, 14−, and 14+, where 11− means values 110 to 114 and 11+ means values 115 to 119, etc. Point out any unusual features of the data that you can see from the stem-and-leaf display. **LO⑤**

```
11 | 0044
11 | 56667899
12 | 123
12 | 679
13 | 01344
13 | 56777889
14 | 01234
14 |
```

15. Hockey. During his 20 seasons in the National Hockey League, Wayne Gretzky scored 50% more points than anyone else who ever played professional hockey. He accomplished this amazing feat while playing in 280 fewer games than Gordie Howe, the previous record holder. Here are the number of games Gretzky played during each season: **LO③, LO⑤**

79, 80, 80, 80, 74, 80, 80, 79, 64, 78, 73, 78, 74, 45, 81, 48, 80, 82, 82, 70

a) Create a stem-and-leaf display.
b) Sketch a boxplot.
c) Briefly describe this distribution.
d) What unusual features do you see in this distribution? What might explain this?

16. Baseball: Mark McGwire. In his 16-year career as a player in major league baseball, Mark McGwire hit 583 home runs, placing him eighth on the all-time home run list (as of 2008). Here are the number of home runs that McGwire hit for each year from 1986 through 2001: **LO③, LO⑤**

3, 49, 32, 33, 39, 22, 42, 9, 9, 39, 52, 58, 70, 65, 32, 29

a) Create a stem-and-leaf display.
b) Sketch a boxplot.
c) Briefly describe this distribution.
d) What unusual features do you see in this distribution? What might explain this?

17. Gretzky returns. Look once more at data of hockey games played each season by Wayne Gretzky, seen in Exercise 15. **LO④**

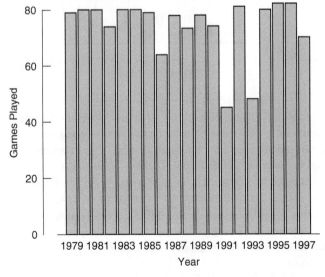

a) Would you use the mean or the median to summarize the centre of this distribution? Why?

b) Without actually finding the mean, would you expect it to be lower or higher than the median? Explain.

c) A student was asked to make a histogram of the data in Exercise 15 and produced the following. Comment.

18. Baseball: Mark McGwire, again. Look once more at data of home runs hit by Mark McGwire during his 16-year career as seen in Exercise 16.

a) Would you use the mean or the median to summarize the centre of this distribution? Why? **LO④**

b) Find the median.

c) Without actually finding the mean, would you expect it to be lower or higher than the median? Explain.

d) A student was asked to make a histogram of the data in Exercise 16 and produced the following. Comment.

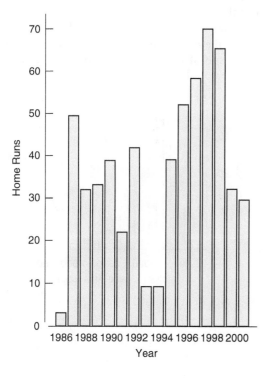

19. Pizza prices. The weekly prices of one brand of frozen pizza over a three-year period in Calgary are provided in the data file. Use the price data to answer the following questions. **LO②, LO③**

a) Find the five-number summary for these data.

b) Find the range and IQR for these data.

c) Create a boxplot for these data.

d) Describe this distribution.

e) Describe any unusual observations.

20. Pizza prices, part 2. The weekly prices of one brand of frozen pizza over a three-year period in Edmonton are provided

in the data file. Use the price data to answer the following questions. **LO②, LO③**

a) Find the five-number summary for these data.

b) Find the range and IQR for these data.

c) Create a boxplot for these data.

d) Describe the shape (centre and spread) of this distribution.

e) Describe any unusual observations.

21. Canadian yearly earnings. Statistics Canada data on the average earnings in 2010 for full-year full-time workers in several census metropolitan areas (CMA) across the country are presented in the following table. There are separate columns for

Census Metropolitan Area	Earnings ($) Females	Earnings ($) Males
St. John's	47 800	67 900
Halifax	45 200	64 200
Québec	47 600	60 600
Sherbrooke	41 300	58 600
Montréal	46 500	60 400
Ottawa-Gatineau	55 500	73 900
Oshawa	45 700	72 600
Toronto	58 200	68 400
Hamilton	49 700	82 200
St. Catharines-Niagara	42 100	64 500
Kitchener-Cambridge-Waterloo	45 800	76 600
London	42 700	64 300
Windsor	46 500	53 400
Winnipeg	43 600	59 500
Regina	54 800	67 800
Saskatoon	46 500	65 200
Calgary	53 200	92 600
Edmonton	50 500	76 600
Vancouver	50 600	64 000
Victoria	48 900	74 300

males and females. Write a report on the earnings by CMA for 2010, for males and females, being sure to include appropriate graphical displays and summary statistics. **LO④, LO⑥**

22. GDP growth. Established in Paris in 1961, the Organisation for Economic Co-operation and Development (OECD) (www.oced.org) collects information on many economic and social aspects of countries around the world. Here are the 2005 gross domestic product (GDP) growth rates (in percentages) of 30 industrialized countries. Write a brief report on the 2005 GDP growth rates of these countries being sure to include appropriate graphical displays and summary statistics. **LO④, LO⑥**

Country	Growth Rate
Turkey	0.074
Czech Republic	0.061
Slovakia	0.061
Iceland	0.055
Ireland	0.055
Hungary	0.041
Korea, Republic of (South Korea)	0.040
Luxembourg	0.040
Greece	0.037
Poland	0.034
Spain	0.034
Denmark	0.032
United States	0.032
Mexico	0.030
Canada	0.029
Finland	0.029
Sweden	0.027
Japan	0.026
Australia	0.025
New Zealand	0.023
Norway	0.023
Austria	0.020
Switzerland	0.019
United Kingdom	0.019
Belgium	0.015
The Netherlands	0.015
France	0.012
Germany	0.009
Portugal	0.004
Italy	0.000

23. Start-up. A start-up company is planning to build a new golf course. For marketing purposes, the company would like to be able to advertise the new course as one of the more difficult courses in British Columbia. One measure of the difficulty of a golf course is its length: the total distance (in yards) from tee to hole for all 18 holes. Here are the histogram and summary statistics for the lengths of all the golf courses in BC.   LO❶, LO❹

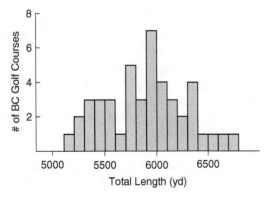

Count	45
Mean	5892.91 yd
StdDev	386.59
Min	5185
Q1	5585.75
Median	5928
Q3	6131
Max	6796

a) What is the range of these lengths?
b) Between what lengths do the central 50% of these courses lie?
c) What summary statistics would you use to describe these data?
d) Write a brief description of these data (shape, centre, and spread).

24. Real estate. A real estate agent has surveyed houses in 20 nearby postal codes in an attempt to put together a comparison for a new property that she would like to put on the market. She knows that the size of the living area of a house is a strong factor in the price, and she'd like to market this house as being one of the biggest in the area. Here is a histogram and summary statistics for the sizes of all the houses in the area.   LO❶, LO❹

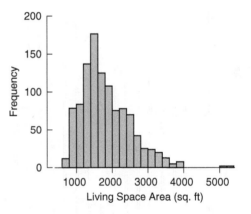

Count	1057
Mean	1819.498 sq. ft
Std Dev	662.9414
Min	672
Q1	1342
Median	1675
Q3	2223
Max	5228
Missing	0

a) What is the range of these sizes?
b) Between what sizes do the central 50% of these houses lie?
c) What summary statistics would you use to describe these data?
d) Write a brief description of these data (shape, centre, and spread).

25. Food sales. Sales (in $) for one week were collected for 18 stores in a food store chain in western Canada. The stores and the towns they are located in vary in size.   LO❸, LO❹, LO❻

a) Make a suitable display of the sales from the data provided.
b) Summarize the central value for sales for this week with a median and mean. Why do they differ?
c) Given what you know about the distribution, which of these measures does the better job of summarizing the stores' sales? Why?
d) Summarize the spread of the sales distribution with a standard deviation and with an IQR.
e) Given what you know about the distribution, which of these measures does the better job of summarizing the spread of stores' sales? Why?
f) If we were to remove the outliers from the data, how would you expect the mean, median, standard deviation, and IQR to change?

26. Insurance profits. Insurance companies don't know whether a policy they've written is profitable until the policy matures (expires). To see how they've performed recently, an analyst looked at mature policies and investigated the net profit to the company (in $).   LO❸, LO❹, LO❻

a) Make a suitable display of the profits from the data provided.
b) Summarize the central value for the profits with a median and mean. Why do they differ?
c) Given what you know about the distribution, which of these measures might do a better job of summarizing the company's profits? Why?
d) Summarize the spread of the profit distribution with a standard deviation and with an IQR.
e) Given what you know about the distribution, which of these measures might do a better job of summarizing the spread in the company's profits? Why?
f) If we were to remove the outliers from the data, how would you expect the mean, median, standard deviation, and IQR to change?

27. iPod failures. MacInTouch (www.macintouch.com/reliability/ipodfailures.html) surveyed readers about the reliability of their iPods. Of the 8926 iPods owned, 7510 were problem-free while the other 1416 failed. Compute the failure rate for each of the 17 iPod models. Produce an appropriate graphical display of the failure rates and briefly describe the distribution. (To calculate the failure rate, divide the number failed by the sum of the number failed and the number OK for each model and then multiply by 100.)   LO❸, LO❻

28. Unemployment. The data set provided contains 2008 unemployment rates for 23 developed countries (www.oecd.org). Produce an appropriate graphical display and briefly describe the distribution of unemployment rates.   LO❸, LO❻

29. Sales. Here are boxplots of the weekly sales (in $) over a two-year period for a regional food store for two locations. Location #1 is a metropolitan area that is known to be residential where shoppers walk to the store. Location #2 is a suburban

area where shoppers drive to the store. Assume that the two locations have similar populations and that the two stores are similar in floor area. Write a brief report discussing what these data show.   LO❶

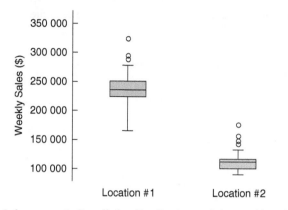

30. Sales, part 2. Recall the distributions of the weekly sales for the regional stores in Exercise 29. Following are boxplots of weekly sales for this same food store chain for three stores of similar size and location for two different provinces: Saskatchewan (SK) and Manitoba (MB). Compare the distribution of sales for the two provinces and describe in a report.   LO❶

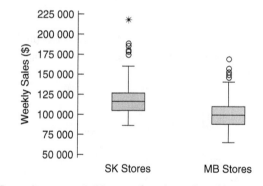

31. Gas prices, part 2. Here are boxplots of weekly gas prices at a service station in Alberta (prices in $ per litre).   LO❶

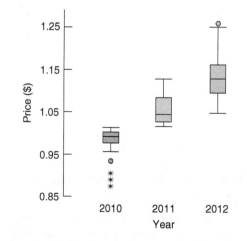

a) Compare the distribution of prices over the three years.
b) In which year were the prices least stable (most volatile)? Explain.

32. Fuel economy. American automobile companies are becoming more motivated to improve the fuel efficiency of the automobiles they produce. It is well known that fuel efficiency is impacted by many characteristics of the car. Describe what these boxplots tell you about the relationship between the number of cylinders a car's engine has and the car's fuel economy (mpg). **LO❶**

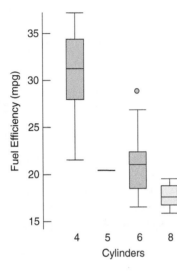

33. Wine prices. The boxplots display case prices (in dollars) of wines produced by vineyards along three of the Finger Lakes in upstate New York. **LO❶**

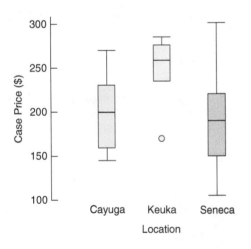

a) Which lake region produces the most expensive wine?
b) Which lake region produces the cheapest wine?
c) In which region are the wines generally more expensive?
d) Write a few sentences describing these prices.

34. Ozone. Ozone levels (in parts per billion, ppb) were recorded at sites in New Jersey monthly between 1926 and 1971. Here are boxplots of the data for each month (over the 46 years) lined up in order (January = 1). **LO❶**

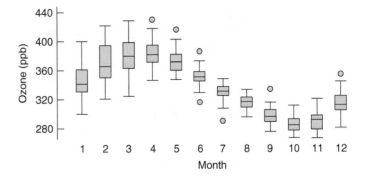

a) In what month was the highest ozone level ever recorded?
b) Which month has the largest IQR?
c) Which month has the smallest range?
d) Write a brief comparison of the ozone levels in January and June.
e) Write a report on the annual patterns you see in the ozone levels.

35. Derby speeds. How fast do horses run? Kentucky Derby winners top 48 kilometres per hour, as shown in the graph. This graph shows the percentage of Kentucky Derby winners that have run *slower* than a given speed. Note that few have won running less than 53 kilometres per hour, but about 95% of the winning horses have run less than 59.5 kilometres per hour. (A cumulative frequency graph like this is called an **ogive**.) **LO❶, LO❸**

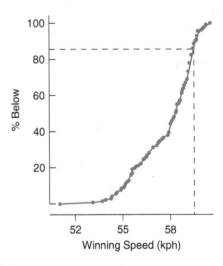

a) Estimate the median winning speed.
b) Estimate the quartiles.
c) Estimate the range and the IQR.
d) Create a boxplot of these speeds.
e) Write a few sentences about the speeds of the Kentucky Derby winners.

36. Mutual funds, part 3. Here is an ogive of the distribution of monthly returns for a group of aggressive (or high growth) mutual funds over a period of 25 years from 1975 to 1999. (Recall from Exercise 35 that an ogive, or cumulative relative frequency graph, shows the percent of cases at or below a certain value. Thus this graph always begins at 0% and ends at 100%.) LO❶, LO❸

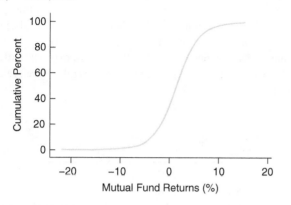

a) Estimate the median.
b) Estimate the quartiles.
c) Estimate the range and the IQR.
d) Create a boxplot of these returns.

37. Test scores. Three Statistics classes all took the same test. Here are histograms of the scores for each class. LO❶

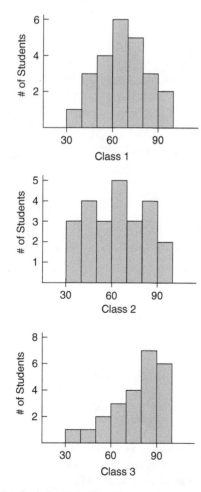

a) Which class had the highest mean score?
b) Which class had the highest median score?

c) For which class are the mean and median most different? Which is higher? Why?
d) Which class had the smallest standard deviation?
e) Which class had the smallest IQR?

38. Test scores, again. Look again at the histograms of test scores for the three Statistics classes in Exercise 37. LO❶

a) Overall, which class do you think performed better on the test? Why?
b) How would you describe the shape of each distribution?
c) Match each class with the corresponding boxplot.

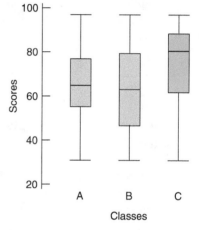

T 39. Quality control. Engineers at a computer production plant tested two methods for accuracy in drilling holes into a PC board. They tested how fast they could set the drilling machine by running 10 boards at each of two different speeds. To assess the results, they measured the distance (in centimetres) from the centre of a target on the board to the centre of the hole. The data and summary statistics are shown in the table. LO❸

	Fast	Slow
	0.000 101	0.000 098
	0.000 102	0.000 096
	0.000 100	0.000 097
	0.000 102	0.000 095
	0.000 101	0.000 094
	0.000 103	0.000 098
	0.000 104	0.000 096
	0.000 102	0.975 600
	0.000 102	0.000 097
	0.000 100	0.000 096
Mean	0.000 102	0.097 647
StdDev	0.000 001	0.308 481

Write a report summarizing the findings of the experiment. Include appropriate visual and verbal displays of the distributions, and make a recommendation to the engineers if they are most interested in the accuracy of the method.

T 40. Fire sale. A real estate agent notices that houses with fireplaces often fetch a premium in the market and wants to assess the difference in sales price of 60 homes that recently sold. The data and summary are shown in the table.   LO❸

No Fireplace	Fireplace
142 212	134 865
206 512	118 007
50 709	138 297
108 794	129 470
68 353	309 808
123 266	157 946
80 248	173 723
135 708	140 510
122 221	151 917
128 440	235 105 000
221 925	259 999
65 325	211 517
87 588	102 068
88 207	115 659
148 246	145 583
205 073	116 289
185 323	238 792
71 904	310 696
199 684	139 079
81 762	109 578
45 004	89 893
62 105	132 311
79 893	131 411
88 770	158 863
115 312	130 490
118 952	178 767
	82 556
	122 221
	84 291
	206 512
	105 363
	103 508
	157 513
	103 861
Mean 116 597.54	7 061 657.74
Median 112 053	136 581

Write a report summarizing the findings of the investigation. Include appropriate visual and verbal displays of the distributions, and make a recommendation to the agent about the average premium that a fireplace is worth in this market.

41. Customer database. A philanthropic organization has a database of millions of donors who they contact by mail to raise money for charities. One of the variables in the database, *Title*, contains the title of the person or persons printed on the address label. The most common are Mr., Ms., Miss, and Mrs., but there are also Ambassador and Mrs., Your Imperial Majesty, and Cardinal, to name a few others. In all there are over 100 different titles, each with a corresponding numeric code. Here are a few of them.

Code	Title
000	MR.
001	MRS.
1002	MR. and MRS.
003	MISS
004	DR.
005	MADAME
006	SERGEANT
009	RABBI
010	PROFESSOR
126	PRINCE
127	PRINCESS
128	CHIEF
129	BARON
130	SHEIK
131	PRINCE AND PRINCESS
132	YOUR IMPERIAL MAJESTY
135	M. ET MME.
210	PROF.
⋮	⋮

An intern who was asked to analyze the organization's fundraising efforts presented these summary statistics for the variable *Title*.   LO❹

Mean	54.41
StdDev	957.62
Median	1
IQR	2
n	94649

a) What does the mean of 54.41 mean?
b) What are the typical reasons that cause measures of centre and spread to be as different as those in this table?
c) Is that why these are so different?

42. CEOs. For each CEO, a code is listed that corresponds to the industry of the CEO's company. Here are a few of the codes and the industries to which they correspond. LO⑦

Industry	Industry Code	Industry	Industry Code
Financial services	1	Energy	12
Food/drink/tobacco	2	Capital goods	14
Health	3	Computers/ communications	16
Insurance	4	Entertainment/ information	17
Retailing	6	Consumer nondurables	18
Forest products	9	Electric utilities	19
Aerospace/defence	11		

A recently hired investment analyst has been assigned to examine the industries and the compensations of the CEOs. To start the analysis, he produces the following histogram of industry codes.

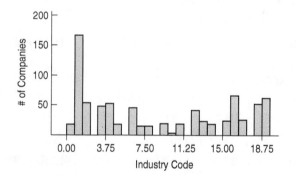

a) What might account for the gaps seen in the histogram?
b) What advice might you give the analyst about the appropriateness of this display?

T 43. Mutual fund types. The 64 mutual funds of Exercise 7 are classified into three types: U.S. Domestic Large Cap Funds, U.S. Domestic Small/Mid Cap Funds, and International Funds. Compare the three-month return of the three types of funds using an appropriate display and write a brief summary of the differences. LO❸

T 44. Car discounts, part 3. The discounts negotiated by the car buyers in Exercise 8 are classified by whether the buyer was Male (code = 0) or Female (code = 1). Compare the discounts of men vs. women using an appropriate display and write a brief summary of the differences. LO❸

45. Houses for sale. Each house listed on the multiple listing service (MLS) is assigned a sequential ID number. A recently hired real estate agent decided to examine the MLS numbers in a recent random sample of homes for sale by one real estate agency in nearby municipalities. To begin the analysis, the agent produces the following histogram of ID numbers. LO⑦

a) What might account for the distribution seen in the histogram?
b) What advice might you give the analyst about the appropriateness of this display?

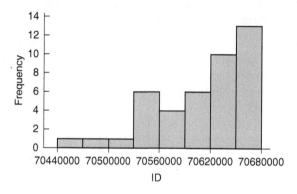

46. Zip codes. Holes-R-Us, an internet company that sells piercing jewelry, keeps transaction records on its sales. At a recent sales meeting, one of the staff presented the following histogram and summary statistics of the zip codes of the last 500 U.S. customers, so that the staff might understand where sales are coming from. Comment on the usefulness and appropriateness of this display. LO⑦

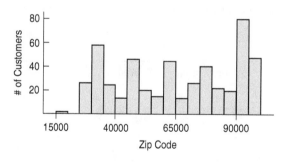

T *47. Hurricanes. Buying insurance for property loss from hurricanes has become increasingly difficult since hurricane Katrina caused record property loss damage. Many companies have refused to renew policies or write new ones. The data set provided contains the total number of hurricanes by every full decade from 1851 to 2000 (from the National Hurricane Center). Some scientists claim that there has been an increase in the number of hurricanes in recent years. LO❻, LO❽

a) Create a histogram of these data.
b) Describe the distribution.

c) Create a time series plot of these data.

d) Discuss the time series plot. Does this graph support the claim of these scientists, at least up to the year 2000?

*48. Hurricanes, part 2. Using the hurricanes data set, examine the number of major hurricanes (category 3, 4, or 5) by every full decade from 1851 to 2000. LO❻, LO❽

a) Create a histogram of these data.

b) Describe the distribution.

c) Create a timeplot of these data.

d) Discuss the timeplot. Does this graph support the claim of scientists that the number of major hurricanes has been increasing (at least up through the year 2000)?

49. Productivity study. The National Center for Productivity releases information on the efficiency of workers. In a recent report, they included the following graph showing a rapid rise in productivity. What questions do you have about this? LO❽

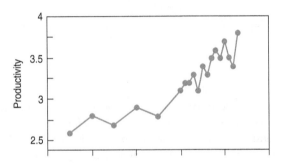

50. Productivity study revisited. A second report by the National Center for Productivity analyzed the relationship between productivity and wages. Comment on the graph they used. LO❽

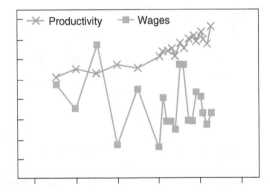

51. Real estate, part 2. The 1057 houses described in Exercise 24 have a mean price of $167 900, with a standard deviation of $77 158. The mean living area is 1819 sq. ft., with a standard deviation of 663 sq. ft. Which is more unusual, a house in that market that sells for $400 000 or a house that has 4000 sq. ft of living area? Explain. LO❾

52. University tuition. The data set provided contains the yearly tuitions in 2012–2013 for undergraduate programs in arts and humanities at 66 universities and colleges, as seen in Exercise 3. Tuition fees are different for Canadian and international students. The mean tuition charged to Canadian students was $5072, with a standard deviation of $939. For international students the mean was $14 427, with a standard deviation of $3758. Which would be more unusual: a university or college with a Canadian student tuition fee of $3000 or one with an international student tuition fee of $7500? Explain. LO❾

53. Food consumption. FAOSTAT, the Food and Agriculture Organization of the United Nations, collects information on the production and consumption of more than 200 food and agricultural products for 200 countries around the world. Here are two tables, one for meat consumption (per capita in kg per year) and one for alcohol consumption (per capita in litres per year). The United States leads in meat consumption with 267.30 kg, while Ireland is the largest alcohol consumer at 55.80 litres. Using z-scores, find which country is the larger consumer of both meat and alcohol together. LO❾

Country	Alcohol	Meat	Country	Alcohol	Meat
Australia	29.56	242.22	Luxembourg	34.32	197.34
Austria	40.46	242.22	Mexico	13.52	126.50
Belgium	34.32	197.34	Netherlands	23.87	201.08
Canada	26.62	219.56	New Zealand	25.22	228.58
Czech Republic	43.81	166.98	Norway	17.58	129.80
Denmark	40.59	256.96	Poland	20.70	155.10
Finland	25.01	146.08	Portugal	33.02	194.92
France	24.88	225.28	Slovakia	26.49	121.88
Germany	37.44	182.82	South Korea	17.60	93.06
Greece	17.68	201.30	Spain	28.05	259.82
Hungary	29.25	179.52	Sweden	20.07	155.32
Iceland	15.94	178.20	Switzerland	25.32	159.72
Ireland	55.80	194.26	Turkey	3.28	42.68
Italy	21.68	200.64	United Kingdom	30.32	171.16
Japan	14.59	93.28	United States	26.36	267.30

54. World Bank. The World Bank, through their Doing Business project (www.doingbusiness.org), ranks nearly 200 economies on the ease of doing business. One of their rankings measures the ease of starting a business and is made up (in part) of the following variables: number of required start-up procedures, average start-up time (in days), and average start-up cost (in % of per capita income). The following table gives the mean and standard deviations of these variables for 95 economies.

	Procedures (#)	Time (Days)	Cost (%)
Mean	7.9	27.9	14.2
SD	2.9	19.6	12.9

Here are the data for three countries.   LO❾

	Procedures	Time	Cost
Spain	10	47	15.1
Guatemala	11	26	47.3
Fiji	8	46	25.3

a) Use z-scores to combine the three measures.
b) Which country has the best environment after combining the three measures? Be careful—a lower rank indicates a better environment to start up a business.

T 55. Personal fitness trainers. Personal fitness training is a growth industry. Trainers' earnings are determined by how many hours a week they train clients. The data set provided gives the number of client-hours per week from two years of records of KIT FIT Personal Training in Vancouver.   LO❹, LO❻

a) Create a histogram of the combined two years of data. Describe the distribution.
b) Create time series plot of the data with a separate line for each year, then describe the trend.
c) Which graphical display seems the more appropriate for these data? Explain.

T 56. Canadian house prices. The MLS Home Price Index (HPI) is a set of indices on residential markets in the territories of participating real estate boards in Canada. The aggregate national index for all home types for the period Jan. 2005 to Dec. 2012 can be found in the data set provided.   LO❻, LO❽

a) Create a histogram of the data and describe the distribution.
*b) Create a time series plot of the data and describe the trend.
c) Which graphical display seems the more appropriate for these data? Explain.

*57. Canadian unemployment rate. The histogram shows the frequency of the monthly Canadian unemployment rates

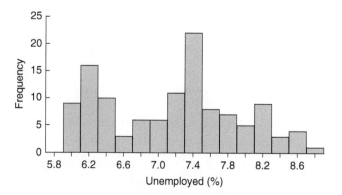

(seasonally adjusted) for the 10-year period from Jan. 2003 to Dec. 2012.   LO❶, LO❽

Here is the time series plot for the same data.

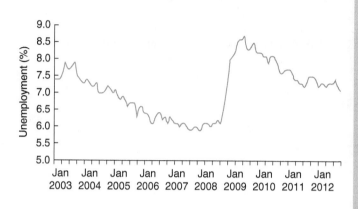

a) What features of the data can you see in the histogram that aren't clear in the time series plot?
b) What features of the data can you see in the time series plot that aren't clear in the histogram?
c) Which graphical display seems the more appropriate for these data? Explain.
d) Write a brief description of unemployment rates in Canada over this time period.

*58. Mutual fund performance. The following histogram displays the monthly returns for a group of mutual funds considered aggressive (or high growth) over a period of 22 years from 1975 to 1997.   LO❻, LO❽

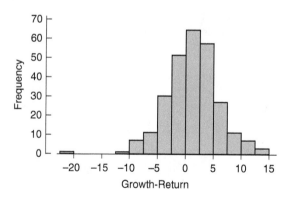

Here is the time series plot for the same data.

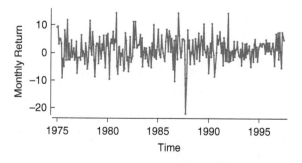

a) What features of the data can you see in the histogram that aren't clear from the time series plot?

b) What features of the data can you see in the time series plot that aren't clear in the histogram?

c) Which graphical display seems the more appropriate for these data? Explain.

d) Write a brief description of monthly returns over this time period.

✔ JUST CHECKING ANSWERS

1. Incomes are probably skewed to the right and not symmetric, making the median the more appropriate measure of centre. The mean will be influenced by the high end of family incomes and not reflect the "typical" family income as well as the median would. It will give the impression that the typical income is higher than it is.

2. An IQR of 9 litres per 100 kilometres would mean that only 50% of the cars get fuel efficiency in an interval 9 litres per 100 kilometres wide. Fuel economy doesn't vary that much; 2 litres per 100 kilometres is reasonable. It seems plausible that 50% of the cars will be within about 8 to 10 litres per 100 kilometres. An IQR of 0.1 litres per 100 kilometres would mean that the fuel efficiency of half the cars varies little from the estimate. It's unlikely that cars, drivers, and driving conditions are that consistent.

3. We'd prefer a standard deviation of two months. Making a consistent product is important for quality. Customers want to be able to count on the MP3 player lasting somewhere close to five years, and a standard deviation of two years would mean that lifespans were highly variable.

Correlation and Linear Regression

6

Niar/Shutterstock

LEARNING OBJECTIVES

1. Analyze a scatterplot to identify possible relationships in bivariate data

2. Calculate and interpret a correlation coefficient

3. Compute and interpret a linear regression equation

4. Use a linear regression equation for prediction

5. Calculate and interpret R-squared

6. Compute and interpret residuals

7. Distinguish between correlation and causation

CONNECTIONS: CHAPTER

In Chapter 5 we learned how to display and describe quantitative data, one variable at a time. In this chapter we learn how to display and assess the relationship between two quantitative variables. This is so important a topic that not only does it have a special name, but it will also be revisited later in the text (Chapter 14). Linear regression is the counterpart to the contingency tables in Chapter 4. You can think of the three Chapters—4, 5, and 6—as a set that cover descriptive statistics for categorical and quantitative data, with one variable or two variables.

RONA

RONA, Inc., Canada's largest retailer of hardware, home renovation, and gardening products, began in 1939, when hardware store operators in Quebec formed a cooperative called Les Marchards en Quincailleries Ltee. to circumvent a monopoly in the hardware supply business. It survived the rise of department store chains through the 1940s and 1950s, and in 1960 a sister company, Quincaillerie Ro-Na Inc., was established. According to popular legend, the name came from the first two letters of the first names of Rolland Dansereau and Napoleon Piotte, the company's first presidents.

Other regional hardware cooperatives sprang up in Canada, but Ro-Na remained inside Quebec. In the 1980s Ro-Na made purchases and alliances, acquiring gardening, interior decorating, and building materials stores, and brought them under one roof as a big-box retailer. Ro-Na and Home Hardware (in Western Canada) formed Alliance RONA Home Inc.

Major changes were also taking place in the U.S. hardware industry, with the rise of Home Depot. The fierce competition between Home Depot and Canadian rivals began in Ontario but only spread to Quebec in 1998.

While Ro-Na's sister company, Home Hardware, continued with small and medium-sized stores, other Canadian chains, such as

Surrey, British Columbia-based Revy Home Centres, Inc., did big-box battle with Home Depot in suburban Toronto. Ro-Na rolled out its own big-box stores (calling them "large surface" stores), but hoped to distinguish them from the competition with great customer service.

During Canada's booming economy in the 1990s home improvement was a flourishing business. Each of the several large Canadian chains needed a strategy to keep market share. Ro-Na chose acquisition. In 1998, the company changed its name to RONA, Inc., opened new stores, and made its first foray into Ontario. By 1999, RONA had almost 500 stores under various banners in eastern Canada, and sales rose to $2.1 billion.

RONA gained a coast-to-coast presence in the 2000s and equalled or surpassed Home Depot in market share, while making sure its stores were noticeably different from the American competitor. RONA, Inc. debuted on the Toronto Stock Exchange in October 2002. The company was now a public corporation, and no longer a cooperative. While RONA and Home Depot were the two biggest contenders in the Canadian hardware market, half the market was still shared by small independent hardware stores, along with the Home Hardware cooperative and Canadian Tire.

RONA's strategy was to have stores in every segment of the market. It would continue to open large-surface stores as well as small neighbourhood stores. It attached RONA to the name of all of its stores. RONA wanted to "take the warehouse out of the warehouse concept." Instead, its stores would offer an enticing shopping experience explained as "Disney meets home improvement." RONA used ideas from other successful chains. And the company strove to please women, who made the majority of home improvement buying decisions. But recent years have also been difficult. A slow recovery following the 2008 world economic crisis, lower consumer confidence, and a slowdown in the housing market have all had a major effect on RONA's growth. The first half of 2011 was a particularly difficult period in the Canadian renovation and construction industry. And in 2012, RONA fended off an unsolicited takeover bid by Lowe's. Currently, RONA has over 800 corporate, franchise, and affiliate retail stores of all sizes, formats, and banners, as well as 14 distribution centres. RONA employed nearly 30 000 people and had sales of $4.9 billion in 2012.

Competition in the sector remains fierce. With new management, store formats, smaller stores, new sales approaches, and a new corporate strategy, the leading company in home renovation is now undergoing its own corporate renovation.

Based on information from www.rona.ca

WHO	Quarter years of financial data
WHAT	RONA's *Sales* and Canadian expenditures on residential *Renovations*
UNITS	Both in $M
WHEN	2002–2012
WHERE	Canada
WHY	To assess RONA's sales relative to the home renovation market

RONA's quarterly sales results fluctuate widely because of the highly seasonal nature of renovation and construction activities. Over 80% of RONA's net annual earnings come from the second and third quarters. Sales in the first quarter are always lowest due to low activity in renovation and construction during the winter. Even in the summer and fall, poor weather has a major impact on sales.

RONA sells to both contractors and homeowners. Perhaps knowing how much Canadians spend on home renovation nationally can help predict RONA's sales. Here's a plot showing RONA's quarterly sales against Statistics Canada's quarterly data on spending for residential renovations.[1]

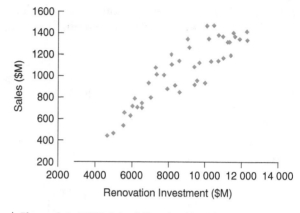

Figure 6.1 RONA's *Sales* ($M) and residential *Renovation Investment*, quarterly, 2002–2012.

If you were asked to summarize this relationship, what would you say? Clearly RONA's sales grew when home renovation spending grew. This plot is an example of a **scatterplot**, which plots one quantitative variable against another. Just by looking at a scatterplot, you can see patterns, trends, relationships, and even the occasional unusual values standing apart from the others. Scatterplots are the best way to start observing the relationship between two *quantitative* variables.

Relationships between variables are often at the heart of what we'd like to learn from data.

◆ *Is consumer confidence related to oil prices?*

◆ *What happens to customer satisfaction as sales increase?*

◆ *Is an increase in money spent on advertising related to sales?*

◆ *What is the relationship between a stock's sales volume and its price?*

Questions such as these relate two quantitative variables and ask whether there is an **association** between them. Scatterplots are the ideal way to *picture* such associations.

Why is this topic the most logical one to follow Chapters 4 and 5? Chapter 4 began with graphs and numerical summaries of categorical data, one variable at a time (the formal term is "univariate"). Then it moved on to contingency tables to examine the association between two categorical variables (called "bivariate" analysis). Similarly, Chapter 5 discussed univariate graphs and numerical summaries of quantitative data, one variable at a time, but stopped short of bivariate descriptive statistics; so there is no analogue to contingency tables. That is the role of scatterplots and correlation and that is why Chapter 6 comes next!

---

[1]http://www5.statcan.gc.ca/cansim/ Table 026–0013 Residential values, by type of investment quarterly

6.1 Looking at Scatterplots

WHO	Years of financial data
WHAT	Official *Exchange Rate* and inflation-adjusted *Price per Barrel* of oil
UNITS	*Exchange Rate* (Canadian $ relative to US $); *Price per Barrel* (US $)
WHEN	1980–2011
WHERE	Canada
WHY	To examine the relationship between exchange rate and price per barrel of oil

The value of the Canadian dollar affects Canadians in a multitude of ways—from pricing of foreign-made products to travel costs to investment returns. For Canadian manufacturers selling products in the United States, a more valuable Canadian dollar can significantly reduce profitability. For example, if the CAD:USD exchange rate is 1.2:1, a $5 USD sale is worth $6 CAD. If the Canadian dollar increases in value to parity (1:1), a $5 USD purchase is now worth only $5 CAD to the manufacturer. This has caused many to argue that the higher Canadian dollar is damaging the Canadian manufacturing sector.

One major driver of the value of the Canadian dollar is oil. Oil from the Alberta oil sands makes up a significant portion of the Canada's total exports. To buy Canadian oil, foreign buyers need to purchase Canadian dollars with foreign

Look for *Direction*: What's the sign—positive, negative, or neither?

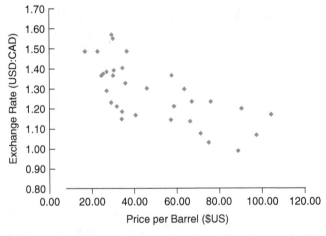

Figure 6.2 Official *Exchange Rate* (Canadian dollar relative to the U.S. dollar; Source: World Bank) vs. Inflation Adjusted *Price Per Barrel* of Oil (in U.S. dollars; Source: U.S. Bureau of Labor Statistics) for the period 1980–2011.

Of course, we could have computed the exchange rate as the U.S. dollar relative to the Canadian dollar. That would mean computing the reciprocal of the exchange rate data presented in Figure 6.2, and then the scatterplot would look like this. It's the same pattern but with positive association. As the price of oil increases, the value of the Canadian dollar increases.

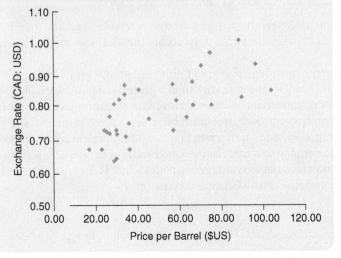

currencies. An increase in the world price of oil increases total exports, subsequently increasing demand for Canadian dollars, driving up the value. To measure the effect of oil prices, we have gathered historical financial data on both oil prices and the value of the Canadian dollar. Figure 6.2 shows a scatterplot of the Inflation Adjusted *Price per Barrel* of Oil (in U.S. dollars) vs. the official *Exchange Rate* (Canadian dollar relative to the U.S. dollar).

Everyone looks at scatterplots. But, if asked, many people would find it hard to say what to look for in a scatterplot. What do *you* see? Try to describe the scatterplot of *Price per Barrel* against *Exchange Rate*.

First, you might say that the **direction** of the association is important. As the price of a barrel of oil goes up, the exchange rate goes down. A pattern that runs from the upper left to the lower right is said to be **negative**.

A pattern running the other way is called **positive**.

The second thing to look for in a scatterplot is its **form**. If there is a straight line relationship, it will appear as a cloud or swarm of points stretched out in a generally consistent, straight form. For example, the scatterplot of oil prices has an underlying **linear** form, although some points stray away from it.

Scatterplots can reveal many different kinds of patterns. Often they will not be straight, but straight line patterns are both the most common and the most useful for statistics.

If the relationship isn't straight, but curves gently, while still increasing or decreasing steadily,  we can often find ways to straighten it out. But

if it curves sharply—up and then down, for example, —then you'll need more advanced methods.

The third feature to look for in a scatterplot is the **strength** of the relationship. At one extreme, do the points appear tightly clustered in a single stream (whether straight, curved, or bending all over the place)? Or, at the other extreme, do the points seem to be so variable and spread out that we can barely discern any trend or pattern? The oil prices plot shows moderate scatter around a generally straight form. That indicates that there's a moderately strong linear relationship between price and exchange rate.

Finally, always look for the unexpected. Often the most interesting discovery in a scatterplot is something you never thought to look for. One example of such a surprise is an unusual observation, or **outlier,** standing away from the overall pattern of the scatterplot. Such a point is almost always interesting and deserves special attention. You may see entire clusters or subgroups that stand away or show a trend in a different direction than the rest of the plot. That should raise questions about why they are different. They may be a clue that you should split the data into subgroups instead of looking at them all together.

> Look for **Form**: Straight, curved, something exotic, or no pattern?

> Look for **Strength**: How much scatter?

> Look for **Unusual Features**: Are there unusual observations or subgroups?

6.2 Assigning Roles to Variables in Scatterplots

Scatterplots were among the first modern mathematical displays. The idea of using two axes at right angles to define a field on which to display values can be traced back to René Descartes (1596–1650), and the playing field he defined in this way is formally called a *Cartesian plane*, in his honour.

The two axes Descartes specified characterize the scatterplot. The axis that runs up and down is, by convention, called the *y*-axis, and the one that runs from side to side is called the *x*-axis. These terms are standard.[2]

To make a scatterplot of two quantitative variables, assign one to the *y*-axis and the other to the *x*-axis. As with any graph, be sure to label the axes clearly, and indicate the scales of the axes with numbers. Scatterplots display *quantitative* variables.

Library of congress

Descartes was a philosopher, famous for his statement *cogito, ergo sum:* I think, therefore I am.

[2] The axes are also called the "ordinate" and the "abscissa"—but we can never remember which is which because statisticians don't generally use these terms. In Statistics (and in all statistics computer programs) the axes are generally called "*x*" (abscissa) and "*y*" (ordinate) and are usually labelled with the names of the corresponding variables.

Each variable has units, and these should appear with the display—usually near each axis. Each point is placed on a scatterplot at a position that corresponds to values of these two variables. Its horizontal location is specified by its x-value, and its vertical location is specified by its y-value variable. Together, these are known as *coordinates* and written (x, y).

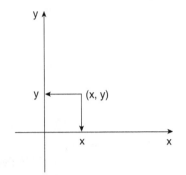

Scatterplots made by computer programs often do not—and usually should not—show the *origin*, the point at $x = 0$, $y = 0$ where the axes meet. If both variables have values near or on both sides of zero, then the origin will be part of the display. If the values are far from zero, though, there's no reason to include the origin. In fact, it's far better to focus on the part of the Cartesian plane that contains the data. In our example about oil prices, the exchange rate was, of course, nowhere near zero, so the scatterplot in Figure 6.2 has axes that don't quite meet.

Which variable should go on the x-axis and which on the y-axis? What we want to know about the relationship can tell us how to make the plot. We often have questions such as:

◆ *Is RONA's employee satisfaction related to productivity?*
◆ *Are increased sales at RONA's reflected in the share price?*
◆ *What other factors besides residential renovations are related to RONA's sales?*

In all of these examples, one variable plays the role of the **explanatory** variable or predictor variable, while the other takes on the role of the **response variable.** We place the explanatory variable on the x-axis and the response variable on the y-axis. When you make a scatterplot, you can assume that those who view it will think this way, so choose which variables to assign to which axes carefully.

The roles that we choose for variables have more to do with how we *think* about them than with the variables themselves. Just placing a variable on the x-axis doesn't necessarily mean that it explains or predicts *anything*, and the variable on the y-axis may not respond to it in any way. We plotted *Exchange Rate* against *Price per Barrel* thinking that as the price per barrel increases, the exchange rate would decrease. But maybe changing the exchange rate would increase the price of oil. If we were examining that option, we might choose to plot *Exchange Rate* as the explanatory variable and *Price per Barrel* as the response variable.

Perhaps an easier example to understand is the relationship between *Height* and *Weight* of young people. As a person grows taller, he/she gains weight. It makes more sense to think of *Height* explaining *Weight* than the other way around. In that case, we would be thinking that gaining weight might increase one's height. That has been a failed experiment in North America, hence the problems with obesity!

The x- and y-variables are sometimes referred to as the **independent** and **dependent** variables, respectively. The idea is that the y-variable *depends* on the

❗ NOTATION ALERT:
So x and y are reserved letters as well, but not just for labelling the axes of a scatterplot. In Statistics, the assignment of variables to the x- and y-axes (and choice of notation for them in formulas) often conveys information about their roles as predictor or response.

Since the y-axis variable will be the outcome, that is, what happened, and the x-axis variable will be the predictor or explanation, here's a suggestion on how to remember which is which: "x" "explains" "why" "y" happened. It's a bit corny, but it works!

x-variable and the *x*-variable acts *independently* to make *y* respond. These names, however, conflict with other uses of the same terms in Statistics. Instead, we'll sometimes use the terms "explanatory" or "predictor variable" and "response variable" when we're discussing roles, but we'll often just say *x-variable* and *y-variable*.

6.3 Understanding Correlation

The Vancouver International Airport Authority (YVR) recently undertook a study to examine how energy usage was related to various factors such as outside temperature, total area of the airport (since airports are always expanding!), and the number of passengers categorized as domestic, transborder (U.S.), and international. Data were collected on a monthly basis and summarized into quarterly totals. Of

WHO	Quarter years of YVR data
WHAT	*Energy Use* and total *Passengers*
UNITS	*Energy Use* (thousands of kWh) and total *Passengers* (thousands)
WHEN	1997–2010
WHERE	YVR (Vancouver International Airport Authority)
WHY	To examine the relationship between energy use and number of passengers in order to forecast and budget future energy costs

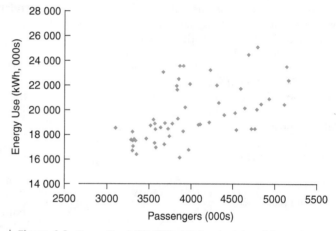

Figure 6.3 *Energy Use* at YVR (kWh, 000s) and number of *Passengers* (000s), 1997 to 2010.

particular interest is how Energy Use and Total Passengers are related to each other. Figure 6.3 shows the scatterplot.

As you might expect, energy use and passenger count tend to rise and fall together. There is a clear positive association and, the scatterplot looks linear. But how strong is the association? If you had to put a number (say, between 0 and 1) on the strength of the association, what would it be? Your measure shouldn't depend on the choice of units for the variables. After all, if the data had been recorded in hundreds of kilowatt hours, or millions of passengers, the scatterplot would look the same. The direction, form, and strength won't change, so neither should our measure of the association's strength.

We saw a way to remove the units in the previous chapter. We can standardize each of the variables finding $z_x = \left(\dfrac{x - \bar{x}}{s_x} \right)$ and $z_y = \left(\dfrac{y - \bar{y}}{s_y} \right)$. With these, we can compute a measure of strength that you've probably heard of: the **correlation coefficient**:

$$r = \frac{\sum z_x z_y}{n - 1}$$

Keep in mind that the *x*'s and *y*'s are paired. For each quarter, we have a measure of energy use and a passenger count. To find the correlation we multiply each standardized value by the standardized value it is paired with and add up those *cross-products*. Then we divide the total by the number of pairs minus one, $n - 1$.[3]

For *Energy Use* and *Passengers*, the correlation coefficient is 0.54.

There are alternative formulas for the correlation in terms of the variables x and y. Here are two of the more common:

$$r = \frac{\sum (x - \bar{x})(y - \bar{y})}{\sqrt{\sum (x - \bar{x})^2 (y - \bar{y})^2}} = \frac{\sum (x - \bar{x})(y - \bar{y})}{(n - 1)s_x s_y}.$$

These formulas can be more convenient for calculating correlation by hand, but the form given using z-scores is best for understanding what correlation means.

Correlation Conditions

Finding the correlation coefficient by hand

To find the correlation coefficient by hand, we'll use a formula in original units, rather than z-scores. This will save us the work of having to standardize each individual data value first. Start with the summary statistics for both variables: $\bar{x}$, $\bar{y}$, s_x, and s_y. Then find the deviations as we did for the standard deviation, but now in both x and y: $(x - \bar{x})$ and $(y - \bar{y})$. For each data pair, multiply these deviations together: $(x - \bar{x}) \times (y - \bar{y})$. Add the products up for all data pairs. Finally, divide the sum by the product of $(n - 1) \times s_x \times s_y$ to get the correlation coefficient.

Here we go.

Suppose the data pairs are:

x	6	10	14	19	21
y	5	3	7	8	12

Then $\bar{x} = 14$, $\bar{y} = 7$, $s_x = 6.20$, and $s_y = 3.39$

Deviations in x	Deviations in y	Product
$6 - 14 = -8$	$5 - 7 = -2$	$-8 \times -2 = 16$
$10 - 14 = -4$	$3 - 7 = -4$	16
$14 - 14 = 0$	$7 - 7 = 0$	0
$19 - 14 = 5$	$8 - 7 = 1$	5
$21 - 14 = 7$	$12 - 7 = 5$	35

Add up the products: $16 + 16 + 0 + 5 + 35 = 72$

Finally, we divide by $(n - 1) \times s_x \times s_y = (5 - 1) \times 6.20 \times 3.39 = 84.07$

The ratio is the correlation coefficient:

$$r = 72/84.07 = 0.856$$

Correlation measures the strength of the *linear* association between two *quantitative* variables. Before you use correlation, you must check three *conditions*:

◆ **Quantitative Variables Condition:** Correlation applies only to quantitative variables. Don't apply correlation to categorical data masquerading as quantitative. Check that you know the variables' units and what they measure.

◆ **Linearity Condition:** Sure, you can *calculate* a correlation coefficient for any pair of variables. But correlation measures the strength only of the *linear* association and will be misleading if the relationship is not straight enough. What is "straight enough"? This question may sound too informal for a statistical condition, but that's really the point. We can't verify whether a relationship is linear or not. Very few relationships between variables are perfectly linear, even in theory, and scatterplots of real data are never perfectly straight. How nonlinear looking would the scatterplot have to be to fail the condition? This is a judgment call that you just have to think about. Do you think that the underlying relationship is curved? If so, then summarizing its strength with a correlation would be misleading.

◆ **Outlier Condition:** Unusual observations can distort the correlation and can make an otherwise small correlation look big or, on the other hand, hide a large correlation. It can even give an otherwise positive association a negative correlation coefficient (and vice versa). When you see an outlier, it's often a good idea to report the correlation both with and without the point.

Each of these conditions is easy to check with a scatterplot. Many correlations are reported without supporting data or plots. You should still think about the conditions. You should be cautious in interpreting (or accepting others' interpretations of) the correlation when you can't check the conditions for yourself.

---

[3] The same $n - 1$ we used for calculating the standard deviation.

✓ JUST CHECKING

For the years 1992 to 2002, the quarterly stock price of the semiconductor companies Cypress and Intel have a correlation of 0.86.

1 Before drawing any conclusions from the correlation, what would you like to see? Why?

2 If your co-worker tracks the same prices in euros, how will this change the correlation? Will you need to know the exchange rate between euros and U.S. dollars to draw conclusions?

3 If you standardize both prices, how will this affect the correlation?

4 In general, if on a given day the price of Intel is relatively low, is the price of Cypress likely to be relatively low as well?

5 If on a given day the price of Intel shares is high, is the price of Cypress shares definitely high as well?

GUIDED EXAMPLE | Customer Spending

A major credit card company sends an incentive to its best customers in hope that the customers will use the card more. They wonder how often they can offer the incentive. Will repeated offerings of the incentive result in repeated increased credit card use?

To examine this question, an analyst took a random sample of 184 customers from their highest use segment and investigated the charges in the two months in which the customers had received the incentive.

PLAN

Setup State the objective. Identify the quantitative variables to examine. Report the time frame over which the data have been collected and define each variable. (State the W's.)

Our objective is to investigate the association between the amount that a customer charges in the two months in which they received an incentive. The customers have been randomly selected from among the highest use segment of customers. The variables measured are the total credit card charges (in $) in the two months of interest.

✓ **Quantitative Variable Condition.** Both variables are quantitative. Both charges are measured in dollars.

Make the scatterplot and clearly label the axes to identify the scale and units.

Because we have two quantitative variables measured on the same cases, we can make a scatterplot.

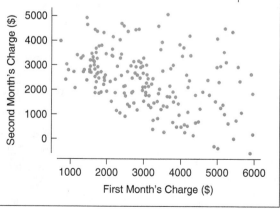

	Check the conditions.	✓ **Linearity Condition.** The scatterplot is straight enough. ✓ **Outlier Condition.** There are no obvious outliers.
DO	**Mechanics** Once the conditions are satisfied, calculate the correlation with technology.	The correlation is −0.391. The negative correlation coefficient confirms the impression from the scatterplot.
REPORT	**Conclusion** Describe the direction, form, and the strength of the plot, along with any unusual points or features. Be sure to state your interpretation in the proper context.	MEMO: **Re: Credit Card Spending** We have examined some of the data from the incentive program. In particular, we looked at the charges made in the first two months of the program. We noted that there was a negative association between charges in the second month and charges in the first month. The correlation was −0.391, which is only moderately strong, and indicates substantial variation. We've concluded that although the observed pattern is negative, these data do not allow us to find the causes of this behaviour. It is likely that some customers were encouraged by the offer to increase their spending in the first month, but then returned to former spending patterns. It is possible that others didn't change their behaviour until the second month of the program, increasing their spending at that time. Without data on the customers' pre-incentive spending patterns it would be hard to say more. We suggest further research, and we suggest that the next trial extend for a longer period of time to help determine whether the patterns seen here persist.

Correlation Properties

Because correlation is so widely used as a measure of association, it's a good idea to remember some of its basic properties. Here's a useful list of facts about the correlation coefficient:

◆ **The sign of a correlation coefficient gives the direction of the association.**

◆ **Correlation is always between −1 and +1.** Correlation *can* be exactly equal to −1.0 or +1.0, but watch out. These values are unusual in real data because they mean that all the data points fall *exactly* on a single straight line.

◆ **Correlation treats *x* and *y* symmetrically.** The correlation of *x* with *y* is the same as the correlation of *y* with *x*.

◆ **Correlation has no units.** This fact can be especially important when the data's units are somewhat vague to begin with (customer satisfaction, worker efficiency, productivity, and so on).

◆ **Correlation is not affected by changes in the centre or scale of either variable.** Changing the units or baseline of either variable has no effect on the correlation coefficient because the correlation depends only on the z-scores.

◆ **Correlation measures the strength of the *linear* association between the two variables.** Variables can be strongly associated but still have a small correlation if the association is not linear.

◆ **Correlation is sensitive to unusual observations.** A single outlier can make a small correlation large or make a large one small.

> **How strong is strong?** Be careful when using the terms "weak," "moderate," or "strong," because there's no agreement on exactly what those terms mean. The same numerical correlation might be strong in one context and weak in another. You might be thrilled to discover a correlation of 0.7 between an economic index and stock market prices, but finding "only" a correlation of 0.7 between a drug treatment and blood pressure might be viewed as a failure by a pharmaceutical company. Using general terms like "weak," "moderate," or "strong" to describe a linear association can be useful, but be sure to report the correlation and show a scatterplot so others can judge for themselves.
>
> It is very difficult to estimate the numerical correlation by eye. See Exercises 7 and 8.

Correlation Tables

Sometimes you'll see the correlations between each pair of variables in a data set arranged in a table. The rows and columns of the table name the variables, and the cells hold the correlations.

Correlation tables are compact and give a lot of summary information at a glance. They can be an efficient way to start to look at a large data set. The diagonal cells of a correlation table always show correlations of exactly 1.000, and the upper half of the table is symmetrically the same as the lower half (can you see why?), so by convention, only the lower half is shown. A table like this can be convenient, but be sure to check for linearity and unusual observations or the correlations in the table may be misleading or meaningless. Can you be sure, looking at Table 6.1, that the variables are linearly associated? Correlation tables are often produced by statistical software packages. Fortunately, these same packages often offer simple ways to make all the scatterplots you need to look at.[4]

You can also call a correlation table a correlation matrix if you want a more impressive-sounding term.

	Volume	Close	Interest Rate	Unemployment Rate
Volume	1.000			
Close	0.187	1.000		
Interest Rate	0.337	0.750	1.000	
Unemployment Rate	−0.381	−0.504	−0.924	1.000

Table 6.1 A correlation table for variables measured monthly during the period 2006 through 2012. Volume = number of shares of RONA traded, Close = closing price of RONA stock, Interest Rate = prevailing Bank of Canada prime interest rate, Unemployment Rate = in Canada, as a percent.

---

[4] A table of scatterplots arranged just like a correlation table is sometimes called a *scatterplot matrix*, or SPLOM, and is easily created using a statistics package.

Crystal Kirk/Shutterstock

6.4 Lurking Variables and Causation

An educational researcher finds a strong association between height and reading ability among elementary school students in a nationwide survey. Taller children tend to have higher reading scores. Does that mean that students' height *causes* their reading scores to go up? No matter how strong the correlation is between two variables, there's no simple way to show from observational data that one variable causes the other. A high correlation just increases the temptation to think and to say that the *x*-variable *causes* the *y*-variable. Just to make sure, let's repeat the point again.

No matter how strong the association, no matter how large the *r* value, no matter how straight the form, there is no way to conclude from a high correlation *alone* that one variable causes the other. There's always the possibility that some third variable—a **lurking variable**—is affecting both of the variables you have observed. In the reading score example, you may have already guessed that the lurking variable is the age of the child. Older children tend to be taller and have stronger reading skills. But even when the lurking variable isn't as obvious, resist the temptation to think that a high correlation implies causation. Here's another example.

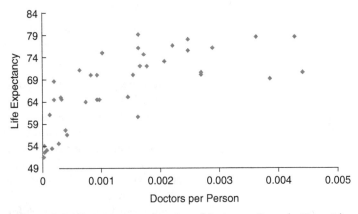

Figure 6.4 Life Expectancy and numbers of Doctors per Person in 40 countries shows a fairly strong, positive linear relationship with a correlation of 0.705.

The scatterplot in Figure 6.4 shows the *Life Expectancy* (average of men and women, in years) for each of 40 countries of the world, plotted against the number of *Doctors per Person* in each country. The strong positive association (*r* = 0.705) seems to confirm our expectation that more *Doctors per Person* improves health care, leading to longer lifetimes and a higher *Life Expectancy*. Perhaps we should send more doctors to developing countries to increase life expectancy.

If we increase the number of doctors, will the life expectancy increase? That is, would adding more doctors *cause* greater life expectancy? Could there be another explanation of the association? Figure 6.5 shows another scatterplot. *Life Expectancy* is still the response, but this time the predictor variable is not the number of doctors, but the number of *Televisions per Person* in each country. The positive association in this scatterplot looks even *stronger* than the association in the previous plot. If we wanted to calculate a correlation, we should straighten the plot first, but even from this plot, it's clear that higher life expectancies are associated with more televisions per person. Should we conclude that increasing the number of televisions extends lifetimes? If so, we should send televisions instead of doctors to developing countries. Not only is the association with life expectancy stronger, but televisions are cheaper than doctors.

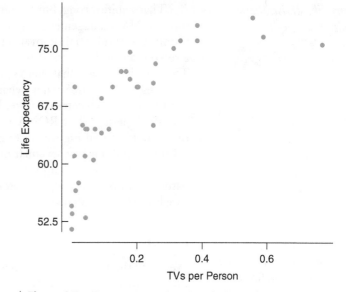

Figure 6.5 Life Expectancy and number of Televisions per Person shows a strong, positive (although clearly not linear) relationship.

What's wrong with this reasoning? Maybe we were a bit hasty earlier when we concluded that doctors *cause* greater life expectancy. Maybe there's a lurking variable here. Countries with higher standards of living have both longer life expectancies *and* more doctors. Could higher living standards cause changes in the other variables? If so, then improving living standards might be expected to prolong lives, increase the number of doctors, and increase the number of televisions. From this example, you can see how easy it is to fall into the trap of mistakenly inferring causality from a correlation. For all we know, doctors (or televisions) *do* increase life expectancy. But we can't tell that from data like these no matter how much we'd like to. Resist the temptation to conclude that *x* causes *y* from a correlation, no matter how obvious that conclusion seems to you.

6.5 The Linear Model

Let's return to the relationship between RONA's sales and home renovation expenditures between 2002 and 2012. In Figure 6.1 (repeated here) we saw a strong, positive, linear relationship, so we can summarize its strength with a correlation. For this relationship, the correlation is 0.885.

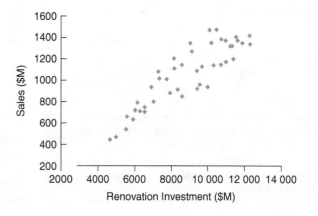

That's quite strong, but the strength of the relationship is only part of the picture. RONA's management might want to predict sales based on Statistics Canada's estimate of residential renovation expenditures for the next four quarters. That's a reasonable business question, but to answer it we'll need a model for the trend. The correlation says that there seems to be a strong linear association between the variables, but it doesn't tell us what that association is.

Of course, we can say more. We can model the relationship with a line and give the equation. For RONA, we can find a linear model to describe the relationship we saw in Figure 6.1 between RONA's *Sales* and residential *Renovations*. A **linear model** is just an equation of a straight line through the data. The points in the scatterplot don't all line up, but a straight line can summarize the general pattern with only a few parameters. This model can help us understand how the variables are associated.

Residuals

> **NOTATION ALERT:**
> "Putting a hat on it" is standard Statistics notation to indicate that something has been predicted by a model. Whenever you see a hat over a variable name or symbol, you can assume it is the predicted version of that variable or symbol.

We know the model won't be perfect. No matter what line we draw, it won't go through many of the points. The best line might not even hit any of the points. Then how can it be the "best" line? We want to find the line that somehow comes *closer* to all the points than any other line. Some of the points will be above the line and some below. A linear model can be written as $\hat{y} = b_0 + b_1 x$, where b_0 and b_1 are numbers estimated from the data and $\hat{y}$ (pronounced y-hat) is the **predicted value**. We use the *hat* to distinguish the predicted value from the observed value y. The difference between these two is called the **residual:**

$$e = y - \hat{y}.$$

> A *negative* residual means the predicted value is too big—an overestimate. A *positive* residual shows the model makes an underestimate. These may seem backwards at first.

The residual value tells us how far the model's prediction is from the observed value at that point. To find the residuals, we always subtract the predicted values from the observed ones.

Our question now is how to find the right line.

The Line of "Best Fit"

When we draw a line through a scatterplot, some residuals are positive, and some are negative. We can't assess how well the line fits by adding up all the residuals—the positive and negative ones would just cancel each other out. We need to find the line that's closest to all the points, and to do that, we need to make all the distances positive. We faced the same issue when we calculated a standard deviation to measure spread. And we deal with it the same way here: by squaring the residuals to make them positive. The sum of all the squared residuals tells us how well the line we drew fits the data— the smaller the sum, the better the fit. A different line will produce a different sum, maybe bigger, maybe smaller. The **line of best fit** is the line for which the sum of the squared residuals is smallest—often called the **least squares line**.

> **Who Was First?**
> French mathematician Adrien-Marie Legendre was the first to publish the "least squares" solution to the problem of fitting a line to data when the points don't all fall exactly on the line. The main challenge was how to distribute the errors "fairly." After considerable thought, he decided to minimize the sum of the squares of what we now call the residuals. After Legendre published his paper in 1805, Carl Friedrich Gauss, the German mathematician and astronomer, claimed he had been using the method since 1795 and, in fact, had used it to calculate the orbit of the asteroid Ceres in 1801. Gauss later referred to the "least squares" solution as *"our* method" (principium *nostrum*), which certainly didn't help his relationship with Legendre.

This line has the special property that the variation of the data around the model, as seen in the residuals, is the smallest it can be for any straight line model for these data. No other line has this property. Speaking mathematically, we say that this line minimizes the sum of the squared residuals. You might think that finding this "least squares line" would be difficult. Surprisingly, it's not, although it was an exciting mathematical discovery when Legendre published it in 1805.

Other criteria for "best fit" are theoretically possible. We have chosen to minimize squared residuals, that is, squared vertical distances from data points to the line. But, mathematically, the shortest distance from a point to a line is the perpendicular. There is also the horizontal distance from a data point to the line. Putting the vertical and horizontal distances together makes a triangle, so a creative criterion would be the minimum area of all the formed triangles. Of course, none of these other criteria work in the context of the linear model we have developed here.

6.6 Correlation and the Line

Any straight line can be written as:

$$y = b_0 + b_1 x.$$

If we were to plot all the (x, y) pairs that satisfy this equation, they'd fall exactly on a straight line. We'll use this form for our linear model. Of course, with real data, the points won't all fall on the line. So, we write our model as $\hat{y} = b_0 + b_1 x$, using $\hat{y}$ for the predicted values, because it's the predicted values (not the data values) that fall on the line. If the model is a good one, the data values will scatter closely around it.

For the RONA sales data, the line is:

$$\widehat{Sales} = 12.13 + 0.117 \, Renovations$$

What does this mean? The **slope** 0.117 says that we can expect a year in which residential renovation spending is 1 million dollars higher to be one in which RONA sales will be about 0.117 $M ($117,000) higher. Slopes are always expressed in y-units per x-units. They tell you how the response variable changes for a one unit step in the predictor variable. So we'd say that the slope is 0.117 million dollars of *Sales* per million dollars of *Renovations*.

The **intercept**, 12.13, is the value of the line when the x-variable is zero. What does it mean here? The intercept often serves just as a starting value for our predictions. We don't interpret it unless a 0 value for the predictor variable would really mean something under the circumstances. The RONA model is based on quarters in which spending on residential renovation is between 4 and 14 billion dollars. It's unlikely to be appropriate if there were no such spending at all. In this case, we wouldn't interpret the intercept.

How do we find the slope and intercept of the least squares line? The formulas are simple. The model is built from the summary statistics we've used before. We'll need the correlation (to tell us the strength of the linear association), the standard deviations (to give us the units), and the means (to tell us where to locate the line).

The slope of the line is computed as:

$$b_1 = r \frac{s_y}{s_x}.$$

We've already seen that the correlation tells us the sign and the strength of the relationship, so it should be no surprise to see that the slope inherits this sign as well. If the correlation is positive, the scatterplot runs from lower left to upper right, and the slope of the line is positive.

Correlations don't have units, but slopes do. How x and y are measured—what units they have—doesn't affect their correlation, but does change the slope. The slope gets its units from the ratio of the two standard deviations. Each standard deviation has the units of its respective variable. So, the units of the slope are a ratio, too, and are always expressed in units of y per unit of x.

✔ JUST CHECKING

A scatterplot of sales per month (in thousands of dollars) vs. number of employees for all the outlets of a large computer chain shows a relationship that is straight, with only moderate scatter and no outliers. The correlation between *Sales* and *Employees* is 0.85, and the equation of the least squares model is:

$$\widehat{Sales} = 9.564 + 122.74 \, Employees$$

6 What does the slope of 122.74 mean?

7 What are the units of the slope?

8 The outlet in Edmonton has 10 more employees than the outlet in Calgary. How much more *Sales* do you expect it to have?

RONA

Summary statistics:

> *Sales*: $\bar{y} = 1049.15$; $s_y = 288.4$
>
> *Improvements*: $\bar{x} = 8833.4$; $s_x = 2175.3$
>
> Correlation = 0.885

So, $b_1 = r \dfrac{s_y}{s_x} = (0.885) \dfrac{288.4}{2175.3}$

> $= 0.117$
>
> ($M Sales per $M Improvement expenditures)

And

$b_0 = \bar{y} - b_1 \bar{x} = 1049.15 - (0.117)8833.4 = 15.64$

The equation from the computer output has slope 0.117 and intercept 12.13. The differences are due to rounding error. We've shown the calculation using rounded summary statistics, but if you are doing this by hand, you should always keep all digits in intermediate steps.

How do we find the intercept? If you had to predict the y-value for a data point whose x-value was average, what would you say? The best fit line predicts $\bar{y}$ for points whose x-value is $\bar{x}$. Putting that into our equation and using the slope we just found gives:

$$\bar{y} = b_0 + b_1 \bar{x}$$

and we can rearrange the terms to find:

$$b_0 = \bar{y} - b_1 \bar{x}$$

It's easy to use the estimated linear model to predict RONA *Sales* for any amount of national spending on residential *Renovations*. For example, in the second quarter of 2012 the total was $12 268(M). To estimate RONA *Sales*, we substitute this value for x in the model:

$$\widehat{Sales} = 12.13 + 0.117 \times 12\,268 = 1447.5$$

Sales actually were 1417.1 ($M), so the residual of $1417.1 - 1447.5 = -30.4$ ($M) tells us how much worse RONA did than the model predicted.

Least squares lines are commonly called **regression lines.** Although this name is an accident of history (as we'll soon see), "regression" almost always means "the linear model fit by least squares." Clearly, regression and correlation are closely related. We'll need to check the same condition for regression as we did for correlation:

1. **Quantitative Variables Condition**

2. **Linearity Condition**

3. **Outlier Condition**

A little later in the chapter we'll add two more.

Understanding Regression from Correlation

The slope of a regression line depends on the units of both x and y. Its units are the units of y per unit of x. The units are expressed in the slope because $b_1 = r \dfrac{s_y}{s_x}$.

The correlation has no units, but each standard deviation contains the units of its respective variable. For our regression of RONA *Sales* on home *Renovations*, the slope was millions of dollars of sales *per* million dollars of renovation expenditure.

It can be useful to see what happens to the regression equation if we were to standardize both the predictor and response variables and regress z_y on z_x. For both these standardized variables, the standard deviation is 1 and the means are zero. That means that the slope is just r, and the intercept is 0 (because both $\bar{y}$ and $\bar{x}$ are now 0).

This gives us the simple equation for the regression of standardized variables:

$$\hat{z}_y = rz_x.$$

Although we don't usually standardize variables for regression, it can be useful to think about what this means. Thinking in z-scores is a good way to understand what the regression equation is doing. The equation says that for every standard deviation we deviate from the mean in x, we predict that y will be r standard deviations away from the mean in y.

Let's be more specific. For the RONA example, the correlation is 0.885. So, we know immediately that:

$$\hat{z}_{Sales} = 0.885\, z_{Renovations}.$$

6.7 Regression to the Mean

Suppose you were told that a new male student was about to join the class and you were asked to guess his height in inches. What would be your guess? A good guess would be the mean height of male students. Now suppose you are also told that this student had a grade point average (GPA) of 3.9—about 2 SDs above the mean GPA. Would that change your guess? Probably not. The correlation between GPA and height is near 0, so knowing the GPA value doesn't tell you anything and doesn't move your guess. (And the standardized regression equation, $\hat{z}_y = rz_x$, tells us that as well, since it says that we should move 0×2 SDs from the mean.)

On the other hand, if you were told that, measured in centimetres, the student's height was 2 SDs above the mean, you'd know his height in inches. There's a perfect correlation between *Height* in inches and *Height* in centimetres ($r = 1$), so you know he's 2 SDs above mean height in inches as well.

What if you were told that the student was 2 SDs above the mean in shoe size? Would you still guess that he's of average height? You might guess that he's taller than average, since there's a positive correlation between height and shoe size. But would you guess that he's 2 SDs above the mean? When there was no correlation, we didn't move away from the mean at all. With a perfect correlation, we moved our guess the full 2 SDs. Any correlation between these extremes should lead us to move somewhere between 0 and 2 SDs above the mean. (To be exact, our best guess would be to move $r \times 2$ SDs away from the mean.)

Notice that if x is 2 SDs above its mean, we won't ever move more than 2 SDs away for y, since r can't be bigger than 1.0. So each predicted y tends to be closer to its mean (in standard deviations) than its corresponding x was. This property of the linear model is called **regression to the mean**. This is why the line is called the regression line.

More on Regression to the Mean

Misinterpretation of "regression to the mean" is a phenomenon that still plagues decision-makers in countless areas. Stephen Senn wrote, "A Victorian eccentric [Francis Galton] . . . made an important discovery of a phenomenon that is so trivial that all should be capable of learning it and so deep that many scientists spend their whole career being fooled by it."

The previous illustrations show that unless the correlation between X and Y is perfect, predictions of Y from X will always appear to be less dramatic than one

Pavel L Photo and Video/Shutterstock

Library of congress

Sir Francis Galton was the first to speak of "regression," although others had fit lines to data by the same method.

might expect. That's because, "A point that is 1 SD above the mean in the X-variable is, on average, *r* SDs above the mean in the Y-variable. Similarly, a point that is 1 SD below the mean in X is, on average, *r* SDs below the mean in Y."

Suppose you missed writing the final exam in a course and wanted to try to predict what grade you might have received based on how you did on the midterm exam in the same course. Results from the rest of the class showed that the midterm had a mean of 75% and SD of 10%, while the final exam had a mean of 70%, also with a SD of 10%. The correlation between midterm and final exam grades was 0.75; that is, students who did well on the midterm generally did well on the final. Suppose you performed exceedingly well on the midterm and received a grade of 95%. That means you were 2 SDs above the average. According to the rule of regression, you would be predicted to get *r* × 2 SDs above the average on the final exam, which would be a grade of 85% (i.e., 70% + (0.75 × 2 × 10%) = 85%). That's still a very good grade, but not as high, even relatively, as your midterm grade. Why not? Because the correlation is not perfect. There are many other explanations for, or predictors of high final grades, such as long hours of studying!

Here is another way to state the main idea of regression: "For each value of X, the regression line passes through average value of Y." Look at the following graph. We know that the regression line will pass through the point of averages $(\overline{x}, \overline{y})$, which is right in the centre of the scatterplot. Can you visualize the slope of the regression line? The answer may surprise you. It is not the line that goes through the main diagonal or "principal axis" of the ellipse. It goes through the average Y at each X. The second graph shows where the regression lies.

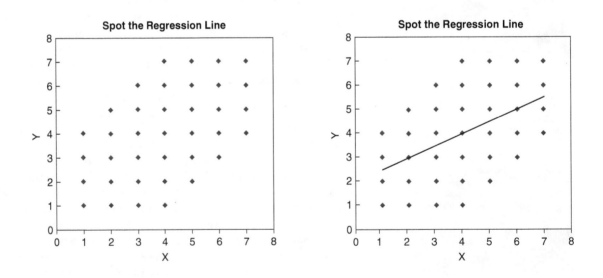

Thus for X = 7, which is 3 units above the average, the regression line predicts a value of 5.5 for Y, which is 1.5 units above average. That's because the correlation here is only 0.5.

Regression to the mean is the tendency for a very high value of a random quantity whose values cluster around an average, to be followed by a value closer to that average, and similarly for a very low value. It is a natural effect. Misinterpretations of this effect lead to regression fallacies, of which there are countless examples. Here are a few.

♦ The "sophomore jinx" in professional sports: a player who has a brilliant rookie (first-year) performance is not quite as brilliant the second year.

◆ *The "cover of Sports Illustrated jinx": an athlete who makes the cover of Sports Illustrated magazine experiences a drop in performance (because he/she only made the cover due to a much better-than-average performance!)*

◆ *The sequel to a movie is rarely ever as good as the original: a really bad movie will not likely have a sequel, so we rarely experience a series of movies that gets better.*

◆ *The "reward and punishment" child-rearing fallacy: Psychologists Amos Tversky and Daniel Kahneman write, "Behaviour is most likely to improve after punishment and deteriorate after reward. Consequently . . . one is most often rewarded for punishing others, and most often punished for rewarding them." Reward a child for angelic behaviour and the next time the behaviour is not exemplary as the child returns to his/her average behaviour. Similarly, punish a child for devilish behaviour and the next time the behaviour is not so bad. It isn't really because of the punishment; it is regression to the mean.*

◆ *The effect of red-light cameras on accidents: when you put cameras in a high-accident-rate intersection the accident rate will decline; at the same time, when you take a camera away from a low-accident intersection the rate will increase!*

Regression to the mean is very often the explanation for many phenomena that so-called experts attribute to something real, not just chance. Don't let yourself be fooled by it!

Regression to the mean was the brilliant observation of the great Victorian era scientist Sir Francis Galton. He was also an explorer, geographer, weather-forecaster, travel-writer, and inventor. He devised the fingerprint classification system for identification used to this day. He had a famous cousin, but it would be accurate to call Galton, "Charles Darwin's smarter cousin!" We celebrated this giant of statistics in 2011, which was the 100th anniversary of Galton's death and the 125th anniversary of his landmark paper that introduced the term "regression to mediocrity" (his term for regression to the mean).

In the paper, Galton related the heights of sons to the height of their fathers. He found that the slope of his line was less than 1. That is, sons of tall fathers were tall, but not as much above their average as their fathers had been above their average. Similarly, sons of short fathers were short, but generally not as far from their mean as their fathers. Galton interpreted the slope correctly, calling it "regression" (i.e., moving back) toward the mean height. The name stuck.

MATH BOX

Where does the equation of the line of best fit come from? To write the equation of any line, we need to know a point on the line and the slope. It's logical to expect that an average x will correspond to an average y, and, in fact, the line does pass through the point $(\overline{x}, \overline{y})$. (This is not hard to show as well.)

To think about the slope, we look once again at the z-scores. We need to remember a few things.

1. The mean of any set of z-scores is 0. This tells us that the line that best fits the z-scores passes through the origin (0, 0).

2. The standard deviation of a set of z-scores is 1, so the variance is also 1. This means that $\dfrac{\sum(z_y - \overline{z}_y)^2}{n-1} = \dfrac{\sum(z_y - 0)^2}{n-1} = \dfrac{\sum z_y^2 n - 1}{= 1}$ a fact that will be important soon.

3. The correlation is $r = \dfrac{\sum z_x z_y}{n-1}$, also important soon.

Remember that our objective is to find the slope of the best fit line. Because it passes through the origin, the equation of the best fit line will be of the form $\hat{z}_y = m z_x$. We want to find the value for m that will minimize the sum of the squared errors. Actually we'll divide that sum by $n - 1$ and minimize this mean squared error (MSE). Here goes:

Minimize: $\qquad MSE = \dfrac{\sum(z_y - \hat{z}_y)^2}{n-1}$

Since $\hat{z}_y = m z_x$: $\qquad MSE = \dfrac{\sum(z_y - m z_x)^2}{n-1}$

Square the binomial:

$$= \frac{\sum(z_y^2 - 2mz_xz_y + m^2z_x^2)}{n-1}$$

Rewrite the summation:

$$= \frac{\sum z_y^2}{n-1} - 2m\frac{\sum z_xz_y}{n-1} + m^2\frac{\sum z_x^2}{n-1}$$

4. Substitute from (2) and (3):

$$= 1 - 2mr + m^2$$

This last expression is a quadratic. A parabola in the form $y = ax^2 + bx + c$ reaches its minimum at its turning point, which occurs when $x = \frac{-b}{2a}$. We can minimize the mean of squared errors by choosing $m = \frac{-(-2r)}{2(1)} = r$.

The slope of the best fit line for z-scores is the correlation, r. This fact leads us immediately to two important additional results:

A slope with value r for z-scores means that a difference of 1 standard deviation in z_x corresponds to a difference of r standard deviations in $\hat{z}_y$. Translate that back to the original x and y values: "Over one standard deviation in x, up r standard deviations in $\hat{y}$."

The slope of the regression line is $b = \dfrac{rs_y}{s_x}$.

We know choosing $m = r$ minimizes the sum of the squared errors (SSE), but how small does that sum get? Equation (4) told us that the mean of the squared errors is $1 - 2mr + m^2$. When $m = r$, $1 - 2mr + m^2 = 1 - 2r^2 + r^2 = 1 - r^2$. This is the percentage of variability *not* explained by the regression line. Since $1 - r^2$ of the variability is *not* explained, the percentage of variability in y that *is* explained by x is r^2. This important fact will help us assess the strength of our models.

And there's still another bonus. Because r^2 is the percent of variability explained by our model, r^2 is at most 100%. If $r^2 \le 1$, then $-1 \le r \le 1$, proving that correlations are always between -1 and $+1$.

Why *r* for *correlation*?

In his original paper on correlation, Galton used r for the "index of correlation"—what we now call the correlation coefficient. He calculated it from the regression of y on x or of x on y after standardizing the variables, just as we have done. It's fairly clear from the text that he used r to stand for (standardized) regression.

6.8 Checking the Model

The linear regression model is perhaps the most widely used model in all of Statistics. It has everything we could want in a model: two easily estimated parameters, a meaningful measure of how well the model fits the data, and the ability to predict new values. It even provides a self-check in plots of the residuals to help us avoid all kinds of mistakes. Most models are useful only when specific assumptions are true. Of course, assumptions are hard—often impossible—to check. That's why we *assume* them. But we should check to see whether the assumptions are *reasonable*. Fortunately, we can often check *conditions* that provide information about the assumptions. For the linear model, we start by checking the same ones we checked earlier in this chapter for using correlation.

Linear Regression Conditions

◆ **Quantitative Data Condition:** Linear models only make sense for quantitative data. Don't be fooled by categorical data recorded as numbers. You probably don't want to predict area codes from credit card account numbers.

Make a Picture

Check the scatterplot. The shape must be linear, or you can't use regression for the variables in their current form. And watch out for outliers. A useful rule of thumb is that the assumptions are probably reasonable if the scatterplot has an approximate oval shape. That doesn't check for independence but it is a quick check on the other assumptions.

- **Linearity Assumption:**   The regression model *assumes* that the relationship between the variables is, in fact, linear. If you try to model a curved relationship with a straight line, you'll usually get what you deserve. We can't ever verify that the underlying relationship between two variables is truly linear, but an examination of the scatterplot will let you decide whether the *Linearity Assumption* is reasonable. The **Linearity Condition** we used for correlation is designed to do precisely that and is satisfied if the scatterplot looks reasonably straight. If the scatterplot is not straight enough, stop. You can't use a linear model for just *any* two variables, even if they are related. The two variables must have a *linear* association, or the model won't mean a thing. Some nonlinear relationships can be saved by re-expressing the data to make the scatterplot more linear.

- **Outlier Condition:**   Watch out for outliers. The linearity assumption also requires that no points lie far enough away to distort the line of best fit. Check to make sure no point needs special attention. Outlying values may have large residuals, and squaring makes their influence that much greater. Outlying points can dramatically change a regression model. Unusual observations can even change the sign of the slope, misleading us about the direction of the underlying relationship between the variables.

- **Independence Assumption:**   Another assumption that is usually made when fitting a linear regression is that the residuals are independent of each other. We don't strictly need this assumption to fit the line, but to generalize from the data it's a crucial assumption and one that we'll come back to when we discuss inference. As with all assumptions, there's no way to be sure that *Independence Assumption* is true. However we could check that the cases are a random sample from the population.

We can also check displays of the regression residuals for evidence of patterns, trends, or clumping, any of which would suggest a failure of independence. In the special case when we have a time series, a common violation of the Independence Assumption is for the errors to be correlated with each other (autocorrelation). The error our model makes today may be similar to the one it made yesterday. We can check this violation by plotting the residuals against time (usually *x* for a time series) and looking for patterns.

When our goal is just to explore and describe the relationship, independence isn't essential (and so we won't insist that the conditions relating to it be formally checked). However, when we want to go beyond the data at hand and make inferences for other situations (in Chapter 14) this will be a crucial assumption, so it's good practice to think about it even now, especially for time series.

Why *e* for *residual*?

The easy answer is that *r* is already taken for correlation, but the truth is that *e* stands for "error." It's not that the data point is a mistake but that statisticians often refer to variability not explained by a model as error.

- **Residuals:**   We always check conditions with a scatterplot of the data, but we can learn even more after we've fit the regression model. There's extra information in the residuals that we can use to help us decide how reasonable our model is and how well the model fits. So, we plot the residuals and check the conditions again.

The residuals are the part of the data that *hasn't* been modelled. We can write

$$Data = Predicted + Residual$$

or, equivalently,

$$Residual = Data - Predicted$$

Or, as we showed earlier, in symbols:

$$e = y - \hat{y}.$$

A scatterplot of the residuals versus the *x*-values should be a plot without patterns. It shouldn't have any interesting features—no direction, no shape. It should stretch horizontally, showing no bends, and it should have no outliers. If you see nonlinearities, outliers, or clusters in the residuals, find out what the regression model missed.

Let's examine the residuals from our regression of RONA *Sales* on residential *Renovations* expenditures.[5]

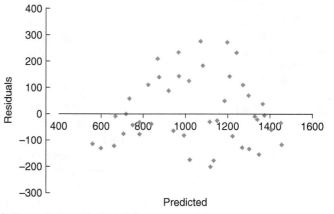

Figure 6.6 Residuals of the regression model predicting RONA *Sales* from residential *Renovation* expenditures 2002–2012.

The residual plot is suitably boring. The only noticeable feature is that at the lower end, the residuals are smaller and mostly negative. The residuals are smaller in the earlier years because the sales are lower in the early years so the error in the predictions must be smaller. The residuals are mostly negative because the speed of growth increased after 2003.

This is a good time to point out a common mistake in the interpretation of residual plots, namely, looking too hard for patterns or unusual features. The residual plots are designed to show major departures from the assumptions. Don't fall victim to over-interpreting them.

Not only can the residuals help check the conditions, but they can also tell us how well the model performs. The better the model fits the data, the less the residuals will vary around the line. The standard deviation of the residuals, s_e, gives us a measure of how much the points spread around the regression line. Of course, for this summary to make sense, the residuals should all share the same underlying spread. So we must *assume* that the standard deviation around the line is the same wherever we want the model to apply.

Equal Spread Condition

This condition requires that the scatter is about equal for all *x*-values. It's often checked using a plot of residuals against predicted values. The underlying assumption of equal variance is also called *homoscedasticity*.

The term comes from the Greek words "*homos*" meaning "same" and "*skedastikos*" meaning able to scatter. So *homoscedasticity* means "same scatter."

◆ **Equal Spread Condition:** This new assumption about the standard deviation around the line gives us a new condition, called the *Equal Spread Condition*. The associated question to ask is does the plot have a consistent spread or does it fan out? We check to make sure that the spread of the residuals is about the same everywhere. We can check that either in the original scatterplot of *y* against *x* or in the scatterplot of residuals (or, preferably, in both plots). We estimate the **standard deviation of the residuals** in almost the way you'd expect:

$$s_e = \sqrt{\frac{\sum e^2}{n - 2}}.$$

---

[5] Most computer statistics packages plot the residuals as we did in Figure 6.6, against the predicted values, rather than against *x*. When the slope is positive, the scatterplots are virtually identical except for the axes labels. When the slope is negative, the two versions are mirror images. Since all we care about is the patterns (or, better, lack of patterns) in the plot, either plot is useful.

We don't need to subtract the mean of the residuals because $\bar{e} = 0$. Why divide by $n - 2$ rather than $n - 1$? We used $n - 1$ for s when we estimated the mean. Now we're estimating both a slope and an intercept. Looks like a pattern—and it is. We subtract one more for each parameter we estimate.

If we predict RONA *Sales* in the third quarter of 2008 when home *Renovation* totalled 10 737.5 $M, the regression model gives a predicted value of 1272.7 $M. The actual value was about 1381.7 $M. So our residual is 1272.7 − 1381.7 = 109.0. The value of s_e from the regression is 135.6, so our residual is only 109.0/135.6 = 0.80 standard deviations away from the actual value. That's a fairly typical size for a residual because it's within 2 standard deviations.

6.9 Variation in the Model and R^2

The variation in the residuals is the key to assessing how well the model fits. Let's compare the variation of the response variable with the variation of the residuals. *Sales* has a standard deviation of 288.4 ($M). The standard deviation of the residuals is only 134.0 ($M). If the correlation were 1.0 and the model predicted the *Sales* values perfectly, the residuals would all be zero and have no variation. We couldn't possibly do any better than that.

On the other hand, if the correlation were zero, the model would simply predict 1049.2 ($M) (the mean) for all menu items. The residuals from that prediction would just be the observed *Sales* values minus their mean. These residuals would have the same variability as the original data because, as we know, just subtracting the mean doesn't change the spread.

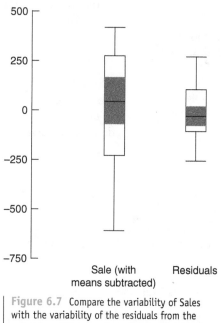

Figure 6.7 Compare the variability of Sales with the variability of the residuals from the regression. The means have been subtracted to make it easier to compare spreads. The variation left in the residuals is unaccounted for by the model, but it's less than the variation in the original data.

How well does the regression model do? Look at the boxplots. The variation in the residuals is smaller than in the data, but bigger than zero. That's nice to know, but how much of the variation is still left in the residuals? If you had to put a

Is a correlation of 0.80 twice as strong as a correlation of 0.40? Not if you think in terms of R^2. A correlation of 0.80 means an R^2 of $0.80^2 = 64\%$. A correlation of 0.40 means an R^2 of $0.40^2 = 16\%$—only a quarter as much of the variability accounted for. A correlation of 0.80 gives an R^2 *four* times as strong as a correlation of 0.40 and accounts for four times as much of the variability.

Some Extreme Tales

One major company developed a method to differentiate between proteins. To do so, they had to distinguish between regressions with R^2 of 99.99% and 99.98%. For this application, 99.98% was not high enough.

The president of a financial services company reports that although his regressions give R^2 below 2%, they are highly successful because those used by his competition are even lower.

number between 0% and 100% on the fraction of the variation left in the residuals, what would you say?

All regression models fall somewhere between the two extremes of zero correlation and perfect correlation. We'd like to gauge where our model falls. Can we use the correlation to do that? Well, a regression model with correlation -0.5 is doing as well as one with correlation $+0.5$. They just have different directions. But if we *square* the correlation coefficient, we'll get a value between 0 and 1, and the direction won't matter. The squared correlation, r^2, gives the fraction of the data's variation accounted for by the model, and $1 - r^2$ is the fraction of the original variation left in the residuals. For the RONA *Sales* model, $r^2 = 0.885^2 = 0.783$ and $1 - r^2$ is 0.216, so only 21.6% of the variability in *Sales* has been left in the residuals.

All regression analyses include this statistic, although by tradition, it is written with a capital letter, R^2, and pronounced "R-squared." An R^2 of 0 means that none of the variance in the data is in the model; all of it is still in the residuals. It would be hard to imagine using that model for anything.

Because R^2 is a fraction of a whole, it is often given as a percentage.[6] For the RONA *Sales* data, R^2 is 78.3%.

When interpreting a regression model, you need to report what R^2 means. According to our linear model, 78.3% of the variability in RONA *Sales* is accounted for by variation in residential *Renovations* expenditures.

◆ **How can we see that R^2 is really the fraction of variance accounted for by the model?** It's a simple calculation. The variance of *Sales* is $288.4^2 = 83\ 175$. If we treat the residuals as data, the variance of the residuals is 17 961.[7] As a fraction of the variance of *Sales*, that's 0.216 or 21.6%. That's the fraction of the variance that is *not* accounted for by the model. The fraction that *is* accounted for is 100% $- 21.6\% = 78.3\%$, just the value we got for R^2.

How Big Should R^2 Be?

The value of R^2 is always between 0% and 100%. But what is a "good" R^2 value? The answer depends on the kind of data you are analyzing and on what you want to do with it. Just as with correlation, there is no value for R^2 that automatically determines that the regression is "good." Data from scientific experiments often

---

✔ **JUST CHECKING**

Let's go back to our regression of sales ($000) on number of employees again.

$$\widehat{Sales} = 9.564 + 122.74\ Employees$$

The R^2 value is reported as 71.4%.

9 What does the R^2 value mean about the relationship of *Sales* and *Employees*?

10 Is the correlation of Sales and Employees positive or negative? How do you know?

11 If we measured the *Sales* in thousands of euros instead of thousands of dollars, would the R^2 value change? How about the slope?

---

[6] By contrast, we usually give correlation coefficients as decimal values between -1.0 and 1.0.

[7] This isn't quite the same as squaring s_e which we discussed previously, but it's very close.

Sum of Squares

The sum of the squared residuals $\sum(y-\hat{y})^2$ is sometimes written as SSE (sum of squared errors). If we call $\sum(y-\bar{y})^2$ SST (for total sum of squares) then

$$R^2 = 1 - \frac{SSE}{SST}.$$

have R^2 in the 80% to 90% range and even higher. Data from observational studies and surveys, though, often show relatively weak associations because it's so difficult to measure reliable responses. An R^2 of 30% to 50% or even lower might be taken as evidence of a useful regression. The standard deviation of the residuals can give us more information about the usefulness of the regression by telling us how much scatter there is around the line.

As we've seen, an R^2 of 100% is a perfect fit, with no scatter around the line. The s_e would be zero. All of the variance would be accounted for by the model with none left in the residuals. This sounds great, but it's too good to be true for real data.[8]

6.10 Reality Check: Is the Regression Reasonable?

Statistics don't come out of nowhere. They are based on data. The results of a statistical analysis should reinforce common sense. If the results are surprising, then either you've learned something new about the world or your analysis is wrong.

Whenever you perform a regression, think about the coefficients and ask whether they make sense. Is the slope reasonable? Does the direction of the slope seem right? The small effort of asking whether the regression equation is plausible will be repaid whenever you catch errors or avoid saying something silly or absurd about the data. It's too easy to take something that comes out of a computer at face value and assume that it makes sense.

Always be skeptical and ask yourself if the answer is reasonable.

GUIDED EXAMPLE | Home Size and Price

Real estate agents know the three most important factors in determining the price of a house are *location*, *location*, and *location*. But what other factors help determine the price at which a house should be listed? Number of bathrooms? Size of the yard? A student amassed publicly available data on thousands of homes. We've drawn a random sample of 1057 homes to examine house pricing. Among the variables she collected were the total living area (in square feet), number of bathrooms, number of bedrooms, size of lot (in acres), and age of house (in years). We will investigate how well the size of the house, as measured by living area, can predict the selling price.

PLAN

Setup State the objective of the study.

Identify the variables and their context.

We want to find out how well the living area of a house can predict its selling price.

We have two quantitative variables: the living area (in square feet) and the selling price ($). These data come from public records in 2006.

---

[8] If you see an R^2 of 100%, it's a good idea to investigate what happened. You may have accidentally regressed two variables that measure the same thing.

Model We need to check the same conditions for regression as we did for correlation. To do that, make a picture. Never fit a regression without looking at the scatterplot first.

✓ **Quantitative Variables Condition**

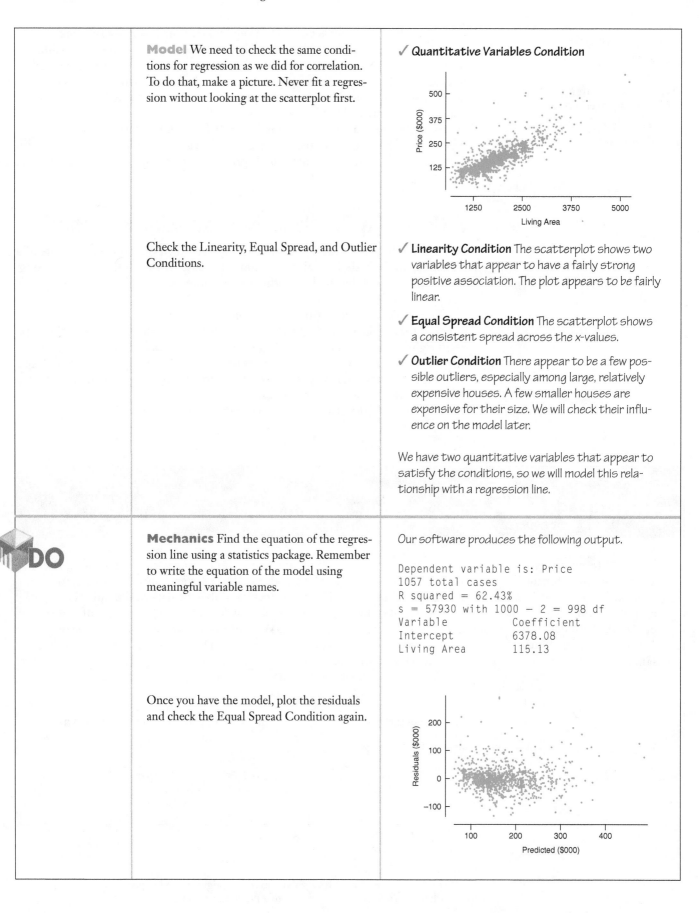

Check the Linearity, Equal Spread, and Outlier Conditions.

✓ **Linearity Condition** The scatterplot shows two variables that appear to have a fairly strong positive association. The plot appears to be fairly linear.

✓ **Equal Spread Condition** The scatterplot shows a consistent spread across the x-values.

✓ **Outlier Condition** There appear to be a few possible outliers, especially among large, relatively expensive houses. A few smaller houses are expensive for their size. We will check their influence on the model later.

We have two quantitative variables that appear to satisfy the conditions, so we will model this relationship with a regression line.

Mechanics Find the equation of the regression line using a statistics package. Remember to write the equation of the model using meaningful variable names.

Our software produces the following output.

```
Dependent variable is: Price
1057 total cases
R squared = 62.43%
s = 57930 with 1000 − 2 = 998 df
Variable          Coefficient
Intercept         6378.08
Living Area       115.13
```

Once you have the model, plot the residuals and check the Equal Spread Condition again.

The residual plot appears generally patternless. The few relatively expensive small houses are evident, but setting them aside and refitting the model did not change either the slope or intercept very much so we left them in. There is a slight tendency for cheaper houses to have less variation, but the spread is roughly the same throughout.

REPORT

Conclusion Interpret what you have found in the proper context.

MEMO:

Re: Report on housing prices.

We examined how well the size of a house could predict its selling price. Data were obtained from recent sales of 1057 homes. The model is:

$$\widehat{Price} = \$6376.08 + 115.13 + \text{Living Area}$$

In other words, from a base of $6376.08, houses cost about $115.13 per square foot.

This model appears reasonable from both a statistical and real estate perspective. Although we know that size is not the only factor in pricing a house, the model accounts for 62.4% of the variation in selling price.

As a reality check, we checked with several real estate pricing sites (www.realestateabc.com, www.zillow.com) and found that houses in this region were averaging $100 to $150 per square foot, so our model is plausible.

Of course, not all house prices are predicted well by the model. We computed the model without several of these houses, but their impact on the regression model was small. We believe that this is a reasonable place to start to assess whether a house is priced correctly for this market. Future analysis might benefit by considering other factors.

WHAT CAN GO WRONG?

- **Don't say "correlation" when you mean "association."** How often have you heard the word "correlation"? Chances are pretty good that when you've heard the term, it's been misused. It's one of the most widely misused Statistics terms, and given how often Statistics are misused, that's saying a lot. One of the problems is that many people use the specific term *correlation* when they really mean the more general term *association*. Association is a deliberately vague term used to describe the relationship between two variables.

  Correlation is a precise term used to describe the strength and direction of a linear relationship between quantitative variables.

(continued)

- **Don't correlate categorical variables.** Be sure to check the Quantitative Variables Condition. It makes no sense to compute a correlation of categorical variables.

- **Make sure the association is linear.** Not all associations between quantitative variables are linear. Correlation can miss even a strong nonlinear association. And linear regression models are never appropriate for relationships that are not linear. A company, concerned that customers might use ovens with imperfect temperature controls, performed a series of experiments[9] to assess the effect of baking temperature on the quality of brownies made from their freeze-dried reconstituted brownies. The company wants to understand the sensitivity of brownie quality to variation in oven temperatures around the recommended baking temperature of 325°F. The lab reported a correlation of −0.05 between the scores awarded by a panel of trained taste-testers and baking temperature and a regression slope of −0.02, so they told management that there is no relationship. Before printing directions on the box telling customers not to worry about the temperature, a savvy intern asks to see the scatterplot.

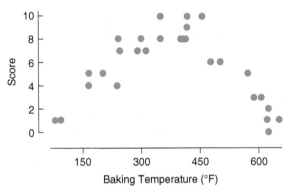

Figure 6.8 The relationship between brownie taste score and baking temperature is strong, but not linear.

The plot actually shows a strong association—but not a linear one. Don't forget to check the Linearity Condition.

- **Beware of outliers.** You can't interpret a correlation coefficient or a regression model safely without a background check for unusual observations. Here's an example. The relationship between IQ and shoe size among comedians shows a surprisingly strong positive correlation of 0.50. To check assumptions, we look at the scatterplot.

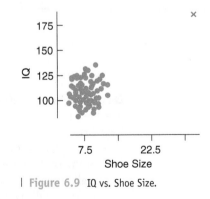

| **Figure 6.9** IQ vs. Shoe Size.

[9] Experiments designed to assess the impact of environmental variables outside the control of the company on the quality of the company's products were advocated by the Japanese quality expert Dr. Genichi Taguchi starting in the 1980s in the United States.

From this "study," what can we say about the relationship between the two? The correlation is 0.50. But who *does* that point in the upper right-hand corner belong to? The outlier is Bozo the Clown, known for his large shoes and widely acknowledged to be a comic "genius." Without Bozo the correlation is near zero.

Even a single unusual observation can dominate the correlation value. That's why you need to check the Unusual Observations Condition.

- **Don't confuse correlation with causation.** Once we have a strong correlation, it's tempting to try to explain it by imagining that the predictor variable has *caused* the response to change. Putting a regression line on a scatterplot tempts us even further. Humans are like that; we tend to see causes and effects in everything. Just because two variables are related does not mean that one *causes* the other.

> **Does cancer cause smoking?** Even if the correlation of two variables is due to a causal relationship, the correlation itself cannot tell us what causes what.
>
> Sir Ronald Aylmer Fisher (1890–1962) was one of the greatest statisticians of the twentieth century. Fisher testified in court (paid by the tobacco companies) that a causal relationship might underlie the correlation of smoking and cancer:
>
> "Is it possible, then, that lung cancer . . . is one of the causes of smoking cigarettes? I don't think it can be excluded . . . the pre-cancerous condition is one involving a certain amount of slight chronic inflammation . . .
>
> A slight cause of irritation . . . is commonly accompanied by pulling out a cigarette, and getting a little compensation for life's minor ills in that way. And . . . is not unlikely to be associated with smoking more frequently."
>
> Ironically, the proof that smoking indeed is the cause of many cancers came from experiments conducted following the principles of experiment design and analysis that Fisher himself developed.

In 2012, the prestigious *New England Journal of Medicine* published research that found countries with higher chocolate consumption win more Nobel prizes. The also-prestigious British journal *Practical Neurology* followed this up with a study that showed a nearly identical link between milk consumption and Nobel prize success. Putting the two results together must mean that chocolate milk (or milk chocolate) is the ultimate brain food! Both studies were, of course, tongue-in-cheek but were undertaken to emphasize the difference between correlation and causation, and that this difference is often overlooked.

A much less serious organization, the Church of the Flying Spaghetti Monster (FSM) published a graph showing a strong negative correlation between the world population of pirates and average global temperatures over the past 200 years (see www.venganza.org). According to the FSM founder, "Global warming, earthquakes, hurricanes, and other natural disasters are a direct effect of the shrinking numbers of pirates since the 1800s." We point out that in recent years the pirate population has begun increasing again (e.g., off the coast of Somalia), and global temperatures are decreasing (which is why the term climate change has superseded the term global warming). Of course, the real reason for global warming is the end of the Cold War!

Scatterplots, correlation coefficients, and regression models *never* prove causation. This is, for example, partly why it took so long for the government to require warning labels on cigarettes. Although there was plenty of evidence that increased smoking was *associated* with increased levels of lung cancer, it took years to provide evidence that smoking actually *causes* lung cancer. (The tobacco companies used this to great advantage.)

- **Watch out for lurking variables.** A scatterplot of the damage (in dollars) caused to a house by fire would show a strong correlation with the number of firefighters at the scene. Surely the damage doesn't cause firefighters. And firefighters actually do cause damage, spraying water all around and chopping holes, but does that mean we shouldn't call the fire department? Of course not. There is an underlying variable that leads to both more damage and more firefighters—the size of the blaze. A hidden variable that stands behind a relationship and determines it by simultaneously affecting the other two variables is called a *lurking variable*. You can often debunk claims made about data by finding a lurking variable behind the scenes.

- **Don't fit a straight line to a nonlinear relationship.** Linear regression is suited only to relationships that are, in fact, linear.

(continued)

- **Beware of extraordinary points.** Data values can be extraordinary or unusual in a regression in two ways. They can have *y*-values that stand off from the linear pattern suggested by the bulk of the data. These are what we have been calling outliers; although with regression, a point can be an outlier by being far from the linear pattern even if it is not the largest or smallest *y*-value. Points can also be extraordinary in their *x*-values. Such points can exert a strong influence on the line. Both kinds of extraordinary points require attention.

- **Don't extrapolate far beyond the data. A linear model will often do a reasonable job of summarizing a relationship in the range of observed *x*-values.** Once we have a working model for the relationship, it's tempting to use it. But beware of predicting *y*-values for *x*-values that lie too far outside the range of the original data. The model may no longer hold there, so such extrapolations too far from the data are dangerous.

- **Don't choose a model based on R^2 alone.** Although R^2 measures the *strength* of the linear association, a high R^2 does not demonstrate the *appropriateness* of the regression. A single unusual observation, or data that separate into two groups, can make the R^2 seem quite large when, in fact, the linear regression model is simply inappropriate. Conversely, a low R^2 value may be due to a single outlier. It may be that most of the data fall roughly along a straight line, with the exception of a single point. Always look at the scatterplot.

- **Beware of the dangers of computing correlation aggregated across different groups.** In Chapter 4 we discussed Simpson's Paradox, and how absurd results can occur when measurements from different groups are combined. The reversals that can happen with categorical data and percentages can also happen with quantitative data and correlation. For example, income is generally accepted to be positively correlated with education. But if a scatterplot were prepared using two groups of people, National Hockey League players and university professors, a negative correlation would be seen. NHL players have much higher salaries, and much lower education than professors!

ETHICS IN ACTION

An ad agency hired by a well-known manufacturer of dental hygiene products (electric toothbrushes, oral irrigators, etc.) put together a creative team to brainstorm ideas for a new ad campaign. Trisha Simes was chosen to lead the team as she has had the most experience with this client to date. At their first meeting, Trisha communicated to her team the client's desire to differentiate themselves from their competitors by not focusing their message on the cosmetic benefits of good dental care. As they brainstormed ideas, one member of the team, Brad Jonns, recalled a recent CNN broadcast that reported a "correlation" between flossing teeth and reduced risk of heart disease. Seeing potential in promoting the health benefits of proper dental care, the team agreed to pursue this idea further. At their next meeting several team members commented on how surprised they were to find so many articles, medical, scientific, and popular, that seemed to claim good dental hygiene resulted in good health. One member noted that he found articles that linked gum disease not only to heart attacks and strokes but to diabetes and even cancer. Although Trisha puzzled over why their client's competitors had not yet capitalized on these research findings, her team was on a roll and had already begun to focus on designing the campaign around this core message.

ETHICAL ISSUE *Correlation does not imply causation. The possibility of lurking variables is not explored. For example, it is likely that those who take better care of themselves would floss regularly and also have less risk of heart disease (related to ASA Ethical Guidelines, Item C, which can be found at http:// www.amstat.org/about/ethicalguidelines.cfm).*

ETHICAL SOLUTION *Refrain from implying cause and effect from correlation results.*

Jill Hathway is looking for a career change and is interested in starting a franchise. After spending the last 20 years working as a mid-level manager for a major corporation, Jill wants to indulge her entrepreneurial spirit and strike out on her own. She is considering a franchise in the health and fitness industry, including *Pilates One*, for which she requested a franchise packet. Included in the packet information were data showing how various regional demographics (age, gender, income) related to franchise success (revenue, profit, return on investment). *Pilates One* is a relatively new franchise with only a few scattered locations. Nonetheless, the company reported various graphs and data analysis results to help prospective franchisers in their decision-making process. Jill was particularly interested in the graph and the regression analysis that related the proportion of women over the age of 40 within a 30-kilometre radius of a *Pilates One* location to return on investment for the franchise. She noticed that there was a positive relationship. With a little research, she discovered that the proportion of women over the age of 40 in her city was higher than for any other *Pilates One* location (attributable, in part, to the large number of retirees relocating to her city). She then used the regression equation to project return on investment for a *Pilates One* located in her city and was very pleased with the result. With such objective data, she felt confident that *Pilates One* was the franchise for her.

ETHICAL ISSUE *Pilates One is reporting analysis based on only a few observations. Jill is extrapolating beyond the range of x-values (related to ASA Ethical Guidelines, Item C, which can be found at http://www.amstat.org/about/ethicalguidelines.cfm).*

ETHICAL SOLUTION *Pilates One should include a disclaimer that the analysis was based on very few observations and that the equation should not be used to predict success at other locations or beyond the range of x-values used in the analysis.*

WHAT HAVE WE LEARNED?

In previous chapters we learned how to listen to the story told by data from a single variable. Now we've turned our attention to the more complicated (and more interesting) story we can discover in the association between two quantitative variables.

We've learned to begin our investigation by looking at a scatterplot. We're interested in the *direction* of the association, the *form* it takes, and its *strength*.

We've learned that, although not every relationship is linear, when the scatterplot is straight enough, the *correlation coefficient* is a useful numerical summary.

- The sign of the correlation tells us the direction of the association.
- The magnitude of the correlation tells us of the *strength* of a linear association. Strong associations have correlations near $+1$ or -1, and very weak associations have correlations near 0.

- Correlation has no units, so shifting or scaling the data, standardizing, or even swapping the variables has no effect on the numerical value.

We've learned that to use correlation we have to check certain conditions for the analysis to be valid.

- Before finding or talking about a correlation, we'll always check the Linearity Condition.
- And, as always, we'll watch out for unusual observations.

We've learned not to make the mistake of assuming that a high correlation or strong association is evidence of a cause-and-effect relationship. Beware of lurking variables!

We've learned that when the relationship between quantitative variables is linear, a linear model can help summarize that relationship and give us insights about it.

- The regression (best fit) line doesn't pass through all the points, but it is the best compromise in the sense that the sum of squares of the residuals is the smallest possible.

We've learned several things the correlation, r, tells us about the regression:

- The slope of the line is based on the correlation, adjusted for the standard deviations of x and y. We've learned to interpret that slope in context.
- For each SD that a case is away from the mean of x, we expect it to be r SDs in y away from the y mean.
- Because r is always between -1 and $+1$, each predicted y is fewer SDs away from its mean than the corresponding x was, a phenomenon called *regression to the mean*.
- The square of the correlation coefficient, R^2, gives us the fraction of the variation of the response accounted for by the regression model. The remaining $1 - R^2$ of the variation is left in the residuals.

Terms

Association

- **Direction:** A **positive** direction or association means that, in general, as one variable increases, so does the other. When increases in one variable generally correspond to decreases in the other, the association is **negative**.
- **Form:** The form we care about most is **linear**, but you should certainly describe other patterns you see in scatterplots.
- **Strength:** A scatterplot is said to show a strong association if there is little scatter around the underlying relationship.

Correlation coefficient

A numerical measure of the direction and strength of a linear association.

$$r = \frac{\sum z_x z_y}{n - 1}$$

Explanatory or independent variable (x-variable)

The variable that accounts for, explains, predicts, or is otherwise responsible for the y-variable.

Intercept

The intercept, b_0, gives a starting value in y-units. It's the $\hat{y}$ value when x is 0.

$$b_0 = \bar{y} - b_1 \bar{x}$$

Least squares	A criterion that specifies the unique line that minimizes the variance of the residuals or, equivalently, the sum of the squared residuals. The resulting line is called the **Least squares line**.
Linear model (Line of best fit)	The linear model of the form $\hat{y} = b_0 + b_1x$ fit by least squares. Also called the regression line. To interpret a linear model, we need to know the variables and their units.
Lurking variable	A variable other than x and y that simultaneously affects both variables, accounting for the correlation between the two.
Outlier	A point that does not fit the overall pattern seen in the scatterplot.
Predicted value	The prediction for y found for each x-value in the data. A predicted value, $\hat{y}$, is found by substituting the x-value in the regression equation. The predicted values are the values on the fitted line; the points $(x, \hat{y})$ lie exactly on the fitted line.
Regression line	The particular linear equation that satisfies the least squares criterion, often called the line of best fit.
Regression to the mean	Because the correlation is always less than 1.0 in magnitude, each predicted y tends to be fewer standard deviations from its mean than its corresponding x is from its mean.
Residual	The difference between the actual data value and the corresponding value predicted by the regression model—or, more generally, predicted by any model.
Response or dependent variable (*y*-variable)	The variable that the scatterplot is meant to explain or predict.
R^2	• The square of the correlation between y and x • The fraction of the variability of y accounted for by the least squares linear regression on x • An overall measure of how successful the regression is in linearly relating y to x
Scatterplot	A graph that shows the relationship between two quantitative variables measured on the same cases.
Standard deviation of the residuals	s_e is found by: $$s_e = \sqrt{\frac{\sum e^2}{n - 2}}.$$
Slope	The slope, b_1, is given in y-units per x-unit. Differences of one unit in x are associated with differences of b_1 units in predicted values of y: $$b_1 = r\frac{s_y}{s_x}.$$

Skills

- Recognize when interest in the pattern of a possible relationship between two quantitative variables suggests making a scatterplot.

- Be able to identify the roles of the variables and to place the response variable on the *y*-axis and the explanatory variable on the *x*-axis.

- Know the conditions for correlation and how to check them.

- Know that correlations are between -1 and $+1$ and that each extreme indicates a perfect linear association.

- Understand how the magnitude of the correlation reflects the strength of a linear association as viewed in a scatterplot.

- Know that the correlation has no units.

- Know that the correlation coefficient is not changed by changing the centre or scale of either variable.

- Understand that causation cannot be demonstrated by a scatterplot or correlation.

- Know how to identify response (*y*) and explanatory (*x*) variables in context.

- Understand how a linear equation summarizes the relationship between two variables.

- Recognize when a regression should be used to summarize a linear relationship between two quantitative variables.

- Know how to judge whether the slope of a regression makes sense.

- Examine a scatterplot of your data for violations of the Linearity, Equal Spread, and Outlier Conditions that would make it inappropriate to compute a regression.

- Understand that the least squares slope is easily affected by extreme values.

- Define residuals as the differences between the data values and the corresponding values predicted by the line, and that the Least Squares Criterion finds the line that minimizes the sum of the squared residuals.

 DO

- Be able to make a scatterplot by hand (for a small set of data) or with technology.

- Know how to compute the correlation of two variables.

- Know how to read a correlation table produced by a statistics program.

- Know how to find the slope and intercept values of a regression.

- Be able to use regression to predict a value of *y* for a given *x*.

- Know how to compute the residual for each data value and how to compute the standard deviation of the residuals.

- Be able to evaluate the Equal Spread Condition with a scatterplot of the residuals after computing the regression.

REPORT

- Be able to describe the direction, form, and strength of a scatterplot.

- Be prepared to identify and describe points that deviate from the overall pattern.

- Be able to use correlation as part of the description of a scatterplot.

- Be alert to misinterpretations of correlation.

- Understand that finding a correlation between two variables does not indicate a causal relationship between them. Beware the dangers of suggesting causal relationships when describing correlations.

- Write a sentence explaining what a linear equation says about the relationship between y and x, basing it on the fact that the slope is given in y-units per x-unit.

- Understand how the correlation coefficient and the regression slope are related. Know that R^2 describes how much of the variation in y is accounted for by its linear relationship with x.

- Be able to describe a prediction made from a regression equation, relating the predicted value to the specified x-value.

TECHNOLOGY HELP: Correlation and Regression

All statistics packages make a table of results for a regression. These tables may differ slightly from one package to another, but all are essentially the same—and all include much more than we need to know for now. Every computer regression table includes a section that looks something like this:

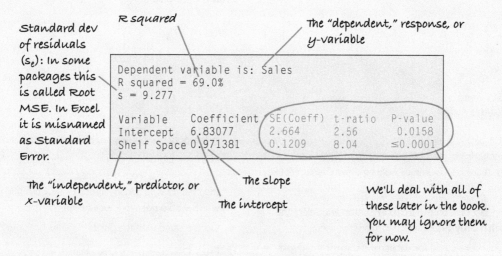

The slope and intercept coefficient are given in a table such as this one. Usually the slope is labelled with the name of the x-variable, and the intercept is labelled "Intercept" or "Constant." So the regression equation shown here is

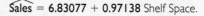

$$\widehat{\text{Sales}} = 6.83077 + 0.97138 \text{ Shelf Space.}$$

EXCEL

To make a scatterplot with the Excel Chart Wizard,

- Click on the **Chart Wizard** Button in the menu bar. Excel opens the Chart Wizard's Chart Type Dialog window.

- Make sure the **Standard Types** tab is selected, and select **XY (Scatter)** from the choices offered.

- Specify the **scatterplot without** lines from the choices offered in the Chart subtype selections. The **Next** button takes you to the Chart Source Data dialog.

- If it is not already frontmost, click on the **Data Range** tab, and enter the data range in the space provided.

- By convention, we always represent variables in columns. The Chart Wizard refers to variables as Series. Be sure the **Column** option is selected.

- Excel places the leftmost column of those you select on the x-axis of the scatterplot. If the column you wish to see on the x-axis is not the leftmost column in your spreadsheet, click on the **Series** tab and edit the specification of the individual axis series.

- Click the **Next** button. The Chart Options dialog appears.

- Select the **Titles** tab. Here you specify the title of the chart and names of the variables displayed on each axis.

- Type the chart title in the **Chart title:** edit box.
- Type the *x*-axis variable name in the **Value (X) Axis:** edit box. Note that you must name the columns correctly here. Naming another variable will not alter the plot, only mislabel it.
- Type the *y*-axis variable name in the **Value (Y) Axis:** edit box.
- Click the **Next** button to open the chart location dialog.
- Select the **As new sheet:** option button.
- Click the **Finish** button.

Often, the resulting scatterplot will require rescaling. By default, Excel includes the origin in the plot even when the data are far from zero. You can adjust the axis scales. To change the scale of a plot axis in Excel,

- Double-click on the axis. The **Format Axis Dialog** appears.
- If the **scale tab** is not the frontmost, select it.

- Enter new minimum or new maximum values in the spaces provided. You can drag the dialog box over the scatterplot as a straightedge to help you read the maximum and minimum values on the axes.
- Click the **OK** button to view the rescaled scatterplot.
- Follow the same steps for the *x*-axis scale.

Compute a correlation in Excel with the **CORREL** function from the drop-down menu of functions. If CORREL is not on the menu, choose **More Functions** and find it among the statistical functions in the browser.

In the dialog box that pops up, enter the range of cells holding one of the variables in the space provided.

Enter the range of cells for the other variable in the space provided. To calculate a regression, make a scatterplot of the data. With the scatterplot front-most, select **Add Trendline . . .** from the **Chart** menu. Click the **Options** tab and select **Display Equation on Chart.** Click **OK.**

EXCEL 2007

To make a scatterplot in Excel 2007:
- Select the columns of data to use in the scatterplot. You can select more than one column by holding down the control key while clicking.

- In the Insert tab, click on the **Scatter** button and select the **Scatter with only Markers** chart from the menu.

To make the plot more useful for data analysis, adjust the display as follows:
- With the chart selected, click on the **Gridlines** button in the Layout tab to cause the Chart Tools tab to appear.
- Within Primary Horizontal Gridlines, select **None.** This will remove the gridlines from the scatterplot.
- To change the axis scaling, click on the numbers of each axis of the chart, and click on the **Format Selection** button in the Layout tab.
- Select the **Fixed** option instead of the Auto option, and type a value more suited for the scatterplot. You can use the popup dialog window as a straightedge to approximate the appropriate values.

Excel 2007 automatically places the leftmost of the two columns you select on the *x*-axis, and the rightmost one on the *y*-axis. If that's not what you'd prefer for your plot, you'll want to switch them.
To switch the X- and Y-variables:
- Click the chart to access the **Chart Tools** tabs.
- Click on the **Select Data** button in the Design tab.

- In the popup window's Legend Entries box, click on **Edit.**
- Highlight and delete everything in the Series X Values line, and select new data from the spreadsheet. (Note that selecting the column would inadvertently select the title of the column, which would not work well here.)
- Do the same with the Series Y Values line.
- Press **OK,** then press **OK** again.

To calculate a correlation coefficient:
- Click on a blank cell in the spreadsheet.
- Go to the **Formulas** tab in the Ribbon and click **More Functions → Statistical.**
- Choose the **CORREL** function from the drop-down menu of functions.
- In the dialog that pops up, enter the range of one of the variables in the space provided.
- Enter the range of the other variable in the space provided.
- Click **OK.**

Comments

The correlation is computed in the selected cell. Correlations computed this way will update if any of the data values are changed. Before you interpret a correlation coefficient, always make a scatterplot to check for nonlinearity and outliers. If the variables are not linearly related, the correlation coefficient cannot be interpreted.

MINI CASE STUDY PROJECTS

Isak55/Shutterstock

Fuel Efficiency

With the ever-increasing price of gasoline, both drivers and auto companies are motivated to raise the fuel efficiency of cars. There are some simple ways to increase fuel efficiency: avoid rapid acceleration, avoid driving over 90 kph, reduce idling, and reduce the vehicle's weight. An extra 50 kilograms can reduce fuel efficiency by up to 2%. A marketing executive is studying the relationship between the fuel efficiency of cars (as measured in litres per 100 kilometres [L/100km]) and their weight to design a new compact car campaign. In the data set **ch06_MCSP_Fuel_Efficiency_Canada.xlsx** you'll find data on the variables below.[10]

- Model of Car
- Engine Size (L)
- Cylinders
- MSRP (Manufacturer's Suggested Retail Price in $)
- City (L/100 km)
- Highway (L/100 km)
- Weight (kilograms)
- Type and Country of manufacturer

Describe the relationship of weight, MSRP, and engine size with fuel efficiency (both city and highway) in a written report. Be sure to plot the residuals.

Energy Use at YVR

In 2013, for the fourth year in a row, the Vancouver International Airport Authority (YVR) was named the Best Airport in North America (and 8th overall worldwide) by Skytrax World Airport Awards. The operation of an airport is a complex undertaking. Budget planning requires being able to forecast costs of energy to operate the airport. With a clear idea of needs, it may be easier to negotiate favourable contracts with energy suppliers.

Earlier in this Chapter, we looked at the scatterplot of energy use versus number of passengers. Now we examine additional factors, and their relationship with energy use. The data file **ch06_MCSP_Energy_Use_YVR.xlsx** has the following variables on a monthly basis from January 1997 to December 2010.

- Date (month and year)
- Energy Use (thousands of kWh = kilowatt hours)
- MeanTemp = Mean monthly temperature (degrees Celsius)
- TotalArea = Total Area of all terminals (sq. m.)
- Pax_Domestic = Domestic passengers (000s)
- Pax_US = U.S (Trans-border) passengers (000s)
- Pax_Intl = International passengers (000s)
- Pax_Total = Total passengers (000s)

Describe the relationships between *Energy Use* and each of *MeanTemp, TotalArea,* and *Pax_Total* (i.e., three separate relationships) in a written report. Based on correlations and linear regression, which data provide the best prediction of *Energy Use*?

Cost of Living

The Mercer Human Resource Consulting website (www.mercerhr.com) lists prices of certain items in selected cities around the world. They also report an overall cost-of-living index for each city compared to the costs of hundreds of items in New York City. For example, London at 110.6 is 10.6% more expensive than New York. You'll find the 2006

---

[10] Data are from the 2004 model year and were compiled from www.Edmonds.com.

data for 16 cities in the data set **ch06_MCSP_Cost_of_Living.xls**. Included are the 2006 cost of living index, cost of a luxury apartment (per month), price of a bus or subway ride, price of a compact disc, price of an international newspaper, price of a cup of coffee (including service), and price of a fast-food hamburger meal. All prices are in U.S. dollars.

Examine the relationship between the overall cost of living and the cost of each of these individual items. Verify the necessary conditions and describe the relationship in as much detail as possible. (Remember to look at direction, form, and strength.) Identify any unusual observations.

Based on the correlations and linear regressions, which item would be the best predictor of overall cost in these cities? Which would be the worst? Are there any surprising relationships? Write a short report detailing your conclusions.

Canadian Banks

The Canadian Bankers Association works on behalf of 54 domestic banks, foreign bank subsidiaries, and foreign bank branches operating in Canada and provides a centralized contact to all banks on matters relating to banking in Canada. The CBA advocates for effective public policies that contribute to a sound, successful banking system, and promotes financial literacy to help Canadians make informed financial decisions. The CBA is involved in financial data collection and analysis, consumer protection efforts, fighting bank fraud, and developing industry consensus on issues impacting banks in Canada.

In addition to policies on financial issues, management must make decisions on infrastructure—how many branches should be opened, and how many bank machines, or automatic teller machines (ABMs) to dispense cash, should be maintained. Each year, the CBA compiles data on the number of ABMs and number of Canadian branches in each province and in the territories for the major banks in Canada: BMO, Royal Bank, TD, Scotiabank, CIBC, HSBC, Laurentian, and National Bank.

The data file **ch06_MCSP_Canadian_Banks.xlsx** has 2011 data on number of branches, number of ABMs, as well as the provincial population (in 000s) and the provincial GDP (in $ millions). The latter two come from Statistics Canada data.

Prepare four scatterplots of: *Branches* against *Population* and *GDP*, and *ABMs* against *Population* and *GDP*. Construct a correlation table from all four variables. Why are the correlation coefficients so high? Which is the better predictor of branches—population or GDP? Which is the better predictor of ABMs—population or GDP? Compute two linear regression equations, one for predicting number of branches from population, the other for predicting number of ABMs from population. Examine the residuals to determine which provinces are "underserved;" that is, have fewer branches and fewer ABMs than would be predicted from your models. Write a short report summarizing your findings.

MyStatLab **Students! Save time, improve your grades with MyStatLab.**
The Exercises marked in red can be found on MyStatLab. You can practice them as often as you want, and most feature step-by-step guided solutions to help you find the right answer. You'll find a personalized Study Plan available to you too! Data Sets for exercises marked **T** are also available on MyStatLab for formatted technologies.

EXERCISES

1. Association. Suppose you were to collect data for each pair of variables. You want to make a scatterplot. Which variable would you use as the explanatory variable and which as the response variable? Why? What would you expect to see in the scatterplot? Discuss the likely direction and form. **LO❶**
a) Cellphone bills: number of text messages, cost.
b) Automobiles: Fuel efficiency (L/100 km), sales volume (number of autos).
c) For each week: Ice cream cone sales, air conditioner sales.
d) Product: Price ($), demand (number sold per day).

2. Association, part 2. Suppose you were to collect data for each pair of variables. You want to make a scatterplot. Which variable would you use as the explanatory variable and which as the response variable? Why? What would you expect to see in the scatterplot? Discuss the likely direction and form. **LO❶**
a) T-shirts at a store: price each, number sold.
b) Real estate: house price, house size (square footage).
c) Economics: Interest rates, number of mortgage applications.
d) Employees: Salary, years of experience.

3. Scatterplots. Which of the scatterplots show: **LO❶**

a) Little or no association?
b) A negative association?
c) A linear association?
d) A moderately strong association?
e) A very strong association?

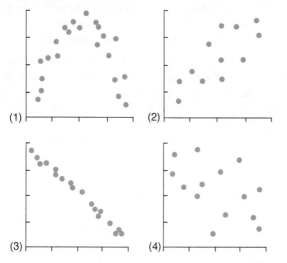

(1) (2)

(3) (4)

4. Scatterplots, part 2. Which of the scatterplots show: **LO❶**

a) Little or no association?
b) A negative association?
c) A linear association?
d) A moderately strong association?
e) A very strong association?

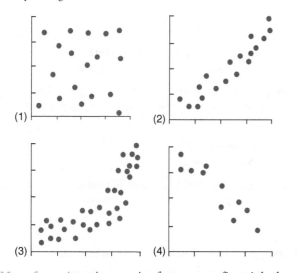

(1) (2)

(3) (4)

5. Manufacturing. A ceramics factory can fire eight large batches of pottery a day. Sometimes a few of the pieces break in the process. In order to understand the problem better, the factory records the number of broken pieces in each batch for three days and then creates the scatterplot shown. **LO❶**

a) Make a histogram showing the distribution of the number of broken pieces in the 24 batches of pottery examined.
b) Describe the distribution as shown in the histogram. What feature of the problem is more apparent in the histogram than in the scatterplot?

c) What aspect of the company's problem is more apparent in the scatterplot?

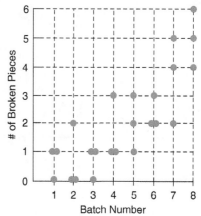

6. Coffee sales. Owners of a new coffee shop tracked sales for the first 20 days and displayed the data in a scatterplot (by day). **LO❶**

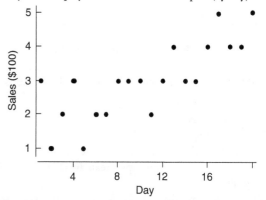

a) Make a histogram of the daily sales since the shop has been in business.
b) State one fact that is obvious from the scatterplot, but not from the histogram.
c) State one fact that is obvious from the histogram, but not from the scatterplot.

7. Matching. Here are several scatterplots. The calculated correlations are −0.923, −0.487, 0.006, and 0.777. Which is which? **LO❶**

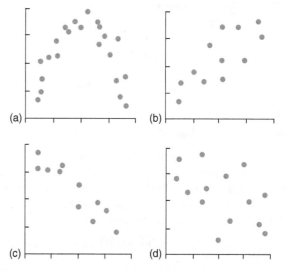

(a) (b)

(c) (d)

8. Matching, part 2. Here are several scatterplots. The calculated correlations are $-0.977, -0.021, 0.736,$ and 0.951. Which is which?   LO❶

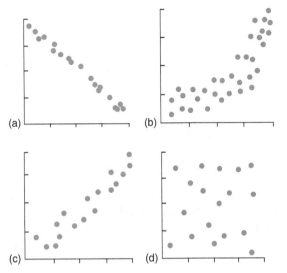

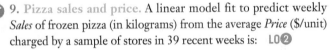

9. Pizza sales and price. A linear model fit to predict weekly *Sales* of frozen pizza (in kilograms) from the average *Price* ($/unit) charged by a sample of stores in 39 recent weeks is: LO❷

$$\widehat{Sales} = 141\,865.53 - 24\,369.49\ Price$$

a) What is the explanatory variable?
b) What is the response variable?
c) What does the slope mean in this context?
d) What does the *y*-intercept mean in this context? Is it meaningful?
e) What do you predict the sales to be if the average price charged was $3.50 for a pizza?
f) If the sales for a price of $3.50 turned out to be 60 000 kilograms, what would the residual be?

10. Used Saab prices. A linear model to predict the *Price* of a 2004 Saab 9-3 (in $) from its *Mileage* (in miles) was fit to 38 cars that were available during the week of January 11, 2008 (Kelly's Blue Book, www.kbb.com). The model was: LO❷

$$\widehat{Price} = 24\,356.15 - 0.0151\ Mileage$$

a) What is the explanatory variable?
b) What is the response variable?
c) What does the slope mean in this context?
d) What does the *y*-intercept mean in this context? Is it meaningful?
e) What do you predict the price to be for a car with 100 000 miles on it?
f) If the price for a car with 100 000 miles on it was $24 000, what would the residual be?

11. Football salaries. Is there a relationship between total team salary and the performance of teams in the National Football League (NFL)? For the 2006 season, a linear model predicting *Wins* (out of 16 regular season games) from the total team *Salary* ($M) for the 32 teams in the league is: LO❷

$$\widehat{Wins} = 1.783 + 0.062\ Salary$$

a) What is the explanatory variable?
b) What is the response variable?
c) What does the slope mean in this context?
d) What does the *y*-intercept mean in this context? Is it meaningful?
e) If one team spends $10 million more than another on salary, how many more games on average would you predict them to win?
f) If a team spent $50 million on salaries and won eight games, would they have done better or worse than predicted?
g) What would the residual of the team in part f be?

12. Baseball salaries. In 2007, the Boston Red Sox won the World Series and spent $143 million on salaries for their players (fathom.info/salaryper). Is there a relationship between salary and team performance in Major League Baseball? For the 2007 season, a linear model fit to the number of *Wins* (out of 162 regular season games) from the team *Salary* ($M) for the 30 teams in the league is: LO❷

$$\widehat{Wins} = 70.097 + 0.132\ Salary$$

a) What is the explanatory variable?
b) What is the response variable?
c) What does the slope mean in this context?
d) What does the *y*-intercept mean in this context? Is it meaningful?
e) If one team spends $10 million more than another on salaries, how many more games on average would you predict them to win?
f) If a team spent $110 million on salaries and won half (81) of their games, would they have done better or worse than predicted?
g) What would the residual of the team in part f be?

13. Pizza sales and price, revisited. For the data in Exercise 9, the average *Sales* was 52,697 kilograms (SD = 10,261 kilograms), and the correlation between *Price* and *Sales* was = −0.547.

If the *Price* in a particular week was 1 SD higher than the mean *Price*, how much pizza would you predict was sold that week?   LO❷

14. Used Saab prices, revisited. The 38 cars in Exercise 10 had an average *Price* of $23 847 (SD = $923), and the correlation between *Price* and *Mileage* was = −0.169.

If the *Mileage* of a 2004 Saab was 1 SD below the average number of miles, what *Price* would you predict for it?   LO❷

15. Packaging. A CEO announces at the annual shareholders meeting that the new see-through packaging for the company's flagship product has been a success. In fact, he says, "There is a strong correlation between packaging and sales." Criticize this statement on statistical grounds.   LO❶

16. Insurance. Insurance companies carefully track claims histories so that they can assess risk and set rates appropriately. The Insurance Bureau of Canada reports that Honda Accords, Honda Civics, and Toyota Camrys are the cars most frequently reported stolen, while Ford Tauruses, Pontiac Vibes, and Buick LeSabres are stolen least often. Is it reasonable to say that there's a correlation between the type of car you own and the risk that it will be stolen?   LO❶

17. Sales by region. A sales manager for a major pharmaceutical company analyzes last year's sales data for her 96 sales representatives, grouping them by region (1 = East Coast U.S.; 2 = Mid West U.S.; 3 = West U.S.; 4 = South U.S.; 5 = Canada; 6 = Rest of World). She plots *Sales* (in $1000) against *Region* (1–6) and sees a strong negative correlation. **LO❶**

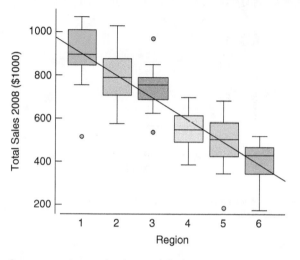

She fits a regression to the data and finds:

$$\widehat{Sales} = 1002.5 - 102.7\ Region.$$

The R^2 is 70.5%.

Write a few sentences interpreting this model and describing what she can conclude from this analysis.

18. Salary by job type. At a small company, the head of human resources wants to examine salary to prepare annual reviews. He selects 28 employees at random with job types ranging from 01 = Stocking clerk to 99 = President. He plots *Salary* ($) against *Job Type* and finds a strong linear relationship with a correlation of 0.96. **LO❶**

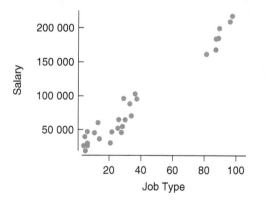

The regression output gives:

$$\widehat{Salary} = 15\ 827.9 + 1939.1\ Job\ Type$$

Write a few sentences interpreting this model and describing what he can conclude from this analysis.

T **19. Carbon footprint.** The scatterplot shows, for 2008 cars, the carbon footprint (tons of CO_2 per year) vs. the new Environ-mental Protection Agency (EPA) highway mileage for 82 family sedans as reported by the U.S. government (www.fueleconomy.gov/feg/findacar.shtml). The car with the highest highway mpg and lowest carbon footprint is the Toyota Prius. **LO❶**

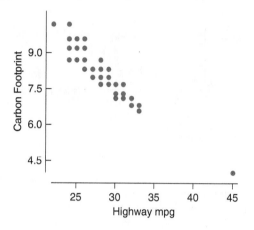

a) The correlation is −0.947. Describe the association.
b) Are the assumptions and conditions met for computing correlation?
c) Using technology, find the correlation of the data when the Prius is not included with the others. Can you explain why it changes in that way?

T **20. EPA mpg.** In 2008, the EPA revised their methods for estimating the fuel efficiency (mpg) of cars—a factor that plays an increasingly important role in car sales. How do the new highway and city estimated mpg values relate to each other? Here's a scatterplot for 83 family sedans as reported by the U.S. government. These are the same cars as in Exercise 19 except that the Toyota Prius has been removed from the data and two other hybrids, the Nissan Altima and Toyota Camry, are included in the data (and are the cars with highest city mpg). **LO❶**

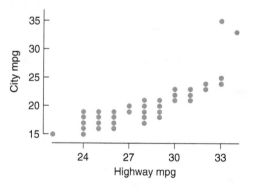

a) The correlation of these two variables is 0.823. Describe the association.
b) If the two hybrids were removed from the data, would you expect the correlation to increase, decrease, or stay the same? Try it using technology. Report and discuss what you find.

T **21. Real estate.** Is the number of total rooms in the house associated with the price of a house? Here is the scatterplot of a random sample of homes for sale: **LO❶**

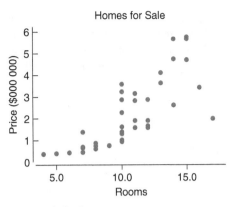

Homes for Sale

a) Is there an association?

b) Check the assumptions and conditions for correlation.

22. WestJet. WestJet is Canada's second largest Canadian air carrier, and the ninth-largest in North America by passengers carried (over 17 million in 2012). Founded in 1996, WestJet is a public company with over 9000 employees, non-unionized, and not part of any airline alliance. Here are two scatterplots of data from 1998–2012. The first shows the growth in annual revenue over time. The second shows the relationship between annual revenue and number of passengers (called "segment guests"). Describe the relationships seen in the two scatterplots. Are they linear? Are there any unusual features or data points? **LO①**

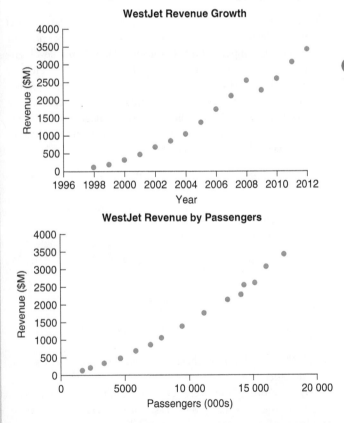

WestJet Revenue Growth

WestJet Revenue by Passengers

T **23. GDP growth.** Is economic growth in the developing world related to growth in the industrialized countries? Here's a scatterplot of the growth (in % of Gross Domestic Product) of the developing countries vs. the growth of developed countries

for 180 countries as grouped by the World Bank. Each point represents one of the years from 1970 to 2007. The output of a regression analysis follows. **LO②**

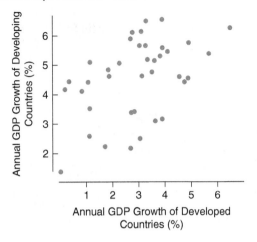

Dependent variable: GDP Growth Developing Countries
$R^2 = 20.81\%$
$s = 1.244$

Variable	Coefficient
Intercept	3.46
GDP Growth Developed Countries	0.433

a) Check the assumptions and conditions for the linear model.

b) Explain the meaning of R^2 in this context.

c) What are the cases in this model?

T **24. European GDP growth.** Is economic growth in Europe related to growth in the United States? Here's a scatterplot of the average growth in 25 European countries (in % of Gross Domestic Product) vs. the growth in the United States. Each point represents one of years from 1970 to 2007. **LO②**

Dependent variable: 25 European Countries GDP Growth
$R^2 = 29.65\%$
$s = 1.156$

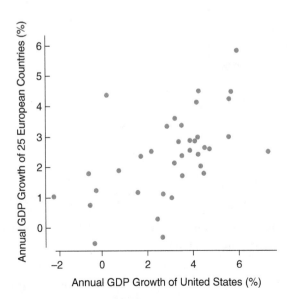

Variable	Coefficient
Intercept	1.330
U.S. GDP Growth	0.3616

a) Check the assumptions and conditions for the linear model.

b) Explain the meaning of R^2 in this context.

T **25. GDP growth part 2.** From the linear model fit to the data on GDP growth of Exercise 23. **LO❷**

a) Write the equation of the regression line.

b) What is the meaning of the intercept? Does it make sense in this context?

c) Interpret the meaning of the slope.

d) In a year in which the developed countries grow 4%, what do you predict for the developing world?

e) In 2007, the developed countries experienced a 2.65% growth, while the developing countries grew at a rate of 6.09%. Is this more or less than you would have predicted?

f) What is the residual for this year?

T **26. European GDP growth part 2.** From the linear model fit to the data on GDP growth of Exercise 24. **LO❷**

a) Write the equation of the regression line.

b) What is the meaning of the intercept? Does it make sense in this context?

c) Interpret the meaning of the slope.

d) In a year in which the United States grows at 0%, what do you predict for European growth?

e) In 2007, the United States experienced a 3.20% growth, while Europe grew at a rate of 2.16%. Is this more or less than you would have predicted?

f) What is the residual for this year?

T **27. Attendance 2006.** American League baseball games are played under the designated hitter rule, meaning that weak-hitting pitchers do not come to bat. Baseball owners believe that the designated hitter rule means more runs scored, which in turn means higher attendance. Is there evidence that more fans attend games if the teams score more runs? Data collected from American League games during the 2006 season have a correlation of 0.667 between *Runs Scored* and the number of people at the game (www.mlb.com). **LO❶**

a) Does the scatterplot indicate that it's appropriate to calculate a correlation? Explain.

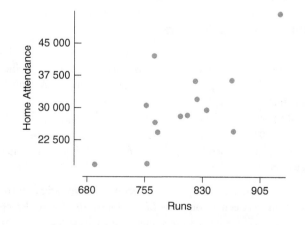

b) Describe the association between attendance and runs scored.

c) Does this association prove that the owners are right that more fans will come to games if the teams score more runs?

28. Second inning 2006. Perhaps fans are just more interested in teams that win. The displays are based on American League teams for the 2006 season (espn.go.com). Are the teams that win necessarily those that score the most runs? **LO❶**

	CORRELATION		
	Wins	Runs	Attend
Wins	1.000		
Runs	0.605	1.000	
Attend	0.697	0.667	1.000

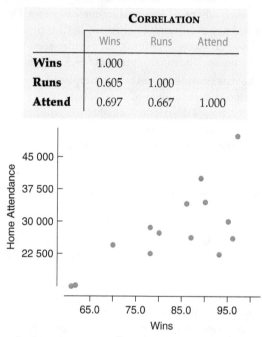

a) Do winning teams generally enjoy greater attendance at their home games? Describe the association.

b) Is attendance more strongly associated with winning or scoring runs? Explain.

c) How strongly is scoring more runs associated with winning more games?

T **29. University tuition.** The data set provided contains the yearly tuitions in 2012–2013 for undergraduate programs in arts and humanities at 66 universities and colleges that are members of the AUCC (Association of Universities and Colleges of Canada. These data were originally used in Chapter 5, Exercises 3 and 52.) Tuition fees are different for Canadian and international students. Would you expect to find a relationship between the tuitions charged by universities and colleges for each type of student? **LO❷**

a) Use the data provided to make a scatterplot of the tuition for international students against the tuition charged for Canadian students. Describe the relationship.

b) Is the direction of the relationship what you expected?

c) What is the regression equation for predicting the tuition for an international student from the tuition for a Canadian student at the same university/college?

d) Is a linear model appropriate?

e) How much more do universities/colleges charge on average in yearly tuition for international students compared to Canadian students according to this model?

f) What is the R^2 value for this model? Explain what it says.

30. NHL salaries. In Exercise 11 you examined the relationship between total team salary and performance of teams in the National Football League (NFL). Here we will examine the relationship in a different professional sports league, the National Hockey League (NHL). In 2005–2006 the NHL instituted a salary cap, the total amount of money that teams are permitted to pay their players. The purpose is to keep teams in larger markets, and therefore with more revenue, from signing all the top players to extend their advantage over smaller-market teams. The data set provided has each team's total *Payroll* ($M) and number of *Points* (based on victories) during the regular season for the 2011–2012 season. The cap that year was $64.3 million. **LO❷**

a) Use the data provided to make a scatterplot of *Points* versus *Payroll*. Describe the relationship.
b) Is the direction of the relationship what you expected?
c) Is a linear model appropriate?
d) What is the regression equation for predicting *Points* from *Payroll*?
e) What does the slope mean in this context?
f) What does the *y*-intercept mean in this context? Is it meaningful?
g) What is the R^2 value for this model? Explain what it says.
h) If one team spends $10 million more than another on salary, how many more points on average would you predict them to get?

31. Mutual funds. As the nature of investing shifted in the 1990s (more day traders and faster flow of information using technology), the relationship between mutual fund monthly performance (*Return*) in percent and money flowing (*Flow*) into mutual funds ($ million) shifted. Using only the values for the 1990s (we'll examine later years in later chapters), answer the following questions. (You may assume that the assumptions and conditions for regression are met.) **LO❷**

The least squares linear regression is:

$$\widehat{Flow} = 9747 + 771 \; Return.$$

a) Interpret the intercept in the linear model.
b) Interpret the slope in the linear model.
c) What is the predicted fund *Flow* for a month that had a market *Return* of 0%?
d) If during this month, the recorded fund *Flow* was $5 billion, what is the residual using this linear model? Did the model provide an underestimate or overestimate for this month?

32. Online clothing purchases. An online clothing retailer examined their transactional database to see if total yearly *Purchases* ($) were related to customers' *Incomes* ($). (You may assume that the assumptions and conditions for regression are met.) **LO❷**

The least squares linear regression is:

$$\widehat{Purchases} = -31.6 + 0.012 \; Income.$$

a) Interpret the intercept in the linear model.
b) Interpret the slope in the linear model.
c) If a customer has an *Income* of $20 000, what is his predicted total yearly *Purchases*?

d) This customer's yearly *Purchases* were actually $100. What is the residual using this linear model? Did the model provide an underestimate or overestimate for this customer?

33. Residual plots. Tell what each of the following residual plots indicates about the appropriateness of the linear model that was fit to the data. **LO❸**

a)   b)   c)

34. Residual plots, again. Tell what each of the following residual plots indicates about the appropriateness of the linear model that was fit to the data. **LO❸**

a)   b)   c)

35. Consumer spending. An analyst at a large credit card bank is looking at the relationship between customers' charges to the bank's card in two successive months. He selects 150 customers at random, regresses charges in *March* ($) on charges in *February* ($), and finds an R^2 of 79%. The intercept is $730.20, and the slope is 0.79. After verifying all the data with the company's CPA, he concludes that the model is a useful one for predicting one month's charges from the other. Examine the data and comment on his conclusions. **LO❷**

36. Insurance policies. An actuary at a mid-sized insurance company is examining the sales performance of the company's sales force. She has data on the average size of the policy ($) written in two consecutive years by 200 salespeople. She fits a linear model and finds the slope to be 3.00 and the R^2 is 99.92%. She concludes that the predictions for next year's policy size will be very accurate. Examine the data and comment on her conclusions. **LO❷**

37. What slope? If you create a regression model for predicting the sales ($ million) from money spent on advertising the prior month ($ thousand), is the slope most likely to be 0.03, 300 or 3000? Explain. **LO❷**

38. What slope, part 2? If you create a regression model for estimating a student's business school GPA (on a scale of 1–5) based on his math SAT (on a scale of 200–800), is the slope most likely to be 0.01, 1, or 10? Explain. **LO❷**

39. Misinterpretations. An advertising agent who created a regression model using amount spent on *Advertising* to predict annual *Sales* for a company made these two statements. Assuming the calculations were done correctly, explain what is wrong with each interpretation. **LO❶**

a) My R^2 of 93% shows that this linear model is appropriate.
b) If this company spends $1.5 million on advertising, then annual sales will be $10 million.

40. More misinterpretations. An economist investigated the association between a country's *Literacy Rate* and *Gross Domestic Product (GDP)* and used the association to draw the following conclusions. Explain why each statement is incorrect. (Assume that all the calculations were done properly.) **LO❶**

a) The *Literacy Rate* determines 64% of the *GDP* for a country.
b) The slope of the line shows that an increase of 5% in *Literacy Rate* will produce a $1 billion improvement in *GDP*.

41. Business admissions. An analyst at a business school's admissions office claims to have developed a valid linear model predicting success (measured by starting salary ($) at time of graduation) from a student's undergraduate performance (measured by GPA). Describe how you would check each of the four regression conditions in this context. **LO❸**

42. School rankings. A popular magazine annually publishes rankings of business programs. The latest issue claims to have developed a linear model predicting the school's ranking (with "1" being the highest ranked school) from its financial resources (as measured by size of the school's endowment). Describe how you would apply each of the four regression conditions in this context. **LO❸**

Ⓣ 43. Used BMW prices. A business student needs cash, so he decides to sell his car. The car is a valuable BMW 840 that was only made over the course of a few years in the late 1990s. He would like to sell it on his own, rather than through a dealer so he'd like to predict the price he'll get for his car's model year. **LO❶**

a) Make a scatterplot for the data on used BMW 840's provided.
b) Describe the association between year and price.
c) Do you think a linear model is appropriate?
d) Computer software says that $R^2 = 57.4\%$. What is the correlation between year and price?
e) Explain the meaning of R^2 in this context.
f) Why doesn't this model explain 100% of the variability in the price of a used BMW 840?

Ⓣ 44. More used BMW prices. Use the advertised prices for BMW 840s given in Exercise 43 to create a linear model for the relationship between a car's *Year* and its *Price*. **LO❷**

a) Find the equation of the regression line.
b) Explain the meaning of the slope of the line.
c) Explain the meaning of the intercept of the line.
d) If you want to sell a 1997 BMW 840, what price seems appropriate?
e) You have a chance to buy one of two cars. They are about the same age and appear to be in equally good condition. Would you rather buy the one with a positive residual or the one with a negative residual? Explain.

Ⓣ 45. Cost of living. Mercer's *Worldwide Cost of Living Survey City Rankings* determine the cost of living in the most expensive cities in the world as an index. The survey covers 214 cities across five continents and measures the comparative cost of over 200 items in each location, including transport, food, clothing, household goods, and entertainment. The cost of housing is also included and, as it is often the biggest expense for expatriates, it plays an important part in determining where cities are ranked. New York is used as the base city and all cities are compared against it. Currency movements are measured against the U.S. dollar. The scatterplot shows the ranking (1 is the most expensive) of the top

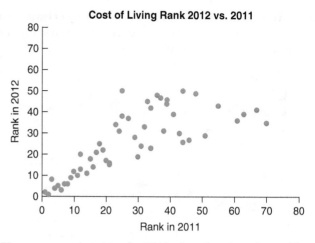

50 most expensive cities for 2012 plotted against the rankings those same cities had in the 2011. **LO❶**

a) Describe the association between the rankings in 2012 and 2011.
b) The R^2 for the regression equation is 0.590. Interpret the value of R^2.
c) Using the data provided, find the correlation.
d) Prepare a plot of the residuals. What does it say about the appropriateness of the linear model?

Ⓣ 46. Lobster prices. Over the past few decades both the demand for lobster and the price of lobster have continued to increase. The scatterplot shows this increase in the *Price* of lobster (*Price/pound*) since 1990. **LO❶**

a) Describe the increase in the *Price* of lobster since 1990.
b) The R^2 for the regression equation is 88.5%. Interpret the value of R^2.

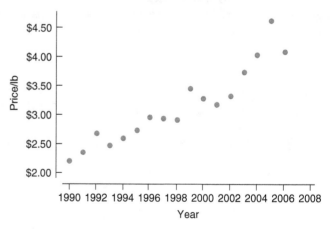

c) Find the correlation.
d) Find the linear model and examine the plot of residuals versus predicted values. Is the Equal Spread Condition satisfied? (Use time starting at 1990 so that 1990 = 0.)

47. El Niño. Concern over the weather associated with El Niño has increased interest in the possibility that the climate on Earth is getting warmer. The most common theory relates an increase in atmospheric levels of carbon dioxide (CO_2), a greenhouse gas, to increases in temperature. Here is a scatterplot showing the mean annual CO_2 concentration in the atmosphere, measured in parts per million (ppm) at the top of Mauna Loa in Hawaii, and the mean annual air temperature over both land and sea across the globe, in degrees Celsius (C). **LO❷**

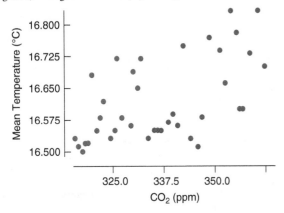

A regression predicting *Mean Temperature* from CO_2 produces the following output table (in part).

Dependent variable: Temperature
R-squared = 33.4%

Variable	Coefficient
Intercept	15.3066
CO2	0.004

a) What is the correlation between CO_2 and *Mean Temperature?*
b) Explain the meaning of *R*-squared in this context.
c) Give the regression equation.
d) What is the meaning of the slope in this equation?
e) What is the meaning of the intercept of this equation?
f) Here is a scatterplot of the residuals vs. CO_2. Does this plot show evidence of the violations of any of the assumptions of the regression model? If so, which ones?
g) CO_2 levels may reach 364 ppm in the near future. What *Mean Temperature* does the model predict for that value?

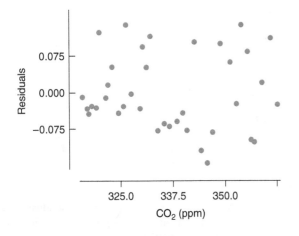

48. Hospital beds. An expert consultant in hospital resource planning states that the number of open beds that a hospital can

use effectively should be estimated by the number of FTEs (full-time equivalent employees) on staff. The consultant collected data on the number of open beds and number of FTEs for 12 hospitals, and computed the means and SDs as follows:

Number of open beds:	Mean = 50	SD = 20
Number of FTEs:	Mean = 140	SD = 40

She computed the least squares regression equation and found that for a hospital with 100 FTEs, the estimated number of open beds was 32. **LO❷**

a) Use this information to compute the value of the correlation coefficient.
b) What is the regression equation she found?
c) From the available data, what would you predict the number of open beds to be for a hospital with an unknown number of FTEs?
d) What fraction of the variation in number of open beds is explained by the number of FTEs?
e) Another expert consultant, this one in hospital administration, claims that the regression was done the wrong way around, and that the number of FTEs required in a hospital should be estimated from the number of open beds in the hospital. What would the value of the correlation coefficient be if the analysis were done this way?

✔ **JUST CHECKING ANSWERS**

1 We know the scores are quantitative. We should check to see if the *Linearity Condition* and the *Outlier Condition* are satisfied by looking at a scatterplot of the two scores.
2 It won't change.
3 It won't change.
4 They are more likely to do poorly. The positive correlation means that low closing prices for Intel are associated with low closing prices for Cypress.
5 No, the general association is positive, but daily closing prices may vary.
6 For each additional employee, monthly sales increase, on average, $122 740.
7 Thousands of $ per employee.
8 $1 227 400 per month.
9 Differences in the number of employees account for about 71.4% of the variation in the monthly sales.
10 It's positive. The correlation and the slope have the same sign.
11 R^2, No. Slope, Yes.

Randomness and Probability

CONNECTIONS: CHAPTER

The previous chapters (2 through 6) dealt with actual data and variation. Now we examine the ideas from another angle, known as probability. That is, we learn how to define and describe the situation that led to the data. In this chapter we learn the definitions of probability and the rules of figuring out probabilities. By the way, this chapter and the next one are much more theoretical than the previous ones, but that doesn't mean they are harder, just different!

Top, Feng Yu/Hemera/360/Getty Images;
bottom, Nyul/Fotolia

LEARNING OBJECTIVES

1 Use the basic rules and multiple definitions of probability

2 Use conditional probability

3 Use a contingency table of probabilities

4 Represent probabilities of multiple events using a probability tree

5 Compute probabilities of multiple events with the addition rule or the multiplication rule for probability

6 Determine if two events are disjoint (mutually exclusive) or independent

7 Identify misinterpretations of the Law of Large Numbers

Credit Reports: Equifax Canada and TransUnion Canada

Is your credit any good? What does that mean? Your credit history and the histories of millions of other people are recorded by at least one of Canada's major credit-reporting agencies, Equifax Canada or TransUnion Canada.

A credit report is a collection of information about financial transactions you have had with banks, finance companies, credit unions, and retailers, and serves as a "snapshot" of your credit history. A credit "score" is a judgment about your financial health at a particular point in time, and it indicates the risk you present for your lenders, compared with other consumers. Whenever you apply for a loan, a credit card, or even a job, your credit score will be used to determine whether you are a good risk.

Equifax and TransUnion use credit scores called FICO scores, developed by the Fair Isaacs Corporation (FICO), a company founded in 1956 with the idea that data, used intelligently, could improve business decision making. A FICO score is a number between 300 and 900, that summarizes your "credit worthiness." The higher your score, the lower the risk for the lenders. It gauges the likelihood that you will pay back borrowed amounts, based on how you handle debts. Higher scores empower you to negotiate lower interest rates on mortgages and personal loans, such as credit cards.

Although there are no established boundaries, generally scores over 750 are considered excellent, and applicants with those scores get the best rates. According to the Financial Consumer Agency of Canada, the average FICO score for Canadians is around 760. About 15% of Canadians have FICO scores below 650, which is generally considered to be a poor risk. Those with very low scores may be denied credit outright or only offered loans at substantially higher rates. It's important that you be able to verify the information that your score is based on, and all Canadians have access to their credit reports. Consumers can request changes to erroneous information and can also check which organizations have accessed their credit report recently.

Based on information from www.consumer.equifax.ca

"Chance is perhaps the pseudonym of God when He did not want to sign." —Anatole France

"The only certainty is that nothing is certain." —Pliny the Elder, Roman scholar, 23–79 CE

"We must believe in luck. For how else can we explain the success of those we don't like?" —Jean Cocteau

"If you bet on a horse, that's gambling; if you bet you can fill an inside straight, that's entertainment; if you bet cotton will go up three points, that's business. See the difference?" —Blackie Sherrod

"If thus all events through all eternity could be repeated, one would find that everything in the world happens from definite causes and according to definite rules, and that we would be forced to assume amongst the most apparently fortuitous things a certain necessity, or so to say, fate." —Jacob Bernoulli

Companies have to manage risk to survive, but by its nature, risk carries uncertainty. A bank can't know for certain that you'll pay your mortgage on time—or at all. What can they do with events they can't predict? They start with the fact that, although individual outcomes cannot be anticipated with certainty, random phenomena do, in the long run, settle into patterns that are consistent and predictable. It's this property of random events that makes Statistics practical.

7.1 Random Phenomena and Probability

When a customer calls the 800 number of a credit card company, he or she is asked for a card number before being connected with an operator. As the connection is made, the purchase records of that card and the demographic information of the customer are retrieved and displayed on the operator's screen. If the customer's FICO score is high enough, the operator may be prompted to "cross-sell" another service—perhaps a new "platinum" card for customers with a credit score of at least 750.

Of course, the company doesn't know which customers are going to call. Call arrivals are an example of a random phenomenon. With **random phenomena**, we can't predict the individual outcomes, but we can hope to understand characteristics of their long-run behaviour. We don't know whether the *next* caller will qualify for the platinum card, but as calls come into the call centre, the company will find that the percentage of platinum-qualified callers who qualify for cross-selling will settle into a pattern, like that shown in the graph in Figure 7.1.

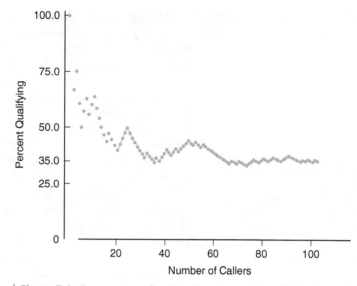

Figure 7.1 The percentage of credit card customers who qualify for the premium card.

As calls come into the call centre, the company might record whether each caller qualifies. The first caller today qualified. Then the next five callers' qualifications were no, yes, yes, no, and no. If we plot the percentage who qualify against the call number, the graph would start at 100% because the first caller qualified (1 out of 1, for 100%). The next caller didn't qualify, so the accumulated percentage dropped to 50% (1 out of 2). The third caller qualified (2 out of 3, or 67%), then yes again (3 out of 4, or 75%), then no twice in a row (3 out of 5, for 60%, and then 3 out of 6, for 50%), and so on (Table 7.1). With each new call, the new datum is a smaller fraction of the accumulated experience, so, in the long run, the graph settles down. As it settles down, it appears that, in fact, the fraction of customers who qualify is about 35%.

Call	FICO Score	Qualify?	% Qualify
1	750	Yes	100
2	640	No	50
3	765	Yes	66.7
4	780	Yes	75
5	680	No	60
6	630	No	50
⋮	⋮	⋮	⋮

Table 7.1 Data on the first six callers showing their FICO score, whether they qualified for the platinum card offer, and a running percentage of number of callers who qualified.

When talking about long-run behaviour, it helps to define our terms. For any random phenomenon, each attempt, or **trial**, generates an **outcome**. For the call centre, each call is a trial. Something happens on each trial, and we call whatever happens the outcome. Here the outcome is whether the caller qualifies or not. We use the more general term **event** to refer to outcomes or combinations of outcomes. For example, suppose we categorize callers into six risk categories and number these outcomes from 1 to 6 (of increasing credit worthiness). The three outcomes 4, 5, or 6 could make up the event "caller is at least a category 4."

A *phenomenon* consists of *trials*. Each trial has an *outcome*. Outcomes combine to make *events*.

We sometimes talk about the collection of *all possible outcomes*, a special event that we'll refer to as the **sample space**. We denote the sample space **S**; you may also see the Greek letter Ω used. But whatever symbol we use, the sample space is the set that contains all the possible outcomes. For the calls, if we let Q = qualified and N = not qualified, the sample space is simple: **S** = {Q, N}. If we look at two calls together, the sample space has four outcomes: **S** = {QQ, QN, NQ, NN}. If we were interested in at least one qualified caller from the two calls, we would be interested in the event (call it **A**) consisting of the three outcomes QQ, QN, and NQ, and we'd write **A** = {QQ, QN, NQ}.

> The *probability* of an event is its long-run relative frequency. A relative frequency is a fraction, so we can write it as $\frac{35}{100}$, as a decimal, 0.35, or as a percentage, 35%.

Although we may not be able to predict a *particular* individual outcome, such as which incoming call represents a potential upgrade sale, we can say a lot about the long-run behaviour. Look back at Figure 7.1. If you were asked for the probability that a random caller will qualify, you might say that it was 35% because, in the *long run*, the percentage of the callers who qualify is about 35%. And, that's exactly what we mean by **probability**.

That seems simple enough, but do random phenomena always behave this well? Couldn't it happen that the frequency of qualified callers never settles down, but just bounces back and forth between two numbers? Maybe it hovers around 45% for awhile, then goes down to 25%, and then back and forth forever. When we think about what happens with a series of trials, it really simplifies things if the individual trials are independent. Roughly speaking, **independence** means that the outcome of one trial doesn't influence or change the outcome of another. Recall, that in Chapter 4, we called two variables *independent* if the value of one categorical variable did not influence the value of another categorical variable. (We checked for independence by comparing relative frequency distributions across variables.) There's no reason to think that whether the one caller qualifies influences whether another caller qualifies, so these are independent trials. We'll see a more formal definition of independence later in the chapter.

> **Law of Large Numbers**
> The *long-run relative frequency* of repeated, independent events eventually produces the *true relative frequency* as the number of trials increases.

Fortunately, for independent events, we can depend on a principle called the **Law of Large Numbers (LLN)**, which states that if the events are independent, then as the number of calls increases, over days or months or years, the long-run relative frequency of qualified calls gets closer and closer to a single value. This gives us the guarantee we need and makes probability a useful concept.

Because the LLN guarantees that relative frequencies settle down in the long run, we know that the value we called the probability is legitimate and the number it settles down to is called the probability of that event. For the call centre, we can write *P*(qualified) = 0.35. Because it is based on repeatedly observing the event's outcome, this definition of probability is often called **empirical probability**.

7.2 The Nonexistent Law of Averages

> *"Slump? I ain't in no slump. I just ain't hittin'."*
>
> —Yogi Berra

The Law of Large Numbers says that the relative frequency of a random event settles down to a single number in the long run. But, it is often misunderstood to be a "law of averages," perhaps because the concept of "long run" is hard to grasp. Many people believe, for example, that an outcome of a random event that hasn't occurred in many trials is "due" to occur. The original "dogs of the Dow" strategy for buying stocks recommended buying the 10 worst performing stocks of the 30 that make up the Dow Jones Industrial Average, figuring that these "dogs" were bound to do better next year. After all, we know that in the long run, the relative frequency will settle down to the probability of that outcome, so now we have some "catching up" to do, right? Wrong. In fact, Louis Rukeyser (the former host of *Wall Street Week*) said of the "dogs of the Dow" strategy, "that theory didn't work as promised."

You may think it's obvious that the frequency of repeated events settles down in the long run to a single number. The discoverer of the Law of Large Numbers thought so, too. The way he put it was: *"For even the most stupid of men is convinced that the more observations have been made, the less danger there is of wandering from one's goal."*

— Jacob Bernoulli, 1713

"In addition, in time, if the roulette-betting fool keeps playing the game, the bad histories [outcomes] will tend to catch up with him."

Excerpt by Nassim Nicholas Taleb from FOOLED BY RANDOMNESS. Published by Random House.

Although we commonly call the two sides of a coin "heads" and "tails," technically speaking, most Canadian quarters are two-headed. The Queen's head (or King if the coin is really old) is on one side and a caribou's head is on the other side!

Actually, we know very little about the behaviour of random events in the short run. The fact that we are seeing independent random events makes each individual result impossible to predict. Relative frequencies even out *only* in the long run. And, according to the LLN, the long run is really long (infinitely long, in fact). The "Large" in the law's name means *infinitely* large. Sequences of random events don't compensate in the short run and don't need to do so to get back to the right long-run probability. Any short-run deviations will be overwhelmed in the long run. If the probability of an outcome doesn't change and the events are independent, the probability of any outcome in another trial is always what it was, no matter what has happened in other trials.

Many people confuse the Law of Large Numbers with the so-called Law of Averages that would say that things have to even out in the short run. But even though the Law of Averages doesn't exist at all, you'll hear people talk about it as if it does. Is a good hitter in baseball who has struck out the last six times due for a hit his next time up? If the stock market has been down for the last three sessions, is it due to increase today? No. This isn't the way random phenomena work. There is no Law of Averages for short runs—no "Law of Small Numbers." A belief in such a "law" can lead to poor business decisions.

You've just flipped a fair coin and seen six heads in a row. Does the coin "owe" you some tails? Suppose you spend that coin and your friend gets it in change. When she starts flipping the coin, should we expect a run of tails? Of course not. Each flip is a new event. The coin can't "remember" what it did in the past, so it can't "owe" any particular outcomes in the future. Just to see how this works in practice, we simulated 100,000 flips of a fair coin on a computer. In our 100,000 "flips," there were 2981 streaks of at least 5 heads. The "Law of Averages" suggests that the next flip after a run of 5 heads should be tails more often to even things out. Actually, the next flip was heads more often than tails: 1550 times to 1431 times. That's 51.9% heads. You can perform a similar simulation easily.

Keno and the Law of Averages.

Of course, sometimes an apparent drift from what we expect means that the probabilities are, in fact, *not* what we thought. If you get 10 heads in a row, maybe the coin has heads on both sides!

Keno is a simple casino game in which numbers from 1 to 80 are chosen. The numbers, as in most lottery games, are supposed to be equally likely. Payoffs are made depending on how many of those numbers you match on your card. A group of graduate students from a Statistics department decided to take a field trip to Reno. They (*very* discreetly) wrote down the outcomes of the games for a couple of days, then drove back to test whether the numbers were, in fact, equally likely. It turned out that some numbers were *more likely* to come up than others. Rather than bet on the Law of Averages and put their money on the numbers that were "due," the students put their faith in the LLN—and all their (and their friends') money on the numbers that had come up before. After they pocketed more than $50,000, they were escorted off the premises and invited never to show their faces in that casino again. Not coincidentally, the ringleader of that group currently makes his living on Wall Street.

✔ **JUST CHECKING**

1 It has been shown that the stock market fluctuates randomly. Nevertheless, some investors believe that they should buy right after a day when the market goes down because it is bound to go up soon. Explain why this is faulty reasoning.

7.3 Different Types of Probability

Model-Based (Theoretical) Probability

We've discussed *empirical probability*—the relative frequency of an event's occurrence as the probability of an event. There are other ways to define probability as well. Probability was first studied extensively by a group of French mathematicians who were interested in games of chance. Rather than experiment with the games and risk losing their money, they developed mathematical models of probability. To make things simple (as we usually do when we build models), they started by looking at games in which the different outcomes were equally likely. Fortunately, many games of chance are like that. Any of 52 cards is equally likely to be the next one dealt from a well-shuffled deck. Each face of a die is equally likely to land up (or at least it should be).

When outcomes are equally likely, their probability is easy to compute—it's just one divided by the number of possible outcomes. So the probability of rolling a three with a fair die is one in six, which we write as 1/6. The probability of picking the ace of spades from the top of a well-shuffled deck is 1/52.

It's almost as simple to find probabilities for events that are made up of several equally likely outcomes. We just count all the outcomes that the event contains. The probability of the event is the number of outcomes in the event divided by the total number of possible outcomes.

The 2011 Canada Census[1] provides data on the composition of private households and how many people live in each situation. For the city of Toronto, the counts are as follows:

We can write:

$$P(\mathbf{A}) = \frac{\# \text{ of outcomes in } \mathbf{A}}{\text{total } \# \text{ of outcomes}}$$

and call this the **(theoretical) probability** of the event.

In an attempt to understand why, an interviewer asked someone who had just purchased a lottery ticket, "What do you think your chances are of winning the lottery?" The reply was, "Oh, about 50–50." The shocked interviewer asked, "How do you get that?" to which the response was, "Well, the way I figure it, either I win or I don't!" The moral of this story is that events are not always equally likely.

	Number of people in Toronto
People living in family households	2 026 450
People living with relatives	81 565
People living with non-relatives only	136 830
People living alone	331 180
Total	**2 576 025**

Suppose family households are the target of telemarketers. If calls are made at random, the probability that the telemarketer reaches a person in a family household is just the number of people living in family households divided by the total number of people: 2 026 450/2 576 025 = 0.7867.

But don't get trapped into thinking that random events are always equally likely. The chance of winning a lottery—especially lotteries with very large payoffs—is small. Regardless, people continue to buy tickets.

The chance of winning the top prize in the Canadian national lottery game Lotto 6/49 is about 1 out of 14 000 000. To put that chance into perspective, that's like trying to pick a particular second out of the next five-and-a-half months!

---

[1]Source: http://www12.statcan.gc.ca/census-recensement/2011/dp-pd/prof/index.cfm?Lang=E

Another common application of probability is in weather forecasting, such as the probability of precipitation or POP. Although it refers to the "likelihood" of precipitation, the definition of POP is quite complicated and very specific. According to Environment Canada, POP is "the chance that measurable precipitation (0.2 mm of rain or 0.2 cm of snow) will fall on any point of the forecast region during the forecast period. For example, a 30% probability of precipitation means that the chance of you getting rained on (or snowed on in winter) is 3 in 10. In other words, there is a 30% chance that rain or snow will fall on you, and, therefore, a 70% chance that it won't. It must also be noted that a low POP does not mean a sunny day: it only means a day where the chance of rain or snow is low." If there is 100% probability of rain covering one side of a city and a 0% probability of rain on the other side of the city, the POP would be 50%. A 50% chance of a rainstorm covering the entire city would also lead to a POP of 50%. Note that POP is meaningless unless it is associated with a period of time. There's lots more to learn about POP; check out the *Guide to Environment Canada's Public Forecasts*, at http://www.ec.gc.ca/meteo-weather.

Personal Probability

What's the probability that gold will sell for more than $1000 an ounce at the end of next year? You may be able to come up with a number that seems reasonable. Of course, no matter how confident you feel about your prediction, your probability should be between 0 and 1. How did you come up with this probability? In our discussion of probability, we've defined probability in two ways: 1) in terms of the relative frequency—or the fraction of times—that an event occurs in the long run or 2) as the number of outcomes in the event divided by the total number of outcomes. Neither situation applies to your assessment of gold's chances of selling for more than $1000.

We use the *language* of probability in everyday speech to express a degree of uncertainty without basing it on long-run relative frequencies. Your personal assessment of an event expresses your uncertainty about the outcome. That uncertainty may be based on your knowledge of commodities markets, but it can't be based on long-run behaviour. We call this kind of probability a subjective, or **personal probability**.

Although personal probabilities may be based on experience, they are not based either on long-run relative frequencies or on equally likely events. Like the two other probabilities we defined, they need to satisfy the same rules as both empirical and theoretical probabilities that we'll discuss in the next section.

7.4 Probability Rules

For some people, the phrase "50/50" means something vague like "I don't know" or "whatever." But when we discuss probabilities, 50/50 has the precise meaning that two outcomes are *equally likely*. Speaking vaguely about probabilities can get you into trouble, so it's wise to develop some formal rules about how probability works. These rules apply to probability whether we're dealing with empirical, theoretical, or personal probability.

Rule 1. If the probability of an event occurring is 0, the event can't occur; likewise if the probability is 1, the event *always* occurs. Even if you think an event is very unlikely, its probability can't be negative, and even if you're sure it will happen, its probability can't be greater than 1. So we require that:

> **A probability is a number between 0 and 1.**
> **For any event A, $0 \leq P(A) \leq 1$.**

Rule 2. If a random phenomenon has only one possible outcome, it's not very interesting (or very random). So we need to distribute the probabilities among all the outcomes a trial can have. How can we do that so that it makes sense? For example, consider the behaviour of a certain stock. The possible daily outcomes might be:

A.   The stock price goes up.

B.   The stock price goes down.

C.   The stock price remains the same.

! **NOTATION ALERT:**
We often represent events with capital letters (such as **A** and **B**), so $P(A)$ means "the probability of event **A**."

"Baseball is 90% mental.
The other half is physical."

—Yogi Berra

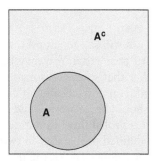

The set A and its complement
A^c. Together, they make up
the entire sample space **S**.

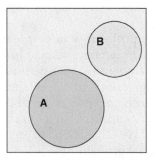

Two disjoint sets, A and B.

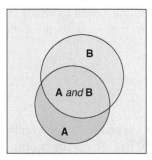

Two sets A and B that are not
disjoint. The event (A and B)
is their intersection.

When we assign probabilities to these outcomes, we should be sure to distribute
all of the available probability. Something always occurs, so the probability of
something happening is 1. This is called the **Probability Assignment Rule**:

The probability of the set of all possible outcomes must be 1.

$$P(S) = 1$$

where **S** represents the set of all possible outcomes and is called the *sample space*.

Rule 3. Suppose the probability that you get to class on time is 0.8. What's the
probability that you don't get to class on time? Yes, it's 0.2. The set of outcomes that
are *not* in the event **A** is called the "complement" of **A**, and is denoted **A**^{C}. This leads
to the **Complement Rule**:

**The probability of an event occurring is 1 minus the probability
that it doesn't occur.**

$$P(A) = 1 - P(A^C)$$

Rule 4. Whether or not a caller qualifies for a platinum card is a random outcome. Suppose the probability of qualifying is 0.35. What's the chance that the next
two callers qualify? The **Multiplication Rule** says that to find the probability that
two independent events occur, we multiply the probabilities:

**For two independent events A and B, the probability that both
A *and* B occur is the product of the probabilities of the two events.**
$$P(A \text{ and } B) = P(A) \times P(B), \text{ provided that A and B are independent.}$$

Thus if **A** = {customer 1 qualifies} and **B** = {customer 2 qualifies}, the chance that
both qualify is:

$$0.35 \times 0.35 = 0.1225$$

Of course, to calculate this probability, we have used the assumption that the two
events are independent. We'll expand the multiplication rule to be more general
later in this chapter.

Rule 5. Suppose the card centre operator has more options. She can **A**: offer a
special travel deal, **B**: offer a platinum card, or **C**: decide to send information about
a new affinity card. If she can do one, but only one, of these, then these outcomes
are **disjoint (or mutually exclusive)**. To see whether two events are disjoint, we
separate them into their component outcomes and check whether they have any
outcomes in common. For example, if the operator can choose to both offer the
travel deal and send the affinity card information, those would not be disjoint.
The **Addition Rule** allows us to add the probabilities of disjoint events to get the
probability that *either* event occurs:

$$P(A \text{ or } B) = P(A) + P(B)$$

Thus the probability that the caller *either* is offered a platinum card or is sent the affinity card information is the sum of the two probabilities, since the events are disjoint.

Rule 6. Suppose we would like to know the probability that either of the next
two callers is qualified for a platinum card? We know $P(A) = P(B) = 0.35$, but
$P(A \text{ or } B)$ is not simply the sum $P(A) + P(B)$ because the events **A** and **B** are
not disjoint in this case. Both customers could qualify. So we need a new probability rule.

✓ **JUST CHECKING**

2 MP3 players have relatively high failure rates for a consumer product, especially those models that contain a disk drive as opposed to those that have less storage but no drive. The worst failure rate for all iPod models was the 40GB Click wheel (as reported by MacIntouch.com) at 30%. If a store sells this model and failures are independent,

  a) What is the probability that the next one they sell will have a failure?
  b) What is the probability that there will be failures on *both* of the next two?
  c) What is the probability that the store's first failure problem will be with the third one they sell?
  d) What is the probability the store will have a failure problem with at least one of the next five that they sell?

We can't simply add the probabilities of **A** and **B** because that would count the outcome of *both* customers qualifying twice. So, if we started by adding the two probabilities, we could compensate by subtracting the probability of that outcome. In other words,

P (customer A *or* customer B qualifies) $= P$ (customer A qualifies) $+ P$ (customer B qualifies) $- P$ (both customers qualify)

$$= (0.35) + (0.35) - (0.35 \times 0.35) \text{ (since events are independent)}$$

$$= (0.35) + (0.35) - (0.1225)$$

$$= 0.5775$$

It turns out that this method works in general. We add the probabilities of two events and then subtract the probability of their intersection. This gives us the **General Addition Rule**, which does not require disjoint events:

$$P(\mathbf{A} \text{ or } \mathbf{B}) = P(\mathbf{A}) + P(\mathbf{B}) - P(\mathbf{A} \text{ and } \mathbf{B})$$

GUIDED EXAMPLE   M&M's Modern Market Research

In 1941, when M&M's milk chocolate candies were introduced, there were six colours: brown, yellow, orange, red, green, and violet. Mars®, the company that manufactures M&M's, has used the introduction of a new colour as a marketing and advertising event several times in the years since then. In 1980, the candy went international adding 16 countries to their markets. In 1995, the company conducted a "worldwide survey" to vote on a new colour. Over 10 million people voted to add blue. They even got the lights of the Empire State Building in New York City to glow blue to help announce the addition. In 2002, they used the internet to help pick a new colour. Children from over 200 countries were invited to respond via the internet, telephone, or mail. Millions of voters chose among purple, pink, and teal. The global winner

was purple, and for a brief time, purple M&M's could be found in packages worldwide (although in 2008, the colours were brown, yellow, red, blue, orange, and green). Overall, 42% of those who voted said purple, 37% said teal, and only 19% said pink. But in Japan the percentages were 38% pink, 36% teal, and only 16% purple. Let's use Japan's percentages to ask some questions.

1. What's the probability that a Japanese M&M's survey respondent selected at random preferred either pink or teal?

2. If we pick two respondents at random, what's the probability that they *both* selected purple?

3. If we pick three respondents at random, what's the probability that *at least one* preferred purple?

PLAN

Setup The probability of an event is its long-term relative frequency. This can be determined in several ways: by looking at many replications of an event, by deducing it from equally likely events, or by using some other information. Here, we are told the relative frequencies of the three responses.

Make sure the probabilities are legitimate. Here, they're not. Either there was a mistake or the other voters must have chosen a colour other than the three given. A check of other countries shows a similar deficit, so probably we're seeing those who had no preference or who wrote in another colour.

The M&M's website reports the proportions of Japanese votes by colour. These give the probability of selecting a voter who preferred each of the colours:

$$P(\text{pink}) = 0.38$$
$$P(\text{teal}) = 0.36$$
$$P(\text{purple}) = 0.16$$

Each is between 0 and 1, but these don't add up to 1. The remaining 10% of the voters must have not expressed a preference or written in another colour. We'll put them together into "other" and add $P(\text{other}) = 0.10$.

With this addition, we have a legitimate assignment of probabilities.

Question 1. What's the probability that a Japanese M&M's survey respondent selected at random preferred either pink or teal?

PLAN

Setup Decide which rules to use and check the conditions they require.

The events "pink" and "teal" are individual outcomes (a respondent can't choose both colours), so they are disjoint. We can apply the General Addition Rule.

DO

Mechanics Show your work.

$$P(\text{pink or teal}) = P(\text{pink}) + P(\text{teal})$$
$$- P(\text{pink and teal})$$
$$= 0.38 + 0.36 - 0 = 0.74$$

The probability that both pink and teal were chosen is zero, since respondents were limited to one choice.

REPORT

Conclusion Interpret your results in the proper context.

The probability that the respondent said pink or teal is 0.74.

Question 2. If we pick two respondents at random, what's the probability that they both said purple?

PLAN

Setup The word "both" suggests we want $P(\mathbf{A}$ and $\mathbf{B})$, which calls for the Multiplication Rule. Check the required condition.

Independence
It's unlikely that the choice made by one respondent affected the choice of the other, so the events seem to be independent. We can use the Multiplication Rule.

DO	**Mechanics** Show your work. For both respondents to pick purple, each one has to pick purple.	$P(\text{both purple})$ $= P(\text{first respondent picks purple and}$ $\quad\quad \text{second respondent picks purple})$ $= P(\text{first respondent picks purple})$ $\quad\quad \times P(\text{second respondent picks purple})$ $= 0.16 \times 0.16 = 0.0256$
REPORT	**Conclusion** Interpret your results in the proper context.	The probability that both respondents pick purple is 0.0256.

Question 3. If we pick three respondents at random, what's the probability that at least one preferred purple?

PLAN	**Setup** The phrase "at least one" often flags a question best answered by looking at the complement, and that's the best approach here. The complement of "at least one preferred purple" is "none of them preferred purple." Check the conditions.	$P(\text{at least one picked purple})$ $= P(\{\text{none picked purple}\}^c)$ $= 1 - P(\text{none picked purple})$ **Independence.** These are independent events because they are choices by three random respondents. We can use the Multiplication Rule.
DO	**Mechanics** We calculate $P(\text{none purple})$ by using the Multiplication Rule. Then we can use the Complement Rule to get the probability we want.	$P(\text{none picked purple}) = P(\text{first not purple})$ $\quad\quad\quad \times P(\text{second not purple})$ $\quad\quad\quad \times P(\text{third not purple})$ $= [P(\text{not purple})]^3$ $P(\text{not purple}) = 1 - P(\text{purple})$ $= 1 - 0.16 = 0.84$ So $P(\text{none picked purple}) = (0.84)^3 = 0.5927$ $\quad\quad\quad P(\text{at least 1 picked purple})$ $= 1 - P(\text{none picked purple})$ $= 1 - 0.5927 = 0.4073$
REPORT	**Conclusion** Interpret your results in the proper context.	There's about a 40.7% chance that at least one of the respondents picked purple.

7.5 Joint Probability and Contingency Tables

As part of a Pick Your Prize Promotion, a chain store invited customers to choose which of three prizes they'd like to win (while providing name, address, phone number, and email address). At one store, the responses could be placed in the contingency table in Table 7.2.

		Prize preference			
		Smartphone	Camera	Bike	Total
Sex	**Man**	117	50	60	**227**
	Woman	130	91	30	**251**
	Total	**247**	**141**	**90**	478

| Table 7.2 Prize preference for 478 customers.

We first encountered contingency tables in Section 4.4 as part of our discussion of categorical data. What's different here? The answer, in practical terms, is: not much. In Chapter 4 we learned how to summarize categorical data, that is, observed counts, by cross-classifying (or cross-tabulating) one categorical variable with another one. And we reported findings as relative frequencies. In this Chapter we use long-run relative frequency as the most common definition of probability.

Previously we computed the relative frequency of a particular cell in a crosstabulation; now we can think of it as the joint probability of two events, namely, the particular combination of row and column. Further, marginal distributions are now marginal probabilities and conditional distributions are conditional probabilities.

So what's different? Our language has changed and the underlying principles are now well-defined. This will allow us to move from simply describing data to describing (and later, understanding) the situation that led to the data.

If the winner is chosen at random from these customers, the probability we select a woman is just the corresponding relative frequency (since we're equally likely to select any of the 478 customers). There are 251 women in the data out of a total of 478, giving a probability of:

$$P(\text{woman}) = 251/478 = 0.525$$

This is called a **marginal probability** because it depends only on totals found in the margins of the table. The same method works for more complicated events. For example, what's the probability of selecting a woman whose preferred prize is the camera? Well, 91 women named the camera as their preference, so the probability is:

$$P(\text{woman and camera}) = 91/478 = 0.190$$

Probabilities such as these are called **joint probabilities** because they give the probability of two events occurring together.

The probability of selecting a customer whose preferred prize is a bike is:

$$P(\text{bike}) = 90/478 = 0.188$$

Since our sample space is these 478 customers, we can recognize the relative frequencies as probabilities. What if we are given the information that the selected customer is a woman? Would that change the probability that the selected customer's preferred prize is a bike? You bet it would! The charts show that women are much less likely to say their preferred prize is a bike than are men. When we restrict our focus to women, we look only at the women's row of the table, which gives the conditional distribution of preferred prizes given "woman." Of the 251 women, only 30 of them said their preferred prize was a bike. We write

> A *marginal probability* uses a marginal frequency (from either the Total row or Total column) to compute the probability.

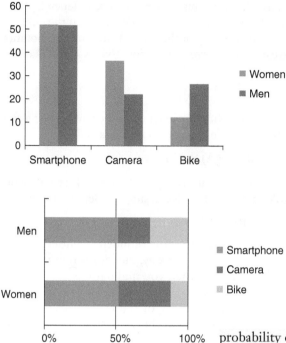

Two different views of the conditional probabilities (i.e., conditional distributions) of Prize Preference for Women and for Men.

Conditional probabilities are closely related to the row and column percentages in Chapter 4, which summarize conditional distributions. A row percentage is computed conditional on the choice of column; a column percentage is computed conditional on the choice of row. In the illustration in Section 7.5, the prize preferences for men and the prize preferences for women would be two conditional distributions based on the gender of the customer.

! **NOTATION ALERT:**
$P(\mathbf{B}|\mathbf{A})$ is the conditional probability of **B** *given* **A**.

the probability that a selected customer wants a bike *given* that we have selected a woman as:

$$P(\text{bike}|\text{woman}) = 30/251 = 0.120$$

For men, we look at the conditional distribution of preferred prizes given "man" shown in the top row of the table. There, of the 227 men, 60 said their preferred prize was a bike. So, $P(\text{bike}|\text{man}) = 60/227 = 0.264$, more than twice the women's probability (see figure at left).

7.6 Conditional Probability

In general, when we want the probability of an event from a *conditional* distribution, we write $P(\mathbf{B}|\mathbf{A})$ and pronounce it "the probability of **B** *given* **A**." A probability that takes into account a given *condition* such as this is called a **conditional probability**.

Let's look at what we did. We worked with the counts, but we could work with the probabilities just as well. There were 30 women who selected a bike as a prize, and there were 251 women customers. So we found the probability to be 30/251. To find the probability of the event **B** *given* the event **A**, we restrict our attention to the outcomes in **A**. We then find in what fraction of *those* outcomes **B** also occurred. Formally, we write:

$$P(\mathbf{B}|\mathbf{A}) = \frac{P(\mathbf{A} \text{ and } \mathbf{B})}{P(\mathbf{A})}$$

We can use the formula directly with the probabilities derived from the contingency table (Table 7.2) to find:

$$P(\text{bike}|\text{woman}) = \frac{P(\text{bike and woman})}{P(\text{woman})} = \frac{30/478}{251/478} = \frac{0.063}{0.525} = 0.120 \text{ as before.}$$

The formula for conditional probability requires one restriction. The formula works only when the event that's given has probability greater than 0. The formula doesn't work if $P(\mathbf{A})$ is 0 because that would mean we had been "given" the fact that **A** was true even though the probability of **A** is 0, which would be a contradiction.

Rule 7. Remember the Multiplication Rule for the probability of **A** *and* **B**? It said

$$P(\mathbf{A} \text{ and } \mathbf{B}) = P(\mathbf{A}) \times P(\mathbf{B})$$

when **A** and **B** are independent. Now we can write a more general rule that doesn't require independence. In fact, we've already written it. We just need to rearrange the equation a bit.

The equation in the definition for conditional probability contains the probability of **A** *and* **B**. Rearranging the equation gives the **General Multiplication Rule** for compound events that does not require the events to be independent:

$$P(\mathbf{A} \text{ and } \mathbf{B}) = P(\mathbf{A}) \times P(\mathbf{B}|\mathbf{A})$$

The probability that two events, **A** and **B**, both occur is the probability that event **A** occurs multiplied by the probability that event **B** *also* occurs—that is, by the probability that event **B** occurs given that event **A** occurs.

Of course, there's nothing special about which event we call **A** and which one we call **B**. We should be able to state this the other way around. Indeed we can. It is equally true that:

$$P(\mathbf{A} \text{ and } \mathbf{B}) = P(\mathbf{B}) \times P(\mathbf{A}|\mathbf{B})$$

Let's return to the question of just what it means for events to be independent. We said informally in Chapter 4 that what we mean by independence is that the outcome of one event does not influence the probability of the other. With our new notation for conditional probabilities, we can write a formal definition. Events **A** and **B** are are **independent** whenever:

$$P(\mathbf{B}\,|\,\mathbf{A}) = P(\mathbf{B})$$

Now we can see that the Multiplication Rule for independent events is just a special case of the General Multiplication Rule. The general rule says

$$P(\mathbf{A}\ and\ \mathbf{B}) = P(\mathbf{A}) \times P(\mathbf{B}\,|\,\mathbf{A})$$

whether the events are independent or not. But when events **A** and **B** are independent, we can write $P(\mathbf{B})$ for $P(\mathbf{B}\,|\,\mathbf{A})$ and we get back our simple rule:

$$P(\mathbf{A}\ and\ \mathbf{B}) = P(\mathbf{A}) \times P(\mathbf{B})$$

Sometimes people use this statement as the definition of independent events, but we find the other definition more intuitive. Either way, the idea is that the probabilities of independent events don't change when you find out that one of them has occurred.

Using our earlier example, is the probability of the event *choosing a bike* independent of the sex of the customer? We need to check whether

$$P(\text{bike}\,|\,\text{man}) = \frac{P(\text{bike } and \text{ man})}{P(\text{man})} = \frac{0.126}{0.475} = 0.265$$

is the same as $P(\text{bike}) = 0.189$.

Because these probabilities aren't equal, we can say that prize preference is *not* independent of the sex of the customer. Whenever at least one of the joint probabilities in the table is *not* equal to the product of the marginal probabilities, we say that the variables are not independent.

◆ **Independent *vs.* Disjoint.** Are disjoint events independent? Both concepts seem to have similar ideas of separation and distinctness about them, but in fact disjoint events *cannot* be independent.[2] Let's see why. Consider the two disjoint events {you get an A in this course} and {you get a B in this course}. They're disjoint because they have no outcomes in common. Suppose you learn that you *did* get an A in the course. Now what is the probability that you got a B? You can't get both grades, so it must be 0.

Think about what that means. Knowing that the first event (getting an A) occurred changed your probability for the second event (down to 0). So these events aren't independent.

Mutually exclusive events can't be independent. They have no outcomes in common, so knowing that one occurred means the other didn't. A common error is to treat disjoint events as if they were independent and apply the Multiplication Rule for independent events. Don't make that mistake.

7.7 Constructing Contingency Tables

Sometimes we're given probabilities without a contingency table. You can often construct a simple table to correspond to the probabilities.

A survey of real estate in Saskatchewan classified homes into two price categories (Low—less than \$250 000 and High—over \$250 000). It also noted whether the

> If we had to pick one key idea in this chapter that you should understand and remember, it's the definition and meaning of *independence*.

LM Productions/Photodisc/Getty Images

---

[2] Technically two disjoint events *can* be independent, but only if the probability of one of the events is 0. For practical purposes, we can ignore this case, since we don't anticipate collecting data about things that can't possibly happen.

houses had at least two bathrooms or not (True or False). We are told that 56% of the houses had at least two bathrooms, 62% of the houses were Low priced, and 22% of the houses were both. That's enough information to fill out the table. Translating the percentages to probabilities, we have:

		At least two Bathrooms		
		True	False	Total
Price	**Low**	0.22		**0.62**
	High			
	Total	**0.56**		**1.00**

The 0.56 and 0.62 are marginal probabilities, so they go in the margins. What about the 22% of houses that were both Low priced and had at least two bathrooms? That's a *joint* probability, so it belongs in the interior of the table.

Because the cells of the table show disjoint events, the probabilities always add to the marginal totals going across rows or down columns.

		At least two Bathrooms		
		True	False	Total
Price	**Low**	0.22	0.40	**0.62**
	High	0.34	0.04	**0.38**
	Total	**0.56**	**0.44**	**1.00**

Now, finding any other probability is straightforward. For example, what's the probability that a high-priced house has at least two bathrooms?

P(at least two bathrooms | high-priced)

$= P$(at least 2 bathrooms *and* high-priced)$/P$(high-priced)

$= 0.34/0.38 = 0.895$ or 89.5%

✔ JUST CHECKING

3 Suppose a supermarket is conducting a survey to find out the busiest time and day for shoppers. Survey respondents are asked 1) whether they shopped at the store on a weekday or on the weekend and 2) whether they shopped at the store before or after 5 p.m. The survey revealed that:

- 48% of shoppers visited the store before 5 p.m.
- 27% of shoppers visited the store on a weekday (Mon.–Fri.)
- 7% of shoppers visited the store before 5 p.m. on a weekday.

a) Make a contingency table for the variables *time of day* and *day of week*.

b) What is the probability that a randomly selected shopper who shops before 5 p.m. also shops on a weekday?

c) Are time and day of the week disjoint events?

d) Are time and day of the week independent events?

Kim Steele/Photodisc/Getty Images

7.8 Probability Trees

Some decisions involve more subtle evaluation of probabilities. Given the probabilities of various states of nature, an analyst can use a picture called a **probability tree** or **tree diagram** to help think through the decision-making process. A tree shows sequences of events as paths that look like branches of a tree. This can enable the analyst to compare several possible scenarios. Here's a manufacturing example.

Personal electronic devices are getting smaller all the time. Manufacturing components for these devices is a challenge, and at the same time, consumers are demanding more and more functionality and increasing sturdiness. Microscopic and even submicroscopic flaws can develop during their fabrication that can blank out pixels on the screens or cause intermittent performance failures. Defects will always occur, so the quality engineer in charge of the production process must monitor the number of defects and take action if the process seems out of control.

Let's suppose that the engineer is called down to the production line because the number of defects has crossed a threshold and the process has been declared to be out of control. She must decide between two possible actions. She knows that a small adjustment to the robots that assemble the components can fix a variety of problems, but for more complex problems, the entire production line needs to be shut down to pinpoint the problem. The adjustment requires that production be stopped for about an hour. But shutting down the line takes at least an entire shift (eight hours). Naturally, her boss would prefer that she make the simple adjustment. But without knowing the source or severity of the problem, she can't be sure whether that will be successful.

If the engineer wants to predict whether the smaller adjustment will work, she can use a probability tree to help make the decision. Based on her experience, the engineer thinks that there are three possible problems: (1) the motherboards could have faulty connections, (2) the memory could be the source of the faulty connections, or (3) some of the cases may simply be seating incorrectly in the assembly line. She knows from past experience how often these types of problem crop up and how likely it is that just making an adjustment will fix each type of problem. *Motherboard* problems are rare (10%), *memory* problems have been showing up about 30% of the time, and *case* alignment issues occur most often (60%). We can put those probabilities on the first set of branches.

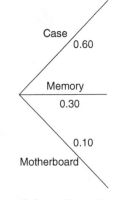

Case
0.60

Memory
0.30

0.10
Motherboard

Figure 7.2 Possible problems and their probabilities.

Notice that we've covered all the possibilities, and so the probabilities sum to one. To this diagram we can now add the *conditional* probabilities that a minor adjustment will fix each type of problem. Most likely the engineer will rely on her experience or assemble a team to help determine these probabilities. For example, the engineer knows that motherboard connection problems are not likely to be fixed with a simple adjustment: P(Fix | Motherboard) = 0.10. After some discussion, she and her team determine that P(Fix | Memory) = 0.50 and P(Fix | Case alignment) = 0.80. At the end of each branch representing the problem type, we draw two possibilities (*Fix* or *Not Fixed*) and write the conditional probabilities on the branches.

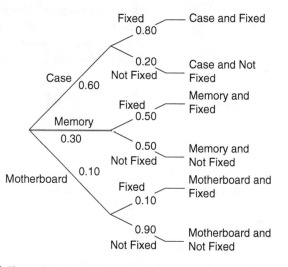

Figure 7.3 Extending the tree diagram, we can show both the problem class and the outcome probabilities. The outcome (Fixed or Not fixed) probabilities are conditional on the problem type, and they change depending on which branch we follow.

At the end of each second branch, we write the *joint event* corresponding to the combination of the two branches. For example, the top branch is the combination of the problem being Case alignment, and the outcome of the small adjustment is that the problem is now Fixed. For each of the joint events, we can use the general multiplication rule to calculate their joint probability. For example:

$$P(\text{Case and Fixed}) = P(\text{Case}) \times P(\text{Fixed} \mid \text{Case})$$
$$= 0.60 \times 0.80 = 0.48$$

We write this probability next to the corresponding event. Doing this for all branch combinations gives the Figure 7.4.

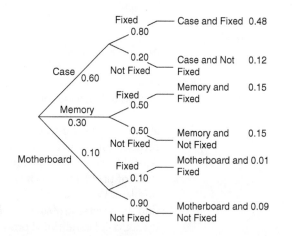

Figure 7.4 We can find the probabilities of compound events by multiplying the probabilities along the branch of the tree that leads to the event, just the way the General Multiplication Rule specifies.

All the outcomes at the far right are disjoint because at every node, all the choices are disjoint alternatives. And those alternatives are *all* the possibilities, so the probabilities on the far right must add up to 1.

Because the final outcomes are disjoint, we can add up any combination of probabilities to find probabilities for compound events. In particular, the engineer can answer her question: What's the probability that the problem will be fixed by a simple adjustment? She finds all the outcomes on the far right in which the problem was fixed. There are three (one corresponding to each type of problem), and she adds their probabilities: $0.48 + 0.15 + 0.01 = 0.64$. So 64% of all problems are fixed by the simple adjustment. The other 36% require a major investigation.

*7.9 Reversing the Conditioning: Bayes' Rule

The engineer in our story decided to try the simple adjustment and, fortunately, it worked. Now she needs to report to the quality engineer on the next shift what she thinks the problem was. Was it more likely to be a case alignment problem or a motherboard problem? We know the probabilities of those problems beforehand, but they change now that we have more information. What are the likelihoods that each of the possible problems was, in fact, the one that occurred?

Unfortunately, we can't read those probabilities from the tree in Figure 7.4. For example, the tree gives us $P(\text{Fixed and Case}) = 0.48$, but we want $P(\text{Case} \,|\, \text{Fixed})$. We know $P(\text{Fixed} \,|\, \text{Case}) = 0.80$, but that's not the same thing. It isn't valid to reverse the order of conditioning in a conditional probability statement. To "turn" the probability around, we need to go back to the definition of conditional probability.

$$P(\text{Case} \,|\, \text{Fixed}) = \frac{P(\text{Case and Fixed})}{P(\text{Fixed})}$$

We can read the probability in the numerator from the tree, and we've already calculated the probability in the denominator by adding all the probabilities on the final branches that correspond to the event *Fixed*. Putting those values in the formula, the engineer finds:

$$P(\text{Case} \,|\, \text{Fixed}) = \frac{0.48}{0.48 + 0.15 + 0.01} = 0.75$$

It is hard to believe that a seemingly innocuous rule about reversing conditional probabilities could have led to a 200-year controversy and a deep philosophical divide about probability. Simply put, Bayes' rule says: update your initial belief with objective new information and get a new and improved belief. The rule led to the field of Bayesian analysis, and the controversy arose over whether you should base your probability on an initial belief (Bayesian inference) or rely solely on new information (empirical probability). The problem is that the initial belief may not be related to the current data.

Sharon Bertsch McGrayne, author of a fascinating book on Bayes' rule called *The Theory That Would Not Die*, notes that Bayesian analysis is used for computer spam filters, locating shipwreck survivors, translating languages, predicting election winners, and breaking codes. Alan Krueger, chair of President Obama's Council of Economic Advisers, said, "It is important in decision-making—how tightly should you hold on to your view and how much should you update your view based on the new information that's coming. We intuitively use Bayes' rule every day."

She knew that 60% of all problems were due to case alignment, but now that she knows the problem has been fixed, she knows more. Given the additional information that a simple adjustment was able to fix the problem, she now can increase the probability that the problem was case alignment to 0.75.

It's usually easiest to solve problems like this by reading the appropriate probabilities from the tree. However, we can write a general formula for finding the reverse conditional probability. To understand it, let's review our example again. Let $\mathbf{A}_1 = \{\text{Case}\}$, $\mathbf{A}_2 = \{\text{Memory}\}$, and $\mathbf{A}_3 = \{\text{Motherboard}\}$ represent the three types of problems. Let $\mathbf{B} = \{\text{Fixed}\}$, meaning that the simple adjustment fixed the problem. We know $P(\mathbf{B} \,|\, \mathbf{A}_1) = 0.80$, $P(\mathbf{B} \,|\, \mathbf{A}_2) = 0.50$, and $P(\mathbf{B} \,|\, \mathbf{A}_3) = 0.10$. We want to find the reverse probabilities, $P(\mathbf{A}_i \,|\, \mathbf{B})$, for the three possible problem types. From the definition of conditional probability, we know (for any of the three types of problems):

$$P(\mathbf{A}_i \,|\, \mathbf{B}) = \frac{P(\mathbf{A}_i \text{ and } \mathbf{B})}{P(\mathbf{B})}$$

We still don't know either of these quantities, but we use the definition of conditional probability again to find $P(A_i \text{ and } B) = P(B|A_i)P(A_i)$, both of which we know. Finally, we find $P(B)$ by adding up the probabilities of the three events.

$$P(B) = P(A_1 \text{ and } B) + P(A_2 \text{ and } B) + P(A_3 \text{ and } B)$$
$$= P(B|A_1)P(A_1) + P(B|A_2)P(A_2) + P(B|A_3)P(A_3)$$

In general, we can write this for n events A_i that are mutually exclusive (each pair is disjoint) and exhaustive (their union is the whole space). Then:

$$P(A_i \mid B) = \frac{P(B|A_i)P(A_i)}{\sum_j P(B|A_j)P(A_j)}$$

This formula is known as Bayes' rule, after the Reverend Thomas Bayes (1702–1761), even though historians doubt that it was actually Bayes who first came up with the reverse conditioning probability. When you need to find reverse conditional probabilities, we recommend drawing a tree and finding the appropriate probabilities as we did at the beginning of the section, but the formula gives the general rule.

The Nobel-Prize winning economist Daniel Kahneman and his collaborator Amos Tversky created the following example to illustrate conditional probabilities and Bayes' rule.

A taxicab was involved in a hit-and-run accident at night. Two cab companies, the Green and the Blue, operate in the city. You are given the following data.

◆ *85% of the cabs in the city are Green and 15% are Blue.*

◆ *A witness identified the cab as Blue. The court tested the reliability of the witness under the same circumstances that existed on the night of the accident and concluded that the witness correctly identified each of the two colours 80% of the time and failed 20% of the time.*

What is the probability that the cab involved in the accident was Blue rather than Green?

The typical answer is around 80%. The correct answer is around 41%. In fact, the hit-and-run cab is more likely to be Green than Blue! Why? Let's apply Bayes' rule to solve this.

Bayes' rule: $P(\text{true Blue} \mid \text{predicted Blue})$

$$= (0.15)(0.80) / [(0.15)(0.80) + (0.85)(0.20)]$$
$$= 0.12 / [0.12 + 0.17] = 0.12 / 0.29 = 0.41 \text{ or } 41\%$$

Here another way to think of it. Suppose there are 100 cabs in the city; 85 are Green and 15 are Blue. Consider the 15 Blue cabs: they are seen as Blue 80% of the time, so we can expect 12 "blue sightings" and 3 "green sightings." So there are 12 correct sightings of blue cabs. Now consider the 85 Green cabs: they are seen as Blue 20% of the time, so we can expect 17 "blue sightings" and 68 "green sightings." So there are 17 incorrect sightings of blue cabs. In total, then, the witness would identify 29 blue cabs (of the 100 cabs), but only 12 of the 29 would actually be blue. And, as above, 12 out of 29 is 41%.

7.10 Fun with Probability!

Probability can be very counterintuitive, but if you follow the rules, you'll get to the correct answer. Here are three famous examples.

Red and White

A statistician tells you he has three cards, the first is red on both sides, the second is white on both sides, and the third is red on one side and white on the other side. You choose one at random; the probability of choosing the all-red card is, of course, 1/3. But suppose that the statistician shows you that one side of the card you chose is red. What is the probability that you have chosen the all-red card?

The standard answer is 1/2, where the reasoning goes as follows. Since you see that one side is red, the card can't be the all-white card. That leaves two cards, one of which is all-red, hence one in two. However, the information you have been given changes the probabilities. The cards are no longer equally likely. The red side you are seeing could be the front of the all-red card, the back of the all-red card, or the red side of the half and half card. That is, there are three red sides and two of them belong to the all-red card, so the probability is 2/3, not 1/2. Counterintuitive? Only if you don't think about conditional probability and update your belief!

The Birthday Problem

What is the minimum number of randomly chosen people so that the probability is greater than one-half that at least two of them share the same birthday?

For simplicity, let's disregard leap years and the fact that real-life birthdays are not distributed evenly. By applying the rules of complements, multiplication, and independent events we get the following.

In order to have no matching birthdays among *n* people, the first person can have a birthday on any of 365 days since they are the first. The second person can have a birthday on any of 364 days, excluding the day of the first person's birthday. The third person's birthday can be on any of 363 days, excluding the first two persons' birthdays. And so on to the *n*th person. Here is the formula:

$$P(\text{at least one match}) = 1 - P(\text{no match}) = 1 - \left(\frac{365}{365}\right) \times \left(\frac{364}{365}\right) \times \left(\frac{363}{365}\right) \times \ldots \times \left(\frac{365 - (n-1)}{365}\right)$$

The probability of at least one match passes 50% when $n = 23$, far fewer than most people might think. With 30 people, the chances are about 70%, with 40 people about 90%, and with 57 people, the chances are 99%. With 100 people, the chances are 99.99997%, essentially a sure thing. Incidentally, there have been 22 Canadian Prime Ministers (as of 2013); Sir John A. Macdonald and Jean Chrétien share a birthday on January 11.

A much tougher question is to figure out how many people are needed to have better than a 50:50 chance that three of them share a birthday! We'll leave that one for you to figure out or research!

The Three Doors Problem (a.k.a. The Monty Hall Puzzle)

Suppose you're on a game show, and you're given the choice of three doors. Behind one door is a car, the others, goats. You pick a door, say #1, and the host, who knows what's behind the doors, opens another door, say #3, which has a goat. He says to you, "Do you want to stay with #1 or do you want to switch to #2?" Is it to your advantage to switch your choice of doors?

The common answer is: No, don't switch. The reasoning is usually like this. If one door is shown to be a loser, that information changes the probability of either remaining choice, neither of which has any reason to be more likely, to 1/2.

It turns out that is the wrong answer! If you switch, you have a 2/3 chance of winning. The 1/3 chance of winning on the first door chosen can't go up just because the host opens a losing door. We can demonstrate it easily as follows. Let's play six games that cover all the possibilities. For the first three games, you choose

#1 and "stay" each time. For the second three games, you choose #1 and "switch" each time, and the host always opens a loser. Here are the results.

	DOOR1	DOOR2	DOOR3	RESULT
Game 1	**Auto**	Goat	Goat	Stay and win
Game 2	Goat	**Auto**	Goat	Stay and lose
Game 3	Goat	Goat	**Auto**	Stay and lose
Game 4	**Auto**	Goat	Goat	Switch and lose
Game 5	Goat	**Auto**	Goat	Switch and win
Game 6	Goat	Goat	**Auto**	Switch and win

When you switch, you win 2/3 of the time! Much has been written about this probability puzzle. It's very counterintuitive but it's true!

By the way, you can win a lot of bets with puzzles like these. One author has had a lot of his drinks paid for by people who don't understand probability!

WHAT CAN GO WRONG?

- **Beware of probabilities that don't add up to 1.** To be a legitimate assignment of probability, the sum of the probabilities for all possible outcomes must total 1. If the sum is less than 1, you may need to add another category ("other") and assign the remaining probability to that outcome. If the sum is more than 1, check that the outcomes are disjoint. If they're not, then you can't assign probabilities by counting relative frequencies.

- **Don't add probabilities of events if they're not disjoint.** Events must be disjoint to use the Addition Rule. The probability of being under 80 *or* a female is not the probability of being under 80 *plus* the probability of being female. That sum may be more than 1.

- **Don't multiply probabilities of events if they're not independent.** The probability of selecting a customer at random who is over 70 years old *and* retired is not the probability the customer is over 70 years old *times* the probability the customer is retired. Knowing that the customer is over 70 changes the probability of his or her being retired. You can't multiply these probabilities. The multiplication of probabilities of events that are not independent is one of the most common errors people make in dealing with probabilities.

- **Don't confuse disjoint and independent.** Disjoint events *can't* be independent. If **A** = {you get a promotion} and **B** = {you don't get a promotion}, **A** and **B** are disjoint. Are they independent? If you find out that **A** is true, does that change the probability of **B**? You bet it does! So they can't be independent.

A national chain of hair salons is considering the inclusion of some spa services. A management team was organized to investigate the possibility of entering the spa market via two offerings: facials or massages. One member of the team, Sherrie Trapper, had found some results published by a spa industry trade journal regarding the probability of salon customers purchasing these types of services. She wasn't quite sure how to interpret the probabilities but reported them this way. There is an 80% chance that a customer visiting a hair salon that offers spa services will be there for hair styling services. Of those, 50% will purchase facials. On the other hand, 90% of customers visiting salons that offer spa services will be there for hair styling

services or massages. Consequently she argued in favour of offering massages rather than facials on their initial spa menu.

ETHICAL ISSUE *Sherrie does not understand what she is reporting and consequently should not use this information to persuade others on the team (related to ASA Ethical Guidelines, Item A, which can be found at http://www.amstat.org/about/ethicalguidelines.cfm).*

ETHICAL SOLUTION *Sherrie should share all details of the published results with the management team. The probabilities she is reporting are not comparable (one is conditional and the other is the probability of a union).*

WHAT HAVE WE LEARNED?

We've learned that probability is based on long-run relative frequencies and that the Law of Large Numbers speaks only of long-run behaviour. Because the long run is a very long time, we need to be careful not to misinterpret the Law of Large Numbers as a law of averages. Even when we've observed a string of heads, we shouldn't expect extra tails in subsequent coin flips.

Also, we've learned some basic rules for combining probabilities of outcomes to find probabilities of more complex events. These include:

1. Probability for any event is between 0 and 1
2. Probability of the sample space, **S**, the set of possible outcomes = 1
3. Complement Rule
4. Multiplication Rule for independent events
5. General Addition Rule
6. General Multiplication Rule

Finally, we've learned how to construct tree diagrams for helping to think through conditional probabilities.

Terms

Addition Rule   If **A** and **B** are disjoint events, then the probability of **A** or **B** is:

$$P(\mathbf{A} \ or \ \mathbf{B}) = P(\mathbf{A}) + P(\mathbf{B})$$

Complement Rule   The probability of an event occurring is 1 minus the probability that it doesn't occur:

$$P(\mathbf{A}) = 1 - P(\mathbf{A}^{\mathbf{C}})$$

Conditional probability	$$P(\mathbf{B}\,|\,\mathbf{A}) = \frac{P(\mathbf{A}\ and\ \mathbf{B})}{P(\mathbf{A})}$$
	$P(\mathbf{B}\,|\,\mathbf{A})$ is read "the probability of $\mathbf{B}$ *given* $\mathbf{A}$."
Disjoint (or Mutually Exclusive) Events	Two events are disjoint if they have no outcomes in common. If $\mathbf{A}$ and $\mathbf{B}$ are disjoint, then knowing that $\mathbf{A}$ occurs tells us that $\mathbf{B}$ cannot occur. Disjoint events are also called "mutually exclusive."
Empirical probability	When the probability comes from the long-run relative frequency of the event's occurrence, it is an empirical probability.
Event	A collection of outcomes. Usually, we identify events so that we can attach probabilities to them. We denote events with bold capital letters such as $\mathbf{A}$, $\mathbf{B}$, or $\mathbf{C}$.
General Addition Rule	For any two events, $\mathbf{A}$ and $\mathbf{B}$, the probability of $\mathbf{A}$ *or* $\mathbf{B}$ is: $$P(\mathbf{A}\ or\ \mathbf{B}) = P(\mathbf{A}) + P(\mathbf{B}) - P(\mathbf{A}\ and\ \mathbf{B})$$
General Multiplication Rule	For any two events, $\mathbf{A}$ and $\mathbf{B}$, the probability of $\mathbf{A}$ and $\mathbf{B}$ is: $$P(\mathbf{A}\ and\ \mathbf{B}) = P(\mathbf{A}) \times P(\mathbf{B}\,|\,\mathbf{A})$$
Independence (used informally)	Two events are *independent* if the fact that one event occurs does not change the probability of the other.
Independence (used formally)	Events $\mathbf{A}$ and $\mathbf{B}$ are independent when $P(\mathbf{B}\,|\,\mathbf{A}) = P(\mathbf{B})$.
Joint probabilities	The probability that two events both occur.
Law of Large Numbers (LLN)	The Law of Large Numbers states that the *long-run relative frequency* of repeated, independent events settles down to the *true relative frequency* as the number of trials increases.
Marginal probability	In a joint probability table a marginal probability is the probability distribution of either variable separately, usually found in the rightmost column or bottom row of the table.
Multiplication Rule	If $\mathbf{A}$ and $\mathbf{B}$ are independent events, then the probability of $\mathbf{A}$ *and* $\mathbf{B}$ is: $$P(\mathbf{A}\ and\ \mathbf{B}) = P(\mathbf{A}) \times P(\mathbf{B})$$
Outcome	The outcome of a trial is the value measured, observed, or reported for an individual instance of that trial.
Personal probability	When the probability is subjective and represents your personal degree of belief, it is called a personal probability.
Probability	The probability of an event is a number between 0 and 1 that reports the likelihood of the event's occurrence. A probability can be derived from a model (such as equally likely outcomes), from the long-run relative frequency of the event's occurrence, or from subjective degrees of belief. We write $P(\mathbf{A})$ for the probability of the event $\mathbf{A}$.
Probability Assignment Rule	The probability of the entire sample space must be 1: $$P(\mathbf{S}) = 1$$

Random phenomenon	A phenomenon is random if we know what outcomes could happen, but not which particular values will happen.
Sample space	The collection of all possible outcome values. The sample space has a probability of 1.
Theoretical probability	When the probability comes from a mathematical model (such as, but not limited to, equally likely outcomes), it is called a theoretical probability.
Tree diagram (or probability tree)	A display of conditional events or probabilities that is helpful in thinking through conditioning.
Trial	A single attempt or realization of a random phenomenon.

Skills

PLAN

- Be able to understand that random phenomena are unpredictable in the short term but show long-run regularity.
- Know how to recognize random outcomes in a real-world situation.
- Know that the relative frequency of an outcome of a random phenomenon settles down as we gather more random outcomes. Be able to state the Law of Large Numbers.
- Know the basic definitions and rules of probability.
- Be able to recognize when events are disjoint and when events are independent. Understand the difference and that disjoint events cannot be independent.

DO

- Be able to use the facts about probability to determine whether an assignment of probabilities is legitimate. Each probability must be a number between 0 and 1, and the sum of the probabilities assigned to all possible outcomes must be 1.
- Know how and when to apply the General Addition Rule. Know when events are disjoint.
- Know how and when to apply the General Multiplication Rule. Be able to use the Multiplication Rule to find probabilities for combinations of both independent and nonindependent events.
- Know how to use the Complement Rule to make calculating probabilities simpler. Recognize that probabilities of "at least" are likely to be simplified in this way.
- Know how to draw a tree diagram to display conditional probabilities.

REPORT

- Be able to use statements about probability in describing a random phenom-enon. You will need this skill soon for making statements about statistical inference.
- Know and be able to use correctly the terms "sample space," "disjoint events," and "independent events."
- Be able to make a statement about a conditional probability that makes clear how the condition affects the probability.
- Avoid making statements that assume independence of events when there is no clear evidence that they are in fact independent.

MINI CASE STUDY PROJECT

Creativa/Shutterstock

Market Segmentation

Marketing managers for department stores want to know how important quality is to their customers. A consultant reports that based on past research, 30% of all consumers nationwide are more interested in quantity than quality.[3] Customers' preferences may vary by store and by age as well. Using conditional probabilities, marginal probabilities, and joint probabilities constructed from the data in the file **ch07_MCSP_Market_Segmentation.xls,**[4] write a report on what you find. Possibilities include focusing on one store, or doing a cross-store comparison.

Keep in mind: The managers may be more interested in the opinions of "frequent" customers than those who never or hardly ever shop at their stores. These "frequent" customers contribute a disproportionate amount of profit to each store. Keep that in mind as you do your analysis and write up your report.

Variable and Question	Categories
Age *Into which of the following age categories do you belong?*	18–24 yrs old 25–34 35–44 45–54 55–64 65 or over
Frequency *How often do you shop for women's clothing at [department store X]?*	Hardly ever 1–2 times per year 3–4 times per year 5 times or more
Quality *For the same amount of money, I will generally buy one good item than several of lower price and quality.*	1. Definitely Disagree 2. Generally Disagree 3. Moderately Disagree 4. Moderately Agree 5. Generally Agree 6. Definitely Agree

---

[3] Original *Market Segmentation Exercise* prepared by K. Matsuno, D. Kopcso, and D. Tigert, Babson College in 1997 (Babson Case Series #133-C97A-U).

[4] For a version with the categories coded as integers see **ch07_MCSP_Market_Segmentation _Coded.**

MyStatLab **Students! Save time, improve your grades with MyStatLab.**
The Exercises marked in red can be found on MyStatLab. You can practice them as often as you want, and most feature step-by-step guided solutions to help you find the right answer. You'll find a personalized Study Plan available to you too! Data Sets for exercises marked **T** are also available on MyStatLab for formatted technologies.

EXERCISES

1. What does it mean? part 1. Respond to the following questions: **LO7**

a) A casino claims that its roulette wheel is truly random. What should that claim mean?

b) A reporter says that there is a 50% chance that the Bank of Canada will cut interest rates by a quarter point at their next meeting. What is the meaning of such a phrase?

2. What does it mean? part 2. Respond to the following questions: **LO7**

a) After an unusually dry autumn, a radio announcer is heard to say, "Watch out! We'll pay for these sunny days later on this winter." Explain what he's trying to say, and comment on the validity of his reasoning.

b) A batter who had failed to get a hit in seven consecutive times at bat then hits a game-winning home run. When talking to reporters afterward, he says he was very confident that last time at bat because he knew he was "due for a hit." Comment on his reasoning.

3. Airline safety. Even though commercial airlines have excellent safety records, in the weeks following a crash, airlines often report a drop in the number of passengers, probably because people are afraid to risk flying. **LO1**

a) A travel agent suggests that since the law of averages makes it highly unlikely to have two plane crashes within a few weeks of each other, flying soon after a crash is the safest time. What do you think?

b) If the airline industry proudly announces that it has set a new record for the longest period of safe flights, would you be reluctant to fly? Are the airlines due to have a crash?

4. Economic predictions. An investment newsletter makes general predictions about the economy to help their clients make sound investment decisions. **LO1**

a) Recently they said that because the stock market had been up for the past three months in a row that it was "due for a correction" and advised their clients to reduce their holdings. What "law" are they applying? Comment.

b) They advised buying a stock that had gone down in the past four sessions because they said that it was clearly "due to bounce back." What "law" are they applying? Comment.

5. Fire insurance. Insurance companies collect annual payments from homeowners in exchange for paying to rebuild houses that burn down. **LO1**

a) Why should you be reluctant to accept a $300 payment from your neighbour to replace his house should it burn down during the coming year?

b) Why can the insurance company make that offer?

6. Casino gambling. Recently, the International Gaming Technology company issued the following press release: **LO1**

(LAS VEGAS, Nev.)—Cynthia Jay was smiling ear to ear as she walked into the news conference at the Desert Inn Resort in Las Vegas today, and well she should. Last night, the 37-year-old cocktail waitress won the world's largest slot jackpot—$34 959 458—on a Megabucks machine. She said she had played $27 in the machine when the jackpot hit. Nevada Megabucks has produced 49 major winners in its 14-year history. The top jackpot builds from a base amount of $7 million and can be won with a 3-coin ($3) bet.

a) How can the Desert Inn afford to give away millions of dollars on a $3 bet?

b) Why did the company issue a press release? Wouldn't most businesses want to keep such a huge loss quiet?

7. Toy company. A toy company manufactures a spinning game and needs to decide what probabilities are involved in the game. The plastic arrow on the spinner stops rotating to point at a colour that will determine what happens next. Knowing these probabilities will help determine how easy or difficult it is for a person to win the game and helps to determine how long the average game will last. Are each of the following probability assignments possible? Why or why not? **LO1**

	Probabilities of . . .			
	Red	**Yellow**	**Green**	**Blue**
a)	0.25	0.25	0.25	0.25
b)	0.10	0.20	0.30	0.40
c)	0.20	0.30	0.40	0.50
d)	0	0	1.00	0
e)	0.10	0.20	1.20	−1.50

8. Store discounts. Many stores run "secret sales": Shoppers receive cards that determine how large a discount they get, but the percentage is revealed by scratching off that silver stuff (what *is* that?) only after the purchase has been totalled at the cash register. The store is required to reveal (in the fine print) the distribution of discounts available. Are each of these probability assignments plausible? Why or why not? **LO1**

	Probabilities of . . .			
	10% off	**20% off**	**30% off**	**50% off**
a)	0.20	0.20	0.20	0.20
b)	0.50	0.30	0.20	0.10
c)	0.80	0.10	0.05	0.05
d)	0.75	0.25	0.25	−0.25
e)	1.00	0	0	0

9. Quality control. A tire manufacturer recently announced a recall because 2% of its tires are defective. If you just bought a new set of four tires from this manufacturer, what is the probability that at least one of your new tires is defective? **LO5**

10. Tim Hortons promotion. One of Canada's favourite annual promotions is the Tim Hortons Roll Up the Rim to Win contest. The company states that the probability of winning a food prize—a free coffee or doughnut—is one in six. If you buy 10 coffees, what is the probability that you win something? **LO5**

11. Auto warranty. In developing their warranty policy, an automobile company estimates that over a one-year period 17% of their new cars will need to be repaired once, 7% will need repairs twice, and 4% will require three or more repairs. If you buy a new car from them, what is the probability that your car will need: **LO5**

a) No repairs?
b) No more than one repair?
c) Some repairs?

12. Consulting team. You work for a large global management consulting company. Of the entire work force of analysts, 55% have had no experience in the telecommunications industry, 32% have had limited experience (less than five years), and the rest have had extensive experience (five years or more). On a recent project, you and two other analysts were chosen at random to constitute a team. It turns out that part of the project involves telecommunications. What is the probability that the first teammate you meet has: LO⑤

a) Extensive telecommunications experience?
b) Some telecommunications experience?
c) No more than limited telecommunications experience?

13. Auto warranty, part 2. Consider again the auto repair rates described in Exercise 11. If you bought two new cars, what is the probability that: LO⑤

a) Neither will need repair?
b) Both will need repair?
c) At least one car will need repair?

14. Consulting team, part 2. You are assigned to be part of a team of three analysts of a global management consulting company as described in Exercise 12. What is the probability that of your other two teammates: LO⑤

a) Neither has any telecommunications experience?
b) Both have some telecommunications experience?
c) At least one has had extensive telecommunications experience?

15. Auto warranty, again. You used the Multiplication Rule to calculate repair probabilities for your cars in Exercise 11. LO⑤

a) What must be true about your cars in order to make that approach valid?
b) Do you think this assumption is reasonable? Explain.

16. Final consulting team project. You used the Multiplication Rule to calculate probabilities about the telecommunications experience of your consulting teammates in Exercise 12. LO⑤

a) What must be true about the groups in order to make that approach valid?
b) Do you think this assumption is reasonable? Explain.

17. Real estate. Real estate ads suggest that 64% of homes for sale have garages, 21% have swimming pools, and 17% have both features. What is the probability that a home for sale has: LO⑤

a) A pool or a garage?
b) Neither a pool nor a garage?
c) A pool but no garage?

18. Human resource data. Employment data at a large company reveal that 72% of the workers are married, 44% are university graduates, and half of the university grads are married. What's the probability that a randomly chosen worker is: LO⑤

a) Neither married nor a university graduate?
b) Married but not a university graduate?
c) Married or a university graduate?

19. Opinions on Canadian oil and gas. An Ipsos Reid poll conducted in 2012 asked 2008 adult Canadians whether they believe it is possible to respect the environment while increasing oil and gas production. Here are the results:

Response	Number
Agree Strongly	530
Agree	790
Disagree	505
Disagree Strongly	183
Total	**2008**

If we select a person at random from this sample of 2008 adults: LO⑤

a) What is the probability that the person responded "Agree Strongly"?
b) What is the probability that the person responded "Disagree" or "Disagree Strongly"?

20. More opinions on Canadian oil and gas. Exercise 19 shows the results of an Ipsos Reid poll about Canadian oil and gas production. Suppose we select three people at random from this sample. LO⑤

a) What is the probability that all three responded "Agree Strongly"?
b) What is the probability that none responded "Disagree" or Disagree Strongly"?
c) What assumption did you make in computing these probabilities?
d) Explain why you think that assumption is reasonable.

21. Telemarketing contact rates. Marketing research firms often contact their respondents by sampling random telephone numbers. Although interviewers currently reach about 76% of selected Canadian and U.S. households, the percentage of those contacted who agree to cooperate with the survey has fallen. Assume that the percentage of those who agree to cooperate in telemarketing surveys is now only 38%. Each household is assumed to be independent of the others. LO⑤

a) What is the probability that the next household on the list will be contacted but will refuse to cooperate?
b) What is the probability of failing to contact a household or of contacting the household but not getting them to agree to the interview?
c) Show another way to calculate the probability in part b.

22. Telemarketing contact rates, part 2. According to Pew Research, the contact rate (probability of contacting a selected household) in 1997 was 69%, and in 2003, it was 76%. However, the cooperation rate (probability of someone at the contacted household agreeing to be interviewed) was 58% in 1997 and dropped to 38% in 2003. LO⑤

a) What is the probability (in 2003) of obtaining an interview with the next household on the sample list? (To obtain an interview, an interviewer must both contact the household and then get agreement for the interview.)
b) Was it more likely to obtain an interview from a randomly selected household in 1997 or in 2003?

23. Mars product information. The Mars company says that before the introduction of purple, yellow made up 20% of their plain M&M candies, red made up another 20%, and orange, blue, and green each made up 10%. The rest were brown. **LO❺**

a) If you picked an M&M at random from a pre-purple bag of candies, what is the probability that it was:

    i. Brown?
    ii. Yellow or orange?
    iii. Not green?
    iv. Striped?

b) Assuming you had an infinite supply of M&M's with the older colour distribution, if you picked three M&M's in a row, what is the probability that:

    i. They are all brown?
    ii. The third one is the first one that's red?
    iii. None is yellow?
    iv. At least one is green?

24. Canadian Blood Services. Canadian Blood Services must track their supply and demand for various blood types. They estimate that about 6% of the Canadian population has Type O blood, 2% Type A, 9% Type B, and the rest Type AB. **LO❺**

a) If someone volunteers to give blood, what is the probability that this donor:

    i. Has Type AB blood?
    ii. Has Type A or Type B blood?
    iii. Is not Type O?

b) Among four potential donors, what is the probability that:

    i. All are Type O?
    ii. None have Type AB blood?
    iii. Not all are Type A?
    iv. At least one person is Type B?

25. More Mars product information. In Exercise 23, you calculated probabilities of getting various colours of M&M. **LO❻**

a) If you draw one M&M, are the events of getting a red one and getting an orange one disjoint or independent or neither?

b) If you draw two M&M one after the other, are the events of getting a red on the first draw and a red on the second disjoint or independent or neither?

c) Can disjoint events ever be independent? Explain.

26. Canadian Blood Services, part 2. In Exercise 24, you calculated probabilities involving various blood types. **LO❻**

a) If you examine one donor, are the events of the donor being Type A and the donor being Type B disjoint or independent or neither? Explain your answer.

b) If you examine two donors, are the events that the first donor is Type A and the second donor is Type B disjoint or independent or neither?

c) Can disjoint events ever be independent? Explain.

27. Airline on-time performance. According to www.flight-stats.com, for the period Jan. 15 to Mar. 15, 2013, Air Canada flights had on-time departures 91% of the time and on-time arrivals 78% of the time. (These statistics were based on tracking a sample of scheduled flights, not all scheduled flights.) Suppose you had taken three Air Canada flights in that period. **LO❺**

a) What is the probability that all three were on-time departures?
b) What is the probability that none were on-time departures?
c) What is the probability that at least one was an on-time departure?
d) Repeat a), b) and c) with on-time arrivals.
e) What did you assume in calculating these probabilities?

28. Casinos. Because gambling is big business, calculating the odds of a gambler winning or losing in every game is crucial to the financial forecasting for a casino. A standard slot machine has three wheels that spin independently. Each has 10 equally likely symbols: 4 bars, 3 lemons, 2 cherries, and a bell. If you play once, what is the probability that you will get: **LO❺**

a) 3 lemons?
b) No fruit symbols?
c) 3 bells (the jackpot)?
d) No bells?
e) At least one bar (an automatic loser)?

29. Information technology. A company has recently replaced their email server because previously mail was interrupted on about 15% of workdays. To see how bad the situation was, calculate the probability that during a five-day work week, there would be an email interruption: **LO❺**

a) On Monday and again on Tuesday
b) For the first time on Thursday
c) Every day
d) At least once during the week

30. Information technology, part 2. At a mid-sized Web design and maintenance company, 57% of the computers are PCs, 29% are Macs, and the rest are Unix-based machines. Assuming that users of each of the machines are equally likely to call in to the information technology help line, what is the probability that of the next three calls: **LO❺**

a) All are Macs?
b) None are PCs?
c) At least one is a Unix machine?
d) All are Unix machines?

31. Casinos, part 2. In addition to slot machines, casinos must understand the probabilities involved in card games. Suppose you are playing at the blackjack table, and the dealer shuffles a deck of cards. The first card shown is red. So is the second and the third. In fact, you are surprised to see five red cards in a row. You start thinking, "The next one is due to be black!" **LO❼**

a) Are you correct in thinking that there's a higher probability that the next card will be black than red? Explain.
b) Is this an example of the Law of Large Numbers? Explain.

32. Inventory. A shipment of road bikes has just arrived at The Spoke, a small bicycle shop, and all the boxes have been placed in the back room. The owner asks her assistant to start bringing in the boxes. The assistant sees 20 identical-looking boxes and starts bringing them into the shop at random. The owner knows that she ordered 10 women's and 10 men's bicycles, and so she's surprised to find that the first six are all women's bikes. As the seventh box is brought in, she starts thinking, "This one is bound to be a men's bike." LO❼

a) Is she correct in thinking that there's a higher probability that the next box will contain a men's bike? Explain.

b) Is this an example of the Law of Large Numbers? Explain.

33. International food survey. A GfK Roper Worldwide survey in 2005 asked consumers in five countries whether they agreed with the statement "I am worried about the safety of the food I eat." Here are the responses classified by the age of the respondent.

	Agree	Neither Agree nor Disagree	Disagree	Don't Know/ No Response	Total
13–19	661	368	452	32	1513
20–29	816	365	336	16	1533
30–39	871	355	290	9	1525
40–49	914	335	266	6	1521
50 +	966	339	283	10	1598
Total	**4228**	**1762**	**1627**	**73**	**7690**

(Age labels along left side)

If we select a person at random from this sample: LO❸

a) What is the probability that the person agreed with the statement?

b) What is the probability that the person is younger than 50 years old?

c) What is the probability that the person is younger than 50 *and* agrees with the statement?

d) What is the probability that the person is younger than 50 *or* agrees with the statement?

34. Cosmetics marketing. A GfK Roper Worldwide survey asked consumers in five countries whether they agreed with the statement "I follow a skin care routine every day." Here are the responses classified by the country of the respondent.

		Response		
	Agree	**Disagree**	**Don't know**	Total
China	361	988	153	**1502**
France	695	763	81	**1539**
India	828	689	18	**1535**
UK	597	898	62	**1557**
USA	668	841	48	**1557**
Total	**3149**	**4179**	**362**	**7690**

(Country labels along left side)

If we select a person at random from this sample: LO❸

a) What is the probability that the person agreed with the statement?

b) What is the probability that the person is from China?

c) What is the probability that the person is from China *and* agrees with the statement?

d) What is the probability that the person is from China *or* agrees with the statement?

35. Ecommerce. Suppose an online business organizes an email survey to find out if online shoppers are concerned with the security of business transactions on the web. Of the 42 individuals who respond, 24 are concerned, and 18 are not concerned. Eight of those concerned about security are male and six of those not concerned are male. If a respondent is selected at random, find each of the following conditional probabilities: LO❷

a) The respondent is male, given that the respondent is not concerned about security.

b) The respondent is not concerned about security, given that it is female.

c) The respondent is female, given that the respondent is concerned about security.

36. Automobile inspection. Twenty percent of cars that are inspected have faulty pollution control systems. The cost of repairing a pollution control system exceeds $300 about 40% of the time. When a driver takes her car in for inspection, what's the probability that she will end up paying more than $300 to repair the pollution control system? LO❷

37. Pharmaceutical company. A pharmaceutical company is considering manufacturing and marketing a pill that will help to lower both an individual's blood pressure and cholesterol. The company is interested in understanding the demand for such a product. The joint probabilities that an adult man has high blood pressure and/or high cholesterol are shown in the table. LO❷

		Blood Pressure	
		High	**OK**
	High	0.11	0.21
	OK	0.16	0.52

(Cholesterol labels along left side)

a) What's the probability that an adult male has both conditions?

b) What's the probability that an adult male has high blood pressure?

c) What's the probability that an adult male with high blood pressure also has high cholesterol?

d) What's the probability that an adult male has high blood pressure if it's known that he has high cholesterol?

38. International relocation. A European department store is developing a new advertising campaign for their new Canadian location, and their marketing managers need to better understand their target market. Based on survey responses, a joint probability table that an adult shops at their new Canadian store classified by their age is shown below. LO❷

a) What's the probability that a survey respondent will shop at the Canadian store?

b) What is the probability that a survey respondent will shop at the store given that they are younger than 20 years old?

c) What is the probability that a survey respondent who is older than 40 shops at the store?

d) What is the probability that a survey respondent is younger than 20 or will shop at the store?

		Shop		
		Yes	**No**	Total
Age	**< 20**	0.26	0.04	0.30
	20–40	0.24	0.10	0.34
	> 40	0.12	0.24	0.36
	Total	**0.62**	**0.38**	**1.00**

39. Pharmaceutical company, again. Given the table of probabilities compiled for marketing managers in Exercise 37, are high blood pressure and high cholesterol independent? Explain. LO❸

		Blood Pressure	
		High	**OK**
Cholesterol	**High**	0.11	0.21
	OK	0.16	0.52

40. International relocation, again. Given the table of probabilities compiled for a department store chain in Exercise 38, are age and shopping at the department store independent? Explain. LO❸

41. International food survey, part 2. Look again at the data from the GfK Roper Worldwide survey on food attitudes in Exercise 33. LO❸

a) If we select a respondent at random, what's the probability we choose a person between 13 and 19 years old who agreed with the statement?
b) Among the 13- to 19-year-olds, what is the probability that a person responded "Agree"?
c) What's the probability that a person who agreed was between 13 and 19?
d) If the person responded "Disagree," what is the probability that they are at least 50 years old?
e) What's the probability that a person 50 years or older disagreed?
f) Are response to the question and age independent?

42. Cosmetics marketing, part 2. Look again at the data from the GfK Roper Worldwide survey on skin care in Exercise 34. LO❸

a) If we select a respondent at random, what's the probability we choose a person from China who agreed with the statement?
b) Among those from the France, what is the probability that a person responded "Agree"?
c) What's the probability that a person who agreed was from India?
d) If the person responded "Disagree," what is the probability that they are from the United Kingdom?
e) What's the probability that a person from the United States disagreed?
f) Are response to the question and Country independent?

43. Real estate, part 2. In the real estate research described in Exercise 17, 64% of homes for sale have garages, 21% have swimming pools, and 17% have both features. LO❸

a) What is the probability that a home for sale has a garage, but not a pool?
b) If a home for sale has a garage, what's the probability that it has a pool, too?
c) Are having a garage and a pool independent events? Explain.
d) Are having a garage and a pool mutually exclusive? Explain.

44. Employee benefits. Fifty-six percent of all North American workers have a workplace retirement plan, 68% have health insurance, and 49% have both benefits. If we select a worker at random: LO❷

a) What's the probability that the worker has neither employer-sponsored health insurance nor a retirement plan?
b) What's the probability that the worker has health insurance if they have a retirement plan?
c) Are having health insurance and a retirement plan independent? Explain.
d) Are having these two benefits mutually exclusive? Explain.

45. Telemarketing. Telemarketers continue to attempt to reach consumers by calling land-line phone numbers. According to a 2012 Residential Telephone Service Survey (a supplement to Statistics Canada's Labour Force Survey) of about 19 000 households, approximately 65% of Canadian households have both a land line in their residence and a cellphone, 13% of Canadian households have only cellphone service but no land line, and 17% use a traditional land line only. The remainder use cable or voice over internet providers exclusively (about 4%) or have no telephone service at all (1%). LO❸

a) Polling agencies won't phone cellphone numbers because customers object to paying for such calls. What proportion of Canadian households can be reached by a land-line call?
b) Are having a cellphone and having a land line independent? Explain.

46. Daily newspapers. NADbank Inc. (www.nadbank.com) is the principal research arm of the Canadian newspaper industry. It carries out an annual telephone survey about daily newspaper readership (print and digital) and other media usage. Their 2011–2012 mid-year survey reported that 49% of Canadians age 18 or over read daily print newspapers, but that only 35% of the 18–34 age group read daily print newspapers. From the 2011 Canada Census, 29% of Canadians are age 18–34. LO❸

a) What percent of the respondents were 35+ years of age and read daily print newspapers?
b) Is daily print newspaper reading independent of age? Explain.

47. Selling cars. A recent ad campaign for a major automobile manufacturer is clearly geared toward an older demographic. You are surprised, so you decide to conduct a quick survey of your own. A random survey of autos parked in the student and staff lots at your university classified the brands by country of origin, as seen in the table. Is country of origin independent of type of driver? LO❸

		Driver	
		Student	**Staff**
Origin	**American**	107	105
	European	33	12
	Asian	55	47

48. Fire sale. In 2006, a survey of 1056 houses in a midsized town in the East found the following relationship between price (in $) and whether the house had a fireplace. Is the price of the house independent of whether it has a fireplace? **LO③**

		Fireplace	
		No	**Yes**
House Price	**Low—less than $112 000**	198	66
	Med Low ($112 to $152K)	133	131
	Med High ($152 to $207K)	65	199
	High—over $207 000	31	233

49. Used cars. A business student is searching for a used car to purchase, so she posts an ad to a website saying she wants to buy a used Jeep between $18 000 and $20 000. From CanadianBlackBook.com, she learns that there are 149 cars matching that description within a 50-kilometre radius of her home. If we assume that those are the people who will call her and that they are equally likely to call her: **LO③**

a) What is the probability that the first caller will be a Jeep Liberty owner?
b) What is the probability that the first caller will own a Jeep Liberty that costs between $18 000 and $18 999?
c) If the first call offers her a Jeep Liberty, what is the probability that it costs less than $19 000?
d) Suppose she decides to ignore calls for cars whose cost is ≥ $19 000. What is the probability that the first call she takes will offer to sell her a Jeep Liberty?

		Price		
Make		**$18 000–$18 999**	**$19 000–$19 999**	Total
Car	**Commander**	3	6	9
	Compass	6	1	7
	Grand Cherokee	33	33	66
	Liberty	17	6	23
	Wrangler	33	11	44
	Total	92	57	149

50. CEO relocation. The CEO of a mid-sized company has to relocate to another part of the country. To make it easier, the company has hired a relocation agency to help purchase a house. The CEO has five children and so has specified that the house have at least five bedrooms, but hasn't put any other constraints on the search. The relocation agency has narrowed the search down to the houses in the table and has selected one house to showcase to the CEO and family on their trip out to the new site. The agency doesn't know it, but the family has its heart set on a Victorian house with a fireplace. If the agency selected the house at random, without regard to this: **LO③**

		Fireplace?		
		No	**Yes**	Total
House Type	**Victorian**	7	2	9
	Ranch	8	14	22
	Other	6	5	11
	Total	21	21	42

a) What is the probability that the selected house is a Victorian?
b) What is the probability that the house is a Ranch with a fireplace?
c) If the house is a Victorian, what is the probability that it has a fireplace?
d) What is the probability that the selected house is what the family wants?

51. Website experiment. Summit Projects provides marketing services and website management for many companies that specialize in outdoor products and services (www.summitprojects.com). To understand customer Web behaviour, the company experiments with different offers and website designs. The results of such experiments can help to maximize the probability that customers purchase products during a visit to a website. Possible actions by the website include offering the customer an instant discount, offering the customer free shipping, or doing nothing. A recent experiment found that customers make purchases 6% of the time when offered the instant discount, 5% when offered free shipping, and 2% when no special offer was given. Suppose 20% of the customers are offered the discount and an additional 30% are offered free shipping. **LO④**

a) Construct a probability tree for this experiment.
b) What percent of customers who visit the site made a purchase?
c) Given that a customer made a purchase, what is the probability that they were offered free shipping?

52. Website experiment, part 2. The company in Exercise 51 performed another experiment in which they tested three website designs to see which one would lead to the highest probability of purchase. The first (design A) used enhanced product information, the second (design B) used extensive iconography, and the third (design C) allowed the customer to submit their own product ratings. After six weeks of testing, the designs delivered probabilities of purchase of 4.5%, 5.2%, and 3.8%, respectively. Equal numbers of customers were sent randomly to each website design. **LO④**

a) Construct a probability tree for this experiment.
b) What percent of customers who visited the site made a purchase?

c) What is the probability that a randomly selected customer was sent to design C?

d) Given that a customer made a purchase, what is the probability that the customer had been sent to design C?

53. Contract bidding. As manager for a construction firm, you are in charge of bidding on two large contracts. You believe the probability you get contract #1 is 0.8. If you get contract #1, the probability you also get contract #2 will be 0.2, and if you do not get #1, the probability you get #2 will be 0.4.   LO❹

a) Sketch the probability tree.

b) What is the probability you will get both contracts?

c) Your competitor hears that you got the second contract but hears nothing about the first contract. Given that you got the second contract, what is the probability that you also got the first contract?

54. Extended warranties. A company that manufactures and sells consumer video cameras sells two versions of their popular hard disk camera, a basic camera for $400 and a deluxe version for $700. About 75% of customers select the basic camera. Of those, 60% purchase the extended warranty for an additional $100. Of the people who buy the deluxe version, 90% purchase the extended warranty.   LO❹

a) Sketch the probability tree for total purchases.

b) What is the percentage of customers who buy an extended warranty?

c) What is the expected revenue of the company from a camera purchase (including warranty if applicable)?

d) Given that a customer purchases an extended warranty, what is the probability that he or she bought the deluxe version?

55. NHL overtime shootouts. In the 2005–2006 season, the National Hockey League (NHL) instituted a shootout if regular season games were still tied after a five-minute overtime period. Three skaters per team take shots on the opposing goalies, and the team with the most goals from their three shots is the winner. If both teams score the same number of goals (out of three chances), a sudden death shootout is begun. The teams alternate taking shots, until one team scores and the other does not, thus producing a winner. The shootout has done away with tie games. The shootout is not used in playoff games.

In the 2011–2012 regular season, home games played by the seven Canadian teams went into overtime 68 times out of 287 games played; 41 of the overtime games went to a shootout. By comparison, home games played by the 23 U.S. teams went into overtime 232 times out of 943 games played; 140 of the overtime games went to a shootout.   LO❹

a) Sketch a probability tree for this situation.

b) What percentage of regular season games in 2011–2012 went to a shootout?

c) What percentage of games that went to a shootout were played in one of the Canadian team cities?

56. Titanic survival. Of the 2201 passengers on the RMS *Titanic*, only 711 survived. The practice of "women and children first" was first used to describe the chivalrous actions of the sailors during the sinking of the HMS *Birkenhead* in 1852, but became popular after the sinking of the *Titanic*, during which 53% of the children and 73% of the women survived, but only 21% of the men survived. Part of the protocol stated that passengers enter lifeboats by ticket class as well. Here is a table showing survival by ticket class.   LO❹

		Class				
		First	**Second**	**Third**	**Crew**	Total
Survival	**Alive**	203	118	178	212	711
		28.6%	16.6%	25.0%	29.8%	100%
	Dead	122	167	528	673	1490
		8.2%	11.2%	35.4%	45.2%	100%

a) Find the conditional probability of survival for each type of ticket.

b) Draw a probability tree for this situation.

c) Given that a passenger survived, what is the probability they had a first-class ticket?

✓ **JUST CHECKING ANSWERS**

1 The probability of going up on the next day is not affected by the previous day's outcome.

2 a) 0.30

b) $0.30(0.30) = 0.09$

c) $(1 - 0.30)^2(0.30) = 0.147$

d) $1 - (1 - 0.30)^5 = 0.832$

3 a)

		Weekday		
		Yes	**No**	Total
Before Five	**Yes**	0.07	0.41	**0.48**
	No	0.20	0.32	**0.52**
	Total	**0.27**	**0.73**	**1.00**

b) $P(\textbf{WD}|\textbf{BF}) = P(\textbf{WD } and \textbf{ BF})/P(\textbf{BF})$

$= 0.07/0.27 = 0.259$

c) No, shoppers can do both (and 7% do).

d) To be independent, we'd need $P(\textbf{BF}|\textbf{WD}) = P(\textbf{BF})$. $P(\textbf{BF}|\textbf{WD}) = 0.259$, but $P(\textbf{BF}) = 0.48$. They do not appear to be independent.

Random Variables and Probability Models

Manulife Real Estate

CONNECTIONS: CHAPTER

With the ideas of probability we discussed in Chapter 7 we now have the tools to create specific models that describe where the data came from. In this chapter we will learn about two types of models—discrete and continuous—that correspond to the two types of data we have worked with—categorical and quantitative. The models will be used all the way through the rest of the text; they are the key to understanding and interpreting data. This is also where the famous bell-shaped curve will be introduced.

LEARNING OBJECTIVES

① Find the expected value and standard deviation of a random variable or combination of random variables

② Use the Binomial and Geometric models to find probabilities

③ Use the 68–95–99.7 Rule to find probabilities or cutoff values

④ Use the Normal model to find probabilities, cutoff values, and the mean and standard deviation

⑤ Compute and use z-scores for comparisons

⑥ Use the Normal model to approximate the Binomial and compute probabilities

Manulife Financial

What company could be more Canadian than one whose first president was the first Prime Minister of Canada, Sir John A. Macdonald? The Manufacturers Life Insurance Company was founded in 1887, and a mere ten years later expanded its operations into China and Hong Kong. Manulife now operates in 21 countries, most notably in the United States, through its subsidiary, John Hancock Insurance.

Manulife Financial is the largest insurance company in Canada, the second largest in the North America (after MetLife, well-known because of their use of Snoopy, the dog from the cartoon strip "Peanuts"), and the world's fifth largest, based on market capitalization. At the end of 2011, its total assets exceeded US$450 billion and total employees surpassed 25 000. Manulife is also a financial services provider and holds Manulife Bank of Canada as a wholly-owned subsidiary.

Manulife changed from a joint stock company to a mutual company, privately owned by its policyholders in 1958. It was demutualized in 1999 and shares of the holding company, Manulife Financial Corporation, began trading on the Toronto Stock Exchange (TSX), New York Stock Exchange (NYSE), and others.

In 2002, China gave approval to Manulife-Sinochem Life Insurance Co. Ltd. to open a branch office in Guangzhou, China,

Choose the appropriate probability model

8 Identify the type and structure of a random variable

9 Use the Poisson model to find probabilities

the first branch licence granted to a foreign invested joint-venture life insurance company. Manulife-Sinochem now has over 1.5 million customers and 12 000 employees in China.

In 2004, Manulife Financial Corporation and John Hancock Financial Services, Inc. (along with its Canadian subsidiary, Maritime Life) completed a stock merger to create a global insurance franchise and give it its number-one ranking by size in Canada. Manulife enhanced its global profile as worldwide sponsor for the 2008 Summer Olympics.

Manulife's corporate giving is based on a model of giving back to communities where it does business, by helping non-profit organizations and supporting volunteerism. In 2012 its Canadian employees donated more than 30 000 volunteer hours. Manulife also sponsors many running, paddling, cycling, and golfing community fundraising events in support of health and environmental projects.

Although Manulife has a major presence in Canada (for example, Edmonton's tallest building is Manulife Place), it now does 75 percent of its business outside Canada and is certainly a global success story. Sir John A. Macdonald would be proud.

Based on information from www.manulife.ca

Fun is like life insurance; the older you get, the more it costs.
– Kin Hubbard

There are worse things in life than death. Have you ever spent an evening with an insurance salesman?
– Quote by Woody Allen from Love and Death. Published by United Artists, © 1975.

I detest life insurance agents; they always argue that I shall some day die, which is not so.
– Stephen Leacock

Insurance: An ingenious modern game of chance in which the player is permitted to enjoy the comfortable conviction that he is beating the man who keeps the table.
– Ambrose Bierce

Insurance companies make bets all the time. For example, they bet that you're going to live a long life. Ironically, you bet that you're going to die sooner. Both you and the insurance company want the company to stay in business, so it's important to find a "fair price" for your bet. Of course, the right price for *you* depends on many factors, and nobody can predict exactly how long you'll live. But when the company averages its bets over enough customers, it can make reasonably accurate estimates of the amount it can expect to collect on a policy before it has to pay out the benefit. To do that effectively, it must model the situation with a probability model. Using the resulting probabilities, the company can find the fair price of almost any situation involving risk and uncertainty.

Here's a simple example. An insurance company offers a "death and disability" policy that pays $100 000 when a client dies or $50 000 if the client is permanently disabled. It charges a premium of only $500 per year for this benefit. Is the company likely to make a profit selling such a plan? To answer this question, the company needs to know the *probability* that a client will die or become disabled in any year. From actuarial information such as this and the appropriate model, the company can calculate the expected value of this policy.

Casinos work in a similar way, but in a casino it is only your financial life that is at stake! Casinos figure out the probability that a player will win a game of chance, and set payouts to be lower than the income produced by the overall wagers. Although the statistical advantage or edge may be very small, when that edge is multiplied by millions of bets made by casino patrons, the casino earns large sums of money.

8.1 Expected Value of a Random Variable

To model the insurance company's risk, we need to define a few terms. The amount the company pays out on an individual policy is an example of a **random variable**, called that because its value is based on the outcome of a random event. We use a

210

What is the difference between a variable and random variable? In algebra, a variable, x, usually represents a single but "hidden" value; solving an equation leads to finding that hidden value. A random variable, X, is more like a rule that connects possible values that a chance process can have with the probabilities of each of those possible values. The confusion comes from the fact that in algebra, $x + x = 2x$, but in probability, $X + X \neq 2X$. In other words you can add values but you can't add rules.

NOTATION ALERT:
The most common letters for random variables are X, Y, and Z, but any capital letter might be used.

capital letter, in this case, X, to denote a random variable. We'll denote a particular *value* that it can have by the corresponding lowercase letter, in this case, x. Once the random event has happened, the value, x, that occurred can also be thought of as a data point. For the insurance company, x can be \$100 000 (if you die that year), \$50 000 (if you are disabled), or \$0 (if neither occurs). Because we can list all the outcomes, we call this random variable a **discrete random variable**. A random variable that can take on any value between two values is called a **continuous random variable**. Continuous random variables are common in business applications for modelling physical quantities like heights and weights, and monetary quantities such as profits, revenues, and spending.

Sometimes it is obvious whether to treat a random variable as discrete or continuous, but at other times the choice is more subtle. Age, for example, might be viewed as discrete if it is measured only to the nearest decade with possible values 10, 20, 30, ... In a scientific context, however, it might be measured more precisely and treated as continuous.

The two types of random variables—discrete and continuous—correspond perfectly to the two types of data—categorical and quantitative—discussed in Chapters 4 and 5. We use different terms to distinguish between what *could* happen (the random variable) and what *did* happen (the data).

For both discrete and continuous variables, the collection of all the possible values and the probabilities associated with them is called the **probability model** for the random variable. For a discrete random variable, we can list the probability of all possible values in a table, or describe it by a formula. For example, to model the possible outcomes of a fair die, we can let X be the number showing on the face. The probability model for X is simply:

$$P(X = x) = \begin{cases} 1/6 & if\ x = 1, 2, 3, 4, 5,\ or\ 6 \\ 0 & otherwise \end{cases}$$

Suppose in our insurance risk example that the death rate in any year is 1 out of every 1000 people and that another 2 out of 1000 suffer some kind of disability. The loss, which we'll denote as X, is a discrete random variable because it takes on only three possible values. We can display the probability model for X in a table, as in Table 8.1.

Policyholder Outcome	Payout x (cost)	Probability $P(X = x)$
Death	100 000	$\dfrac{1}{1000}$
Disability	50 000	$\dfrac{2}{1000}$
Neither	0	$\dfrac{997}{1000}$

| **Table 8.1**   Probability model for an insurance policy.

Of course, we can't predict exactly what *will* happen during any given year, but we can say what we *expect* to happen—in this case, what we expect the profit of a policy will be. The expected value of a policy is a **parameter** of the probability model. In fact, it's the mean. We'll signify this with the notation $E(X)$, for expected value (or sometimes EV, or sometimes μ). We use the term "mean" for this quantity just as we did for data, but be careful. This isn't an average of data values, so we won't estimate it. Instead, we calculate it directly from the probability model for the random variable. Because it comes from a model and not data, we use the parameter μ to denote it (and *not* $\bar{y}$ or $\bar{x}$.) In general, Greek letters are used to denote characteristics or parameters from a model. But like most generalizations, there are exceptions, as we shall see.

To see what the insurance company can expect, think about some (convenient) number of outcomes. For example, imagine that they have exactly 1000 clients and that the outcomes in one year followed the probability model exactly: 1 died, 2 were disabled, and 997 survived unscathed. Then our expected payout would be:

$$\mu = E(X) = \frac{100\,000(1) + 50\,000(2) + 0(997)}{1000} = 200$$

So our expected payout comes to $200 per policy.

Instead of writing the expected value as one big fraction, we can rewrite it as separate terms, each divided by 1000.

$$\mu = E(X) = \$100\,000\left(\frac{1}{1000}\right) + \$50\,000\left(\frac{2}{1000}\right) + \$0\left(\frac{997}{1000}\right)$$

$$= \$200$$

Writing it this way, we can see that for each policy, there's a $1/1000$ chance that we'll have to pay $100\,000$ for a death and a $2/1000$ chance that we'll have to pay $50\,000$ for a disability. Of course, there's a $997/1000$ chance that we won't have to pay anything.

So the **expected value** of a (discrete) random variable is found by multiplying each possible value of the random variable by the probability that it occurs and then summing all those products. This gives the general formula for the expected value of a discrete random variable[1]:

$$E(X) = \Sigma x \cdot P(x)$$

Here we have used $P(x)$ as an abbreviation for $P(X = x)$. We'll use it again to simplify some of the formulas.

Be sure that *every* possible outcome is included in the sum. Verify that you have a valid probability model to start with—the probabilities should each be between 0 and 1 and should sum to one. (Recall the rules of probability in Chapter 7.)

8.2 Standard Deviation of a Random Variable

Of course, this expected value (or mean) is not what actually happens to any *particular* policyholder. No individual policy actually costs the company $200. We are dealing with random events, so some policyholders receive big payouts and others nothing. Because the insurance company must anticipate this variability, it needs to know the standard deviation of the random variable.

For data, we calculate the standard deviation by first computing the deviation of each data value from the mean and squaring it. We perform a similar calculation when we compute the **standard deviation of a** (discrete) **random variable** as well. First, we find the deviation of each payout from the mean (expected value). (See Table 8.2.)

Next, we square each deviation. The **variance** is the expected value of those squared deviations. To find it, we multiply each by the appropriate probability and sum those products:

$$Var(X) = 99\,800^2\left(\frac{1}{1000}\right) + 49\,800^2\left(\frac{2}{1000}\right) + (-200)^2\left(\frac{997}{1000}\right)$$

$$= 14\,960\,000$$

Note the similarity to how we compute the standard deviation of a set of data values. Each value is equally likely, so the probability of each one is $1/n$. We sum the squared deviations from each x value to $\bar{x}$ and then multiply by $1/n$ (i.e., divide by n). Except for needing a small modification, namely that we divide by $n - 1$, the computation with data is the same as the computation with a random variable.

---

[1] The concept of expected values for continuous random variables is similar, but the calculation requires calculus and is beyond the scope of this text. Instead of summation, we use integration to find "area under the curve."

Policyholder Outcome	Payout x (cost)	Probability $P(X = x)$	Deviation $X - E(X)$
Death	100 000	$\frac{1}{1000}$	$(100\ 000 - 200) = 99\ 800$
Disability	50 000	$\frac{2}{1000}$	$(50\ 000 - 200) = 49\ 800$
Neither	0	$\frac{997}{1000}$	$(0 - 200) = -200$

| **Table 8.2** Deviations between the expected value and each payout (cost).

Finally, we take the square root to get the standard deviation:

$$SD(X) = \sqrt{14\ 960\ 000} \approx \$3867.82$$

The insurance company can expect an average payout of \$200 per policy, with a standard deviation of \$3867.82.

Think about that. The company charges \$500 for each policy and expects to pay out \$200 per policy. Sounds like an easy way to make \$300. (In fact, most of the time—probability 997/1000—the company pockets the entire \$500.) But would you be willing to take on this risk yourself and sell all your friends policies like this? The problem is that occasionally the company loses big. With a probability of 1/1000, it will pay out \$100 000, and with a probability of 2/1000, it will pay out \$50 000. That may be more risk than you're willing to take on. The standard deviation of \$3867.82 gives an indication of the uncertainty of the profit, and that seems like a pretty big spread (and risk) for an average profit of \$300. A large standard deviation also happens with lottery winnings. There is a very small probability of winning a large amount and a very large probability of losing.

Here are the formulas for these arguments. Because these are parameters of our probability model, the variance and standard deviation can also be written as σ^2 and σ, respectively (sometimes with the name of the random variable as a subscript). You should recognize both kinds of notation:

$$\sigma^2 = Var(X) = \Sigma(x - E(X))^2 P(x) = \Sigma(x - \mu)^2 P(x), \text{ and}$$
$$\sigma = SD(X) = \sqrt{Var(X)}.$$

GUIDED EXAMPLE | Computer Inventory

As the head of inventory for a computer company, you've had a challenging couple of weeks. One of your warehouses recently had a fire, and you had to flag all the computers stored there to be recycled. On the positive side, you were thrilled that you had managed to ship two computers to your biggest client last week. But then you discovered that your assistant hadn't heard about the fire and had mistakenly transported a whole truckload of computers from the damaged warehouse into the shipping centre. It turns out that 30% of all the computers shipped last week were damaged.

You don't know whether your biggest client received two damaged computers, two undamaged ones, or one of each. Computers were selected at random from the shipping centre for delivery.

If your client received two undamaged computers, everything is fine. If the client gets one damaged computer, it will be returned at your expense—\$100—and you can replace it. However, if both computers are damaged, the client will cancel all other orders this month, and you'll lose \$10 000. What are the expected value and the standard deviation of your loss under this scenario?

PLAN

Setup State the problem.

We want to analyze the potential consequences of shipping damaged computers to a large client. We'll look at the expected value and standard deviation of the amount we'll lose.

Let $X =$ amount of loss. We'll denote the receipt of an undamaged computer by **U** and the receipt of a damaged computer by **D**. The three possibilities are: two undamaged computers (**U** and **U**), two damaged computers (**D** and **D**), and one of each (**UD** or **DU**). Because the computers were selected randomly and the number in the warehouse is large, we can assume independence.

DO

Model List the possible values of the random variable, and compute all the values you'll need to determine the probability model.

Because the events are independent, we can use the multiplication rule (Chapter 7) and find:

$$P(\textbf{UU}) = P(\textbf{U}) \times P(\textbf{U})$$
$$= 0.7 \times 0.7 = 0.49$$
$$P(\textbf{DD}) = P(\textbf{D}) \times P(\textbf{D})$$
$$= 0.3 \times 0.3 = 0.09$$

So, $P(\textbf{UD} \text{ or } \textbf{DU}) = 1 - (0.49 + 0.09) = 0.42$

We have the following model for all possible values of X.

Outcome	x	$P(X = x)$
Two damaged	10 000	$P(\textbf{DD}) = 0.09$
One damaged	100	$P(\textbf{UD} \text{ or } \textbf{DU}) = 0.42$
Neither damaged	0	$P(\textbf{UU}) = 0.49$

Mechanics Find the expected value.

$$E(X) = 0(0.49) + 100(0.42) + 10\,000(0.09)$$
$$= \$942.00$$

Find the variance.

$$Var(X) = (0 - 942)^2 \times (0.49)$$
$$+ (100 - 942)^2 \times (0.42)$$
$$+ (10\,000 - 942)^2 \times (0.09)$$
$$= 8\,116\,836$$

Find the standard deviation.

$$SD(X) = \sqrt{8\,116\,836} = \$2849.01$$

REPORT

Conclusion Interpret your results in context.

REALITY CHECK

MEMO:

Re: Damaged Computers

The recent shipment of two computers to our large client may have some serious negative impact. Even though there is about a 50% chance that they will receive two perfectly good computers, there is a 9% chance that they will receive two damaged computers and will cancel the rest of their monthly order. We have analyzed the expected loss to the firm as $942 with a standard deviation of $2849.01. The large standard deviation reflects the fact that there is real possibility of losing $10 000 from the mistake.

Both numbers seem reasonable. The expected value of $942 is between the extremes of $0 and $10 000, and there's great variability in the outcome values.

8.3 Properties of Expected Values, Variances, and Standard Deviations

Our example insurance company expected to pay out an average of $200 per policy, with a standard deviation of about $3868. The expected profit then was $500 − $200 = $300 per policy. Suppose that the company decides to lower the price of the premium by $50 to $450. It's pretty clear that the expected profit would drop an average of $50 per policy, to $450 − $200 = $250.

What about the standard deviation? We know that adding or subtracting a constant from data shifts the mean but doesn't change the variance or standard deviation. The same is true of random variables[2]:

$$E(X \pm c) = E(X) \pm c,$$

$$Var(X \pm c) = Var(X), \text{ and}$$

$$SD(X \pm c) = SD(X)$$

What if the company decides to *double* all the payouts—that is, pay $200 000 for death and $100 000 for disability? This would double the average payout per policy and also increase the variability in payouts. In general, multiplying each value of a random variable by a constant multiplies the mean by that constant and multiplies the variance by the *square* of the constant:

$$E(aX) = aE(X), \text{ and}$$

$$Var(aX) = a^2 Var(X)$$

---

[2]The rules in this section are true for both discrete *and* continuous random variables.

Taking square roots of the last equation shows that the standard deviation is multiplied by the absolute value of the constant:

$$SD(aX) = |a|SD(X)$$

So now we know the effect of **changing a random variable by a constant**.

This insurance company sells policies to more than just one person. We've just seen how to compute means and variances for one person at a time. What happens to the mean and variance when we have a collection of customers? The profit on a group of customers is the *sum* of the individual profits, so we'll need to know how to find expected values and variances for sums. To start, consider a simple case with just two customers who we'll call Mr. Ecks and Ms. Wye. With an expected payout of $200 on each policy, we might expect a total of $200 + $200 = $400 to be paid out on the two policies—nothing surprising there. In other words, we have the **Addition Rule for Expected Values of Random Variables**: *The expected value of the sum (or difference) of random variables is the sum (or difference) of their expected values:*

$$E(X \pm Y) = E(X) \pm E(Y).$$

The variability is another matter. Is the risk of insuring two people the same as the risk of insuring one person for twice as much? We wouldn't expect both clients to die or become disabled in the same year. In fact, because we've spread the risk, the standard deviation should be smaller. Indeed, this is the fundamental principle behind insurance. By spreading the risk among many policies, a company can keep the standard deviation quite small and predict costs more accurately. It's much less risky to insure thousands of customers than one customer when the total expected payout is the same, assuming that the events are independent. Catastrophic events such as hurricanes or earthquakes that affect large numbers of customers at the same time destroy the independence assumption, and often the insurance company along with it.

But how much smaller is the standard deviation of the sum? It turns out that, if the random variables are independent, we have the **Addition Rule for Variances of (Independent) Random Variables**: *The variance of the sum or difference of two independent random variables is the sum of their individual variances:*

$$Var(X \pm Y) = Var(X) + Var(Y)$$

if X and Y are independent.

Recall the basic algebraic expansion: $(a \pm b)^2 = a^2 + b^2 \pm 2ab$. Let's call $2ab$ the "cross-product" term. Variance is based on squares, so the variance of sum or difference of two random variables should have a cross-product term. It does, and it is based on correlation. If the two random variables are independent, the correlation, and hence the cross-product, is zero. That's why independence is needed in order to be able to add variances. To see what happens when the random variables are dependent, read on.

Just as a data value, x, is a specific result of a random variable X, the sample mean, $\bar{x}$, can be thought of as the mean of a set of random variables. If the random variables are independent, the data will be a random sample, as we discussed in Chapter 3. The randomness of the sample is crucial for decision-making.

MATH BOX

Pythagorean Theorem of Statistics

We often use the standard deviation to measure variability, but when we add independent random variables, we use their variances. Think of the Pythagorean Theorem. In a right triangle (only), the *square* of the length of the hypotenuse is the sum of the *squares* of the lengths of the other two sides:

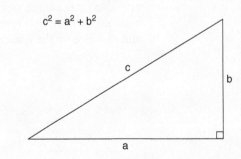

$$c^2 = a^2 + b^2$$

For independent random variables (only), the *square* of the standard deviation of their sum is the sum of the *squares* of their standard deviations:

$$SD^2(X+Y) = SD^2(X) + SD^2(Y).$$

It's simpler to write this with *variances*:

$$Var(X+Y) = Var(X) + Var(Y),$$

but we'll use the standard deviation formula often as well:

$$SD(X+Y) = \sqrt{Var(X) + Var(Y)}.$$

For Mr. Ecks and Ms. Wye, the insurance company can expect their outcomes to be independent, so (using X for Mr. Ecks's payout and Y for Ms. Wye's):

$$Var(X+Y) = Var(X) + Var(Y)$$
$$= 14\,960\,000 + 14\,960\,000$$
$$= 29\,920\,000$$

Let's compare the variance of writing two independent policies to the variance of writing only one for twice the size. If the company had insured only Mr. Ecks for twice as much, the variance would have been

$$Var(2X) = 2^2 Var(X) = 4 \times 14\,960\,000 = 59\,840\,00$$

or

twice as big as with two independent policies, even though the expected payout is the same.

Of course, variances are in squared units. The company would prefer to know standard deviations, which are in dollars. The standard deviation of the payout for two independent policies is $SD(X+Y) = \sqrt{Var(X+Y)} = \sqrt{29\,920\,000} = \$5469.92$. But the standard deviation of the payout for a single policy of twice the size is twice the standard deviation of a single policy: $SD(2X) = 2SD(X) = 2(\$3867.82) = \$7735.64$, or about 40% more than the standard deviation of the sum of the two independent policies, $\$5469.92$.

If the company has two customers, then it will have an expected annual total payout (cost) of $400 with a standard deviation of about $5470. If they write one policy with an expected annual payout of $400, they increase the standard deviation by about 40%. Spreading risk by insuring many independent customers is one of the fundamental principles in insurance and finance.

Let's review the rules of expected values and variances for sums and differences.

◆ *The expected value of the sum of two random variables is the sum of the expected values.*

◆ *The expected value of the difference of two random variables is the difference of the expected values:*

$$E(X \pm Y) = E(X) \pm E(Y)$$

◆ *If the random variables are independent, the variance of their sum or difference is always the sum of the variances:*

$$Var(X \pm Y) = Var(X) + Var(Y)$$

Do we always *add* variances? Even when we take the *difference* of two random quantities? Yes! Think about the two insurance policies. Suppose we want to know the mean and standard deviation of the *difference* in payouts to the two clients. Since each policy has an expected payout of $200, the expected difference is $200 − $200 = $0. If we computed the variance of the difference by subtracting variances, we would get $0 for the variance. But that doesn't make sense. Their difference won't always be exactly $0. In fact, the difference in payouts could range from $100 000 to −$100 000, a spread of $200 000. The variability in differences *increases* as much as the variability in sums. If the company has two customers, the difference in payouts has a mean of $0 and a standard deviation of about $5470.

◆ **For random variables, does $X + X + X = 3X$?** Maybe, but be careful. As we've just seen, insuring one person for $300 000 is not the same risk as insuring three people for $100 000 each. When each instance represents a different outcome for the same random variable, though, it's easy to fall into the trap of writing all of them with the same symbol. Don't make this common mistake. Make sure you write each instance as a *different* random variable. Just because each random variable describes a similar situation doesn't mean that each random outcome will be the same. What you really mean is $X_1 + X_2 + X_3$. Written this way, it's clear that the sum shouldn't necessarily equal three times *anything*.

*Dependent Random Variables

Not all situations have independent random variables. In fact, any two variables usually do have some correlation and so are dependent. An important example of this occurs in finance with the idea of portfolio diversification. Investors try to manage their risk by using a portfolio, that is, a collection of various investments such as stocks. The strategy of diversification was developed mathematically by Harry Markowitz in 1952; modern portfolio theory is the concept behind mutual funds. The main idea is that the correlation between investments can lead to a smaller variance (and hence risk) from a combination of investments when compared with the variance or risk from a single investment. This is the financial version of "Don't put all your eggs in one basket."

Here is the formula for the variance of a sum or difference of two *dependent* random variables:

$$Var(X \pm Y) = Var(X) + Var(Y) \pm 2\,SD(X) \times SD(Y) \times r$$
where r is the correlation between X and Y.

And, of course, the SD is still the square root of the Variance.

But this would only apply if you had one share in stock X and one share in stock Y. That's not really investing. The challenge is to decide in what proportions should the investments be made. For example, suppose you decide to invest 75% of your funds in stock X and 25% in stock Y. What happens now? The portfolio return could be written as $0.75X + 0.25Y$, or more generally, $aX + bY$. This is called a linear combination of two random variables. And here are the formulas for the mean and variance.

$$E(aX + bY) = aE(X) + bE(Y)$$

Note that independence or dependence is of no concern here.

$$Var(aX + bY) = a^2Var(X) + b^2Var(Y) \pm 2ab \times SD(X) \times SD(Y) \times r$$
where r is the correlation between X and Y.

Here is an example to illustrate.

In 2008, a musician invested in two stocks; he put 25% of his portfolio in RIM/Research in Motion (call it R) and 75% in Barrick Gold (call it B); that's a true R&B investment!

(Note: In 2013, RIM officially changed its name to BlackBerry, so this would now be a B&B investment.)

From 30 trading days on the TSX in 2008, the results are:

	RIM share price	Barrick share price
Mean ($)	50.73	36.88
Variance ($²)	12.38	26.48

$$\text{Correlation} = -0.5689$$

What are the mean, variance, and standard deviation of his portfolio (PF)?

$$\text{Mean}(PF) = \text{Mean}(0.25R + 0.75B) = 0.25(50.73) + 0.75(36.88) = 40.3425$$

$$\text{Variance}(PF) = 0.25^2(12.38) + 0.75^2(26.48)$$

$$+ 2(0.25)(0.75)\sqrt{12.38}\sqrt{26.48}$$

$$(-0.5689)$$

$$= 11.80609$$

$$\text{SD}(PF) = 3.436$$

Note that the SD of the portfolio is smaller than the SD of either stock: $\sqrt{12.38} = 3.519$ and $\sqrt{26.48} = 5.146$)

We'll leave further discussion of this topic for finance textbooks.

✓ JUST CHECKING

1 Suppose that the time it takes a customer to get and pay for seats at the ticket window of a baseball park is a random variable with a mean of 100 seconds and a standard deviation of 50 seconds. When you get there, you find only two people in line in front of you.

   a) How long do you expect to wait for your turn to get tickets?

   b) What's the standard deviation of your wait time?

   c) What assumption did you make about the two customers in finding the standard deviation?

8.4 Discrete Probability Models

We've seen how to compute means and standard deviations of random variables. But plans based just on averages are, on average, wrong. At least that's what Sam Savage, Professor at Stanford University says in his book, *The Flaw of Averages*. Unfortunately, many business owners make decisions based solely on averages—the average amount sold last year, the average number of customers seen last month, etc. Instead of relying on averages, the business decisionmaker can incorporate much more by modelling the situation with a probability model. Probability models can play an important and pivotal role in helping decisionmakers better predict both the outcome and the consequences of their decisions. In this section we'll see that some fairly simple models provide a framework for thinking about how to model a wide variety of business phenomena.

The Uniform Model

When we first studied probability in Chapter 7, we saw that equally likely events were the simplest case. For example, a single die can turn up 1, 2, ... , 6 on one toss. A probability model for the toss is Uniform because each of the outcomes has the same probability (1/6) of occurring. Similarly if X is a random variable with possible outcomes $1, 2, \ldots, n$ and $P(X = i) = 1/n$ for each value of i, then we say X has a discrete **Uniform distribution, U[1, … , n]**.

Bernoulli Trials

In September 2008, Google Inc. announced the release of their web browser *Chrome*, designed to compete with Microsoft's *Internet Explorer*, Apple's *Safari*, and others. One of the goals of *Chrome* was to insulate the browser from websites that fail to display. The developers of *Chrome* worked hard to minimize the probability that their browser will have trouble displaying a website. Before releasing the product, they had to test many websites to discover those that might fail. Although web browsers are relatively new, *quality control inspection* such as this is common throughout manufacturing worldwide and has been in use in industry for nearly 100 years.

The developers of *Chrome* sampled websites, recording whether the browser displayed the website correctly or had a problem. We call the act of inspecting a website a trial. There are two possible outcomes—either the website renders correctly or it doesn't. By convention, one of the outcomes is denoted a "success" and the other a "failure." Which one is called a success is arbitrary, but often the less common outcome or the one that calls for action is called a success. Here, that would mean that a website that *doesn't* work would be a "success." (That may seem strange, but if you're a quality inspector, you'll want to find problems so you can fix them. This happens in medicine and medical diagnostics too. A negative test result is a good thing since no problem was identified; however, a positive test result means something is wrong. So a "success" means that the test was successful in identifying a problem. Mortality rates are another backwards use of success. A person is either alive or dead; to compute a mortality rate, a success is a death!) At least early in this work, the probability of a success didn't change from trial to trial. Situations like this occur often and are called **Bernoulli trials**. To summarize, trials are Bernoulli if:

Calvin and Hobbes © 1993 Watterson/
Distributed by Universal Uclick.

◆ *There are only two possible outcomes (called success and failure) for each trial. For example, either you get a website that fails to display correctly (success), or you don't (failure).*

◆ *The probability of success, denoted p, is the same on every trial. (The probability of failure, $1 - p$ is often denoted q.)*

◆ *The trials are independent. Finding that one website does not display correctly does not change what might happen with the next website.*

Common examples of Bernoulli trials include tossing a coin, collecting responses on Yes/No questions from surveys, or even shooting free throws in a basketball game. Bernoulli trials are remarkably versatile and can be used to model a wide variety of real-life situations. The specific question you might ask in different situations will give rise to different random variables that, in turn, have different probability models.

The Geometric Model

Elk-Opid/Photos12/Alamy

Daniel Bernoulli (1700–1782) was the nephew of Jakob, whom you saw in Chapter 7. He was the first to work out the mathematics for what we now call Bernoulli trials.

What's the probability that the first website that fails to display is the second one that we test? Let X denote the number of trials (websites) until the first such "success." For X to be 2, the first website must have displayed correctly (which has probability $1 - p$), and then the second one must have failed to display correctly—a success, with probability p. Since the trials are independent, these probabilities can be multiplied, and so $P(X = 2) = (1 - p)(p)$ or qp. Maybe you won't find a success until the fifth trial. What are the chances of that? You'd have to fail four times in a row and then succeed, so $P(X = 5) = (1 - p)^4(p) = q^4 p$. See the Math Box for an extension and more explanation.

Whenever we want to know how long (how many trials) it will take us to achieve the first success, the model that tells us this probability is called the **geometric probability model**. Geometric models are completely specified by one parameter, p, the probability of success, and are denoted Geom(p).

The geometric model can tell Google something important about its software. No large complex program is entirely free of bugs. So before releasing a program or upgrade, developers typically ask not whether it is free of bugs, but how long it is likely to be until the next bug is discovered. If the expected number of pages displayed until the next failure is high enough, then the program is ready to ship.

> **Geometric probability model for Bernoulli trials: Geom(p)**
>
> p = probability of success (and $q = 1 - p$ = probability of failure)
>
> X = number of trials until the first success occurs
>
> $$P(X = x) = q^{x-1}p$$
>
> Expected value: $\mu = \dfrac{1}{p}$
>
> Standard deviation: $\sigma = \sqrt{\dfrac{q}{p^2}}$

MATH BOX

We want to find the mean (expected value) of random variable X, using a geometric method with probability of success p.

First write the probabilities:

x	1	2	3	4	$\cdots$
$P(X = x)$	p	qp	q^2p	q^3p	$\cdots$

The expected value is: $E(X) = 1p + 2qp + 3q^2p + 4q^3p + \cdots$

Let $p = 1 - q$: $\qquad = (1 - q) + 2q(1 - q) + 3q^2(1 - q) + 4q^3(1 - q) + \cdots$

Simplify: $\qquad = 1 - q + 2q - 2q^2 + 3q^2 - 3q^3 + 4q^3 - 4q^4 + \cdots$

That's an infinite geometric series, with first term 1 and common ratio q:

$\qquad = 1 + q + q^2 + q^3 + \cdots$

$\qquad = \dfrac{1}{1 - q}$

So, finally: $\qquad E(X) = \dfrac{1}{p}$

Independence

One of the important requirements for Bernoulli trials is that the trials be independent. Sometimes that's a reasonable assumption. Is it true for our example? It's easy to imagine that related sites might have similar problems, but if the sites are selected at random, whether one has a problem should be independent of others.

The 10% Condition: Bernoulli trials must be independent. In theory, we need to sample from a population that's infinitely big. However, if the population is finite, it's still okay to proceed as long as the sample is smaller than 10% of the population. Be careful. The 10% Condition doesn't mean that smaller samples are better. The reverse is true. It refers to the relative sizes of the sample and the population. So another way to think of the 10% Condition is that the population should be more than 10 times as large as the sample. In Google's case, they just happened to have a directory of millions of websites, so most samples would easily satisfy the 10% Condition.

The Binomial Model

Suppose Google tests five websites. What's the probability that *exactly* two of them have problems (two "successes")? When we studied the geometric model, we asked how long it would take until our first success. Now we want to find the probability of getting exactly two successes among the five trials. We are still talking about Bernoulli trials, but we're asking a different question.

This time we're interested in the *number of successes* in the five trials, which we'll denote by Y. We want to find $P(Y = 2)$. Whenever the random variable of interest is the number of successes in a series of Bernoulli trials, it's called a Binomial random variable. It takes two parameters to define this **Binomial probability model**: the number of trials, n, and the probability of success, p. We denote this model Binom(n, p).

Suppose that in this phase of development, 10% of the sites exhibited some sort of problem so that $p = 0.10$. (Early in the development phase of a product, it is not uncommon for the number of defects to be much higher than it is when the product is released.) Exactly two successes in five trials means two successes and three failures. It seems logical that the probability should be $(p)^2(1 - p)^3$. Unfortunately, it's not *quite* that easy. That calculation would give you the probability of finding two successes and then three failures—*in that order*. But you could find the two successes in a lot of other ways, for example in the second and fourth website you test. The probability of that sequence is $(1 - p)p(1 - p)(p)(1 - p)$ which is also $p^2(1 - p)^3$. In fact, as long as there are two successes and three failures, the probability will always be the same, regardless of the order of the sequence of successes and failures. The probability will be $p^2(1 - p)^3$. To find the probability of getting two successes in five trials in any order, we just need to know how many ways that outcome can occur.

Fortunately, all the possible sequences that lead to the same number of successes are *disjoint*. (For example, if your successes came on the first two trials, they couldn't come on the last two.) So once we find all the different sequences, we can add up their probabilities. And since the probabilities are all the same, we just need to find how many sequences there are and multiply $p^2(1 - p)^3$ by that number.

Each different order in which we can have k successes in n trials is called a "combination." The total number of ways this can happen is written $\binom{n}{k}$ or $_nC_k$ and pronounced "n choose k:"

$$\binom{n}{k} = {_nC_k} = \frac{n!}{k!\,(n - k)!} \text{ where } n! = n \times (n - 1) \times \cdots \times 1$$

For two successes in five trials,

$$\binom{5}{2} = \frac{5!}{2!\,(5 - 2)!} = \frac{(5 \times 4 \times 3 \times 2 \times 1)}{(2 \times 1 \times 3 \times 2 \times 1)} = \frac{(5 \times 4)}{(2 \times 1)} = 10$$

So there are 10 ways to get two successes in five websites, and the probability of each is $p^2(1 - p)^3$. To find the probability of exactly two successes in five trials, we multiply the probability of any particular order by this number:

$P(\textit{exactly 2 successes in 5 trials}) = 10p^2(1 - p)^3 = 10(0.10)^2(0.90)^3 = 0.0729$

In general, we can write the probability of exactly k successes in n trials as

$$P(Y = k) = \binom{n}{k} p^k q^{n-k}$$

If the probability that any single website has a display problem is 0.10, what's the expected number of websites with problems if we test 100 sites? You probably said 10. We suspect you didn't use the formula for expected value that involves multiplying each value times its probability and adding them up. In fact, there is an easier way to find the expected value for a Binomial random variable. You just multiply the probability of success by n. In other words, $E(Y) = np$. We prove this in the next Math Box.

The standard deviation is less obvious and you can't just rely on your intuition. Fortunately, the formula for the standard deviation also boils down to something simple: $SD(Y) = \sqrt{npq}$. If you're curious to know where that comes from, it's in the Math Box, too.

In our website example, with $n = 100$, $E(Y) = np = 100(0.10) = 10$, so we expect to find 10 successes out of the 100 trials. The standard deviation is:

$$\sqrt{100 \times 0.10 \times 0.90} = 3 \text{ websites}$$

To summarize, a Binomial probability model describes the distribution of the number of successes in a specified number of trials.

Binomial model for Bernoulli trials: Binom(n, p)

n = number of trials
p = probability of success (and $q = 1 - p$ = probability of failure)
X = number of successes in n trials

$$P(X = x) = \binom{n}{x} p^x q^{n-x}, \text{ where } \binom{n}{x} = \frac{n!}{x!(n-x)!}$$

Mean: $\mu = np$
Standard deviation: $\sigma = \sqrt{npq}$

MATH BOX

To derive the formulas for the mean and standard deviation of the Binomial model, we start with the most basic situation.

Consider a single Bernoulli trial with probability of success p. Let's find the mean and variance of the number of successes.

Here's the probability model for the number of successes:

x	0	1
$P(X) = x$	q	p

Find the expected value:

$$E(X) = 0q + 1p$$
$$E(X) = p$$

Now the variance:

$$Var(X) = (0 - p)^2 q + (1 - p)^2 p$$
$$= p^2 q + q^2 p$$
$$= pq(p + q)$$
$$= pq(1)$$
$$Var(X) = pq$$

What happens when there is more than one trial? A Binomial model simply counts the number of successes in a series of n independent Bernoulli trials. That makes it easy to find the mean and standard deviation of a binomial random variable, Y.

$$\text{Let } Y = X_1 + X_2 + X_3 + \cdots + X_n$$

$$\begin{aligned} E(Y) &= E(X_1 + X_2 + X_3 + \cdots + X_n) \\ &= E(X_1) + E(X_2) + E(X_3) + \cdots + E(X_n) \\ &= p + p + p + \cdots + p \ (\text{There are } n \text{ terms.}) \end{aligned}$$

So, as we thought, the mean is $E(Y) = np$.

And since the trials are independent, the variances add:

$$\begin{aligned} Var(Y) &= Var(X_1 + X_2 + X_3 + \cdots + X_n) \\ &= Var(X_1) + Var(X_2) + Var(X_3) + \cdots + Var(X_n) \\ &= pq + pq + pq + \cdots + pq \ (\text{Again, } n \text{ terms.}) \end{aligned}$$

$$Var(Y) = npq$$

Voila! The standard deviation is $SD(Y) = \sqrt{npq}$.

GUIDED EXAMPLE | Canadian Blood Services

Keith Brofsky/Photodisc/Getty Images

Every minute, on average, someone in Canada needs blood or a blood product. It takes only one hour to donate enough blood. And each donation can save three lives since blood is separated into three components: red cells, plasma, and platelets. Canadian Blood Services is a not-for-profit, charitable organization that manages the blood and blood products supply for Canadians. It collects about 850 000 units of blood annually from 43 permanent collection sites and more than 20 000 donor clinics; and it serves over 800 hospitals across the country. Provincial and territorial ministries of health provide the funding and Health Canada handles the regulatory side.[3]

The balancing of supply and demand is complicated not only by the logistics of finding donors that meet health criteria, but by the fact that the blood type of donor and patient must be matched. People with O-negative blood are called "universal donors" because O-negative blood can be given to patients with any blood type. Only about 6% of people have O-negative blood, which presents a challenge in managing and planning. This is especially true, since, unlike a manufacturer who can balance supply by planning to produce or to purchase more or less of a key item, the Canadian Blood Services gets its supply from volunteer donors who show up more-or-less at random (at least in terms of blood type). Modelling the arrival of samples with various blood types helps Canadian Blood Services managers to plan their blood allocations.

---

[3]Source: www.bloodservices.ca

Here's a small example of the kind of planning required. Of the next 20 donors to arrive at a blood donation centre, how many universal donors can be expected? Specifically, what are the mean and standard deviation of the number of universal donors? What is the probability that there are two or three universal donors?

Question 1: What are the mean and standard deviation of the number of universal donors?

Question 2: What is the probability that there are exactly two or three universal donors out of the 20 donors?

PLAN	**Setup** State the question. Check to see that these are Bernoulli trials. **Variable** Define the random variable. **Model** Specify the model.	We want to know the mean and standard deviation of the number of universal donors among 20 people and the probability that there are two or three of them. ✓ There are two outcomes: success = O-negative failure = other blood types ✓ $p = 0.06$ ✓ **10% Condition:** Fewer than 10% of all possible donors have shown up. Let $X =$ number of O-negative donors among $n = 20$ people. We can model X with a Binom(20, 0.06) model.
DO	**Mechanics** Find the expected value and standard deviation. Calculate the probability of two or three successes.	$E(X) = np = 20(0.060) = 1.2$ $SD(X) = \sqrt{npq} = \sqrt{20(0.06)(0.94)} \approx 1.06$ $P(X = 2 \text{ or } 3) = P(X = 2) + P(X = 3)$ $= \binom{20}{2}(0.06)^2(0.94)^{18}$ $+ \binom{20}{3}(0.06)^3(0.94)^{17}$ $\approx 0.2246 + 0.0860$ $= 0.3106$
REPORT	**Conclusion** Interpret your results in context.	MEMO: **Re: Blood Drive** In groups of 20 randomly selected blood donors, we'd expect to find an average of 1.2 universal donors, with a standard deviation of 1.06. About 31% of the time, we'd expect to find exactly two or three universal donors among the 20 people.

Simeon Denis Poisson was a French mathematician interested in rare events. He originally derived his model to approximate the Binomial model when the probability of a success, *p*, is very small and the number of trials, *n*, is very large. Poisson's contribution was providing a simple approximation to find that probability. When you see the formula, however, you won't necessarily see the connection to the Binomial.

W. S. Gosset, the quality control chemist at the Guinness brewery in the early twentieth century who developed the methods of Chapter 12, was one of the first to use the Poisson in industry. He used it to model and predict the number of yeast cells so he'd know how much to add to the stock. The Poisson is a good model to consider whenever your data consist of counts of occurrences. It requires only that the events be independent and that the mean number of occurrences stays constant.

*The Poisson Model

Not all discrete events can be modelled as Bernoulli trials. Sometimes we're interested simply in the number of events that occur over a given interval of time or space. For example, we might want to model the number of customers arriving in our store in the next ten minutes, the number of visitors to our website in the next minute, or the number of defects that occur in a computer monitor of a certain size. In cases like these, the number of occurrences can be modelled by a Poisson random variable. The Poisson's parameter, the mean of the distribution, is usually denoted by λ, the Greek letter lambda.

For example, data show an average of about four hits per minute to a small business website during the afternoon hours from 1:00 to 5:00 p.m. We can use the **Poisson model** to find the probability that any number of hits

---

Poisson probability model for occurrences: Poisson (λ)

λ = mean number of occurrences

X = number of occurrences

$$P(X = x) = \frac{e^{-\lambda}\lambda^x}{x!}$$

Expected value: $E(X) = \lambda$

Standard deviation: $SD(X) = \sqrt{\lambda}$

---

will arrive. For example, if we let X be the number of hits arriving in the next minute,

then $P(X = x) = \dfrac{e^{-\lambda}\lambda^x}{x!} = \dfrac{e^{-4}4^x}{x!}$, using the given average rate of four per minute. So,

the probability of no hits during the next minute would be

$P(X = 0) = \dfrac{e^{-4}4^0}{0!} = e^{-4} = 0.0183$ (where $e \approx 2.71828$, the base of the natural logarithm).

One interesting and useful feature of the Poisson model is that it scales according to the interval size. For example, suppose we want to know the probability of no hits to our website in the next 30 seconds. Since the mean rate is four hits per minute, it's two hits per 30 seconds, so we can use the model with $\lambda = 2$ instead. If we let Y be the number of hits arriving in the next 30 seconds, then:

$$P(Y = 0) = \frac{e^{-2}2^0}{0!} = e^{-2} = 0.1353$$

The Poisson model has been used to model phenomena such as customer arrivals, hot streaks in sports, and disease clusters.

Whenever or wherever rare events happen closely together, people want to know whether the occurrence

---

AF archive/Alamy

The Poisson distribution was the model used in the famous 1982 Woburn toxic waste trial when eight families from Woburn, Massachusetts, sued W. R. Grace & Company, alleging that the company contaminated the public water supplies by dumping toxic materials near city wells. The families argued that eight recent cases of leukemia were the result of the company's actions. The resulting trial was the basis for the book and movie *A Civil Action*. For the Woburn case, the probability (based on national averages) for eight leukemia cases in a town of that size in the given time period was determined to be about 0.04. That's a small chance, but not strikingly unusual.

happened by chance or whether an underlying change caused the unusual occurrence. The Poisson model can be used to find the probability of the occurrence and can be the basis for making the judgment.

8.5 Continuous Random Variables and the Normal Model

Discrete random variables are great for modelling occurrences, categories, or small counts. But in industry we often measure quantities that a discrete variable just can't handle. For example, the time until a computer battery needs to be charged might take on any value between two and four hours.

When a random variable can take on any value in an interval, we can no longer model it using a discrete probability model and must use a continuous probability model instead. For any continuous random variable, the distribution of its probability can be shown with a curve. That curve is called the **probability density function (pdf)**, usually denoted as $f(x)$. You've probably seen the Normal or bell-shaped curve. Technically, that is known as the Normal probability density function.

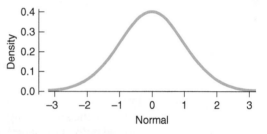

Figure 8.1 The standard Normal density function (a normal with mean 0 and standard deviation 1). The probability of finding a z-score in any interval is the area over that interval under the curve. For example, the probability that the z-score falls between −1 and 1 is about 68%, which can be seen approximately from the density function or found more precisely from a table or technology.

Density functions must satisfy two requirements. They must stay nonnegative for every possible value, and the total area under the curve must be exactly 1.0. This last requirement corresponds to the Probability Assignment Rule of Chapter 7, which said that the total probability (equal to 1.0) must be assigned somewhere.

Any density function can give the probability that the random variable lies in an interval. But remember, the probability that X lies in the interval from a to b is the *area* under the density function, $f(x)$, between the values a and b and not the value $f(a)$ or $f(b)$. In general, finding that area requires calculus or numerical analysis, and is beyond the scope of this text. But for the models we'll discuss, the probabilities are found either from tables (the Normal) or simple computations (Uniform).

There are many (in fact, there are an infinite number of) possible continuous distributions, but we'll explore only two of the most commonly used to model business phenomena: the **Uniform model** and the **Normal model**.

The Uniform Model

We've already seen the discrete version of the uniform model. A continuous uniform shares the principle that all events should be equally likely, but with a continuous model, we can't talk about the probability of a particular value because each value has probability zero. Instead, for a continuous random variable X, we say that the probability that X lies in any interval depends only on the length of that interval. Not surprisingly the density function of a continuous uniform random variable looks flat (see Figure 8.2).

The density function of a continuous uniform random variable defined on the interval a to b can be defined by the formula (see also Figure 8.2)

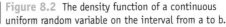

$$f(x) = \begin{cases} \dfrac{1}{b-a} & if \quad a \le x \le b \\ 0 & otherwise \end{cases}$$

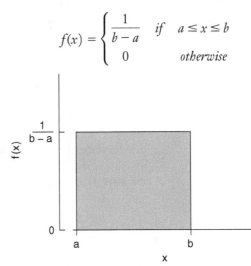

Figure 8.2 The density function of a continuous uniform random variable on the interval from a to b.

From Figure 8.2, it's easy to see that the probability that X lies in any interval between a and b is the same as any other interval of the same length. In fact, the probability is just the ratio of the length of the interval to the total length: $b - a$. In other words:

For values c and d ($c \le d$) both within the interval $[a, b]$:

$$P(c \le X \le d) = \frac{(d-c)}{(b-a)}$$

As an example, suppose you arrive at a bus stop and want to model how long you'll wait for the next bus. The sign says that buses arrive about every 20 minutes, but no other information is given. You might assume that the arrival is equally likely to be anywhere in the next 20 minutes, and so the density function would be

$$f(x) = \begin{cases} \dfrac{1}{20} & if \quad 0 \le x \le 20 \\ 0 & otherwise \end{cases}$$

and would look as shown in Figure 8.3.

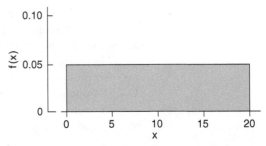

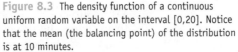

Figure 8.3 The density function of a continuous uniform random variable on the interval [0,20]. Notice that the mean (the balancing point) of the distribution is at 10 minutes.

Just as the mean of a data distribution is the balancing point of a histogram, the mean of any continuous random variable is the balancing point of the density function. Looking at Figure 8.3, we can see that the balancing point is halfway between the end points at 10 minutes. In general, the expected value is:

$$E(X) = \frac{a+b}{2}$$

for a uniform distribution on the interval (a, b). With $a = 0$ and $b = 20$ the expected value would be 10 minutes.

The variance and standard deviation are less intuitive:

$$Var(X) = \frac{(b-a)^2}{12}; \ SD(X) = \sqrt{\frac{(b-a)^2}{12}}$$

Using these formulas, our bus wait will have an expected value of 10 minutes with a standard deviation of $\sqrt{\frac{(20-0)^2}{12}} = 5.77$ minutes.

How can *every* value have probability 0?

At first it may seem illogical that every value of a continuous random variable has probability 0. Let's look at the standard Normal random variable, Z. The Normal model is a continuous model. We could find (from a table, website, or computer program) that the probability that Z lies between 0 and 1 is 0.3413,

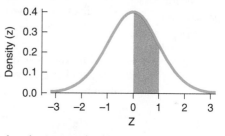

which is the area under the Normal pdf (in red) between the values 0 and 1. So, what's the probability that Z is between 0 and 1/10?

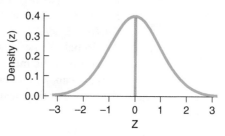

That area is only 0.0398. What is the chance then that Z will fall between 0 and 1/100? There's not much area—the probability is only 0.0040. If we kept going, the probability would keep getting smaller. The probability that Z is between 0 and 1/100,000 is less than 0.0001.

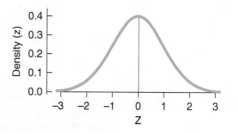

No one knows for sure why the bell-shaped curve got the name "normal." The word comes from the Latin *normalis*. A "*norma*" was a carpenter's square, so *normalis* meant perpendicular, and that is still one of the meanings of the word normal. But in statistics, "normal" is not a value judgment. In statistics the opposite of normal is non-normal, not abnormal—that's psychology! Incidentally, there is a town in Illinois called Normal; perhaps not surprisingly it is in the centre of the state!

> **NOTATION ALERT:**
> $N(\mu, \sigma)$ always denotes a Normal model. The μ, pronounced "mew," is the Greek letter for "m," and always represents the mean in a model. The σ, sigma, is the lowercase Greek letter for "s," and always represents the standard deviation in a model.

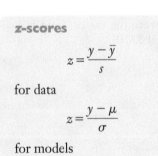

z-scores

$$z = \frac{y - \bar{y}}{s}$$

for data

$$z = \frac{y - \mu}{\sigma}$$

for models

So, what's the probability that Z is *exactly* 0? Well, there's *no* area under the curve right at $x = 0$, so the probability is 0. It's only intervals that have positive probability, but that's OK. In real life we never mean exactly 0.0000000000 or any other value. If you say "exactly 164 pounds," you might really mean between 163.5 and 164.5 pounds or even between 163.99 and 164.01 pounds, but realistically not 164.000000000 . . . pounds.

The Normal Model

Normal models show up throughout Statistics. Normal models are appropriate for distributions whose shapes are unimodal and roughly symmetric. You've probably seen Normal models before, and if you've seen a "bell-shaped curve," chances are it was a Normal model. Normal models are defined by two parameters, a mean and a standard deviation. By convention, we denote parameters with Greek letters. For example, we denote the mean of such a model with the Greek letter μ, which is the Greek equivalent of "m," for *m*ean, and the standard deviation with the Greek letter σ, the Greek equivalent of "s," for *s*tandard deviation. So we write $N(\mu, \sigma)$ to represent a Normal model with mean μ and standard deviation σ.

There's a different Normal model for every combination of μ and σ, but if we standardize our data first as we did in Chapter 5, creating z-scores by subtracting the mean to make the mean 0 and dividing by the standard deviation to make the standard deviation 1, then we'll need only the model with mean 0 and standard deviation 1. We call this the **standard Normal model** (or the **standard Normal distribution**, shown in Figure 8.1).

Of course, we shouldn't use a Normal model for every data set. If the histogram isn't unimodal and symmetric to begin with, the z-scores won't be well modelled by the Normal model. And standardizing won't help because standardizing doesn't change the shape of the distribution. So always check the histogram of the data before using the Normal model.

The 68-95-99.7 Rule

Normal models are useful because they can give us an idea of how extreme a value is by telling us how likely we are to find one that far from the mean. We'll soon see how to find these values for any z-score, but for now, there's a simple rule, called the **68-95-99.7 Rule**, that tells us roughly how the values are distributed.

In bell-shaped distributions, about 68% of the values fall within one standard deviation of the mean, about 95% of the values fall within two standard deviations of the mean, and about 99.7%—almost all—of the values fall within three standard deviations of the mean (Figure 8.4).[4]

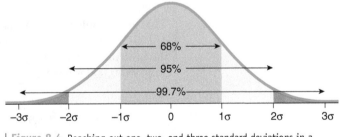

Figure 8.4 Reaching out one, two, and three standard deviations in a bell-shaped distribution gives the 68-95-99.7 Rule.

---

[4] This rule was first recognized by the mathematician Abraham De Moivre in 1733, based on empirical observations of data, so it is sometimes called the **Empirical Rule**. But it's a better mnemonic to call it the 68-95-99.7 Rule, for the three numbers that define it.

Finding Other Percentiles

Finding the probability that a proportion is at least one SD above the mean is easy. We know that 68% of the values lie within one SD of the mean, so 32% lie farther away. Since the Normal model is symmetric, half of those 32% (or 16%) are more than one SD above the mean. But what if we want to know the percentage of observations that fall more than 1.8 SD above the mean? We already know that no more than 16% of observations have z-scores above one. By similar reasoning, no more than 2.5% of the observations have a z-score above two. Can we be more precise with our answer than "between 16% and 2.5%"?

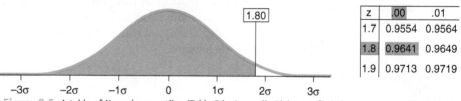

z	.00	.01
1.7	0.9554	0.9564
1.8	0.9641	0.9649
1.9	0.9713	0.9719

Figure 8.5 A table of Normal percentiles (Table Z in Appendix B) lets us find the percentage of individuals in a standard Normal distribution falling below any specified z-score value.

When the value doesn't fall exactly 0, 1, 2, or 3 standard deviations from the mean, we can look it up in a table of **Normal percentiles**.[5] Tables use the standard Normal model, so we'll have to convert our data to z-scores before using the table. If our data value was 1.8 standard deviations above the mean, we would standardize it to a z-score of 1.80, and then find the value associated with a z-score of 1.80. If we use a table, as shown in Figure 8.5, we find the z-score by looking down the left column for the first two digits (1.8) and across the top row for the third digit, 0. The table gives the percentile as 0.9641. That means that 96.4% of the z-scores are less than 1.80. Since the total area is always 1, and 1 − 0.9641 = 0.0359 we know that only 3.6% of all observations from a Normal model have z-scores higher than 1.80.

> These days, finding percentiles from a Normal table is rarely necessary. Most of the time, we can use a calculator, a computer, or a website. But learning how to find percentiles from the table helps in understanding the Normal model.

Practice with Normal Distribution Calculations

Finding the percentiles associated with any value in a Normal model isn't hard, but a little practice might be useful. Most of you have taken standardized tests of one kind or another, and you probably focused as much on the "percentile" of your performance as on the raw score. The scores from most standardized tests, such as SATs, GMATs, and LSATs, are well modelled by a Normal and are often reported both as raw scores and percentiles. For practice, let's see how we can convert SAT scores to percentiles.

> We strongly recommend that you draw a little sketch of the distribution and mark off the area of interest. This will help you avoid simple but critical errors, whether you use the Normal table of percentiles, a calculator, or a computer. All of these sources are good at calculating but terrible at thinking!

---

[5] See Table Z in Appendix B. Many calculators and statistics computer packages do this as well.

Here is a summary of the three kinds of Normal distribution calculations as demonstrated in Examples I, II, and III, and in the Guided Example that follows. All three are based on $z = \dfrac{y - \mu}{\sigma}$ and the probability P related to z.

1. Start with y, μ, and σ; compute z, and find P correspond to z (table, calculator, or computer).

2. Start with P, y, and σ; find z corresponding to P, and compute μ, from $\mu = y + z\sigma$.

3. Start with P, y, and μ; find z corresponding to P, and compute σ from $\sigma = \dfrac{y - \mu}{z}$.

Note that #1 goes from z to P, while #2 and #3 go from P to z.

Example I

Problem: Each SAT Reasoning Test (SAT) has a distribution that is roughly unimodal and symmetric and is designed to have an overall mean of 500 and a standard deviation of 100. In any one year, the mean and standard deviation may differ from these target values by a small amount, but we can use these values as good overall approximations.

Suppose you earned a 600 on an SAT test. From that information and the 68-95-99.7 Rule, where do you stand among all students who took the SAT?

Solution: Because we're told that the distribution is unimodal and symmetric, we can model the distribution with a Normal model. We are also told the scores have a mean of 500 and an SD of 100. So, we'll use a $N(500,100)$ model. It's good practice at this point to draw the distribution. Find the score whose percentile you want to know and locate it on the picture. When you finish the calculation, you should check to make sure that it's a reasonable percentile from the picture.

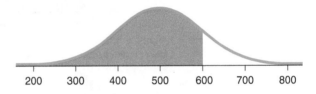

A score of 600 is 1 SD above the mean. That corresponds to one of the points in the 68-95-99.7% Rule. About 32% (100% − 68%) of those who took the test were more than one standard deviation from the mean, but only half of those were on the high side. So about 16% (half of 32%) of the test scores were better than 600.

Example II

Problem: Assuming the SAT scores are nearly normal with $N(500,100)$, what proportion of SAT scores falls between 450 and 600?

Solution: *The first step is to find the z-scores associated with each value.* Standardizing the scores we are given, we find that for 600, $z = (600 - 500)/100 = 1.0$ and for 450, $z = (450 - 500)/100 = -0.50$. We can label the axis below the picture either in the original values or the z-scores or even use both scales as the following picture shows.

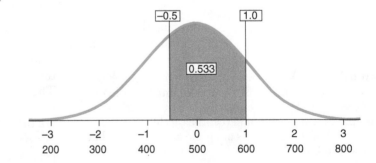

From Table Z, we find the area $z \le 1.0 = 0.8413$, which means that 84.13% of scores fall below 1.0, and the area $z \le -0.50 = 0.3085$, which means that 30.85% of the values fall below −0.5, so the proportion of z-scores *between* them is 84.13% − 30.85% = 53.28%. So, the Normal model estimates that about 53.3% of SAT scores fall between 450 and 600.

Finding areas from z-scores is the simplest way to work with the Normal model. But sometimes we start with areas and are asked to work backward to find the corresponding z-score or even the original data value. For instance, what z-score represents the first quartile, Q1, in a Normal model? In our first set of examples, we knew the z-score and used the table or technology to find the percentile. Now we want to find the cut point for the 25th percentile. Make a picture, shading the leftmost 25% of the area. Look in Table Z for an area of 0.2500. The exact area is not there, but 0.2514 is the closest number. That shows up in the table with −0.6 in the left margin and .07 in the top margin. The z-score for Q1, then, is approximately $z = -0.67$. Computers and calculators can determine the cut point more precisely (and more easily).[6]

Example III

Problem: Suppose a university says it admits only people with SAT scores among the top 10%. How high an SAT score does it take to be eligible?

Solution: The university takes the top 10%, so their cutoff score is the 90th percentile. Draw an approximate picture like this one.

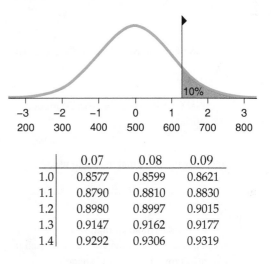

	0.07	0.08	0.09
1.0	0.8577	0.8599	0.8621
1.1	0.8790	0.8810	0.8830
1.2	0.8980	0.8997	0.9015
1.3	0.9147	0.9162	0.9177
1.4	0.9292	0.9306	0.9319

From our picture we can see that the z-value is between 1 and 1.5 (if we've judged 10% of the area correctly), and so the cutoff score is between 600 and 650 or so. Using technology, you may be able to select the 10% area and find the z-value directly. Using a table, such as Table Z, locate 0.90 (or as close to it as you can; here 0.8997 is closer than 0.9015) in the *interior* of the table and find the corresponding z-value (see table above). Here the 1.2 is in the left margin, and the 0.08 is in the margin above the entry. Putting them together gives 1.28. Now, convert the z-score back to the original units. From Table Z, the cut point is $z = 1.28$. A z-value of 1.28 is 1.28 standard deviations above the mean. Since the standard deviation is 100, that's 128 SAT points. The cutoff is 128 points above the mean of 500, or 628. Because the school wants SAT scores in the top 10%, the cutoff is 628. (Actually since SAT scores are reported only in multiples of 10, you'd have to score at least a 630.)

---

[6] We'll often use those more precise values in our examples. If you're finding the values from the table you may not get *exactly* the same number to all decimal places as your classmate who's using a computer package.

GUIDED EXAMPLE Cereal Company

David Buffington/Blend Images/Getty Images

A cereal manufacturer has a machine that fills the boxes. Boxes are labelled "16 oz," so the company wants to have that much cereal in each box. But since no packaging process is perfect, there will be minor variations. If the machine is set at exactly 16 oz and the Normal model applies (or at least the distribution is roughly symmetric), then about half of the boxes will be underweight, making consumers unhappy and exposing the company to bad publicity and possible lawsuits. To prevent underweight boxes, the manufacturer has to set the mean a little higher than 16.0 oz. Based on their experience with the packaging machine, the company believes that the amount of cereal in the boxes fits a Normal model with a standard deviation of 0.2 oz. The manufacturer decides to set the machine to put an average of 16.3 oz in each box. Let's use that model to answer a series of questions about these cereal boxes.

Question 1. What fraction of the boxes will be underweight?

PLAN		
	Setup State the variable and the objective.	The variable is weight of cereal in a box. We want to determine what fraction of the boxes risk being underweight.
	Model Check to see if a Normal model is appropriate.	We have no data, so we cannot make a histogram. But we are told that the company believes the distribution of weights from the machine is Normal.
	Specify which Normal model to use.	We use an $N(16.3, 0.2)$ model.

DO

Mechanics Make a graph of this Normal model. Locate the value you're interested in on the picture, label it, and shade the appropriate region.

REALITY CHECK Estimate from the picture the percentage of boxes that are underweight. (This will be useful later to check that your answer makes sense.)

| 15.7 | 15.9 **16.0** 16.1 | 16.3 | 16.5 | 16.7 | 16.9 |

(It looks like a low percentage—maybe less than 10%.)

We want to know what fraction of the boxes will weigh less than 16 oz.

Convert your cutoff value into a z-score.

$$z = \frac{y - \mu}{\sigma} = \frac{16 - 16.3}{0.2} = -1.50.$$

Look up the area in the Normal table, or use your calculator, or software.

Area $(y < 16)$ = Area $(z < -1.50)$ = 0.0668.

 **REPORT**

Conclusion State your conclusion in the context of the problem.

We estimate that approximately 6.7% of the boxes will contain less than 16 oz of cereal.

Question 2. The company's lawyers say that 6.7% is too high. They insist that no more than 4% of the boxes can be underweight. So the company needs to set the machine to put a little more cereal in each box. What mean setting do they need?

PLAN

Setup State the variable and the objective.

The variable is weight of cereal in a box. We want to determine a setting for the machine.

Model Check to see if a Normal model is appropriate.

We have no data, so we cannot make a histogram. But we are told that a Normal model applies.

Specify which Normal model to use. This time you are not given a value for the mean!

We don't know μ, the mean amount of cereal. The standard deviation for this machine is 0.2 oz. The model, then, is $N(\mu, 0.2)$.

REALITY CHECK

We found out earlier that setting the machine to $\mu = 16.3$ oz made 6.7% of the boxes too light. We'll need to raise the mean a bit to reduce this fraction.

We are told that no more than 4% of the boxes can be below 16 oz.

DO

Mechanics Make a graph of this Normal model. Centre it at μ (since you don't know the mean) and shade the region below 16 oz.

Using the Normal table, a calculator, or software, find the z-score that cuts off the lowest 4%.
Use this information to find μ. It's located 1.75 standard deviations to the right of 16.

The z-score that has 0.04 area to the left of it is $z = -1.75$.

Since 16 must be 1.75 standard deviations below the mean, we need to set the mean at $16 + 1.75 \times 0.2 = 16.35$.

REPORT

Conclusion State your conclusion in the context of the problem.

The company must set the machine to average 16.35 oz of cereal per box.

Question 3. The company president vetoes that plan, saying the company should give away less free cereal, not more. Her goal is to set the machine no higher than 16.2 oz and still have only 4% underweight boxes. The only way to accomplish this is to reduce the standard deviation. What standard deviation must the company achieve, and what does that mean about the machine?

PLAN

Setup State the variable and the objective.

The variable is weight of cereal in a box. We want to determine the necessary standard deviation to have only 4% of boxes underweight.

Model Check that a Normal model is appropriate.

The company believes that the weights are described by a Normal model.

Specify which Normal model to use. This time you don't know σ.

Now we know the mean, but we don't know the standard deviation. The model is therefore $N(16.2, \sigma)$.

REALITY CHECK

We know the new standard deviation must be less than 0.2 oz.

DO

Mechanics Make a graph of this Normal model. Centre it at 16.2, and shade the area you're interested in. We want 4% of the area to the left of 16 oz.

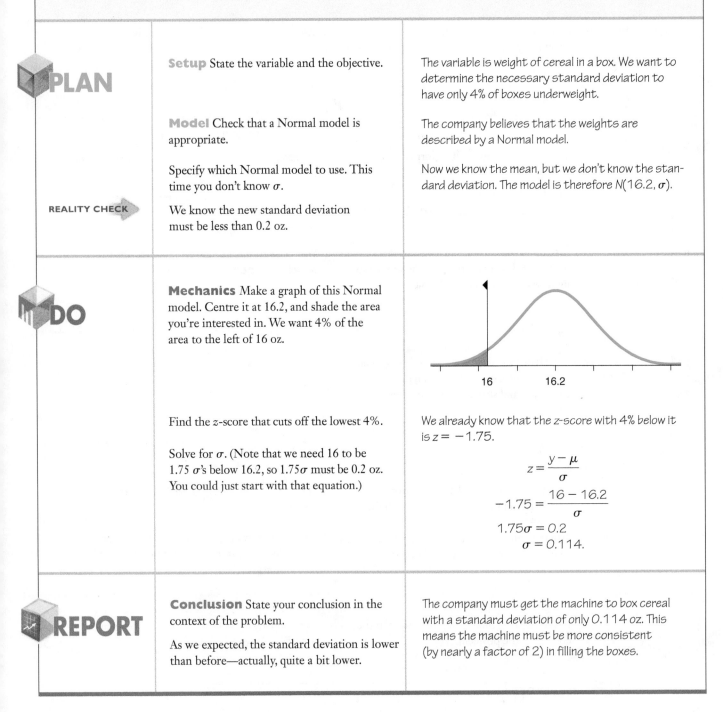

Find the z-score that cuts off the lowest 4%.

Solve for σ. (Note that we need 16 to be 1.75 σ's below 16.2, so 1.75σ must be 0.2 oz. You could just start with that equation.)

We already know that the z-score with 4% below it is $z = -1.75$.

$$z = \frac{y - \mu}{\sigma}$$

$$-1.75 = \frac{16 - 16.2}{\sigma}$$

$$1.75\sigma = 0.2$$

$$\sigma = 0.114.$$

REPORT

Conclusion State your conclusion in the context of the problem.

As we expected, the standard deviation is lower than before—actually, quite a bit lower.

The company must get the machine to box cereal with a standard deviation of only 0.114 oz. This means the machine must be more consistent (by nearly a factor of 2) in filling the boxes.

Walter Hodges/Digital Vision/Getty Images

Sums of Normals

Another reason normal models show up so often is that they have some special properties. An important one is that the sum or difference of two independent Normal random variables is also Normal.

A company manufactures small stereo systems. At the end of the production line, the stereos are packaged and prepared for shipping. Stage 1 of this process is called "packing." Workers must collect all the system components (a main unit, two speakers, a power cord, an antenna, and some wires), put each in plastic bags, and then place everything inside a protective form. The packed form then moves on to Stage 2, called "boxing," in which workers place the form and a packet of instructions in a cardboard box and then close, seal, and label the box for shipping.

Because the times required for packing and boxing can take on any value, they must be modelled by a continuous random variable. In particular, the company says that times required for the packing stage are unimodal and symmetric and can be described by a Normal model with a mean of 9 minutes and standard deviation of 1.5 minutes. (See Figure 8.6.) The times for the boxing stage can also be modelled as Normal, with a mean of 6 minutes and standard deviation of 1 minute.

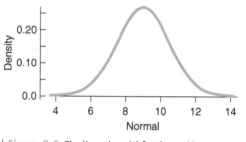

Figure 8.6 The Normal model for the packing stage with a mean of 9 minutes and standard deviation of 1.5 minutes.

The company is interested in the total time that it takes to get a system through both packing and boxing, so they want to model the sum of the two random variables. Fortunately, the special property that adding independent Normals yields another Normal model allows us to apply our knowledge of Normal probabilities to questions about the sum or difference of independent random variables. To use this property of Normals, we'll need to check two assumptions: that the variables are Independent and that they can be modelled by the Normal distribution.

GUIDED EXAMPLE | Packaging Stereos

Consider the company that manufactures and ships small stereo systems that we discussed previously.

If the time required to pack the stereos can be described by a Normal model, with a mean of 9 minutes and standard deviation of 1.5 minutes, and the times for the boxing stage can also be modelled as Normal, with a mean of 6 minutes and standard deviation of 1 minute, what is the probability that packing an order of two systems takes over 20 minutes? What percentage of the stereo systems takes longer to pack than to box?

Question 1: What is the probability that packing an order of two systems takes over 20 minutes?

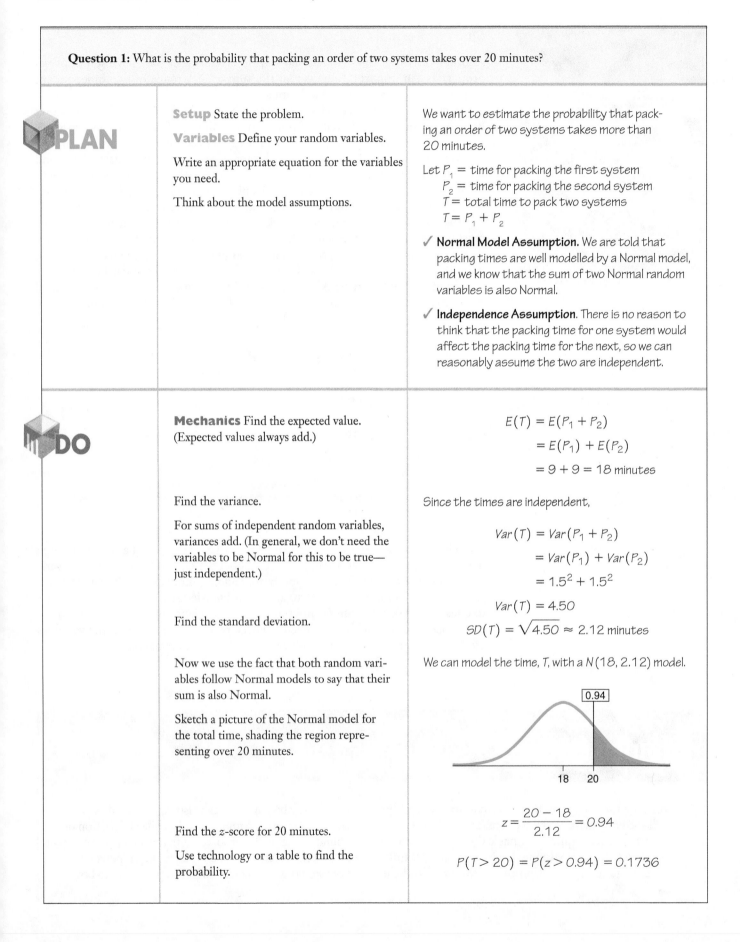

PLAN

Setup State the problem.

Variables Define your random variables.

Write an appropriate equation for the variables you need.

Think about the model assumptions.

We want to estimate the probability that packing an order of two systems takes more than 20 minutes.

Let P_1 = time for packing the first system
P_2 = time for packing the second system
T = total time to pack two systems
$T = P_1 + P_2$

✓ **Normal Model Assumption.** We are told that packing times are well modelled by a Normal model, and we know that the sum of two Normal random variables is also Normal.

✓ **Independence Assumption.** There is no reason to think that the packing time for one system would affect the packing time for the next, so we can reasonably assume the two are independent.

DO

Mechanics Find the expected value. (Expected values always add.)

$$E(T) = E(P_1 + P_2)$$
$$= E(P_1) + E(P_2)$$
$$= 9 + 9 = 18 \text{ minutes}$$

Find the variance.

For sums of independent random variables, variances add. (In general, we don't need the variables to be Normal for this to be true—just independent.)

Since the times are independent,

$$Var(T) = Var(P_1 + P_2)$$
$$= Var(P_1) + Var(P_2)$$
$$= 1.5^2 + 1.5^2$$
$$Var(T) = 4.50$$

Find the standard deviation.

$$SD(T) = \sqrt{4.50} \approx 2.12 \text{ minutes}$$

Now we use the fact that both random variables follow Normal models to say that their sum is also Normal.

Sketch a picture of the Normal model for the total time, shading the region representing over 20 minutes.

We can model the time, T, with a $N(18, 2.12)$ model.

Find the z-score for 20 minutes.

Use technology or a table to find the probability.

$$z = \frac{20 - 18}{2.12} = 0.94$$

$$P(T > 20) = P(z > 0.94) = 0.1736$$

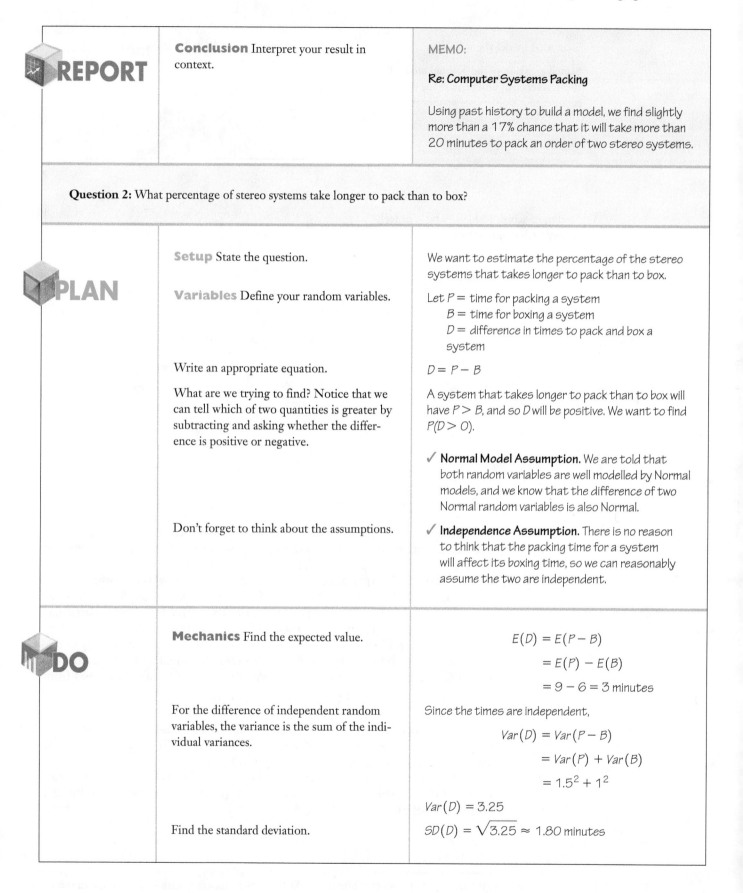

REPORT

Conclusion Interpret your result in context.

MEMO:

Re: Computer Systems Packing

Using past history to build a model, we find slightly more than a 17% chance that it will take more than 20 minutes to pack an order of two stereo systems.

Question 2: What percentage of stereo systems take longer to pack than to box?

PLAN

Setup State the question.

We want to estimate the percentage of the stereo systems that takes longer to pack than to box.

Variables Define your random variables.

Let P = time for packing a system
B = time for boxing a system
D = difference in times to pack and box a system

Write an appropriate equation.

$D = P - B$

What are we trying to find? Notice that we can tell which of two quantities is greater by subtracting and asking whether the difference is positive or negative.

A system that takes longer to pack than to box will have $P > B$, and so D will be positive. We want to find $P(D > 0)$.

✓ **Normal Model Assumption.** We are told that both random variables are well modelled by Normal models, and we know that the difference of two Normal random variables is also Normal.

Don't forget to think about the assumptions.

✓ **Independence Assumption.** There is no reason to think that the packing time for a system will affect its boxing time, so we can reasonably assume the two are independent.

DO

Mechanics Find the expected value.

$$E(D) = E(P - B)$$
$$= E(P) - E(B)$$
$$= 9 - 6 = 3 \text{ minutes}$$

For the difference of independent random variables, the variance is the sum of the individual variances.

Since the times are independent,

$$Var(D) = Var(P - B)$$
$$= Var(P) + Var(B)$$
$$= 1.5^2 + 1^2$$

$$Var(D) = 3.25$$

Find the standard deviation.

$$SD(D) = \sqrt{3.25} \approx 1.80 \text{ minutes}$$

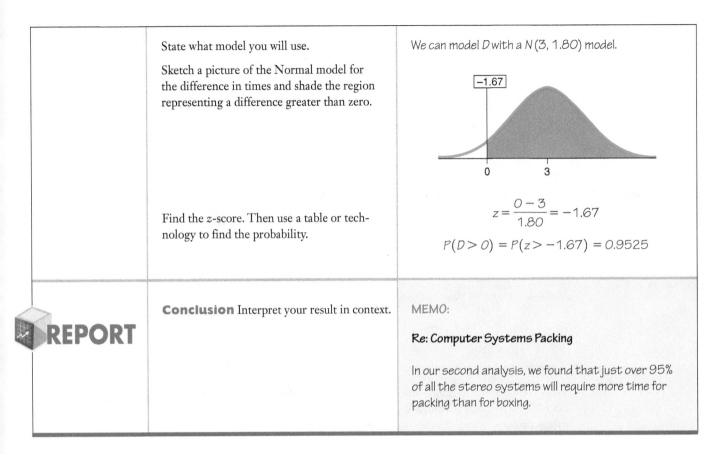

State what model you will use.	We can model D with a $N(3, 1.80)$ model.
Sketch a picture of the Normal model for the difference in times and shade the region representing a difference greater than zero.	
Find the z-score. Then use a table or technology to find the probability.	$z = \dfrac{0-3}{1.80} = -1.67$ $P(D > 0) = P(z > -1.67) = 0.9525$

Conclusion Interpret your result in context.

MEMO:

Re: Computer Systems Packing

In our second analysis, we found that just over 95% of all the stereo systems will require more time for packing than for boxing.

The Normal Model for the Binomial

Even though the Normal is a continuous model, it is often used as an approximation for discrete events when the number of possible events is large. In particular, it is a good model for sums of independent random variables of which a Binomial random variable is a special case. Here's an example of how the Normal can be used to calculate binomial probabilities. Suppose that Canadian Blood Services anticipates the need for at least 1850 units of O-negative blood for a particular region this year. It estimates that it will collect blood from 32 000 donors. How likely is Canadian Blood Services to meet its need? We've just learned how to calculate such probabilities. We could use the binomial model with $n = 32\,000$ and $p = 0.06$. The probability of getting *exactly* 1850 units of O-negative blood from 32 000 donors is $\binom{32\,000}{1850} \times 0.06^{1850} \times 0.94^{30\,150}$. No calculator on earth can calculate that first term (it has more than 100 000 digits).[7] And that's just the beginning. The problem said *at least* 1850, so we would have to do it again for 1851, for 1852, and all the way up to 32 000. (No thanks.)

When we're dealing with a large number of trials like this, making direct calculations of the probabilities becomes tedious (or outright impossible). But the Normal model can come to the rescue.

---

[7] If your calculator *can* find Binom(32000, 0.06), then apparently it's smart enough to use an approximation.

The Binomial model has mean $np = 1920$ and standard deviation $\sqrt{npq} \approx 42.48$. We could try approximating its distribution with a Normal model, using the same mean and standard deviation. Remarkably enough, that turns out to be a very good approximation. Using that mean and standard deviation, we can find the *probability:*

$$P(X \geq 1850) = P\left(z \geq \frac{1850 - 1920}{42.48}\right) \approx P(z \geq -1.65) \approx 0.95$$

There seems to be about a 95% chance that Canadian Blood Services will have enough O-negative blood.

The Continuity Correction

When we use a continuous model to model a set of discrete events, we may need to make an adjustment called the **continuity correction**. We approximated the Binomial distribution (50, 0.2) with a Normal model. But what does the Normal model say about the probability that $X = 10$? Every specific value in the Normal probability model has probability 0. That's not the answer we want.

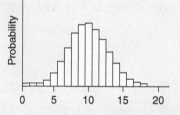

Because X is really discrete, it takes on the exact values 0, 1, 2, ... , 50, each with positive probability. The histogram holds the secret to the correction. Look at the bin corresponding to $X = 10$ in the histogram. It goes from 9.5 to 10.5. What we really want is to find the area under the normal curve *between* 9.5 and 10.5. So when we use the Normal model to approximate discrete events, we go halfway to the next value on the left and/or the right. We approximate $P(X = 10)$ by finding $P(9.5 \leq X \leq 10.5)$. For a Binomial (50, 0.2), $\mu = 10$ and $\sigma = 2.83$.

So $P(9.5 \leq X \leq 10.5) \approx P\left(\dfrac{9.5 - 10}{2.83} \leq z \leq \dfrac{10.5 - 10}{2.83}\right)$

$$= P(-0.177 \leq z \leq 0.177)$$

$$= 0.1405$$

By comparison, the *exact* Binomial probability is 0.1398.

Can we always use a Normal model to make estimates of Binomial probabilities? No. It depends on the sample size. Suppose we are searching for a prize in cereal boxes, where the probability of finding a prize is 20%. If we buy five boxes, the actual Binomial probabilities that we get 0, 1, 2, 3, 4, or 5 prizes are 33%, 41%, 20%, 5%, 1%, and 0.03%, respectively. The histogram just below shows that this probability model is skewed. That makes it clear that we should not try to estimate these probabilities by using a Normal model.

If we open 50 boxes of this cereal and count the number of prizes we find, we get the histogram below. It is centred at $np = 50(0.2) = 10$ prizes, as expected, and it appears to be fairly symmetric around that centre.

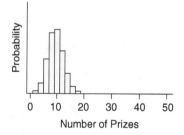

Let's have a closer look. The third histogram (in the side bar above) shows the same distribution, but this time magnified somewhat and centred at the expected value of 10 prizes. It looks close to Normal for sure. With this larger sample size, it appears that a Normal model might be a useful approximation.

A Normal model is a close enough approximation to the Binomial only for a large enough number of trials. And what we mean by "large enough" depends on the probability of success. We'd need a larger sample if the probability of success were very low (or very high). It turns out that a Normal model works pretty well if we expect to see at least 10 successes and 10 failures. That is, we check the Success/Failure Condition.

Success/Failure Condition: A Binomial model is approximately Normal if we expect at least 10 successes and 10 failures:

$$np \geq 10 \text{ and } nq \geq 10$$

Why 10? Well, actually it's 9, as revealed in the following Math Box.

MATH BOX

It's easy to see where the magic number 10 comes from. You just need to remember how Normal models work. The problem is that a Normal model extends infinitely in both directions. But a Binomial model must have between 0 and *n* successes, so if we use a Normal to approximate a Binomial, we have to cut off its tails. That's not very important if the centre of the Normal model is so far from 0 and *n* that the lost tails have only a negligible area. More than three standard deviations should do it because a Normal model has little probability past that.

So the mean needs to be at least three standard deviations from 0 and at least three standard deviations from *n*. Let's look at the 0 end.

We require:	$\mu - 3\sigma > 0$
Or, in other words:	$\mu > 3\sigma$
For a Binomial that's:	$np > 3\sqrt{npq}$
Squaring yields:	$n^2p^2 > 9npq$
Now simplify:	$np > 9q$
Since $q \leq 1$, we require:	$np > 9$

For simplicity we usually demand that *np* (and *nq* for the other tail) be at least 10 to use the Normal approximation which gives the Success/Failure Condition.[8]

✓ **JUST CHECKING**

Roper Worldwide reports that they are able to contact 76% of the randomly selected households drawn for a telephone survey.

2 Explain why these phone calls can be considered Bernoulli trials.

3 Which of the models of this chapter (Binomial, Normal, or Uniform) would you use to model the number of successful contacts from a list of 1000 sampled households?

---

[8] Looking at the final step, we see that we need $np > 9$ in the worst case, when *q* (or *p*) is near 1, making the Binomial model quite skewed. When *q* and *p* are near 0.5—for example, between 0.4 and 0.6—the Binomial model is nearly symmetric, and $np > 5$ ought to be safe enough. Although we'll always check for 10 expected successes and failures, keep in mind that for values of *p* near 0.5, we can be somewhat more forgiving.

WHAT CAN GO WRONG?

- **Probability models are still just models.** Models can be useful, but they are not reality. Think about the assumptions behind your models. Question probabilities as you would data.

- **If the model is wrong, so is everything else.** Before you try to find the mean or standard deviation of a random variable, check to make sure the probability model is reasonable. As a start, the probabilities in your model should all be between 0 and 1 and they should add up to 1. If not, you may have calculated a probability incorrectly or left out a value of the random variable.

- **Don't assume everything's Normal.** Just because a random variable is continuous or you happen to know a mean and standard deviation doesn't mean that a Normal model will be useful. You must think about whether the **Normality Assumption** is justified. Using a Normal model when it really does not apply will lead to wrong answers and misleading conclusions.

- **Watch out for variables that aren't independent.** You can add expected values of *any* two random variables, but you can only add variances of independent random variables. Suppose a survey includes questions about the number of hours of sleep people get each night and also the number of hours they are awake each day. From their answers, we find the mean and standard deviation of hours asleep and hours awake. The expected total must be 24 hours; after all, people are either asleep or awake. The means still add just fine. Since all the totals are exactly 24 hours, however, the standard deviation of the total will be 0. We can't add variances here because the number of hours you're awake depends on the number of hours you're asleep. Be sure to check for independence before adding variances.

- **Don't write independent instances of a random variable with notation that looks like they are the same variables.** Make sure you write each instance as a different random variable. Just because each random variable describes a similar situation doesn't mean that each random outcome will be the same. These are *random* variables, not the variables you saw in Algebra. Write $X_1 + X_2 + X_3$ rather than $X + X + X$.

- **Don't forget:** Variances of independent random variables add. Standard deviations don't.

- **Don't forget:** Variances of independent random variables add, even when you're looking at the difference between them.

- **Be sure you have Bernoulli trials.** Be sure to check the requirements first: two possible outcomes per trial ("success" and "failure"), a constant probability of success, and independence. Remember that the 10% Condition provides a reasonable substitute for independence.

- **Don't use the Normal approximation with small *n*.** To use a Normal approximation in place of a Binomial model, there must be at least 10 expected successes and 10 expected failures.

ETHICS IN ACTION

Although e-government services are available online, many Canadians, especially those who are older, prefer to deal with government agencies in person. For this reason, Service Canada has local offices distributed across the country. Joel Payton is the office manager for one of the two Service Canada offices in Victoria, B.C. The government expects most people to use the Service Canada website so the office is small. Yet, because of the number of retirees in the area, his office is one of the busiest. Although there have been no formal complaints, Joel expects that customer waiting times have increased. He decides to keep track of customer wait times for a one-month period in the hopes of making a case for hiring additional staff. He finds that the average wait time is 5 minutes with a standard deviation of 6 minutes. He reasons that 50% of customers who visit his office wait longer than 5 minutes for service. The target wait time is

10 minutes or less. Applying the Normal probability model, Joel finds that more than 20% of customers will have to wait longer than 10 minutes! He has uncovered what he suspected. His next step is to request additional staff based on his findings.

ETHICAL ISSUE *Waiting times are generally skewed and therefore not usually modeled using the Normal distribution. Pat should have checked the data to see if a Normal model was appropriate. Using the Normal for data that are highly skewed to the right will inflate the probability a customer will have to wait longer than 10 minutes. Related to ASA Ethical Guidelines, Item A, which can be found at http://www.amstat.org/about/ethicalguidelines.cfm.*

ETHICAL SOLUTION *Check reasonableness of applying the Normal probability model.*

WHAT HAVE WE LEARNED?

We've learned to work with random variables. We can use the probability model for a discrete random variable to find its expected value and its standard deviation.

We've learned that the mean of the sum or difference of two random variables, discrete or continuous, is just the sum or difference of their means. And we've learned the Pythagorean Theorem of Statistics: *For independent random variables, the variance of their sum or difference is always the sum of their variances.* We have also learned that Normal models are once again special: sums or differences of Normally distributed random variables also follow Normal models.

Finally, we've learned that Bernoulli trials show up in lots of places. When we're interested in the probability of the number of successes in a certain number of Bernoulli trials, we can use the Binomial model. When we expect at least 10 successes and 10 failures we can use the Normal model to approximate the Binomial model.

Terms

68-95-99.7 Rule (or Empirical Rule)   In a Normal model, 68% of values fall within one standard deviation of the mean, 95% fall within two standard deviations of the mean, and 99.7% fall within three standard deviations of the mean.

Addition Rule for Expected Values of Random Variables $E(X \pm Y) = E(X) \pm E(Y)$

Addition Rule for Variances of Random Variables   (Pythagorean Theorem of Statistics)

If X and Y are *independent*: $Var(X \pm Y) = Var(X) + Var(Y)$,

and $SD(X \pm Y) = \sqrt{Var(X) + Var(Y)}$.

Bernoulli trials	A sequence of trials are called Bernoulli trials if:
	1. There are exactly two possible outcomes (usually denoted *success* and *failure*).
	2. The probability of success is constant (that is, the same from trial to trial).
	3. The trials are independent.
Binomial probability model	A Binomial model is appropriate for a random variable that counts the number of successes in a fixed number of Bernoulli trials.
Changing a random variable by a constant	$E(X \pm c) = E(X) \pm c \quad Var(X \pm c) = Var(X) \quad SD(X \pm c) = SD(X)$
	$E(aX) = aE(X) \qquad Var(aX) = a^2 Var(X) \qquad SD(aX) = |a| SD(X)$
Continuity correction	An adjustment made when a continuous model is used to model discrete events, such as the Normal model to approximate the Binomial.
Continuous random variable	A random variable that can take any numeric value within a range of values. The range may be infinite or bounded at either or both ends.
Discrete random variable	A random variable that can take one of a finite number[9] of distinct outcomes.
Expected value	The expected value of a random variable is its theoretical long-run average value, the centre of its model. Denoted μ, $E(X)$ or sometimes EV, it is found (if the random variable is discrete) by summing the products of variable values and probabilities:
	$$\mu = EV = E(X) = \sum x \cdot P(x)$$
Geometric probability model	A model appropriate for a random variable that counts the number of Bernoulli trials until the first success.
Normal model	The most famous continuous probability model, the Normal is used to model a wide variety of phenomena whose distributions are unimodal and symmetric. The Normal model is also used as an approximation to the Binomial model for large n, when np and $nq \geq 10$, and is used as the model for distributions of sums and means under a wide variety of conditions.
Normal percentile	A percentile corresponding to a z-score that gives the percentage of values in a standard Normal distribution found at that z-score or below.
Parameter	A numerically valued attribute of a model, such as the values of μ and σ in a $N(\mu, \sigma)$ model.
*Poisson model	A discrete model often used to model the number of arrivals of events such as customers arriving in a queue or calls arriving into a call centre.
Probability density function (pdf)	A function $f(x)$ that represents the probability distribution of a random variable X. The probability that X is in an interval A is the area under the curve $f(x)$ over A.
Probability model	A function that associates a probability P with each value of a discrete random variable X, denoted $P(X = x)$, or with any interval of values of a continuous random variable.
Random variable	Assumes any of several different values as a result of some random event. Random variables are denoted by a capital letter, such as X.

---

[9] Technically, there could be an infinite number of outcomes as long as they're *countable*. Essentially, that means we can imagine listing them all in order, like the counting numbers $1, 2, 3, 4, 5, \ldots$.

Standard deviation of a random variable	Describes the spread in the model and is the square root of the variance.
Standard Normal model or Standard Normal distribution	A Normal model, $N(\mu, \sigma)$ with mean $\mu = 0$ and standard deviation $\sigma = 1$. A Standard Normal random variable is usually denoted by Z.
Uniform distribution	For a discrete uniform model over a set of n values, each value has probability $1/n$. For a continuous uniform random variable over an interval $[a, b]$, the probability that X lies in any subinterval within $[a, b]$ is the same and is just equal to the length of the interval divided by the length of $[a, b]$ which is $b - a$.
Variance	The variance of a random variable is the expected value of the squared deviations from the mean. For discrete random variables, it can be calculated as:

$$\sigma^2 = Var(X) = \sum (x - \mu)^2 P(x).$$

Skills

When you complete this lesson, you should:

 PLAN

- Be able to recognize random variables.
- Understand that random variables must be independent in order to determine the variability of their sum or difference by adding variances.

DO

- Be able to find the probability model for a discrete random variable.
- Know how to find the mean (expected value) and the variance of a random variable.
- Always use the proper notation for these population parameters: μ or $E(X)$ for the mean and σ, $SD(X)$, σ^2, or $Var(X)$ when discussing variability.
- Know how to determine the new mean and standard deviation after adding a constant, multiplying by a constant, or adding or subtracting two independent random variables.

REPORT

- Be able to interpret the meaning of the expected value and standard deviation of a random variable in the proper context.

MINI CASE STUDY PROJECT

Lester Balajadia/Shutterstock

Investment Options

A young entrepreneur has just raised a sum of money ($30 000) from investors, and she would like to invest it while she continues her fundraising in hopes of starting her company one year from now. She wants to do due diligence and understand the risk of each of her investment options. After speaking with her colleagues in finance, she believes that she has three choices: (1) she can purchase a $30 000 certificate of deposit (CD); (2) she can invest in a mutual fund with a balanced portfolio; or (3) she can invest in a growth stock that has a greater potential payback but also has greater volatility. Each of her options will yield a different payback on her $30 000, depending on the state of the economy.

During the next year, she knows that the CD yields a constant annual percentage rate, regardless of the state of the economy. If she invests in a balanced mutual fund, she estimates that she will earn 9% if the economy remains strong, but earn only 3% if the economy takes a downturn. Finally, if she invests all $30 000 in a growth stock, experienced investors tell her that she can earn as much as 50% in a strong economy, but may *lose* as much as 50% in a poor economy.

Estimating these returns, along with the likelihood of a strong economy, is challenging. Therefore, often a "sensitivity analysis" is conducted, where figures are computed using a range of values for each of the uncertain parameters in the problem. Following this advice, this investor decides to compute measures for a range of interest rates for CDs, a range of returns for the mutual fund, and a range of returns for the growth stock. In addition, the likelihood of a strong economy is unknown, so she will vary these probabilities as well.

Assume that the probability of a strong economy over the next year is either 0.5, 0.3, or 0.7. To help this investor make an informed decision, evaluate the expected value and volatility of each of her investments using the following ranges of rates of growth:

CD: Look up the current annual rate for the return on a three-year CD and use this value $\pm$ 0.5%.

Mutual Fund: Use values of 8%, 10%, and 12% for a strong economy and values of 2%, 0%, and −4% for a weak economy.

Growth Stock: Use values of 15%, 20%, and 25% in a strong economy and values of −25%, −15%, and −10% in a weak economy.

Discuss the expected returns and uncertainty of each of the alternative investment options for this investor in each of the scenarios you analyzed. Be sure to compare the volatility of each of her options.

EXERCISES

1. New website. You have just launched the website for your company that sells nutritional products online. Suppose X = the number of different pages that a customer hits during a visit to the website.   LO❽

a) Assuming that there are n different pages in total on your website, what are the possible values that this random variable may take on?

b) Is the random variable discrete or continuous?

2. New website, part 2. For the website described in Exercise 1, let Y = the total time (in minutes) that a customer spends during a visit to the website.   LO❽

a) What are the possible values of this random variable?

b) Is the random variable discrete or continuous?

3. Job interviews. Through the career services office, you have arranged preliminary interviews at four companies for summer jobs. Each company will either ask you to come to their site for a follow-up interview or not. Let X be the random variable equal to the total number of follow-up interviews that you might have.   LO❽

a) List all the possible values of X.

b) Is the random variable discrete or continuous?

c) Do you think a uniform distribution might be appropriate as a model for this random variable? Explain briefly.

4. Help desk. The computer help desk is staffed by students during the 7:00 p.m. to 11:00 p.m. shift. Let Y denote the random variable that represents the number of students seeking help during the 15-minute time slot 10:00 to 10:15 p.m.   LO❽

a) What are the possible values of Y?

b) Is the random variable discrete or continuous?

5. Orthodontist. An orthodontist has three financing packages, and each has a different service charge. He estimates that 30% of patients use the first plan which has a $10 finance charge; 50% use the second plan which has a $20 finance charge; and 20% use the third plan which has a $30 finance charge.   LO❶

a) Find the expected value of the service charge.

b) Find the standard deviation of the service charge.

6. Timeshare. A marketing agency has developed three vacation packages to promote a timeshare plan at a new resort. They estimate that 20% of potential customers will choose the Day Plan, which does not include overnight accommodations; 40% will choose the Overnight Plan, which includes one night at the resort; and 40% will choose the Weekend Plan, which includes two nights.   LO❶

a) Find the expected value of the number of nights potential customers will need.

b) Find the standard deviation of the number of nights potential customers will need.

7. Concepts I. Given independent random variables, X and Y, with means and standard deviations as shown, find the mean and standard deviation of each of the variables in parts a) to d). **LO❶**

a) $3X$
b) $Y + 6$
c) $X + Y$
d) $X - Y$

	Mean	SD
X	10	2
Y	20	5

8. Concepts II. Given independent random variables, X and Y, with means and standard deviations as shown, find the mean and standard deviation of each of the variables in parts a) to d). **LO❶**

a) $X - 20$
b) $0.5Y$
c) $X + Y$
d) $X - Y$

	Mean	SD
X	80	12
Y	12	3

9. Lottery. The Western Canada Lottery Corporation (WCLC) has a lottery game called Pick 3 in which customers buy a ticket for $1 and choose three numbers, each from zero to nine. They also must select the play type, which determines what combinations are winners. In one type of play, called the "Straight/Box," they win if they match the three numbers in any order, but the payout is greater if the order is exact. For the case where all three of the numbers selected are different, the WCLC reports that the probabilities and payouts are: **LO❶**

	Probability	Payout
Straight (Exact)	1 in 1000	$500
Box (Any Order)	6 in 1000	$80

a) Find the amount a Straight/Box player can expect to win.
b) Find the standard deviation of the player's winnings.
c) Tickets to play this game cost $1 each. If you subtract $1 from the result in part a, what is the expected result of playing this game?

10. Software company. A small software company will bid on a major contract. It anticipates a profit of $50 000 if it gets it, but thinks there is only a 30% chance of that happening. **LO❶**

a) What's the expected profit?
b) Find the standard deviation for the profit.

11. Commuting to work. A commuter must pass through five traffic lights on her way to work and will have to stop at each one that is red. After keeping records for several months, she developed the following probability model for the number of red lights she hits: **LO❶**

X = # of red	0	1	2	3	4	5
$P(X=x)$	0.05	0.25	0.35	0.15	0.15	0.05

a) How many red lights should she expect to hit each day?
b) What's the standard deviation?

12. Defects. A consumer organization inspecting new cars found that many had appearance defects (dents, scratches, paint chips, etc.). While none had more than three of these defects, 7% had three, 11% had two, and 21% had one defect. **LO❶**

a) Find the expected number of appearance defects in a new car.
b) What is the standard deviation?

13. Fishing tournament. A sporting goods manufacturer was asked to sponsor a local boy in two fishing tournaments. They claim the probability that he will win the first tournament is 0.4. If he wins the first tournament, they estimate the probability that he will also win the second is 0.2. They guess that if he loses the first tournament, the probability that he will win the second is 0.3. **LO❶**

a) According to their estimates, are the two tournaments independent? Explain your answer.
b) What's the probability that he loses both tournaments?
c) What's the probability he wins both tournaments?
d) Let random variable X be the number of tournaments he wins. Find the probability model for X.
e) What are the expected value and standard deviation of X?

14. Contracts. Your company bids for two contracts. You believe the probability that you get contract #1 is 0.8. If you get contract #1, the probability that you also get contract #2 will be 0.2, and if you do not get contract #1, the probability that you get contract #2 will be 0.3. **LO❶**

a) Are the outcomes of the two contract bids independent? Explain.
b) Find the probability you get both contracts.
c) Find the probability you get neither contract.
d) Let X be the number of contracts you get. Find the probability model for X.
e) Find the expected value and standard deviation of X.

15. Battery recall. A company has discovered that a recent batch of batteries had manufacturing flaws, and has issued a recall. You have 10 batteries covered by the recall, and 3 are dead. You choose 2 batteries at random from your package of 10. **LO❶**

a) Has the assumption of independence been met? Explain.
b) Create a probability model for the number of good batteries chosen.
c) What's the expected number of good batteries?
d) What's the standard deviation?

16. Grocery supplier. A grocery supplier believes that the mean number of broken eggs per dozen is 0.6, with a standard deviation of 0.5. You buy three dozen eggs without checking them. **LO❶**

a) How many broken eggs do you expect to get?
b) What's the standard deviation?
c) Is it necessary to assume the cartons of eggs are independent? Why?

17. Commuting, part 2. A commuter finds that she waits an average of 14.8 seconds at each of five stoplights, with a standard deviation of 9.2 seconds. Find the mean and the standard deviation of the total amount of time she waits at all five lights. What, if anything, did you assume? **LO①**

18. Repair calls. A small engine shop receives an average of 1.7 repair calls per hour, with a standard deviation of 0.6. What is the mean and standard deviation of the number of calls they receive for an eight-hour day? What, if anything, did you assume? **LO①**

19. Insurance company. An insurance company estimates that it should make an annual profit of $150 on each homeowner's policy written, with a standard deviation of $6000. **LO①**
a) Why is the standard deviation so large?
b) If the company writes only two of these policies, what are the mean and standard deviation of the annual profit?
c) If the company writes 1000 of these policies, what are the mean and standard deviation of the annual profit?
d) What is the probability that the company will make money if they write 1000 policies?
e) What circumstances could violate the assumption of independence of the policies?

20. Casino. At a casino, people play the slot machines in hopes of hitting the jackpot, but most of the time, they lose their money. A certain machine pays out an average of $0.92 (for every dollar played), with a standard deviation of $120. **LO①**
a) Why is the standard deviation so large?
b) If a gambler plays five times, what are the mean and standard deviation of the casino's profit?
c) If gamblers play this machine 1000 times in a day, what are the mean and standard deviation of the casino's profit?

21. Bike sale. A bicycle shop plans to offer two specially priced children's models at a sidewalk sale. The basic model will return a profit of $120 and the deluxe model $150. Past experience indicates that sales of the basic model will have a mean of 5.4 bikes with a standard deviation of 1.2, and sales of the deluxe model will have a mean of 3.2 bikes with a standard deviation of 0.8 bikes. The cost of setting up for the sidewalk sale is $200. **LO①**
a) Define random variables and use them to express the bicycle shop's net profit.
b) What's the mean of the net profit?
c) What's the standard deviation of the net profit?
d) Do you need to make any assumptions in calculating the mean? How about the standard deviation?

22. Farmers' market. A farmer has 100 kg of apples and 50 kg of potatoes for sale. The market price for apples (per kilogram) each day is a random variable with a mean of 0.5 dollars and a standard deviation of 0.2 dollars. Similarly, for a kilogram of potatoes, the mean price is 0.3 dollars and the standard deviation is 0.1 dollars. It also costs him two dollars to bring all the apples and potatoes to the market. The market is busy with eager shoppers, so we can assume that he'll be able to sell all of each type of produce at that day's price. **LO①**
a) Define your random variables, and use them to express the farmer's net income.
b) Find the mean of the net income.

c) Find the standard deviation of the net income.
d) Do you need to make any assumptions in calculating the mean? How about the standard deviation?

23. NASCAR. For a new type of tire, a NASCAR team found the average distance a set of tires would run during a race is 168 miles, with a standard deviation of 14 miles. Assume that tire mileage is independent and follows a Normal model. **LO①**
a) If the team plans to change tires twice during a 500-mile race, what is the expected value and standard deviation of miles remaining after two changes?
b) What is the probability they won't have to change tires a third time before the end of a 500-mile race?

24. Swimming medley. In the 4×100 medley relay event, four swimmers swim 100 metres, each using a different stroke. A university team preparing for a national championship looks at the times their swimmers have posted and creates a model based on the following assumptions: **LO①**
• The swimmers' performances are independent.
• Each swimmer's times follow a Normal model.
• The means and standard deviations of the times (in seconds) are as shown here.

Swimmer	Mean	SD
1 (backstroke)	50.72	0.24
2 (breaststroke)	55.51	0.22
3 (butterfly)	49.43	0.25
4 (freestyle)	44.91	0.21

a) What are the mean and standard deviation for the relay team's total time in this event?
b) The team's best time so far this season was 3:19.48. (That's 199.48 seconds.) What is the probability that they will beat that time in the next event?

25. Movie rentals. To compete with Netflix, the owner of a movie rental shop decided to try sending DVDs through the mail. In order to determine how many copies of newly released titles he should purchase, he carefully observed turnaround times. Since nearly all of his customers were in his local community, he tested delivery times by sending DVDs to his friends. He found the mean delivery time was 1.3 days, with a standard deviation of 0.5 days. He also noted that the times were the same whether going to the customer or coming back to the shop. **LO①**
a) Find the mean and standard deviation of the round-trip delivery times for a DVD (mailed to the customer and then mailed back to the shop).
b) The shop owner tries to process a DVD that is returned to him and get it back in the mail in one day, but circumstances sometimes prevent it. His mean turnaround time is 1.1 days, with a standard deviation of 0.3 days. Find the mean and standard deviation of the turnaround times combined with the round-trip times in part a.

c) The complete rent cycle is the time from when a DVD is placed in the mail until it is returned, processed, and placed back in the mail. Initially, the shop owner estimated the rent cycle would take 9.0 days. If the time customers hold DVDs has a mean of 3.7 days and a standard deviation of 2.0 days, combine customer times with round-trip and process times in part b and determine what proportion of DVD rentals would take longer than 9 days to complete the cycle. (Assume the distribution of rent cycle time has a Normal model.)

26. Online applications. Researchers for an online marketing company suggest that new customers who have to become a member before they can check out on the website are very intolerant of long applications. One way to rate an application is by the total number of keystrokes required to fill it out. **LO❶**

a) One common frustration is having to enter an email address twice. If the mean length of email addresses is 13.3 characters, with a standard deviation of 2.8 characters, what is the mean and standard deviation of total characters typed if entered twice?

b) The company found the mean and standard deviation of the length of customers' names (including spaces) were 13.4 and 2.4 characters, respectively, and for addresses, 30.8 and 6.3 characters. What is the mean and standard deviation of the combined lengths of entering the email addresses twice and then the name and the address?

c) The store's researchers suggested the frustration limit is 80 characters, beyond which a potential customer is likely to close the application without completing the purchase. What proportion of applications found in part b will exceed that? (Assume the distribution of application lengths has a Normal model.)

27. eBay. A collector purchased a quantity of action figures and is going to sell them on eBay. He has 19 Hulk figures. In recent auctions, the mean selling price of similar figures has been $12.11, with a standard deviation of $1.38. He also has 13 Iron Man figures which have had a mean selling price of $10.19, with a standard deviation of $0.77. His insertion fee will be $0.55 on each item, and the closing fee will be 8.75% of the selling price. He assumes all will sell without having to be relisted. **LO❶**

a) Define your random variables, and use them to create a random variable for the collector's net income.

b) Find the mean (expected value) of the net income.

c) Find the standard deviation of the net income.

d) Do you have to assume independence for the sales on eBay? Explain.

28. Real estate. A real estate broker purchased three two-bedroom houses in a depressed market for a combined cost of $71 000. He expects the cleaning and repair costs on each house to average $3700, with a standard deviation of $1450. When he sells them, after subtracting taxes and other closing costs, he expects to realize an average of $39 000 per house, with a standard deviation of $1100. **LO❶**

a) Define your random variables, and use them to create a random variable for the broker's net profit.

b) Find the mean (expected value) of the net profit.

c) Find the standard deviation of the net profit.

d) Do you have to assume independence for the repairs and sale prices of the houses? Explain.

29. Bernoulli. Can we use probability models based on Bernoulli trials to investigate the following situations? Explain. **LO❷**

a) Each week a doctor rolls a single die to determine which of his six office staff members gets the preferred parking space.

b) A medical research lab has samples of blood collected from 120 different individuals. How likely is it that the majority of them are Type A blood, given that Type A is found in 42% of the population?

c) From a workforce of 13 men and 23 women, all five promotions go to men. How likely is that, if promotions are based on qualifications rather than gender?

d) We poll 500 of the 3000 stockholders to see how likely it is that the proposed budget will pass.

e) A company realizes that about 10% of its packages are not being sealed properly. In a case of 24 packages, how likely is it that more than three are unsealed?

30. Bernoulli, part 2. Can we use probability models based on Bernoulli trials to investigate the following situations? Explain. **LO❷**

a) You are rolling five dice. How likely is it to get at least two sixes to win the game?

b) You survey 500 potential customers to determine their colour preference.

c) A manufacturer recalls a doll because about 3% have buttons that are not properly attached. Customers return 37 of these dolls to the local toy store. How likely are they to find any buttons not properly attached?

d) A city council of 11 Conservatives and 8 Liberals picks a committee of 4 at random. How likely are they to choose all Liberals?

e) An executive reads that 74% of employees in his industry are dissatisfied with their jobs. How many dissatisfied employees can he expect to find among the 481 employees in his company?

31. Closing sales. A salesman normally makes a sale (closes) on 80% of his presentations. Assuming the presentations are independent, find the probability of each of the following. **LO❷**

a) He fails to close for the first time on his fifth attempt.

b) He closes his first presentation on his fourth attempt.

c) The first presentation he closes will be on his second attempt.

d) The first presentation he closes will be on one of his first three attempts.

32. Computer chip manufacturer. Suppose a computer chip manufacturer rejects 2% of the chips produced because they fail presale testing. Assuming the bad chips are independent, find the probability of each of the following. **LO❷**

a) The fifth chip they test is the first bad one they find.

b) They find a bad one within the first 10 they examine.

c) The first bad chip they find will be the fourth one they test.

d) The first bad chip they find will be one of the first three they test.

33. *Side effects.* Researchers testing a new medication find that 7% of users have side effects. To how many patients would a doctor expect to prescribe the medication before finding the first one who has side effects? LO❷

34. *Credit cards.* University students are a major target for advertisements for credit cards. At a university, 65% of students surveyed said they had opened a new credit card account within the past year. If that percentage is accurate, how many students would you expect to survey before finding one who had not opened a new account in the past year? LO❷

*35. *Missing pixels.* A company that manufactures large LCD screens knows that not all pixels on their screen light, even if they spend great care when making them. In a sheet 6 ft by 10 ft (72 in. by 120 in.) that will be cut into smaller screens, they find an average of 4.7 blank pixels. They believe that the occurrences of blank pixels are independent. Their warranty policy states that they will replace any screen sold that shows more than two blank pixels. LO❾

a) What is the mean number of blank pixels per square foot?
b) What is the standard deviation of blank pixels per square foot?
c) What is the probability that a 2 ft by 3 ft screen will have at least one defect?
d) What is the probability that a 2 ft by 3 ft screen will be replaced because it has too many defects?

*36. *Bean bags.* Cellophane that is going to be formed into bags for items such as dried beans or bird seed is passed over a light sensor to test if the alignment is correct before it passes through the heating units that seal the edges. Small adjustments can be made by the machine automatically. But if the alignment is too bad, the process is stopped and an operator has to manually adjust it. These misalignment stops occur randomly and independently. On one line, the average number of stops is 52 per 8-hour shift. LO❾

a) What is the mean number of stops per hour?
b) What is the standard deviation of stops per hour?
c) When the machine is restarted after a stop, what is the probability it will run at least 15 minutes before the next stop?

*37. *Hurricane insurance.* An insurance company needs to assess the risks associated with providing hurricane insurance. Between 1990 and 2006, Florida was hit by 22 tropical storms or hurricanes. If tropical storms and hurricanes are independent and the mean has not changed, what is the probability of having a year in Florida with each of the following. (Note that 1990 to 2006 is 17 years.) LO❾

a) No hits?
b) Exactly one hit?
c) More than three hits?

*38. *Hurricane insurance, part 2.* Between 1965 and 2007, there were 95 major hurricanes (category 3 or more) in the Atlantic basin. Assume that hurricanes are independent and the mean has not changed. LO❾

a) What is the mean number of major hurricanes per year? (There are 43 years from 1965 to 2007.)

b) What is the standard deviation of the frequency of major hurricanes?
c) What is the probability of having a year with no major hurricanes?
d) What is the probability of going three years in a row without a major hurricane?

39. *Professional tennis.* Serena Williams made a successful first serve 67% of the time in a Wimbledon finals match against her sister Venus. If she continues to serve at the same rate the next time they play and serves six times in the first game, determine the following probabilities. (Assume that each serve is independent of the others.) LO❷

a) All six first serves will be in.
b) Exactly four first serves will be in.
c) At least four first serves will be in.

40. *Canadian Blood Services.* Only 3% of people have Type AB blood. A bloodmobile has 12 vials of blood on a rack. If the distribution of blood types at this location is consistent with the general population, what's the probability they find AB blood in:
a) None of the 12 samples? LO❷
b) At least two samples?
c) Three or four samples?

For Exercises 41–48, use the 68-95-99.7 Rule to approximate the probabilities rather than using technology to find the values more precisely. Answers given for probabilities or percentages from Exercise 49 and on assume that a calculator or software has been used. Answers found from using Z-tables may vary slightly.

Ⓣ **41.** *Mutual fund returns.* In the last quarter of a recent year, a group of 64 mutual funds had a mean return of 2.4% with a standard deviation of 5.6%. If a Normal model can be used to model them, what percent of the funds would you expect to be in each region? LO❸

Be sure to draw a picture first.
a) Returns of 8.0% or more
b) Returns of 2.4% or less
c) Returns between -8.8% and 13.6%
d) Returns of more than 19.2%

42. *Human resource testing.* Although controversial and the subject of some recent law suits in the United States (e.g., *Satchell et al. vs. FedEx Express*), some human resource departments administer standard IQ tests to all employees. The Stanford-Binet test scores are well modelled by a Normal model with mean 100 and standard deviation 16. If the applicant pool is well modelled by this distribution, a randomly selected applicant would have what probability of scoring in the following regions? LO❸

a) 100 or below
b) Above 148
c) Between 84 and 116
d) Above 132

43. *Mutual funds, again.* From the 64 mutual funds in Exercise 41 with quarterly returns that are well modelled by a Normal model with a mean of 2.4% and a standard deviation of 5.6%, find the cutoff return value(s) that would separate the LO❸

a) highest 50%.

b) highest 16%.

c) lowest 2.5%.

d) middle 68%.

44. Human resource testing, again. For the IQ test administered by human resources and discussed in Exercise 42, what cutoff value would separate the LO❸

a) lowest 0.15% of all applicants?

b) lowest 16%?

c) middle 95%?

d) highest 2.5%?

45. Currency exchange rates. The daily exchange rates for the five-year period 2003 to 2008 between the euro (EUR) and the British pound (GBP) are well modelled by a Normal distribution with mean 1.459 euros (to pounds) and standard deviation 0.033 euros. Given this model, what is the probability that on a randomly selected day during this period, the pound was worth LO❸

a) less than 1.459 euros?

b) more than 1.492 euros?

c) less than 1.393 euros?

d) Which would be more unusual, a day on which the pound was worth less than 1.410 euros or more than 1.542 euros?

46. Stock prices. For the 600 trading days from January 2011 through May 2013, the daily closing price of TD Canada Trust stock (in $CAD) is well modelled by a Normal model with mean $79.80 and standard deviation $3.75. According to this model, what is the probability that on a randomly selected day in this period the stock price closed LO❸

a) above $83.55?

b) below $87.30?

c) between $72.30 and $87.30?

d) Which would be more unusual, a day on which the stock price closed above $85 or below $70?

47. Currency exchange rates, again. For the model of the EUR/GBP exchange rate discussed in Exercise 45, what would the cutoff rates be that would separate the LO❸

a) highest 16% of EUR/GBP rates?

b) lowest 50%?

c) middle 95%?

d) lowest 2.5%?

48. Stock prices, again. According to the model in Exercise 46, what cutoff value of price would separate the LO❸

a) lowest 16% of the days?

b) highest 0.15%?

c) middle 68%?

d) highest 50%?

49. Mutual fund probabilities. According to the Normal model N(0.024, 0.056) describing mutual fund returns in the fourth

quarter of 2007 in Exercise 41, what percent of this group of funds would you expect to have return LO❸

a) over 6.8%?

b) between 0% and 7.6%?

c) more than 1%?

d) less than 0%?

50. Normal IQs. Based on the Normal model N(100, 16) describing IQ scores from Exercise 42, what percent of applicants would you expect to have scores LO❹

a) over 80?

b) under 90?

c) between 112 and 132?

d) over 125?

51. Mutual funds, once more. Based on the model N(0.024, 0.056) for quarterly returns from Exercise 41, what are the cutoff values for the LO❹

a) highest 10% of these funds?

b) lowest 20%?

c) middle 40%?

d) highest 80%?

52. More IQs. In the Normal model N(100, 16) for IQ scores from Exercise 42, what cutoff value bounds the LO❹

a) highest 5% of all IQs?

b) lowest 30% of the IQs?

c) middle 80% of the IQs?

d) lowest 90% of all IQs?

53. Mutual funds, finis. Consider the Normal model N(0.024, 0.056) for returns of mutual funds in Exercise 41 one last time. LO❹

a) What value represents the 40th percentile of these returns?

b) What value represents the 99th percentile?

c) What's the IQR of the quarterly returns for this group of funds?

54. IQs, finis. Consider the IQ model N(100, 16) one last time. LO❹

a) What IQ represents the 15th percentile?

b) What IQ represents the 98th percentile?

c) What's the IQR of the IQs?

55. Parameters. Every Normal model is defined by its parameters, the mean and the standard deviation. For each model described here, find the missing parameter. As always, start by drawing a picture. LO❹

a) $\mu = 20$, 45% above 30; $\sigma = ?$

b) $\mu = 88$, 2% below 50; $\sigma = ?$

c) $\sigma = 5$, 80% below 100; $\mu = ?$

d) $\sigma = 15.6$, 10% above 17.2; $\mu = ?$

56. Parameters, again. Every Normal model is defined by its parameters, the mean and the standard deviation. For each model described here, find the missing parameter. Don't forget to draw a picture. LO❹

a) $\mu = 1250$, 35% below 1200; $\sigma = ?$

b) $\mu = 0.64$, 12% above 0.70; $\sigma = ?$
c) $\sigma = 0.5$, 90% above 10.0; $\mu = ?$
d) $\sigma = 220$, 3% below 202; $\mu = ?$

57. SAT or ACT? Each year thousands of high school students take either the SAT or ACT, standardized tests used in the university admissions process. Combined SAT scores can go as high as 1600, while the maximum ACT composite score is 36. Since the two exams use very different scales, comparisons of performance are difficult. (A convenient rule of thumb is $SAT = 40 \times ACT + 150$; that is, multiply an ACT score by 40 and add 150 points to estimate the equivalent SAT score.) Assume that one year the combined SAT can be modelled by $N(1000, 200)$ and the ACT can be modelled by $N(27, 3)$. If an applicant to a university has taken the SAT and scored 1260 and another student has taken the ACT and scored 33, compare these students scores using z-values. Which one has a higher relative score? Explain. **LO⑤**

58. Economics. Anna, a business major, took final exams in both Microeconomics and Macroeconomics and scored 83 on both. Her roommate Megan, also taking both courses, scored 77 on the Micro exam and 95 on the Macro exam. Overall, student scores on the Micro exam had a mean of 81 and a standard deviation of 5, and the Macro scores had a mean of 74 and a standard deviation of 15. Which student's overall performance was better? Explain. **LO⑤**

59. Claims. Two companies make batteries for cell phone manufacturers. One company claims a mean life span of 2.0 years, while the other company claims a mean life span of 2.5 years (assuming average use of minutes/month for the cell phone). **LO⑤**
a) Explain why you would also like to know the standard deviations of the battery life spans before deciding which brand to buy.
b) Suppose those standard deviations are 1.5 months for the first company and 9 months for the second company. Does this change your opinion of the batteries? Explain.

Ⓣ 60. Car speeds. The police department of a major city needs to update its budget. For this purpose, they need to understand the variation in their fines collected from motorists for speeding. As a sample, they recorded the speeds of cars driving past a location with a 40 kph speed limit, a place that in the past has been known for producing fines. The mean of 100 readings was 46.7 kph, with a standard deviation of 6.2 kph. (The police actually recorded every car for a two-month period. These are 100 representative readings.) **LO⑤**
a) How many standard deviations from the mean would a car going the speed limit be?
b) Which would be more unusual, a car travelling 60 kph or one going 25 kph?

61. CEOs. A business publication recently released a study on the total number of years of experience in industry among CEOs. The mean is provided in the article, but not the standard deviation. Is the standard deviation most likely to be 6 months, 6 years, or 16 years? Explain which standard deviation is correct and why. **LO④**

62. Stocks. A newsletter for investors recently reported that the average stock price for a blue chip stock over the past 12 months was $72. No standard deviation was given. Is the standard deviation more likely to be $6, $16, or $60? Explain. **LO④**

63. Fuel economy. Recent Environmental Protection Agency (EPA) fuel economy estimates for automobile models tested predicted a mean of 9.6 l/100 km mpg and a standard deviation of 2.4 l/100 km for highway driving. Assume that a Normal model can be applied. **LO④**
a) Draw the model for auto fuel economy. Clearly label it, showing what the 68-95-99.7 Rule predicts about fuel efficiency.
b) In what interval would you expect the central 68% of autos to be found?
c) About what percent of autos should require more than 12 l/100 km?
d) About what percent of cars should require between 12 and 14.4 l/100 km?
e) Describe the fuel efficiency of the worst 2.5% of all cars.

64. Job satisfaction. Some job satisfaction assessments are standardized to a Normal model with a mean of 100 and a standard deviation of 12. **LO④**
a) Draw the model for these job satisfaction scores. Clearly label it, showing what the 68-95-99.7 Rule predicts about the scores.
b) In what interval would you expect the central 95% of job satisfaction scores to be found?
c) About what percent of people should have job satisfaction scores above 112?
d) About what percent of people should have job satisfaction scores between 64 and 76?
e) About what percent of people should have job satisfaction scores above 124?

65. Low job satisfaction. Exercise 64 proposes modelling job satisfaction scores with $N(100, 12)$. Human resource departments of corporations are generally concerned if the job satisfaction drops below a certain score. What score would you consider to be unusually low? Explain. **LO④**

66. Low return. Exercise 41 proposes modelling quarterly returns of a group of mutual funds with $N(0.024, 0.056)$. The manager of this group of funds would like to flag any fund whose return is unusually low for a quarter. What level of return would you consider to be unusually low? Explain. **LO④**

67. Management survey. A survey of 200 middle managers showed a distribution of the number of hours of exercise they participated in per week with a mean of 3.66 hours and a standard deviation of 4.93 hours. **LO④**
a) According to the Normal model, what percent of managers will exercise fewer than one standard deviation below the mean number of hours?
b) For these data, what does that mean? Explain.
c) Explain the problem in using the Normal model for these data.

68. Customer database. A large philanthropic organization keeps records on the people who have contributed to their cause. In addition to keeping records of past giving, the organization gets demographic data on neighbourhoods from Statistics Canada. Eighteen of these variables concern the ethnicity of the neighbourhood of the donor. Here is a histogram and summary statistics for the percentage of Caucasians in the neighbourhoods of 500 donors. **LO4**

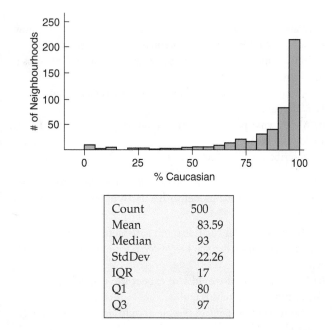

Count	500
Mean	83.59
Median	93
StdDev	22.26
IQR	17
Q1	80
Q3	97

a) Which is a better summary of the percentage of Caucasian residents in the neighbourhoods, the mean or the median? Explain.
b) Which is a better summary of the spread, the IQR or the standard deviation? Explain.
c) From a Normal model, about what percentage of neighbourhoods should have a percent Caucasian residents within one standard deviation of the mean?
d) What percentage of neighbourhoods actually have a percent Caucasian within one standard deviation of the mean?
e) Explain the problem in using the Normal model for these data.

69. Drug company. Manufacturing and selling drugs that claim to reduce an individual's cholesterol level is big business. A company would like to market their drug to women if their cholesterol is in the top 15%. Assume the cholesterol levels of adult Canadian women can be described by a Normal model with a mean of 188 mg/dL and a standard deviation of 24. **LO4**

a) Draw and label the Normal model.
b) What percent of adult women do you expect to have cholesterol levels over 200 mg/dL?
c) What percent of adult women do you expect to have cholesterol levels between 150 and 170 mg/dL?
d) Estimate the interquartile range of the cholesterol levels.
e) Above what value are the highest 15% of women's cholesterol levels?

70. Tire company. A tire manufacturer believes that the tread life of its snow tires can be described by a Normal model with a mean of 50 000 kilometres and a standard deviation of 4000 kilometres. **LO4**

a) If you buy a set of these tires, would it be reasonable for you to hope that they'll last 64 000 kilometres? Explain.
b) Approximately what fraction of these tires can be expected to last less than 48 000 kilometres?
c) Approximately what fraction of these tires can be expected to last between 48 000 and 56 000 kilometres?
d) Estimate the IQR for these data.
e) In planning a marketing strategy, a local tire dealer wants to offer a refund to any customer whose tires fail to last a certain number of kilometres. However, the dealer does not want to take too big a risk. If the dealer is willing to give refunds to no more than 1 of every 25 customers, for what kilometrage can he guarantee these tires to last?

71. Professional tennis, part 2. Suppose Serena continues to make 67% of her first serves as in Exercise 39 and serves 80 times in a match. **LO6**

a) What's the mean and standard deviation of the number of good first serves expected?
b) Justify why you can use a Normal model to approximate the distribution of the number of good first serves.
c) Use the 68-95-99.7 Rule to describe this distribution.
d) What's the probability she makes at least 65 first serves in the 80 attempts?

72. Canadian Blood Services, part 2. The bloodmobile in Exercise 40 received 400 donations in one day. **LO6**

a) Assuming the frequency of AB blood is 3%, determine the mean and standard deviation of the number of donors who are AB.
b) Justify why you can use a Normal model to approximate the distribution of Type AB blood.
c) How likely would it be to find 10 or more samples with type AB blood in 400 samples?

73. No-shows. Because many passengers who make reservations do not show up, airlines often overbooks flights (sell more tickets than there are seats). A Boeing 767-400ER holds 245 passengers. If the airline believes the rate of passenger no-shows is 5% and sells 255 tickets, is it likely they will not have enough seats and someone will get bumped? **LO6**

a) Use the Normal model to approximate the Binomial to determine the probability of at least 246 passengers showing up.
b) Should the airline change the number of tickets they sell for this flight? Explain.

74. Euro. Shortly after the introduction of the Belgian euro coin, newspapers around the world published articles claiming the coin was biased. The stories were based on reports that someone had spun the coin 250 times and gotten 140 heads—that's 56% heads. **LO6**

a) Use the Normal model to approximate the Binomial to determine the probability of spinning a fair coin 250 times and getting at least 140 heads.

b) Do you think this is evidence that spinning a Belgian euro is unfair? Would you be willing to use it at the beginning of a sports event? Explain.

75. Satisfaction survey. A cable provider wants to contact customers in a particular telephone exchange to see how satisfied they are with the new digital TV service the company has provided. All numbers are in the 452 exchange, so there are 10 000 possible numbers from 452-0000 to 452-9999. If they select the numbers with equal probability: **LO⑦**

a) What distribution would they use to model the selection?
b) What is the probability the number selected will be an even number?
c) What is the probability the number selected will end in 000?

76. Manufacturing quality. In an effort to check the quality of their cell phones, a manufacturing manager decides to take a random sample of 10 cell phones from yesterday's production run, which produced cell phones with serial numbers ranging (according to when they were produced) from 43005000 to 43005999. If each of the 1000 phones is equally likely to be selected: **LO⑦**

a) What distribution would they use to model the selection?
b) What is the probability that a randomly selected cell phone will be one of the last 100 to be produced?
c) What is the probability that the first cell phone selected is either from the last 200 to be produced or from the first 50 to be produced?
d) What is the probability that the first two cell phones are both from the last 100 to be produced?

*77. Web visitors. A website manager has noticed that during the evening hours, about three people per minute check out from their shopping cart and make an online purchase. She believes that each purchase is independent of the others and wants to model the number of purchases per minute.   **LO⑦**

a) What model might you suggest to model the number of purchases per minute?
b) What is the probability that in any one minute at least one purchase is made?
c) What is the probability that no one makes a purchase in the next two minutes?

*78. Quality control. The manufacturer in Exercise 76 has noticed that the number of faulty cell phones in a production run of cell phones is usually small and that the quality of one day's run seems to have no bearing on the next day.   **LO⑦**

a) What model might you use to model the number of faulty cell phones produced in one day.
b) If the mean number of faulty cell phones is two per day, what is the probability that no faulty cell phones will be produced tomorrow?
c) If the mean number of faulty cell phones is two per day, what is the probability that three or more faulty cell phones were produced in today's run?

79. Golf. Two close friends, Fred and Neil, are playing in a golf tournament. Record-keeping from previous years show that Fred's scores are normally distributed with mean 110 and standard deviation 10, and that Neil's scores are normally distributed with mean 100 and standard deviation 8. They play independently. What is the probability that Fred will beat Neil?   **LO①, LO④**

80. Elevator loads. A sign in an elevator states that the load limit is 1200 kilograms and that no more than 16 persons may occupy the elevator at one time. Assume that the weights of elevator riders follows a Normal distribution, with mean 70.0 kilograms and standard deviation 6.25 kilograms.   **LO①, LO④**

a) What is the chance of exceeding the load limit with 16 randomly chosen riders?
b) A limit of 1200 kilograms for 16 riders is equivalent to an average of 75 kilograms per rider. What is the chance of a single elevator rider weighing more than 75 kilograms?
c) Explain why the probability in part a is so much smaller than the probability in part b. What does this tell you about managing risk by diversification?

✔️ **JUST CHECKING ANSWERS**

1 a) $100 + 100 = 200$ seconds
   b) $\sqrt{50^2 + 50^2} = 70.7$ seconds
   c) The times for the two customers are independent.

2 There are two outcomes (contact, no contact), the probability of contact stays constant at 0.76, and random calls should be independent.

3 Binomial (or Normal approximation)

Sampling Distributions and Confidence Intervals for Proportions

CHAPTER 9

CONNECTIONS: CHAPTER

The probability models of Chapter 8 will now be put to work to create the framework for statistical inference. In this chapter we will learn what might be the single most difficult concept in statistics—sampling distributions. They are the foundations needed to tell us not only how to make good estimates but also how to assess the uncertainty in those estimates. We introduce the most important theorem in all of statistics. And we begin our development of techniques of inference, with our first confidence interval.

M Itani/Alamy

LEARNING OBJECTIVES

1. Use the Normal model to find probability and parameters

2. Apply the Normal model to the sampling distribution of the sample proportion

3. Compute and interpret the margin of error

4. Check whether conditions for confidence intervals are satisfied

5. Give correct explanations and interpretations of a confidence interval

6. Construct and interpret the confidence interval for a proportion

7. Find the sample size required for a given level of precision

8. Find the level of confidence from a given confidence interval

Credit Cards in Canada and the MBNA Story

So you want to get a credit card. Where do you apply? How should you make the decision about which one to get? After all, there are nearly 200 credit cards available in Canada. What resources are available to help you?

You could check the website of the Financial Consumer Agency of Canada (FCAC), a Government of Canada database with information on card fees, features, interest rates, and reward programs. It has an interactive tool that builds a profile of the user's credit card habits and needs, and presents a small number of suitable choices on which to do detailed comparisons. You can visit CreditCards.ca, a free internet resource that lists credit card offers from the leading Canadian card issuers and major banks, lets you compare them and even apply online. You will learn that cards come in various categories: Low Interest, Balance Transfer, Cash Back, Rewards, Airlines, Business, and, perhaps most relevant for readers of this textbook, Student.

For many of the issuers or banks it is obvious who the sponsoring company is; for example, BMO, CIBC, and Scotiabank are three of the major banks in Canada. American Express and Capital One have strong corporate images and identities. But what is MBNA, and what do the letters stand for?

When Delaware substantially raised its interest rate ceiling in 1981, the Maryland Bank National Association was one of the banks that rushed to establish corporate headquarters there. It established a credit card branch using the acronym MBNA. It underwent explosive growth and at its peak had more than 50 million cardholders, making it the third-largest U.S. credit card bank. Bank of America bought MBNA in 2005, for $35 billion. In 2011, the Toronto-Dominion Bank Group acquired MBNA's Canadian credit card business from Bank of America. In doing so, TD Bank Group added the largest issuer of MasterCard in Canada to its portfolio of Visa accounts. It continues to operate under the MBNA name.

Based on information from www.fcac-acfc.gc.ca/ and www.bankofamerica.com

In Chapter 8 we learned about discrete and continuous probability distributions or models, which correspond to categorical and quantitative data (discussed in Chapters 2, 4, and 5). Beginning in this chapter we will use those distributions to model data and explain the uncertainty that comes from having only samples of data rather than complete populations.

A great deal of data collected in business comes from surveys and is categorical in nature. The most common categorical data have only two possible values; we call these binary data. So that's where we will begin. Remember the Binomial distribution from Chapter 8? That's what we'll use to model binary data.

Unlike the early days of the credit card industry when MBNA established itself, the environment today is intensely competitive, with companies constantly looking for ways to attract new customers and to maximize the profitability of the customers they already have. Many of the large companies have millions of customers, so instead of trying out a new idea with all their customers, they almost always conduct a pilot study or trial first, conducting a survey or an experiment on a sample of their customers.

Credit card companies make money on their cards in three ways: they earn a percentage of every transaction, they charge interest on balances that are not paid in full, and they collect fees (yearly fees, late fees, etc.). To generate all three types of revenue, the marketing departments of credit card banks constantly seek ways to encourage customers to increase the use of their cards.

A marketing specialist at one company had an idea of offering double air miles to their customers with an airline-affiliated card if they increased their spending by at least $800 in the month following the offer. In order to forecast the cost and revenue of the offer, the finance department needed to know what percentage of customers would actually qualify for the double miles. The marketer decided to send the offer to a random sample of 1000 customers to find out. In that sample, she found that 211 (21.1%) of the cardholders increased their spending by more than the required $800. But, another analyst drew a different sample of 1000 customers of whom 202 (20.2%) of the cardholders exceeded $800.

WHO	Cardholders of a bank's credit card
WHAT	Whether cardholders increased their spending by at least $800 in the subsequent month
WHEN	February 2013
WHERE	Canada
WHY	To predict costs and benefits of a program offer

Imagine

We see only the sample we actually drew, but if we *imagine* the results of all the other possible samples we could have drawn (by modelling or simulating them), we can learn more.

The two samples don't agree. We know that observations vary, but how much variability among samples should we expect to see?

Why do sample proportions vary at all? How can two samples of the same population measuring the same quantity get different results? The answer is fundamental to statistical inference. Each proportion is based on a *different* sample of cardholders. The proportions vary from sample to sample because the samples comprise different people.

We'd like to know how much proportions can vary from sample to sample. We've talked about *Plan*, *Do*, and *Report*, but to learn more about the variability, we have to add *Imagine*. When we sample, we see only the results from the actual sample that we draw, but we can *imagine* what we might have seen had we drawn *all* other possible random samples. What would the histogram of all those sample proportions look like?

If we could take many random samples of 1000 cardholders, we would find the proportion of each sample who spent more than $800 and collect all of those proportions into a histogram. Where would you expect the centre of that histogram to be? Of course, we don't *know* the answer, but it is reasonable to think that it will be at the true proportion in the population. We probably will never know the value of the true proportion. But it is important to us, so we'll give it a label, p for "true proportion." Remember that a numerical characteristic of a population is called a population parameter, or simply, a parameter (see Chapter 3).

9.1 Simulations

In fact, we can do better than just imagining. We can *simulate*. We can't really take all those different random samples of size 1000, but we can use a computer to pretend to draw random samples of 1000 individuals from some population of values over and over. In this way, we can model the process of drawing many samples from a real population. A *simulation* can help us understand how sample proportions vary due to random sampling.

When we have only two possible outcomes for an event, the convention in Statistics is to arbitrarily label one of them "success" and the other "failure." The terms "success" and "failure" first appeared as the two possible outcomes of a Bernoulli trial, and then the Binomial distribution, in Chapter 8. Here, a "success" would be that a customer increases card charges by at least $800, and a "failure" would be that the customer didn't. In the simulation, we'll set the true proportion of successes to a known value, draw random samples, and then record the sample proportion of successes, which we'll denote by $\hat{p}$, for each sample. That is, $\hat{p}$ is a sample statistic, which serves as an estimate of the population parameter p. Placing a "caret" or "hat" on a parameter is common statistical notation for a sample statistic.

The proportion of successes in each of our simulated samples will vary from one sample to the next, but the *way* in which the proportions vary shows us how the proportions of real samples would vary. Because we can specify the true proportion of successes, we can see how close each sample comes to estimating that true value. Suppose we simulate 2000 independent samples of 1000 cardholders, where the true proportion is $p = 0.21$. (We know this is the true value of p because in a simulation we can control it.) For each sample compute the proportion of cardholders who increased spending by at least $800. That will produce 2000 values of $\hat{p}$. Here is a histogram of the 2000 $\hat{p}$'s.

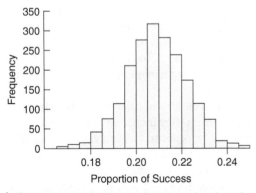
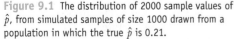

Figure 9.1 The distribution of 2000 sample values of $\hat{p}$, from simulated samples of size 1000 drawn from a population in which the true $\hat{p}$ is 0.21.

It should be no surprise that we don't get the same proportion for each sample we draw, even though the underlying true value, p, stays the same at $p = 0.21$. Since each $\hat{p}$ comes from a random sample, we don't expect them to all be equal to p. And since each comes from a *different* independent random sample, we don't expect them to be equal to each other, either. The remarkable thing is that even though the $\hat{p}$'s vary from sample to sample, they do so in a way that we can model and understand.

9.2 The Sampling Distribution for Proportions

The collection of $\hat{p}$'s may be better behaved than you expected. The histogram in Figure 9.1 is unimodal, symmetric, and bell-shaped. In order to make general statements about how often values occur in histograms like this, statisticians make models for distributions. The distribution of proportions over many independent samples from the same population is called the **sampling distribution** of a proportion. Section 9.1 showed a simulation in which that distribution was bell-shaped and centred at the true proportion, p. If we knew that the sampling distribution of proportions always followed a bell-shaped distribution, we could use the Normal model to describe the behaviour of proportions. With the Normal model, we could find the percentage of values falling between any two values. But to make that work, we need to know one more thing. Normal models are determined by their mean and standard deviation, and we only know that the mean is p, the true proportion. What about the standard deviation?

An amazing fact about proportions is that (unlike quantitative data) once we know the mean, p, and the sample size, n, we also know the standard deviation of the sampling distribution as you can see from its formula:

$$SD(\hat{p}) = \sqrt{\frac{p(1-p)}{n}} = \sqrt{\frac{pq}{n}}$$

If the true proportion of credit cardholders who increased their spending by more than \$800 is 0.21, then for samples of size 1000, we expect the distribution of sample proportions to have a standard deviation of:

$$SD(\hat{p}) = \sqrt{\frac{p(1-p)}{n}} = \sqrt{\frac{0.21(1-0.21)}{1000}} = 0.0129, \text{ or about } 1.3\%$$

Remember that the two samples of size 1000 had proportions of 21.1% and 20.2%. Since the standard deviation of proportions is 1.3%, these two proportions are not even a full standard deviation apart. In other words, the two samples don't really disagree. Proportions of 21.1% and 20.2% from samples of 1000 are both *consistent* with a true proportion of 21%. We know from Chapter 3 that this difference between sample proportions is referred to as **sampling error**. But it's not really an *error*. It's just the *variability* you'd expect to see from one sample to another. A better term might be *sampling variability*.

Warning! Do not confuse "sampling distribution" with "sample distribution." There is a huge difference. In this situation the sample distribution shows how many successes and failures there are in the actual data. The sampling distribution shows what values of the sample statistic could happen if many samples were taken. This is such an important distinction we will discuss it more fully at the end of Section 9.4.

Here's a hint on how you can remember the difference. Words that end in "-ing" indicate an action or process that is ongoing or incomplete. So "sampling" means the ongoing action of taking a sample and computing something with it. In this case, you compute $\hat{p}$ each time you take a sample. But, as we'll point out again, this repeated sampling is actually only hypothetical or imaginary. We won't need to do the repeated sampling once we figure out what is expected to occur.

NOTATION ALERT:
We use p for the proportion in the population and $\hat{p}$ for the observed proportion in a sample. We'll also use q for the proportion of failures ($q = 1 - p$), and $\hat{q}$ for its observed value, just to simplify some formulas.

We have now answered the question raised at the start of the chapter. To discover how variable a sample proportion is, we need to know the proportion and the size of the sample. That's all.

Effect of Sample Size

Because n is in the denominator of $SD(\hat{p})$, the larger the sample, the smaller the standard deviation. We need a small standard deviation to make sound business decisions, but larger samples cost more. That tension is a fundamental issue in statistics. The second effect of sample size is a result of the square root sign. We'll discuss that later.

Look back at Figure 9.1 to see how well the model worked in our simulation. If $p = 0.21$, we now know that the standard deviation should be about 0.013. The 68-95-99.7 Rule from the Normal model says that 68% of the samples will have proportions within 1 SD of the mean of 0.21. How closely does our simulation match the predictions? The actual standard deviation of our 2000 *sample* proportions is 0.0129 or 1.29%. And, of the 2000 simulated samples, 1346 of them had proportions between 0.197 and 0.223 (one standard deviation on either side of 0.21). The 68-95-99.7 Rule predicts 68%—the actual number is 1346/2000 or 67.3%.

Now we know everything we need to know to model the sampling distribution. We know the mean and standard deviation of the sampling distribution of proportions: they're p, the true population proportion, and $\sqrt{\dfrac{pq}{n}}$. So the particular Normal model, $N\left(p, \sqrt{\dfrac{pq}{n}}\right)$, is a **sampling distribution model for the sample proportion**.

We saw this worked well in a simulation, but can we rely on it in all situations? It turns out that this model can be justified theoretically with just a little mathematics. It won't work for *all* situations, but it works for most situations that you'll encounter in practice. We'll provide conditions to check so you'll know when the model is useful.

> **The Sampling Distribution Model for a Proportion**
>
> Provided that the sampled values are independent and the sample size is large enough, the sampling distribution of $\hat{p}$ is modelled by a Normal model centred at mean $\mu(\hat{p}) = p$ and standard deviation $SD(\hat{p}) = \sqrt{\dfrac{pq}{n}}$.

There is one unanswered question in the previous statement. How large is "large enough?" We'll address that later.

✔ **JUST CHECKING**

1 You want to poll a random sample of 100 shopping mall customers about whether they like the proposed location for the new coffee shop on the third floor, with a panoramic view of the food court. Of course, you'll get just one number, your sample proportion, $\hat{p}$. But if you imagined all the possible samples of 100 customers you could draw and imagined the histogram of all the sample proportions from these samples, what shape would it have?

2 Where would the centre of that histogram be?

3 If you think that about half the customers are in favour of the plan, what would the standard deviation of the sample proportions be?

Here's a simple illustration of how we will use this result. How unlikely would it be to get 70 or more heads in 100 tosses of a fair coin? We have $p = 0.5$, $q = 0.5$, and $n = 100$ and $\hat{p} = 0.70$. $SD(\hat{p}) = \sqrt{(0.5)(0.5)/100} = 0.05$. Thus $\hat{p} = 0.70$ is 4 SDs away from $p = 0.5$. From the 68–95-99.7 Rule, this is extremely unlikely (about 3 chances in 100 000). There is a 95% chance that $\hat{p}$ will be within ± 2 $SD(\hat{p})$; that means between 0.4 and 0.6. In other words, we expect between 40% and 60% heads in 100 tosses of a fair coin.

The sampling distribution model for $\hat{p}$ is valuable for a number of reasons. First, because it is known from mathematics to be a good model (and one that gets better and better as the sample size gets larger), we don't need to actually draw many samples and accumulate all those sample proportions, or even to simulate them. The Normal sampling distribution model tells us what the distribution of sample proportions would look like. Second, because the Normal model is a mathematical model, we can calculate what fraction of the distribution will be found in any region. You can find the fraction of the distribution in *any* interval of values using Table Z at the back of the book or with technology.

How Good Is the Normal Model?

We've seen that the simulated proportions follow the 68-95-99.7 Rule well. But do all sample proportions really work like this? Stop and think for a minute about what we're claiming. We've said that if we draw repeated random samples of the same size, n, from some population and measure the proportion, $\hat{p}$, we get for each sample, then the collection of these proportions will pile up around the underlying population proportion, p, in such a way that a histogram of the sample proportions can be modelled well by a Normal model.

There must be a catch. Suppose the samples were of size 2, for example. Then the only possible numbers of successes could be 0, 1, or 2, and the proportion values would be 0, 0.5, and 1. There's no way the histogram could ever look like a Normal model with only three possible values for the variable (Figure 9.2).

Well, there *is* a catch. The claim is only approximately true. (But, that's fine. Models are *supposed* to be only approximately true.) And the model becomes a better and better representation of the distribution of the sample proportions as the sample size gets bigger.[1] Samples of size one or two just aren't going to work very well, but the distributions of proportions of many larger samples do have histograms that are remarkably close to a Normal model.

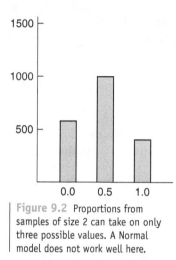

Figure 9.2 Proportions from samples of size 2 can take on only three possible values. A Normal model does not work well here.

9.3 Assumptions and Conditions

Most models are useful only when specific assumptions are true. In the case of the model for the distribution of sample proportions, there are two assumptions:

> **Independence Assumption**: The sampled values must be *independent* of each other.

> **Sample Size Assumption:** The sample size, n, must be *large* enough.

Of course, the best we can do with assumptions is to think about whether they are likely to be true, and we should do so. However, we often can check corresponding *conditions* that provide information about the assumptions as well. Think about the Independence Assumption and check the following corresponding conditions before using the Normal model to model the distribution of sample proportions:

> **Randomization Condition:** If your data come from an experiment, subjects should have been randomly assigned to each of the experimental groups. If you have a survey, your sample should be a simple random sample of the population. If some other sampling design was used, be sure the sampling method was not biased and that the data are representative of the population.

> **10% Condition:** If sampling has not been made with replacement (that is, returning each sampled individual to the population before drawing the next individual), then the sample size, n, must be no larger than 10% of the population. If

---

[1] Formally, we say the claim is true in the limit as the sample size (n) grows.

it is larger, you must make adjustments with methods more advanced than those found in this book. Be careful. The 10% Condition doesn't mean that smaller samples are better. The reverse is true. It refers to the relative sizes of the sample and the population. So another way to think of the 10% Condition is that the population should be more than 10 times as large as the sample.

Success/Failure Condition: The Success/Failure condition says that the sample size must be big enough so that both the number of "successes," np, and the number of "failures," nq, are expected to be at least 10.[2] This is the same Condition required for Bernoulli trials and the Binomial model discussed in Section 8.4. Expressed without the symbols, this condition just says that we need to expect at least 10 successes and at least 10 failures to have enough data for sound conclusions. For the bank's credit card promotion example, we labelled as a "success" a cardholder who increases monthly spending by at least $800 during the trial. The bank observed 211 successes and 789 failures. Both are at least 10, so there are certainly enough successes and enough failures for the condition to be satisfied.[3]

These last two conditions seem to contradict each other. The Success/Failure condition wants a big sample size. How big depends on p. If p is near 0.5, we need a sample of only 20 or so. If p is only 0.01, however, we'd need 1000. But the 10% condition says that the sample size can't be too large a fraction of the population. Fortunately, the tension between them isn't usually a problem in practice. Often, as in polls that sample from all Canadian adults, or industrial samples from a day's production, the populations are much larger than 10 times the sample size.

GUIDED EXAMPLE   Foreclosures

Gary yim/Shutterstock

During the global economic downturn in 2008–2009, an analyst at a home loan lender was looking at a package of 90 mortgages that the company had recently purchased in Atlantic Canada. The analyst was aware that in that region about 13% of the homeowners with current mortgages would default on their loans in the next year and the house would go into foreclosure. In deciding to buy the collection of mortgages, the finance department assumed that no more than 15 of the mortgages would go into default. Any amount above that would result in losses for the company. In the package of 90 mortgages, what's the probability that there would be more than 15 foreclosures?

PLAN 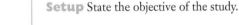	**Setup** State the objective of the study.	We want to find the probability that in a group of 90 mortgages, more than 15 will default. Since 15 out of 90 is 16.7%, we need the probability of finding more than 16.7% defaults out of a sample of 90, if the proportion of defaults is 13%.

---

[2] Why 10? This is actually a little conservative, but if you have 10 successes and 10 failures, you can safely use the Normal model.

[3] The Success/Failure condition is about the number of successes and failures we *expect*, but if the number of successes and failures that *occurred* is ≥ 10, then you can use that instead.

	Model Check the conditions.	✓ **Independence Assumption** If the mortgages come from a wide geographical area, one homeowner defaulting should not affect the probability that another does. However, if the mortgages come from the same neighbourhood(s), the independence assumption may fail and our estimates of the default probabilities may be wrong.
		✓ **Randomization Condition.** The 90 mortgages in the package can be considered as a random sample of mortgages in the region.
		✓ **10% Condition.** The 90 mortgages are less than 10% of the population.
		✓ **Success/Failure Condition** $$np = 90(0.13) = 11.7 \geq 10$$ $$nq = 90(0.87) = 78.3 \geq 10$$
	State the parameters and the sampling distribution model.	The population proportion is $p = 0.13$. The conditions are satisfied, so we'll model the sampling distribution of $\hat{p}$ with a Normal model, with mean 0.13 and standard deviation $$SD(\hat{p}) = \sqrt{\frac{pq}{n}} = \sqrt{\frac{(0.13)(0.87)}{90}} \approx 0.035.$$ Our model for $\hat{p}$ is $N(0.13, 0.035)$. We want to find $P(\hat{p} > 0.167)$.
	Plot Make a picture. Sketch the model and shade the area we're interested in, in this case the area to the right of 16.7%.	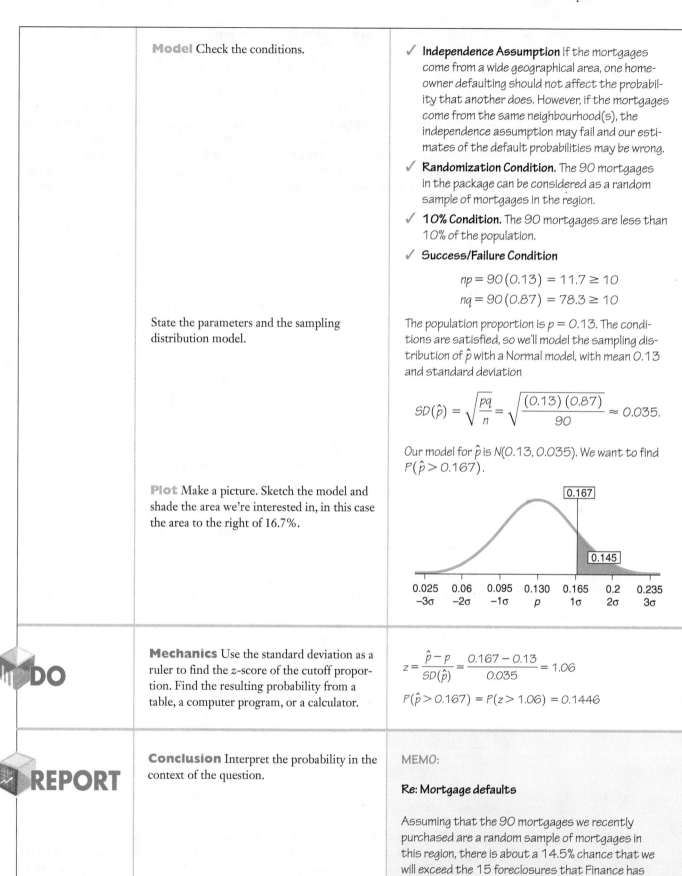

DO	**Mechanics** Use the standard deviation as a ruler to find the z-score of the cutoff proportion. Find the resulting probability from a table, a computer program, or a calculator.	$z = \dfrac{\hat{p} - p}{SD(\hat{p})} = \dfrac{0.167 - 0.13}{0.035} = 1.06$ $P(\hat{p} > 0.167) = P(z > 1.06) = 0.1446$	

REPORT	**Conclusion** Interpret the probability in the context of the question.	MEMO: **Re: Mortgage defaults** Assuming that the 90 mortgages we recently purchased are a random sample of mortgages in this region, there is about a 14.5% chance that we will exceed the 15 foreclosures that Finance has determined as the break-even point.

9.4 The Central Limit Theorem—The Fundamental Theorem of Statistics

Proportions summarize categorical variables, and, in particular, binary (two-category) variables. When we sample at random, the results we get will vary from sample to sample. The Normal model seems an incredibly simple way to summarize all that variation. Could something that simple work for means? Although we won't discuss the full details until Chapter 12, we won't keep you in suspense. It turns out that means have a sampling distribution that we can model with a Normal model as well. For now, we'll get some insight from a simulation.

Simulating the Sampling Distribution of a Mean

Here's a simple simulation with a quantitative variable. Let's start with one fair die. If we toss this die 10 000 times, what should the histogram of the numbers on the face of the die look like? Here are the results of a simulated 10 000 tosses:

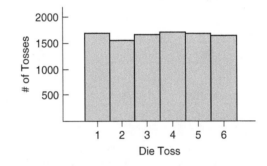

That's called the *uniform distribution* (see Section 8.5), and it's certainly not Normal. Now let's toss a *pair* of dice and record the average of the two. If we repeat this (or at least simulate repeating it) 10 000 times, recording the average of each pair, what will the histogram of these 10 000 averages look like? Before you look, think a minute. Is getting an average of 1 on *two* dice as likely as getting an average of 3 or 3.5? Let's see:

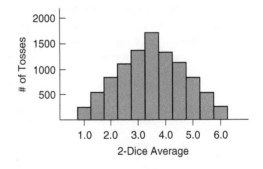

We're much more likely to get an average near 3.5 than we are to get one near 1 or 6. Without calculating those probabilities exactly, it's fairly easy to see that the *only* way to get an average of 1 is to get two 1s. To get a total of 7 (for an average of 3.5), though, there are many more possibilities. This distribution even has a name—the *triangular distribution*.

What if we average three dice? We'll simulate 10 000 tosses of three dice and take their average.

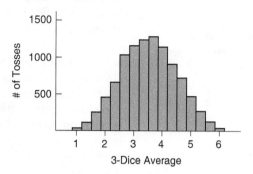

What's happening? First notice that it's getting harder to have averages near the ends. Getting an average of 1 or 6 with three dice requires all three to come up 1 or 6, respectively. That's less likely than for two dice to come up both 1 or both 6. The distribution is being pushed toward the middle. But what's happening to the shape?

Let's continue this simulation to see what happens with larger samples. Here's a histogram of the averages for 10 000 tosses of five dice.

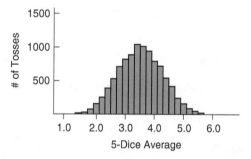

The pattern is becoming clearer. Two things are happening. The first fact we knew already from the Law of Large Numbers, which we saw in Chapter 7. It says that as the sample size (number of dice) gets larger, each sample average tends to become closer to the population mean. So we see the shape continuing to tighten around 3.5. But the shape of the distribution is the surprising part. It's becoming bell-shaped. In fact, it's approaching the Normal model.

Are you convinced? Let's skip ahead and try 20 dice. The histogram of averages for 10 000 throws of 20 dice looks like this.

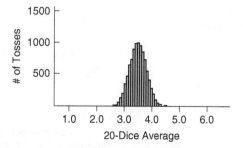

Elk-opid/Photos12/Alamy
Pierre-Simon Laplace, 1749–1827.

Now we see the Normal shape again (and notice how much smaller the spread is). But can we count on this happening for situations other than dice throws? What kinds of sample means have sampling distributions that we can model with a Normal model? It turns out that Normal models work well amazingly often.

The Central Limit Theorem

The dice simulation may look like a special situation. But it turns out that what we saw with dice is true for means of repeated samples for almost every situation. When we looked at the sampling distribution of a proportion, we had to check only a few conditions. For means, the result is even more remarkable. There are almost no conditions at all.

"The theory of probabilities is at bottom nothing but common sense reduced to calculus."

—Laplace, in Théorie Analytique des Probabilités, 1812

Let's say that again: The sampling distribution of *any* mean becomes Normal as the sample size grows. All we need is for the observations to be independent and collected with randomization. We don't even care about the shape of the population distribution![4] This surprising fact was proved in a fairly general form in 1810 by Pierre-Simon Laplace, and caused quite a stir (at least in mathematics circles) because it is so unintuitive. Laplace's result is called the **Central Limit Theorem**[5] (CLT).

This subsection heading is in green font, just like all the other subsection headings. But truly it should be in flashing neon lights. This result may be the most important result in all statistical theory, and is certainly the most important result in this book.

The development of the CLT involved many of the great minds of mathematics and science, beginning in 1733 with Abraham de Moivre (one of the first people to work with the normal distribution). It took 80 years for Pierre-Simon Laplace (see sidebar) to rescue it from obscurity, and another 90 years for the Russian mathematician Aleksandr Lyapunov to define it and prove it mathematically. It didn't get its name until 1920, when it was used by the great mathematician George Pólya in the title of a paper. Henk Tijms wrote, "Nowadays, the CLT is considered to be the unofficial sovereign of probability theory."

Sir Francis Galton (the originator of regression, who we met in Chapter 6) described the Central Limit Theorem this way:

Laplace was one of the greatest scientists and mathematicians of his time. In addition to his contributions to probability and statistics, he published many new results in mathematics, physics, and astronomy (where his nebular theory was one of the first to describe the formation of the solar system in much the way it is understood today). He also played a leading role in establishing the metric system of measurement.

His brilliance, though, sometimes got him into trouble. A visitor to the Académie des Sciences in Paris reported that Laplace let it be known widely that he considered himself the best mathematician in France. The effect of this on his colleagues was not eased by the fact that Laplace was right.

I know of scarcely anything so apt to impress the imagination as the wonderful form of cosmic order expressed by the "Law of Frequency of Error." The law would have been personified by the Greeks and deified, if they had known of it. It reigns with serenity and in complete self-effacement, amidst the wildest confusion. The huger the mob, and the greater the apparent anarchy, the more perfect is its sway. It is the supreme law of Unreason. Whenever a large sample of chaotic elements are taken in hand and marshaled in the order of their magnitude, an unsuspected and most beautiful form of regularity proves to have been latent all along.

Here's an odd footnote: Alan Turing provided a proof in 1934 for his dissertation at University of Cambridge, but he did not know that the theorem had been proved already in 1922. So Turing's dissertation was never published. Too bad he didn't have the internet available!

Not only does the distribution of means of many random samples get closer and closer to a Normal model as the sample size grows, but *this is true regardless of the shape of the population distribution!* Even if we sample from a skewed or bimodal population, the Central Limit Theorem tells us that means of repeated random samples will tend to follow a Normal model as the sample size grows. Of course, you won't be surprised to learn that it works better and faster the closer the

---

[4] Technically, the data must come from a population with a finite variance.

[5] In Pólya's 1920 paper, he used the word "central" in the name of the theorem to mean "fundamental" for its role in probability theory. It sounds even better in German: "zentraler Grenzwertsatz." But according to Lucien Le Cam, the French school of probability interprets "central" to mean the movement, or piling up, of the distribution to the centre rather than the tails. If you want to read the exciting history of the CLT, try William J. Adams' 1974 monograph titled, *The Life and Times of the Central Limit Theorem.* Trust us, it's a page-turner!

population distribution is to a Normal model. And it works better for larger samples. If the data come from a population that's exactly Normal to start with, then the observations themselves are Normal. If we take samples of size 1, their "means" are just the observations—so, of course, they have a Normal sampling distribution. But now suppose the population distribution is very skewed (as, for example, the annual compensation for CEOs of the Fortune 500 might be). The CLT works, although it may take a sample size of dozens or even hundreds of observations for the Normal model to work well.

For example, think about a real bimodal population, one that consists of only 0s and 1s. The CLT says that even means of samples from this population will follow a Normal sampling distribution model. But wait. Suppose we have a categorical variable and we assign a 1 to each individual in the category and a 0 to each individual not in the category. Then we find the mean of these 0s and 1s. That's the same as counting the number of individuals who are in the category and dividing by n. That mean will be the *sample proportion*, $\hat{p}$, of individuals who are in the category (a "success"). So maybe it wasn't so surprising after all that proportions, like means, have Normal sampling distribution models; proportions are actually just a special case of Laplace's remarkable theorem. Of course, for such an extremely bimodal population, we need a reasonably large sample size—and that's where the Success/Failure condition for proportions comes in.

> ## The Central Limit Theorem (CLT)
>
> The mean of a random sample has a sampling distribution whose shape can be approximated by a Normal model. The larger the sample, the better the approximation will be.

Be careful. The concept of sampling distributions has bedevilled students of statistics for decades. Here's why it is such a challenge to understand. We have been slipping smoothly between the real world, in which we draw random samples of data, and a model world, in which we describe how the sample means and proportions we observe in the real world might behave if we could see the results from every random sample that we might have drawn. Now we have *two* distributions to deal with. The first is the real-world distribution of the sample, which we might display with a histogram (for quantitative data) or with a bar chart or table (for categorical data). The second is the math-world *sampling distribution* of the statistic, which we model with a Normal model based on the Central Limit Theorem. Don't confuse the two.

For example, don't mistakenly think the CLT says that the *data* are Normally distributed as long as the sample is large enough. In fact, as samples get larger, we expect the distribution of the data to look more and more like the distribution of the population from which it is drawn—skewed, bimodal, whatever—but not necessarily Normal. You can collect a sample of CEO salaries for the next 1000 years, but the histogram will never look Normal. It will be skewed to the right. The Central Limit Theorem doesn't talk about the distribution of the data from the sample. It talks about the sample *means* and sample *proportions* of many different random samples drawn from the same population. Of course, we never actually draw all those samples, so the CLT is talking about an imaginary distribution—the sampling distribution model.

The CLT does require that the sample be big enough when the population shape is not unimodal and symmetric. But it is still a very surprising and powerful result. The CLT is the basis for our work on dealing with variation both for proportions and for means. We won't put the CLT for means to work until Chapter 12.

But it is so important we couldn't wait until then to show it to you. In Chapter 12 we will also discuss the details of the sampling distribution of a mean.

Sample Size–Diminishing Returns

The standard deviation of the sampling distribution declines only with the square root of the sample size. Because it's four times bigger, a sample of 100 has a sample proportion whose standard deviation is only half $\left(\dfrac{1}{\sqrt{4}} = \dfrac{1}{2}\right)$ the standard deviation of the sample proportion of a sample of 25. To cut the standard deviation in half again, we'd need a sample of 400 and a sample of 1600 to halve it once more. This is the power of averaging and the mathematical reason why we want as large a sample as we can afford.

Of course, sampling four times as many people costs more (either in time or money or both). The fact that this cuts the standard deviation of the sample proportion only in half is an example of something that's known as the Law of Diminishing Returns. We'll put this idea to work later in the chapter.

9.5 A Confidence Interval

What is the probability that $\hat{p}$, your sample statistic is exactly equal to (please excuse the redundancy of that phrase) p, the population parameter? Actually, the probability is zero, since the area under the normal curve at the single point, $\hat{p}$, is zero. So how can you come up with an estimate that has a high chance of being correct instead of an estimate that has a 100% chance of being wrong? The answer is to use an interval instead of a single point. That's what we will develop here. For example, if a physician gives a pregnant woman her "due date" as a single day, the chance of a correct prediction is very small. But if, instead, the woman is given two-week range as a due date, the chance of a correct prediction is very high.

In order to plan their inventory and production needs, businesses use a variety of forecasts about the economy. One important attribute is consumer confidence in the overall economy. Tracking changes in consumer confidence over time can help businesses gauge whether the demand for their products is on an upswing or about to experience a downturn. The Angus Reid Public Opinion poll periodically asks a random sample of Canadian adults whether they think Canada's economy will improve, remain the same, or decline over the next six months. When they polled 1502 respondents in September 2012, only 195 thought the economy would improve—a sample proportion of $\hat{p} = 195/1502 = 13\%$.[6] We (and Angus Reid) hope that this observed proportion is close to the population proportion, p, but we know that a second sample of 1502 adults wouldn't have a sample proportion of exactly 13.0%.

We know it isn't surprising that two random samples give slightly different results. We'd like to say something, not about different random *samples*, but about the proportion of *all* adults who thought that Canada's economy would improve in the six months after September 2012. The sampling distribution will be the key to our ability to generalize from our sample to the population.

What do we know about our sampling distribution model? We know that it's centred at the true proportion, p, of all Canadian adults who think the economy will improve. But we don't know p. It isn't 13.0%. That's the $\hat{p}$ from our sample. What we do know is that the sampling distribution model of $\hat{p}$ is centred at p, and we know that the standard deviation of the sampling distribution is $\sqrt{\dfrac{pq}{n}}$. We also

WHO	Canadian adults
WHAT	Proportion who think economy will improve in the next six months
WHEN	September 2012
WHY	To measure expectations about the economy

---

[6] You may see proportions expressed either as numbers between 0 and 1, or, as is often the case in business, as percentages.

know, from the Central Limit Theorem, that the shape of the sampling distribution is approximately Normal, when the sample is large enough.

We don't know p, so we can't find the true standard deviation of the sampling distribution model. Instead, we'll use $\hat{p}$-*hat* and $\hat{q}$-*hat* in the formula and rather than calling it standard deviation, we will call it standard error and denote it by SE. Thus:

$$SE(\hat{p}) = \sqrt{\frac{\hat{p}\hat{q}}{n}} = \sqrt{\frac{(0.13)(1 - 0.13)}{1502}} = 0.009$$

Since the Angus Reid sample of 1502 is large, we know that the sampling distribution model for $\hat{p}$ should look approximately like the one shown in Figure 9.3. Whenever we estimate the standard deviation of a sampling distribution, we call it a **standard error (SE)**.

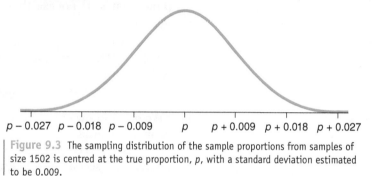

$$p - 0.027 \quad p - 0.018 \quad p - 0.009 \quad\quad p \quad\quad p + 0.009 \quad p + 0.018 \quad p + 0.027$$

Figure 9.3 The sampling distribution of the sample proportions from samples of size 1502 is centred at the true proportion, p, with a standard deviation estimated to be 0.009.

The sampling distribution model for $\hat{p}$ is Normal with a mean of p and a standard deviation we estimate to be $\sqrt{\frac{\hat{p}\hat{q}}{n}}$. Because the distribution is Normal, we'd expect that about 68% of all samples of 1502 Canadian adults taken in September 2012 would have had sample proportions within 1 standard deviation of p. And about 95% of all these samples will have proportions within $p \pm 2$ SEs. But where is *our* sample proportion in this picture? And what value does p have? We still don't know!

We do know that for 95% of random samples, $\hat{p}$ will be no more than 2 SEs away from p. So let's reverse it and look at it from $\hat{p}$'s point of view. If I'm $\hat{p}$, there's a 95% chance that p is no more than 2 SEs away from me. If I reach out 2 SEs, or 2×0.009, away from me on both sides, I'm 95% sure that p will be within my grasp. Of course, I won't know, and even if my interval does catch p, I still don't know its true value. The best I can do is state a probability that I've covered the true value in our interval.

$$\hat{p} - 2\,SE \quad\quad\quad \hat{p} \quad\quad\quad \hat{p} + 2\,SE$$

Figure 9.4 Reaching out 2 SEs on either side of $\hat{p}$ makes us 95% confident we'll trap the true proportion, p.

What Can We Say about a Proportion?

So what can we really say about *p*? Here's a list of things we'd like to be able to say and the reasons we can't say most of them:

1. **"13.0% of *all* Canadian adults thought the economy would improve."** It would be nice to be able to make absolute statements about population values with certainty, but we just don't have enough information to do that. There's no way to be sure that the population proportion is the same as the sample proportion; in fact, it almost certainly isn't. Observations vary. Another sample would yield a different sample proportion.

2. **"It is *probably* true that 13.0% of *all* Canadian adults thought the economy would improve."** No. In fact, we can be pretty sure that whatever the true proportion is, it's not exactly 13.0%, so the statement is not true.

3. **"We don't know exactly what proportion of Canadian adults thought the economy would improve, but we *know* that it's within the interval 13.0% ± 2 × 0.9%. That is, it's between 11.2% and 14.8%."** This is getting closer, but we still can't be certain. We can't know for sure that the true proportion is in this interval—or in any particular range.

4. **"We don't know exactly what proportion of Canadian adults thought the economy would improve, but the interval from 11.2% to 14.8% *probably* contains the true proportion."** We've now fudged twice—first by giving an interval and second by admitting that we only think the interval "probably" contains the true value.

That last statement may be true, but it's a bit wishy-washy. We can tighten it up by quantifying what we mean by "probably." We saw that 95% of the time when we reach out 2 SEs from $\hat{p}$, we capture *p*, *so we can be 95% confident that this is one of those times*. After putting a number on the probability that this interval covers the true proportion, we've given our best guess of where the parameter is and how certain we are that it's within some range.

5. **"We are 95% confident that between 11.2% and 14.8% of Canadian adults thought the economy would improve."** This is now an appropriate interpretation of our confidence intervals. It's not perfect, but it's about the best we can do.

Each **confidence interval** discussed in the book has a name. You'll see many different kinds of confidence intervals in the following chapters. Some will be about more than *one* sample, some will be about statistics other than *proportions*, and some will use models other than the Normal. The interval calculated and interpreted here is an example of a **one-proportion z-interval**.[7] (We prefer this term instead of the more frequently used "one-sample confidence interval for a proportion" because it reminds the reader that it is based on the Normal (*z*) model.) We'll lay out the formal definition in the next few pages.

What Does "95% Confidence" Really Mean?

What do we mean when we say we have 95% confidence that our interval contains the true proportion? Formally, what we mean is that "95% of samples of this size will produce confidence intervals that capture the true proportion." This is correct but a little long-winded, so we sometimes say "we are 95% confident that the true proportion lies in our interval." Our uncertainty is about whether the particular

"Far better an approximate answer to the right question, … than an exact answer to the wrong question."

—John W. Tukey

---

[7] In fact, this confidence interval is so standard for a single proportion that you may see it simply called a "confidence interval for the proportion."

As a visual analogy, think about tossing a Frisbee at a small target, say a dime, that is affixed to a flat surface. A "95% confident Frisbee thrower" would mean that 95 of 100 tosses of the Frisbee would cover the dime. Each toss is like a sample, and just as each sample gives a different confidence interval; each toss lands in a different position. But just as the true population proportion (i.e., the parameter) does not change, neither does the position of the dime. Five tosses in 100 would be expected to miss the target completely.

sample we have at hand is one of the successful ones or one of the 5% that fail to produce an interval that captures the true value. Earlier in the chapter we saw how proportions vary from sample to sample. If other pollsters had selected their own samples of adults, they would have found some who thought the economy would improve, but each sample proportion would almost certainly differ from ours. When they each tried to estimate the true proportion, they'd centre their confidence intervals at the proportions they observed in their own samples. Each would have ended up with a different interval.

Figure 9.5 shows the confidence intervals produced by simulating 20 samples. The purple dots are the simulated proportions of adults in each sample who thought the economy would improve, and the orange segments show the confidence intervals found for each simulated sample. The green line represents the true percentage of adults who thought the economy would improve. You can see that most of the simulated confidence intervals include the true value—but one missed. (Note that it is the *intervals* that vary from sample to sample; the green line doesn't move.)

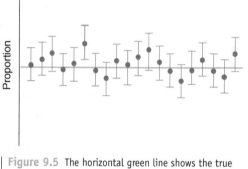

Figure 9.5 The horizontal green line shows the true proportion of people in September 2012 who thought the economy would improve. Most of the 20 simulated samples shown here produced 95% confidence intervals that captured the true value, but one missed.

Of course, a huge number of possible samples *could* be drawn, each with its own sample proportion. This simulation approximates just some of them. Each sample can be used to make a confidence interval. That's a large pile of possible confidence intervals, and ours is just one of those in the pile. Did *our* confidence interval "work"? We can never be sure because we'll never know the true proportion of all Canadian adults who thought in September 2012 that the economy would improve. However, the Central Limit Theorem assures us that 95% of the intervals in the pile are winners, covering the true value, and only 5% on average, miss the target. That's why we're 95% *confident* that our interval is a winner.

9.6 Margin of Error: Certainty vs. Precision

We've just claimed that at a certain confidence level we've captured the true proportion of all Canadian adults who thought in September 2012 that the economy would improve. Our confidence interval stretched out the same distance on either side of the estimated proportion with the form:

$$\hat{p} \pm 2\ SE(\hat{p})$$

The *extent* of that interval on either side of $\hat{p}$ is called the **margin of error (ME)**. In general, confidence intervals look like this:

$$estimate \pm ME$$

Confidence Intervals

We'll see many confidence intervals in this book. All have the form:

estimate $\pm$ ME.
For proportions at 95% confidence:

ME $\approx 2SE(\hat{p})$.

The margin of error for our 95% confidence interval was 2 SEs. What if we wanted to be more confident? To be more confident, we'd need to capture *p* more often, and to do that, we'd need to make the interval wider. For example, if we want to be 99.7% confident, the margin of error will have to be 3 SEs.

> In our Frisbee analogy, to be more confident of covering the coin with a Frisbee toss we would need a larger Frisbee.

Figure 9.6 Reaching out 3 SEs on either side of $\hat{p}$ makes us 99.7% confident we'll trap the true proportion *p*. Compare the width of this interval with the interval in Figure 9.4.

The more confident we want to be, the larger the margin of error must be. We can be 100% confident that any proportion is between 0% and 100%, but that's not very useful. Or we could give a narrow confidence interval, say, from 12.98% to 13.02%. But we couldn't be very confident about a statement this precise. Every confidence interval is a balance between certainty and precision.

The tension between certainty and precision is always there. There is no simple answer to the conflict. Fortunately, in most cases we can be both sufficiently certain and sufficiently precise to make useful statements. The choice of confidence level is somewhat arbitrary, but you must choose the level yourself. The data can't do it for you. The most commonly chosen confidence levels are 90%, 95%, and 99%, but any percentage can be used. (In practice, though, using something like 92.9% or 97.2% might be viewed with suspicion.)

Universal Uclick

> **NOTATION ALERT:**
> We put an asterisk on a letter to indicate a critical value. We usually use "*z*" when we talk about Normal models, so z^* is always a critical value from a Normal model.

9.7 Critical Values

In the polling example, our margin of error was 2 SEs, which produced a 95% confidence interval. To change the confidence level, we'll need to change the *number* of SEs to correspond to the new level. A wider confidence interval means more confidence. For any confidence level the number of SEs we must stretch out on either

Some common confidence levels and their associated critical values:

CI	z^*
90%	1.645
95%	1.960
99%	2.576

side of $\hat{p}$ is called the **critical value**. Because it is based on the Normal model, we denote it z^*. For any confidence level, we can find the corresponding critical value from a computer, a calculator, or a Normal probability table, such as Table Z in the back of the book.

For a 95% confidence interval, the precise critical value is $z^* = 1.96$. That is, 95% of a Normal model is found within $\pm$ 1.96 standard deviations of the mean. We've been using $z^* = 2$ from the 68-95-99.7 Rule because 2 is very close to 1.96 and is easier to remember. Usually, the difference is negligible, but if you want to be precise, use 1.96.[8]

Suppose we could be satisfied with 90% confidence. What critical value would we need? We can use a smaller margin of error. Our greater precision is offset by our acceptance of being wrong more often (that is, having a confidence interval that misses the true value). Specifically, for a 90% confidence interval, the critical value is only 1.645 because for a Normal model, 90% of the values are within 1.645 standard deviations from the mean. By contrast, suppose your boss demands more confidence. If she wants an interval in which she can have 99% confidence, she'll need to include values within 2.576 standard deviations, creating a wider confidence interval.

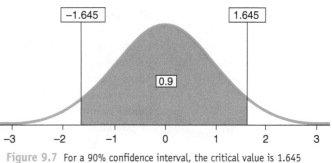

Figure 9.7 For a 90% confidence interval, the critical value is 1.645 because for a Normal model, 90% of the values fall within 1.645 standard deviations of the mean.

9.8 Assumptions and Conditions for a Confidence Interval

The statements we made about what all Canadian adults thought about the economy were possible because we used a Normal model for the sampling distribution. But is that model appropriate?

As we've seen, all statistical models make assumptions. If those assumptions are not true, the model might be inappropriate, and our conclusions based on it may be wrong. Because the confidence interval is built on the Normal model for the sampling distribution, the assumptions and conditions are the same as those we discussed in Section 9.3. But, because they are so important, we'll go over them again.

You can never be certain that an assumption is true, but you can decide intelligently whether it is reasonable. When you have data, you can often decide whether an assumption is plausible by checking a related condition in the data. However,

---

[8] It's been suggested that since 1.96 is both an unusual value and so important in Statistics, you can recognize someone who's had a Statistics course by just saying "1.96" and seeing whether they react.

you'll want to make a statement about the world at large, not just about the data. So the assumptions you make are not just about how the data look, but about how representative they are.

Here are the assumptions and the corresponding conditions to check before creating (or believing) a confidence interval about a proportion.

Independence Assumption

You first need to think about whether the independence assumption is plausible. You can look for reasons to suspect that it fails. You might wonder whether there is any reason to believe that the data values somehow affect each other. (For example, might any of the adults in the sample be related?) This condition depends on your knowledge of the situation. It's not one you can check by looking at the data. However, now that you have data, there are two conditions that you can check:

◆ **Randomization Condition:** Were the data sampled at random or generated from a properly randomized experiment? Proper randomization can help ensure independence.

◆ **10% Condition:** Samples are almost always drawn without replacement. Usually, you'd like to have as large a sample as you can. But if you sample from a small population, the probability of success may be different for the last few individuals you draw than it was for the first few. For example, if most of the women have already been sampled, the chance of drawing a woman from the remaining population is lower. If the sample exceeds 10% of the population, the probability of a success changes so much during the sampling that a Normal model may no longer be appropriate. But if less than 10% of the population is sampled, it is safe to assume it to have independence.

Sample Size Assumption

The model we use for inference is based on the Central Limit Theorem. So, the sample must be large enough for the Normal sampling model to be appropriate. It turns out that we need more data when the proportion is close to either extreme (0 or 1). This requirement is easy to check with the following condition:

◆ **Success/Failure Condition:** We must expect our sample to contain at least 10 "successes" and at least 10 "failures." Recall that by tradition we arbitrarily label one alternative (usually the outcome being counted) as a "success" even if it's something bad. The other alternative is then a "failure." So we check that both $n\hat{p} \geq 10$ and $n\hat{q} \geq 10$. This is equivalent to the Condition required for the Normal model to apply to the sampling distribution of a proportion (see Section 9.3). But here we use $\hat{p}$ and $\hat{q}$ instead of p and q (since the latter two are unknown parameters.

One-proportion z-interval

When the conditions are met, we are ready to find the confidence interval for the population proportion, p. The confidence interval is $\hat{p} \pm z^* \times SE(\hat{p})$, where the standard deviation of the proportion is estimated by the standard error

$$SE(\hat{p}) = \sqrt{\frac{\hat{p}\hat{q}}{n}}.$$

GUIDED EXAMPLE | Public Opinion: Fighting in Hockey

Mark Spowart/Alamy

Very few topics lead to more heated debate in Canada than whether on-ice fighting (or the gentler sounding official term, "fisticuffs") is an essential component of the game of hockey. Hockey is the only one of the four major sports in North America that allows two players to fight without severe consequences.

Reasons given for banning fighting are that violence in sports has no place in today's world, that it is a bad example for youth, that it is bad for players' health (specifically, three recent deaths of hockey enforcers), and that on-ice violence leads to off-ice violence.

There are two main reasons for allowing fighting, beyond the traditional, "It's been part of the game forever." First, fighting creates fans; sports are entertainment and business, and fan revenue is how players' salary demands are met. Second, fighting actually helps keep players safe by helping them self-police the game, and keeping cheap shots to a minimum.

It is commonly believed that the majority of people calling for fighting to be banned are people outside the sport, but that the majority of people in the sport think it needs to stay. To check this, in February 2013, Angus Reid Public Opinion conducted an online survey of 502 randomly selected Canadians who regularly attend, listen to, or watch hockey. They were asked, "Would you support or oppose eliminating on-ice fights from professional hockey. Of these adult hockey fans, 68% responded that they support eliminating on-ice fights. (In a larger random sample of 1013 Canadian adults, not just hockey fans, 67% supported taking fighting out of the game.) What can we conclude from this survey?

To answer this question, we'll build a confidence interval for the proportion of all Canadian adult hockey fans who think that on-ice fights should be eliminated from professional hockey. As with other procedures, there are three steps to building and summarizing a confidence interval for proportions: Plan, Do, and Report.

WHO	Adult hockey fans in Canada
WHAT	Proportion who think on-ice fights should be eliminated from professional hockey
WHEN	February 22–26, 2013
WHERE	Canada
HOW	502 adults were randomly sampled by Angus Reid Public Opinion
WHY	To investigate public opinion about fighting in professional hockey

PLAN

Setup State the context of the question.

Identify the *parameter* you wish to estimate. Identify the *population* about which you wish to make statements.

Choose and state a confidence level.

Model Think about the assumptions and check the conditions to decide whether we can use the Normal model.

We want to find an interval that is likely with 95% confidence to contain the true proportion, p, of Canadian adult hockey fans who think fighting should be eliminated from professional hockey. We have a random sample of 502 Canadian adult hockey fans, with a sample proportion of 68%.

✓ **Independence Assumption:** Angus Reid contacted a random sample of Canadian adult hockey fans. It is unlikely that any respondent influenced another.

✓ **Randomization Condition:** Angus Reid drew a random sample. We don't have details of their randomization but assume that we can trust it.

✓ **10% Condition:** Although sampling was necessarily without replacement, there are many more adult hockey fans in Canada than were sampled. The sample is certainly less than 10% of the population.

✓ **Success/Failure Condition:**
$n\hat{p} = 502 \times 0.67 = 336 \geq 10$ and
$n\hat{q} = 502 \times 0.33 = 166 \geq 10$,
so the sample is large enough.

State the sampling distribution model for the statistic. Choose your method.

The conditions are satisfied, so I can use a Normal model to find a one-proportion z-interval.

DO

Mechanics Construct the confidence interval. First, find the standard error. (Remember: It's called the "standard error" because we don't know *p* and have to use $\hat{p}$ instead.)

$n = 502, \hat{p} = 0.67$, so

$$SE(\hat{p}) = \sqrt{\frac{0.67 \times 0.33}{502}} = 0.021$$

Next, find the margin of error. We could informally use 2 for our critical value, but 1.96 is more accurate.

Because the sampling model is Normal, for a 95% confidence interval, the critical value $z^* = 1.96$. The margin of error is:

$$ME = z^* \times SE(\hat{p}) = 1.96 \times 0.021 = 0.041$$

Write the confidence interval.

So the 95% confidence interval is:

$$0.67 \pm 0.041 \text{ or } (0.629, 0.711)$$

REALITY CHECK Check that the interval is plausible. We may not have a strong expectation for the centre, but the width of the interval depends primarily on the sample size—especially when the estimated proportion is near 0.5.

The confidence interval covers a range of nearly 10%, but that's about the width we might expect for a sample of 500 (when $\hat{p}$ is close to 0.5).

REPORT

Conclusion Interpret the confidence interval in the proper context. We're 95% confident that our interval captured the true proportion.

MEMO:

Re: Fighting in Hockey

Angus Reid Public Opinion surveyed 502 Canadian adult hockey fans and asked their opinion about fighting in professional hockey. Although we can't know the true proportion of Canadian adult hockey fans who support eliminating on-ice fights, based on Angus Reid's results, we can be 95% confident that between 62.9% and 71.1% thought that fighting should be eliminated. However, opinions change frequently, especially when there are tragic consequences from a hockey fight, so additional and regular examination of public opinion is needed.

✔ **JUST CHECKING**

Think some more about the 95% confidence interval we just created for the proportion of Canadian adult hockey fans who support eliminating on-ice fights in professional hockey.

4 If we wanted to be 98% confident, would our confidence interval need to be wider or narrower?

5 Our margin of error was about ± 4%. If we wanted to reduce it to ± 3% without increasing the sample size, would our level of confidence be higher or lower?

6 If Angus Reid Public Opinion had polled more people, would the interval's margin of error have likely been larger or smaller?

9.9 Choosing the Sample Size

What $\hat{p}$ should we use?

Often you'll have an estimate of the population proportion based on experience or perhaps on a previous study. If so, use that value as $\hat{p}$ in calculating what size sample you need. If not, the cautious approach is to use $\hat{p} = 0.5$. That will determine the largest sample necessary regardless of the true proportion. It's the *worst case* scenario. The product $\hat{p}\hat{q}$ is maximized when $\hat{p} = \hat{q}$, in the same way that a rectangle of fixed perimeter has maximum area if the length equals the width. It's simple calculus in action!

Every confidence interval must balance precision—the width of the interval—against confidence. Although it is good to be precise and comforting to be confident, there is a trade-off between the two. A confidence interval that says that the percentage is between 10% and 90% wouldn't be of much use, although you could be quite confident that it covered the true proportion. An interval from 43% to 44% is reassuringly precise, but not if it carries a confidence level of 35%. It's a rare study that reports confidence levels lower than 80%. Levels of 95% or 99% are more common.

The time to decide whether the margin of error is small enough to be useful is when you design your study. Don't wait until you compute your confidence interval. To get a narrower interval without giving up confidence, you need to have less variability in your sample proportion. How can you do that? Choose a larger sample.

Consider a company planning to offer a new service to their customers. Product managers want to estimate the proportion of customers who are likely to purchase this new service to within 3% with 95% confidence. How large a sample do they need?

Let's look at the margin of error:

$$ME = z^* \sqrt{\frac{\hat{p}\hat{q}}{n}}$$

$$0.03 = 1.96 \sqrt{\frac{\hat{p}\hat{q}}{n}}$$

Here's a very handy rule of thumb: For 95% confidence, use $z^* = 2$ (instead of 1.96), and use $\hat{p} = 0.5$ (the worst-case scenario).

Then, $ME \approx 2\sqrt{\frac{\hat{p}\hat{q}}{n}} = 2\sqrt{\frac{(0.5)(0.5)}{n}} = \frac{1}{\sqrt{n}}$, or

equivalently, $n \approx 1/(ME)^2$

Sample sizes required for various margins of error.

- $E \approx \pm 10\%$, n ≈ 100
- $E \approx \pm 5\%$, n ≈ 400
- $E \approx \pm 3\%$, n ≈ 1000 (it is closer to 1100, but it is easier to remember 1000)
- $E \approx \pm 2\%$, n ≈ 2500

They want to find n, the sample size. To find n, they need a value for $\hat{p}$. They don't know $\hat{p}$ because they don't have a sample yet, but they can probably guess a value. The worst case—the value that makes the SD (and therefore n) largest—is 0.50, so if they use that value for $\hat{p}$, they'll certainly be safe.

The company's equation, then, is:

$$0.03 = 1.96 \sqrt{\frac{(0.5)(0.5)}{n}}$$

To solve for n, just multiply both sides of the equation by $\sqrt{n}$ and divide by 0.03:

$$0.03 \sqrt{n} = 1.96 \sqrt{(0.5)(0.5)}$$

$$\sqrt{n} = \frac{1.96 \sqrt{(0.5)(0.5)}}{0.03} \approx 32.67$$

Then square the result to find *n*:

$$n \approx (32.67)^2 \approx 1067.1$$

That method will probably give a value with a fraction. To be safe, always round up. The company will need at least 1068 respondents to keep the margin of error as small as 3% with a confidence level of 95%.

Unfortunately, bigger samples cost more money and require more effort. Because the standard error declines only with the *square root* of the sample size, to cut the standard error (and thus the ME) in half, you must *quadruple* the sample size.

Generally a margin of error of 5% or less is acceptable, but different circumstances call for different standards. The size of the margin of error may be a marketing decision or one determined by the amount of financial risk you (or the company) are willing to accept. Drawing a large sample to get a smaller ME, however, can run into trouble. It takes time to survey 2400 people, and a survey that extends over a week or more may be trying to hit a target that moves during the time of the survey. A news event or new product announcement can change opinions in the middle of the survey process.

Keep in mind that the sample size for a survey is the number of respondents, not the number of people to whom questionnaires were sent or whose phone numbers were dialed. Also keep in mind that a low response rate turns any study essentially into a voluntary response study, which is of little value for inferring population values. It's almost always better to spend resources on increasing the response rate than on surveying a larger group. A complete or nearly complete response by a modest-size sample can yield useful results.

Surveys are not the only place where proportions pop up. Credit card banks sample huge mailing lists to estimate what proportion of people will accept a credit card offer. Even pilot studies may be mailed to 50 000 customers or more. Most of these customers don't respond. But in this case, that doesn't make the sample smaller. In fact, they did respond in a way—they just said "No thanks." To the bank, the response rate[9] is $\hat{p}$. With a typical success rate below 1%, the bank needs a very small margin of error—often as low as 0.1%—to make a sound business decision. That calls for a large sample, and the bank should take care when estimating the size needed. For our survey of consumer confidence, we used $p = 0.5$, both because it's safe and because we honestly believed *p* to be near 0.5. If the bank used 0.5, they'd get an absurd answer. Instead they base their calculation on a value of *p* that they expect to find from their experience.

There's one more aspect to notice. The population size is not part of this calculation. As long as the population is very large compared to the sample, the population size is not relevant. Precision, or sampling variability, is determined mainly by the size of the sample. So a random sample of 1000 Canadians and a random sample of 1000 Americans would lead to, all other things being equal, the same margin of error, even though the population of the United States is ten times the population of Canada. This seems counterintuitive, but imagine you are tasting chicken soup to see if it has enough salt. Whether you are making a small pot at home or an industrial-sized vat at a soup kitchen, a tablespoon from either size container would be sufficient. You don't need to taste a pailful from the vat just because it is a bigger container!

Public opinion polls often use a sample size of 1000, which gives an ME of about 3% (at 95% confidence) when *p* is near 0.5. But businesses and nonprofit organizations often use much larger samples to estimate the response to a direct mail campaign. Why? Because the proportion of people who respond to these mailings is very low, often 5% or even less. An ME of 3% may not be precise enough if the response rate is that low. Instead, an ME like 0.1% would be more useful, and that requires a very large sample size.

---

[9] Be careful. In marketing studies like this *every* mailing yields a response—"yes" or "no"—and response rate means the success rate, the proportion of customers who accept the offer. That's a different use of the term response rate from the one used in survey response.

Michael Blann/Photodisc/Getty Images

How Much of a Difference Can It Make?

A credit card company is about to send out a mailing to test the market for a new credit card. From that sample, they want to estimate the true proportion of people who will sign up for the card nationwide. To be within a tenth of a percentage point, or 0.001 of the true acquisition rate with 95% confidence, how big does the test mailing have to be? Similar mailings in the past lead them to expect that about 0.5% of the people receiving the offer will accept it. Using those values, they find:

$$ME = 0.001 = z^* \sqrt{\frac{\hat{p}\hat{q}}{n}} = 1.96 \sqrt{\frac{(0.005)(0.995)}{n}}$$

$$(0.001)^2 = 1.96^2 \frac{(0.005)(0.995)}{n} \Rightarrow n = \frac{1.96^2(0.005)(0.995)}{(0.001)^2}$$

$$= 19\ 111.96\ or\ 19\ 112$$

That's a perfectly reasonable size for a trial mailing. But if they had used 0.50 as their proposed value of p they would have found:

$$ME = 0.001 = z^* \sqrt{\frac{pq}{n}} = 1.96 \sqrt{\frac{(0.5)(0.5)}{n}}$$

$$(0.001)^2 = 1.96^2 \frac{(0.5)(0.5)}{n} \Rightarrow n = \frac{1.96^2(0.5)(0.5)}{(0.001)^2} = 960\ 400$$

Quite a different result!

WHAT CAN GO WRONG?

- **Don't use Normal models when the distribution is not unimodal and symmetric.** Normal models are so easy and useful that it is tempting to use them even when they don't describe the data very well. That can lead to wrong conclusions. Don't use a Normal model without first looking at a picture of the data to check that it is unimodal and symmetric. A histogram, or boxplot, can help you tell whether a Normal model is appropriate.

- **Don't confuse the sampling distribution with the distribution of the sample.** When you take a sample, you always look at the distribution of the values, usually with a histogram, and you may calculate summary statistics. Examining the distribution of the sample like this is wise. But that's not the sampling distribution. The sampling distribution is an imaginary collection of the values that a statistic might have taken for all the random samples—the one you got and the ones that you didn't get. Use the sampling distribution model to make statements about how the statistic varies.

- **Beware of observations that are not independent.** The CLT depends crucially on the assumption of independence. Unfortunately, this isn't something you can check in your data. You have to think about how the data were gathered. Good sampling practice and well-designed randomized experiments ensure independence.

Confidence intervals are powerful tools. Not only do they tell us what is known about the parameter value, but—more important—they also tell us what we *don't* know. In order to use confidence intervals effectively, you must be clear about what you say about them. Don't misstate what the interval means.

What *Can* I Say?

Confidence intervals are based on random samples, so the interval is random, too. The Central Limit Theorem tells us that 95% of the random samples will yield intervals that capture the true value. That's what we mean by being 95% confident.

Technically, we should say "I am 95% confident that the interval from 11.2% to 14.8% captures the true proportion of Canadian adults who thought the economy would improve in the six months following September 2012." That formal phrasing emphasizes that *our confidence (and our uncertainty) is about the interval, not the true proportion.* But you may choose a more casual phrasing like "I am 95% confident that between 11.2% and 14.8% of Canadian adults thought the economy would improve in the six months following September 2012." Because you've made it clear that the uncertainty is yours and you didn't suggest that the randomness is in the true proportion, this is OK. Keep in mind that it's the interval that's random. It's the focus of both our confidence and our doubt.

- **Don't suggest that the parameter varies.** A statement like "there is a 95% chance that the true proportion is between 11.2% and 14.8%" sounds as though you think the population proportion wanders around and sometimes happens to fall between 11.2% and 14.8%. When you interpret a confidence interval, make it clear that *you* know that the population parameter is fixed and that it is the interval that varies from sample to sample.

- **Don't claim that other samples will agree with yours.** Keep in mind that the confidence interval makes a statement about the true population proportion. An interpretation such as "in 95% of samples of Canadian adults the proportion who thought the economy would improve in the six months following September 2012 will be between 11.2% and 14.8%" is just wrong. The interval isn't about sample proportions but about the population proportion. There is nothing special about the sample we happen to have; it doesn't establish a standard for other samples.

- **Don't be certain about the parameter.** Saying "between 11.2% and 14.8% of Canadian adults thought the economy would improve in the six months following September 2012" asserts that the population proportion cannot be outside that interval. Of course, you can't be absolutely certain of that (just pretty sure).

- **Don't forget: It's about the parameter.** Don't say "I'm 95% confident that $\hat{p}$ is between 11.2% and 14.8%." Of course, you are—in fact, we calculated that our sample proportion was 13.0%. So we already *know* the sample proportion. The confidence interval is about the (unknown) population parameter, p.

- **Don't claim to know too much.** Don't say "I'm 95% confident that between 11.2% and 14.8% of all Canadian adults think the economy will improve." Angus Reid sampled adults during September 2012, and public opinion shifts over time.

- **Do take responsibility.** Confidence intervals are about *un*certainty. *You* are the one who is uncertain, not the parameter. You have to accept the responsibility and consequences of the fact that not all the intervals you compute will capture the true value. In fact, about 5% of the 95% confidence intervals you find will fail to capture the true value of the parameter. You *can* say "I am 95% confident that between 11.2% and 14.8% of Canadian adults thought the economy would improve in the six months following September 2012."

Violations of Assumptions

Confidence intervals and margins of error are often reported along with poll results and other analyses. But it's easy to misuse them and wise to be aware of the ways things can go wrong.

- **Watch out for biased sampling.** Don't forget about the potential sources of bias in surveys that we discussed in Chapter 3. Just because we have more statistical machinery now doesn't mean we can forget what we've already learned. A questionnaire that finds that 85% of people enjoy filling out surveys still suffers from nonresponse bias even though now we're able to put confidence intervals around this (biased) estimate.

♦ **Think about independence.** The assumption that the values in a sample are mutually independent is one that you usually cannot check. It always pays to think about it, though.

♦ **Be careful of sample size.** The validity of the confidence interval for proportions may be affected by sample size. Avoid using the confidence interval on "small" samples.

ETHICS IN ACTION

Home Illusions, a national retailer of contemporary furniture and home décor, has recently experienced customer complaints about the delivery of its products. This retailer uses different carriers depending on the order destination. Its policy with regard to most items it sells and ships is to simply deliver to the customer's doorstep. However, its policy with regard to furniture is to "deliver, unpack, and place furniture in the intended area of the home." Most of their recent complaints have been from customers in Southern Ontario who were dissatisfied because their furniture deliveries were not unpacked and placed in their homes. Since the retailer uses different carriers, it is important for them to label their packages correctly so the delivery company can distinguish between furniture and nonfurniture deliveries. Home Illusions sets as a target "1% or less" for incorrect labelling of packages. Joe Zangard, V.P. Logistics, was asked to look into the problem. The retailer's largest warehouse in Southern Ontario prepares about 1000 items per week for shipping. Joe's initial attention was directed at this facility, not only because of its large volume, but also because he had some reservations about the newly hired warehouse manager, Brent Mossir. Packages at the warehouse were randomly selected and examined over a period of several weeks. Out of 1000 packages, 13 were labelled incorrectly. Since Joe had expected the count to be 10 or fewer, he was confident that he had now pinpointed the problem. His next step was to set up a meeting with Brent in order to discuss the ways in which he can improve the labelling process at his warehouse.

ETHICAL ISSUE *Joe is treating the sample proportion as if it were the true fixed value. By not recognizing that this sample proportion varies from sample to sample, he has unfairly judged the labelling process at Brent's warehouse. This is consistent with his initial misgivings about Brent being hired as warehouse manager (related to ASA Ethical Guidelines, Item A, which can be found at http://www.amstat.org/about/ethicalguidelines.cfm).*

ETHICAL SOLUTION *Joe Zangard needs to use the normal distribution to model the sampling distribution for the sample proportion. In this way, he would realize that the sample proportion observed is less than one standard deviation away from*

1% (the upper limit of the target) and thus not conclusively larger than the limit.

One of Tim Solsby's major responsibilities at CanCity Credit Union is managing online services and website content. In an effort to better serve CanCity members, Tim routinely visits the sites of other financial institutions to get ideas on how he can improve CanCity's online presence. One of the features that caught his attention was a "teen network" that focused on educating teenagers about personal finances. He thought that this was a novel idea and one that could help build a stronger online community among CanCity's members. The executive board of CanCity was meeting next month to consider proposals for improving credit union services, and Tim was eager to present his idea for adding an online teen network. To strengthen his proposal, he decided to poll current credit union members. On the CanCity Credit Union website, he posted an online survey. Among the questions he asked are "Do you have teenage children in your household?" and "Would you encourage your teenage children to learn more about managing personal finances?" Based on 850 responses, Tim constructed a 95% confidence interval and was able to estimate (with 95% confidence) that between 69% and 75% of CanCity members had teenage children at home and that between 62% and 68% would encourage their teenagers to learn more about managing personal finances. Tim believed these results would help convince the executive board that CanCity should add this feature to its website.

ETHICAL ISSUE *The sampling method introduces bias because it is a voluntary response sample and not a random sample. Customers who do have teenagers are more likely to respond than those that do not (related to ASA Ethical Guidelines, Item A, which can be found at http://www.amstat.org/about/ethicalguidelines.cfm).*

ETHICAL SOLUTION *Tim should revise his sampling methods. He might draw a simple random sample of credit union customers and try and contact them by mail or telephone. Whatever method he uses, Tim needs to disclose the sampling procedure to the Board and discuss possible sources of bias.*

WHAT HAVE WE LEARNED?

In Chapter 1, we said that Statistics is about variation. We know that no sample fully and exactly describes the population; sample proportions and means will vary from sample to sample. That's sampling error (or, better, sampling variability). We know it will always be present—indeed, the world would be a boring place if variability didn't exist. You might think that sampling variability would prevent us from learning anything reliable about a population by looking at a sample, but that's just not so. The fortunate fact is that sampling variability is not just unavoidable—it's predictable!

We've learned how the Central Limit Theorem describes the behaviour of sample proportions (and means)—shape, centre, and spread—as long as certain conditions are met. The sample must be random, of course, and large enough that we expect at least 10 successes and 10 failures. Then:

- The sampling distribution (the imagined histogram of the proportions from all possible samples) is shaped like a Normal model.
- The mean of the sampling model is the true proportion in the population.
- The standard deviation of the sample proportions is $\sqrt{\dfrac{pq}{n}}$.

The first few chapters of the book explored graphical and numerical ways of summarizing and presenting sample data. We've learned to use the sample we have at hand to say something about the *world at large*. This process, called *statistical inference*, is based on our understanding of sampling models and will be our focus for the rest of the book.

As our first step in statistical inference, we've learned to use our sample to make a *confidence interval* that estimates what proportion of a population has a certain characteristic.

We've learned that:

- Our best estimate of the true population proportion is the proportion we observed in the sample, so we centre our confidence interval there.
- Samples don't represent the population perfectly, so we create our interval with a *margin of error*. This method successfully captures the true population proportion most of the time, providing us with a level of confidence in our interval.
- For a given sample size, the higher the level of confidence we want, the *wider* our confidence interval becomes.
- For a given level of confidence, the larger the sample size we have, the *narrower* our confidence interval can be.
- When designing a study, we can calculate the sample size we'll need to enable us to reach conclusions that have a desired margin of error and level of confidence.
- There are important assumptions and conditions we must check before using this (or any) statistical inference procedure.

We've learned to interpret a confidence interval by reporting what we believe is true in the entire population from which we took our random sample. Of course, we can't be *certain*. We've learned not to overstate or misinterpret what the confidence interval says.

Terms

Central Limit Theorem   The Central Limit Theorem (CLT) states that the sampling distribution model of the sample proportions (and means) is approximately Normal for large n, regardless of the distribution of the population, as long as the observations are independent.

Confidence interval	An interval of values usually of the form $$estimate \pm margin\ of\ error$$ found from data in such a way that a percentage of all random samples can be expected to yield intervals that capture the true parameter value.
Critical value	The number of standard errors to move away from the mean of the sampling distribution to correspond to the specified level of confidence. The critical value, denoted by an asterisk (e.g., z^* for a Normal critical value), is usually found from a table or with technology.
Margin of error (ME)	In a confidence interval, the extent of the interval on either side of the observed statistic value. A margin of error is typically the product of a critical value from the sampling distribution and a standard error from the data. A small margin of error corresponds to a confidence interval that pins down the parameter precisely. A large margin of error corresponds to a confidence interval that gives relatively little information about the estimated parameter.
One-proportion z-interval	A confidence interval for the true value of a proportion. The confidence interval is $$\hat{p} \pm z^* SE(\hat{p})$$ where z^* is a critical value from the Standard Normal model corresponding to the specified confidence level.
Sampling distribution	The distribution of a statistic over many independent samples of the same size from the same population.
Sampling distribution model for a proportion	If the independence assumption and randomization condition are met and we expect at least 10 successes and 10 failures, then the sampling distribution of a proportion is well modelled by a Normal model with a mean equal to the true proportion value, p, and a standard deviation equal to $\sqrt{\dfrac{pq}{n}}$.
Sampling error	The variability we expect to see from sample to sample is often called the sampling error, although sampling variability is a better term.
Standard error	When the standard deviation of the sampling distribution of a statistic is estimated from the data, the resulting statistic is called a standard error (SE). So $SD(\hat{p}) = \sqrt{\dfrac{pq}{n}}$ and $SE(\hat{p}) = \sqrt{\dfrac{\hat{p}\hat{q}}{n}}$

Skills

PLAN

- Understand that the variability of a statistic (as measured by the standard deviation of its sampling distribution) depends on the size of the sample. Statistics based on larger samples are less variable.
- Understand confidence intervals as a balance between the precision and the certainty of a statement about a model parameter.
- Understand that the margin of error of a confidence interval for a proportion changes with the sample size and the level of confidence.
- Know how to examine your data for violations of conditions that would make inference about a population proportion unwise or invalid.

DO

- Be able to use a sampling distribution model to make simple statements about the distribution of a proportion under repeated sampling.
- Be able to construct a one-proportion z-interval.

REPORT

- Be able to interpret a sampling distribution model as describing the values taken by a statistic in all possible realizations of a sample or randomized experiment under the same conditions.

- Know how to interpret a one-proportion z-interval in a simple sentence or two. Be able to write such an interpretation so that it does not state or suggest that the parameter of interest is itself random, but rather that the bounds of the confidence interval are the random quantities about which we state our degree of confidence.

TECHNOLOGY HELP: Confidence Intervals for Proportions

Confidence intervals for proportions are so easy and natural that many statistics packages don't offer special commands for them. Most statistics programs want the "raw data" for computations. For proportions, the raw data are the "success" and "failure" status for each case. Usually, these are given as 1 or 0, but they might be category names like "yes" and "no." Often we just know the proportion of successes, $\hat{p}$, and the total count, n. Computer packages don't usually deal with summary data like this easily, but the statistics routines found on many graphing calculators allow you to create confidence intervals from summaries of the data—usually all you need to enter are the number of successes and the sample size.

In some programs you can reconstruct variables of 0's and 1's with the given proportions. But even when you have (or can reconstruct) the raw data values, you may not get *exactly* the same margin of error from a computer package as you would find working by hand. The reason is that some packages make approximations or use other methods. The result is very close but not exactly the same. Fortunately, Statistics means never having to say you're certain, so the approximate result is good enough.

EXCEL

Inference methods for proportions are not part of the standard Excel tool set.

MINI CASE STUDY PROJECTS

Santiago Cornejo/Shutterstock

Real Estate Simulation

Many variables important to the real estate market are skewed, limited to only a few values, or considered as categorical variables. Yet, marketing and business decisions are often made based on proportions calculated over many homes. One reason these statistics are useful is the Central Limit Theorem.

Data on 1265 houses sold during the spring of 2013 in the Fraser Valley region of British Columbia are in the file **ch09_MCSP_Real_Estate.xlsx**. Let's investigate how the CLT guarantees that the sampling distribution of proportions approaches Normal.

The variable *View* is a dichotomous variable where $1 = has\ a\ view$ and $0 = does\ not\ have\ a\ view$.

- Calculate the proportion of homes that have views for all 1265 homes. Using this value, calculate what the standard error of the sample proportion would be for a sample of size 50.

- Using the software of your choice, draw 100 samples of size 50 from this population of homes, find the proportion of homes with views in each of these samples, and make a histogram of these proportions.
- Compare the mean and standard deviation of this (sampling) distribution to what you previously calculated.

Investor Sentiment

Jenny Thompson/Fotolia

A national survey conducted by Head Research was commissioned by TD Investor Insights Index to study investor sentiment. The survey took place during the period April 8–12, 2013, and targeted adult Canadian investors who had purchased or sold investments in the previous 12 months and who had owned at least one investment product at the time of the survey. Three of the questions asked were:

1. "Do you expect an improvement in your personal portfolio over the next 12 months?" Of the 1002 respondents, 41% said yes.
2. "Do you expect to see economic improvements in the <u>Canadian</u> economy over the next 12 months?" Of the 1002 respondents, 26% said yes.
3. "Do you expect to see economic improvements in the <u>world</u> economy over the next 12 months? Of the 1002 respondents, 10% said yes.

Compute the standard error for each sample proportion. Compute and describe the 95% confidence intervals in the context of the question. What would the size of the sample need to be for the margin of error to be 2%?

Find a recent survey about investment optimism and write up a short report on your findings.

EXERCISES

1. Fidelity funds. Fidelity offers its customers many different investment options, depending on the risk each investor would like to take. For example, the Fidelity Aggressive International Fund is known to invest in more volatile stocks. Over the past 10 years, the mean annual return for this high-growth fund is 10.47%, and the standard deviation is 25.90%. Assume that the distribution is normally distributed and find the probability that the annual return for this fund is   **LO❶**

a) greater than 0%.
b) greater than 5%.
c) greater than 10%.
d) less than –5%.

2. Fidelity funds, part 2. Fidelity also offers the Fidelity Mid-Cap Growth Fund, which specializes in mid-growth stocks. Many investors believe that both the average return and the volatility of a mid-growth fund will be less than that of a high-growth fund. The mean annual return for this fund over the past 10 years is reported to be 7.98%, with a standard deviation of 21.13%. Assume the distribution is normally distributed and find the probability that the annual return for this fund is   **LO❶**

a) greater than 0%.
b) greater than 5%.
c) greater than 10%.
d) less than –5%.
e) Compare your answers above to your answers in Exercise 1 for the high-growth fund.

3. Quality control. A farmer is concerned about the number of eggs he has been collecting that are "below weight" because this impacts his bottom line. Hens usually begin laying eggs when they are about six months old. Young hens tend to lay smaller eggs, often weighing less than the desired minimum weight of 54 grams.   **LO❶**

a) The average weight of the eggs produced by the young hens is 50.9 grams, and only 28% of their eggs exceed the desired minimum weight. If a Normal model is appropriate, what would the standard deviation of the egg weights be?

b) By the time these hens have reached the age of one year, the eggs they produce average 67.1 grams, and 98% of them are above the minimum weight. What is the standard deviation for the appropriate Normal model for these older hens?

c) Are egg sizes more consistent for the younger hens or the older ones? Explain.

d) A certain poultry farmer finds that 8% of his eggs are underweight and that 12% weigh over 70 grams. Estimate the mean and standard deviation of his eggs.

4. Selling tomatoes. Agricultural scientists are working on developing an improved variety of Roma tomatoes. Marketing research indicates that customers are likely to bypass Romas that weigh less than 70 grams. The current variety of Roma plants produces fruit that average 74 grams, but 11% of the tomatoes are too small. It is reasonable to assume that a Normal model applies. **LO❶**

a) What is the standard deviation of the weights of Romas now being grown?

b) Scientists hope to reduce the frequency of undersized tomatoes to no more than 4%. One way to accomplish this is to raise the average size of the fruit. If the standard deviation remains the same, what target mean should they have as a goal?

c) The researchers produce a new variety with a mean weight of 75 grams, which meets the 4% goal. What is the standard deviation of the weights of these new Romas?

d) Based on their standard deviations, compare the tomatoes produced by the two varieties.

5. Loans. Based on past experience, a bank believes that 7% of the people who receive loans will not make payments on time. The bank has recently approved 200 loans. **LO❷**

a) What are the mean and standard deviation of the proportion of clients in this group who may not make timely payments?

b) What assumptions underlie your model? Are the conditions met? Explain.

c) What's the probability that over 10% of these clients will not make timely payments?

6. Stock market. Assume that 30% of all business students at a university invest in the stock market. **LO❷**

a) We randomly pick 100 students. Let $\hat{p}$ represent the proportion of students in this sample who buy and sell shares. What's the appropriate model for the distribution of $\hat{p}$? Specify the name of the distribution, the mean, and the standard deviation. Be sure to verify that the conditions are met.

b) What's the approximate probability that more than one third of this sample invests in the stock market?

7. Polling. Just before a referendum on a harmonized sales tax, a local newspaper polls 400 voters in an attempt to predict whether the proposition will pass. Suppose that the proposition actually has the support of 52% of the voters. What's the probability the newspaper's sample will lead them to predict defeat? Be sure to

verify that the assumptions and conditions necessary for your analysis are met. **LO❷**

8. Selling seeds. Information on a packet of seeds claims that the germination rate is 92%. The manufacturer needs to understand the likelihood of this claim. What's the probability that more than 95% of the 160 seeds in the packet will germinate? Be sure to discuss your assumptions and check the conditions that support your model. **LO❷**

9. Apples. When a truckload of apples arrives at a packing plant, a random sample of 150 is selected and examined for bruises, discoloration, and other defects. The whole truckload will be rejected if more than 5% of the sample is unsatisfactory. Suppose that in fact 8% of the apples on the truck do not meet the desired standard. What's the probability that the shipment will be accepted anyway? **LO❷**

10. Equipment testing. It's believed that 4% of children have a gene that may be linked to juvenile diabetes. Researchers at a firm would like to test new monitoring equipment for diabetes. Hoping to have 20 children with the gene for their study, the researchers test 732 newborns for the presence of the gene linked to diabetes. What's the probability that they find enough subjects for their study? **LO❷**

11. Game show. A Canadian television game show auditions contestants by using a 100-question, multiple choice, general knowledge quiz. Each question has four response choices, exactly one of which is correct. In other words, the proportion of correct answers in the population is 25%. The producer wants to set the threshold for passing the audition high enough so that the probability of passing just by guessing randomly on each question is "very small." Based on a probability of 0.25 of guessing the correct answer for each question, what number of correct answers should be set as the threshold? Be sure to comment on the assumptions and conditions that support your model, and explain what "very small" means to you. **LO❷**

12. Customer demand. A restaurateur anticipates serving about 180 people on a Friday evening and believes that about 20% of the patrons will order the chef's steak special.

How many of those meals should he plan on serving in order to be pretty sure of having enough steaks on hand to meet customer demand?

Justify your answer, including an explanation of what "pretty sure" means to you. **LO❷**

13. Margin of error. A corporate executive reports the results of an employee satisfaction survey, stating that 52% of employees say they are either "satisfied" or "extremely satisfied" with their jobs, and then says "the margin of error is plus or minus 4%." Explain carefully what that means. **LO❸**

14. Margin of error, again. A market researcher estimates the percentage of adults between the ages of 21 and 39 who will see their television ad is 15%, adding that he believes his estimate has a margin of error of about 3%. Explain what the margin of error means. **LO❸**

15. Conditions. Consider each situation described below. Identify the population and the sample, explain what p and $\hat{p}$ represent, and tell whether the methods of this chapter can be used to create a confidence interval. **LO④**

a) Police set up an auto checkpoint at which drivers are stopped and their cars inspected for safety problems. They find that 14 of the 134 cars stopped have at least one safety violation. They want to estimate the proportion of all cars in this area that may be unsafe.

b) A CBC news program asks viewers in Quebec to register their opinions about political corruption in the province by logging onto a website. Of the 602 people who voted, 488 were very or moderately concerned about corruption. The news program wants to estimate the level of concern about corruption among the general public in Quebec.

16. More conditions. Consider each situation described below. Identify the population and the sample, explain what p and $\hat{p}$ represent, and tell whether the methods of this chapter can be used to create a confidence interval. **LO④**

a) A large company with 10 000 employees at their main research site is considering moving its day care centre off-site to save money. Human resources gathers employees' opinions by sending a questionnaire home with all employees; 380 surveys are returned, with 228 employees in favour of the change.

b) A company sold 1632 ereaders last month, and within a week, 1388 of the customers had registered their products online at the company website. The company wants to estimate the percentage of all their customers who enroll their products.

17. Conditions, again. Consider each situation described. Identify the population and the sample, explain what p and $\hat{p}$ represent, and tell whether the methods of this chapter can be used to create a confidence interval. **LO④**

a) A consumer group hoping to assess customer experiences with auto dealers surveys 167 people who recently bought new cars; 3% of them expressed dissatisfaction with the salesperson.

b) A cellphone service provider wants to know what percent of Canadian university students have smartphones. A total of 883 students were questioned as they entered a sports arena, and 768 indicated they had smartphones.

18. Final conditions. Consider each situation described. Identify the population and the sample, explain what p and $\hat{p}$ represent, and tell whether the methods of this chapter can be used to create a confidence interval. **LO④**

a) A total of 240 potato plants in a field in Prince Edward Island are randomly checked, and only 7 show signs of blight. How severe is the blight problem for the Canadian potato industry?

b) Concerned about workers' compensation costs, a small company decided to investigate on-the-job injuries. The company reported that 12 of their 309 employees suffered an injury on the job last year. What can the company expect in future years?

19. Catalogue sales. A catalogue sales company promises to deliver orders placed on the internet within three days.

Follow-up calls to a few randomly selected customers show that a 95% confidence interval for the proportion of all orders that arrive on time is 88% $\pm$ 6%. What does this mean? Are the conclusions in parts a–e correct? Explain. **LO⑤**

a) Between 82% and 94% of all orders arrive on time.

b) 95% of all random samples of customers will show that 88% of orders arrive on time.

c) 95% of all random samples of customers will show that 82% to 94% of orders arrive on time.

d) The company is 95% sure that between 82% and 94% of the orders placed by the customers in this sample arrived on time.

e) On 95% of the days, between 82% and 94% of the orders will arrive on time.

20. Belgian euro. Recently, two students made worldwide headlines by spinning a Belgian euro 250 times and getting 140 heads—that's 56%. That makes the 90% confidence interval (51%, 61%). What does this mean? Are the conclusions in parts a–e correct? Explain your answers. **LO⑤**

a) Between 51% and 61% of all euros are unfair.

b) We are 90% sure that in this experiment this euro landed heads on between 51% and 61% of the spins.

c) We are 90% sure that spun euros will land heads between 51% and 61% of the time.

d) If you spin a euro many times, you can be 90% sure of getting between 51% and 61% heads.

e) 90% of all spun euros will land heads between 51% and 61% of the time.

21. Confidence intervals. Several factors are involved in the creation of a confidence interval. Among them are the sample size, the level of confidence, and the margin of error. Which statements are true? **LO⑤**

a) For a given sample size, higher confidence means a smaller margin of error.

b) For a specified confidence level, larger samples provide smaller margins of error.

c) For a fixed margin of error, larger samples provide greater confidence.

d) For a given confidence level, halving the margin of error requires a sample twice as large.

22. Confidence intervals, again. Several factors are involved in the creation of a confidence interval. Among them are the sample size, the level of confidence, and the margin of error. Which statements are true? **LO⑤**

a) For a given sample size, reducing the margin of error will mean lower confidence.

b) For a certain confidence level, you can get a smaller margin of error by selecting a bigger sample.

c) For a fixed margin of error, smaller samples will mean lower confidence.

d) For a given confidence level, a sample nine times as large will make a margin of error one third as big.

23. Cars. A student is considering publishing a new magazine aimed directly at owners of Japanese automobiles. He wants to estimate the fraction of cars in Canada that are made in Japan. The computer output summarizes the results of a random sample of 50 autos. Explain carefully what it tells you.   LO❺

```
z-interval for proportion
With 90.00% confidence
0.29938661 < p(japan) < 0.46984416
```

24. Quality control. For quality control purposes, 900 ceramic tiles were inspected to determine the proportion of defective (e.g., cracked, uneven finish, etc.) tiles. Assuming that these tiles are representative of all tiles manufactured by an Italian tile company, what can you conclude based on the computer output?   LO❺

```
z-interval for proportion
With 95.00% confidence
0.025 < p(defective) < 0.035
```

25. Social media. A researcher in digital culture is interested in statistics concerning the use of social media. A poll found that 32% of a random sample of 1012 Anglophone Canadians who are internet users check their social media feeds every single day.   LO❸

a) Find the margin of error for this poll if we want 90% confidence in our estimate of the percent of Anglophone Canadian internet users who check social media every day.

b) Explain what that margin of error means.

c) If we want to be 99% confident, will the margin of error be larger or smaller? Explain.

d) Find that margin of error.

e) In general, if all other aspects of the situation remain the same, will smaller margins of error involve greater or less confidence in the interval?

26. Biotechnology. A biotechnology firm is planning its investment strategy for future products and research labs. A poll found that only 8% of a random sample of 1012 Canadian adults approved of attempts to clone a human.   LO❸

a) Find the margin of error for this poll if we want 95% confidence in our estimate of the percent of Canadian adults who approve of cloning humans.

b) Explain what that margin of error means.

c) If we only need to be 90% confident, will the margin of error be larger or smaller? Explain.

d) Find that margin of error.

e) In general, if all other aspects of the situation remain the same, would smaller samples produce smaller or larger margins of error?

27. Teenage drivers. An insurance company checks police records on 582 accidents selected at random and notes that teenagers were at the wheel in 91 of them.   LO❻

a) Create a 95% confidence interval for the percentage of all auto accidents that involve teenage drivers.

b) Explain what your interval means.

c) Explain what "95% confidence" means.

d) A politician urging tighter restrictions on drivers' licences issued to teens says, "In one of every five auto accidents, a teenager is behind the wheel." Does your confidence interval support or contradict this statement? Explain.

28. Advertisers. Direct mail advertisers send solicitations ("junk mail") to thousands of potential customers in the hope that some will buy the company's product. The response rate is usually quite low. Suppose a company wants to test the response to a new flyer and sends it to 1000 people randomly selected from their mailing list of over 200 000 people. They get orders from 123 of the recipients.   LO❻

a) Create a 90% confidence interval for the percentage of people the company contacts who may buy something.

b) Explain what this interval means.

c) Explain what "90% confidence" means.

d) The company must decide whether to do a mass mailing. The mailing won't be cost-effective unless it produces at least a 5% return. What does your confidence interval suggest? Explain.

29. Retailers. Some food retailers propose subjecting food to a low level of radiation in order to improve safety, but sale of such "irradiated" food is opposed by many people. Suppose a grocer wants to find out what his customers think. He has cashiers distribute surveys at checkout and ask customers to fill them out and drop them in a box near the front door. He gets responses from 122 customers, of whom 78 oppose the radiation treatments. What can the grocer conclude about the opinions of all his customers?   LO❻

30. Local news. The mayor of a small city has suggested that the province locate a new prison there, arguing that the construction project and resulting jobs will be good for the local economy. A total of 183 residents show up for a public hearing on the proposal, and a show of hands finds 31 in favour of the prison project. What can the city council conclude about public support for the mayor's initiative?   LO❻

31. Internet music. In a survey on downloading music, the Gallup Poll asked 703 internet users if they "ever downloaded music from an internet site that was not authorized by a record company, or not", and 18% responded "yes." Construct a 95% confidence interval for the true proportion of internet users who have downloaded music from an internet site that was not authorized.   LO❻

32. Economic confidence. In 2013, Angus Reid Public Opinion studied opinions of adults about economic conditions in three countries. Polls were conducted from April 18 to April 28, 2013, among 1001 Canadians, 1005 American adults, and 2003 Britons. Results showed that 55% of Canadians, compared with only 27% of Americans and only 12% of Britons rate the economic conditions in their country as "very good " or good." Construct 95% confidence intervals for the true proportion in each country who rated their economy as Very Good/Good.   LO❻

33. International business. In Canada, the vast majority (90%) of companies in the chemical industry are ISO 14001 certified. The ISO 14001 is an international standard for environmental management systems. An environmental group wished to estimate the percentage of U.S. chemical companies that are ISO 14001 certified. Of the 550 chemical companies sampled, 385 are certified. **LO❻**

a) What proportion of the sample reported being certified?

b) Create a 95% confidence interval for the proportion of U.S. chemical companies with ISO 14001 certification. (Be sure to check conditions.) Compare to the Canadian proportion.

34. Worldwide survey. In Chapter 4, Exercise 17, we learned that GfK Roper surveyed people worldwide asking them "how important is acquiring wealth to you." Of 1535 respondents in India, 1168 said that it was of more than average importance. In the United States of 1317 respondents, 596 said it was of more than average importance. **LO❻**

a) What proportion thought acquiring wealth was of more than average importance in each country's sample?

b) Create a 95% confidence interval for the proportion who thought it was of more than average importance in India. (Be sure to test conditions.) Compare that to a confidence interval for the U.S. population.

35. Business ethics. In a survey on corporate ethics, a poll split a simple random sample of 1076 faculty and corporate recruiters into two halves, asking 538 respondents the question, "Generally, do you believe that MBAs are more or less aware of ethical issues in business today than five years ago?" The other half were asked: "Generally, do you believe that MBAs are less or more aware of ethical issues in business today than five years ago?" These may seem like the same questions, but sometimes the order of the choices matters. In response to the first question, 53% thought MBA graduates were more aware of ethical issues, but when the question was phrased differently, this proportion dropped to 44%. **LO❺**

a) What kind of bias may be present here?

b) Each group consisted of 538 respondents. If we combine them, considering the overall group to be one larger random sample, what is a 95% confidence interval for the proportion of the faculty and corporate recruiters that believe MBAs are more aware of ethical issues today?

c) How does the margin of error based on this pooled sample compare with the margins of error from the separate groups? Why?

36. Media survey. In 2007, a Gallup Poll conducted face-to-face interviews with 1006 adults in Saudi Arabia, aged 15 and older, asking them questions about how they get information. Among them was the question: "Is international television very important in keeping you well-informed about events in your country?" Gallup reported that 82% answered "yes" and noted that at 95% confidence there was a 3% margin of error and that "in addition to sampling error, question wording and practical difficulties in conducting surveys can introduce error or bias into the findings of public opinion polls." **LO❺**

a) What kinds of bias might they be referring to?

b) Do you agree with their margin of error? Explain.

37. Gambling. A city ballot includes a local initiative that would expand gambling. The issue is hotly contested, and two groups decide to conduct polls to predict the outcome. The local newspaper finds that 53% of 1200 randomly selected voters plan to vote "yes," while a university Statistics class finds 54% of 450 randomly selected voters in support. Both groups will create 95% confidence intervals. **LO❻**

a) Without finding the confidence intervals, explain which one will have the larger margin of error.

b) Find both confidence intervals.

c) Which group concludes that the outcome is too close to call? Why?

38. Climate change. In December 2011, Canada formally withdrew from the Kyoto Protocol on climate change, which was the world's only legally binding plan to address global warming. CBC News website has an *Inside Politics* blog that carries a regular "question of the day." The website question immediately after the announcement was, "Do you support Canada's decision to withdraw from the Kyoto Protocol?" When the internet poll was closed, a total of 8540 votes had been cast, of which 61.5% supported the decision. **LO❻**

a) Find a 95% confidence interval for the proportion of Canadians who would support the decision to withdraw.

b) Are the assumptions and conditions satisfied? Explain.

39. Pharmaceutical company. A pharmaceutical company is considering investing in a "new and improved" vitamin D supplement for children. Vitamin D, whether ingested as a dietary supplement or produced naturally when sunlight falls upon the skin, is essential for strong, healthy bones. The bone disease rickets was largely eliminated in England during the 1950s, but now there is concern that a generation of children more likely to watch TV or play computer games than spend time outdoors is at increased risk. A recent study of 2700 children randomly selected from all parts of England found 20% of them deficient in vitamin D. **LO❻**

a) Find a 98% confidence interval for the proportion of children in England who are deficient in vitamin D.

b) Explain carefully what your interval means.

c) Explain what "98% confidence" means.

d) Does the study show that computer games are a likely cause of rickets? Explain.

40. Smartphone use. In Chapter 4, Exercise 26, we saw that in 2012 Angus Reid carried out a survey for Rogers about smartphones. Of 1040 Canadian smartphone users surveyed, 431 said that at night they keep their phone either in bed or on the nightstand beside their bed. **LO❻**

a) Find a 98% confidence interval for the proportion of all Canadian smartphone users who keep their phone in or beside their bed at night.

b) Explain carefully what your interval means.

c) Explain what "98% confidence" means.

41. Banks. Each year the *Financial Post Magazine* publishes information on Canada's largest 500 corporations. In 2013, 25% of the top 20 corporations ranked by revenue were in the banking industry. LO❻

a) Check the assumptions and conditions for inference on proportions.

b) Would your conclusions change if the reported percentage were based on the top 100 corporations instead of the top 20?

42. Real estate survey. A real estate agent looks over the 15 listings she has in a particular postal code in Toronto and finds that 80% of them have swimming pools. LO❻

a) Check the assumptions and conditions for inference on proportions.

b) If it's appropriate, find a 90% confidence interval for the proportion of houses in this postal code that have swimming pools.

43. CRA. In a random survey of 226 self-employed individuals, 20 reported having had their tax returns audited by the CRA in the past year. Estimate the proportion of self-employed individuals nationwide who've been audited by the CRA in the past year. LO❻

a) Check the assumptions and conditions (to the extent you can) for constructing a confidence interval.

b) Construct a 95% confidence interval.

c) Interpret your interval.

d) Explain what "95% confidence" means in this context.

44. ACT, Inc. In 2004, ACT, Inc. reported that 74% of 1644 randomly selected U.S. college freshmen returned to college the next year. Estimate the national freshman-to-sophomore retention rate in the United States. LO❻

a) Check that the assumptions and conditions are met for inference on proportions.

b) Construct a 98% confidence interval.

c) Interpret your interval.

d) Explain what "98% confidence" means in this context.

e) In Canada there is nothing on a national scope about retention rates. At most Ontario universities the retention rates are high; in 2008, between 80% and 90% of first-year students continued on to their second year. Compare this to the ACT results; is there evidence that Ontario is different?

45. Internet music, again. A Gallup Poll (Exercise 31) asked internet users if the fact that they can make copies of songs on the internet for free made them more likely—or less likely—to buy a performer's CD. Only 13% responded that it made them "less likely." The poll was based on a random sample of 703 internet users. LO❻

a) Check that the assumptions and conditions are met for inference on proportions.

b) Find the 95% confidence interval for the true proportion of all internet users who are "less likely" to buy CDs.

46. ACT, Inc., again. The ACT, Inc. study described in Exercise 44 was actually stratified by type of U.S. college—public or private. The retention rates were 71.9% among 505 students enrolled in public colleges and 74.9% among 1139 students enrolled in private colleges. LO❻

a) Will the 95% confidence interval for the true national retention rate in private colleges be wider or narrower than the 95% confidence interval for the retention rate in public colleges? Explain.

b) Find the 95% confidence interval for the public college retention rate.

c) Should a public college whose retention rate is 75% proclaim that they do a better job than other public colleges of keeping freshmen in school? Explain.

47. Credit card safety. A news release in February 2013 stated that an online survey found 45% of 18–34 year olds reported taking risks with payment card information, such as loaning their card to someone or sharing card information, such as the PIN, over email, phone, or text. This compared with 32% of respondents aged 35 and older. The article stated that the survey was conducted by the market research firm Fabrizio Ward with 1000 major credit and debit cardholders in December 2012. LO❻

a) Is there enough information to create a 95% confidence interval for the true proportion of 18–34 years who take risks with payment care information? If not, what additional information is needed?

b) Are all the conditions for a confidence interval satisfied?

c) The article did not state a margin of error. What margin of error could they have reported?

48. Smartphone use, part 2. The survey in Exercise 40 asking about users' smartphone location at night also classified the 1040 respondents by age. LO❻

Phone location at night	Age			
	18–34	**35–54**	**55+**	Total
In bed or on nightstand	186	149	96	431
Same room or next room	57	120	162	339
Another floor/Other	27	85	158	270
Total	**270**	**354**	**416**	**1040**

a) Do you expect the 95% confidence interval for the true proportion of all users in the 18–34 age group who have their smartphone with them in bed or on the nightstand to be wider or narrower than the 95% confidence interval for the true proportion in the 55+ age group? Explain briefly.

b) Find the 95% confidence interval for the true proportion of all users in the 18–34 age group who keep their smartphone with them in bed or on the nightstand.

49. More internet music. A random sample of 168 students was asked how many songs were in their digital music library and what fraction of them was legally purchased. Overall, they

reported having a total of 117 079 songs, of which 23.1% were legal. The music industry would like a good estimate of the proportion of songs in students' digital music libraries that are legal. **LO⑥**
a) Think carefully. What is the parameter being estimated? What is the population? What is the sample size?
b) Check the conditions for making a confidence interval.
c) Construct a 95% confidence interval for the fraction of legal digital music.
d) Explain what this interval means. Do you believe that you can be this confident about your result? Why or why not?

50. Trade agreement. The Asia Pacific Foundation of Canada commissioned Angus Reid to survey public opinion about free trade agreements (FTA) with countries around the world. Results from a February 2012 survey of 3129 Canadian adults showed 69% of respondents supported a FTA with the European Union, and 63% with Japan, but only 46% with India and 45% with South Korea. According to the Angus Reid, the sample was representative of the entire adult population of Canada. **LO⑥**
a) What parameters are being estimated? What is the population?
b) Check the conditions for making a confidence interval.
c) Construct 95% confidence intervals for the proportion of Canadians who support a FTA, one for each of the four partners.

51. CDs. A company manufacturing CDs is working on a new technology. A random sample of 703 internet users were asked: "As you may know, some CDs are being manufactured so that you can only make one copy of the CD after you purchase it. Would you buy a CD with this technology, or would you refuse to buy it even if it were one you would normally buy?" Of these users, 64% responded that they would buy the CD. **LO⑥**
a) Create a 90% confidence interval for this percentage.
b) If the company wants to cut the margin of error in half, how many users must they survey?

52. Internet music, last time. The research group that conducted the survey in Exercise 49 wants to provide the music industry with definitive information, but they believe that they could use a smaller sample next time. If the group is willing to have twice as big a margin of error, how many songs must be included? **LO⑦**

53. High school graduation. A report by The Conference Board of Canada notes that between 1997 and 2010 Canada's high school completion rate increased from 78% to 88%. Statistics Canada reports that in 2010 the rate for the 55–64 age group was a bit lower, 82%, than the overall rate. We wish to see if this percentage is the same as the percentage among the 20–24 age group. **LO⑦**
a) How many of this younger age group must we survey in order to estimate the proportion of grads to within 6% with 90% confidence?
b) Suppose we want to cut the margin of error to 4%. What's the necessary sample size?
c) What sample size would produce a margin of error of 3%?

54. Hiring. In preparing a report on the economy, we need to estimate the percentage of businesses that plan to hire additional employees in the next 60 days. **LO⑦**
a) How many randomly selected employers must we contact in order to create an estimate in which we are 98% confident with a margin of error of 5%?
b) Suppose we want to reduce the margin of error to 3%. What sample size will suffice?
c) Why might it not be worth the effort to try to get an interval with a margin of error of only 1%?

55. High school graduation, again. As in Exercise 53, we hope to estimate the percentage of adults aged 20 to 24 who never graduated from high school. What sample size would allow us to increase our confidence level to 95% while reducing the margin of error to only 2%? **LO⑦**

56. Better hiring info. Editors of the business report in Exercise 54 are willing to accept a margin of error of 4% but want 99% confidence. How many randomly selected employers will they need to contact? **LO⑦**

57. Pilot study. An environmental agency worries that a large percentage of cars may be violating clean air emissions standards. The agency hopes to check a sample of vehicles in order to estimate that percentage with a margin of error of 3% and 90% confidence. To gauge the size of the problem, the agency first picks 60 cars and finds nine with faulty emissions systems. How many should be sampled for a full investigation? **LO⑦**

58. Another pilot study. During routine conversations, the CEO of a new start-up reports that 22% of adults between the ages of 21 and 39 will purchase her new product. Hearing this, some investors decide to conduct a large-scale study, hoping to estimate the proportion to within 4% with 98% confidence. How many randomly selected adults between the ages of 21 and 39 must they survey? **LO⑦**

59. Approval rating. A newspaper reports that a premier's approval rating stands at 65%. The article adds that the poll is based on a random sample of 972 adults and has a margin of error of 2.5%. What level of confidence did the pollsters use? **LO⑧**

60. Amendment. The Board of Directors of a publicly traded company says that a proposed amendment to their bylaws is likely to win approval in the upcoming shareholder meeting because a poll of 1505 share owners indicated that 52% would vote in favour. The Board goes on to say that the margin of error for this poll was 3%. **LO⑧**
a) Explain why the poll is actually inconclusive.
b) What confidence level did the pollsters use?

T 61. Customer spending. The data set provided contains last month's credit card purchases of 500 customers randomly chosen from a segment of a major credit card issuer. The marketing department is considering a special offer for customers who spend more than $1000 per month on their card. From these data construct a 95% confidence interval for the proportion of customers in this segment who will qualify.   LO**6**

62. *Advertising.* A philanthropic organization knows that its donors have an average age near 60 and is considering taking out an ad in the Canadian Association of Retired People (CARP) magazine. An analyst wonders what proportion of their donors are actually 50 years old or older. He takes a random sample of the records of 500 donors. From the data provided, construct a 95% confidence interval for the proportion of donors who are 50 years old or older.   LO**6**

63. *Cross-border shopping.* Based on an Ipsos-Reid 2012 survey of 2477 adult British Columbians, 66% have gone shopping across the U.S. border within the past year.   LO**6**

a) Examine the conditions for constructing a confidence interval for the proportion of British Columbian adults who have cross-border shopped in the past year.

b) Find the 95% confidence interval.

c) Interpret your confidence interval.

64. *Cross-border shopping, part 2.* Using the same survey and data as in Exercise 63, 15% of those who had gone shopping across the border in the past year responded affirmatively that they had ever lied to a customs agent about how much they spent on a cross-border shopping trip.   LO**6**

a) Examine the conditions for constructing a confidence interval for the proportion of British Columbians who have ever lied to a customs agent about how much spent on a cross-border shopping trip.

b) Find the 95% confidence interval. Be careful about the denominator for this interval.

c) Interpret your confidence interval.

JUST CHECKING ANSWERS

1 A Normal model (approximately).

2 At the actual proportion of all customers who like the new location.

3 $SD(\hat{p}) = \sqrt{\dfrac{(0.5)(0.5)}{100}} = 0.05$

4 Wider

5 Lower

6 Smaller

Testing Hypotheses about Proportions

Rick Chard/TSX

In Chapter 9 we developed a confidence interval for a single proportion. In this chapter we discuss the companion technique called hypothesis testing and develop a test of a single proportion. We'll leave the confidence interval and hypothesis test for a single mean for the next chapter.

LEARNING OBJECTIVES

1. Write the null and alternative hypotheses

2. Use P-values to make conclusions about the hypotheses

3. Use a confidence interval to make conclusions about hypotheses

4. Choose and interpret alpha levels

5. Find and correct mistakes in an incorrectly performed hypothesis test

6. Identify and carry out all parts (hypotheses, test statistic, P-value, conclusion) of a hypothesis test for proportion

7. Use z-score and critical value to make conclusions about hypotheses

8. Explain the two types of error and determine the power of the test

Dow Jones Industrial Average

ore than a hundred years ago Charles Dow changed the way people look at the stock market. Surprisingly, he wasn't an investment wizard or a venture capitalist. He was a journalist who wanted to make investing understandable to ordinary people. Although he died at the relatively young age of 51 in 1902, his impact on how we track the stock market has been both long-lasting and far-reaching.

In the late 1800s, when Charles Dow reported on Wall Street, investors preferred bonds, not stocks. Bonds were reliable, backed by the real machinery and other hard assets the company owned. What's more, bonds were predictable; the bond owner knew when the bond would mature and so, knew when and how much the bond would pay. Stocks simply represented "shares" of ownership, which were risky and erratic. In May 1896, Dow and Edward Jones, whom he had known since their days as reporters for the *Providence Evening Press*, launched the now-famous Dow Jones Industrial Average (DJIA) to help the public understand stock market trends. The original DJIA averaged 11 stock prices. Of those original industrial stocks, only General Electric is still in the DJIA.

Since then, the DJIA has become synonymous with overall market performance and is often referred to simply as the Dow. Today the Dow is a weighted average of 30 industrial stocks, with weights used to account for splits and other adjustments.

The "Industrial" part of the name is largely historic. Today's DJIA includes the service industry and financial companies and is much broader than just heavy industry. It is still one of the most watched indicators of the global economy.

Dow Jones also maintains a family of international equity indices (Dow Jones Global Indexes or DJGI) including world, region, and country indices and various market sector and industry group sub-indices. The indices cover 95 percent of market capitalization in a country.

There are Canadian indices focusing on growth stocks and value stocks in large, medium, and small companies. Some, such as the Canada Total Market Index provide a broad perspective on the Canadian equity market as a whole. Others, such as the Canada Select Dividend Index focus on stocks that have dividends that are more than the Canadian average. For a stock to be included in the index, it must have a high enough size of dividend per share, but also demonstrate long-term sustainability and high trading volume. Dow Jones provides investors with a range of indices that can be used as benchmarks for tracking the performance of the full range of Canadian companies.

Based on information from www.dowjones.com/history.asp

WHO	Days on which the stock market was open ("trading days")
WHAT	Closing price of the Dow Jones Industrial Average (*Close*)
UNITS	Points
WHEN	August 1982 to December 1986
WHY	To test theory of stock market behaviour

How does the stock market move? Here are the DJIA closing prices for the bull market that ran from mid 1982 to the end of 1986.

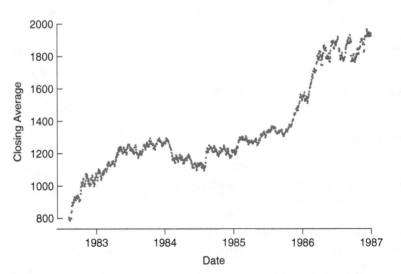

Figure 10.1 Daily closing prices of the Dow Jones Industrials from mid 1982 to the end of 1986.

The DJIA clearly increased during this famous bull market, more than doubling in value in less than five years. One common theory of market behaviour says that on a given day, the market is just as likely to move up as down. Another way of phrasing this is that the daily behaviour of the stock market is random. Can that be true during such periods of obvious increase? Let's investigate if the Dow is just as likely to move higher or lower on any given day. Out of the 1112 trading days in that period, the average increased on 573 days, a sample proportion of 0.5153 or 51.53%. That *is* more "up" days than "down" days, but is it far enough from 50% to cast doubt on the assumption of equally likely up or down movement?

10.1 Hypotheses

How can we state and test a hypothesis about daily changes in the DJIA? Hypotheses are working models that we adopt temporarily. To test whether the daily fluctuations are equally likely to be up as down, we assume that they are, and that any apparent difference from 50% is just random fluctuation. So, our starting hypothesis, called the null hypothesis, is that the proportion of days on which the DJIA increases is 50%. The **null hypothesis**, which we denote by H_0, specifies a population model parameter and proposes a value for that parameter. We usually write down a null hypothesis about a proportion in the form $H_0: p = p_0$. This is a concise way to specify the two things we need most: the identity of the parameter we hope to learn about (the true proportion) and a specific hypothesized value for that parameter (in this case, 50%). We need a hypothesized value so we can compare our observed statistic to it. Which value to use for the hypothesis is not a statistical question. It may be obvious from the context of the data, but sometimes it takes a bit of thinking to translate the question we hope to answer into a hypothesis about a parameter. For our hypothesis about whether the DJIA moves up or down with equal likelihood, it's pretty clear that we need to test $H_0: p = 0.5$.

The **alternative hypothesis**, which we denote by H_A, contains the values of the parameter that we consider plausible if we reject the null hypothesis. In our example, our null hypothesis is that the proportion, p, of "up" days is 0.5. What's the alternative? During a bull market, you might expect more up days than down, but we'll assume that we're interested in a deviation in either direction from the null hypothesis, so our alternative is $H_A: p \neq 0.5$.

What would convince you that the proportion of up days was not 50%? If on 95% of the days, the DJIA closed up, most people would be convinced that up and down days were not equally likely. But if the sample proportion of up days were only slightly higher than 50%, you'd be skeptical. After all, observations do vary, so we wouldn't be surprised to see some difference. How different from 50% must the proportion be before we *are* convinced that it has changed? Whenever we ask about the size of a statistical difference, we naturally think of the standard deviation. So let's start by finding the standard deviation of the sample proportion of days on which the DJIA increased.

We've seen 51.53% up days out of 1112 trading days. The sample size of 1112 is certainly big enough to satisfy the Success/Failure condition. (We expect $0.50 \times 1112 = 556$ daily increases.) We suspect that the daily price changes are random and independent. And we know what hypothesis we are testing. To test a hypothesis we (temporarily) *assume* that it is true so we can see whether that description of the world is plausible. If we assume that the Dow increases or decreases with equal likelihood, we'll need to centre our Normal sampling model at a mean of 0.5. Then, we can find the standard deviation of the sampling model as

$$SD(\hat{p}) = \sqrt{\frac{pq}{n}} = \sqrt{\frac{(0.5)(1-0.5)}{1112}} = 0.015$$

Hypothesis n.;

pl. {Hypotheses}.

A supposition; a proposition or principle which is supposed or taken for granted, in order to draw a conclusion or inference for proof of the point in question; something not proved, but assumed for the purpose of argument.

—Webster's Unabridged Dictionary, 1913

! **NOTATION ALERT:**

Capital H is the standard letter for hypotheses. H_0 labels the null hypothesis, and H_A labels the alternative. How do you pronounce H_0? Traditionally, we say "H-nought" rather than H-zero, out of respect for the British statisticians who developed these techniques. And "nought" is a British English word for "zero." So to be proper you should say "H-nought" with a British accent. H_A is just "H-aye" or as we say in Canada, "H-eh?"

In a standard deck of playing cards, half the cards are red and the other half are black; that is, the proportion of red cards is 50% (or $p = 0.5$), just like the proportion of up days for the DJIA. Suppose a deck is shuffled so that the cards are in random order. Deal them out one at a time. How many red cards in a row would you need to see before you become suspicious that the proportion is not 50%, and that perhaps the deck was not properly shuffled or perhaps not a proper deck? This is an excellent analogy to up days and down days for the DJIA.

◆ **Why is this a standard deviation and not a standard error?** This is a standard deviation because we haven't estimated anything. Once we assume that the null hypothesis is true, it gives us a value for the model parameter p. With proportions, if we know p then we also automatically know its standard deviation. Because we find the standard deviation from the model parameter, this is a standard deviation and not a standard error. When we found a confidence interval for p, we could not assume that we knew its value, so we estimated the standard deviation from the sample value, $\hat{p}$.

Now we know both parameters of the Normal sampling distribution model for our null hypothesis. For the mean, μ, we use $p = 0.50$, and for σ we use the standard deviation of the sample proportions $SD(\hat{p}) = 0.015$. We want to know how likely it would be to see the observed value $\hat{p}$ as far away from 50% as the value of 51.53% that we actually have observed. Looking first at a picture (Figure 10.2), we can see that 51.53% doesn't look very surprising. The more exact answer (from a calculator, computer program, or the Normal table) is that the probability is about 0.308. This is the probability of observing more than 51.53% up days (or more than 51.53% down days) if the null model were true. In other words, if the chance of an up day for the Dow is 50%, we'd expect to see stretches of 1112 trading days with as many as 51.53% up days about 15.4% of the time and with as many as 51.53% down days about 15.4% of the time. That's not terribly unusual, so there's really no convincing evidence that the market did not act randomly.

> To remind us that the parameter value comes from the null hypothesis, it is sometimes written as p_0 and the standard deviation as
>
> $$SD(\hat{p}) = \sqrt{\frac{p_0 q_0}{n}}.$$

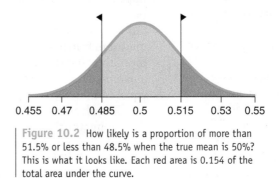

0.455 0.47 0.485 0.5 0.515 0.53 0.55

Figure 10.2 How likely is a proportion of more than 51.5% or less than 48.5% when the true mean is 50%? This is what it looks like. Each red area is 0.154 of the total area under the curve.

It may surprise you that even during a bull market, the direction of daily movements is random. But, the probability that any given day will end up or down appears to be about 0.5 regardless of the longer-term trends. It may be that when the stock market has a long run up (or possibly down, although we haven't checked that), it does so not by having more days of increasing or decreasing value, but by the actual amounts of the increases or decreases being unequal.

10.2 A Trial as a Hypothesis Test

We started by assuming that the probability of an up day was 50%. Then we looked at the data and concluded that we couldn't say otherwise because the proportion that we actually observed wasn't far enough from 50%. Does this reasoning of hypothesis tests seem backwards? That could be because we usually prefer to think about getting things right rather than getting them wrong. But, you've seen this reasoning before in a different context. This is the logic of jury trials.

Let's suppose a defendant has been accused of robbery. In British common law and those systems derived from it (including Canadian and U.S. law), the null hypothesis is that the defendant is innocent. Instructions to juries are quite explicit about this.

IE235/Image Source Plus/Alamy

Here's the correspondence in roles:

Defendant's plea of "not guilty" = Null hypothesis

Prosecutor's claim of "guilty" = Alternative hypothesis

"Burden of proof" = Evidence for rejecting the null hypothesis

Prosecutor = Investigator

(The onus for the burden of proof is on the prosecutor (innocent until proven guilty) or the investigator (keep the status quo until refuted)

Is the evidence more consistent with a verdict of "not guilty" or "guilty"? = Are the data that occurred more consistent with the null hypothesis or alternative hypothesis?

The verdict = the conclusion

Reasonable doubt has also been defined as "moral certainty." For Jacob Bernoulli, who we encountered previously, moral certainty meant less than one time in 1000 (or 0.001). But the definition is very personal and depends on both the context and the judge or jury member!

Beyond a Reasonable Doubt

We ask whether the data were unlikely beyond a reasonable doubt. We've just calculated that probability. The probability that the observed statistic value (or an even more extreme value) could occur if the null model were true—in this case, 0.308—is the P-value.

The evidence takes the form of facts that seem to contradict the presumption of innocence. For us, this means collecting data. In the trial, the prosecutor presents evidence. ("If the defendant were innocent, wouldn't it be remarkable that the police found him at the scene of the crime with a bag full of money in his hand, a mask on his face, and a getaway car parked outside?") The next step is to judge the evidence. Evaluating the evidence is the responsibility of the jury in a trial, but it falls on your shoulders in hypothesis testing. The jury considers the evidence in light of the *presumption* of innocence and judges whether the evidence against the defendant would be plausible *if the defendant were in fact innocent*.

Like the jury, we ask: "Could these data plausibly have happened by chance if the null hypothesis were true?" If they are very unlikely to have occurred, then the evidence raises a reasonable doubt about the null hypothesis. Ultimately, *you* must make a decision. The standard of "beyond a reasonable doubt" is purposefully ambiguous because it leaves the jury to decide the degree to which the evidence contradicts the hypothesis of innocence. Juries don't explicitly use probability to help them decide whether to reject that hypothesis. But when you ask the same question of your null hypothesis, you have the advantage of being able to quantify exactly how surprising the evidence would be if the null hypothesis were true.

How unlikely is unlikely? Some people set rigid standards. Levels like 1 time out of 20 (0.05) or 1 time out of 100 (0.01) are common. But if *you* have to make the decision, you must judge for yourself in each situation whether the probability of observing your data is small enough to constitute "reasonable doubt."

10.3 P-Values

The fundamental step in our reasoning is the question: "Are the data surprising, given the null hypothesis?" And the key calculation is to determine exactly how likely the data we observed would be if the null hypothesis were the true model of the world. So we need a *probability*. Specifically, we want to find the probability of seeing data like these (or something even less likely) *given* the null hypothesis. This probability is the value on which we base our decision, so statisticians give this probability a special name. It's called the **P-value**. (The P just stands for probability; we know, it's not very imaginative.)

A low enough P-value says that the data we have observed would be very unlikely if our null hypothesis were true. We started with a model, and now that same model tells us that the data we have are unlikely to have happened. That's surprising. In this case, the model and data are at odds with each other, so we have to make a choice. Either the null hypothesis is correct and we've just seen something remarkable, or the null hypothesis is wrong, (and, in fact, we were wrong to use it as the basis for computing our P-value). If you believe in data more than in assumptions, then, given that choice, when you see a low P-value you should reject the null hypothesis.

When the P-value is *high* (or just not low *enough*), what do we conclude? In that case, we haven't seen anything unlikely or surprising at all. The data are consistent with the model from the null hypothesis, and we have no reason to reject the null hypothesis. Events that have a high probability of happening happen all the time. So, when the P-value is high does that mean we've proved the null hypothesis is

In Chapter 9, we thought about tossing a Frisbee at a fixed target as an analogy to a confidence interval for estimating a fixed parameter. Each toss of a Frisbee lands in a slightly different place but the target doesn't move. Confidence refers to the proportion of times the Frisbee lands covering the target. Confidence is a probability about the Frisbee, not the target. In the same way, a P-value is a probability about the data, not the hypothesis.

true? No! We realize that many other similar hypotheses could also account for the data we've seen. The most we can say is that it doesn't appear to be false. Formally, we say that we "fail to reject" the null hypothesis. That may seem to be a pretty weak conclusion, but it's all we can say when the P-value is not low enough. All that means is that the data are consistent with the model that we started with.

The logic of hypothesis testing parallels "proof by contradiction" in mathematics or logic. To prove a statement using the method of contradiction, assume the converse or opposite and then show that the opposite leads to an impossibility. If the converse is impossible the original proposition must be true.

For example, prove $\sqrt{a} + \sqrt{b} \neq \sqrt{a+b}$, for a and $b > 0$ (this is the alternative hypothesis).

Assume the opposite; that is, assume $\sqrt{a} + \sqrt{b} = \sqrt{a+b}$ (this is the null hypothesis).

Square both sides: $(\sqrt{a} + \sqrt{b})^2 = (\sqrt{a+b})^2$

$$=> a + b + 2\sqrt{a}\sqrt{b} = a + b$$

$$=> 2\sqrt{a}\sqrt{b} = 0$$

But this is impossible since a and b are both greater than 0 and the product of two positive numbers cannot be 0. That is a contradiction.

Since the assumption (H_0) is wrong, the original statement (H_A) must be true. Q.E.D.

"If the People fail to satisfy their burden of proof, you must find the defendant not guilty."
—Excerpt from New York State Jury Instructions. Published by The Law of Self Defence.

What to Do with an "Innocent" Defendant

In the context of a jury trial, what does it mean to say that "the data are consistent with the model that we started with"? If the evidence is not strong enough to reject the defendant's presumption of innocence, what verdict does the jury return? They do not say that the defendant is innocent. They say "not guilty." All they are saying is that they have not seen sufficient evidence to reject innocence and convict the defendant. The defendant may, in fact, be innocent, but the jury has no way to be sure.

Said statistically, the jury's null hypothesis is: innocent defendant. If the evidence is too unlikely (the P-value is low) then, given the assumption of innocence, the jury rejects the null hypothesis and finds the defendant guilty. But—and this is an important distinction—if there is *insufficient evidence* to convict the defendant (if the P-value is *not* low), the jury does not conclude that the null hypothesis is true and declare that the defendant is innocent. Juries can only *fail to reject* the null hypothesis and declare the defendant "not guilty."

In the same way, if the data are not particularly unlikely under the assumption that the null hypothesis is true, then the most we can do is to "fail to reject" our null hypothesis. We never declare the null hypothesis to be true. In fact we simply do not know whether it's true or not. (After all, more evidence may come along later.)

Don't We Want to Reject the Null?

Often the people who collect the data or perform the experiment hope to reject the null. They hope the new drug is better than the placebo; they hope the new ad campaign is better than the old one; or they hope their candidate is ahead of the opponent. But when we practise Statistics, we can't allow that hope to affect our decision. The essential attitude for a hypothesis tester is skepticism. Until we become convinced otherwise, we cling to the null's assertion that there's nothing unusual, nothing unexpected, no effect, no difference, etc. As in a jury trial, the burden of proof rests with the alternative hypothesis—innocent until proven guilty. When you test a hypothesis, you must act as judge and jury, but you are not the prosecutor.

Conclusion

If the P-value is "low", reject H_0 and conclude H_A.

If the P-value is not "low enough" then fail to reject H_0 and the test is inconclusive.

Imagine a test of whether a company's new website design encourages a higher percentage of visitors to make a purchase (as compared to the site the company has used for years). The null hypothesis is that the new site is no more effective at stimulating purchases than the old one. The test sends visitors randomly to one version of the website or the other. Of course, some will make a purchase, and others won't. If we compare the two websites on only 10 customers each, the results are likely *not to be clear*, and we'll be unable to reject the hypothesis. Does this mean the new design is a complete bust? Not necessarily. It simply means that we don't have enough evidence to reject our null hypothesis. That's why we don't start by assuming that the new design is *more* effective. If we were to do that, then we could test just a few customers, find that the results aren't clear, and claim that since we've been unable to reject our original assumption the redesign must be effective. The Board of Directors is unlikely to be impressed by that argument.

✔️ **JUST CHECKING**

1 A pharmaceutical firm wants to know whether aspirin helps to thin blood. The null hypothesis says that it doesn't. The firm's researchers test 12 patients, observe the proportion with thinner blood, and get a P-value of 0.32. They proclaim that aspirin doesn't work. What would you say?

2 An allergy drug has been tested and found to give relief to 75% of the patients in a large clinical trial. Now the scientists want to see whether a new, "improved" version works even better. What would the null hypothesis be?

3 The new allergy drug is tested, and the P-value is 0.0001. What would you conclude about the new drug?

> Warning: The P-value IS NOT the probability that the null hypothesis is correct. The P-value IS a probability about the data. The P-value is computed under the assumption that H_0 is true. You can't say something is true and then ask, "Is it true?" Since this is a very common error, it is also a very common exam question.

> Sometimes you'll see the four distinct sections described a little differently: hypotheses, test statistic, P-value, and conclusion. It doesn't matter whether you use the terms "model" and "mechanics" or "test statistic" and "P-value." But note that there must always be hypotheses to start and a conclusion to, well, conclude!

10.4 The Reasoning of Hypothesis Testing

Hypothesis tests follow a carefully structured path. To avoid getting lost as we navigate down it, we divide that path into four distinct sections: hypotheses, model, mechanics, and conclusion.

Hypotheses

First, state the null hypothesis. That's usually the skeptical claim that nothing's different. The null hypothesis assumes the default (often the status quo) is true (the defendant is innocent, the new method is no better than the old, customer preferences haven't changed since last year, etc.).

In statistical hypothesis testing, hypotheses are almost always about model parameters. To assess how unlikely our data may be, we need a null model. The null hypothesis specifies a particular parameter value to use in our model. In the usual notation, we write H_0: *parameter = hypothesized value*. The alternative hypothesis, H_A, contains the values of the parameter we consider plausible when we reject the null.

Model

To plan a statistical hypothesis test, specify the *model* for the sampling distribution of the statistic you will use to test the null hypothesis and the parameter of interest. The statistic is called, not surprisingly, the *test statistic*. For proportions, we use the Normal model for the sampling distribution. Of course, all models require assumptions, so you will need to state them and check any corresponding conditions. For a test of a proportion, the assumptions and conditions are the same as for a one-proportion *z*-interval (see page 261).

Your model step should end with a statement such as: *Because the conditions are satisfied, we can model the sampling distribution of the proportion with a Normal model.* Watch out, though. Your Model step could end with: *Because the conditions are not satisfied, we can't proceed with the test.* (If that's the case, stop and reconsider.)

When the Conditions Fail ...

You might proceed with caution, explicitly stating your concerns. Or you may need to do the analysis with and without an outlier, or on different subgroups, or after re-expressing the response variable. Or you may not be able to proceed at all.

Conditional Probability

Did you notice that a P-value results from what we referred to as a "conditional distribution" in Chapter 7? A P-value is a "conditional probability" because it's based on—or is conditional on—another event being true: It's the probability that the observed results could have happened *if the null hypothesis is true.*

Rido/Fotolia

Each test we discuss in this book has a name that you should include in your report. We'll see many tests in the following chapters. Some will be about more than one sample, some will involve statistics other than proportions, and some will use models other than the Normal (and so will not use z-scores). The test about proportions is called a **one-proportion z-test**.[1]

One-proportion z-test

The conditions for the one-proportion z-test are the same as for the one-proportion z-interval. We test the hypothesis $H_0: p = p_0$ using the statistic

$$z = \frac{(\hat{p} - p_0)}{SD(\hat{p})}$$

We use the hypothesized proportion to find the standard deviation: $SD(\hat{p}) = \sqrt{\frac{p_0 q_0}{n}}$. When the conditions are met and the null hypothesis is true, this statistic follows the standard Normal model, so we can use that model to obtain a P-value.

Mechanics

Under "Mechanics" we perform the actual calculation of our test statistic from the data. Different tests we encounter will have different formulas and different test statistics. Usually, the mechanics are handled by a statistics program or calculator. The ultimate goal of the calculation is to obtain a P-value—the probability that the observed statistic value (or an even more extreme value) could occur if the null model were correct. If the P-value is small enough, we'll reject the null hypothesis.

Conclusions and Decisions

The primary conclusion in a formal hypothesis test is only a statement about the null hypothesis. It simply states whether we reject or fail to reject that hypothesis. But it should never simply be "reject the null hypothesis" or "fail to reject the null hypothesis." The conclusion must be stated in the context of the question; it should be correct from the statistical, grammatical, and subject matter perspectives. In our analogy to a trial, it is not a sufficient conclusion for the foreperson of the jury to announce, simply, "Guilty!" Rather, the foreperson should restate the charge (i.e., the null hypothesis) and the verdict; for example, "On the charge of murder in the first degree, we find the defendant guilty." But your conclusion about the null hypothesis should never be the end of the process. You can't make a decision based solely on a P-value. Business decisions have consequences, with actions to take or policies to change. The conclusions of a hypothesis test can help *inform* your decision, but they shouldn't be the only basis for it.

Business decisions should always take into consideration three things: the statistical significance of the test, the *cost* of the proposed action, and the *effect size* of the statistic they observed. For example, a cellular telephone provider finds that 30% of their customers switch providers (or *churn*) when their two-year subscription contract expires. They try a small experiment and offer a random sample of customers a free $350 top-of-the-line phone if they renew their contracts for another two

---

[1]It's also called the "one-sample z-test for a proportion."

years. Not surprisingly, they find that the new switching rate is lower by a statistically significant amount (i.e., the lower rate cannot be explained as a chance occurrence). Should they offer these free phones to all their customers? Obviously, the answer depends on more than the P-value of the hypothesis test. Even if the P-value is statistically significant, the correct business decision also depends on the cost of the free phones and by how much the churn rate is lowered (the effect size). It's rare that a hypothesis test alone is enough to make a sound business decision. We'll give a full explanation of "statistical significance" in Section 10.6.

10.5 Alternative Hypotheses

In our example about the DJIA, we were equally interested in proportions that deviate from 50% in *either* direction. So we wrote our alternative hypothesis as $H_A: p \neq 0.5$. Such an alternative hypothesis is known as a **two-sided alternative** because we are equally interested in deviations on either side of the null hypothesis value. For two-sided alternatives, the P-value is the probability of deviating in *either* direction from the null hypothesis value.

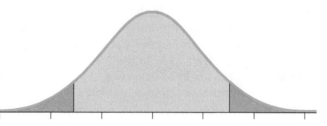

Figure 10.3 The P-value for a two-sided alternative adds the probabilities in both tails of the sampling distribution model outside the value that corresponds to the test statistic.

Alternative Hypotheses

Two-sided:
$H_0: p = p_0$
$H_A: p \neq p_0$
One-sided:
$H_0: p = p_0$
$H_A: p < p_0 \text{ or } p > p_0$
Remember that the "equal sign" always goes in the null hypothesis.

Suppose we want to test whether the proportion of customers returning merchandise has decreased under our new quality monitoring program. We know the quality has improved, so we can be pretty sure things haven't gotten worse. But have the customers noticed? We would only be interested in a sample proportion *smaller* than the null hypothesis value. We'd write our alternative hypothesis as $H_A: p < p_0$. An alternative hypothesis that focuses on deviations from the null hypothesis value in only one direction is called a **one-sided alternative** (or sometimes a one-tailed alternative).

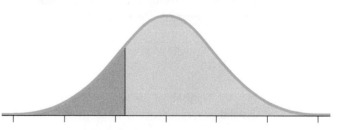

Figure 10.4 The P-value for a one-sided alternative considers only the probability of values beyond the test statistic value in the specified direction.

For a hypothesis test with a one-sided alternative, the P-value is the probability of deviating *only in the direction of the alternative* away from the null hypothesis value.

GUIDED EXAMPLE | Home Field Advantage

Actionpics/Fotolia

Major league sports are big business. And the fans are more likely to come out to root for the team if the home team has a good chance of winning. Anyone who follows or plays sports has heard of the "home field advantage." It is said that teams are more likely to win when they play at home. That *would* be good for encouraging the fans to come to the games. But is it true?

According to the book *Scorecasting: The Hidden Influences Behind How Sports Are Played and Games Are Won* (Moskowitz and Wertheim), in the past 10 years (2003–2012) the percentage of home games won in each of the four major sports leagues was 53.9% in MLB, 55.7% in the NHL, 57.3% in the NFL, and 60.5% in the NBA. (You might be interested to know that Moskowitz is a professor of Finance at the University of Chicago.)

To take one specific case, consider the 2006 Major League Baseball (MLB) season, which had 2429 regular season games. (One rained-out game was never made up.) It turns out that the home team won 1327 of the 2429 games, or 54.63% of the time. If there were no home field advantage, the home teams would win about half of all games played. Could this deviation from 50% be explained just from natural sampling variability, or does this evidence suggest that there really is a home field advantage, at least in professional baseball?

To test the hypothesis, we will ask whether the observed rate of home team victories, 54.63%, is so much greater than 50% that we cannot explain it away as just chance variation.

Remember the four main steps to performing a hypothesis test—hypotheses, model, mechanics, and conclusion? Let's put them to work and see what this will tell us about the home team's chances of winning a baseball game.

PLAN

Setup State what we want to know. Define the variables and discuss their context.

We want to know whether the home team in professional baseball is more likely to win. The data are all 2429 games from the 2006 Major League Baseball season. The variable is whether or not the home team won. The parameter of interest is the proportion of home team wins. If there is an advantage, we'd expect that proportion to be greater than 0.50.

$$H_0: p = 0.50$$

Hypotheses The null hypothesis makes the claim of no home field advantage.

We are interested only in a home field *advantage*, so the alternative hypothesis is one-sided.

$$H_A: p > 0.50$$

Model Think about the assumptions and check the appropriate conditions.

✓ **Independence** Assumption. Generally, the outcome of one game has no effect on the outcome of another game. But this may not always be strictly true. For example, if a key player is injured, the probability that the team will win in the next couple of games may decrease slightly, but independence is still roughly true.

Consider the time frame carefully.

✓ **Randomization Condition.** We have results for all 2429 games of the 2006 season. But we're not just interested in 2006. While these games were not randomly selected, they *may* be reasonably representative of all recent professional baseball games.

✓ **10% Condition.** This is not a random sample, but these 2429 games are fewer than 10% of all games played over the years.

✓ **Success/Failure Condition.** Both
$np_0 = 2429(0.50) = 1214.5$ and
$nq_0 = 2429(0.50) = 1214.5$ are at least 10.

Specify the sampling distribution model.

Tell what test you plan to use.

Because the conditions are satisfied, we'll use a Normal model for the sampling distribution of the proportion and do a one-proportion z-test.

DO

Mechanics The null model gives us the mean, and (because we are working with proportions) the mean gives us the standard deviation.

The null model is a Normal distribution with a mean of 0.50 and a standard deviation of:

$$SD(\hat{p}) = \sqrt{\frac{p_0 q_0}{n}} = \sqrt{\frac{(0.5)(1-0.5)}{2429}} = 0.01015$$

The observed proportion $\hat{p}$ is 0.5463.

From technology, we can find the P-value, which tells us the probability of observing a value that extreme (or more).

The probability of observing a $\hat{p}$ of 0.5463 or more in our Normal model can be found by computer, calculator, or table to be <0.001.

The corresponding P-value is <0.001.

REPORT

Conclusion State your conclusion about the parameter—in context.

MEMO:

Re: Home field advantage

Our analysis of outcomes during the 2006 Major League Baseball season showed an advantage to the home team that cannot be explained by chance alone. We can be quite confident that playing at home gives a baseball team an advantage.

10.6 Alpha Levels and Significance

Sometimes we need to make a firm decision about whether or not to reject the null hypothesis. A jury must *decide* whether the evidence reaches the level of "beyond a reasonable doubt." A business must *select* a web design. You need to decide which section of a Statistics course to enroll in.

When the P-value is small, it tells us that our data are rare *given the null hypothesis*. As humans, we are suspicious of rare events. If the data are "rare enough," we just don't think that could have happened due to chance. Since the data *did* happen, something must be wrong. All we can do now is to reject the null hypothesis.

But how rare is "rare"? How low does the P-value have to be?

We can define "rare event" arbitrarily by setting a threshold for our P-value. If our P-value falls below that point, we'll reject the null hypothesis. We call such results *statistically significant*. The threshold is called an **alpha level**. Not surprisingly, it's labelled with the Greek letter α. Common α-levels are 0.10, 0.05, and 0.01. You have the option—almost the *obligation*—to consider your alpha level carefully and choose an appropriate one for the situation. If you're assessing the safety of air bags, you'll want a low alpha level; even 0.01 might not be low enough. If you're just wondering whether folks prefer their pizza with or without pepperoni, you might be happy with $\alpha = 0.10$. It can be hard to justify your choice of α, though, so often we arbitrarily choose 0.05.

A. Barrington Brown/Science Source/
Photo Researchers

Sir Ronald Fisher (1890–1962) was one of the founders of modern Statistics.

◆ **Where did the value 0.05 come from?** In 1931, in a famous book called *The Design of Experiments*, Sir Ronald Fisher discussed the amount of evidence needed to reject a null hypothesis. He said that it was *situation dependent*, but remarked, somewhat casually, that for many scientific applications, 1 out of 20 *might be* a reasonable value, especially in a *first* experiment—one that will be followed by confirmation. Since then, some people—indeed some entire disciplines—have acted as if the number 0.05 were sacrosanct. An alpha level of 0.05 (or 5%) is consistent with a confidence level of 95%. That is, if we consider 95% to be a sufficiently high confidence level, then 5% would be a sufficiently low alpha level. We'll discuss this in detail in Section 10.8.

The alpha level is also called the **significance level**. When we reject the null hypothesis, we say that the test is "significant at that level." For example, we might say that we reject the null hypothesis "at the 5% level of significance." You must select the alpha level *before* you look at the data. Otherwise you can be accused of finagling the conclusions by tuning the alpha level to the results after you've seen the data. It would be like moving the football goalposts after a field goal kicker has kicked the ball, in order to make sure the ball goes between the posts.

What can you say if the P-value does not fall below α? When you have not found sufficient evidence to reject the null according to the standard you have established, you should say: "The data have failed to provide sufficient evidence to reject the null hypothesis." Don't say: "We accept the null hypothesis." You certainly haven't proven or established the null hypothesis; it was assumed to begin with. You *could* say that you have *retained* the null hypothesis, but it's better to say that you've failed to reject it. Similarly, the verdict of a trial is guilty or not guilty,

> **NOTATION ALERT:**
> The first Greek letter, α, is used in Statistics for the threshold value of a hypothesis test. You'll hear it referred to as the alpha level. Common values are 0.10, 0.05, 0.01, and 0.001.

It could happen to you!

Of course, if the null hypothesis *is* true, no matter what alpha level you choose, you still have a probability α of rejecting the null hypothesis by mistake. When we do reject the null hypothesis, no one ever thinks that *this* is one of those rare times. As statistician Stu Hunter notes, "The statistician says 'rare events do happen—but not to me!'"

rather than guilty or innocent. A verdict of not guilty means there was not sufficient evidence to convict the defendant; it doesn't mean the defendant was innocent of the crime.

Look again at the home field advantage example. The P-value was <0.001. This is so much smaller than any reasonable alpha level that we can reject H_0. We concluded: "We reject the null hypothesis. There is sufficient evidence to conclude that there is a home field advantage over and above what we expect with random variation."

The automatic nature of the reject/fail-to-reject decision when we use an alpha level may make you uncomfortable. If your P-value falls just slightly above your alpha level, you're not allowed to reject the null. Yet a P-value just barely below the alpha level leads to rejection. If this bothers you, you're in good company. Many statisticians think it better to report the P-value than to choose an alpha level and carry the decision through to a final reject/fail-to-reject verdict. So when you declare your decision, it's always a good idea to report the P-value as an indication of the strength of the evidence.

◆ **It's in the stars.** Some disciplines carry the idea further and code P-values by their size. In this scheme, a P-value between 0.05 and 0.01 gets highlighted by a single asterisk (*). A P-value between 0.01 and 0.001 gets two asterisks (**), and a P-value less than 0.001 gets three (***). This can be a convenient summary of the weight of evidence against the null hypothesis, but it isn't wise to take the distinctions too seriously and make black-and-white decisions near the boundaries. The boundaries are a matter of tradition, not science; there is nothing special about 0.05. A P-value of 0.051 should be looked at seriously and not casually thrown away just because it's larger than 0.05, and one that's 0.009 is not very different from one that's 0.011.

Sometimes it's best to report that the conclusion is not yet clear and to suggest that more data be gathered. (In a trial, a jury may "hang" and be unable to return a verdict.) In such cases, it's an especially good idea to report the P-value, since it is the best summary we have of what the data say or fail to say about the null hypothesis.

What do we mean when we say that a test is statistically significant? All we mean is that the test statistic had a P-value lower than our alpha level. Don't be lulled into thinking that "statistical significance" necessarily carries with it any practical importance or impact.

For large samples, even small, unimportant ("insignificant") deviations from the null hypothesis can be statistically significant. On the other hand, if the sample is not large enough, even large, financially or scientifically important differences may not be statistically significant.

It's good practice to report the magnitude of the difference between the observed statistic value and the null hypothesis value (in the data units) along with the P-value on which you have based your decision about statistical significance.

10.7 Critical Values

When building a confidence interval, we found a **critical value**, z^*, to correspond to our selected confidence level. Critical values can also be used as a shortcut for hypothesis tests. Before computers and calculators were common, P-values were hard to find. It was easier to select a few common alpha levels (0.05, 0.01, 0.001, for example) and learn the corresponding critical values for the Normal model (that is, the critical values corresponding to confidence levels 0.95, 0.99, and 0.999, respectively). Rather than find the probability that corresponded to your observed statistic, you'd just calculate how many standard deviations it was away from the hypothesized value and compare that value directly against these z^* values. (Remember that when ever we measure the distance of a value from the mean in standard deviations, we are finding a z-score.) Any z-score larger in magnitude (that is, more extreme) than a particular critical value has to be less likely, so it will have a P-value smaller than the corresponding alpha.

If we were willing to settle for a flat reject/fail-to-reject decision, comparing an observed z-score with the critical value for a specified alpha level would give a shortcut path to that decision. For the home field advantage example, if we choose $\alpha = 0.05$, then in order to reject H_0, our z-score has to be larger than the one-sided critical value of 1.645. The observed proportion was actually 4.56 standard deviations above 0.5, so we clearly reject the null hypothesis. This is perfectly correct and does give us a yes/no decision, but it gives us less information about the hypothesis because we don't have the P-value to think about. With technology, P-values are easy to find. And since they give more information about the strength of the evidence, you should report them.

Here are the traditional z^* critical values from the Normal model[2]:

α	1-sided	2-sided
0.10	1.28	1.645
0.05	1.645	1.96
0.01	2.33	2.576
0.001	3.09	3.29

If you need to make a decision on the fly with no technology, remember "2." That's our old friend from the 68-95-99.7 Rule. It's roughly the critical value for testing a hypothesis against a two-sided alternative at $\alpha = 0.05$. The exact critical value is 1.96, but 2 is close enough for most decisions.

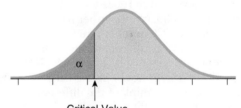

Figure 10.5 When the alternative is one-sided, the critical value puts all of α on one side.

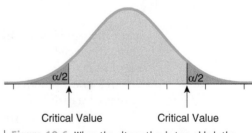

Figure 10.6 When the alternative is two-sided, the critical value splits α equally into two tails.

[2]In a sense, these are the flip side of the 68-95-99.7 Rule. There we chose simple statistical distances from the mean and recalled the areas of the tails. Here we select convenient tail areas (0.05, 0.01, and 0.001, either on one side or adding both together), and record the corresponding statistical distances.

As we saw in Chapter 9, it is not *exactly* true that hypothesis tests and confidence intervals are equivalent for proportions. For a confidence interval, we estimate the standard deviation of $\hat{p}$ from $\hat{p}$ itself, making it a *standard error*. For the corresponding hypothesis test, we use the model's *standard deviation* for $\hat{p}$ based on the null hypothesis value p_0. When $\hat{p}$ and p_0 are close, these calculations give similar results. When they differ, you're likely to reject H_0 (because the observed proportion is far from your hypothesized value). In that case, you're better off building your confidence interval with a standard error estimated from the data rather than rely on the model you just rejected. Happily, in all the other situations we will encounter, the equivalence between hypothesis tests and confidence intervals is indeed exactly true.

"Extraordinary claims require extraordinary proof."

—Carl Sagan

10.8 Confidence Intervals and Hypothesis Tests

Confidence intervals and hypothesis tests are built from the same calculations. They have the same assumptions and conditions. As we have just seen, you can approximate a hypothesis test by examining the confidence interval. Just ask whether the null hypothesis value is consistent with a confidence interval for the parameter at the corresponding confidence level. Because confidence intervals are naturally two-sided, they correspond to two-sided tests. For example, a 95% confidence interval corresponds to a two-sided hypothesis test at $\alpha = 5\%$. In general, a confidence interval with a confidence level of $C\%$ corresponds to a two-sided hypothesis test with an α level of $100 - C\%$.

The relationship between confidence intervals and one-sided hypothesis tests gives us a choice. For a one-sided test with $\alpha = 5\%$, you could construct a one-sided confidence level of 95%, leaving 5% in one tail.

A one-sided confidence interval leaves one side unbounded. For example, in the home field example, we wondered whether the home field gave the home team an *advantage*, so our test was naturally one-sided. A 95% one-sided confidence interval would be constructed from one side of the associated two-sided confidence interval:

$$0.5463 - 1.645 \times 0.0101 = 0.530$$

In order to leave 5% on one side, we used the z^* value 1.645 that leaves 5% in one tail. Writing the one-sided interval as $(0.530, \infty)$ allows us to say with 95% confidence that we know the home team will win, on average, at least 53.0% of the time. To test the hypothesis H_0: $p = 0.50$ we note that the value 0.50 is not in this interval. The lower bound of 0.53 is clearly above 0.50, showing the connection between hypothesis and confidence intervals.

For convenience, and to provide more information, however, we sometimes report a two-sided confidence interval even though we are interested in a one-sided test. For the home field example, we could report a 90% confidence interval:

$$0.5463 \pm 1.645 \times 0.0101 = (0.530, 0.563)$$

Notice that we *matched* the left end point by leaving α in *both* sides, which made the corresponding confidence level 90%. We can still see the correspondence that since the 95% (two-sided) confidence interval for $\hat{p}$ doesn't contain 0.50, we reject the null hypothesis, but it also tells us that the home team winning percentage is unlikely to be greater than 56.3%, an added benefit to understanding. You can see the relationship between the two confidence intervals in Figure 10.7.

There's another good reason for finding a confidence interval along with a hypothesis test. Although the test can tell us whether the observed statistic differs from the hypothesized value, it doesn't say by how much. Often, business decisions depend not only on whether there is a statistically significant difference, but also on whether the difference is meaningful. For the home field advantage, the corresponding confidence interval shows that over a full season, home field advantage adds an average of about two to six extra victories for a team. That could make a meaningful difference in both the team's standing and in the size of the crowd.

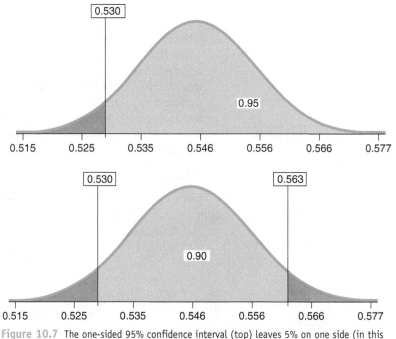

Figure 10.7 The one-sided 95% confidence interval (top) leaves 5% on one side (in this case the left), but leaves the other side unbounded. The 90% confidence interval is symmetric and matches the one-sided interval on the side of interest. Both intervals indicate that a one-sided test of $p = 0.50$ would be rejected at $\alpha = 0.05$ for any value of $\hat{p}$ greater than 0.530.

✓ JUST CHECKING

4 A bank is testing a new method for getting delinquent customers to pay their past-due credit card bills. The standard way was to send a letter (costing about $0.60 each) asking the customer to pay. That worked 30% of the time. The bank wants to test a new method that involves sending a DVD to the customer encouraging them to contact the bank and set up a payment plan. Developing and sending the DVD costs about $10.00 per customer. What is the parameter of interest? What are the null and alternative hypotheses?

5 The bank sets up an experiment to test the effectiveness of the DVD. The DVD is mailed to several randomly selected delinquent customers, and employees keep track of how many customers then contact the bank to arrange payments. The bank just got back the results on their test of the DVD strategy. A 90% confidence interval for the success rate is (0.29, 0.45). Their old send-a-letter method had worked 30% of the time. Can you reject the null hypothesis and conclude that the method increases the proportion at $\alpha = 0.05$? Explain.

6 Given the confidence interval the bank found in the trial of the DVD mailing, what would you recommend be done? Should the bank scrap the DVD strategy?

GUIDED EXAMPLE | Credit Card Promotion

A credit card company plans to offer a special incentive program to customers who charge at least $500 next month. The marketing department has pulled a sample of 500 customers from the same month last year and noted that the mean amount charged was $478.19 and the median amount was $216.48. The finance department says that the only relevant quantity is the proportion of customers who spend more than $500. If that proportion is less than 25%, the program will lose money.

Among the 500 customers, 148 or 29.6% of them charged $500 or more. Can we use a confidence interval to test whether the goal of 25% for all customers was met?

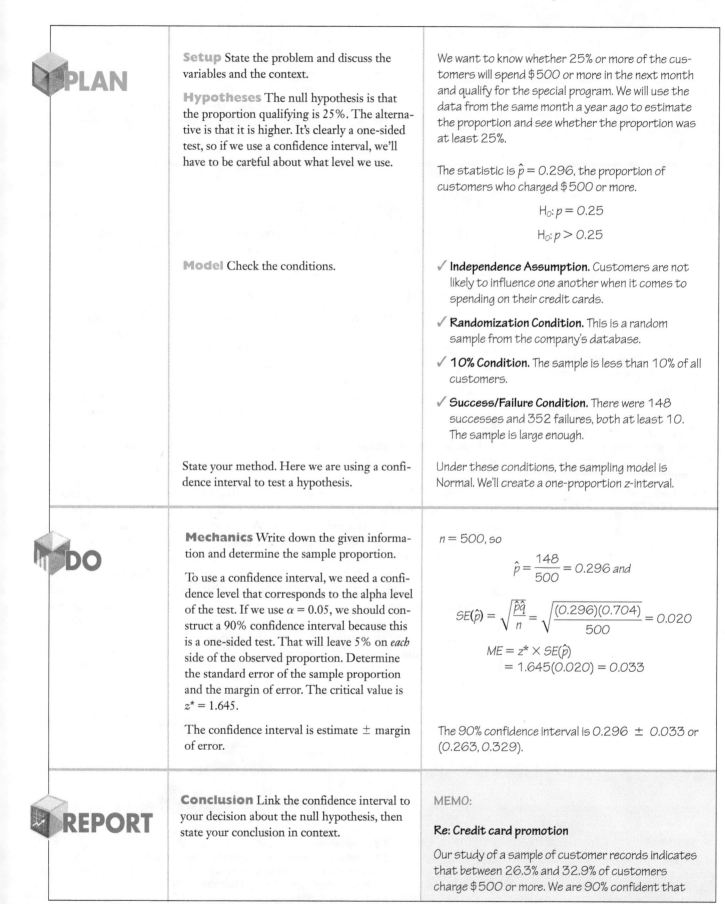

PLAN

Setup State the problem and discuss the variables and the context.

Hypotheses The null hypothesis is that the proportion qualifying is 25%. The alternative is that it is higher. It's clearly a one-sided test, so if we use a confidence interval, we'll have to be careful about what level we use.

We want to know whether 25% or more of the customers will spend $500 or more in the next month and qualify for the special program. We will use the data from the same month a year ago to estimate the proportion and see whether the proportion was at least 25%.

The statistic is $\hat{p} = 0.296$, the proportion of customers who charged $500 or more.

$$H_0: p = 0.25$$
$$H_0: p > 0.25$$

Model Check the conditions.

✓ **Independence Assumption.** Customers are not likely to influence one another when it comes to spending on their credit cards.

✓ **Randomization Condition.** This is a random sample from the company's database.

✓ **10% Condition.** The sample is less than 10% of all customers.

✓ **Success/Failure Condition.** There were 148 successes and 352 failures, both at least 10. The sample is large enough.

State your method. Here we are using a confidence interval to test a hypothesis.

Under these conditions, the sampling model is Normal. We'll create a one-proportion z-interval.

DO

Mechanics Write down the given information and determine the sample proportion.

To use a confidence interval, we need a confidence level that corresponds to the alpha level of the test. If we use $\alpha = 0.05$, we should construct a 90% confidence interval because this is a one-sided test. That will leave 5% on *each* side of the observed proportion. Determine the standard error of the sample proportion and the margin of error. The critical value is $z^* = 1.645$.

The confidence interval is estimate ± margin of error.

$n = 500$, so

$$\hat{p} = \frac{148}{500} = 0.296 \text{ and}$$

$$SE(\hat{p}) = \sqrt{\frac{\hat{p}\hat{q}}{n}} = \sqrt{\frac{(0.296)(0.704)}{500}} = 0.020$$

$$ME = z^* \times SE(\hat{p})$$
$$= 1.645(0.020) = 0.033$$

The 90% confidence interval is 0.296 ± 0.033 or $(0.263, 0.329)$.

REPORT

Conclusion Link the confidence interval to your decision about the null hypothesis, then state your conclusion in context.

MEMO:

Re: Credit card promotion

Our study of a sample of customer records indicates that between 26.3% and 32.9% of customers charge $500 or more. We are 90% confident that this interval includes the true value. Because the minimum suitable value of 25% is below this interval, we conclude that it is not a plausible value, and so we reject the null hypothesis that only 25% of the customers charge more than $500 a month. The goal appears to have been met assuming that the month we studied is typical.

10.9   Two Types of Errors

Nobody's perfect. Even with lots of evidence, we can still make the wrong decision. In fact, when we perform a hypothesis test, we can make mistakes in *two* ways:

I. The null hypothesis is true, but we mistakenly reject it.

II. The null hypothesis is false, but we fail to reject it.

These two types of errors are known as **Type I** and **Type II errors** respectively. On behalf of all statisticians, we apologize that the names are not more imaginative or memorable. One way to keep the names straight is to remember that we start by assuming the null hypothesis is true, so a Type I error is the first kind of error we could make.

In medical disease testing, the null hypothesis is usually the assumption that a person is healthy. The alternative is that he or she has the disease we're testing for. So a Type I error is a *false positive*—a healthy person is diagnosed with the disease. A Type II error, in which an infected person is diagnosed as disease free, is a *false negative*. These errors have other names, depending on the particular discipline and context.

Which type of error is more serious depends on the situation. In a jury trial, a Type I error occurs if the jury convicts an innocent person. A Type II error occurs if the jury fails to convict a guilty person. Which seems more serious? In medical diagnosis, a false negative could mean that a sick patient goes untreated. A false positive might mean that the person must undergo further tests.

In business planning, a false positive result could mean that money will be invested in a project that turns out not to be profitable. A false negative result might mean that money won't be invested in a project that would have been profitable. Which error is worse, the lost investment or the lost opportunity? The answer always depends on the situation, the cost, and your point of view.

Here's an illustration of the situations:

> In an ideal world you wouldn't make any errors. Unfortunately, when the chance of one type of error is very small, the other is very large. Never convicting an innocent person (a Type I error) means acquitting some guilty people. Conversely, never acquitting a guilty person, means accidentally convicting some innocent people. So, some errors will be made.

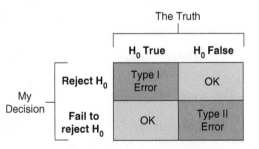

Figure 10.8 The two types of errors occur on the diagonal where the truth and decision don't match. Remember that we start by assuming H_0 to be true, so an error made (rejecting it) when H_0 is true is called a Type I error. A Type II error is made when H_0 is false (and we fail to reject it).

The null hypothesis specifies a single value for the parameter. So it's easy to calculate the probability of a Type I error. But the alternative gives a whole range of possible values, and we may want to find a β for several of them.

We have seen ways to find a sample size by specifying the margin of error. Choosing the sample size to achieve a specified β (for a particular alternative value) is sometimes more appropriate, but the calculation is more complex and lies beyond the scope of this book.

How often will a Type I error occur? It happens when the null hypothesis is true but we've had the bad luck to draw an unusual sample. To reject H_0, the P-value must fall below α. When H_0 is true, that happens *exactly* with probability α. So when you choose level α, you're setting the probability of a Type I error to α.

What if H_0 is not true? Then we can't possibly make a Type I error. You can't get a false positive from a sick person. A Type I error can happen only when H_0 is true.

When H_0 is false and we reject it, we have done the right thing. A test's ability to detect a false hypothesis is called the **power** of the test. In a jury trial, power is a measure of the ability of the criminal justice system to convict people who are guilty. We'll have a lot more to say about power soon.

When H_0 is false but we fail to reject it, we have made a Type II error. We assign the letter β to the probability of this mistake. What's the value of β? That's harder to assess than α because we don't know what the value of the parameter really is. When H_0 is true, it specifies a single parameter value. But when H_0 is false, we don't have a specific one; we have many possible values. We can compute the probability β for any parameter value in H_A, but the choice of which one to pick is not always clear.

One way to focus our attention is by thinking about the *effect size*. That is, ask: "How big a difference would matter?" Suppose a charity wants to test whether placing personalized address labels in the envelope along with a request for a donation increases the response rate above the baseline of 5%. If the minimum response that would pay for the address labels is 6%, they would calculate β for the alternative $p = 0.06$.

Of course, we could reduce β for *all* alternative parameter values by increasing α. By making it easier to reject the null, we'd be more likely to reject it whether it's true or not. The only way to reduce *both* types of error is to collect more evidence or, in statistical terms, to collect more data. Otherwise, we just wind up trading off one kind of error against the other. Whenever you design a survey or experiment, it's a good idea to calculate β (for a reasonable α level). Use a parameter value in the alternative that corresponds to an effect size that you want to be able to detect. Too often, studies fail because their sample sizes are too small to detect the change they are looking for.

✔ **JUST CHECKING**

7 Remember our bank that's sending out DVDs to try to get customers to make payments on delinquent loans? It is looking for evidence that the costlier DVD strategy produces a higher success rate than the letters it has been sending. Explain what a Type I error is in this context and what the consequences would be to the bank.

8 What's a Type II error in the bank experiment context and what would the consequences be?

9 If the DVD strategy *really* works well—actually getting 60% of the people to pay off their balances—would the power of the test be higher or lower compared to a 32% payoff rate? Explain briefly.

*10.10 Power

Remember, we can never prove a null hypothesis true. We can only fail to reject it. But when we fail to reject a null hypothesis, it's natural to wonder whether we looked hard enough. Might the null hypothesis actually be false and our test too weak to tell?

When the null hypothesis actually *is* false, we hope our test is strong enough to reject it. We'd like to know how likely we are to succeed. The power of the test gives us a way to think about that. The power of a test is the probability that it

Power can be thought of as magnification, as with a microscope or telescope. The greater the magnification, the more powerful the instrument is at being able to detect things that are very small or very far away. Perhaps you've heard the expression, "It's as difficult as looking for a needle in a haystack." That's difficult because the needle is very small and the haystack is very large. The combination is the effect size. With a very small effect size like this, the power to find the needle will be low. To increase the power you will need to spend more time looking. If you are looking for an elephant in a haystack you will have much higher power because the effect size will be much larger, and you won't need to look long. How long you look is like how much data you have.

correctly rejects a false null hypothesis. When the power is high, we can be confident that we've looked hard enough. We know that β is the probability that a test *fails* to reject a false null hypothesis, so the power of the test is the complement, $1 - \beta$. We might have just written $1 - \beta$, but power is such an important concept that it gets its own name.

Whenever a study fails to reject its null hypothesis, the test's power comes into question. Was the sample size big enough to detect an effect had there been one? Might we have missed an effect large enough to be interesting just because we failed to gather sufficient data or because there was too much variability in the data we could gather? Might the problem be that the experiment simply lacked adequate power to detect their ability?

When we calculate power, we imagine that the null hypothesis is false. The value of the power depends on how far the truth lies from the null hypothesis value. We call the distance between the null hypothesis value, p_0, and the truth, p, the **effect size**. The power depends directly on the effect size. It's easier to see larger effects, so the further p_0 is from p, the greater the power.

How can we decide what power we need? Choice of power is more a financial or scientific decision than a statistical one because to calculate the power, we need to specify the "true" parameter value we're interested in. In other words, power is calculated for a particular effect size, and it changes depending on the size of the effect we want to detect.

Graph It!

It makes intuitive sense that the larger the effect size, the easier it should be to see it. Obtaining a larger sample size decreases the probability of a Type II error, so it increases the power. It also makes sense that the more we're willing to accept a Type I error, the less likely we will be to make a Type II error.

Figure 10.9 may help you visualize the relationships among these concepts. Suppose we are testing $H_0: p = p_0$ against the alternative $H_A: p > p_0$. We'll reject

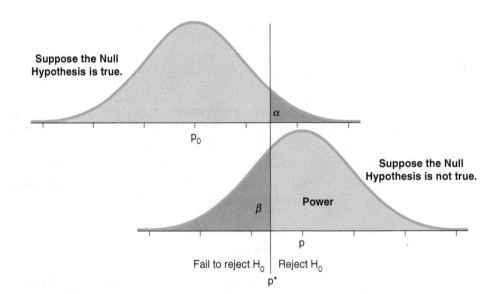

Figure 10.9 The power of a test is the probability that it rejects a false null hypothesis. The upper figure shows the null hypothesis model. We'd reject the null in a one-sided test if we observed a value in the red region to the right of the critical value, p*. The lower figure shows the true model. If the true value of p is greater than p_0, then we're more likely to observe a value that exceeds the critical value and make the correct decision to reject the null hypothesis. The power of the test is the green region on the right of the lower figure. Of course, even drawing samples whose observed proportions are distributed around p, we'll sometimes get a value in the red region on the left and make a Type II error of failing to reject the null.

the null if the observed proportion, $\hat{p}$ is big enough. By *big enough*, we mean $\hat{p} > p^*$ for some critical value p^* (shown as the red region in the right tail of the upper curve). The upper model shows a picture of the sampling distribution model for the proportion when the null hypothesis is true. If the null were true, then this would be a picture of that truth. We'd make a Type I error whenever the sample gave us $\hat{p} > p^*$ because we would reject the (true) null hypothesis. Unusual samples like that would happen only with probability α.

In reality, though, the null hypothesis is rarely *exactly* true. The lower probability model supposes that H_0 is not true. In particular, it supposes that the true value is p, not p_0. It shows a distribution of possible observed $\hat{p}$ values around this true value. Because of sampling variability, sometimes $\hat{p} < p^*$ and we fail to reject the (false) null hypothesis. Then we'd make a Type II error. The area under the curve to the left of p^* in the bottom model represents how often this happens. The probability is β. In this picture, β is less than half, so most of the time we *do* make the right decision. The *power* of the test—the probability that we make the right decision—is shown as the region to the right of p^*. It's $1 - \beta$.

We calculate p^* based on the upper model because p^* depends only on the null model and the alpha level. No matter what the true proportion turns out to be, p^* doesn't change. After all, we don't *know* the truth, so we can't use it to determine the critical value. But we always reject H_0 when $\hat{p} > p^*$.

How often we reject H_0 when it's *false* depends on the effect size. We can see from the picture that if the true proportion were further from the hypothesized value, the bottom curve would shift to the right, making the power greater.

We can see several important relationships from this figure:

◆ Power = $1 - \beta$.

◆ Moving the critical value, p^*, to the right, reduces α, the probability of a Type I error, but increases β, the probability of a Type II error. It correspondingly reduces the power.

◆ The larger the true effect size, the real difference between the hypothesized value, p_0, and the true population value, p, the smaller the chance of making a Type II error and the greater the power of the test.

If the two proportions are very far apart, the two models will barely overlap, and we would not be likely to make any Type II errors at all—but then, we are unlikely to really need a formal hypothesis testing procedure to see such an obvious difference.

Reducing Both Type I and Type II Errors

Figure 10.9 seems to show that if we reduce Type I error, we automatically must increase Type II error. But there is a way to reduce both. Can you think of it?

If we can make both curves narrower, as shown in Figure 10.10, then the probability of both Type I errors and Type II errors will decrease, and the power of the test will increase.

How can we do that? The only way is to reduce the standard deviations by increasing the sample size. (Remember, these are pictures of sampling distribution models, not of data.) Increasing the sample size works regardless of the true population parameters. But recall the curse of diminishing returns. The standard deviation of the sampling distribution model decreases only as the *square root* of the sample size, so to halve the standard deviations, we must *quadruple* the sample size.

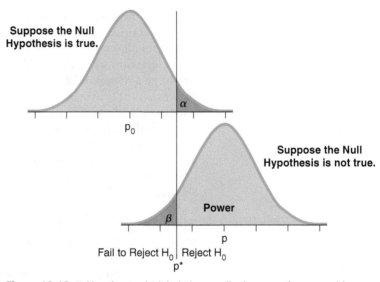

Figure 10.10 Making the standard deviations smaller increases the power without changing the alpha level or the corresponding *z*-critical value. The means are just as far apart as in Figure 10.9, but the error rates are reduced.

WHAT CAN GO WRONG?

- **Don't base your null hypotheses on what you see in the data.** You are not allowed to look at the data first and then adjust your null hypothesis so that it will be rejected. If your sample value turns out to be $\hat{p} = 51.8\%$ with a standard deviation of 1%, don't form a null hypothesis like $H_0: p = 49.8\%$, knowing that will enable you to reject it. Your null hypothesis describes the "nothing interesting" or "nothing has changed" scenario and should not be based on the data you collect.

- **Don't base your alternative hypothesis on the data either.** You should always think about the situation you are investigating and base your alternative hypothesis on that. Are you interested only in knowing whether something has *increased*? Then write a one-tail (upper tail) alternative. Or would you be equally interested in a change in either direction? Then you want a two-tailed alternative. You should decide whether to do a one- or two-tailed test based on what results would be of interest to you, not on what you might see in the data.

- **Don't make your null hypothesis what you want to show to be true.** Remember, the null hypothesis is the status quo, the nothing-is-strange-here position a skeptic would take. You wonder whether the data cast doubt on that. You can reject the null hypothesis, but you can never "accept" or "prove" the null.

- **Don't forget to check the conditions.** The reasoning of inference depends on randomization. No amount of care in calculating a test result can save you from a biased sample. The probabilities you compute depend on the independence assumption. And your sample must be large enough to justify your use of a Normal model.

- **Don't believe too strongly in arbitrary alpha levels.** There's not really much difference between a P-value of 0.051 and a P-value of 0.049, but sometimes it's regarded as the difference between night (having to retain H_0) and day (being able to shout to the world that your results are "statistically significant"). It may just be better to report the P-value and a confidence interval and let the world (perhaps your manager or client) decide along with you.

- **Don't interpret the P-value as the probability that the null hypothesis is correct.** It isn't. It is the probability that the data could have occurred if the null hypothesis really were true.

- **Don't confuse practical and statistical significance.** A large sample size can make it easy to discern even a trivial change from a null hypothesis value. In other words, a trivial change can still be statistically significant. But after finding statistical significance you need to determine whether the change is important. Does it matter in real life? That's practical significance. Without sufficient power a difference that would be important might be missed (i.e., would not be statistically significant).

- **Don't forget that in spite of all your care, you might make a wrong decision.** No one can ever reduce the probability of a Type I error (α) or of a Type II error (β) to zero (but increasing the sample size helps).

ETHICS IN ACTION

Many retailers have recognized the importance of staying connected to their in-store customers via the internet. Retailers not only use the internet to inform their customers about specials and promotions, but also to send them ecoupons redeemable for discounts. Shellie Cooper, longtime owner of a small organic food store, specializes in locally produced organic foods and products. Over the years Shellie's customer base has been quite stable, consisting mainly of health-conscious individuals who tend not to be very price sensitive, opting to pay higher prices for better-quality local, organic products. However, faced with increasing competition from grocery chains offering more organic choices, Shellie is now thinking of offering coupons. She needs to decide between the newspaper and the internet. She recently read that the percentage of consumers who use printable internet coupons is on the rise but, at 15%, is much less than the 40% who clip and redeem newspaper coupons. Nonetheless, she's interested in learning more about the internet and sets up a meeting with Jack Kasor, a web consultant. She discovers that for an initial investment and continuing monthly fee, Jack would design Shellie's website, host it on his server, and broadcast ecoupons to her customers at regular intervals. While she was concerned about the difference in redemption rates for ecoupons vs. newspaper coupons, Jack assured her that ecoupon redemptions are continuing to rise and that she should expect between 15% and 40% of her customers to redeem them. Shellie agreed to give it a try. After the first six months, Jack informed Shellie that the proportion of her customers who redeemed ecoupons was significantly greater than 15%. He determined this by selecting several broadcasts at random and found the number redeemed (483) out of the total number sent (3000). Shellie thought that this was positive and made up her mind to continue the use of ecoupons.

ETHICAL ISSUE *Statistical vs. practical significance. While it is true that the percentage of Shellie's customers redeeming ecoupons is significantly greater than 15% statistically, in fact, the percentage is just over 16%. This difference amounts to about 33 customers more than 15%, which may not be of practical significance to Shellie (related to ASA Ethical Guidelines, Item A, which can be found at http://www.amstat .org/about/ethicalguidelines.cfm). Mentioning a range of 15% to 40% may mislead Shellie into expecting a value somewhere in the middle.*

ETHICAL SOLUTION *Jack should report the difference between the observed value and the hypothesized value to Shellie, especially since there are costs associated with continuing ecoupons. Perhaps he should recommend that she reconsider using the newspaper.*

WHAT HAVE WE LEARNED?

We've learned to use what we see in a random sample to test a particular hypothesis about the world. This is our second step in statistical inference, complementing our use of confidence intervals.

We've learned that testing a hypothesis involves proposing a model and then seeing whether the data we observe are consistent with that model or so unusual that we must reject it. We do this by finding a P-value—the probability that data like ours could have occurred if the model is correct. If the data are out of line with the null hypothesis model, the P-value will be small, and we will reject the null hypothesis. If the data are consistent with the null hypothesis model, the P-value will be large, and we will not reject the null hypothesis.

We've learned that:

- We start with a *null hypothesis* specifying the parameter of a model we'll test using our data.

- Our *alternative hypothesis* can be one- or two-sided, depending on what we want to learn.

- We must check the appropriate *assumptions* and *conditions* before proceeding with our test.

- The *significance level* of the test establishes the level of proof we'll require. That determines the critical value of z that will lead us to reject the null hypothesis.

- *Hypothesis tests* and *confidence intervals* are really two ways of looking at the same question. The hypothesis test gives us the answer to a decision about a parameter; the confidence interval tells us the plausible values of that parameter.

- If the null hypothesis is really true and we reject it, that's a *Type I error*; the alpha level of the test is the probability that this happens.

- If the null hypothesis is really false but we fail to reject it, that's a *Type II error*.

*Optional Sections

- The *power* of the test is the probability that we reject the null hypothesis when it's false. The larger the size of the effect we're testing for, the greater the power of the test in detecting it.

- Tests with a greater likelihood of Type I error have more power and less chance of a Type II error. We can increase power while reducing the chances of both kinds of error by increasing the sample size.

Terms

Alpha level
The threshold P-value that determines when we reject a null hypothesis. Using an alpha level of α, if we observe a statistic whose P-value based on the null hypothesis is less than α, we reject that null hypothesis.

Alternative hypothesis
The hypothesis that proposes what we should conclude if we find the null hypothesis to be unlikely.

Critical value
The value in the sampling distribution model of the statistic whose P-value is equal to the alpha level. Any statistic value further from the null hypothesis value than the critical value will have a smaller P-value than α and will lead to rejecting the null hypothesis. The critical value is often denoted with an asterisk, as z^*, for example.

Effect size The difference between the null hypothesis value and the true value of a model parameter.

Null hypothesis The claim being assessed in a hypothesis test. Usually, the null hypothesis is a statement of "no change from the traditional value," "no effect," "no difference," or "no relationship." For a claim to be a testable null hypothesis, it must specify a value for some population parameter that can form the basis for assuming a sampling distribution for a test statistic.

One-proportion z-test A test of the null hypothesis that the proportion of a single sample equals a specified value

$(H_0: p = p_0)$ by comparing the statistic $z = \dfrac{\hat{p} - p_0}{SD(\hat{p})}$ to a standard Normal model.

One-sided alternative An alternative hypothesis is one-sided (e.g., $H_A: p > p_0$ or $H_A: p < p_0$) when we are interested in deviations in *only one* direction away from the hypothesized parameter value.

P-value The probability of observing a value for a test statistic at least as far from the hypothesized value as the statistic value actually observed if the null hypothesis is true. A small P-value indicates that the observation obtained is improbable given the null hypothesis and thus provides evidence against the null hypothesis.

Power The probability that a hypothesis test will correctly reject a false null hypothesis. To find the power of a test, we must specify a particular alternative parameter value as the "true" value. For any specific value in the alternative, the power is $1 - \beta$.

Significance level Another term for the alpha level, used most often in a phrase such as "at the 5% significance level."

Two-sided alternative An alternative hypothesis is two-sided $(H_A: p \neq p_0)$ when we are interested in deviations in *either* direction away from the hypothesized parameter value.

Type I error The error of rejecting a null hypothesis when in fact it is true (also called a "false positive"). The probability of a Type I error is α.

Type II error The error of failing to reject a null hypothesis when in fact it is false (also called a "false negative"). The probability of a Type II error is commonly denoted β and depends on the effect size.

Skills

PLAN

- Be able to state the null and alternative hypotheses for a one-proportion z-test.
- Know how to think about the assumptions and their associated conditions. Examine your data for violations of those conditions.
- Be able to identify and use the alternative hypothesis when testing hypotheses. Understand how to choose between a one-sided and two-sided alternative hypothesis and be able to explain your choice.

DO

- Know how to perform a one-proportion z-test.
- Be able to interpret the results of a one-proportion z-test.

REPORT

- Be able to interpret the meaning of a P-value in nontechnical language, making clear that the probability claim is about computed values under the assumption that the null model is true and not about the population parameter of interest.

TECHNOLOGY HELP

Hypothesis tests for proportions are so easy and natural that many statistics packages don't offer special commands for them. Most statistics programs want to know the "success" and "failure" status for each case. Usually these are given as 1 or 0, but they might be category names like "yes" and "no." Often we just know the proportion of successes, $\hat{p}$, and the total count, n. Computer packages don't usually deal naturally with summary data like this.

In some programs you can reconstruct the original values. But even when you have reconstructed (or can reconstruct) the raw data values, often you won't get *exactly* the same test statistic from a computer package as you would find working by hand. The reason is that when the packages treat the proportion as a mean, they make some approximations. The result is very close, but not exactly the same. If you use a computer package, you may notice slight discrepancies between your answers and the answers in the back of the book, but they're not important.

Reports about hypothesis tests generated by technologies don't follow a standard form. Most will name the test and provide the test statistic value, its standard deviation, and the P-value. But these elements may not be labelled clearly. For example, the expression "Prob > |z|" means the probability (the "Prob") of observing a test statistic whose magnitude (the absolute value tells

us this) is larger than that of the one (the "z") found in the data (which, because it is written as "z," we know follows a Normal model). That is a fancy (and not very clear) way of saying P-value. In some packages, you can specify that the test be one-sided. Others might report three P-values, covering the ground for both one-sided tests and two-sided tests.

Sometimes a confidence interval and hypothesis test are automatically given together. The confidence interval ought to be for the corresponding confidence level: $1 - \alpha$.

Often, the standard deviation of the statistic is called the "standard error," and usually that's appropriate because we've had to estimate its value from the data. That's not the case for proportions, however: we get the standard deviation for a proportion from the null hypothesis value. Nevertheless, you may see the standard deviation called a "standard error" even for tests with proportions.

It's common for statistics packages and calculators to report more digits of "precision" than could possibly have been found from the data. You can safely ignore them. Round values such as the standard deviation to one digit more than the number of digits reported in your data.

Here are the kind of results you might see in typical computer output.

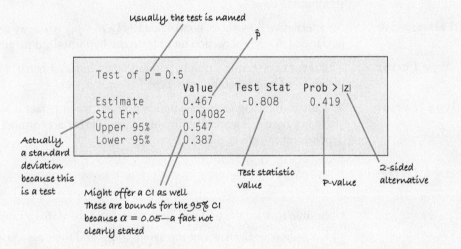

EXCEL

Inference methods for proportions are not part of the standard Excel tool set.

MINI CASE STUDY PROJECTS

Left; Jordache/Shutterstock,
Right; Jag_cz/Shutterstock

Metal Production

Ingots are huge pieces of metal, often weighing in excess of 10 000 kilograms, made in a giant mold. They must be cast in one large piece for use in fabricating large structural parts for cars and planes. If they crack while being made, the crack may propagate into the zone required for the part, compromising its integrity. Airplane manufacturers insist that metal for their planes be defect-free, so the ingot must be made over if any cracking is detected.

Even though the metal from the cracked ingot is recycled, the scrap cost runs into the tens of thousands of dollars. Metal manufacturers would like to avoid cracking if at all possible. But the casting process is complicated, and not everything can be controlled completely. In one plant, only about 75% of the ingots have been free of cracks. In an attempt to reduce the cracking proportion, the plant engineers and chemists recently (January 2006) made changes to the casting process. The data from 5000 ingots produced since the changes are found in the file **ch10_MCSP_Ingots.xls**. The variable *Crack* indicates whether a crack was found (1) or not (0). Select a random sample of 100 ingots and test the claim that the cracking rate has decreased from 25%. Find a confidence interval for the cracking rate as well. Now select a random sample of 1000 ingots and test the claim and find the confidence interval again. Compare the two tests and intervals and prepare a short report about your findings including the differences (if any) that you see from the two samples.

Loyalty Program

A marketing manager has sent out 10 000 mail pieces to a random sample of customers to test a new web-based loyalty program. The customers either received nothing (No Offer), a free companion airline ticket (Free Flight), or free flight insurance on their next flight (Free Insurance). The person in charge of selecting the 10 000 customers has assured the marketing manager that the sample is representative of the various marketing segments in the customer base. However, the manager is worried that the offer was not sent out to enough customers in the *Travel* segment, which represents 25% of the entire customer base (variable *Spending.Segment*). In addition, he is worried that fewer than 1/3 of customers in that segment actually received no offer. Using the data found in **ch10_MCSP_Loyalty_Program.xls**, write a short report to the manager testing the appropriate hypotheses and summarizing your findings. Include in your report a 95% confidence interval for the proportion of customers who responded to the offer by signing up for the loyalty program. (The variable *Response* indicates a 1 for responders and 0 for non-responders.)

EXERCISES

1. Hypotheses. Write the null and alternative hypotheses to test each of the following situations. **LO❶**

a) An online clothing company is concerned about the timeliness of the delivery of their products. The VP of Operations and Marketing recently stated that she wanted the percentage of products delivered on time to be at least 90%, and she wants to know if the company has succeeded.

b) A realty company recently announced that the proportion of houses taking more than three months to sell is now greater than 50%.

c) A financial firm's accounting reports have an error rate below 2%.

2. More hypotheses. Write the null and alternative hypotheses to test each of the following situations. **LO❶**

a) A business magazine article reports that, in 1990, 35% of CEOs had an MBA degree. Has the percentage changed?

b) Recently, 20% of cars of a certain model have needed costly transmission work after being driven between 80 000 and 160 000 kilometres. The car manufacturer hopes that the redesign of a transmission component has solved this problem.

c) A market researcher for a beverage company decides to field test a new flavour soft drink, planning to market it only if he is sure that over 60% of the people like the flavour.

3. Deliveries. The clothing company in Exercise 1a looks at a sample of delivery reports. They test the hypothesis that 90% of the deliveries are on time against the alternative that greater than 90% are on time and find a P-value of 0.22. Which of these conclusions is appropriate? **LO❷**

a) There's a 22% chance that 90% of the deliveries are on time.

b) There's a 78% chance than 90% of the deliveries are on time.

c) There's a 22% chance that the sample they drew shows the correct percentage of on-time deliveries.

d) There's a 22% chance that natural sampling variation could produce a sample with an observed proportion of on-time deliveries such as the one they obtained if, in fact, 90% of deliveries are on time.

4. House sales. The realty company in Exercise 1b looks at a recent sample of houses that have sold. On testing the null hypothesis that 50% of the houses take more than three months to sell against the hypothesis that more than 50% of the houses take more than three months to sell, they find a P-value of 0.034. Which of these conclusions is appropriate? **LO❷**

a) There's a 3.4% chance that 50% of the houses take more than three months to sell.

b) If 50% of the houses take more than three months to sell, there's a 3.4% chance that a random sample would produce a sample proportion as high as the one they obtained.

c) There's a 3.4% chance that the null hypothesis is correct.

d) There's a 96.6% chance that 50% of the houses take more than three months to sell.

5. P-value. Have harsher penalties and ad campaigns increased seat belt use among drivers and passengers? Observations of commuter traffic have failed to find evidence of a significant change compared with three years ago. Explain what the study's P-value of 0.17 means in this context. **LO❷**

6. Another P-value. A company developing scanners to search for hidden weapons at airports has concluded that a new device is significantly better than the current scanner. The company made this decision based on a P-value of 0.03. Explain the meaning of the P-value in this context. **LO❷**

7. Ad campaign. An information technology analyst believes that they are losing customers on their website who find the checkout and purchase system too complicated. She adds a one-click feature to the website to make it easier, but finds that only about 10% of the customers are using it. She decides to launch an ad awareness campaign to tell customers about the new feature in the hope of increasing the percentage. She doesn't see much of a difference, so she hires a consultant to help her. The consultant selects a random sample of recent purchases, tests the hypothesis that the ads produced no change against the alternative that the percent who use the one-click feature is now greater than 10%, and finds a P-value of 0.22. Which conclusion is appropriate? Explain. **LO❷**

a) There's a 22% chance that the ads worked.

b) There's a 78% chance that the ads worked.

c) There's a 22% chance that the null hypothesis is true.

d) There's a 22% chance that natural sampling variation could produce poll results like these if the use of the one-click feature has increased.

e) There's a 22% chance that natural sampling variation could produce poll results like these if there's really no change in website use.

8. Mutual funds. A mutual fund manager claims that at least 70% of the stocks she selects will increase in price over the next year. We examined a sample of 200 of her selections over the past three years. Our P-value turns out to be 0.03. Test an appropriate hypothesis. Which conclusion is appropriate? Explain. **LO❷**

a) There's a 3% chance that the fund manager is correct.

b) There's a 97% chance that the fund manager is correct.

c) There's a 3% chance that a random sample could produce the results we observed, so it's reasonable to conclude that the fund manager is correct.

d) There's a 3% chance that a random sample could produce the results we observed if $p = 0.7$, so it's reasonable to conclude that the fund manager is not correct.

e) There's a 3% chance that the null hypothesis is correct.

9. Product effectiveness. A pharmaceutical company's old antacid formula provided relief for 70% of the people who used it. The company tests a new formula to see if it is better and gets a P-value of 0.27. Is it reasonable to conclude that the new formula and the old one are equally effective? Explain **LO❷**

10. Car sales. A German automobile company is counting on selling more cars to the younger market segment—drivers under the age of 20. The company's market researchers survey to investigate whether or not the proportion of today's Grade 12 students who own their own cars is higher than it was a decade ago. They find a P-value of 0.017. Is it reasonable to conclude that more Grade 12 students have cars? Explain. **LO❷**

11. False claims? A candy company claims that in a large bag of holiday M&M's® half the candies are red and half the candies are green. You pick candies at random from a bag and discover that of the first 20 you eat, 12 are red. **LO❷**

a) If it were true that half are red and half are green, what is the probability you would have found that at least 12 out of 20 were red?

b) Do you think that half of the M&M's® candies in the bag are really red? Explain.

12. Scratch off. A retail company offers a "scratch off" promotion. Upon entering the store, you are given a card. When you pay, you may scratch off the coating. The company advertises that half the cards are winners and have immediate cash-back savings of $5 (the others offer $1 off any future purchase of coffee in the cafe). You aren't sure the percentage is really 50% winners. **LO❷**

a) The first time you shop there, you get the coffee coupon. You try again and again get the coffee coupon. Do two failures in a row convince you that the true fraction of winners isn't 50%? Explain.

b) You try a third time. You get coffee again! What's the probability of not getting a cash savings three times in a row if half the cards really do offer cash savings?

c) Would three losses in a row convince you that the store is cheating?

d) How many times in a row would you have to get the coffee coupon instead of cash savings to be pretty sure that the company isn't living up to its advertised percentage of winners? Justify your answer by calculating a probability and explaining what it means.

13. Financial literacy. In July 2011, Harris/Decima research carried out an online survey for the Canadian Institute of Chartered Accountants. A total of 1209 respondents aged 16–22 were asked how confident they were in managing their money well overall; 41% said very confident and 47% said only somewhat confident. The remaining 12% were not very or not at all confident. **LO❸**

a) Estimate the percentage of all Canadian youth aged 16–22 who feel very or somewhat confident in managing their money well overall. Use a 98% confidence interval. Don't forget to check the conditions first.

b) Suppose we wished to conduct a hypothesis test to see if the percentage who are very or somewhat confident is less than 90%. What does your confidence interval indicate? Explain.

c) What is the significance level of this test? Explain.

14. Stocks. A young investor in the stock market is concerned that investing in the stock market is actually gambling, since the chance of the stock market going up on any given day is 50%. She decides to track her favourite stock for 250 days and finds that on 140 days the stock was "up." **LO❸**

a) Find a 95% confidence interval for the proportion of days the stock is "up." Don't forget to check the conditions first.

b) Does your confidence interval provide any evidence that the market is not random? Explain.

c) What is the significance level of this test? Explain.

15. Economic confidence. In 2013, Angus Reid Public Opinion studied opinions of adults about economic conditions. A poll conducted from April 18 to April 28, 2013, among 1001 Canadians showed that 55% rate the economic conditions in Canada as "very good " or "good." A journalist would like to state that the majority of Canadians have this opinion. Does the poll support this claim? **LO❸**

a) Test the appropriate hypothesis. Find a 95% confidence interval for the true proportion of Canadian adults who rated the economy as Very Good/Good. Check conditions.

b) Does your confidence interval provide evidence to support the claim?

c) What is the significance level of the test in part b? Explain.

16. Physical fitness. According to the 2005 Canadian Community Health Survey (CCHS), 38% of Canadians aged 18 to 24 were active (energy expenditure of three or more kilocalories per kilogram of body weight per day; e.g., walking an hour a day or jogging 20 minutes a day) in their self-reported leisure-time pursuits. However, a survey of 614 undergraduate business students at a large Canadian university found that only 26% spent at least an hour a day in physical activity. Assume that the CCHS definition of physical activity is equivalent to an hour a day. Are business students as physically active as the general Canadian population of the same age? **LO❸**

a) Test the appropriate hypothesis. Find a 95% confidence interval for the true proportion of undergraduate business students who are active at least one hour a day. Check conditions.

b) Does your confidence interval provide evidence to support the claim?

c) What is the significance level of the test in part b? Explain.

17. Convenient alpha. An enthusiastic junior executive has run a test of his new marketing program. He reports that it resulted in a "significant" increase in sales. A footnote on his report explains that he used an alpha level of 7.2% for his test. Presumably, he performed a hypothesis test against the null hypothesis of no change in sales. **LO❹**

a) If instead he had used an alpha level of 5%, is it more or less likely that he would have rejected his null hypothesis? Explain.

b) If he chose the alpha level 7.2% so that he could claim statistical significance, explain why this is not an ethical use of statistics.

18. Safety. The manufacturer of a new sleeping pill suspects that it may increase the risk of sleepwalking (or *somnambulism*, to use the technical term), which could be dangerous. A test of the drug fails to reject the null hypothesis of no increased sleepwalking when tested at alpha = 0.01. **LO④**

a) If the test had been performed at alpha = 0.05 would the test have been more or less likely to reject the null hypothesis of no increase in sleepwalking?

b) Which alpha level do you think the company should use? Why?

19. Product testing. Home espresso machines have gained wide popularity across Canada. They vary widely in their ease of use, and many people have trouble learning how to operate them. One leading company has developed what it hopes will be easier instructions. The goal is to have at least 96% of customers succeed at being able to make the perfect espresso. The company tests the new system on 200 people, 188 of whom were successful. Is this strong evidence that the new system fails to meet the company's goal? A student's test of this hypothesis is shown here. How many mistakes can you find? **LO⑤**

$$H_0 : \hat{p} = 0.96$$

$$H_A : \hat{p} \neq 0.96$$

$$SRS, \ 0.96(200) > 10$$

$$\frac{188}{200} = 0.94; \ SD(\hat{p}) = \sqrt{\frac{(0.94)(0.06)}{200}} = 0.017$$

$$z = \frac{0.96 - 0.94}{0.017} = 1.18$$

$$P = P(z > 1.18) = 0.12$$

There is strong evidence that the new system does not work.

20. Marketing. A nutrition newsletter reported that 90% of adults drink milk. A regional farmers organization planning a new marketing campaign across its multicounty area polls a random sample of 750 adults living there. In this sample, 657 people said that they drink milk. Do these responses provide strong evidence that the 90% figure is not accurate for this region? Correct the mistakes you find in the following student's attempt to test an appropriate hypothesis. **LO⑤**

$$H_0 : \hat{p} = 0.9$$

$$H_A : \hat{p} < 0.9$$

$$SRS, \ 750 > 10$$

$$\frac{657}{750} = 0.876; \ SD(\hat{p}) = \sqrt{\frac{(0.88)(0.12)}{750}} = 0.012$$

$$z = \frac{0.876 - 0.94}{0.012} = -2$$

$$P = P(z > -2) = 0.977$$

There is more than a 97% chance that the stated percentage is correct for this region.

21. Environment. In the 1980s, it was generally believed that congenital abnormalities affected about 5% of Canadian children. Some people believe that the increase in the number of chemicals in the environment has led to an increase in the incidence of abnormalities. A recent study examined 384 children and found that 46 of them showed signs of an abnormality. Is this strong

evidence that the risk has increased? (We consider a P-value of around 5% to represent reasonable evidence.) **LO⑥**

a) Write appropriate hypotheses.
b) Check the necessary assumptions.
c) Perform the mechanics of the test. What is the P-value?
d) Explain carefully what the P-value means in this context.
e) What's your conclusion?
f) Do environmental chemicals cause congenital abnormalities?

22. Airline performance. FlightStats.com tracks real-time flight status, departures and arrivals, and airport delays, and provides historical on-time performance ratings. How did Air Canada do, for the two months from April 15 to June 15, 2013? For the 20 most active routes in this period, Air Canada operated 9039 flights, 78% had on-time arrivals. Suppose Air Canada's target is 80% on-time arrivals. Is there evidence that Air Canada is falling short of its target? Assume that the flights in the time period are representative of all Air Canada flights. **LO⑥**

a) Write appropriate hypotheses.
b) Check the assumptions and conditions.
c) Perform the test and find the P-value.
d) State your conclusion.
e) Do you think this difference is meaningful? Explain.

23. Alcohol consumption. The 2004 Canadian Campus Survey, which focused on risky behaviours and health concerns of Canadian university students, found that 86% of undergraduate students had consumed alcohol within the past year. The survey of undergraduate business students reported in Exercise 16 included a question about alcohol consumption. Of the 625 respondents, 553 reported drinking alcohol at least occasionally. Is the rate among business students the same as the rate reported in the Canadian Campus Survey? **LO⑥**

a) Write appropriate hypotheses.
b) Check the assumptions and conditions.
c) Perform the test and find the P-value.
d) State your conclusion.
e) Do you think this difference is meaningful? Explain.

24. Alcohol consumption, part 2. A 2008 Statistics Canada study revealed that within the Prairie Provinces (Alberta, Saskatchewan, and Manitoba), 50% of young adults who drank alcohol in the past year reported risky drinking at least monthly. The survey reported in Exercise 23 also asked about risky alcohol consumption. There were 625 respondents but only 553 reported any alcohol consumption. Of these 553, 126 reported regular consumption sometimes to excess; we will define that as risky behaviour for the purpose of this comparison. Is the rate of risky drinking behaviour among business students the same as the rate among the Prairie Provinces as reported in the Statistics Canada study? **LO⑥**

a) Write appropriate hypotheses.
b) Check the assumptions and conditions.
c) Perform the test and find the P-value.
d) State your conclusion.
e) Do you think this difference is meaningful? Explain.

25. Retirement savings. According to a 2012 Bank of Montreal RRSP study of 1000 Canadians 18 years of age and older, 67% of Canadians have a registered retirement savings plan (RRSP). A

Statistics Canada study reported that in 1999, 57% of Canadians had an RRSP. **LO❸**

a) Create a 95% confidence interval for the proportion of Canadian adults who have invested in an RRSP based on the survey.

b) Does this provide evidence of a change from 1999 in RRSP investing among Canadians? Using your confidence interval, test an appropriate hypothesis and state your conclusion.

26. Customer satisfaction. A company hopes to improve customer satisfaction, setting as a goal no more than 5% negative comments. A random survey of 350 customers found only 10 with complaints. **LO❸**

a) Create a 95% confidence interval for the true level of dissatisfaction among customers.

b) Does this provide evidence that the company has reached its goal? Using your confidence interval, test an appropriate hypothesis and state your conclusion.

27. Maintenance costs. A limousine company is concerned with increasing costs of maintaining their fleet of 150 cars. After testing, the company found that the emissions systems of 7 out of the 22 cars they tested failed to meet pollution control guidelines. They had forecasted costs assuming that a total of 30 cars would need updating to meet the latest guidelines. Is this strong evidence that more than 20% of the fleet might be out of compliance? Test an appropriate hypothesis and state your conclusion. Be sure the appropriate assumptions and conditions are satisfied before you proceed. **LO❻**

28. Damaged goods. An appliance manufacturer stockpiles washers and dryers in a large warehouse for shipment to retail stores. Sometimes in handling them the appliances get damaged. Even though the damage may be minor, the company must sell those machines at drastically reduced prices. The company goal is to keep the proportion of damaged machines below 2%. One day an inspector randomly checks 60 washers and finds that 5 of them have scratches or dents. Is this strong evidence that the warehouse is failing to meet the company goal? Test an appropriate hypothesis and state your conclusion. Be sure the appropriate assumptions and conditions are satisfied before you proceed. **LO❻**

29. Defective products. An internal report from a manufacturing company indicated that about 3% of all products were defective. Data from one batch found only 7 defective products out of 469 products. Is this consistent with the report? Test an appropriate hypothesis and state your conclusion. Be sure the appropriate assumptions and conditions are satisfied before you proceed. **LO❻**

30. Jobs. A large Canadian business school would like to advertise that more than 50% of its graduates obtained a job offer prior to graduation. A sample of 240 recent graduates indicated that 138 of these graduates had a job offer prior to graduation. Test an appropriate hypothesis and state your conclusion. Be sure the appropriate assumptions and conditions are satisfied before you proceed. **LO❻**

31. Online magazine. A magazine called *Vital Statistics* is considering the launch of an online edition. The magazine plans to go ahead only if it's convinced that more than 25% of current readers would subscribe. The magazine contacts a simple random sample of 500 current subscribers, and 137 of those surveyed expressed interest. What should the magazine do? Test an appropriate hypothesis and state your conclusion. Be sure the appropriate assumptions and conditions are satisfied before you proceed. **LO❻**

32. Truth in advertising. A garden centre wants to store leftover packets of vegetable seeds for sale the following spring, but the centre is concerned that the seeds may not germinate at the same rate a year later. The manager finds a packet of last year's green bean seeds and plants them as a test. Although the packet claims a germination rate of 92%, only 171 of 200 test seeds sprout. Is this evidence that the seeds have lost viability during a year in storage? Test an appropriate hypothesis and state your conclusion. Be sure the appropriate assumptions and conditions are satisfied before you proceed. **LO❻**

33. Women executives. A company is criticized because only 13 of 43 people in executive-level positions are women. The company explains that although this proportion is lower than it might wish, it's not surprising given that only 40% of their employees are women. What do you think? Test an appropriate hypothesis and state your conclusion. Be sure the appropriate assumptions and conditions are satisfied before you proceed. **LO❻**

34. Jury selection. According to Canadian Criminal Procedure and Practice / Trials / Juries / Jury Selection, juries are to consist of a "representative cross-section of Canadian society." The underrepresentation of individuals from First Nations communities on jury rolls is a serious concern in a number of provinces across Canada. According to Canada Census, 14% of Manitobans are Aboriginal people. Suppose 84 people are called for jury duty, and only 9 of them are Aboriginal people. Does this apparent underrepresentation call into question the fairness of the jury selection system? Explain. **LO❻**

35. High school. High school drop-out rates in Canada have decreased from nearly 17% in 1990–1991 to 9% in 2008–2009. However the rate in rural areas is 16%, nearly double. A pilot program aimed at keeping students in school in rural Canada reported that in the first year of operation 250 of the 1782 students that participated in the program had dropped out of high school. Does this provide evidence that the pilot program has been effective? Explain. **LO❻**

36. Real estate. A national real estate magazine advertised that 15% of first home buyers had a family income below $60 000. A national real estate firm believes this percentage is too low and samples 100 of its records. The firm finds that 25 of its first home buyers did have a family income below $60 000. Does the sample suggest that the proportion of first home buyers with an income less than $60 000 is more than 15%? Comment and write up your own conclusions based on an appropriate confidence interval as well as a hypothesis test. Include any assumptions you made about the data. **LO❻**

37. Public relations. An airline's public relations department says that their airline rarely loses luggage. Furthermore, it claims that when it does, 90% of the time the bags are recovered and delivered within 24 hours. A consumer group surveys a large number of air travellers and finds that 103 of 122 people who lost luggage were reunited with their missing items within 24 hours. Does this cast doubt on the airline's claim? Explain. **LO❻**

38. TV ads. A start-up company is about to market a new mobile device. It decides to gamble by running commercials during the Super Bowl. The company hopes that name recognition will be worth the high cost of the ads. The goal of the company is that over 40% of the public recognize its brand name and associate it with mobile devices. The day after the game, a pollster contacts 420 randomly chosen adults and finds that 181 of them know that this company manufactures mobile devices. Would you recom mend that the company continue to advertise during the Super Bowl? Explain. **LO❻**

39. Business ethics. One study reports that 30% of newly hired MBAs are confronted with unethical business practices during their first year of employment. One business school dean wondered if her MBA graduates had similar experiences. She surveyed recent graduates from her school's MBA program to find that 27% of the 120 graduates from the previous year claim to have encountered unethical business practices in the workplace. Can she conclude that her graduates' experiences are different? **LO❻**

40. Stocks, part 2. A young investor believes that he can beat the market by picking stocks that will increase in value. Assume that on average 50% of the stocks selected by a portfolio manager will increase over 12 months. Of the 25 stocks that the young investor bought over the last 12 months, 14 have increased. Can he claim that he is better at predicting increases than the typical portfolio manager? **LO❻**

41. Voting. Voter turnout in Canada has dropped from over 75% in the 1960s to 60% in the most recent federal elections. A national sample of 2645 Canadians, aged 18 and older, surveyed over the telephone (using both landlines and cellphones) in September 2009 in an EKOS poll asked Canadians whether they would support legislation making it a legal requirement for all citizens to vote. The poll reported that 49% would support and 36% would oppose; 15% said neither. Legislation would require two-thirds support. Does the survey provide evidence that the percentage who would oppose such legislation is greater than 33%? **LO❼**

a) Find the z-score of the observed proportion.
b) Compare the z-score to the critical value for a 0.1% significance level using a one-sided alternative.
c) Explain your conclusion.

42. iPod reliability. MacInTouch reported that several versions of the iPod reported failure rates of 20% or more. From a customer survey, the colour iPod, first released in 2004, showed 64 failures out of 517. Is there any evidence that the failure rate for this model may be lower than the 20% rate of previous models? **LO❼**

a) Find the z-score of the observed proportion.

b) Compare the z-score to the critical value for a 0.1% significance level using a one-sided alternative.
c) Explain your conclusion.

43. Testing cars. A clean air standard requires that vehicle exhaust emissions not exceed specified limits for various pollutants. Some provinces require that cars be tested annually to be sure they meet these standards. Suppose provincial regulators double-check a random sample of cars that a suspect repair shop has certified as okay. They will revoke the shop's licence if they find significant evidence that the shop is certifying vehicles that do not meet standards. **LO❽**

a) In this context, what is a Type I error?
b) In this context, what is a Type II error?
c) Which type of error would the shop's owner consider more serious?
d) Which type of error might environmentalists consider more serious?

44. Quality control. Production managers on an assembly line must monitor the output to be sure that the level of defective products remains small (1% or less). They periodically inspect a random sample of the items produced. If they find a significant increase in the proportion of items that must be rejected, they will halt the assembly process until the problem can be identified and repaired. **LO❽**

a) Write null and alternative hypothesis for this problem.
b) What is the Type I and Type II error in this context?
c) Which type of error would the factory owner consider more serious?
d) Which type of error might customers consider more serious?

45. Testing cars, again. As in Exercise 43, provincial regulators are checking up on repair shops to see if they are certifying vehicles that do not meet pollution standards. **LO❽**

a) In this context, what is meant by the power of the test the regulators are conducting?
b) Will the power be greater if they test 20 or 40 cars? Why?
c) Will the power be greater if they use a 5% or a 10% level of significance? Why?
d) Will the power be greater if the repair shop's inspectors are only a little out of compliance or a lot? Why?

46. Quality control, part 2. Consider again the task of the quality control inspectors in Exercise 44. **LO❽**

a) In this context, what is meant by the power of the test the inspectors conduct?
b) They are currently testing 5 items each hour. Someone has proposed they test 10 items each hour instead. What are the advantages and disadvantages of such a change?
c) Their test currently uses a 5% level of significance. What are the advantages and disadvantages of changing to a significance level of 1%?
d) Suppose that as a day passes one of the machines on the assembly line produces more and more items that are defective. How will this affect the power of the test?

47. Statistics software. A Statistics professor has observed that for several years about 13% of the students who initially enroll in his Introductory Statistics course withdraw before the end of the course. A salesperson suggests that he try a statistics software package that gives students more practice, feedback, and advice on a study plan, predicting that it will cut the dropout rate, and the salesperson offers to let the professor use it for a course to see if the dropout rate goes down significantly. The professor will have to pay for the software only if he chooses to continue using it. LO❽

a) Is this a one-tailed or two-tailed test? Explain.
b) Write the null and alternative hypotheses.
c) In this context, explain what would happen if the professor makes a Type I error.
d) In this context, explain what would happen if the professor makes a Type II error.
e) What is meant by the power of this test?

48. Radio ads. A company is willing to renew its advertising contract with a local radio station only if the station can prove that more than 20% of the residents of the city have heard the ad and recognize the company's product. The radio station conducts a random phone survey of 400 people. LO❽

a) What are the hypotheses?
b) The station plans to conduct this test using a 10% level of significance, but the company wants the significance level lowered to 5%. Why?
c) What is meant by the power of this test?
d) For which level of significance will the power of this test be higher? Why?
e) They finally agree to use $\alpha = 0.05$, but the company proposes that the station call 600 people instead of the 400 initially proposed. Will that make the risk of Type II error higher or lower? Explain.

49. Statistics software, part 2. Initially, 203 students signed up for the Statistics course in Exercise 47. They used the software suggested by the salesperson, and only 11 dropped out of the course. LO❻

a) Should the professor spend the money for this software? Support your recommendation with an appropriate test.
b) Explain what your P-value means in this context.

50. Radio ads, part 2. The company in Exercise 48 contacts 600 people selected at random, and 133 can remember the ad. LO❻

a) Should the company renew the contract? Support your recommendation with an appropriate test.
b) Explain carefully what your P-value means in this context.

ⓣ 51. Customer spending, part 2. In Chapter 9, Exercise 61 constructed a confidence interval for the proportion of customers who qualified for a special offer by spending more than $1000 a

month on their credit card. Historically, the percentage has been 11%, and the finance department wonders if it has increased. Test the appropriate hypothesis and write up a few sentences with your conclusions. LO❻

ⓣ 52. Fund-raising. In Chapter 9, Exercise 62 found a confidence interval for the proportion of donors that were 50 years old or older. The head of finance says that the Canadian Association of Retired Persons (CARP) advertisement won't be worth the money unless at least 2/3 of the donors are 50 years old or older. Test the appropriate hypothesis and write up a few sentences with your conclusions. LO❻

✓ **JUST CHECKING ANSWERS**

1 You can't conclude that the null hypothesis is true. You can conclude only that the experiment was unable to reject the null hypothesis. They were unable, on the basis of 12 patients, to show that aspirin was effective.

2 The null hypothesis is $H_0: p = 0.75$.

3 With a P-value of 0.0001, this is very strong evidence against the null hypothesis. We can reject H_0 and conclude that the improved version of the drug gives relief to a higher proportion of patients.

4 The parameter of interest is the proportion, p, of all delinquent customers who will pay their bills. $H_0: p = 0.30$ and $H_A: p > 0.30$

5 At $\alpha = 0.05$, you can't reject the null hypothesis because 0.30 is contained in the 90% confidence interval—it's plausible that sending the DVDs is no more effective than sending letters.

6 The confidence interval is from 29% to 45%. The DVD strategy is more expensive and may not be worth it. We can't distinguish the success rate from 30% given the results of this experiment, but 45% would represent a large improvement. The bank should consider another trial, increasing the sample size to get a narrower confidence interval.

7 A Type I error would mean deciding that the DVD success rate is higher than 30%, when it isn't. The bank would adopt a more expensive method for collecting payments that's no better than its original, less expensive strategy.

8 A Type II error would mean deciding that there's not enough evidence to say the DVD strategy works when in fact it does. The bank would fail to discover an effective method for increasing revenue from delinquent accounts.

9 Higher; the larger the effect size, the greater the power. It's easier to detect an improvement to a 60% success rate than to a 32% rate.

Confidence Intervals and Hypothesis Tests for Means

Left, Getty Images Publicity/Arthur Guinness/Getty Images; right top, Routier/Turiot/photocuisine/Corbis; right bottom, Bert Hardy/Hulton Archive/Getty Images

LEARNING OBJECTIVES

1. Apply the Normal model to the sampling distribution of the sample mean

2. Find critical values and P-values for *t*-distributions

3. Calculate, check assumptions, and interpret a confidence interval (and margin of error) for the mean

4. Choose the alternative hypothesis and explain types of error (I and II) and power in the context of the question

5. Test a claim using a one-sample *t*-test or *t*-interval, and check assumptions

CONNECTIONS: CHAPTER

In Chapters 9 and 10 we developed a confidence interval and a hypothesis test for a single proportion. Now that we know the logic of these methods we can speed things up. In this chapter we discuss the confidence interval and hypothesis test for a single mean.

Guinness & Co.

ost beer drinkers will recognize the brand name Guinness. But most do not know its history, nor its connection with Statistics.

In 1759, when Arthur Guinness was 34 years old, he took an incredible gamble, signing a 9000-year lease on a run-down, abandoned brewery in Dublin. The brewery covered four acres and consisted of a mill, two malt houses, stabling for 12 horses, and a loft that could hold 200 tons of hay. At the time, brewing was a difficult and competitive market. Gin, whiskey, and the traditional London porter were the drinks of choice.

In addition to the lighter ales that Dublin was known for, Guinness began to brew dark porters to compete directly with those of the English brewers. Forty years later, Guinness stopped brewing light Dublin ales altogether to concentrate on his stouts and porters. Upon his death in 1803, his son Arthur Guinness II took over the business, and a few years later the company began to export Guinness stout to other parts of Europe. By the 1830s, the Guinness St. James's Gate Brewery had become the largest in Ireland. In 1886, the Guinness Brewery, with an annual production of 1.2 million barrels, was the first major brewery to be incorporated as a public company on the London Stock Exchange. During the 1890s, the company began to employ scientists. One of those, William S. Gosset, was hired as a chemist to test the quality of the brewing process. Gosset was not only an early pioneer of quality control methods in industry but his statistical work made modern statistical inference possible.[1]

Based on information from www.guinness.com

> What does Guinness have to do with Statistics? Look closely at the word: GU-INN-ESS. When you're at an INN drinking a Guinness, you're surrounded by a GUESS, which is an informal name for a statistical estimate!

As a chemist at the Guinness Brewery in Dublin, William S. Gosset was in charge of quality control. His job was to make sure that the stout (a thick, dark beer) leaving the brewery was of high enough quality to meet the standards of the brewery's many discerning customers. It's easy to imagine, when testing stout, why testing a large amount of stout might be undesirable, not to mention dangerous to one's health. So to test for quality Gosset often used a sample of only three or four observations per batch. But he noticed that with samples of this size, his tests for quality weren't quite right. He knew this because when the batches that he rejected were sent back to the laboratory for more extensive testing, too often the test results turned out to be wrong. As a practising statistician, Gosset knew he had to be wrong *some* of the time, but he hated being wrong more often than the theory predicted. One result of Gosset's frustrations was the development of a test to handle small samples, the main subject of this chapter.

11.1 The Sampling Distribution for Means

The CLT says that the sampling distribution of any mean or proportion will become Normal as the sample size grows. But which Normal? We know that any Normal model is specified by its mean and standard deviation. For proportions, the sampling distribution is centred at the population proportion. For means, it's centred at the population mean. What else would we expect?

> ### The Central Limit Theorem (CLT)
> The mean of a random sample has a sampling distribution whose shape can be approximated by a Normal model. The larger the sample, the better the approximation will be.

What about the standard deviations? We noticed in the dice simulation from Chapter 9 that the histograms got narrower as the number of dice we averaged increased. This shouldn't be surprising because means vary less than the individual observations. Think about it for a minute. Which would be more surprising, having *one* person in your Statistics class who is over 6′9″ tall or having the *mean* of 100 students taking the course be over 6′9″? The first event is fairly rare.[2] You may have seen somebody this tall in one of your classes sometime. But finding a class

---

[1] Source: Guinness & Co. 2009, www.guinness.com/en-ca/thestory

[2] If students are a random sample of adults, fewer than 1 out of 10 000 should be taller than 6′9″. Why might university students not really be a random sample with respect to height? Even if they're not a perfectly random sample, a university student over 6′9″ tall is still rare.

"The n's justify the means."

—Apocryphal statistical saying

of 100 whose mean height is over 6′9″ tall just won't happen. Why? *Means have smaller standard deviations than individuals.*

More precisely, the Normal model for the sampling distribution of the mean has a standard deviation equal to $SD(\bar{y}) = \dfrac{\sigma}{\sqrt{n}}$ where σ is the standard deviation of the population. To emphasize that this is a standard deviation *parameter* of the sampling distribution model for the sample mean, $\bar{y}$, we write $SD(\bar{y})$ or $\sigma(\bar{y})$.

> ### The Sampling Distribution Model for a Mean
>
> When a random sample is drawn from any population with mean μ and standard deviation σ, its sample mean, $\bar{y}$, has a sampling distribution with the same mean, μ, but whose standard deviation is $\dfrac{\sigma}{\sqrt{n}}$ $\left(\text{and we write } \sigma(\bar{y}) = SD(\bar{y}) = \dfrac{\sigma}{\sqrt{n}}\right).$
> No matter what population the random sample comes from, the shape of the sampling distribution is approximately Normal as long as the sample size is large enough and the observations are independent. The larger the sample used, the more closely the Normal approximates the **sampling distribution model for the mean**. Guidelines for what is considered "large" are discussed later.

We now have two closely related sampling distribution models. Which one we use depends on which kind of data we have.

◆ When we have categorical data, we calculate a sample proportion, $\hat{p}$. Its sampling distribution has a Normal model with a mean at the population proportion, p, and a standard deviation $SD(\hat{p}) = \sqrt{\dfrac{pq}{n}} = \dfrac{\sqrt{pq}}{\sqrt{n}}.$

◆ When we have quantitative data, we calculate a sample mean, $\bar{y}$. Its sampling distribution has a Normal model with a mean at the population mean, μ, and a standard deviation $SD(\bar{y}) = \dfrac{\sigma}{\sqrt{n}}.$

The means of these models are easy to remember, so all you need to be careful about is the standard deviations. Remember that these are standard deviations of the *statistics* $\hat{p}$ and $\bar{y}$. They both have a square root of n in the denominator. That tells us that the larger the sample, the less either statistic will vary. The only difference is in the numerator. If you just start by writing $SD(\bar{y})$ for quantitative data and $SD(\hat{p})$ for categorical data, you'll be able to remember which formula to use.

> ### Example
> **Problem:** Suppose that the mean weight of boxes shipped by a company is 12 kgs, with a standard deviation of 4 kgs. Boxes are shipped in palettes of 10 boxes. The shipper has a limit of 150 kgs for such shipments. What's the probability that a palette will exceed that limit?
>
> **Solution:** Asking the probability that the total weight of a sample of 10 boxes exceeds 150 kgs is the same as asking the probability that the *mean* weight exceeds 15 kgs. First we'll check the conditions. We will assume that the 10 boxes on the palette are a random sample from the population of boxes and that their weights are mutually independent.
> Under these conditions, the CLT says that the sampling distribution of $\bar{y}$ has a Normal model with mean 12 and standard deviation
> $$SD(\bar{y}) = \frac{\sigma}{\sqrt{n}} = \frac{4}{\sqrt{10}} = 1.26 \text{ and } z = \frac{\bar{y}-\mu}{SD(\bar{y})} = \frac{15-12}{1.26} = 2.38$$
> $$P(\bar{y} > 15) = P(z > 2.38) = 0.0087$$

So the chance that the shipper will reject a palette is only 0.0087—less than 1%. That's probably good enough for the company.

11.2 How Sampling Distribution Models Work

Both of the sampling distributions we've looked at (for proportions and means) are Normal. We know for proportions, $SD(\hat{p}) = \sqrt{\frac{pq}{n}}$, and for means, $SD(\bar{y}) = \frac{\sigma}{\sqrt{n}}$. These are great if we know, or can pretend that we know, p or σ, and sometimes we'll do that. But if they are not known we need to replace them with estimates. In Chapter 9 we introduced the term "standard error" (SE) as the estimated standard deviation of a sampling distribution. There we found the SE for a sample proportion; now we have the SE for a sample mean.

Remember that for the sample proportion, $\hat{p}$, the standard error is:

$$SE(\hat{p}) = \sqrt{\frac{\hat{p}\hat{q}}{n}}$$

For the sample mean, $\bar{y}$, the standard error is:

$$SE(\bar{y}) = \frac{s}{\sqrt{n}}$$

You may see a "standard error" reported by a computer program in a summary or offered by a calculator. It's safe to assume that if no statistic is specified, what was meant is $SE(\bar{y})$, the standard error of the mean.

The term "standard error" can be very confusing because the words "standard" and "error" have non-statistical meanings too. "Standard error" sounds like a mistake you always make, as in, "Oh, that error—I make it all the time; it is my standard error." Remember that the statistical meaning of the word "error" is the difference between an estimated value and the true value.

One way to remember the difference between SD (standard deviation) and SE (standard error) is that the D suggests "data," as in, how much does one *data value* differ from the truth, while the E suggests "estimate," as in how much does one *estimate* differ from the truth. Here, one data value, y, is about s units from μ, while the estimate $\bar{y}$ is about $\frac{s}{\sqrt{n}}$ units from μ, on average.

✓ JUST CHECKING

1 The entrance exam for business schools, the GMAT, given to 100 students had a mean of 520 and a standard deviation of 120. What was the standard error for the mean of this sample of students?

2 As the sample size increases, what happens to the standard error, assuming the standard deviation remains constant?

3 If the sample size is doubled, what is the impact on the standard error?

To keep track of how the concepts we've seen combine, we can draw a diagram relating them. At the heart is the idea that *the statistic itself (the proportion or the mean) is a random quantity*. We can't know what our statistic will be because it comes from a random sample. A different random sample would have given a different result. This sample-to-sample variability is what generates the sampling distribution, the distribution of all the possible values that the statistic could have had.

We could simulate that distribution by pretending to take lots of samples. Fortunately, for the mean and the proportion, the CLT tells us that we can model their sampling distribution directly with a Normal model.

The two basic truths about sampling distributions are:

1. Sampling distributions arise because samples vary. Each random sample will contain different cases and, so, a different value of the statistic.

2. Although we can always simulate a sampling distribution, the Central Limit Theorem saves us the trouble for means and proportions.

Figure 11.1 diagrams the process.

Figure 11.1 We start with a population model, which can have any shape. It can even be bimodal or skewed (as this one is). We label the mean of this model μ and its standard deviation, σ.

We draw one real sample (solid line) of size n and show its histogram and summary statistics. We imagine (or simulate) drawing many other samples (dotted lines), which have their own histograms and summary statistics.

We (imagine) gathering all the means into a histogram.

The CLT tells us we can model the shape of this histogram with a Normal model. The mean of this Normal is μ, and the standard deviation is $SD(\bar{y}) = \dfrac{\sigma}{\sqrt{n}}$.

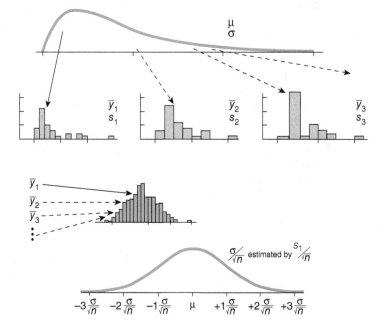

When we don't know σ, we estimate it with the standard deviation of the one real sample. That gives us the standard error, $SE(\bar{y}) = \dfrac{s}{\sqrt{n}}$.

11.3 Gossett and the *t*-Distribution

You know how to create confidence intervals and test hypotheses about proportions. Now we want to do the same thing for means. For proportions we found the confidence interval as

$$\hat{p} \pm ME$$

The Margin of Error, or ME, was equal to a critical value, z^*, times $SE(\hat{p})$. Our confidence interval for means will be

$$\bar{y} \pm ME$$

and our ME will be a critical value times $SE(\bar{y})$. So let's put the pieces together. The Central Limit Theorem tells us that the sampling distribution for means becomes Normal as the sample size increases, and we know the standard deviation of the mean is $\dfrac{\sigma}{\sqrt{n}}$. All we need is a random sample of quantitative data and the true value of the the population standard deviation σ.

But wait. That could be a problem. To compute $\sigma/\sqrt{n}$ we need to know σ. How are we supposed to know σ? Suppose we told you that for 25 young executives the mean value of their stock portfolios is \$125 672. Would that tell you the value of σ? No, the standard deviation depends on how *similarly* the executives invest, not on how well they invested (the mean tells us that). But we need σ because it's the numerator of the standard deviation of the sample mean: $SD(\bar{y}) = \dfrac{\sigma}{\sqrt{n}}$. So what can we do? The obvious answer is to use the sample standard deviation, s, from the data instead of σ. The result is the standard error: $SE(\bar{y}) = \dfrac{s}{\sqrt{n}}$.

International Statistical Institute (ISI)

To find the sampling distribution of $\dfrac{\bar{y}}{s/\sqrt{n}}$, Gosset simulated it by hand. He drew paper slips of small samples from a hat hundreds of times and computed the means and standard deviations with a mechanically cranked calculator. Today you could repeat in seconds on a computer the experiment that took him over a year. Gosset's work was so meticulous that not only did he get the shape of the new histogram approximately right, but he even figured out the exact formula for it from his sample. The formula was not confirmed mathematically until years later by Sir R. A. Fisher.

> **! NOTATION ALERT:**
> Ever since Gosset, the letter t has been reserved in Statistics for his distribution.

A century ago, people just plugged the standard error into the Normal model, assuming it would work. And for large sample sizes it *did* work pretty well. But they began to notice problems with smaller samples. The extra variation in the standard error was wreaking havoc with the P-values and margins of error.

William S. Gosset was the first to investigate this phenomenon. He realized that not only do we need to allow for the extra variation with larger margins of error and P-values, but we also need a new sampling distribution model. In fact, we need a whole *family* of models, depending on the sample size, n. These models are unimodal, symmetric, and bell-shaped, but the smaller our sample, the more we must stretch out the tails. Gosset's work transformed Statistics, but most people who use his work don't even know his name.

Gosset checked the stout's quality at Guinness by performing hypothesis tests. He knew that if he set $\alpha = 0.05$ the test would make some Type I errors by rejecting about 5% of the good batches of stout. However, the lab told him that he was in fact rejecting about 15% of the good batches. Gosset knew something was wrong, and it bothered him.

Gosset took time off from his job to study the problem and earn a graduate degree in the emerging field of Statistics. He figured out that when he used the standard error $\dfrac{s}{\sqrt{n}}$, the shape of the sampling model was no longer Normal. He even figured out what the new model was and called it a t-distribution.

The Guinness Company didn't give Gosset a lot of support for his work. In fact, it had a policy against publishing results. Gosset had to convince the company that he was not publishing an industrial secret and (as part of getting permission to publish) had to use a pseudonym. The pseudonym he chose was "Student," and ever since, the model he found has been known as **Student's t.** However, nowadays we are more likely to call it, simply, the t, since we know who the "Student" was. Gosset published his landmark paper in 1908, so we celebrated the centennial just a few years ago, in 2008. Sadly, it was not sponsored by Guinness!

Gosset's model is always bell-shaped, but the details change with the sample sizes. So the Student's t-models form a family of related distributions that depend on a parameter known as **degrees of freedom**. We often denote degrees of freedom as df and the model as t_{df}, with the numerical value of the degrees of freedom as a subscript.

11.4 A Confidence Interval for Means

To make confidence intervals or to test hypotheses for means, we need to use Gosset's model. Which one? Well, for means, it turns out the right value for degrees of freedom is df $= n - 1$. You've seen $n - 1$ before. It is the denominator in the formula for s, which is used in Gosset's model as a replacement for σ. We'll see this correspondence between degrees of freedom and standard deviation in later chapters.

> **Practical Sampling Distribution Model for Means**
>
> When certain conditions are met, the standardized sample mean,
>
> $$t = \frac{\bar{y} - \mu}{SE(\bar{y})}$$
>
> follows a Student's t-model with $n - 1$ degrees of freedom. We find the standard error from:
>
> $$SE(\bar{y}) = \frac{s}{\sqrt{n}}$$

When Gosset corrected the Normal model for the extra uncertainty, the margin of error got bigger, as you might have guessed. When you use Gosset's model instead of the Normal model, your confidence intervals will be just a bit wider and your P-values just a bit larger (Figure 11.2). That's just the correction you need. By using the *t*-model, you've compensated for the extra variability in precisely the right way.

One-sample *t*-interval for the mean

When the assumptions and conditions are met, we are ready to find the **confidence interval (CI) for the population mean, μ**. The confidence interval is:

$$\bar{y} \pm t^*_{n-1} \times SE(\bar{y})$$

where the standard error of the mean is:

$$SE(\bar{y}) = \frac{s}{\sqrt{n}}$$

The critical value t^*_{n-1} depends on the particular confidence level, C, that you specify and on the number of degrees of freedom, $n - 1$, which we get from the sample size.

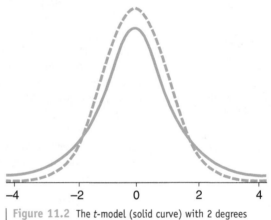

Figure 11.2 The *t*-model (solid curve) with 2 degrees of freedom has fatter tails than the Normal model (dashed curve). So the 68-95-99.7 Rule doesn't work for *t*-models with only a few degrees of freedom.

z or t?

If you know σ, use z. (That's rare!) Whenever you use s to estimate σ, use t. So a very useful rule of thumb is: Use t for the CI for a mean and use z for the CI for a proportion.

Student's *t*-models are unimodal, symmetric, and bell-shaped, just like the Normal model. But *t*-models with only a few degrees of freedom have a narrower peak than the Normal model and have much fatter tails. (That's what makes the margin of error bigger.) As the degrees of freedom increase, the *t*-models look more and more like the Normal model. In fact, the *t*-model with infinite degrees of freedom is exactly Normal.[3] This is great news if you happen to have an infinite number of data values. Unfortunately, that's not practical. Fortunately, above a few hundred degrees of freedom it's very hard to tell the difference. Of course, in the rare situation that we *know* σ, it would be foolish not to use that information. If we don't have to estimate σ, we can use the Normal model. Typically that value of σ would be based on (lots of) experience, or on a theoretical model. Usually, however, we estimate σ by s from the data and use the *t*-model.

---

[3] Formally, in the limit as the number of degrees of freedom goes to infinity.

11.5 Assumptions and Conditions

Gosset found the *t*-model by simulation. Years later, when Sir Ronald Fisher showed mathematically that Gosset was right, he needed to make some assumptions to make the proof work. These are the assumptions we need in order to use the Student's *t*-models.

Independence Assumption

Independence Assumption: The data values should be independent. That is, the measurement of one data point should not influence the measurement of another data point. There's really no way to check the independence of the data by looking at the sample, but we should think about whether the assumption is reasonable.

Randomization Condition: The data arise from a random sample or suitably randomized experiment. Randomly sampled data—and especially data from a Simple Random Sample (SRS)—are ideal.

When a sample is drawn without replacement, technically we ought to confirm that we haven't sampled a large fraction of the population, which would threaten the independence of our selections.

10% Condition: The sample size should be no more than 10% of the population. In practice, though, we often don't mention the 10% Condition when estimating means. Why not? When we made inferences about proportions, this condition was crucial because we usually had large samples. But for means our samples are generally smaller, so this problem arises only if we're sampling from a small population (and then there's a correction formula we could use).

Normal Population Assumption

Student's *t*-models won't work for data that are badly skewed. We can't rely on the Central Limit Theorem for small sample sizes. How skewed is too skewed? Well, formally, we assume that the data are from a population that follows a Normal model. Practically speaking, there's no way to be certain this is true.

And it's almost certainly *not* true. Models are idealized; real data are, well, real. The good news, however, is that even for small samples, it's sufficient to check a condition.

Nearly Normal Condition. The data come from a distribution that is unimodal and symmetric. This is a much more practical condition and one we can check by making a histogram.[4] For small samples, it can be hard to see any distribution shape in the histogram. Unfortunately, the condition matters most when it's hardest to check.[5]

For very small samples (*n* < 15 or so), the data should follow a Normal model pretty closely. Of course, with so little data, it's rather hard to tell. But if you do find outliers or strong skewness, don't use these methods.

For moderate sample sizes (*n* between 15 and 40 or so), the *t* methods will work well as long as the data are unimodal and reasonably symmetric. Make a histogram to check.

When the sample size is larger than 40 or 50, the *t* methods are safe to use unless the data are extremely skewed. Make a histogram anyway. If you find outliers in the data and they aren't errors that are easy to fix, it's always a good idea to perform the analysis twice, once with and once without the outliers, even for large

---

We Don't *Want* to Stop

We check conditions hoping that we can make a meaningful analysis of our data. The conditions serve as *disqualifiers*—we keep going unless there's a serious problem. If we find minor issues, we note them and express caution about our results. If the sample is not an SRS, (i.e., a simple random sample) but we believe it's representative of some populations, we limit our conclusions accordingly. If there are outliers, rather than stop, we perform the analysis both with and without them. If the sample looks bimodal, we try to analyze subgroups separately. The mean is only useful if the sample is unimodal. Only when there's major trouble—like a strongly skewed small sample or an obviously non-representative sample—are we unable to proceed at all.

NOTATION ALERT:
When we found critical values from a Normal model, we called them *z**. When we use a Student's *t*-model, we denote the critical values *t**.

---

[4] Or we could check a more sensitive display called a normal probability plot, discussed in Chapter 15.

[5] There are formal tests of Normality, but they don't really help. When we have a small sample—just when we really care about checking Normality—these tests don't perform well. So it doesn't make much sense to use them in deciding whether to use a *t*-test.

samples. The outliers may well hold additional information about the data, so they deserve special attention. If you find multiple modes, you may well have different groups that should be analyzed and understood separately.

If the data are extremely skewed (like the CEO data in Figure 11.3), the mean may not be the most appropriate summary. But in business we often are concerned with costs and profits. When our data consist of a collection of instances whose *total* is the business consequence—as when we add up the profits (or losses) from many transactions or the costs of many supplies—then the mean is just that total divided by *n*. And that's the value with a business consequence. Fortunately, in this instance, the Central Limit Theorem comes to our rescue. Even when we must sample from a very skewed distribution, the sampling distribution of our sample mean will be close to Normal, so we can use Student's *t* methods without much worry as long as the sample size is *large enough*.

How large is large enough? Here's the histogram of CEO compensations ($000).

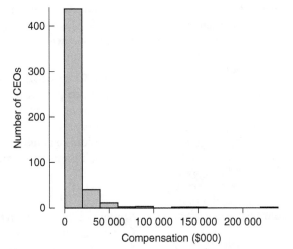

Figure 11.3 It's hard to imagine a distribution more skewed than these annual compensations from the Fortune 500 CEOs.

Although this distribution is very skewed, the Central Limit Theorem will make the sampling distribution of the means of samples from this distribution more and more Normal as the sample size grows. Here's a histogram of the means of samples of size 100 CEOs:

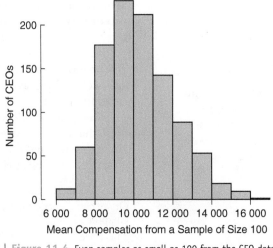

Figure 11.4 Even samples as small as 100 from the CEO data set produce means whose sampling distribution is nearly normal. Larger samples will have sampling distributions even more Normal.

Often, in modern business applications, we have samples of many hundreds, or thousands. We should still be on guard for outliers and multiple modes and we should be sure that the observations are independent. But if the mean is of interest, the Central Limit Theorem works quite well in ensuring that the sampling distribution of the mean will be close to the Normal for samples of this size.

✓ **JUST CHECKING**

Every five years, Statistics Canada takes a nationwide census that tries to count every resident. In addition, the census collects information on a variety of economic and social questions. Businesses of all types use census data to plan sales and marketing strategies and to understand the underlying demographics of the areas that they serve.

Prior to 2011, the Canada Census consisted of a "short form" census questionnaire distributed to 80% of the population and a "long form" distributed to the remaining 20%, chosen at random. Completion of the form was mandatory, regardless of which form you received. The short form covered basic population demographics and housing questions. The long form added socioeconomic questions.

Beginning in 2011, the mandatory long form was replaced with a voluntary National Household Survey. The change from mandatory to voluntary was met with much criticism and controversy. The Census Bureau in the United States, which carries out its national census every 10 years, currently still has a mandatory long form, but this is also under debate, as it is in the United Kingdom.

It is generally agreed that the data from the NHS is not of the same calibre as the mandatory census, although the results are probably sound at the national and provincial level. The problem lies in the results for small communities' populations and small geographical areas. Some say the NHS data are worthless because they are not a random sample, and so the representativeness of the sample is not known. The key issue is response rate; do all population groups answer the NHS at the same rate or are some groups under-represented?

Opinion is mixed on how big a loss has been incurred. Some say the long-form census wasn't perfect either, and that it had a high non-response rate in the populations that critics are most worried about losing. As Darrell Bricker, CEO of Ipsos Public Affairs noted, "Poor people were always hard to reach." But Ivan Fellegi, a former chief statistician of Statistics Canada says, " the long-form census is still a better representation of the Canadian population than the National Household Survey." He says that it will be tough to assess the quality of the survey data, and advocates great caution, especially with detailed data at the neighbourhood level and with comparisons to prior years.

One possible solution is to add a few questions on income, education, immigration, and Aboriginal status to the short form. As of this writing a decision has not been made about the format of the 2016 census.

When the long form was mandatory and used a "one household in five" random sample, confidence intervals were computed for each estimate. Details can be found on the Statistics Canada website (www.statcan.gc.ca).

4 Prior to 2011, why did Statistics Canada need a confidence interval for long-form information, but not for the questions that appear on both the long and short forms?

5 Prior to 2011, why did Statistics Canada base these confidence intervals on t-models?

An examination of the computed confidence intervals shows that the smaller the population or the less frequent the characteristic in the geographic area being studied (e.g., income under $1000 in the Census Metropolitan Area (CMA) Winnipeg), the wider the confidence interval.

6 Why is this so? For example, why should a confidence interval for the mean amount families spend monthly on housing be wider for a sparsely populated area of farms in Saskatchewan than for a densely populated area of Toronto? How does the formula for the one-sample t-interval show this will happen?

Statistics Canada's *2006 Census Technical Report* states, "Sampling is now an accepted and integral part of census-taking. The effect of sampling is most important for small census figures. As a general rule of thumb for the 2006 Census, figures of size 100 or less that are based on sample [long-form] data are of very low reliability...."

7 Suppose Statistics Canada had determined that 200 completed long forms was the minimum number to produce good quality estimates; that is, confidence intervals narrow enough to be useful. What effect would changing the minimum to 50 completed long forms have on a 95% confidence interval for, say, the mean cost of housing? Specifically, which values used in the formula for the margin of error would change? Which values would change a lot, and which values would change only slightly? Approximately how much wider would that confidence interval based on 50 forms be than the one based on 200 forms?

GUIDED EXAMPLE | Insurance Profits

Sapsiwai/Shutterstock

Insurance companies take risks. When they insure a property or a life, they must price the policy in such a way that their expected profit enables them to survive. They can base their projections on actuarial tables, but the reality of the insurance business often demands that they discount policies to a variety of customers and situations. Managing this risk is made even more difficult by the fact that until the policy expires, the company won't know if they've made a profit, no matter what premium they charge.

A manager wanted to see how well one of her sales representatives was doing, so she selected 30 matured policies that had been sold by the sales rep and computed the (net) profit (premium charged minus paid claims), for each of the 30 policies.

The manager would like you, as a consultant, to construct a 95% confidence interval for the mean profit of the policies sold by this sales rep.

Profit (in $) from 30 Policies		
222.80	463.35	2089.40
1756.23	−66.20	2692.75
1100.85	57.90	2495.70
3340.66	833.95	2172.70
1006.50	1390.70	3249.65
445.50	2447.50	−397.70
3255.60	1847.50	−397.31
3701.85	865.40	186.25
−803.35	1415.65	590.85
3865.90	2756.34	578.95

PLAN

Setup State what we want to know. Identify the variables and their context.

Make a picture. Check the distribution shape and look for skewness, multiple modes, and outliers.

We wish to find a 95% confidence interval for the mean profit of policies sold by this sales rep. We have data for 30 matured policies.

Here's a boxplot and histogram of these values.

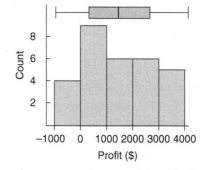

The sample appears to be unimodal and fairly symmetric with profit values between −$1000 and $4000 and no outliers.

Model Think about the assumptions and check the conditions.

✓ **Independence Assumption**

This is a random sample so observations should be independent.

✓ **Randomization Condition**

This sample was selected randomly from the matured policies sold by the sales representative of the company.

✓ **Nearly Normal Condition**

The distribution of profits is unimodal and fairly symmetric without strong skewness.

State the sampling distribution model for the statistic.

Since σ, the population standard deviation, is unknown, use s, the sample standard deviation, and a Student's t-model with $n - 1 = 30 - 1 = 29$ degrees of freedom and find a one-sample t-interval for the mean.

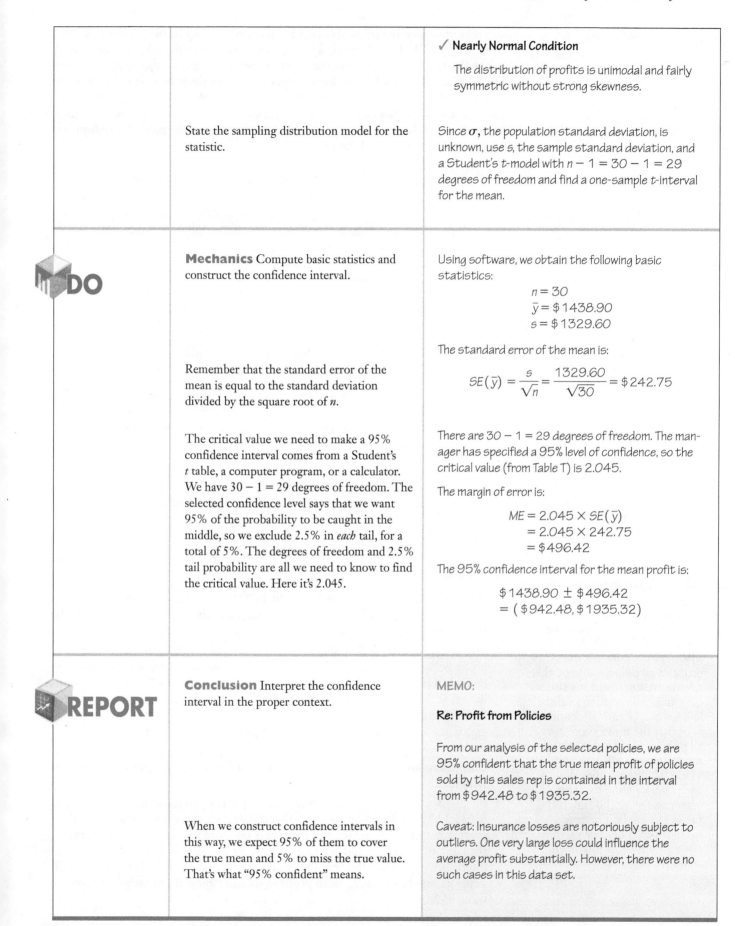

DO

Mechanics Compute basic statistics and construct the confidence interval.

Using software, we obtain the following basic statistics:

$$n = 30$$
$$\bar{y} = \$1438.90$$
$$s = \$1329.60$$

Remember that the standard error of the mean is equal to the standard deviation divided by the square root of *n*.

The standard error of the mean is:

$$SE(\bar{y}) = \frac{s}{\sqrt{n}} = \frac{1329.60}{\sqrt{30}} = \$242.75$$

The critical value we need to make a 95% confidence interval comes from a Student's *t* table, a computer program, or a calculator. We have $30 - 1 = 29$ degrees of freedom. The selected confidence level says that we want 95% of the probability to be caught in the middle, so we exclude 2.5% in *each* tail, for a total of 5%. The degrees of freedom and 2.5% tail probability are all we need to know to find the critical value. Here it's 2.045.

There are $30 - 1 = 29$ degrees of freedom. The manager has specified a 95% level of confidence, so the critical value (from Table T) is 2.045.

The margin of error is:

$$ME = 2.045 \times SE(\bar{y})$$
$$= 2.045 \times 242.75$$
$$= \$496.42$$

The 95% confidence interval for the mean profit is:

$$\$1438.90 \pm \$496.42$$
$$= (\$942.48, \$1935.32)$$

REPORT

Conclusion Interpret the confidence interval in the proper context.

MEMO:

Re: Profit from Policies

From our analysis of the selected policies, we are 95% confident that the true mean profit of policies sold by this sales rep is contained in the interval from $942.48 to $1935.32.

When we construct confidence intervals in this way, we expect 95% of them to cover the true mean and 5% to miss the true value. That's what "95% confident" means.

Caveat: Insurance losses are notoriously subject to outliers. One very large loss could influence the average profit substantially. However, there were no such cases in this data set.

The critical value in the Guided Example was found in the Student's *t* Table in Appendix B. To find the critical value, locate the row of the table corresponding to the degrees of freedom and the column corresponding to the probability you want. Since a 95% confidence interval leaves 2.5% of the values on either side, we look for 0.025 at the top of the column or look for 95% confidence directly in the bottom row of the table. The value in the table at that intersection is the critical value we need. In the Guided Example, the number of degrees of freedom was $30 - 1 = 29$, so we located the value of 2.045.

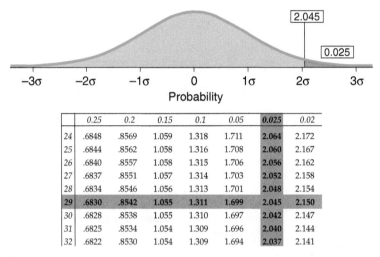

	0.25	0.2	0.15	0.1	0.05	**0.025**	0.02
24	.6848	.8569	1.059	1.318	1.711	**2.064**	2.172
25	.6844	.8562	1.058	1.316	1.708	**2.060**	2.167
26	.6840	.8557	1.058	1.315	1.706	**2.056**	2.162
27	.6837	.8551	1.057	1.314	1.703	**2.052**	2.158
28	.6834	.8546	1.056	1.313	1.701	**2.048**	2.154
29	**.6830**	**.8542**	**1.055**	**1.311**	**1.699**	**2.045**	**2.150**
30	.6828	.8538	1.055	1.310	1.697	**2.042**	2.147
31	.6825	.8534	1.054	1.309	1.696	**2.040**	2.144
32	.6822	.8530	1.054	1.309	1.694	**2.037**	2.141

Figure 11.5 Using Table T to look up the critical value *t** for a 95% confidence level with 29 degrees of freedom.

11.6 Cautions About Interpreting Confidence Intervals

Confidence intervals for means offer new, tempting wrong interpretations. Here are some ways to keep from going astray:

◆ ***Don't say,*** "*95% of all the policies* sold by this sales rep have profits between $942.48 and $1935.32." The confidence interval is about the *mean*, not about the measurements of individual policies.

◆ ***Don't say,*** "We are 95% confident that *a randomly selected policy* will have a net profit between $942.48 and $1935.32." This false interpretation is also about individual policies rather than about the *mean* of the policies. We are 95% confident that the *mean* profit of all (similar) policies sold by this sales rep is between $942.48 and $1935.32.

◆ ***Don't say,*** "The mean profit is $1438.90 in 95% *of the time*." That's about means, but still wrong. It implies that the true mean varies, when in fact it is the confidence interval that would have been different had we gotten a different sample.

◆ Finally, ***don't say,*** "*95% of all samples* will have mean profits between $942.48 and $1935.32." That statement suggests that *this* interval somehow sets a standard for every other interval. In fact, this interval is no more (or less) likely to be correct than any other. You could say that 95% of all possible samples would produce intervals that contain the true mean profit. (The problem is that because we'll never know what the true mean profit is, we can't know if our sample was one of those 95%.)

11.7 One-Sample *t*-Test

The manager has a more specific concern. Company policy states that if a sales rep's mean profit is below $1500, the sales rep has been discounting too much and will have to adjust his pricing strategy. Is there evidence from this sample that the mean is really less than $1500? This question calls for a hypothesis test called the **one-sample *t*-test for the mean**.

You already know enough to construct this test. The test statistic looks just like the others we've seen. We've always compared the difference between the observed statistic and a hypothesized value to the standard error. For means that looks like: $\dfrac{\bar{y} - \mu_0}{SE(\bar{y})}$. We already know that the appropriate probability model to use is Student's *t* with $n - 1$ degrees of freedom.

One-sample *t*-test for the mean

The conditions for the one-sample *t*-test for the mean are the same as for the one-sample *t*-interval. We test the hypothesis $H_0: \mu = \mu_0$ using the statistic

$$t_{n-1} = \frac{\bar{y} - \mu_0}{SE(\bar{y})},$$

where the standard error of $\bar{y}$ is: $SE(\bar{y}) = \dfrac{s}{\sqrt{n}}$.

When the conditions are met and the null hypothesis is true, this statistic follows a Student's *t*-model with $n - 1$ degrees of freedom. We use that model to obtain a P-value.

GUIDED EXAMPLE | Insurance Profits Revisited

Let's apply the one-sample *t*-test to the 30 mature policies sampled by the manager. From these 30 policies, the management would like to know if there's evidence that the mean profit of policies sold by this sales rep is less than $1500.

PLAN	**Setup** State what we want to know. Make clear what the population and parameter are.	We want to test whether the mean profit of the sales rep's policies is less than $1500. We have a random sample of 30 mature policies from which to judge.
	Identify the variables and context.	
	Hypotheses We give benefit of the doubt to the sales rep. The null hypothesis is that the true mean profit is equal to $1500. Because we're interested in whether the profit is less, the alternative is one-sided.	$H_O: \mu = \$1500$ $H_A: \mu < \$1500$
	Make a graph. Check the distribution for skewness, multiple modes, and outliers.	We checked the histogram of these data in the previous Guided Example and saw that they had a unimodal, symmetric distribution.

	Model Check the conditions.	We checked the Randomization and Nearly Normal Conditions in the previous Guided Example.
	State the sampling distribution model. Choose your method.	The conditions are satisfied, so we'll use a Student's t-model with $n - 1 = 29$ degrees of freedom and a one-sample t-test for the mean.
DO	**Mechanics** Compute the sample statistics. Be sure to include the units when you write down what you know from the data.	Using software, we obtain the following basic statistics: $n = 30$ Mean = \$1438.90 StDev = \$1329.60
	The t-statistic calculation is just a standardized value. We subtract the hypothesized mean and divide by the standard error.	$$t = \frac{1438.90 - 1500}{1329.60/\sqrt{30}} = -0.2517$$
	We assume the null model is true to find the P-value. Make a picture of the t-model, centred at μ_0. Since this is a lower-tail test, shade the region to the left of the observed average profit.	(The observed mean is less than one standard error below the hypothesized value.)
	The P-value is the probability of observing a sample mean as small as \$1438.90 (or smaller) *if* the true mean were \$1500, as the null hypothesis states. We can find this P-value from a table, calculator, or computer program.	 1438.9 771 1014 1257 1500 1743 1986 2229 P-value $= P(t_{29} < -0.2517) = 0.4015$ (or from a table $0.1 < P < 0.5$)
REPORT	**Conclusion** Link the P-value to your decision about H_0, and state your conclusion in context.	MEMO: **Re: Sales Performance** The mean profit on 30 sampled contracts closed by the sales rep in question has fallen below our standard of \$1500, but there is not enough evidence in this sample of policies to indicate that the true mean is below \$1500. If the mean were \$1500, we would expect a sample of size 30 to have a mean this low about 40.15% of the time.

Notice that the way this hypothesis was set up, the sales rep's mean profit would have to be well below \$1500 to reject the null hypothesis. Because the null hypothesis was that the mean was \$1500 and the alternative was that it was less, this set up gave some benefit of the doubt to the sales rep. There's nothing intrinsically wrong with that, but keep in mind that it's always a good idea to make sure that the hypotheses are stated in ways that will guide you to make the right business decision.

Finding *t*-Values by Hand

The Student's *t*-model is different for each value of degrees of freedom. We might print a table like Table Z (in Appendix B) for each degrees of freedom value, but that's a lot of pages and not likely to be a bestseller. One way to shorten the book is to limit ourselves to 80%, 90%, 95% and 99% confidence levels. So Statistics books usually have one table of *t*-model critical values for a selected set of confidence levels. This one does, too; see Table T in Appendix B. (You can also find tables on the internet.)

The *t*-tables run down the page for as many degrees of freedom as can fit, and they are much easier to use than the Normal tables (Figure 11.6). Then they get to the bottom of the page and run out of room. Of course, for *enough* degrees of freedom, the *t*-model gets closer and closer to the Normal, so the tables give a final row with the critical values from the Normal model and label it "∞ df."

The degrees of freedom column also shows when the *t*-model is practically different from the normal *z*-model, and thus what sample size is considered "large." For df > 30, look at the gaps between the reported df values: 32, 35, 40, 45, 50, 60, 75, 100, 120, 140, 180, 250, 400, 1000, and infinity. These are increments greater than one. Beginning at 30 df, the changes are in increments of one, and that is where the critical values begin to change in meaningful amounts. If the values at the 95% confidence level were rounded to one decimal point, they would change from 2.0 to 2.1 at 27 df. In the confidence interval formula that change would represent about a 5% increase in the margin of error.

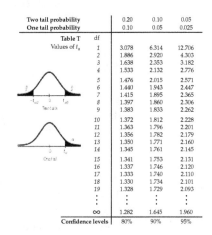

Two tail probability		0.20	0.10	0.05
One tail probability		0.10	0.05	0.025
Table T	df			
Values of t_α	1	3.078	6.314	12.706
	2	1.886	2.920	4.303
	3	1.638	2.353	3.182
	4	1.533	2.132	2.776
	5	1.476	2.015	2.571
	6	1.440	1.943	2.447
	7	1.415	1.895	2.365
	8	1.397	1.860	2.306
	9	1.383	1.833	2.262
	10	1.372	1.812	2.228
	11	1.363	1.796	2.201
	12	1.356	1.782	2.179
	13	1.350	1.771	2.160
	14	1.345	1.761	2.145
	15	1.341	1.753	2.131
	16	1.337	1.746	2.120
	17	1.333	1.740	2.110
	18	1.330	1.734	2.101
	19	1.328	1.729	2.093
	⋮	⋮	⋮	⋮
	∞	1.282	1.645	1.960
Confidence levels		80%	90%	95%

| **Figure 11.6** Part of Table T in Appendix B.

✔ **JUST CHECKING**

The *Statistics Canada 2006 Census Technical Report* states, "The price paid for these advantages [of sampling] is the introduction of sampling error to census figures that are based on the sample." The U.S. Census Bureau concurs that estimates of characteristics reported on both the short form and long form will not match, because of sampling error.

The short-form estimates are values from a complete census, so they are the "true" values—something we don't usually have when we do inference.

8 Suppose we use long-form data to make 100 95% confidence intervals for the mean age of residents, one for each of 100 of the census-defined areas. How many of these 100 intervals should we expect will *fail* to include the true mean age (as determined from the complete short-form census data)?

9 Based on the long-form sample, we might test the null hypothesis that the mean household income in a region was the same as in the previous census. Would the standard error for such a test be likely to increase or decrease if we used an area with more long-form respondents?

For example, suppose we've performed a one-sample *t*-test finding for large degrees of freedom, with 19 df and want the upper-tail P-value. From the table we see that 1.639 falls between 1.328 and 1.729. All we can say is that the P-value lies between the P-values of these two critical values, so $0.05 < P < 0.10$.

Or we can use technology. Calculators or statistics programs can give critical values for a *t*-model for any number of degrees of freedom and for any confidence

For large degrees of freedom, the shape of Student's *t*-models changes more gradually. Table T in Appendix B includes degrees of freedom between 100 and 1000 so you can pin down the P-value for just about any df. If your df's aren't listed, take the cautious approach by using the next lower value or use technology to find the exact value.

level you need. And they can go straight to P-values when you test a hypothesis. With tables we can only approximate P-values by pinning them down between two of the columns. Usually that's good enough. More precision won't necessarily help make a good business decision.

Did we need to perform a one-sample *t*-test to know that we would fail to reject a null hypothesis that the mean was $1500?

After all, we saw that the interval $942.48 to $1935.32 contained all the plausible values for the mean profit at 95% confidence. Since $1500 was one of those plausible values, we have no evidence to suggest that the mean is not $1500.

Because we wanted a one-sided test, our α level from the 95% confidence interval would be 0.025, corresponding to only one side of the confidence interval. If we wanted an α level of 0.05 we could look at the narrower 90% confidence interval: ($1022.26, $1855.54). Because $1500 is also in this interval we would come to the same conclusion and fail to reject the hypothesis that the mean is $1500.

11.8 Sample Size

How large a sample do we need? The simple answer is always "larger." But more data cost money, effort, and time. So how much is enough? Suppose your computer took an hour to download a movie you wanted to watch. You wouldn't be happy. Then you hear about a program that claims to download movies in under a half hour. You're interested enough to spend $29.95 for it, but only if it really delivers. So you get the free evaluation copy and test it by downloading a movie 10 times. Of course, the mean download time is not exactly 30 minutes as claimed. Observations vary. If the margin of error were eight minutes, though, you'd probably be able to decide whether the software was worth the money. Doubling the sample size would require another five or so hours of testing and would reduce your margin of error to a bit under six minutes. You'd need to decide whether that's worth the effort.

As we make plans to collect data, we should have some idea of how small a margin of error is required to be able to draw a conclusion or detect a difference we want to see. If the size of the effect we're studying is large, then we may be able to tolerate a larger ME. If we need great precision, however, we'll want a smaller ME, and, of course, that means a larger sample size.

Armed with the ME and confidence level, we can find the sample size we'll need. Almost.

We know that for a mean, $ME = t^*_{n-1} \times SE(\bar{y})$ and that $SE(\bar{y}) = \dfrac{s}{\sqrt{n}}$, so we can determine the sample size by solving this equation for *n*:

$$ME = t^*_{n-1} \times \frac{s}{\sqrt{n}}$$

The good news is that we have an equation; the bad news is that we won't know most of the values we need to compute it. When we thought about sample size for proportions, we ran into a similar problem. There we had to guess a working value for *p* to compute a sample size. Here, we need to know *s*. We don't know *s* until we get some data, but we want to calculate the sample size *before* collecting the data. We might be able to make a good guess, and that is often good enough for this purpose. If we have no idea what the standard deviation might be or if the sample size really matters (for example, because each additional individual is very expensive to sample or experiment on), it might be a good idea to run a small *pilot study* to get some feeling for the size of the standard deviation.

Sample size calculations by hand

Let's give the sample size formula a spin. Suppose we want an ME of 8 minutes and we think the standard deviation of download times is about 10 minutes. Using a 95% confidence interval and $z* = 1.96$, we solve for n:

$$8 = 1.96 \frac{10}{\sqrt{n}}$$

$$\sqrt{n} = \frac{1.96 \times 10}{8} = 2.45$$

$$n = (2.45)^2 = 6.0025$$

That's a small sample size, so we use $(6 - 1) = 5$ degrees of freedom to substitute an appropriate $t*$ value. At 95%, $t*_5 = 2.571$. Now we can solve the equation one more time:

$$8 = 2.571 \frac{10}{\sqrt{n}}$$

$$\sqrt{n} = \frac{2.571 \times 10}{8} \approx 3.214$$

$$n = (3.214)^2 \approx 10.33$$

To make sure the ME is no larger than you want, you should always round *up*, which gives $n = 11$ runs. So, to get an ME of 8 minutes, we should find the downloading times for $n = 11$ movies.

How did we come up with 10 minutes as a good guess at the standard deviation? One answer comes from remembering that the standard deviation is the typical distance between data values. Here it means that we expect one download time to differ from another by about 10 minutes. A second answer is to use the rule of thumb that for reasonably symmetric, unimodal distributions, the standard deviation is approximately equal to the range divided by four (for small samples). The minimum and maximum download times could reasonably be expected to be 10 and 50 minutes respectively; that's a range of 40 (50 minus 10). Divide by 4 to get the estimated standard deviation of 10 minutes.

Here's another way to illustrate the $n - 1$ degrees of freedom. Suppose you are asked to choose five numbers. You can pick any numbers you like, except that the mean must be 10. Your first four choices are completely free and unconstrained, but the last choice is predetermined. It must be the number that, when added to the first four, gives a mean of 10. In other words, you have four free choices, or four degrees of freedom, not five. In the t-model, the same data that you use to compute the standard deviation have a constraint; their mean is $\bar{y}$.

That's not all. Without knowing n, we don't know the degrees of freedom, and we can't find the critical value, $t*_{n-1}$. One common approach is to use the corresponding $z*$ value from the Normal model. If you've chosen a 95% confidence level, then just use 2, following the 68-95-99.7 Rule, or 1.96 to be more precise. If your estimated sample size is 60 or more, it's probably okay—$z*$ was a good guess. If it's smaller than that, you may want to add a step, using $z*$ at first, finding n, and then replacing $z*$ with the corresponding $t*_{n-1}$ and calculating the sample size once more.

Sample size calculations are *never* exact. The margin of error you find *after* collecting the data won't match exactly the one you used to find n. The sample size formula depends on quantities that you won't have until you collect the data, but using it is an important first step. Before you collect data, it's always a good idea to know whether the sample size is large enough to give you a good chance of being able to tell you what you want to know.

*11.9 Degrees of Freedom—Why $n - 1$?

In Section 11.4 we observed that the number of degrees of freedom $(n - 1)$ might have reminded you of the value we divide by to find the standard deviation of the data (since, after all, it's the same number). We promised back when we introduced that formula to say a bit more about why we divide by $n - 1$ rather than by n. The reason is closely tied to the reasoning of the t-distribution.

If only we knew the true population mean, μ, we would find the sample standard deviation using n instead of $n - 1$ as:

$$s = \sqrt{\frac{\sum (y - \mu)^2}{n}} \text{ and we'd call it } s.$$

We use $\bar{y}$ instead of μ, though, and that causes a problem. For any sample, $\bar{y}$ will be as close to the data values as possible. Generally the population mean, μ, will be farther away. Think about it. GMAT scores have a population mean of 525. If you took a random sample of 5 students who took the test, their sample mean wouldn't be 525. The five data values will be closer to their own $\bar{y}$ than to 525. So if we use $\sum (y - \bar{y})^2$ instead of $\sum (y - \mu)^2$ in the equation to calculate s, our standard deviation estimate will be too small. The amazing mathematical fact is that we can compensate for the fact that $\sum (y - \bar{y})^2$ is too small just by dividing by $n - 1$ instead of by n. So that's all the $n - 1$ is doing in the denominator of s. We call $n - 1$ the degrees of freedom.

WHAT CAN GO WRONG?

First, you must decide when to use Student's *t* methods.

- **Don't confuse proportions and means.** When you treat your data as categorical, counting successes and summarizing with a sample proportion, make inferences using the Normal model methods. When you treat your data as quantitative, summarizing with a sample mean, make your inferences using Student's *t* methods. Remember: *z* for proportions, *t* for means.

- **Be careful of interpretation when confidence intervals overlap.** If confidence intervals for the means from two groups overlap, don't jump to the conclusion that the means are equal. It can be the case that two means are significantly different, and yet their confidence intervals will overlap. We'll see in the next chapter how to test the difference between two means directly. If the confidence intervals don't overlap, we are safe in rejecting the null hypothesis, but the methods in the next chapter are more powerful.

  Student's *t* methods work only when the Normal Population Assumption is true. Naturally, many of the ways things can go wrong turn out to be ways that the Normal Population Assumption can fail. It's always a good idea to look for the most common kinds of failure. It turns out that you can even fix some of them.

- **Beware of multimodality.** The Nearly Normal Condition clearly fails if a histogram of the data has two or more modes. When you see this, look for the possibility that your data come from two groups. If so, your best bet is to try to separate the data into groups. (Use the variables to help distinguish the modes, if possible. For example, if the modes seem to be composed mostly of men in one and women in the other, split the data according to the person's sex.) Then you can analyze each group separately.

- **Beware of skewed data.** The CLT assures us that the sampling distribution model is Normal if *n* is large enough. If the population is nearly Normal, even small samples may work. If the population is very skewed, then *n* will have to be large before the Normal model will work well. If we sampled 50 or even 100 CEOs and used that sample to make a statement about the mean of all CEOs' compensation, we'd likely get into trouble because the underlying data distribution is so skewed. Unfortunately, there's no good rule to handle this. It just depends on how skewed the data distribution is. Always plot the data to check.

> As tempting as it is to get rid of annoying values, you can't just throw away outliers and not discuss them. It is not appropriate to lop off the highest or lowest values just to improve your results.

- **Investigate outliers.** The Nearly Normal Condition also fails if the data have outliers. If you find outliers in the data, you need to investigate them. Sometimes, it's obvious that a data value is wrong and the justification for removing or correcting it is clear. When there's no clear justification for removing an outlier, you might want to run the analysis both with and without the outlier and note any differences in your conclusions. Any time data values are set aside, you *must* report on them individually. Often they will turn out to be the most informative part of your report on the data.[6]

---

[6] This suggestion may be controversial in some disciplines. Setting aside outliers is seen by some as unethical because the result is likely to be a narrower confidence interval or a smaller P-value. But an analysis of data with outliers left in place is *always* wrong. The outliers violate the Nearly Normal Condition and also the implicit assumption of a homogeneous population, so they invalidate inference procedures. An analysis of the non-outlying points, along with a separate discussion of the outliers, is often much more informative, and can reveal important aspects of the data.

Of course, Normality issues aren't the only risks you face when doing inferences about means.

- **Watch out for bias.** Measurements of all kinds can be biased. If your observations differ from the true mean in a systematic way, your confidence interval may not capture the true mean. And there is no sample size that will save you. A bathroom scale that's two kilograms off will be two kilograms off even if you weigh yourself 100 times and take the average. We've seen several sources of bias in surveys, but measurements can be biased, too. Be sure to think about possible sources of bias in your measurements.

- **Make sure data are independent.** Student's *t* methods also require the sampled values to be mutually independent. We check for random sampling and the 10% Condition. You should also think hard about whether there are likely violations of independence in the data collection method. If there are, be very cautious about using these methods.

- **Make sure that data are from an appropriately randomized sample.** Ideally, all data that we analyze are drawn from a simple random sample or generated by a randomized experiment. When they're not, be careful about making inferences from them. You may still compute a confidence interval correctly or get the mechanics of the P-value right, but this can't save you from making a serious mistake in inference.

ETHICS IN ACTION

The Fraser Institute 2011 report on wait times for elective medical treatment in Canada[7] indicated a total wait time of 19.0 weeks between referral from a general practitioner and receiving elective treatment, the longest total wait time recorded since their measurement began in 1993. Wait time has two components: the wait from GP to specialist and the wait from specialist to treatment.

The report also found that the wait time between consulting a specialist and receiving treatment, across Canada, was 9.5 weeks in 2011, up from 9.3 weeks in 2010. Physicians believe that Canadians wait nearly three weeks longer than what they consider to be clinically reasonable. Ontario reported the shortest wait time of 7.1 weeks and Saskatchewan the longest at 19.0 weeks. These increases are despite considerable effort and initiatives aimed at reducing wait time.

To compare itself with other hospitals in the province, a hospital in Saskatchewan monitors its wait time between specialist consultation and receipt of treatment. After collecting data for a random sample of 30 patients, they found an average wait time of 15.3 weeks with a standard deviation of 1.6 weeks. Further statistical analysis yielded a 95% confidence interval of 14.7 to 15.9 weeks, a clear indication that patients wait less than 19 weeks to get treatment. The hospital issued a press release stating, "95% of our patients wait three weeks less than the provincial average to get treatment."

ETHICAL ISSUE *Interpretation of the confidence interval is incorrect and misleading (related to ASA Ethical Guidelines, Item C, which can be found at http://www.amstat.org/about/ethicalguidelines.cfm). The confidence interval does not provide results for individual patients. So, it is incorrect to state that 95% of patients wait less (or can expect to wait less) than 16 weeks to get treatment.*

ETHICAL SOLUTION *Interpret the results of the confidence interval correctly, in terms of the mean wait time and not individual patients.*

---

[7] B. Barua, M. Rovere, & B. J. Skinner, "Waiting Your Turn: Wait Times for Health Care in Canada 2011 Report" (Vancouver: Fraser Institute Studies in Health Care Policy, December 2011).

WHAT HAVE WE LEARNED?

We've learned that the behaviour of sample means, like proportions, is also based on the Central Limit Theorem—the Fundamental Theorem of Statistics. Again the sample must be random and needs to be larger if our data come from a population that's not roughly unimodal and symmetric. Then:

- Regardless of the shape of the original population, the shape of the distribution of the means of all possible samples can be described by a Normal model, provided the samples are large enough.

- The centre of the sampling model will be the true mean of the population from which we took the sample.

- The standard deviation of the sample means is the population's standard deviation divided by the square root of the sample size, $\frac{\sigma}{\sqrt{n}}$.

We first learned to create confidence intervals (in Chapter 9) and test hypotheses (in Chapter 10) about proportions. Now we've turned our attention to means and learned that statistical inference for means relies on the same concepts; only the mechanics and our model have changed.

- We've learned that what we can say about a population mean is inferred from data, using the mean and standard deviation of a representative random sample.

- We've learned to describe the sampling distribution of sample means using a new model we select from the Student's *t* family based on our degrees of freedom.

- We've learned that our ruler for measuring the variability in sample means is the standard error:

$$SE(\bar{y}) = \frac{s}{\sqrt{n}}$$

- We've learned to find the margin of error for a confidence interval using that standard error ruler and a critical value based on a Student's *t*-model.

- We've also learned to use that ruler to test hypotheses about the population mean.

Above all, we've learned that the reasoning of inference, the need to verify that the appropriate assumptions are met, and the proper interpretation of confidence intervals and P-values all remain the same regardless of whether we are investigating means or proportions.

Terms

Degrees of freedom (df)

A parameter of the Student's *t*-distribution that depends upon the sample size. Typically, more degrees of freedom reflects increasing information from the sample.

One-sample *t*-interval for the mean (also called Confidence interval for the mean)

A one-sample *t*-interval for the population mean is:

$$\bar{y} \pm t^*_{n-1} \times SE(\bar{y}) \text{ where } SE(\bar{y}) = \frac{s}{\sqrt{n}}$$

The critical value t^*_{n-1} depends on the particular confidence level, C, that you specify and on the number of degrees of freedom, $n - 1$.

One-sample *t*-test for the mean

A one-sample t-test for the mean tests the hypothesis H_0: $\mu = \mu_0$ using the statistic $t_{n-1} = \dfrac{\bar{y} - \mu_0}{SE(\bar{y})}$, where $SE(\bar{y}) = \dfrac{s}{\sqrt{n}}$.

Sampling distribution model for a mean

If the independence assumption and randomization condition are met and the sample size is large enough, the sampling distribution of the sample mean is well modelled by a Normal model with a mean equal to the population mean, and a standard deviation equal to $\dfrac{\sigma}{\sqrt{n}}$.

Student's *t*

A family of distributions indexed by its degrees of freedom. The t-models are unimodal, symmetric, and bell-shaped, but generally have fatter tails and a narrower centre than the Normal model. As the degrees of freedom increase, t-distributions approach the Normal model.

Skills

PLAN

- Understand that the Central Limit Theorem gives the sampling distribution model of the mean for sufficiently large samples regardless of the underlying population.

- Be able to state the assumptions required for t-tests and t-based confidence intervals.

- Know to examine your data for violations of conditions that would make inference about the population mean unwise or invalid.

- Understand that a hypothesis test can be performed with an appropriately chosen confidence interval.

DO

- Know how to compute and interpret a t-test for the population mean using a statistics software package or by working from summary statistics for a sample.

- Know how to compute and interpret a t-based confidence interval for the population mean using a statistics software package or by working from summary statistics for a sample.

REPORT

- Be able to explain the meaning of a confidence interval for a population mean. Make clear that the randomness associated with the confidence level is a statement about the interval bounds and not about the population parameter value.

- Understand that a 95% confidence interval does not trap 95% of the sample values.

- Be able to interpret the result of a test of a hypothesis about a population mean.

- Know that we do not "accept" a null hypothesis if we cannot reject it. We say that we fail to reject it.

- Understand that the P-value of a test does not give the probability that the null hypothesis is correct. It gives the probability of getting the data you got if, in fact, the null hypothesis were correct.

TECHNOLOGY HELP: Inference for Means

Statistics packages offer convenient ways to make histograms of the data. That means you have no excuse for skipping the check that the data are nearly Normal.

Any standard statistics package can compute a hypothesis test. Here's what the package output might look like in general (although no package we know gives the results in exactly this form).

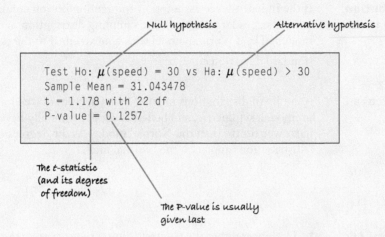

Null hypothesis   Alternative hypothesis

```
Test Ho: μ(speed) = 30 vs Ha: μ(speed) > 30
Sample Mean = 31.043478
t = 1.178 with 22 df
P-value = 0.1257
```

The *t*-statistic
(and its degrees
of freedom)

The P-value is usually
given last

The package computes the sample mean and sample standard deviation of the variable and finds the P-value from the *t*-distribution based on the appropriate number of degrees of freedom. All modern statistics packages report P-values. The package may also provide additional information such as the sample mean, sample standard deviation, *t*-statistic value, and degrees of freedom. These are useful for interpreting the resulting P-value and telling the difference between a meaningful result and one that is merely statistically significant. Statistics packages that report the estimated standard deviation of the sampling distribution usually label it "standard error" or "SE."

Inference results are also sometimes reported in a table. You may have to read carefully to find the values you need. Often, test results and the corresponding confidence interval bounds are given together. And often you must read carefully to find the alternative hypotheses. Below is an example of that kind of output.

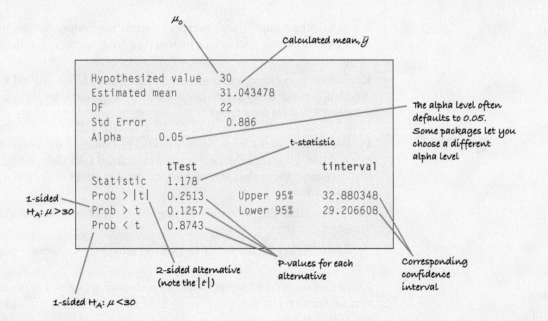

μ_0

Calculated mean, $\bar{y}$

```
Hypothesized value    30
Estimated mean        31.043478
DF                    22
Std Error              0.886
Alpha        0.05
```

The alpha level often
defaults to 0.05.
Some packages let you
choose a different
alpha level

t-statistic

```
              tTest                    tinterval
Statistic     1.178
Prob > |t|    0.2513    Upper 95%      32.880348
Prob > t      0.1257    Lower 95%      29.206608
Prob < t      0.8743
```

1-sided
$H_A: \mu > 30$

1-sided $H_A: \mu < 30$

2-sided alternative
(note the $|t|$)

P-values for each
alternative

Corresponding
confidence
interval

The commands to do inference for means on common statistics programs and calculators are not always obvious. (By contrast, the resulting output is usually clearly labelled and easy to read.) The guides for each program can help you start navigating.

MINI CASE STUDY PROJECTS

Real Estate

Andy Dean Photography/Shutterstock

A real estate agent is trying to understand the pricing of homes in her area, a region
comprising small to midsize towns and a small city. For each of 1200 homes recently
sold in the region, the file **ch11_MCSP_Real_Estate.xls** holds the following
variables:

- *Sale Price* (in $)
- *Lot size* (size of the lot in acres)
- *Waterfront* (Yes, No)
- *Age* (in years)
- *Central Air* (Yes, No)
- *Fuel Type* (Wood, Oil, Gas, Electric, Propane, Solar, Other)
- *Condition* (1 to 5, 1 = Poor, 5 = Excellent)
- *Living Area* (living area in square feet)
- *Pct University* (% in postal code who attend a four-year university program)
- *Full Baths* (number of full bathrooms)
- *Half Baths* (number of half bathrooms)
- *Bedrooms* (number of bedrooms)
- *Fireplaces* (number of fireplaces)

The agent has a family interested in a four bedroom house. Using confidence intervals, how should she advise the family on what the average price of a four bedroom house
might be in this area? Compare that to a confidence interval for two bedroom homes.
How does the presence of central air conditioning affect the mean price of houses in this
area? Use confidence intervals and graphics to help answer that question.

Explore other questions that might be useful for the real estate agent in knowing
how different categorical factors affect the sale price and write up a short report on your
findings.

Social Media

Social media websites generate revenue by collecting data on their users and presenting ads to users based upon their preferences. Some social media companies also
offer premium paid content to supplement their revenue stream. The full database of a
popular social media company amounts to more than 10 million users, but the data set
ch11_MCSP_Social_Media.xlsx has a sample of 916 users and includes the variables:

- *Age* (in years)
- *Relationship Status* (Y = Yes, in a relationship, N = No, not in a relationship/
  Unknown)

- *Gender* (F = Female, M = Male, U = Unknown)
- *Advertising Revenues* (ordered categories of total advertising revenue from user, ranging from 0 = Lowest, 9 = Highest)
- *Family* (Number of family members using the same social network)
- *Last Purchase* (0 = No purchases in the past year, 1 = Purchased premium services in the past year)
- *Last Purchase Amount* ($ amount of last purchase)

The young CIO (Chief Information Officer) of the organization wants to know how much users spend on average per year, and what factors might influence that amount. Compare the confidence intervals for the mean *Last Purchase Amount* for the two categories of *Relationship Status*. Redo the comparison for the two categories of *Gender* (exclude Unknown). Finally, compare the groups that produce very high *Advertising Revenue* (use category 9) and very low *Advertising Revenue* (use category 1). Write a short report using graphics and confidence intervals to summarize what you have found. (Be careful not to make inferences directly about the differences between groups. We'll discuss that in the next chapter, but for now your inferences should be about single groups.)

(The distribution of *Last Purchase Amount* is highly skewed to the right, and so the median might be thought to be the appropriate summary. But the median is $0.00, so the analysts must use the mean. From simulations, they have ascertained that the sampling distribution for the mean is unimodal and symmetric for samples larger than 250 or so. Note that small differences in the mean could result in millions of dollars of added revenue nationwide. The average cost to solicit members for purchases is $0.67 per person, per year.)

MyStatLab **Students! Save time, improve your grades with MyStatLab.**
The Exercises marked in red can be found on MyStatLab. You can practice them as often as you want, and most feature step-by-step guided solutions to help you find the right answer. You'll find a personalized Study Plan available to you too! Data Sets for exercises marked **T** are also available on MyStatLab for formatted technologies.

EXERCISES

1. Sampling. A sample is chosen randomly from a population that can be described by a Normal model. **LO❶**

a) What's the sampling distribution model for the sample mean? Describe shape, centre, and spread.

b) If we choose a larger sample, what's the effect on this sampling distribution model?

2. Sampling, part 2. A sample is chosen randomly from a population that was strongly skewed to the left. **LO❶**

a) Describe the sampling distribution model for the sample mean if the sample size is small.

b) If we make the sample larger, what happens to the sampling distribution model's shape, centre, and spread?

c) As we make the sample larger, what happens to the expected distribution of the data in the sample?

3. Home values. Assessment records indicate that the value of homes in a small city is skewed right, with a mean of $140 000 and a standard deviation of $60 000. To check the accuracy of the assessment data, officials plan to conduct a detailed appraisal of 100 homes selected at random. Using the 68-95-99.7 Rule, draw

and label an appropriate sampling model for the mean value of the homes selected. **LO❶**

4. Fidelity funds. Statistics for the closing price of the Fidelity Aggressive International Fund in a recent year indicate that the average closing price was $39.01, with a standard deviation of $2.86. Assume that this will be indicative of performance next year and assume that a Normal model applies. Using the 68-95-99.7 Rule, draw and label an appropriate sampling model for the mean closing price of 35 funds selected at random. **LO❶**

5. At work. Some business analysts estimate that the length of time people work at a job has a mean of 6.2 years and a standard deviation of 4.5 years. **LO❶**

a) Explain why you suspect this distribution may be skewed to the right.

b) Explain why you could estimate the probability that 100 people selected at random had worked for their employers an average of 10 years or more, but you could not estimate the probability that an individual had done so.

6. Store receipts. Grocery store receipts show that customer purchases have a skewed distribution with a mean of $32 and a standard deviation of $20. **LO❶**

a) Explain why you cannot determine the probability that the next customer will spend at least $40.
b) Can you estimate the probability that the next 10 customers will spend an average of at least $40? Explain.
c) Is it likely that the next 50 customers will spend an average of at least $40? Explain.

7. Quality control. The weight of sugar in a medium-size bag is stated to be 10 kilograms. The amount that the packaging machine puts in these bags is believed to have a Normal model with a mean of 10.2 kilograms and a standard deviation of 0.12 kilograms. **LO❶**

a) What fraction of all bags sold are underweight?
b) Some of the sugar is sold in "bargain packs" of three bags. What's the probability that none of the three is underweight?
c) What's the probability that the mean weight of the three bags is below the stated amount?
d) What's the probability that the mean weight of a 24-bag case of sugar chips is below 10 kilograms?

8. Milk production. Although most of us buy milk by the litre, quart, or gallon, farmers measure daily production in pounds. Ayrshire cows average 47 pounds of milk a day, with a standard deviation of 6 pounds. For Jersey cows, the mean daily production is 43 pounds, with a standard deviation of 5 pounds. Assume that Normal models describe milk production for these breeds. **LO❶**

a) We select an Ayrshire at random. What's the probability that she averages more than 50 pounds of milk a day?
b) What's the probability that a randomly selected Ayrshire gives more milk than a randomly selected Jersey?
c) A farmer has 20 Jerseys. What's the probability that the average production for this small herd exceeds 45 pounds of milk a day?

9. t-models. Using the *t* tables, software, or a calculator, estimate: **LO❷**

a) the critical value of *t* for a 90% confidence interval with df = 17.
b) the critical value of *t* for a 98% confidence interval with df = 88.
c) the P-value for $t \geq 2.09$ with 4 degrees of freedom.
d) the P-value for $|t| > 1.78$ with 22 degrees of freedom.

10. t-models, part 2. Using the *t* tables, software, or a calculator, estimate: **LO❷**

a) the critical value of *t* for a 95% confidence interval with df = 7.
b) the critical value of *t* for a 99% confidence interval with df = 102.
c) the P-value for $t \leq 2.19$ with 41 degrees of freedom.
d) the P-value for $|t| > 2.33$ with 12 degrees of freedom.

11. Confidence intervals. Describe how the width of a 95% confidence interval for a mean changes as the standard deviation (*s*) of a sample increases, assuming sample size remains the same. **LO❸**

12. Confidence intervals, part 2. Describe how the width of a 95% confidence interval for a mean changes as the sample size (*n*) increases, assuming the standard deviation remains the same. **LO❸**

13. Confidence intervals and sample size. A confidence interval for the price of a litre of gasoline from a random sample of 30 gas stations in a region gives the following statistics: **LO❸**

$$\bar{y} = \$1.40 \quad s = \$0.18$$

a) Find a 95% confidence interval for the mean price of regular gasoline in that region.
b) Find the 90% confidence interval for the mean.
c) If we had the same statistics from a sample of 60 stations, what would the 95% confidence interval be now?

14. Confidence intervals and sample size, part 2. A confidence interval for the price of a litre of gasoline from a random sample of 30 gas stations in a region gives the following statistics: **LO❸**

$$\bar{y} = \$1.40 \quad SE(\bar{y}) = \$0.06$$

a) Find a 95% confidence interval for the mean price of regular gasoline in that region.
b) Find the 90% confidence interval for the mean.
c) If we had the same statistics from a sample of 60 stations, what would the 95% confidence interval be now?

15. Marketing livestock feed. A feed supply company has developed a special feed supplement to see if it will promote weight gain in livestock. Their researchers report that the 77 cows studied gained an average of 25 kilograms and that a 95% confidence interval for the mean weight gain this supplement produces has a margin of error of ±5 kilograms. Staff in their marketing department wrote the following conclusions. Did anyone interpret the interval correctly? Explain any misinterpretations. **LO❸**

a) 95% of the cows studied gained between 20 and 30 kilograms.
b) We're 95% sure that a cow fed this supplement will gain between 20 and 30 kilograms.
c) We're 95% sure that the average weight gain among the cows in this study was between 20 and 30 kilograms.
d) The average weight gain of cows fed this supplement is between 20 and 30 kilograms 95% of the time.
e) If this supplement is tested on another sample of cows, there is a 95% chance that their average weight gain will be between 20 and 30 kilograms.

16. Meal costs. A company is interested in estimating the costs of lunch in their cafeteria. After surveying employees, the staff calculated that a 95% confidence interval for the mean amount of money spent for lunch over a period of six months is ($780, $920). Now the organization is trying to write its report and considering the following interpretations. Comment on each. **LO❸**

a) 95% of all employees pay between $780 and $920 for lunch.
b) 95% of the sampled employees paid between $780 and $920 for lunch.

c) We're 95% sure that employees in this sample averaged between $780 and $920 for lunch.

d) 95% of all samples of employees will have average lunch costs between $780 and $920.

e) We're 95% sure that the average amount all employees pay for lunch is between $780 and $920.

17. CEO compensation. A sample of 20 CEOs from the Forbes 500 shows total annual compensations ranging from a minimum of $0.1 to $62.24 million. The average for these 20 CEOs is $7.946 million. The histogram and boxplot are as follows: LO ❸

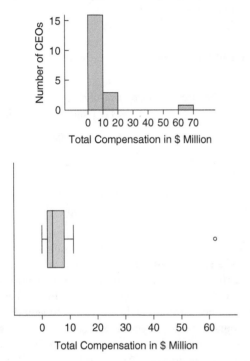

Total Compensation in $ Million

Based on these data, a computer program found that a 95% confidence interval for the mean annual compensation of all Forbes 500 CEOs is (1.69, 14.20) $M. Why should you be hesitant to trust this confidence interval?

18. Credit card charges. A credit card company takes a random sample of 100 cardholders to see how much they charged on their card in a recent month. A histogram and boxplot are as follows: LO ❸

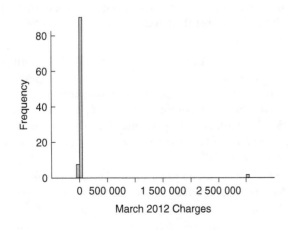

March 2012 Charges

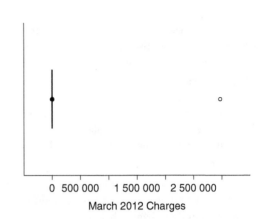

March 2012 Charges

A computer program found that the 95% confidence interval for the mean amount spent in March 2012 is (−$28 366.84, $90 691.49). Explain why the analysts didn't find the confidence interval useful, and explain what went wrong.

19. Parking. Hoping to lure more shoppers downtown, a city builds a new public parking garage in the central business district. The city plans to pay for the structure through parking fees. For a random sample of 44 weekdays, daily fees collected averaged $126, with a standard deviation of $15. LO ❸

a) What assumptions must you make in order to use these statistics for inference?

b) Find a 90% confidence interval for the mean daily income this parking garage will generate.

c) Explain in context what this confidence interval means.

d) Explain what 90% confidence means in this context.

e) The consultant who advised the city on this project predicted that parking revenues would average $128 per day. Based on your confidence interval, what do you think of the consultant's prediction? Why?

20. Housing. 2008 was a difficult year for the economy globally, and the United States in particular, where there were a large number of foreclosures of family homes. In one large community, realtors randomly sampled 36 bids from potential buyers to determine the average loss in home value. The sample showed the average loss was $11 560 with a standard deviation of $1500. LO ❸

a) What assumptions and conditions must be checked before finding a confidence interval? How would you check them?

b) Find a 95% confidence interval for the mean loss in value per home.

c) Interpret this interval and explain what 95% confidence means.

d) Suppose that across the United States, the average loss in home values at this time was $10 000. Do you think the loss in the sampled community differs significantly from the U.S. national average? Explain.

21. Parking, part 2. Suppose that for budget planning purposes the city in Exercise 19 needs a better estimate of the mean daily income from parking fees. LO ❸

a) Someone suggests that the city use its data to create a 95% confidence interval instead of the 90% interval first created.

How would this interval be better for the city? (You need not actually create the new interval.)

b) How would the 95% confidence interval be worse for the planners?

c) How could they achieve a confidence interval estimate that would better serve their planning needs?

22. Housing, part 2. In Exercise 20, we found a 95% confidence interval to estimate the loss in home values.   LO❸

a) Suppose the standard deviation of the losses was $3000 instead of the $1500 used for that interval. What effect would the larger standard deviation have on the width of the confidence interval (assuming the same level of confidence)?

b) Your classmate suggests that the margin of error in the interval could be reduced if the confidence level were changed to 90% instead of 95%. Do you agree with this statement? Why or why not?

c) Instead of changing the level of confidence, would it be more statistically appropriate to draw a bigger sample?

23. Provincial budgets. Provinces that rely on sales tax for revenue to fund education, public safety, and other programs often end up with budget surpluses during economic growth periods (when people spend more on consumer goods) and budget deficits during recessions (when people spend less on consumer goods). Fifty-one small retailers in a province with a growing economy were recently sampled. The sample showed a mean increase of $2350 in additional sales tax revenue collected per retailer compared to the previous quarter. The sample standard deviation = $425.   LO❸

a) Find a 95% confidence interval for the mean increase in sales tax revenue.

b) What assumptions have you made in this inference? Do you think the appropriate conditions have been satisfied?

c) Explain what your interval means and provide an example of what it does not mean.

24. Provincial budgets, part 2. Suppose the province in Exercise 23 sampled 16 small retailers instead of 51, and for the sample of 16, the sample mean increase again equaled $2350 in additional sales tax revenue collected per retailer compared to the previous quarter. Also assume the sample standard deviation = $425.   LO❸

a) What is the standard error of the mean increase in sales tax revenue collected?

b) What happens to the accuracy of the estimate when the interval is constructed using the smaller sample size?

c) Find and interpret a 95% confidence interval.

d) How does the margin of error for the interval constructed in Exercise 23 compare with the margin of error constructed in this exercise? Explain statistically how sample size changes the accuracy of the constructed interval. Which sample would you prefer if you were a provincial budget planner? Why?

25. Departures. What are the chances your flight will leave on time? The U.S. Bureau of Transportation Statistics of the Department of Transportation publishes information about

airline performance. Here are a histogram and summary statistics for the percentage of flights departing on time each month from 1995 through 2006.   LO❸

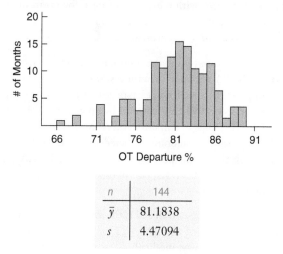

n	144
$\bar{y}$	81.1838
s	4.47094

There is no evidence of a trend over time. (The correlation of On Time Departure% with time is $r = -0.016$.)

a) Check the assumptions and conditions for inference.

b) Find a 90% confidence interval for the true percentage of flights that depart on time.

c) Interpret this interval for a traveller planning to fly.

26. Late arrivals. Will your flight get you to your destination on time? The U.S. Bureau of Transportation Statistics reported the percentage of flights that were late each month from 1995 through 2006. Here's a histogram, along with some summary statistics: LO❸

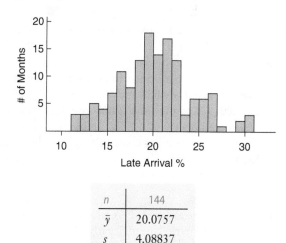

n	144
$\bar{y}$	20.0757
s	4.08837

We can consider these data to be a representative sample of all months. There is no evidence of a time trend ($r = -0.07$).

a) Check the assumptions and conditions for inference about the mean.

b) Find a 99% confidence interval for the true percentage of flights that arrive late.

c) Interpret this interval for a traveller planning to fly.

27. Ecommerce. A market researcher at a major clothing company decides to investigate whether the amount of online sales has changed. She compares the mean monthly online sales of the past several months with a historical figure for mean monthly sales for online purchases. She gets a P-value of 0.01. Explain in this context what the 1% represents. **LO⑤**

28. Performance standards. The United States Golf Association (USGA) sets performance standards for golf balls. For example, the initial velocity of the ball may not exceed 250 feet per second when measured by an apparatus approved by the USGA. Suppose a manufacturer introduces a new kind of ball and provides a randomly selected sample of balls for testing. Based on the mean speed in the sample, the USGA comes up with a P-value of 0.34. Explain in this context what the 34% represents. **LO⑤**

29. Canadian income tax. In 2011, the average Canadian family earned cash income of about $74 233 and paid total taxes (on income, social security, medical, sales, property, fuel, liquor, etc.) of about $31 000, or 41.5% of cash income (*Taxes versus the Necessities of Life: The Canadian Consumer Tax Index, 2012 edition*. www.fraserinstitute.org). Here we focus on income tax only. Each province has a different tax rate so taxes vary by region of the country as well as on earnings. For example, if you earned a taxable income of $30 000 in 2011, you would have paid $4000 income tax if you lived in British Columbia, and about $5500 (the highest) if you lived in Quebec.

Suppose you want to test the hypothesis that Albertans have a different tax bill than British Columbians. To do this, you randomly sample 100 tax returns of Albertans who were at the $30 000 taxable income level in 2011 and find the sample mean to be $3825 with a standard deviation of $635. **LO③**

a) Find and interpret a 95% confidence interval estimate for the true mean 2011 tax bill for Albertans with $30 000 taxable income.

b) In a hypothesis test performed to determine whether the Alberta's average tax bill was different, the test was rejected with a P-value = 0.007 (using the same sample results shown above and a level of significance = 0.05). Explain how the confidence interval constructed in part a is consistent with the hypothesis test results. Your discussion should include the level of confidence, the interval bounds, the P-value, and the hypothesis test decision.

30. Canadian income tax, part 2. A taxation advocate claims that the tax bill in Ontario is significantly higher than that in British Columbia. To test his claim you take a random sample of 100 tax returns of Ontarians who were at the $30 000 taxable income level in 2011, and this time find a sample mean of $4050 with a standard deviation of $700. **LO③**

a) Find and interpret a 95% confidence interval estimate for the true mean 2011 tax bill of Ontarians with $30 000 taxable income.

b) Is the taxation advocate correct that Ontario has a significantly higher tax bill than British Columbia for earners at the $30 000 level?

31. TV safety. The manufacturer of a metal stand for home TV sets must be sure that its product will not fail under the weight of a typical TV set. Since some larger sets weigh nearly 50 kilograms, the company's safety inspectors have set a standard of ensuring that the stands can support an average of 50 kilograms. Their inspectors regularly subject a random sample of the stands to increasing weight until they fail. They test the hypothesis $H_0: \mu = 80$ against $H_A: \mu > 80$, using the level of significance $\alpha = 0.01$. If the sample of stands fails this safety test, the inspectors will not certify the product for sale to the general public. **LO④**

a) Is this an upper-tail or lower-tail test? In the context of the problem, why do you think this is important?

b) Explain what will happen if the inspectors commit a Type I error.

c) Explain what will happen if the inspectors commit a Type II error.

32. Quality control. During an angiogram, heart problems can be examined via a small tube (a catheter) threaded into the heart from a vein in the patient's leg. It's important that the company who manufactures the catheter maintain a catheter diameter of 2.00 mm. (The standard deviation is quite small.) Each day, quality control personnel make several measurements to test $H_0: \mu = 2.00$ against $H_A: \mu \neq 2.00$ at a significance level of $\alpha = 0.05$. If they discover a problem, they will stop the manufacturing process until it is corrected. **LO④**

a) Is this a one-sided or two-sided test? In the context of the problem, why do you think this is important?

b) Explain in this context what happens if the quality control people commit a Type I error.

c) Explain in this context what happens if the quality control people commit a Type II error.

33. TV safety, revisited. The manufacturer of the metal TV stands in Exercise 31 is thinking of revising its safety test. **LO④**

a) If the company's lawyers are worried about being sued for selling an unsafe product, should they increase or decrease the value of α? Explain.

b. In this context, what is meant by the power of the test?

c) If the company wants to increase the power of the test, what options does it have? Explain the advantages and disadvantages of each option.

34. Quality control, part 2. The catheter company in Exercise 32 is reviewing its testing procedure. **LO④**

a) Suppose the significance level is changed to $\alpha = 0.01$. Will the probability of Type II error increase, decrease, or remain the same?

b) What is meant by the power of the test the company conducts?

c) Suppose the manufacturing process is slipping out of proper adjustment. As the actual mean diameter of the catheters produced gets farther and farther above the desired 2.00 mm, will the power of the quality control test increase, decrease, or remain the same?

d) What could they do to improve the power of the test?

35. Ecommerce, part 2. The average age of online consumers a few years ago was 23.3 years. As older individuals gain confidence with the internet, it is believed that the average age has increased. We would like to test this belief. **LO⑤**

a) Write appropriate hypotheses.

b) We plan to test the null hypothesis by selecting a random sample of 40 individuals who have made an online purchase during 2012. Do you think the necessary assumptions for inference are satisfied? Explain.

c) The online shoppers in our sample had an average age of 24.2 years, with a standard deviation of 5.3 years. What's the P-value for this result?

d) Explain (in context) what this P-value means.

e) What's your conclusion?

36. Fuel economy. A company with a large fleet of cars hopes to keep gasoline costs down and sets a goal of attaining a fleet average of at least 8.4 litres per 100 kilometres. To see if the goal is being met, they check the gasoline usage for 50 company trips chosen at random, finding a mean of 0.08 l/100 km and a standard deviation of 1.56 l/100 km. Is this strong evidence that they have failed to attain their fuel economy goal? **LO⑤**

a) Write appropriate hypotheses.

b) Are the necessary assumptions to perform inference satisfied?

c) Test the hypothesis and find the P-value.

d) Explain what the P-value means in this context.

e) State an appropriate conclusion.

37. Pricing for competitiveness. SLIX wax is developing a new high-performance fluorocarbon wax for cross country ski racing designed to be used under a wide variety of conditions. In order to justify the price marketing wants, the wax needs to be very fast. Specifically, the mean time to finish their standard test course should be less than 55 seconds for the former Olympic champion who is now their consultant. To test it, the consultant will ski the course eight times. **LO⑤**

a) The champion's times are 56.3, 65.9, 50.5, 52.4, 46.5, 57.8, 52.2, and 43.2 seconds to complete the test course. Should they market the wax? Explain.

b) Suppose they decide not to market the wax after the test, but it turns out that the wax really does lower the champion's average time to less than 55 seconds. What kind of error have they made? Explain the impact to the company of such an error.

38. Popcorn. Pop's Popcorn, Inc. needs to determine the optimum power and time settings for their new licorice-flavored microwave popcorn. They want to find a combination of power and time that delivers high-quality popcorn with less than 10% of the kernels left unpopped, on average—a value that their market research says is demanded by their customers. Their research department experiments with several settings and determines that power 9 at 4 minutes is optimum. Their tests confirm that this setting meets the less than 10% requirement. They change the instructions on the box and promote a new money back guarantee of less than 10% unpopped kernels. **LO⑤**

a) If, in fact, the setting results in more than 10% kernels unpopped, what kind of error have they made? What will the consequence be for the company?

b) To reduce the risk of making an error, the president (Pop himself) tells them to test eight more bags of popcorn (selected at random) at the specified setting. They find the following percentage of unpopped kernels: 7, 13.2, 10, 6, 7.8, 2.8, 2.2, 5.2. Does this provide evidence that the setting meets their goal of less than 10% unpopped? Explain.

39. False claims? A manufacturer claims that a new design for a portable phone has increased the range to 50 metres, allowing many customers to use the phone throughout their homes and yards. An independent testing laboratory found that a random sample of 44 of these phones worked over an average distance of 47.5 metres, with a standard deviation of 4 metres. Is there evidence that the manufacturer's claim is false? **LO⑤**

40. False claims? part 2. The makers of *Abolator*, a portable exercise device that sells for $149.95, claim that using their machine for only six minutes a day results in an average weight loss of 4 kilograms during the first week. A consumer organization recruits 30 volunteers to use the product according to the manufacturer's recommendations and finds an average weight loss of 2.5 kilograms with a standard deviation of 2.8 kilograms. Is there evidence that the makers of the *Abolator* claim is false? **LO⑤**

T 41. Chips Ahoy! In 1998, as an advertising campaign, the Nabisco Company announced a "1000 Chips Challenge," claiming that every 18-ounce bag of their Chips Ahoy! cookies contained at least 1000 chocolate chips. Dedicated Statistics students at the Air Force Academy (no kidding) purchased some randomly selected bags of cookies, and counted the chocolate chips. Some of their data are given below. (*Chance*, 12, no. 1 [1999]) **LO❸, LO⑤**

1219 1214 1087 1200 1419 1121 1325 1345
1244 1258 1356 1132 1191 1270 1295 1135

a) Check the assumptions and conditions for inference. Comment on any concerns you have.

b) Create a 95% confidence interval for the average number of chips in bags of Chips Ahoy! cookies.

c) What does this evidence say about Nabisco's claim? Use your confidence interval to test an appropriate hypothesis and state your conclusion.

T 42. Consumer Reports. *Consumer Reports* tested 14 brands of vanilla yogurt and found the following numbers of calories per serving: 160, 200, 220, 230, 120, 180, 140, 130, 170, 190, 80, 120, 100, and 170. **LO❸, LO⑤**

a) Check the assumptions and conditions for inference.

b) Create a 95% confidence interval for the average calorie content of vanilla yogurt.

c) A diet guide claims that you will get 120 calories from a serving of vanilla yogurt. What does this evidence indicate? Use your confidence interval to test an appropriate hypothesis and state your conclusion.

43. Investment. Investment style plays a role in constructing a mutual fund. Many individual stocks can be grouped into two distinct groups: Growth and Value. A Growth stock is one with high earning potential and often pays little or no dividends to shareholders. Conversely, Value stocks are commonly viewed as steady or more conservative stocks with a lower earning potential. A family is trying to decide what type of funds to invest in. An independent advisor claims that Value Mutual Funds provided an annualized return of greater than 8% over a recent five-year period. Below are the summary statistics for the five-year return for a random sample of such Value funds.

Variable	N	Mean	SE Mean	StDev
5 yr Return	35	8.418	0.493	2.916

	Minimum	Q1	Median	Q3	Maximum
	2.190	6.040	7.980	10.840	14.320

Test the hypothesis that the mean five-year return for value funds is greater than 8%, assuming a significance level of 5%. What does this evidence say about the portfolio managers' claim that the annualized five-year return was greater than 8%? State your conclusion. LO❺

44. Manufacturing. A tire manufacturer is considering a newly designed tread pattern for its all-weather tires. Tests have indicated that these tires will provide better fuel economy and longer tread life. The last remaining test is for braking effectiveness. The company hopes the tire will allow a car travelling at 90 kph to come to a complete stop within an average of 43 metres after the brakes are applied. They will adopt the new tread pattern unless there is strong evidence that the tires do not meet this objective. The distances (in metres) for 10 stops on a test track were 44.3, 44.0, 44.6, 45.2, 46.1, 42.5, 36.1, 43.1, 44.0, and 44.6. Should the company adopt the new tread pattern? Test an appropriate hypothesis and state your conclusion. Explain how you dealt with the outlier and why you made the recommendation you did. LO❺

45. Collections. Credit card companies lose money on cardholders who fail to pay their minimum payments. They use a variety of methods to encourage their delinquent cardholders to pay their credit card balances, such as letters, phone calls, and eventually the hiring of a collection agency. To justify the cost of using the collection agency, the agency must collect an average of at least $200 per customer. After a trial period during which the agency attempted to collect from a random sample of 100 delinquent cardholders, the 90% confidence interval on the mean collected amount was reported as ($190.25, $250.75). Given this, what recommendation(s) would you make to the credit card company about using the collection agency? LO❸

46. Free gift. A philanthropic organization sends out "free gifts" to people on their mailing list in the hope that the receiver will respond by sending back a donation. Typical gifts are mailing labels, greeting cards, or post cards. They want to test out a new gift that costs $0.50 per item to produce and mail. They mail it

to a "small" sample of 2000 customers and find a 90% confidence interval of the mean donation to be ($0.489, $0.879). As a consultant, what recommendation(s) would you make to the organization about using this gift? LO❸

47. Collections, part 2. The owner of the collection agency in Exercise 45 is quite certain that they can collect more than $200 per customer on average. He urges that the credit card company run a larger trial. Do you think a larger trial might help the company make a better decision? Explain. LO❸

48. Free gift, part 2. The philanthropic organization of Exercise 46 decided to go ahead with the new gift. In mailings to 98 000 prospects, the new mailing yielded an average of $0.78. If they had decided based on their initial trial *not* to use this gift, what kind of error would they have made? What aspects of their initial trial might have suggested to you (as their consultant) that a larger trial would be worthwhile? LO❹

49. Batteries. A battery company claims that its batteries last an average of 100 hours under normal use. There have been several complaints that the batteries don't last that long, so an independent testing agency is engaged to test them. For the 16 batteries they tested, the mean lifetime was 97 hours with a standard deviation of 12 hours. LO❺

a) What are the null and alternative hypotheses?
b) A consumer advocate (who does not know statistics) says that 97 hours is a lot less than the advertised 100 hours, so we should reject the company's claim. Explain to him the problem with doing that.
c) What assumptions must we make in order to proceed with inference?
d) At a 5% level of significance, what do you conclude?
e) Suppose that, in fact, the average life of the company's batteries is only 98 hours. Has an error been made in part d? If so, what kind?

50. Pet breeding. Fancy pets are big business, so a young entrepreneur (age 12) decided to breed golden hamsters, a type well known to pet stores and collectors. (Oddly enough, nearly all the golden hamsters in captivity are descendants of one litter found in Syria in 1930.) Of 47 recent litters, there were an average of 7.27 baby hamsters with a standard deviation of 2.5 hamsters per litter. LO❸

a) Find and interpret a 90% confidence interval for the mean litter size.
b) How much smaller or larger would the margin of error be for a 99% confidence interval? Explain.
c) Based on these statistics, how many litters would we need to estimate the mean litter size to within one baby hamster with 95% confidence?

51. Fish production. Farmed salmon is much cheaper to bring to market than salmon caught in the wild, but consumers are concerned about several issues recently publicized about farmed salmon including the type of food they are fed and the contaminants found in their meat (see www.healthcastle.com). Among the contaminants are such compounds as polychlorinated biphenyls (PCBs), dioxins, toxaphene, dieldrin, hexachlorobenzene, lindane, heptachlor epoxide, cis-nonachlor, trans-nonachlor, gamma-chlordane, alpha-chlordane, Mirex, endrin, and DDT.

The EPA recommends that salmon contain no more than 0.08 ppm of the insecticide Mirex. A local environmental group is considering a boycott of salmon if it exceeds 0.08 ppm. A 95% confidence interval from a sample of farmed salmon from a random sample of 150 different salmon farms (*Science*, 9, January 2004) is found to be (0.0834 to 0.0992) ppm. The data were unimodal and symmetric with no outliers. **LO⑤**

a) Is there evidence that the farms are producing salmon with mean Mirex contamination higher than the EPA recommended amount? Your explanation should discuss the confidence level, P-value, and the decision.

b) Discuss the two types of errors that can be made in this decision in the context of a business decision of whether to prohibit the producers from selling their salmon.

52. Downloading speed. A student recently bought an antispyware program for her computer to help increase performance. Before she installed the program, her mean download speed was 14 Mbps (megabits per second). The program cost $29.95 and she wants to see if her speed has increased.

She tried a band width speed test (www.bandwidthplace.com) 16 different times and found a 90% confidence interval to be (14.08, 14.76) Mbps. She plotted the 16 speeds and found the data to be unimodal and roughly symmetric with no obvious outliers. **LO⑤**

a) Is there evidence to suggest that the computer's downloading speed is greater than 14 Mbps? Your explanation should discuss the confidence level, P-value, and the decision.

b) If she finds out later that the mean is really 13.5 Mbps, what kind of error has she made?

c) Do you think her decision to buy the software was the right one based on the data?

T **53. Computer lab fees.** The technology committee has stated that the average time spent by students per lab visit has increased, and the increase supports the need for increased lab fees. To substantiate this claim, the committee randomly samples 12 student lab visits and notes the amount of time spent using the computer. The times in minutes are as follows: **LO⑤**

Time	Time
52	74
57	53
54	136
76	73
62	8
52	62

a) Plot the data. Are any of the observations outliers? Explain.

b) The previous mean amount of time spent using the lab computer was 55 minutes. Test the hypothesis that the mean is now higher than 55 minutes at $\alpha = 0.05$. What is your conclusion?

c) If outliers exist, eliminate the outlier(s) and retest the hypothesis. What is your conclusion?

d) Discuss the statistical implications of eliminating outliers. Why might some researchers disagree with deleting outlying observations from a data set?

T **54. Cell phone batteries.** A company that produces cell phones claims its standard phone battery lasts longer on average than other batteries in the market. To support this claim, the company publishes an ad reporting the results of a recent experiment showing that under normal usage, their batteries last at least 35 hours. To investigate this claim, a consumer advocacy group asked the company for the raw data. The company sends the group the following results: **LO⑤**

35, 34, 32, 31, 34, 34, 32, 33, 35, 55, 32, 31

a) Test an appropriate hypothesis and state your conclusion.

b) Explain how you dealt with the outlier, and why you made the recommendation you did.

55. Growth and air pollution. Government officials have difficulty attracting new business to communities with troubled reputations. Nevada has been one of the fastest growing states in the United States for a number of years. Accompanying the rapid growth are massive new construction projects. Since Nevada has a dry climate, the construction creates visible dust pollution. High pollution levels may paint a less than attractive picture of the area, and can also result in fines levied by the federal government. As required by government regulation, researchers continually monitor pollution levels. In the most recent test of pollution levels, 121 air samples were collected. The dust particulate levels must be reported to the federal regulatory agencies. In the report sent to the federal agency, it was noted that the mean particulate level = 57.6 μg/cubic litre of air, and the 95% confidence interval estimate is (52.06 μg to 63.07 μg). A graph of the distribution of the particulate amounts was also included and is shown below. **LO⑤**

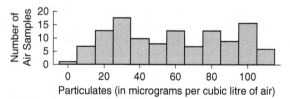

a) Discuss the assumptions and conditions for using Student's *t* inference methods with these data.

b) Do you think the confidence interval noted in the report is valid? Briefly explain why or why not.

56. Convention revenues. At one time, Nevada was the only U.S. state that allowed gambling. Although gambling continues to be one of the major industries in Nevada, the proliferation of legalized gambling in other areas of the United States has required state and local governments to look at other growth possibilities. The convention and visitor's authorities in many Nevada cities actively recruit national conventions that bring thousands of visitors to the state. Various demographic and economic data are collected from surveys given to convention attendees. One statistic of interest is the amount visitors spend on slot machine gambling. Nevada often reports the slot machine expenditure as amount spent per hotel guest room. A recent survey of 500 visitors asked how much they spent on gambling. The average expenditure per room was $180.   LO❸

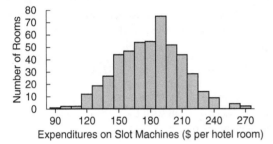

Casinos will use the information reported in the survey to estimate slot machine expenditure per hotel room. Do you think the estimates produced by the survey will accurately represent expenditures? Explain using the statistics reported and graph shown.

57. Traffic speed. Police departments often try to control traffic speed by placing speed-measuring machines on roads that tell motorists how fast they are driving. Traffic safety experts must determine where machines should be placed. In one recent test, police recorded the average speed clocked by cars driving on one busy street close to an elementary school. For a sample of 25 speeds, it was determined that the average amount over the speed limit for the 25 clocked speeds was 11.6 kilometres per hour (kph) with a standard deviation of 8 kph. The 95% confidence interval estimate for this sample is 8.30 kph to 14.90 kph.   LO❸

a) What is the margin of error for this problem?
b) The researchers commented that the interval was too wide. Explain specifically what should be done to reduce the margin of error to no more than ±2 kph.

58. Traffic speed, part 2. The speed-measuring machines must measure accurately to maximize effectiveness in slowing traffic. The accuracy of the machines will be tested before placement on city streets. To ensure that error rates are estimated accurately, the researchers want to take a large enough sample that will ensure usable and accurate interval estimates of how much the machines may be off in measuring actual speeds. Specially, the researchers want the margin of error for a single speed measurement to be no more than ±1.5 kph.   LO❸

a) Discuss how the researchers may obtain a reasonable estimate of the standard deviation of error in the measured speeds.
b) Suppose the standard deviation for the error in the measured speeds equals 4 kph. At 95% confidence, what sample size should

be taken to ensure that the margin of error is no larger than ±1.0 kph?

59. Tax audits. Certified public accountants are often required to appear with clients if the Canada Revenue Agency audits the client's tax return. Some accounting firms give the client an option to pay a fee when the tax return is completed that guarantees tax advice and support from the accountant if the client were audited. The fee is charged up front like an insurance premium and is less than the amount that would be charged if the client were later audited and then decided to ask the firm for assistance during the audit. A large accounting firm is trying to determine what fee to charge for next year's returns. In previous years, the actual mean cost to the firm for attending a client audit session was $650. To determine if this cost has changed, the firm randomly samples 32 client audit fees. The sample mean audit cost was $680 with a standard deviation of $75.   LO❸, LO❺

a) Develop a 95% confidence interval estimate for the mean audit cost.
b) Perform the appropriate test to determine if the mean audit cost is now different from the historical mean of $650. Use a .05 level of significance.
c) Comment on how the confidence interval estimate supports the results of the hypothesis test.

Ⓣ 60. Tax audits, part 2. While reviewing the sample of audit fees, a senior accountant for the firm notes that the fee charged by the firm's accountants depends on the complexity of the return. A comparison of actual charges therefore might not provide the information needed to set next year's fees. To better understand the fee structure, the senior accountant requests a new sample that measures the time the accountants spent on the audit. Last year, the average hours charged per client audit was 3.25 hours. A new sample of 10 audit times shows the following times in hours: LO❸, LO❺

4.2, 3.7, 4.8, 2.9, 3.1, 4.5, 4.2, 4.1, 5.0, 3.4

a) Assume the conditions necessary for inference are met. Find a 90% confidence interval estimate for the mean audit time.
b) Perform the appropriate test to determine if the mean audit time for this year's audits is significantly different from last year's 3.25 hours. Use α = 0.10.
c) Comment on how the confidence interval estimate supports the results of the hypothesis test.

Ⓣ 61. Wind power. Should you generate electricity with your own personal wind turbine? That depends on whether you have enough wind on your site. To produce enough energy, your site should have an annual average wind speed of at least 8 kilometres per hour, according to the Canadian Wind Energy Association. One candidate site was monitored for a year, with wind speeds recorded every 6 hours. A total of 1114 readings of wind speed averaged 8.019 kph with a standard deviation of 3.813 kph. You've been asked to make a statistical report to help the landowner decide whether to place a wind turbine at this site.   LO❺

a) Discuss the assumptions and conditions for using Student's *t* inference methods with these data. Here are some plots that may help you decide whether the methods can be used:

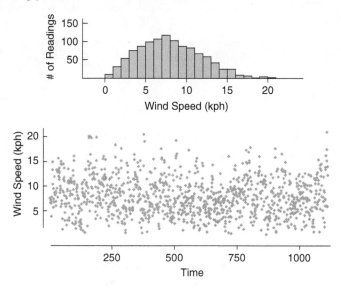

b) What would you tell the landowner about whether this site is suitable for a small wind turbine? Explain.

62. *Real estate crash?* After the sub-prime crisis of late 2007, real estate prices fell almost everywhere in the United States. In 2006–2007 before the crisis, the average selling price of homes in a region in upstate New York was $191 300. A real estate agency wants to know how much the prices have fallen since then. They collect a sample of 1231 homes in the region and find the average asking price to be $178 613.50 with a standard deviation of $92 701.56. You have been retained by the real estate agency to report on the current situation. **LO❺**

a) Discuss the assumptions and conditions for using *t*-methods for inference with these data. Here are some plots that may help you decide what to do.

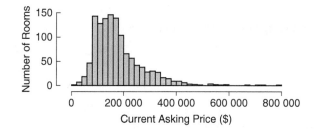

b) What would you report to the real estate agency about the current situation?

Comparing Two Groups

Top to bottom, Chris Hondros/Getty Images, Stephen Chernin/Getty Images News/Getty Images, B Christopher/Alamy

CONNECTIONS: CHAPTER

In Chapters 9, 10, and 11 we dealt with inference (confidence intervals and hypothesis tests) for a single mean and a single proportion. In this chapter we extend the methods to compare two groups. We will develop confidence intervals and hypothesis tests to compare two means and two proportions. By the end of this chapter we will have a complete set of methods for one and two means, and one and two proportions.

Visa Global and Visa Canada

To most people, a "visa" is a credit card, not an authorization to enter a foreign country. According to Wikinvest.com, there are more than 1.7 billion Visa-branded cards worldwide. Operating the world's largest retail electronic-payment network, Visa's operating revenue surpassed $8 billion in 2010. According to the Canadian Bankers Association, there were 75 million Visa and MasterCard cards in circulation in Canada by the end of 2011; a large percentage of these were Visa cards. However, Visa does not offer cards directly to consumers. Instead, it provides financial institutions with payment products that allow them to offer credit, debit, prepaid, and commercial cards, as well as cash-access programs.

Visa's origins date back to 1958, when Bank of America pioneered its BankAmericard program in Fresno, California, and American Express issued the first plastic card in 1959. The idea of a credit "card" really gained momentum a decade later when a group of banks formed a joint venture to create a centralized system of payment, and National BankAmericard, Inc. (NBI) was created.

During the 1960s it also expanded to Canada, where Toronto-Dominion Bank, Canadian Imperial Bank of Commerce, Royal Bank of Canada, Banque Canadienne Nationale, and Bank of Nova Scotia issued credit cards under the Chargex name from 1968–1977. Other names were used in other countries, but by

LEARNING OBJECTIVES

1. Check assumptions and conditions for a two-sample *t*-test

2. Create and interpret a confidence interval for the difference of two means

3. Interpret output and written results from two-sample *t*-tests

4. Test a hypothesis about the difference of two means of independent populations

5. Determine whether to use a two-sample *t*-test or a paired *t*-test

6. Create a confidence interval and test a hypothesis about means based on paired data

7. Create a confidence interval and test a hypothesis about the difference of two proportions

1986, for simplicity and marketability, the international networks were united under the name "Visa." (The name "Visa" is pronounced nearly the same way in every language.)

That year, Visa processed 679 000 transactions—a volume that is processed on average every four minutes today. Visa has the capacity to handle more than 10 000 transactions a second, and processed about 75 billion transactions in 2011.

Visa did not become a publicly traded company until 2008, when Visa Canada, Visa International, and Visa USA merged to form Visa Inc., which had the largest IPO in U.S. history, raising $17.9 billion. Visa employs nearly 7000 people in its global organization comprising seven regional entities, one of which is Visa Canada. In Canada today, Visa cards are issued by CIBC, Desjardins, Laurentian Bank, Royal Bank of Canada, Scotiabank, and TD Canada Trust, among others.

In return for Visa's support of the Olympic and Paralympic games, it is the only form of electronic payment accepted at Olympic venues. It provides financial support to the Canadian bobsleigh and skeleton teams and individual athletes, and supports a mentoring program that pairs up young athletes with former Olympians. As well, Visa is an official partner of the NHL and NHLPA in Canada. The value of that support? Priceless! Oops, that's MasterCard's slogan![1]

Based on information from www.bankofamerica.com and www.wikinvest.com and www.visa.ca

The credit card business can be extremely profitable. As far back as 2003, card issuers worldwide made $2.5 billion per month before taxes. The typical American household has six cards while the typical Canadian household has two, with a total of $16 000 debt on them, usually at rates much higher than conventional loans and mortgages. Not surprisingly, the credit card business is also intensely competitive. Rival banks and lending agencies are constantly trying to create new products and offers to win new customers, keep current customers, and provide incentives for current customers to charge more on their cards.

Are some credit card promotions more effective than others? For example, do customers spend more using their credit card if they know they will be given "double miles" or "double points" toward flights, hotel stays, or store purchases? To answer questions such as this, credit card issuers often perform experiments on a sample of customers, making them an *offer* of an incentive, while other customers receive no offer. Promotions cost the company money, so the company needs to estimate the size of any increased revenue to judge whether it is sufficient to cover

---

[1] Sources: www.visa.ca, www.visa.com; http://canada.creditcards.com

their expenses. By comparing the performance of the two offers on the sample, they can decide whether the new offer would provide enough potential profit if they were to "roll it out" and offer it to their entire customer base.

Experiments that compare two groups are common throughout both science and industry. Other applications include comparing the effects of a new drug with the traditional therapy, the fuel efficiency of two car engine designs, or the sales of new products on two different customer segments. Usually the experiment is carried out on a subset of the population, often a much smaller subset. Using statistics, we can make statements about whether the means of the two groups differ in the population at large, and how large that difference might be.

12.1 Comparing Two Means

The natural display for comparing the means of two groups is side-by-side boxplots (see Figure 12.1). For the credit card promotion, the company judges performance by comparing the *mean* spend lift (the change in spending from before receiving the promotion to after receiving it) for the two samples. (Note the optimism in the terminology. Even if spending decreases after the promotion, it is still called spend lift, but it would be negative.) If the difference in spend lift between the group that received the promotion and the group that didn't is high enough, this will be viewed as evidence that the promotion worked. Looking at the two boxplots, it's not obvious that there's much of a difference. Can we conclude that the slight increase seen for those who received the promotion is more than just random fluctuation? We'll need statistical inference.

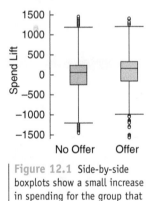

Figure 12.1 Side-by-side boxplots show a small increase in spending for the group that received the promotion.

For two groups, the statistic of interest is the difference in the observed means of the offer and no offer groups: $\bar{y}_o - \bar{y}_n$. (Here we have used subscripts o and n to signify *offer* and *no offer*. Generally the subscripts will be 1 and 2.) We've offered the promotion to a random sample of cardholders and used another sample of cardholders, who got no special offer, as a control group. We know what happened in our samples, but what we'd really like to know is the difference of the means in the population at large: $\mu_o - \mu_n$.

We compare two means in much the same way as we compared a single mean to a hypothesized value. But now the population model parameter of interest is the *difference* between the means. In our example, it's the true difference between the mean spend lift for customers offered the promotion and for customers for whom no offer was made. We estimate the difference with $\bar{y}_o - \bar{y}_n$. How can we tell if a difference we observe in the sample means indicates a real difference in the underlying population means? We'll need to know the sampling distribution model and standard deviation of the difference. Once we know those, we can build a confidence interval and test a hypothesis just as we did for a single mean.

We have data on 500 randomly selected customers who were offered the promotion and another randomly selected 500 who were not. It's easy to find the mean and standard deviation of the spend lift for each of these groups. From these, we can find the standard deviations of the means, but that's not what we want. We need the standard deviation of the *difference* in their means. For that, we can use a simple rule: *If the sample means come from independent samples, the variance of their sum or difference is the sum of their variances.* (See Chapter 8.)

Variances Add for Sums *and* Differences At first, it may seem that this can't be true for differences as well as for sums. Here's some intuition about why variation increases even when we subtract two random quantities. Grab a full box of cereal. The label claims that it contains 500 grams of cereal. We know that's not exact. There's a random quantity of cereal in the box with a mean (presumably) of 500 grams and some variation from box to box. Now pour a 50 gram serving of cereal into a bowl. Of course, your serving isn't exactly 50 grams. There's some variation there, too. How much cereal would you guess was left in the box? Can you guess as accurately as you could for the full box? The mean should be 450 grams. But does the amount left in the box have *less* variation than it did before you poured your serving? Almost, certainly not! *After* you pour your bowl, the amount of cereal in the box is still a random quantity (with a smaller mean than before), but you've made it *more variable* because of the uncertainty in the amount you poured. However, notice that we don't add the *standard deviations* of these two random quantities. As we'll see, it's the *variance* of the amount of cereal left in the box that's the sum of the two variances.

Peter Cade/Photodisc/Getty Images

As long as the two groups are independent, we find the standard deviation of the *difference* between the two sample means by adding their variances and then taking the square root:

$$SD(\bar{y}_1 - \bar{y}_2) = \sqrt{Var(\bar{y}_1) + Var(\bar{y}_2)}$$
$$= \sqrt{\left(\frac{\sigma_1}{\sqrt{n_1}}\right)^2 + \left(\frac{\sigma_2}{\sqrt{n_2}}\right)^2}$$
$$= \sqrt{\frac{\sigma_1^2}{n_1} + \frac{\sigma_2^2}{n_2}}$$

An Easier Rule?
The formula for the degrees of freedom of the sampling distribution of the difference between two means is complicated. So some books teach an easier rule: The number of degrees of freedom is always at *least* the smaller of $n_1 - 1$ and $n_2 - 1$ and at most $n_1 + n_2 - 2$. The problem is that if you need to perform a two-sample *t*-test and don't have the formula at hand to find the correct degrees of freedom, you have to be conservative and use the lower value. And *that* approximation can be a poor choice because it can give less than *half* the degrees of freedom you're entitled to from the correct formula. Of course, this only really matters for small samples, not for large ones. For example, the two-sided 0.05 critical value at 50 df is 2.009 and at 100 df is 1.984, a very small difference indeed.

Of course, usually we don't know the true standard deviations of the two groups, σ_1 and σ_2, so we substitute the estimates, s_1 and s_2, and find a *standard error*:

$$SE(\bar{y}_1 - \bar{y}_2) = \sqrt{\frac{s_1^2}{n_1} + \frac{s_2^2}{n_2}}$$

Just as we did for one mean, we'll use the standard error to see how big the difference really is. You shouldn't be surprised that, just as for a single mean, the ratio of the difference in the means to the standard error of that difference has a sampling model that follows a Student's *t* distribution.

What else do we need? Only the degrees of freedom for the Student's *t*-model. Unfortunately, *that* formula isn't as simple as $n - 1$. The problem is that the sampling model isn't *really* Student's *t*, but only something close. The reason is that we estimated two different variances (s_1^2 and s_2^2) and they may be different. That extra variability makes the distribution even more variable than the Student's *t* for either of the means. But by using a special, adjusted degrees of freedom value, we can find a Student's *t*-model that is so close to the right sampling distribution model that nobody can tell the difference. The adjustment formula is straightforward but doesn't help our understanding much, so we leave it to the computer or calculator. (If you are curious and really want to see the formula, look in the footnote.[2])

A Sampling Distribution for the Difference Between Two Means

When the conditions are met (see Section 12.3), the standardized sample difference between the means of two independent groups,

$$t = \frac{(\bar{y}_1 - \bar{y}_2) - (\mu_1 - \mu_2)}{SE\,(\bar{y}_1 - \bar{y}_2)}$$

can be modelled by a Student's *t*-model with a number of degrees of freedom found with a special formula. We estimate the standard error with:

$$SE\,(\bar{y}_1 - \bar{y}_2) = \sqrt{\frac{s_1^2}{n_1} + \frac{s_2^2}{n_2}}$$

NOTATION ALERT:

Δ_0 (pronounced "delta naught") isn't so standard that you can assume everyone will understand it. We use it because it's the capital Greek letter "D" for "difference."

12.2 The Two-Sample *t*-Test

Now we've got everything we need to construct the hypothesis test, and you already know how to do it. It's the same idea we used when testing one mean against a hypothesized value. Here, we start by hypothesizing a value for the true difference of the means. We'll call that hypothesized difference Δ_0. (It's so common for that hypothesized difference to be zero that we often just assume $\Delta_0 = 0$.) We then take the ratio of the difference in the means from our samples to its standard error and compare that ratio to a critical value from a Student's *t*-model. The test is called the **two-sample *t*-test**.

---

[2] The result is due to Satterthwaite and Welch.
Satterthwaite, F. E. (1946). "An Approximate Distribution of Estimates of Variance Components," *Biometrics Bulletin* 2: 110–114.
Welch, B. L. (1947). "The Generalization of 'Student's' Problem when Several Different Population Variances are Involved," *Biometrika* 34: 28–35.

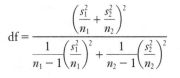

$$df = \frac{\left(\dfrac{s_1^2}{n_1} + \dfrac{s_2^2}{n_2}\right)^2}{\dfrac{1}{n_1 - 1}\left(\dfrac{s_1^2}{n_1}\right)^2 + \dfrac{1}{n_2 - 1}\left(\dfrac{s_2^2}{n_2}\right)^2}$$

This approximation formula usually doesn't even give a whole number. If you are using a table, you'll need a whole number, so round down to be safe. If you are using technology, the approximation formulas that computers and calculators use for the Student's *t*-distribution can deal with fractional degrees of freedom.

The two-sample *t*-methods

Two-sample *t*-methods assume that the two groups are independent. This is a crucial assumption. If it's not met, it is not safe to use these methods. One common way for groups to fail independence is when each observation in one group is related to one (and only one) observation in the other group. For example, if we test the *same* subjects before and after an event, or if we measure a variable on both husbands and wives. In that case, the observations are said to be **paired** and you'll need to use the paired *t*-methods discussed in Section 12.7. Thus independence means no connection between observations in the two groups.

Sometimes you may see the two-sample *t*-methods referred to as the two-sample **independent** *t*-methods for emphasis. In this book, however, when we say two-sample, we'll always assume that the groups are independent.

Two-sample *t*-test

When the appropriate assumptions and conditions are met, we test the hypothesis:

$$H_0: \mu_1 - \mu_2 = \Delta_0$$

where the hypothesized difference Δ_0 is almost always 0. We use the statistic:

$$t = \frac{(\bar{y}_1 - \bar{y}_2) - \Delta_0}{SE(\bar{y}_1 - \bar{y}_2)}$$

The standard error of $\bar{y}_1 - \bar{y}_2$ is:

$$SE(\bar{y}_1 - \bar{y}_2) = \sqrt{\frac{s_1^2}{n_1} + \frac{s_2^2}{n_2}}$$

When the null hypothesis is true, the statistic can be closely modelled by a Student's *t*-model with a number of degrees of freedom given by a special formula. We use that model to compare our *t* ratio with a critical value for *t* or to obtain a P-value.

12.3 Assumptions and Conditions

Before we can perform a two-sample *t*-test, we have to check the assumptions and conditions.

Independence Assumption

The data in each group must be drawn independently and at random from each group's own homogeneous population or generated by a randomized comparative experiment. We can't expect that the data, taken as one big group, come from a homogeneous population because that's what we're trying to test. But without randomization of some sort, there are no sampling distribution models and inference. We should think about whether the independence assumption is reasonable. We can also check two conditions:

Randomization Condition: Were the data collected with suitable randomization? For surveys, are they a representative random sample? For experiments, was the experiment randomized?

10% Condition: We usually don't check this condition for differences of means. We'll check it only if we have a very small population or an extremely large sample. We needn't worry about it at all for randomized experiments.

Normal Population Assumption

As we did before with Student's *t*-models, we need the assumption that the underlying populations are *each* Normally distributed. So we check one condition.

Nearly Normal Condition: We must check this for *both* groups; a violation by either one violates the condition. As we saw for single sample means, the Normality Assumption matters most when sample sizes are small. When either group is small ($n < 15$), you should not use these methods if the histogram or Normal probability plot (see Chapter 14) shows skewness. For *n*'s closer to 40, a mildly skewed histogram is OK, but you should remark on any outliers you find and not work with severely skewed data. When both groups are bigger than that, the Central Limit Theorem starts to work unless the data are severely skewed or there are extreme outliers, so the Nearly Normal Condition for the data matters less. Even in large samples, however, you should still be on the lookout for outliers, extreme skewness, and multiple modes.

Independent Groups Assumption

To use the two-sample *t* methods, the two groups we are comparing must be independent of each other. In fact, the test is sometimes called the two *independent samples t*-test. No statistical test can verify that the groups are independent. You have to think about how the data were collected. Independent groups arise in two main ways, either as two separate unrelated groups (e.g., Canadians and Americans), or as two separate groups created by random assignment (e.g., offer and no offer). The assumption would be violated, for example, if one group comprised husbands and the other group, their wives. Whatever we measure on one might naturally be related to the other. Similarly, if we compared subjects' performances before some treatment with their performances afterward, we'd expect a relationship of each "before" measurement with its corresponding "after" measurement. Measurements taken for two groups over time when the observations are taken at the same time may be related—especially if they share, for example, the chance they were influenced by the overall economy or world events. In cases such as these, where the observational units in the two groups are related or matched, *the two-sample methods of this chapter can't be applied*. When this happens, we need a different procedure, discussed in Section 12.7.

GUIDED EXAMPLE	Credit Card Promotions and Spending

Our preliminary market research has suggested that a new incentive may increase customer spending. However, before we invest in this promotion on the entire population of cardholders, let's test a hypothesis on a sample. To judge whether the incentive works, we will examine the change in spending (called the *spend lift*) over a six-month period. We will see whether the *spend lift* for the group that received the offer was greater than the *spend lift* for the group that received no offer. If we observe differences, how will we know whether these differences are important (or real) enough to justify our costs?

PLAN

Setup State what we want to know.

Identify the *parameter* we wish to estimate. Here our parameter is the difference in the means, not the individual group means.

Identify the *population(s)* about which we wish to make statements.

Identify the variables and context.

We want to know if cardholders who are offered a promotion spend more on their credit card. We have the spend lift (in $) for a random sample of 500 cardholders who were offered the promotion and for a random sample of 500 customers who were *not*. H_0: The mean *spend lift* for the group who received the offer is the same as for the group who did not:

$H_0: \mu_{Offer} = \mu_{No\ Offer}$

H_A: The mean *spend lift* for the group who received the offer is higher:

H_A: $\mu_{Offer} > \mu_{No\,Offer}$

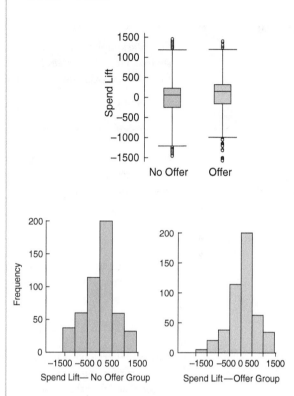

Make a graph to compare the two groups and check the distribution of each group. For completeness, we should report any outliers. If any outliers are extreme enough, we should consider performing the test both with and without the outliers and reporting the difference.

Model Check the assumptions and conditions.

For large samples like these with quantitative data, we often don't worry about the 10% Condition.

The boxplots and histograms show the distribution of both groups. It looks like the distribution for each group is fairly symmetric.

The boxplots indicate several outliers in each group, but we have no reason to delete them, and their impact is minimal.

✓ **Independence** Assumption. We have no reason to believe that the spending behaviour of one customer would influence the spending behaviour of another customer in the same group. The data report the "spend lift" for each customer for the same time period.

✓ **Randomization Condition.** The customers who were offered the promotion were selected at random.

✓ **Nearly Normal Condition.** The samples are large, so we are not overly concerned with this condition, and the boxplots and histograms show symmetric distributions for both groups.

✓ **Independent Groups Assumption.** Customers were assigned to groups at random. There's no reason to think that those in one group can affect the spending behaviour of those in the other group.

State the sampling distribution model for the statistic. Here the degrees of freedom will come from the approximation formula in footnote 2.

Specify your method.

Under these conditions, it's appropriate to use a Student's *t*-model.

We will use a two-sample *t*-test.

Mechanics List the summary statistics. Be sure to include the units along with the statistics. Use meaningful subscripts to identify the groups.

We know $n_{No\ Offer} = 500$ and $n_{Offer} = 500$.

From technology, we find:

$$\bar{y}_{No\ Offer} = \$7.69 \qquad \bar{y}_{Offer} = \$127.61$$

$$s_{No\ Offer} = \$611.62 \qquad s_{Offer} = \$566.05$$

The observed difference in the two means is:

$$\bar{y}_{Offer} - \bar{y}_{No\ Offer} = \$127.61 - \$7.69 = \$119.92$$

Use the sample standard deviations to find the standard error of the sampling distribution.

The groups are independent, so:

$$SE(\bar{y}_{Offer} - \bar{y}_{No\ Offer}) = \sqrt{\frac{(611.62)^2}{500} + \frac{(566.05)^2}{500}}$$

$$= \$37.27$$

The best alternative is to let the computer use the approximation formula for the degrees of freedom and find the P-value.

The observed *t*-value is:

$$t = 119.92/37.27 = 3.218$$

with 992.0 df (from technology).

(To use critical values, we could find that the one-sided 0.01 critical value for a *t* with 992.0 df is $t^* = 2.33$.

Our observed *t*-value is larger than this, so we could reject the null hypothesis at the 0.01 level.)

Even if you use the simpler but more conservative choice of df, namely 499 (= 500 − 1), the critical value is still 2.33 to two decimal places. That's because the sample size is so large.

Using software to obtain the P-value, we get:

```
Promotional Group    N      Mean     StDev
No                 500      7.69    611.62
Yes                500    127.61    566.05

Difference = mu(1) − mu(0)
Estimate for difference: 119.9231
t = 3.2178, df = 992.007
One-sided P-value = 0.0006669
```

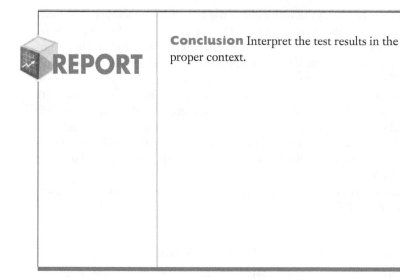

REPORT

Conclusion Interpret the test results in the proper context.

MEMO:

Re: Credit Card Promotion

Our analysis of the credit card promotion experiment found that customers offered the promotion spent more than those not offered the promotion. The difference was statistically significant, with a P-value < 0.001. So we conclude that this promotion will increase spending. The difference in spend lift averaged $ 119.92, but our analyses so far have not determined how much income this will generate for the company and thus whether the estimated increase in spending is worth the cost of the offer.

✔ JUST CHECKING

Top to bottom, Accord/Shutterstock, AleksKey/Shutterstock, BESTWEB/Shutterstock, Jorg Hackemann/Shutterstock, Jason Stitt/Shutterstock

Many office "coffee stations" collect voluntary payments for the food consumed. Researchers at the University of Newcastle upon Tyne performed an experiment to see whether the image of eyes watching would change employee behaviour.[3] They alternated pictures of eyes looking at the viewer with pictures of flowers each week on the cupboard behind the "honesty box." They measured the consumption of milk to approximate the amount of food consumed and recorded the contributions (in £) each week per litre of milk. The table summarizes their results.

	Eyes	Flowers
n(# weeks)	5	5
$\bar{y}$	0.417 £/litre	0.151 £/litre
s	0.1811	0.067

1 What null hypothesis were the researchers testing?

2 Check the assumptions and conditions needed to test whether there really is a difference in behaviour due to the difference in pictures.

12.4 A Confidence Interval for the Difference Between Two Means

We rejected the null hypothesis that customers' mean spending would not change when offered a promotion. Because the company took a random sample of customers for each group, and our P-value was convincingly small, we concluded this difference is not zero for the population. Does this mean that we should offer the promotion to all customers?

---

[3] Melissa Bateson, Daniel Nettle, and Gilbert Roberts, "Cues of Being Watched Enhance Cooperation in a Real-World Setting," *Biol. Lett.* Doi:10.1098/rsbl.2006.0509.

A hypothesis test really says nothing about the size of the difference. All it says is that the observed difference is large enough that we can be confident it isn't zero. That's what the term "statistically significant" means. It doesn't say that the difference is important, financially significant, or interesting. Rejecting a null hypothesis simply says that the observed statistic was unlikely to have been observed if the null hypothesis had been true. See the discussion of practical significance in Chapter 10.

So, what recommendations can we make to the company? Almost every business decision will depend on looking at a range of likely scenarios—precisely the kind of information a confidence interval gives. We construct the confidence interval for the difference in means in the usual way, starting with our observed statistic, in this case $(\bar{y}_1 - \bar{y}_2)$. We then add and subtract a multiple of the standard error $SE(\bar{y}_1 - \bar{y}_2)$ where the multiple is based on the Student's t distribution with the same df formula we saw before.

Confidence Interval for the Difference Between Two Means

When the conditions are met, we are ready to find a **two-sample t-interval** for the difference between means of two independent groups, $\mu_1 - \mu_2$. The confidence interval is:

$$(\bar{y}_1 - \bar{y}_2) \pm t^*_{\text{df}} \times SE(\bar{y}_1 - \bar{y}_2)$$

where the standard error of the difference of the means is:

$$SE(\bar{y}_1 - \bar{y}_2) = \sqrt{\frac{s_1^2}{n_1} + \frac{s_2^2}{n_2}}$$

The critical value t^*_{df} depends on the particular confidence level, and on the number of degrees of freedom.

GUIDED EXAMPLE — Confidence Interval for Credit Card Spending

We rejected the null hypothesis that the mean spending in the two groups was equal. But, to find out whether we should consider offering the promotion nationwide, we need to estimate the magnitude and variability of the spend lift.

PLAN	
Setup State what we want to know.	We want to find a 95% confidence interval for the mean difference in spending between those who are offered a promotion and those who aren't.
Identify the *parameter* we wish to estimate. Here our parameter is the difference in the means, not the individual group means.	
Identify the *population(s)* about which we wish to make statements.	We looked at the boxplots and histograms of the groups and checked the conditions before. The same assumptions and conditions are appropriate here, so we can proceed directly to the confidence interval.
Identify the variables and context.	
Specify the method.	We will use a two-sample t-interval.

Mechanics Construct the confidence interval. Be sure to include the units along with the statistics. Use meaningful subscripts to identify the groups.

Use the sample standard deviations to find the standard error of the sampling distribution.

In our previous analysis, we found:

$$\bar{y}_{No\ Offer} = \$7.69 \qquad \bar{y}_{Offer} = \$127.61$$
$$s_{No\ Offer} = \$611.62 \qquad s_{Offer} = \$566.05$$

The observed difference in the two means is:

$$\bar{y}_{Offer} - \bar{y}_{No\ Offer} = \$127.61 - \$7.69 = \$119.92$$

and the standard error is:

$$SE(\bar{y}_{Offer} - \bar{y}_{No\ Offer}) = \$37.27$$

The best alternative is to let the computer use the approximation formula for the degrees of freedom and find the confidence interval.

From technology, the df is 992.007, and the 0.025 critical value for t with 992.007 df is 1.96. So the 95% confidence interval is:

$$119.92 \pm 1.96(37.27) = (\$46.87, \$192.97)$$

Ordinarily, we rely on technology for the calculations. In our hand calculations, we rounded values at intermediate steps to show the steps more clearly. The computer keeps full precision and is the one you should report. The difference between the hand and computer calculations is about $0.08.

Using software to obtain these computations, we get:

```
95 percent confidence interval:
 46.78784, 193.05837
sample means:
No Offer  Offer
7.690882 127.613987
```

Conclusion Interpret the test results in the proper context.

MEMO:

Re: Credit Card Promotion Experiment

In our experiment, the promotion resulted in an increased spend lift of $119.92 on average. Further analysis gives a 95% confidence interval of ($46.79, $193.06). In other words, we expect with 95% confidence that under similar conditions, the mean spend lift that we achieve when we roll out the offer to all similar customers will be in this interval. We recommend that the company consider whether the values in this interval will justify the cost of the promotion program.

12.5 The Pooled *t*-Test

If you bought a used camera in good condition from a friend, would you pay the same as you would if you bought the same item from a stranger? A researcher at Cornell University[4] wanted to know how friendship might affect simple sales such as this. She randomly divided subjects into two groups and gave each group descriptions of items they might want to buy. One group was told to imagine buying from a friend whom they expected to see again. The other group was told to imagine buying from a stranger.

lenaer/Shutterstock

[4] J. J. Halpern (1997). "The Transaction Index: A Method for Standardizing Comparisons of Transaction Characteristics Across Different Contexts," *Group Decision and Negotiation*, 6, no. 6: 557–572.

WHO	University students
WHAT	Prices offered to pay for a used camera ($)
WHEN	1990s
WHERE	Cornell University
WHY	To study the effects of friendship on transactions

Here are the prices they offered to pay for a used camera in good condition.

PRICE OFFERED FOR A USED CAMERA ($)	
Buying from a Friend	Buying from a Stranger
275	260
300	250
260	175
300	130
255	200
275	225
290	240
300	

The researcher who designed the friendship study was interested in testing the impact of friendship on negotiations. Previous theories had doubted that friendship had a measurable effect on pricing, but she hoped to find such an effect. The usual null hypothesis is that there's no difference in means and that's what we'll use for the camera purchase prices.

When we performed the t-test earlier in the chapter, we used an approximation formula that adjusts the degrees of freedom to a lower value. When $n_1 + n_2$ is only 15, as it is here, we don't really want to lose any degrees of freedom. Because this is an experiment, we might be willing to make another assumption. The null hypothesis says that whether you buy from a friend or a stranger should have no effect on the mean amount you're willing to pay for a camera. If it has no effect on the means, should it affect the variance of the transactions?

If we're willing to *assume* that the variances of the groups are equal (at least when the null hypothesis is true), then we can save some degrees of freedom. Further, since s_1^2 and s_2^2 are two separate estimates of the same quantity, we get a better estimate by combining them. To do that, we *pool* the two sample variances into one common, or **pooled**, estimate of the variance:

$$s_{\text{pooled}}^2 = \frac{(n_1 - 1)s_1^2 + (n_2 - 1)s_2^2}{(n_1 - 1) + (n_2 - 1)}$$

(If the two sample sizes are equal, this is just the average of the two variances.)

Now we just substitute this pooled variance in place of each of the variances in the standard error formula. Remember, the standard error formula for the difference of two independent means is:

$$SE(\bar{y}_1 - \bar{y}_2) = \sqrt{\frac{s_1^2}{n_1} + \frac{s_2^2}{n_2}}$$

We substitute the common pooled variance for each of the two variances in this formula, making the pooled standard error formula simpler:

$$SE_{\text{pooled}}(\bar{y}_1 - \bar{y}_2) = \sqrt{\frac{s_{\text{pooled}}^2}{n_1} + \frac{s_{\text{pooled}}^2}{n_2}} = s_{\text{pooled}}\sqrt{\frac{1}{n_1} + \frac{1}{n_2}}$$

The formula for degrees of freedom for the Student's t-model is simpler, too. It was so complicated for the two-sample t that we stuck it in a footnote. Now it's just df $= (n_1 - 1) + (n_2 - 1)$.

Substitute the pooled-t estimate of the standard error and its degrees of freedom into the steps of the confidence interval or hypothesis test and you'll be using

How close do the two sample variances need to be in order to be able to defend the assumption of equal population variances? It turns out that if the larger variance is not more than four times as large as the smaller variance (or if the larger standard deviation is not more than twice as large as the smaller standard deviation), it is safe to assume equality. Remember, however, that this is just a rule of thumb. It is preferable to justify the assumption based on the design of the study and where the two groups come from.

pooled-*t* methods. Of course, if you decide to use a pooled-*t* method, you must defend your assumption that the variances of the two groups are equal.

To use the pooled-*t* methods, you'll need to add the **Equal Variance Assumption** that the variances of the two populations from which the samples have been drawn are equal. That is, $\sigma_1^2 = \sigma_2^2$. (Of course, we can think about the standard deviations being equal instead.)

Pooled *t*-Test and Confidence Interval for the Difference Between Means

The conditions for the **pooled *t*-test** for the difference between the means of two independent groups (commonly called a pooled *t*-test) are the same as for the two-sample *t*-test, with the additional assumption that the variances of the two groups are the same. We test the hypothesis:

$$H_0: \mu_1 - \mu_2 = \Delta_0$$

where the hypothesized difference Δ_0 is almost always 0, using the statistic:

$$t = \frac{(\bar{y}_1 - \bar{y}_2) - \Delta_0}{SE_{\text{pooled}}(\bar{y}_1 - \bar{y}_2)}$$

The standard error of $\bar{y}_1 - \bar{y}_2$ is:

$$SE_{\text{pooled}}(\bar{y}_1 - \bar{y}_2) = s_{\text{pooled}}\sqrt{\frac{1}{n_1} + \frac{1}{n_2}}$$

where the pooled variance is:

$$s_{\text{pooled}}^2 = \frac{(n_1 - 1)s_1^2 + (n_2 - 1)s_2^2}{(n_1 - 1) + (n_2 - 1)}$$

When the conditions are met and the null hypothesis is true, we can model this statistic's sampling distribution with a Student's *t*-model with $(n_1 - 1) + (n_2 - 1)$ degrees of freedom. We use that model to obtain a P-value for a test or a margin of error for a confidence interval.

The corresponding **pooled *t*-interval** is:

$$(\bar{y}_1 - \bar{y}_2) \pm t_{\text{df}}^* \times SE_{\text{pooled}}(\bar{y}_1 - \bar{y}_2)$$

where the critical value t^* depends on the confidence level and is found with $(n_1 - 1) + (n_2 - 1)$ degrees of freedom.

GUIDED EXAMPLE   Role of Friendship in Negotiations

Monkey Business Images/Shutterstock

The usual null hypothesis in a pooled *t*-test is that there's no difference in means and that's what we'll use for the camera purchase prices.

PLAN

Setup State what we want to know.

Identify the *parameter* we wish to estimate. Here our parameter is the difference in the means, not the individual group means. Identify the variables and context.

We want to know whether people are likely to offer a different amount for a used camera when buying from a friend than when buying from a stranger. We wonder whether the difference between mean amounts is zero. We have bid prices from eight subjects buying from a friend and seven subjects buying from a stranger, found in a randomized experiment.

Hypotheses State the null and alternative hypotheses.

The research claim is that friendship changes what people are willing to pay.[5] The natural null hypothesis is that friendship makes no difference.

H_O: The difference in mean price offered to friends and the mean price offered to strangers is zero:

$$\mu_F - \mu_S = 0$$

H_A: The difference in mean prices is not zero:

$$\mu_F - \mu_S \neq 0$$

We didn't start with any knowledge of whether friendship might increase or decrease the price, so we choose a two-sided alternative.

Make a graph. Boxplots are the display of choice for comparing groups. We'll also want to check the distribution of each group. Histograms may do a better job.

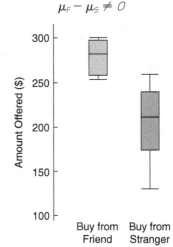

REALITY CHECK

Looks like the prices are higher if you buy from a friend. The two ranges barely overlap, so we'll be pretty surprised if we don't reject the null hypothesis.

Model Think about the assumptions and check the conditions. (Because this is a randomized experiment, we haven't sampled at all, so the 10% Condition doesn't apply.)

✓ **Independence Assumption.** There is no reason to think that the behaviour of one person will influence the behaviour of another.

✓ **Randomization Condition.** The experiment was randomized. Subjects were assigned to treatment groups at random.

✓ **Independent Groups Assumption.** Randomizing the experiment gives independent groups.

✓ **Nearly Normal Condition.** Histograms of the two sets of prices show no evidence of skewness or extreme outliers.

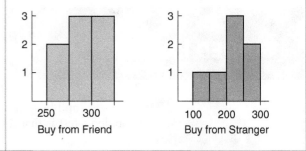

---

[5] This claim is a good example of what is called a "research hypothesis" in many social sciences. The only way to check it is to deny that it's true and see where the resulting null hypothesis leads us.

State the sampling distribution model.

Specify the method.

Because this is a randomized experiment with a null hypothesis of no difference in means, we can make the Equal Variance Assumption. If, as we are assuming from the null hypothesis, the treatment doesn't change the means, then it is reasonable to assume that it also doesn't change the variances. The nature of the study design takes precedence over the failure of the rule of thumb that the two standard deviations should be within a factor of two of one another. Under these assumptions and conditions, we can use a Student's *t*-model to perform a pooled *t*-test.

Mechanics List the summary statistics. Be sure to use proper notation.

From the data:

$$n_F = 8 \qquad n_S = 7$$
$$\bar{y}_F = \$281.88 \qquad \bar{y}_S = \$211.43$$
$$s_F = \$18.31 \qquad s_S = \$46.43$$

Use the null model to find the P-value. First determine the standard error of the difference between sample means.

The pooled variance estimate is:

$$s_p^2 = \frac{(n_F - 1)s_F^2 + (n_S - 1)s_S^2}{n_F + n_S - 2}$$

$$= \frac{(8 - 1)(18.31)^2 + (7 - 1)(46.43)^2}{8 + 7 - 2}$$

$$= 1175.48$$

The standard error of the difference becomes:

$$SE_{pooled}(\bar{y}_F - \bar{y}_S) = \sqrt{\frac{s_p^2}{n_F} + \frac{s_p^2}{n_S}}$$

$$= 17.744$$

Make a graph. Sketch the *t*-model centred at the hypothesized difference of zero. Because this is a two-tailed test, shade the region to the right of the observed difference and the corresponding region in the other tail.

The observed difference in means is:

$$(\bar{y}_F - \bar{y}_S) = 281.88 - 211.43 = \$70.45$$

which results in a *t*-ratio

$$t = \frac{(\bar{y}_F - \bar{y}_S) - (0)}{SE_{pooled}(\bar{y}_F - \bar{y}_S)} = \frac{70.45}{17.744} = 3.97$$

Find the *t*-value.

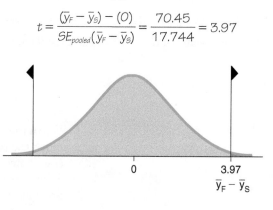

A statistics program can find the P-value.

The computer output for a pooled *t*-test appears here.

Pooled T Test for Friend vs. Stranger

```
            N     Mean    StDev    SE Mean
Friend      8     281.9   18.3     6.5
Stranger    7     211.4   46.4     18
t = 3.9699, df = 13, P-value = 0.001600
Alternative hypothesis: true difference in
means is not equal to 0
95 percent confidence interval:
32.11047 108.78238
```

REPORT

Conclusion Link the P-value to your decision about the null hypothesis and state the conclusion in context.

Be cautious about generalizing to items whose prices are outside the range of those in this study. The confidence interval can reveal more detailed information about the size of the difference. In the original article (referenced in footnote 4 in this chapter), the researcher tested several items and proposed a model relating the size of the difference to the price of the items.

MEMO:

Re: Role of friendship in negotiations.

Results of a small experiment show that people are likely to offer a different amount for a used camera when bargaining with a friend than when bargaining with a stranger. The difference in mean offers was statistically significant ($P = 0.0016$).

The confidence interval suggests that people tend to offer more to a friend than they would to a stranger. For the camera, the 95% confidence interval for the mean difference in price was $32.11 to $108.78, but we suspect that the actual difference may vary with the price of the item purchased.

✓ **JUST CHECKING**

Recall the experiment to see whether pictures of eyes would improve compliance in voluntary contributions at an office coffee station.

3 What alternative hypothesis would you test?

4 The P-value of the test was less than 0.05. State a brief conclusion.

When Should You Use the Pooled *t*-Test?

When the variances of the two groups are in fact equal, the two methods give pretty much the same result. Pooled methods have a small advantage (slightly narrower confidence intervals, slightly more powerful tests) mostly because they usually have a few more degrees of freedom, but the advantage is slight. To illustrate, if the previous example were done using the two-sample t-test, it would give a t-ratio of 3.77, with a P-value of 0.0055, and a 95% confidence interval of $26.94 to $113.96.

When the variances are *not* equal, the pooled methods are just not valid and can give poor results. You have to use the two-sample methods instead.

As the sample sizes get bigger, the advantages that come from a few more degrees of freedom make less and less difference. So the advantage (such as it is) of the pooled method is greatest when the samples are small—just when it's hardest to check the conditions. And the difference in the degrees of freedom is greatest when the variances are not equal—just when you can't use the pooled method anyway. Our advice is to use the two-sample (i.e., unpooled) *t* methods to compare means.

Why did we devote a whole section to a method that we don't recommend using? That's a good question. The answer is that pooled methods are actually very important in Statistics, especially in the case of designed experiments, where we start by assigning subjects to treatments at random. We know that at the start of the experiment each treatment group is a random sample from the same population,[6] so each treatment group begins with the same population variance. In this case, assuming the variances are equal after we apply the treatment is the same as assuming that the treatment doesn't change the variance. When we test whether the true means are equal, we may be willing to go a bit farther and say that the treatments made no difference *at all*. That's what we did in the friendship and bargaining experiment. Then it's not much of a stretch to assume that the variances have remained equal.

The other reason to discuss the pooled *t*-test is historical. Until recently, many software packages offered the pooled *t*-test as the default for comparing means of two groups and required you to specifically request the *two-sample t-test* (or sometimes the misleadingly named "unequal variance *t*-test") as an option. That's changing, but be careful when using software to specify the right test.

There is also a hypothesis test that you could use to test the assumption of equal variances. However, it is sensitive to failures of the assumptions and works poorly for small sample sizes—just the situation in which we might care about a difference in the methods. We recommend not using it. When the choice between two-sample *t* and pooled *t* methods makes a difference (that is, when the sample sizes are small), the test for whether the variances are equal hardly works at all.

Even though pooled methods are important in Statistics, the ones for comparing two means have good alternatives that don't require the extra assumption. The two-sample methods apply to more situations and are safer to use. If you are very cautious, a good piece of advice is to try both methods and see if, and how, the conclusions change. But if they do change don't just take the one you like; investigate why they change. Perhaps you failed to notice extreme outliers or vastly different variances, in which case the more interesting question is why the variances are so different.

*12.6 Tukey's Quick Test

If you think that the *t*-test is a lot of work for what seemed like an easy comparison, you're not alone. The famous statistician John Tukey[7] was once challenged to come up with a simpler alternative to the two-sample *t*-test that, like the 68-95-99.7 Rule, had critical values that could be remembered easily. The test he came up with asks you only to count and to remember three numbers: 7, 10, and 13.

Because the advantages of pooling are small, and you are allowed to pool only rarely (when the equal variances assumption is met), our advice is: *don't*. **It's never wrong *not* to pool.**

The statistician George Box commented that using the test for equal variances prior to comparing means was like sending a rowboat out into the ocean to see whether it is calm enough for an ocean liner.

It is remarkable that so few people know about, and even fewer use, this simple and effective test. This test is a "keeper" even though the section is marked as optional.

---

[6] That is, the population of experimental subjects. Remember that to be valid, experiments do not need a representative sample drawn from a population because we are not trying to estimate a population model parameter.

[7] Famous seems like an understatement for John Tukey. The *New York Times* called Tukey "one of the most influential statisticians" of the twentieth century and noted that he is credited with inventing the words "software" and "bit." He also invented both the stem-and-leaf display and the boxplot.

When you first looked at the boxplots of the friendship data, you might have noticed that they didn't overlap very much. That's the basis for Tukey's test. To use Tukey's test, one group must have the highest value, and the other must have the lowest. We just count how many values in the high group are higher than *all* the values of the lower group. Add to this the number of values in the low group that are lower than *all* the values of the higher group. (You can count ties as $\frac{1}{2}$.) If the total of these exceedences is 7 or more, we can reject the null hypothesis of equal means at $\alpha = 0.05$. The "critical values" of 10 and 13 correspond to α's of 0.01 and 0.001.

Let's try it. The "Friend" group has the highest value ($300), and the "Stranger" group has the lowest value ($130). Six of the values in the Friend group are higher than the highest value of the Stranger group ($260), and one is a tie. Six of the Stranger values are lower than the lowest value for the Friend group. That's a total of $12\frac{1}{2}$ exceedences. That's more than 10, but less than 13. So the P-value is between 0.01 and 0.001—just what we found with the pooled t.

This is a remarkably good test. The only assumption it requires is that the two samples be independent. It's so simple to do that there's no reason not to do one to check your two-sample t results. If they disagree, check the assumptions. Tukey's quick test, however, is not as widely known or accepted as the two-sample t-test, so you still need to know and use the two-sample t.

12.7 Paired Data

The two sample t-test depends crucially on the assumption that the cases in the two groups are independent of each other. When is that assumption violated? Most commonly, it's when we have data on the *same* cases in two different circumstances. For example, we might want to compare the same customers' spending at our website last January to this January, or we might have each participant in a focus group rate two different product designs. Data such as these are called **paired**. When pairs arise from an experiment, we compare measurements before and after a treatment, and the pairing is a type of *blocking*. When they arise from an observational study, it is called *matching*. All the terms—pairing, blocking, and matching—share the idea of a linkage between measurements in each pair of data values.

When the data are paired, you *should not* use the two-sample (or pooled two-sample) method. You must decide, from the way the data were collected, whether the data are paired. Be careful. There is no statistical test to determine whether the data are paired. You must decide whether the data are paired from understanding how they were collected and what they mean (check the W's).

Once we recognize that our data are matched pairs, it makes sense to concentrate on the *difference* between the two measurements for each individual. That is, we look at the collection of pairwise differences in the measured variable. For, example, if studying customer spending, we would analyze the *difference* between this January's and last January's spending for each customer. Because it is the *differences* we care about, we can treat them as if there was a single variable of interest holding those differences. With only one variable to consider, we can use a simple one-sample t-test. A **paired t-test** is just a one-sample t-test for the mean of the pairwise differences. The sample size is the number of pairs. Another way to think about the pairwise differences is as "changes." For example, how much change in spending was there from last January to this January?

Note that it doesn't matter in which direction you compute the differences, as long as you are consistent throughout all the pairs. Make your decision on what is easiest to interpret. For example, if differences are computed as this January's

This is a good time to remind you that Statistics addresses not only the analysis of data but the design of the study that produced the data. Each design has advantages and disadvantages; the choice depends on the question of interest and what is feasible. Understanding the distinction between paired samples and two independent samples illustrates the importance of thinking about design prior to analysis.

spending minus last January's spending, then positive numbers indicate increased spending.

Because the paired *t*-test is mechanically just the same as a one sample *t*-test of the pairwise differences for each case, the assumptions and conditions for those differences are exactly the same as the ones we used for the one sample *t*-test. However, because the paired *t*-test is used so often, it's a good idea to go over how the assumptions and conditions apply to this new setting.

Paired Data Assumption

The data must actually be paired. You can't just decide to pair data from independent groups. When you have two groups with the same number of observations, it may be tempting to match them up, but that's not valid. You can't pair data just because they "seem to go together." To use paired methods you must determine from knowing how the data were collected whether the two groups are paired or independent. Usually the context will make it clear.

Be sure to recognize paired data when you have them. Remember, two-sample *t*-methods aren't valid unless the groups are independent, and paired groups aren't independent. This is a very important distinction!

Independence Assumption

For these methods, it's the *differences* that must be independent of each other. This is just the one-sample *t*-test assumption of independence, now applied to the differences. As always, randomization helps to ensure independence. Don't confuse this meaning of independence with the Independent Groups assumption needed for the two-sample *t*-test.

Randomization Condition. Randomness can arise in many ways. The *pairs* may be a random sample. For example, we may be comparing opinions of husbands and wives from a random selection of couples. In an experiment, the order of the two treatments may be randomly assigned, or the treatments may be randomly assigned to one member of each pair. In a before-and-after study, like this one, we may believe that the observed differences are a representative sample from a population of interest. If we have any doubts, we'll need to include a control group to be able to draw conclusions. What we want to know usually focuses our attention on where the randomness should be.

10% Condition. When we sample from a finite population, we should be careful not to sample more than 10% of that population. Sampling too large a fraction of the population calls the independence assumption into question. As with other quantitative data situations, we don't usually explicitly check the 10% condition, but be sure to think about it.

Normal Population Assumption

We need to assume that the population of *differences* follows a Normal model. We don't need to check the data in each of the two individual groups. In fact, the data from each group can be quite skewed, but the differences can still be unimodal and symmetric.

Nearly Normal Condition. This condition can be checked with a histogram of the differences. As with the one-sample *t*-methods, this assumption matters less as we have more pairs to consider. You may be pleasantly surprised when you check this condition. Even if your original measurements are skewed or bimodal, the *differences* may be nearly Normal. After all, the individual who was way out in the tail on an initial measurement is likely to still be out there on the second one, giving a perfectly ordinary difference.

12.8 The Paired *t*-Test

Alert! This alert is not about notation, but about terminology. Do not confuse the Pooled *t*-test from Section 12.5 with the Paired *t*-test in Section 12.8. The two words—pooled and paired—look and sound somewhat similar, but are very different. Pooled refers to "pooled variance," while paired refers to "paired data values."

The paired *t*-test is mechanically a one-sample *t*-test. We treat the differences as our variable. We simply compare the mean difference to its standard error. If the *t*-statistic is large enough, we reject the null hypothesis.

Paired *t*-test

When the conditions are met, we are ready to test whether the mean paired difference is significantly different from a hypothesized value (called Δ_0). We test the hypothesis:

$$H_0: \mu_d = \Delta_0$$

where the d's are the pairwise differences and Δ_0 is almost always 0.

We use the statistic:

$$t = \frac{\bar{d} - \Delta_0}{SE(\bar{d})}$$

where $\bar{d}$ is the mean of the pairwise differences, n is the number of *pairs*, and

$$SE(\bar{d}) = \frac{s_d}{\sqrt{n}}$$

where s_d is the standard deviation of the pairwise differences.

When the conditions are met and the null hypothesis is true, the sampling distribution of this statistic is a Student's *t*-model with $n - 1$ degrees of freedom and we use that model to obtain the P-value.

Similarly, we can construct a confidence interval for the true difference. As in a one-sample *t*-interval, we centre our estimate at the mean difference in our data. The margin of error on either side is the standard error multiplied by a critical *t*-value (based on our confidence level and the number of pairs we have).

Paired *t*-interval

When the conditions are met, we are ready to find the **paired *t*-interval** for the mean of the paired differences. The confidence interval is:

$$\bar{d} \pm t^*_{n-1} \times SE(\bar{d})$$

where the standard error of the mean difference is $SE(\bar{d}) = \frac{s_d}{\sqrt{n}}$.

The critical value t^* from the Student's *t*-model depends on the particular confidence level that you specify and on the degrees of freedom, $n - 1$, which is based on the number of pairs, n.

✔ JUST CHECKING

Think about each of the following situations. Would you use a two-sample t or paired t-method (or neither)? Why?

5 Random samples of 50 men and 50 women are surveyed on the amount they invest on average in the stock market on an annual basis. We want to estimate any gender difference in how much they invest.

6 Random samples of students were surveyed on their perception of ethical and community service issues both in their first year and fourth year at a university. The university wants to know whether their required programs in ethical decision-making and service learning change student perceptions.

7 A random sample of work groups within a company was identified. Within each work group, one male and one female worker were selected at random. Each was asked to rate the secretarial support that their workgroup received. When rating the same support staff, do men and women rate them equally on average?

8 A total of 50 companies are surveyed about business practices. They are categorized by industry, and we wish to investigate differences across industries.

9 These same 50 companies are surveyed again one year later to see if their perceptions, business practices, and R&D investment have changed.

GUIDED EXAMPLE | Seasonal Spending

Ariel Skelley/Blend Images/Getty Images

In Canada, retail sales are markedly higher for December than the average for the rest of year. For example, retail sales in December 2011 were $44.8 billion, compared with $38.9 billion in November and $32.3 billion in January 2012 (*Source:* www.statcan.gc.ca.). That's one reason why Statistics Canada generally reports seasonally adjusted data to display change from month to month. In the United States, sales in the few days after American Thanksgiving (the fourth Thursday of November) give an indication of the strength of the holiday season sales and an early look at the strength of the American economy in general.

Because credit card banks receive a percentage of each transaction, they need to forecast how much the average spending will increase or decrease from month to month. How much less do people tend to spend in January than December? For any particular segment of cardholders, a credit card bank could select two random samples—one for each month—and simply compare the average amount spent in January with that in December. A more sensible approach might be to select a single random sample and compare the spending between the two months for *each cardholder*. Designing the study in this way and examining the paired differences gives a more precise estimate of the actual change in spending.

Here we have a sample of cardholders from a particular market segment and the amount they charged on their credit card in both December 2011 and January 2012. (There were 1000 cardholders in the original sample, but 89 of them had at least one month missing leaving a sample of $n = 911$.) We can test whether the mean difference in spending is 0 by using a paired t-test and create a paired t-confidence interval to estimate the true mean difference in spending between the two months.

WHO	Cardholders in a particular market segment of a major credit card issuer
WHAT	Amount charged on their credit card in December and January
WHEN	2011–2012
WHERE	Canada
WHY	To estimate the amount of decrease in spending one could expect after the holiday shopping season

---

PLAN

Setup State what we want to know.

Identify the *parameter* we wish to estimate and the sample size.

We want to know how much we can expect credit card charges to change, on average, from December to January for this market segment. We have the total amount charged in December 2011 and January 2012 for $n = 911$ cardholders in this segment. We want to test whether the mean spending is the same for customers in the two months and find a confidence interval for the true mean difference in charges between these two months for all cardholders in this segment. Because we know that people tend to spend more in December, we will look at the difference: *December spend − January spend* and use a one-sided test. A positive difference will mean a *decrease* in spending.

Hypotheses State the null and alternative hypotheses.

H_0: Mean spending was the same in December and January; the mean difference is zero: $\mu_d = 0$.

H_A: Mean spending was greater in December than January; the mean difference was greater than zero: $\mu_d > 0$.

Model Check the conditions.

State why the data are paired. Simply having the same number of individuals in each group or displaying them in side-by-side columns, doesn't make them paired.

✓ **Paired Data Assumption:** The data are paired because they are measurements on the same cardholders in two different months.

✓ **Independence Assumption:** The behaviour of any individual is independent of the behaviour of the others, so the differences are mutually independent.

Think about what we hope to learn and where the randomization comes from.

✓ **Randomization Condition:** This was a random sample from a large market segment.

Make a picture of the differences. Don't plot separate distributions of the two groups—that would entirely miss the pairing. For paired data, it's the Normality of the differences that we care about. Treat those paired differences as you would a single variable, and check the Nearly Normal condition.

✓ **Nearly Normal Condition:** The distribution of the differences is unimodal and symmetric. Although there are many observations nominated by the boxplot as outliers, the distributions are symmetric. (This is typical of the behaviour of credit card spending.) There are no isolated cases that would unduly dominate the mean difference, so we will leave all observations in the study.

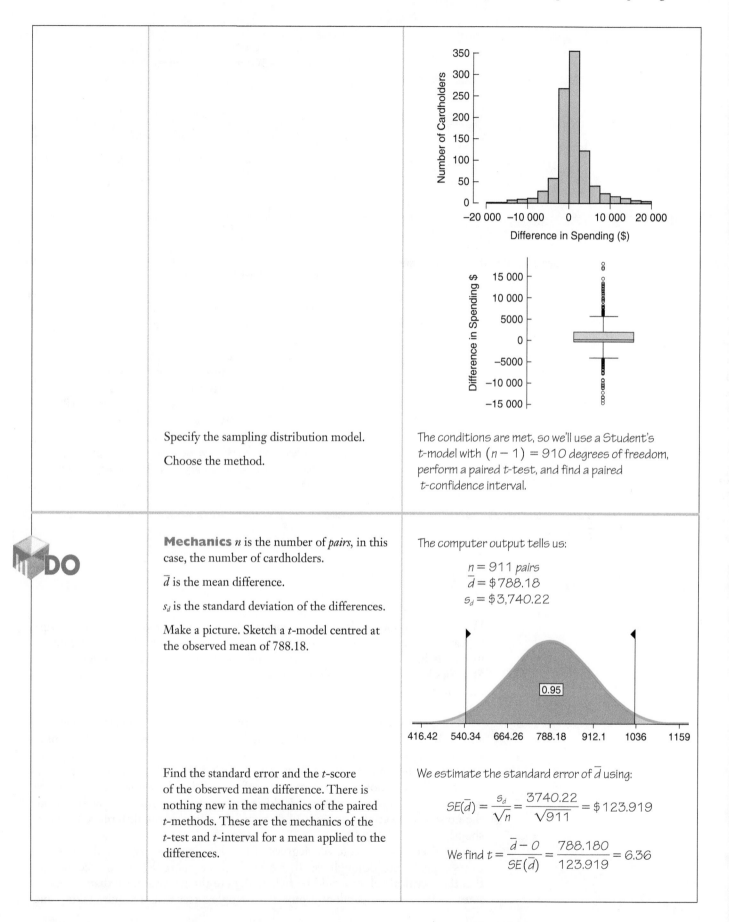

Specify the sampling distribution model.

Choose the method.

The conditions are met, so we'll use a Student's *t*-model with $(n - 1) = 910$ degrees of freedom, perform a paired *t*-test, and find a paired *t*-confidence interval.

Mechanics *n* is the number of *pairs*, in this case, the number of cardholders.

$\bar{d}$ is the mean difference.

s_d is the standard deviation of the differences.

Make a picture. Sketch a *t*-model centred at the observed mean of 788.18.

The computer output tells us:

$$n = 911 \text{ pairs}$$
$$\bar{d} = \$788.18$$
$$s_d = \$3{,}740.22$$

Find the standard error and the *t*-score of the observed mean difference. There is nothing new in the mechanics of the paired *t*-methods. These are the mechanics of the *t*-test and *t*-interval for a mean applied to the differences.

We estimate the standard error of $\bar{d}$ using:

$$SE(\bar{d}) = \frac{s_d}{\sqrt{n}} = \frac{3740.22}{\sqrt{911}} = \$123.919$$

We find $t = \dfrac{\bar{d} - 0}{SE(\bar{d})} = \dfrac{788.180}{123.919} = 6.36$

A *t*-statistic with 910 degrees of freedom and a value of 6.36 has a one-sided P-value < 0.001.

The critical value is:

$$t^*_{910} = 1.96$$

The margin of error, $ME = t^*_{910} \times SE(\bar{d})$

$$= 1.96 \times 123.919 = 242.88$$

So a 95% CI is $\bar{d} \pm ME = (\$545.30, \$1031.06)$.

REPORT

Conclusion Link the results of the confidence interval to the context of the problem.

MEMO:

Re: Credit Card Expenditure Changes

In the sample of cardholders studied, the change in expenditures between December and January averaged $788.18, which means that, on average, cardholders spend $788.18 *less* in January than the month before. There is strong evidence to suggest that the mean difference is not zero and that customers really do spend more in December than January. Although we didn't measure the change for all cardholders in the segment, we can be 95% confident that the true *mean decrease* in spending from December to January was between $545.30 to $1031.06.

How the Paired *t*-Test Works

When data are paired, it is quite conceivable that the paired *t*-test can find significant differences while a two-sample *t*-test cannot, especially when the measurements have great variability (i.e., large standard deviations). Remember that Statistics is about understanding sources of variation. By removing or controlling one source of variation, other sources come into focus; the pairing removes one source.

For example, suppose insurance adjusters investigate car repair costs at two autobody shops by taking each of 15 cars involved in accidents to both shops A and B for separate estimates of repair costs. By examining differences, the effect of unequal amounts of damage from car to car is removed, allowing comparison between the two shops. Engineers often refer to a "signal-to-noise" ratio. If there is too much background noise, it is difficult to detect a signal. In this situation, the noise is the variable amount of damage; the signal is the difference between shops.

A paired design has fewer degrees of freedom (approximately half) than the two-sample *t*-test. Although usually we would prefer more degrees of freedom (so that the *t*-critical values would be reduced), here the pairing more than compensates. In fact, an independent groups two-sample *t*-test would require taking one set of 15 cars to one shop and a different 15 cars to the other shop—that would require 30 cars! So the paired design is more efficient and more sensible.

12.9 Comparing Two Proportions

At the beginning of the book (Chapter 2) we talked about the two main types of data, quantitative and categorical. We also know that a key parameter about quantitative data is the mean, while a key parameter about categorical data is the proportion. To remind you of our discussion in Chapter 9, categorical data are often binary; that is, we have only two possible outcomes for an event, and we arbitrarily label them as "success" and "failure." "Success" doesn't necessarily mean "something good;" it means something we are interested in tracking. A proportion is, therefore, the rate of successes in a population.

In Chapters 9 and 10 we developed confidence intervals and hypothesis tests for a single proportion. In Chapter 11 we developed confidence intervals and hypothesis tests for a single mean. In this chapter we have already developed confidence intervals and hypothesis tests for comparing two means (either two-sample or paired). To complete the set and to finish this chapter on comparing two groups, we have one more situation to address, namely, comparing two proportions.

Time magazine named Facebook founder Mark Zuckerberg "Person of the Year" in 2010. According to a 2011 opinion poll by Ipsos Public Affairs, 75% of American teens have a Facebook page. It also found that 30% of girls and 24% of boys (27% overall) admitted to accessing their Facebook page continuously throughout the day; they are termed "super users." The results were based on a survey of 1009 randomly selected teenagers interviewed on the Ipsos U.S. Online Teen omnibus. (A similar survey product has recently been started in Canada.) Should we conclude that girls are more likely than boys to be "super users" of Facebook?

Here is a table of the counts from which the percentages were computed.

> In case you're thinking ahead, we will only address the comparison of two independent proportions, not proportions with paired data. Taking differences of binary data is very limited; a separate procedure is required and will not be discussed in this book.

Bloomberg/Getty Images

	Girls	Boys	Total
Super user	149	123	272
Not-so-super user	352	385	737
Total	501	508	1009

Table 12.1 Numbers of teenage girls and boys who access their Facebook page continuously throughout the day, in a sample of 1009 Americans aged 12–17.

Just as we did with the two-sample *t*-test, we start by hypothesizing a value for the true difference of the proportions, and once again we call that hypothesized difference Δ_0. (And once again, it's so common for the hypothesized difference to be zero that we often just assume that $\Delta_0 = 0$.) We take the ratio of the difference in the sample proportions to its standard error and compare the ratio to a critical value from a Normal model. The test is called the **two-sample z-test**. If this seems very familiar, check back to Section 12.2.

Two-sample *z*-test for comparing two proportions $p_1 - p_2$

When the appropriate assumptions and conditions are met, we test the hypothesis
$$H_0: p_1 - p_2 = \Delta_0$$

where the hypothesized difference Δ_0 is almost always 0. (When $\Delta_0 = 0$ it is common to write the hypothesis as $H_0 : p_1 = p_2$[8]). We use the statistic: $z = \dfrac{(\hat{p}_1 - \hat{p}_2) - \Delta_0}{SE(\hat{p}_1 - \hat{p}_2)}$ where $\hat{p}_1 = \dfrac{X_1}{n_1}$ and $\hat{p}_2 = \dfrac{X_2}{n_2}$ (X_1 and X_2 are the count of successes in each group, n_1 and n_2 are the sample sizes of each group).

The standard error[9] of $(\hat{p}_1 - \hat{p}_2)$ is:

$$SE(\hat{p}_1 - \hat{p}_2) = \sqrt{\frac{\hat{p}_1 \hat{q}_1}{n_1} + \frac{\hat{p}_2 \hat{q}_2}{n_2}}$$

Compare the z-ratio with a critical value for z or find a P-value.

Let's carry out this test with the Facebook super user comparison. Let p_1 be the proportion of girls who are super-users and p_2 be the proportion of boys who are super-users. Then:
$\hat{p}_1 = 149/501 = 0.2974$, $\hat{p}_2 = 123/508 = 0.2424$ and the standard error is 0.0278.

The z-ratio is: $z = \dfrac{0.2974 - 0.2424}{0.0278} = 1.979$

The P-value for a two-sided alternative is 0.0479, so there is sufficient evidence to conclude that girls are more likely than boys to be super users of Facebook.

As with the two-sample t-test, there is an accompanying confidence interval that tells the magnitude of the difference. In the previous example, it would be more useful to know how large a difference there is in the percentage of super users among girls and boys. The confidence interval follows the usual form; we have all the components we need.

Confidence Interval for the Difference of Two Proportions

When the conditions are met, we can find the **two-sample z-interval** for difference of two proportions, $p_1 - p_2$.

The confidence interval is:

$$(\hat{p}_1 - \hat{p}_2) \pm z^* \times SE(\hat{p}_1 - \hat{p}_2)$$

where we find the standard error of the difference as:

$$SE(\hat{p}_1 - \hat{p}_2) = \sqrt{\frac{\hat{p}_1 \hat{q}_1}{n_1} + \frac{\hat{p}_2 \hat{q}_2}{n_2}}$$

from the observed proportions.

The critical value z* depends on the particular confidence level that you specify.

---

[8] A small improvement in the z-ratio is possible if $\Delta_0 = 0$; that is, you want to test whether the two proportions are equal. Since the two sample proportions are estimates of the same quantity under the null hypothesis, pool them into a single combined estimate, $\hat{p} = \dfrac{X_1 + X_2}{n_1 + n_2}$, and replace $\hat{p}_1$ and $\hat{p}_2$ in the standard error. The modified SE is:

$$SE(\hat{p}_1 - \hat{p}_2) = \sqrt{\hat{p}\hat{q}\left(\frac{1}{n_1} + \frac{1}{n_2}\right)}$$

The z-ratio and the remainder of the test are unchanged.

[9] As we saw in Chapter 8, the standard error of the difference is found from the general fact that the variance of a difference of two independent quantities is the *sum* of their variances.

For the Facebook example, a 95% confidence interval for the true difference between rates for girls and boys is:

$$(0.2974 - 0.2424) \pm 1.96 \times \sqrt{\frac{(0.2974)(0.7026)}{501} + \frac{(0.2424)(0.7576)}{508}}$$

$$= 0.0550 \pm 0.0545 = (0.0005, 0.1095), \text{ or } 0.05\% \text{ to } 10.95\%$$

Assumptions and Conditions

Counted Data Condition. The data must be counts for the two categories of a binary categorical variable. If the categorical variable starts with more than two categories, identify the one that is of interest, and then combine all the other ones into the second category. Here "super users" are compared to "all others" and "all others" includes the categories: once a day, a few times a week, once week, etc.

Independence Assumption

Independence. The counts should be independent of each other. If the data are a random sample you simply need to check the randomization condition.

Randomization Condition. The individuals counted should be a random sample from some population. We need this in order to be able to generalize our conditions to that population. Here we took a random sample of 1009 teens; the randomness ensures that one teen's Facebook behaviour is independent of another's behaviour.

Sample Size Assumption. We must have enough data for the methods to work. Proportions based on too small a sample are not useful. You would never carry out an opinion poll based on only 10 people.

WHAT CAN GO WRONG?

- **Watch out for paired data when using the two-sample *t*-test.** The Independent Groups Assumption deserves special attention. Some researchers *deliberately* violate the Independent Groups Assumption. For example, suppose you wanted to test a diet program. You select 10 people at random to take part in your diet. You measure their weights at the beginning of the diet and after 10 weeks of the diet. So, you have two columns of weights, one for *before* and one for *after*. Can you use these methods to test whether the mean has gone down? No! The data are related; each "after" weight goes naturally with the "before" weight for the *same* person. If the samples are *not* independent, you can't use two-sample methods. This is probably the main thing that can go wrong when using these two-sample methods. Certainly, someone's weight before and after the 10 weeks will be related (whether the diet works or not). The two sample *t*-methods can be used *only* if the observations in the two groups are *independent*. (If the data are paired use paired *t*-methods.)

- **Don't use individual confidence intervals for each group to test the difference between their means.** If you make 95% confidence intervals for the means of two groups separately and you find that the intervals don't overlap, you can reject the hypothesis that the means are equal (at the corresponding α level). But, if the intervals do overlap, that doesn't mean that you *can't* reject the null hypothesis. The margin of error for the difference between the means is smaller than the sum of the individual confidence interval margins of error. Comparing the individual confidence intervals is like adding the standard deviations. But we know that it's the variances that we add, and when we do it right, we actually get a more powerful test. That's because the sum of two square roots is greater than the square root of a sum. So, don't test the difference between group means by looking at separate confidence intervals. Always make a two sample *t*-interval or perform a two sample *t*-test.

- **Look at the plots.** The usual (by now) cautions about checking for outliers and non-Normal distributions apply. The simple defence is to make and examine plots (side by side boxplots and histograms for two independent samples, histograms of the differences for paired data). You may be surprised how often this simple step saves you from the wrong or even absurd conclusions that can be generated by a single undetected outlier. You don't want to conclude that two methods have very different means just because one observation is atypical.

- **Don't use a paired *t*-method when the samples aren't paired.** When two groups don't have the same number of values, it's easy to see that they can't be paired. But just because two groups have the same number of observations doesn't mean they can be paired, even if they are shown side-by-side in a table. We might have 25 men and 25 women in our study, but they might be completely independent of one another. If they were siblings or spouses, we might consider them paired. Remember that you cannot *choose* which method to use based on your preferences. Only if the data are from an experiment or study in which observations were paired, can you use a paired method.

- **Don't forget to look for outliers when using paired methods.** For two-sample *t*-methods watch out for outliers in *either* group. For paired *t*-methods, the outliers we care about now are in the differences. A subject who is extraordinary both before and after a treatment may still have a perfectly typical difference. But one outlying difference can completely distort your conclusions. Be sure to plot the differences (even if you also plot the data) when using paired methods.

- **Make the correct choice of degrees of freedom.** Remember that the degrees of freedom in a paired *t*-test is "number of pairs minus 1." Once you have computed the differences from the paired data, you have only a single sample.

- ***t*-test or *z*-test.** Remember the general rule for choosing the model. Use a *t*-test or *t*-interval for means of quantitative data; use a *z*-test or *z*-interval for proportions of count data.

- **Do what we say, not what we do.** Precision machines used in industry often have a bewildering number of parameters that have to be set, so experiments are performed in an attempt to try to find the best settings. Such was the case for a hole-punching machine used by a well-known computer manufacturer to make printed circuit boards. The data were analyzed by one of the authors, but because he was in a hurry, he didn't look at the boxplots first and just performed *t*-tests on the experimental factors. When he found extremely small P-values even for factors that made no sense, he plotted the data. Sure enough, there was one observation 1 000 000 times bigger than the others. It turns out that it had been recorded in microns (millionths of an inch), while all the rest were in inches.

ETHICS IN ACTION

Advocacy groups for equity and diversity in the workplace often cite middle managers as an obstacle to many organizations' efforts to be more inclusive. In response to this concern, Michael Schrute, the CEO for a large manufacturing company, asked Albert Fredericks, VP of Human Resources, to look into the possibility of instituting some type of diversity training for the company's middle managers. One option under consideration was an online education program that focused on cultural diversity, gender equity, and disability awareness. Although cost-effective, Albert suspected that an online program would not be as effective as traditional training for middle managers. In order to evaluate the online program under consideration, 20 middle managers were selected to participate. Before beginning, they were given a test to assess their knowledge of and sensitivity to various diversity and equity issues. Out of a possible perfect score of 100, the test average was 63.65. Each of the 20 managers then completed the six-week online diversity education program

and was retested. The average on the test after completing the online program was 69.15. Although the group achieved a higher mean test score after completing the program, the two-sample *t*-test revealed that this average test score was not significantly higher than the average prior to completing the online program ($t = -0.94$, P-value $= 0.176$). Albert was not surprised and began to explore more traditional diversity educational programs.

ETHICAL ISSUE *The pretest and posttest design violates independence and therefore the two-sample t-test is not appropriate (related to ASA Ethical Guidelines, Item A, which can be found at http://www.amstat.org/about/ethicalguidelines.cfm).*

ETHICAL SOLUTION *Use the correct test. The two-sample t-test is not appropriate for these data. Use a paired t-test instead. Using the correct test shows that the online diversity education program was effective.*

WHAT HAVE WE LEARNED?

Are the means of two groups equal? Are the proportions of two groups equal? If not, how different are they? We've learned to use statistical inference to compare the means and proportions of two independent groups and we have learned that:

- Confidence intervals and hypothesis tests about the difference between two means, like those for an individual mean, use *t*-models.

- Confidence intervals and hypothesis tests about the difference between two proportions, like those for an individual proportion, use *z*-models.

- Checking assumptions that tell us whether our method will work is important.

- The standard error for the difference in sample means and sample proportions relies on the assumption that our data come from independent groups. Pooled methods should be used cautiously, especially with means.

- We can add variances of independent random variables to find the standard deviation of the difference in two independent means and two independent proportions.

For quantitative variables, pairing can be an effective strategy. Because pairing can help control variability between individual subjects, paired methods are usually more powerful than methods that compare independent groups. Now we've learned that analyzing data from matched pairs requires different inference procedures.

- We've learned that paired t-methods look at pairwise differences of quantitative data. Based on these differences, we test hypotheses and generate confidence intervals. Our procedures are mechanically identical to the one-sample t-methods.

- We've also learned to think about the design of the study that collected the data before we proceed with inference. We must be careful to recognize pairing when it is present but not assume it when it is not. Making the correct decision about whether to use independent t-procedures or paired t-methods is the first critical step in analyzing the data.

Terms

Paired data
Data are paired when the observations are collected in pairs or the observations in one group are naturally related to observations in the other. The simplest form of pairing is to measure each subject twice—often before and after a treatment is applied. Pairing in experiments is a form of blocking and arises in other contexts. Pairing in observational and survey data is a form of matching.

Paired t-test
A hypothesis test for the mean of the pairwise differences of two groups. It tests the null hypothesis $H_0: \mu_d = \Delta_0$, where the hypothesized difference is almost always 0, using the statistic $t = \dfrac{\bar{d} - \Delta_0}{SE(\bar{d})}$ with $n - 1$ degrees of freedom, where $SE(\bar{d}) = \dfrac{s_d}{\sqrt{n}}$ and n is the number of pairs.

Paired t-confidence interval
A confidence interval for the mean of the pairwise differences between paired groups found as $\bar{d} \pm t^*_{n-1} \times SE(\bar{d})$, where $SE(\bar{d}) = \dfrac{s_d}{\sqrt{n}}$ and n is the number of pairs.

*Pooled t-interval
A confidence interval for the difference in the means of two independent groups used when we are willing and able to make the additional assumption that the variances of the groups are equal. It is found as:

$$(\bar{y}_1 - \bar{y}_2) \pm t^*_{df} \times SE_{pooled}(\bar{y}_1 - \bar{y}_2)$$

$$\text{where } SE_{pooled}(\bar{y}_1 - \bar{y}_2) = s_{pooled}\sqrt{\frac{1}{n_1} + \frac{1}{n_2}}$$

and the pooled variance is

$$s^2_{pooled} = \frac{(n_1 - 1)s_1^2 + (n_2 - 1)s_2^2}{(n_1 - 1) + (n_2 - 1)}$$

The number of degrees of freedom is $(n_1 - 1) + (n_2 - 1)$.

Pooled
Data from two or more populations may sometimes be combined, or *pooled*, to estimate a statistic (typically a pooled variance) when we are willing to assume that the estimated value is the same in both populations. The resulting larger sample size may lead to an estimate with lower sample variance. However, pooled estimates are appropriate only when the required assumptions are true.

Pooled *t*-test A hypothesis test for the difference in the means of two independent groups when we are willing and able to assume that the variances of the groups are equal. It tests the null hypothesis:

$$H_0: \mu_1 - \mu_2 = \Delta_0$$

where the hypothesized difference Δ_0 is almost always 0, using the statistic:

$$t_{df} = \frac{(\bar{y}_1 - \bar{y}_2) - \Delta_0}{SE_{pooled}(\bar{y}_1 - \bar{y}_2)}$$

where the pooled standard error is defined as for the pooled interval and the degrees of freedom is $(n_1 - 1) + (n_2 - 1)$.

Two-sample *t*-interval A confidence interval for the difference in the means of two independent groups found as

$$(\bar{y}_1 - \bar{y}_2) \pm t^*_{df} \times SE(\bar{y}_1 - \bar{y}_2), \text{ where}$$

$$SE(\bar{y}_1 - \bar{y}_2) = \sqrt{\frac{s_1^2}{n_1} + \frac{s_2^2}{n_2}}$$

and the number of degrees of freedom is given by the approximation formula in footnote 2 of this chapter, or with technology.

Two-sample *t*-test A hypothesis test for the difference in the means of two independent groups. It tests the null hypothesis:

$$H_0: \mu_1 - \mu_2 = \Delta_0$$

where the hypothesized difference Δ_0 is almost always 0, using the statistic:

$$t_{df} = \frac{(\bar{y}_1 - \bar{y}_2) - \Delta_0}{SE(\bar{y}_1 - \bar{y}_2)}$$

with the number of degrees of freedom given by the approximation formula in footnote 2 of this chapter, or with technology.

Two-sample *z*-interval A confidence interval for the difference in the proportions of two independent groups. It is found as:

$$(\hat{p}_1 - \hat{p}_2) \pm z^* \times SE(\hat{p}_1 - \hat{p}_2), \text{ where}$$

$$SE(\hat{p}_1 - \hat{p}_2) = \sqrt{\frac{\hat{p}_1\hat{q}_1}{n_1} + \frac{\hat{p}_2\hat{q}_2}{n_2}}$$

Two-sample *z*-test A hypothesis test for the difference in the proportions of two independent groups. It tests the null hypothesis: $H_0: p_1 - p_2 = \Delta_0$

where the hypothesized difference Δ_0 is almost always 0, using the statistic:

$$z = \frac{(\hat{p}_1 - \hat{p}_2) - \Delta_0}{SE(\hat{p}_1 - \hat{p}_2)}$$

Skills

PLAN

- Be able to recognize situations in which we want to do inference on the difference between the means or proportions of two independent groups.

- Know how to examine your data for violations of conditions that would make inference about the difference between two population means or proportions unwise or invalid.
- Recognize whether a design that compares two groups is paired or not.

DO

- Be able to perform a two-sample *t*-test and confidence interval for the difference in means, using a statistics package or calculator (at least for finding the degrees of freedom).
- Be able to perform a paired *t*-test and find a paired confidence interval, recognizing that they are mechanically equivalent to a one-sample *t*-test and confidence interval applied to the differences.
- Be able to perform a two-sample *z*-test and confidence interval for the difference in proportions, using a statistics package or calculator.

REPORT

- Be able to interpret a test of the null hypothesis that the means of two independent groups are equal. (If the test is a pooled *t*-test, your interpretation should include a defence of your assumption of equal variances.)
- Know how to interpret a paired *t*-test, recognizing that the hypothesis tested is about the mean of the differences between paired values rather than about the differences between the means of two independent groups.
- Know how to interpret a paired *t*-interval, recognizing that it gives an interval for the mean difference in the pairs.
- Be able to interpret a test of the null hypothesis that the proportions of two independent groups are equal.

TECHNOLOGY HELP: Two-Sample Methods

Here's some typical computer package output with comments:

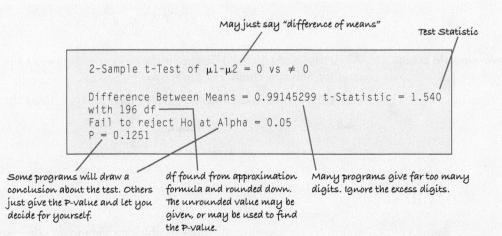

Most statistics packages compute the test statistic for you and report a P-value corresponding to that statistic. And statistics packages make it easy to examine the boxplots of the two groups, so you have no excuse for skipping the important check of the Nearly Normal Condition.

Some statistics software automatically tries to test whether the variances of the two groups are equal. Some automatically offer both the two-sample-t and pooled-t results. Ignore the test for the variances; it has little power in any situation in which its results could matter. If the pooled and two-sample methods differ in any important way, you should stick with the two-sample method. Most likely, the Equal Variance Assumption needed for the pooled method has failed.

The degrees of freedom approximation usually gives a fractional value. Most packages seem to round the approximate value down to the next smallest integer (although they may actually compute the P-value with the fractional value, gaining a tiny amount of power).

There are two ways to organize data when we want to compare two independent groups. The first, called **unstacked data,** lists the data in two columns, one for each group. Each list can be thought of as a variable. In this method, the variables in the credit card example would be "Offer" and "No Offer." Graphing calculators usually prefer this form, and some computer programs can use it as well.

The alternative way to organize the data is as **stacked data.** What is the response variable for the credit card experiment? It's the "Spend Lift"—the amount by which customers increased their spending. But the values of this variable in the unstacked lists are in both columns, and actually there's an experiment factor here, too—namely, whether the customer was offered the promotion or not. So we could put the data into two different columns, one with the "Spend Lift"s in it and one with a "Yes" for those who were offered the promotion and a "No" for those who weren't. The stacked data would look like this:

Spend Lift	Offer
969.74	Yes
915.04	Yes
197.57	No
77.31	No
196.27	Yes
…	…

This way of organizing the data makes sense as well. Now the factor and the response variables are clearly visible. You'll have to see which method your program requires. Some packages even allow you to structure the data either way.

The commands to do inference for two independent groups on common statistics technology are not always found in obvious places. Here are some starting guidelines.

EXCEL

From the Data Tab, Analysis Group, choose Data Analysis and select either t-Test: Two-Sample Assuming Unequal Variances or t-Test: Two-Sample Assuming Equal Variances. Fill in the cell ranges for the two groups, the hypothesized difference, and the alpha level.

Alternatively (if the Data Analysis Tool Pack is not installed), in the Formulas Tab, choose More functions, Statistical, TTEST, fill in the cell ranges and number of tails and specify Type 3 in the resulting dialogue. TTEST returns only the P-value.

Comments

Excel expects the two groups to be in separate cell ranges. Notice that, contrary to Excel's wording, we do not need to assume that the variances are *not* equal; we simply choose not to assume that they *are* equal.

TECHNOLOGY HELP: Paired *t*

Most statistics programs can compute paired-t analyses. Some may want you to find the differences yourself and use the one-sample t-methods. Those that perform the entire procedure will need to know the two variables to compare. The computer, of course, cannot verify that the variables are naturally paired. Most programs will check whether the two variables have the same number of observations, but some stop there, and that can cause trouble.

Most programs will automatically omit any pair that is missing a value for either variable. You must look carefully to see whether that has happened.

As we've seen with other inference results, some packages pack a lot of information into a simple table, but you must locate what you want for yourself. Here's a generic example with comments.

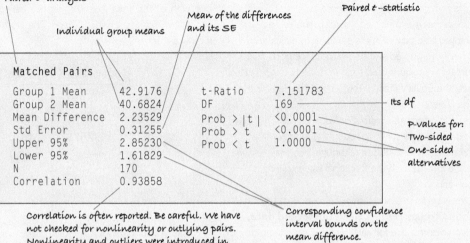

Could be called "Matched Pair" or "Paired-*t*" analysis

Individual group means

Mean of the differences and its SE

Paired *t*-statistic

Its df

P-values for: Two-sided One-sided alternatives

Corresponding confidence interval bounds on the mean difference.

Correlation is often reported. Be careful. We have not checked for nonlinearity or outlying pairs. Nonlinearity and outliers were introduced in Chapters 6 and 7 and will be discussed again in Chapter 14. Either could make the correlation meaningless, even though the paired was still appropriate.

Other packages try to be more descriptive. It may be easier to find the results, but you may get less information from the output table.

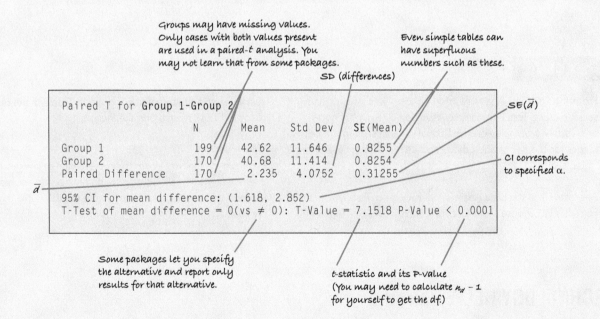

Groups may have missing values. Only cases with both values present are used in a paired-*t* analysis. You may not learn that from some packages.

SD (differences)

Even simple tables can have superfluous numbers such as these.

SE($\bar{d}$)

CI corresponds to specified α.

Some packages let you specify the alternative and report only results for that alternative.

t-statistic and its P-value (You may need to calculate $n_d - 1$ for yourself to get the df.)

Computers make it easy to examine the boxplots of the two groups and the histogram of the differences—both important steps. Some programs offer a scatterplot of the two variables. That can be helpful. In terms of the scatterplot, a paired *t*-test is about whether the points tend to be above or below the 45° line y = x. (Note that pairing says nothing about whether the scatterplot should be straight. That doesn't matter for our *t*-methods.)

EXCEL

From the Data Tab, Analysis Group, choose Data Analysis and select t-Test: Paired Two Sample for Means. (Don't let the words Two Sample distract you; the key word is Paired.) Fill in the cell ranges for the two groups, the hypothesized difference, and the alpha level.

Alternatively (if the Data Analysis Tool Pack is not installed), in the Formulas Tab, choose More functions, Statistical, TTEST, fill in the cell ranges and number of tails, and specify Type 1 in the resulting dialogue. TTEST returns only the P-value.

Comments

Excel expects the two groups to be in separate cell ranges.

Warning: Do not compute this test in Excel without checking for missing values. If there are any missing values (empty cells), Excel will usually give a wrong answer. Excel compacts each list, pushing values up to cover the missing cells, and then checks only that it has the same number of values in each list. The result is mismatched pairs and an entirely wrong analysis.

MINI CASE STUDY PROJECTS

Breadmaker/Shutterstock

Real Estate

In Chapter 6 we examined the regression of the sales price of a home on its size and saw that larger homes generally fetch a higher price. How much can we learn about a house from the fact that it has a fireplace or more than the average number of bedrooms? Data for a random sample of 1047 homes can be found in the file **ch12_MCSP_Real_Estate.xls**. There are six quantitative variables: *Price ($)*, *Living Area (sq.ft)*, *Bathrooms(#)*, *Bedrooms(#)*, *Lot Size(Acres)*, and *Age(years)*, and one categorical variable, *Fireplace?(1= Yes; 0 =No)* denoting whether the house has at least one fireplace. We can use *t*-methods to see, for example, whether homes with fireplaces sell for more, on average, and by how much. For the quantitative variables, create new categorical variables by splitting them at the median or some other splitting point of your choice, and compare home prices above and below this value. For example, the median number of *Bedrooms* of these homes is two. You might compare the prices of homes with one or two bedrooms to those with more than two. Write up a short report summarizing the differences in mean price based on the categorical variables that you created.

Stanley Cup Fatigue (Data Analysis)

There is a persistent rumor in the world of professional hockey that winning a Stanley Cup will decrease a team's performance in the following year's regular season. The data set **ch12_MCSP_Stanley_Cup.xlsx** contains information about 50 Stanley Cup winners from 1961 to 2011 (with 2005 excluded because of the lockout year when the league suspended operations due to a labour dispute). The file has the number of regular season points in the year of winning the Cup and in the year immediately following their win. There is also a binary variable that records whether the team is based in Canada (*Canadian Team* =1) or in the United States (*Canadian Team* = 0). (Note for hockey aficionados: The 1994–95 season was abbreviated to 48 games. The data values for the New York Rangers and New Jersey Devils for that season were adjusted by extrapolating their performances to a full season.)

Analyze these data to determine if, in fact, winning a Stanley Cup has an effect on a team's performance in the next regular season. Then split the data set into two groups—Canadian and American teams—and redo the analysis for each group separately. Are the results the same as for the full data set? Include hypothesis tests and confidence intervals in your report. Explain why it is important to use paired data in this analysis. If you had failed to realize that these are paired data, what difference would that have made in your reported confidence intervals and tests.

MyStatLab **Students! Save time, improve your grades with MyStatLab.**
The Exercises marked in red can be found on MyStatLab. You can practice them as often as you want, and most feature step-by-step guided solutions to help you find the right answer. You'll find a personalized Study Plan available to you too! Data Sets for exercises marked 🅣 are also available on MyStatLab for formatted technologies.

EXERCISES

1. Hot dogs and calories. Consumers increasingly make food purchases based on nutrition values. In the July 2007 issue, *Consumer Reports* examined the calorie content of two kinds of hot dogs: meat (usually a mixture of pork, turkey, and chicken) and all beef. The researchers purchased samples of several different brands. The meat hot dogs averaged 111.7 calories, compared to 135.4 for the beef hot dogs. A test of the null hypothesis that there's no difference in mean calorie content yields a P-value of 0.124. State the hypotheses and what you would conclude. **LO①**

2. Hot dogs and sodium. The *Consumer Reports* article described in Exercise 1 also listed the sodium content (in mg) for the various hot dogs tested. A test of the null hypothesis that beef hot dogs and meat hot dogs don't differ in the mean amounts of sodium yields a P-value of 0.110. State the hypotheses and what you would conclude. **LO①**

3. Learning math. The Core Plus Mathematics Project (CPMP) is an innovative approach to teaching mathematics that engages students in group investigations and mathematical modelling. After field tests in 36 high schools over a three-year period, researchers compared the performances of CPMP students with those taught using a traditional curriculum. In one test, students had to solve applied algebra problems using calculators. Scores for 320 CPMP students were compared with those of a control group of 273 students in a traditional math program. Computer software was used to create a confidence interval for the difference in mean scores (*Journal for Research in Mathematics Education*, 31, no. 3, 2000). **LO②**

Conf. level: 95%
Variable: μ (CPMP)− μ(Ctrl)
Interval: (5.573, 11.427)

a) What is the margin of error for this confidence interval?
b) If we had created a 98% confidence interval, would the margin of error be larger or smaller?
c) Explain what the calculated interval means in this context.
d) Does this result suggest that students who learn mathematics with CPMP will have significantly higher mean scores in applied algebra than those in traditional programs? Explain.

4. Sales performance. A chain that specializes in healthy and organic food would like to compare the sales performance of two of its primary stores in urban, residential areas with similar demographics. A comparison of the weekly sales randomly sampled over a period of nearly two years for these two stores yields the following information: **LO③**

Store	N	Mean	StDev	Minimum	Median	Maximum
Store #1	9	242170	23937	211225	232901	292381
Store #2	9	235338	29690	187475	232070	287838

a) Create a 95% confidence interval for the difference in the mean store weekly sales.
b) Interpret your interval in context.
c) Does it appear that one store sells more on average than the other store?
d) What is the margin of error for this interval?
e) Would you expect a 99% confidence interval to be wider or narrower? Explain.
f) If you computed a 99% confidence interval, would your conclusion in part c change? Explain.

5. CPMP, again. During the study described in Exercise 3, students in both CPMP and traditional classes took another algebra test that did not allow them to use calculators. The table shows the results. Are the mean scores of the two groups significantly different? Assume that the assumptions for inference are satisfied. **LO①**

Math Program	n	Mean	SD
CPMP	312	29.0	18.8
Traditional	265	38.4	16.2

a) Write an appropriate hypothesis.
b) Here is computer output for this hypothesis test. Explain what the P-value means in this context.

2-Sample t-Test of $\mu 1 - \mu 2 \neq 0$
t-Statistic = −6.451 w/574.8761 df
P < 0.0001

c) State a conclusion about the CPMP program.

6. IT training costs. An accounting firm is trying to decide between IT training conducted in-house and the use of third party consultants. To get some preliminary cost data, each type of training was implemented at two of the firm's offices located in different cities. The table below shows the average annual training cost per employee at each location. Are the mean costs significantly different? Assume that the assumptions for inference are satisfied. LO❶

IT Training	n	Mean	SD
In-House	210	$490.00	$32.00
Consultants	180	$500.00	$48.00

a) Write the appropriate hypotheses.
b) Below is computer output for this hypothesis test. Explain what the P-value means in this context.

    2-Sample t-Test of μ1 − μ2 ≠ 0
    t-Statistic = −2.38 w/303df
    P = 0.018

c) State a conclusion about IT training costs.

7. CPMP and word problems. The study of the new CPMP mathematics methodology described in Exercise 3 also tested students' abilities to solve word problems. This table shows how the CPMP and traditional groups performed. What do you conclude? (Assume that the assumptions for inference are met.) LO❹

Math Program	n	Mean	SD
CPMP	320	57.4	32.1
Traditional	273	53.9	28.5

8. Statistical training. The accounting firm described in Exercise 6 is interested in providing opportunities for its auditors to gain more expertise in statistical sampling methods. They wish to compare traditional classroom instruction with online self-paced tutorials. Auditors were assigned at random to one type of instruction, and the auditors were then given an exam. The table shows how the two groups performed. What do you conclude? (Assume the assumptions for inference are met.) LO❹

Program	n	Mean	SD
Traditional	296	74.5	11.2
Online	275	72.9	12.3

9. Trucking company. A trucking company would like to compare two different routes for efficiency. Truckers are randomly assigned to two different routes. Twenty truckers following Route A report an average of 40 minutes, with a standard deviation of 3 minutes. Twenty truckers following Route B report an

average of 43 minutes, with a standard deviation of 2 minutes. Histograms of travel times for the routes are roughly symmetric and show no outliers. LO❸

a) Find a 95% confidence interval for the difference in average time for the two routes.
b) Will the company save time by always driving one of the routes? Explain.

10. Change in sales. Suppose the specialty food chain from Exercise 4 wants to now compare the change in sales across different regions. An examination of the difference in sales over a 37-week period in a recent year for 8 stores in British Columbia compared to 12 stores in Ontario reveals the following descriptive statistics for relative increase in sales. (If these means are multiplied by 100, they show % increase in sales.) LO❸

Province	N	Mean	StDev
BC	8	0.0738	0.0666
Other	12	0.0559	0.0503

a) Find the 90% confidence interval for the difference in relative increase in sales over this time period.
b) Is there a significant difference in increase in sales between these two groups of stores? Explain.
c) What would you like to see to check the conditions?

11. Cereal company. A food company is concerned about recent criticism of the sugar content of their children's cereals. The data show the sugar content (as a percentage of weight) of several national brands of children's and adults' cereals. LO❹

Children's cereals: 40.3, 55, 45.7, 43.3, 50.3, 45.9, 53.5, 43, 44.2, 44, 47.4, 44, 33.6, 55.1, 48.8, 50.4, 37.8, 60.3, 46.6
Adults' cereals: 20, 30.2 , 2.2, 7.5, 4.4, 22.2, 16.6, 14.5, 21.4, 3.3, 6.6, 7.8, 10.6, 16.2, 14.5, 4.1, 15.8, 4.1, 2.4, 3.5, 8.5, 10, 1, 4.4, 1.3, 8.1, 4.7, 18.4

a) Write the null and alternative hypotheses.
b) Check the conditions.
c) Find the 95% confidence interval for the difference in means.
d) Is there a significant difference in mean sugar content between these two types of cereals? Explain.

12. Foreclosure rates. According to reports, home foreclosures were up 47% in March 2008 compared to the previous year (realestate.msn.com; April 2008). The data show home foreclosure rates (as % change from the previous year) for a sample of cities in two regions of the United States, the Northeast and the Southwest. LO❹

Northeast: 2.99, −2.36, 3.03, 1.01, 5.77, 9.95, −3.52, 7.16, −3.34, 4.75, 5.25, 6.21, 1.67, −2.45, −0.55, 3.45, 4.50, 1.87, −2.15, −0.75

Southwest: 10.15, 23.05, 18.95, 21.16, 17.45, 12.67, 13.75, 29.42, 11.45, 16.77, 12.67, 13.69, 25.81, 21.16, 19.67, 11.88, 13.67, 18.00, 12.88

a) Write the null and alternative hypotheses.
b) Check the conditions.

c) Test the hypothesis and find the P-value.
d) Is there a significant difference in the mean home foreclosure rates between these two regions of the United States? Explain.

13. Investment. Investment style plays a role in constructing a mutual fund. Each individual stock is grouped into one of two distinct groups: "Growth" and "Value." A Growth stock is one with high earning potential and often pays little or no dividends to shareholders. Conversely, Value stocks are commonly viewed as steady, or more conservative, with a lower earning potential. You are trying to decide what type of funds to invest in. Because you are saving toward your retirement, if you invest in a Value fund, you hope that the fund remains conservative. We would call such a fund "consistent." If the fund did not remain consistent and became higher risk, that could impact your retirement savings. The funds in this data set have been identified as either being "style consistent" or "style drifter." Portfolio managers wonder whether consistency provides the optimal chance for successful retirement, so they believe that style-consistent funds outperform style drifters. Out of a sample of 140 funds, 66 were identified as style consistent, while 74 were identified as style drifters. Their statistics for their average return over five years are given below: LO❹

Type	N	Mean	StDev	Minimum	Q1	Q3	Maximum 5-yr Return
Consistent	66	9.382	2.675	1.750	7.675	11.110	15.920
Drifter	74	8.563	3.719	−0.870	5.928	11.288	17.870

a) Write the null and alternative hypotheses.
b) Find the 95% confidence interval of the difference in mean return between style-consistent and style-drifter funds.
c) Is there a significant difference in five-year return for these two types of funds? Explain.

14. Technology adoption. The Pew Internet & American Life Project (www.pewinternet.org/) conducts surveys to gauge how the internet and technology impact daily life of individuals, families, and communities. In a recent survey Pew asked respondents if they thought that computers and technology give people more or less control over their lives. Companies that are involved in innovative technologies use the survey results to better understand their target market. One might suspect that younger and older respondents might differ in their opinions of whether computers and technology give them more control over their lives. A subset of the data from this survey (*February–March 2007 Tracking Data Set*) shows the mean ages of two groups of respondents, those who reported that they believed that computers and technology give them "more" control and those that reported "less" control. LO❹

Group	N	Mean	StDev	Min	Q1	Med	Q3	Max
More	74	54.42	19.65	18	41.5	53.5	68.5	99.0
Less	29	54.34	18.57	20	41.0	58.0	70.0	84.0

a) Write the null and alternative hypotheses.
b) Find the 95% confidence interval for the difference in mean age between the two groups of respondents.
c) Is there a significant difference in the mean ages between these two groups? Explain.

T 15. Product testing. A company is producing and marketing new reading activities for elementary school children that it believes will improve reading comprehension scores. A researcher randomly assigns third graders to an eight-week program in which some will use these activities and others will experience traditional teaching methods. At the end of the experiment, both groups take a reading comprehension exam. Their scores are shown in the back-to-back stem-and-leaf display. Do these results suggest that the new activities are better? Test an appropriate hypothesis and state your conclusion.

New Activities		Control
	1	07
4	2	068
3	3	377
96333	4	12222238
9876432	5	355
721	6	02
1	7	
	8	5

T 16. Product placement. The owner of a small organic food store was concerned about her sales of a specialty yogurt manufactured in Greece. As a result of increasing fuel costs, she recently had to increase its price. To help boost sales, she decided to place the product on a different shelf (near eye level for most consumers) and in a location near other popular international products. She kept track of sales (number of containers sold per week) for six months after she made the change. These values are shown below, along with the sales numbers for the six months prior to making the change, in stem-and-leaf displays. LO❹

After Change			**Before Change**
3	2	2	0
3	9	2	899
4	23	3	224
4	589	3	7789
5	0012	4	0000223
5	55558	4	5567
6	00123	5	0
6	67	5	6
7	0		

Do these results suggest that sales are better after the change in product placement? Test an appropriate hypothesis and state your conclusion. Be sure to check assumptions and conditions.

T 17. Acid rain. Researchers collected samples of water from streams to investigate the effects of acid rain. They measured the pH (acidity) of the water and classified the streams with respect to the kind of substrate (type of rock) over which they flow. A lower pH means the water is more acidic. Here is a plot of the pH of the streams by substrate (limestone, mixed, or shale): **LO❸**

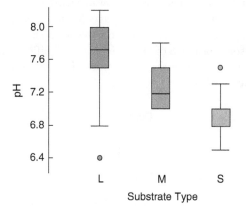

Here are selected parts of a software analysis comparing the pH of streams with limestone and shale substrates:

2-Sample t-Test of $\mu_1 - \mu_2 = 0$
Difference Between Means = 0.735
t-Statistic = 16.30 w/133 df
P ≤ 0.0001

a) State the null and alternative hypotheses for this test.
b) From the information you have, do the assumptions and conditions appear to be met?
c) What conclusion would you draw?

T 18. Hurricanes. It has been suggested that global warming may increase the frequency of hurricanes. The data show the number of major Atlantic hurricanes recorded annually before and after 1970. Has the frequency of hurricanes increased since 1970? **LO❹**

Before (1944–1969)	After (1970–2010)
3, 3, 1, 2, 4, 3, 8, 5, 3, 4, 2,	2, 1, 0, 1, 2, 3, 2, 1, 2, 2, 2,
6, 2, 2, 5, 2, 2, 7, 1, 2, 6, 1,	3, 1, 1, 1, 3, 0, 1, 3, 2, 1, 2,
3, 1, 0, 5	1, 1, 0, 5, 6, 1, 3, 5, 3, 4, 2,
	3, 6, 7, 2, 2, 5, 2, 5

a) Write the null and alternative hypotheses.
b) Are the conditions for hypothesis testing satisfied?
c) If so, test the hypothesis.

T 19. Product testing, part 2. A pharmaceutical company is producing and marketing a ginkgo biloba supplement to enhance memory. In an experiment to test the product, subjects were assigned randomly to take ginkgo biloba supplements or a placebo. Their memory was tested to see whether it improved. Here

are boxplots comparing the two groups and some computer output from a two-sample *t*-test computed for the data. **LO❹**

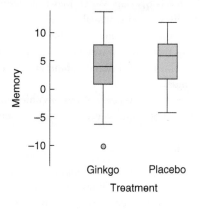

2-Sample t-Test of $\mu_G - \mu_P > 0$
Difference Between Means = −0.9914
t-Statistic = −1.540 w/196 df
P = 0.9374

a) Explain in this context what the P-value means.
b) State your conclusion about the effectiveness of ginkgo biloba.
c) Proponents of ginkgo biloba continue to insist that it works. What type of error do they claim your conclusion makes?

T 20. Baseball 2007. American League baseball teams play their games with the designated hitter rule, meaning that pitchers do not bat. The league believes that replacing the pitcher, traditionally a weak hitter, with another player in the batting order produces more runs and generates more interest among fans. The data provided include the average numbers of runs scored per game (*Runs per game*) by American League and National League teams for almost the complete first half of the 2007 season. **LO❸**

a) Create an appropriate display of these data. What do you see?
b) With a 95% confidence interval, estimate the mean number of runs scored by American League teams.
c) With a 95% confidence interval, estimate the mean number of runs scored by National League teams.
d) Explain why you should not use two separate confidence intervals to decide whether the two leagues differ in average number of runs scored.

21. Productivity. A factory hiring people to work on an assembly line gives job applicants a test of manual agility. This test counts how many strangely shaped pegs the applicant can fit into matching holes in a one-minute period. The table summarizes the data by gender of the job applicant. Assume that all conditions necessary for inference are met. **LO❸**

	Male	Female
Number of subjects	50	50
Pegs placed:		
Mean	19.39	17.91
SD	2.52	3.39

a) Find 95% confidence intervals for the average number of pegs that males and females can each place.

b) Those intervals overlap. What does this suggest about any gender-based difference in manual agility?

c) Find a 95% confidence interval for the difference in the mean number of pegs that could be placed by men and women.

d) What does this interval suggest about any gender-based difference in manual agility?

e) The two results seem contradictory. Which method is correct: doing two-sample inference, or doing one-sample inference twice?

f) Why don't the results agree?

22. Online shopping. Online shopping statistics are routinely reported by www.shop.org. Of interest to many online retailers are gender-based differences in shopping preferences and behaviours. The average monthly online expenditures are reported for males and females: **LO❸**

		Male	Female
	n	45	45
Group	**Mean**	$352	$310
	StDev	$95	$80

a) Find 95% confidence intervals for the average monthly online expenditures for males and females.

b) These intervals overlap. What does this suggest about any gender-based difference in monthly online expenditures?

c) Find a 95% confidence interval for the *difference* in average monthly online expenditures between males and females.

d) The two results seem contradictory. Which method is correct: doing two-sample inference, or doing one-sample inference twice?

23. Double header. Do the data in Exercise 20 suggest that the American League's designated hitter rule may lead to more runs? **LO❹**

a) Write the null and alternative hypothesis.

b) Find a 95% confidence interval for the difference in mean Runs per game and interpret your interval.

c) Test the hypothesis stated above in part a and find the P-value.

d) Interpret the P-value and state your conclusion. Does the test suggest that the American League scores more runs on average?

24. Online shopping, again. In 2004, it was reported that the average male spends more money shopping online per month than the average female, $204 compared to $186 (www.shop.org; accessed April 2008). Do the data reported in Exercise 22 indicate that this is still true? **LO❹**

a) Write the null and alternative hypothesis.

b) Test the hypothesis stated in part a and find the P-value.

c) Interpret the P-value and state your conclusion. Does the test suggest that males continue to spend more online on average than females?

Ⓣ 25. Drinking water. In an investigation of environmental causes of disease, data were collected on the annual mortality rate (deaths per 100 000) for males in 61 large towns in England and Wales. In addition, the water hardness was recorded as the calcium concentration (parts per million, ppm) in the drinking water. The data set also notes for each town whether it was south or north of Derby. Is there a significant difference in mortality rates in the two regions? Here are the summary statistics. **LO❺**

Summary of:	mortality
For categories in:	Derby

Group	Count	Mean	Median	StdDev
North	34	1631.59	1631	138.470
South	27	1388.85	1369	151.114

a) Test appropriate hypotheses and state your conclusion.

b) The boxplots of the two distributions show an outlier among the data north of Derby. What effect might that have had on your test?

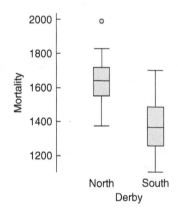

26. Sustainable stocks. The earnings per share ratio (EPS) is one of several important indicators of a company's profitability. There are several categories of "sustainable" stocks including natural foods/health and green energy/bio fuels. Below are earnings per share for a sample of stocks from both of these categories (Yahoo Financial, April 6, 2008). Is there a significant difference in earnings per share values for these two groups of sustainable stocks? **LO❹**

Group	Count	Mean	Median	StDev
Foods/Health	15	0.862	1.140	0.745
Energy/Fuel	16	−0.320	−0.545	0.918

a) Test appropriate hypotheses and state your conclusion.
b) Based upon the boxplots of the two distributions shown below, what might you suspect about your test? Explain.

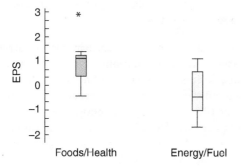

T **27. Job satisfaction.** A company institutes an exercise break for its workers to see if this will improve job satisfaction, as measured by a questionnaire that assesses workers' satisfaction. Scores for 10 randomly selected workers before and after implementation of the exercise program are shown. The company wants to assess the effectiveness of the exercise program. Explain why you can't use the methods discussed in this chapter to do that. (Don't worry, we'll give you another chance to do this the right way.) LO⑤

Worker Number	Job Satisfaction Index	
	Before	**After**
1	34	33
2	28	36
3	29	50
4	45	41
5	26	37
6	27	41
7	24	39
8	15	21
9	15	20
10	27	37

28. ERP effectiveness. When implementing a packaged Enterprise Resource Planning (ERP) system, many companies report that the module they first install is Financial Accounting. Among the measures used to gauge the effectiveness of their ERP system implementation is acceleration of the financial close process. Below is a sample of eight companies that report their average time (in weeks) to financial close before and after the implementation of their ERP system. LO⑤

Company	Before	After
1	6.5	4.2
2	7.0	5.9
3	8.0	8.0
4	4.5	4.0
5	5.2	3.8
6	4.9	4.1
7	5.2	6.0
8	6.5	4.2

Check the assumptions and conditions for using two-sample *t*-methods. Can you proceed with them? If not, why not?

29. Delivery time. A small appliance company is interested in comparing delivery times of their product during two months. They are concerned that the summer slow-downs in August cause delivery times to lag during this month. Given the following delivery times (in days) of their appliances to the customer for a random sample of six orders each month, test if delivery times differ across these two months. LO④

June	54	49	68	66	62	62
August	50	65	74	64	68	72

30. Branding. In June 2002, the *Journal of Applied Psychology* reported on a study that examined whether the content of TV shows influenced the ability of viewers to recall brand names of items featured in the commercials. The researchers randomly assigned volunteers to watch one of three programs, each containing the same nine commercials. One of the programs had violent content, another sexual content, and the third neutral content. After the shows ended, the subjects were asked to recall the brands of products that were advertised. LO⑤

		Program Type		
		Violent	**Sexual**	**Neutral**
Brands Recalled	**n**	108	108	108
	Mean	2.08	1.71	3.17
	SD	1.87	1.76	1.77

a) Do these results indicate that viewer memory for ads may differ depending on program content? Test the hypothesis that there is no difference in ad memory between programs with sexual content and those with violent content. State your conclusion.

b) Is there evidence that viewer memory for ads may differ between programs with sexual content and those with neutral content? Test an appropriate hypothesis and state your conclusion.

31. Ad campaign. You are a consultant to the marketing department of a business preparing to launch an ad campaign for a new product. The company can afford to run ads during one TV show, and has decided not to sponsor a show with sexual content. You read the study described in Exercise 30 and then use a computer to create a confidence interval for the difference in mean number of brand names remembered between the groups watching violent shows and those watching neutral shows. LO❺

> Two-Sample t
> 95% CI for $\mu_{viol} - \mu_{neut}$: [−1.578, −0.602]

a) At the meeting of the marketing staff, you have to explain what this output means. What will you say?
b) What advice would you give the company about the upcoming ad campaign?

32. Branding, part 2. In the study described in Exercise 30, the researchers also contacted the subjects again, 24 hours later, and asked them to recall the brands advertised. Results for the number of brands recalled are summarized in the table. LO❹

| | Program Type | | |
	Violent	Sexual	Neutral
No. of subjects	101	106	103
Mean	3.02	2.72	4.65
SD	1.61	1.85	1.62

a) Is there a significant difference in viewers' abilities to remember brands advertised in shows with violent vs. neutral content?
b) Find a 95% confidence interval for the difference in mean number of brand names remembered between the groups watching shows with sexual content and those watching neutral shows. Interpret your interval in this context.

33. Ad recall. In Exercises 30 and 32, we see the number of advertised brand names people recalled immediately after watching TV shows and 24 hours later. Strangely enough, it appears that they remembered more about the ads the next day. Should we conclude this is true in general about people's memory of TV ads? LO❺

a) Suppose one analyst conducts a two-sample hypothesis test to see if memory of brands advertised during violent TV shows is higher 24 hours later. The P-value is 0.00013. What might she conclude?

b) Explain why her procedure was inappropriate. Which of the assumptions for inference was violated?
c) How might the design of this experiment have tainted these results?
d) Suggest a design that could compare immediate brand name recall with recall one day later.

34. Wireless carriers. A major Canadian wireless carrier is trying to maximize revenue and profit by moving more people to smartphone devices. The carrier will need to decide how large a subsidy to offer on smartphones. A random sample of existing contracts of 100 non-smartphone customers showed an average revenue per user (ARPU) of $59 per month with a standard deviation of $25. Another random sample of 100 smartphone customers showed an average ARPU of $80 per month with a standard deviation of $40. LO❺

a) Compute a 95% confidence interval to estimate the difference in mean ARPU between the two groups of customers.
b) Suggest a design that could compare the ARPU for people who have already switched from non-smartphone to smartphone.

35. Science scores. Newspaper headlines recently announced a decline in science scores among U.S. high school seniors. In 2000, 15 109 seniors tested by the National Assessment in Education Program (NAEP) scored a mean of 147 points. Four years earlier, 7537 seniors had averaged 150 points. The standard error of the difference in the mean scores for the two groups was 1.22. LO❺

a) Have the science scores declined significantly? Cite appropriate statistical evidence to support your conclusion.
b) The sample size in 2000 was almost double that in 1996. Does this make the results more convincing or less? Explain.

36. Credit card debt. The average household credit card debt has been reported to be between $8000 and $10 000. Often of interest is the average credit card debt carried by university students. In 2008, the average credit card debt for university students was reported to be $2200 based on 12 500 responses. A year earlier it was reported to be $2190 based on survey of 8200 university students. The standard error of the difference in mean credit card balances was $1.75. LO❺

a) Has the average credit card balance carried by university students increased significantly? Cite appropriate statistical evidence to support your conclusion.
b) Is this a meaningful difference to the typical student? Is it meaningful to a credit card company?
c) The sample size in 2008 is one and a half times that in 2007. Does this make the results more or less convincing? Explain.

37. The internet. The NAEP report described in Exercise 35 compared science scores for students who had home internet access with the scores of those who did not, as shown in the graph. They report that the differences are statistically significant. LO❺

a) Explain what "statistically significant" means in this context.

b) If their conclusion is incorrect, which type of error did the researchers commit?

c) Does this prove that using the internet at home can improve a student's performance in science?

d) What companies might be interested in this information?

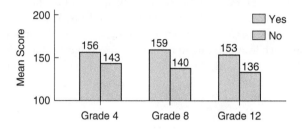

38. Credit card debt public or private. The average credit card debt carried by students was compared at public versus private universities. It was reported that a significant difference existed between the two types of institutions and that students at private universities carried higher credit card debt. LO❺

a) Explain what "statistically significant" means in this context.

b) If this conclusion is incorrect, which type of error was committed?

c) Does this prove that students who choose to attend public institutions will carry lower credit card debt?

39. Pizza sales. A national food product company believes that it sells more frozen pizza during the winter months than during the summer months. Average weekly sales for a sample of stores over a three-year period provided the following data for sales volume (in kilograms) during the two seasons. LO❹

Season	N	Mean	StDev	Minimum	Maximum
Winter	38	31234	13500	15312	73841
Summer	40	22475	8442	12743	54706

a) How much difference is there between the mean amount of this brand of frozen pizza sold (in kilograms) between the two seasons? (Assume that this time frame represents typical sales in the area.)

b) Construct and interpret a 95% confidence interval for the difference between weekly sales during the winter and summer months.

c) Suggest factors that might have influenced the sales of the frozen pizza during the winter months.

40. More pizza sales. Here's some additional information about the pizza sales data presented in Exercise 39. It is generally thought that sales spike in the weeks of the National Football League (NFL) playoffs leading up to the Super Bowl at the end of January each year. If we omit those six weeks of sales from this three-year period of weekly sales, the summary statistics look like this. Do sales appear to be higher during the winter months

after omitting those weeks most influenced by football playoff games? LO❹

Season	N	Mean	StDev	Minimum	Maximum
Winter	32	28995	9913	15312	48354
Summer	40	22475	8442	12743	54706

a) Write the null and alternative hypotheses.

b) Test the null hypotheses and state your conclusion.

c) Suggest additional factors that may influence pizza sales not accounted for in this exercise.

T 41. Olympic heats. In Olympic running events, preliminary heats are determined by random draw, so we should expect that the ability level of runners in the various heats to be about the same, on average. Here are the times (in seconds) for the 400-m women's run in the 2004 Olympics in Athens for preliminary heats 2 and 5. Is there any evidence that the mean time to finish is different for randomized heats? Explain. Be sure to include a discussion of assumptions and conditions for your analysis. LO❹

Country	Name	Heat	Time
USA	HENNAGAN Monique	2	51.02
BUL	DIMITROVA Mariyana	2	51.29
CHA	NADJINA Kaltouma	2	51.50
JAM	DAVY Nadia	2	52.04
BRA	ALMIRAO Maria Laura	2	52.10
FIN	MYKKANEN Kirsi	2	52.53
CHN	BO Fanfang	2	56.01
BAH	WILLIAMS-DARLING Tonique	5	51.20
BLR	USOVICH Svetlana	5	51.37
UKR	YEFREMOVA Antonina	5	51.53
CMR	NGUIMGO Mireille	5	51.90
JAM	BECKFORD Allison	5	52.85
TOG	THIEBAUD-KANGNI Sandrine	5	52.87
SRI	DHARSHA K V Damayanthi	5	54.58

T 42. Swimming heats. In Exercise 41 we looked at the times in two different heats for the 400-m women's run from the 2004 Olympics. Unlike track events, swimming heats are *not* determined at random. Instead, swimmers are seeded so that better swimmers are placed in later heats. Here are the times (in seconds) for the women's 400-m freestyle from heats 2 and 5. Do these results suggest that the mean times of seeded heats are not equal? Explain. Include a discussion of assumptions and conditions for your analysis.   LO❹

Country	Name	Heat	Time
ARG	BIAGIOLI Cecilia Elizabeth	2	256.42
SLO	CARMAN Anja	2	257.79
CHI	KOBRICH Kristel	2	258.68
MKD	STOJANOVSKA Vesna	2	259.39
JAM	ATKINSON Janelle	2	260.00
NZL	LINTON Rebecca	2	261.58
KOR	HA Eun-Ju	2	261.65
UKR	BERESNYEVA Olga	2	266.30
FRA	MANAUDOU Laure	5	246.76
JPN	YAMADA Sachiko	5	249.10
ROM	PADURARU Simona	5	250.39
GER	STOCKBAUER Hannah	5	250.46
AUS	GRAHAM Elka	5	251.67
CHN	PANG Jiaying	5	251.81
CAN	REIMER Brittany	5	252.33
BRA	FERREIRA Monique	5	253.75

43. Tee tests. Does it matter what kind of tee a golfer places the ball on? The company that manufactures "Stinger" tees claims that the thinner shaft and smaller head will lessen resistance and drag, reducing spin and allowing the ball to travel farther. In August 2003, Golf Laboratories, Inc. compared the distance travelled by golf balls hit off regular wooden tees to those hit off Stinger tees. All the balls were struck by the same golf club using a robotic device set to swing the club head at approximately 95 miles per hour. Summary statistics from the test are shown in the table. Assume that six balls were hit off each tee and that the data were suitable for inference. (Note: Golf, like many other sports, still uses units in the imperial system, not the metric system.)   LO❹

		Total Distance (yards)	Ball Velocity (mph)	Club Velocity (mph)
Regular	**Avg.**	227.17	127.00	96.17
tee	**SD**	2.14	0.89	0.41
Stinger	**Avg.**	241.00	128.83	96.17
tee	**SD**	2.76	0.41	0.52

Is there evidence that balls hit off the Stinger tees would have a higher initial velocity?

44. Tee tests, again. Given the test results on golf tees described in Exercise 43, is there evidence that balls hit off Stinger tees would travel farther? Again assume that six balls were hit off each tee and that the data were suitable for inference.   LO❹

45. Marketing slogan. A company is considering marketing their classical music as "music to study by." Is this a valid slogan? In a study conducted by some Statistics students, 62 people were randomly assigned to listen to rap music, music by Mozart, or no music while attempting to memorize objects pictured on a page. They were then asked to list all the objects they could remember. Here are summary statistics for each group.   LO❹

	Rap	Mozart	No Music
Count	29	20	13
Mean	10.72	10.00	12.77
SD	3.99	3.19	4.73

a) Does it appear that it is better to study while listening to Mozart than to rap music? Test an appropriate hypothesis and state your conclusion.
b) Create a 90% confidence interval for the mean difference in memory score between students who study to Mozart and those who listen to no music at all. Interpret your interval.

46. Marketing slogan, part 2. Using the results of the experiment described in Exercise 45, does it matter whether one listens to rap music while studying, or is it better to study without music at all?   LO❹

a) Test an appropriate hypothesis and state your conclusion.
b) If you concluded there is a difference, estimate the size of that difference with a 90% confidence interval and explain what your interval means.

T 47. Mutual funds. You have heard that if you leave your money in mutual funds for a longer period of time, you will see a greater return. So you would like to compare the three-year and five-year returns of a random sample of mutual funds to see if indeed, your return is expected to be greater if you leave your money in the funds for five years.   LO❹

a) Using the data provided, check the conditions for this test.
b) Write the null and alternative hypothesis for this test.
c) Test the hypothesis and find the P-value if appropriate.
d) What is your conclusion?

48. Mutual funds, part 2. An investor now tells you that if you leave your money in as long as 10 years, you will see an even greater return, so you would like to compare the 5-year and 10-year returns of a random sample of mutual funds to see if your return is expected to be greater if you leave your money in the funds for 10 years.   LO❹

a) Using the data provided, check the conditions for this test.
b) Write the null and alternative hypothesis for this test.

c) Test the hypothesis and find the P-value if appropriate.
d) What is your conclusion?

Ⓣ 49. Real estate. Residents of neighbouring towns have an ongoing disagreement over who lays claim to the higher average price of a single-family home. Since you live in one of these towns, you decide to obtain a random sample of homes listed for sale with a major local realtor to investigate if there is actually any difference in the average home price. **LO④**
a) Using the data provided on the CD, check the conditions for this test.
b) Write the null and alternative hypothesis for this test.
c) Test the hypothesis and find the P-value.
d) What is your conclusion?

Ⓣ 50. Real estate, part 2. Residents of one of the towns discussed in Exercise 49 claim that since their town is much smaller, the sample size should be increased. Instead of random sampling 30 homes, you decide to sample 42 homes from the database to test the difference in the mean price of single-family homes in these two towns. **LO④**
a) Using the data provided on the CD, check the conditions for this test.
b) Write the null and alternative hypothesis for this test.
c) Test the hypothesis and find the P-value.
d) What is your conclusion? Did the sample size make a difference?

51. Home run. For the same reasons identified in Exercise 20, a friend of yours claims that the average number of home runs hit per game is higher in the American League than in the National League. Using the same 2007 data as in Exercises 20 and 23, you decide to test your friend's theory. **LO④**
a) Using the data provided, check the conditions for this test.
b) Write the null and alternative hypothesis for this test.
c) Test the hypothesis and find the P-value.
d) What is your conclusion?

52. Statistics journals. When a professional statistician has information to share with colleagues, he or she will submit an article to one of several Statistics journals for publication. This can be a lengthy process; typically, the article must be circulated for "peer review" and perhaps edited before being accepted for publication. Then the article must wait in line with other articles before actually appearing in print. In the Winter 1998 issue of *Chance* magazine, Eric Bradlow and Howard Wainer reported on this delay for several journals between 1990 and 1994. For 288 articles published in *The American Statistician*, the mean length of time between initial submission and publication was 21 months, with a standard deviation of 8 months. For 209 *Applied Statistics* articles, the mean time to publication was 31 months, with a standard deviation of 12 months. Create and interpret a 90% confidence interval for the difference in mean delay, and comment on the assumptions that underlie your analysis. **LO③**

53. Labour force. Values for the labour force participation rate (proportion) of women (LFPR) are published by the U.S. Bureau of Labor Statistics. We are interested in whether there was a difference between female participation in 1968 and 1972, a time of rapid change for women. We check LFPR values for 19 randomly selected cities for 1968 and 1972. Here is software output for two possible tests. **LO⑤**

> Paired t-Test of $\mu(1-2)$
> Test Ho: $\mu(1972-1968) = 0$ vs Ha: $\mu(1972-1968) \neq 0$
> Mean of Paired Differences = 0.0337
>
> t-Statistic = 2.458 w/18 df
> p = 0.0244
> 2-Sample t-Test of $\mu1 - \mu2$
> Ho: $\mu1 - \mu2 = 0$ Ha: $\mu1 - \mu2 \neq 0$
> Test Ho: $\mu(1972) - \mu(1968) = 0$ vs
> Ha: $\mu(1972) - \mu(1968) \neq 0$
> Difference Between Means = 0.0337
> t-Statistic = 1.496 w/35 df
> p = 0.1434

a) Which of these tests is appropriate for these data? Explain.
b) Using the test you selected, state your conclusion.

54. Rain. It has long been a dream of farmers to summon rain when it is needed for their crops. Crop losses to drought have significant economic impact. One possibility is cloud seeding in which chemicals are dropped into clouds in an attempt to induce rain. Simpson, Alsen, and Eden (*Technometrics*, 1975) report the results of trials in which clouds were seeded and the amount of rainfall recorded. The authors report on 26 seeded (Group 2) and 26 unseeded (Group 1) clouds. Each group has been sorted in order of the amount of rainfall, largest amount first. Here are two possible tests to study the question of whether cloud seeding works. **LO⑤**

> Paired t-Test of $\mu(1-2)$
> Mean of Paired Differences = -277.4
> t-Statistic = -3.641 w/25 df p = 0.0012
> 2-Sample t-Test of $\mu1 - \mu2$
> Difference Between Means = -277.4
> t-Statistic = -1.998 w/33 df p = 0.0538

a) Which of these tests is appropriate for these data? Explain.
b) Using the test you selected, state your conclusion.

Ⓣ 55. Online insurance. After seeing countless commercials claiming one can get cheaper car insurance from an online company, a local insurance agent was concerned that he might lose some customers. To investigate, he randomly selected profiles (type of car, coverage, driving record, etc.) for 10 of his clients and checked online price quotes for their policies. The comparisons are shown in the table. His statistical software produced the following summaries (where *PriceDiff = Local – Online*): **LO④**

Variable	Count	Mean	StdDev
Local	10	799.200	229.281
Online	10	753.300	256.267
PriceDiff	10	45.900	175.663

Local	Online	PriceDiff
568	391	177
872	602	270
451	488	−37
1229	903	326
605	677	−72
1021	1270	−249
783	703	80
844	789	55
907	1008	−101
712	702	10

At first, the insurance agent wondered whether there was some kind of mistake in this output. He thought the Pythagorean Theorem of Statistics should work for finding the standard deviation of the price differences—in other words, that $SD(Local - Online) = \sqrt{SD^2(Local) + SD^2(Online)}$. But when he checked, he found that $\sqrt{(229.281)^2 + (256.267)^2} = 343.864$, not 175.663 as given by the software. Tell him where his mistake is.

T 56. Windy. Alternative sources of energy are of increasing interest throughout the energy industry. Wind energy has great potential. But appropriate sites must be found for the turbines. To select the site for an electricity-generating wind turbine, wind speeds were recorded at several potential sites every six hours for a year. Two sites not far from each other looked good. Each had a mean wind speed high enough to qualify, but we should choose the site with a higher average daily wind speed. Because the sites are near each other and the wind speeds were recorded at the same times, we should view the speeds as paired. Here are the summaries of the speeds (in kilometres per hour): **LO❹**

Variable	Count	Mean	StdDev
site2	1114	7.452	3.586
site4	1114	7.248	3.421
site2 − site4	1114	0.204	2.551

Is there a mistake in this output? Why doesn't the Pythagorean Theorem of Statistics work here? In other words, shouldn't $SD(site2 - site4) = \sqrt{SD^2(site2) + SD^2(site4)}$? But $\sqrt{(3.586)^2 + (3.421)^2} = 4.956$, not 2.551 as given by the software. Explain why this happened.

T 57. Online insurance, part 2. In Exercise 55, we saw summary statistics for 10 drivers' car insurance premiums quoted by a local

agent and an online company. Here are displays for each company's quotes and for the difference (*Local – Online*): **LO❹**

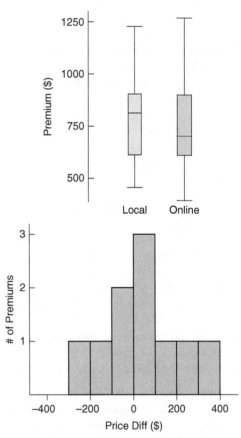

a) Which of the summaries would help you decide whether the online company offers cheaper insurance? Why?
b) The standard deviation of *PriceDiff* is quite a bit smaller than the standard deviation of prices quoted by either the local or online companies. Discuss why.
c) Using the information you have, discuss the assumptions and conditions for inference with these data.

T 58. Windy, part 2. In Exercise 56, we saw summary statistics for wind speeds at two sites near each other, both being considered as locations for an electricity-generating wind turbine. The data, recorded every six hours for a year, showed each of the sites had a mean wind speed high enough to qualify, but how can we tell which site is best? Here are some displays: **LO❹**

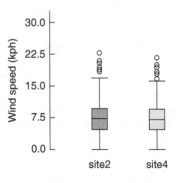

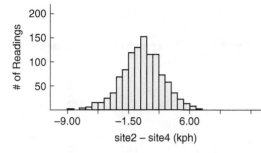

a) The boxplots show outliers for each site, yet the histogram shows none. Discuss why.

b) Which of the summaries would you use to select between these sites? Why?

c) Using the information you have, discuss the assumptions and conditions for paired *t* inference for these data. (*Hint:* Think hard about the independence assumption in particular.)

59. Online insurance, part 3. Exercises 55 and 57 give summaries and displays for car insurance premiums quoted by a local agent and an online company. Test an appropriate hypothesis to see if there is evidence that drivers might save money by switching to the online company. **LO④**

T 60. Windy, part 3. Exercises 56 and 58 give summaries and displays for two potential sites for a wind turbine. Test an appropriate hypothesis to see if there is evidence that either of these sites has a higher average wind speed. **LO④**

61. Employee athletes. An ergonomics consultant is engaged by a large consumer products company to see what they can do to increase productivity. The consultant recommends an "employee athlete" program, encouraging every employee to devote five minutes an hour to physical activity. The company worries that the gains in productivity will be offset by the loss in time on the job. They'd like to know if the program increases or decreases productivity. To measure it, they monitor a random sample of 145 employees who word process, measuring their hourly key strokes both before and after the program is instituted. Here are the data: **LO④**

	Keystrokes per Hour		
	Before	**After**	**Difference (After − Before)**
Mean	1534.2	1556.9	22.7
SD	168.5	149.5	113.6
N	145	145	145

a) What are the null and alternative hypotheses?

b) What can you conclude? Explain.

c) Give a 95% confidence interval for the mean change in productivity (as measured by keystrokes per hour).

62. Employee athletes, part 2. A small company, on hearing about the employee athlete program (see Exercise 61) at the large company down the street, decides to try it as well. To measure the difference in productivity, they measure the average number of keystrokes per hour of 23 employees before and after the five-minutes-per-hour program is instituted. The data follow: **LO③**

	Keystrokes per Hour		
	Before	**After**	**Difference (After − Before)**
Mean	1497.3	1544.8	47.5
SD	155.4	136.7	122.8
N	23	23	23

a) Is there evidence to suggest that the program increases productivity?

b) Give a 95% confidence interval for the mean change in productivity (as measured by keystrokes per hour).

c) Given this information and the results of Exercise 61, what recommendations would you make to the company about the effectiveness of the program?

T 63. Exercise equipment. A leading manufacturer of exercise equipment wanted to collect data on the effectiveness of their equipment. An August 2001 article in the journal *Medicine and Science in Sports and Exercise* compared how long it would take men and women to burn 200 calories during light or heavy workouts on various kinds of exercise equipment. The results summarized in the following table are the average times for a group of physically active young men and women whose performances were measured on a representative sample of exercise equipment: **LO③**

	AVERAGE MINUTES TO BURN 200 CALORIES			
	Hard Exertion		Light Exertion	
	Men	**Women**	**Men**	**Women**
Treadmill	12	17	14	22
X-C skier	12	16	16	23
Stair climber	13	18	20	37
Rowing machine	14	16	21	25
Exercise rider	22	24	27	36
Exercise bike	16	20	29	44

(left axis label: Machine Type)

a) On average, how many minutes longer than a man must a woman exercise at a light exertion rate in order to burn 200 calories? Find a 95% confidence interval.

b) Estimate the average number of minutes longer a woman must work out at light exertion than at heavy exertion to get the same benefit. Find a 95% confidence interval.

c) These data are actually averages rather than individual times. How might this affect the margins of error in these confidence intervals?

64. Market value. Real estate agents want to set the price of a house that's about to go on the real estate market correctly. They must choose a price that strikes a balance between one that is so high that the house takes too long to sell and one that's so low that not enough value will go to the homeowner. One appraisal method is the "Comparative Market Analysis" approach by which the market value of a house is based on recent sales of similar homes in the neighbourhood. Because no two houses are exactly the same, appraisers have to adjust comparable homes for such features as extra square footage, bedrooms, fireplaces, upgrading, parking facilities, swimming pool, lot size, location, and so on. The appraised market values and the selling prices of 45 homes from the same region are found in the data set. **LO❹**

a) Test the hypothesis that on average, the market value and the sale price of homes from this region are the same.
b) Find a 95% confidence interval for the mean difference.
c) Explain your findings in a sentence or two in context.

65. Quality control. In an experiment on braking performance, a U.S. tire manufacturer measured the stopping distance for one of its tire models. On a test track, a car made repeated stops from 60 miles per hour. Twenty tests were run, 10 each on both dry and wet pavement, with results shown in the following table. (Note that actual *braking distance*, which takes into account the driver's reaction time, is much longer, typically nearly 300 feet at 60 mph!) **LO❸**

a) Find a 95% confidence interval for the mean dry pavement stopping distance. Be sure to check the appropriate assumptions and conditions, and explain what your interval means.
b) Find a 95% confidence interval for the mean increase in stopping distance on wet pavement. Be sure to check the appropriate assumptions and conditions, and explain what your interval means.

Stopping Distance (ft)

Dry Pavement	Wet Pavement
145	211
152	191
141	220
143	207
131	198
148	208
126	206
140	177
135	183
133	223

66. Quality control, part 2. For another test of the tires in Exercise 65, the company tried them on 10 different cars, recording the stopping distance for each car on both wet and dry pavement. Results are shown in the following table. **LO❸**

Stopping Distance (ft)

Car #	Dry Pavement	Wet Pavement
1	150	201
2	147	220
3	136	192
4	134	146
5	130	182
6	134	173
7	134	202
8	128	180
9	136	192
10	158	206

a) Find a 95% confidence interval for the mean dry pavement stopping distance. Be sure to check the appropriate assumptions and conditions, and explain what your interval means.
b) Find a 95% confidence interval for the mean increase in stopping distance on wet pavement. Be sure to check the appropriate assumptions and conditions, and explain what your interval means.

67. Airlines. In recent years, the airline industry has been severely criticized for a variety of service-related issues including poor on-time performance, cancelled flights, and lost luggage. Some believe airline service is declining while the price of airline fares is increasing. A sample of 10 second-quarter changes in average domestic airfares is shown below. **LO❺**

Origin	Second Quarter 2010	Second Quarter 2011	Percent Change from 2nd Qtr 2010
Calgary	163.70	178.50	9.0
Edmonton	160.30	174.00	8.5
Halifax	168.20	179.70	6.8
Montreal	190.60	202.10	6.0
Ottawa	195.50	202.10	3.4
Regina	168.70	183.40	8.7
Saskatoon	165.40	179.80	8.7
Toronto	199.60	221.60	11.0
Vancouver	188.50	209.20	11.0
Winnipeg	176.90	193.80	9.6

Source: "A Sample of 10 Second Quarter Changes" from Statistics Canada. Used by permission of Statistics Canada.

a) Does the percent change in airfare from the second-quarter 2010 column represent paired data? Why or why not?
b) Was there an actual change, on average, in airline fares between the two quarters? Perform the test on both the actual and percentage differences. Discuss the results of the test and

explain how you chose between the fares and the percent differences as the data to test.

T **68. Grocery prices.** WinCo Foods, a large discount grocery retailer in the western United States, promotes itself as the lowest priced grocery retailer. In newspaper ads printed and distributed during January 2008, WinCo Foods published a price comparison for products between WinCo and several competing grocery retailers. One of the retailers compared against WinCo was Walmart, also known as a low price competitor. WinCo selected a variety of products, listed the price of the product charges at each retailer, and showed the sales receipt to prove the prices at WinCo were the lowest in the area. A sample of the product and their price comparison at both WinCo and Walmart are shown in the following table: **LO❺**

Item	WinCo Price	Walmart Price
Bananas (lb)	0.42	0.56
Red Onions (lb)	0.58	0.98
Mini Peeled Carrots (1 lb bag)	0.98	1.48
Roma Tomatoes (lb)	0.98	2.67
Deli Tater Wedges (lb)	1.18	1.78
Beef Cube Steak (lb)	3.83	4.118
Beef Top Round London Broil (lb)	3.48	4.12
Pillsbury Devils Food Cake Mix (18.25 oz)	0.88	0.88
Lipton Rice and Sauce Mix (5.6 oz)	0.88	1.06
Sierra Nevada Pale Ale (12 - 12 oz bottles)	12.68	12.84
GM Cheerios Oat Clusters (11.3 oz)	1.98	2.74
Charmin Bathroom Tissue (12 roll)	5.98	7.48
Bumble Bee Pink Salmon (14.75 oz)	1.58	1.98
Pace Thick & Chunky Salsa, Mild (24 oz)	2.28	2.78
Nalley Chili, Regular w/Beans (15 oz)	0.78	0.78
Challenge Butter (lb quarters)	2.18	2.58
Kraft American Singles (12 oz)	2.27	2.27
Yuban Coffee FAC (36 oz)	5.98	7.56
Totino's Pizza Rolls, Pepperoni (19.8 oz)	2.38	2.42
Rosarita Refried Beans, Original (16 oz)	0.68	0.73
Barilla Spaghetti (16 oz)	0.78	1.23
Sun-Maid Mini Raisins (14 - .5 oz)	1.18	1.36
Jif Peanut Butter, Creamy (28 oz)	2.54	2.72
Dole Fruit Bowl, Mixed Fruit (4 - 4 oz)	1.68	1.98
Progresso Chicken Noodle Soup (19 oz)	1.28	1.38
Precious Mozzarella Ball, Part Skim (16 oz)	3.28	4.23
Mrs. Cubbison Seasoned Croutons (6 oz)	0.88	1.12
Kellogg's Raisin Bran (20 oz)	1.98	2.50
Campbell's Soup at Hand, Cream of Tomato (10.75 oz)	1.18	1.26

a) Do the prices listed indicate that, on average, prices at WinCo are lower than prices at Walmart?

b) At the bottom of the price list, the following statement appears: "Though this list is not intended to represent a typical weekly grocery order or a random list of grocery items, WinCo continues to be the area's low price leader." Why do you think WinCo added this statement?

c) What other comments could be made about the statistical validity of the test on price comparisons given in the ad?

69. Fast food. GfK Roper Consulting gathers information on consumer preferences around the world to help companies monitor attitudes about health, food, and health care products. They asked people in many different cultures how they felt about the following statement: *I try to avoid eating fast foods.*

In a random sample of 800 respondents, 411 people were 35 years old or younger, and, of those, 197 agreed (completely or somewhat) with the statement. Of the 389 people over 35 years old, 246 people agreed with the statement. Are the percentages of people avoiding fast food different in the two age groups? **LO❻**

a) Write the appropriate null and alternative hypothesis.

b) Test the hypothesis stated in part a, find the P-value, and state your conclusion.

c) Give a 95% confidence interval for the difference in proportions.

70. Computer gaming. In order to effectively market electronic games, a manager wanted to know what age group of boys played more. A recent survey found that 154 of 223 boys aged 12–14 said they "played computer or console games like Xbox or PlayStation ... or games online." Of 248 boys aged 15–17, 154 also said they played these games. Is the percentage of boys who play these types of games different in the two age groups? **LO❻**

a) Write the appropriate null and alternative hypothesis.

b) Test the hypothesis stated in part a, find the P-value, and state your conclusion.

c) Give a 95% confidence interval for the difference in proportions.

71. Titanic. Newspaper headlines at the time and traditional wisdom in the succeeding decades have held that women and children escaped the *Titanic* in greater proportion than men. Here's a table with the relevant data. **LO❻**

	Female	Male	Total
Alive	343	367	**710**
Dead	127	1364	**1491**
Total	**470**	**1731**	**2201**

a) Do you think that the chance of survival was the same for males and females? Use an appropriate test to defend your conclusion.

b) Find a 95% confidence interval for the difference in the proportion of women who survived and the proportion of men who survived.

72. Twitter use. A Mini Case Study Project in Chapter 2 described a survey of students in a large undergraduate business statistics course. One question on the survey asked whether students were Twitter users. Responses were received by 574 students. Of the 294 males responding, 62 reported being Twitter users compared with 74 of 280 females responding. Assume that the responding students are a random sample of Canadian undergraduate business students. **LO❻**

a) Is there evidence of a difference between males and females with respect to the proportion who are Twitter users?
b) Find a 95% confidence interval for the difference in proportions.
c) Is the assumption of randomness a sensible one here? If not, how might that change your conclusions, if at all?

73. Statistics course outlook. Another question on the survey referred to in Exercise 72 asked students to rate their outlook concerning the Statistics course they were about to take, using the following five-point rating scale.

1= I'm dreading it
2= I'm not looking forward to it but I'll survive
3= I'm moderately excited about the course
4= I'm very excited about the course
5= It will be the most important and thrilling experience of my life

Assume that the responding students are a random sample of Canadian undergraduate business students. Here is a table of the data, split by gender. **LO❻**

| | Outlook | | | | | |
	1 Dreading it	2 Will survive	3 Mod. excited	4 Very excited	5 Most thrilling	Total
Male	4	60	155	64	11	294
Female	7	91	132	42	8	280
Total	11	151	287	106	19	574

In Chapter 13, we will learn how to use all five categories of the variable Outlook in a comparison of males of females. But for now, we can only compare two categories, so combine levels 1 and 2 into a category called Unexcited and combine levels 3, 4, and 5 into a category called Excited.

a) Construct a 2×2 table with Males and Females as the rows and Unexcited and Excited as the columns.

b) Test the claim that males and females were equally likely to be Excited about the upcoming course.
c) Find a 95% confidence interval for the difference in proportions of males and females who were Unexcited. (Be careful; part c asks about the Unexcited group.) How does this confidence interval confirm the findings in part b?

✔

JUST CHECKING ANSWERS

1 $H_0: \mu_{eyes} - \mu_{flowers} = 0$

2   ✓ **Independence Assumption**: The amount paid by one person should be independent of the amount paid by others.

 ✓ **Randomization Condition:** This study was observational. Treatments alternated a week at a time and were applied to the same group of office workers.

 ✓ **Nearly Normal Condition:** We don't have the data to check, but it seems unlikely there would be outliers in either group.

 ✓ **Independent Groups Assumptions:** The same workers were recorded each week, but week-to-week independence is plausible.

3 $H_A: \mu_{eyes} - \mu_{flowers} \neq 0$. An argument could be made for a one-sided test because the research hypothesis was that eyes would improve honest compliance.

4   Office workers' compliance in leaving money to pay for food at an office coffee station was different when a picture of eyes was placed behind the "honesty box" than when the picture was one of flowers.

5   These are independent groups sampled at random, so use a two-sample *t* confidence interval to estimate the size of the difference.

6   If the same random sample of students was sampled both in the first year and again in the fourth year of their university experience, then this would be a paired *t*-test.

7   A male and female are selected from each work group. The question calls for a paired *t*-test.

8   Since the sample of companies is different in each of the industries, this would be a two-sample test.

9   Since the same 50 companies are surveyed twice to examine a change in variables over time, this would be a paired *t*-test.

Inference for Counts: Chi-Square Tests

13

In Chapter 4 we discussed the relationship between two categorical variables, in a descriptive way, using contingency tables. In the current chapter we develop hypothesis tests for these tables and related tests for categorical data, also known as count data. These methods are also our first generalization beyond the one- and two-sample methods of Chapters 9 through 12.

Top, Henry Georgi/All Canada Photos/Alamy; bottom, Jonathan Kirn/Getty Images

LEARNING OBJECTIVES

1. Choose the most appropriate type of chi-square test

2. Test a hypothesis about the distribution of a categorical variable

3. Use standardized residuals to examine the conclusion of a chi-square test

4. Use the appropriate chi-square test to determine evidence of an association between two categorical variables

5. Use expected counts to check assumptions for chi-square tests

Eric Sprott

In 2011, investor Eric Sprott was ranked by Bloomberg Markets as a "hidden billionaire" with wealth of at least $1.3 billion (U.S.). In 2001, he established Sprott Asset Management, one of Canada's largest independently-owned securities firms. As its chairman, CEO, and Portfolio Manager, he manages over $10 billion in investments. He has won many awards, including Ernst and Young's Entrepreneur of the Year (2006), Investment Executive Fund Manager of the Year (2007), and Advisor.ca's Top Financial Visionary (2011). He is widely respected for foreseeing the dangers of excessive leverage, the resulting collapse, and current economic crisis. His *Markets at a Glance* newsletter is widely distributed and highly regarded in the financial community. His name is also well-known in academic circles through the Sprott School of Business at Carleton University in Ottawa.

Among other activities, Sprott Asset Management manages a number of award-winning hedge funds, such as the Sprott Capital LP, which won Absolute Return's Hedge Fund of the Year in 2010. Hedge funds, like mutual funds and pension funds, pool investors' money in an attempt to make profits. Unlike these other funds, however, hedge funds are privately-offered investments that use non-traditional strategies to offset risk, an approach called "hedging." Most hedge funds require a minimum investment of

$1 million but there are a growing number of "lite" hedge funds with more affordable minimum investments. Typically, hedge funds use multiple, often complex, strategies to exploit inefficiencies in the market. However, they are not immune to risk, and Wall Street has had some massive hedge fund failures. But the Sprott Hedge Fund is one of the successful hedge funds, and one of a number of investment funds available through Sprott's companies.

Question: What is a long-term investment?

Answer: A short-term investment that failed!

In a business as competitive as hedge fund management, information is gold. Being the first to have information and knowing how to act on it can mean the difference between success and failure. Hedge fund managers look for small advantages everywhere, hoping to exploit inefficiencies in the market and to turn those inefficiencies into profit.

Wall Street has plenty of "wisdom" about market patterns. For example, investors are advised to watch for "calendar effects," certain times of year or days of the week that are particularly good or bad: "As goes January, so goes the year" and "Sell in May and go away." Some analysts claim that the "bad period" for holding stocks is from the sixth trading day of June to the fifth-to-last trading day of October. Of course, there is also Mark Twain's advice.

"October. This is one of the peculiarly dangerous months to speculate in stocks. The others are July, January, September, April, November, May, March, June, December, August, and February."

—Pudd'nhead Wilson's Calendar

One common claim is that stocks show a weekly pattern. For example, some argue that there is a *weekend effect* in which stock returns on Mondays are often lower than those of the immediately preceding Friday. Are patterns such as this real? We have the data, so we can check. Between October 1, 1928, and June 6, 2007, there were 19 755 trading sessions. Let's first see how many trading days fell on each day of the week. It's not exactly 20% for each day because of holidays. The distribution of days is shown in Table 13.1.

Day of Week	Count	% of Days
Monday	3820	19.34%
Tuesday	4002	20.26
Wednesday	4024	20.37
Thursday	3963	20.06
Friday	3946	19.97

Table 13.1 The distribution of days of the week among the 19 755 trading days from October 1, 1928, to June 6, 2007. We expect about 20% to fall in each day, with minor variations due to holidays and other events.

Of these 19 755 trading sessions, 10 272, or about 52% of the days, saw a gain in the Dow Jones Industrial Average (DJIA). To test for a pattern, we need a model. The model comes from the supposition that any day is as likely to show a gain as any other. In any sample of positive or "up" days, we should expect to see the same distribution of days as in Table 13.1—in other words, about 19.34% of "up" days would be Mondays, 20.26% would be Tuesdays, and so on. Here is the distribution of days in one such random sample of 1000 "up" days.

Day of Week	Count	% of Days in the Sample of "up" Days
Monday	192	19.2%
Tuesday	189	18.9
Wednesday	202	20.2
Thursday	199	19.9
Friday	218	21.8

Table 13.2 The distribution of days of the week for a sample of 1000 "up" trading days selected at random from October 1, 1928, to June 6, 2007. If there is no pattern, we would expect the proportions here to match fairly closely the proportions observed among all trading days in Table 13.1.

Of course, we expect some variation. We wouldn't expect the proportions of days in the two tables to match exactly. In our sample, the percentage of Mondays in Table 13.2 is slightly lower than in Table 13.1, and the proportion of Fridays is a little higher. Are these deviations enough for us to declare that there is a recognizable pattern?

In Chapter 9 we learned how to compare a single proportion to a hypothesized value. In Chapter 11 we learned how to compare two proportions, one to another. But neither of those procedures will allow us to compare multiple proportions to multiple hypothesized values. We need a brand-new procedure.

13.1 Goodness-of-Fit Tests

To address this question, we test the table's **goodness-of-fit**, where *fit* refers to the null model proposed. Here, the null model is that there is no pattern, that the distribution of *up* days should be the same as the distribution of trading days overall. (If there were no holidays or other closings, that would just be 20% for each day of the week.)

Assumptions and Conditions

Data for a goodness-of-fit test are organized in tables, and the assumptions and conditions reflect that. Rather than having an observation for each individual, we typically work with summary counts in categories. Here, the individuals are trading days, but rather than list all 1000 trading days in the sample, we have totals for each weekday.

Counted Data Condition.   The data must be counts for the categories of a categorical variable. This might seem a silly condition to check. But many kinds of values can be assigned to categories, and it is unfortunately common to find the methods of this chapter applied incorrectly (even by business professionals) to

Expected Cell Frequencies

Companies often want to assess the relative successes of their products in different regions. However, a company whose sales regions had 100, 200, 300, and 400 representatives might not expect equal sales in all regions. They might expect observed sales to be proportional to the size of the sales force. The null hypothesis in that case would be that the proportions of sales were 1/10, 2/10, 3/10, and 4/10, respectively. With 500 total sales, their expected counts would be 50, 100, 150, and 200.

proportions or quantities just because they happen to be organized in a two-way table. So check to be sure that you really have counts.

Independence Assumption

Independence Assumption.   The counts in the **cells** should be independent of each other. You should think about whether that's reasonable. If the data are a random sample you can simply check the randomization condition.

Randomization Condition.   The individuals counted in the table should be a random sample from some population. We need this condition if we want to generalize our conclusions to that population. We took a random sample of 1000 trading days on which the DJIA rose. That lets us assume that the market's performance on any one day is independent of performance on another. If we had selected 1000 consecutive trading days, there would be a risk that market performance on one day could affect performance on the next, or that an external event could affect performance for several consecutive days.

Sample Size Assumption

Sample Size Assumption.   We must have enough data for the methods to work. We usually just check the following condition:

Expected Cell Frequency Condition.   We should expect to see at least 5 individuals in each cell. The expected cell frequency condition should remind you of—and is, in fact, quite similar to—the condition that np and nq be at least 10 when we test proportions.

Chi-Square Model

We have observed a count in each category (weekday). We can compute the number of up days we'd *expect* to see for each weekday if the null model were true. For the trading days example, the expected counts come from the null hypothesis that the up days are distributed among weekdays just as trading days are. Of course, we could imagine almost any kind of model and base a null hypothesis on that model.

To decide whether the null model is plausible, we look at the differences between the expected values from the model and the counts we observe. We wonder: Are these differences so large that they call the model into question, or could they have arisen from natural sampling variability? We denote the *differences* between these observed and expected counts $(Obs - Exp)$. As we did with variance, we square them. That gives us positive values and focuses attention on any cells with large differences. Because the differences between observed and expected counts generally get larger the more data we have, we also need to get an idea of the *relative* sizes of the differences. To do that, we divide each squared difference by the expected count for that cell.

The test statistic, called the **chi-square (or chi-squared) statistic**, is found by adding up the sum of the squares of the deviations between the observed and expected counts divided by the expected counts:

$$\chi^2 = \sum_{all\ cells} \frac{(Obs - Exp)^2}{Exp}$$

The chi-square statistic is denoted χ^2, where χ is the Greek letter chi (pronounced kī). Warning: Many statisticians have a pet peeve about mispronunciations and misspellings of this test's name. Do not pronounce the "ch" as in "child." Do not

> **NOTATION ALERT:**
> We compare the counts *observed* in each cell with the counts we *expect* to find. The usual notation uses *Obs* and *Exp* as we've used here. The expected counts are found from the null model.

> **NOTATION ALERT:**
> The only use of the Greek letter χ in Statistics is to represent the chi-square statistic and the associated sampling distribution. This is another violation of the general rule that Greek letters represent population parameters. Here we are using a Greek letter simply to name a family of distribution models and a statistic.

confuse it with the Chinese word *chi* (also spelled or *ch'i* or *qi*) which means "vital energy." Do not confuse chi with *chai*, which is a form of Indian tea. Finally, do not confuse chi with *chai*, which is the Hebrew word for life. Whew! Remember that chi rhymes with pie and you'll be fine. The resulting family of sampling distribution models is called the **chi-square models.**

The members of this family of models differ in the number of degrees of freedom. The number of degrees of freedom for a goodness-of-fit test is $k - 1$, where k is the number of cells—in this example, five weekdays.

We will use the chi-square statistic only for testing hypotheses, not for constructing confidence intervals. A small chi-square statistic means that our model fits the data well, so a small value gives us no reason to doubt the null hypothesis. If the observed counts don't match the expected counts, the statistic will be large. If the calculated statistic value is large enough, we'll reject the null hypothesis. So the chi-square test is always one-sided. What could be simpler? Let's see how it works.

The Chi-Square Calculation

Here are the steps to calculate the chi-square statistic:

1. **Find the expected values.** These come from the null hypothesis model. Every null model gives a hypothesized proportion for each cell. The expected value is the product of the total number of observations times this proportion. (The result need not be an integer.)

2. **Compute the residuals.** Once you have expected values for each cell, find the residuals, Obs − Exp.

3. **Square the residuals.** $(\text{Obs} - \text{Exp})^2$

4. **Compute the components.** Find $\dfrac{(\text{Obs} - \text{Exp})^2}{\text{Exp}}$ for each cell.

5. **Find the sum of the components.** That's the chi-square statistic, $\chi^2 = \displaystyle\sum_{\text{all cells}} \dfrac{(\text{Obs} - \text{Exp})^2}{\text{Exp}}$.

6. **Find the degrees of freedom.** It's equal to the number of cells minus one.

7. **Test the hypothesis.** Large chi-square values mean lots of deviation from the hypothesized model, so they give small P-values. Look up the critical value from a table of chi-square values such as Table X in Appendix B, or use technology to find the P-value directly.

The steps of the chi-square calculations are often laid out in tables. Use one row for each category, and columns for observed counts, expected counts, residuals, squared residuals, and the contributions to the chi-square total:

	Observed	Expected	Residual = (Obs − Exp)	(Obs − Exp)²	Component = (Obs − Exp)² / Exp
Monday	192	193.369	−1.369	1.874	0.0097
Tuesday	189	202.582	−13.582	184.471	0.9106
Wednesday	202	203.695	−1.695	2.873	0.0141
Thursday	199	200.607	−1.607	2.582	0.0129
Friday	218	199.747	18.253	333.172	1.6680

Table 13.3 Calculations for the chi-square statistic in the trading days example. Table X has a layout similar to Table T (for the *t*-distribution). But it is simpler to read since there is only a right-tail probability to consider; there is no need to decide between one-tail and two-tail probabilities. Simply find the row corresponding to the number of degrees of freedom you have and find the critical value in the appropriate column, or locate where the computed chi-square statistic lies in relation to the given entries.

GUIDED EXAMPLE | Stock Market Patterns

We have counts of the "up" days for each day of the week. The economic theory we want to investigate is whether there is a pattern in "up" days. So, our null hypothesis is that across all days in which the DJIA rose, the days of the week are distributed as they are across all trading days. (As we saw, the trading days are not quite *evenly* distributed because of holidays, so we use the *trading days* percentages as the null model.) We refer to this as *uniform*, accounting for holidays. The alternative hypothesis is that the observed percentages are *not* uniform. The test statistic looks at how closely the observed data match this idealized situation.

PLAN

Setup State what you want to know.

Identify the variables and context.

We want to know whether the distribution for "up" days differs from the null model (the trading days distribution). We have the number of times each weekday appeared among a random sample of 1000 "up" days.

Hypotheses State the null and alternative hypotheses. For χ^2 tests, it's usually easier to state the hypotheses in words than in symbols.

H_0: The days of the work week are distributed among the up days as they are among all trading days.

H_A: The trading days model does not fit the up days distribution.

Model Think about the assumptions and check the conditions.

✓ **Counted Data Condition** We have counts of the days of the week for all trading days and for the "up" days.

✓ **Independence Assumption** We have no reason to expect that one day's performance will affect another's, but to be safe we've taken a random sample of days. The randomization should make them far enough apart to alleviate any concerns about dependence.

✓ **Randomization Condition** We have a random sample of 1000 days from the time period.

✓ **Expected Cell Frequency Condition** All the expected cell frequencies are much larger than 5.

Specify the sampling distribution model.

Name the test you will use.

The conditions are satisfied, so we'll use a χ^2 model with $5 - 1 = 4$ degrees of freedom and do a **chi-square goodness-of-fit test**.

DO

Mechanics Each cell contributes a value equal to $\dfrac{(Obs - Exp)^2}{Exp}$ to the chi-square sum.

To find the expected number of days, we take the fraction of each weekday from *all* days and multiply by the number of "up" days.

For example, there were $3820/19\,755$ Mondays overall, or 19.34%.

So, we'd expect there would be $1000 \times 19.34\%$ or 193.4 Mondays among the 1000 "up" days.

The expected values are:

Monday: 193.4
Tuesday: 202.6
Wednesday: 203.7
Thursday: 200.6
Friday: 199.7

And we observe:
Monday: 192
Tuesday: 189
Wednesday: 202
Thursday: 199
Friday: 218

Add up these components. If you do it by hand, it can be helpful to arrange the calculation in a table.

$$\chi^2 = \frac{(192 - 193.4)^2}{193.4} + \cdots + \frac{(218 - 199.7)^2}{199.7} = 2.62$$

The P-value is the probability in the upper tail of the χ^2 model. It can be found using software or a table (see Table X in Appendix B).

Using Table X in Appendix B, we find that for a significance level of 5% and 4 degrees of freedom, we'd need a value of 9.488 or more to have a P-value less than 0.05. Our value of 2.62 is less than that.

The χ^2 models are skewed to the high end. Large χ^2 statistic values correspond to small P-values, which would lead us to reject the null hypothesis.

Using a computer to generate the P-value, we find:

$$\text{P-value} = P(\chi^2 > 2.62) = 0.62$$

REPORT

Conclusion Link the P-value to your decision. Be sure to say more than a fact about the distribution of counts. State your conclusion in terms of what the data mean.

MEMO:

Re: Stock Market Patterns

Our investigation of whether there are day-of-the-week patterns in the behaviour of the DJIA in which one day or another is more likely to be an "up" day found no evidence of such a pattern. Our statistical test indicated that a pattern such as the one found in our sample of trading days would happen by chance about 62% of the time.

We conclude that there is, unfortunately, no evidence of a pattern that could be used to guide investment in the market. We were unable to detect a "weekend" or other day of the week effect in the market.

A goodness-of-fit test can be thought of as an expansion of the one-proportion z-test to more than two categories. A z-test would only be able to examine one day at a time to check if, for example, the proportion of Friday up days is the same as the proportion of all Friday trading days. Just as the z-test null hypothesis value Δ_0 comes from theory, so does the entire null hypothesis model.

13.2 Interpreting Chi-Square Values

When we calculated χ^2 for the trading days example, we got 2.62. That value was not large for 4 degrees of freedom, so we were unable to reject the null hypothesis. In general, what *is* big for a χ^2 statistic?

Think about how χ^2 is calculated. In every cell any deviation from the expected count contributes to the sum. Large deviations generally contribute more, but if there are a lot of cells, even small deviations can add up, making the χ^2 value larger. So the more cells there are, the higher the value of χ^2 has to be before it becomes significant. For χ^2, the decision about how big is big depends on the number of degrees of freedom.

Unlike the Normal and *t* families, χ^2 models are skewed. Curves in the χ^2 family change both shape and centre as the number of degrees of freedom grows. Here, for example, are the χ^2 curves for five and for nine degrees of freedom.

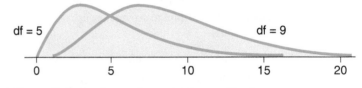

| Figure 13.1 The χ^2 curves for 5 and 9 degrees of freedom.

Notice that the value $\chi^2 = 10$ might seem somewhat extreme when there are five degrees of freedom, but appears to be rather ordinary for nine degrees of freedom. Here are two simple facts to help you think about χ^2 models:

◆ The mode is at $\chi^2 = df - 2$. (Look at the curves; their peaks are at 3 and 7.)

◆ The expected value (mean) of a χ^2 model is its number of degrees of freedom. That's a bit to the right of the mode—as we would expect for a skewed distribution.

Why Can't We Prove the Null?

A student claims that it really makes no difference to your starting salary how well you do in your Statistics class. He surveys recent graduates, categorizes them according to whether they earned an A, B, or C in Statistics, and according to whether their starting salary is above or below the median for their class. He calculates the proportion above the median salary for each grade. His null model is that in each grade category, 50% of students are above the median. With 40 respondents, he gets a P-value of 0.07 and declares that Statistics grades don't matter. But then more questionnaires are returned, and he finds that with a sample size of 70, his P-value is 0.04. Can he ignore the second batch of data? Of course not. If he could do that, he could claim almost any null model was true just by having too little data to refute it.

Goodness-of-fit tests are often performed by people who have a theory of what the proportions *should* be in each category and who believe their theory to be true. In some cases, unlike our market example, there isn't an obvious null hypothesis against which to test the proposed model. So, unfortunately, in those cases, the only *null* hypothesis available is that the proposed theory is true. And as we know, the hypothesis testing procedure allows us only to reject the null or fail to reject it. We can never confirm that a theory is in fact true; we can never confirm the null hypothesis.

At best, we can point out that the data are consistent with the proposed theory. But this doesn't prove the theory. The data *could* be consistent with the model even if the theory were wrong. In that case, we fail to reject the null hypothesis but can't conclude anything for sure about whether the theory is true.

13.3 Examining the Residuals

Chi-square tests are always one-sided. The chi-square statistic is always positive, and a large value provides evidence against the null hypothesis (because it shows that the fit to the model is *not* good), while small values provide little evidence that the model doesn't fit. In another sense, however, chi-square tests are really many-sided; a large statistic doesn't tell us *how* the null model doesn't fit. In our market theory example, if we had rejected the uniform model, we wouldn't have known *how* it failed. Was it because there were not enough Mondays represented, or was it that all five days showed some deviation from the uniform?

When we reject a null hypothesis in a goodness-of-fit test, we can examine the residuals in each cell to learn more. In fact, whenever we reject a null hypothesis, it's a good idea to examine the residuals. (We don't need to do that when we fail to reject because when the χ^2 value is small, all of its components must have been small.)

Because we want to compare residuals for cells that may have very different counts, we standardize the residuals. We know the mean residual is zero,[1] but we need to know each residual's standard deviation. When we tested proportions, we saw a link between the expected proportion and its standard deviation. For counts, there's a similar link. To standardize a cell's residual, we divide by the square root of its expected value[2]:

$$\frac{(Obs - Exp)}{\sqrt{Exp}}$$

Notice that these **standardized residuals** are the square roots of the components we calculated for each cell, with the plus (+) or the minus (−) sign indicating whether we observed more or fewer cases than we expected.

The standardized residuals give us a chance to think about the underlying patterns and to consider how the distribution differs from the model. Now that we've divided each residual by its standard deviation, they are *z*-scores. If the null hypothesis was true, we could even use the 68-95-99.7 Rule to judge how extraordinary the large ones are.

Here are the standardized residuals for the trading days data:

	Standardized Residual $= \dfrac{(Obs - Exp)}{\sqrt{Exp}}$
Monday	−0.0984
Tuesday	−0.9542
Wednesday	−0.1188
Thursday	−0.1135
Friday	1.292

Table 13.4 Standardized residuals.

None of these values is remarkable. The largest, Friday, at 1.292, is not impressive when viewed as a *z*-score. The deviations are in the direction suggested by the "weekend effect," but they aren't quite large enough for us to conclude that they are real.

13.4 Chi-Square Tests of Two-Way Tables

In Section 12.9, we studied whether girls and boys were equally likely to be Facebook super users; that is, people who access their Facebook page continuously throughout the day.

The data we used for the comparison of two proportions were displayed in a two-by-two table. (Remember that we don't include the Row and Column

---

[1]Residual = observed − expected. Because the total of the expected values is the same as the observed total, the residuals must sum to zero.

[2]It can be shown mathematically that the square root of the expected value estimates the appropriate standard deviation.

Totals, i.e., the marginal distributions, when we state the dimensions of the table.) The table looked like this:

	Girls	Boys	Total
Super user	149	123	272
Not-so-super user	352	385	737
Total	501	508	1009

A more general layout for a two-by-two table would be:

	Sample 1	Sample 2	Row Total
"Success"	X_1	X_2	$X_1 + X_2$
"Failure"	$n_1 - X_1$	$X_2 - X_2$	$n_1 + n_2 - (X_1 + X_2)$
Column Total	n_1	n_2	$n_1 + n_2$

where $\hat{p}_1 = \dfrac{X_1}{n_1}$, $\hat{p}_2 = \dfrac{X_2}{n_2}$, $\hat{q}_1 = \dfrac{n_1 - X_1}{n_1}$, and $\hat{q}_2 = \dfrac{n_2 - X_2}{n_2}$.

But what if we wanted to compare two-year age groups (12 or 13, 14 or 15, 16 or 17) rather than sexes? Then the table would be:

	12–13	14–15	16–17	Total
Super user	50	99	123	272
Not-so-super user	263	242	232	737
Total	313	341	355	1009

And what if we wanted further differentiation among levels of usage?

	12–13	14–15	16–17	Total
Super user	50	99	123	272
Regular user	104	155	144	403
Occasional/Rare user	28	29	31	88
Non-user	131	58	57	246
Total	313	341	355	1009

Now, it is not possible to carry out a z-test to compare the three age groups or to contrast all four usage levels simultaneously. Instead we need to use another version of a chi-square test.

A two-way table goes by many names. In Chapter 4 we called it a **contingency table** because the table shows how individuals are distributed along each variable depending on, or contingent on, the value of the other variable. It is also commonly called a cross tabulation, or simply a crosstab, since individuals are classified or tabulated in two dimensions, across and down.

Two-way tables arise in two main ways, depending on the design of the study and how the data are collected.

One study design aims to determine whether two or more subgroups of population share the same distribution of a single categorical variable. The technical term is **homogeneity**; that is, are the responses on the categorical variables homogeneous (i.e., the same) for each of the subgroups. A test of homogeneity is a logical expansion of the two-sample z-test of two proportions, but it is an expansion in two

A bit of statistical history. The chi-square test was introduced by Karl Pearson in 1900 in a journal called *Philosophical Magazine*. The article had a very catchy title: "On the Criterion that a Given System of Deviations from the Probable in the Case of a Correlated System of Variables is such that it can be Reasonably Supposed to have Arisen from Random Sampling." It makes you want to read the original article! In view of its creator, the test is sometimes called the Pearson chi-square. Pearson used the capital chi (χ) in his notation of the normal distribution. In 1924, Sir Ronald Fisher showed how the chi-square distribution was part of a whole family of distributions related to the normal.

ways. It applies if there are more than two groups, and/or if there are more than two categories. Thus, a 2×2 table is expanded to any number of rows and columns.

The other study design aims to determine whether two categorical variables are associated with one another in the population. The technical term is **independence**; that is, are the individuals' responses on one categorical variable independent of, or unrelated to, the responses on another categorical variable. A test of independence is analogous to the idea of correlation and regression with two quantitative variables.

Let's revisit the Facebook and teens example one more time. As a test of homogeneity, the question is whether the proportions in each usage level are the same for each of the three age groups. As a test of independence, the question is whether usage level is independent of age among a population of teens.

I know what you're thinking: homogeneity and independence sound suspiciously similar. What is the difference? In a test of homogeneity, the individuals in each subgroup come from a separate random sample. In a test of independence the individuals are a random sample from a population and two categorical variables are observed for each individual.

So which design is the Facebook situation? The latter. It is a test of independence since Ipsos collected a random sample of 1009 teens and afterward cross-tabulated the sample by age and usage level.

But here's the great news. Mechanically and computationally, the chi-square tests for both situations are identical. The only difference is a subtle one in how we word the hypotheses and the conclusions.

We will provide examples of both situations.

A Chi-Square Test of Homogeneity

WHO	Respondents in the GfK Roper Reports Worldwide Survey
WHAT	Responses to questions relating to perceptions of food and health
WHEN	Fall 2005; published in 2006
WHERE	Worldwide
HOW	Data collected by GfK Roper Consulting using a multistage design
WHY	To understand cultural differences in the perception of the food and beauty products we buy and how they affect our health

Skin care products are big business. Growth in the skin care market in China during 2006 was 15%, fueled by its population size and massive economic growth. But not all cultures and markets are the same. Global companies must understand cultural differences in the importance of various skin care products in order to compete effectively.

The GfK Roper Reports Worldwide Survey, which we first saw in Chapter 4, asked 30 000 consumers in 23 countries about their attitudes on health, beauty, and other personal values. One question participants were asked was how important is: "Seeking the utmost attractive appearance" to you? Responses were a scale with 1 = Not at all important and 7 = Extremely important. Is agreement with this question the same across the five countries for which we have data (China, France, India, U.K., and the United States)? Here is a table with the counts.

		Country					
		China	France	India	U.K.	U.S.	Total
Appearance	**7—Extremely important**	197	274	642	210	197	**1520**
	6	257	405	304	252	203	**1421**
	5	315	364	196	348	250	**1473**
	4—Average importance	480	326	263	486	478	**2033**
	3	98	82	41	125	100	**446**
	2	63	46	36	70	58	**273**
	1—Not at all important	92	38	53	62	29	**274**
	Total	**1502**	**1535**	**1535**	**1553**	**1315**	**7440**

Table 13.5 Responses to how important is: "Seeking the utmost attractive appearance."

We can compare the countries more easily by examining the column percentages.

		Country					
		China	France	India	U.K.	U.S.	Row %
Appearance	7—Extremely important	13.12%	17.85	41.82	13.52	14.98	**20.43%**
	6	17.11	26.38	19.80	16.23	15.44	**19.10**
	5	20.97	23.71	12.77	22.41	19.01	**19.80**
	4—Average importance	31.96	21.24	17.13	31.29	36.35	**27.33**
	3	6.52	5.34	2.67	8.05	7.60	**5.99**
	2	4.19	3.00	2.35	4.51	4.41	**3.67**
	1—Not at all important	6.13	2.48	3.45	3.99	2.21	**3.68**
	Total	**1502**	**1535**	**1535**	**1553**	**1315**	**7440**

| Table 13.6 Responses as a percentage of respondents by country.

The stacked barchart of the responses by country shows the patterns more vividly:

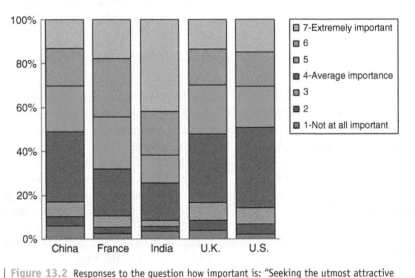

Figure 13.2 Responses to the question how important is: "Seeking the utmost attractive appearance" by country. India stands out for the proportion of respondents who said Important or Extremely important. (Chart created in Excel.)

It seems that India stands out from the other countries. There is a much larger proportion of respondents from India who responded *Extremely Important*. But are the observed differences in the percentages real or just natural sampling variation?

Table 13.6 is a two-way table with seven rows and five columns, so a chi-square test of a two-way table is appropriate. Note that each of the five countries is a separate random sample. Our null hypothesis is that the proportions choosing each alternative are the same for each country (i.e., homogeneous), so this chi-square test is formally a test of homogeneity.

Note that if we considered the table to be a single sample of individuals who are cross-tabulated by "importance of appearance rating" and "country of residence," that would make it a test of independence. We told you the difference was subtle!

It turns out that the mechanics of the chi-square test needed here are nearly identical to the chi-square goodness-of-fit test we just saw in Section 13.1. The difference is that the goodness-of-fit test compared our observed counts to the expected counts from a *given* model. Here the null hypothesis is that the distributions are the same for all the groups. The test examines the differences between the observed counts and what we'd expect under that assumption of homogeneity.

For example, 20.43% (the row %) of *all* 7440 respondents said that looking good was extremely important to them. If the distributions were homogenous across the five countries (as the null hypothesis asserts), then that proportion should be the same for all five countries. So 20.43% of the 1315 U.S. respondents, or 268.66, would have said that looking good was extremely important. That's the number we'd *expect* under the null hypothesis.

Working in this way, we (or, more likely, the computer) can fill in expected values for each cell. The following table shows these expected values for each response and each country.

| | | Country | | | | | |
		China	France	India	U.K.	U.S.	Row %
Appearance	7—Extremely important	306.86	313.60	313.60	317.28	268.66	**20.43%**
	6	286.87	293.18	293.18	296.61	251.16	**19.10**
	5	297.37	303.91	303.91	307.47	260.35	**19.80**
	4—Average importance	410.43	419.44	419.44	424.36	359.33	**27.33**
	3	90.04	92.02	92.02	93.10	78.83	**5.99**
	2	55.11	56.32	56.32	56.99	48.25	**3.67**
	1—Not at all important	55.32	56.53	56.53	57.19	48.43	**3.68**
	Total	**1502**	**1535**	**1535**	**1553**	**1315**	**7440**

Table 13.7 Expected values for the responses. Because these are theoretical values, they don't have to be integers.

The term *homogeneity* means that things are the same. Here, we ask whether the distribution of responses about the importance of looking good is the same across the five countries. The chi-square test looks for differences large enough to step beyond what we might expect from random sample-to-sample variation. It can reveal a large deviation in a single category or small but persistent differences over all the categories—or anything in between.

Assumptions and Conditions

The assumptions and conditions are the same as for the chi-square test for goodness-of-fit. The **Counted Data Condition** says that these data must be counts. You can never perform a chi-square test on a quantitative variable. For example, if Roper had recorded how much respondents spent on skin care products, you wouldn't be able to use a chi-square test to determine whether the mean expenditures in the five countries were the same.[3]

Independence Assumption. So that we can generalize, we need the counts to be independent of each other. We can check the **Randomization Condition**. Here, we have random samples, so we *can* assume that the observations are independent

---

[3]To do that, you'd use a method called Analysis of Variance.

How to Find Expected Values

In a contingency table we need to find the expected values when the null hypothesis is true. To find the expected value for row i and column j, we take:

$$\text{Exp}_{ij} = \frac{\text{Total}_{\text{Row }i} \times \text{Total}_{\text{Col }j}}{\text{Table Total}}$$

Here's an example:

Suppose we ask 100 people, 40 men and 60 women, to name their magazine preference: *Sports Illustrated*, *Cosmopolitan*, or *The Economist* with the following result:

Magazine Preference

	Sports Illustrated	Cosmopolitan	Economist	**Total**
Men	25	5	10	**40**
Women	10	45	5	**60**
Total	**35**	**50**	**15**	**100**

Then, for example, the expected value under the null hypothesis for *Men* who prefer *The Economist* would be:

$$\text{Exp}_{13} = \frac{40 \times 15}{100} = 6$$

Performing similar calculations for all cells gives the expected values:

	Sports Illustrated	Cosmopolitan	Economist	
Men	14	20	6	40
Women	21	30	9	60
	35	50	15	100

and draw a conclusion comparing the populations from which the samples were taken.

We must be sure we have enough data for this method to work. The **Sample Size Assumption** can be checked with the **Expected Cell Frequency Condition,** which says that the expected count in each cell must be at least five. Here, our samples are certainly large enough.

Following the pattern of the goodness-of-fit test, we compute the component for each cell of the table:

$$\textbf{Component} = \frac{(\textit{Obs} - \textit{Exp})^2}{\textit{Exp}}$$

Summing these components across all cells gives the chi-square value:

$$\chi^2 = \sum_{\text{all cells}} \frac{(\textit{Obs} - \textit{Exp})^2}{\textit{Exp}}$$

The degrees of freedom are different than they were for the goodness-of-fit test. For a chi-square test of a two-way table, there are $(R - 1) \times (C - 1)$ degrees of freedom, where R is the number of rows and C is the number of columns.

In our example, we have $6 \times 4 = 24$ degrees of freedom. We'll need the degrees of freedom to find a P-value for the chi-square statistic.

GUIDED EXAMPLE	Attitudes on Appearance

PLAN

Setup State what you want to know. Identify the variables and context.	We want to know whether the distribution of responses to how important is "Seeking the utmost attractive appearance" is the same for the five countries for which we have data: China, France, India, U.K., and U.S.
Hypotheses State the null and alternative hypotheses.	H_0: The responses have the same distribution for all five countries (i.e., are homogeneous). H_A: The responses do not have the same distribution for all five countries (i.e., are not homogeneous).
Model Think about the assumptions and check the conditions.	We have counts of the number of respondents in each country who choose each response.

		✓ **Counted Data Condition** The data are counts of the number of people choosing each possible response.
		✓ **Randomization Condition** The data were obtained from a random sample by a professional global marketing company.
		✓ **Expected Cell Frequency Condition** The expected values in each cell are all at least five.
	State the sampling distribution model. Name the test you will use.	The conditions seem to be met, so we can use a χ^2 model with $(7-1) \times (5-1) = 24$ degrees of freedom and use a **chi-square test**.

DO

Mechanics Show the expected counts for each cell of the data table. You could make separate tables for the observed and expected counts or put both counts in each cell. A segmented bar chart is often a good way to display the data.

The observed and expected counts are in Tables 13.5 and 13.7. The bar graph shows the column percentages:

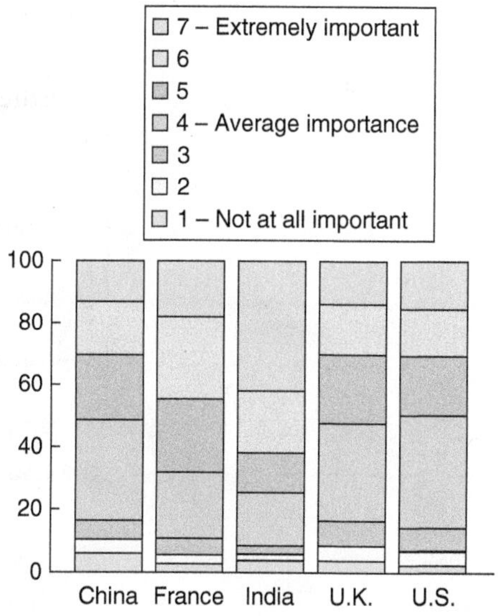

$$\chi^2 = 810.65$$

Use software to calculate χ^2 and the associated P-value.

Here, the calculated value of the χ^2 statistic is extremely high, so the P-value is quite small.

The P-value is very small in part because of the large sample size, which gives the test considerable power to detect even small differences.

P-value $= P(\chi^2_{24} > 810.65) < 0.001$, so we reject the null hypothesis.

REPORT

Conclusion State your conclusion in the context of the data. Discuss whether the distributions for the groups appear to be different. For a small table, examine the residuals.

MEMO:

Re: Importance of Appearance

Our analysis of the Roper data shows large differences across countries in the distribution of how important respondents say it is for them to look attractive. Marketers of cosmetics are advised to take notice of these differences, especially when selling products to India.

If you find that simply rejecting the hypothesis of homogeneity is a bit unsatisfying, you're in good company. It's hardly a shock that responses to this question differ from country to country. What we'd really like to know is where the differences were and how big they were. The test for homogeneity doesn't answer these interesting questions, but it does provide some evidence that can help us. A look at the standardized residuals can help identify cells that don't match the homogeneity pattern.

A Chi-Square Test of Independence

We saw that the importance people place on their personal appearance varies a great deal from one country to another, a fact that might be crucial for the marketing department of a global cosmetics company. Suppose the marketing department wants to know whether the age of the person matters as well. That might affect the kind of media channels they use to advertise their products. Do older people feel as strongly as younger people that personal appearance is important?

		Age						
		13–19	20–29	30–39	40–49	50–59	60+	Total
Appearance	7—Extremely important	396	337	300	252	142	93	**1520**
	6	325	326	307	254	123	86	**1421**
	5	318	312	317	270	150	106	**1473**
	4—Average importance	397	376	403	423	224	210	**2033**
	3	83	83	88	93	54	45	**446**
	2	37	43	53	58	37	45	**273**
	1—Not at all important	40	37	53	56	36	52	**274**
	Total	**1596**	**1514**	**1521**	**1406**	**766**	**637**	**7440**

| **Table 13.10** Responses to the question about personal appearance by age group.

Table 13.10 is a two-way table with seven rows and six columns, so once again a chi-square test of a two-way table is appropriate.

When we examined the five countries, we thought of the countries as five different groups, rather than as levels of a variable. But here, we can (and probably should) think of *Age* as a second variable whose value has been measured for each respondent along with his or her response to the appearance question. Asking whether the distribution of responses changes with *Age* now raises the question of whether the variables personal *Appearance* and *Age* are independent.

Our null hypothesis is that the response to the personal appearance question is independent of age, so this chi-square test is formally a test of independence.

Note that if we considered the table to be a set of random samples of individuals from each age group who are cross-tabulated by "importance of appearance rating" and "age group," that would make it a test of homogeneity. We'll tell you again that the difference is subtle!

What is meant by "independence" of two variables? Two events, A and B, are independent if the probability of event A given that event B occurred must be the same as the probability of event A. In other words, knowing that event B has (or hasn't) happened doesn't change your assessment of how likely it is for A to happen. So "independent" means "unrelated" or "unassociated." Here, this means the probability that a randomly selected respondent thinks personal appearance

> The only difference between the test for homogeneity and the test for independence is in how you state the conclusion. Everything about the computations is the same!

In the previous example, we showed how to find expected values from a table of gender by magazine preference. Here, again, is the table.

Magazine Preference

	Sports Illustrated	Cosmopolitan	Economist	Row Total
Men	25	5	10	40
Women	10	45	5	60
Column Total	35	50	15	100

Recall the multiplication rule from Chapter 7:

If A and B are independent events, $P(A \text{ and } B) = P(A) \times P(B)$.

To illustrate, consider the top left cell. When the null hypothesis is true,

$P(\text{Male and Sports Illustrated}) = P(\text{Male}) \times P(\text{Sports Illustrated})$

$P(\text{Male}) = 40/100$, since 40 of the 100 individuals are male,

$P(\text{Sports Illustrated}) = 35/100$ since 35 of the 100 preferences are for *Sports Illustrated*.

Therefore, $P(\text{Male and Sports Illustrated}) = \left(\frac{40}{100}\right) \times \left(\frac{35}{100}\right)$

There are 100 individuals, each with this probability, so the expected number of individuals in the top left cell is $100 \times P(\text{Male and Sports Illustrated}) = 100 \times \left(\frac{40}{100}\right) \times \left(\frac{35}{100}\right) = \frac{40 \times 35}{100}$

Thus, to find the expected value for the cell identified by row i and column j, we take:

$$Exp_{ij} = \frac{Total\ Row\ i \times Total\ Column\ j}{Overall\ Total}$$

is extremely important is the same for all age groups. That would show that the response to the personal *Appearance* question is independent of that respondent's *Age*. Of course, from a table based on data, the probabilities will never be exactly the same. But to tell whether they are different enough, we use a chi-square test of independence.

The mechanics of the chi-square test of independence are identical to those of a test of a chi-square test of homogeneity. The expected values are computed with the same formula, and the test statistic, degrees of freedom, and P-value are the same.

Assumptions and Conditions

Of course, we still need counts and enough data so that the expected counts are at least five in each cell.

If we're interested in the independence of variables, we usually want to generalize from the data to some population. In that case, we'll need to check that the data are a representative random sample from that population.

GUIDED EXAMPLE   Personal Appearance and Age

PLAN

Setup State what you want to know.

Identify the variables and context.

Hypotheses State the null and alternative hypotheses.

We perform a test of independence when we suspect the variables may not be independent. We are making the claim that knowing the respondents' age will change the distribution of their response to the question about personal *Appearance*, and testing the null hypothesis that it is *not* true.

We want to know whether the categorical variables personal *Appearance* and *Age* are statistically independent. We have a contingency table of 7440 respondents from a sample of five countries.

H_O: personal *Appearance* and *Age* are independent.[4]

H_A: personal *Appearance* and *Age* are not independent.

---

[4]As in other chi-square tests, the hypotheses are usually expressed in words, without parameters. The hypothesis of independence itself tells us how to find expected values for each cell of the contingency table. That's all we need.

Model Check the conditions.

✓ **Counted Data Condition** We have counts of individuals categorized on two categorical variables.

✓ **Randomization Condition** These data are from a randomized survey conducted in 30 countries. We have data from five of them. Although they are not an SRS, they were selected to avoid biases.

This table shows the expected counts below for each cell. The expected counts are calculated exactly as they were for a test of homogeneity; in the first cell, for example, we expect $\frac{1520}{7440} = 20.43\%$ of 1596 which is 326.06.

✓ **Expected Cell Frequency Condition** The expected values are all much larger than five.

Expected Values

	Age					
	13–19	20–29	30–39	40–49	50–59	60+
7—Extremely important	326.065	309.312	310.742	287.247	156.495	130.140
6	304.827	289.166	290.503	268.538	146.302	121.664
5	315.982	299.748	301.133	278.365	151.656	126.116
4—Average importance	436.111	413.705	415.617	384.193	209.312	174.062
3	95.674	90.759	91.178	84.284	45.919	38.186
2	58.563	55.554	55.811	51.591	28.107	23.374
1—Not at all important	58.777	55.758	56.015	51.780	28.210	23.459

(row label on the left: *Appearance*)

The stacked bar graph shows that the response seems to be dependent on Age. Older people tend to think personal appearance is less important than younger people.

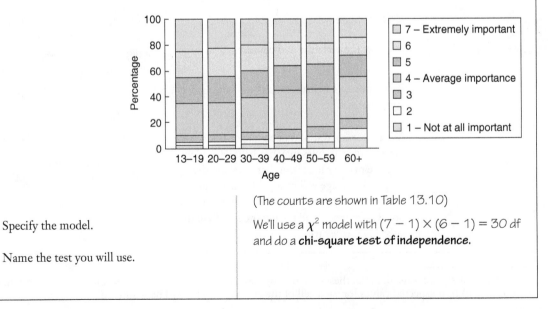

(The counts are shown in Table 13.10)

Specify the model.

Name the test you will use.

We'll use a χ^2 model with $(7 - 1) \times (6 - 1) = 30$ df and do a **chi-square test of independence**.

DO	**Mechanics** Calculate χ^2 and find the P-value using software. The shape of a chi-square model depends on its degrees of freedom. Even with 30 df, this chi-square statistic is extremely large, so the resulting P-value is small.	$\chi^2 = \sum_{all\ cells} \dfrac{(Obs - Exp)^2}{Exp} = 170.7762$ P-value $= P(\chi^2_{30} > 170.7762) < 0.001$
REPORT	**Conclusion** Link the P-value to your decision. State your conclusion.	MEMO: **Re: Investigation of the relationship between age of consumer and attitudes about personal appearance.** It appears from our analysis of the Roper survey that attitudes on personal *Appearance* are not independent of *Age*. It seems that older people find personal appearance less important than younger people do.

We rejected the null hypothesis of independence between *Age* and attitudes about personal *Appearance*. With a sample size this large, we can detect very small deviations from independence, so it's almost guaranteed that the chi-square test will reject the null hypothesis. Examining the residuals can help you see the cells that deviate farthest from independence. To make a meaningful business decision, you'll have to look at effect sizes as well.

Suppose the company was specifically interested in deciding how to split advertising resources between the teen market and the 30- to 39-year-old market. How much of a difference are the proportions of those in each age group that rated personal *Appearance* as very important (responding either 6 or 7)?

✓ **JUST CHECKING**

For each of the following situations, decide whether you should use a chi-square goodness-of-fit test or a chi-square test of a two-way table. If it is the latter, decide whether the hypotheses are more appropriately formulated as a test of homogeneity or independence.

1 A restaurant manager wonders whether customers who dine on Friday nights have the same preferences among the chef's four special entrées as those who dine on Saturday nights. One weekend he has the wait staff record which entrées were ordered each night. Assuming these customers to be typical of all weekend diners, he'll compare the distributions of meals chosen Friday and Saturday.

2 Company policy calls for parking spaces to be assigned to everyone at random, but you suspect that may not be so. There are three lots of equal size: lot A, next to the building; lot B, a bit farther away; and lot C on the other side of the highway. You gather data about employees at middle management level and above to see how many were assigned parking in each lot.

3 Is a student's social life affected by where the student lives? A campus survey asked a random sample of students whether they lived in a dormitory, in off-campus housing, or at home and whether they had been out on a date 0, 1–2, 3–4, or 5 or more times in the past two weeks.

There is a close connection between the chi-square test and the z-test for two proportions. For a 2×2 table, which has only 1 df, the chi-square test is equivalent to testing whether two proportions are equal, that is, the z-test. The two tests give the same P-value. So which test should you use? The z-test has the important advantage of also giving a confidence interval, while the chi-square test can be used for bigger tables. If you have quite a few two-way tables to analyze, it might be more efficient to do them all the same way; so use the chi-square test. But remember that you may still need to use z-intervals for follow-up analysis.

Mathematically, the test statistics are related as follows. The chi-square test statistic equals the square of the z-ratio in the two-sample z-test of H_0: $p_1 - p_2 = 0$, that is, when $\Delta_0 = 0$, where the pooled estimate,
$\hat{p} = \dfrac{X_1 + X_2}{n_1 + n_2}$, is used in the standard error.

For that we'll need to construct a confidence interval on the difference. Unlike the z-tests and t-tests, a chi-square test is difficult to state in terms of parameters. The result is that there is no accompanying confidence interval as there is with the other tests. Once a chi-square test identifies a significant lack of homogeneity or lack of independence, the follow-up questions are about where the heterogeneity or dependence comes from. This is a job for the two-sample z-interval.

From Table 13.10, we find that the percentages of those answering 6 and 7 are 45.17% and 39.91% for the teen and 30- to 39-year-old groups, respectively. The 95% confidence interval is:

$$(\hat{p}_1 - \hat{p}_2) \pm z^* SE(\hat{p}_1 - \hat{p}_2)$$
$$= (0.4517 - 0.3991) \pm 1.96 \times \sqrt{\frac{(0.4517)(0.5483)}{1596} + \frac{(0.3991)(0.6009)}{1521}}$$
$$= (0.018, 0.087), \text{ or } (1.8\% \text{ to } 8.7\%)$$

This is a statistically significant difference, but now we can see that the difference may be as small as 1.8%. When deciding how to allocate advertising expenditures, it is important to keep these estimates of the effect size in mind.

Chi-Square Tests and Causation

Chi-square tests are widespread, especially as tests for independence. Unfortunately, many people interpret a small P-value as proof of causation. We know better. Just as correlation between quantitative variables does not demonstrate causation, a failure of independence between two categorical variables does not show a cause-and-effect relationship between them, nor should we say that one variable *depends* on the other.

The chi-square test for independence treats the two variables symmetrically. There is no way to differentiate the direction of any possible causation from one variable to the other. While we can see that attitudes on personal *Appearance* and *Age* are related, we can't say that getting older *causes* you to change attitudes. And certainly it's not correct to say that changing attitudes on personal appearance makes you older.

Of course, there's never any way to eliminate the possibility that a lurking variable is responsible for the observed lack of independence. In some sense, a failure of independence between two categorical variables is less impressive than a strong, consistent, linear association between quantitative variables. Two categorical variables can fail the test of independence in many ways, including ways that show no consistent pattern of failure. Examination of the chi-square standardized residuals can help you think about the underlying patterns.

? WHAT CAN GO WRONG?

- **Don't use chi-square methods unless you have counts.** All chi-square tests apply only to counts. Other kinds of data can be arrayed in two-way tables. Just because numbers are in a two-way table doesn't make them suitable for chi-square analysis. Data reported as proportions or percentages can be suitable for chi-square procedures, *but only after they are converted to counts.* If you try to do the calculations without first finding the counts, your results will be wrong.

- **Beware large samples.** Beware *large* samples? That's not the advice you're used to hearing. The chi-square tests, however, are unusual. You should be wary of chi-square tests performed on very large samples. No hypothesized distribution fits perfectly, no two groups are exactly homogeneous, and two variables are rarely perfectly independent. The degrees of freedom for chi-square tests don't grow with the sample size. With a sufficiently large sample size, a chi-square test can always reject the null hypothesis. But we have no measure of how far the data are from the null model. There are no confidence intervals to help us judge the effect size except in the case of two proportions.

- **Don't say that one variable "depends" on the other just because they're not independent.** "Depend" can suggest a model or a pattern, but variables can fail to be independent in many different ways. When variables fail the test for independence, it may be better to say they are "associated."

ETHICS IN ACTION

Deliberately Different specializes in unique accessories for the home such as hand-painted switch plates and hand-embroidered linens, offered through a catalogue and a website. Its customers tend to be women, generally older, with relatively high household incomes. Although the number of customer visits to the site has remained the same, management noticed that the proportion of customers visiting the site who make a purchase has been declining. Megan Cally, the product manager for Deliberately Different, was in charge of working with the market research firm hired to examine this problem. In her first meeting with Jason Esgro, the firm's consultant, she directed the conversation toward website design. Jason mentioned several reasons for consumers abandoning online purchases, the two most common being concerns about transaction security and unanticipated shipping/handling charges. Because Deliberately Different's shipping charges are reasonable, Megan asked him to look further into the issue of security concerns. They developed a survey that randomly sampled customers who had visited the website. They contacted these customers by e-mail and asked them to respond to a brief survey, offering the chance of winning a prize, which would be awarded at random among the respondents. A total of 2450 responses were received. The analysis of the responses included chi-square tests for independence, checking to see if responses on the security question were independent of gender and income category. Both tests were significant, rejecting the null hypothesis of independence. Megan reported to management that concerns about online transaction security were dependent on gender, and income, so Deliberately Different began to explore ways in which they could assure their older female customers that transactions on the website are indeed secure. As product manager, Megan was relieved that the decline in purchases was not related to product offerings.

ETHICAL ISSUE *The chance of rejecting the null hypothesis in a chi-square test for independence increases with sample size. Here the sample size is very large. In addition, it is misleading to state that concerns about security depend on gender, age, and income. Furthermore, patterns of association were not examined (for instance, with varying age categories). Finally, as product manager, Megan intentionally steered attention away from examining the product offerings, which could be a factor in declining purchases. Instead she reported to management that they have pinpointed the problem without noting that they had not explored other potential factors (related to ASA Ethical Guidelines, Items A and H, which can be found at http://www.amstat.org/about/ethicalguidelines.cfm).*

ETHICAL SOLUTION *Interpret results correctly, cautioning about the large sample size and looking for any patterns of association, realizing that there is no way to estimate the effect size.*

We've learned how to test hypotheses about categorical variables. Data are counts in categories, and we use chi-square models, a new family indexed by degrees of freedom.

- Goodness-of-fit tests compare the observed distribution of a single categorical variable to an expected distribution based on a theory or model.

- Tests of homogeneity or independence are both tests of two-way tables (also known as contingency tables or crosstabs). They are identical in computation and differ only in the wording of the hypothesis and the conclusion.

- Tests of homogeneity compare the distribution of several groups for the same categorical variable.

- Tests of independence examine counts from a single group for evidence of an association between two categorical variables. This is the most common design. In general, when you read about a chi-square test, it is usually a test of independence.

Although the tests appear to be one-sided, we've learned that conceptually they are many-sided because there are many ways that a table of counts can deviate significantly from what we hypothesized. When that happens and we reject the null hypothesis, we've learned to examine standardized residuals in order to better understand the patterns in the table.

Terms

Cell
A cell of a two-way table is one element of the table corresponding to a specific row and a specific column. Table cells can hold counts, percentages, or measurements on other variables, or they can hold several values.

Chi-square models
Chi-square models are skewed to the right. They are parameterized by their degrees of freedom and become less skewed with increasing degrees of freedom.

Chi-square (or chi-squared) statistic
The chi-square statistic is found by summing the chi-square components. Chi-square tests can be used to test goodness-of-fit, homogeneity, or independence.

Contingency table
A two-way table that classifies individuals according to two categorical variables.

Goodness-of-fit
A test of whether the distribution of counts in one categorical variable matches the distribution predicted by a model. A chi-square test of goodness-of-fit finds

$$\chi^2 = \sum_{all\ cells} \frac{(Obs - Exp)^2}{Exp}$$

where the expected counts come from the predicting model. It finds a P-value from a chi-square model with $n - 1$ degrees of freedom, where n is the number of categories in the categorical variable.

Homogeneity
A test comparing the distribution of counts for two or more groups on the same categorical variable. A chi-square test of homogeneity finds

$$\chi^2 = \sum_{all\ cells} \frac{(Obs - Exp)^2}{Exp}$$

where the expected counts are based on the overall frequencies, adjusted for the totals in each group. We find a P-value from a chi-square distribution with $(R - 1) \times (C - 1)$ degrees of freedom, where R gives the number of categories (rows) and C gives the number of independent groups (columns).

Independence

A test of whether two categorical variables are independent. It examines the distribution of counts for one group of individuals classified according to both variables. A chi-square test of *independence* uses the same calculation as a test of homogeneity. We find a P-value from a chi-square distribution with $(R - 1) \times (C - 1)$ degrees of freedom, where R gives the number of categories in one variable and C gives the number of categories in the other.

Standardized residual

In each cell of a two-way table, a standardized residual is the square root of the chi-square component for that cell with the sign of the *Observed – Expected* difference:

$$\frac{(Obs - Exp)}{\sqrt{Exp}}$$

When we reject a chi-square test, an examination of the standardized residuals can sometimes reveal more about how the data deviate from the null model.

Skills

PLAN

- Be able to recognize when a test of goodness-of-fit, or a test of a two-way table would be appropriate for a table of counts.
- Understand that the degrees of freedom for a chi-square test depend on the dimensions of the table and not on the sample size. Understand that this means that increasing the sample size increases the ability of chi-square procedures to reject the null hypothesis.

DO

- Be able to display and interpret counts in a two-way table.
- Know how to use the chi-square tables to perform chi-square tests.
- Know how to perform a chi-square test using statistics software or a calculator.
- Be able to examine the standardized residuals to explain the nature of the deviations from the null hypothesis.

REPORT

- Know how to communicate the results of chi-square tests, whether goodness-of-fit, homogeneity, or independence, in a few sentences.

TECHNOLOGY HELP: Chi-Square

Most statistics packages associate chi-square tests with contingency tables. Often chi-square is available as an option only when you make a contingency table. This organization can make it hard to locate the chi-square test and may confuse the different roles that the chi-square test can take. In particular, chi-square tests for goodness-of-fit may be hard to find or missing entirely. Remember that the distinction between homogeneity and independence does not matter in the computation of the chi-square test.

Most statistics packages work with data on individuals rather than with the summary counts. If the only information you have is the table of counts, you may find it more difficult to get a statistics package to compute chi-square. Some packages offer a way to reconstruct the data from the summary counts so that they can then be passed back through the chi-square calculation, finding the cell counts again. Many packages offer chi-square standardized residuals (although they may be called something else).

Excel offers the function **CHITEST (actual_range, expected_range)**, which computes a chi-square P-value. Both ranges are of the form UpperLeftCell: LowerRightCell, specifying two rectangular tables that must hold counts (although Excel will not check for integer values). The two tables must be of the same size and shape.

find expected counts, so the function is not particularly useful for testing independence. You can use this function only if you already know the expected values or are willing to program additional calculations. It is indeed surprising that such a widely used procedure is not readily available in Excel. Direct your complaints to Microsoft.

Comments

Excel's documentation claims this is a test for independence and labels the input ranges accordingly, but Excel offers no way to

MINI CASE STUDY PROJECTS

Sripfoto/Fotolia

Coffee Consumption in Canada

Canada has certainly embraced the coffee culture. According to a survey carried out by Ipsos Reid on behalf of McDonald's Canada,[5] 88% of Canadians surveyed stated that they drink at least one cup of coffee in a typical day, with those drinkers averaging 3.2 cups per day. Further, more than half (53%) describe themselves as having a confirmed or potential caffeine addiction. The survey used a national sample of 2101 adults from Ipsos' Canadian online panel.

One survey question asked, "What type of coffee drinker would you describe yourself as?" Response choices were: Serial Drinker / Addict (I can't live without the stuff), Borderline Problem (I'd sure miss it if I couldn't have it), and Casual Consumer (I can take it or leave it). The following tables present crosstabs of type of drinker by region, gender, and age. Use chi-square tests and the statistics software of your choice to examine any relationships between type of drinker and these three demographic variables. Don't forget to include some analysis of the residuals. Be sure to discuss your assumptions, methods, results, and conclusions.

Type of Drinker	Region				
	West	Ontario	Quebec	Atlantic	Total
Serial Drinker	74	113	45	19	**251**
Borderline Problem	258	346	204	65	**873**
Casual Consumer	298	361	255	63	**977**
Total	**630**	**820**	**504**	**147**	**2101**

---

[5]www.ipsos-na.com/news-polls/pressrelease.aspx?id=5016

Gender			
Type of Drinker	**Male**	**Female**	Total
Serial Drinker	99	152	**251**
Borderline Problem	370	503	**873**
Casual Consumer	545	432	**977**
Total	**1014**	**1087**	**2101**

Age Groups				
Type of Drinker	**18–34**	**35–54**	**55 +**	Total
Serial Drinker	94	113	44	**251**
Borderline Problem	211	375	287	**873**
Casual Consumer	264	345	368	**977**
Total	**569**	**833**	**699**	**2101**

Loyalty Program

A marketing executive tested two incentives to see what percentage of customers would enroll in a new web-based loyalty program. The customers were asked to log on to their accounts on the web and provide some demographic and spending information. As an incentive, they were offered either Nothing (No Offer), Free flight insurance on their next flight (Free Insurance), or a free companion Airline ticket (Free Flight). The customers were segmented according to their past year's spending patterns as spending primarily in one of five areas: *Travel, Entertainment, Dining, Household,* or *Balanced.* The executive wanted to know whether the incentives resulted in different enrollment rates (*Response*). Specifically, she wanted to know how much higher the enrollment rate for the free flight was compared to the free insurance. She also wanted to see whether *Spending Segment* was associated with *Response.* Using the data **ch13_MCSP_Loyalty_Program.xls,** write up a report for the marketing executive using appropriate graphics, summary statistics, statistical tests, and confidence intervals.

MyStatLab **Students! Save time, improve your grades with MyStatLab.** The Exercises marked in red can be found on MyStatLab. You can practice them as often as you want, and most feature step-by-step guided solutions to help you find the right answer. You'll find a personalized Study Plan available to you too! Data Sets for exercises marked ⊤ are also available on MyStatLab for formatted technologies.

EXERCISES

1. Concepts. For each of the following situations, decide whether you should use a chi-square goodness-of-fit test or a chi-square test of a two-way table. If it is the latter, decide whether the hypotheses are more appropriately formulated as a test of homogeneity or independence. **LO❶**

a) A brokerage firm wants to see whether the type of account a customer has (Silver, Gold, or Platinum) affects the type of trades that customer makes (in person, by phone, or on the internet). It collects a random sample of trades made for its customers over the past year and performs a test.

b) That brokerage firm also wants to know if the type of account affects the size of the account (in dollars). It performs a test to see if the mean size of the account is the same for the three account types.

c) The academic research office at a large community college wants to see whether the distribution of courses chosen (Humanities, Social Science, or Science) is different for its residential and nonresidential students. It assembles last semester's data and performs a test.

2. Concepts, part 2. For each of the following situations, decide whether you should use a chi-square goodness-of-fit test or a chi-square test of a two-way table. If it is the latter, decide whether the hypotheses are more appropriately formulated as a test of homogeneity or independence. **LO❶**

a) Is the quality of a car affected by what day it was built? A car manufacturer examines a random sample of the warranty claims filed over the past two years to test whether defects are randomly distributed across days of the work week.

b) A researcher for the Canadian Booksellers Association wants to know if retail sales per square metre is related to serving coffee or snacks on the premises. She examines a database of 300 independently owned bookstores testing whether retail sales (dollars per square metre) is related to whether or not the store has a coffee bar.

c) A researcher wants to find out whether education level (some high school, high school graduate, university graduate, advanced degree) is related to the type of transaction most likely to be conducted using the internet (shopping, banking, travel reservations, auctions). He surveys 500 randomly chosen adults and performs a test.

3. Dice. After getting trounced by your little brother in a children's game, you suspect that the die he gave you is unfair. To check, you roll it 60 times, recording the number of times each face appears in the table below. Do these results cast doubt on the die's fairness? **LO②**

a) If the die is fair, how many times would you expect each face to show?

b) To see if these results are unusual, will you test goodness-of-fit, homogeneity, or independence?

c) State your hypotheses.

d) Check the conditions.

e) How many degrees of freedom are there?

f) Find χ^2 and the P-value.

g) State your conclusion.

Face	Count
1	11
2	7
3	9
4	15
5	12
6	6

4. Quality control. Mars, Inc. says that the colours of its M&M's candies are 14% yellow, 13% red, 20% orange, 24% blue, 16% green and 13% brown. On his way home from work the day he was writing these exercises, one of the authors bought a bag of plain M&M's. He got 29 yellow, 23 red, 12 orange, 14 blue, 8 green, and 20 brown. Is this sample consistent with the company's advertised proportions? Test an appropriate hypothesis and state your conclusion. **LO②**

a) If the M&M's are packaged in the advertised proportions, how many of each colour should the author have expected in his bag of M&M's?

b) To see if his bag was unusual, should he test goodness-of-fit, homogeneity, or independence?

c) State the hypotheses.

d) Check the conditions.

e) How many degrees of freedom are there?

f) Find χ^2 and the P-value.

g) State a conclusion.

5. Quality control, part 2. A company advertises that its premium mixture of nuts contains 10% Brazil nuts, 20% cashews, 20% almonds, 10% hazelnuts, and that the rest are peanuts. You buy a large can and separate the various kinds of nuts. Upon weighing them, you find there are 112 grams of Brazil nuts, 183 grams of cashews, 207 grams of almonds, 71 grams of hazelnuts, and 446 grams of peanuts. You wonder whether your mix is significantly different from what the company advertises. **LO①**

a) Explain why the chi-square goodness-of-fit test is not an appropriate way to find out.

b) What might you do instead of weighing the nuts in order to use a χ^2 test?

6. Sales rep travel. A sales representative who is on the road visiting clients thinks that, on average, he drives the same distance each day of the week. He keeps track of his kilometrage for several weeks and discovers that he averages 122 kilometres on Mondays, 203 kilometres on Tuesdays, 176 kilometres on Wednesdays, 181 kilometres on Thursdays, and 108 kilometres on Fridays. He wonders if this evidence contradicts his belief in a uniform distribution of kilometres across the days of the week. Is it appropriate to test his hypothesis using the chi-square goodness-of-fit test? Explain. **LO①**

7. Maryland lottery. For a lottery to be successful, the public must have confidence in its fairness. One of the lotteries in Maryland is Pick-3 Lottery, where three random digits are drawn each day.[6] A fair game depends on every value (0 to 9) being equally likely at each of the three positions. If not, then someone detecting a pattern could take advantage of that and beat the lottery. To investigate the randomness, we'll look at data collected over a recent 32-week period. Although the winning numbers look like three-digit numbers, in fact, each digit is a randomly drawn numeral. We have 654 random digits in all. Are each of the digits from 0 to 9 equally likely? Here is a table of the frequencies. **LO②**

Group	Count	%
0	62	9.480
1	55	8.410
2	66	10.092
3	64	9.786
4	75	11.468
5	57	8.716
6	71	10.856
7	74	11.315
8	69	10.550
9	61	9.327

a) Select the appropriate procedure.

b) Check the assumptions.

_____

[6]Source: Maryland State Lottery Agency, www.mdlottery.com.

c) State the hypotheses.

d) Test an appropriate hypothesis and state your results.

e) Interpret the meaning of the results and state a conclusion.

8. Employment discrimination? Census data for New York City indicate that 29.2% of the under-18 population is white, 28.2% black, 31.5% Hispanic, 9.1% Asian, and 2% are of other ethnicities. The New York Civil Liberties Union points out that of 26 181 police officers, 64.8% are white, 14.5% black, 19.1% Hispanic, and 1.4% Asian. Do the police officers reflect the ethnic composition of the city's youth?

a) Select the appropriate procedure.

b) Check the assumptions.

c) State the hypotheses.

d) Test an appropriate hypothesis and state your results.

e) Interpret the meaning of the results and state a conclusion.

T 9. Titanic. Here is a table showing who survived the sinking of the *Titanic* based on whether they were crew members or passengers booked in first-, second-, or third-class staterooms. LO❷

	Crew	First	Second	Third	Total
Alive	212	202	118	178	**710**
Dead	673	123	167	528	**1491**
Total	**885**	**325**	**285**	**706**	**2201**

a) If we draw an individual at random from this table, what's the probability that we will draw a member of the crew?

b) What's the probability of randomly selecting a third-class passenger who survived?

c) What's the probability of a randomly selected passenger surviving, given that the passenger was in a first-class stateroom?

d) If someone's chances of surviving were the same regardless of their status on the ship, how many members of the crew would you expect to have lived?

e) State the null and alternative hypotheses we would test here.

f) Give the degrees of freedom for the test.

g) The chi-square value for the table is 187.8, and the corresponding P-value is barely greater than 0. State your conclusions about the hypotheses.

T 10. Promotion discrimination? The table shows the rank attained by male and female officers in the New York City Police Department (NYPD). Do these data indicate that men and women are equitably represented at all levels of the department? LO❷

		Male	Female
Rank	**Officer**	21 900	4281
	Detective	4058	806
	Sergeant	3898	415
	Lieutenant	1333	89
	Captain	359	12
	Higher ranks	218	10

a) What's the probability that a person selected at random from the NYPD is a female?

b) What's the probability that a person selected at random from the NYPD is a detective?

c) Assuming no bias in promotions, how many female detectives would you expect the NYPD to have?

d) To see if there is evidence of differences in ranks attained by males and females, will you test goodness-of-fit, homogeneity, or independence?

e) State the hypotheses.

f) Test the conditions.

g) How many degrees of freedom are there?

h) Find the chi-square value and the associated P-value.

i) State your conclusion.

j) If you concluded that the distributions are not the same, analyze the differences using the standardized residuals of your calculations.

11. Birth order and program choice. Students in an Introductory Statistics class at a large university were classified by birth order and by their program area of study. LO❸

	Birth Order (1 = oldest or only child)				
	1	**2**	**3**	**4 or more**	Total
Arts and Sciences	34	14	6	3	57
Agriculture	52	27	5	9	93
Social Science	15	17	8	3	43
Professional	13	11	1	6	31
Total	**114**	**69**	**20**	**21**	**224**

Program

	Expected Values			
	Birth Order (1 = oldest or only child)			
	1	**2**	**3**	**4 or more**
Arts and Sciences	29.0089	17.5580	5.0893	5.3438
Agriculture	47.3304	28.6473	8.3036	8.7188
Social Science	21.8839	13.2455	3.8393	4.0313
Professional	15.7768	9.5491	2.7679	2.9063

Program

a) What kind of chi-square test is appropriate—goodness-of-fit, homogeneity, or independence?

b) State your hypotheses.

c) State and check the conditions.

d) How many degrees of freedom are there?

e) The calculation yields $\chi^2 = 17.78$, with P = 0.0378. State your conclusion.

f) Examine and comment on the standardized residuals. Do they challenge your conclusion? Explain.

	Standardized Residuals Birth Order (1 = oldest or only child)			
	1	**2**	**3**	**4 or more**
Arts and Sciences	0.92667	−0.84913	0.40370	−1.01388
Agriculture	0.67876	−0.30778	−1.14640	0.09525
Social Science	−1.47155	1.03160	2.12350	−0.51362
Professional	−0.69909	0.46952	−1.06261	1.81476

(Program)

12. Automobile manufacturers. *Consumer Reports* uses surveys given to subscribers of its magazine and website (www.ConsumerReports.org) to measure reliability in automobiles. This annual survey asks about problems that consumers have had with their cars, vans, SUVs, or trucks during the previous 12 months. Each analysis is based on the number of problems per 100 vehicles. LO❷

	Origin of Manufacturer			
	Asia	**Europe**	**U.S.**	Total
No Problems	88	79	83	250
Problems	12	21	17	50
Total	**100**	**100**	**100**	**300**

	Expected Values		
	Asia	**Europe**	**U.S.**
No Problems	83.33	83.33	83.33
Problems	16.67	16.67	16.67

a) State your hypotheses.
b) State and check the conditions.
c) How many degrees of freedom are there?
d) The calculation yields $\chi^2 = 2.928$, with P = 0.231. State your conclusion.
e) Would you expect that a larger sample might find statistical significance? Explain.

T 13. Cranberry juice. It's common folk wisdom that cranberries can help prevent urinary tract infections in women. A leading producer of cranberry juice would like to use this information in their next ad campaign, so they need evidence of this claim. In 2001, the *British Medical Journal* reported the results of a Finnish study in which three groups of 50 women were monitored for these infections over six months. One group drank cranberry juice daily, another group drank a lactobacillus drink, and the third group drank neither of those beverages, serving as a control group. In the control group, 18 women developed at least one infection compared with 20 of those who consumed the lactobacillus drink and only 8 of those who drank cranberry juice. Does this study provide supporting evidence for the value of cranberry juice in warding off urinary tract infections in women? LO❸

a) Select the appropriate procedure.
b) Check the assumptions.
c) State the hypotheses.
d) Test an appropriate hypothesis and state your results.
e) Interpret the meaning of the results and state a conclusion.
f) If you concluded that the groups are not the same, analyze the differences using the standardized residuals of your calculations.

T 14. Car company. A European manufacturer of automobiles claims that their cars are preferred by the younger generation and would like to target university students in their next ad campaign. Suppose we test their claim with our own survey. A random survey of autos parked in the student lot and the staff lot at a large university classified the brands by country of origin, as seen in the following table. Are there differences in the national origins of cars driven by students and staff? LO❷

	Driver	
	Student	**Staff**
American	107	105
European	33	12
Asian	55	47

(Origin)

a) Is this a test of independence or homogeneity?
b) Write appropriate hypotheses.
c) Check the necessary assumptions and conditions.
d) Find the P-value of your test.
e) State your conclusion and analysis.

T 15. Market segmentation. Surveys of retail customers are very useful for market segmentation. The data presented here are from a survey of characteristics of "frequent" shoppers at different department stores in a large city. (The original study was part of the Chicago Female Fashion Study.[7]) Suppose you are a marketing manager at one of the department stores. You would like to know if a customer's shopping frequency and her age are related. Here are the data: LO❸

	Age			
	18–24	**25–44**	**45–54**	**55 or over**
Never/Hardly Ever	32	171	45	24
1–2 times/yr	18	134	40	37
3–4 times/yr	21	109	48	27
≥ 5 times/yr	39	134	71	50

(Shopping Frequency)

[7]Original *Market Segmentation Exercise* prepared by K. Matsuno, D. Kopcso, and D. Tigert, Babson College in 1997 (Babson Case Series #133-C97A-U).

Shopping Frequency	Standardized Residuals Age			
	18–24	**25–44**	**45–54**	**55 or over**
Never/Hardly Ever	0.3803	1.7974	−1.4080	−2.2094
1–2 times/yr	−1.4326	0.7595	−0.9826	0.9602
3–4 times/yr	−0.3264	−0.3151	0.9556	−0.2425
≥ 5 times/yr	1.1711	−2.1360	1.4235	1.4802

a) Is this a test of homogeneity or independence?

b) Write an appropriate hypothesis.

c) Are the conditions for inference satisfied?

d) The calculation yields $\chi^2 = 26.084$, P-value = 0.002. State your conclusion.

e) Given the standardized residuals in the table, state a complete conclusion.

16. Seafood company. A large company in the Maritimes that buys fish from local fishermen and distributes them to major companies and restaurants is considering launching a new ad campaign on the health benefits of fish. As evidence, they would like to cite the following study. Medical researchers followed 6272 Swedish men for 30 years to see if there was any association between the amount of fish in their diet and prostate cancer ("Fatty Fish Consumption and Risk of Prostate Cancer," *Lancet*, June 2001). LO④

Fish Consumption	Prostate Cancer	
	No	**Yes**
Never/seldom	110	14
Small part of diet	2420	201
Moderate part	2769	209
Large part	507	42

a) Is this a survey, a retrospective study, a prospective study, or an experiment? Explain.

b) Is this a test of homogeneity or independence?

c) Do you see evidence of an association between the amount of fish in a man's diet and his risk of developing prostate cancer?

d) Does this study prove that eating fish does not prevent prostate cancer? Explain.

For questions 17–22, parts denoted with an asterisk (*) use material from Chapter 12: a confidence interval for the difference of two proportions.

17. Shopping. A survey of 430 randomly chosen adults finds that 47 of 222 men and 37 of 208 women had purchased books online. LO④

a) Is there evidence that the sex of the person and whether they buy books online are associated?

b) If your conclusion in fact proves to be wrong, did you make a Type I or Type II error?

*c) Give a 95% confidence interval for the difference in proportions of buying online for men and women.

18. Information technology. A recent report suggests that Chief Information Officers (CIOs) who report directly to Chief Financial Officers (CFOs) rather than Chief Executive Officers (CEOs) are more likely to have IT agendas that deal with cost cutting and compliance (SearchCIO.com, March 14, 2006). In a random sample of 535 companies, it was found that CIOs reported directly to CFOs in 173 out of 335 service firms and in 95 out of 200 manufacturing companies. LO④

a) Is there evidence that type of business (service versus manufacturing) and whether or not the CIO reports directly to the CFO are associated?

b) If your conclusion proves to be wrong, did you make a Type I or Type II error?

*c) Give a 95% confidence interval for the difference in proportions of companies in which the CIO reports directly to the CFO between service and manufacturing firms.

19. Mobile banking. Ipsos Canadian Inter@ctive Reid Report looked at online Canadians' use of web-based financial services. They asked whether respondents had conducted any online banking transaction in the past three months. In 2012, 658 of 843 respondents said yes, compared with 609 of 834 respondents in 2011. LO②

a) Is there evidence that the percentage of online Canadians who use web-based financial services has changed from 2011 to 2012?

*b) Give a 90% confidence interval for the difference in proportions.

20. Mobile banking, part 2. The survey described in Exercise 19 also asked respondents whether they had conducted banking from a mobile phone. Only a small minority used mobile banking, but the minority is growing. In 2011, 67 of 834 respondents reported using mobile banking; this rose to 101 of 843 respondents in 2012. LO②

a) Is there evidence that the percentage of online Canadians who use mobile banking has changed from 2011 to 2012?

*b) Give a 90% confidence interval for the difference in proportions.

21. Foreclosure rates. The two U.S. states with the highest home foreclosure rates in March 2008 were Nevada and Colorado (realestate.msn.com, April 2008). In the second quarter of 2008, there were 8 foreclosures in a random sample of 1098 homes in Nevada, and 6 in a sample of 1460 homes in Colorado. LO④

a) Is there evidence that the percentage of foreclosures is different in the two states?

*b) Give a 90% confidence interval for the difference in proportions.

22. Small and medium enterprise (SME). According to Cathy Pin, VP Commercial Banking, BMO Bank of Montreal, "Small businesses account for almost one-third of Canada's GDP annually. Many of the newest small and medium-sized businesses are among the most successful, productive and fastest growing enterprises in Canada." A survey carried out by Leger Marketing's online panel LegerWeb for BMO in 2012 showed that 71%

of Canadian women and 82% of Canadian men "would become their own boss if they had the opportunity." The LegerWeb panel is a sample of 1523 Canadians. Since details of the composition of the panel are proprietary, let's assume that the percentages were computed based on 540 of 760 females in the sample and 626 of 763 males in the sample. LO④

a) Is there evidence that the percentage of Canadians who would become their own boss if given the opportunity differs between females and males?

*b) Give a 90% confidence interval for the difference in proportions.

T **23. Market segmentation, part 2.** The survey described in Exercise 15 also investigated the customers' marital status. Using the same definitions for *Shopping Frequency* as in Exercise 15, the calculations yielded the following table. Test an appropriate hypothesis for the relationship between marital status and the frequency of shopping at the same department store as in Exercise 15, and state your conclusions. LO④

Counts	Single	Widowed	Married	Total
Never/Hardly Ever	105	5	162	272
1–2 times/yr	53	15	161	229
3–4 times/yr	57	8	140	205
≥ 5 times/yr	72	15	207	294
Total	**287**	**43**	**670**	**1000**

24. Investment options. The economic slowdown in early 2008 and the possibility of future inflation prompted a full service brokerage firm to gauge the level of interest in inflation-beating investment options among its clients. It surveyed a random sample of 1200 clients asking them to indicate the likelihood that they would add inflation-linked annuities and bonds to their portfolios within the next year. The table below shows the distribution of responses by the investors' tolerance for risk. Test an appropriate hypothesis for the relationship between risk tolerance and the likelihood of investing in inflation-linked options. LO④

Likelihood of Investing in Inflation-Linked Options	Risk Tolerance: Averse	Neutral	Seeking	Total
Certain Will Invest	191	93	40	**324**
Likely to Invest	82	106	123	**311**
Not Likely to Invest	64	110	101	**275**
Certain Will Not Invest	63	91	136	**290**
Total	**400**	**400**	**400**	**1200**

25. Accounting. The Sarbanes-Oxley (SOX) Act was passed in the United States in 2002 as a result of corporate scandals and in an attempt to regain public trust in accounting and reporting practices. Two random samples of 1015 executives were surveyed and asked their opinion about accounting practices in both 2000 and in 2006. The table below summarizes all 2030 responses to the question, "Which of the following do you consider most critical to establishing ethical and legal accounting and reporting practices?" Did the distribution of responses change from 2000 to 2006? LO④

Responses	2000	2006
Training	142	131
IT Security	274	244
Audit Trails	152	173
IT Policies	396	416
No Opinion	51	51

a) Select the appropriate procedure.
b) Check the assumptions.
c) State the hypotheses.
d) Test an appropriate hypothesis and state your results.
e) Interpret the meaning of the results and state a conclusion.

26. Entrepreneurial executives. A leading CEO mentoring organization offers a program for chief executives, presidents, and business owners with a focus on developing entrepreneurial skills. Women and men executives that recently completed the program rated its value. Are perceptions of the program's value the same for men and women? LO⑤

Perceived Value	Men	Women
Excellent	3	9
Good	11	12
Average	14	8
Marginal	9	2
Poor	3	1

a) Will you test goodness-of-fit, homogeneity, or independence?
b) Write appropriate hypotheses.
c) Find the expected counts for each cell, and explain why the chi-square procedures are not appropriate for this table.

T **27. Market segmentation, again.** The survey described in Exercise 15 also investigated the customers' emphasis on *Quality* by asking them the question: "For the same amount of money, I will generally buy one good item rather than several of lower price and quality." Using the same definitions for *Shopping Frequency* as in Exercise 15, the calculations yielded the following table. Test an appropriate hypothesis for the relationship between a customer's emphasis on *Quality* and the *Shopping Frequency* at this department store. LO④

a) Select the appropriate procedure.
b) Check the assumptions.
c) State the hypotheses.
d) Test an appropriate hypothesis and state your results.
e) Interpret the meaning of the results and state a conclusion.

Counts

	Disagree	Moderately Disagree/Agree	Agree	Total
Never/Hardly Ever	15	97	160	**272**
1–2 times/yr	28	107	94	**229**
3–4 times/yr	30	90	85	**205**
≥ 5 times/yr	35	140	119	**294**
Total	**108**	**434**	**458**	**1000**

28. Online shopping. A recent report concludes that while internet users like the convenience of online shopping, they do have concerns about privacy and security (*Online Shopping*, Washington, DC, Pew Internet & American Life Project, February 2008). Respondents were asked to indicate their level of agreement with the statement "I don't like giving my credit card number or personal information online." The table gives a subset of responses. Test an appropriate hypothesis for the relationship between age and level of concern about privacy and security online. LO④

Age Category	Strongly Agree	Agree	Disagree	Strongly Disagree	Total
Ages 18–29	127	147	138	10	422
Ages 30–49	141	129	78	55	403
Ages 50–64	178	102	64	51	395
Ages 65+	180	132	54	14	380
Total	626	510	334	130	1600

a) Select the appropriate procedure.
b) Check the assumptions.
c) State the hypotheses.
d) Test an appropriate hypothesis and state your results.
e) Interpret the meaning of the results and state a conclusion.

29. Entrepreneurial executives again. In some situations where the expected counts are too small, as in Exercise 26, we can complete an analysis anyway. We can often proceed after combining cells in some way that makes sense and also produces a table in which the conditions are satisfied. Here is a new table displaying the same data, but combining "Marginal" and "Poor" into a new category called "Below Average." LO⑤

Perceived Value	Men	Women
Excellent	3	9
Good	11	12
Average	14	8
Below Average	12	3

a) Find the expected counts for each cell in this new table, and explain why a chi-square procedure is now appropriate.
b) With this change in the table, what has happened to the number of degrees of freedom?
c) Test your hypothesis about the two groups and state an appropriate conclusion.

30. Small business. The director of a small business development centre located in a mid-sized city is reviewing data about its clients. In particular, she is interested in examining if the distribution of business owners across the various stages of the business life cycle is the same for white-owned and visible-minority-owned businesses. The data are shown below. LO⑤

Stage in Business	White-Owned	Visible-Minority-Owned
Planning	11	9
Starting	14	11
Managing	20	2
Getting Out	15	1

a) Will you test goodness-of-fit, homogeneity, or independence?
b) Write the appropriate hypotheses.
c) Find the expected counts for each cell and explain why chi-square procedures are not appropriate for this table.
d) Create a new table by combining categories so that a chi-square procedure can be used.
e) With this change in the table, what has happened to the number of degrees of freedom?
f) Test your hypothesis about the two groups and state an appropriate conclusion.

31. Racial steering. A subtle form of racial discrimination in housing is "racial steering." Racial steering occurs when real estate agents show prospective buyers only homes in neighbourhoods already dominated by that family's race. According to an article in *Chance* magazine (Vol. 14, no. 2, 2001), tenants at a large apartment complex recently filed a lawsuit alleging racial steering. The complex is divided into two parts: Section A and Section B. The plaintiffs claimed that white potential renters were steered to Section A, while African-Americans were steered to Section B. The following table displays the data that were presented in court to show the locations of recently rented apartments. Do you think there is evidence of racial steering? LO④

New Renters			
	White	**Black**	Total
Section A	87	8	**95**
Section B	83	34	**117**
Total	**170**	**42**	**212**

32. E-readers. An e-reader survey was conducted as part of a survey of student technology use at Queens College, City University of New York. (Foasberg, Nancy. Adoption of E-Book Readers among College Students: A Survey. *Information Technology and Libraries*, Sept. 2011). Of the sample of 1705 respondents, 401 said they read e-books. However, most of the readers used a device other than a dedicated e-reader, despite the ergonomic disadvantages. The following table compared the amount of reading done with e-books by type of user. **LO❹**

Amount of reading	Ereader users	Other users	Total
About two-thirds or all	27	65	**92**
About a third	14	90	**104**
Less than a third	22	183	**205**
Total	**63**	**338**	**401**

Do you think the amount of reading is independent of the type of user? Test your hypothesis and state your results.

Questions 33 and 34, denoted with an asterisk (*), use material from Chapter 12: a confidence interval for the difference of two proportions.

*33. Racial steering, revisited. Find a 95% confidence interval for the difference in the proportions of Black renters in the two sections for the data in Exercise 31. **LO❹**

*34. E-readers, part 2. Refer to Exercise 32. Combine the top two rows to create a category of "frequent e-readers." Rename the third row as a category called "infrequent e-readers." Compare the proportion of frequent e-readers among the two types of users by constructing a 95% confidence interval for the difference of two proportions. How do these results compare with the findings of Exercise 32? **LO❹**

35. Industry sector and outsourcing. Many companies have chosen to outsource segments of their business to external providers in order to cut costs and improve quality and/or efficiencies. Common business segments that are outsourced include Information Technology (IT) and Human Resources (HR). The data below show the types of outsourcing decisions made (no outsourcing, IT only, HR only, both IT and HR) by a sample of companies from various industry sectors. **LO❹**

Industry Sector	No Outsourcing	IT Only	HR Only	Both IT and HR
Healthcare	810	6429	4725	1127
Financial	263	1598	549	117
Industrial Goods	1031	1269	412	99
Consumer Goods	66	341	305	197

Do these data highlight significant differences in outsourcing by industry sector?
a) Select the appropriate procedure.
b) Check the assumptions.
c) State the hypotheses.
d) Test an appropriate hypothesis and state your results.
e) Interpret the meaning of the results and state a conclusion.

36. Industry sector and outsourcing, part 2. Consider only the companies that have outsourced their IT and HR business segments. Do these data suggest significant differences between companies in the financial and industrial goods sectors with regard to their outsourcing decisions? **LO❷**

Industry Sector	IT Only	HR Only	Both IT and HR
Financial	1598	549	117
Industrial Goods	1269	412	99

a) Select the appropriate procedure.
b) Check the assumptions.
c) State the hypotheses.
d) Test an appropriate hypothesis and state your results.
e) Interpret the meaning of the results and state the conclusion.

37. Management styles. Use the survey results in the table at the top of the page to investigate differences in employee job satisfaction among organizations with different management styles. **LO❷**

Employee Job Satisfaction	Management Styles				
	Exploitative Authoritarian	Benevolent Authoritarian	Laissez Faire	Consultative	Participative
Very Satisfied	27	50	52	71	101
Satisfied	82	19	88	83	59
Somewhat Satisfied	43	56	26	20	20
Not Satisfied	48	75	34	26	20

a) Select the appropriate procedure.
b) Check the assumptions.
c) State the hypotheses.
d) Test an appropriate hypothesis and state your results.
e) Interpret the meaning of the results and state a conclusion.

38. Ranking companies. Every year *Fortune* magazine lists the 100 best companies to work for, based on criteria such as pay, benefits, turnover rate, and diversity. In 2008, the top three were Google, Quicken Loans, and Wegmans Food Markets (*Fortune*, February 4, 2008). Of the best 100 companies to work for, 33 experienced double digit job growth (10%–68%), 49 experienced single digit job growth (1%–9%), and 18 experienced no growth or a decline. A closer examination of the top 30 showed that 15 had job growth in the double digits, 11 in the single digits, and only 4 had no growth or a decline. Is there anything unusual about job growth among the 30 top companies? **LO❷**

a) Select the appropriate procedure.
b) Check the assumptions.
c) State the hypotheses.
d) Test an appropriate hypothesis and state your results.
e) Interpret the meaning of the results and state a conclusion.

39. Businesses and blogs. The Pew Internet & American Life Project routinely conducts surveys to gauge the impact of the internet and technology on daily life. A recent survey asked respondents if they read online journals or blogs, an internet activity of potential interest to many businesses. A subset of the data from this survey (*February–March 2007 Tracking Data Set*) shows responses to this question. Test whether reading online journals or blogs is independent of generation. **LO❹**

	Read Online Journal or Blog			
	Yes, Yesterday	Yes, but not Yesterday	No	Total
Gen-Y (18–30)	29	35	62	**126**
Gen X (31–42)	12	34	137	**183**
Trailing Boomers (43–52)	15	34	132	**181**
Leading Boomers (53–61)	7	22	83	**112**
Matures (62+)	6	21	111	**138**
Total	**69**	**146**	**525**	**740**

Generation (row label)

40. Businesses and blogs again. The Pew Internet & American Life Project survey described in Exercise 39 also asked respondents if they ever created or worked on their own online journal or blog. Again, a subset of the data from this survey (*February–March 2007 Tracking Data Set*) shows responses to this question. Test whether creating online journals or blogs is independent of generation. **LO❹**

	Create Online Journal or Blog ...			
	Yes/ Yesterday	Yes/ Not Yesterday	No	Total
Gen Y (18–30)	18	24	85	**127**
Gen X (31–42)	6	15	162	**183**
Boomers (43–61)	5	15	273	**293**
Matures (62+)	3	3	132	**138**
Total	**32**	**57**	**652**	**741**

Generation (row label)

41. Information systems. In a recent study of enterprise resource planning (ERP) system effectiveness, researchers asked companies about how they assessed the success of their ERP systems. Out of 335 manufacturing companies surveyed, they found that 201 used return on investment (ROI), 100 used reductions in inventory levels, 28 used improved data quality, and 6 used on-time delivery. In a survey of 200 service firms, 40 used ROI, 40 used inventory levels, 100 used improved data quality, and 20 used on-time delivery. Is there evidence that the measures used to assess ERP system effectiveness differ between service and manufacturing firms? Perform the appropriate test and state your conclusion. **LO❷**

42. Alcohol use on Canadian campuses. The 2004 Canadian Campus Survey aimed to learn about individual, social, and environmental factors related to alcohol use, other drug use, mental health, and gambling problems among Canadian undergraduates. The survey comprised a random sample of 6282 full-time university undergraduates from 64 universities across Canada. Use the data in the following table to examine if there is independence of alcohol use and region of the country. **LO❹**

Alcohol use in the past month	British Columbia	Prairies	Ontario	Quebec	Atlantic	Total
Yes	560	397	1570	1729	660	**4916**
No	233	116	537	347	133	**1366**
Total	**793**	**513**	**2107**	**2076**	**793**	**6282**

43. Alcohol use on Canadian campuses, part 2. The survey described in Exercise 42 compared level of alcohol consumption between males and females. Use the data in the following table to look for any differences between level of consumption (i.e., drinking status) between the sexes. **LO❹**

Drinking Status	Male	Female	Total
Abstainer	204	366	**570**
Former	133	153	**286**
Monthly	817	2169	**2986**
Weekly+	1094	1346	**2440**
Total	**2248**	**4034**	**6282**

44. Cell phones and driving. An Angus Reid Public Opinion survey of 1001 Canadian adults addressed opinions about the use of hand-held cellphones while driving. The report noted that a large proportion of Canadians have seen the practice even though all Canadian provinces have enacted legislation to restrain this use. Survey respondents were asked whether they would support or oppose a federal regulation to ban the use of hand-held cellphones while driving. The results are as follows: **LO❹**

	BC	AB	MB/SK	ON	PQ	ATL	Total
Support	91%	84%	90%	92%	84%	92%	**89%**
Oppose/ not sure	9%	16%	10%	8%	16%	8%	**11%**

Note that the small number of "not sure" responses were combined with those opposed.

Many reports of surveys that are publicly available present only percentages, not counts, just as in this table. In order to be able to carry out a chi-square test, we need to convert the percentages to counts. Since the composition of the total sample is not known,

we must first assume that the sample is distributed among the provinces in the same percentages as the populations of the provinces are distributed among the Canadian total.

BC	AB	MB/SK	ON	PQ	ATL
13%	11%	7%	39%	23%	7%

We can then calculate the number of respondents in each cell of the table as follows:

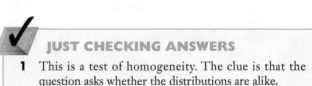

	BC	AB	MB/SK	ON	PQ	ATL	Total
Support	118	92	63	360	193	64	**890**
Oppose/ not sure	12	18	7	31	37	6	**111**
Total	**130**	**110**	**70**	**391**	**230**	**70**	**1001**

Use the table of counts to determine whether there is any difference among the provinces with respect to their support for a federal ban.

Source: "Most Canadians Have Seen Drivers Using Hand-held Cell Phones." Angus Reid Public Opinion 2012.

✓ **JUST CHECKING ANSWERS**

1 This is a test of homogeneity. The clue is that the question asks whether the distributions are alike.

2 This is a test of goodness-of-fit. We want to test the model of equal assignment to all lots against what actually happened.

3 This is a test of independence. We have responses on two variables for the same individuals.

Inference for Regression

CONNECTIONS: CHAPTER 14

In Chapter 6 we discussed the relationship between two quantitative variables in a descriptive way, using scatterplots and linear regression. In the current chapter we extend our study of linear regression to add techniques of inference based on a statistical model. Chapter 14 follows logically from Chapter 13; both chapters address relationships between two variables; the distinction is due to the type of variables (categorical or quantitative) being related.

Canada Goose

CANADA GOOSE

How do you get down from an elephant? You don't, you get down from a goose. It's a groaner, but a great way to introduce Canada Goose Inc., founded in Toronto in 1957 to make clothing and eventually down-filled coats for people in the coldest places on Earth. The company has an international reputation "as one of the world's leading manufacturers of extreme weather outerwear." A key part of their strategy, and branding, is their commitment to keep production in Canada. This is a rarity in the textile industry where most production is done in foreign countries. But Canada Goose makes its parkas in two wholly-owned factories (Winnipeg and Toronto) and up to 20 contract factories across Canada. Sales have grown more than 4000% in the past decade and in 2013, they had sales near $150 million. In December 2013, Canada Goose announced the sale of a majority stake to Bain Capital.

Quality is a key goal of the company. Known as "the down experts", they have four proprietary blends of down, each of which uses some down from Hutterite farmers in rural

LEARNING OBJECTIVES

1 Determine whether a linear model is appropriate

2 Interpret linear regression software output

3 Find and interpret a confidence interval for slope

4 Carry out a regression analysis (with or without technology)

5 Examine residuals to check assumptions

6 Find outliers and influential and high leverage points, and assess their effect

7 Identify cause-and-effect relationships

communities in Alberta. Hutterite down plumes are larger, so they're better at trapping warm air. But that makes it more expensive too, and accordingly also exclusive.

Canada Goose products focus not only on quality, but also on form and function. Their parkas not only keep you warm, they also allow you to perform your job or sport at a high level. It is this functionality and quality, combined with sophisticated styling, that have made Canada Goose jackets popular in the global fashion community. They are found on the racks of high-end clothing retailers in Canada, and also in London, Stockholm, Tokyo, Milan, New York and Paris. Available in more than 50 countries, the parkas have become high status merchandise, like Rolex is to watches. The parkas are just as likely to be worn by movie stars and fashion models, as by oil riggers, polar explorers, dogsled racers, policemen, and bouncers at popular nightclubs.

Based on information from www.canada-goose.com/story

Canada Goose garments come in many different styles and have gone through various changes in design. They cost more because they use the best materials and take great care in manufacturing their jackets; they also pay employees a higher wage because they are made in Canada. Setting prices depends not only on materials used but on the production time. To assist the pricing process management examined the design, preparation, and assembly times of a sample of 59 different items. Here's a scatterplot showing the wholesale price of the items and the total amount of time (in hours) from start to finish of production of an item (Figure 14.1).

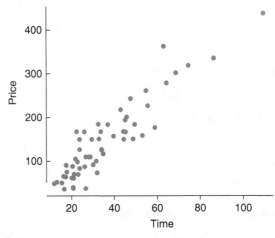

Figure 14.1 A scatterplot of Price ($) against production Time (hours) for Canada Goose products shows that the items that take longer to produce cost more, on average.

Note that the data are the authors' conception, not actual data from Canada Goose. They were created to illustrate the techniques in this chapter, but are a realistic approximation of actual price and production time data.

Back in Chapter 6 we modelled relationships like this by fitting a straight line. The equation of the least squares line for these data is:

$$\widehat{\text{Price}} = -4.871 + 4.200 \times \textit{Time}$$

The slope says that, on average, the price increases by \$4.20 for every extra hour of production time.

How useful is this model? When we fit linear models before, we used them to describe the relationship between the variables, and we interpreted the slope and intercept as descriptions of the data. Now we'd like to know what the regression model can tell us beyond the sample we used to generate this regression. To do that, we'll want to make confidence intervals and test hypotheses about the slope and intercept of the regression line.

This development parallels what we did in the previous few chapters on inference. We used the descriptions of data—the mean for quantitative data and the proportion for binary categorical data—to say something about the larger population from where the data came. The sample mean, $\bar{x}$, and sample proportion, $\hat{p}$, were "promoted" to be estimates of the population parameters μ and p. In the same way we will use the estimate b_0 and b_1 to say something about the relationship between variables in the larger population. This seems sensible when one realizes that the scatterplot introduced in Chapter 6 was based only on a sample of data, not the entire population.

14.1 The Population and the Sample

Our data are a sample of 59 items. If we take another sample, we hope the regression line will be similar to the one we found here, but we know it won't be exactly the same. Observations vary from sample to sample. But we can imagine a true line that summarizes the relationship between *Price* and *Time*. Following our usual conventions, we write the idealized line with Greek letters and consider the coefficients (slope and intercept) to be parameters: β_0 is the intercept, and β_1 is the slope. Corresponding to our fitted line of $\hat{y} = b_0 + b_1 x$, we write $\mu_y = \beta_0 + \beta_1 x$. We write μ_y instead of y because the regression line assumes that the *means* of the y values for each value of x fall exactly on the line. We can picture the relationship as in Figure 14.2. The means fall exactly on the line (for our idealized model), and the y values at each x are distributed around them.

> **NOTATION ALERT:**
> We use lowercase Greek betas (β) to denote the coefficients in the regression model. We estimate them with the b's in the fitted regression equation. We used β earlier for the probability of a Type II error, but β here is not related to its earlier use. And the lowercase Greek epsilon (ϵ) is estimated by the residual, e (ϵ is the Greek equivalent of e).

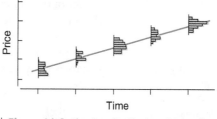

Figure 14.2 There's a distribution of Prices for each value of production Time. The regression model assumes that the means line up perfectly like this.

Now, if only we had all the values in the population, we could find the slope and intercept of this *idealized regression line* explicitly by using least squares.

Of course, not all the individual y's are at these means. In fact, the line will miss most—and usually all—of the plotted points. Some y's lie above the line and some below the line, so like all models, this one makes errors. If we want to account for each individual value of y in our model, we have to include these errors, which we denote by ε:

$$y = \beta_0 + \beta_1 x + \varepsilon$$

This equation has an ε to soak up the deviation at each point, so the model gives a value of y for each value of x.

We estimate the β's by finding a regression line, $\hat{y} = b_0 + b_1 x$ as we did in Chapter 6. The residuals, $e = y - \hat{y}$, are the sample-based versions of the errors, ε. We'll use them to help us assess the regression model.

We know that least squares regression will give us reasonable estimates of the parameters of this model from a random sample of data. We also know that our estimates won't be equal to the parameters in the idealized or "true" model. Our challenge is to account for the uncertainty in our estimates by making confidence intervals as we've done for means and proportions. For that, we need to make some assumptions about the model and the errors.

14.2 Assumptions and Conditions

Back in Chapter 6 when we fit lines to data, we needed both the **Linearity** and the **Equal Variance Assumptions**, and so we checked four conditions. Now, when we want to make inferences about the coefficients of the line, we'll have to assume more, so we'll add more conditions.

Also, we need to be careful about the order in which we check conditions. So we number the assumptions, and check conditions for each in order: (1) Linearity Assumption, (2) Independence Assumption, (3) Equal Variance Assumption, and (4) Normal Population Assumption.

1. Linearity Assumption

> What situations would you expect *not* to satisfy the Linearity Assumption? Examples include: a) sales of ice cream by month of the year—parabolic: highest in July and August, lowest in December and January; b) number of new internet connections by time—exponential growth; c) energy needs by temperature—probably parabolic.

If the true relationship of two quantitative variables is far from linear and we use a straight line to fit the data, our entire analysis will be useless, so we always check linearity first (and we check the **Quantitative Variable Condition** for both variables as well).

The **Linearity Condition** is satisfied if a scatterplot looks straight. It's generally not a good idea to draw a line through the scatterplot when checking. That can fool your eye into seeing the plot as straighter than it really is. Recall the errors, or residuals, we computed in Chapter 6 for each observation. Sometimes it's easier to see violations of this condition by looking at a scatterplot of the residuals against x or against the predicted values, $\hat{y}$. That plot should have no pattern if the condition is satisfied.

If the scatterplot of the residuals is straight enough, we can go on to some assumptions about the errors. If not, we stop here, or consider transforming the variables to make the scatterplot more linear.

2. Independence Assumption

> What situations would you expect *not* to satisfy the Independence Assumption? It happens most often when data are collected at various time points; for example, monthly sales records over a number of years—next month depends on this month and November sales one year depend on what happened the previous November.

The errors in the true underlying regression model (the ε's) must be independent of each other. As usual, there's no way to be sure that the Independence Assumption is true.

When we care about inference for the regression parameters, it's often because we think our regression model might apply to a larger population. In such cases, we can check the **Randomization Condition** that the individuals are a random sample from that population.

We can also check displays of the regression residuals for evidence of patterns, trends, or clumping, any of which would suggest a failure of independence. In the special case when we have a time series, a common violation of the Independence Assumption is for the errors to be correlated with each other (autocorrelated). (The error our model makes today may be similar to the one it made yesterday.) We can check this violation by plotting the residuals against time (usually the x-variable for a time series) and looking for patterns.

3. Equal Variance Assumption

The variability of y should be about the same for all values of x. In Chapter 6, we looked at the standard deviation of the residuals (s_e) to measure the size of the scatter. Now we'll need this standard deviation to build confidence intervals and test hypotheses. The standard deviation of the residuals is the building block for the standard errors of all the regression parameters. But it only makes sense if the scatter of the residuals is the same everywhere. In effect, the standard deviation of the residuals "pools" information across all of the individual distributions of y at each x-value, and pooled estimates are appropriate only when they combine information for groups with the same variance. The idea of pooling first appeared with the Pooled t-test in Chapter 12. A scatterplot of residuals against predicted values can help us see if the spread changes in any way. (You can also plot the residuals against x.)

We always check the **Equal Spread Condition** by looking at a scatterplot of residuals against x or $\hat{y}$. Make sure the spread around the line is nearly constant. Be alert for a "fan" shape or other tendency for the variation to grow or shrink in one part of the scatterplot. A belt or rectangular band shape is ideal.

If the plot is straight enough, the data are independent, and the spread doesn't change, we can move on to the final assumption and its associated condition.

4. Normal Population Assumption

We assume the errors around the idealized regression line at each value of x follow a Normal model. We need this assumption so that we can use a Student's t-model for inference.

As with other times when we've used Student's t, we'll settle for the residuals satisfying the **Nearly Normal Condition**.[1] As we have noted before, the Normality Assumption becomes less important as the sample size grows because the model is about means and the Central Limit Theorem takes over. A histogram of the residuals is one way to check whether they are nearly Normal. Alternatively, we can look at a **Normal probability plot** of the residuals (see Figure 14.3). It finds deviations from the Normal model more efficiently than a histogram. If the distribution of the data is Normal, the Normal probability plot will look roughly like a diagonal straight line. Deviations from a straight line indicate that the distribution is not Normal. This plot is usually able to show deviations from Normality more clearly than the corresponding histogram, but it's usually easier to understand *how* a distribution fails to be Normal by looking at its histogram. Another common failure of Normality is the presence of an outlier. So, we still

What situations would you expect *not* to satisfy the Equal Variance Assumption? Examples include: a) length of hospital stay (days) by size of the hospital (number of beds)—larger hospitals will see more varied medical situations; b) sales revenue by size of store (floor space)—small stores are likely to be more similar to one another; c) executive salary by years of experience— with more experience there is greater variability in salaries.

What situations would you expect *not* to satisfy the Normal Population Assumption? Very often it is the same situations that do not satisfy the Equal Variance Assumption. Examples include: a) length of hospital stay (days) by size of the hospital (number of beds); b) water usage by household income; c) executive salary by years of experience—in all three examples the y variable is skewed to the right.

---

[1] *This* is why we check the conditions in order. We check that the residuals are independent and that the variation is the same for all x's before we can lump all the residuals together to check the Normal Condition.

check the **Outlier Condition** to ensure that no point is exerting too much influence on the fitted model.

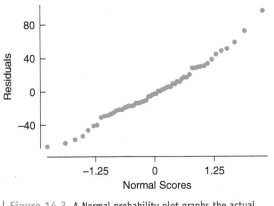

Figure 14.3 A Normal probability plot graphs the actual standardized residuals against those expected (Normal Scores) for a sample from a standard Normal containing the same number of observations.

The idea behind a normal probability plot is similar to that behind a log-scale plot. Imagine the growth rate of the powers of 10: $10^1, 10^2, 10^3, 10^4, 10^5$. It would look "exponential." But if you took the log (base 10), you'd have 1, 2, 3, 4, 5, and the plot (called a log-scale plot) would look like a straight line. Similarly, on a Normal plot the growth rate of normal probability follows a straight line.

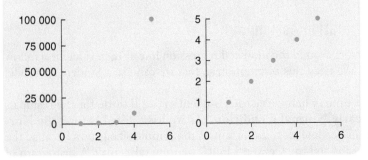

The best advice on using a Normal probability plot is to check whether it is straight. If it is, then your data look like data from a Normal model. If not, make a histogram to understand how they differ from the model.

◆   **How does the Normal probability plot work?**
A Normal probability plot compares each value (in our case each of the 59 residuals) with the value we would have *expected* to get if we'd just drawn a sample of 59 values from a Standard Normal model. The key is to match our numbers in order to the expected Normal values in order.

It helps to think in terms of standardized values. For example, the lowest (most negative) residual in our example has a value of −$69.48. Standardizing, we find that it is 2.03 standard deviations below the mean giving a *z*-score of −2.03. We can learn from theory that if we draw a sample of 59 values at random from a standard Normal model, we'd expect the smallest of them to have a value of −2.39. We're drawing from a standard Normal, so that's already a *z*-score. We can see, then, that our lowest residual isn't quite as far from the mean as we might have expected (had the residuals been perfectly Normal).

We can continue in this way, comparing each observed value with the value we'd expect from a Normal model. The easiest way to make the comparison, of course, is to graph it. If our observed values look like a sample from a Normal model, then the probability plot stretches out in a straight line from lower left to upper right. But if our values deviate from what we'd expect, the plot will bend or have jumps in it.

The values we'd expect from a Normal model are called **Normal scores**, or sometimes nscores. Statistics programs haven't agreed on whether to plot the normal scores on the *x*-axis or the *y*-axis, so you need to look to be sure. But since you usually just want to check whether the plot is straight or not, it really doesn't matter.

A Normal probability plot is a great way to check whether the distribution is nearly Normal. But when it isn't straight, it is often a good idea to make a histogram of the values as well to get a sense of just how the data are distributed.

Summary of Assumptions and Conditions

If all four assumptions were true, the idealized regression model would look like Figure 14.4.

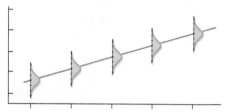

Figure 14.4 The regression model has a distribution of y-values for each x-value. These distributions follow a Normal model with means lined up along the line and the same standard deviations.

At each value of x, there is a distribution of y-values that follows a Normal model, and each of these Normal models is centred on the line and has the same standard deviation. Of course, we don't expect the assumptions to be exactly true. As George Box said, "all models are wrong." But the linear model is often close enough to be useful.

In regression, there's a little catch; an example of circular reasoning. The best way to check many of the conditions is with the residuals, but we get the residuals only *after* we compute the regression. Before we compute the regression, however, we should check at least one of the conditions.

So we work in this order:

1. **Make a scatterplot of the data** to check the Linearity Condition (and always check that the variables are quantitative as well). (This checks the **Linearity Assumption**.)
2. If the data are straight enough, **fit a regression and find the residuals, e, and predicted values, $\hat{y}$.**
3. If you know when the measurements were made, **plot the residuals against time** to check for evidence of patterns that suggest they may not be independent (**Independence Assumption**).
4. **Make a scatterplot of the residuals against x or the predicted values.** This plot should have no pattern. Check in particular for any bend (which would suggest that the data weren't that straight after all), for any thickening (or thinning), and, of course, for any unusual observations. (If you discover any errors, correct them or omit those points, and go back to step 1. Otherwise, consider performing two regressions—one with and one without the unusual observations.) (**Equal Variance Assumption**)
5. If the scatterplots look OK, then **make a histogram and Normal probability plot of the residuals** to check the **Nearly Normal** and **Outlier Conditions** (**Normal Population Assumption**).

Here's a helpful shortcut hint. Oval-shaped scatterplots usually satisfy the assumptions of regression (except perhaps the Independence Assumption).

14.3 Regression Inference

There's only one regression model for the population. Sample regressions try to estimate the parameters, β_0 and β_1. We expect the estimated slope for any sample, b_1, to be close to—but not actually equal to—the model slope, β_1. If we could see

Actually, the full quotation is, "All models are wrong, but some are useful." It is, of course, the "usefulness" part that we are most interested in! George Box died at the age of 93 in March 2013. He was a giant among twentieth century statisticians and was certainly famous for thinking outside the "box!"

"Truth will emerge more readily from error than from confusion."
—Francis Bacon (1561–1626)

the collection of slopes from many samples (imagined or real) we would see a distribution of values around the true slope. That's the sampling distribution of the slope. This follows logically from our work with the sampling distributions of $\bar{x}$ and $\hat{p}$ where we imagined the distribution of values that the sample mean or sample proportion could have if we took many samples. We need the sampling distribution of the slope in order to make inferences.

What is the standard deviation of this distribution? What aspects of the data affect how much the slopes vary from sample to sample?

◆ **Spread around the line.** Figure 14.5 shows samples from two populations. Which underlying population would give rise to the more consistent slopes?

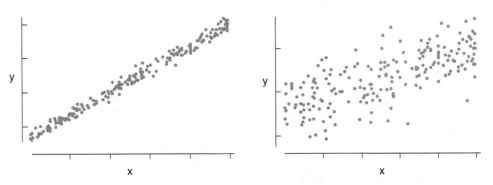

Figure 14.5 Which of these scatterplots would give the more consistent regression slope estimate if we were to sample repeatedly from its underlying population?

Less scatter around the line means the slope will be more consistent from sample to sample. Recall that we measure the spread around the line with the **residual standard deviation:**

$$s_e = \sqrt{\frac{\sum (y - \hat{y})^2}{n - 2}}$$

The less scatter around the line, the smaller the residual standard deviation and the stronger the relationship between x and y.

◆ **Spread of the x's:** Here are samples from two more populations (Figure 14.6). Which of these would yield more consistent slopes?

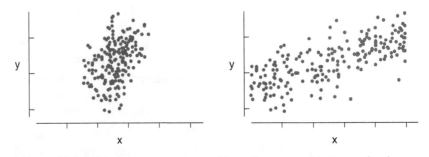

Figure 14.6 Which of these scatterplots would give the more consistent regression slope estimate if we were to sample repeatedly from the underlying population?

A plot like the one on the right has a broader range of x-values, so it gives a more stable base for the slope. We might expect the slopes of samples from situations like that to vary less from sample to sample. A large standard deviation of x, s_x, as in the figure on the right, provides a more stable regression.

◆ **Sample size.** What about the two scatterplots in Figure 14.7?

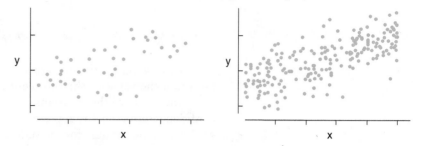

Figure 14.7 Which of these scatterplots would give the more consistent regression slope estimate if we were to sample repeatedly from the underlying population?

It shouldn't shock you that a larger sample size (scatterplot on the right), n, gives more consistent estimates from sample to sample.

Let's summarize what we've seen in these three figures:

> Don't confuse s_e and s_x. Where is s_y? It is hiding as part of s_e.
>
> Here is another version of the formula for the standard error of the slope:
>
> $$SE(b_1) = \frac{s_e}{\sqrt{\sum (x - \bar{x})^2}}$$

The standard error of the regression slope

Three aspects of the scatterplot that affect the standard error of the regression slope are:

- Spread around the line: s_e
- Spread of x values: s_x
- Sample size: n

These are in fact the *only* things that affect the standard error of the slope. The formula for the standard error of the slope is:

$$SE(b_1) = \frac{s_e}{s_x \sqrt{n - 1}}$$

The error standard deviation, s_e, is in the *numerator*, since a larger spread around the line *increases* the slope's standard error. On the other hand, the *denominator* has both a sample size term ($\sqrt{n - 1}$) and s_x because increasing either of these *decreases* the slope's standard error.

To find the standard error of the slope, think about fitting a straight line to different samples from the same population. We know b_1 varies from sample to sample. As you'd expect, its sampling distribution model is centred at β_1, the slope of the idealized regression line. Now we can estimate its standard deviation with $SE(b_1)$. What about its shape? Here the Central Limit Theorem and Gosset come to the rescue again. When we standardize the slopes by subtracting the model mean and dividing by their standard error, we get a Student's t-model, this time with $n - 2$ degrees of freedom:

$$\frac{b_1 - \beta_1}{SE(b_1)} \sim t_{n-2}$$

The sampling distribution for the regression slope (β_1)

When the conditions are met, the standardized estimated regression slope

$$t = \frac{b_1 - \beta_1}{SE(b_1)}$$

follows a Student's t-model with $n - 2$ degrees of freedom. We estimate the standard error with $SE(b_1) = \dfrac{s_e}{s_x \sqrt{n - 1}}$, where $s_e = \sqrt{\dfrac{\sum (y - \hat{y})^2}{n - 2}}$, n is the number of data values, and s_x is the standard deviation of the x-values.

The same reasoning applies for the intercept. We write:

$$\frac{b_0 - \beta_0}{SE(b_0)} \sim t_{n-2}$$

We could use this statistic to construct confidence intervals and test hypotheses, but often the value of the intercept isn't interesting. In fact, it is meaningless when the range of the *x* variable does not include 0. Most hypothesis tests and confidence intervals for regression are about the slope. But in case you really want to see the formula for the standard error of the intercept, we've parked it in a footnote.[2]

Now that we have the standard error of the slope and its sampling distribution, we can test a hypothesis about it and make confidence intervals. The usual null hypothesis about the slope is that it's equal to 0. Why? Well, a slope of zero would say that *y* doesn't tend to change linearly when *x* changes—in other words, that there is no linear association between the two variables. If the slope were zero, there wouldn't be much left of our regression equation.

A null hypothesis of a zero slope questions the entire claim of a linear relationship between the two variables, and often that's just what we want to know. In fact, every software package or calculator that does regression simply assumes that you want to test the null hypothesis that the slope is really zero.

What if the slope is 0?

If $b_1 = 0$, our prediction is $\hat{y} = b_0 + 0x$, and the equation collapses to just $\hat{y} = b_0$. Now *x* is nowhere in sight, so *y* doesn't depend on *x* at all.

In this case, b_0 would turn out to be $\bar{y}$. Why? Because we know that $b_0 = \bar{y} - b_1\bar{x}$, and when $b_1 = 0$, that becomes simply $b_0 = \bar{y}$. It turns out, that when the slope is 0, the entire regression equation is just $\hat{y} = \bar{y}$, so for every value of *x*, we predict the mean value $(\bar{y})$ for *y*. In other words, if you have no information about the predictor variable, then predict the mean for every case!

The *t*-test for the regression slope

When the assumptions and conditions are met, we can test the hypothesis $H_0: \beta_1 = 0$ vs. $H_A: \beta_1 \neq 0$ (or a one-sided alternative hypothesis) using the standardized estimated regression slope:

$$t = \frac{b_1 - \beta_1}{SE(b_1)}$$

which follows a Student's *t*-model with $n - 2$ degrees of freedom. We can use the *t*-model to find the P-value of the test.

This is just like every other *t*-test we've seen: a difference between the statistic and its hypothesized value divided by its standard error. This test is the *t*-test that the regression slope is 0, usually referred to as the *t*-**test for the regression slope**.

Another use of these values might be to make a confidence interval for the slope. We can build a confidence interval in the usual way, as an estimate plus or minus a margin of error. As always, the margin of error is just the product of the standard error and a critical value.

Very occasionally you may need to test whether the slope is equal to, or different from, some value other than zero. For example, in finance, the market model uses simple regression to explain variation in a particular stock by variation in the market as a whole. The slope, which is called the "beta" of a stock, determines whether the stock is more volatile (beta > 1) or less volatile (beta < 1) than the market. In that case the hypothesized value of β_1 is 1 and is the value subtracted in the numerator of the test statistic.

---

[2] $SE(b_0) = s_e \sqrt{\dfrac{1}{n} + \dfrac{\bar{x}^2}{\sum (x - \bar{x})^2}}$ or $SE(b_0) = s_e \sqrt{\dfrac{1}{n} + \dfrac{\bar{x}^2}{(n-1)s_x^2}}$

> ### The confidence interval for the regression slope
> When the assumptions and conditions are met, we can find a confidence interval for β_1 from
>
> $$b_1 \pm t^*_{n-2} \times SE(b_1)$$
>
> where the critical value t^* depends on the confidence level and has $n - 2$ degrees of freedom.

As we pointed out before, the confidence interval is more flexible and therefore more useful than the hypothesis test. The confidence interval can be used to test whether β_1 is 0 or whether it is some non-zero value, as in the market model application.

GUIDED EXAMPLE — Canada Goose

Now that we have a method to draw inferences from our regression equation, let's try it out on the Canada Goose data. The slope of the regression gives the impact of *Time* on *Price*. Let's test the hypothesis that the slope is different from zero.

PLAN

Setup State the objectives.

Identify the parameter you wish to estimate. Here our parameter is the slope.

Identify the variables and their context.

Hypotheses Write the null and alternative hypotheses.

Model Check the assumptions and conditions.

We want to test the theory that the wholesale price of a particular item at Canada Goose is related to the time it takes to produce it. We have data for 59 items made by Canada Goose. The slope of this relationship will indicate the impact of *Time* on *Price*. Our null hypothesis will be that the slope of the regression is 0.

H_0: The *Price* of an item is not related to the production *Time*: $\beta_1 = 0$.

H_A: The *Price* is, in fact, related to the *Time*: $\beta_1 \neq 0$.

✓ **Linearity Condition:** There is no obvious curve in the scatterplot of *y* versus *x*.

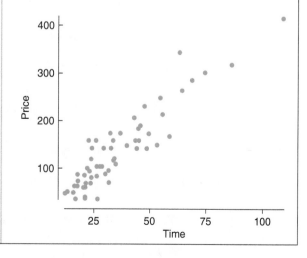

Make graphs. Because our scatterplot of *y* versus *x* seems straight enough, we can find the least squares regression and plot the residuals.

Usually, we check for suggestions that the Independence Assumption fails by plotting the residuals against time. Patterns or trends in that plot raise our suspicions.

✓ **Independence Assumption:** These data are on 59 different items produced by the company. There is no reason to suggest that the error in price of one item should be influenced by another.

✓ **Randomization Condition:** The data are *not a random sample*, but we assume they are representative of the prices and production times of Canada Goose items.

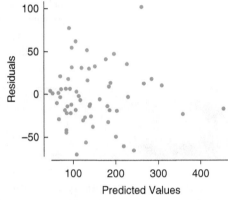

✓ **Equal Spread Condition:** The plot of residuals against the predicted values shows no obvious patterns. The spread is about the same for all predicted values, and the scatter appears random.

✓ **Nearly Normal Condition:** A histogram of the residuals is unimodal and symmetric, and the normal probability plot is reasonably straight.

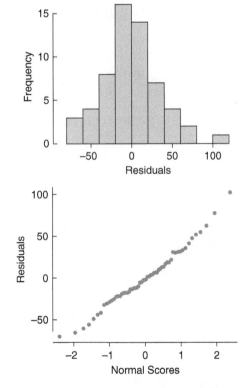

	State the sampling distribution model. Choose the method.	Under these conditions, the sampling distribution of the regression slope can be modelled by a Student's t-model with $(n-2) = 59 - 2 = 57$ degrees of freedom, so we'll proceed with a regression slope t-test.
DO	**Mechanics** The regression equation can be found from the formulas in Chapter 6, but regressions are almost always found from a computer program or calculator.	Here's the computer output for this regression. ``` Variable Coefficient SE(Coeff) t-ratio P-value Intercept -4.871 9.654 -0.50 0.6159 Time 4.200 0.2385 17.61 <0.0001 S = 32.54 R-Sq = 84.5% ```
	The P-values given in the regression output table are from the Student's *t*-distribution on $(n-2) = 57$ degrees of freedom. They are appropriate for two-sided alternatives.	The P-value < 0.0001 means that the association we see in the data is unlikely to have occurred by chance. Therefore, we reject the null hypothesis and conclude that there is strong evidence that the *Price* is linearly related to the production *Time*.
	Create a confidence interval for the true slope. To obtain the *t*-value for 57 degrees of freedom, use the *t*-table at the back of your textbook. The estimated slope and SE for the slope are obtained from the regression output. Interpret the interval. Simply rejecting the standard null hypothesis doesn't guarantee that the size of the effect is large enough to be important.	A 95% confidence interval for β_1 is: $$b_1 \pm t^*_{n-2} \times SE(b_1) = (3.722, 4.678) \, \$/hour$$ I am 95% confident that the price increases, on average, between \$3.72 and \$4.68 for each additional hour of production time. (Technically: I am 95% confident that the interval from \$3.72 to \$4.68 per hour captures the true rate at which the *Price* increases with production *Time*.)
REPORT	**Conclusion** State the conclusion in the proper context.	MEMO: **Re: Canada Goose Pricing** We investigated the relationship between production time and pricing of 59 Canada Goose items. The regression analysis showed that, on average, the price increased \$4.20 for every additional hour of production time. Assuming that these items are representative, we are 95% confident that the actual price of an item produced by Canada Goose increases, on average, between \$3.72 and \$4.68 for each additional hour of production work required.

✔ JUST CHECKING

General economic theory suggests that as unemployment rises and jobs become harder to find, more students will enrol in universities. Researchers analyzed enrolment at the University of New Mexico and unemployment data in New Mexico to determine whether or not there is any statistical relationship between the two variables. The data were collected by the University of New Mexico over a period of 29 years, starting with 1961 and ending with 1989. The variable *Enrolment* is in number of students and the variable *Unemp* is a percentage. Here is some regression output for these data.

Predictor	Coefficient	SE(Coeff)	t-ratio	P-value
Intercept	3957	4000	0.99	0.331
Unemp	1133.8	513.1	2.21	0.036

S = 3049.50   R-Sq = 15.3%

1 What would you like to see before proceeding with inference on this regression? Why?

2 Assuming the assumptions and conditions for regression are met, find the 95% confidence interval for the slope.

3 Clearly state the null and alternative hypothesis for the slope. Interpret the P-value.

4 Is there a strong relationship between enrolment and unemployment?

5 Interpret the value of R-Sq in the output.

14.4 Standard Errors for Predicted Values

We've seen how to construct the confidence interval for a slope or intercept, but we're often interested in prediction. We know how to compute predicted values of *y* for any value of *x*. We first did that in Chapter 6. This predicted value would be our best estimate, but it's still just an informed guess. Now, however, we have standard errors. We can use those SE's to construct confidence intervals for the predictions and to report our uncertainty honestly.

From our model of Canada Goose items, we can use production *Time* to get a reasonable estimate of *Price*. Suppose we want to predict the *Price* of an item that takes 40 hours of *Time* to produce. A confidence interval can tell us how precise that prediction is. The precision depends on the question we ask, however, and there are two different questions we could ask:

Do we want to know the mean *Price* for *all items* that have a production *Time* of 40 hours?

or,

Do we want to estimate the *Price* for a *particular* item whose production *Time* is 40 hours?

What's the difference between the two questions? If we were the manufacturer, we might be more naturally interested in the *mean Price* of all items that take a certain *Time* to produce. On the other hand, if we're interested in purchasing an item, we might be more interested in knowing how much an *individual* item's *Price* will vary at that production *Time*. Both questions are interesting. The predicted *Price* value is the same for both, but one question leads to a much more precise interval than the other. If your intuition says that it's easier to be more precise about the mean than about the individuals, you're on the right track. Because individual items vary much more than means, we can predict the *mean Price* for all items with a lot more precision than we can predict the *Price* of a particular item with the same production *Time*.

We chose this notation on purpose: ν is the Greek letter nu. It is pronounced "new," which reminds us that we are predicting a new value of y at an x of our choosing.

Let's start by predicting the *Price* for a new *Time*, one that was not necessarily part of the original data set. To emphasize this, we'll call this x-value "x sub new" and write it x_ν. As an example, we'll take x_ν to be 40 hours. The regression equation predicts *Price* by $\hat{y}_\nu = b_0 + b_1 x_\nu$. Now that we have the predicted value, we can construct intervals around this number. Both intervals take the form:

$$\hat{y}_\nu \pm t^*_{n-2} \times SE$$

Even the t^* value is the same for both. It's the critical value (from Table T or technology) for $n - 2$ degrees of freedom and the specified confidence level. The difference between the two intervals is in the standard errors.

> ### The confidence interval for the predicted mean value
> When the conditions are met, we find the confidence interval for the predicted mean value μ_ν at a value x_ν as
>
> $$\hat{y}_\nu \pm t^*_{n-2} \times SE$$
>
> where the standard error is
>
> $$SE(\hat{\mu}_\nu) = \sqrt{SE^2(b_1) \times (x_\nu - \bar{x})^2 + \frac{s_e^2}{n}}$$
>
> An alternative formula is given as a footnote on page 462.

The details behind the standard error can be found in the Math Box on pages 461–462, but the ideas behind the interval are best understood by looking at an example. Figure 14.8 shows the confidence interval for the mean predictions. In this plot, the intervals for all the mean *Prices* at all values of *Time* are shown together as confidence bands. Notice that the bands get wider as we attempt to predict values that lie farther away from the mean *Time* (35.82 minutes). (That's the $(x_\nu - \bar{x})^2$ term in the SE formula.) As we move away from the mean

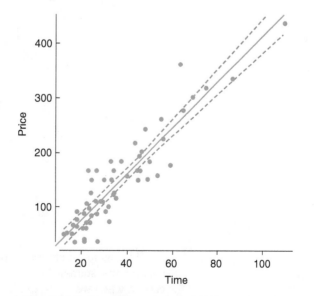

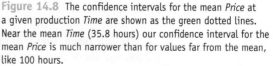

Figure 14.8 The confidence intervals for the mean *Price* at a given production *Time* are shown as the green dotted lines. Near the mean *Time* (35.8 hours) our confidence interval for the mean *Price* is much narrower than for values far from the mean, like 100 hours.

Suppose a linear model is appropriate to describe the relationship between number of study hours and grade on a final exam. A confidence interval would be used to predict the average grade for all students who studied 10 hours, say. A prediction interval would be used to predict the grade for one student who studied 10 hours. If you are only interested in "you," use the prediction interval. If you have a more general interest in what grade would result from 10 hours of studying, use the confidence interval.

x value, there is more uncertainty associated with our prediction. We can see, for example, that a 95% confidence interval for the mean *Price* of an item that takes 40 hours to produce would go from about $150 to $170. (It's actually $153.90 to $172.34.) The interval is much wider for items that take 100 hours to produce.

Like all confidence intervals, the width of these confidence intervals varies with the sample size. A sample larger than 59 items would result in narrower intervals. A regression on 10 000 items would have much narrower bands. The last factor affecting our confidence intervals is the spread of the data around the line. If there is more spread around the line, predictions are less certain, and the confidence interval bands are wider.

From Figure 14.8, it's easy to see that most *points* don't fall within the confidence interval bands—and we shouldn't expect them to. These bands show confidence intervals for the *mean*. An even larger sample would have given even narrower bands. Then we'd expect an even smaller percentage of the points to fall within them.

If we want to capture an individual price, we need to use a wider interval, called a **prediction interval (also known as a prediction interval for a future observation)**. Figure 14.9 shows these prediction intervals for the Canada Goose data. Prediction intervals are based on the same quantities as the confidence intervals, but to capture a percentage of all the future predictions, they include an extra term for the spread around the line. As we can see in Figure 14.9, these bands also widen as we move from the mean of *x*, but it's less obvious because the extra width across the entire range of *x* makes the change harder to see.

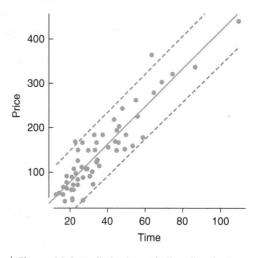

Figure 14.9 Prediction intervals (in red) estimate the interval that contains say, 95% of the distribution of the y values that might be observed at a given value of x. If the assumptions and conditions hold, then there's about a 95% chance that a particular y-value at x$_v$ will be covered by the interval.

The standard errors for prediction depend on the same kinds of things as the coefficients' standard errors. If there is more spread around the line, we'll be less certain when we try to predict the response. Of course, if we're less certain of the slope, we'll be less certain of our prediction. If we have more data, our estimate will be more precise. And there's one more piece. If we're farther from the centre of our data, our prediction will be less precise. It's a lot easier to predict a data point near the middle of the data set than to extrapolate far from the centre.

The prediction interval for an individual value

When the conditions are met, we can find the prediction interval for all values of y at a value x_ν as

$$\hat{y}_\nu \pm t^*_{n-2} \times SE$$

where the standard error is

$$SE(\hat{y}_\nu) = \sqrt{SE^2(b_1) \times (x_\nu - \bar{x})^2 + \frac{s_e^2}{n} + s_e^2}$$

An alternative formula is given as a footnote on page 462.

The critical value t^* depends on the confidence level that you specify.

Let's have a closer look at the terms under the long square root sign. The first term is responsible for the curvature in the prediction interval band around the regression line. It is sometimes called the "extrapolation penalty." But if you make predictions near the mean of x, this term is quite small compared with s_e^2. And if the sample size is reasonably large, the second term s_e^2/n is also small compared with s_e^2.

In that case, the square root sign reduces to $\sqrt{s_e^2}$ or simply s_e. Since we are already approximating, let's go one step further and use a 95% level of confidence; that means t^*_{n-2} is about 2. So we have a very simple and useful approximation. An approximate 95% prediction interval is:

$\hat{y}_\nu \pm 2s_e$, where s_e is always readily available from regression software output.

But remember, it's only an approximation, and only applies when n is large **and** the prediction is not too far from the middle of the x-values **and** at 95% confidence.

Remember to keep the distinction between the two kinds of intervals when looking at computer output. The narrower ones are confidence intervals for the *mean* and the wider ones are prediction intervals for *individual* values.

Prediction intervals are to observations as confidence intervals are to parameters.

MATH BOX

Some insight into the differences between the two intervals can be gained by looking at the formulas for their standard errors and how they're derived.

To predict a y-value for a new value of x, x_ν, we'd have:

$\hat{y}_\nu = b_0 + b_1 x_\nu$, which, because $b_0 = \bar{y} - b_1\bar{x}$, can be written $\hat{y}_\nu = b_1(x_\nu - \bar{x}) + \bar{y}$.

We use $\hat{y}_\nu$ in two ways. First, we use it to estimate the mean value of all the y's at x_ν, in which case we *call* it $\hat{\mu}^\nu$.

To create a confidence interval for the mean value, we need to measure the variability in this prediction:

$$Var(\hat{\mu}_\nu) = Var(b_1(x_\nu - \bar{x}) + \bar{y})$$

We now call on the Pythagorean Theorem of Statistics: The slope, b_1, and mean, $\bar{y}$, are independent, so their variances add:

$$Var(\hat{\mu}_\nu) = Var(b_1(x_\nu - \bar{x})) + Var(\bar{y})$$

The horizontal distance from our specific x-value to the mean, $x_\nu - \bar{x}$, is a constant, so it comes "out" of the variance:

$$Var(\hat{\mu}_\nu) = (Var(b_1))(x_\nu - \bar{x})^2 + Var(\bar{y})$$

Let's write that equation in terms of standard deviations:

$$SD(\hat{\mu}_v) = \sqrt{(SD^2(b_1))\ (x_v - \bar{x})^2 + SD^2(\bar{y})}$$

Because we'll need to estimate these standard deviations using sample statistics, we're really dealing with standard errors:

$$SE(\hat{\mu}_v) = \sqrt{(SE^2(b_1))\ (x_v - \bar{x})^2 + SE^2(\bar{y})}$$

We know that the standard deviation of a mean, $\bar{y}$, is $\dfrac{\sigma}{\sqrt{n}}$. Here we'll estimate σ using s_e, which describes the variability in how far the line we drew through our sample mean may lie above or below the true mean:

$$SE(\hat{\mu}_v) = \sqrt{(SE^2(b_1))\ (x_v - \bar{x})^2 + \left(\frac{s_e}{\sqrt{n}}\right)^2}$$

$$= \sqrt{(SE^2(b_1))\ (x_v - \bar{x})^2 + \frac{s_e^2}{n}}$$

And there it is—the standard error we need to create a confidence interval for a predicted mean value.[3]

When we try to predict an *individual* value of y, we also must worry about how far the true point may lie above or below the regression line. We represent that uncertainty by adding another term, e, to the original equation to get:

$$y = \hat{\mu}_v + e = b_1(x_v - \bar{x}) + \bar{y} + e$$

To make a long story short (and the equation just a bit longer), that additional term simply adds one more standard error to the sum of the variances:

$$SE(\hat{y}_v) = \sqrt{(SE^2(b_1))\ (x_v - \bar{x})^2 + \frac{s_e^2}{n} + s_e^2}$$

We've written the predicted value as $\hat{y}_v$ instead of $\hat{\mu}_v$ this time, not because it's a different value, but to emphasize that we're *using* it to predict an individual now and not the mean of all y values at x_v.

14.5 Using Confidence and Prediction Intervals

Now that we have standard errors, we can ask how well our analysis can predict the mean price for objects that take 25 hours to produce. The regression output table provides most of the numbers we need.

Variable	Coefficient	SE(coeff)	t-ratio	P-value
Intercept	−4.871	9.654	−0.50	0.6159
Time	4.200	0.2385	17.61	< 0.0001

$S = 32.54$ $R\text{-}Sq = 84.5\%$

---

[3] You may see the standard error expressions written in other, equivalent ways. The most common alternatives are:

$$SE(\hat{\mu}_v) = s_e\sqrt{\frac{1}{n} + \frac{(x_v - \bar{x})^2}{\sum(x - \bar{x})^2}} \quad \text{and} \quad SE(\hat{y}_v) = s_e\sqrt{1 + \frac{1}{n} + \frac{(x_v - \bar{x})^2}{\sum(x - \bar{x})^2}}$$

The regression model gives a predicted value at $x_\nu = 25$ hours of:

$$-4.871 + 4.200\,(25) = \$100.13$$

Using this, we'll first find the 95% confidence interval for the mean *Price* for all objects whose production *Time* is 25 hours. We find the standard error from the formula using the values in the regression output.

$$SE(\hat{\mu}_\nu) = \sqrt{(SE^2(b_1))\,(x_\nu - \bar{x})^2 + \left(\frac{s_e}{\sqrt{n}}\right)^2}$$

$$= \sqrt{(0.2385)^2\,(25 - 35.82)^2 + \left(\frac{32.54}{\sqrt{59}}\right)^2} = \$4.96$$

The t^* value that excludes 2.5% in either tail with $59 - 2 = 57$ df is (according to the tables) 2.002.

Putting it all together, we find the margin of error as:

$$ME = 2.002(4.96) = \$9.93$$

So, we are 95% confident that the interval

$$\$100.13 \pm 9.93 = (\$90.20, \$110.06)$$

includes the true mean *Price* of objects whose *Time* is 25 hours.

Suppose, however, that instead of the mean price, we want to know how much an item that needs 25 hours of production will cost. The confidence interval we just found is too narrow. It may contain the mean price, but it's unlikely to cover many of the individual price values. To make a prediction interval for an *individual* item's price with a production time of 25 hours, we need the larger standard error formula to account for the greater variability. Using the formula

$$SE(\hat{y}_\nu) = \sqrt{(SE^2(b_1))\,(x_\nu - \bar{x})^2 + \frac{s_e^2}{n} + s_e^2} = \$32.92$$

we find the ME to be

$$ME = t^*SE(\hat{y}_\nu) = 2.002 \times 32.92 = \$65.91$$

and so the prediction interval is

$$\hat{y} \pm ME = 100.13 \pm 65.91 = (\$34.22, \$166.04)$$

Notice how much wider this interval is than the 95% confidence interval. Most of the time we will use a software package to compute and display these intervals. Most packages generate displays that show the regression line along with both the 95% confidence and prediction intervals (combining what we've shown in Figures 14.8 and 14.9). This makes it easier to see how much wider the prediction intervals are than the corresponding confidence intervals (see Figure 14.10).

A useful mnemonic to distinguish between a Confidence Interval and Prediction Interval:

The "C" reminds us that we are estimating *y* for *all* cases having a **C**ommon *x*-value.

The "P" reminds us that we are estimating *y* for *one* **P**articular case at a given *x*-value.

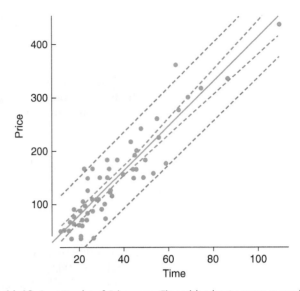

Figure 14.10 A scatterplot of *Price* versus *Time* with a least squares regression line. The inner lines (green) near the regression line show the extent of the 95% confidence intervals, and the outer lines (red) show the prediction intervals. Most of the points are contained within the prediction intervals (as they should be), but not within the confidence interval for the means.

14.6 Extrapolation and Prediction

Heather A. Craig/Shutterstock

Linear models give a predicted value for each case in the data. Put a new *x*-value into the equation, and it gives a predicted value, $\hat{y}$, to go with it. But when the new *x*-value lies far from the data we used to build the regression, how trustworthy is the prediction?

The simple answer is that the farther the new *x*-value is from $\bar{x}$, the centre of the *x*-values, the less trust we should place in the predicted value. Once we venture into new *x* territory, such a prediction is called an **extrapolation**. Extrapolations are dangerous because they require the additional—and questionable—assumption that nothing about the relationship between *x* and *y* changes, even at extreme values of *x* and beyond. Extrapolations can get us into deep trouble, especially if we try to predict far into the future.

As a cautionary example, let's examine oil prices from 1972 to 1981 in constant (2005) dollars.[4] In the mid 1970s, in the midst of an energy crisis, oil prices surged, and long lines at gas stations, particularly in the United States, were common. In 1970, the price of oil was about $3 a barrel. A few years later, it had surged to $15. In 1975, a survey of 15 top econometric forecasting models (built by groups that included Nobel prize-winning economists) found predictions for 1985 oil prices that ranged from $50 to $200 a barrel (or $181 to $726(!) dollars a barrel in 2005 dollars). How close were these forecasts? Let's look at Figure 14.11.

The regression model for the *Price* of oil against *Time* (Years since 1970) for these data is

$$\widehat{Price} = -0.85 + 7.39 \; Time$$

which says that prices increased, on average, $7.39 per year, or nearly $75 in 10 years. If they continued to increase linearly, it would have been easy to predict

---

[4] There are special methods, called time series methods, for fitting data when *x* is time, that lie outside the scope of this book. But simple regression models are often used as well. Even when using more sophisticated methods, the dangers of extrapolation don't disappear.

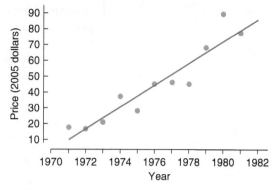

Figure 14.11 The price of oil per barrel in constant (2005) dollars from 1971 to 1982 shows a linear trend increasing at about $7 a year.

oil prices. And indeed, many forecasters made that assumption. So, how well did they do? Well, in the period from 1982 to 1998, oil prices didn't exactly continue that steady increase. In fact, they went down so much that by 1998, prices (adjusted for inflation) were the lowest they'd been since before World War II (Figure 14.12).

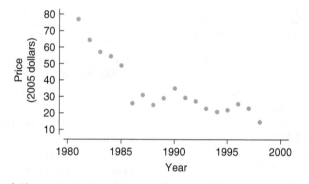

Figure 14.12 Time series plot of price of oil in constant (2005) dollars shows a fairly constant decrease over time.

For example, the average price of oil in 1985 turned out to be less than $30 per barrel—not quite the $100 predicted by the model. Extrapolating out beyond the original data by just four years produced some vastly inaccurate forecasts. While the time series plot in Figure 14.12 shows a fairly steady decline, this pattern clearly didn't continue (or oil would be free by now).

In the 1990s, the U.S. government decided to include scenarios in their forecasts. The result was that the Energy Information Administration (EIA) offered *two* 20-year forecasts for oil prices after 1998 in their Annual Energy Outlook (AEO). Both of these scenarios, however, called for relatively modest increases in oil prices (Figure 14.13).

In 1993, *The New York Times* reported that the cow population of New York State had dropped to the lowest level (749 000) since 1924 when record-keeping began. However the remaining cows produced more milk than ever (11.6 billion pounds). The correlation between number of cows and amount of milk produced is –0.76. A linear regression gives: $\hat{y} = 16\,200 - 0.6x$, where x is thousands of cows and y is millions of pounds. If we extrapolate downward we find that 0 cows would produce 16.2 billion pounds of milk. That's udder nonsense (sorry about that)!

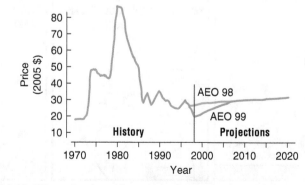

Figure 14.13 This graph, adapted from one by the Energy Information Administration, shows oil prices from 1970 to 1998 with two sets of forecasts for the period 1999 to 2020.

So, how accurate have these forecasts been? Let's compare these predictions to the actual prices in constant (2005) dollars (Figure 14.14).

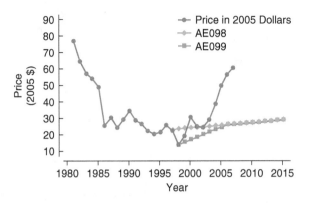

Figure 14.14 Here are the same EIA forecasts as in Figure 14.13, together with the actual prices from 1981 to 2007. Neither forecast predicted the sharp run-up in the past few years.

Return to the earlier example about the number of study hours as a predictor of grade on a final exam. Whatever the fitted model is, we shouldn't use it for wild extrapolation. For example, studying 20 hours will lead to a higher grade than studying 10 hours, on average. But not studying 200 hours; that will fry your brain cells!

The experts seem to have missed the sharp run-up in oil prices in the first decade of the twenty-first century. Where do you think oil prices will go in the *next* decade? Your guess may be as good as anyone's. Clearly, these forecasts did not take into account many of the unforeseen global and economic events that occurred since 2000. Providing accurate long-term forecasts is extremely difficult.

Extrapolation far from the data is dangerous. Linear models are based on the *x*-values of the data at hand and cannot be trusted beyond that span. The irony is that predictions are most reliable and most accurate at the place where you have the most data, and that's where you already know what is likely to happen. Some phenomena do exhibit a kind of inertia that allows us to guess that the currently observed systematic behaviour will continue outside this range. When *x* is time, you should be especially wary. Such regularity can't be counted on in phenomena such as stock prices, sales figures, hurricane tracks, or public opinion.

Extrapolating from current trends is a mistake made not only by regression beginners or the naïve. Professional forecasters are prone to the same mistakes, and sometimes the errors are striking. However, because the temptation to predict the future is so strong, our more realistic advice is this:

If you extrapolate far into the future, be prepared for the actual values to be (possibly quite) different from your predictions.

"Prediction is difficult, especially about the future."

—Niels Bohr, Danish physicist

FOXTROT © 2002 Bill Amend. Reprinted with permission of UNIVERSAL PRESS SYNDICATE. All rights reserved.

14.7 Unusual and Extraordinary Observations

Your credit card company makes money each time you use your card. To encourage you to use your card, the card issuer may offer you an incentive such as airline miles, rebates, or gifts.[5] Of course, this is profitable to the company only if the increased use brings in enough revenue to offset the cost of the incentives. New ideas for offers (referred to as "creatives") are typically tested on a sample of cardholders before they are rolled out to the entire segment or population, a process referred to as a "campaign." Typically, the new offer (the "challenger") is tested against a control group who may be offered nothing or the current best offer ("the champion").

One campaign offered one of the highest-performing market segments an incentive for three months: one redeemable anytime air mile for each dollar spent. They hoped that the cardholders would increase their spending enough to pay for the campaign, but they feared that some cardholders would move spending forward into the incentive period, with a resulting drop in spending afterward.

For this particular segment, the typical cardholder charged about $1700 a month. During the campaign period, the group averaged around $1919.61 a month, a difference that was both statistically and financially significant. But analysts were surprised to see that the increase in spending continued well beyond the offer period. To investigate it, they made a scatterplot like the one shown in Figure 14.15.

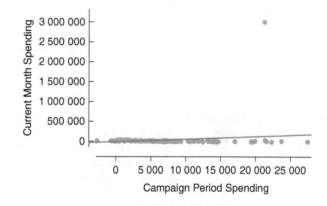

Figure 14.15 Spending after the campaign plotted against spending during the campaign period reveals a surprising value and a positive regression slope.

The outlying point, at the top of the graph, represents a cardholder who charged nearly $3 million in the month after the free miles period ended. Remarkably, the point was verified to be a real purchase! Nevertheless, this cardholder is clearly not typical of the rest of the segment. To answer the company's question, we need to examine the plot without the outlying point (Figure 14.16).

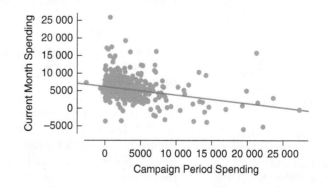

Figure 14.16 A plot of current spending against the spending during the campaign period, with the outlier set aside. Now the slope is negative, and significantly so.

---

[5] There are websites dedicated to finding credit card "deals." Search "credit card rewards." "Air miles" is one place where Canada has not gone metric. No one collects air kilometres.

The plot does show that those with the largest charges during the campaign spent less in the month after the campaign. Just one outlier was capable of changing the slope's direction from strongly negative to strongly positive. On the basis of this finding, the analysts decided to focus only on people whose spending during *both* periods was less than $10,000 a month, figuring that if someone decides to spend more than $10,000 on their credit card, their primary motivation is probably not the airline miles incentive.

Outliers, Leverage, and Influence

By providing a simple description of how data behave, models help us see when and how data values are unusual. In regression, a point can stand out in two ways. A case can have a large residual, as our $3 million spender certainly did. Because they are not like the other cases, points with large residuals always deserve special attention and are called **outliers**.

A data point can also be unusual if its *x*-value is far from the mean of the *x*-values. Such a point is said to have high **leverage**. The physical image of a lever is exactly right. The least squares line must pass through $(\bar{x}, \bar{y})$, so you can picture that point as the fulcrum of the lever. Just as sitting farther from the centre of a seesaw gives you more leverage, points with values far from $\bar{x}$ pull more strongly on the regression line.

A point with high leverage has the potential to change the regression line but it doesn't always use that potential. If the point lines up with the pattern of the other points, it doesn't change our estimate of the line. By sitting so far from $\bar{x}$ though, it may appear to strengthen the relationship, inflating the correlation and R^2.

World History Archive/Alamy

"Give me a place to stand and I will move the Earth."
—Archimedes (287–211 BCE)

One of the most-loved films in American cinema is also an example of influential points. *It's a Wonderful Life* (1946) stars James Stewart as George Bailey, a man who has given up his dreams to help others and who is planning suicide on Christmas Eve. His guardian angel intervenes and shows how different the life of his family and community would be if he had never been born. That's what we do in linear regression. Check what the result would be with and without a data point. What would life have been like with and without George Bailey?

How can you tell if a high-leverage point changes the model? Just fit the linear model twice, both with and without the point in question. We say that a point is **influential** if omitting it from the analysis gives a very different model (as the high spender did in our example).[6]

Unusual points in a regression often tell us more about the data and the model than any other cases. Whenever you have—or suspect that you have—influential points, you should fit the linear model to the other cases alone and then compare the two regression models to understand how they differ. A model dominated by a single point is unlikely to be useful for understanding the rest of the cases. The best way to understand unusual points is against the background of the model established by the other data values. Don't give in to the temptation to delete points simply because they don't fit the line. That can give a false picture of how well the model fits the data. But often the best way to identify interesting cases and subgroups is to note that they are influential and to find out what makes them special. There is a saying that Nobel prizes come not from identifying outliers but from figuring out why they are outliers.

Influence depends on both the leverage and the residual; a case with high leverage whose *y*-value sits right on the line fit to the rest of the data is not influential. A case with low leverage but a very large residual can be influential. The only way to be sure is to fit the regression with and without the potential influential point.

Not all points with large influence have large residuals. Sometimes, their influence pulls the regression line so close that it makes the residual deceptively small. Influential points like that can have a shocking effect on the regression. Figure 14.17 shows IQ plotted against shoe size from a fanciful study of intelligence and foot size. The outlier is Bozo the clown, known for his large feet and hailed as a comic genius.

---

[6] Some textbooks use the term *influential point* for any observation that influences the slope, intercept, or R^2. We'll reserve the term for points that influence the slope.

"For whoever knows the ways of Nature will more easily notice her deviations; and, on the other hand, whoever knows her deviations will more accurately describe her ways."

—Francis Bacon (1561–1626)

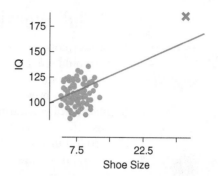

Figure 14.17 Bozo the clown's extraordinarily large shoes give his data point high-leverage in the regression of: IQ = 93.3 + 2.08 Shoe Size, even though the R^2 is 25%. Wherever Bozo's IQ happens to be, the regression line will follow.

Although this is a silly example, it illustrates an important and common potential problem. Almost all of the variance accounted for $(R^2 = 25\%)$ is due to *one* point, namely, Bozo. Without Bozo, there is little correlation between shoe size and IQ. If we run the regression after omitting Bozo, we get an R^2 of only 0.7%—a weak linear relationship (as one might expect). One single point exhibits a great influence on the regression analysis.

✔ **JUST CHECKING**

Each of these scatterplots shows an unusual point. For each, tell whether the point is a high-leverage point, would have a large residual, and/or is influential.

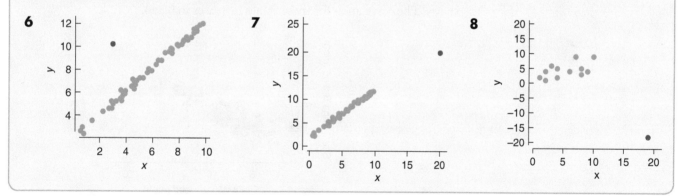

What should you do with a high-leverage point? Sometimes these values are important (they may be customers with extremely high incomes or employees with unusually long service to the company), and they may say more about the relationship between *y* and *x* than any of the other data values. However, at other times, high-leverage points are values that really don't belong with the rest of the data. Such points should probably be omitted, and a linear model found without them for comparison. When in doubt, it's usually best to fit regressions both with and without the points and compare the two models.

◆ **Warning:** Influential points can hide in plots of residuals. Points with high leverage pull the line close to them, so they often have small residuals. You'll see influential points more easily in scatterplots of the original data, and you'll see their effects by finding a regression model with and without the points.

Michael Betts/Digital Vision/Getty Images

*14.8 Working with Summary Values

Scatterplots of statistics summarized over groups tend to show less variability than we would see if we measured the same variables on individuals. This is because the summary statistics themselves vary less than the data on the individuals.

Wind power is getting increasing attention as an alternative, carbon-free method of generating electricity. Of course, there must be enough wind to make it cost-effective. In a study to find a site for a wind generator, wind speeds were collected four times a day (at 6:00 a.m., noon, 6:00 p.m., and midnight) for a year at several possible sites. Figure 14.18 plots the wind speeds for two of these sites. The correlation is 0.736.

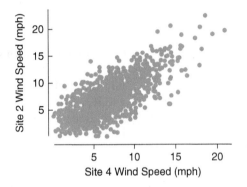

| Figure 14.18 The wind speed at sites 2 and 4 are correlated.

What would happen to the correlation if we used only one measurement per day? If, instead of plotting four data points for each day, we record an average speed for each day, the resulting scatterplot shows less variation, as Figure 14.19 shows. The correlation for these values increases to 0.844.

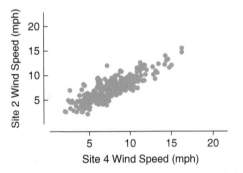

| Figure 14.19 Daily average wind speeds show less variation.

Let's average over an even longer time period. Figure 14.20 shows *monthly* averages for the year (plotted on the same scale). Now the correlation is 0.942.

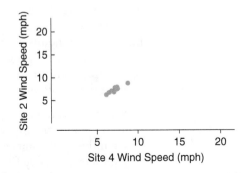

| Figure 14.20 Monthly averages are even less variable.

What these scatterplots show is that summary statistics exhibit less scatter than the data on individuals on which they're based and can give us a false impression of how well a line summarizes the data. There's no simple correction for this phenomenon. If we're given summary data, we usually can't get the original values back. You should be a bit suspicious of conclusions based on regressions of summary data. They may look better than they really are.

Another way to reduce the number of points in a data set is to select or sample points rather than average them. This can be especially important with data, such as the wind speeds, that are measured over time. For example, if instead of finding the *mean* for each day, we select just one of the four daily measurements—say the one made at noon on each day. We would have just as many points as in Figure 14.19, but the correlation is 0.730—essentially the same as for the full data. Figure 14.21 shows the relationship.

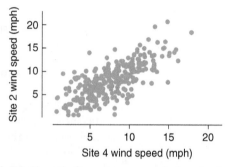

Figure 14.21 Selecting only the noon measurements doesn't reduce the variation. Compare this scatterplot to Figures 14.18 and 14.19.

*14.9 Linearity

Increasing gas prices and concern for the environment have lead to increased attention to automobile fuel efficiency. In the United States, this is measured in miles per gallon (mpg). The most important factor in fuel efficiency is the weight of the car.

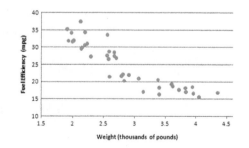

Figure 14.22 Fuel Efficiency (mpg) vs. Weight (thousands of pounds) shows a strong, apparently linear, negative trend.

The relationship is strong ($R^2 = 81.6\%$), clearly negative, and apparently linear. The regression equation

$$\widehat{Fuel\ Efficiency} = 48.7 - 8.4\ Weight$$

says that fuel efficiency drops by 8.4 mpg per 1000 pounds, starting from a value of 48.7 mpg. We check the **Linearity Condition** by plotting the residuals versus either the *x* variable or the predicted values.

The scatterplot of the residuals against *Weight* (Figure 14.23) holds a surprise. Residual plots should have no pattern, but this one has a bend. Look back at the original scatterplot. The scatter of points isn't really straight. There's a slight bend to the plot, but the bend is much easier to see in the residuals. That's because the linear trend, which is shown along with the curvature in the scatterplot, has been removed for the residual plot. It has the effect of magnifying the curvature.

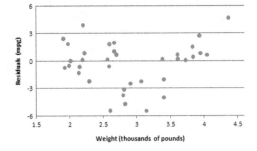

Figure 14.23 Plotting residuals against weight reveals a bend. The bend can be seen if you look carefully at the original scatterplot, but here it's easier to see.

When the relationship isn't straight, we shouldn't fit a regression or summarize the strength of the association with correlation. But often we can make the relationship straighter. All we have to do is re-express (or transform) one or both of the variables with a simple function. In this case, there's a natural function. As we mentioned, in the United States, automobile fuel efficiency is measured in miles per gallon. But in Canada and many other countries, things are different. Not only do we use metric measures, and thus kilometres and litres, but we measure fuel efficiency in litres per 100 kilometres. That's the *reciprocal* of miles per gallon (times a scale constant). That is, the gas amount (gallons or litres) is in the numerator, and the distance (miles or kilometres) is now in the denominator.

There's no reason to prefer one form or the other, so let's try the (negative) reciprocal form.

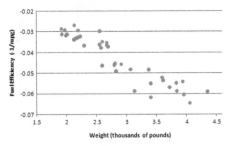

Figure 14.24 The reciprocal of Fuel Efficiency vs. Weight is straighter.

The residuals look better as well.

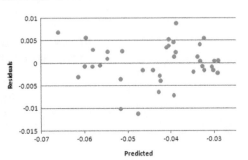

Figure 14.25 Residuals from the regression of Fuel Efficiency (−1/mpg) *on* Weight show less bend.

There's a clear improvement using the reciprocal, so we should use the reciprocal as the response in our regression model. (More information on how to transform variables effectively can be found in the optional topic Re-expressing Data, on MyStatLab.)

14.10 A Hypothesis Test for Correlation

We just tested whether the slope, β_1, was zero. To test it, we estimated the slope from the data and then, using its standard error and the t-distribution, measured how far the slope was from zero: $t = \dfrac{b_1 - 0}{SE(b_1)}$.

What if we wanted to test whether the *correlation* between x and y is zero? We write ρ for the parameter (true population value) of the correlation, so we're testing H_0: $\rho = 0$. Note that ρ is the Greek letter rho, the equivalent of the English r, which is the corresponding sample statistic. Be careful to write neatly and do not mistake ρ for p, which represents proportion, among other things.

Remember that the regression slope estimate is $b_1 = r\dfrac{s_y}{s_x}$. The same is true for the parameter versions of these statistics: $\beta_1 = \rho\dfrac{\sigma_y}{\sigma_x}$. That means that if the slope really is zero, then the correlation has to be zero, too. So if we test H_0: $\beta_1 = 0$, that's really the same as testing H_0: $\rho = 0$. Sometimes, however, a researcher might want to test correlation without fitting a regression, so you'll see the test of correlation as a separate test (it's also slightly more general), but the results are mathematically the same even though the form looks a little different. Here's the t-test for the correlation coefficient.

The *t*-Test for the Correlation Coefficient

When the conditions are met, we can test the hypotheses H_0: $\rho = 0$ vs. H_A: $\rho \neq 0$ using the test statistic:

$$t = r\sqrt{\frac{n-2}{1-r^2}}$$

which follows a Student's t-model with $n - 2$ degrees of freedom. We can use the t-model to find the P-value of the test.

One word of warning. When you read that a correlation is statistically significant, remember that it is just a test of whether or not the correlation is different from zero (just like zero or non-zero slope). It doesn't say anything about the strength of the association; it just means that some correlation is present. For example, suppose two variables have a correlation, $r = 0.08$, based on 1000 data values. Then $t = 0.08\sqrt{\dfrac{1000-2}{1-(0.08)^2}} = 2.54$. The P-value is less than 0.001. So the correlation of 0.08 is statistically significant but not practically significant.

14.11 ANOVA and the F-statistic

The term "simple regression" is something of a misnomer, especially the simple part. There are many aspects to linear regression: model specification, assumptions/conditions, least squares estimates, confidence interval and hypothesis test for the parameters (especially the slope), confidence intervals and prediction intervals for future values, and checking residuals for outliers, leverage, and influential points. The word "simple" doesn't mean easy, it means there is only one predictor variable, x. A better term would be "single regression." That's a big hint at what is to come in the next chapter, multiple regression, where we build models with more than one predictor variable.

The key question in simple regression is whether the slope is zero, and we developed a hypothesis test for $\beta_1 = 0$. If the null hypothesis is rejected it means that the predictor variable has a significant (i.e., real) relationship with the outcome variable. But this approach does not generalize perfectly in multiple regression, and so we will we need another approach, called **Analysis of Variance (ANOVA) for Regression**.

Since it is easier to understand in the simple regression situation we introduce it here and then use it to fuller advantage in Chapter 15.

To start with, you can think of this as another test for β_1. But instead of stating the test in terms of the parameter, we will restate it in terms of the model, in a very general way: Is the regression worthwhile? In other words, does the predictor variable contain useful information about the response variable?

Analysis of Variance for Regression

To answer this more general question, we will divide up and explain the sources of variation in the response variable. And that's why this approach is called "analysis of variance." It really should be called "analysis of variation" but nobody asked us!

Consider what variation means here. Ask yourself the question, "Why don't all the *y*-values equal the mean value of *x*?" The answer is twofold. First, some *y*-values have different *x*-values; and second, even if two *y*-values have the same *x*-value, there may be other variables, or simply random error, that explain the difference.

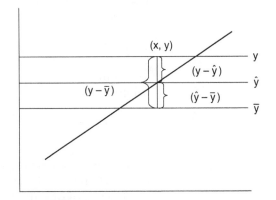

Figure 14.26 The point (*x,y*) is a typical point on the scatterplot. The vertical line from the point to the lowest horizontal line is the deviation—the distance from the actual *y* to the mean *y*. The height represented by the bracket on the left side of the vertical line is the sum of the heights represented by the two brackets on the right side of the vertical line. This demonstrates how the deviation is partitioned into two parts.

A residual, *e*, is the difference between an actual *y* and its predicted value, $\hat{y}$. That difference can be written as the sum of two parts: $y - \bar{y} = (\hat{y} - \bar{y}) + (y - \hat{y})$. We have "partitioned" the residual to correspond to the twofold answer above.

If we define "variation" as the square of a deviation (distance from a data value to its mean), then the total variation of *y* is defined as the sum of the squared deviations: $\sum (y - \bar{y})^2$. But this is also equal to $(n - 1)s_y^2$, so variation and variance are closely related; variation is $(n - 1)$ multiplied by variance.

Summing and squaring the left hand side of the equation: $y - \bar{y} = (\hat{y} - \bar{y}) + (y - \hat{y})$, gives the total variation $\sum (y - \bar{y})^2$. Let's sum and square the right hand side, using the algebraic expansion $(a + b)^2 = a^2 + b^2 + 2ab$ that you learned long ago.

A remarkable thing happens. The right hand side becomes $\sum (\hat{y} - \bar{y})^2 + \sum (y - \hat{y})^2$. What happened to the cross-product? It sums to zero. That's one of the great consequences of the decision we made long ago to define variance using squared differences from the mean rather than the absolute value of differences from the mean. (It's a tedious calculation, but not difficult; we won't bore you with it here.)

So we have an elegant partition of variation $\sum (y - \bar{y})^2 = \sum (\hat{y} - \bar{y})^2 + \sum (y - \hat{y})^2$, which can express in words and acronyms as:

Sum of Squares Total (SST) = Sum of Squares Model (SSM)
+ Sum of Squares Error (SSE)

In many books and software (including Excel), the words "Model" and "Error" are replaced by Regression and Residual, but then we can't distinguish between SSR (for Regression) and SSR (for Residual). So we prefer SSM and SSE.

Each of the sums of squares is associated with a number of degrees of freedom, and if you notice that $\text{SST} = \sum (y - \bar{y})^2 = (n-1)s_y^2$, and $\text{SSE} = \sum (y - \hat{y})^2 = \sum e^2 = (n-2)s_e^2$, you might have an idea of what the degrees of freedom are: $(n-1)$ for SST, and $(n-2)$ for SSE. What about SSM? That's the easy part—it's 1, the number of predictor variables, which, in a simple regression, is 1.

When we calculate the variance of sample data (think back to Chapter 5), we divide the total sum of squares by degrees of freedom $(n-1)$, giving the mean sum of squares. We can do the same thing for the other sums of squares, and we get:

Mean Square Model, $\text{MSM} = \dfrac{SSM}{1}$

Mean Square Error, $\text{MSE} = \dfrac{SSE}{(n-2)}$

We don't bother defining the Mean Square Total, MST, since we already have a name for it—the variance of y, s_y^2—and since we won't need it for the rest of the ANOVA table.

There's one more thing to compute, something called the F-statistic. More about that in a moment. But first, let's summarize all the previous calculations in an <u>A</u>nalysis of <u>V</u>ariance table. The underlined letters lead to the convenient and clever acronym ANOVA, coined by John Tukey of stem-and-leaf display and boxplot fame, among other things. Remember that he also coined the term "software."

ANOVA Table

Source of Variation	Sum of Squares	Degrees of Freedom	Mean Square	F-statistic
Model†	SSM	1	$MSM = \dfrac{SSM}{1}$	$F = \dfrac{MSM}{MSE}$
Error†	SSE	$n-2$	$MSE = \dfrac{SSE}{n-2}$	
Total	SST	$n-1$		

† Remember that "Model" means "variation explained by the regression model" and "Error" means "residual or leftover or unexplained variation due to other sources including random error."

The sharp-eyed among you might have already noticed that $MSE = \dfrac{SSE}{(n-2)} = s_e^2$, the key component in our earlier regression inference formulas.

Just as the z-statistic has a z-distribution, a t-statistic has a t-distribution and a chi-square statistic has a chi-square distribution, the F-statistic in the ANOVA table has an F-distribution. It is called F in honour of Sir Ronald Fisher, possibly the greatest statistician in the first half of the twentieth century.

$$F = \frac{MSM}{MSE} = \frac{(Explained)}{(Unexplained)}$$

The *F*-distribution is skewed (like the chi-square distribution), is anchored at 0 on the left end, and has two values of degrees of freedom, one corresponding to the numerator and the other corresponding to the denominator of the ratio that makes up the *F*-statistic.

The *F*-statistic is the ratio of explained and unexplained mean squares. So when we see a high value for the *F*-statistic, we know that a lot of the variability in the original data has been explained by the regression. In ANOVA tables from software, a P-value is also given, indicating whether the *F*-statistic is high enough to imply that the regression is significant overall. In other words: Is the regression worthwhile?

The null hypothesis is that the regression model predicts no better than the mean; that is, the model is not worthwhile. The alternative is that it does; that is, the model is worthwhile. If the null hypothesis were true, the *F*-statistic would be near 1.

The *F*-Test for Regression

When the conditions are met, we can test the hypotheses $H_0: \beta_1 = 0$ vs. $H_A: \beta_1 \neq 0$ using a test statistic called the **F-test for regression**:

$$F = \frac{MSM}{MSE}$$

which follows an *F*-model with 1 and $n - 2$ degrees of freedom. We can use the *F*-model to find the P-value of the test.

So now we have two test statistics to test whether $\beta_1 = 0$. It shouldn't surprise you that they have a close relationship. When the numerator degrees of freedom is 1, $F_{1,k} = t_k^2$, so the *t*-stat for testing $\beta_1 = 0$ is the square root of the *F*-stat for testing $\beta_1 = 0$.

R^2 revisited

In Chapter 6 we learned that R^2 is a measure of how much variation in our data is explained by the regression model, and that it is the square of the correlation, *r*. In other words, $r^2 = R^2$! There is another way to compute it:

$$R^2 = \frac{SSM}{SST} = \frac{(explained)}{(total)}$$

In other words, using an *F*-test to see whether the model is worthwhile is the same as testing whether the R^2 is different from zero. Rejecting either version of the hypothesis means the predictor accounts for enough variation in *y* to distinguish it from noise. It is a "worthwhile predictor."

Let's return to the Canada Goose case we discussed earlier. In the Guided Example the computer output for the regression was displayed as follows.

Predictor	Coefficient	SE(Coeff)	t-ratio	P-value
Intercept	−4.871	9.654	−0.50	0.6159
Time	4.200	0.2385	17.61	<0.0001

$S_e = 32.54$ R − sq = 84.5%

Here is the ANOVA Table for the same data.

Source of Variation	Sum of Squares	Degrees of Freedom	Mean Square	F-statistic
Model	328359.97	1	328359.97	310.11
Error	60354.45	57	1058.85	
Total	388714.42	58		

Notice three equivalences:

1. MSE = $1058.85 = (32.54)^2 = S_e^2$

2. SSM/SST = $328\,359.97/388\,714.42 = 0.845 = R^2$.

3. F-statistic = $310.11 = (17.61)^2 = $ (t-ratio for slope)^2

From software, the P-value for the F-statistic (with 1 and 57 degrees of freedom) is <0.0001, which must be the same as the P-value for the *t*-test of slope.

? WHAT CAN GO WRONG?

With inference, we've put numbers on our estimates and predictions, but these numbers are only as good as the model. Here are the main things to watch out for:

- **Don't fit a linear regression to data that aren't straight.** This is the most fundamental assumption. If the relationship between x and y isn't approximately linear, there's no sense in fitting a straight line to it.

- **Watch out for a changing spread.** The common part of confidence and prediction intervals is the estimate of the error standard deviation, the spread around the line. If it changes with x, the estimate won't make sense. Imagine making a prediction interval for these data:

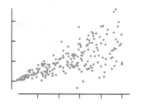

When x is small, we can predict y precisely, but as x gets larger, it's much harder to pin y down. Unfortunately, if the spread changes, the single value of s_e won't pick that up. The prediction interval will use the average spread around the line, with the result that we'll be too pessimistic about our precision for low x-values and too optimistic for high x-values. A re-expression of y is often a good fix for changing spread.

- **Watch out for non-Normal errors.** When we make a prediction interval for an individual y-value, the Central Limit Theorem can't come to our rescue. For us to believe the prediction interval, the errors must follow the Normal model. Check the histogram and Normal probability plot of the residuals to see if this assumption looks reasonable.

- **Watch out for one-tailed tests.** Because tests of hypotheses about regression coefficients are usually two-tailed, software packages report two-tailed P-values. If you are using that type of software to conduct a one-tailed test about the slope, you'll need to divide the reported P-value by two. However, the need to do this is very rare.

- **Beware of extrapolating.** Beware of extrapolation beyond the x-values that were used to fit the model. Although it's common to use linear models to extrapolate, be cautious.

(continued)

- **Beware of extrapolating far into the future.** Be especially cautious about extrapolating far into the future with linear models, especially when the x variable is time. A linear model assumes that changes over time will continue forever at the same rate you've observed in the past. Predicting the future is particularly tempting and particularly dangerous.

- **Look for unusual points.** Unusual points always deserve attention and may well reveal more about your data than the rest of the points combined. Always look for them and try to understand why they stand apart. Making a scatterplot of the data is a good way to reveal high-leverage and influential points. A scatterplot of the residuals against the predicted values is a good tool for finding points with large residuals.

- **Beware of high-leverage points, especially of those that are influential.** Influential points can alter the regression model a great deal. The resulting model may say more about one or two points than about the overall relationship.

- **Consider setting aside outliers and re-running the regression.** To see the impact of outliers on a regression, try running two regressions, one with and one without the extraordinary points, and then discuss the differences.

- **Treat unusual points honestly.** If you remove enough carefully selected points, you will eventually get a regression with a high R^2. But it won't get you very far. Some data are not simple enough for a linear model to fit very well. When that happens, report the failure and stop.

- **Significant correlation does not necessarily mean strong correlation.** A statistically significant correlation means the correlation is not zero. It doesn't say anything about the strength of the association.

- **Don't confuse sums of squares and mean squares.** The F-statistic is the ratio of mean squares (MSM to MSE), but R^2 is the ratio of sums of squares (SSM to SST). The numerators both come from the Model line of the ANOVA table but the denominators are from different lines.

ETHICS IN ACTION

Peter Teller/Photodisc/
Getty Images

The need for elder care businesses that offer companionship and non-medical home services is increasing as the Canadian population continues to age. One such franchise, Independent Elder Care, tries to set itself apart from its competitors by offering an additional service to prospective franchisees. In addition to standard information packets that provide tools, training, and mentorship opportunities, Independent Elder Care has an analyst on staff, Allen Ackman, to help prospective franchisees evaluate the feasibility of opening an elder care business in their area. Allen was contacted recently by Kyle Sennefeld, a recent business school graduate with a minor in gerontology, who is interested in starting a elder care franchise in southwestern Ontario. Allen decides to use a regression model that relates annual profit to the number of residents over the age of 65 that live within a 150-kilometre radius of a franchise location. Even though the

R^2 for this model is small, the variable is statistically significant, and the model is easy to explain to prospective franchisees. Allen sends Kyle a report that estimates the annual profit at Kyle's proposed location. Kyle was excited to see that opening an Independent Elder Care franchise in southwestern Ontario would be a good business decision.

ETHICAL ISSUE *The regression model has a small R^2, so its predictive ability is questionable. Related to ASA Ethical Guidelines, Items A and B, which can be found at http://www .amstat.org/about/ethicalguidelines.cfm.*

ETHICAL SOLUTION *Disclose the value of R^2 along with the prediction results and disclose if the regression is being used to extrapolate outside the range of x values. Allen should provide a prediction interval as well as an estimate of the profit. Because Kyle will be assessing his franchise's chances for profit from this interval, Allen should make sure it is a prediction interval and not a confidence interval for the mean profit at all similar locations.*

WHAT HAVE WE LEARNED?

In this chapter, we have extended our study of inference methods by applying them to regression models. We've found that the same methods we used for means—Student's *t*-models—work for regression in much the same way they did for means. And we've seen that although this makes the mechanics familiar, we need to check new conditions and be careful when describing the hypotheses we test and the confidence intervals we construct.

- We've learned that under certain assumptions, the sampling distribution for the slope of a regression line can be modelled by a Student's *t*-model with $n - 2$ degrees of freedom.

- We've learned to check four conditions before we proceed with inference. We've learned the importance of checking these conditions in order, and we've seen that most of the checks can be made by graphing the data and the residuals.

- We've learned to use the appropriate *t*-model to test a hypothesis about the slope. If the slope of our regression line is significantly different from zero, we have strong evidence that there is an association between the two variables.

- We've learned to use an alternative method, the *F*-model and ANOVA, for testing a hypothesis about slope. The *F*-test examines whether the model is worthwhile, and will be used for the more general situation of multiple regression in the next chapter. We've also seen another derivation of R^2, based on the ANOVA table calculations.

- We've learned to use the *t*-model to test for correlation when a linear regression is not available. It is equivalent to the *t*-model for slope, and a significant test means there is a linear association between the two variables.

We've also learned to create and interpret a confidence interval for the true slope. We've learned that there are many ways in which a data set may be unsuitable for a regression analysis:

- The **Linearity Condition** says that the relationship should be reasonably straight to fit a regression. Paradoxically, it may be easier to see that the relationship is not straight *after* you fit the regression and examine the residuals.

- The **Outlier Condition** refers to two ways in which cases can be extraordinary. They can have large residuals or high leverage (or, of course, both). Cases with either kind of extraordinary behavior can influence the regression model significantly.

Terms

Analysis for Variance (ANOVA) for regression

The total variation of *y* values from the mean is partitioned into sums of squares that represent explained and unexplained variation. Adjust the sums of squared by their degrees of freedom to get mean squares and compute the ratio of the mean square to get an *F*-statistic that assesses the worth of the model. It is an alternative to the *t*-test for regression slope. See *F*-test for regression, below.

Confidence interval for the regression slope

When the assumptions are satisfied, we can find a confidence interval for the slope parameter from $b_1 \pm t^*_{n-2} \times SE(b_1)$. The critical value, t^*_{n-2}, depends on the confidence interval specified and on the Student's *t*-model with $n - 2$ degrees of freedom.

Confidence interval for the predicted mean value	Different samples will give different estimates of the regression model and, so, different predicted values for the same value of x. We find a confidence interval for the mean of these predicted values at a specified x-value, x_ν, as

$$\hat{y}_\nu \pm t^*_{n-2} \times SE(\hat{\mu}_\nu)$$

where

$$SE(\hat{\mu}_\nu) = \sqrt{SE^2(b_1) \times (x_\nu - \bar{x})^2 + \frac{s_e^2}{n}}$$

The critical value, t^*_{n-2}, depends on the specified confidence level and the Student's t-model with $n - 2$ degrees of freedom.

Extrapolation	Although linear models provide an easy way to predict values of y for a given value of x, it is unsafe to predict for values of x far from the ones used to find the linear model equation. Be cautious when extrapolating.
F-test for regression	An alternative test of the null hypothesis of whether the slope is zero can also be thought of as a test of whether the regression model is worthwhile. It is based on a ratio of mean squares. To test $H_0: \beta_1 = 0$ use $F = \dfrac{MSM}{MSE}$ where MSM and MSE come from the ANOVA table. We find the P-value values from the F-model with 1 and $n - 2$ degrees of freedom.
Influential	If omitting a point from the data changes the regression model substantially, that point is considered influential.
Leverage	Data points whose x-values are far from the mean of x are said to exert leverage on a linear model. High-leverage points pull the line close to them, so they can have a large effect on the line, sometimes completely determining the slope and intercept. Points with high enough leverage can have deceptively small residuals.
Outlier	Any data point that stands away from the regression line by having a large residual is called an outlier.
Prediction interval for a future observation	A confidence interval for individual values. Prediction intervals are to observations as confidence intervals are to parameters. They predict the distribution of individual values, while confidence intervals specify likely values for a true parameter. The prediction interval takes the form

$$\hat{y}_\nu \pm t^*_{n-2} \times SE(\hat{y}_\nu)$$

where

$$SE(\hat{y}_\nu) = \sqrt{SE^2(b_1) \times (x_\nu - \bar{x})^2 + \frac{s_e^2}{n} + s_e^2}$$

The critical value, t^*_{n-2}, depends on the specified confidence level and the Student's t-model with $n - 2$ degrees of freedom. The extra s_e^2 in $SE(\hat{y}_\nu)$ makes the interval wider than the corresponding confidence interval for the mean.

Residual standard deviation	The measure, denoted s_e, of the spread of the data around the regression line:

$$s_e = \sqrt{\frac{\sum (y - \hat{y})^2}{n - 2}} = \sqrt{\frac{\sum e^2}{n - 2}}$$

t-test for the regression slope
The usual null hypothesis is that the true value of the slope is zero. The alternative is that it is not. A slope of zero indicates a complete lack of linear relationship between y and x.

To test $H_0: \beta_1 = 0$ we find

$$t = \frac{b_1 - 0}{SE(b_1)}$$

where $SE(b_1) = \dfrac{s_e}{s_x\sqrt{n-1}}$, $s_e = \sqrt{\dfrac{\sum(y - \hat{y})^2}{n-2}}$, n is the number of cases, and s_x is the standard deviation of the x-values. We find the P-value from the Student's t-model with $n - 2$ degrees of freedom.

Skills

PLAN

- Understand that the "true" regression line does not fit the population data perfectly, but rather is an idealized summary of that data.

- Know how to examine your data and a scatterplot of y vs. x for violations of assumptions that would make inference for regression unwise or invalid.

- Know how to examine displays of the residuals from a regression to double-check that the conditions required for regression have been met. In particular, know how to judge linearity and constant variance from a scatterplot of residuals against predicted values. Know how to judge Normality from a histogram and Normal probability plot.

- Remember to be especially careful to check for failures of the Independence Assumption when working with data recorded over time. To search for patterns, examine scatterplots both of x against time and of the residuals against time.

- Know the danger of extrapolating beyond the range of the x-values used to find the linear model, especially when the extrapolation tries to predict into the future.

- Understand that points can be unusual by having a large residual or by having high leverage.

- Understand that an influential point can change the slope and intercept of the regression line.

DO

- Know how to test the standard hypothesis that the true regression slope is zero. Be able to state the null and alternative hypotheses. Know where to find the relevant numbers in standard computer regression output.

- Be able to find a confidence interval for the slope of a regression based on the values reported in a standard regression output table.

- Know how to look for high-leverage and influential points by examining a scatterplot of the data. Know how to look for points with large residuals by examining a scatterplot of the residuals against the predicted values or against the x-variable. Understand how fitting a regression line with and without influential points can add to understanding of the regression model.

- Know how to look for high-leverage points by examining the distribution of the x-values or by recognizing them.

REPORT

- Be able to summarize a regression in words. In particular, be able to state the meaning of the true regression slope, the standard error of the estimated slope, and the standard deviation of the errors.

- Be able to interpret the P-value of the *t*-statistic for the slope to test the standard null hypothesis.
- Be able to interpret a confidence interval for the slope of a regression.
- Include diagnostic information such as plots of residuals and leverages as part of your report of a regression.
- Report any high-leverage points.
- Report any outliers. Consider reporting analyses with and without outliers included to assess their influence on the regression.
- Include appropriate cautions about extrapolation when reporting predictions from a linear model.
- Be able to test for zero correlation.
- Be able to interpret an ANOVA table and *F*-statistic in simple linear regression.

TECHNOLOGY HELP: Regression Analysis

All statistics packages make a table of results for a regression. These tables differ slightly from one package to another, but all are essentially the same. We've seen two examples of such tables already.

All packages offer analyses of the residuals. With some, you must request plots of the residuals as you request the regression. Others let you find the regression first and then analyze the residuals afterward. Either way, your analysis is not complete if you don't check the residuals with a histogram or Normal probability plot and a scatterplot of the residuals against *x* or the predicted values.

You should, of course, always look at the scatterplot of your two variables before computing a regression.

Regressions are almost always found with a computer or calculator. The calculations are too long to do conveniently by hand for data sets of any reasonable size. No matter how the regression is computed, the results are usually presented in a table that has a standard form. Here's a portion of a typical regression results table, along with annotations showing where the numbers come from.

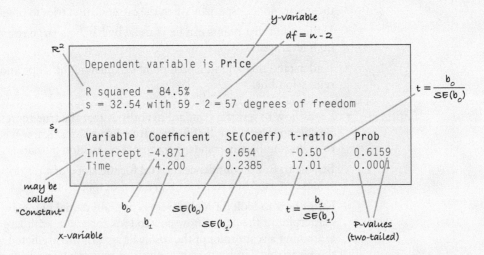

The regression table gives the coefficients (once you find them in the middle of all this other information). This regression predicts *Price* from *Time*. The regression equation is

$$\widehat{Price} = -4.871 + 4.200\,Time$$

and the R^2 for the regression is 84.5%.

The column of *t*-ratios gives the test statistics for the respective null hypotheses that the true values of the coefficients are zero. The corresponding P-values are also usually reported.

EXCEL

- In Excel 2003 and earlier, select **Data Analysis** from the **Tools** menu. In Excel 2007, select **Data Analysis** from the **Analysis Group** on the Data Tab.
- Select Regression from the **Analysis Tools** list.
- Click the **OK** button.
- Enter the data range holding the Y-variable in the box labelled "Y-range."
- Enter the range of cells holding the X-variable in the box labelled "X-range."
- Select the **New Worksheet Ply** option.
- Select **Residuals** options. Click the **OK** button.

Comments

The Y and X ranges do not need to be in the same rows of the spreadsheet, although they must cover the same number of cells. But it is a good idea to arrange your data in parallel columns as in a data table.

Although the dialogue offers a Normal probability plot of the residuals, the data analysis add-in does not make a correct probability plot, so don't use this option.

MINI CASE STUDY PROJECTS

Left: Larry Crowe/AP Images,
Right: Evlakhov Valeriy/Shutterstock

Frozen Pizza

The product manager at a major food distributor is interested in learning how sensitive sales are to changes in the unit price of a frozen pizza in Winnipeg, Edmonton, Toronto, and Calgary. The product manager has been provided data on both *Price* and *Sales* volume every fourth week over a period of nearly four years for the four cities (**ch14_MCSP_Frozen_Pizza.xlsx**).

Examine the relationship between *Price* and *Sales* for each city. Be sure to discuss the nature and validity of this relationship. Is it linear? Is it negative? Is it significant? Are the conditions of regression met? Some individuals in the product manager's division suspect that frozen pizza sales are more sensitive to price in some cities than in others. Is there any evidence to suggest that? Write up a short report on what you find. Include 95% confidence intervals for the mean *Sales* if the *Price* is $2.50 and discuss how that interval changes if the *Price* is $3.50.

Global Warming?

Every spring, Nenana, Alaska, hosts a contest in which participants try to guess the exact minute that a wooden tripod placed on the frozen Tanana River will fall through the breaking ice. The contest started in 1917 as a diversion for railroad engineers, with a jackpot of $800 for the closest guess. It has grown into an event in which hundreds of thousands of entrants enter their guesses on the Internet and vie for more than $300 000.

Because so much money and interest depends on the time of the ice breakup, it has been recorded to the nearest minute with great accuracy ever since 1917 (**ch14_MCSP_Global_Warming.xls**). And because a standard measure of breakup has been used throughout this time, the data are consistent. An article in *Science* ("Climate Change in Nontraditional Data Sets," *Science* 294, October 2001) used the data to investigate global warming. Researchers are interested in the following questions. What is the rate of change in the date of breakup over time (if any)? If the ice is breaking up earlier, what is your conclusion? Does this necessarily suggest global warming? What could be other reasons for this trend? What is the predicted breakup date for the year 2015? (Be sure to include an appropriate prediction or confidence interval.) Write up a short report with your answers.

EXERCISES

⊤ **1. Marriage age 2008.** Weddings are one of the fastest growing businesses; about $4 billion is spent on weddings in Canada each year. But demographics may be changing, and this could affect wedding retailers' marketing plans. Is there evidence that the age at which women get married has changed over the past 100 years? The graph shows the trend in age at first marriage for Canadian women. (www4.hrsdc.gc.ca) **LO❶**

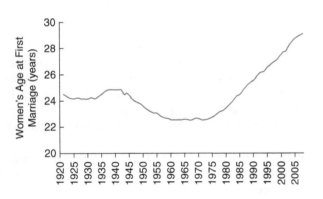

a) Do you think there is a clear pattern? Describe the trend.
b) Is the association strong?
c) Is the correlation high? Explain.
d) Do you think a linear model is appropriate for these data? Explain.

⊤ **2. Smoking 2011.** The Canadian Tobacco Use Monitoring Survey (CTUMS) was developed in 1999 by Health Canada and Statistics Canada to provide timely, reliable, and continual data on tobacco use and related issues. Before 1999, smoking behaviour was assessed by Statistics Canada's General Social Survey and the National Population Health Survey. CTUMS revealed that the overall current smoking rate among Canadians aged 15 years and older declined from 25% in 1999 to 17% in 2011. Among 20–24 year olds, the rate declined from 35% to 21%. How has the percentage of 20–24 year olds who smoke changed since the danger became clear during the last half of the twentieth century? The following scatterplot shows percentages of smokers among all Canadians 20–24 years of age, as estimated by surveys from 1965 to 2011 (http://www.hc-sc.gc.ca/hc-ps/tobac-tabac/research-recherche/stat/ctums-esutc_2011-eng.php. **LO❶**

a) Do you think there is a clear pattern? Describe the trend.
b) Is the association strong?
c) Is a linear model appropriate for these data? Explain.

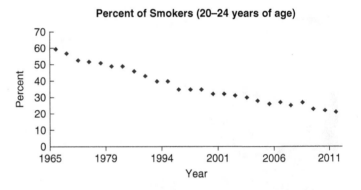

⊤ **3. Human Development Index.** The United Nations Development Programme (UNDP) collects data in the developing world to help countries solve global and national development challenges. In the UNDP annual Human Development Report, you can find data on over 100 variables for each of 177 countries worldwide. One summary measure used by the agency is the Human Development Index (HDI), which attempts to summarize in a single number the progress in health, education, and economics of a country. In 2006, the HDI was as high as 0.965 for Norway and as low as 0.331 for Niger. The gross domestic product per capita (GDPPC), by contrast, is often used to summarize the *overall* economic strength of a country. Is the HDI related to the GDPPC? Here is a scatterplot of *HDI* against *GDPPC*. **LO❶**

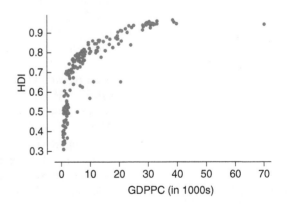

a) Explain why fitting a linear model to these data would be misleading.

b) If you fit a linear model to the data, what do you think a scatterplot of residuals versus predicted *HDI* will look like?

c) There is an outlier (Luxembourg) with a *GDPPC* of around $70 000. Will setting this point aside improve the model substantially? Explain.

T 4. HDI, part 2. The United Nations Development Programme (UNDP) uses the Human Development Index (HDI) in an attempt to summarize in one number the progress in health, education, and economics of a country. The number of cell phone subscribers per 1000 people is positively associated with economic progress in a country. Can the number of cell phone subscribers be used to predict the HDI? Here is a scatterplot of HDI against cell phone subscribers: **LO❶**

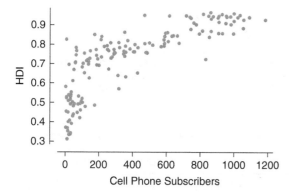

a) Explain why fitting a linear model to these data might be misleading.

b) If you fit a linear model to the data, what do you think a scatterplot of residuals versus predicted *HDI* will look like?

5. Good model? In justifying his choice of a model, a consultant says "I know this is the correct model because $R^2 = 99.4\%$." **LO❶**

a) Is this reasoning correct? Explain.

b) Does this model allow the consultant to make accurate predictions? Explain.

6. Bad model? An intern who has created a linear model is disappointed to find that her R^2 value is a very low 13%.

a) Does this mean that a linear model is not appropriate? Explain.

b) Does this model allow the intern to make accurate predictions? Explain. **LO❶**

T 7. Online shopping. Several studies have found that the frequency with which shoppers browse internet retailers is related to the frequency with which they actually purchase products and/or services online. Here are data showing the age of respondents and their answer to the question "how many minutes do you browse online retailers per week?" **LO❶, LO❹**

Age	Browsing Time (min/wk)
22	492
50	186
44	180
32	384
55	120
60	120
38	276
22	480
21	510
45	252
52	126
33	360
19	570
17	588
21	498

a) Make a scatterplot for these data.

b) Do you think a linear model is appropriate? Explain.

c) Find the equation of the regression line.

d) Check the residuals to see if the conditions for inference are met.

T 8. El Niño. Concern over the weather associated with El Niño has increased interest in the possibility that the climate on Earth is getting warmer. The most common theory relates an increase in atmospheric levels of carbon dioxide (CO_2), a greenhouse gas, to increases in temperature. Here is part of a regression analysis of the mean annual CO_2 concentration in the atmosphere, measured in parts per thousand (ppt), at the top of Mauna Loa in Hawaii and the mean annual air temperature over both land and sea across the globe, in degrees Celsius. The scatterplots and residuals plots indicated that the data were appropriate for inference and the response variable is *Temp*. **LO❷, LO❾**

Variable	Coefficient	SE(Coeff)
Intercept	16.4328	0.0557
CO_2	0.0405	0.0116

R squared = 25.8%

s = 0.0854 with 37 − 2 = 35 degrees of freedom

a) Write the equation of the regression line.

b) Find the value of the correlation and test whether the true correlation is zero. Is there evidence of an association between CO_2 level and global temperature?

c) Find the *t*-value and P-value for the slope. Is there evidence of an association between CO_2 level and global temperature? What do you know from the slope and *t*-test that you might not have known from testing the correlation?

d) Do you think predictions made by this regression will be very accurate? Explain.

9. Movie budgets. How does the cost of a movie depend on its length? Data on the cost (millions of dollars) and the running time (minutes) for major release films of 2005 are summarized in these plots and computer output: **LO②**

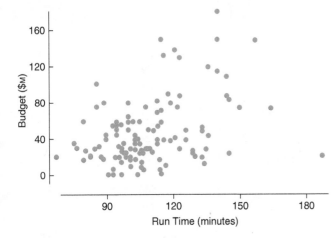

Dependent variable is: Budget($M)
R squared = 15.4%
s = 32.95 with 120 − 2 = 118 degrees of freedom

Variable	Coefficient	SE(Coeff)	t-ratio	P-value
Intercept	−31.39	17.12	−1.83	0.0693
Run Time	0.71	0.15	4.64	≤0.0001

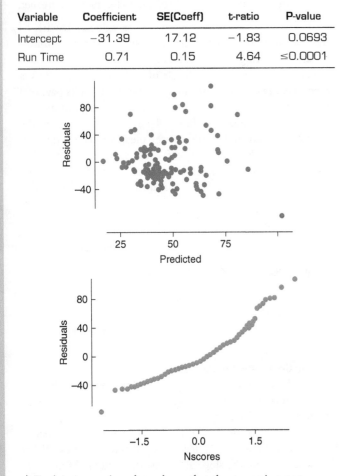

a) Explain in words and numbers what the regression says.
b) The intercept is negative. Discuss its value, taking note of the P-value.

c) The output reports $s = 32.95$. Explain what that means in this context.
d) What's the value of the standard error of the slope of the regression line?
e) Explain what that means in this context.

10. House prices. How does the price of a house depend on its size? Data on 1064 randomly selected houses that had been sold include data on price ($1000s) and size (1000s ft²), producing the following graphs and computer output: **LO②**

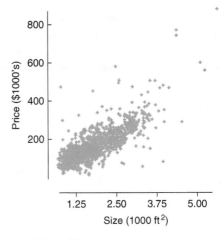

Dependent variable is: Price
R squared = 59.5%
s = 53.79 with 1064 − 2 = 1062 degrees of freedom

Variable	Coefficient	SE(Coeff)	t-ratio	P-value
Intercept	−3.1169	4.688	−0.665	0.5063
Size	94.4539	2.393	39.465	≤0.0001

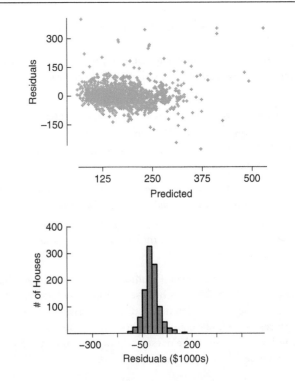

a) Explain in words and numbers what the regression says.

b) The intercept is negative. Discuss its value, taking note of its P-value.

c) The output reports $s = 53.79$. Explain what that means in this context.

d) What's the value of the standard error of the slope of the regression line?

e) Explain what that means in this context.

T 11. Movie budgets: the sequel. Exercise 9 shows computer output examining the association between the length of a movie and its cost. LO❸

a) Check the assumptions and conditions for inference.

b) Find a 95% confidence interval for the slope and interpret it.

T 12. Second home. Exercise 10 shows computer output examining the association between the sizes of houses and their sale prices. LO❸

a) Check the assumptions and conditions for inference.

b) Find a 95% confidence interval for the slope and interpret it.

T 13. Water hardness. In an investigation of environmental causes of disease, data were collected on the annual mortality rate (deaths per 100 000) for males in 61 large towns in England and Wales. In addition, the water hardness was recorded as the calcium concentration (parts per million, or ppm) in the drinking water. Here are the scatterplot and regression analysis of the relationship between mortality and calcium concentration, where the dependent variable is *Mortality*. LO❷, LO❸

Variable	Coefficient	SE(Coeff)
Intercept	1676.36	29.30
Calcium	-3.226	0.485

R squared = 42.9%
s = 143.0 with 61 − 2 = 59 degrees of freedom

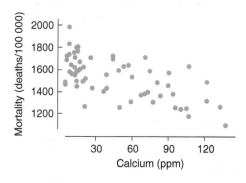

a) Is there an association between the hardness of the water and the mortality rate? Write the appropriate hypothesis.

b) Assuming the assumptions for regression inference are met, what do you conclude?

c) Create a 95% confidence interval for the slope of the true line relating calcium concentration and mortality.

d) Interpret your interval in context.

T 14. Mutual funds. A recent issue of *Consumer Reports* listed the rate of return for several large cap mutual funds over the previous 3-year and 5-year periods. (Here, "large cap" refers to companies worth over $10 billion.) It's common for advertisements to carry the disclaimer that "past returns may not be indicative of future performance." Do these data indicate that there was an association between 3-year and 5-year rates of return? LO❹

	Annualized Returns (%)	
Fund Name	**3-year**	**5-year**
Ameristock	7.9	17.1
Clipper	14.1	18.2
Credit Suisse Strategic Value	5.5	11.5
Dodge & Cox Stock	15.2	15.7
Excelsior Value	13.1	16.4
Harbor Large Cap Value	6.3	11.5
ICAP Discretionary Equity	6.6	11.4
ICAP Equity	7.6	12.4
Neuberger Berman Focus	9.8	13.2
PBHG Large Cap Value	10.7	18.1
Pelican	7.7	12.1
Price Equity Income	6.1	10.9
USAA Cornerstone Strategy	2.5	4.9
Vanguard Equity Income	3.5	11.3
Vanguard Windsor	11.0	11.0

T 15. Youth unemployment. The United Nations has developed a set of millennium goals for countries, and the United Nations Statistics Division (UNSD) maintains databases to measure economic progress toward these goals (unstats.un.org/unsd/mdg). Data extracted from this source are on MyStatLab. One measure that is tracked is the youth (ages 15–24) unemployment rate in different countries. Is the unemployment rate for the male youth related to the unemployment rate for the female youth? LO❹, LO❺

a) Find a regression model predicting *Male Rate* from the *Female Rate* in 2005 for the sample of 57 countries provided by UNSD.

b) Examine the residuals to determine if a linear regression is appropriate.

c) Test an appropriate hypothesis to determine if the association is significant.

d) What percentage of the variability in the *Male Rate* is accounted for by the regression model?

T 16. Male unemployment. Using the unemployment data provided by the United Nations, investigate the association between the male unemployment rate in 2004 and 2005 for a sample of 52 countries. (The sample is smaller than in Exercise 15, since not all countries reported rates in both years.) LO❹, LO❺

a) Find a regression model predicting the *2005-Male* rate from the *2004-Male* rate.

b) Examine the residuals to determine if a linear regression is appropriate.

c) Test an appropriate hypothesis to determine if the association is significant.

d) What percentage of the variability in the *2005-Male* rate is accounted for by the *regression model*?

17. Unusual points. Each of the four scatterplots a–d that follow shows a cluster of points and one "stray" point. For each, answer questions 1–4:   LO**6**

1) In what way is the point unusual? Does it have high leverage, a large residual, or both?

2) Do you think that point is an influential point?

3) If that point were removed from the data, would the correlation become stronger or weaker? Explain.

4) If that point were removed from the data, would the slope of the regression line increase, decrease, or remain the same? Explain.

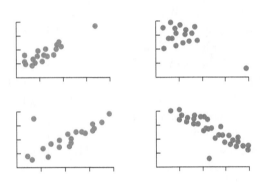

18. More unusual points. Each of the following scatterplots a–d shows a cluster of points and one "stray" point. For each, answer questions 1–4:   LO**6**

1) In what way is the point unusual? Does it have high leverage, a large residual, or both?

2) Do you think that point is an influential point?

3) If that point were removed from the data, would the correlation become stronger or weaker? Explain.

4) If that point were removed from the data, would the slope of the regression line increase, decrease, or remain the same? Explain.

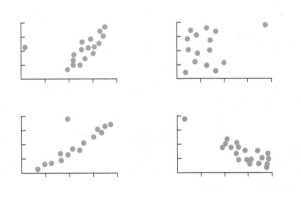

19. The extra point. The scatterplot shows five blue data points at the left. Not surprisingly, the correlation for these points is $r = 0$. Suppose *one* additional data point is added at one of the five positions suggested below in green. Match each point (a–e) with the correct new correlation from the list given.   LO**6**

1) −0.90
2) −0.40
3) 0.00
4) 0.05
5) 0.75

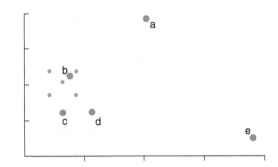

20. The extra point, part 2. The original five points in Exercise 19 produce a regression line with slope 0. Match each of the green points (a–e) with the slope of the line after that one point is added: LO**6**

1) −0.45
2) −0.30
3) 0.00
4) 0.05
5) 0.85

21. What's the cause? A researcher gathering data for a pharmaceutical firm measures blood pressure and the percentage of body fat for several adult males and finds a strong positive association. Describe three different possible cause-and-effect relationships that might be present.   LO**7**

22. What's the effect? Published reports about violence in computer games have become a concern to developers and distributors of these games. One firm commissioned a study of violent behaviour in elementary-school children. The researcher asked the children's parents how much time each child spent playing computer games and had their teachers rate each child's level of aggressiveness when playing with other children. The researcher found a moderately strong positive correlation between computer game time and aggressiveness score. But does this mean that playing computer games increases aggression in children? Describe three different possible cause-and-effect explanations for this relationship.   LO**7**

T 23. Used cars. Classified ads in a newspaper offered several used Toyota Corollas for sale. Listed below are the ages of the cars and the advertised prices.   LO**4**, LO**5**

Age (yr)	Prices Advertised ($)
1	13 990
1	13 495
3	12 999
4	9 500
4	10 495
5	8 995
5	9 495
6	6 999
7	6 950
7	7 850
8	6 999
8	5 995
10	4 950
10	4 495
13	2 850

a) Make a scatterplot for these data.
b) Do you think a linear model is appropriate? Explain.
c) Find the equation of the regression line.
d) Check the residuals to see if the conditions for inference are met.

24. Property assessments. The following software outputs provide information about the size (in square feet) of 18 homes, and the city's assessed value of those homes, where the response variable is *Assessment*. **LO②**

Predictor	Coefficient	SE(Coeff)	t-ratio	P-value
Intercept	37108.85	8664.33	4.28	0.0006
Size	11.90	4.29	2.77	0.0136

s = 4682.10   R-Sq = 32.5%

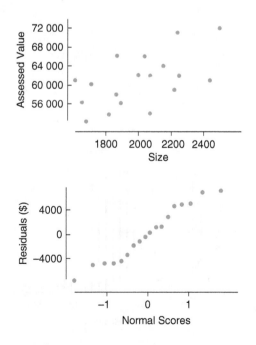

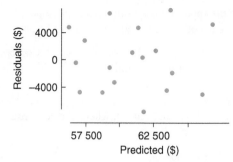

a) Explain why inference for linear regression is appropriate with these data.
b) Is there a significant linear association between the *Size* of a home and its *Assessment*? Test an appropriate hypothesis and state your conclusion.
c) What percentage of the variability in assessed value is accounted for by this regression?
d) Give a 90% confidence interval for the slope of the true regression line, and explain its meaning in the proper context.
e) From this analysis, can we conclude that adding a room to your house will increase its assessed value? Why or why not?
f) The owner of a home measuring 2100 square feet files an appeal, claiming that the $70 200 assessed value is too high. Do you agree? Explain your reasoning.

25. Used cars, again. Based on the analysis of used car prices you did for Exercise 23, if appropriate, create a 95% confidence interval for the slope of the regression line and explain what your interval means in context. **LO③**

26. Assets and sales. A business analyst is looking at a company's assets and sales to determine the relationship (if any) between the two measures. She has data (in $million) from a random sample of 79 Fortune 500 companies, and obtained the linear regression below: **LO③**

The regression equation is Assets = 1867.4 + 0.975 Sales

Predictor	Coefficient	SE(Coeff)	t-ratio	P-value
Constant	1867.4	804.5	2.32	0.0230
Sales	0.975	0.099	9.84	≤0.0001

s = 6132.59   R-Sq = 55.7%   R-Sq(adj) = 55.1%

Use the data provided to find a 95% confidence interval, if appropriate, for the slope of the regression line and interpret your interval in context.

27. Fuel economy. A consumer organization has reported test data for 50 car models. We will examine the association between the weight of the car (in thousands of pounds) and the fuel efficiency (in miles per gallon). Use the data provided MyStatLab to answer the following questions, where the response variable is *Fuel Efficiency* (mpg). **LO④**

a) Create the scatterplot and obtain the regression equation.
b) Are the assumptions for regression satisfied?

c) Write the appropriate hypotheses for the slope.

d) Test the hypotheses and state your conclusion.

28. Consumer Reports. In a recent issue of, *Consumer Reports* listed the price (in dollars) and power (in cold cranking amps) of auto batteries. We want to know if more expensive batteries are generally better in terms of starting power. Here are the regression and residual output, where the response variable is *Power*.   LO❷, LO❸, LO❺

Dependent variable is: Power

R squared = 25.2%

s = 116.0 with 33 − 2 = 31 degrees of freedom

Variable	Coefficient	SE(Coeff)	t-ratio	P-value
Intercept	384.594	93.55	4.11	0.0003
Cost	4.146	1.282	3.23	0.0029

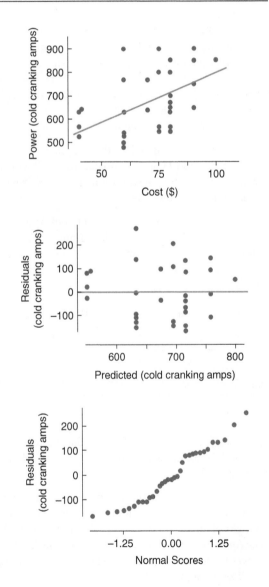

a) How many batteries were tested?

b) Are the conditions for inference satisfied? Explain.

c) Is there evidence of a linear association between the cost and cranking power of auto batteries? Test an appropriate hypothesis and state your conclusion.

d) Is the association strong? Explain.

e) What is the equation of the regression line?

f) Create a 90% confidence interval for the slope of the true line.

g) Interpret your interval in this context.

T 29. SAT scores. How strong was the association between student scores on the Math and Verbal sections of the old SAT? Scores on this exam ranged from 200 to 800 and were widely used by U.S. college admissions offices. Here are summary statistics, regression analysis, and plots of the scores for a graduating class of 162 high school students, where the response variable is *Math Score*.   LO❷, LO❺

Predictor	Coefficient	SE(Coeff)	t-ratio	P-value
Intercept	209.55	34.35	6.10	<0.0001
Verbal	0.675	0.057	11.88	<0.0001

s = 71.75   R-Sq = 46.9%

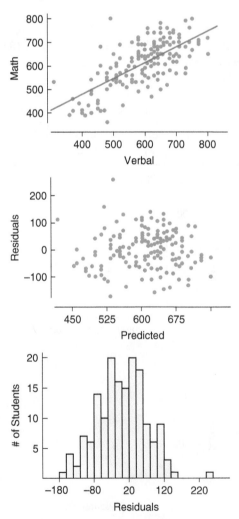

a) Is there evidence of a linear association between *Math* and *Verbal* scores? Write an appropriate hypothesis.
b) Discuss the assumptions for inference.
c) Test your hypothesis and state an appropriate conclusion.

T 30. **Productivity.** How strong is the association between labour productivity and labour costs? Statistics Canada provides seasonally adjusted quarterly indexes of labour productivity and related variables, using 2007 index values as the base year (i.e., 2007 = 100) by industry based on the North American Industry Classification System (NAICS). Data for labour productivity and unit labour costs across 18 industries, from the fourth quarter of 2012, are used to examine this relationship (CANSIM Table 383–0012). Here are the results of a regression analysis where the response variable is *Labour Productivity*. **LO❷**

Predictor	Coefficient	SE(Coeff)	t-ratio	P-value
Intercept	178.40	11.63	15.34	<0.0001
Unit Labour Cost	−0.679	0.101	−6.70	<0.0001

s = 14.39   R-Sq = 73.7%

a) Is there evidence of a linear association between *Labour Productivity* and Unit Labour Costs? Write appropriate hypotheses.
b) Test your null hypothesis and state an appropriate conclusion (assume that assumptions and conditions are met).

T 31. **Football salaries.** Football owners are constantly in competition for good players. The better the winning percentage, the more likely that the team will provide good business returns for the owners. Of course, the resources that each of the 32 teams has in the National Football League (NFL) vary. Does the size of the payroll matter? Here is a scatterplot and regression showing the association between team salaries in the NFL in 2006 and winning percentage. **LO❷**

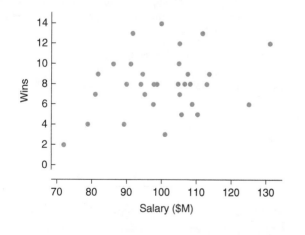

Predictor	Coefficient	SE(Coeff)	t-ratio	P-value
Intercept	1.783	3.964	0.45	0.6560
Salary ($M)	0.062	0.039	1.58	0.1244

s = 2.82   R-Sq = 7.7%

a) State the hypotheses about the slope.
b) Perform the hypothesis test and state your conclusion in context.

T 32. **Beer sales.** According to Statistics Canada, beer's market share of consumption of alcoholic beverages in our country fell from 50% in 2002 to 44% in 2012 while wine's market share grew from 24% to 31% over that same period. Spirits' market share stayed the same at about 25%. They report that "beer remained the alcoholic drink of choice for Canadians, but preferences are changing." However, Canadians are not drinking less; total sales of beer, wine, and spirits in 2012 compared with the previous year were up in total dollar value (to $20.9 billion) and in total volume (to 233 million litres). Using annual per capita volume of beer sales (in litres) from 1989 through 2012, we carried out a regression to examine whether there has been a consistent change over time. Assume that the conditions for inference are satisfied and that the response variable is *Per Capita Volume*. **LO❷**

Predictor	Coefficient	SE(Coeff)	t-ratio	P-value
Intercept	1195.413	170.945	6.99	0.0001
Year	−0.5544	0.0855	−6.49	0.0001

s = 2.90   R-Sq = 65.7%

a) State the hypotheses about the slope (both numerically and in words) that describes how per capita volume of beer sales has changed over time.
b) Assuming that the assumptions for inference are satisfied, perform the hypothesis test and state your conclusion.
c) Examine the scatterplot corresponding to the regression of *Per Capita Volume*. How does it change your opinion of the trend in beer sales? Is a linear regression the appropriate model to use here? What aspects of the scatterplot are noteworthy?

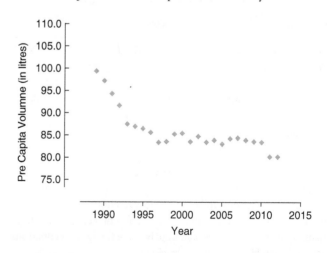

T 33. **Fuel economy, part 2.** Consider again the data in Exercise 27 about the fuel economy and weights of cars. **LO❸**
a) Create a 95% confidence interval for the slope of the regression line.
b) Explain in this context what your confidence interval means.

34. SAT scores, part 2. Consider the high school SAT scores data from Exercise 29. LO❸

a) Find a 90% confidence interval for the slope of the true line describing the association between Math and Verbal scores.

b) Explain in this context what your confidence interval means.

35. Mutual funds. It is common economic theory that the money flowing into and out of mutual funds (fund flows) is related to the performance of the stock market. Another way of stating this is that investors are more likely to place money into mutual funds when the market is performing well. One way to measure market performance is the Wilshire 5000 Total Market Return (%), which is a value-weighted return. (The return of each stock in the index is weighted by its percent of market value for all stocks.) Here are the scatterplot and regression analysis, where the response variable is *Fund Flows* ($ million) and the explanatory variable is *Market Return* (%), using data from January 1990 to October 2002. LO❷

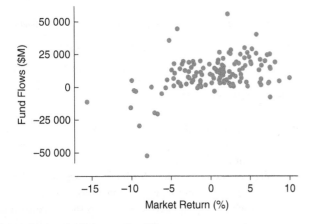

Dependent variable is: Fund Flows
R squared = 17.9%
s = 10999 with 154 − 2 = 152 degrees of freedom

Variable	Coefficient	SE(Coeff)	t-ratio	P-value
Intercept	9599.10	896.9	10.7	≤ 0.0001
Market Return	1156.40	201.1	5.75	≤ 0.0001

a) State the null and alternative hypotheses under investigation.

b) Assuming that the assumptions for regression inference are reasonable, test the hypothesis.

c) State your conclusion.

36. Marketing managers. Are wages for various marketing managerial positions related? One way to determine this is to examine the relationship between the mean hourly wages for two managerial occupations in marketing: sales managers and advertising managers. The average hourly wage for both occupations are analyzed. Here are the regression analysis results. LO❷

Predictor	Coefficient	SE(Coeff)	t-ratio	P-value
Constant	10.317	4.382	2.35	0.0227
Sales Mgr Avg Hourly Wage	0.56349	0.09786	5.76	< 0.0001

a) State the null and alternative hypothesis under investigation.

b) Assuming that the assumptions for regression inference are reasonable, test the null hypothesis.

c) State your conclusion.

37. Cost index. Recall the *Worldwide Cost of Living Survey* from Chapter 6 that determined the cost of living in the most expensive cities in the world as an index. This index scales New York City as 100 and expresses the cost of living in other cities as a percentage of the New York cost. For example, in 2007 the cost of living index in Tokyo was 122.1, which means that it was 22% higher than New York. The output shows the regression of the 2006 on the 2007 index for the most expensive cities in 2007, where *Index 2007* is the response variable. A recent update: In 2012, Vancouver rose to 21st in the world and the highest in North America–a dubious honour! LO❷

Predictor	Coefficient	SE(Coeff)	t-ratio	P-value
Intercept	12.02	12.25	0.98	0.3446
Index 2006	0.943	0.115	8.17	< 0.0001

s = 4.45   R-Sq = 83.7%

a) State the hypotheses about the slope (both numerically and in words).

b) Perform the hypothesis test and state your conclusion in context.

c) Explain what the *R*-squared in this regression means.

d) Do these results indicate that, in general, cities with a higher index in 2006 will also have a higher index in 2007? Explain.

38. Job growth. *Fortune* Magazine publishes the top 100 companies to work for every year. Among the information listed is the percentage growth in jobs at each company. The output below shows the regression of the 2008 job growth (%) on the 2006 job growth for a sample of 29 companies. Note that *Job Growth 2008* is the response variable. (money.cnn.com/magazines/fortune/bestcompanies/full_list; accessed May, 2008). LO❷

Dependent variable is: Job Growth 2008
R squared = 25.6%   R squared (adjusted) = 22.9%
s = 6.129 with 29 − 2 = 27 degrees of freedom

Variable	Coefficient	SE(Coeff)	t-ratio	P-value
Intercept	2.993	1.441	2.08	0.0475
Job Growth 2006	0.399	0.131	3.05	0.0051

a) State the hypotheses about the slope (both numerically and in words).

b) Assuming that the assumptions for inference are satisfied, perform the hypothesis test and state your conclusion in context.

c) Explain what the *R*-squared in this regression means.

d) Do these results indicate that, in general, companies with a higher job growth in 2006 will also have a higher job growth in 2008? Explain.

39. Oil prices. The Organization of Petroleum Exporting Countries (OPEC) is a cartel, so it artificially sets prices. But are prices related to production? Using the data provided on MyStatLab for crude oil prices ($/barrel) and oil production (thousand barrels per day) between 2001 and 2007, answer the following questions. Use the *Crude price* as the response variable and *Production* as the predictor variable. **LO❹**

a) Examine a scatterplot for the two variables and test the conditions for regression.

b) Do you think there is a linear association between oil prices and production? Explain.

40. NHL attendance 2011–2012. Traditionally, athletic teams that perform better grow their fan base and generate greater attendance at games or matches. This should hold true regardless of the sport—whether it's soccer, football, baseball, or hockey. Data on the number of points and home attendance for the 30 teams in the 2011–2012 National Hockey League season are provided. Use *Home Attendance* as the dependent variable and *Points* as the explanatory variable to answer the following questions. **LO❹**

a) Examine a scatterplot for the two variables and test the conditions for regression.

b) Do you think there is a linear association between *Home Attendance* and *Points*? Explain.

41. Printers. In March 2002, *Consumer Reports* reviewed several models of inkjet printers. The following table shows the speed of the printer (in pages per minute) and the cost per page printed. Is there evidence of an association between *Speed* and *Cost*? Test an appropriate hypothesis and state your conclusion. **LO❹**

Speed (ppm)	Cost (cents/page)
4.6	12.0
5.5	8.5
4.5	6.2
3.8	3.4
4.6	2.6
3.7	4.0
4.7	5.8
4.7	8.1
4.0	9.4
3.1	14.9
1.9	2.6
2.2	4.3
1.8	4.6
2.0	14.8
2.0	4.4

42. Product testing. Ads for a video claimed that the techniques shown would improve the performances of Little League pitchers. To test this claim, 20 Little Leaguers threw 50 pitches each, and we recorded the number of strikes. After the players participated

in the training program, we repeated the test. The following table shows the number of strikes each player threw before and after the training. A test of paired differences failed to show that this training was effective in improving a player's ability to throw strikes. Is there any evidence that the *Effectiveness (After−Before)* of the video depends on the player's *Initial Ability (Before)* to throw strikes? Test an appropriate hypothesis and state your conclusion. Propose an explanation for what you find. **LO❹**

\multicolumn{4}{c}{Number of Strikes (out of 50)}
Before	**After**	**Before**	**After**
28	35	33	33
29	36	33	35
30	32	34	32
32	28	34	30
32	30	34	33
32	31	35	34
32	32	36	37
32	34	36	33
32	35	37	35
33	36	37	32

43. Fuel economy, revisited. Consider again the data in Exercise 27 about the fuel economy and weights of cars. **LO❽**

a) Create a 95% confidence interval for the average fuel efficiency among cars weighing 2500 pounds, and explain what your interval means.

b) Create a 95% prediction interval for the fuel efficiency you might get driving your new 3450-pound SUV, and explain what that interval means.

44. SAT scores, again. Consider the high school SAT scores data from Exercise 29 once more. The mean Verbal score was 596.30. **LO❽**

a) Find a 90% confidence interval for the mean SAT Math score for all students with an SAT Verbal score of 500.

b) Find a 90% prediction interval for the Math score of the grad class president, if you know she scored 710 on the Verbal section.

45. Mutual funds part 2. Using the same mutual fund flow data provided in Exercise 35, answer the following questions. **LO❽**

a) Find the 95% prediction interval for month that reports a market return of 8%.

b) Do you think predictions made by this regression will be very accurate? Explain.

c) Would your prediction be more or less precise if you were to omit the points noted in Exercise 35?

46. Assets and sales, revisited. A business analyst was interested in the relationship between a company's assets and its sales. She collected data (in millions of dollars) from a random sample of 79 Fortune 500 companies and created the following regression analysis. Economists commonly take the logarithm of these variables to make the relationship more nearly linear, and she did too. The dependent variable is *LogSales*. The assumptions for regression inference appeared to be satisfied. **LO❷**

Dependent variable is: LogSales
R squared = 33.9%
s = 0.4278 with 79 − 2 = 77 degrees of freedom

Variable	Coefficient	SE(Coeff)	t-ratio	P-value
Intercept	1.303	0.3211	4.06	0.0001
LogAssets	0.578	0.0919	6.28	≤ 0.0001

a) Is there a significant linear association between *LogAssets* and *LogSales*? Find the *t*-value and P-value to test an appropriate hypothesis and state your conclusion in context.
b) Do you think that a company's assets serve as a useful predictor of their sales?

T 47. All the efficiency money can buy. A sample of 84 model-2004 cars from an online information service was examined to see how fuel efficiency (as highway mpg) relates to the cost (Manufacturer's Suggested Retail Price in dollars) of cars. Here are displays and computer output: **LO❷**

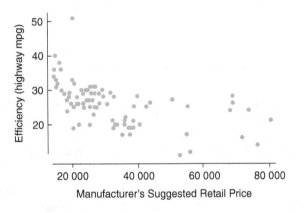

Dependent variable is: Highway MPG
R squared = 30.1%
s = 5.298 with 84 − 2 = 82 degrees of freedom

Variable	Coefficient	SE(Coeff)	t-ratio	P-value
Constant	33.06	1.299	25.5	≤0.0001
MSRP	−2.165e-4	3.639e-5	−5.95	≤0.0001

a) State what you want to know, identify the variables, and give the appropriate hypotheses.
b) Check the assumptions and conditions.
c) If the conditions are met, complete the analysis.

T 48. Energy use. Based on data collected from the United Nations Millennium Indicators Database related to measuring the goal of *ensuring environmental sustainability*, investigate the association between energy use (kg oil equivalent per $1000 GDP) in 1990 and 2004 for a sample of 96 countries (unstats.un.org/unsd/mi/mi_goals.asp; accessed May 2008). **LO❹, LO❺**

a) Find a regression model showing the relationship between *2004 Energy Use* (response variable) and *1990 Energy Use* (predictor variable).
b) Examine the residuals to determine if a linear regression is appropriate.
c) Test an appropriate hypothesis to determine if the association is significant.
d) What percentage of the variability in *2004 Energy Use* is explained by *1990 Energy Use*?

T 49. Youth unemployment, part 2. Refer to the United Nations data referenced in Exercise 15. Here is a scatterplot showing the regression line, 95% confidence interval, and 95% prediction interval, using 2005 youth unemployment data for a sample of 57 nations. The response variable is the *Male Rate*, and the predictor variable is the *Female Rate*. **LO❹, LO❺**

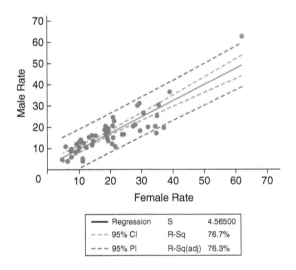

—— Regression	S	4.56500	
- - - 95% CI	R-Sq	76.7%	
- - - 95% PI	R-Sq(adj)	76.3%	

a) Explain the meaning of the 95% prediction interval in this context.
b) Explain the meaning of the 95% confidence interval in this context.
c) Identify the unusual observation, and discuss its potential impact on the regression.

T 50. Male unemployment, part 2. Refer to the United Nations data referenced in Exercise 16. Here is a scatterplot showing the regression line, 95% confidence interval, and 95% prediction interval, using 2005 and 2004 male unemployment data for a sample of 52 nations. The response variable is the *2005-Male Rate*, and the predictor variable is the *2004-Male Rate*. LO❽, LO❻

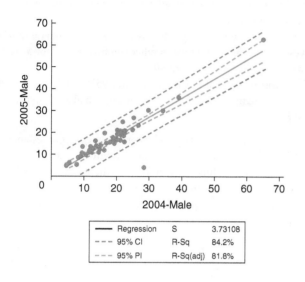

a) Explain the meaning of the 95% prediction interval in this context.
b) Explain the meaning of the 95% confidence interval in this context.
c) Identify the unusual observation, and discuss its potential impact on the regression.

51. Energy use again. Examine the regression and scatterplot showing the regression line, 95% confidence interval, and 95% prediction interval using *1990* and *2004 energy use* (kg oil equivalent per $1000 GDP) for a sample of 96 countries. The response variable is *2004 Energy Use*. LO❽

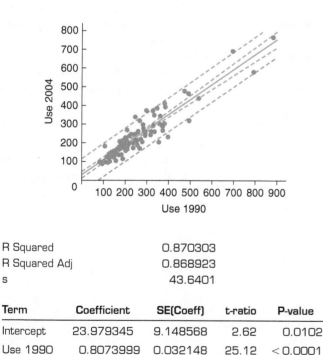

R Squared	0.870303
R Squared Adj	0.868923
s	43.6401

Term	Coefficient	SE(Coeff)	t-ratio	P-value
Intercept	23.979345	9.148568	2.62	0.0102
Use 1990	0.8073999	0.032148	25.12	<0.0001

a) Explain the meaning of the 95% prediction interval in this context.
b) Explain the meaning of the 95% confidence interval in this context.

52. Global reach. The internet has revolutionized business and offers unprecedented opportunities for globalization. However, the ability to access the internet varies greatly among different regions of the world. One of the variables the United Nations collects data on each year is *Personal Computers per 100 Population* (http://mdgs.un.org/unsd/mdg/default.aspx) for various countries. Below is a scatterplot showing the regression line, 95% confidence interval, and 95% prediction interval using 2000 and 2004 computer adoption (personal computers per 100 population) for a sample of 85 countries. The response variable is *PC/100 2004*. LO❹, LO❽

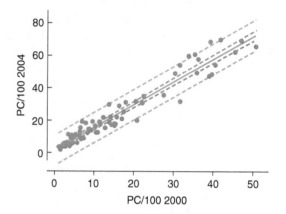

a) Find a regression model showing the relationship between personal computer adoption in 2004 *PC/100 2000* (the response variable) and personal computer adoption in 2000 *PC/100 2000* (the predictor variable).
b) Explain the meaning of the 95% prediction interval in this context.
c) Explain the meaning of the 95% confidence interval in this context.

53. Seasonal spending revisited. Spending on credit cards decreases after the Christmas spending season (as measured by amount charged on a credit card in December). The data set on MyStatLab contains the monthly credit card charges of a random sample of 99 cardholders. LO❹, LO❽

a) Build a regression model to predict January spending from December's spending.
b) How much, on average, will cardholders who charged $2000 in December charge in January?
c) Give a 95% confidence interval for the average January charges of cardholders who charged $2000 in December.
d) From part c, give a 95% confidence interval for the average decrease in the charges of cardholders who charged $2000 in December.
e) What reservations, if any, do you have about the confidence intervals you made in parts c and d?

54. Seasonal spending revisited part 2. Financial analysts know that January credit card charges will generally be much lower than those of the month before. What about the difference between January and the next month? Does the trend continue? The data set on MyStatLab contains the monthly credit card charges of a random sample of 99 cardholders. LO❹, LO❽

a) Build a regression model to predict February charges from January's charges.

b) How much, on average, will cardholders who charged $2000 in January charge in February?

c) Give a 95% confidence interval for the average February charges of cardholders who charged $2000 in January.

d) From part c, give a 95% confidence interval for the average decrease in the charges of cardholders who charged $2000 in January.

e) What reservations, if any, do you have about the confidence intervals you made in parts c and d?

T **55.** Exam grades. Student stress at final exam time comes partly from the uncertainty of grades and the consequences of those grades. Can knowledge of a mid-term grade be used to predict a final exam grade? At University of British Columbia's Sauder School of Business thousands of students have taken an undergraduate course in business statistics. A random sample of 200 students from the past three years was taken and their percentage grades on a single mid-term exam and a final exam were recorded. LO❹, LO❽, LO❿

Results from a regression are shown; the dependent variable is *FinalExam*.

Dependent variable is: *FinalExam*
R squared = 57.3%
s = 9.488 with 200 − 2 = 198 df

Variable	Coefficient	SE(Coeff)
Intercept	2.9781	4.1115
Mid-term	0.8861	0.0544

a) Is the relationship between final exam grade and mid-term exam grade significant?
Assuming the conditions for inference are satisfied, find the *t*-value and P-value to test the appropriate hypothesis. State your conclusion in context.

b) Here is part of the ANOVA Table. Find the *F*-statistic and P-value and state your conclusion in context. How does it compare with part a?

Anova

Source	Sum of Squares	Degrees of Freedom	Mean Square
Model	23875.86	1	23875.86
Error	17823.82	198	90.02
Total	41699.68	199	

c) How useful a predictor of final exam grade is mid-term grade? Use the values of both R^2 and *s* in your explanation.

d) Give and interpret a 95% confidence interval for the increase in final exam grade associated with each percent increase in mid-term exam grade.

e) The mean mid-term grade was 75. Using an interval in which you have 95% confidence, predict the final grade for a student who had mid-term grade of 80.

f) Using an interval in which you have 95% confidence, predict the average final grade for all students who had a mid-term grade of 80.

T **56.** Exam grades, part 2. The spreadsheet of grades analyzed in Exercise 55 also has the total assignment grade. Now consider the relationship between Assignment grade and Final Exam grade for the same sample of 200 students. LO❹, LO❽, LO❿

a) Fill in the missing cells in the regression output template below.

Variable	Coefficient	SE(Coeff)	t-stat	P-value
Intercept	41.7308	4.1238	_____	_____
Assignment	0.3481	_____	6.795	

Anova

Source	Sum of Squares	Degrees of Freedom	Mean Square	F-stat
Model	_____	_____	7885.44	_____
Error	_____	_____	_____	
Total	41699.68	_____		

b) Find the values of R^2 and *s*.

c) Assume the conditions for inference are satisfied. Using two different test statistics, test whether the relationship between final exam grade and the assignment grade is significant. Don't forget to state your conclusion in context.

d) Considering both Exercise 55 and 56, which grade—assignment or mid-term—is a better predictor of final exam grade?

PREVIEW OF COMING ATTRACTIONS: How much better a prediction of final exam grade could you make if you used both the mid-term grade *and* the assignment grade? To find out how to do this kind of analysis, turn the page and begin Chapter 15!

JUST CHECKING ANSWERS

1 I would need to see a scatterplot to see if the linearity assumption is reasonable, to make sure that there are no outliers, and a residual plot to check the equal spread condition. I'd also like to see a histogram or Normal probability plot of the residuals to make sure the nearly Normal condition is satisfied. Finally, I'd like to see the residuals plotted in time to see if the residuals appear independent. Without verifying these conditions, I wouldn't know whether my analysis is valid.

2 The 95% CI for the slope is $1133.8 \pm 2.052(513.1)$, or $(80.9, 2186.7)$.

3 H_0: The slope $\beta_1 = 0$. H_A: The slope $\beta_1 \neq 0$. Since the P-value $= 0.036$, we reject the null hypothesis (at $\alpha = 0.05$) and conclude that there is a linear relationship between enrolment and unemployment.

4 Strength is a judgment call, but I'd be hesitant to call a relationship with an R^2 value of only 15% strong.

5 Approximately 15% of the variation in enrolment at the University of New Mexico is accounted for by variation in the unemployment rate in New Mexico.

6 Not high-leverage, not influential, large residual

7 High-leverage, not influential, small residual

8 High-leverage, influential, not large residual

Multiple Regression

RSnapshotPhotos/Shutterstock

LEARNING OBJECTIVES

1. Check regression assumptions and R^2

2. Interpret coefficients, test statistic computations, and hypothesis tests

3. Check assumptions using residual plots

4. Interpret complete regression output

5. Carry out multiple regression analysis with software

6. Use the fitted model for making prediction

7. Communicate conclusions of regression analysis

8. Compare models with F-test for change in R^2

9. Extend regression models to include polynomial terms and indicator variables

CONNECTIONS: CHAPTER 15

Chapter 14 examined the relationship between one quantitative predictor or explanatory variable and one quantitative response or outcome variable using a simple linear model. In the current chapter we extend the linear model to multiple predictor variables. Multiple regression is one of the most powerful and widely used statistical tools.

CREA—Canadian Real Estate Association

For most people the most expensive purchase they will ever make will be a new home. In February 2013, average house prices in Canada ranged from about $150 000–$200 000 in the Maritimes to over $500 000 in British Columbia. The Canadian Real Estate Association (CREA) is one of the largest single-industry trade associations in Canada, with over 100 000 members. For years, information on listings data was only available to its members—real estate brokers and agents. If you are a member you can access the RealtorLink.ca website, a subscription service that compiles all historical MLS (Multiple Listing Service) data for various regions. But it is not freely available. Instead, consumers are directed to Realtor.ca to look for listings. In 2011, in response to growing market pressure, CREA began to develop a program to do what Zillow.com and Redfin.com do in the United States. The plan was to let agents and others build feature-heavy sites using CREA's data.

One such site is Zoocasa.com where you can carry out a home search and then get connected with real estate agents. Zoocasa's CEO Butch Langlois stated, "The Canadian real estate industry has spent a lot of effort on keeping that data to itself. But everyone now sees how powerful it can be as a lead channel for the agents who are trying to sell the houses. The Ontario-based company Teranet operates Purview For Lenders, a national automated service through which you can determine property valuation, get an equity estimate, and view comparable sales. BuzzBuzzHome.com is another Toronto-based company, founded in 2009, that provides a free wiki-powered listing service for new residential developments. Information includes pricing, floor plans, renderings, and builder/developer. Page-views have grown by 10 percent per month and the site now receives over 175 000 unique visitors per month.

An important aspect of real estate data is the ability is to estimate a home's worth, based on a variety of predictor variables such as past history of the home's sales, location, and house characteristics (lot size, floor space area, number of bedrooms and bathrooms).

The tools for people to be able to analyze real estate trends have been growing substantially. With advances in mobile technology, real time mapping, and data acquisition, home buyers will be even better prepared to make purchase decisions. But no matter how much data is available a home purchase will still be expensive!

By the way, the word Realtor® is capitalized because it is a trademark. To be a Realtor® in Canada you must be a member of your local real estate board and CREA.

Based on information from www.crea.ca/organization

WHO:	Houses
WHAT:	Sale price and other facts about the houses
WHEN:	2011–2012
WHERE:	"Somewhere in Canada"
WHY:	To understand what influences housing prices and how to predict them

How would CREA or any of these other real estate sites figure out the worth of a house? The answer is, not surprisingly, to collect a huge amount of data and build a model. For example, the Zillow.com site computes a Zestimate (the proper pronunciation is unclear: in Canada it's "zed-estimate", in the United States "zee-estimate", or perhaps it's just "zest-imate"). According to the Zillow.com site, "We compute this figure by taking zillions of data points—much of this data is public—and entering them into a formula. This formula is built using what our statisticians call 'a proprietary algorithm'—big words for 'secret formula.' When our statisticians developed the model to determine home values, they explored how homes in certain areas were similar (i.e., number of bedrooms and baths, and a myriad of other details) and then looked at the relationships between actual sale prices and those home details." These relationships form a pattern, and they use that pattern to develop a model to estimate a market value for a home. In other words, real estate statisticians would use a model, most likely a regression model, to predict home value from the characteristics of the house. We've seen how to predict a response variable based on a single predictor. That's been useful, but the types of business decisions we'll want to make are often too complex for simple regression.[1] In this chapter, we'll expand the power of the regression model to take into account many predictor variables into what's called a multiple regression model. With our understanding of simple regression as a base, getting to multiple regression isn't a big step, but it's an important and worthwhile one. Multiple regression is probably the most powerful and widely used statistical tool today.

[1] When we need to note the difference, a regression with a single predictor is called a *simple regression*. Remember that, in regression "simple" means "single," not "easy."

As anyone who's ever looked at house prices knows, house prices depend on the local market. To control for that, we will restrict our attention to a single market. We have a random sample of 1057 home sales from the public records of sales. The first thing often mentioned in describing a house for sale is the number of bedrooms. Let's start with just one predictor variable. Can we use *Bedrooms* to predict home *Price*?

The number of *Bedrooms* is a quantitative variable, but it holds only a few values (from 1 to 5 in this data set). So a scatterplot may not be the best way to examine the relationship between *Bedrooms* and *Price*. In fact, at each value for *Bedrooms* there is a whole distribution of prices. Side-by-side boxplots of *Price* against *Bedrooms* (Figure 15.1) show a general increase in price with more bedrooms, and an approximately linear growth.

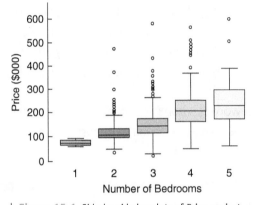

Figure 15.1 Side-by-side boxplots of Price against Bedrooms show that price increases, on average, with more bedrooms.

Figure 15.1 also shows a clearly increasing spread from left to right, violating the Equal Spread Condition, and that's a possible sign of trouble. For now, we'll proceed cautiously. We'll fit the regression model, but we will be cautious about using inference methods for the model. Later we'll add more variables to increase the power and usefulness of the model.

The output from a linear regression model of *Price* on *Bedrooms* shows:

```
Response variable: Price

R² = 21.4%
s = 68432.21 with 1057 − 2 = 1055 degrees of freedom
```

Variable	Coeff	SE(Coeff)	t-ratio	P-value
Intercept	14349.48	9297.69	1.54	0.1230
Bedrooms	48218.91	2843.88	16.96	≤ 0.0001

Table 15.1 Linear regression of Price on Bedrooms.

Apparently, just knowing the number of bedrooms gives us some useful information about the sale price. The model tells us that, on average, we'd expect the price to increase by almost \$50 000 for each additional bedroom in the house, as we can see from the slope value of \$48 219.90:

$$\widehat{Price} = 14349.48 + 48218.91 \times Bedrooms$$

Even though the model does tell us something, notice that the R^2 for this regression is only 21.4%. The variation in the number of bedrooms accounts for only 21% of the variation in house prices. Perhaps some of the other facts about these houses can account for portions of the remaining variation.

15.1 The Multiple Regression Model

For simple regression, we wrote the predicted values in terms of one predictor variable:

$$\hat{y} = b_0 + b_1 x$$

To include more predictors in the model, we just write the regression model with more predictor variables. The resulting **multiple regression** looks like this:

$$\hat{y} = b_0 + b_1 x_1 + b_2 x_2 + \ldots + b_k x_k$$

where b_0 is still the intercept and each b_k is the estimated coefficient of its corresponding predictor x_k. Although the model doesn't look much more complicated than a simple regression, it isn't practical to determine a multiple regression by hand. This is a job for a statistics program on a computer. Remember that for simple regression, we found the coefficients for the model using the **least squares** solution, the one whose coefficients made the sum of the squared residuals as small as possible. For multiple regression, a statistics package does the same thing and can find the coefficients of the least squares model easily.

If you know how to find the regression of *Price* on *Bedrooms* using a statistics package, you can probably just add another variable to the list of predictors in your program to compute a multiple regression. Statistics software usually uses the same macros for simple and multiple regression. A multiple regression of *Price* on the two variables *Bedrooms* and *Living Area* generates a multiple regression table like this one.

```
Response variable: Price

R² = 57.8%
s = 50142.4 with 1057 − 3 = 1054 degrees of freedom
```

Variable	Coeff	SE(Coeff)	t-ratio	P-value
Intercept	20986.09	6816.3	3.08	0.0021
Bedrooms	−7483.10	2783.5	−2.69	0.0073
Living Area	93.84	3.11	30.18	≤ 0.0001

Table 15.2 Multiple regression output for the linear model predicting Price from Bedrooms and Living Area.

You should recognize most of the numbers in this table, and most of them mean what you expect them to. The value of R^2 for a regression on two variables gives the fraction of the variability of *Price* accounted for by both predictor variables together. With *Bedrooms* alone predicting *Price*, the R^2 value was 22.1%, but this model accounts for 57.8% of the variability in *Price*. We shouldn't be surprised that the variability explained by the model has gone up. It was for this reason—the hope of accounting for some of that leftover variability—that we tried a second predictor. We also shouldn't be surprised that the size of the house, as measured by *Living Area*, also contributes to a good prediction of house prices. Collecting the coefficients of the multiple regression of *Price* on *Bedrooms* and *Living Area* from Table 15.2, we can write the estimated regression as:

$$\widehat{Price} = 20\,986.09 - 7483.10\,Bedrooms + 93.84\,Living\,Area$$

In simple regression, finding the least squares solution requires simple calculus (partial derivatives) and solving two equations in two unknowns; the algebra is very easy. But in multiple regression, the solution requires solving *k+1* equations in *k+1* unknowns. That's not easy, and requires matrix algebra, so we leave it to the computer.

Why can we not draw a scatterplot of the data, as we did in simple regression? By adding predictor variables we have increased the number of dimensions we would need to display. With one predictor variable (*y* vs. *x*), least squares means finding the best-fitting line through a two-dimensional (i.e., oval) cloud of points. If there are two predictor variables, we look for the best-fitting plane through a three-dimensional (i.e., ovate or egg-shaped) cloud of points. That's the furthest we can go visually, because adding a third predictor variable would mean finding the best-fitting solid through four-dimensional space, and so on. It makes your brain hurt to think about what happens in 10 dimensions!

As before, we define the residuals as:

$$e = y - \hat{y}$$

The standard deviation of the residuals is still denoted as *s* (or also sometimes as *se* as in simple regression—for the same reason—to distinguish it from the standard deviation, s_y, of *y*). The degrees of freedom calculation comes right from our definition. The degrees of freedom is the number of observations ($n = 1057$) minus one for each coefficient estimated:

$$df = n - k - 1$$

where *k* is the number of predictor variables and *n* is the number of cases. For this model, we subtract three (the two coefficients and the intercept). To find the standard deviation of the residuals, we use that number of degrees of freedom in the denominator:

$$s_e = \sqrt{\frac{\sum (y - \hat{y})^2}{n - k - 1}}$$

For each predictor, the regression output shows a coefficient, its standard error, a ***t*-ratio for the coefficient**, and the corresponding P-value. As with simple regression, the *t*-ratio measures how many standard errors the coefficient is away from 0. Using a Student's *t*-model, we can use its P-value to test the null hypothesis that the true value of the coefficient is 0.

What's different? With so much of the multiple regression looking just like simple regression, why devote an entire chapter to the subject?

There are several answers to this question. First, and most important, is that the meaning of the coefficients in the regression model has changed in a subtle, but important, way. Because that change is not obvious, multiple regression coefficients are often misinterpreted. We'll show some examples to explain this change in meaning.

Second, the analysis is much more complex. Analysis of the simple regression model tests one key hypothesis, namely, does the single predictor explain variation in *y* more than just chance alone? Analysis of the multiple regression model goes far beyond that. Once it is determined that the model as a whole is useful, the question turns to which of the whole set of *x*-variables in the model are the contributors to that usefulness. A team may be a winner but that doesn't mean every team member was a contributing member.

Third, multiple regression is an extraordinarily versatile model, underlying many widely used statistics methods. A sound understanding of the multiple regression model will help you to understand these other applications as well.

Fourth, multiple regression offers you a first glimpse into statistical models that use more than two quantitative variables. The real world is complex. Simple models of the kind we've shown so far are a great start, but they're not detailed enough to be useful for understanding, predicting, and making business decisions in many real-world situations. Models that use several variables can be a big step toward realistic and useful modelling of complex phenomena and relationships.

15.2 Interpreting Multiple Regression Coefficients

It makes sense that both the number of bedrooms and the size of the living area would influence the price of a house. We'd expect both variables to have a positive effect on price—houses with more bedrooms typically sell for more money, as do larger houses. But look at the coefficient for *Bedrooms* in the multiple regression equation. It's negative: -7483.09. How can it be that the coefficient of *Bedrooms* in the multiple regression is negative? And not just slightly negative, its *t*-ratio is large

enough for us to be quite confident that the true value is really negative. Yet from Table 15.1, we saw the coefficient was equally clearly positive when *Bedrooms* was the sole predictor in the model (see Figure 15.2).

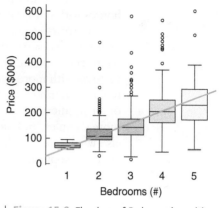

Figure 15.2 The slope of Bedrooms is positive. For each additional bedroom, we would predict an additional $48 000 in the price of a house from the simple regression model of Table 15.1.

The explanation of this apparent paradox is that in a multiple regression, coefficients have a more subtle meaning. Each coefficient takes into account the other predictor(s) in the model.

Think about a group of houses of about the same size. For the *same size* living area, a house with more bedrooms is likely to have smaller rooms. That might actually make it *less* valuable. To see this in the data, let's look at a group of similarly sized homes from 2500 to 3000 square feet of living area, and examine the relationship between *Bedrooms* and *Price* just for houses in this size range (see Figure 15.3).

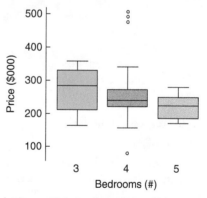

Figure 15.3 For the 96 houses with Living Area between 2500 and 3000 square feet, the slope of Price on Bedrooms is negative. For each additional bedroom, restricting data to homes of this size, we would predict that the house's Price was about $17 800 lower.

For houses with between 2500 and 3000 square feet of living area, it appears that homes with *fewer* bedrooms have a higher price, on average, than those with more bedrooms. When we think about houses in terms of *both* variables, we can see that this makes sense. A 2500-square-foot house with five bedrooms would have either relatively small, cramped bedrooms or not much common living space. The same size house with only three bedrooms could have larger, more attractive bedrooms and still have adequate common living space. What the coefficient of *Bedrooms* is saying in the multiple regression is that, after accounting for living area, houses with more bedrooms tend to sell for a *lower* price. In other words, what we saw by *restricting* our attention to homes of a certain size and seeing that additional bedrooms had a negative impact on price was generally true across all sizes. What seems confusing at first is that without taking *Living Area* into account, *Price* tends to go *up* with more bedrooms. But that's because *Living Area* and *Bedrooms* are also related. Multiple regression coefficients must always be interpreted in terms of the other predictors in the model. That can make their interpretation more subtle, more complex, and more challenging than when we had only one predictor. This is also what makes multiple regression so versatile and effective. The interpretations are more sophisticated and more appropriate.

✔ **JUST CHECKING**

Body fat percentage is an important health indicator, but it is difficult to measure accurately. One way to do so is to take an MRI (magnetic resonance image) at a cost of about $1000 per image. Insurance companies want to know if body fat percentage can be estimated from easier to measure characteristics such as *Height* and *Weight*. A scatterplot of *Percent Body Fat* against *Height* shows no pattern, and the correlation is −0.03 and is not statistically significant. A multiple regression using *Height (centimetres)*, *Age (years)*, and *Weight (kilograms)* finds the following model:

	Coeff	SE(Coeff)	t-ratio	P-value
Intercept	57.27217	10.39897	5.507	<0.0001
Height	−0.50164	0.06221	−8.064	<0.0001
Weight	0.55805	0.03262	17.110	<0.0001
Age	0.13732	0.02806	4.895	<0.0001

$s = 5.382$ on 246 degrees of freedom
Multiple R-squared: 0.584
F-statistic: 115.1 on 3 and 246 DF, P-value: <0.0001

1 Interpret the R^2 of this regression model.

2 Interpret the coefficient of *Age*.

3 How can the coefficient of *Height* have such a small P-value in the multiple regression when the correlation between *Height* and *Percent Body Fat* was not statistically distinguishable from zero?

Your spellchecker won't pick it up, but there's a big difference between a causal relationship and a casual relationship. One's between variables, the other's between people!

There's a second common pitfall in interpreting coefficients. Be careful not to interpret the coefficients causally. For example, this analysis cannot tell a homeowner how much the price of his home will change if he combines two of his four bedrooms into a new master bedroom. And it can't be used to predict whether adding a 100-square-foot child's bedroom onto the house would increase or decrease its value. The model simply reports the relationship between the number of *Bedrooms* and *Living Area* and *Price* for existing houses. As always with regression, we should be careful not to assume causation between the predictor variables and the response.

15.3 Assumptions and Conditions for the Multiple Regression Model

We can write the multiple regression model like this, numbering the predictors arbitrarily (the order doesn't matter), writing betas for the model coefficients (which we will estimate from the data), and including the errors in the model:

$$y = \beta_0 + \beta_1 x_1 + \beta_2 x_2 + \ldots + \beta_k x_k + \varepsilon$$

The assumptions and conditions for the multiple regression model are nearly the same as for simple regression, but with more variables in the model, we'll have to make a few changes, as described in the following sections.

Linearity Assumption

We are fitting a linear model.[2] For that to be the right kind of model for this analysis, we need to verify an underlying linear relationship. But now we're thinking about several predictors. To confirm that the assumption is reasonable, we'll check the Linearity Condition for *each* of the predictors.

Linearity Condition. Scatterplots of y against each of the predictors are reasonably straight. The scatterplots need not show a strong (or any) slope; we just check to make sure that there isn't a bend or other nonlinearity. For the real estate data, the scatterplot is linear in both *Bedrooms* and *Living Area*.

As in simple regression, it's a good idea to check the residual plot for any violations of the linearity condition. We can fit the regression and plot the residuals against the predicted values (Figure 15.4), checking to make sure we don't find patterns—especially bends or other nonlinearities.

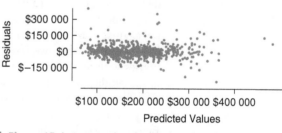

Figure 15.4 A scatterplot of residuals against the predicted values shows no obvious pattern.

Independence Assumption

As with simple regression, the errors in the true underlying regression model must be independent of each other. As usual, there's no way to be sure that the Independence Assumption is true, but we should think about how the data were collected to see if that assumption is reasonable. We should check the randomization condition as well.

---

[2] By *linear* we mean that each x appears simply multiplied by its coefficient and added to the model, and that no x appears in an exponent or some other more complicated function. That ensures that as we move along any x-variable, our prediction for y will change at a constant rate (given by the coefficient) if nothing else changes. This use of *linear* comes from mathematical terminology where a model of this form is called a *linear combination*.

To assess the assumptions in simple regression, there is little difference between plotting the residuals against the predicted values or against the x-values. But in multiple regression there is a big difference. Plotting residuals against the predicted values captures the combined effect of all variables in the model. That's different from separate plots of the residuals against each x-variable.

Randomization Condition. Ideally, the data should arise from a random sample or randomized experiment. Randomization assures us that the data are representative of some identifiable population. If you can't identify the population, you can interpret the regression model as a description of the data you have, but you can't interpret the hypothesis tests at all because such tests are about a regression model for a specific population. Regression methods are often applied to data that were not collected with randomization. Regression models fit to such data may still do a good job of modelling the data at hand, but without some reason to believe that the data are representative of a particular population, you should be reluctant to believe that the model generalizes to other situations.

We also check the regression residuals for evidence of patterns, trends, or clumping, any of which would suggest a failure of independence. In the special case when one of the *x*-variables is related to time (or *is* itself *Time*), be sure that the residuals do not have a pattern when plotted against that variable. In addition to checking the plot of residuals against the predicted values, we recommend that you check the individual plots of the residuals against each of the explanatory, or *x*, variables in the model. These individual plots can yield important information on necessary transformations, or re-expressions, for the predictor variables.

The real estate data were sampled from a larger set of public records for sales during a limited period of time. The houses were not related in any way, so we can be fairly confident that their measurements are independent.

Equal Variance Assumption

The variability of the errors should be about the same for all values of *each* predictor. To see whether this assumption is valid, we look at scatterplots and check the Equal Spread Condition.

Equal Spread Condition. The same scatterplot of residuals against the predicted values (Figure 15.4) is a good check of the consistency of the spread. We saw what appeared to be a violation of the equal spread condition when *Price* was plotted against *Bedrooms* (Figure 15.2). But here in the multiple regression, the problem has dissipated when we look at the residuals. Apparently, much of the tendency of houses with more bedrooms to have greater variability in prices was accounted for in the model when we included *Living Area* as a predictor.

If residual plots show no pattern, if the data are plausibly independent, and if the plots don't thicken, we can feel good about interpreting the regression model. Before we test hypotheses, however, we must check one final assumption: the normality assumption.

Normality Assumption

We assume that the errors around the idealized regression model at any specified values of the *x*-variables follow a Normal model. We need this assumption so that we can use a Student's *t*-model for inference. As with other times when we've used Student's *t*, we'll settle for the residuals satisfying the Nearly Normal Condition. As with means, the assumption is less important as the sample size grows. Our inference methods will work well even when the residuals are moderately skewed, if the sample size is large. If the distribution of residuals is unimodal and symmetric, there is little to worry about.[3]

---

[3] The only procedure that needs strict adherence to Normality of the errors is finding prediction intervals for individuals in multiple regression. Because they are based on Normal probabilities, the errors must closely follow a Normal model.

Nearly Normal Condition. Because we have only one set of residuals, this is the same set of conditions we had for simple regression. Look at a histogram or Normal probability plot of the residuals.

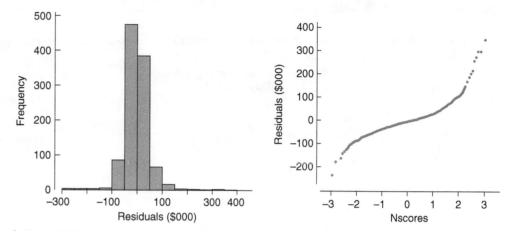

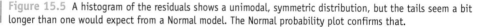

Figure 15.5 A histogram of the residuals shows a unimodal, symmetric distribution, but the tails seem a bit longer than one would expect from a Normal model. The Normal probability plot confirms that.

The histogram of residuals in the real estate example certainly looks unimodal and symmetric. The Normal probability plot has some bend on both sides, which indicates that there are more residuals in the tails than Normally distributed data would have. However, as we have said before, the Normality Assumption becomes less important as the sample size grows, and here we have no skewness and more than 1000 cases. (The Central Limit Theorem will help our confidence intervals and tests based on the *t*-statistic with large samples.)

Let's summarize all the checks of conditions that we've made and the order in which we've made them.

1. Check the Linearity Condition with scatterplots of the *y*-variable against each *x*-variable.

2. If the scatterplots are straight enough, fit a multiple regression model to the data. (Otherwise, either stop or consider re-expressing an *x*-variable or the *y*-variable.)

3. Find the residuals and predicted values.

4. Make a scatterplot of the residuals against the predicted values (and ideally against each predictor variable separately). These plots should look patternless. Check, in particular, for any bend (which would suggest that the data weren't all that straight after all) and for any thickening. If there's a bend, consider re-expressing the *y*- and/or the *x*-variables. If the variation in the plot grows from one side to the other, consider re-expressing the *y*-variable. If you re-express a variable, start the model fitting over.

5. Think about how the data were collected. Should they be independent? Was suitable randomization used? Are the data representative of some identifiable population? If the data are measured over time, check for evidence of patterns that might suggest they are not independent by plotting the residuals against time to look for patterns.

6. If the conditions check out up to here, feel free to interpret the regression model and use it for prediction.

7. Make a histogram and Normal probability plot of the residuals to check the Nearly Normal Condition. If the sample size is large, the Normality is less important for inference, but always be on the lookout for skewness or outliers.

CREA attracts many thousands of users each month who are interested in finding out how much their house is worth. Let's see how well a multiple regression model can do. The variables available include:

Price   The price of the house as sold in 2012

Living Area   The size of the living area of the house in square feet

Bedrooms   The number of bedrooms

Bathrooms   The number of bathrooms (a half bath is a toilet and sink only)

Age   Age of the house in years

Fireplaces   Number of fireplaces in the house

PLAN

Setup State the objective of the study. Identify the variables.

We want to build a model to predict house prices for a region "somewhere in Canada". We have data on *Price* ($), *Living Area* (sq ft), *Bedrooms* (#), *Bathrooms* (#), *Fireplaces* (#) , and *Age* (in years).

Model Think about the assumptions and check the conditions.

Linearity Condition

To fit a regression model, we first require linearity. Scatterplots (or side-by-side boxplots) of *Price* against all potential predictor variables are shown.

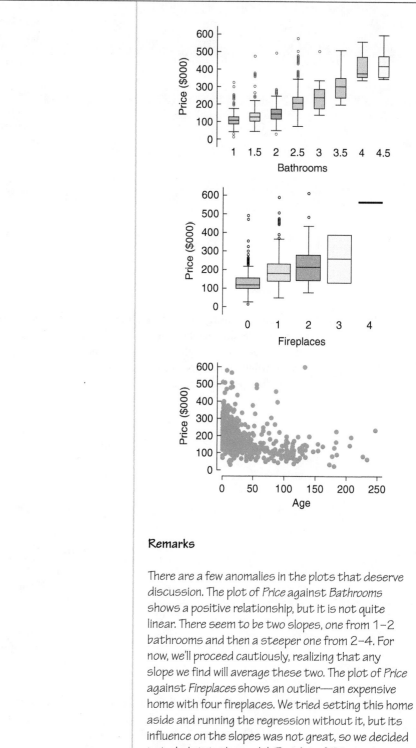

Remarks

There are a few anomalies in the plots that deserve discussion. The plot of *Price* against *Bathrooms* shows a positive relationship, but it is not quite linear. There seem to be two slopes, one from 1–2 bathrooms and then a steeper one from 2–4. For now, we'll proceed cautiously, realizing that any slope we find will average these two. The plot of *Price* against *Fireplaces* shows an outlier—an expensive home with four fireplaces. We tried setting this home aside and running the regression without it, but its influence on the slopes was not great, so we decided to include it in the model. The plot of *Price* against *Age* shows that there may be some curvature. We should be cautious in interpreting the slope, especially for newer homes.

✓ **Independence Assumption.** We can regard the house prices as being independent of one another since they are from a fairly large geographic area.

✓ **Randomization Condition.** These 1057 houses are a random sample of a much larger set.

✓ **Equal Spread Condition.** A scatterplot of residuals *vs.* predicted values shows no evidence of changing spread. There is a group of homes whose residuals are larger (both negative and positive) than the vast majority. This is also seen in the long tails of the histogram of residuals.

We need the Nearly Normal Condition only if we want to do inference and the sample size is not large. If the sample size is large, we need the distribution to be Normal only if we plan to produce prediction intervals.

✓ **Nearly Normal Condition, Outlier Condition.** The histogram of residuals is unimodal and symmetric, but long tailed. The Normal probability plot supports that.

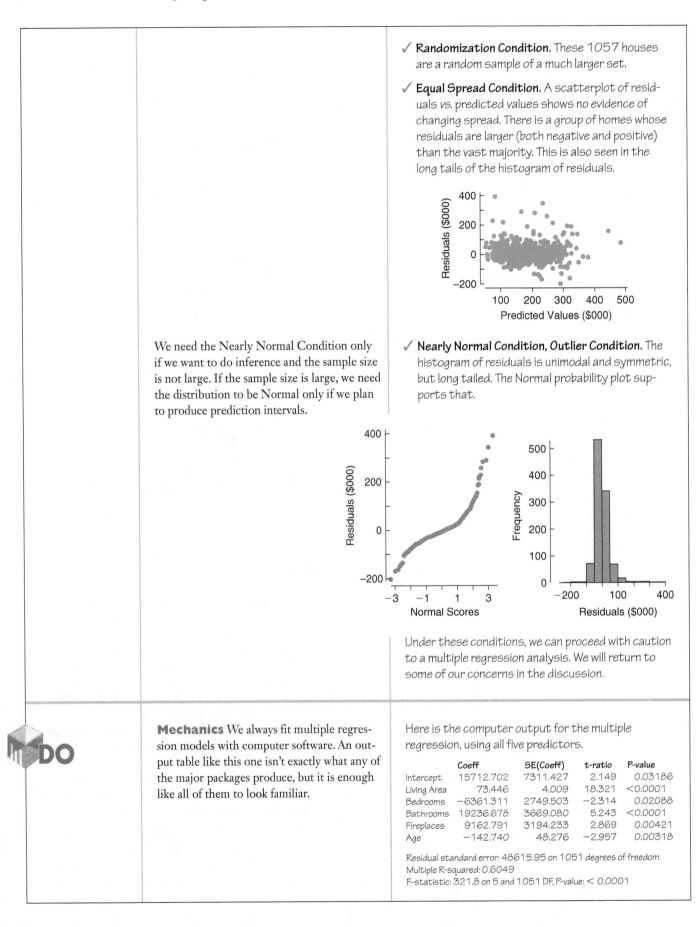

Under these conditions, we can proceed with caution to a multiple regression analysis. We will return to some of our concerns in the discussion.

Mechanics We always fit multiple regression models with computer software. An output table like this one isn't exactly what any of the major packages produce, but it is enough like all of them to look familiar.

Here is the computer output for the multiple regression, using all five predictors.

	Coeff	SE(Coeff)	t-ratio	P-value
Intercept	15712.702	7311.427	2.149	0.03186
Living Area	73.446	4.009	18.321	<0.0001
Bedrooms	−6361.311	2749.503	−2.314	0.02088
Bathrooms	19236.678	3669.080	5.243	<0.0001
Fireplaces	9162.791	3194.233	2.869	0.00421
Age	−142.740	48.276	−2.957	0.00318

Residual standard error: 48615.95 on 1051 degrees of freedom
Multiple R-squared: 0.6049
F-statistic: 321.8 on 5 and 1051 DF, P-value: < 0.0001

The estimated equation is:

$$\widehat{Price} = 15\,712.70 + 73.45 Living\ Area - 6361.31 Bedrooms + 19\,236.68 Bathrooms + 9162.79 Fireplaces - 142.74 Age$$

All of the P-values are small which indicates that even with five predictors in the model, all are contributing. The R^2 value of 60.49% indicates that more than 60% of the overall variation in house prices has been accounted for by this model. The residual standard error of $48\,620$ gives us a rough indication that we can predict the price of a home to within about $2 \times \$48\,620 = \$97\,240$. If that's close enough to be useful, then our model is potentially useful as a price guide.

 **REPORT**

Summary and Conclusions Summarize your results and state any limitations of your model in the context of your original objectives.

MEMO:

Re: Regression Analysis of Home Price Predictions

A regression model of *Price* on *Living Area, Bedrooms, Bathrooms, Fireplaces,* and *Age* accounts for 60.5% of the variation in the price of homes. A statistical test of each coefficient shows that each one is almost certainly not zero, so each of these variables appears to be a contributor of the price of a house.

This model reflects the common wisdom in real estate about the importance of various aspects of a home. An important variable not included is the location, which every real estate agent knows is crucial to pricing a house. This is ameliorated by the fact that all these houses are in the same general area. However, knowing more specific information about where they are located would almost certainly help the model. The price found from this model is to be used as a starting point for comparing a home with comparable homes in the area.

The model may be improved by re-expressing one or more of the predictors, especially *Age* and *Bathrooms*. We recommend caution in interpreting the slopes across the entire range of these predictors.

15.4 Testing the Multiple Regression Model

There are several hypothesis tests in the section of the multiple regression output we have seen, but all of them talk about the same thing. Each is concerned with whether the underlying model parameters (the slopes and intercept) are actually zero. The first of these hypotheses is one we introduced in simple regression and promised then would be much more useful in multiple regression. Now you'll see why.

Now that we have more than one predictor, there's an overall test we should perform before we consider inference for the coefficients. We ask the global question: Is this multiple regression model any good at all? If home prices were set randomly or based on other factors than those we have as predictors, then the best estimate would just be the mean price.

To address the overall question, we'll test the null hypothesis that all the slope coefficients are zero:

$$H_0: \beta_1 = \ldots = \beta_k = 0 \; vs \; H_A: \text{at least one } \beta \neq 0$$

Notice how we wrote the alternative hypothesis. We *did not* write $H_A: \beta_1 \neq \beta_2 \neq \ldots \neq \beta_k \neq 0$. That would mean every one of the coefficients was significant, and further, that they were all different from one another. This notation is just plain wrong—don't ever write it!

Another way to think of, or write, the hypotheses is to say:

H_0: The model is not worthwhile (i.e., it has no predictive value)

vs. H_A: The model is worthwhile (i.e., it has some predictive value).

We can test this hypothesis with an **F-test**. We introduced the F-test in Chapter 14, but we'll review it here. (It's the generalization of the t-test to more than one predictor.) The sampling distribution of the statistic is labelled with the letter F (in honour of Sir Ronald Fisher). The F-distribution has two degrees of freedom, k, the number of predictors, and $n - k - 1$. In our Guided Example, we have $k = 5$ predictors and $n = 1057$ homes, which means that the F-value of 321.8 has 5 predictors and $1057 - 5 - 1 = 1051$ degrees of freedom. The regression output shows that it has a P-value < 0.0001. The null hypothesis is that the regression model predicts no better than the mean. The alternative is that it does. The test is one-sided—bigger F-values mean smaller P-values. If the null hypothesis were true, the F-statistic would be near 1. The F-statistic here is quite large, so we can easily reject the null hypothesis and conclude that the multiple regression model for predicting house prices with these five variables is better than just using the mean.[4]

Once we check the F-test and reject its null hypothesis—and, if we are being careful, *only* if we reject that hypothesis—we can move on to checking the test statistics for the individual coefficients. Those tests look like what we did for the slope of a simple regression in Chapter 14. For each coefficient, we test the null hypothesis that the slope is zero against the (two-sided) alternative that it isn't zero. The regression table gives a standard error for each coefficient and the ratio of the estimated coefficient to its standard error. If the assumptions and conditions are met (and now we need the Nearly Normal Condition or a large sample), these ratios follow a Student's t-distribution:

$$t_{n-k-1} = \frac{b_j - 0}{SE(b_j)}$$

Where did the degrees of freedom $n - k - 1$ come from? We have a rule of thumb that works here. The degrees of freedom value is the number of data values minus the number of estimated parameters (including the intercept). For the house price regression on five predictors, that's $n - 5 - 1$. Almost every regression report includes both the t-statistics and their corresponding P-values.

We can build a confidence interval in the usual way, with an estimate plus or minus a margin of error. As always, the margin of error is the product of the standard error and a critical value. Here the critical value comes from the t-distribution

---

F-test for Simple Regression?

When you do a simple regression with statistics software, you'll see the F-statistic in the output. But for simple regression, it gives the same information as the t-test for the slope. It tests the null hypothesis that the slope coefficient is zero, and we already test that with the t-statistic for the slope. As we saw in Chapter 14 the square of that t-statistic is equal to the F-statistic for the simple regression, so it really is the identical test.

---

[4] There are F tables in the back of the book, and most regression tables include a P-value for the F-statistic.

on $n - k - 1$ degrees of freedom, and the standard errors are in the regression table. So a confidence interval for each slope β_j is:

$$b_j \pm t^*_{n-k-1} \times SE(b_j)$$

The tricky parts of these tests are that the standard errors of the coefficients now require harder calculations (so we leave it to technology), and the meaning of a coefficient, as we have seen, depends on all the other predictors in the multiple regression model.

That last point is important. If we fail to reject the null hypothesis for a multiple regression coefficient, it does *not* mean that the corresponding predictor variable has no linear relationship to y. It means that the corresponding predictor contributes nothing to modelling y *after allowing for all the other predictors*.

The multiple regression model looks so simple and straightforward. It *looks* like each β_j tells us the effect of its associated predictor, x_j, on the response variable, y. But that is not true. This is, without a doubt, the most common error that people make with multiple regression. In fact:

- ◆ *The coefficient β_j in a multiple regression can be quite different from zero even when it is possible there is no simple linear relationship between y and x_j.*
- ◆ *It is even possible that the multiple regression slope changes sign when a new variable enters the regression. We saw this for the Price on Bedrooms real estate example when Living Area was added to the regression.*

So we'll say it once more: the coefficient of x_j in a multiple regression depends as much on the *other* predictors as it does on x_j. Failing to interpret coefficients properly is the most common error in working with regression models.

15.5 ANOVA Table, *F*-statistic, R^2, and Adjusted R^2

In Chapter 14, for simple linear regression, we interpreted R^2 as the variation in y accounted for by the model. The same interpretation holds for multiple regression, where now the model contains more than one predictor variable. The R^2 value tells us how much (as a fraction or percentage) of the variation in y is accounted for by the model with all the predictor variables included.

There are some relationships among the standard error of the residuals, s_e, the *F*-statistic, and R^2, that are useful for understanding how to assess the value of the multiple regression model.

In Chapter 14 we also introduced the ANOVA Table; we'll revisit it here, now in the context of multiple regression.

We define the total variation of the response variable, y, as the **Sum of Squares Total**, $SST = \sum(y - \bar{y})^2$. The total variation can be split into two parts; the **Sum of Squares Model** (or Regression), $SSM = \sum(\hat{y} - \bar{y})^2$ and the **Sum of Squares Error** (or Residual), $SSE = \sum(y - \hat{y})^2$. To see a visual explanation of this in the simple regression situation, see Chapter 14.

SSM comes from the predictor variables and tells us how much of the total variation in the response is due to the regression model. SSE is the leftover or unexplained variation. We can write an equation that relates the three sums of squares:

$$SST = SSM + SSE$$

For any regression model, we have no control over SST (since it is not based on the choice of model), but we'd like SSE to be as small as we can make it by finding predictor variables that account for as much of that variation as possible.

> In many books and software (including Excel), the words "Model" and "Error" are replaced by Regression and Residual, but then we can't distinguish between SSR (for Regression) and SSR (for Residual). So we prefer SSM and SSE.

For a model to account for a large portion of the variability in y, we need SSM to be large and SSE to be small relative to SST. In fact, R^2 is just the ratio of SSM to SST:

$$R^2 = \frac{SSM}{SST} = 1 - \frac{SSE}{SST}$$

When the SSE is nearly 0, the R^2 value will be close to 1.

Another relationship to note is that, since $SSE = \Sigma(y - \hat{y})^2 = \Sigma e^2$, the standard error of the residuals is: $s_e = \sqrt{\dfrac{SSE}{n - k - 1}}$. As we know, a larger s_e (and thus SSE) means that the residuals are more variable and that our predictions will be correspondingly less precise.

Once we have the sums of squares, the next step is to compute mean squares. Whenever a sum of squares is divided by its degrees of freedom, the result is called a mean square.

The Mean Square Error, which you may see written as MSE, is found as $SSE/(n - k - 1)$. It estimates the variance of the errors; in fact, $MSE = s_e^2$. Similarly $SST/(n - 1)$ divides the total sum of squares by *its* degrees of freedom. That is sometimes called the Mean Square Total and denoted MST. We've seen this one before; the MST is just the variance of y. But it's not needed for our hypothesis test so regression software output doesn't report it

Just as the model and error sums of squares add up to the total sum of squares, so do the degrees of freedom. By subtraction, that leaves k degrees of freedom for SSM, so the Mean Square Model is $MSM = SSM/k$. It's easy to remember this one since there are k predictor variables in the model.

There is a standard display of all these items—sums of squares, degrees of freedom, and mean squares; it is called the ANOVA Table. ANOVA comes from the first letter or two of each word in the phrase "analysis of variance." The technique is called that because the mean squares are really just variances, and as we will see in a moment, the F-statistic is based on these variances.

		ANOVA Table		
Source of Variation	Sum of Squares	Degrees of Freedom	Mean Square	F-statistic
Model (*)	SSM	k	MSM	$F = \dfrac{MSM}{MSE}$
Error (*)	SSE	$n - k - 1$	MSE	
Total	SST	$n - 1$		

* Remember that "Model" means "variation explained by the regression model" and "Error" means "residual or leftover or unexplained variation due to other sources including random error."

Compare this with the ANOVA Table in Chapter 14. Most entries are the same; only the Model and Error degrees of freedom look different.

The F-statistic is the ratio of explained and unexplained mean squares: $F = \dfrac{MSM}{MSE}$

A high value for the F-statistic means that the model is statistically significantly better than using the mean alone.

The *F*-Test for Regression

When the conditions are met, we can test the hypotheses $H_0: \beta_1 = \beta_2 = \ldots = \beta_k = 0$ vs. H_A: at least one $\beta \neq 0$, using

$$F = \frac{MSM}{MSE}$$

which follows an F-model with k and $n - k - 1$ degrees of freedom. We can use the F-model to find the P-value of the test.

In simple linear regression, testing the standard null hypothesis about the slope, H_0: $\beta_1 = 0$ is also a test of the model, testing whether x has any ability to predict y. In fact, the test is equivalent to testing whether the correlation between the two variables is zero. A similar result holds here for multiple regression. Testing the overall hypothesis tested by the F-statistic, H_0: $\beta_1 = \beta_2 = \ldots = \beta_k = \beta_k = 0$, is equivalent to testing whether the true multiple regression R^2 is zero. In fact, the F-statistic for testing that all the slopes are zero can also be found as:

$$F = \frac{\dfrac{R^2}{k}}{\dfrac{1 - R^2}{n - k - 1}} = \frac{\dfrac{SSM}{SST}\dfrac{1}{k}}{\dfrac{SSE}{SST}\dfrac{1}{n - k - 1}} = \frac{\dfrac{SSM}{k}}{\dfrac{SSE}{n - k - 1}} = \frac{MSM}{MSE}$$

In other words, using an F-test to see whether any of the true coefficients is different from zero is equivalent to testing whether the R^2 value is different from zero. A rejection of either hypothesis says that at least one of the predictors accounts for enough variation in y to distinguish it from noise. Unfortunately, the test doesn't say which slope is responsible. You need to look at individual t-tests on the slopes to determine that. Because removing one predictor variable from the regression equation can change any number of slope coefficients, it is not straightforward to determine the right subset of predictors to use.

R^2 and Adjusted R^2

Adding a predictor variable to a multiple regression equation does not always increase the amount of variation accounted for by the model, but it can never reduce it. Adding new predictor variables will always keep the R^2 value the same or increase it. It can never decrease it. But, even if the R^2 value grows, that doesn't mean that the resulting model is a better model or that it has greater predictive ability. If we have a model with k predictors (all of which have statistically significant coefficients at some α level) and want to see if including a new variable, x_{k+1}, is warranted, we could fit the model with all $k + 1$ variables and simply test the slope of the added variable with a t-test of the slope.

This method can test whether the last added variable adds significantly to the model, but choosing the "best" subset of predictors is not necessarily straightforward. The trade-off between a small (parsimonious) model and one that fits the data well is one of the great challenges of any serious model-building effort. Various statistics have been proposed to provide guidance for this search, and one of the most common is called adjusted R^2. **Adjusted R^2** imposes a "penalty" for each new term that's added to the model in an attempt to make models of different sizes (numbers of predictors) comparable. It differs from R^2 because it can shrink when a predictor is added to the regression model or grow when a predictor is removed if the predictor in question doesn't contribute usefully to the model. In fact, it can even be negative.

For a multiple regression with k predictor variables and n cases, it is defined as

$$R^2_{adj} = 1 - (1 - R^2)\frac{n - 1}{n - k - 1} = 1 - \frac{SSE/(n - k - 1)}{SST/(n - 1)}$$

In the Guided Example, we saw that the regression of *Price* on *Bedrooms, Bathrooms, Living Area, Fireplaces,* and *Age* resulted in an R^2 of 0.6049. All the coefficients had P-values well below 0.05. The adjusted R^2 value for this model is 0.6030. If we add the variable *Lot Size* to the model, we get the following regression model:

	Coeff	SE(Coeff)	t-ratio	P-value
Intercept	15360.011	7334.804	2.094	0.03649
Living Area	73.388	4.043	18.154	<0.00001
Bedrooms	−6096.387	2757.736	−2.211	0.02728
Bathrooms	18824.069	3676.582	5.120	<0.00001
Fireplaces	9226.356	3191.788	2.891	0.00392
Age	−152.615	48.224	−3.165	0.00160
Lot Size	847.764	1989.112	0.426	0.67005

```
Residual standard error: 48440 on 1041 degrees of freedom
Multiple R-squared: 0.6081, Adjusted R-squared: 0.6059
F-statistic: 269.3 on 6 and 1041 DF, P-value: <0.0001
```

The most striking feature of this output, as compared to the output in the Guided Example on page 510, is that although most of the coefficients have changed very little, the coefficient of *Lot Size* is far from significant, with a P-value of 0.670. Yet, the adjusted R^2 value is actually higher than for the previous model. This is why we warn against putting too much faith in this statistic. Especially for large samples, the adjusted R^2 does not always adjust downward enough to make sensible model choices. The other problem with comparing these two models is that nine homes had missing values for *Lot Size*, which means that we're not comparing the models on exactly the same data set. When we matched the two models on the smaller data set, the adjusted R^2 value actually did "make the right decision" but just barely—0.6059 versus 0.6060 for the model without *Lot Size*. One might expect a larger difference considering we added a variable whose *t*-ratio is much less than 1.

The lesson to be learned here is that there is no "correct" set of predictors to use for any real business decision problem, and finding a reasonable model is a process that takes a combination of science, art, business knowledge, and common sense. Look at the adjusted R^2 value for any multiple regression model you fit, but be sure to think about all the other reasons for including or not including any given predictor variable.

15.6 Building, Comparing, and Using Models

Principle of Parsimony—Why Simpler Is Better

We said in the previous section that the trade-off between a parsimonious model and one that fits the data well is one of the great challenges of model-building. Parsimony means "thrifty," or "economy in the use of means to an end."

This is well expressed classically as Occam's razor, a principle that states that among competing hypotheses, the one with the fewest assumptions should be chosen. In other words, the simplest explanation is usually the correct one. Einstein expressed this view as Einstein's Constraint: "It can scarcely be denied that the supreme goal of all theory is to make the irreducible basic elements as simple and as few as possible without having to surrender the adequate representation of a single datum of experience." An often-quoted version (but probably not actually said by Einstein exactly this way) is, "Everything should be made as simple as possible, but not simpler."

Science prefers the simplest explanation that is consistent with the data available at a given time, but the simplest explanation may be ruled out as new data become available. Simplest need not be the most accurate. (In fact, there are examples where Occam's razor would have picked the wrong theory.) So start with the simpler theory until simplicity should be traded for greater explanatory power.

Why is parsimony important? A complex model could fit existing data perfectly, but fail badly when new data are available. This series of three plots shows what we mean. In each of the first two, the four data points can be fit exactly with a polynomial. But the curve that is exactly correct for one plot is exactly wrong for the other plot. If both sets of data are combined, a simpler model, a straight line, gives an adequate fit. It's not perfect, but it is pretty good for each set of four points. As John Tukey said, "Better the approximate answer to the right question than the exact answer to the wrong one."

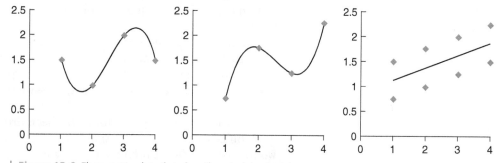

| Figure 15.6 Three scatterplots that show the principle of parsimony.

Dangers of Over-fitting

There can be negative consequences from overly complex models. We said earlier that adding a predictor variable will usually increase the R^2 value, and hence will seem to indicate a better model. How do you reconcile this with the principle of parsimony? Should you aim for the smallest adequate model or the model that gives you the largest R^2?

Here's a very simple illustration having with two predictors and four data points.

x_1	x_2	y
2	6	23
8	9	83
6	8	63
10	10	103

Consider each of the following two possible estimated regression models:

◆ $\hat{y} = -87 + x_1 + 18x_2$

◆ $\hat{y} = -7 + 9x_1 + 2x_2$

Both models give the same computed predicted values of y. For example, for the first row $(x_1 = 2, x_2 = 6): \hat{y} = -87 + 2 + 18(6) = 23 = y$, and $\hat{y} = -7 + 9(2) + 2(6) = 23 = y$. (You can try out the other ones yourself.) So the R^2 is 100% for each model—two perfect fits, yet two completely different models. Why do both regression equations fit the data perfectly? Because x_1 and x_2 are perfectly correlated: $x_2 = 5 + 0.5x_1$. All the information in x_1 is duplicated in x_2. The result is that the estimated coefficients cannot be trusted.

In practice, *x*-variables are unlikely to be perfectly correlated, but they can have very high correlations. That is, much of the information in one predictor variable is contained in another one or combination of other ones. (The technical term for this is *collinearity* or the even fancier *multicollinearity*. See the supplemental material on MyStatLab.) A good model, therefore, is one where each of the predictor variables adds unique predictive information. Predictor variables should only be added to the model if they contain sufficient predictive information not already supplied by the existing variables. Redundancy might be useful in engineering systems, but not in regression models!

Comparing Models

Individual *t*-tests on the slopes in multiple regression are tests of each variable as "the last predictor into the model;" that is, they test how much new or extra information comes from adding a particular variable given that all the other variables are in the model.

Testing one variable at a time is a correct but time-consuming method. Is there a way to compare two models where one is a much smaller subset of the other? In other words, can you test whether two or more predictor variables can be dropped at the same time? The short answer is, yes—we can use a new version of an *F*-test.

Let's call the larger model with *k* predictors the Full Model, and the subset model, where *q* of the predictors have been dropped, the Reduced Model. Our question is whether we are justified in dropping these *q* predictors or whether we would lose significant predictive ability in doing so. The Full Model will have a larger R^2 than the Reduced Model, so our *F*-test will examine whether the change in R^2 is significant.

> There is an old saying, "Don't throw the baby out with the bath water." It means "Don't discard something valuable along with something undesirable." If the null hypothesis is rejected here you will have done just that. This is one of the few times that the researcher is "cheering" against the alternative hypothesis! It's the opposite from what we hoped for the overall *F*-test we did previously.

F-test to compare Full and Reduced Models:

H_0: The reduced model *is* adequate.

(The extra variables in the full model that are not in the reduced model do not provide a significant improvement in the model's predictive ability.)

H_a: The reduced model *is not* adequate.

(At least one of the extra predictors is worthwhile, so the reduced model discards some worthwhile predictors; therefore, it is better to keep the full model rather than this reduced model.)

The test statistic is:

$$F = \left(\frac{n-k-1}{q}\right)\left(\frac{R^2(Full) - R^2(Reduced)}{1 - R^2(Full)}\right)$$

where k = number of *x*-variables in the Full Model, and q = number of variables dropped from the Full Model to get the Reduced Model. (Remember: *q is not* the number of *x*-variables in the Reduced Model!)

The degrees of freedom are q for the numerator, and $n - k - 1$ for the denominator. To determine statistical significance, compare the *F*-statistic with the critical value $F^*_{q,n-k-1}$.

You will need to compute this *F*-statistic yourself—software can't do it because it depends on your choice of Reduced Model. In fact, you need two regression outputs to compute this. You need the R^2 from the Full Model and the R^2 from the Reduced Model. Some assembly is required!

Using the Model for Prediction

As in simple regression, the fitted regression model can be used very easily for prediction. Simply substitute the values of the predictor variables into the equation, multiply by the coefficients, and add the intercept to get the predicted value. But how do you compute a confidence interval or a prediction interval? The formulas for the standard errors are complex, require software to compute, and are beyond the scope of this text. But all is not lost. The same simple useful approximation for the prediction interval that we developed in simple linear regression works here too.

An approximate 95% prediction interval for a new value of y is: $\hat{y} \pm 2S_e$, where S_e is the residual standard deviation which is always readily available from regression software output.

So even in multiple regression your predictions should come with a margin of error. But remember, it's only an approximation, and only applies when n is large *and* the prediction is made where you have data; extrapolation is as much a hazard as ever.

15.7 Extending Multiple Regression

You may have noticed that in this book we like to quote other people. Now we'll quote ourselves. At the beginning of this chapter we stated, "Multiple regression is probably the most powerful and widely used statistical tool today." That is because it can be extended beyond the situations we have discussed so far. We will discuss briefly two of these important extensions.

1. Adding Curvature

Has a voice in your head been saying, "The world is not flat, so how can all the models be linear?" Is there a way to model smooth curved relationships between a response variable and a predictor?

Suppose you create x-variables for a multiple regression model as powers of a single x-variable: $x_1 = x, x_2 = x^2, \ldots, x_k = x^k$. Then the multiple regression model $y = \beta_0 + \beta_1 x_1 + \beta_2 x_2 + \ldots + \beta_k x_k + \varepsilon$ becomes $y = \beta_0 + \beta_1 x^1 + \beta_2 x^2 + \ldots + \beta_k x^k + \varepsilon$. On the surface it just looks like the "subscripts" on the x-variables have become "superscripts." But in fact we have a new set of predictor variables. So if you have an x-y scatterplot with curvature you could fit a quadratic model $y = \beta_0 + \beta_1 x + \beta_2 x^2 + \varepsilon$ just by using $x_1 = x$ and $x_2 = x^2$.

Second-order (i.e., quadratic) terms can also be included when there are several independent variables. For example, here is a "complete" second-order model in two predictor variables, including an "interaction" term that multiplies x_1 and x_2:

$$y = \beta_0 + \beta_1 x_1 + \beta_2 x_2 + \beta_2 x_1^2 + \beta_4 x_2^2 + \beta_5 x_1 x_2 + \varepsilon$$

(If you're curious, this surface would look like a saddle.)

To illustrate, here is scatterplot showing the number of crimes over a 15-year period.

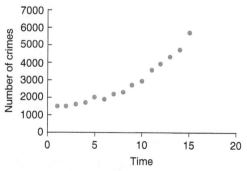

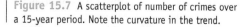

Figure 15.7 A scatterplot of number of crimes over a 15-year period. Note the curvature in the trend.

Simple linear regression gives an equation: $\hat{y} = 607 + 281\,Time$ and $R^2 = 90.4\%$. But there is clear curvature, and using multiple regression with a quadratic term gives an equation $\hat{y} = 1641 - 84\,Time + 23\,Time^2$ and $R^2 = 99.1\%$.

2. Adding Categorical Predictors

Many potentially useful predictors are not quantitative variables and do not have a linear relationship with the response. For example, in a human resources study, gender is likely a useful predictor. It is very simple to include it in a multiple regression model; simply code Males as 0 and Females as 1 (or vice versa if you prefer), and then run the regression analysis as usual. If the coefficient on this variable is significantly different from zero, then gender is a useful predictor.

Categorical variables can be incorporated into the multiple regression model using **indicator variables**. Indicator variables (also called "dummy" variables) are just binary (0/1) variables. It's easy when the categorical variable only has two categories because it's already binary; you just need to make sure it is coded as 0 and 1 (not 1 and 2, for example).

It takes a little more work if there are more than two categories. Three categories require two indicator variables—let's call them Z_1 and Z_2. For example, job status could be classified as full-time, part-time, and casual. Let $Z_1 = 1$ for full-time and 0 otherwise, and let $Z_2 = 1$ for part-time and 0 otherwise. Why don't we need Z_3? Because if you are not full-time and not part-time, you must be casual—it is the "leftover category. In general, if a categorical variable has k categories, then $k - 1$ indicator variables are needed.

To illustrate, consider the Boston Marathon, the world's oldest annual marathon, first run in 1897 with 18 entrants (now there are between 20 000 and 30 000 runners). In 1966, the first woman completed the run, but women were not allowed official entry until 1972, and now make up nearly half of the entrants. Winning times have improved over the years as can be seen in the scatterplot below. Notice the two distinct groups of points; the lower, more horizontal, group consists of times for men, the upper, more vertical group which starts in 1966, has times for women.

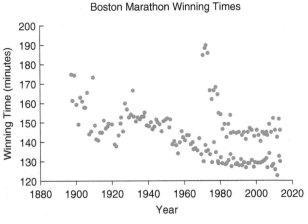

Figure 15.8 A scatterplot of winning times at the Boston Marathon. The lower set are for men; the upper (and to the right) set are for women.

Fitting a simple linear regression model $y = \beta_0 + \beta_1 Year + \varepsilon$ with *Year* as the predictor gives a fitted equation of: $\hat{y} = 500 - 0.18\,Year$ and R^2 of only 14.3%. But this equation doesn't apply either to men or to women; you wouldn't want to use it for prediction.

Let's add *Gender* as an indicator variable (0 = Male, 1 = Female) and fit a multiple regression model $y = \beta_0 + \beta_1 Year + \beta_2 Gender + \varepsilon$. The fitted equation becomes: $\hat{y} = 824 - 0.35 Year + 26.41 Gender$ and R^2 is 59.0%.

If you are male, *Gender* is 0, and the equation is $\hat{y} = 824 - 0.35 Year$; but if you are female, *Gender* is 1, and the equation is $\hat{y} = 851 - 0.35 Year$. So there are different intercepts but the same slope. However, the scatterplot shows that the slopes should be different too. How can that be incorporated in the model? Create one more predictor variable that is the product of *Year* and *Gender*. The model is $y = \beta_0 + \beta_1 Year + \beta_2 Gender + \beta_2 Year \times Gender + \varepsilon$; the fitted equation becomes: $\hat{y} = 728 - 0.30 Year + 1546 Gender - 0.76 Year \times Gender$ and R^2 is 71.2%.

With this enhanced model, if you are male, *Gender* is 0, and the equation is $\hat{y} = 728 - 0.30 Year$; but if you are female, *Gender* is 1, and the equation is $\hat{y} = 2274 - 1.06 Year$. For women, the intercept is higher and the slope more negative than for men, just as the scatterplot shows.

These examples show the power and richness of multiple regression models and how widely applicable they can be.

WHAT CAN GO WRONG?
Interpreting Coefficients

- **Don't claim to "hold everything else constant" for a single individual.** It's often meaningless to say that a regression coefficient says what we expect to happen if all variables but one were held constant for an individual and the predictor in question changed. While it's mathematically correct, it often just doesn't make any sense. For example, in a regression of salary on years of experience, years of education, and age, subjects can't gain a year of experience or get another year of education without getting a year older. Instead, we *can* think about all those who fit given criteria on some predictors and ask about the conditional relationship between *y* and one *x* for those individuals.

- **Don't interpret regression causally.** Regressions are usually applied to observational data. Without deliberately assigned treatments, randomization, and control, we can't draw conclusions about causes and effects. We can never be certain that there are no variables lurking in the background, causing everything we've seen. Don't interpret b_1, the coefficient of x_1 in the multiple regression, by saying: "If we were to change an individual's x_1 by one unit (holding the other *x*'s constant), it would change his *y* by b_1 units." We have no way of knowing what applying a change to an individual would do.

- **Be cautious about interpreting a regression model as predictive.** Yes, we do call the *x*'s predictors, and you can certainly plug in values for each of the *x*'s and find a corresponding *predicted value*, $\hat{y}$. But the term "prediction" suggests extrapolation into the future or beyond the data, and we know that we can get into trouble when we use models to estimate $\hat{y}$ values for *x*'s not in the range of the data. Be careful not to extrapolate very far from the span of your data. In simple regression, it was easy to tell when you extrapolated. With many predictor variables, it's often harder to know when you are

(continued)

outside the bounds of your original data.[5] We usually think of fitting models to the data more as modelling than as prediction, so that's often a more appropriate term.

- **Don't think that the sign of a coefficient is special.** Sometimes our primary interest in a predictor is whether it has a positive or negative association with *y*. As we have seen, though, the sign of the coefficient also depends on the other predictors in the model. Don't look at the sign in isolation and conclude that "the direction of the relationship is positive (or negative)." Just like the value of the coefficient, the sign is about the relationship after allowing for the linear effects of the other predictors. The sign of a variable can change depending on which other predictors are in or out of the model. For example, in the regression model for house prices, we saw the coefficient of *Bedrooms* change sign when *Living Area* was added to the model as a predictor. It isn't correct to say either that houses with more bedrooms sell for more on average or that they sell for less. The truth is more subtle and requires that we understand the multiple regression model.

- **If a coefficient's *t*-statistic is not significant, don't interpret it at all.** You can't be sure that the value of the corresponding parameter in the underlying regression model isn't really zero.

WHAT ELSE CAN GO WRONG?

- **Don't fit a linear regression to data that aren't straight.** This is the most fundamental regression assumption. If the relationship between the *x*'s and *y*'s isn't approximately linear, there's no sense in fitting a linear model to it. What we mean by "linear" is a model of the form we have been writing for the regression. When we have two predictors, this is the equation of a plane, which is linear in the sense of being flat in all directions. With more predictors, the geometry is harder to visualize, but the simple structure of the model is consistent; the predicted values change consistently with equal size changes in any predictor.

  Usually we're satisfied when plots of *y* against each of the *x*'s are straight enough. We'll also check a scatterplot of the residuals against the predicted values for signs of nonlinearity.

  This first warning is not strictly true. In Section 15.7 we learned that we can add indicator variables as predictors. In that case, the relationship between *y* and *x* is certainly not linear, since there are only two *x*-values, 0 and 1. We also learned that if the relationship between *y* and *x* has curvature, all is not lost; we can add a second-order (quadratic) term to the model.

- **Watch out for the plot thickening.** The estimate of the error standard deviation shows up in all the inference formulas. But that estimate assumes that the error standard deviation is the same throughout the range of the *x*'s so that we can combine all the residuals when we estimate it. If s_e changes with any *x*,

[5] With several predictors we can wander beyond the data because of the *combination* of values even when individual values are not extraordinary. For example, houses with one bathroom and houses with five bedrooms can both be found in the real estate records, but a single house with five bedrooms and only one bathroom would be quite unusual. The model we found is not appropriate for predicting the price of such an extraordinary house.

these estimates won't make sense. The most common check is a plot of the residuals against the predicted values. If plots of residuals against several of the predictors all show a thickening and especially if they also show a bend, then consider re-expressing y. If the scatterplot against only one predictor shows thickening, consider re-expressing that predictor.

- **Make sure the errors are nearly Normal.** All of our inferences require that the true errors be modelled well by a Normal model. Check the histogram and Normal probability plot of the residuals to see whether this assumption looks reasonable.

- **Watch out for high-influence points and outliers.** We always have to be on the lookout for a few points that have undue influence on our model, and regression is certainly no exception.

ETHICS IN ACTION

Alpine Medical Systems, Inc. is a large provider of medical equipment and supplies to hospitals, doctors, clinics, and other health care professionals. Alpine's VP of Marketing and Sales, Kenneth Jadik, asked one of the company's analysts, Nicole Haly, to develop a model that could be used to predict the performance of the company's sales force. Based on data collected over the past year, as well as records kept by Human Resources, she considered five potential independent variables: (1) gender, (2) starting base salary, (3) years of sales experience, (4) personality test score, and (5) high school grade point average. The dependent variable (sales performance) is measured as the sales dollars generated per quarter. In discussing the results with Nicole, Kenneth asks to see the full regression model with all five independent variables included. Kenneth notes that a t-test for the coefficient of gender shows no significant effect on sales performance and recommends that it be eliminated from the model. Nicole reminds him of the company's history of offering lower starting base salaries to women, recently corrected under court order. If instead, starting base salary is removed from the model, gender is statistically significant, and

its coefficient indicates that women on the sales force outperform men (taking into account the other variables). Kenneth argues that because gender is not significant when all predictors are included, it is the variable that should be omitted.

ISSUE *The choice of predictors for the regression model is politically motivated. Because gender and base salary are related, it is impossible to separate their effects on sales performance, and inappropriate to conclude that one or the other is irrelevant. Related to ASA Ethical Guidelines, Item A, which can be found at http://www.amstat.org/about/ethicalguidelines.cfm.*

ETHICAL SOLUTION *The situation is more complex than a single model can explain. Both the model with gender but not base salary and the one with base salary but not gender should be reported. Then the discussion of these models should point out that the two variables are related because of previous company policy and note that the conclusion that those with lower base salary have better sales and the conclusion that women tend to have better sales performance are equivalent as far as these data are concerned.*

WHAT HAVE WE LEARNED?

In Chapter 14, we learned to apply our inference methods to linear regression models. Now we've seen that much of what we know about those models is also true for multiple regression.

- The assumptions and conditions are the same: linearity (checked now with scatterplots of y against each x), independence (think about it), constant variance (checked with the scatterplot of residuals against predicted values), and nearly Normal residuals (checked with a histogram or probability plot).

- R^2 is still the fraction of the variation in y accounted for by the regression model.
- s_e is still the standard deviation of the residuals—a good indication of the precision of the model.
- The degrees of freedom (in the denominator of s_e and for each of the t-tests) follows the same rule: n minus the *number of parameters estimated*.
- The regression table produced by any statistics package shows a row for each coefficient, giving its estimate, a standard error, a t-statistic, and a P-value.
- If all the conditions are met, we can test each coefficient against the null hypothesis that its parameter value is zero with a Student's t-test.

And we've learned some new things that are useful now that we have multiple predictors.

- We can perform an overall test of whether the multiple regression model provides a better summary for y than its mean by using the F-distribution.
- We learned that R^2 may not be appropriate for comparing multiple regression models with different numbers of predictors. Adjusted R^2 is one approach to this problem.
- We've learned that the goal of multiple regression is to find the simplest model that provides an adequate fit; in other words, no useless or redundant predictor variables should be retained.
- We've learned how to compare models, dropping more than one predictor at a time, using an F-test to compare full and reduced models.

We've learned that multiple regression models extend our ability to model the world to many more situations but that we must take great care when we interpret its coefficients. To interpret a coefficient of a multiple regression model, remember that it estimates the linear relationship between y and that predictor *after accounting for two things*: 1) the linear effects of all the other predictors on y and 2) the linear relationship between that predictor and all other x's.

- We've learned how multiple regression can be used to account for curvature, using polynomial terms, and categorical predictors, using indicator variables.

Terms

Adjusted R^2   An adjustment to the R^2 statistic that attempts to allow for the number of predictors in the model. It is sometimes used when comparing regression models with different numbers of predictors:

$$R^2_{adj} = 1 - (1 - R^2)\frac{n-1}{n-k-1} = 1 - \frac{SSE/(n-k-1)}{SST/(n-1)}$$

F-test   The F-test is used to test the null hypothesis that the overall regression is no improvement over just modelling y with its mean:

$$H_0: \beta_1 = \ldots = \beta_k = 0 \; vs \; H_A: \text{at least one } \beta \neq 0$$

If this null hypothesis is not rejected, then you should not proceed to test the individual coefficients.

F-test to compare models   A test based on another version of an F-statistic of whether the difference in R^2 between a full model and a subset model is significant. If the null hypothesis is not rejected, the smaller model is considered adequate and is preferred over the larger model. It is different from examining *t*-statistics of each coefficient because it allows the removal of more than one predictor at a time.

Indicator variable	A binary (0/1) variable that is used to incorporate categorical predictor variables. One indicator variable is needed if there are two categories, two if there are three categories, and so on. In general, if a categorical variable has k categories, then $k-$ indicator variables are needed.
Least squares	We still fit multiple regression models by choosing the coefficients that make the sum of the squared residuals as small as possible. This is called the *method of least squares*.
Multiple regression	A linear regression with two or more predictors whose coefficients are found by least squares. When the distinction is needed, a least squares linear regression with a single predictor is called a *simple regression*. The multiple regression model is: $y = \beta_0 + \beta_1 x_1 + \ldots + \beta_k x_k + \varepsilon$.
Sum of Squares Model (a.k.a. Regression), SSM	A measure of the total variation in the response variable due to the model. $SSM = \sum (\hat{y} - \bar{y})^2$
Sum of Squares Error (a.k.a. Residual), SSE	A measure of the variation in the residuals. $SSE = \sum (y - \hat{y})^2$
Sum of Squares Total, SST	A measure of the variation in the response variable. $SST = \sum (y - \bar{y})^2$. Note that $\frac{SST}{n-1} = Var(y)$.
t-ratio for the coefficients	The *t*-ratios for the coefficients can be used to test the null hypotheses that the true value of each coefficient is zero against the alternative that it is not. The *t* distribution is also used in the construction of confidence intervals for each slope coefficient.

Skills

PLAN

- Understand that the "true" regression model is an idealized summary of the data.
- Know how to examine scatterplots of *y* vs. each *x* for violations of assumptions that would make inference for regression unwise or invalid.
- Know how to examine displays of the residuals from a multiple regression to check that the conditions have been satisfied. In particular, know how to judge linearity and constant variance from a scatterplot of residuals against predicted values. Know how to judge normality from a histogram and Normal probability plot.
- Remember to be especially careful to check for failures of the independence assumption when working with data recorded over time. Examine scatterplots of the residuals against time and look for patterns.

 DO

- Be able to use a statistics package to perform the calculations and make the displays for multiple regression, including a scatterplot of the response against each predictor, a scatterplot of residuals against predicted values, and a histogram and Normal probability plot of the residuals.

- Know how to use the *F*-test to check that the overall regression model is better than just using the mean of *y*.

- Know how to test the standard hypotheses that each regression coefficient is really zero. Be able to state the null and alternative hypotheses. Know where to find the relevant numbers in standard computer regression output.

- Know how to use an *F*-test to compare full and reduced models.

- Know how to add curvature to the model and how to add categorical predictors to the model.

REPORT

- Be able to summarize a regression in words. In particular, be able to state the meaning of the regression coefficients, taking full account of the effects of the other predictors in the model.

- Be able to interpret the *F*-statistic and R^2 for the overall regression.

- Be able to interpret the P-value of the *t*-statistics for the coefficients to test the standard null hypotheses.

TECHNOLOGY HELP: Regression Analysis

All statistics packages make a table of results for a regression. The table for multiple regression looks very similar to the table for simple regression. You'll want to look at the Analysis of Variance (ANOVA) table, and you'll see information for each of the coefficients.

Most packages offer to plot residuals against predicted values. Some will also plot residuals against the *x*'s. With some packages, you must request plots of the residuals when you request the regression. Others let you find the regression first and then analyze the residuals afterward. Either way, your analysis is not complete if you don't check the residuals with a histogram or Normal probability plot and a scatterplot of the residuals against the *x*'s or the predicted values.

One good way to check assumptions before embarking on a multiple regression analysis is with a scatterplot matrix. This is sometimes abbreviated SPLOM (or Matrix Plot) in commands.

Multiple regressions are always found with a computer or programmable calculator. Before computers were available, a full multiple regression analysis could take months or even years of work.

EXCEL

- In Excel 2003 and earlier, select **Data Analysis** from the **Tools** menu.
- In Excel 2007, select **Data Analysis** from the **Analysis Group** on the Data Tab.
- Select **Regression** from the **Analysis Tools** list.
- Click the **OK** button.
- Enter the data range holding the Y-variable in the box labelled "Y-range."
- Enter the range of cells holding the X-variables in the box labelled "X-range."
- Select the **New Worksheet Ply** option.
- Select **Residuals** options. Click the **OK** button.

Comments

The Y- and X-ranges do not need to be in the same rows of the spreadsheet, although they must cover the same number of cells. But it is a good idea to arrange your data in parallel columns as in a data table. IMPORTANT: The X-variables must be in adjacent columns. No cells in the data range may hold non-numeric values or be left blank.

Although the dialogue offers a Normal probability plot of the residuals, the data analysis add-in does not make a correct probability plot, so don't use this option.

MINI CASE STUDY PROJECTS

Golf Success

Left, Mikael Damkier/Shutterstock;
Right, Petr Jilek/Shutterstock

Professional sports, like many other professions, require a variety of skills for success. That makes it difficult to evaluate and predict success. Fortunately, sports provide examples we can use to learn about modelling success because of the vast amount of data which are available. Here's an example.

What makes a golfer successful? The game of golf requires many skills. Putting well or hitting long drives will not, by themselves, lead to success. Success in golf requires a combination of skills. That makes multiple regression a good candidate for modelling golf achievement.

A number of internet sites post statistics for the current PGA players. We have compiled data from the ESPN website (http://espn.go.com/golf/statistics/_/year/2012) for 191 top players of 2012 in the file **ch15_MCSP_Golfers.xlsx**.

All of these players earned money on the tour, but they didn't all play the same number of events. And the distribution of earnings is quite skewed. (Rory McIlroy earned $503 000 per event. In second place, Tiger Woods earned only (!) $323 000 per event. Median earnings per event were $42 650.) So it's a good idea to take logs of Earnings/Event as the response variable.

The variables in the data file include:

Log$/E   The logarithm of earnings per event.

GIR   Greens in Regulation. Percentage of holes played in which the ball is on the green with two or more strokes left for par.

Putts   Average number of putts per hole in which the green was reached in regulation.

Save%   Each time a golfer hits a bunker by the side of a green but needs only one or two additional shots to reach the hole, he is credited with a save. This is the percentage of opportunities for saves that are realized.

DDist   Average Drive Distance (yards). Measured as averages over pairs of drives in opposite directions (to account for wind).

DAcc   Drive Accuracy. Percent of drives landing on the fairway.

Investigate these data. Find a regression model to predict golfers' success (measured in log earnings per event). Write a report presenting your model including an assessment of its limitations. Note: Although you may consider several intermediate models, a good report is about the model you think best, not necessarily about all the models you tried along the way while searching for it.

Rating School Performance

The Fraser Institute is an independent, non-partisan Canadian research and educational organization that publishes peer-reviewed research on economic and public policy issues. One annual project of note is their report on school performance in British Columbia, Alberta, Ontario, and Quebec. They produce school "reports cards" based on objective, publicly available data. For secondary schools these include provincial exam results, grade-to-grade transition rates and graduation rates, among other things. The report card also provides the percent of students enrolled in ESL programs, French immersion programs, the percent with special needs students, and the parents' average income. Each school receives a overall rating out of 10.

The data set provided in the file **ch15_MSCP_School_Performance.xlsx** was compiled from 85 public secondary schools in the Lower Mainland of British Columbia in 2012. School Name, Region, and measurements of the gender gap (difference in male and female scores) in math and English are not included in the data set. Here is a description of the variables:

- *ID*—Sequential ID from 1 to 85
- *ESLPct*—Percentage of students enrolled in English-as-a-Second-Language programs
- *SpecNeedsPct*—Percentage of special needs students
- *FrenchImmPct*—Percentage of students enrolled in French Immersion programs at the school
- *ParentIncome*—Parents' average employment income ($000s)
- *AveExamMark*—Average provincial mark (%) of all students in Grades 10, 11, and 12 courses with a mandatory provincial exam
- *PctExamsFailed*—Percent of all mandatory Grades 10, 11, and 12 provincial exams that received a failing grade
- *SchoolExamDiff*—The difference between the school mark and provincial exam mark in courses where the provincial exam is mandatory. A large difference indicates grades "inflation"
- *GraduationRate*—Percentage of eligible graduates who graduate in the same school year
- *DelayedAdvancementRate*—Estimated percentage of Grade 10 students who will not complete Grade 12 within three years
- *OverallRating*—rating on a 0–10 scale, based on standardized scores (which makes it a relative rating)

Investigate these data by building the following regression models. Use appropriate techniques of model-building. Don't forget to check assumptions and examine residuals. Summarize the findings of each model in a brief report.

a. Use the provincial *AveExamMark* as the response variable, and *ESLPct*, *SpecNeedsPct*, *FrenchImmPct*, and *ParentIncome* as predictor variables.

b. Use the Fraser Institute's *Overall Rating* as the response variable, and *ESLPct*, *SpecNeedsPct*, *FrenchImmPct*, and *ParentIncome* as predictor variables.

c. Use the Fraser Institute's *Overall Rating* as the response variable, and *AveExamMark*, *PctExamsFailed*, *SchoolExamDiff*, *GraduationRate*, and *DelayedAdvancementRate* as predictor variables.

d. Finally, use the Fraser Institute's *Overall Rating* as the response variable, and all of the following: *ESLPct*, *SpecNeedsPct*, *FrenchImmPct*, *ParentIncome*, *AveExamMark*, *PctExamsFailed*, *SchoolExamDiff*, *GraduationRate*, and *DelayedAdvancementRate* as predictor variables.

MyStatLab **Students! Save time, improve your grades with MyStatLab.**
The Exercises marked in red can be found on MyStatLab. You can practice them as often as you want, and most feature step-by-step guided solutions to help you find the right answer. You'll find a personalized Study Plan available to you too! Data Sets for exercises marked **T** are also available on MyStatLab for formatted technologies.

EXERCISES

The first 12 exercises consist of two sets of six (one even-numbered, one odd-numbered). Each set guides you through a multiple regression analysis. We suggest that you do all six exercises in a set. Remember that the answers to the odd-numbered exercises can be found in the back of the book.

T 1. **Police salaries.** Is the amount of violent crime related to what police officers are paid? The U.S. Bureau of Labor Statistics

publishes data on occupational employment and wage estimates (www.bls.gov/oes/). Here are data on those states for which 2006 data were available. The variables are:

Violent Crime (crimes per 100 000 population)

Police Officer Wage (mean $/hr)

Graduation Rate (%)

One natural question to ask of these data is how police officer wages are related to violent crime across these states. **LO❶**

First, here are plots and background information.

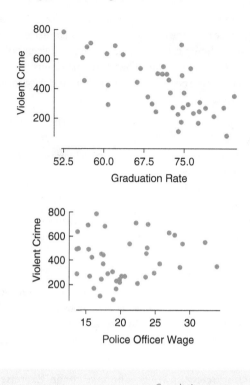

Correlations			
	Violent Crime	Graduation Rate	Police Officer Wage
Violent Crime	1.000		
Graduation Rate	−0.682	1.000	
Police Officer Wage	0.103	0.213	1.000

a) Name and check (to the extent possible) the regression assumptions and their corresponding conditions.

b) If we found a regression to predict *Violent Crime* just from *Police Officer Wage*, what would the R^2 of that regression be?

T 2. Ticket prices. On a typical night in New York, about 25 000 people attend a Broadway show, paying an average price of more than $75 per ticket. *Variety* (www.variety.com), a news weekly that reports on the entertainment industry, publishes statistics about the Broadway show business. The data file on the MyStatLab holds data about shows on Broadway for most weeks of 2006–2008. (A few weeks are missing data.) The following variables are available for each week:

> *Receipts* ($ million)
>
> *Paid Attendance* (thousands)
>
> *# Shows*
>
> *Average Ticket Price* ($)

Viewing this as a business, we'd like to model *Receipts* in terms of the other variables.

First, here are plots and background information. **LO❶**

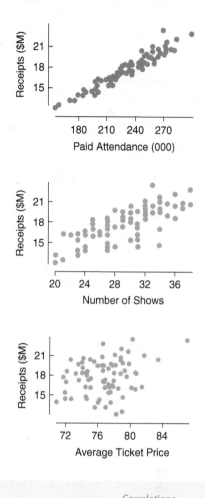

Correlations				
	Receipts	Paid Attendance	# Shows	Average Ticket Price
Receipts ($M)	1.000			
Paid Attendance	0.961	1.000		
# Shows	0.745	0.640	1.000	
Average Ticket Price	0.258	0.331	−0.160	1.000

a) Name and check (to the extent possible) the regression assumptions and their corresponding conditions.

b) If we found a regression to predict *Receipts* only from *Paid Attendance*, what would the R^2 of that regression be?

T 3. Police salaries, part 2. Here's a multiple regression model for the variables considered in Exercise 1. **LO❷, LO❻**

Dependent variable is: Violent Crime
R squared = 53.0% R squared (adjusted) = 50.5%
s = 129.6 with 37 degrees of freedom

Source	Sum of Squares	df	Mean Square	F-ratio
Regression	701648	2	350824	20.9
Residual	621060	37	16785.4	

Variable	Coeff	SE(Coeff)	t-ratio	P-value
Intercept	1390.83	185.9	7.48	<0.0001
Police Officer Wage	9.33	4.125	2.26	0.0297
Graduation Rate	−16.64	2.600	−6.40	<0.0001

a) Write the regression model.

b) What does the coefficient of *Police Officer Wage* mean in the context of this regression model?

c) In a state in which the average police officer wage is $20/hour and the high school graduation rate is 70%, what does this model estimate the violent crime rate would be?

d) Is this likely to be a good prediction? Why do you think that?

T 4. Ticket prices, part 2. Here's a multiple regression model for the variables considered in Exercise 2:[6] LO❷, LO❻

Dependent variable is: Receipts($M)
R squared = 99.9%   R squared (adjusted) = 99.9%
s = 0.0931 with 74 degrees of freedom

Source	Sum of Squares	df	Mean Square	F-ratio
Regression	484.789	3	161.596	18634
Residual	0.641736	74	0.008672	

Variable	Coeff	SE(Coeff)	t-ratio	P-value
Intercept	−18.320	0.3127	−58.6	<0.0001
Paid Attendance	0.076	0.0006	126.7	<0.0001
# Shows	0.0070	0.0044	1.59	0.116
Average Ticket Price	0.24	0.0039	61.5	<0.0001

a) Write the regression model.

b) What does the coefficient of *Paid Attendance* mean in this regression? Does that make sense?

c) In a week in which the paid attendance was 200 000 customers attending 30 shows at an average ticket price of $70, what would you estimate the receipts would be?

d) Is this likely to be a good prediction? Why do you think that?

T 5. Police salaries, part 3. Using the regression table in Exercise 3, answer the following questions. LO❷

a) How was the *t*-ratio of 2.26 found for *Police Officer Wage*? (Show what is computed using numbers from the table.)

b) How many states are used in this model. How do you know?

c) The *t*-ratio for *Graduation Rate* is negative. What does that mean?

T 6. Ticket prices, part 3. Using the regression table in Exercise 4, answer the following questions. LO❷

a) How was the *t*-ratio of 126.7 found for *Paid Attendance*? (Show what is computed using numbers found in the table.)

b) How many weeks are included in this regression? How can you tell?

c) The *t*-ratio for the intercept is negative. What does that mean?

T 7. Police salaries, part 4. Consider the coefficient of *Police Officer Wage*. LO❷

---
[6] Some values are rounded to simplify the exercises. If you recompute the analysis with your statistics software you may see slightly different numbers.

a) State the standard null and alternative hypotheses for the true coefficient of *Police Officer Wage*.

b) Test the null hypothesis (at $\alpha = 0.05$) and state your conclusion.

c) A state senate aide challenges your conclusion. She points out that we can see from the scatterplot and correlation (see Exercise 1) that there is almost no linear relationship between police officer wages and violent crime. Therefore, she claims, your conclusion in part a must be mistaken. Explain to her why this is not a contradiction.

T 8. Ticket prices, part 4. Consider the coefficient of *# Shows*. LO❷

a) State the standard null and alternative hypotheses for the true coefficient of *# Shows*.

b) Test the null hypothesis (at $\alpha = 0.05$) and state your conclusion.

c) A Broadway investor challenges your analysis. He points out that the scatterplot of *Receipts* vs. *# Shows* in Exercise 2 shows a strong linear relationship and claims that your result in part a can't be correct. Explain to him why this is not a contradiction.

T 9. Police salaries, part 5. The Senate aide in Exercise 7 now accepts your analysis but claims that it demonstrates that if the state pays police more, it will actually *increase* the rate of violent crime. Explain why this interpretation is not a valid use of this regression model. Offer some alternative explanations. LO❷, LO❼

T 10. Ticket prices, part 5. The investor in Exercise 8 now accepts your analysis but claims that it demonstrates that it doesn't matter how many shows are playing on Broadway; receipts will be essentially the same. Explain why this interpretation is not a valid use of this regression model. Be specific. LO❷, LO❼

T 11. Police salaries, part 6. Here are some plots of residuals for the regression of Exercise 3. LO❸

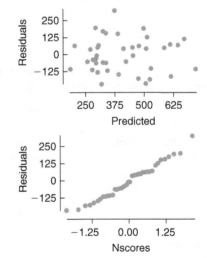

Which of the regression conditions can you check with these plots?

Do you find that those conditions are met?

T 12. Ticket prices, part 6. Here are some plots of residuals for the regression of Exercise 4. LO❸

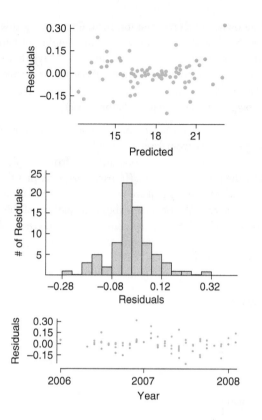

Which of the regression conditions can you check with these plots?

Do you find that those conditions are met?

13. Real estate prices. A regression was performed to predict selling price of houses based on *Price* in dollars, *Area* in square feet, *Lotsize* in square feet, and *Age* in years. The R^2 is 92%. The equation from this regression is given here.

$$Price = 169\,328 + 35.3\ Area + 0.718\ Lotsize - 6543\ Age$$

One of the following interpretations is correct. Which is it? Explain what's wrong with the others. LO❷

a) Each year a house ages, it is worth $6543 less.

b) Every extra square foot of area is associated with an additional $35.30 in average price, for houses with a given lot size and age.

c) Every additional dollar in price means lot size increases 0.718 square feet.

d) This model fits 92% of the data points exactly.

14. Wine prices. Many factors affect the price of wine, including such qualitative characteristics as the variety of grape, location of winery, and label. Researchers developed a regression model considering two quantitative variables: the tasting score of the wine and the age of the wine (in years) when released to market. They found the following regression equation, with an R^2 of 65%, to predict the price (in dollars) of a bottle of wine.

$$Price = 6.25 + 1.22\ Tasting\ Score + 0.55\ Age$$

One of the following interpretations is correct. Which is it? Explain what's wrong with the others. LO❷

a) Each year a bottle of wine ages, its price increases about $0.55.

b) This model fits 65% of the points exactly.

c) For a unit increase in tasting score, the price of a bottle of wine increases about $1.22.

d) After allowing for the age of a bottle of wine, a wine with a one unit higher tasting score can be expected to cost about $1.22 more.

15. Appliance sales. A household appliance manufacturer wants to analyze the relationship between total sales and the company's three primary means of advertising (television, magazines, and radio). All values were in millions of dollars. They found the following regression equation.

$$Sales = 250 + 6.75\ TV + 3.5\ Radio + 2.3\ Magazine$$

One of the following interpretations is correct. Which is it? Explain what's wrong with the others. LO❷

a) If they did no advertising, their income would be $250 million.

b) Every million dollars spent on radio makes sales increase $3.5 million, all other things being equal.

c) Every million dollars spent on magazines increases TV spending $2.3 million.

d) Sales increase on average about $6.75 million for each million spent on TV, after allowing for the effects of the other kinds of advertising.

16. Wine prices, part 2. Here are some more interpretations of the regression model to predict the price of wine developed in Exercise 14. One of these interpretations is correct. Which is it? Explain what is wrong with the others. LO❷

a) The minimum price for a bottle of wine that has not aged is $6.25.

b) The price for a bottle of wine increases on average about $0.55 for each year it ages, after allowing for the effects of tasting score.

c) Each year a bottle of wine ages, its tasting score increases by 1.22.

d) Each dollar increase in the price of wine increases its tasting score by 1.22.

17. Canadian executives' stock options. Corporate social responsibility (CSR) refers to how a business complies with the spirit of the law, ethical standards, and international norms, and sometimes goes beyond the interests of the business and the law to further some social good. Is there a relationship between the salary and stock options paid to a Canadian company executive and the company's CSR rating? A study of 77 Canadian companies found the following (adapted) regression equation:

$$CSR\ Rating = -0.163 \times Salary + 0.320 \times Options + Several\ Other\ Factors$$

All variables are transformed to *z*-scores (i.e., standardized to have a mean of zero and a standard deviation of one). For *Salary*, the *t*-statistic and P-value are -1.196 and 0.235. For *Options*, the *t*-statistic and P-value are -2.921 and 0.0046. The *F*-statistic is 4.811 and has a P-value < 0.01. LO❷

(Source: L.S. Mahoney and L. Thorn, "An Examination of the Structure of Executive Compensation and Corporate Social Responsibility: A Canadian Investigation," *Journal of Business Ethics* 69 (2006): 149–162, Table VI)

a) Based on the information provided, is this regression a good model of how *Salary* and *Options* impact CSR Rating?

b) What other steps would you take to determine whether this is a good model?

c) Interpret the *t*-statistics for the coefficients of *Salary* and *Options*.

d) What does it mean that the coefficient for *Salary* is negative?

e) What effect do you think raising executive options by 0.25 standard deviations would have on the CSR rating for a particular company?

18. OECD economic regulations. A study by the U.S. Small Business Administration modelled the GDP per capita of 24 of the countries in the Organization for Economic Cooperation and Development (OECD) (Crain, M. W., *The Impact of Regulatory Costs on Small Firms*, available at www.sba.gov/sites/default/files/The Impact of Regulatory Costs on Small Firms (Summary).pdf). One analysis estimated the effect on GDP of economic regulations, using an index of the degree of OECD economic regulation and other variables. They found the following regression model.

$$GDP(1998–2002) = 10487 - 1343 \text{ } OECD \text{ } Economic \text{ } Regulation$$
$$Index + 1.078 \text{ } GDP/Capita(1988) - 69.99 \text{ } Ethno\text{-}linguistic$$
$$Diversity \text{ } Index + 44.71 \text{ } Trade \text{ } as \text{ } share \text{ } of \text{ } GDP \text{ } (1998–2002)$$
$$- 58.4 \text{ } Primary \text{ } Education(\%Eligible \text{ } Population)$$

All *t*-statistics on the individual coefficients have P-values < 0.05, except the coefficient of *Primary Education*. **LO❷**

a) Does the coefficient of the OECD Economic Regulation Index indicate that more regulation leads to lower GDP? Explain.

b) The *F*-statistic for this model is 129.61 (5, 17 *df*). What do you conclude about the model?

c) If *GDP/Capita(1988)* is removed as a predictor, then the *F*-statistic drops to 0.694 and none of the *t*-statistics is significant (all P-values > 0.22). Reconsider your interpretation in (a).

19. Home prices. Many variables have an impact on determining the price of a house. A few of these are size of the house (square feet), lot size, and number of bathrooms. Information for a random sample of homes for sale was obtained from the internet. Regression output modelling the asking price with square footage and number of bathrooms gave the following result. **LO❹, LO❼**

Dependent Variable is: Asking Price
s = 67013 R-Sq = 71.1% R-Sq(adj) = 64.6%

Predictor	Coeff	SE(Coeff)	t-ratio	P-value
Intercept	−152037	85619	−1.78	0.110
Baths	9530	40826	0.23	0.821
Area	139.87	46.67	3.00	0.015

Analysis of Variance

Source	DF	SS	MS	F	P-value
Regression	2	99303550067	49651775033	11.06	0.004
Residual	9	40416679100	4490742122		
Total	11	1.39720E + 11			

a) Write the regression equation.

b) How much of the variation in home asking prices is accounted for by the model?

c) Explain in context what the coefficient of *Area* means.

d) The owner of a construction firm, upon seeing this model, objects because the model says that the number of bathrooms has no effect on the price of the home. He says that when *he* adds another bathroom, it increases the value. Is it true that the number of bathrooms is unrelated to house price? (*Hint:* Do you think bigger houses have more bathrooms?)

20. Home prices, part 2. Here are some diagnostic plots for the home prices data from Exercise 19. These were generated by a computer package and may look different from the plots generated by the packages you use. (In particular, note that the axes of the Normal probability plot are swapped relative to the plots we've made in the text. We only care about the pattern of this plot, so it shouldn't affect your interpretation.) Examine these plots and discuss whether the assumptions and conditions for the multiple regression seem reasonable. **LO❸**

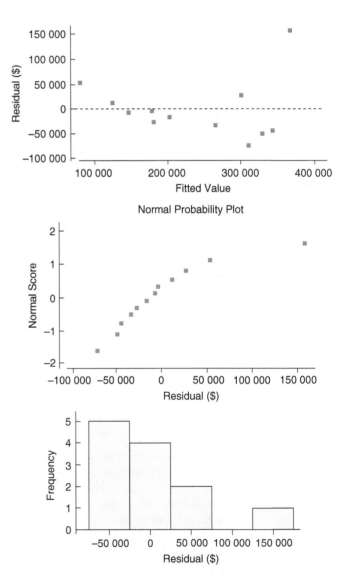

21. Secretary performance. A Canadian labour union has undertaken a study of 30 secretaries' yearly salaries (in thousands of dollars). The organization wants to predict salaries from several other variables. The variables to be considered potential predictors of salary are:

X1 = months of service
X2 = years of education
X3 = score on standardized test
X4 = words per minute (wpm) typing speed
X5 = ability to take dictation in words per minute

A multiple regression model with all five variables was run on a computer package, resulting in the following output. LO❹

Variable	Coeff	Std. Error	t-value
Intercept	9.788	0.377	25.960
X1	0.110	0.019	5.178
X2	0.053	0.038	1.369
X3	0.071	0.064	1.119
X4	0.004	0.0307	0.013
X5	0.065	0.038	1.734

s = 0.430   R-sq = 0.863

Assume that the residual plots show no violations of the conditions for using a linear regression model.

a) What is the regression equation?
b) From this model, what is the predicted salary (in thousands of dollars) of a secretary with 10 years (120 months) of experience, 9th grade education (9 years of education), 50 on the standardized test, 60 wpm typing speed, and the ability to take 30 wpm dictation?
c) Test whether the coefficient for words per minute of typing speed (X4) is significantly different from zero at $\alpha = 0.05$.
d) How might this model be improved?
e) A correlation of age with salary finds $r = 0.682$, and the scatterplot shows a moderately strong positive linear association. However, if X6 = Age is added to the multiple regression, the estimated coefficient of age turns out to be $b_6 = -0.154$. Explain some possible causes for this apparent change of direction in the relationship between age and salary.

Ⓣ 22. Walmart revenue. Here's a regression of monthly revenue of Walmart Corp, relating that revenue to the Total U.S. Retail Sales, the Personal Consumption Index, and the Consumer Price Index. LO❹

Dependent variable is: Walmart_Revenue
R squared = 66.7% R squared (adjusted) = 63.8%
s = 2.327 with 39 − 4 = 35 degrees of freedom

Source	Sum of Squares	df	Mean Square	F-ratio
Regression	378.749	3	126.250	23.3
Residual	189.474	35	5.41354	

Variable	Coeff	SE(Coeff)	t-ratio	P-value
Intercept	87.0089	33.60	2.59	0.0139
Retail Sales	0.000103	0.000015	6.67	< 0.0001
Persnl Consmp	0.00001108	0.000004	2.52	0.0165
CPI	−0.344795	0.1203	−2.87	0.0070

a) Write the regression model.
b) Interpret the coefficient of the Consumer Price Index (CPI). Does it surprise you that the sign of this coefficient is negative? Explain.

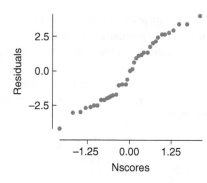

c) Test the standard null hypothesis for the coefficient of CPI and state your conclusions.

Ⓣ 23. Mutual funds returns. Chapter 14, Exercise 35 considered the relationship between the Wilshire 5000 Total Market Return and the amount of money flowing into and out of mutual funds (fund flows) monthly from January 1990 through October of 2002. The data file included data on the unemployment rate in each of the months. The original model looked like this. LO❹

Dependent variable is: Fund_Flows
R squared = 17.9%   R squared (adjusted) = 17.3%
s = 10999 with 154 − 2 = 152 degrees of freedom

Source	Sum of Squares	df	Mean Square	F-ratio
Regression	4002044231	1	4002044231	33.1
Residual	18389954453	152	120986542	

Variable	Coeff	SE(Coeff)	t-ratio	P-value
Intercept	9599.10	896.9	10.7	< 0.0001
Wilshire	1156.40	201.1	5.75	< 0.0001

Adding the *Unemployment Rate* to the model yields:

Dependent variable is: Fund_Flows
R squared = 28.8%   R squared (adjusted) = 27.8%
s = 10276 with 154 − 3 = 151 degrees of freedom

Source	Sum of Squares	df	Mean Square	F-ratio
Regression	6446800389	2	3223400194	30.5
Residual	15945198295	151	105597340	

Variable	Coeff	SE(Coeff)	t-ratio	P-value
Intercept	30212.2	4365	6.92	≤ 0.0001
Wilshire	1183.29	187.9	6.30	< 0.0001
Unemployment	−3719.55	773.0	−4.81	< 0.0001

a) Interpret the coefficient of the *Unemployment Rate*.
b) The *t*-ratio for the *Unemployment Rate* is negative. Explain why.
c) State and complete the standard hypothesis test for the *Unemployment Rate*.

Ⓣ 24. Price of beef. How is the price of beef related to other factors? The data below give information on the price of beef (*PBE*) and the possible explanatory variables: consumption of beef per capita (*CBE*), retail food price index (*PFO*), food consumption per capita index (*CFO*), and an index of real disposable income per capita (*RDINC*) for the years 1925 to 1941 in the United States. LO❹

a) Use computer software to find the regression equation for predicting the price of beef based on all of the given explanatory variables. What is the regression equation?

b) Produce the appropriate residual plots to check the assumptions. Is this inference appropriate for this model? Explain.

c) How much variation in the price of beef can be explained by this model?

d) Consider the coefficient of beef consumption per capita (*CBE*). Does it say that that price of beef goes up when people eat less beef? Explain.

Year	PBE	CBE	PFO	CFO	RDINC
1925	59.7	58.6	65.8	90.9	68.5
1926	59.7	59.4	68	92.1	69.6
1927	63	53.7	65.5	90.9	70.2
1928	71	48.1	64.8	90.9	71.9
1929	71	49	65.6	91.1	75.2
1930	74.2	48.2	62.4	90.7	68.3
1931	72.1	47.9	51.4	90	64
1932	79	46	42.8	87.8	53.9
1933	73.1	50.8	41.6	88	53.2
1934	70.2	55.2	46.4	89.1	58
1935	82.2	52.2	49.7	87.3	63.2
1936	68.4	57.3	50.1	90.5	70.5
1937	73	54.4	52.1	90.4	72.5
1938	70.2	53.6	48.4	90.6	67.8
1939	67.8	53.9	47.1	93.8	73.2
1940	63.4	54.2	47.8	95.5	77.6
1941	56	60	52.2	97.5	89.5

T **25.** Walmart revenue, part 2. Walmart is the second largest retailer in the world. The data file on MyStatLab holds monthly data on Walmart's revenue, along with several possibly related economic variables. **LO❺**

a) Using computer software, find the regression equation predicting Walmart revenues from the *Retail Index*, the Consumer Price index (*CPI*), and *Personal Consumption*.

b) Does it seem that Walmart's revenue is closely related to the general state of the economy?

T **26.** Walmart revenue, part 3. Consider the model you fit in Exercise 27 to predict Walmart's revenue from the Retail Index, CPI, and Personal Consumption index. **LO❺**

a) Plot the residuals against the predicted values and comment on what you see.

b) Identify and remove the four cases corresponding to December revenue and find the regression with December results removed.

c) Does it seem that Walmart's revenue is closely related to the general state of the economy?

T **27.** Motorcycles. More than one million motorcycles are sold annually (www.webbikeworld.com). Off-road motorcycles (often called "dirt bikes") are a market segment (about 18%) that is highly specialized and offers great variation in features.

This makes it a good segment to study to learn about which features account for the cost (manufacturer's suggested retail price, MSRP) of a dirt bike. Researchers collected data on 2005 model dirt bikes (lib.stat.cmu.edu/datasets/dirtbike_aug.csv). Their original goal was to study market differentiation among brands (*The Dirt on Bikes: An Illustration of CART Models for Brand Differentiation*, Jiang Lu, Joseph B. Kadane, and Peter Boatwright, server1.tepper.cmu.edu/gsiadoc/WP/2006-E57.pdf), but we can use these to predict msrp from other variables.

Here are scatterplots of three potential predictors, *Wheelbase (in)*, *Displacement (cu in)*, and *Bore (in)*.

Which of these variables would you choose first as a predictor in a regression to model *MSRP*? Explain. **LO❺**

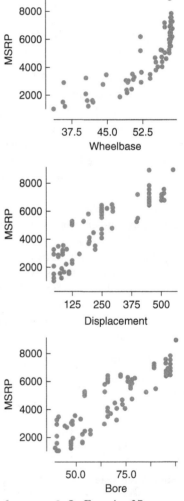

T **28.** Motorcycles, part 2. In Exercise 27, we saw data on off-road motorcycles and examined scatterplots. Review those scatterplots. Here's a regression of *MSRP* on both *Displacement* and *Bore*. Both of the predictors are measures of the size of the engine. The displacement is the total volume of air and fuel mixture that an engine can draw in during one cycle. The bore is the diameter of the cylinders. **LO❺**

Dependent variable is: MSRP
R squared = 77.0% R squared (adjusted) = 76.5%
s = 979.8 with 98 − 3 = 95 degrees of freedom

Variable	Coeff	SE(Coeff)	t-ratio	P-value
Intercept	318.352	1002	0.318	0.7515
Bore	41.1650	25.37	1.62	0.1080
Displacement	6.57069	3.232	2.03	0.0449

a) State and test the standard null hypothesis for the coefficient of *Bore*.

b) Both of these predictors seem to be linearly related to *MSRP*. Explain what your result in part a means.

(T) 29. Motorcycles, part 3. Here's another model for the *MSRP* of off-road motorcycles. **LO❻**

Dependent variable is: MSRP
R squared = 90.9% R squared (adjusted) = 90.6%
s = 617.8 with 95 − 4 = 91 degrees of freedom

Source	Sum of Squares	df	Mean Square	F-ratio
Regression	346795061	3	115598354	303
Residual	34733372	91	381685	

Variable	Coeff	SE(Coeff)	t-ratio	P-value
Intercept	−2682.38	371.9	−7.21	< 0.0001
Bore	86.5217	5.450	15.9	< 0.0001
Clearance	237.731	30.94	7.68	< 0.0001
Engine strokes	−455.897	89.88	−5.07	< 0.0001

a) Would this be a good model to use to predict the price of an off-road motorcycle if you knew its bore, clearance, and engine strokes? Explain.

b) The Suzuki DR650SE had an *MSRP* of $4999 and a 4-stroke engine, with a bore of 100 inches. Can you use this model to estimate its *Clearance*? Explain.

(T) 30. Exam grades, revisited. Chapter 14, Exercises 55 and 56 looked separately at the relationships between mid-term grades and final exam grades, and between assignment grades and final exam grades. Data were a random sample of 200 students from the Sauder School of Business at the University of British Columbia. Now let's examine the combined effect of mid-term and assignment grades on final exam grades. **LO❷**

The original models looked like this.
Using *Midterm* as the predictor variable:

Dependent variable is: *FinalExam*
R squared = 57.3%
s = 9.488 with 200 − 2 = 198 df

Variable	Coeff	SE(Coeff)	t-ratio	P-value
Intercept	2.9781	4.1115	0.72	<0.0001
Midterm	0.8861	0.0544	16.29	<0.0001

Source	Sum of Squares	df	Mean Square	F-ratio
Model	23875.86	1	23875.86	265.23
Error	17823.82	198	90.02	
Total	41699.68	199		

Using *Assignment* as the predictor variable:

Dependent variable is: *FinalExam*
R squared = 18.9%
s = 13.068 with 200 − 2 = 198 df

Variable	Coeff	SE(Coeff)	t-ratio	P-value
Intercept	41.7308	4.1238	10.12	<0.0001
Assignment	0.3481	0.0512	6.80	<0.0001

Source	Sum of Squares	df	Mean Square	F-ratio
Model	7885.44	1	7885.44	46.17
Error	33814.24	198	170.78	
Total	41699.68	199		

Putting both predictors in the model yields:

Dependent variable is: *FinalExam*
R squared = 58.9%
s = 9.322 with 200 − 2 = 198 df

Variable	Coeff	SE(Coeff)	t-ratio	P-value
Intercept	0.7837	4.2496	−0.18	0.8539
Midterm	0.8159	0.0589	13.86	<0.0001
Assignment	0.1147	0.0402	2.85	0.0048

Source	Sum of Squares	df	Mean Square	F-ratio
Model	24581.68	2	12290.84	141.45
Error	17118.00	197	86.89	
Total	41699.68	199		

a) Does the multiple regression model provide an improvement over each of the two simple regression models?

b) The R^2 increases from 57.3% using only *Midterm* to 58.9% with the addition of *Assignment*. Compute the appropriate *F*-statistic to test whether the increase in R^2 is significant. If it is, explain why a seemingly small increase turns out to be statistically significant?

c) Use the full model to predict the final exam grade for a student who gets a mid-term grade of 85 and an assignment grade of 90. Be sure to provide an approximate 95% prediction interval. Comment on the width of the interval.

(T) 31. Burger King nutrition. Like many fast-food restaurant chains, Burger King (BK) provides data on the nutrition content of its menu items on its website. Here's a multiple regression predicting calories for Burger King foods from *Protein* content (g), *Total Fat* (g), *Carbohydrate* (g), *and Sodium* (mg) per serving. **LO❺, LO❻**

Dependent variable is: Calories
R-squared = 100.0% R-squared [adjusted] = 100.0%
s = 3.140 with 31 − 5 = 26 degrees of freedom

Source	Sum of Squares	df	Mean Square	F-ratio
Regression	1419311	4	354828	35994
Residual	256.307	26	9.85796	

Variable	Coeff	SE(Coeff)	t-ratio	P-value
Intercept	6.53412	2.425	2.69	0.0122
Protein	3.83855	0.0859	44.7	<0.0001
Total fat	9.14121	0.0779	117	<0.0001
Carbs	3.94033	0.0338	117	<0.0001
Na/Serv.	−0.69155	0.2970	−2.33	0.0279

a) Do you think this model would do a good job of predicting calories for a new BK menu item? Why or why not?

b) The mean of *Calories* is 455.5 with a standard deviation of 217.5. Discuss what the value of *s* in the regression means about how well the model fits the data.

c) Does the R^2 value of 100.0% mean that the residuals are all actually equal to zero?

32. Forestry industry. Measurement of tree volume is a key activity in the forestry industry in Canada. Estimating the volume of standing trees is needed to determine whether it will be profitable to log a particular region in view of lumber prices as well as stumpage fees and royalties paid to provincial ministries of forests. Volume tables for each species are based on non-destructive measurements of standing trees; the most common ones are DBH (diameter at breast height, set at 1.3 metres above the ground) and total height. **LO❺**

To obtain tree volumes, measurements may be obtained from felled trees on logging operations. A random sample of 40 yellow-poplar trees provided the following data set:

Tree #	Volume (cu m)	DBH (cm)	Height (m)	Tree #	Volume (cu m)	DBH (cm)	Height (m)
1	0.133	15.2	19.8	21	1.685	40.9	29.9
2	0.150	16.0	19.2	22	1.368	41.1	26.2
3	0.198	18.3	21.0	23	2.158	42.7	32.0
4	0.210	18.8	19.2	24	1.662	43.7	29.9
5	0.354	20.3	23.8	25	2.144	44.7	32.3
6	0.297	21.6	20.1	26	2.234	46.7	30.8
7	0.408	23.6	22.6	27	2.523	49.0	33.8
8	0.379	21.8	24.4	28	2.418	47.5	31.1
9	0.614	25.9	25.3	29	2.953	51.8	33.2
10	0.496	24.9	23.5	30	2.619	50.3	31.4
11	0.651	29.2	22.6	31	2.914	52.6	32.9
12	0.697	29.0	25.6	32	3.203	54.1	30.8
13	1.079	31.0	29.9	33	3.259	56.9	32.3
14	0.900	30.5	29.9	34	3.831	56.4	36.6
15	1.178	34.0	29.3	35	3.557	56.4	32.9
16	0.991	32.5	27.4	36	4.315	58.4	39.0
17	1.220	35.6	29.0	37	4.754	59.4	35.1
18	1.175	35.8	27.7	38	4.349	61.7	37.8
19	1.297	37.8	26.5	39	3.922	64.3	32.6
20	1.557	39.1	29.9	40	5.021	65.5	36.0

a) Fit a simple linear regression of *Volume* vs. *DBH*. From the scatterplot and residual plot, is this an appropriate model to fit? Are you surprised by the value of R^2?
b) Add *Height* to the model and refit using multiple regression. What happens to R^2? Is *Height* needed in the model?
c) Create a new variable called *DBHSQ* by squaring each *DBH* value. (This variable is included already on the spreadsheet.) Fit a

multiple regression model using *DBH*, *Height*, and *DBHSQ*. Comment on the new value of R^2.
d) Determine whether all three predictor variables are required to adequately predict tree volume. If not, provide the final model. Compare the three-predictor model to a model using only *DBHSQ*. Make sure to carry out appropriate hypothesis tests to support your choice of final model.

33. Real estate, B.C. We began this chapter with a vignette about real estate data and models to predict sale price from various home characteristics. We'll end the chapter the same way, but now it's your turn to do the analysis. The data set has information on a selection of 1086 home sales in 2013 from the Fraser Valley in British Columbia. The data were provided by the Fraser Valley Real Estate Board.

We have selected some variables for you to consider in your model: number of bedrooms, number of bathrooms, floor area, lot size, age, and whether or not it was a view property. The response variable is, of course, sale price. **LO❺**

a) Use the techniques we have learned in this chapter to build a regression model to predict sale price from any or all of the available predictor variables. Remember that the binary variable, *View*, can be analyzed in the same way as the quantitative predictor variables. Don't forget to check assumptions.
b) Write a short report of your findings; explain your model and how to use it, in a way that a prospective home buyer could understand. Make sure to include a discussion of the margin of error in prediction.
c) Can you suggest other variables, not provided here or perhaps not even collected, that could improve the accuracy and precision of the model?

JUST CHECKING ANSWERS

1 58.4% of the variation in *Percent Body Fat* can be accounted for by the multiple regression model using *Height*, *Age*, and *Weight* as predictors.

2 For a given *Height* and *Weight*, an increase of one year in *Age* is associated with an increase of 0.137% in *Body Fat* on average.

3 The multiple regression coefficient is interpreted for *given* values of the other variables. That is, for people of the *same Weight* and *Age*, an increase of one centimetre of *Height* is associated with, on average, a *decrease* of 0.502% in *Body Fat*. The same cannot be said when looking at people of all *Weights* and *Ages*.

Statistical Modelling and the World of Business Statistics

CHAPTER 16

Mark Blinch/Reuters Pictures

CONNECTIONS CHAPTER

In Chapters 9 through 15 we developed a large set of methods of inference, z-tests, t-tests, chi-square tests, and linear regression. In the current chapter we develop a framework into which all these tests can fit, and a way to choose the appropriate procedure for a given data analysis situation. We also provide a little taste of the wide world of business statistics methods beyond where we end our study.

LEARNING OBJECTIVES

1. Form a statistical model to address a research question

2. Choose an appropriate statistical technique for a specific research question

3. Recognize the need for other techniques beyond this book

Rogers Communications Inc.

This book is about communication. What do data communicate to us and how do we communicate to others what we learn from the data? So our story to begin this chapter is about Rogers, a diversified public telecommunications and mass media company.

Rogers began in 1924 as the Standard Radio Manufacturing Corporation when Edward Rogers Sr. invented the world's first alternating current (AC) radio tube, which enabled radios to be powered by ordinary household electric currents. The invention was a technological breakthrough that helped popularize radios around the world. Rogers died very young at 38; his son E.S. "Ted" Rogers Jr. later carried on his father's business, acquiring CHFI-FM in 1960, then creating Rogers Broadcasting Limited from Rogers Radio Broadcasting in 1962. The business continued to evolve, to Rogers Cablesystems, Cantel, and then Rogers Communications Inc. in 1986. Following the death of Ted Rogers in 2008, control of Rogers Communications passed to the Rogers Control Trust, which operates, in part, for the benefit of current and future generations of the Rogers family.

With headquarters in Toronto, Rogers has three primary business lines. Rogers Cable is the largest cable television provider in Canada; it offers analog and digital television, high-speed internet access, residential telephony services, and home service monitoring. One division is Rogers Business Solutions, which provides voice communications services, data networking, and broadband internet connectivity to small, medium, and large businesses.

Rogers Media is Canada's premier collection of category-leading media assets with businesses in radio and television broadcasting, televised shopping, publishing, and sports entertainment. Rogers Wireless entered the mobile phone market in 1985 and is Canada's largest voice and data communications services provider. They launched the Apple iPhone in Canada in 2008. In 2011, Rogers launched a home monitoring service using both its wireless network and cable network. The service lets one manage multiple utilities at home, including security sensors and cameras, the thermostat, appliances, and lighting.

Rogers is also well-known for its leading role in Canadian sports. They acquired the Toronto Blue Jays Baseball Club in 2000 and the Skydome in 2004, renaming it the Rogers Centre. Rogers also purchased the naming rights to Rogers Arena, home of the Vancouver Canucks. They sponsor the Rogers Cup of Tennis Canada. Along with their chief competitor, Bell Canada, Rogers bought a majority stake in Maple Leaf Sports & Entertainment, the parent company of the Toronto Maple Leafs. In 2013, Rogers signed a landmark 12-year $5.2 billion agreement with the NHL for complete broadcast and multimedia rights on all platforms in all languages.

Rogers is listed on the TSX and NYSE, and with revenues exceeding $12 billion in 2011 and nearly 30 000 employees, Rogers is a leading name on the Canadian communications landscape.

S uch a diversified company as Rogers collects massive amounts of data, and not just what their subscribers upload and download through their cellular phone data plans! Here are a few examples:

- ◆ Financial performance data, of interest to shareholders
- ◆ Surveys of customer satisfaction with wireless service, outlet stores, and technical assistance through their Canadian-based call centres
- ◆ Employee productivity: sales records, response times, absenteeism
- ◆ Wireless contract renewal rates
- ◆ Internet connectivity and usage statistics
- ◆ Magazine subscriptions and readership
- ◆ Television viewer and radio listener numbers

All the statistical techniques presented in this textbook, and many more, can be applied to help Rogers draw conclusions from data, to understand and grow the activities of the company.

Even Rogers' current logo has a mathematical aspect. The symbol is a Mobius strip that has amazing mathematical properties. Look them up!

Now that we've reached the final chapter, we will look at how the wide range of techniques fits together. Is there a framework that makes it possible to see the common features of the techniques and, more importantly, how to decide which ones to use in which situations? Let's review the main headlines.

We began with a discussion of data—types, quality, sources, and sample surveys. Next we learned how to display and describe data, one variable at a time, and then in relationship with one another. We built some foundations on random variables and probability models and, in particular, the normal model. That was the first half of the book and it set the stage for statistical inference. That's been the second half of the book: confidence intervals and hypothesis tests for proportions and means with one sample, two independent samples and two related samples. And finally, we developed inference for simple and multiple regression to investigate more fully the relationships among two or more variables.

One word that showed up repeatedly was "model." We defined a **model** as a mathematical description of a real-world phenomenon. For example, the normal model is an equation that describes a common distribution displayed as a bell-shaped histogram. The z-model and t-model describe the distributions of the sample proportion and sample mean, respectively. The simple linear regression model describes a straight-line relationship between two quantitative variables. And so on. Let's look more deeply at what makes a statistical model and how statistical modelling is the key to understanding data.

16.1 Statistical Models

Science and scientists have developed countless models to explain physical situations. The models are mathematical representations that used data to estimate parameters. For example, Hooke's Law explains the relationship between the length of an extended spring and the mass hanging from the end of it. Newton's laws include the famous "force = mass $\times$ acceleration." Boyle's law in physics says that, at constant temperature, "pressure $\times$ volume = constant" for a given quantity of gas. In each of these examples there is a systematic relationship between the outcome and the predictors. Possibly the most famous model of all (no, not Gisele Bundchen, Channing Tatum, or Naomi Campbell) is Einstein's $E = mc^2$.

These are all examples of deterministic models, because the left-hand side of the equation is completely determined or explained by the right-hand side. The relationship is exact.

Statistical models are a little different. A **statistical model** has an added component. In addition to the systematic component there is a random component (also called "error," or a "stochastic" component if you want to impress people). The random component happens for a variety of reasons: measurement error, unaccounted-for factors, and natural variability between experimental units. For example, consider the height of people. Different people have different heights, because people are different! That's natural variability. But even if you measured the same person twice you would get slightly different results. That's measurement error.

Let's visualize a statistical model as a mathematical equation, as follows: write an "equal" sign. The variable(s) to the left are the outcome(s) or response(s); variables to the right are predictors or explanatory factors. But the right-hand side has one more term, representing the random component.

$$\text{Outcome} = \text{Math function of (Predictors)} + \text{Error}$$
$$= (\text{Systematic component}) + (\text{Random component})$$

Imagine how much less impressive Einstein's model would look if it were:

$$E = mc^2 + \{\text{some other things I haven't figured out}\}.$$

We mentioned previously George Box's famous observation that, "All models are wrong, but some are useful." It is impossible to represent a real-world system exactly by a simple mathematical model. But a carefully constructed model can provide a good approximation to both the systematic and random components. That is, it can explain how the predictors affect the outcome and how big the uncertainty is. That's what we did in our study of regression.

What are the objectives of model building? Christopher Chatfield summarized them as follows:

◆ To provide a simple but adequate description of data

◆ To compare different sets of data

◆ To test a theory about a relationship

◆ To make predictions

◆ To give margins of error around estimates, predictions, and conclusions

◆ To understand the process that generated the data

Note that this list *does not* include getting the best fit to the observed data. Recall our Chapter 15 discussion of over-fitting a model. Chatfield cautioned that the procedure of trying lots of different models until a good-looking fit is obtained is a dubious one. The purpose of model-building is not just to get the "best" fit, but rather to construct a model that is consistent, not only with the data, but also with background knowledge and with any earlier data sets. Remember, the model must apply not only to the data you have already collected but any other data that might be collected using the same procedures. In our text we have addressed the three stages in model building: formulation, estimation, and validation (checking assumptions and conditions).

Let's look at one famous and tragic illustration of how a good graph and a properly-built model could have saved lives.

The NASA Space Shuttle program operated from 1981 to 2011 and ran 135 missions to launch satellites, interplanetary probes, and the Hubble Space Telescope, to conduct science experiments in orbit, and to construct and service the International Space Station. The first orbiter, Enterprise, was built for testing and not for orbit. The original four fully functional orbiters were: Columbia, Challenger, Discovery, and Atlantis; Endeavour was added in 1991 to replace Challenger. Challenger and Columbia were lost in mission accidents in 1986 and 2003. We will investigate the Challenger disaster here.

The shuttle had a number of components: the orbiter vehicle, a pair of recoverable solid rocket boosters, and an expendable external tank. The shuttle was launched vertically, using the boosters and the orbiter vehicle's main engines fuelled by the external tank. The boosters were jettisoned before the vehicle reached orbit, and the external tank just before orbit insertion. Each booster rocket consisted of several pieces whose joints were sealed with rubber O-rings (think of them as giant rubber washers), designed to prevent the release of hot gases during combustion. Each booster contained three primary O-rings (for a total of six for the craft).

On January 28, 1986, Challenger took off, as the twenty-fifth flight in the space shuttle program. Two minutes into the flight, the spacecraft exploded, killing all on board. A presidential commission that included the late Nobel-prize-winning physicist Richard Feynman determined the cause of the accident and wrote a two-volume report.

The key issue was the forecasted temperature on launch day, a chilly 31°F (just below 0°C). The coldest previous launch temperature was 53°F. After each of the 23 previous flights for which there were data, the O-rings were examined for damage. The sensitivity of O-rings to temperature was well-known; a warm O-ring had greater elasticity so it would quickly recover its shape after being compressed, but a cold one would not. The inability of the O-ring to recover its shape would lead to

Nasa

joints not being sealed and might result in a gas leak. The commission determined that this was the cause of the Challenger explosion.

Could this have been foreseen? Engineers discussed whether the flight should go on as planned (no statisticians were involved). Here is a simplified version of one of the arguments.

The following table gives the ambient temperature at launch and number of primary O-rings damaged during the flight.

Ambient temp. at launch (°F): 53° 57° 58° 63° 70° 70° 75°
Number of O-rings damaged: 2   1   1   1   1   1   2

The table and a scatterplot (graph it yourself) shows no apparent relationship between temperature and the number of O-rings damaged; higher damage occurred at both lower and higher temperatures. Hence, just because it was cold the day of the flight doesn't imply that the flight should have been postponed or cancelled.

This is an inappropriate analysis! It ignores the 16 flights when zero O-rings were damaged. When those are included the scatterplot looks quite different, and in fact, shows a strong relationship between the number of O-rings damaged and temperature. Here is the complete data set:

Temp. (°F): 53 57 58 63 66 67 67 67 68 69 70 70 70 70 72 73 75 75 76 76 78 79 81
damaged: 2 1 1 1 0 0 0 0 0 0 0 0 0 0 1 1 0 0 0 2 0 0 0 0

Here is a scatterplot of the data.

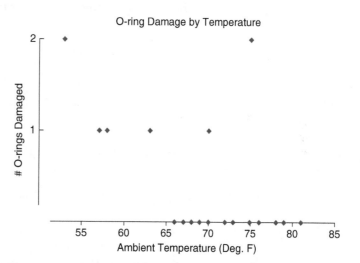

Except for the single observation in the upper right, there is a clear inverse relationship between the probability of O-ring damage and ambient temperature. Unfortunately, this plot was never made! The flaw in the analysis was not to include flights in which there was no O-ring damage.

On January 28, 1986, the ambient (outside) temperature was 31°F. Since this is off the scale of available data, extrapolation is needed. An appropriate statistical model (using a technique called logistic regression, discussed at the end of this chapter) estimates the probability of an O-ring failure at 31°F to be 96%! If you were in charge and knew that the probability of an O-ring failure was 96% would you have given go-ahead to launch?

There is a postscript to this illustration. One of the Commission's recommendations was that a statistician must be part of the ground control team for all flights.

Not only does this story emphasize the importance of graphing and using all available data, it also points out the vital role of a good statistical model. How was that model chosen? By first examining the data types. The outcome variable was binary—was there an O-ring failure, yes or no? The predictor variable was quantitative—temperature. Logistic regression (see the following section) was a suitable model for a situation where the outcome is binary and the predictor is measurement.

Perhaps this approach of classifying the role and type of variable can be applied to our other techniques and models.

16.2 A Modelling Framework

Let's look at a gender equity study that compares salaries of men and women, using a two-sample t-test. The following "data" table has five males and five females, with letters standing in for dollar values. A t-test compares the mean of the male salaries, *Mean(M)* to the mean of the female salaries, *Mean(F)*.

Male Salary	Female Salary
A	F
B	G
C	H
D	I
E	J
Mean(M)	*Mean(F)*

But we can rearrange the data as follows:

Salary ($)	Gender (0=M,1=F)
A	0
B	0
C	0
D	0
E	0
F	1
G	1
H	1
I	1
J	1

We can model the relationship by treating salary as the outcome variable and gender as the predictor variable. Salary is quantitative and gender is binary, so a two-sample t-test can be thought of as a model with a quantitative outcome variable and a binary predictor variable.

Let's try another situation: are male and female drivers equally likely to use a cellphone while driving? We can use a two-sample z-test of two proportions. Here is a data table, again for five males and five females. A z-test compares the proportion of male Yes responses, *Proportion(M)*, to the proportion of female Yes responses, *Proportion(F)*.

Male Driver Cell User	Female Driver Cell User
Yes	Yes
No	No
No	Yes
Yes	Yes
No	Yes
Proportion(M)	*Proportion(F)*

Again, we can rearrange the data as follows:

Cell Phone While Driving (Y/N)	Gender (0=M,1=F)
Yes	0
No	0
No	0
Yes	0
No	0
Yes	1
No	1
Yes	1
Yes	1
Yes	1

We can model the relationship by treating cell phone use as the outcome variable and gender as the predictor variable. Cell phone use is binary and gender is binary, so a two-sample z-test can be thought of as a model with a binary outcome variable and a binary predictor variable.

It is easy to extend this to categorical variables with more than two categories. For example, is ethnicity a predictor of smoking status (never, former, current)? We can use a chi-square test of independence to model this relationship, where smoking status is a categorical outcome variable and ethnicity is a categorical predictor variable.

Let's summarize these three situations in the following table.

Outcome Variable	Predictor Variable	Model or Technique
Quantitative	Binary	Two-sample t-test of means
Binary	Binary	Two-sample z-test of proportions
Categorical (2+ categories)	Categorical (2+ categories)	Chi-square test of independence

Now you can see how simple linear regression fits into this framework. The outcome variable and the predictor variable are each quantitative. If we allow more than one predictor variable, that's multiple regression.

Here is the previous table, expanded to include these and three possibilities we haven't yet considered.

One of the authors calls this his Grand Unified Theory of Statistics, which has the acronym G.U.T.S.! As the saying goes, "No guts, no glory."

Outcome Variable	Predictor Variable(s)	Model or Technique
Quantitative	Binary	Two-sample t-test of means
Binary	Binary	Two-sample z-test of proportions
Categorical (2+ categories)	Categorical (2+ categories)	Chi-square test of independence
Quantitative	Quantitative	Simple linear regression
Quantitative	Any combination of quantitative or categorical	Multiple linear regression
Binary	Quantitative	Simple logistic regression
Binary	Any combination of quantitative or categorical	Multiple logistic regression
Quantitative	Categorical (2+ categories)	One-way analysis of variance

The techniques called simple and multiple logistic regression and one-way analysis of variance have not been discussed. We will address them briefly in the next section. (And a fuller explanation of logistic regression is available on MyStatLab.)

However, the framework is not perfect. One-sample tests don't quite fit into this framework. Neither do situations like the paired *t*-test that has linkage between observations, or repeated measuring of subjects. Oh well, every theory has its limitations.

Outcome Variable	Predictor Variable	Model or Technique
Quantitative	None—compare to an external target instead	One-sample *t*-test of a single mean
Binary	None—compare to an external target instead	One-sample *z*-test of a single proportion

So we're right back where we started in Chapter 2. We wrote, "Section 2.2 is the most important section in the whole book. Why? ... A statistical analysis cannot be done without knowing the type of variables or type of data to be analyzed." We also wrote, "Variables play different roles, and knowing the variable's *type* is crucial to knowing what to do with it and what it can tell us. The simplest and most important way to classify variables (and data) is either as *categorical* or *quantitative*."

There you have it. If you can figure out each variable's role, that is, which variable is the outcome and which is/are the predictor(s), and then decide whether they are categorical (including the simple two-category version called binary), you can pick a technique. It's that easy! The framework shows what all the important statistical modelling techniques have in common and, more importantly, how to choose an appropriate one. Let's try it out with a Mini Case Study Project from Chapter 2.

An anonymous online survey of a large undergraduate business statistics course gathered information for research about student life. Questions were asked about demographic characteristics, grades, study habits, and leisure activities. Here are some of the variables for which data were collected (they are labeled V1 through V9, for convenience—V for variable). Assume that the quantitative variables are normally distributed.

◆ V1 Gender (0=Male, 1=Female)
◆ V2 First-year overall grade (Percent)
◆ V3 Second-year overall grade (Percent)
◆ V4 Opinion of campus support services (1=Poor, 2=Fair, 3=Good, 4=Excellent)
◆ V5 Any paid part-time work (1=Yes, 0=No)
◆ V6 Total study time per week (Hours)
◆ V7 Mode of travel to campus (1=Car, 2=Transit, 3=Bicycle, 4=Walk/live on campus)
◆ V8 Regular Facebook user (1=Yes, 0=No)
◆ V9 Monthly amount spent on recreational activities (Dollars)

For each of the following research questions, suggest which of the techniques we have studied could be used. Here is a list of techniques to choose from. Consult the framework.

1. Is the average study time (V6) the same for males and females (V1)?

   Answer: Outcome variable is quantitative (study time); explanatory variable is binary (gender); = two-sample t-test of independent means

2. Is gender (V1) related to opinion about campus support services (V4)?

   Answer: Outcome variable is categorical (support services); explanatory variable is binary (gender); = chi-square test of independence

3. Can second-year overall grade (V3) be explained by study hours (V6), amount spent on recreational activities (V9), and paid part-time work (V5)?

   Answer: Outcome variable is quantitative (overall grade); explanatory variables are quantitative (study hours, recreational spending) and binary (part-time work); = multiple regression

4. Are there equal percentages of males and females (V1) who do paid part-time work (V5)?

   Answer: There are two possibilities here. Outcome variable is binary (paid part-time work—Yes/No); explanatory variable is binary (gender); = two-sample z-test of proportions OR chi-square test of independence

5. Do males and females (V1) achieve different first-year overall grades (V2)?

   Answer: Outcome variable is quantitative (overall grade); explanatory variable is binary (gender); = two-sample t-test of independent means

6. Is the rate of Facebook users (V8) different from the Canadian percentage?

   Answer: There is only one sample here and the variable is binary (Facebook user—Yes/No). Compare the estimate from the single sample with the external target; = one-sample z-test of a single proportion

7. Does monthly expenditure on recreational activities (V9) exceed $250?

   Answer: There is only one sample here and the variable is quantitative (recreational expenditure). Compare the estimate from the single sample with the external target; =one-sample t-test of a single mean

8. Are first-year overall grades (V2) and second-year overall grades (V3) different on average?

   Answer: Each respondent's first-year data value is matched with his/her second-year data value. Hence the outcome variable is the difference between first-year and second-year overall grade, so this is a one-sample test of the differences; = matched pairs t-test

9. Is second-year overall grade (V3) related to study hours (V6)?

   Answer: Outcome variable is quantitative (overall grade); explanatory variable is quantitative (study hours); = linear regression

   Bonus. Is mode of travel (V7) related to study hours (V6)?

   Answer: Outcome variable is quantitative (study hours); explanatory variable is categorical (mode of travel, 4 categories); = one-way analysis of variance (see Section 16.3)

16.3 A Short Tour of Other Statistical Methods in Business

Our book is titled *Business Statistics: A First Course*. That suggests the possibility of a second course, and perhaps more beyond that. What topics and techniques might be found in such a book? Let's look briefly at a few of them, especially the ones identified in our modelling framework, and illustrate them with plausible research questions that might be of interest to Rogers Communications Inc.

One-Way Analysis of Variance (ANOVA) (a.k.a. comparison of multiple means)

Rogers' Human Resources Division wonders whether the average level of employee satisfaction is the same for full-time, part-time, and casual employees. A two-sample *t*-test compares the means of two independent populations. How could you compare the means of three independent populations? A crude solution would be to compare each pair of means with a series of three two-sample *t*-tests—that is, compare full-time to part-time, full-time to casual, and part-time to casual (i.e., 1 to 2, 1 to 3, and 2 to 3). But that's inefficient and prone to misinterpretation. A better solution would be to use multiple regression with two dummy predictor variables. There is a third solution: **one-way analysis of variance**, a method for comparing more than two means.

The hypotheses are: $H_0: \mu_1 = \mu_2 = \cdots = \mu_k$ vs. H_a: at least one μ is different from the others. The test statistic is based on an *F*-ratio (which is why it is called ANOVA) that compares the variance *across* the means of the samples with the variance *within* the samples.

Why is one-way ANOVA preferred over a series of two-sample *t*-tests?

1. You get a single test that answers the question, "Is there ANY difference among group means?" If the answer is no, you are done. Only if you reject the null hypothesis would you go further to locate the source of the difference. So there are gains in efficiency.

2. When multiple tests are performed, each at a 5% significance level (and therefore a 0.05 chance of a Type I error), the overall chance of a Type I error increases dramatically. For example, if you had 10 means to compare, you would need 45 two-sample *t*-tests! The more tests you run, the greater the chance of finding a false positive. So you could be quite likely to get spurious significance; that is, conclude that a difference is real, when, in fact, it isn't.

3. When two-sample *t*-tests are used, the pooled variance estimate of the error variance uses only the two samples being compared, and this estimate will change in the next *t*-test. One-way ANOVA uses a pooled estimate of the error variance from *all* of the samples. So the standard error, P-values, and confidence intervals are more trustworthy because they are based on more data.

Warning #1: A common error is to confuse One-Way ANOVA with ANOVA in Regression. The common part of the name—ANOVA—represents the analysis of variance table that summarizes the computations. The "one-way" refers to the fact that we have classified the observations in one "way," according to one categorical variable.

Warning #2: The technique is really designed for experimental situations, not observational data. We'll discuss the difference below.

One-Way ANOVA can also be thought of as a statistical model with one quantitative outcome variable and one categorical predictor variable (with two or more categories). We can extend this further to have two categorical predictor variables. Not surprisingly, it is called Two-Way ANOVA. And it leads to the idea of Design of Experiments.

Design of Experiments

A full discussion of design of experiments could fill its own textbook. Except for our work on sample survey design in Chapter 3, we have focused on the analysis of data.

Data come from two main types of situations. They can come from observational studies, so-called because the studies simply observe and record the behaviour or response of subjects. Surveys are the prime example of observational studies. Data can also come from experiments: studies in which the experimenter manipulates or controls attributes of what is being studied and sees the consequences. Each controlled attribute is called a factor. But if the experimenter is to manipulate things, he or she must make decisions about how many groups are to be compared, how the subjects should be assigned to each group, and how many factors are of interest; this is the **design of the experiment**.

Experiments are often harder to set up and carry out, but the conclusions that can be drawn by assessing cause and effect are stronger than observational studies, which can only look for correlations. Observational studies usually go backward in time (and so are called retrospective), for example, by asking respondents for opinions or recollections of things that have happened. Experiments usually go forward in time (and so are called prospective).

Here is an example of an experimental design. Rogers selects 30 stores to display a particular product using different types of packaging: 10 stores will get Packaging A, 10 stores will get Packaging B, and 10 stores will get Packaging C. The sales for each type of packaging are recorded. In this design, Packaging is the factor, with three levels. Sales volume is the response. If different packaging and different pricing levels are used, there would be two factors: *Packaging* and *Pricing*, and various combinations of the two would be analyzed.

Here's a more complicated design. Suppose a study is undertaken to examine the separate and combined effects of length of break during a class and the class start time on the attentiveness of university students. Three lengths of break (5, 10, and 15 minutes) are tested with two start times (8:30 a.m. and 10:30 a.m.). For nine lectures with each start time, three are taught with each length of break (i.e., three lectures use 5-minute breaks, three use 10-minute breaks, and three use 15-minute breaks). Random samples of 20 students in each of the lectures are given a test of "attentiveness." Two-way analysis of variance will compare the mean attentiveness for each of the break durations, compare mean attentiveness for early and late start times, and then assess whether the means for each break duration are dependent on the start time. A two-way analysis of variance is better than two one-way analyses of variance precisely because of the ability to test for the connection between factors. It may be that a 15-minute break is best only for the early class, while a 5-minute break is best for the later class, perhaps because the caffeine is already in effect!

Logistic Regression

How could Rogers model the likelihood of a wireless subscriber renewing a contract once it expires? That's a typical situation for **logistic regression**, an advanced statistical procedure that looks a great deal like regular linear regression, except that the response variable is binary. It takes only two values, such as success or failure, accept or reject, yes or no, or in Rogers' case, renew or not renew. If the values are denoted by 1 and 0, then the mean value of y is actually just the proportion of 1s, which we denoted by p, just as before.

There are three main reasons why the usual least squares regression is not suitable here. First, the outcome variable is obviously not normally distributed. How can it be? There are only two values! Second, the variance of the outcome variable depends on the value(s) of the predictor variables(s), thus violating the equal spread condition. And third, there is no guarantee that the least squares estimated value of p will fall between 0 and 1; but it has to, because it represents a probability, namely, the probability of getting a "yes" or "success" outcome!

Instead of using proportions, logistic regression works with odds. The odds equal the proportion of one outcome divided by the proportion of the other outcome. Gamblers are all too familiar with the concept of odds. $Odds = \frac{\hat{p}}{1 - \hat{p}}$

The odds gives us a convenient way to model the relationship between p and the predictor variables: x_1 to x_k. For Rogers, the predictor variables could include customer characteristics such as: age, gender, years as a Rogers' customer, number of calls/texts/instant messages, employment status, and so on. We take the logarithm of the odds and set it equal to the linear combination of the x-variables to get the logistic regression model: $log\left(\frac{p}{1 - p}\right) = \beta_0 + \beta_1 x_1 + \beta_2 x_2 + \cdots \beta_k x_k$.

If there is only one x-variable it is called simple logistic regression; with more than one x-variable it is called multiple logistic regression.

Unlike linear regression, which uses least squares to estimate the parameters $\beta_0, \beta_1, \cdots, \beta_k$, logistic regression uses a method called maximum likelihood. The details are not necessary for you to use this technique. Simply rely on your software package. The software will also produce confidence intervals and hypothesis tests of the parameters, just as in linear regression. And the hypothesis tests are interpreted pretty much the same way. That is, rejecting a null hypothesis of $\beta_i = 0$ means that there is a statistically significant relationship between that x-variable and the binary outcome y-variable.

Once the model has been fit and tested it can be used to estimate the probability of a "success" for any given value of x, by solving for $\hat{p}$ as follows.

$$\hat{p} = \frac{1}{1 + \exp\left[-(b_0 + b_1 x_1 + \cdots b_k x_k)\right]} = \frac{\exp(b_0 + b_1 x_1 + \cdots b_k x_k)}{1 + \exp(b_0 + b_1 x_1 + \cdots b_k x_k)}$$

A special case happens when x_i is also a binary (0/1) variable. In that case $exp(b_i)$ can be interpreted as an odds ratio. For example, if the outcome is contract renewal (yes or no, coded as 1 or 0) and the predictor is "discount offered" (yes or no, coded as 1 or 0), then $exp(b_i)$ can be interpreted as the number of times higher the chance of a renewal is when a discount is offered as when there is no discount.

Logistic regression is a powerful modelling technique for assessing the joint effect of many predictor variables (quantitative and categorical) on a binary outcome.

Factor Analysis

Rogers' Human Resources Division carries out a survey of employee attitudes about working at Rogers. The survey has 50 questions about different aspects of the workplace. How can you best group them into categories and compute summary scores?

That's a job for **factor analysis**, a technique that comes under the general heading of "methods of data reduction." It was developed as a method of uncovering a smaller number of concepts or "factors" from a larger set of measured variables. These concepts cannot easily be measured directly so they are measured indirectly instead.

For example, the Rogers' survey may ask employees to rate a series of items, using a five-point scale from "very dissatisfied" to "very satisfied." By summing up all 50 items you can get an overall measure of attitude. But there may also be subscales of interest. Some items may refer to physical environment, some to interpersonal interactions with staff, some to communications with management, some to a sense of shared decision-making and autonomy, and so on. Factor analysis is a technique to find those subscales. The basic idea is to collect variables that are most highly correlated with one another. The thinking is that if high scores on one variable go along with high scores on another, perhaps they are measuring the same thing. Factor analysis is different from our other techniques because it makes no distinction between response and predictor variables. And the computational procedures feel a bit like magic!

Cluster Analysis

Rogers' Marketing Division is interested in developing targeted advertising campaigns, and needs to know how to divide customers into identifiable subgroups or segments. This is known as market segmentation.

Cluster analysis is a set of methods designed to find similarities among cases (in this case, people) based on a set of variables, such as demographic characteristics and past customer behaviour information. It is a little like factor analysis because it, too, is a data reduction technique that makes no distinction between response and predictor variables, and because the computational procedures are complex.

If anyone ever asks you for a one-sentence description of what these two techniques can do, just tell them: Factor analysis reduces the number of variables by grouping them into a smaller set of factors, while cluster analysis reduces the number of cases by grouping them into a small set of clusters.

Nonparametric Methods

The confidence intervals and hypothesis tests for measurement data discussed in our text are based on the assumption that the populations from which the data are drawn are normally distributed. The *t*-distribution procedures are very popular because they work well even with a moderate lack of normality, as long as the samples are reasonably large. What can be done with severe non-normality, especially with small samples?

There are procedures that make no assumptions at all about the distribution of the populations. These are called **nonparametric methods** (and also distribution-free methods), because there are no distributional parameters, such as the mean or standard deviation of the normal. The tests are also known as rank tests, because they are based on the relative position of each data value in a sample, rather than the actual magnitude of each data value. For example, we know the ranking of the three Olympic medals—gold, silver, bronze—but we don't worry about the difference in actual performance that won the gold and the silver. The gold medallist could have beaten the silver medallist by a fraction of a second or by a minute; all that matters is that the gold medallist was ahead and was therefore ranked number one.

While a two-sample t-test can only compare means of two populations, there are non-parametric tests that can compare medians or even the entire distributions of two populations.

Just to introduce them to you by name, here is a short list of nonparametric procedures that correspond to the parametric procedures we developed.

Parametric (normal distribution test)	Nonparametric (rank) Test
One-sample *t*-test	Wilcoxon signed-rank test
Two-sample *t*-test for independent samples	Wilcoxon rank-sum (a.k.a. Mann-Whitney) test; and Tukey's quick test
Paired *t*-test for dependent samples	Wilcoxon signed-rank test
One-way ANOVA	Kruskal-Wallis test
… and many others!	… and many others!

Nonparametric procedures are a very handy addition to the statistical toolkit.

16.4 The Future of Business Statistics

Statistics has always been a crossover field. Its foundations are in mathematics. In economics, it is called econometrics; in psychology, it's psychometrics. Graphical displays of data include aspects of visual perception, art, and perspective, not to mention computing. We call it biostatistics if people are the cases and health care is the subject. Another separate field is epidemiology—statistical methods that deal with the incidence, distribution, and control of disease in a population. Courses in introductory statistics are taught as part of a wide range of academic programs, from accounting to zoology, from A to Z. Statistics is everywhere.

Where is Statistics headed and what new crossover fields is it encountering? New terms now in vogue are: data mining, big data, business analytics, business intelligence, data visualization, machine learning, and artificial intelligence. Very often they concern the collection of data sets so large and complex that traditional data processing applications are overwhelmed.

What is **data mining**? It is the name for a process that uses a variety of data analysis tools to discover patterns and relationships in data to help build useful models and make predictions. In particular, its purpose is to extract useful information hidden in very large databases. Many of the modelling techniques that we've covered in this book—especially multiple regression and logistic regression—are used in data mining. But because data mining has benefited from work in machine learning, computer science, and artificial intelligence, as well as statistics, it has a much richer set of tools than those we've discussed in this book. Data mining is similar to traditional statistical analysis in that it involves exploratory data analysis and modelling. But it has some different aspects too. The most important ones include: the size of the databases, the exploratory nature, the lack of a designed experiment or survey, and the automatic nature of modelling. Surprisingly, perhaps, there is no consensus on exactly what constitutes data mining.

What is business analytics? An excellent definition appears in Wikipedia. **Business analytics** "refers to the skills, technologies, applications and practices for continuous iterative exploration and investigation of past business performance to gain insight and drive business planning." It is based on data and statistical methods, and explanatory and predictive modelling. In other words, it is really just a new term for the techniques we have discussed in this textbook, and more.

The underlying theme is that business decision making (financial, managerial, policy, etc.) is improved considerably by an understanding of statistical concepts and statistical methods.

The traditional challenge facing statisticians has been *not enough data*. Today the challenge is a new one, *too much data*. Imagine the volume of data collected by Google, Facebook, Twitter, Wikipedia, Amazon, Netflix, and the GPS application Waze. In online commerce, meteorology, genomics, biological and environmental research, internet searching, finance, business informatics, remote sensing, software logs, etc. investigators regularly encounter limitations due to large data sets. According to IBM, as of 2012, 2.5 quintillion (2.5×10^{18}) bytes (10^{18} bytes is a million million MB) were created every day!

The size of a typical data warehouse makes any analysis challenging. The ability to store data is growing faster than the ability to use it effectively. Commercial data warehouses often contain terabytes (TB)—more than 1 000 000 000 000 (1 trillion) bytes or a million MB—of data (one TB is equivalent to about 260 000 digitized songs), and warehouses containing petabytes (PB—one PB = 1000 TB) are now common. The digital size of all 33 000 000 books in the U.S. Library of Congress is about 15 TB. According to *Wired* magazine, about 20 TB of photos are uploaded to Facebook every month. It's estimated that the servers at *Google* process a petabyte of data every 72 minutes. One key challenge of statistics and all its related fields is how to uncover important strategic information lying hidden within these massive collections of data.

As the statistician William G. Hunter observed more than 30 years ago, "We live not in a time of information explosion but in a time of data inundation." Statistics is how we turn all the data into information!

(Famous) Last Words

The year 2013 was designated The International Year of Statistics, a worldwide campaign promoting the power and impact of statistics on everyday life.

A special resolution in the U.S. Senate, introduced by Senator Kay Hagan, recognizes that "the science of statistics is vital to the improvement of human life because of the power of statistics to improve, enlighten, and understand" and that "statisticians contribute to the vital and excellent of myriad aspects of United States society, including the economy, health care, security, commerce, education, and research." The same is true in Canada and around the world.

We live in a data-centric world, and the future depends on data, not just their collection, but analysis, interpretation, and communication. We hope this textbook has succeeded in showing you the power and possibility that comes with knowledge of statistical thinking, and that we added quality to quantity!

We'll end by repeating the words of the great Canadian humourist, Stephen Leacock:

"I've been reading some very interesting statistics," he was saying to the other thinker.

"Ah, statistics!" said the other, "Wonderful things, sir, statistics; very fond of them myself."

WHAT HAVE WE LEARNED?

In this chapter we developed a framework that ties together the common features of the inference methods we have studied. We extended the idea of a model to a statistical model. We developed a method for choosing an appropriate inference technique by identifying the roles played by each variable and the type of data represented by each variable. We also provided brief introductions to many other statistical methods used in business applications.

- We learned that a statistical model connects an outcome variable to one or more predictor variables (the systematic component), but recognizes that there are also factors that we can't identify or measure (the random component).

- We learned that the main objective of statistical modelling is to build a model that is consistent with background knowledge, existing data, and future data. It is not simply an attempt to get the best fit to the observed data.

- We learned that statistical modelling has three stages: formulation, estimation, and validation (checking assumptions and conditions).

- We learned how each of the methods—two-sample t-test of means, two-sample z-test of proportions, chi-square test of independence, simple linear regression, and multiple regression—are examples of statistical models.

- We learned how to identify the appropriate inference method to use by determining which variable is the outcome, which variable(s) is/are the predictor variables, and whether each variable is binary, categorical, or quantitative.

Terms

Business analytics   A new term for the techniques discussed in this book. It has also been defined as "the skills, technologies, applications, and practices for continuous iterative exploration and investigation of past business performance to gain insight and drive business planning."

Cluster Analysis	A set of methods for finding similarities among cases based on a set of variables. It is used extensively in market segmentation.
Data Mining	A process that uses a variety of data analysis tools to discover patterns and relationships in data to help build useful models and make predictions. In particular, its purpose is to extract useful information hidden in very large databases.
Design of Experiments	Experiments are studies where the experimenter manipulates attributes of what is being studied. In that way they are different from observational studies. Designing experiments is a complex field in itself.
Factor Analysis	A technique for discovering a smaller number of concepts or "factors" from a larger set of measured variables. It is used frequently in developing measurement tools.
Logistic Regression	A method similar to regular linear regression, but where the model has a binary outcome variable. Simple logistic regression has one predictor; multiple logistic regression has multiple predictors, and they can be any combination of quantitative and categorical variables.
Model	A mathematical description of a real-world phenomenon.
Nonparametric Methods	These are procedures that make no assumptions about the population distributions and so don't involve testing parameters such as the mean or proportion. They are based on comparing ranks, rather than the actual data values.
One-Way Analysis of Variance	A method for comparing more than two means. The model has one quantitative outcome variable and one categorical predictor variable.
Statistical Model	A model with an added component. It identifies a mathematical relationship between an outcome variable and one or more predictor variables plus a random error term.

Chapter 2

1. Answers will vary.

3. *Who*—tankers having recent oil spills; *What*—date, spillage amount (no specified unit), and cause of puncture; *When*—recent years; *Where*—not specified; *Why*—not specified, but probably to determine whether or not spillage amount per oil spill has decreased as a result of improvements in new tanker design; *How*—not specified, although it is mentioned that the data are online; *Variables*—there are three variables: the date, the spillage amount (which is quantitative), and the cause of the puncture (which is categorical); *Concerns*—more detail needed on the specifics of the study.

5. *Who*—existing stores; *What*—weekly sales ($), town population (thousands), median age of town (years), median income of town ($), and whether or not the stores sell beer/wine; *When*—not specified; *Where*—Canada (assumed); *Why*—the food retailer is interested in understanding if there is an association among these variables to help determine where to open the next store; *How*—data collected from their stores; *Variables*—sales ($), town population (thousands), median age of town (years), median income of town ($), which are all quantitative. Whether or not the stores sell beer/wine is categorical.

7. *Who*—Subway sandwiches; *What*—type of meat, number of calories (in calories), and serving size (in ounces); *When*—not specified; *Where*—Subway restaurants; *Why*—assess the nutritional value of the different sandwiches; *How*—information gathered on each of the sandwiches offered on the menu; *Variables*—the number of calories and serving size (grams) (which are quantitative), and the type of meat (which is categorical).

9. *Who*—385 species of flowers; *What*—date of first flowering (in days); *When*—over a period of 47 years; *Where*—southern England; *Why*—the researchers believe that this indicates a warming of the overall climate; *How*—not specified; *Variables*—date of first flowering is a quantitative variable; *Concerns*—hopefully, date of first flowering was measured in days from January 1, or some other convention, to avoid problems with leap years.

11. *Who*—students; *What*—age (years or years and months), number of days absent, grade level, reading score, math score, and any disabilities/special needs; *When*—ongoing and current; *Where*—a Canadian province; *Why*—keeping this information is a provincial requirement; *How*—data collected and stored as part of school records; *Variables*—there are six variables. Grade level and disabilities/special needs are categorical variables. Number of absences, age (years or years and months), reading scores, and math scores are quantitative variables; *Concerns*—what tests are used to measure reading and math ability and what are the units of measurement?

13. *Who*—customers of a start-up company; *What*—customer name, ID number, region of the country, date of last purchased, amount of purchase ($), and item purchased; *When*—present day; *Where*—Canada (assumed); *Why*—the company is building a database of customers and sales information; *How*—assumed that the company records the needed information from each new customer; *Variables*—there are six variables: name, ID number, region of the country, and item purchased are categorical, and date and amount of purchase ($) are quantitative; *Concerns*—although region is coded as a number, it is still a categorical variable.

15. *Who*—vineyards; *What*—size (hectares), number of years in existence, state, varieties of grapes grown, average case price ($), gross sales ($), and percent profit; *When*—not specified; *Where*—assume Canada since province is recorded; *Why*—business analysts hope to provide information that would be helpful to grape growers in Canada; *How*—not specified; *Variables*—size of vineyard (hectares), number of years in existence, average case price ($), gross sales ($), and percent profit are quantitative variables. Province and variety of grapes grown are categorical variables.

17. *Who*—1180 Canadian voters; *What*—region (West, Prairies, etc.), age (in years), party affiliation, whether or not the person owned any shares of stock, and their attitude (scale 1 to 5) toward unions; *When*—not specified; *Where*—Canada; *Why*—the information was gathered as part of an Environics public opinion poll; *How*—telephone survey; *Variables*—there are five variables. Region (West, Prairies, etc.), party affiliation, and whether or not the person owned any shares of stock are categorical variables. Age (in years), and their attitude (scale 1 to 5) toward unions are quantitative variables.

19. *Who*—every cellphone user in Canada; *What*—cellphone manufacturer and model, and demographic characteristics of the users; *When*—the information is currently collected; *Where*—Canada; *Why*—all companies involved in telecommunications sales and marketing will use the information to design advertising campaigns, pricing, applications, etc.; *How*—the Print Measurement Bureau collects the data; *Variables*—there are six variables. Cellphone manufacturer and model are categorical variables. Some demographic characteristics will be categorical (e.g., gender, marital status, education, place of residence) and others will be quantitative (e.g., income, age). Others could be either depending on how they are collected (e.g., income).

21. *Who*—major Canadian cities; *What*—city name, average price of unleaded gasoline ($ per litre) per city per month for a year; *When*—current year (assumed); *Where*—Canada; *Why*—not specified, but likely to examine geographical disparity in price and changes over time; *How*—not specified, but data were collected by Statistics Canada; *Variables*—City name is an identifier variable; each of the monthly prices ($ per litre) is a quantitative variable.

23. *Who*—students in an MBA statistics class; *What*—total personal investment in stock market ($), number of different stocks held, total invested in mutual funds ($), and the name of each mutual fund; *When*—not specified; *Where*—a business school in Ontario; *Why*—the information was collected for use in classroom illustrations; *How*—an online survey was conducted, participation was probably required for all members of the class; *Variables*—there are four variables. Total personal investment in stock market ($), number of different stocks held, total invested in mutual funds ($) are quantitative variables. The name of each mutual fund is a categorical variable.

25. *Who*—Indy 500 races; *What*—year, winner, car model, time (hrs), speed (mph), and car number; *When*—1911–2011; *Where*—Indianapolis, Indiana; *Why*—examine trends in Indy 500 race winners; *How*—official statistics kept for each race every year; *Variables*—there are six variables. Winner, car model, and car number are categorical variables. Year, time (hrs), and speed (mph) are quantitative variables.

27. Each row should be a single mortgage loan. Columns hold the borrower name (which identifies the rows) and amount.
29. Each row is a week. Columns hold week number (to identify the row), sales prediction, sales, and difference.
31. Cross-sectional.
33. Time series.
35. "Bullying" is a broad term, and is not defined here. Two decimal places in the reported percentage is spurious accuracy; report the percentage to the nearest whole number (40%).

Chapter 3

1. a) No. It would be nearly impossible to get exactly 500 males and 500 females by random chance.
   b) A stratified sample, stratified by whether the respondent is male or female.
3. a) Voluntary response.
   b) We have no confidence at all in estimates from such studies.
5. a) The population of interest is all adults in Canada aged 18 and older.
   b) The sampling frame is Canadian adults with telephones. If the numbers are drawn from telephone directories, then only adults with landline telephones will be in the sampling frame.
   c) Some members of the population, especially among the younger age groups, do not have landline phones with numbers listed in directories. That could create a bias.
7. a) Population—Human resources directors of Fortune 500 companies.
   b) Parameter—Proportion who don't feel surveys intruded on their workday.
   c) Sampling Frame—List of HR directors at Fortune 500 companies.
   d) Sample—23% who responded.
   e) Method—Questionnaire mailed to all (nonrandom).
   f) Bias—Nonresponse. Hard to generalize because who responds is related to the question itself.
9. a) Population—Consumers Union subscribers.
   b) Parameter—Proportion who have used and benefited from alternative medicine.
   c) Sampling Frame—All Consumers Union subscribers.
   d) Sample—Those who responded (random).
   e) Method—Questionnaire to all (nonrandom).
   f) Bias—Nonresponse. Those who respond may have strong feelings one way or another.
11. a) Population—Adults.
   b) Parameter—Proportion who think drinking and driving is a serious problem.
   c) Sampling Frame—Bar patrons.
   d) Sample—Every 10th person leaving the bar.
   e) Method—Systematic sampling.
   f) Bias—Those interviewed had just left a bar. They probably think drinking and driving is less of a problem than do adults in general.
13. a) Population—Soil around a former waste dump.
   b) Parameter—Concentrations of toxic chemicals.
   c) Sampling Frame—Accessible soil around the dump.
   d) Sample—16 soil samples.
   e) Method—Not clear.

   f) Bias—Don't know if soil samples were randomly chosen. If not, may be biased toward more or less polluted soil.
15. a) Population—Snack food bags.
   b) Parameter—Weight of bags, proportion passing inspection.
   c) Sampling Frame—All bags produced each day.
   d) Sample—10 randomly selected cases, one bag from each case for inspection.
   e) Method—Multistage sampling.
   f) Bias—Should be unbiased.
17. Bias. Only people watching the news will respond, and their preference may differ from that of other voters. The sampling method may systematically produce samples that don't represent the population of interest.
19. a) Voluntary response. Only those who both see the ad *and* feel strongly enough will respond.
   b) Cluster sampling. One town may not be typical of all.
   c) Attempted census. Will have nonresponse bias.
   d) Stratified sampling with follow-up. Should be unbiased.
21. a) This is a multistage design, with a cluster sample at the first stage and a simple random sample for each cluster.
   b) If any of the three churches you pick at random is not representative of all churches, then you'll introduce sampling error by the choice of that church.
23. a) This is a systematic sample.
   b) It is likely to be representative of those waiting for the roller coaster. Indeed, it may do quite well if those at the front of the line respond differently (after their long wait) than those at the back of the line.
   c) The sampling frame is patrons willing to wait for the roller coaster on that day at that time. It should be representative of the people in line, but not of all people at the amusement park.
25. Answers will vary. a) Question 1 is the more neutrally worded question. b) Question 2 is biased in its wording.
27. Only those who think it worth the wait are likely to be in line. Those who don't like roller coasters are unlikely to be in the sampling frame, so the poll won't get a fair picture of whether park patrons overall would favour still more roller coasters.
29. a) Biased toward yes because of "pollute." "Should companies be responsible for any costs of environmental cleanup?"
   b) Biased toward no because of "enforce" and "strict." "Should companies have dress codes?"
31. a) Not everyone has an equal chance. People with unlisted numbers, people without phones, and those at work cannot be reached.
   b) Generate random numbers and call at random times.
   c) Under the original plan, those families in which one person stays home are more likely to be included. Under the second plan, many more are included. People without phones are still excluded.
   d) It improves the chance of selected households being included.
   e) This takes care of phone numbers. Time of day may be an issue. People without phones are still excluded.
33. a) Answers will vary.
   b) The amount of change you typically carry. Parameter is the true mean amount of change. Population is the amount on each day around noon.
   c) Population is now the amount of change carried by your friends. The average estimates the mean of these amounts.

d) Possibly for your class. Probably not for larger groups. Your friends are likely to have similar needs for change during the day.

35. a) Assign numbers 001 to 120 to each order. Use random numbers to select 10 transactions to examine.

   b) Sample proportionately within each type. (Do a stratified random sample.)

37. a) Select three cases at random; then select one jar randomly from each case.

   b) Use random numbers to choose 3 cases from numbers 61 through 80; then use random numbers between 1 and 12 to select the jar from each case.

   c) No. Multistage sampling.

39. a) Depends on the Yellow Page listings used. If from regular (line) listings, this is fair if all family doctors are listed. If from ads, probably not, as those family doctors may not be typical.

   b) Not appropriate. This cluster sample will probably contain listings for only one or two business types.

Chapter 4

1. Answers will vary.
3. Answers will vary.
5. a) Yes, all categories of type of non-alcoholic beverage are displayed. The categories divide the whole, while the category *Other* combines the smaller shares.

   b) Carbonated soft drinks have the same market share as coffee, and both are only slightly larger than milk and tea, with bottled water ranked fifth.

   c) The *All Others* category is slightly less than 25%.

7. a) The pie chart does a better job of showing portions of a whole.

   b) There is no bar for "All Others."

9. a) Yes, it is reasonable to conclude that deaths due to heart OR respiratory diseases is equal to 25.3% (20.7% plus 4.6%). The percentages can be added because the categories do not overlap. There can only be one cause of death.

   b) The percentages listed only add up to 65.3%; other causes must account for 34.7% of Canadian deaths.

   c) A bar graph or a pie graph would be appropriate if an *Other* category for 34.7% were added.

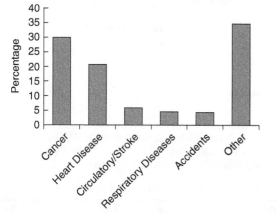

11. WebEx Communications, Inc. has the majority of the market share for web conferencing (58.4%), and Microsoft has approximately a quarter of the market share. There appears to be room for both to grow, because other companies comprise about 15% of market share. A pie chart or bar chart would be appropriate.

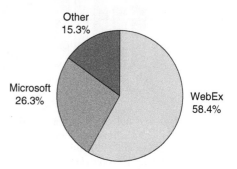

13. a) They total more than 100%; overlapping categories.

   b)

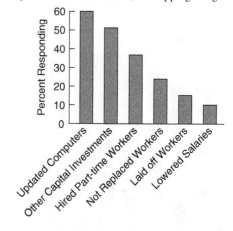

   c) No because the percentages do not total 100%.

   d) (Answers will vary). More than 50% of business owners say that they have either updated their computers or made other non-computer capital investments (or both). Smaller percentages of business owners (from 10 to 37%) made changes in either their hiring or salary structure.

15. The bar chart shows that grounding is the most frequent cause of oil spillage (149) for these 455 spills, while collisions (134) are ranked a close second. The other causes were due to hull failures, fires and explosions, equipment failures, and other or unknown causes. In order to differentiate between close counts, a bar chart is easier to read. Even with the actual percentages the bar chart is easier to read. It is difficult to determine differences between similar areas in the pie chart. To showcase the causes of oil spills as a fraction of all 455 spills, the pie chart could be a reasonable choice.

17. a) 31%

   b) It looks like India's percentage is about 6 times as big, but it's not even twice as big.

   c) Start the percentages at 0% on the vertical axis, not 40%.

d)

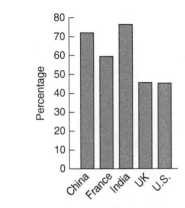

e) The percentage of people who say that wealth is important to them is highest in China and India (around 70%), followed by France (around 60%) and then the U.S. and U.K. where the percentage was only about 45%.

19. a) These are column percentages because the column sums add up to 100% and the row percentages add up to more than 100%.

b) A stacked bar chart is appropriate.

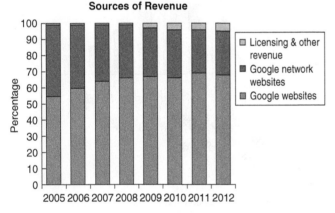

c) The main source of revenue for Google is from their own websites, which in 2005 was 55%, rising to 66% in 2008 and then staying fairly stable through 2012. The second largest source of revenue is from other network websites. While the Google websites have remained the main source of revenue, the revenue from the Google network websites has been decreasing. Licensing and other revenue has risen from 1% in 2005 to 5% in 2012.

21. a) 62.5%
   b) 35%
   c) 15%
   d) 50%
   e) 61%
   f) 65%
   g) There does not appear to be any relationship between the performance of a stock on a single day and its performance over the prior year.

23. a) 25.3%; 30.2%
   b) 5.9%; 6.7%
   c) Sales increased by 1.4%.

25. a) 11.4% G; 14.3% PG; 48.6% PG-13; 25.7% R
   b) 0% G; 0% PG%; 57.9% PG-13; 42.1% R

c)

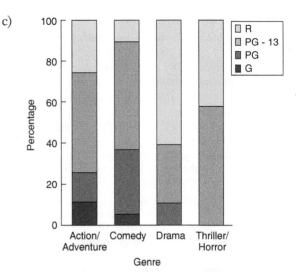

d) *Genre* and *Rating* are not independent. Thriller/Horror movie are all PG-13 or R and Drama are nearly so. Comedy moves are nearly 40% G and PG and only 10% R. Action/Adventure movies are nearly 15% G and 15% PG.

27. a) 47.6%
   b) 45.2%
   c) 52.3%
   d) Marginal distribution of region of birth: 47.6% North America; 36.6% Asia/Pacific Rim; 8.7% Europe; 3.8% Middle East; 3.2% Other.
   e) The column percentages:

	Full-time	**Part-time**	Total
North America	45.4	52.3	47.6
Asia/Pacific Rim	41.0	27.1	36.6
Europe	8.0	10.3	8.7
Middle East	1.8	8.4	3.8
Other	3.8	1.9	3.2
Total	**100.0**	**100.0**	**100.0**

f) They are not independent. Compared with the full-time program, the part-time program has a higher percentage of students born in North America and in the Middle East, but a lower percentage of students born in Asia/Pacific Rim. Knowing the type of MBA program does affect the likelihood of the region of birth of the MBA student.

29. a) 5.5%
   b) 5.0%
   c) 6.5%
   d) 54.2%
   e) 58.8%
   f) Overall, differences between the two periods are small. However, PG-13 films increased from 21.3% in 2003–2006 to 28.3% in 2007–2013 while PG films decreased from 58.8% in 2003–2006 to 54.2% in 2007–2013.

	G	**PG**	**PG-13**	**R**	Total
2007–2012	5.8%	28.3%	54.2%	11.7%	100.0%
2003–2006	5.0%	21.3%	58.8%	15.0%	100.0%

PG-13 films increased from 36.3% in 1996–1999 to 57.5% in 2000–2005 and R-rated films decreased from 36.3% to 15.8%.

31. The study by the University of Texas Southwestern Medical Center provides evidence of an association between having a tattoo and contracting hepatitis C. Around 33% of the subjects who were tattooed in a commercial parlor had hepatitis C, compared with 13% of those tattooed elsewhere, and only 3.5% of those with no tattoo. If having a tattoo and having hepatitis C were independent, we would have expected these percentages to be roughly the same.

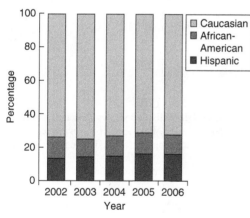

33. a) 8%
    b) No, because we're not given counts or totals.
    c) 92%
    d) There appears to be little, if any, relationship between revenue category and education level of the women CEOs.

35. a) 14.5% Hispanic, 12.5% African-American, and 73.0% Caucasian.
    b) For 2006, 15.7% Hispanic, 12.0% African-American, 72.3% Caucasian.
    c)

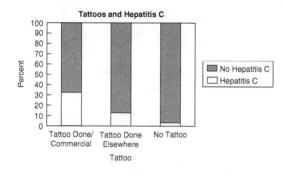

    d) The (conditional) distribution of *Ethnicity* is almost the same across the five *Years*, however there seems to be a slight increase in the percentage of Hispanics who go to the movies from 13.1% in 2002 to 15.7% in 2006.

37. a) Row percentages.
    b) A slightly higher percentage of urban women's business centres are established (at least 5 years old).

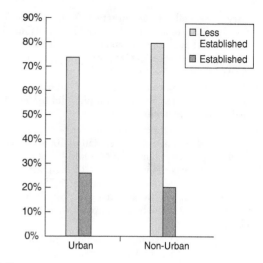

39. a) Row percentages.
    b) No. We are given only the conditional distributions. We have no idea how much are sold in either Europe or America.
    c)

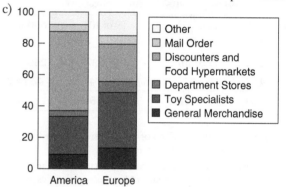

    d) In America more than 50% of all toys are sold by large mass merchant discounters and food hypermarkets and only 25% are sold in toy specialty stores. In Europe 36% of all toys are sold in toy specialty stores while a relatively small 24% are sold in the large discount and hypermarket chains.

41. a) The marginal totals have been added to the table:

		Hospital Size		
		Large	**Small**	Total
Procedure	**Major surgery**	120 of 800	10 of 50	**130 of 850**
	Minor surgery	10 of 200	20 of 250	**30 of 450**
	Total	130 of 1000	30 of 300	**160 of 1300**

160 of 1300, or about 12.3% of the patients had a delayed discharge.

    b) Major surgery patients were delayed 15.3% of the time. Minor surgery patients were delayed 6.7% of the time.
    c) Large Hospital had a delay rate of 13%. Small Hospital had a delay rate of 10%. The small hospital has the lower overall rate of delayed discharge.

d) Large Hospital: Major Surgery 15% and Minor Surgery 5%. Small Hospital: Major Surgery 20% and Minor Surgery 8%. Even though small hospital had the lower overall rate of delayed discharge, the large hospital had a lower rate of delayed discharge for each type of surgery.

e) Yes. While the overall rate of delayed discharge is lower for the small hospital, the large hospital did better with *both* major surgery and minor surgery.

f) The small hospital performs a higher percentage of minor surgeries than major surgeries. 250 of 300 surgeries at the small hospital were minor (83%). Only 200 of the large hospital's 1000 surgeries were minor (20%). Minor surgery had a lower delay rate than major surgery (6.7% to 15.3%), so the small hospital's overall rate was artificially inflated. The larger hospital is the better hospital when comparing discharge delay rates.

43. a) 1284 applicants were admitted out of a total of 3014 applicants. 1284/3014 = 42.6%

		Males Accepted (of applicants)	Females Accepted (of applicants)	Total
Program	**1**	511 of 825	89 of 108	**600 of 933**
	2	352 of 560	17 of 25	**369 of 585**
	3	137 of 407	132 of 375	**269 of 782**
	4	22 of 373	24 of 341	**46 of 714**
	Total	**1022 of 2165**	**262 of 849**	**1284 of 3014**

b) 1022 of 2165 (47.2%) of males were admitted. 262 of 849 (30.9%) of females were admitted.

c) Because there are four comparisons to make, the table below organizes the percentages of males and females accepted in each program. Females are accepted at a higher rate in every program.

Program	Males	Females
1	61.9%	82.4%
2	62.9%	68.0%
3	33.7%	35.2%
4	5.9%	7.0%

d) The comparison of acceptance rate within each program is most valid. The overall percentage is an unfair average. It fails to take the different numbers of applicants and different acceptance rates of each program. Women tended to apply to the programs in which gaining acceptance was difficult for everyone. This is an example of Simpson's Paradox.

Chapter 5

1. Answers will vary.
3. This distribution is nearly symmetric and unimodal, centred at around $5500. The range is about $6000. Most of the tuitions lie between $4000 and $6000.
5. a) The distribution is skewed to the right. There are a few negative values. The spread is about $6000.
   b) The mean will be larger because the distribution is right skewed.
   c) Because of the skewness, the median is a better summary.

7. The distribution is unimodal and skewed to the right with two high outliers. The median is near 10%.
9. a) Five-Number Summary (Answers may vary depending on software.)

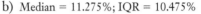

Min.	1st Qu.	Median	3rd Qu.	Max.
−10.820	6.965	11.275	17.440	94.940

b) Median = 11.275%; IQR = 10.475%
c)

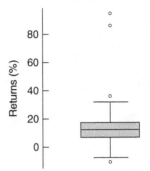

d) The histogram makes the skewness of the distribution clear.
11. a) Skewed to the right, since the mean is much greater than the median.
    b) Yes, at least one high outlier, since 250 is far greater than Q3 + 1.5 IQRs.
    c) We don't know how far the high whisker should go because we don't know the largest value inside the fence.

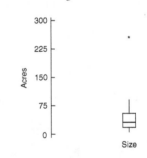

13. The stem-and-leaf display shows that many of the acreage values end in 0 or 5. Perhaps this is evidence that they are rounding or estimating the value. There is a high outlier near 240.

```
24 | 0
22 |
20 |
18 |
16 |
14 | 0
12 | 0
10 | 0
 8 | 0
 6 | 920
 4 | 553500
 2 | 8655210987520
 0 | 751000086
```

Key: 8 | 0 = 80 acres

15. a)

**Wayne Gretzky–Games
played per season**

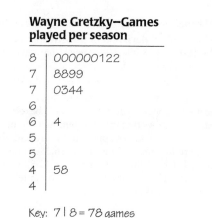

8	000000122
7	8899
7	0344
6	
6	4
5	
5	
4	58
4	

Key: 7 | 8 = 78 games

b)

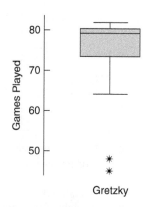

c) The distribution of the number of games played per season by Wayne Gretzky is skewed to the low end and has low outliers. The median is 78, and the range is 37 games.

d) There are two outlier seasons with 45 and 48 games. He may have been injured. The season with 64 games is also separated by a gap.

17. a) The median because the distribution is skewed.

b) Lower, because the distribution is skewed toward the low end.

c) That display is not a histogram. It's a time series plot using bars to represent each point. The histogram should split up the number of games played into bins, not display the number of games played over time.

19. a) Descriptive Statistics: Price ($)

Minimum	Q1	Median	Q3	Maximum
2.21	2.51	2.61	2.72	3.05

b) Range = max − min = 3.05 − 2.21 = $0.84; IQR = Q3 − Q1 = 2.72 − 2.51 = $0.21

c)

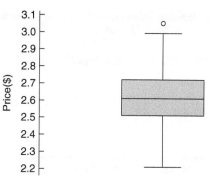

d) Symmetric with one high outlier. The mean is $2.62, with a standard deviation of $0.156.

e) There is one unusually high price that is greater than $3.00 per frozen pizza.

21. The histogram for males is approximately symmetric, with an outlier corresponding to Calgary. The histogram for females is slightly right-skewed, with the highest averages in Toronto, Ottawa, and Regina. The average across all CMAs is about $20 000 higher for males. That does not mean that males earn $20 000 more than females for the Canadian population of full-time full-year workers; that would require a weighted average, taking into account the size of each CMA.

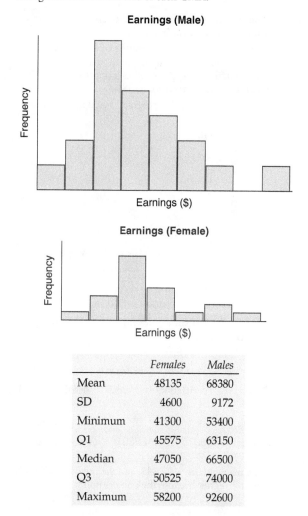

Earnings (Male)

Earnings (Female)

	Females	Males
Mean	48135	68380
SD	4600	9172
Minimum	41300	53400
Q1	45575	63150
Median	47050	66500
Q3	50525	74000
Maximum	58200	92600

The boxplots below show the comparison of females and males across the 20 CMAs very clearly.

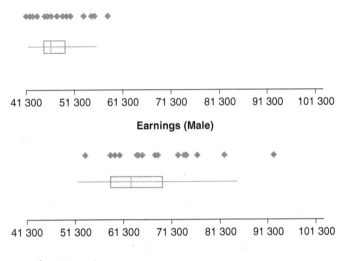

Earnings (Female)

41 300 | 51 300 | 61 300 | 71 300 | 81 300 | 91 300 | 101 300

Earnings (Male)

41 300 | 51 300 | 61 300 | 71 300 | 81 300 | 91 300 | 101 300

23. a) 1611 yards.
  b) Between Quartile 1 = 5585.75 yards, and Quartile 3 = 6131 yards.
  c) The distribution of golf course lengths appears roughly symmetric, so the mean and SD are appropriate.
  d) The distribution of the lengths of all the golf courses in British Columbia is roughly unimodal and symmetric. The mean length of the golf courses is approximately 5900 yards and the standard deviation is 386.6 yd.

25. a) A boxplot is shown. A histogram would also be appropriate.

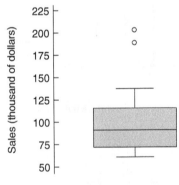

  b) Descriptive Statistics: Sales ($) (Different statistics software may yield different results.)

Variable	N	Mean	SE Mean	StDev	Minimum
Sales ($)	18	107845	11069	46962	62006

Q1	Median	Q3		Maximum
173422.5	95975	112330.0		224504

The mean sale is $107 845, and the median is $95 975. The mean is higher because the outliers pull it up.

c) The median because the distribution has outliers.
  d) The standard deviation of the distribution is $46 962, and the IQR is $38 907.50 (answers may vary due to different quartile algorithms).
  e) The IQR because the outliers inflate the standard deviation.
  f) The mean would decrease. The standard deviation would decrease. The median and IQR would be relatively unaffected.

27. A histogram shows that the distribution is unimodal and skewed to the left. There do not appear to be any outliers. The median failure rate for these 17 models is 16.2%. The middle 50% of the models have failure rates between 10.87% and 21.2%. The best rate is 3.17% for the 60GB Video model, and the worst is the 40GB Click Wheel at 29.85%.

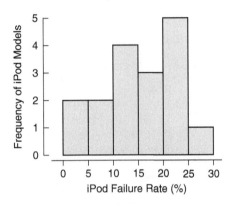

29. Sales in Location #1 were higher than sales in Location #2 in every week. The company might want to compare other stores in locations like these to see if this phenomenon holds true for other locations.

31. a) Gas prices increased over the three-year period, and the spread increased as well. The distribution of prices in 2010 was skewed to the left with several low outliers. Since then, the distribution has been increasingly skewed to the right. There is a high outlier in 2012, although it appears to be pretty close to the upper fence.
  b) The distribution of gas prices in 2012 shows the greatest range and the biggest IQR, so the prices varied a great deal.

33. a) Seneca Lake.
  b) Seneca Lake.
  c) Keuka Lake.
  d) Cayuga Lake vineyards and Seneca Lake vineyards have approximately the same median case price, of about $200, while a typical Keuka Lake vineyard has a case price of about $260. Keuka Lake vineyards have consistently high case prices, between $240 and $280, with one low outlier at about $170 per case. Cayuga Lake vineyards have case prices from $140 to $270, and Seneca Lake vineyards have highly variable case prices, from $100 to $300.

35. a) The median speed is the speed at which 50% of the winning horses ran slower. Find 50% on the left, move straight over to the graph and down to a speed of about 58 kph.
  b) Q1 = 55.5 kph, and Q3 = 58.5 kph.
  c) Range = 10 kph
     IQR = 3 kph

d)

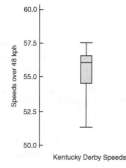

Kentucky Derby Speeds

e) The distribution of winning speeds in the Kentucky Derby is skewed to the left. The lowest winning speed is just under 50 kph, and the fastest speed is about 60 kph. The median speed is approximately 58 kph, and 75% of winning speeds are above 58.5 kph. Only a few percent of winners have had speeds below 53 kph.

37. a) Class 3
    b) Class 3
    c) Class 3 because it is the most highly skewed.
    d) Class 1
    e) Probably Class 1. But without the actual scores, it is impossible to calculate the exact IQRs.

39. There is an extreme outlier for the slow speed drilling. One hole was drilled almost an inch away from the centre of the target! If that distance is correct, the engineers at the computer production plant should investigate the slow speed drilling process closely. It may be plagued by extreme, intermittent inaccuracy. The outlier in the slow speed drilling process is so extreme that no graphical display can display the distribution in a meaningful way while including that outlier. That distance should be removed before looking at a plot of the drilling distances.

    With the outlier removed, we can see that the slow drilling process is more accurate. The greatest distance from the target for the slow drilling process, 0.000098 cm, is still more accurate than the smallest distance for the fast drilling process, 0.000100 cm.

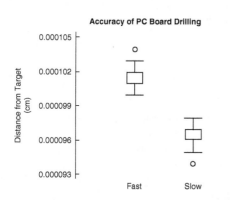

Accuracy of PC Board Drilling

41. a) The mean of 54.41 is meaningless. These are categorical values.
    b) Typically, the mean and standard deviation are influenced by outliers and skewness.
    c) No. Summary statistics are only appropriate for quantitative data.

43. Over this 3-month period, International Funds generally outperformed the other two. Almost half of the International Funds outperformed all the funds in the other two categories. U.S. Domestic Large Cap Funds did better than U.S. Domestic Small/Mid Cap Funds in general. Large Cap funds had the least variation of the three types.

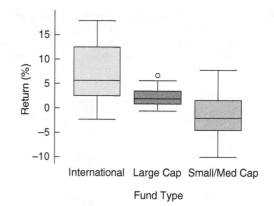

45. a) Even though MLS ID numbers are categorical identifiers, they are assigned sequentially, so this graph has some information. Most of the houses listed long ago have sold and are no longer listed.
    b) A histogram is generally not an appropriate display for categorical data.

47. a)

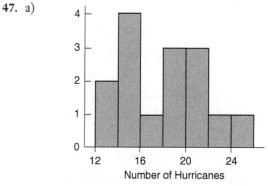

    b) The distribution is fairly uniform. There do not appear to be any decades that would be considered to be outliers.
    c)

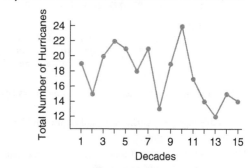

    d) This graph does not support the claim that the number of hurricanes has increased in recent decades.

49. What is the *x*-axis? If it is time, what are the units? Months? Years? Decades? How is "productivity" measured?

51. The house that sells for $400 000 has a *z*-score of (400 000 − 167 900)/77 158 = 3.01, but the house with 4000 sq. ft. of living space has a *z*-score of (4000 − 1819)/663 = 3.29. So it's even more unusual.

53. U.S. *z*-scores are −0.04 and 1.63, total = 1.59. Ireland *z*-scores are 0.25 and 2.77, total 3.02. So Ireland "wins" the consumption battle.

55. a) The histogram is symmetric with outliers at the left end. There are four weeks with 10 or fewer hours. Likely these are vacation weeks or the December holiday season. Most weeks have between 18 and 30 hours of client training.

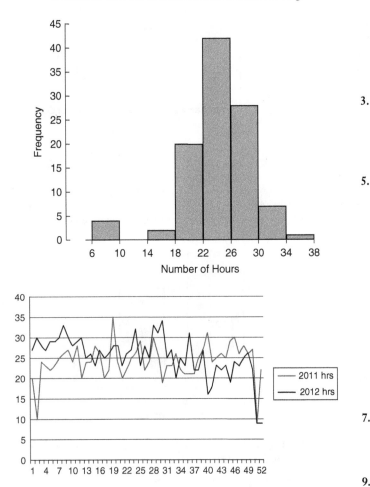

b) Hours are relatively stable throughout the year, except for expected slowdowns in late December and early January. Other drops likely correspond to vacation times. Both years show very similar work patterns.

c) The time series plot because the training hours change over time.

57. a) Possible skewness to the right and definitely bimodal.

b) The trend over time.

c) The time series plot shows more of the data structure, and how the data change over time.

d) Unemployment decreased steadily from approximately 7.5–8.0% in 2003 to just below 6.0% at the start of 2008. Then the rate increased sharply over the next year (world economic meltdown), rising to 8.5% before beginning another steady decline through 2012, to a level of 7.0%–7.5%.

Chapter 6

1. a) Number of text messages: explanatory; cost: response. To predict cost from number of text messages. Positive direction. Linear shape. Possibly an outlier for contracts with fixed cost for texting.

b) Fuel efficiency: explanatory; sales volume: response. To predict sales from fuel efficiency. There may be no association between mpg and sales volume. Environmentalists hope that a higher mpg will encourage higher sales, which would be a positive association. We have no information about the shape of the relationship.

c) Neither variable is explanatory. Both are responses to the lurking variable of temperature.

d) Price: explanatory variable; demand: response variable. To predict demand from price. Negative direction. Linear shape in a narrow range, but curved over a larger range of prices.

3. a) None

b) 3 and 4

c) 2, 3, and 4

d) 2

e) 3 and 1

5. a)

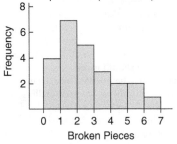

b) Unimodal, skewed to the right. The skewness.

c) The positive, somewhat linear relation between batch number and broken pieces.

7. a) 0.006

b) 0.777

c) −0.923

d) −0.487

9. a) *Price*

b) *Sales*

c) Sales decrease by 24 369.49 kilograms per dollar.

d) It is just a base value. It means nothing because stores won't set their price to $0.

e) 56 572.32 kilograms

f) 3427.69 kilograms

11. a) *Salary*

b) *Wins*

c) On average teams win 0.062 more games per million dollars in salary.

d) Number of wins predicted for a team that spends $0 on salaries. This is not meaningful here.

e) 0.62 games more

f) 4.883 games. Better.

g) 3.117 games.

13. 47 084.23 kilograms
15. "Packaging" isn't a variable. At best, it is a category. There's no basis for computing a correlation.
17. The model is meaningless because the variable *Region* is not quantitative. The slope makes no sense because *Region* has no units. The boxplot comparisons are fine, but the regression is meaningless.
19. a) There is a strong negative linear association between *Carbon Footprint* and *Highway* mpg.
    b) Quantitative variables, straight enough. The Prius is far from the rest of the data. But it is in line with the linear pattern. It is correct to regard it as an outlier or not; that's a matter of judgment.
    c) $r = -0.94$; Removing the Prius reduces the correlation. Data values far from the main body of the data and in line with the linear trend tend to increase correlation and may make it misleading.
21. a) Positive association.
    b) Plot is not linear, violating the linearity condition. There may be an outlier at 17 rooms.
23. a) The variables are both quantitative (with units % of GDP), the plot is reasonably straight, there are no outliers, and the spread is roughly constant (although the spread is large).
    b) About 21% of the variation in the growth rates of developing countries is accounted for by the growth rates of developed countries.
    c) Years 1970–2007
25. a) $\overline{Growth\ (Developing\ Countries)} = 3.46 + 0.433\ Growth\ (Developed\ Countries)$
    b) The predicted growth of developing countries in years of 0 growth in developed countries. Yes, this makes sense.
    c) On average, GDP in developed countries increased 0.433% for a 1% increase in growth in developed countries.
    d) 5.192%
    e) More; we would predict 4.61%.
    f) 1.48%
27. a) Yes, the scatterplot is straight enough, variables are quantitative, and there are no outliers.
    b) Teams that score more runs generally have higher attendance.
    c) There is a positive association, but correlation doesn't imply causation.
29. a) Weak positive relationship; data points are very spread out.

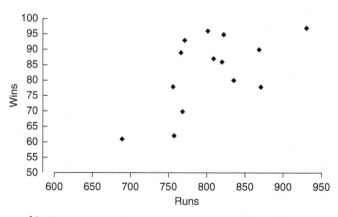

    b) The relationship is expected. Institutions with higher tuitions should be higher both for Canadian and International students.

c) *International Tuition* = 7238.7 + 1.4172 *Canadian Tuition*
d) Yes
e) From a starting point of $7238.70, on average, every increase of $1 in Canadian tuition leads to an increase of $1.417 in International tuition.
f) 12.53% of the variation in International tuitions is accounted for by the regression on Canadian tuitions.
31. a) The predicted value of the money *Flow* if the *Return* was 0%.
    b) An increase of 1% in mutual fund return was associated with an increase of $771 million in money flowing into mutual funds.
    c) $9747 million
    d) −$4747 million; Overestimated.
33. a) Model seems appropriate. Residual plot looks fine.
    b) Model not appropriate. Relationship is nonlinear.
    c) Model not appropriate. Spread is increasing.
35. There are two outliers that inflate the R^2 value and affect the slope and intercept. Without those two points, the R^2 drops from 79% to about 31%. The analyst should set aside those two customers and refit the model.
37. 0.03
39. a) R^2 is an indication of the strength of the model, not the appropriateness of the model.
    b) The student should have said, "The model predicts that quarterly sales will be $10 million when $1.5 million is spent on advertising."
41. a) Quantitative variable condition: Both variables are quantitative (*GPA* and *Starting Salary*).
    b) Linearity condition: Examine a scatterplot of *Starting Salary* by *GPA*.
    c) Outlier condition: Examine the scatterplot.
    d) Equal spread condition: A plot the regression residuals versus predicted values.
43. a)

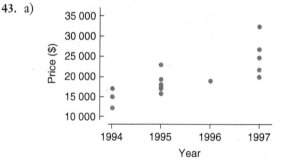

    b) There is a strong, positive, linear association between *Price* and *Year* of used BMW 840s.
    c) Yes
    d) 0.757
    e) 57.4% of the variability in *Price* of a used BMW 840 can be accounted for by the *Year* the car was made.
    f) The relationship is not perfect. Other factors, such as options, condition, and mileage, may account for some of the variability in price.
45. a) The association between the cost of living rank in 2012 and 2011 is linear, positive, and strong. The linearity of the scatterplot indicates that the linear model is appropriate.
    b) 59.0% of the variability in cost of living rank in 2012 can be explained by the cost of living rank in 2011.
    c) 0.768

d) The residual plot shows greater spread in the higher rankings; there is more movement in the list for cities not near the top. There may also be some curvature, from the predicted ranks at the far right (cities ranked lower on the top 50). The data points at the top of the plot (Victoria, Seychelles) and at the far right (Yangon, Myanmar /Burma) are outliers.

47. a) 0.578
    b) CO_2 levels account for 33.4% of the variation in mean temperature.
    c) $\overline{Mean\ Temperature} = 15.3066 + 0.004\ CO_2$
    d) The predicted mean temperature has been increasing at an average rate of 0.004 degrees (C)/ppm of CO_2.
    e) One *could* say that with no CO_2 in the atmosphere, there would be a temperature of 15.3066 degrees Celsius, but this is extrapolation to a nonsensical point.
    f) No
    g) Predicted 16.7626 degrees C.

Chapter 7

1. a) Outcomes are equally likely and independent.
   b) This is likely a personal probability expressing his degree of belief that there will be a rate cut.
3. a) There is no such thing as the "law of averages." The overall probability of an airplane crash does not change due to recent crashes.
   b) There is no such thing as the "law of averages." The overall probability of an airplane crash does not change due to a period in which there were no crashes.
5. a) It would be foolish to insure your neighbour's house for $300. Although you would probably simply collect $300, there is a chance you could end up paying much more than $300. That risk is not worth the $300.
   b) The insurance company insures many people. The overwhelming majority of customers pay and never have a claim. The few customers who do have a claim are offset by the many who simply send their premiums without a claim. The relative risk to the insurance company is low.
7. a) yes
   b) yes
   c) no, probabilities sum to more than 1
   d) yes
   e) no, sum isn't 1 and one value is negative
9. 0.078
11. The events are disjoint. Use the addition rule.
    a) 0.72
    b) 0.89
    c) 0.28
13. a) 0.5184
    b) 0.0784
    c) 0.4816
15. a) The repair needs for the two cars must be independent of one another.
    b) This may not be reasonable. An owner may treat the two cars similarly, taking good (or poor) care of both. This may decrease (or increase) the likelihood that each needs to be repaired.
17. a) 0.68

b) 0.32
c) 0.04
19. a) 0.264
    b) 0.343
21. a) 0.4712
    b) 0.7112
    c) $1 - P(\text{interview}) = 1 - 0.2888 = 0.7112$
23. a) The events are disjoint (an M&M can't be two colours at once), so use the addition rule where applicable.
    i) 0.30
    ii) 0.30
    iii) 0.90
    iv) 0
    b) The events are independent (picking out one M&M doesn't affect the outcome of the next pick), so use the multiplication rule.
    i) 0.027
    ii) 0.128
    iii) 0.512
    iv) 0.271
25. a) disjoint
    b) independent
    c) No. Once you know that one of a pair of disjoint events has occurred, the other one cannot occur, so its probability has become zero.
27. a) 0.754
    b) 0.0007
    c) 0.999
    d) 0.475, 0.011, 0.989
    e) independence
29. a) 0.0225
    b) 0.092
    c) 0.00008
    d) 0.556
31. a) Your thinking is correct. There are 47 cards left in the deck, 26 black and only 21 red.
    b) This is not an example of the Law of Large Numbers. The card draws are not independent.
33. a) 0.550
    b) 0.792
    c) 0.424
    d) 0.918
35. a) 0.333
    b) 0.429
    c) 0.667
37. a) 0.11
    b) 0.27
    c) 0.407
    d) 0.344
39. No. 28.8% of men with OK blood pressure have high cholesterol, but 40.7% of men with high blood pressure have high cholesterol.
41. a) 0.086
    b) 0.437
    c) 0.156
    d) 0.174
    e) 0.177
    f) No.

43. a) 0.47

b) 0.266

c) Having a garage and a pool are not independent events.

d) Having a garage and a pool are not disjoint events.

45. a) 82%

b) Among Canadian adults, the probability of having a cell phone is 78%. The probability of having a cell phone, given that they have a landline, is 79%. It appears that having a cell phone and having a land line are independent since the probabilities are roughly the same.

47. No. 12.5% of the cars were of European origin, but about 16.9% of the students drive European cars.

49. a) 15.4%

b) 11.4%

c) 73.9%

d) 18.5%

51. a)

b) 3.7%

c) 0.405

53. a)

b)

Number good	0	1	2
P (number good)	$\left(\frac{3}{10}\right)\left(\frac{2}{9}\right) = \frac{6}{90}$	$\left(\frac{3}{10}\right)\left(\frac{7}{9}\right) + \left(\frac{7}{10}\right)\left(\frac{3}{9}\right) = \frac{42}{90}$	$\left(\frac{7}{10}\right)\left(\frac{6}{9}\right) = \frac{42}{90}$

b) 0.16

c) 0.667

55. a)

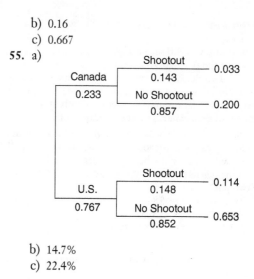

b) 14.7%

c) 22.4%

Chapter 8

1. a) $1, 2, \dots, n$

b) Discrete

3. a) $0, 1, 2, 3, 4$

b) Discrete

c) No, the outcomes are not equally likely.

5. a) $19

b) $7

7. a) $\mu = 30; \sigma = 6$

b) $\mu = 26; \sigma = 5$

c) $\mu = 30; \sigma = 5.39$

d) $\mu = -10; \sigma = 5.39$

9. a) $0.98

b) $16.93

c) $-$0.02

11. a) 2.25 lights

b) 1.26 lights

13. a) No, the probability he wins the second changes depending on whether he won the first.

b) 0.42

c) 0.08

d)

x	0	1	2
$P (X = x)$	0.42	0.50	0.08

e) $E(X) = 0.66$ tournaments; $\sigma = 0.62$ tournaments

15. a) No, the probability of one battery being dead will depend on the state of the other one since there are only 10 batteries.

c) $\mu = 1.4$ batteries
d) $\sigma = 0.61$ batteries

17. $\mu = E(\text{total wait time}) = 74.0$ seconds
$\sigma = SD(\text{total wait time}) \approx 20.57$ seconds
(Answers to standard deviation may vary slightly due to rounding of the standard deviation of the number of red lights each day.) The standard deviation may be calculated only if the days are independent of each other. This seems reasonable.

19. a) The standard deviation is large because the profits on insurance are highly variable. Although there will be many small gains, there will occasionally be large losses when the insurance company has to pay a claim.
b) $\mu = E(\text{two policies}) = \$300$
$\sigma = SD(\text{two policies}) \approx \$8485.28$
c) $\mu = E(1000 \text{ policies}) = \$150,000$
$\sigma = SD(1000 \text{ policies}) = \$189\,736.66$
d) 0.785
e) A natural disaster affecting many policyholders such as a large fire or hurricane

21. a) $B = $ number basic; $D = $ number deluxe Net Profit $= 120B + 150D - 200$
b) $928.00
c) $187.45
d) Mean—no; SD—yes (sales are independent)

23. a) $\mu = E(\text{miles remaining}) = 164$ miles
$\sigma = SD(\text{miles remaining}) \approx 19.799$ miles
b) 0.580

25. a) $\mu = E(\text{time}) = 2.6$ days
$\sigma = SD(\text{time}) \approx 0.707$ days
b) $\mu = E(\text{combined time}) = 3.7$ days
$\sigma = SD(\text{combined time}) \approx 0.768$ days
c) 22.76% (22.66% from tables)

27. a) Let $X_i = $ price of ith Hulk figure sold; $Y_i = $ price of ith Iron Man figure sold; Insertion Fee $= \$0.55$; $T = $ Closing Fee $= 0.875(X_1 + X_2 + \ldots + X_{19} + Y_1 + \ldots + Y_{13})$
Net Income $= (X_1 + X_2 + \ldots + X_{19} + Y_1 + \ldots + Y_{13}) - 32(0.55) - 0.0875(X_1 + X_2 + \ldots + X_{19} + Y_1 + \ldots + Y_{13})$
b) $\mu = E(\text{net income}) = \$313.24$
c) $\sigma = SD(\text{net income}) = \$6.25$
d) Yes, to compute the standard deviation

29. a) No, these are not Bernoulli trials. The possible outcomes are 1, 2, 3, 4, 5, and 6. There are more than two possible outcomes.
b) Yes, these may be considered Bernoulli trials. There are only two possible outcomes: Type A and not Type A. Assuming the 120 donors are representative of the population, the probability of having Type A blood is 42%. The trials are not independent because the population is finite, but the 120 donors represent less than 10% of all possible donors.
c) No, these are not Bernoulli trials. The probability of choosing a man changes after each promotion and the 10% condition is violated.
d) No, these are not Bernoulli trials. We are sampling without replacement, so the trials are not independent. Samples without replacement may be considered Bernoulli trials if the sample size is less than 10% of the population, but 500 is more than 10% of 3000.
e) Yes, these may be considered Bernoulli trials. There are only two possible outcomes: sealed properly and not sealed properly. The probability that a package is unsealed is constant at about 10%, as long as the packages checked are a representative sample of all packages.

31. a) 0.0819
b) 0.0064
c) 0.16
d) 0.992

33. $E(X) = 14.28$, so 15 patients

35. a) 0.078 pixels
b) 0.280 pixels
c) 0.375
d) 0.012

37. a) 0.274
b) 0.355
c) 0.043

*39. a) 0.090
b) 0.329
c) 0.687

*41. a) 16%
b) 50%
c) 95%
d) 0.15%

43. a) 2.4%
b) 8.0%
c) −8.8%
d) $(-3.2\% < x < 8.0\%)$

45. a) 50%
b) 16%
c) 2.5%
d) More than 1.542 is more unusual.

47. a) $x > 1.492$
b) $x < 1.459$
c) $(1.393 < x < 1.525)$
d) $x < 1.393$

49. a) 21.6% (using technology)
b) 48.9%
c) 59.9%
d) 33.4%

51. a) $x > 9.58\%$
b) $x < -2.31\%$
c) $(-0.54\% < x < 5.34\%)$
d) $x > -2.31\%$

53. a) 0.98%
b) 15.4%
c) 7.56%

55. a) 79.58
b) 18.50
c) 95.79
d) −2.79

57. $z_{\text{SAT}} = 1.30$; $z_{\text{ACT}} = 2$. The ACT score is the better score because it is farther above the mean in standard deviation units than the SAT score.

59. a) To know about their consistency and how long they might last. Standard deviation measures variability, which translates to consistency in everyday use. A type of battery with a small standard deviation would be more likely to have life spans close to their mean life span than a type of battery with a larger standard deviation.
b) The second company's batteries have a higher mean life span, but a larger standard deviation, so they have more variability. The decision is not clear-cut. The first company's

batteries are not likely to fail in less than 21 months, but that wouldn't be surprising for the second company. But the second company's batteries could easily last longer than 39 months—a span very unlikely for the first company.

61. CEOs can have between 0 and maybe 40 (or possibly 50) years' experience. A standard deviation of $1/2$ year is impossible because many CEOs would be 10 or 20 SDs away from the mean, whatever it is. An SD of 16 years would mean that 2 SDs on either side of the mean is plus or minus 32, for a range of 64 years. That's too high. So, the SD must be 6 years.

63. a)

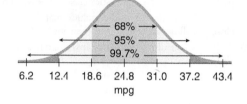

b) Between 7.2 and 12.0 l/100km

c) 16%

d) 13.5%

e) Below 4.8 1/100km

65. Any Job Satisfaction score more than 2 standard deviations below the mean or less than $100 - 2(12) = 76$ might be considered unusually low. We would expect to find someone with a Job Satisfaction score less than $100 - 3(12) = 64$ very rarely.

67. a) About 16%

b) One standard deviation below the mean is -1.27 hours, which is impossible.

c) Because the standard deviation is larger than the mean, the distribution is strongly skewed to the right, not symmetric.

69. a)

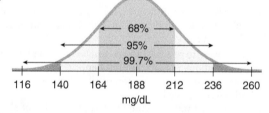

b) 30.85%

c) 17.00%

d) IQR = Q3 − Q1 = 32.38

e) Above 212.87 points

71. a) $\mu = 53.6$ serves
$\sigma = 4.2$ serves

b) $np > 10$; $nq > 10$; serves assumed to be independent.

c) According to the Normal model, in matches with 80 serves, she is expected to make between 49.4 and 57.8 first serves approximately 68% of the time, between 45.2 and 62.0 first serves approximately 95% of the time, and between 41.0 and 66.2 first serves approximately 99.7% of the time.

d) 0.0034 (0.0048 with continuity correction)

73. a) 0.141 (0.175 with continuity correction)

b) Answers may vary. That's a fairly high proportion, but the decision depends on the relative costs of not selling seats and bumping passengers.

75. a) A uniform; all numbers should be equally likely to be selected.

b) 0.5

c) 0.001

*77. a) The Poisson model

b) 0.9502

c) 0.0025

79. X = Fred's score, Y = Neil's score. Find $P(X - Y < 0)$; in golf, low score wins $E(X - Y) = 10$; $Var(X - Y) = 164$; $SD(X - Y) = 12.81$, $X - Y$ is normal.
$P(X - Y < 0) = 0.2177$. There is about a 22% chance that Fred wins.

Chapter 9

1. a) 0.657

b) 0.584

c) 0.507

d) 0.275

3. a) 5.3 grams

b) 6.4 grams

c) Since 5.3 < 6.4, the younger hens lay eggs that have more consistent weights than the eggs laid by the older hens.

d) According to the Normal model, the mean weight of the eggs is 62.7 grams, with a standard deviation of 6.2 grams.

5. a) $\mu(\hat{p}) = p = 7\%$ and $SD(\hat{p}) \approx 1.8\%$

b) $N(0.07, 0.018)$ Assume that these new clients are a random sample from same population on which the default percentage is based. This is not necessarily true. Assume independence—seems reasonable. Sample size condition is met.

c) 0.048

7. 0.212; reasonable that those polled are independent of each other and represent less than 10% of all potential voters. We assume the sample was selected at random. Success/Failure condition met: $np = 208 \geq 10$ and $nq = 192 \geq 10$.

9. 0.088 using $N(0.08, 0.022)$ model

11. Assume the questions are independent of each other and a random sample, and represent less than 10% of all potential questions; $np = 25$ and $nq = 75$ so the $N(0.25, 0.0433)$ model is reasonable. Answers may vary. Using $\mu + 3\sigma$ above the expected proportion of correct answers, the contestant should score at least 38 on the test. To "virtually guarantee" that no one will pass by guessing, set the threshold at 40 out of 100. That probability is less than 3 in 10 000.

13. He believes the true proportion is within 4% of his estimate, with some (probably 95%) degree of confidence.

15. a) *Population*—all cars in the local area; *sample*—134 cars actually stopped at the checkpoint; *p*—population proportion of all cars with safety problems; $\hat{p}$—proportion of cars in the sample that actually have safety problems (10.4%); if sample (a cluster sample) is representative, then the methods of the chapter will apply.

b) *Population*—general public in Quebec; *sample*—602 viewers that logged on to the website; *p*—population proportion of the general public who are very or moderately concerned about political corruption; proportion that logged onto the website and voted that they are very or moderately concerned about political corruption (81.1%); can't use the methods of the chapter—sample is biased and non-random.

17. a) *Population*—all customers who recently bought new cars; *sample*—167 people surveyed about their experience; *p*—proportion of all new car buyers who are dissatisfied with the salesperson; $\hat{p}$—proportion of new car buyers surveyed who are dissatisfied with the salesperson (3%); can't use the methods of the chapter because only 5 people were dissatisfied.

b) *Population*—all university students; *sample*—883 who were asked at a sports arena whether they had smartphones; *p*—proportion of all college students with cell phones; proportion of university students at the sports arena who had a smartphone (87.0%). Be cautious—students at the sports arena may not represent all university students; the sample may be biased.

19. a) Not correct. This implies certainty.
    b) Not correct. Different samples will give different results. Most likely, none of the samples will have *exactly* 88% on-time orders.
    c) Not correct. A confidence interval says something about the unknown population proportion, not the sample proportion in different samples.
    d) Not correct. In this sample, we *know* that 88% arrived on time.
    e) Not correct. The interval is about the parameter, not about the days.

21. a) False
    b) True
    c) True
    d) False

23. We are 90% confident that between 29.9% and 47.0% of U.S. cars are made in Japan.

25. a) 0.024
    b) The pollsters are 90% confident that the true proportion of adults who check their social media feeds every day is within 2.4% of the estimated 32%.
    c) A 99% confidence interval requires a larger margin of error. In order to increase confidence, the interval must be wider.
    d) 0.038 or 3.8%
    e) Smaller margins of error will give us less confidence in the interval.

27. a) (12.7%, 18.6%)
    b) We are 95% confident that between 12.7% and 18.6% of all accidents involve teenage drivers.
    c) About 95% of all random samples of size 582 will produce intervals that contain the true proportion of accidents involving teenage drivers.
    d) Contradicts—the interval is completely below 20%.

29. Probably nothing. Those who bothered to fill out the survey may be a biased sample.

31. This was a random sample of less than 10% of all Internet users; there were $703 \times 0.18 = 127$ successes and 576 failures, both at least 10. We are 95% confident that between 15.2% and 20.8% of Internet users have downloaded music from a site that was not authorized. (Answer could be 15.2% to 20.9% if $n = 127$ is used instead of 0.18).

33. a) $385/550 = 0.70$; 70% of U.S. chemical companies in the sample are certified.
    b) This was a random sample, but we don't know if it is less than 10% of all U.S. chemical companies; there were $550(0.70) = 385$ successes and 165 failures, both at least 10. We are 95% confident that between 66.2% and 73.8% of the chemical companies in the United States are certified. It appears that the proportion of companies certified in the United States is less than in Canada.

35. a) There may be response bias based on the wording of the question.
    b) (45.5%, 51.5%)

c) The margin of error based on the pooled sample is smaller, since the sample size is larger.

37. a) The interval based on the survey conducted by the university Statistics class will have the larger margin of error, since the sample size is smaller.
    b) Both samples are random and are probably less than 10% of the city's voters (provided the city has more than 12 000 voters); there were 636 successes and 564 failures for the newspaper, both at least 10; there were 243 successes and 207 failures for the Statistics class, both at least 10; Newspaper poll: (50.2%, 55.8%); Statistics class: (49.4%, 58.6%).
    c) The Statistics class should conclude that the outcome is too close to call because 50% is in their interval.

39. a) This was a random sample of less than 10% of all English children; there were $2700(0.20) = 540$ successes and 2160 failures, both at least 10; (18.2%, 21.8%).
    b) We are 98% confident that between 18.2% and 21.8% of English children are deficient in vitamin D.
    c) About 98% of random samples of size 2700 will produce confidence intervals that contain the true proportion of English children that are deficient in vitamin D.
    d) No. The interval says nothing about causation.

41. a) This is not a random sample, so no generalization can be made. There are only 5 successes which is not greater than 10, so the sample is not large enough.
    b) Increasing the sample size does not address the problem that this is not a random sample. Do not construct a confidence interval in this situation.

43. a) This was a random sample of less than 10% of all self-employed taxpayers; there were 20 successes and 206 failures, both at least 10.
    b) (5.1%, 12.6%)
    c) We are 95% confident that between 5.1% and 12.6% of all self-employed individuals had their tax returns audited in the past year.
    d) If we were to select repeated samples of 226 individuals, we'd expect about 95% of the confidence intervals we created to contain the true proportion of all self-employed individuals who were audited.

45. a) This was a random sample of less than 10% of all internet users; there were $703 \times 0.13 = 91$ successes and 612 failures, both at least 10.
    b) (10.5%, 15.5%)

47. a) The article states the total sample size but not the numbers in the 18–34 or over 35 age groups. So the sample proportion for 18–34 year olds is based on an unknown denominator. If equally sized age groups is assumed, a confidence interval could be computed.
    b) The responses are likely independent, but the article does not say whether the respondents were randomly selected. 1000 cardholders are less than 10% of all Canadian cardholders. The success/failure condition cannot be checked since the number of 18–34 year olds is not given. However, if is about half of the 1000 respondents, there would be about 225 successes and 275 failures, both greater than 10, so the sample is large enough.
    c) The rule of thumb for margin of error $(1/\sqrt{n})$ gives about 3.2% at the 95% confidence level.

49. a) The parameter is the proportion of digital songs in student libraries that are legal. The population is all songs held in digital libraries. The sample size is 117 079 songs, not 168 students.

b) This was a cluster sample (168 clusters of songs in the digital libraries); 117 079 is less than 10% of all digital songs; the number of legal songs and illegal songs in the sample are both much greater than 10.

c) We are 95% confident that between 22.9% and 23.3% of digital songs were legally purchased.

d) The very large sample size has made the confidence interval unreasonably narrow. It is hard to believe that such a narrow interval really captures the parameter of interest. Additionally, these data were collected in a cluster sample of only 168 students. This gives us less certainty about our ability to capture the true parameter.

51. a) This was a random sample of less than 10% of all internet users; there were $703(0.64) = 450$ successes and 253 failures, both at least 10. We are 90% confident that between 61.0% and 67.0% of internet users would still buy a CD.

b) In order to cut the margin of error in half, they must sample 4 times as many users; $4 \times 703 = 2812$ users.

53. a) 111
   b) 250
   c) 444

55. 1418

57. 384 total, using $\hat{p} = 0.15$

59. Since $z^* \approx 1.634$, which is close to 1.645, the pollsters were probably using 90% confidence.

61. This was a random sample of less than 10% of all customers; there were 67 successes and 433 failures, both at least 10. From the data set, $\hat{p} = 67/500 = 0.134$. We are 95% confident that the true proportion of customers who spend $1000 per month or more is between 10.4% and 16.4%.

63. a) This was a random sample of less than 10% of all British Columbian adults; there were 1635 successes and 842 failures, both at least 10.

b) $(0.641, 0.679)$

c) We are 95% confident that between 64.1% and 67.9% of British Columbian adults have gone cross-border shopping in the past year.

Chapter 10

1. a) Let p be the percentage of products delivered on time. $H_0: p = 0.90$ vs. $H_A: p > 0.90$

b) Let p be the proportion of houses taking more than three months to sell. $H_0: p = 0.50$ vs. $H_A: p > 0.50$

c) Let p be the error rate. $H_0: p = 0.02$ vs. $H_A: p < 0.02$

3. Statement d is correct.

5. If the rate of seat belt usage after the campaign is the same as the rate of seat belt usage before the campaign, there is a 17% chance of observing a rate of seat belt usage after the campaign this large or larger in a sample of the same size by natural sampling variation alone.

7. Statement e is correct.

9. No, we can say only that there is a 27% chance of seeing the observed effectiveness just from natural sampling if $p = 0.7$. There is no *evidence* that the new formula is more effective, but we can't conclude that they are equally effective.

11. a) 0.186 (using the normal model); 0.252 using exact probabilities.

b) It seems reasonable to think there really may have been half of each. We would expect to get 12 or more reds out of 20 more than 15% of the time, so there's no real evidence that the company's claim is not true. The two-sided P-value is greater than 0.30.

13. a) Conditions are satisfied: random sample; less than 10% of population; more than 10 successes and failures; (85.8%, 90.2%)

b) Since 90% is in the interval, there is not sufficient evidence that fewer than 90% of all Canadian youth aged 16–22 are very or somewhat confident in managing their money well overall.

c) $\alpha = 0.01$; it's a lower tail test based on a 98% confidence interval.

15. a) Conditions are satisfied: random sample; less than 10% of population; more than 10 successes and failures; (0.519, 0.581); we are 95% confident that the true proportion of Canadian adults who rate the economic conditions as Very Good/Good is between 0.519 and 0.581.

b) Yes. Since 0.50 is not within the interval, there is evidence that the proportion is not 50%.

c) $\alpha = 0.05$; it's a two-tail test based on a 95% confidence interval.

17. a) Less likely

b) Alpha levels must be chosen *before* examining the data. Otherwise the alpha level could always be selected to reject the null hypothesis.

19. 1. Use p, not $\hat{p}$, in hypotheses.

2. The question is about *failing* to meet the goal. H_A should be $p < 0.96$.

3. Did not check $nq = (200)(0.04) = 8$. Since $nq < 10$, the Success/Failure condition is violated. Didn't check the 10% condition.

4. $\hat{p} = \dfrac{188}{200} = 0.94$; $SD(\hat{p}) = \sqrt{\dfrac{pq}{n}} = \sqrt{\dfrac{(0.96)(0.04)}{200}} \approx 0.014$
The student used $\hat{p}$ and $\hat{q}$.

5. z is incorrect; should be $z = \dfrac{0.94 - 0.96}{0.014} \approx -1.43$

6. $P = P(z < -1.43) = 0.076$

7. There is only weak evidence that the new system has failed to meet the goal.

21. a) Let p = the percentage of children with genetic abnormalities. $H_0: p = 0.05$ vs. $H_A: p > 0.05$

b) SRS (not clear from information provided); $384 < 10\%$ of all children; $np = (384)(0.05) = 19.2 > 10$ and $nq = (384)(0.95) = 364.8 > 10$.

c) $z = 6.28, P < 0.0001$.

d) If 5% of children have genetic abnormalities, the chance of observing 46 children with genetic abnormalities in a random sample of 384 children is essentially 0.

e) Reject H_0. There is strong evidence that more than 5% of children have genetic abnormalities.

f) We don't know that environmental chemicals cause genetic abnormalities, only that the rate is higher now than in the past.

23. a) Let p = the proportion of undergraduate business students who have consumed alcohol within the past year. $H_0: p = 0.86$ vs. $H_A: p \neq 0.86$.

b) Students' decisions about drinking are assumed to be independent of one another. Although not stated, treat the survey as a random sample of undergraduate business students. The sample is less than 10% of all students. $np = 538 > 10$, $nq = 88 > 10$.

c) $z = 1.80$, P-value = 0.072.

d) Do not reject H_0 at $\alpha = 0.05$. There is insufficient evidence to suggest that the percentage of undergraduate business students who drink alcohol is different from all university students as reported by the 2004 Canadian Campus Survey.

e) Since the result is not statistically significant at $\alpha = 0.05$ it is not relevant to discuss practical significance. The difference in percentages 88.5% vs. 86% can be explained by sampling variability. If the result had been statistically significant it is not clear whether the difference would have any practical significance.

25. a) SRS (not clear from information provided); $1000 < 10\%$ of all Canadian adults; $n\hat{p} = 670 > 10$ and $n\hat{q} = 330 > 10$; (0.641, 0.699); we are 95% confident that between 64.1% and 69.9% of Canadian adults have invested in an RRSP.

b) Let p = the percentage of workers who have invested. $H_0: p = 0.57$ vs. $H_A: p \neq 0.57$; since 57% is not in the 95% confidence interval, we reject H_0 at $\alpha = 0.05$. There is strong evidence that the percentage of Canadians who have invested in RRSPs was not 57%. In fact, our sample indicates an increase in the percentage of Canadian adults who invest in an RRSP.

27. Let p = the percentage of cars with faulty emissions. $H_0: p = 0.20$ vs. $H_A: p > 0.20$; two conditions are not satisfied: $22 > 10\%$ of the population of 150 cars and $np = (22)(0.20) = 4.4 < 10$. It's not a good idea to proceed with a hypothesis test.

29. Let p = the percentage of defective products. $H_0: p = 0.03$ vs. $H_A: p \neq 0.03$; SRS (not clear from information provided); $469 < 10\%$ of all products; $np = (469)(0.03) = 14.07 > 10$ and $nq = (469)(0.97) = 454.93 > 10$; $z = -1.91$, $P = 0.0556$; since the P-value = 0.0556 is technically greater than 0.05, we do not reject H_0.

31. Let p = the percentage of readers interested in an online edition. $H_0: p = 0.25$ vs. $H_A: p > 0.25$; SRS; $500 < 10\%$ of all potential subscribers; $np = (500)(0.25) = 125 > 10$ and $np = (500)(0.75) = 375 > 10$; $z = 1.24$, $P = 0.1076$. Since the P-value is high, we fail to reject H_0. There is insufficient evidence to suggest that the proportion of interested readers is greater than 25%. The magazine should not publish the online edition.

33. Let p = the proportion of female executives. $H_0: p = 0.40$ vs. $H_A: p < 0.40$; data are for all executives in this company and may not be able to be generalized to all companies; $np = (43)(0.40) = 17.2 > 10$ and $nq = (43)(0.60) = 25.8 > 10$; $z = -1.31$, $P = 0.0951$. Since the P-value is high, we fail to reject H_0. There is insufficient evidence to suggest proportion of female executives is any different from the overall proportion of 40% female employees at the company.

35. Let p = the proportion of rural high school dropouts in 2009 (0.16). $H_0: p = 0.16$ vs. $H_A: p < 0.16$. Assume that the students in the program are representative of all rural students. Rejecting H_0 will provide evidence that the dropout rate at rural high schools is no longer close to the national rate. 1782 students are less than 10% of all students nationally. $np = (1782)(0.16) = 285 > 10$ and $nq = (1782)(0.84) = 1497 > 10$. Test statistic: $z = -2.26$; P-value = 0.012. Since the P-value < 0.05, there is sufficient evidence at $\alpha = 0.05$ to say that there is a decrease in the dropout rate from 16%.

37. Let p = the proportion of lost luggage returned the next day. $H_0: p = 0.90$ vs. $H_A: p < 0.90$; it is reasonable to think that the people surveyed were independent with regard to their luggage woes; although not stated, we will hope that the survey was conducted randomly, or at least that these air travellers are representative of all air travellers for that airline; $122 < 10\%$ of all air travellers on the airline; $np = (122)(0.90) = 109.8 > 10$ and $nq = (122)(0.10) = 12.2 > 10$; $z = -2.05$, $P = 0.0201$. Since the P-value is low, we reject H_0. There is evidence that the proportion of lost luggage returned the next day is lower than the 90% claimed by the airline.

39. H_0: These MBA students are exposed to unethical practices at a similar rate to others in the program ($p = 0.30$). H_A: These students are exposed to unethical practices at a different rate from other students ($p \neq 0.30$). There is no reason to believe that students' rates would influence others; the professor considers this class typical of other classes; $120 < 10\%$ of all students in the MBA program; 27% of 120 = 32.4—use 32 graduates; $np = 36 > 10$ and $nq = 84 > 10$; $z = -0.717$, $P = 0.4733$. Since the P-value is > 0.05, we fail to reject the null hypothesis. There is little evidence that the rate at which these students are exposed to unethical business practices is different from that reported in the study.

41. a) $z = 3.28$

b) $3.28 > 3.29$, if we assume a two-sided 0.1% significance level.

c) We conclude that the percent of Canadian adults who would oppose legislation for mandatory voting is greater than 33%.

43. a) The regulators decide that the shop is not meeting standards when it actually is.

b) The regulators certify the shop when it is not meeting the standards.

c) Type I

d) Type II

45. a) The probability of detecting that the shop is not meeting standards when they are not.

b) 40 cars; larger n

c) 10%; more chance to reject H_0

d) A lot; larger problems are easier to detect.

47. a) One-tailed; we are testing to see if a decrease in the dropout rate is associated with the software.

b) H_0: The dropout rate does not change following the use of the software ($p = 0.13$). H_A: The dropout rate decreases following the use of the software ($p < 0.13$).

c) The professor buys the software when the dropout rate has not actually decreased.

d) The professor doesn't buy the software when the dropout rate has actually decreased.

e) The probability of buying the software when the dropout rate has actually decreased.

49. a) H_0: The dropout rate does not change following the use of the software ($p = 0.13$). H_A: The dropout rate decreases following the use of the software ($p < 0.13$). One student's decision about dropping out should not influence another's decision; this year's class of 203 students is probably representative of all statistics students; $203 < 10\%$ of all students; $np = (203)(0.13) = 26.39 > 10$ and $nq = (203)(0.87) = 176.61 > 10$; $z = -3.21$, $P = 0.0007$. Since the P-value is very low, we reject H_0. There is strong evidence that the dropout rate has dropped since use of the software program was implemented. As long as the professor feels confident that this class of statistics students is representative of all potential students, then he should buy the program.

b) The chance of observing 11 or fewer dropouts in a class of 203 is only 0.07% if the dropout rate is really 13%.

51. $\hat{p} = \dfrac{67}{500} \approx 0.134$; $z = 1.715$, $P = 0.043$; reject H_0. However, the finance department might also look at the 95% confidence interval (10.4%, 16.4%) and make calculations based on this

range of possible proportions to see the potential financial impact.

Chapter 11

1. a) $N\left(\mu, \dfrac{\sigma}{\sqrt{n}}\right)$

    b) Standard deviation will be smaller. Centre will remain the same.

3.

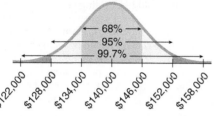

The sampling distribution model for the sample mean of home values is approximately N (140 000, 6000).

5. a) Some people work far longer than the mean plus 2 or 3 SDs.
    b) The CLT says $\bar{y}$ is approximately Normal for large sample sizes, but not for samples of size 1 (individuals). Besides, people can't work fewer than 0 hours.

7. a) 0.0478
    b) 0.863
    c) 0.0019
    d) Essentially 0

9. a) 1.74
    b) 2.37
    c) 0.0524
    d) 0.0889

11. As the variability of a sample increases, the width of a 95% confidence interval increases, assuming that sample size re mains the same.

13. a) $1.333, $1.467
    b) $1.344, $1.456
    c) $1.354, $1.446

15. a) Not correct. A confidence interval is for the mean weight gain of the population of all cows. It says nothing about individual cows.
    b) Not correct. A confidence interval is for the mean weight gain of the population of all cows, not individual cows.
    c) Not correct. We don't need a confidence interval about the average weight gain for cows in this study. We are certain that the mean weight gain of the cows in this study is 25 kilograms.
    d) Not correct. This statement implies that the average weight gain varies. It doesn't.
    e) Not correct. This statement implies that there is something special about our interval, when this interval is actually one of many that could have been generated, depending on the cows that were chosen for the sample.

17. The assumptions and conditions for a t-interval are not met. With a sample size of only 20, the distribution is too skewed. There is also a large outlier that is pulling the mean higher.

19. a) The data are a random sample of all days; the distribution is unimodal and symmetric with no outliers.
    b) ($122.20, $129.80)

c) We are 90% confident that the interval $122.20 to $129.80 contains the true mean daily income of the parking garage.

d) 90% of all random samples of size 44 will produce intervals that contain the true mean daily income of the parking garage.

e) $128 is a plausible value.

21. a) We can be more confident that our interval contains the mean parking revenue.

    b) Wider (and less precise) interval

    c) By collecting a larger sample, they could create a more precise interval without sacrificing confidence.

23. a) 2350 ± 2.009 (59.51)   Interval: (2230.4, 2469.6)

    b) The assumptions and conditions that must be satisfied are:
       1) Independence: probably OK.
       2) Nearly Normal condition: can't tell.
       3) Sample size of 51 is large enough.

    c) We are 95% confident the interval $2230.40 to $2469.60 contains the true mean increase in sales tax revenue. Examples of what the interval *does not* mean: The mean increase in sales tax revenue is $2350 95% of the time. 95% of all increases in sales tax revenue increases will be between $2230.40 and $2469.60. There's 95% confidence the next small retailer will have an increase in sales tax revenue between $2230.40 and $2469.60.

25. a) Given no time trend, the monthly on-time departure rates should be independent. Though not a random sample, these months should be representative, and they're fewer than 10% of all months. The histogram looks unimodal, but slightly left-skewed; not a concern with this large sample.

    b) (80.57%, 81.80%)

    c) We can be 90% confident that the interval from 80.57% to 81.80% holds the true mean monthly percentage of on-time flight departures.

27. If in fact the mean monthly sales due to online purchases has not changed, then only 1 out of every 100 samples would be expected to have mean sales as different from the historical figure as the mean sales observed in the sample.

29. a) ($3699, $3951) We are 95% confident that the interval $3699 to $3951 contains the true mean tax bill for Albertans with $30 000 taxable income.

    b) With a P-value of 0.007, the hypothesis test results are significant and we reject the null hypothesis at $\alpha = 0.05$. We conclude that the mean tax bill for Albertans is different from the British Columbia mean of $4000. Since the 95% confidence interval estimate of $3699 to $3951 does not contain the hypothesized value of $4000, we have evidence that the mean is unlikely to be $4000.

31. a) Upper-tail. They need to prove that the stands will support 80 kilograms (or more) easily.

    b) The inspectors certify the stands as safe, when they are not.
    c) The inspectors decide the stands are not safe when they are.

33. a) Decrease α. This means a smaller chance of declaring the stands safe if they are not.

    b) The probability of correctly detecting that the stands can safely hold over 80 kilograms

    c) Decrease the standard deviation—probably costly. Increase the number of stands tested—takes more time for testing and is costly. Increase α—more Type I errors. Make the stands stronger—costly.

35. a) $H_0: \mu = 23.3$; $H_A: \mu > 23.3$

b) **Randomization condition:** The 40 online shoppers were selected randomly. **Nearly Normal condition:** We should examine the distribution of the sample to check for serious skewness and outliers, but with a large sample of 40 shoppers, it should be safe to proceed.

c) 0.145

d) If the mean age of shoppers is still 23.3 years, there is a 14.5% chance of getting a sample mean of 24.2 years or older simply from natural sampling variation.

e) There is no evidence to suggest that the mean age of online shoppers has increased from the mean of 23.3 years.

37. a) $H_0: \mu = 55$; $H_A: \mu < 55$; **Independence assumption:** Since the times are not randomly selected, we will assume that the times are independent and representative of all the champion's times. **Nearly Normal condition:** The histogram of the times is unimodal and roughly symmetric; P-value = 0.235; fail to reject H_0. There is insufficient evidence to conclude the mean time is less than 55 seconds. They should not market the new ski wax.

b) Type II error. They won't market a competitive wax and thus lose the potential profit from having done so.

39. $H_0: \mu = 50$; $H_A: \mu < 50$; **Randomization condition:** The 44 phones in the sample were randomly selected. **Nearly Normal condition:** We don't have the actual data, so we cannot look at a graphical display. But since the sample is fairly large, it is safe to proceed. $t = -4.146$; P-value < 0.00008; reject H_0. There is strong evidence to reject the null hypothesis. Our evidence suggests that the mean range is actually less than 50 metres.

41. a) Random sample; the Nearly Normal Condition seems reasonable from a Normal probability plot. The histogram is roughly unimodal and symmetric with no outliers.

b) (1187.9, 1288.4) chips

c) Based on this sample, the mean number of chips in an 18-ounce bag is between 1187.9 and 1288.4, with 95% confidence. The *mean* number of chips is clearly greater than 1000. However, if the claim is about individual bags, then it's not necessarily true. If the mean is 1188 and the SD is near 94, then 2.5% of the bags will have fewer than 1000 chips, using the Normal model. If in fact the mean is 1288, the proportion below 1000 will be less than 0.1%, but the claim is still false.

43. **Independence assumption:** We assume that these mutual funds were selected at random and that 35 funds are less than 10% of all value funds. **Nearly Normal condition:** A histogram shows a nearly normal distribution.
$H_0: \mu = 8$; $H_A: \mu > 8$; P-value = 0.201; fail to reject H_0. There is insufficient evidence that the mean 5-year return is greater than 8% for value funds.

45. Given this confidence interval, we cannot reject the null hypothesis of a mean $200 collection using $\alpha = 0.05$. However, the confidence interval suggests that there may be a large upside potential. The collection agency may be collecting as much as $250 per customer on average, or as little as $190 on average. If the possibility of collecting $250 on average is of interest to them, they may want to collect more data.

47. Yes, there is a large ($50) upside potential. The larger trial will likely narrow the confidence interval and make the decision clearer.

49. a) $H_0: \mu = 100$; $H_A: \mu < 100$

b) Different samples give different means; this is a fairly small sample. The difference may be due to natural sampling variation.

c) Batteries selected are an SRS (representative); fewer than 10% of the company's batteries; lifetimes are approximately Normal.

d) $t = -1.0$; P-value = 0.167; do not reject H_0. This sample does not show that the average life of the batteries is significantly less than 100 hours.

e) Yes; Type II.

51. a) The sample is random and the data are alleged to be nearly normal, so at $\alpha = 0.025$ we can reject the null hypothesis that the mean is 0.08 ppm and conclude that it is greater.

b) A type I error would be deciding (as we did) that the mean Mirex contamination level is greater than 0.08 ppm when in fact it isn't. The boycott might harm the salmon producers needlessly. A type II error would be failing to reject the null hypothesis when it's false. In this case, the boycott would likely not take place, but the public would be exposed to the risk of eating salmon with elevated levels of Mirex.

53. a) The histogram of the lab fees shows 2 extreme outliers, so the conditions for inference are violated.

b) $H_0: \mu = 55$
$H_A: \mu > 55$
$t = (63.25 - 55)/8.35 = 0.99$; $P = 0.172$
Do not reject H_0 because $0.172 > 0.05$. We do not have evidence (at $\alpha = 0.05$) to conclude that the average time spent by students in the lab is greater than 55 minutes.

c) $t = (61.5 - 55)/3.03 = 2.14$; $P = 0.030$
When the 2 outliers are deleted, the decision is reject H_0 because $0.03 < 0.05$ We have evidence at $\alpha < 0.05$ that the average time spent by students in the lab is greater than 55 minutes.

d) Outliers, especially extreme outliers, are troublesome for inference because their presence violates the Nearly Normal Condition and assumption of a homogeneous population. When extreme outliers are present, the results of estimation and hypothesis testing can change dramatically. Testing and estimation should therefore be conducted both with and without outliers to see if changes do occur in the statistical results. When an outlier is deleted, an observation from the population is eliminated, so some researchers question whether it is appropriate to delete outliers. Addressing outliers and performing the analysis both with and without those outliers provides a more thorough analysis of the data.

55. a) The assumptions and conditions that must be satisfied are:
The data come from a nearly normal distribution.
The air samples were selected randomly, and there is no bias present in the sample.

b) The histogram of air samples is not nearly normal, but the sample size is large, so inference is OK.

57. a) $14.90 - 11.6$ or ± 3.3 kilometres per hour

b) The sample size for ME = 2 should be increased to
$1.96 \times 8/2 = 7.84$
$(7.84)^2 = 61.466 \Rightarrow$ use 62

59. a) Interval: $653 to $707

b) $H_0: \mu = 650$
$H_A: \mu \neq 650$
$P = 0.031$
Reject H_0. There is strong evidence that the mean audit cost is significantly different from $650.

c) The confidence interval does not contain the hypothesized mean of $650. This provides evidence that the current year's mean audit cost is significantly different from $650.

61. a) The timeplot shows no pattern, so it seems that the measurements are independent. Although this is not a random

sample, an entire year is measured, so it is likely that we have representative values. We certainly have fewer than 10% of all possible wind readings. The histogram appears nearly normal.

b) Testing H_0: $\mu = 8$ kph vs. H_A: $\mu > 8$ kph with 1113 df gives $t = 0.1663$ for a P-value of about 0.43. Even though the observed mean wind speed is over 8 kph, we can't be confident that the true annual mean wind speed exceeds 8 kph. We would not recommend building a turbine at this site.

Chapter 12

1. The P-value is too high to reject H_0 at any reasonable α-level.

3. a) 2.927 points

   b) Larger

   c) We are 95% confident that the mean score for the CPMP math students will be between 5.573 and 11.427 points higher on this assessment than the mean score of the traditional students.

   d) Since the entire interval is above 0, there is strong evidence that students who learn with CPMP will have higher mean scores in applied algebra than those in traditional programs.

5. a) H_0: $\mu_C - \mu_T = 0$; H_A: $\mu_C - \mu_T \neq 0$

   b) If the mean scores for the CPMP and traditional students are really equal, there is less than a 1 in 10 000 chance of seeing a difference as large or larger than the observed difference of 9.4 points just from natural sampling variation.

   c) There is strong evidence that the CPMP students have a different mean score than the traditional students. The evidence suggests that the CPMP students have a higher mean score.

7. H_0: $\mu_C - \mu_T = 0$; H_A: $\mu_C - \mu_T \neq 0$
   $P = 0.1602$; fail to reject H_0. There is no evidence that the CPMP students have a different mean score on the word problems test than the traditional students.

9. a) (1.36, 4.64); df = 33.1

   b) Since the CI does not contain 0, there is evidence that Route A is faster on average.

11. a) H_0: $\mu_C - \mu_A = 0$; H_A: $\mu_C - \mu_A \neq 0$

    b) Independent groups assumption: The percentage of sugar in the children's cereals is unrelated to the percentage of sugar in adult cereals. Randomization condition: It is reasonable to assume that the cereals are representative of all children's cereals and adult cereals, in regard to sugar content. Nearly Normal condition: The histogram of adult cereal sugar content is skewed to the right, but the sample sizes are reasonably large. The Central Limit Theorem allows us to proceed.

    c) (32.15, 40.82)%

    d) Since the 95% confidence interval does not contain 0, we can conclude that the mean sugar content for the two cereals is significantly different at the 5% level of significance.

13. a) H_0: $\mu_C - \mu_D = 0$; H_A: $\mu_C - \mu_D \neq 0$

    b) (−0.256, 1.894)

    c) Since the confidence interval contains 0, there is insufficient evidence to conclude that the mean return over a five-year period is different for consistent style funds as opposed to style drifters.

15. H_0: $\mu_N - \mu_C = 0$; H_A: $\mu_N - \mu_C > 0$ Independent groups assumption: Student scores in one group should not have an impact on the scores of students in the other group. Randomization condition: Students were randomly assigned to classes. Nearly Normal condition: The histograms of the scores are unimodal

and symmetric. $P = 0.023$; reject H_0. There is evidence that the students taught using the new activities have a higher mean score on the reading comprehension test than the students taught using traditional methods.

17. a) H_0: $\mu_L - \mu_S = 0$; H_A: $\mu_L - \mu_S \neq 0$

    b) Independent groups assumption: pH levels from the two types of streams are independent. Independence assumption: Since we don't know if the streams were chosen randomly, assume that the pH level of one stream does not affect the pH of another stream. This seems reasonable. Nearly Normal condition: The boxplots provided show that the pH levels of the streams may be skewed (since the median is either the upper or lower quartile for the shale streams and the lower whisker of the limestone streams is stretched out), and there are outliers. However, since there are 133 degrees of freedom, we know that the sample sizes are large. It should be safe to proceed.

    c) $P \leq 0.0001$; reject H_0. There is strong evidence that the streams with limestone substrates have mean pH levels different than those of streams with shale substrates. The limestone streams are less acidic on average.

19. a) If the mean memory scores for people taking ginkgo biloba and people not taking it are the same, there is a 93.74% chance of seeing a difference in mean memory score this large or larger simply from natural sampling variability.

    b) Since the P-value is so high, there is no evidence that the mean memory test score for ginkgo biloba users is higher than the mean memory test score for non-users.

    c) Type II

21. a) Males: (18.67, 20.11) pegs; females: (16.95, 18.87) pegs

    b) It may appear to suggest that there is no difference in the mean number of pegs placed by males and females, but a two-sample t-interval should be constructed to assess the difference in mean number of pegs placed.

    c) (0.29, 2.67) pegs

    d) We are 95% confident that the mean number of pegs placed by males is between 0.29 and 2.67 pegs higher than the mean number of pegs placed by females.

    e) Two-sample t-interval.

    f) If you attempt to use two confidence intervals to assess a difference in means, you are actually adding standard deviations. But it's the variances that add, not the standard deviations. The two-sample difference of means procedure takes this into account.

23. a) H_0: $\mu_A - \mu_N = 0$; H_A: $\mu_A - \mu_N > 0$

    b) We are 95% confident that the mean number of runs scored by American League teams is between 0.62 and 0.40 runs higher than the mean number of runs scored by National League teams.

    c) $t = 2.42$; $P = 0.013$; Reject H_0.

    d) There is evidence that the mean number of runs scored per game by the AL is greater than in the NL.

25. a) H_0: $\mu_N - \mu_S = 0$; H_A: $\mu_N - \mu_S \neq 0$. $t = 6.47$,   df = 53.49, $P < 0.001$
    Since the P-value is low, we reject H_0. There is strong evidence that the mean mortality rate is different for towns north and south of Derby. There is evidence that the mortality rate north of Derby is higher.

    b) Since there is an outlier in the data north of Derby, the conditions for inference are not satisfied, and it is risky to use the two-sample t-test. The outlier should be removed, and the test should be performed again.

27. A two-sample *t*-procedure is not appropriate for these data because the two groups are not independent. They are before and after satisfaction scores for the same workers.

29. Independent groups assumption: assume that orders in June are independent of orders in August. Independence assumption: orders were a random sample. Nearly normal condition hard to check with small sample, but no outliers.
$H_0: \mu_J - \mu_A = 0$; $H_A: \mu_J - \mu_A \neq 0$; $t = -1.17$; $P = 0.274$; fail to reject H_0. Thus, although the mean delivery time during August is higher, the difference in delivery time from June is not significant. A larger sample may produce a different result.

31. a) We are 95% confident that the mean number of ads remembered by viewers of shows with violent content will be between 1.6 and 0.6 lower than the mean number of brand names remembered by viewers of shows with neutral content.

   b) If they want viewers to remember their brand names, they should consider advertising on shows with neutral content, as opposed to shows with violent content.

33. a) She might attempt to conclude that the mean number of brand names recalled is greater after 24 hours.

   b) The groups are not independent. They are the same people, asked at two different time periods.

   c) A person with high recall right after the show might tend to have high recall 24 hours later as well. Also, the first interview may have helped the people to remember the brand names for a longer period of time than they would have otherwise.

   d) Randomly assign half of the group watching that type of content to be interviewed immediately after watching, and assign the other half to be interviewed 24 hours later.

35. a) Using df ≥ 7536, we are 95% confident that the mean score in 2000 was between 0.61 and 5.39 points lower than the mean score in 1996. Since 0 is not contained in the interval, this provides evidence that the mean score has decreased from 1996 to 2000.

   b) Both sample sizes are very large, which will make the standard errors of these samples very small. They are both likely to be very accurate. The difference in sample size shouldn't make you any more certain or any less certain.

37. a) The differences that were observed between the group of students with internet access and those without were too great to be attributed to natural sampling variation.

   b) Type I

   c) No. There may be many other factors.

   d) It might be used to market computer services to parents.

39. a) 8759 kilograms

   b) Independent groups assumption: sales in different seasons should be independent. Randomization Condition: Not a random sample of weeks, but it is of stores. Nearly Normal condition: can't verify, but we will proceed cautiously. We are 95% confident that the interval 3630.54 to 13 887.39 kilograms contains the true difference in mean sales between winter and summer.

   c) Weather and sporting events may impact pizza sales.

41. $H_0: \mu_2 - \mu_5 = 0$; $H_A: \mu_2 - \mu_5 \neq 0$ Independent groups assumption: The two heats were independent. Randomization condition: Runners were randomly assigned. Nearly Normal condition: Boxplots show an outlier in the distribution of times in heat 2. Perform the test twice, once with the outlier and once without. With outlier: $t = 0.035$; df $= 10.82$; $P = 0.972$; fail to reject H_0. Without the outlier in heat 2: $t = -1.141$; df $= 8.83$; $P = 0.287$; fail to reject H_0. Regardless of whether the outlier is included or excluded, there is no evidence that the mean time to finish differs between the two heats.

43. $H_0: \mu_S - \mu_R = 0$; $H_A: \mu_S - \mu_R > 0$. Assuming the conditions are satisfied, it is appropriate to model the sampling distribution of the difference in means with a Student's *t*-model, with 7.03 degrees of freedom (from the approximation formula). $t = 4.57$; $P = 0.0013$; reject H_0. There is strong evidence that the mean ball velocity for Stinger tees is higher than the mean velocity for regular tees.

45. a) $H_0: \mu_M - \mu_R = 0$; $H_A: \mu_M - \mu_R > 0$. Independent groups assumption: The groups are not related in regards to memory score. Randomization condition: Subjects were randomly assigned to groups. Nearly Normal condition: We don't have the actual data. We will assume that the distributions of the populations of memory test scores are Normal. $t = -0.70$; df $= 45.88$; $P = 0.7563$; fail to reject H_0. There is no evidence that the mean number of objects remembered by those who listen to Mozart is higher than the mean number of objects remembered by those who listen to rap music.

   b) We are 90% confident that the mean number of objects remembered by those who listen to Mozart is between 0.189 and 5.352 objects lower than the mean of those who listened to no music.

47. a) Independent groups assumption: 3- and 5-year returns are not independent. These data are paired and not suited for a two-sample *t*-test. Randomization Condition: random sample of funds. Nearly Normal condition: histograms are unimodal and symmetric with no outliers.

   b) $H_0: \mu_5 - \mu_3 = 0$; $H_A: \mu_5 - \mu_3 > 0$

   c) Not appropriate for a two-sample *t*-test.

   d) None. Can't use the methods of this chapter on these data.

49. a) Independent groups assumption: the prices in the two towns are not related. Randomization condition: each sample was a random sample of prices. Nearly Normal condition: both histograms are reasonably unimodal and symmetric with no outliers, so will use the two-sample *t*-test.

   b) $H_0: \mu_1 = \mu_2$; $H_A: \mu_1 \neq \mu_2$

   c) $t = -0.58$; $P = 0.567$; fail to reject H_0

   d) We conclude that the mean price of homes in these two towns is not significantly different.

51. a) Independent groups assumption: the home runs hit in different leagues are independent. Randomization condition: not a random sample, but we will assume it's representative. Nearly Normal condition: both histograms are reasonably symmetric with no outliers. Unimodality is questionable, but we will proceed with caution. We will use the two-sample *t*-test.

   b) $H_0: \mu_{AL} - \mu_{NL} = 0$; $H_A: \mu_{AL} - \mu_{NL} > 0$

   c) $t = 0.90$; $P = 0.376$

   d) There is insufficient evidence to conclude that the mean number of home runs is different in the two leagues. We fail to reject the null hypothesis.

53. a) The paired *t*-test is appropriate. The labour force participation rate for two different years was paired by city.

   b) Since the P-value $= 0.0244$, there is evidence of a difference in the average labour force participation rate for women between 1968 and 1972. The evidence suggests an increase in the participation rate for women.

55. Adding variances requires that the variables be independent. These price quotes are for the same cars, so they are paired. Drivers quoted high insurance premiums by the local company will be likely to get a high rate from the online company, too.

57. a) The histogram—we care about differences in price.

b) Insurance cost is based on risk, so drivers are likely to see similar quotes from each company, making the differences relatively smaller.

c) The price quotes are paired; they were for a random sample of fewer than 10% of the agent's customers; the histogram of differences looks approximately Normal.

59. $H_0: \mu(\text{Local} - \text{Online}) = 0$ vs. $H_A: \mu(\text{Local} - \text{Online}) > 0$
$t = 0.826$ with 9 df. With a P-value of 0.215, we cannot reject the null hypothesis. These data don't provide evidence that online premiums are lower, on average.

61. a) $H_0: \mu_d = 0$ vs. $H_A: \mu_d \neq 0$

b) $t_{144} = \dfrac{22.7}{113.6/\sqrt{145}} = 2.406$ 2-sided P = 0.017

We are able to reject the null hypothesis (with a P-value of 0.017) and conclude that mean number of keystrokes per hour has changed.

c) 95% CI for mean keystrokes per hour
$22.7 \pm t_{0.025,\,144}\ s/\sqrt{n} = (4.05, 41.35)$

63. a) Paired data assumption: The data are paired by type of exercise machine. Randomization condition: Assume that the men and women participating are representative of all men and women in terms of number of minutes of exercise required to burn 200 calories. Nearly Normal condition: The histogram of differences between women's and men's times is roughly unimodal and symmetric. We are 95% confident that women take an average of 4.8 to 15.2 minutes longer to burn 200 calories than men when exercising at a light exertion rate.

b) Nearly Normal condition: There is no reason to think that this histogram does not represent differences drawn from a Normal population. We are 95% confident that women exercising with light exertion take an average of 4.9 to 20.4 minutes longer to burn 200 calories than women exercising with hard exertion.

c) Since these data are averages, we expect the individual times to be more variable. Our standard error would be larger, resulting in a larger margin of error.

65. a) Randomization condition: These stops are probably representative of all such stops for this type of car, but not for all cars. Nearly Normal condition: A histogram of the stopping distances is roughly unimodal and symmetric. We are 95% confident that the mean dry pavement stopping distance for this type of car is between 133.6 and 145.2 feet.

b) Independent groups assumption: The wet pavement stops and dry pavement stops were made under different conditions and not paired in any way. Randomization condition: These stops are probably representative of all such stops for this type of car, but not for all cars. Nearly Normal condition: The histogram of wet pavement stopping distances is more uniform than unimodal, but no outliers. We are 95% confident that the mean stopping distance on wet pavement is between 51.4 and 74.6 feet longer than the mean stopping distance on dry pavement.

67. a) Yes. The percent change is computed using paired data. Same cities both years.

b) Data are paired. Differences (both actual and percent change) are roughly unimodal and symmetric. Actual differences: $H_0: \mu_d = 0$; $H_A: \mu_d \neq 0$
Mean difference: $(2Q2011 - 2Q2010) = 14.68$; $t = -10.34$; P-value < 0.0001; reject H_0. There is extremely strong evidence the second quarter 2010 domestic airfares are significantly different from the second quarter 2011 domestic airfares.

t-test on the percent change:
$H_0: \mu = 0$; $H_A: \mu \neq 0$
For percentage differences, $t = -11.25$, and P-value < 0.0001

Both tests provide the same statistical conclusion. However, in general if there were extreme or outlying paired observations that skewed the mean difference, then the mean percent change might be a more appropriate test because it would eliminate the variability due to extreme differences.

69. a) $H_0: p_{Older} - p_{Younger} = 0$ vs. $H_A: p_{Older} - p_{Younger} \neq 0$
b) $\hat{p}_1 = 0.6323$ (Older), $\hat{p}_2 = 0.4793$, $z = 4.409$, two-tailed P-value $< 0.000\,01$. There is strong evidence that the percentage of people avoiding fast food is different for the two age groups. The older group is more likely to avoid fast food.
c) (8.5%, 22.1%)

71. a) $H_0: p_{Female} - p_{Male} = 0$ vs. $H_A: p_{Female} - p_{Male} \neq 0$
b) $\hat{p}_1 = 0.730$ (Female), $\hat{p}_2 = 0.212$; $z = 22.82$; two-tailed P-value is extremely small, less than 0.000 01. There is very strong evidence that females had a higher chance of survival. The same conclusion could be drawn from the confidence interval in part c).
c) (47.35%, 56.25%)

73. a)

	Outlook		
	1 Unexcited	**2 Excited**	Total
Male	64	230	294
Female	98	182	280
Total	162	412	574

b) $H_0: p_{Male} - p_{Female} = 0$ vs. $H_A: p_{Male} - p_{Female} \neq 0$
$\hat{p}_1 = 0.7823$ (Males excited about the course), $\hat{p}_2 = 0.6500$, $z = 3.547$, two-tailed P-value = 0.000 39. There is evidence that the percentage of males who are excited about the course is different from the percentage of females who are excited about the course.

c) $\hat{p}_1 = 0.2177$ (Males unexcited about the course), $\hat{p}_2 = 0.3500$; the 95% confidence interval is (–20.2%, –6.3%). Since the interval does not include zero, there is evidence of a difference. Further, since the entire interval is negative, the percentage of males who are unexcited is lower, hence the percentage who are excited is higher than the percentage of females.

Chapter 13

1. a) Chi-square test of two-way table, specifically, independence; One sample, two variables. We want to see if the variable *Account type* is independent of the variable *Trade type*.
b) Some other statistical test; the variable *Account size* is quantitative, not counts.
c) Chi-square test of two-way table, specifically, homogeneity; we have two samples (residential and nonresidential students) and one variable, *Courses*. We want to see if the distribution of *Courses* is the same for the two groups.

3. a) 10
b) Goodness-of-fit
c) H_0: The die is fair. (All faces have $p = 1/6$.)

d) Count data; rolls are random and independent of each other; expected frequencies are all greater than 5.

e) 5

f) $\chi^2 = 5.600$; $P = 0.3471$

g) Since $P = 0.3471$ is high, fail to reject H_0. There is not enough evidence to conclude that the die is unfair.

5. a) Weights are quantitative, not counts.

b) Count the number of each type of nut, assuming the company's percentages are based on counts rather than weights (which is not clear).

7. a) Goodness-of-fit

b) Count data; assume the lottery mechanism uses randomization and guarantees independence; expected frequencies are all greater than 5.

c) H_0: Likelihood of drawing each numeral is equal.
H_A: Likelihood of drawing each numeral is *not* equal.

d) $\chi^2 = 6.46$; df = 9; $P = 0.693$; fail to reject H_0.

e) The P-value says that if the drawings were in fact fair, an observed chi-square value of 6.46 or higher would occur about 69% of the time. This is not unusual at all, so we won't reject the null hypothesis that the values are uniformly distributed. The variation that we observed seems typical of that ex pected if the digits were drawn equally likely.

9. a) 40.2%   b) 8.1%   c) 62.2%   d) 285.48

e) H_0: Survival was independent of status on the ship.
H_A: Survival was not independent of the status.

f) 3

g) We reject the null hypothesis. Survival depended on status. We can see that first-class passengers were more likely to survive than passengers of any other class.

11. a) Independence

b) H_0: Program choice is independent of birth order.
H_A: There is an association between program choice and birth order.

c) Count data; not a random sample of students, but assume that it is representative; expected counts are low for both the Social Science and Professional programs for both third and fourth or higher birth order. We'll keep an eye on these when we calculate the standardized residuals.

d) 9

e) With a P-value this low, we reject the null hypothesis. There is some evidence of an association between birth order and program choice.

f) Unfortunately, 3 of the 4 largest standardized residuals are in cells with expected counts less than 5. We should be very wary of drawing conclusions from this test.

13. a) Chi-square test for homogeneity

b) Count data; assume random assignment to treatments (although not stated); expected counts are all greater than 5.

c) H_0: The proportion of infection is the same for each group.
H_A: The proportion of infection is different among the groups.

d) $\chi^2 = 7.776$; *df* = 2; $P = 0.02$; reject H_0.

e) Since the P-value is low, we reject the null hypothesis. There is strong evidence of difference in the proportion of urinary tract infections for cranberry juice drinkers, lactobacillus drinkers, and women that drink neither of the two beverages.

f) The standardized residuals are:
The significant difference appears to be primarily due to the success of cranberry juice.

	Cranberry	**Lactobacillus**	**Control**
Infection	−1.87276	1.191759	0.681005
No infection	1.245505	−0.79259	−0.45291

15. a) Independence

b) H_0: Age is independent of frequency of shopping at this department store.
H_A: Age is not independent of frequency of shopping at this department store.

c) Count data; assume survey was conducted randomly (not specifically stated); expected counts are all greater than 5.

d) Since the P-value is low, we reject the null hypothesis. There is evidence of an association between age and frequency of shopping at this department store.

e) Given the negative residuals for the low frequency categories among the older women and the positive residuals for the higher frequency categories among the older women, we conclude that older women in this survey shop more frequently at this department store than expected.

17. a) $P = 0.3766$. With a P-value this high, we fail to reject. There is not enough evidence to conclude that either men or women are more likely to make online purchases of books.

b) Type II.

c) $(-4.09\%, 10.86\%)$

19. a) $\chi^2 = 5.749$ with 1 df; P-value = 0.0165. At the 5% level, there is evidence that the percentage of online Canadians who use Web-based financial services has changed from 2011 to 2012.

b) (0.0158, 0.0848). The percentage has increased from 2011 to 2012 by anywhere from 1.6% to 8.5%.

21. a) No, the P-value = 0.281.

b) 90% confidence interval is $(-0.19, 0.82\%)$.

23. H_0: Marital status is independent of frequency of shopping.
H_A: Marital status is not independent of frequency of shopping.
Count data; assume survey was conducted randomly (not specifically stated); expected counts are all greater than 5.
$\chi^2 = 23.858$; df = 6; P-value = 0.001
Since the P-value is low, reject the null hypothesis. There is strong evidence of an association between marital status and frequency of shopping at this department store. Based on the residuals, married customers shopped at this store more frequently than expected, and more single women shopped never/hardly ever than expected.

25. a) Chi-square test for homogeneity.

b) Count data; executives were surveyed randomly; expected counts are all greater than 5.

c) H_0: The distribution of attitudes about critical factors affecting ethical and legal accounting practices was the same in 2000 and 2006.
H_A: The distribution of attitudes about critical factors affecting ethical and legal accounting practices was not the same in 2000 and 2006.

d) $\chi^2 = 4.030$; df = 4; $P = 0.4019$

e) Since the P-value is high, we fail to reject the null hypothesis. There is no evidence of a change in the distribution of attitudes about factors affecting ethical and legal accounting practices between 2000 and 2006.

27. a) Chi-square test of independence.
    b) Count data; assume survey was conducted randomly (not specifically stated); expected counts are all greater than 5.
    c) H_0: Emphasis on quality is independent of frequency of shopping.
       H_A: Emphasis on quality is not independent of frequency of shopping.
    d) $\chi^2 = 30.007$; df = 6; P < 0.001
    e) Since the P-value is low, reject the null hypothesis. There is strong evidence of an association between emphasis on quality and frequency of shopping at this department store.

29. a)

	Men	**Women**
Excellent	6.667	5.333
Good	12.778	10.222
Average	12.222	9.778
Below Average	8.333	6.667

Count data; assume that these executives are representative of all executives that have ever completed the program; expected counts are all greater than 5.
    b) Decreased from 4 to 3.
    c) $\chi^2 = 9.306$; P = 0.0255. Since the P-value is low, we reject the null hypothesis. There is evidence that the distributions of responses about the value of the program for men and women executives are different.

31. H_0: There is no association between race and the section of the apartment complex in which people live.
    H_A: There is an association between race and the section of the apartment complex in which people live.
    Count data; assume that the recently rented apartments are representative of all apartments in the complex; expected counts are all greater than 5.
    $\chi^2 = 14.058$; df = 1; P < 0.001
    Since the P-value is low, we reject the null hypothesis. There is strong evidence of an association between race and the section of the apartment complex in which people live. An examination of the components shows us that whites are more likely to rent in Section A (component = 6.2215) and that blacks are more likely to rent in Section B (component = 5.0517).

33. $\hat{p}_B - \hat{p}_A = 0.206$
    95% CI = (0.107, 0.306)

35. a) Chi-square test for independence.
    b) Count data; assume that the sample was taken randomly; expected counts are all greater than 5.
    c) H_0: Outsourcing is independent of industry sector.
       H_A: There is an association between outsourcing and industry sector.
    d) $\chi^2 = 2815.968$; df = 9; P-value is essentially 0.
    e) Since the P-value is so low, we reject the null hypothesis. There is strong evidence of an association between outsourcing and industry sector.

37. a) Chi-square test for homogeneity. (Could be independence if the categories are considered exhaustive.)
    b) Count data; assume that the sample was taken randomly; expected counts are all greater than 5.

c) H_0: The distribution of employee job satisfaction level attained is the same for different management styles.
   H_A: The distribution of employee job satisfaction level attained is different for different management styles.
d) $\chi^2 = 178.453$; df = 12; P-value is essentially 0.
e) Since the P-value is so low, we reject the null hypothesis. There is strong evidence that the distribution of employee job satisfaction level attained is different across management styles. Generally, exploitative authoritarian management is more likely to have lower levels of employee job satisfaction than consultative or participative styles.

39. Assumptions and conditions for test of independence satisfied. H_0: Reading online journals or blogs is independent of generation. H_A: There is an association between reading online journals or blogs and generation. $\chi^2 = 48.408$; df = 8; P < 0.001. We reject the null hypothesis and conclude that reading online journals or blogs is not independent of generational age.

41. Chi-square test of homogeneity (unless these two types of firms are considered the only two types in which case it's a test of independence).
    Count data; assume that the sample was random; expected counts are all greater than 5.
    H_0: Systems used have same distribution for both types of industry.
    H_A: Distribution of type of system differs in the two industries.
    $\chi^2 = 157.256$; df = 3; P-value is essentially 0.
    Since the P-value is low, we can reject the null hypothesis and conclude that the type of ERP system used differs across industry type. Those in manufacturing appear to use more of the inventory management and ROI systems.

43. Chi-square test of independence. Data are counts; random sample from the population of Canadian undergraduates; expected counts are all greater than five.
    H_0: Drinking status is independent of gender.
    H_A: Drinking status is not independent of gender.
    $\chi^2 = 193.50$ with 3 df; P-value is essentially zero so reject the null hypothesis and conclude there is strong evidence that drinking status is different for male and female undergraduates in Canada. Males are much more likely to be frequent drinkers (at least weekly). About the same proportions of males and females are abstainers, or are former drinkers.

Drinking status	**Male**	**Female**
Abstainer	9.1%	9.1%
Former	5.9%	3.8%
Monthly	36.4%	43.8%
Weekly+	48.7%	33.4%

Chapter 14

1. a) The trend appears to be somewhat linear up to about 1940, but from 1940 to about 1970 the trend appears to be nonlinear. From 1975 or so to about 2008, the trend appears to be linear.
   b) Strong from 1975 but much weaker for the 50 years preceding.
   c) No, as a whole the graph is clearly nonlinear. Within certain periods (1975 to about 2008) the correlation is high.

d) Overall, no. You could fit a linear model to the period from 1975 to about 2008, but why? You don't need to interpolate, since every year is reported, and extrapolation seems dangerous.

3. a) The relationship is not straight.
   b) It will be curved downward.
   c) No. The relationship will still be curved.

5. a) No. We need to see the scatterplot first to see if the conditions are satisfied.
   b) No, the linear model might not fit the data at all.

7. a)

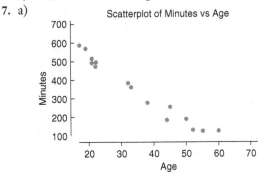

Scatterplot of Minutes vs Age

b) This scatterplot appears to have curvature at both ends of the age distribution so a linear regression may not be completely appropriate.
c) The regression equation is $\widehat{Minutes} = 750 - 11.5(Age)$
d) The residual plots are:

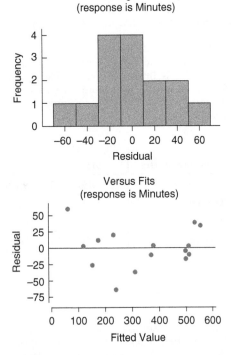

Histogram
(response is Minutes)

Versus Fits
(response is Minutes)

The nearly normal condition is satisfied. There may be some curvature to the residual plot.

9. a) $\widehat{Budget} = -31.39 + 0.71\ Run\ Time$. The model suggests that movies cost about $710 000 per minute to make.
   b) A negative starting value makes no sense, but the P-value of 0.07 indicates that we can't discern a difference between

our estimated value and zero. The statement that a movie of zero length should cost $0 makes sense.

c) Amounts by which movie costs differ from predictions made by this model vary, with a standard deviation of about $33 million.
d) $0.15 m/min
e) If we constructed other models based on different samples of movies, we'd expect the slopes of the regression lines to vary, with a standard deviation of about $150 000 per minute.

11. a) The scatterplot looks straight enough, the residuals look random and roughly normal, and the residuals don't display any clear change in variability although there may be some increasing spread.
   b) I'm 95% confident that the cost of making longer movies increases at a rate of between 0.41 and 1.01 million dollars per minute. (CI is 0.41 to 1.02 using raw data.)

13. a) H_0: There is no linear relationship between calcium concentration in water and mortality rates for males. ($\beta_1 = 0$)
   H_A: There is a linear relationship between calcium concentration in water and mortality rates for males. ($\beta_1 \neq 0$)
   b) $t = -6.65$, $P < 0.0001$; reject the null hypothesis. There is strong evidence of a linear relationship between calcium concentration and mortality. Towns with higher calcium concentrations tend to have lower mortality rates.
   c) For 95% confidence, use $t^*_{59} \approx 2.001$, or estimate from the table $t^*_{50} \approx 2.009$; $(-4.19, -2.27)$.
   d) We are 95% confident that the average mortality rate decreases by between 2.27 and 4.19 deaths per 100 000 for each additional part per million of calcium in drinking water.

15. a) $\widehat{male\ rate} = 2.376 + 0.755\ 64 \times (female\ rate)$
   b) The scatterplot shows a high-leverage point. The residual plot suggests that it may not fit with the other points, so the regression should be run both with and without that point to examine its impact.
   c) H_0: There is no linear relationship between male and female unemployment rate. ($\beta_1 = 0$)
   H_A: There is a linear relationship between male and female unemployment rate. ($\beta_1 \neq 0$)
   $t = 13.46$, df $= 55$, $P < 0.001$; reject the null hypothesis. There is strong evidence of a positive linear relationship between the male and female unemployment rate
   d) 76.7%

17. a) 1) High leverage, small residual.
   2) No, not influential for the slope.
   3) Correlation would decrease because outlier has large z_x and z_y, increasing correlation.
   4) Slope wouldn't change much because the outlier is in line with other points.
   b) 1) High leverage, probably small residual.
   2) Yes, influential.
   3) Correlation would weaken and become less negative because scatter would increase.
   4) Slope would increase toward 0, since outlier makes it negative.
   c) 1) Some leverage, large residual.
   2) Yes, somewhat influential.
   3) Correlation would strengthen, since scatter would decrease.
   4) Slope would increase slightly.
   d) 1) Little leverage, large residual.
   2) No, not influential.

3) Correlation would become stronger and become more negative because scatter would decrease.

4) Slope would change very little.

19. 1. e 2. d 3. c 4. b 5. a

21. Perhaps high blood pressure causes high body fat, high body fat causes high blood pressure, or both could be caused by a lurking variable such as a genetic or lifestyle issue.

23. a)

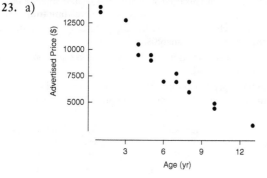

b) Yes, the plot seems linear.

c) $\widehat{Advertised\ Price} = 14\,286 - 959 \times Age$

d)

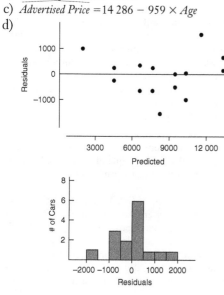

The residual plot shows some possible curvature. Inference may not be valid here, but we will proceed (with caution).

25. Based on these data, we are 95% confident that a used car's *Price* decreases between \$819.50 and \$1098.50 per year.

27. a)

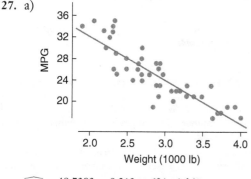

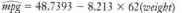
$\widehat{mpg} = 48.7393 - 8.213 \times 62(weight)$

b) Yes, the conditions seem satisfied. Histogram of residuals is unimodal and symmetric; residual plot looks okay, but some "thickening" of the plot with increasing values. There may be one possible outlier.

c) H_0: There is no linear relationship between the weight of a car and its fuel efficiency. ($\beta_1 = 0$)
H_A: There is a linear relationship between the weight of a car and its mileage. ($\beta_1 \neq 0$)

d) $t = -12.2$, df $= 48$, P < 0.0001; reject the null hypothesis. There is strong evidence of a linear relationship between weight of a car and its mileage. Cars that weigh more tend to have lower gas mileage.

29. a) H_0: There is no linear relationship between SAT Verbal and Math scores. ($\beta_1 = 0$)
H_A: There is a linear relationship between SAT Verbal and Math scores. ($\beta_1 \neq 0$)

b) Assumptions seem reasonable, since conditions are satisfied. Residual plot shows no patterns (one outlier); histogram is unimodal and roughly symmetric.

c) $t = 11.9$, df $= 160$, P < 0.0001; reject the null hypothesis. There is strong evidence of a linear relationship between SAT Verbal and Math scores. Students with higher SAT Verbal scores tend to have higher SAT Math scores.

31. a) H_0: There is no linear relationship between team salaries and number of wins. ($\beta_1 = 0$)
H_A: There is a linear relationship between team salaries and wins. ($\beta_1 \neq 0$)

b) $t = 1.58$; P $= 0.124$; we fail to reject the null hypothesis. There is no evidence of a linear relationship between team salary and team wins in 2006.

33. a) $(-9.57, -6.86)$ mpg per 1000 pounds

b) We are 95% confident that the mean fuel efficiency of cars decreases by between 6.86 and 9.57 miles per gallon for each additional 1000 pounds of weight.

35. a) H_0: There is no linear relationship between market return and fund flows. ($\beta_1 = 0$)
H_A: There is a linear relationship between market return and fund flows. ($\beta_1 \neq 0$)

b) $t = 5.75$, P < 0.001; reject the null hypothesis. There is strong evidence of a linear relationship between money invested in mutual funds and market performance.

c) Greater investment in mutual funds tends to be associated with higher market return. I would suggest investigating the unusual observations and finding out when and why they occurred.

37. a) H_0: There is no linear association between the Index in 2006 and 2007. ($\beta_1 = 0$)
H_A: There is a linear association between the Index in 2006 and 2007. ($\beta_1 \neq 0$)

b) $t = 8.17$; P < 0.001. The association is not likely to occur by chance. We reject the null hypothesis. There is strong evidence of a linear relationship between the Index in 2006 and 2007.

c) 83.7% of the variation in the 2007 Index is accounted for by the 2006 Index.

d) On average, as one increases, so does the other. However, this does not mean if the index is high in one year, it will necessarily be high in the other.

39. a)

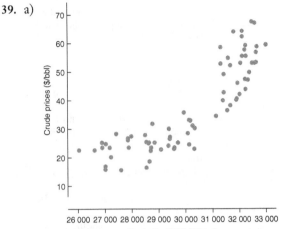

The conditions for regression fail, since the scatterplot bends.

b) No, the relationship does not appear to be linear.

41. H_0: There is no linear relationship between speed and cost of printers. $(\beta_1 = 0)$
H_A: There is a linear relationship between speed and cost of printers. $(\beta_1 \neq 0)$

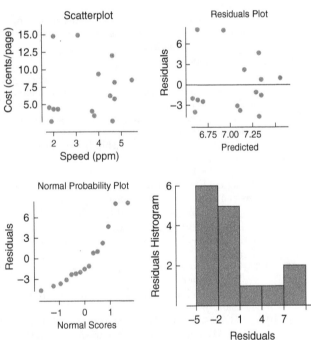

Assumptions do not seem reasonable. Scatterplot isn't straight. The histogram of the residuals is skewed to the right. The conditions are not met, so inference is not appropriate.

43. a) We are 95% confident that the mean fuel efficiency of cars that weigh 2500 pounds is between 27.34 and 29.07 miles per gallon.

b) We are 95% confident that a car weighing 3450 pounds will have fuel efficiency between 15.44 and 25.37 miles per gallon.

45. a) $(-3145, 40\ 845)$

b) Since the SE for the slope is relatively large and the R^2 is relatively small (18%), predictions using this regression will be imprecise.

c) Omitting outlying values makes the SE smaller and the R^2 larger, so predictions should be more precise.

47. a) We'd like to know if there is a linear association between *Price* and *Fuel Efficiency* in cars. We have data on 2004 model-year cars giving their highway mpg and retail price. H_0: $\beta_1 = 0$ (no linear relationship between *Price* and *Fuel Efficiency*); H_A: $\beta_1 \neq 0$.

b) The scatterplot fails the Linearity condition. It shows a bend and it has an outlier. There is also some spreading from right to left, which would violate the Equal Spread condition. We cannot continue the analysis.

c) The conditions are not met; the regression equation should not be interpreted.

49. a) The 95% prediction interval shows the interval of uncertainty for a single predicted male unemployment rate, given a specific female unemployment rate.

b) The 95% confidence interval shows the interval of uncertainty for the mean male unemployment rate given a sample of female unemployment rates. Because this is an interval for an average, the variation or uncertainty is less, so the interval is narrower.

c) The unusual observation is the former Yugoslav Republic of Macedonia. Besides being an outlier, it is also a potential leverage value because its female rate is so removed from the average female rate for this sample of countries. Without this leverage value, $\widehat{male\ rate} = 4.459 + 0.629\ 51 \times (female\ rate)$. Note that the slope remains significant (P < 0.001), and the R^2 decreases slightly compared to the output in Exercise 15 without this leverage value.

51. a) The 95% prediction interval shows the interval of uncertainty for the predicted energy use in 2004 based on energy use in 1990 for a single country.

b) The 95% confidence interval shows the interval of uncertainty for the mean energy use in 2004 based on the same energy use in 1990 for a sample of countries. Because this is an interval for an average, the variation or uncertainty is less, so the interval is narrower.

53. a) $\widehat{Jan} = 120.73 + 0.6695 \times Dec$. We are told this is an SRS. One cardholders' spending should not affect another's. These are quantitative data with no apparent bend in the scatterplot. The residual plot shows some increased spread for larger values of January charges. A histogram of residuals is unimodal and slightly skewed to the right with several high outliers. We will proceed cautiously.

b) $1519.73

c) ($1330.24, $1709.24)

d) ($290.76, $669.76)

e) The residuals show increasing spread, so the confidence intervals may not be valid. I would be skeptical of interpreting them too literally.

55. a) H_0: There is no linear relationship between *Midterm Grade* and *Final Exam Grade*. $(\beta_1 = 0)$
H_A: There is a positive linear relationship between *Midterm Grade* and *Final Exam Grade*. $(\beta_1 > 0)$
$t = 16.28$, P-value < 0.0001; reject the null hypothesis. There is strong evidence of a positive linear relationship between *Final Exam Grade* and *Midterm Grade*. As expected, students with higher midterm grades have higher final exam grades, on average.

b) F = 265.23, P-value < 0.0001. There is very strong evidence that *Midterm Grade* is a useful predictor of *Final Exam Grade* (the same conclusion as in part a).

c) *Midterm Grade* is a good predictor of *Final Exam Grade*. It explains 57% (R^2) of the variation in *Final Exam Grade* and s is just about 9.5 marks.

d) Confidence interval for slope: (0.7788, 0.9934)
We are 95% confident that each additional percent on the midterm will increase the final exam grade by between 0.78 and 0.99 marks.

e) Final Exam = 2.9781 + 0.8861(80) = 73.87
The 95% prediction interval: 73.87 ± 18.77 or (55.10, 92.64)
We are 95% confident that a student who gets a midterm grade of 80 will get a final exam mark between 55 and 93.

f) The same prediction as in e) but the standard error changes.
The 95% confidence interval: 73.87 ± 1.43 or (72.44, 75.30)
We are 95% confident that the average final grade of all students who get a midterm grade of 80 will be between 72 and 75.

Chapter 15

1. a) Linearity: The scatterplots appear linear.
Independence: States are not a random sample, but they may be independent of each other.
Equal variance: The scatterplot of *Violent Crime* vs. *Police Officer Wage* may become less spread to the right, or maybe that's just fewer data points.
Normality: To check the Nearly Normal condition, we'll need to look at the residuals; we can't check it with these plots.

b) 1.1%

3. a) $\widehat{Violent\ Crime}$ = 1390.83 + 9.33 *Police Officer Wage* − 16.64 *Graduation Rate*

b) After allowing for the effects of graduation rate (or, alternatively, among states with similar graduation rates), states with higher police officer wages have more crime at the rate of 9.3 crimes per 100 000 for each dollar per hour of average wage.

c) 412.63 crimes per 100 000

d) Not very good; R^2 is only 53%.

5. a) $2.26 = \dfrac{9.33}{4.125}$

b) 40, the degrees of freedom is 37, and that's equal to $n - k - 1$. With two predictors, $40 - 2 - 1 = 37$.

c) The t-ratio is negative because the coefficient is negative.

7. a) $H_0: \beta_{Officer} = 0$ vs. $H_A: \beta_{Officer} \neq 0$

b) P = 0.0297; that's small enough to reject the null hypothesis at $\alpha = 0.05$ and conclude that the coefficient is discernibly different from zero.

c) The coefficient of *Police Officer Wage* reports the relationship after allowing for the effects of *Graduation Rate*. The scatterplot and correlation were only concerned with the two-variable relationship.

9. This is a causal interpretation, which is not supported by regression. For example, among states with high graduation rates, it may be that those with higher violent crime rates choose (or are obliged) to spend more to hire police officers, or that states with higher costs of living must pay more to attract qualified police officers but also have higher crime rates.

11. Constant variance condition: met by the residuals vs. predicted plot
Nearly Normal condition: met by the Normal probability plot

13. a) Doesn't mention other predictors; suggests direct relationship

b) Correct

c) Can't predict *x* from *y*

d) Incorrect interpretation of R^2

15. a) Extrapolates far from the data

b) Suggests a perfect relationship

c) Can't predict one explanatory variable from another

d) Correct

17. a) Since the P-value for the *F*-statistic is small, the regression is significant.

b) Check residuals plotted against predicted values and the histogram of the residuals.

c) Salary is not a significant contributor to CSR rating at the 5% or 10% significance level, since the P-value of the coefficient is > 0.10 (i.e., 0.235). Options is a significant contributor to CSE rating at the 5% level since the P-value is < 0.05 (i.e., 0.0046).

d) No interpretation for the coefficient is needed since it is not significantly different from zero.

e) We would expect the CSR rating to increase by 0.08 standard deviations (0.32 × 0.25) = 0.08).

19. a) $\widehat{Price}$ = 152 037 + 9530 *Baths* + 139.87 *Area*

b) R^2 = 71.1%

c) For houses with the same number of bathrooms, each square foot of area is associated with an increase of $139.87 in the price of the house, on average.

d) The regression model says that for houses of the same size, those with more bathrooms are not priced higher. It says nothing about what would happen if a bathroom were added to a house. That would be a predictive interpretation, which is not supported by regression.

21. a) The regression equation is: $\widehat{Salary}$ = 9.788 + 0.110 *Service* + 0.053 *Education* + 0.071 *Test Score* + 0.004 *Typing wpm* + 0.065 *Dictation wpm*

b) *Salary* = 29.205 or $29 205

c) The *t*-value is 0.013 with 24 df. P-value = 0.4949, which is not significant at $\alpha = 0.05$.

d) Take out the explanatory variable for typing speed since it is not significant.

e) *Age* is likely to be collinear with several of the other predictors already in the model. For example, secretaries with longer terms of *Service* will naturally also be older.

23. a) After allowing for the effects measured by the Wilshire 5000 index, an increase of one point in the *Unemployment Rate* is associated with a decrease on average of about $3719.55 million in the *Funds flow*.

b) The *t*-ratio divides the coefficient by its standard error. The coefficient here is negative.

c) $H_0: \beta = 0$, $H_A: \beta \neq 0$; P-value < 0.0001 is very small, so reject the null hypothesis.

25. a) *R* squared = 66.7% *R* squared (adjusted) = 63.8%
s = 2.327 with $39 - 4 = 35$ degrees of freedom

Variable	Coeff	SE(Coeff)	t-ratio	P-value
Intercept	87.0089	33.60	2.59	0.0139
CPI	−0.344795	0.1203	−2.87	0.0070
Personal Consumption	1.10842e-5	0.0000	2.52	0.0165
Retail Sales	1.03152e-4	0.0000	6.67	≤ 0.0001

$\widehat{Revenue}$ = 87.0 − 0.344 *CPI* + 0.000 011 *Personal Consumption* + 0.0001 *Retail Sales*

b) R^2 is 66.7%, and all t-ratios are significant. It looks like these variables can account for much of the variation in Walmart revenue.

27. *Displacement* and *Bore* would be good predictors. Relationship with *Wheelbase* isn't linear.

29. a) Yes, R^2 of 90.9% says that most of the variability of *MSRP* is accounted for by this model.

b) No, a regression model may not be inverted in this way.

31. a) Yes, R^2 is very large.

b) The value of s, 3.140 calories, is very small compared with the initial standard deviation of *Calories*. This indicates that the model fits the data quite well, leaving very little variation unaccounted for.

c) A true value of 100% would indicate zero residuals, but with real data such as these, it is likely that the computed value of 100% is rounded up from a slightly lower value.

33. a) Scatterplots of *Sale Price* vs. each of the predictors (except *View*) are somewhat linear but with a lot of scatter. Homes are a sample but only from one period of time so not truly random; however they are independent of each other. The scatterplots show some evidence of differing spreads. Residual plots confirm some variation in spread, but it doesn't look too serious. A histogram of sales prices shows some right skewness but mostly just a few outliers (a few homes with very large price tags). Because of the large sample size the effect of the outliers will likely be minor.
Full model with all predictor variables:

Regression Statistics	
Multiple R	0.704
R Square	0.495
Adjusted R Square	0.493
Standard Error	180655
Observations	1086

F-statistic = 176.60; P-value < 0.0001

	Coefficients	Standard Error	t Stat	P-value
Intercept	226 082.49	34 143.26	6.622	0.0000
Bedrooms (#)	−71 306.51	6 587.48	−10.825	0.0000
Bathrooms (#)	17 586.39	9 472.65	1.857	0.0636
FloorArea (sq ft)	201.44	11.25	17.906	0.0000
Age (yrs)	−1 031.11	571.50	−1.804	0.0715
Lot Size (sq ft)	15.78	2.74	5.754	0.0000
View	−8 393.68	12 281.81	−0.683	0.4945

Residuals plot against predicted values:

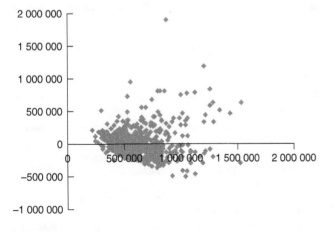

Full model R^2 is only 49.5%. The coefficient of *View* is the least significant and is the first candidate to be dropped. Other predictors for possible removal are *Age* and *# Bathrooms*.
Model with *View* and *Age* removed:

Regression Statistics	
Multiple R	0.7027
R Square	0.4937
Adjusted R Square	0.4919
Standard Error	180799
Observations	1086

F-statistic = 263.55; P-value < 0.0001

	Coefficients	Standard Error	t Stat	P-value
Intercept	190 812.91	28 100.27	6.790	0.0000
Bedrooms (#)	−72 954.80	6 488.98	−11.243	0.0000
Bathrooms (#)	24 224.44	8 754.85	2.767	0.0058
FloorArea (sq ft)	205.68	10.66	19.304	0.0000
LotSize (sq ft)	13.30	2.39	5.561	0.0000

R^2 only changes by a minuscule amount, from 49.5% to 49.3%. The coefficient of *Bathrooms* is now significant, as are all the predictors in the model. This appears to be the best choice of model. Residual plots (not shown here) confirm that the model at least somewhat satisfies the assumptions. Future work could examine how the model might change if the 17 high-priced homes (over $1.5 million) are removed.

b) Report: Of the potential variables considered for predicting sale price, the best model includes four significant predictor variables: *Floor Area*, *# of Bedrooms*, *# of Bathrooms*, and *Lot Size*. Approximately linear relationships between each predictor and sale price were observed. The fitted model is: *Sale Price = 190 813 + 205.68 Floor Area − 72 955 Bedrooms + 24 225 Bathrooms + 13.30 Lot Size*, but the explanatory power is only moderate, with an R^2 of about 50%. Examination of the residuals plotted against fitted values indicates that the equal spread condition is reasonably satisfied, but the histogram of residuals is skewed right with some outliers, indicating problems with the nearly normal condition.

c) Other possible predictors: location, type of dwelling (ranch, two-story, basement, etc.), area on the main floor separated from the total finished area, finished basement (full finished, full unfinished, crawl space, none), frontage, type of construction.

ROW	TABLE OF RANDOM DIGITS									
1	96299	07196	98642	20639	23185	56282	69929	14125	38872	94168
2	71622	35940	81807	59225	18192	08710	80777	84395	69563	86280
3	03272	41230	81739	74797	70406	18564	69273	72532	78340	36699
4	46376	58596	14365	63685	56555	42974	72944	96463	63533	24152
5	47352	42853	42903	97504	56655	70355	88606	61406	38757	70657
6	20064	04266	74017	79319	70170	96572	08523	56025	89077	57678
7	73184	95907	05179	51002	83374	52297	07769	99792	78365	93487
8	72753	36216	07230	35793	71907	65571	66784	25548	91861	15725
9	03939	30763	06138	80062	02537	23561	93136	61260	77935	93159
10	75998	37203	07959	38264	78120	77525	86481	54986	33042	70648
11	94435	97441	90998	25104	49761	14967	70724	67030	53887	81293
12	04362	40989	69167	38894	00172	02999	97377	33305	60782	29810
13	89059	43528	10547	40115	82234	86902	04121	83889	76208	31076
14	87736	04666	75145	49175	76754	07884	92564	80793	22573	67902
15	76488	88899	15860	07370	13431	84041	69202	18912	83173	11983
16	36460	53772	66634	25045	79007	78518	73580	14191	50353	32064
17	13205	69237	21820	20952	16635	58867	97650	82983	64865	93298
18	51242	12215	90739	36812	00436	31609	80333	96606	30430	31803
19	67819	00354	91439	91073	49258	15992	41277	75111	67496	68430
20	09875	08990	27656	15871	23637	00952	97818	64234	50199	05715
21	18192	95308	72975	01191	29958	09275	89141	19558	50524	32041
22	02763	33701	66188	50226	35813	72951	11638	01876	93664	37001
23	13349	46328	01856	29935	80563	03742	49470	67749	08578	21956
24	69238	92878	80067	80807	45096	22936	64325	19265	37755	69794
25	92207	63527	59398	29818	24789	94309	88380	57000	50171	17891
26	66679	99100	37072	30593	29665	84286	44458	60180	81451	58273
27	31087	42430	60322	34765	15757	53300	97392	98035	05228	68970
28	84432	04916	52949	78533	31666	62350	20584	56367	19701	60584
29	72042	12287	21081	48426	44321	58765	41760	43304	13399	02043
30	94534	73559	82135	70260	87936	85162	11937	18263	54138	69564
31	63971	97198	40974	45301	60177	35604	21580	68107	25184	42810
32	11227	58474	17272	37619	69517	62964	67962	34510	12607	52255
33	28541	02029	08068	96656	17795	21484	57722	76511	27849	61738
34	11282	43632	49531	78981	81980	08530	08629	32279	29478	50228
35	42907	15137	21918	13248	39129	49559	94540	24070	88151	36782
36	47119	76651	21732	32364	58545	50277	57558	30390	18771	72703
37	11232	99884	05087	76839	65142	19994	91397	29350	83852	04905
38	64725	06719	86262	53356	57999	50193	79936	97230	52073	94467
39	77007	26962	55466	12521	48125	12280	54985	26239	76044	54398
40	18375	19310	59796	89832	59417	18553	17238	05474	33259	50595

Table Z	Second decimal place in z										
Areas under the standard Normal curve	0.09	0.08	0.07	0.06	0.05	0.04	0.03	0.02	0.01	0.00	z
										0.0000†	−3.9
	0.0001	0.0001	0.0001	0.0001	0.0001	0.0001	0.0001	0.0001	0.0001	0.0001	−3.8
	0.0001	0.0001	0.0001	0.0001	0.0001	0.0001	0.0001	0.0001	0.0001	0.0001	−3.7
	0.0001	0.0001	0.0001	0.0001	0.0001	0.0001	0.0001	0.0001	0.0002	0.0002	−3.6
	0.0002	0.0002	0.0002	0.0002	0.0002	0.0002	0.0002	0.0002	0.0002	0.0002	−3.5
	0.0002	0.0003	0.0003	0.0003	0.0003	0.0003	0.0003	0.0003	0.0003	0.0003	−3.4
	0.0003	0.0004	0.0004	0.0004	0.0004	0.0004	0.0004	0.0005	0.0005	0.0005	−3.3
	0.0005	0.0005	0.0005	0.0006	0.0006	0.0006	0.0006	0.0006	0.0007	0.0007	−3.2
	0.0007	0.0007	0.0008	0.0008	0.0008	0.0008	0.0009	0.0009	0.0009	0.0010	−3.1
	0.0010	0.0010	0.0011	0.0011	0.0011	0.0012	0.0012	0.0013	0.0013	0.0013	−3.0
	0.0014	0.0014	0.0015	0.0015	0.0016	0.0016	0.0017	0.0018	0.0018	0.0019	−2.9
	0.0019	0.0020	0.0021	0.0021	0.0022	0.0023	0.0023	0.0024	0.0025	0.0026	−2.8
	0.0026	0.0027	0.0028	0.0029	0.0030	0.0031	0.0032	0.0033	0.0034	0.0035	−2.7
	0.0036	0.0037	0.0038	0.0039	0.0040	0.0041	0.0043	0.0044	0.0045	0.0047	−2.6
	0.0048	0.0049	0.0051	0.0052	0.0054	0.0055	0.0057	0.0059	0.0060	0.0062	−2.5
	0.0064	0.0066	0.0068	0.0069	0.0071	0.0073	0.0075	0.0078	0.0080	0.0082	−2.4
	0.0084	0.0087	0.0089	0.0091	0.0094	0.0096	0.0099	0.0102	0.0104	0.0107	−2.3
	0.0110	0.0113	0.0116	0.0119	0.0122	0.0125	0.0129	0.0132	0.0136	0.0139	−2.2
	0.0143	0.0146	0.0150	0.0154	0.0158	0.0162	0.0166	0.0170	0.0174	0.0179	−2.1
	0.0183	0.0188	0.0192	0.0197	0.0202	0.0207	0.0212	0.0217	0.0222	0.0228	−2.0
	0.0233	0.0239	0.0244	0.0250	0.0256	0.0262	0.0268	0.0274	0.0281	0.0287	−1.9
	0.0294	0.0301	0.0307	0.0314	0.0322	0.0329	0.0336	0.0344	0.0351	0.0359	−1.8
	0.0367	0.0375	0.0384	0.0392	0.0401	0.0409	0.0418	0.0427	0.0436	0.0446	−1.7
	0.0455	0.0465	0.0475	0.0485	0.0495	0.0505	0.0516	0.0526	0.0537	0.0548	−1.6
	0.0559	0.0571	0.0582	0.0594	0.0606	0.0618	0.0630	0.0643	0.0655	0.0668	−1.5
	0.0681	0.0694	0.0708	0.0721	0.0735	0.0749	0.0764	0.0778	0.0793	0.0808	−1.4
	0.0823	0.0838	0.0853	0.0869	0.0885	0.0901	0.0918	0.0934	0.0951	0.0968	−1.3
	0.0985	0.1003	0.1020	0.1038	0.1056	0.1075	0.1093	0.1112	0.1131	0.1151	−1.2
	0.1170	0.1190	0.1210	0.1230	0.1251	0.1271	0.1292	0.1314	0.1335	0.1357	−1.1
	0.1379	0.1401	0.1423	0.1446	0.1469	0.1492	0.1515	0.1539	0.1562	0.1587	−1.0
	0.1611	0.1635	0.1660	0.1685	0.1711	0.1736	0.1762	0.1788	0.1814	0.1841	−0.9
	0.1867	0.1894	0.1922	0.1949	0.1977	0.2005	0.2033	0.2061	0.2090	0.2119	−0.8
	0.2148	0.2177	0.2206	0.2236	0.2266	0.2296	0.2327	0.2358	0.2389	0.2420	−0.7
	0.2451	0.2483	0.2514	0.2546	0.2578	0.2611	0.2643	0.2676	0.2709	0.2743	−0.6
	0.2776	0.2810	0.2843	0.2877	0.2912	0.2946	0.2981	0.3015	0.3050	0.3085	−0.5
	0.3121	0.3156	0.3192	0.3228	0.3264	0.3300	0.3336	0.3372	0.3409	0.3446	−0.4
	0.3483	0.3520	0.3557	0.3594	0.3632	0.3669	0.3707	0.3745	0.3783	0.3821	−0.3
	0.3859	0.3897	0.3936	0.3974	0.4013	0.4052	0.4090	0.4129	0.4168	0.4207	−0.2
	0.4247	0.4286	0.4325	0.4364	0.4404	0.4443	0.4483	0.4522	0.4562	0.4602	−0.1
	0.4641	0.4681	0.4721	0.4761	0.4801	0.4840	0.4880	0.4920	0.4960	0.5000	−0.0

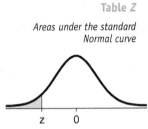

† For z ≤ 3.90 the areas are 0.0000 to four decimal places.

Table Z (cont.)

Areas under the standard Normal curve

z	0.00	0.01	0.02	0.03	0.04	0.05	0.06	0.07	0.08	0.09
0.0	0.5000	0.5040	0.5080	0.5120	0.5160	0.5199	0.5239	0.5279	0.5319	0.5359
0.1	0.5398	0.5438	0.5478	0.5517	0.5557	0.5596	0.5636	0.5675	0.5714	0.5753
0.2	0.5793	0.5832	0.5871	0.5910	0.5948	0.5987	0.6026	0.6064	0.6103	0.6141
0.3	0.6179	0.6217	0.6255	0.6293	0.6331	0.6368	0.6406	0.6443	0.6480	0.6517
0.4	0.6554	0.6591	0.6628	0.6664	0.6700	0.6736	0.6772	0.6808	0.6844	0.6879
0.5	0.6915	0.6950	0.6985	0.7019	0.7054	0.7088	0.7123	0.7157	0.7190	0.7224
0.6	0.7257	0.7291	0.7324	0.7357	0.7389	0.7422	0.7454	0.7486	0.7517	0.7549
0.7	0.7580	0.7611	0.7642	0.7673	0.7704	0.7734	0.7764	0.7794	0.7823	0.7852
0.8	0.7881	0.7910	0.7939	0.7967	0.7995	0.8023	0.8051	0.8078	0.8106	0.8133
0.9	0.8159	0.8186	0.8212	0.8238	0.8264	0.8289	0.8315	0.8340	0.8365	0.8389
1.0	0.8413	0.8438	0.8461	0.8485	0.8508	0.8531	0.8554	0.8577	0.8599	0.8621
1.1	0.8643	0.8665	0.8686	0.8708	0.8729	0.8749	0.8770	0.8790	0.8810	0.8830
1.2	0.8849	0.8869	0.8888	0.8907	0.8925	0.8944	0.8962	0.8980	0.8997	0.9015
1.3	0.9032	0.9049	0.9066	0.9082	0.9099	0.9115	0.9131	0.9147	0.9162	0.9177
1.4	0.9192	0.9207	0.9222	0.9236	0.9251	0.9265	0.9279	0.9292	0.9306	0.9319
1.5	0.9332	0.9345	0.9357	0.9370	0.9382	0.9394	0.9406	0.9418	0.9429	0.9441
1.6	0.9452	0.9463	0.9474	0.9484	0.9495	0.9505	0.9515	0.9525	0.9535	0.9545
1.7	0.9554	0.9564	0.9573	0.9582	0.9591	0.9599	0.9608	0.9616	0.9625	0.9633
1.8	0.9641	0.9649	0.9656	0.9664	0.9671	0.9678	0.9686	0.9693	0.9699	0.9706
1.9	0.9713	0.9719	0.9726	0.9732	0.9738	0.9744	0.9750	0.9756	0.9761	0.9767
2.0	0.9772	0.9778	0.9783	0.9788	0.9793	0.9798	0.9803	0.9808	0.9812	0.9817
2.1	0.9821	0.9826	0.9830	0.9834	0.9838	0.9842	0.9846	0.9850	0.9854	0.9857
2.2	0.9861	0.9864	0.9868	0.9871	0.9875	0.9878	0.9881	0.9884	0.9887	0.9890
2.3	0.9893	0.9896	0.9898	0.9901	0.9904	0.9906	0.9909	0.9911	0.9913	0.9916
2.4	0.9918	0.9920	0.9922	0.9925	0.9927	0.9929	0.9931	0.9932	0.9934	0.9936
2.5	0.9938	0.9940	0.9941	0.9943	0.9945	0.9946	0.9948	0.9949	0.9951	0.9952
2.6	0.9953	0.9955	0.9956	0.9957	0.9959	0.9960	0.9961	0.9962	0.9963	0.9964
2.7	0.9965	0.9966	0.9967	0.9968	0.9969	0.9970	0.9971	0.9972	0.9973	0.9974
2.8	0.9974	0.9975	0.9976	0.9977	0.9977	0.9978	0.9979	0.9979	0.9980	0.9981
2.9	0.9981	0.9982	0.9982	0.9983	0.9984	0.9984	0.9985	0.9985	0.9986	0.9986
3.0	0.9987	0.9987	0.9987	0.9988	0.9988	0.9989	0.9989	0.9989	0.9990	0.9990
3.1	0.9990	0.9991	0.9991	0.9991	0.9992	0.9992	0.9992	0.9992	0.9993	0.9993
3.2	0.9993	0.9993	0.9994	0.9994	0.9994	0.9994	0.9994	0.9995	0.9995	0.9995
3.3	0.9995	0.9995	0.9995	0.9996	0.9996	0.9996	0.9996	0.9996	0.9996	0.9997
3.4	0.9997	0.9997	0.9997	0.9997	0.9997	0.9997	0.9997	0.9997	0.9997	0.9998
3.5	0.9998	0.9998	0.9998	0.9998	0.9998	0.9998	0.9998	0.9998	0.9998	0.9998
3.6	0.9998	0.9998	0.9999	0.9999	0.9999	0.9999	0.9999	0.9999	0.9999	0.9999
3.7	0.9999	0.9999	0.9999	0.9999	0.9999	0.9999	0.9999	0.9999	0.9999	0.9999
3.8	0.9999	0.9999	0.9999	0.9999	0.9999	0.9999	0.9999	0.9999	0.9999	0.9999
3.9	1.0000[†]									

[†] For $z \geq 3.90$, the areas are 1.0000 to four decimal places.

Two-tail probability		0.20	0.10	0.05	0.02	0.01	
One-tail probability		0.10	0.05	0.025	0.01	0.005	
	df						df
Table T Values of t_α	1	3.078	6.314	12.706	31.821	63.657	1
	2	1.886	2.920	4.303	6.965	9.925	2
	3	1.638	2.353	3.182	4.541	5.841	3
	4	1.533	2.132	2.776	3.747	4.604	4
	5	1.476	2.015	2.571	3.365	4.032	5
	6	1.440	1.943	2.447	3.143	3.707	6
	7	1.415	1.895	2.365	2.998	3.499	7
	8	1.397	1.860	2.306	2.896	3.355	8
	9	1.383	1.833	2.262	2.821	3.250	9
	10	1.372	1.812	2.228	2.764	3.169	10
	11	1.363	1.796	2.201	2.718	3.106	11
	12	1.356	1.782	2.179	2.681	3.055	12
	13	1.350	1.771	2.160	2.650	3.012	13
	14	1.345	1.761	2.145	2.624	2.977	14
	15	1.341	1.753	2.131	2.602	2.947	15
	16	1.337	1.746	2.120	2.583	2.921	16
	17	1.333	1.740	2.110	2.567	2.898	17
	18	1.330	1.734	2.101	2.552	2.878	18
	19	1.328	1.729	2.093	2.539	2.861	19
	20	1.325	1.725	2.086	2.528	2.845	20
	21	1.323	1.721	2.080	2.518	2.831	21
	22	1.321	1.717	2.074	2.508	2.819	22
	23	1.319	1.714	2.069	2.500	2.807	23
	24	1.318	1.711	2.064	2.492	2.797	24
	25	1.316	1.708	2.060	2.485	2.787	25
	26	1.315	1.706	2.056	2.479	2.779	26
	27	1.314	1.703	2.052	2.473	2.771	27
	28	1.313	1.701	2.048	2.467	2.763	28
	29	1.311	1.699	2.045	2.462	2.756	29
	30	1.310	1.697	2.042	2.457	2.750	30
	32	1.309	1.694	2.037	2.449	2.738	32
	35	1.306	1.690	2.030	2.438	2.725	35
	40	1.303	1.684	2.021	2.423	2.704	40
	45	1.301	1.679	2.014	2.412	2.690	45
	50	1.299	1.676	2.009	2.403	2.678	50
	60	1.296	1.671	2.000	2.390	2.660	60
	75	1.293	1.665	1.992	2.377	2.643	75
	100	1.290	1.660	1.984	2.364	2.626	100
	120	1.289	1.658	1.980	2.358	2.617	120
	140	1.288	1.656	1.977	2.353	2.611	140
	180	1.286	1.653	1.973	2.347	2.603	180
	250	1.285	1.651	1.969	2.341	2.596	250
	400	1.284	1.649	1.966	2.336	2.588	400
	1000	1.282	1.646	1.962	2.330	2.581	1000
	∞	1.282	1.645	1.960	2.326	2.576	∞
Confidence levels		80%	90%	95%	98%	99%	

Two tails: $-t_{\alpha/2}$ 0 $t_{\alpha/2}$ $\frac{\alpha}{2}$ $\frac{\alpha}{2}$

One tail: 0 t_α α

Right-tail probability		0.10	0.05	0.025	0.01	0.005
	df					
Table X	1	2.706	3.841	5.024	6.635	7.879
Values of χ^2_α	2	4.605	5.991	7.378	9.210	10.597
	3	6.251	7.815	9.348	11.345	12.838
	4	7.779	9.488	11.143	13.277	14.860
	5	9.236	11.070	12.833	15.086	16.750
	6	10.645	12.592	14.449	16.812	18.548
	7	12.017	14.067	16.013	18.475	20.278
	8	13.362	15.507	17.535	20.090	21.955
	9	14.684	16.919	19.023	21.666	23.589
	10	15.987	18.307	20.483	23.209	25.188
	11	17.275	19.675	21.920	24.725	26.757
	12	18.549	21.026	23.337	26.217	28.300
	13	19.812	22.362	24.736	27.688	29.819
	14	21.064	23.685	26.119	29.141	31.319
	15	22.307	24.996	27.488	30.578	32.801
	16	23.542	26.296	28.845	32.000	34.267
	17	24.769	27.587	30.191	33.409	35.718
	18	25.989	28.869	31.526	34.805	37.156
	19	27.204	30.143	32.852	36.191	38.582
	20	28.412	31.410	34.170	37.566	39.997
	21	29.615	32.671	35.479	38.932	41.401
	22	30.813	33.924	36.781	40.290	42.796
	23	32.007	35.172	38.076	41.638	44.181
	24	33.196	36.415	39.364	42.980	45.559
	25	34.382	37.653	40.647	44.314	46.928
	26	35.563	38.885	41.923	45.642	48.290
	27	36.741	40.113	43.195	46.963	49.645
	28	37.916	41.337	44.461	48.278	50.994
	29	39.087	42.557	45.722	59.588	52.336
	30	40.256	43.773	46.979	50.892	53.672
	40	51.805	55.759	59.342	63.691	66.767
	50	63.167	67.505	71.420	76.154	79.490
	60	74.397	79.082	83.298	88.381	91.955
	70	85.527	90.531	95.023	100.424	104.213
	80	96.578	101.879	106.628	112.328	116.320
	90	107.565	113.145	118.135	124.115	128.296
	100	118.499	124.343	129.563	135.811	140.177

Selected Formulas

$Range = Max - Min$

$IQR = Q3 - Q1$

Outlier Rule-of-Thumb: $y < Q1 - 1.5 \times IQR$ or $y > Q3 + 1.5 \times IQR$

$$\bar{y} = \frac{\sum y}{n}$$

$$s = \sqrt{\frac{\sum (y - \bar{y})^2}{n - 1}}$$

$$z = \frac{y - \mu}{\sigma} \text{ (model based)} \qquad z = \frac{y - \bar{y}}{s} \text{ (data based)}$$

$$r = \frac{\sum z_x z_y}{n - 1}$$

$$\hat{y} = b_0 + b_1 x \qquad \text{where } b_1 = r \frac{s_y}{s_x} \text{ and } b_0 = \bar{y} - b_1 \bar{x}$$

$P(\mathbf{A}) = 1 - P(\mathbf{A}^C)$

$P(\mathbf{A} \text{ or } \mathbf{B}) = P(\mathbf{A}) + P(\mathbf{B}) - P(\mathbf{A} \text{ and } \mathbf{B})$

$P(\mathbf{A} \text{ and } \mathbf{B}) = P(\mathbf{A}) \times P(\mathbf{B}|\mathbf{A})$

$$P(\mathbf{B}|\mathbf{A}) = \frac{P(\mathbf{A} \text{ and } \mathbf{B})}{P(\mathbf{A})}$$

If $\mathbf{A}$ and $\mathbf{B}$ are independent, $P(\mathbf{B}|\mathbf{A}) = P(\mathbf{B})$

$$E(X) = \mu = \sum x \cdot P(x) \qquad Var(X) = \sigma^2 = \sum (x - \mu)^2 P(x)$$

$$E(X \pm c) = E(X) \pm c \qquad Var(X \pm c) = Var(X)$$

$$E(aX) = aE(X) \qquad Var(aX) = a^2 Var(X)$$

$$E(X \pm Y) = E(X) \pm E(Y) \qquad Var(X \pm Y) = Var(X) + Var(Y)$$

$$\text{if } X \text{ and } Y \text{ are independent}$$

Geometric: $\quad P(x) = q^{x-1} p \qquad \mu = \frac{1}{p} \qquad \sigma = \sqrt{\frac{q}{p^2}}$

Binomial: $\quad P(x) = {_nC_x} p^x q^{n-x} \qquad \mu = np \qquad \sigma = \sqrt{npq}$

$$\hat{p} = \frac{x}{n} \qquad \mu(\hat{p}) = p \qquad SD(\hat{p}) = \sqrt{\frac{pq}{n}}$$

Poisson probability model for successes: Poisson (λ)

λ = mean number of successes

X = number of successes

$$P(X = x) = \frac{e^{-\lambda} \lambda^x}{x!}$$

Expected value: $\quad E(X) = \lambda$

Standard deviation: $\quad SD(X) = \sqrt{\lambda}$

Sampling distribution of $\bar{y}$:

(CLT) As n grows, the sampling distribution approaches the Normal model with

$$\mu(\bar{y}) = \mu_y \qquad SD(\bar{y}) = \frac{\sigma}{\sqrt{n}}$$

Inference

Confidence interval for parameter = **statistic ± critical value × SE (statistic)**

$$\text{Test statistic} = \frac{statistic - parameter}{SD\,(statistic)}$$

Parameter	Statistic	SD(statistic)	SE(statistic)
p	$\hat{p}$	$\sqrt{\dfrac{pq}{n}}$	$\sqrt{\dfrac{\hat{p}\hat{q}}{n}}$
μ	$\bar{y}$	$\dfrac{\sigma}{\sqrt{n}}$	$\dfrac{s}{\sqrt{n}}$
$\mu_1 - \mu_2$	$y_1 - y_2$	$\sqrt{\dfrac{\sigma_1^2}{n_1} + \dfrac{\sigma_2^2}{n_2}}$	$\sqrt{\dfrac{s_1^2}{n_1} + \dfrac{s_2^2}{n_2}}$
μ_d	$\bar{d}$	$\dfrac{\sigma_d}{\sqrt{n}}$	$\dfrac{s_d}{\sqrt{n}}$
σ_ϵ	$s_e = \sqrt{\dfrac{\sum (y - \hat{y})^2}{n - 2}}$	(divide by $n - k - 1$ in multiple regression)	
β_1	b_1	(in simple regression)	$\dfrac{s_e}{s_x \sqrt{n - 1}}$
μ_ν	$\hat{y}_\nu$	(in simple regression)	$\sqrt{SE^2(b_1) \cdot (x_\nu - \bar{x})^2 + \dfrac{s_e^2}{n}}$
y_ν	$\hat{y}_\nu$	(in simple regression)	$\sqrt{SE^2(b_1) \cdot (x_\nu - \bar{x})^2 + \dfrac{s_e^2}{n} + s_e^2}$

Pooling: For testing difference between proportions: $\hat{p}_{pooled} = \dfrac{y_1 + y_2}{n_1 + n_2}$

For testing difference between means: $s_p = \sqrt{\dfrac{(n_1 - 1)s_1^2 + (n_2 - 1)s_2^2}{n_1 + n_2 - 2}}$

Substitute these pooled estimates in the respective SE formulas for both groups when assumptions and conditions are met.

Chi-square: $\chi^2 = \sum \dfrac{(Obs - Exp)^2}{Exp}$

Assumptions for Inference	And the Conditions That Support or Override Them

Proportions (z)

- **One sample**
  1. Individuals are independent.
  2. Sample is sufficiently large.

  1. SRS and $n < 10\%$ of the population.
  2. Successes and failures each ≥ 10.

Means (t)

- **One Sample** (df $= n - 1$)
  1. Individuals are independent.
  2. Population has a Normal model.

  1. SRS and $n < 10\%$ of the population.
  2. Histogram is unimodal and symmetric.*

- **Matched pairs** (df $= n - 1$)
  1. Data are matched.
  2. Individuals are independent.
  3. Population of differences is Normal.

  1. (Think about the design.)
  2. SRS and $n < 10\%$ OR random allocation.
  3. Histogram of differences is unimodal and symmetric.*

- **Two independent samples** (df from technology)
  1. Groups are independent.
  2. Data in each group are independent.
  3. Both populations are Normal.

  1. (Think about the design.)
  2. SRSs and $n < 10\%$ OR random allocation.
  3. Both histograms are unimodal and symmetric.*

Distributions/Association (χ^2)

- **Goodness of fit** (df $=$ # of cells $- 1$; one variable, one sample compared with population model)
  1. Data are counts.
  2. Data in sample are independent.
  3. Sample is sufficiently large.

  1. (Are they?)
  2. SRS and $n < 10\%$ of the population.
  3. All expected counts ≥ 5.

- **Homogeneity** [df $= (r - 1)(c - 1)$; many groups compared on one variable]
  1. Data are counts.
  2. Data in groups are independent.
  3. Groups are sufficiently large.

  1. (Are they?)
  2. SRSs and $n < 10\%$ OR random allocation.
  3. All expected counts ≥ 5.

- **Independence** [df $= (r - 1)(c - 1)$; sample from one population classified on two variables]
  1. Data are counts.
  2. Data are independent.
  3. Sample is sufficiently large.

  1. (Are they?)
  2. SRSs and $n < 10\%$ of the population.
  3. All expected counts ≥ 5.

Regression with k predictors (t, df $= n - k - 1$)

- **Association** of each quantitative predictor with the response variable
  1. Form of relationship is linear.

  2. Errors are independent.
  3. Variability of errors is constant.

  4. Errors follow a Normal model.

  1. Scatterplots of y against each x are straight enough. Scatterplot of residuals against predicted values shows no special structure.
  2. No apparent pattern in plot of residuals against predicted values.
  3. Plot of residuals against predicted values has constant spread, doesn't "thicken."
  4. Histogram of residuals is approximately unimodal and symmetric, or Normal probability plot is reasonably straight.*

(*Less critical as n increases)

Quick Guide to Inference							
Plan				**Do**			**Report**
Inference about?	**One group or two?**	**Procedure**	**Model**	**Parameter**	**Estimate**	**SE**	**Chapter**
Proportions	One sample	1-Proportion z-Interval	z	p	$\hat{p}$	$\sqrt{\dfrac{\hat{p}\hat{q}}{n}}$	9
		1-Proportion z-Test				$\sqrt{\dfrac{p_0 q_0}{n}}$	10
	Two samples	2-Sample z-Test 2-Sample z-Interval	z	$p_1 - p_2$	$\hat{p}_1 - \hat{p}_2$	$\sqrt{\dfrac{\hat{p}_1\hat{q}_1}{n_1} + \dfrac{\hat{p}_2\hat{q}_2}{n_2}}$	12
Means	One sample	t-Interval t-Test	t df $= n-1$	μ	$\bar{y}$	$\dfrac{s}{\sqrt{n}}$	11
	Two independent groups	2-Sample t-Test 2-Sample t-Interval	t df from technology	$\mu_1 - \mu_2$	$\bar{y}_1 - \bar{y}_2$	$\sqrt{\dfrac{s_1^2}{n_1} + \dfrac{s_2^2}{n_2}}$	12
	Matched pairs	Paired t-Test Paired t-Interval	t df $= n-1$	μ_d	$\bar{d}$	$\dfrac{s_d}{\sqrt{n}}$	12
Distributions (one categorical variable)	One sample	Goodness of-Fit	χ^2 df $= cells - 1$			$\sum \dfrac{(Obs - Exp)^2}{Exp}$	13
	Many independent groups	Homogeneity χ^2 Test	χ^2 df $= (r-1)(c-1)$				
Independence (two categorical variables)	One sample	Independence χ^2 Test					
Association (two quantitative variables)	One sample	Linear Regression t-Test or Confidence Interval for β	t df $= n-2$	β_1	b_1	$\dfrac{s_e}{s_x\sqrt{n-1}}$ (compute with technology)	14
		*Confidence Interval for μ_ν		μ_ν	$\hat{y}_\nu$	$\sqrt{SE^2(b_1) \cdot (x_\nu - \bar{x})^2 + \dfrac{s_e^2}{n}}$	
		*Prediction Interval for y_ν		y_ν	$\hat{y}_\nu$	$\sqrt{SE^2(b_1) \cdot (x_\nu - \bar{x})^2 + \dfrac{s_e^2}{n} + s_e^2}$	
Association (one quantitative variable fit modelled by K quantitative variables)	One sample	Multiple Regression t-test or Confidence interval for each β_j	t df $= n - (k+1)$	β_j	b_j	(from technology)	15
		F test for regression model	F df $= k$ and $n - (k+1)$			MSM/MSE	15

NAME INDEX

BE = Boxed Example; E = Exercises; EIA = Ethics in Action; GE = Guided Example; IE = In-Text Example; JC = Just Checking; P = Project; TH = Technology Help

Consumers

Demographics

Distribution and Operations Management

E-Commerce

Economics

Education

Technology

Transportation

SUBJECT INDEX